TIMETABLES OF WORLD LITERATURE

George Thomas Kurian

Facts On File, Inc.

Timetables of World Literature

Facts On File, Inc.
132 West 31st Street
New York NY 10001

Library of Congress Cataloging-in-Publication Data
Kurian, George Thomas.
     Timetables of world literature / George Thomas Kurian.
        p. cm.
     Summary: Chronicles world literature from the Classical Age through the twentieth century, discussing literary developments and the relationship between literature and the political and social climate of each historical period.
     Includes bibliographical references and indexes.
     ISBN 0-8160-4197-0 (alk. paper)
     1. Literature—Chronology—Juvenile literature. [1. Literature—Chronology.] I. Title.
PN524 .K87 2002
809' .002'02—dc21   2002003891

Facts On File books are available at special discounts when purchased in bulk quantities for businesses, associations, institutions, or sales promotions. Please call our Special Sales Department in New York at (212) 967-8800 or (800) 322-8755.

You can find Facts On File on the World Wide Web at http://www.factsonfile.com

Text design adapted by Erika K. Arroyo
Cover illustration by Smart Graphics
Cover design by Cathy Rincon

Printed in the United States of America

VB FOF 10 9 8 7 6 5 4 3 2

This book is printed on acid-free paper.

CONTENTS

PREFACE

Which authors were contemporaries of Charles Dickens? Which books, plays, and poems were published during World War II? Who won the Pulitzer Prize in the year you were born? *Timetables of World Literature* is a chronicle of literary works from the earliest times through the year 2000. It answers the question Who wrote what when? and allows readers to place authors and their works in the context of their times.

This chronology lists more than 12,000 titles and 9,800 authors. It includes all genres of literature—novels, plays, poems, autobiography and biography, essays, meditations, romance, science fiction, mystery, and history—from more than 58 countries and in 41 languages, ranging from classical Greek and Latin to the so-called imperial European languages (English, French, Dutch, and Spanish) to Arabic and the major languages of Asia.

One of the functions of a chronology is to separate the wheat from the chaff. Which are the outstanding works of every century in every language? The selections for this timetable are comprehensive but not exhaustive. They include but are not limited to what is known as the canon: books accepted by literary scholars as constituting the core, as represented in major anthologies and encyclopedias of national and world literatures. Even so, not all works by all authors cited in these anthologies or encyclopedias have been included, because not even the works of great authors are uniformly noteworthy or outstanding.

Timetables of World Literature is divided into seven periods: The Classical Age (to A.D. 100), the Middle Ages (100–1500), the Sixteenth Century, the Seventeenth Century, the Eighteenth Century, the Nineteenth Century, and the Twentieth Century. Each section begins with a brief discussion of literary developments of the age and the relationship of literature to the general political and social climate. This is followed by short profiles of the major writers

of the era, in order of prominence. Ranking is always subjective to a certain degree, but an effort has been made to base the ranking on the influence the selected writers have had on succeeding generations and the number of their works that have been translated into other languages. A timeline of key historical events concludes the introduction to each section.

The first author listed in *Timetables of World Literature* is from the seventh century B.C. In the centuries between that date and the 15th century, when printing was invented, books had to be copied by hand, and this task limited the circulation of books. Lack of schooling and marginal rates of literacy in even civilized countries also did not stimulate writing. In fact, during these years, writers were a rare breed. (The number of writers in the first 13 centuries of the modern era is estimated at fewer than 7,000.) For the classical period and the early Middle Ages, the chronology lists only the years of notable literary events. For every year after 1500, *Timetables* provides annual chronologies.

The information for each year includes up to four sections: Births, Deaths, Literary Events, and Publications. The Births and Deaths sections include the nationality of the writers. The Literary Events section generally highlights the founding of major literary magazines or societies, and in the Twentieth Century chapter, it also consists of literary prizes and awards such as the Nobel Prize in literature and the Pulitzer Prizes.

The Publications list is arranged alphabetically by language, then by nationality. For example, a novel written in English by a South African writer is listed under the main heading English and the subheading South African. Indian authors writing in English are similarly listed, but those writing in any of the native languages (Assamese, Bengali, Gujarathi, Hindi, Kannada, Malayalam, Marathi, Oriya, Punjabi, Rajasthani, Tamil, Telugu, Urdu) are listed under

those languages. Sometimes nationality and language converge and sometimes they overlap. In the modern world, emigrés and expatriates pose a particularly difficult problem in classification: They may be born in one country but reside for part of their lives in another and write in a language not their own. There are writers of hyphenated national origins who do not fall into any discrete category in terms of language or nationality.

Works of authors who write in more than one language are listed under the language of the specific work. Vladimir Nabokov's early books, therefore, are listed under Russian, and his later ones under English. The works of most African authors are listed under French, English, or Portuguese, the main literary languages of postcolonial Africa.

To aid in research, the book has four indexes. Authors are indexed by last name and by nationality. Publications are indexed by title and by language, grouped by genre.

THE CLASSICAL AGE
(TO A.D. 100)

It is not known with any certainty when literature first appeared on the human scene, but alphabets exist from as long ago as the third millennium B.C., and oral traditions predate written literature by many hundreds of years. The earliest author known by name was Enheduanna, an Akkadian princess born about 2300 B.C. Her father was Sargon, the conqueror of Sumer and the first emperor known by name, who appointed her as priestess at the temple of the moon god in Ur. Two clay tablets signed with Enheduanna's name have survived. Both contain poems in honor of Inanna, the goddess of war and fertility.

The first literature for children was found on Sumerian clay tablets from the period of the Third Dynasty in the city of Ur (2100–2004 B.C.) These texts fall into five categories: lullabies, proverbs and fables, stories of children's lives, writing exercises, and dialogs or debates.

Bards, or tribal poet-singers who declaimed heroic poetry, were the earliest compilers of books, and the books they compiled were mostly epics. They were written on clay tablets, which predate parchment. The most ancient epic is that of *Gilgamesh,* which relates the futile search for immortality of a Sumerian king of the same name who ruled the city of Uruch around 2200 B.C. Gilgamesh is also the first important literary hero. Other fragments of Sumerian literature include hymns to Sumerian gods and lamentations by unknown bards of the destruction of the ancient Sumer and Nippur.

Religion was the primary source of literature before the rise of ancient Greece. The Hebrew Bible was written about 1000 B.C., although scholars have speculated that the Book of Job, the oldest of the books of the Old Testament, was written many centuries earlier. Regarding its literary and poetic quality, the Bible reveals a high degree of linguistic sophistication and refinement, and its evocative cadences have continued to inspire generations of believers and nonbelievers alike. The oldest Hebrew book is the Gezer Calendar, a description of the agricultural year written in Gezer, Israel, in the late 10th century, in the era of King Solomon.

Religious literature has an ancient history in India and China. The Indian Rig-Veda (Wisdom of the Verses), a collection of 1,028 verses recited by priests during fire sacrifices, is divided into 10 books, each composed by a different sage. Books 2 through 7 date from 1200 B.C. The Upanishad mystical scriptures appeared between 1000 and 500 B.C. The world's first grammar, *Astadhyayi,* also came from India. It was written by Panini in the fifth century B.C. The Buddhist sacred text Tripitaka was written between the fifth and first centuries B.C. The oldest surviving Chinese prose work is the *Yijing* (Book of Changes), a collection of 64 hexagrams intended as an aid to divination. It is said to have been written between 1144 and 1141 B.C. by Wenwang, ruler of the ancient state of Zhou. The first book of poetry in the Chinese language was the *Shijing* (Book of Songs), a collection of 305 poems drawn from the oral tradition, written around the fifth century B.C. The first poet in the Chinese language was Qu Yuan, a courtier from a noble family in the southern state of Chu. He died in 278 B.C. Ancient China produced a number of female poets; among the first was Cai Yan (Cai Wenji), who lived at the turn of the first century B.C.

Classical Literature

Greece produced the first corpus of literature that has survived more or less intact to the present day. Classical Greek literature is familiar to most Western readers, and some of its great names are as well known as those of Shakespeare and Goethe. What distinguishes Greek literature is its great range, extending from drama and poetry to history, sciences, biography, and philosophy. The earliest recorded work apart from law codes is a cosmographical work, *Heptamychos,* by Pherecydes of Syros, one of the Seven Wise Men (the other six being Bias, Chilon, Cleobulus, Pittacus, Solon, and Thales) who lived in the mid-sixth century B.C. Pherecydes is said to have been the teacher of the great mathematician Pythagoras.

Although influenced by the religious myths of Mesopotamia and Egypt, Greek literature has no direct literary ancestry. On the other hand, Greece is at the head of a transmission line of literary genres and themes that passed through Rome into the Middle Ages and then on to modern times. Roman writers looked to Greece for themes, forms, and choice of meter and verse. All the major forms of literature—including epic, tragedy, comedy, lyric, satire, history, biography, and prose narrative—were established by the Greeks and Romans. (The only modern literary development is the novel, which did not come into vogue until the 16th century.) The Greek epics of Homer were models for the Latin epics of Virgil; the lyric fragments of Alcaeus and Sappho were echoed in the works of Catullus and Ovid; the histories of Thucydides and Herodotus were succeeded by those of Livy and Tacitus. Roman literature had no match for the great Athenian playwrights of the fifth century, however, and it also lacked philosophers equal to the great Athenians such as Plato and Aristotle.

Major Greek Authors

Homer (9th or 8th century B.C.) Author of the *Iliad* and *Odyssey,* the two greatest epic poems of ancient Greece. Virtually nothing is known of his life, except that he was possibly blind. His great epics formed part of the moral education of generations of Greeks and the literary education of most modern writers.

Pindar (522/518–446/438 B.C.) The greatest lyric poet of ancient Greece, the master of epinicia (triumphal odes), choral odes, and hymns in honor of gods or that celebrated victories in games as well as battles. Seventeen volumes of his poetry were known to the ancient world, but of these only four volumes with 44 fragments have survived. The extant fragments fall into four divisions: Olympian, Pythian, Isthmian, and Nemean, named after the games, each in honor of the god whose festival was being celebrated. Pindar's metrical range is exceptionally wide, and he shows consummate mastery of intricate techniques.

Xenophon (431–350 B.C.) Greek historian. He grew up in ancient Greece during the great war between Athens and Sparta and served in the elite cavalry force. Around 400 B.C. he was exiled and thereafter served as a mercenary in Persia under Cyrus, an experience he memorialized in *Anabasis.* Later he served in Asia Minor under the Spartan king Agesilaus II, who at the Battle of Coronea defeated Athens. Xenophon's banishment was revoked around 365, and he returned to Athens. In addition to *Anabasis,* the eyewitness history for which he is known, he also wrote *On Horsemanship, Cavalry Officer, On Hunting, Cyropaedia* (on Emperor Cyrus), *Hieron* (a fictitious dialogue between a king and a poet), and *The Constitution of Sparta.*

Aeschylus (525/524–456/455 B.C.) The first of the classical Greek dramatists, he transformed tragic drama from a static and choral recitation to its present form. He developed dialogue, introduced action, and used dramatic form to express a tragic vision of life. After fighting in the Persian wars, he entered many dramatic competitions and won for the first time in 484 B.C. Twelve years later he produced his first play, *Persians,* based on his experiences on the battlefields. He was at the court of King Hieron I at Syracuse, Sicily, twice during the next 29 years. During the Dionysian festival of 467 B.C. he produced the Oedipus trilogy, including *Seven Against Thebes;* he wrote the *Oresteia* trilogy (comprising *Agamemnon, Libation Bearers,* and *Eumenides*) in 458. He wrote approximately 90 plays, of which 80 are known and seven (*Persians, Seven Against Thebes, Suppliants, Oresteia,* and *Prometheus Bound*) have survived in their entirety. Aeschylus's plays are marked by their majestic, emotionally intense and lyrical language, the intricate architecture of the plots, and universal themes.

Euripides (484–406 B.C.) One of the three great Greek playwrights. He competed in all of the 22 dramatic festivals held in honor of Dionysus and won his first victory in 441 B.C. In 408 he left for the court of Archelaus, king of Macedonia, and died two years later. He is believed to have composed 92 plays, of which 19 have survived, including *Medea* (431), *Hippolytus* (428), *Electra* (418), *Trojan Women* (415), *Ion* (413), *Iphigenia at Aulis* (406), and *Bacchae* (406). In his plays Euripides transformed mythological figures into ordinary people responding to crises and tragedies. He was both rationalistic and iconoclastic, depicting gods as petulant and capricious. Most of the suffering in his plays stems from flaws of character (hamartia), uncontrolled passion, and hubris. His plays are characterized by some structural innovations such as the use of prologues, the providential ap-

pearance of a god (deus ex machina), a monologue at the beginning and an epilogue at the end. Toward the end of his career, he dispensed with the use of a chorus in his plays. After 415 B.C. his lyrics became emotionally luxuriant and unsurpassed in beauty and power.

Sophocles (496–406 B.C.) One of the three great Greek playwrights. His career began with his first victory in a poetic contest in 468 B.C., defeating Aeschylus. He wrote 123 plays and won major dramatic competitions. Only seven of his tragedies—*Ajax, Antigone, Trachiniae, Oedipus Rex, Electra, Philoctetes,* and *Oedipus at Colonus,*—have survived in their entirety. All seven represent his mature years, but only the last two have certain dates. Sophocles introduced many innovations to Greek drama, such as the addition of a third actor on the stage and a larger chorus. Sophocles was a well-loved public figure who took an active part in Athenian politics as a colleague of the statesman Pericles. Many of his plays are marked by supple language, superb artistry, and vivid characterizations that make them the epitome of Greek drama.

Aristophanes (450–388 B.C.) Greatest comic dramatist of ancient Greece. He began his career in 427 B.C. and wrote about 40 plays in all, of which 11—*Acharnians, Clouds, Wasps, Peace, Birds, Lysistrata, Women at the Thesmophoria, Frogs, Knights, Women at the Ecclesia,* and *Wealth*—have survived intact. An early comedy, *Babylonians,* exists in fragments. Most of Aristophanes' plays deal with the Peloponnesian War and its aftermath. They are the best representatives of the Old Comedy characterized by chorus, mime, burlesque, fantasy, invective, licentious political humor, and satire. The brilliance of his comic scenes and witty dialogue have rarely been equaled.

Herodotus (484–430/420 B.C.) First Greek historian of note. His celebrated *History* of the Greek-Persian wars was probably published in 425 B.C. He was a resident of Athens but is believed to have left for Thurii, a Greek colony in southern Italy. Despite its many factual errors, his *History* is the best source of information on a critical period of Greek history between 550 and 479 B.C.

Thucydides (454–399 B.C.) Greatest historian of the ancient world and author of *History of the Peloponnesian War,* recounting the struggle between Athens and Sparta. Although he fought in that war, upon his failure to thwart the capture of Amphipolis by the Spartan general Brasidas, he was recalled from the field, tried, and exiled. He later joined Sparta, and his exile ended 20 years later with the fall of Athens and the peace of 404. He spent most of his exile writing his monumental history, which is not merely a record of events but also a personal memoir and a detailed chronicle.

Aristotle (384–322 B.C.) Philosopher, one of the towering intellectuals of the ancient world, whose influence was transmitted from the classical period to medieval and modern times. Born in Stagira in Chalcidice (thus he was dubbed "the Stagirite"), he was associated with the Athenian Academy of Plato for 20 years, from 367. On Plato's death he began his peripatetic journeys, establishing new academies in Assus and Mytilene. For three years he lived at Pella, the capital of Macedonia, where he tutored Alexander the Great. In 335 he returned to Athens, where he opened the Lyceum, an institution modeled on Plato's Academy. In the field of literature his most influential work was *Poetics,* a long treatise on poetry and drama in which he codified Greek poetic traditions.

Plato (428/427–348/347 B.C.) Philosopher who developed a system of philosophic thought now known as Platonism. A disciple of Socrates, he fled Athens after the execution of his mentor in 399 but returned in 387 to found the famous Academy at Athens, which trained a generation of philosophers. He presided over the Academy for the rest of his life except for a brief period when he went to Sicily as the tutor of Dionysius II. Most of his writings are in the form of dialogues that tend to emphasize the moral aspects of a text. He was also the first literary critic, providing a commentary on other writers and teachers. His works, listed in their traditional order, are *Euthyphoron, Apology, Crito, Phaedo, Cratylus, Theaetetus, Sophist, Statesman, Parmedides, Philebus, Symposium, Phaedrus, Alcibiades, Hipparchus, Lovers, Charmides, Laches, Lysis, Euthymdemus, Protagoras, Gorgias, Meno, Hippias Major, Hippias Minor, Menexeums, Republic, Timeaus, Critias, Nomoi,* and *Epinomis.*

Menander (342–292 B.C.) Athenian playwright, considered the chief representative of the New Comedy, which featured characters from ordinary life such as stern fathers, young lovers, greedy prostitutes, and plotting slaves. Actors' masks were retained but the chorus performed only during interludes. Menander wrote more than 100 plays, of which the titles of more than 80 are known, and he enjoyed eight victories in Athenian dramatic festivals. His career began with his first play, *Anger,* in 321 B.C. He won his first prize in 316 with *Misanthrope* (also known as *Dyskolos,* his only play for which the complete text exists) and gained his first victory at the Dionysian festival the following year. Fragments of many of Menander's plays have been recovered and published, including *The Woman of Samos, The Shield,* and *The Man She Hated.* Through the Roman playwrights Plautus (254–184) and Terence, Menander influenced the modern comedies of manners.

Callimachus (305–240 B.C.) Poet of the Alexandrian school and librarian of the great Alexandrian Library in Egypt. Of his voluminous writings, only fragments survive. His

most famous poetical work is *Causes* (270 B.C.), a narrative elegy in four books containing a medley of obscure mythological tales. Of his elegies the best known is the *Lock of Berenice*. His other works include *Iambi,* containing 13 short poems; *Hecale,* an epic; *Ibis,* a polemical poem; *Hymns,* modeled on the Homeric hymns; and the *Epigrams,* of which some 60 survive. Of his prose works, the most famous is the *Tablets* in 120 books. It is an elaborate catalog of the authors of the works held in the Library of Alexandria.

Theocritus (310–250 B.C.) The creator of pastoral poetry, Theocritus was born in Sicily but lived at various times in Rhodes, Cos, and Alexandria. His surviving corpus consists of bucolics (writings on shepherds and herdsmen, typical of rural life) set in the country and epics, lyrics, and epigrams set in towns. His bucolics were the precursors of Virgil's *Eclogues* and much of the poetry and drama of the Renaissance as well as more modern poems such as John Milton's *Lycidas,* Percy Bysshe Shelley's *Adonais,* and Matthew Arnold's *Thyrsis.* Two of his idylls are still read: *Thyrsis,* a lament for Daphnis, and *Harvest Festival,* set in Cos.

Sappho of Lesbos (610–580 B.C.) Celebrated lyric poet much admired for the beauty of her language. The principal themes of her poems are love, jealousy, and hate, usually among a select circle of women. Her works include wedding songs and erotic poems. In the third or second centuries B.C. her poems were published in nine volumes, but they have not survived. Some of her poems are available in fragments, but she is read mostly in quotations by other ancient Greek authors.

Major Roman Authors

Virgil or **Vergil (Publius Vergilius Maro)** (70–19 B.C.) Greatest Roman poet, best known for his epic *Aeneid.* His first major work was the *Eclogues* (42–37 B.C.), a collection of 10 pastoral poems that glorified the Augustan Age. It was followed by *Georgics* (37–30 B.C.), a vision of a new golden age of Rome. His masterpiece, *Aeneid,* celebrates the birth of Rome and is also a tribute to Augustus.

Horace (Quintus Horatius Flaccus) (65–8 B.C.) Outstanding Roman lyric poet, best known for his *Odes* and *Epistles.* Horace was deeply involved in Roman politics at the time between the murder of Julius Caesar and the rise of Emperor Augustus. During this period Horace wrote Book I of the *Satires,* 10 poems in hexameter verse published in 35 B.C. He published *Epodes* in 31 and a second book of eight *Satires* in 30–29. Then he turned to the *Odes,* publishing three

books, containing 88 short poems in 23. The third, the *Epistle to the Pisos,* was known subsequently as *Ars poetica.* By this time Horace had established his reputation as the poet laureate of Rome. In 17 B.C. he composed his *Secular Hymns* and in the next four years he completed a fourth book of 15 *Odes.* The *Odes* and the *Ars poetica* were greatly admired in the Middle Ages and have exerted a profound influence on Western poets.

Ovid (Publius Ovidius Naso) (43 B.C.–A.D. 17) Roman poet noted for *Ars amatoria* (The Art of Love) and *Metamorphoses. Ars amatoria* comprises three books of mock didactic elegiacs on the art of seduction and intrigue. *Metamorphoses* was a poetical collection in 15 books of mythological and legendary stories in which transformation plays a role. Ovid described his life in his autobiographical poems *Tristia* (Sorrows), an apt title that captured the vicissitudes of a life that began auspiciously in Rome and ended in Tomi, on the Black Sea, where he was exiled on the orders of Emperor Augustus in A.D. 8. His first work, *Amores* (Loves), a series of short poems, was followed by *Epistle to the Heroines,* dramatic monologues, *Ars amatoria,* and *Remedia amoris.* By this time Ovid was recognized as the leading poet of his day, and he turned to his last masterpieces, *Metamorphoses* and *Fasti.* Ovid was an accomplished poet whose imaginative interpretations of classical myths have had immense influence on the Western mind.

Juvenal (Decimus Junius Juvenalis) (A.D. 55/60–127) Roman satiric poet. Juvenal's 16 *Satires* dealt mainly with life in Rome under the Roman emperors from Domitian to Hadrian. They were published at intervals in five books. Forgotten after the decline of Rome, Juvenal's work was revived by Christian writers and thereafter has been studied and admired.

Cicero (Marcus Tullius Cicero) (106–43 B.C.) Roman statesman, orator, lawyer, and writer. Although better known as the greatest Roman orator, Cicero was a prolific writer whose works include books of rhetoric, philosophical and political treatises, and letters. He was also a staunch republican, and he paid the price for his political principles when he was executed by Octavian, later Emperor Augustus. Cicero's writings include *De oratore* (On the Orator) (55 B.C.), *On the State* (52), *Brutus* and *Orator* (46), *On the Different Conceptions of the Chief Good and Evil* (45), and *The Tusculan Disputations, On the Nature of Gods,* and *On Duties* (44). Some 900 of his letters, 58 speeches, and fragments of his poems have also survived.

Seneca (Lucius Annaeus) (4 B.C.–A.D. 65) Roman philosopher and tragedian, the leading intellectual and one of the towering political figures in the post–Augustan Age. In

A.D. 31 he began a career in politics and law but was banished by Emperor Claudius to Corsica on charges of adultery with the emperor's niece. He was recalled to Rome in 59 to become tutor to the future emperor Nero. The murder of Claudius in 54 pushed Seneca to the forefront as a favorite of Nero, the new emperor, and for the next eight years he was a virtual coruler of Rome. He retired in 62 and in his remaining three years wrote the works for which he is known. In A.D. 65 he was denounced as a party to the conspiracy of Piso to assassinate Nero and was forced to commit suicide. Apart from one political skit (*The Pumpkinification of the Divine Claudius*), Seneca mainly wrote brilliant essays on a range of moral problems. They include *De ira* (On Anger), *De clementia* (On Clemency), *De tranquillitate animi* (On Tranquility of the Soul), *De otio* (On Leisure), *De beneficiis* (On Benefits), and 124 essays called *Moral Epistles*. He also wrote nine tragedies, of which *Thyestes* is the best known.

Terence (195–159 B.C.) One of the greatest Roman playwrights, the father of the comedy of manners. During his short life he produced six plays: *The Woman of Andros* (166 B.C.), *The Mother-in-Law* (165), *The Self-Tormentor* (163), *The Eunuch* and *Phormio* (161), and *The Brothers* (160). Although he drew most of his themes from the Greek playwrights, he shows both originality and skill in his dialogue and psychological insights.

Tacitus (**Publius** or **Gaius Cornelius Tacitus**) (A.D. 56–120) Greatest Roman historian. Tacitus's fame is based on four works: *The Life of Julius Agricola* (his father-in-law), *Germania*, *Historiae* (Histories), and *Annales* (Annals). *Germania* describes the people of the Roman frontier on the Rhine. *Histories* originally contained 12 books, of which only five survive, that dealt with the history of Rome from Nero to Domitian. *Annals* covered the earlier period from Augustus to Nero. Tacitus's writings are marked by vigor, rhythm, and color.

Lucan (**Marcus Annaeus Lucanus**) (A.D. 39–65) Poet, the author of *Pharsalia*, major Latin epic poem that eschewed mythology. He was for a time a favorite of Nero, but when Nero banned him from reciting his poetry, Lucan became one of the leaders of a conspiracy to assassinate Nero. When the conspiracy was discovered, Lucan committed suicide. *Pharsalia* is his only poem. It deals with the Battle of Pharsalus between Julius Caesar and Pompey the Great. Lucan was immensely popular in the Middle Ages.

Catullus (**Gaius Valerius Catullus**) (84–54 B.C.) One of the finest poets in ancient Rome, he is the author of some 40 poems recording his emotional crises, such as the death of a brother, a passionate love affair with a woman called Claudia, and an affair with a male youth named Juventius. His lyrics display an extraordinary versatility and passion.

Key World Events of the Classical Age

B.C.

553-529 Cyrus the Great of Persia conquers Lydia, the Medes, and Babylonia, transforming Persia into a vast empire; his successor, Darius, divides empire into 20 satrapies
c. 510 Rome is declared a republic
500 High point of Etruscan civilization
480 Siddhārtha Gautama founds Buddhism
449 Greek states defeat Persia at Salamis
c. 450 Beginning of the Gupta Empire in India. The Periclean age blooms in Greece
431–404 Peloponnesian War between Athens and Sparta
356 Alexander the Great is born
335 Alexander the Great begins his conquests in Asia and extends the Greek Empire up to the Indus River
319 Candragupta Maurya founds the Maurya dynasty in India
264–241 The First Punic War between Rome and Carthage marks the ascendancy of Rome
221–206 The Qin dynasty in China
202 Liu Bang assumes imperial title in China and founds Han dynasty
146 Rome destroys Carthage at the end of the Punic War. Greece comes under Roman control
90 Civil war in Rome between Marius and Sulla
49–47 Rivalry between Pompey and Julius Caesar for Rome ends in defeat of Pompey
45 Caesar becomes dictator and adopts Gaius Octavius (Octavian) as heir
44 Caesar is assassinated by conspirators led by Brutus and Cassius Longinus
42 Brutus and Cassius are defeated by the Second Triumvirate led by Mark Antony, Marcus Aemilius Lepidus, and Octavian
31 In the Battle of Actium, Mark Antony and Cleopatra, queen of Egypt, are defeated by Octavian; Egypt is annexed by the Romans
6 Judea is annexed by Rome
4 Birth of Jesus at Bethlehem

A.D.

25 Later Han dynasty is founded in China
33 Crucifixion of Jesus
43 Romans invade and conquer Britain
45 St. Paul sets out on his missionary travels
58 Emperor Mingdi introduces Buddhism into China
98 Under Emperor Trajan (98–116) the Roman Empire reaches its greatest extent with the conquest of Dacia

9TH/8TH CENTURY B.C.

BIRTH/DEATH
Homer, Greek poet

675 B.C.

BIRTH
Archilocus, Greek poet

635

DEATH
Archilocus, Greek poet

620

BIRTH
Alcaeus, Greek lyric poet

610

BIRTH
Sappho of Lesbos, Greek lyric poet

580

DEATHS
Alcaeus, Greek lyric poet
Sappho, Greek lyric poet

560

BIRTH
Xenophanes, Greek playwright

525/524

BIRTH
Aeschylus, Greek playwright

522/518

BIRTH
Pindar, Greek lyric poet

496

BIRTH
Sophocles, Greek playwright

484

BIRTHS
Euripides, Greek playwright
Herodotus, Greek historian

478

DEATH
Xenophanes, Greek playwright

463

PUBLICATION
                                    GREEK
Suppliants Play by Aeschylus

458

PUBLICATION
                                    GREEK
Oresteia Play by playwright Aeschylus

456/455

DEATH
Aeschylus, Greek playwright

454

BIRTH
Thucydides, Greek historian

450

BIRTH
Aristophanes, Greek playwright

446/438

DEATH
Pindar, Greek lyric poet

445

BIRTH
Agathon, Greek tragic poet and playwright

431

BIRTH
Xenophon, Greek historian

PUBLICATION
GREEK
Medea Play by Euripides

430/420

DEATH
Herodotus, Greek historian

428

BIRTH
Plato, Greek philosopher

PUBLICATION
GREEK
Hippolytus Play by Euripides

423

PUBLICATION
GREEK
Clouds Play by Aristophanes

421

PUBLICATION
GREEK
Peace Comedy by Aristophanes

418

PUBLICATION
GREEK
Electra Play by Euripides

415

PUBLICATION
GREEK
Trojan Women Play by Euripides

413

PUBLICATION
GREEK
Ion Play by Euripides

412

PUBLICATION
GREEK
Helen Play by Euripides

409

PUBLICATION
GREEK
Philoctetes Play by Sophocles

408

PUBLICATION

GREEK

Orestes Play by Euripides

406

DEATHS

Euripides, Greek playwright
Sophocles, Greek playwright

PUBLICATION

GREEK

Iphigenia at Aulis, Bacchae Plays by Euripides

405

BIRTH

Ephorus, Greek historian

400

DEATH

Agathon, Greek tragic poet and playwright

399

DEATH

Thucydides, Greek historian

388

DEATH

Aristophanes, Greek playwright

384

BIRTH

Aristotle, Greek philosopher

350

DEATH

Xenophon, Greek historian

348/347

DEATH

Plato, Greek philosopher

343

BIRTH

Qu Yuan, Chinese poet

342

BIRTH

Menander, Greek playwright

330

DEATH

Ephorus, Greek historian

322

DEATH

Aristotle, Greek philosopher

310

BIRTH

Theocritus, Greek poet

305

BIRTH

Callimachus, Greek poet

295

BIRTH
Apollonius of Rhodes, Greek poet

292

DEATH
Menander, Greek playwright

284

BIRTH
Livius Andronicus, Roman poet and playwright

278

DEATH
Qu Yuan, Chinese poet

254

BIRTH
Plautus, Roman playwright

250

DEATH
Theocritus, Greek poet

240

DEATH
Callimachus, Greek poet

239

BIRTH
Quintus Ennius, Roman poet and playwright

217

BIRTH
Aristarchus, Greek critic

204

DEATH
Livius Andronicus, Roman poet and playwright

195

BIRTH
Terence, Roman comic playwright

184

DEATH
Plautus, Roman playwright

170

BIRTH
Lucius Accius, Roman tragic playwright

169

DEATH
Quintus Ennius, Roman poet

166

PUBLICATION
LATIN
The Woman of Andros Play by Terence

159

DEATH
Terence, Roman comic playwright

145

DEATH
Aristarchus, Greek critic

116

BIRTH
Marcus Terentius Varro, Roman scholar

109

BIRTH
Titus Pomponius Atticus, Roman patron and man of letters

106

BIRTH
Cicero, Roman writer and orator

86

BIRTH
Sallust, Roman historian

DEATH
Lucius Accius, Roman tragic poet

84

BIRTH
Catullus, Roman poet

70

BIRTH
Virgil, Roman poet

65

BIRTH
Horace, Roman poet

59

BIRTH
Livy, Roman historian

55

BIRTHS
Tibullus, Roman poet
Sextus Propertius, Roman poet

PUBLICATION

LATIN
On the Orator by Cicero

54

DEATH
Catullus, Roman poet

52

PUBLICATION

LATIN
On the State Treatise by Roman statesman Cicero

43

BIRTH
Ovid, Roman poet

DEATH
Cicero, Roman orator and writer

35

DEATH
Sallust, Roman historian

32

DEATH
Titus Pomponius Atticus, Roman patron of letters

29/19

PUBLICATION

LATIN

Aeneid Epic poem by Roman poet Virgil

27

DEATH

Marcus Terentius Varro, Roman scholar

19

DEATHS

Tibullus, Roman poet
Virgil, Roman poet

PUBLICATION

LATIN

Ars poetica by Roman poet Horace

16

DEATH

Sextus Propertius, Roman poet

8

DEATH

Horace, Roman poet

4

BIRTH

Seneca, Roman moral philosopher

1 B.C.

PUBLICATION

LATIN

Ars amatoria Poem by Roman poet Ovid

A.D. 17

DEATHS

Livy, Roman historian
Ovid, Roman poet

23

BIRTH

Pliny the Elder, Roman scholar

35

BIRTH

Quintilian, Roman writer

39

BIRTH

Lucan, Roman poet

40

BIRTH

Martial, Roman poet

45

BIRTH

Publius Papinius Statius, Roman poet

46

BIRTH

Plutarch, Greek historian

55/60

BIRTH

Juvenal, Roman poet

56

BIRTH
Tacitus, Roman historian

60

PUBLICATION

LATIN

Thyestes Play by Seneca

61/62

BIRTH
Pliny the Younger, Roman writer and statesman

65

DEATHS
Lucan, Roman poet
Seneca, Roman philosopher

69

BIRTH
Suetonius, Roman historian

79

DEATH
Pliny the Elder, Roman scholar

80

BIRTH
Aśvaghosa, Indian philosopher and poet

96

DEATH
Publius Papinius Statius, Roman poet

100

DEATH
Quintilian, Roman writer

THE MIDDLE AGES
(100–1500)

The dates for the Middle Ages are somewhat fluid, but generally the period spans roughly from the end of the Augustan Age in Rome to the end of the 15th century. The establishment of Christianity throughout Europe during this period meant that the moral underpinnings of society and culture shifted dramatically in relation to the classical age. In the West, the fusion of Christian theology and classical philosophy formed the basis of the medieval habit of interpreting life symbolically. Through the writings of St. Augustine, platonic and Christian thought were reconciled, and the world of Greek and Roman literature, in which natural emotions and passions were dominant, was displaced to make room for the Christian ideal of sacramental life serving as a symbol of eternal spiritual truths. The exegetical, or interpretative, methods the early Christians applied to the Scriptures were extended to all forms of literature. Thus Virgil's *Aeneid* became a narrative of the soul's journey to paradise and was reborn in Dante's own journey (with Virgil as a guide during his journey through the inferno) in the *Divine Comedy.*

The Christian church not only established the purpose of literature but also preserved it through its monastic copyists. Saint Benedict's monastery in Monte Cassino, Italy, was established in 529, and other centers of scholarship followed, particularly after the sixth- and seventh-century Irish missions to the Rhine and England, and Gothic missions up the Danube were established. These monasteries preserved the only classical literature then available to the West, especially because Latin literature took precedence over vernacular literature during most of the period. Saint Augustine's *City of God,* the Venerable Bede's *Ecclesiastical History of the English Nation,* and the *Danish History* of Saxo Grammaticus were all written in Latin, as were the few works in philosophy, theology, history, and science.

The main literary achievements of the period are found in the vernacular works. The pre-Christian literature of Europe belonged to an oral tradition that grew out of the *Poetic Edda*

and sagas, 13th-century heroic epics of Iceland. The *Prose Edda* (*Younger Edda*) and the *Poetic Edda* (*Elder Edda*) are the fullest and most detailed sources for modern knowledge of Germanic mythology. The Anglo-Saxon *Beowulf* and the German *Song of Hildebrand* belonged to a common Germanic poetic tradition but were first recorded by Christian scribes at dates later than the historical events they relate. Their pagan elements were fused with an overlay of Christian thought and feeling. Numerous ballads in different countries also reflect an earlier native tradition of oral recitation. Among the best known of the many genres that arose in medieval vernacular literatures were the romance and the courtly love lyrics, mostly French in origin. Romances such as *Song of Roland* used classical or Arthurian sources in poetic narrative, replacing the heroic epics with a chivalrous tale of knightly valor. In them complex themes of love and loyalty were interwoven with the theme of a spiritual quest. The love lyric, similarly, has a heterogeneous background. The idealized lady and her languishing lover are found, imitated, and interpreted in every European culture, from the French troubadours to the German minnesingers.

Medieval drama grew out of the religious ceremonies of the Catholic Church, and the dramatic nature of Mass lent itself to elaboration in the form of gestures and mime, and later of dramatic interpolations. The elaboration gradually increased until drama became a secular affair performed on stages or carts in town streets or open squares. (The players were guild craftsmen who were engaged in other, more lucrative jobs when not acting.) Three types of plays developed: the mystery of salvation, the miracle of healing, and the morality play. One of the best-known morality plays, *Everyman,* was actually translated from the Dutch. The majority of medieval literature was written anonymously and not easily dated. The great names of medieval literature are important not merely in themselves but as precursors of the literary blossoming of the 16th century.

Much of the literature in the Middle and later Middle Ages came from outside Europe. Muslims consider the medieval period their golden age, since their culture, which included well-known scholars, philosophers, and poets, went into a steep decline after the rise of European powers in the 16th century. In India, Hindu literature flourished in the early centuries of the Christian era before Muslim power was firmly established in the north. In both Japan and China, important literary traditions were established and new genres took shape in poetry and drama.

Major Authors of the Middle Ages

Dante Alighieri (1265–1321) The greatest Italian poet and perhaps the greatest Christian poet, Dante is best known for his monumental epic poem the *Divine Comedy* (c. 1308–21). His writings reveal much about his life. He was born in Florence and began writing sonnets in his late 20s. In 1302 he was exiled from Florence by his enemies and spent much of his remaining life in Ravenna. The turning point in his life came when—already married to Gemma Donati—he discovered a spiritual love for Beatrice Portinari: Although Beatrice died in 1290, she remained his ideal and the inspiration for his poetry. The three-part *Divine Comedy* (at first called simply *Comedy; Divine* was added much later, around 1555) was possibly begun about 1308 and completed just before his death in 1321. It is a story of a man's journey through hell, purgatory, and paradise, led by two guides: Virgil through *Inferno* and *Purgatory* and Beatrice through *Paradise*. By 1400 the work was acknowledged as that of a supreme genius, and Dante himself became known as the divine poet. Besides *Divine Comedy,* Dante wrote two collections of verse, *The New Life* (1293) and the *Banquet* (1304–7); a treatise on language, *Concerning Vernacular Eloquence* (1304–7); and *On Monarchy* (1313).

Geoffrey Chaucer (1342/43–1400) English poet whose *The Canterbury Tales* is one of the outstanding poetic works in Middle English. Little is known of his early life except that he served in the army in France with Edward III, who ransomed him after he was captured at the Siege of Reims in 1359. Thereafter Chaucer held a succession of diplomatic and government positions. His first book of poems was *Book of the Duchess* (1369), an elegy for Blanche, the duchess of Lancaster and the first wife of John of Gaunt. A number of dream visions and poems followed: *Hous of Fame,* a narrative poem; *The Parlement of Foules,* a poem in which the narrator falls asleep and dreams about a courtly love among eagles; *Troilus and Creseyde,* a romance; and *Legend of Good Women,* a dream vision. During the 1390s he began *The Canterbury Tales,* a collection of 24 tales told by pilgrims on their way to the shrine of Thomas à Becket in Canterbury. It was unfinished at his death.

Petrarch (Francesco Petrarca) (1304–74) Italian poet and humanist, considered the greatest scholar of his age. After his father's death he moved to Avignon, where he took minor ecclesiastical orders and entered the household of a cardinal. This period marks the beginning of his chaste love for a woman named Laura, who inspired many of his later poems. In 1337 he left Avignon for Vaucluse, where he produced many of his masterpieces. In 1341 he went to Rome to be crowned as a poet but continued to travel for the next 16 years before settling near Padua. For his combining humanism and Christianity, Petrarch is hailed as a forerunner of the Renaissance. His most important works include the Latin poem *Africa* (1338); the autobiographical *Petrarch's Secret* (1342–58); *On Illustrious Men* (1337); *Books on Matters to Be Remembered* (1342–43); *On Religious Idleness* (1345–47); *Bucolic Song* (1345–47); *The Life of Solitude* (1345–47); and *Metrical Epistles* (1345).

Giovanni Boccaccio (1313–1375) Italian poet, best known as the author of the *Decameron*. From 1328 to 1345 he was in Naples, where he wrote the poems *Diana's Hunt, Love Struck* (1338), *The Amorous Vision* (1342–43), and *Tale of the Fiesole Nymph* (1344–45) and the prose works *Elegy on Madonna Fiammetta* (1343–44), *Ameto's Story of the Nymphs* (1341–45), and *The Love Afflicted* (1336). He composed the *Decameron,* a group of 100 stories told by 10 characters fleeing plague-stricken Florence, between 1349 and 1353. It is one of the best examples of classic Italian prose. Boccaccio met the poet Petrarch in Florence in 1350, and thereafter he no longer wrote in Italian but instead turned to Latin. His Latin works include *On the Genealogy of the Gods of the Gentiles* (1350), *Bucolicum carmen* (1351–66), *Concerning Famous Women* (1360–74), and *On the Fates of Famous Men* (1355–74). Later in life he wrote a biography of Dante.

Bede, the Venerable (672/673–735) Anglo-Saxon historian, best known for his *Ecclesiastical History of the English Nation,* the first history of the Anglo-Saxon people and their conversion to Christianity. Bede was a priest at the Monastery of St. Paul at Jarrow. He completed his *Ecclesiastical History* in 731–32. Divided into five books, it recorded English history from the time of Julius Caesar and was based on the "traditions of our forefathers" and his own knowledge of contemporary events. Besides this major work, he wrote two works on chronology, *On Time* and *On the Reckoning of Time.*

Kālidāsa (c. 5th century) Sanskrit poet and dramatist, the greatest Indian writer up to the 20th century. He is believed to have lived sometime before 634. Many works are traditionally ascribed to him, but only six are accepted as genuine: *Abhijñānaśakuntala* (The Recognition of Śakuntalā), *Vikramorvaśī* (Urvasi Won by Valor), *Mālavikāgnimitra* (Malavika and Agnimitra), *Raghuvamśa* (The Dynasty of

Raghu), *Kumarāsambhava* (Birth of the War God), and "Meghadūta," (Cloud Messenger). Of these, the play *Abhijñānaśakuntala* was his supreme achievement and became the standard by which all later Indian works were judged. Kālidāsa was a master of the literary genre *kavya,* metrical stanzas replete with rich imagery.

Jalāl ad-Dīn ar-Rūmī (1207–1273) The greatest Sufi mystic and poet in the Persian language, best known for his didactic epic *Spiritual Couplets,* which widely influenced Muslim culture through the centuries. After his death, his followers were organized as the Mawlawīyah Order, known as the Whirling Dervishes in the West. Rūmī was a theologian and teacher in Anatolia, a part of modern-day Turkey. In 1244 he met the wandering dervish Shams ad-Dīn of Tabriz, who revealed to him divine mysteries and became his mentor. When Shams was murdered, Rūmī turned to poetry to fill the loss and composed, while in states of trance or ecstasy, 30,000 verses and a large number of rubaiyat (quatrains) under the title *Divan-e-Shams* (The Collected Poetry of Shams), in honor of his mentor and lover. He formed similar attachments to two other illiterate teachers, Salah ad-Dīn Zarkub and Husam ad-Dīn Chelebi. *Spiritual Couplets,* which contains 26,000 couplets, was composed under the latter's influence.

Du Fu (Tu Fu) (712–770) The greatest Chinese poet of all time, Du Fu spent much of his life as a traveler and minor court official. His early poetry celebrated the beauties of the natural world, but his personal hardships and the national turmoil of his times led him to write bitterly later about war and the senselessness of violence. Du Fu's commanding position in Chinese letters is due to his mastery of the medium and the techniques, including the use of all the connotative overtones of a phrase and the intonational potentials of individual words as spoken. His *lushi,* or "regulated verse," has a glowing intensity that few other Chinese poets have been able to match. Because his multilayered and rich imagery cannot be properly translated from Chinese, however, he has not received his due recognition in the West.

Zeami Motokiyo (1363/1364–1443) Japanese Nō playwright, the greatest theorist of the Nō theater and the creator of the Nō drama in its present form. Working under the patronage of the shogun Ashikaga Yoshimitsu, Zeami directed the Kanze theatrical school that his father had established. Zeami both wrote the plays and performed in them. He is credited with 90 of the 230 plays in the present Nō repertoire. In 1422 he became a Zen monk. Zeami wrote a manual for Nō theater known as *The Transmission of the Flower of Acting Style* (1400–18), which sets forth the guiding principles of the Nō drama. Foremost among these principles was *yugen,* an ineffable and ethereal beauty of language, as found, for example, in Zeami's *Wind in the Pines.*

Murasaki Shikibu (978–1026?) Japanese courtier who authored of *Tales of the Genji,* generally considered one of the world's oldest and greatest novels. Murasaki (also the name of the heroine in the novel) was a lady at the court of the empress Akiko. The story, written between 1001 and 1005, focuses on the loves of Prince Genji with the various women in his life. Pervading the work is the Buddhist sense of the vanity of this world.

Key World Events of the Middle Ages

105	Cai Lun invents the world's first lightweight writing material, later known as paper
132	Bar Kokhba leads the last great Jewish revolt against the Romans
150	Ptolemy, the Alexandrian mathematician, completes the *Almagest,* a cosmology
220	Civil wars bring to an end the Han dynasty in China
224	Sassanids conquer Persia after capturing Ctesiphon and overthrowing the Parthians
285	Emperor Diocletian divides the Roman Empire into the Eastern Empire and the Western Empire
313	Edict of Milan makes Christianity lawful throughout the Roman Empire
320	Gupta dynasty is founded in the Ganges Valley
330	Constantinople is made capital of the Roman Empire
350	Pallava dynasty is established in southern India with Kanchipuram as capital
c. 390	Jerome prepares the Vulgate, the oldest complete version of the Bible, translated into Latin from Greek
432	Saint Patrick arrives in Ireland
451	Huns invade Gaul, but Attila is repulsed after failing to capture Rome
476	The Western Roman Empire collapses as the last emperor, Romulus, is deposed by the invading Ostrogoths
496	Clovis, king of the Franks, and all his subjects are baptized, laying the foundation of European Christendom
527	Justinian becomes Byzantine emperor
529	First Benedictine monastery is founded at Monte Cassino in Italy
563	Columba founds celebrated monastery at Iona
568	The Lombards invade Italy, the last Barbarian tribe to do so
581	Sui dynasty reunites China under Yang Jian
590	Gregory the Great is elected pope
597	Augustine begins Christian mission in England and is consecrated the first Archbishop of Canterbury
618	The Tang dynasty is founded in China
622	Muhammad flees from Mecca to Medina with his followers, marking the beginning of Islam
637	Arab armies overrun Persia, Egypt, Palestine, Syria, Mesopotamia, and all Roman provinces in Asia and Africa
661	Umayyad caliphate is founded

710	Japan builds a permanent capital at Nara
711	Muslims overthrow the Visigothic kingdom in Spain
732	Charles Martel defeats the Arabs at Poitiers
750	Abbasid caliphate takes control of the Arab Empire after Abu al-Abbas murders the last Umayyad caliph
768	Charlemagne the Great ascends to the Carolingian throne on the death of Pepin the Short
794	Heian period opens in Japan as the Fujiwara clan seizes imperial power
800	Charlemagne is crowned Roman emperor; Holy Roman Empire begins
843	Treaty of Verdun breaks up the Carolingian Empire
868	China produces the first printed book, the *Diamond Sutra*, made from movable type engraved on clay blocks
875	Vikings discover Iceland
888	Chola dynasty replaces the Pallavas in southern India
900	Toltecs gain ascendancy in Mexico after the fall of Teotihuacán
910	Burgundian Abbey is founded at Cluny, an important landmark in Western monasticism
960	Song dynasty under Zhao Kuangyin brings peace to China; Confucianism triumphs over Buddhism and Taoism
969	Fātimids found an independent caliphate in Egypt
980	Vladimir, prince of Kiev, is baptized as a Christian, marking the foundation of the Russian Orthodox Church
987	Hugh Capet becomes king of France, marking the beginning of modern France
1001	Stephen of Hungary is crowned, an act symbolizing the birth of modern Hungary
1010	Fātimid caliph Hākim the Mad destroys the Church of the Holy Sepulcher in Jerusalem, provoking the Crusades
1031	Caliphate of Cordoba collapses and Muslim Spain is fragmented into small, independent states
1066	Normans under William the Conqueror win the Battle of Hastings, thus establishing modern England
1071	At the Battle of Manzikert, Seljuk Turks rout the Byzantine army, capture the emperor, and gain control of Asia Minor
1085	Reconquest of Spain begins as Alfonso VI captures Toledo
1086	Normans undertake the first English census, compiling the Domesday Book
1095	Council of Claremont heeds Pope Urban II's call for a holy war, or crusade to recover Jerusalem
1098	Cistercian monastic order is founded
1147	National independence of Portugal is secured as Alfonso Henriques drives the Moors from Lisbon
1167	Italian cities defy Emperor Frederick Barbarossa and form the Lombard League
1169	Normans arrive in Ireland as Henry II lays claim to English overlordship of the island
1185	Kamakura period opens in Japan as power passes to the Minamoto military family
1206	First Muslim kingdom is established in India under Muhammad Ghūrī
1215	King John signs the Magna Carta at Runnymede, marking the beginning of the rule of law
1223	Pope Honorius III approves the Franciscan Order with Francis of Assisi as head
1241	Hanseatic League, a loose association of German merchant cities, is formed
1260	Kublai Khan establishes the Yuan dynasty in China, marking the greatest extent of the Mongol Empire
1260	Mamluks defeat the Mongols at Goliath Springs and take over Egypt and Syria
1271	Marco Polo sets out on his journey to China
1282	Edward I of England subdues and annexes Wales
1309	French popes make Avignon in France their headquarters, as papacy enters its Babylonian Captivity
1325	Aztecs make Tenochtitlán the capital of a new Mesoamerican empire that replaces the Toltecs
1334	Black Plague begins to sweep through Europe
1368	Zhu Yuanzhang drives the Mongols from Beijing and establishes the Ming dynasty
1389	Turks defeat a force of Serbians, Bulgarians, Bosnians, and Montenegrins at Kosovo Field in Serbia
1438	Habsburgs, the ruling house of Austria, inherit the imperial title of the Holy Roman Emperor
1438	Pachacuti establishes the Inca Empire in Peru
1453	Constantinople falls to the Ottomans after a long and bloody siege
1455	Wars of the Roses begin between the houses of York and Lancaster for mastery of England
1469	Aragon and Castile in Spain are united by the marriage of Ferdinand I of Aragon and Isabella of Castile, called the "Most Catholic Majesties"
1472	Ivan the Great, the grand duke of Moscow, takes the title of czar of all Russia
1480	Inquisition, an ecclesiastical tribunal against heretics, is established in Spain by Pope Sixtus IV at the request of Ferdinand and Isabella
1492	Christopher Columbus reaches the New World
1494	Treaty of Tordesillas divides the New World between Spain and Portugal
1497	John Cabot lands in Newfoundland, the first recorded landfall on North America
1498	Vasco da Gama, Portuguese navigator, reaches Calicut to become the first European to reach India by sea

103

DEATH
Martial, Roman poet

113

DEATH
Pliny the Younger, Roman writer

119

DEATH
Plutarch, Greek historian

120

BIRTH
Lucian, Greek satirist

DEATH
Tacitus, Roman historian

122

DEATH
Suetonius, Roman historian

127

DEATH
Juvenal, Roman poet

150

DEATH
Aśvaghosa, Indian philosopher and poet

170

BIRTH
Aelian, Roman writer

180

DEATH
Lucian, Greek satirist

192

BIRTH
Cao Zhi, Chinese poet

232

DEATH
Cao Zhi, Chinese poet

235

DEATH
Aelian, Roman writer

261

BIRTH
Lu Ji, Chinese literary critic

303

DEATH
Lu Ji, Chinese literary critic

348

BIRTH
Aurelius Clemens Prudentius, Roman Christian writer

353

BIRTH
Saint Paulinus of Nola, Roman Christian poet

354

BIRTH
Saint Augustine (Aurelius Augustinus), North African Christian
   theologian

365

BIRTH
Tao Qian, Chinese poet

370

BIRTH
Claudian, Roman poet

c. 400

Kālidāsa, Indian poet and dramatist

404

DEATH
Claudian, Roman poet

405

DEATH
Aurelius Clemens Prudentius, Roman Christian poet

413–426

PUBLICATION

LATIN
City of God Theological treatise by Saint Augustine

427

DEATH
Tao Qian, Chinese poet

430

DEATH
Saint Augustine, North African Christian theologian

431

DEATH
Saint Paulinus of Nola, Roman Christian poet

520

BIRTH
Zuhayr, Arab poet

540

BIRTH
Venantius Fortunatus, Roman poet

600

DEATH
Venantius Fortunatus, Roman poet

609

DEATH
Zuhayr, Arab poet

644

BIRTH
'Umar ibn Abī Rabī'ah, Arab poet

650

BIRTH
Jarīr (Jarīr ibn 'Atīyah ibn al-Khatafā), Arab poet

672

BIRTH
Bede (the Venerable Bede), English monk and historian

680

BIRTH
Kakinomoto Hitomaro, Japanese poet

710

DEATH
Kakinomoto Hitomaro, Japanese poet

712

BIRTH
Du Fu, Chinese poet

712/719

DEATH
'Umar ibn Abī Rabī'ah, Arab poet

715

BIRTH
Cen Shen, Chinese poet

729

DEATH
Jarīr (Jarīr ibn 'Atīyah ibn al-Khatfā), Arab poet

731/732

PUBLICATION
ENGLISH
Ecclesiastical History of the English Nation History by Bede (the Venerable Bede)

735

DEATH
Bede (the Venerable Bede), English monk and historian

c. 750

PUBLICATION
ENGLISH
Beowulf Anglo-Saxon epic poem of unknown authorship

768

BIRTH
Han Yu, Chinese writer

770

DEATHS
Cen Shen, Chinese poet
Du Fu, Chinese poet

772

BIRTH
Bo Juyi, Chinese poet

808

BIRTH
Walafrid Strabo, German poet and monk

824

DEATH
Han Yu, Chinese writer

835

PUBLICATION
ARABIC
Hamāsah Anthology by Arab poet Abū Tammām

846

DEATH
Bo Juyi, Chinese poet

849

DEATH
Walafrid Strabo, German monk and poet

859

BIRTH
Rūdakī, Persian poet

905

PUBLICATION
JAPANESE
Kokinshu Anthology of poems by Tsurayuki Ki

910

BIRTH
Egill Skallagrimsson, Icelandic poet

911

BIRTH
Minamoto Shitago, Japanese poet

915

BIRTHS
Hisdai ibn Shaprut, Spanish Jewish man of letters
al-Mutanabbī, Arab poet

935

BIRTH
Firdawsī, Persian poet

940/941

DEATH
Rūdakī, Persian poet

961

PUBLICATION
ICELANDIC
Loss of Sons Poem by Egill Skallagrimsson

965

DEATH
al-Mutanabbī, Arab poet

973

BIRTHS
al-Bīrūnī, Persian scholar
al-Ma'arrī, Arab poet

975

DEATH
Hisdai ibn Shaprut, Spanish Jewish man of letters

978

BIRTH
Murasaki Shikibu, Japanese writer

983

DEATH
Minamoto Shitago, Japanese poet

990

DEATH
Egill Skallagrimsson, Icelandic poet

1007

BIRTH
Ouyang Xiu, Chinese poet and historian

1010

PUBLICATION
PERSIAN
Shāh-nāmeh Epic poem by Firdawsī

1020

DEATH
Firdawsī, Persian poet

1021

BIRTH
Ibn Gabirol, Spanish Jewish poet

1026

DEATH
Murasaki Shikibu, Japanese writer

1036

BIRTH
Su Dongpo (Su Shi), Chinese poet and essayist

1048

DEATH
al-Bīrūnī, Persian scholar

1150

BIRTH
Sanā'ī (Abū al-Majd Majdud ibn Adam), Persian poet

1057

DEATH
al-Ma'arrī, Arab poet

1058

DEATH
Ibn Gabirol, Spanish Jewish poet

1072

DEATH
Ouyang Xiu, Chinese poet and historian

1075

BIRTH
Judah ha-Levi, Spanish Jewish philosopher

1098

BIRTH
Saint Hildegard (Hildegard von Bingen), German abbess and mystic

c. 1100

PUBLICATION

FRENCH
La Chanson de Roland (*Song of Roland*) Epic poem of unknown authorship

1101

DEATH
Su Dongpo (Su Shi), Chinese poet and essayist

1106

BIRTH
Khāqānī, Persian poet

1118

BIRTH
Saigyo, Japanese poet

1125

BIRTH
Lu You, Chinese poet

1126

BIRTH

Anvarī (Awhad ad-Dīn ibn Vāhid ad-Dīn Muhammad Khāvarānī), Persian poet

1131

DEATH

Sanā'ī (Abū al-Majd Majdud ibn Adam), Persian poet

1136

PUBLICATION

FRENCH

Sic et Non (Yes and No) Theological treatise by Pierre Abélard, philosopher

1141

BIRTH

Nezāmī, Persian poet

DEATH

Judah ha-Levi, Spanish Jewish philosopher

1142

BIRTH

Farīd od-Din 'Attār, Persian poet

1150–1160

PUBLICATION

GERMAN

Memento Mori Poem by Heinrich von Melk

1155

BIRTH

Kamo Chomei, Japanese poet

1162

BIRTH

Fujiwara Sadaie, Japanese poet

1170–1189

PUBLICATION

GERMAN

Eneit Epic poem by Heinrich von Veldeke

1172

BIRTH

Shota Rustaveli, Georgian poet

1179

DEATH

Saint Hildegard (Hildegard von Bingen), German abbess and mystic

1180

BIRTH

Kavicakravarti Kamban, Tamil poet

1185

DEATH

Khāqānī, Persian poet

1189

DEATH

Anvarī (Awhad ad-Dīn ibn Vāhid ad-Dīn Muhammad Khāvarānī), Persian poet

1190

DEATH

Saigyo, Japanese poet

1198

DEATH
Khāqānī, Persian poet

1200

PUBLICATIONS

FRENCH
Play of St. Nicholas Religious drama by Jean Bodel

GERMAN
Iwein Epic poem by Hartmann von Aue

1203/1217

DEATH
Nezāmī, Persian poet

1207

BIRTH
Jalāl ad-Dīn ar-Rūmī, Persian mystic and poet

1210

DEATH
Lu You, Chinese poet

PUBLICATION

GERMAN
Tristan und Isolde Epic poem by Gottfried von Strassburg

1212

PUBLICATION

JAPANESE
An Account of My Hut Poetic diary by Kamo Chomei

1213

BIRTH
Saʿdī (Mosharref od-Dīn ibn Mosleh od-Dīn Saʿdi), Persian poet

1216

DEATHS
Kamo Chomei, Japanese poet
Shota Rustaveli, Georgian poet

1220

DEATH
Farīd od-Dīn ʿAttār, Persian poet

1230

BIRTH
Jacopone da Todi, Italian religious poet

1241

DEATH
Fujiwara Sadaie, Japanese poet

1250

BIRTH
Wang Shifu, Chinese playwright

DEATH
Kamban, Tamil poet

1253

BIRTH
Amīr Khosrow, Indian court poet

1255

BIRTH
Guido Cavalcanti, Italian poet

1257

PUBLICATION

PERSIAN
The Orchard Poems by Saʿdī

1258

PUBLICATION

PERSIAN
The Rose Garden Poems by Sa'dī

1265

BIRTH
Dante Alighieri, Italian poet

PUBLICATION

ITALIAN
Golden Legend Hagiography by Jacobus de Voragine

1272

BIRTH
Asik Pasha, Turkish poet

1273

DEATH
Jalāl ad-Dīn ar-Rūmī, Persian mystic and poet

1283

BIRTHS
Juan Ruiz, Spanish poet
Yoshida Kenko, Japanese poet and essayist

1287

PUBLICATION

ITALIAN
History of the Destruction of Troy Poem by Guido delle Colonno

1292

DEATH
Sa'dī (Mosharref od-Dīn ibn Mosleh od-Dīn Sa'di), Persian poet

1293

PUBLICATION

ITALIAN
The New Life Prose and poems by Dante Alighieri

1300

DEATH
Guido Cavalcanti, Italian poet

1304

BIRTH
Petrarch, Italian poet and humanist

1306

DEATH
Jacopone da Todi, Italian religious poet

1308–1321

PUBLICATION

ITALIAN
Divine Comedy Epic poem by Dante Alighieri

1313

BIRTH
Giovanni Boccaccio, Italian writer

1321

DEATH
Dante Alighieri, Italian poet

1325

BIRTH
Hāfez, Persian poet

DEATH
Amīr Khosrow, Indian poet

1330

PUBLICATION

SPANISH
The Book of Good Love Poem by Juan Ruiz

1333

BIRTHS
Jean Froissart, French poet
Kanami, Japanese poet

DEATH
Asik Pasha, Turkish poet

1334/1335

BIRTH
Taceddin Ahmedi, Turkish poet

1337

DEATH
Wang Shifu, Chinese playwright

PUBLICATION

ITALIAN
On Illustrious Men Biography by Petrarch

1342/1343

BIRTH
Geoffrey Chaucer, English poet

PUBLICATION

LATIN
Books on Matters to Be Remembered Work by Petrarch

1345–1347

PUBLICATION

LATIN
On Religious Idleness, Bucolic Song, The Life of Solitude, Metrical Letters General works by Italian writer Petrarch

1349

PUBLICATION

ITALIAN
Decameron Collection of tales by Giovanni Boccaccio

1350

DEATHS
Juan Ruiz, Spanish poet
Yoshida Kenko, Japanese poet and essayist

1351

BIRTH
Süleyman Çelebi, Turkish poet

1363/64

BIRTH
Zeami Motokiyo, Japanese playwright

1364

BIRTH
Christine de Pisan, French poet

c. 1373

BIRTH
Margery Kempe, English mystic

1374

DEATH
Petrarch, Italian poet

1375

DEATH
Giovanni Boccaccio, Italian storyteller

1376

PUBLICATION

SCOTTISH
The Bruce National epic by poet John Barbour

1380–1390

PUBLICATION

ENGLISH
The Parlement of Foules Poem by Geoffrey Chaucer

1384

DEATH
Kanami, Japanese playwright

1386

PUBLICATION

LATIN
Confessio Amantis Tales by English writer John Gower

1387

PUBLICATION

ENGLISH
The Canterbury Tales Stories by Geoffrey Chaucer

1389

DEATH
Hāfez, Persian poet

1398

BIRTH
Iñigo López de Mendoza, marqués de Santillana, Spanish poet and humanist

1400

DEATH
Geoffrey Chaucer, English poet

PUBLICATION

GERMAN
Death and the Ploughman Dialogue by Bohemian writer Johannes von Tepl

1405

PUBLICATION

ITALIAN
Book of the City of Ladies Prose work by Christine de Pisan

1405/1410

DEATH
Jean Froissart, French poet

1412/1413

DEATH
Taceddin Ahmedi, Turkish poet

1414

BIRTH
Jāmī (Mowlanā Nūr od-Dīn 'Abd or-Rahmān ebn Ahmad), Persian scholar, poet, and mystic

1418

DEATH
Seyid Imadeddin Nesimi, Turkish poet

1421

BIRTH
Sogi, Japanese poet

1429

DEATH
Süleyman Çelebi, Turkish poet

1430

DEATH
Christine de Pisan, French poet

1431

BIRTH
François Villon, French lyric poet

1432

PUBLICATION
ENGLISH
Book of Margery Kempe Devotional autobiography by Margery Kempe

1440

DEATH
Margery Kempe, English mystic

1441

BIRTH
Mir Ali Shir Nava'i, Turkish poet and scholar

1443

DEATH
Zeami Motokiyo, Japanese playwright

1450

BIRTH
Marko Marulić, Croatian poet and philosopher

PUBLICATION
SINHALESE
Guttilaya Narrative poem by monk Vetteve

1454

BIRTH
Politian (Angelo Ambrogini), Italian poet and humanist

PUBLICATION
RAJASTHANI
Kanhadade Prabandha Poem by Padmanabhan, Indian Brahmin poet

1456

PUBLICATION
FRENCH
Le Petit Testament Poem by François Villon

1458

DEATH
Iñigo López de Mendoza, marqués de Santillana, Spanish poet

1461

PUBLICATION
FRENCH
Le Grand Testament Lyric poem by François Villon

1463

DEATH
François Villon, French lyric poet

PUBLICATION
ITALIAN
Carmina de Laudibus Estensium Collection of poems by Matteo Maria Boiardo

1465

BIRTH
Gil Vicente, Portuguese playwright

1468

PUBLICATION
PERSIAN
Haft Owrang (Seven Thrones) Collection of seven poetic idylls (*masnavi*) by Jāmī

1469

BIRTH

Desiderius Erasmus, Dutch humanist and philosopher

1470

PUBLICATION

ENGLISH

Le Morte d'Arthur Romance cycle of King Arthur legends by Sir Thomas Malory

1474

BIRTH

Ludovico Ariosto, Italian poet

1475–1478

PUBLICATION

ITALIAN

Stanzas Begun for the Tournament of the Magnificent Giuliano de Medici Poem by Politian

1476

PUBLICATION

PERSIAN

Nahafat al-Uns (Breath of Familiarity) Biographies by poet Jāmī

1479

PUBLICATION

PERSIAN

Salaman u Absal (Salaman and Absal) Allegory by Jāmī

1480

PUBLICATION

ITALIAN

Orpheus Dramatic composition by Politian

1483

PUBLICATION

PERSIAN

Yusuf u Zulaikha (Joseph and Zulaikha) Poem by Jāmī

1484

BIRTH

Bartolomé de Torres, Spanish playwright

PUBLICATION

BURMESE

Bhuridat Lingagyi Poem of the *pyo* form by Shin Maha Rahtathara

1486

PUBLICATION

PERSIAN

Sayahatnameye Hateme Tai (The Travels of Hateme Tai) Collection of fairy tales by Hussain Vaeze Kashefi

1487

PUBLICATION

PERSIAN

Tazkerat Osh-sho-Ara (The Record of Poets) Literary history by Alaoddoule Bakhtishah Samarqandi Daulatshah

1488

PUBLICATION

JAPANESE

A Poem of One Hundred Links Composed by Three Poets at Minase Poem by Sogi

1491

BIRTH

Bach Van (Nguyen Bin Khiem), Vietnamese poet

1492

BIRTH
Pietro Aretino, Italian poet and playwright

DEATH
Jāmī (Mowlanā Nūr od-Dīn 'Abd or-Rahmān ebn Ahmad), Persian, mystic, poet, and scholar

PUBLICATIONS
SPANISH
La cárcel de amor (The Prison of Love) Novel by Diego San Pedro
Stanzas for the Death of His Father Lyric poem by Jorge Manrique

1493

PUBLICATIONS
CHAGATAI TURKISH
Mizan al-Awzan (Scales of Poetic Meters) Poems by Turkish writer Mir Ali Shir Nava'i

GERMAN
The Nuremberg Chronicle Outline of world history by Hartmann Schedel

1494

BIRTH
François Rabelais, French writer

DEATH
Politian (Angelo Ambrogini), Italian poet and humanist

PUBLICATIONS
BURMESE
Bhuridat Zatpaung Pyo Poem by monk Shin Maha Rahtathara

ENGLISH
The Fall of Princes Thirty-six-thousand-line poem by John Lydgate

GERMAN
Das Narrenschiff (The Ship of Fools) Satire by Sebastian Brant

1495

BIRTH
Fuzûlî (Mehmed ibn Suleyman), Turkish poet

PUBLICATION
DUTCH
Den Spieghel der Salicheit van Elckerlijk (*Everyman*) Morality play by Peter Dorland van Diest

1496

BIRTH
Clément Marot, French poet

PUBLICATIONS
BURMESE
Tada uti Mawgun Collection of verse by Shin Maha Rahtathara

LATIN
Sergius Dramatic comedy by German humanist Johannes Reuchlin

PERSIAN
Aklake Mohseni (Morals of the Beneficent) Prose and verse by Hussain Vaeze Kashefi

SPANISH
Cancionero One-act play by Juan del Encino

1498

BIRTH
Nawade I, Burmese poet

PUBLICATIONS
CHAGATAI TURKISH
Char Divan (Four Divans) Collection of lyric poems by Mir Ali Shir Nava'i

DUTCH
Reinke de Vos (Reynard the Fox) Animal epic poem by Hinrek van Alkmaar

FRENCH
Memoires Autobiography by statesman Philippe de Comines

LATIN
Henno Satiric comedy by German writer Johannes Reuchlin

1499

PUBLICATIONS
ENGLISH
The Bouge of Court Allegorical poem by John Skelton

LATIN

Bellus Helveticum (The Swiss War) History by Swiss intellectual and scholar Willibald Pirkheimer

SPANISH

La Celestina Prose drama by Fernando de Rojas

La comedia de Calisto y Melibea Play by Fernando de Rojas

THE SIXTEENTH CENTURY

The 16th century represents the first phase of the Renaissance, the historical period immediately following the Middle Ages marked by the stirring of a new spirit of artistic and intellectual inquiry and the restoration of the spirit of ancient Greece and Rome. Printing, introduced in the mid-15th century, became widespread throughout Europe and opened a floodgate of books and other printed materials that official censors could neither shut nor control. Printing also led to a new interest in and revival of classical writers who provided the models and source materials for playwrights and poets. The new spirit was best exemplified in the historical Spanish voyages to the New World and Portuguese voyages to India.

Almost every western European country shared in the great flowering of literature. In England, poetic drama dominated the age, especially the works of Christopher Marlowe, Ben Jonson, John Webster, and, above all, William Shakespeare, whose works spanned the late 16th and early 17th centuries. In Portugal, the poet Luis Camões occupies the same place as Shakespeare does in England, as do Lope de Vega in imperial Spain and Gil Vicente in Spain and Portugal. The century also produced Miguel de Cervantes Saavedra, Spain's greatest novelist. In France the group of seven poets known as the Pléiade (literally, the constellation) and the essayist Michel de Montaigne stand at the vanguard of a vast army of writers that followed in the centuries to come. Philosopher Desiderius Erasmus's work was representative of the period's shift from Christian to secular learning. A rising tide of dissent within the Catholic Church led to several great translations of the Bible, including one by Erasmus, into vernacular languages, setting new standards for prose writing. Latin was a dying language, and displacing it were the many national languages, such as English, French, Italian, and German, each heralding the new age with creative works of enduring worth. Europe no longer had a lingua franca, and national literatures developed independent traditions and protocols.

Major Writers of the Sixteenth Century

William Shakespeare (1564–1616) The Bard of Avon; English poet, dramatist, and actor; national poet and playwright of England; considered by most scholars as the greatest dramatist of all time. Shakespeare's active career spanned 28 years, from 1582 to 1610, when he was a member of the Lord Chamberlain's company in London's Globe Theatre. Most of his plays were written in the 16th century, but his tragedies—considered his masterpieces—were written in the first decade of the 17th century, before he retired in 1610. The exact order of his plays is not known with certainty, and all that is available is the date when they were first performed. From 1590 to 1595 he wrote mainly comedies, including *The Comedy of Errors* (1592–93), *The Taming of the Shrew* (1593), *Love's Labour's Lost* (1594–95), *A Midsummer Night's Dream* (1595–96), as well as histories such as *Henry VI, Part I* (1589–92), *Richard III* (1592–93), and *Richard II* (1595–96) and the early tragedy *Romeo and Juliet* (1594–95). In the last years of the century he wrote two comedies, *The Merchant of Venice* (1596–97) and *Much Ado About Nothing* (1598–99), and two histories, *Henry IV, Part I* and *Julius Caesar* (1599–1600). In the first decade of the 17th century came *Hamlet* (1600–1), *Othello* (1604–5), *King Lear* (1605–6), and *Macbeth* (1605–6). His last plays were *The Winter's Tale* (1610–11) and *The Tempest* (1611). The first collected edition of his plays, known as the First Folio, was issued in 1623. In addition to his plays Shakespeare wrote 154 sonnets and two heroic narrative poems, *Venus and Adonis* (1593) and *Lucrece* (1594).

Lope de Vega (Lope Félix de Vega Carpio) (1562–1635) Known as the Phoenix of Spain, Lope de Vega was the most important Spanish dramatist of the Spanish Golden Age, the author of 1,800 plays and several hundred shorter dramatic pieces of which 43 plays and 50 shorter pieces survive. Vega was a master of the Spanish *comedia,* the then-new verse drama of love and intrigue that presented characters as exaggerated personifications of a vice or flaw. Vega's output was phenomenal and his range vast, but his plays fall into two categories: historical plays and cloak-and-dagger dramas of intrigue. The best examples of his historical plays are *Peribanez and the Commander of Ocana, The King, The Greatest Alcalde, All Citizens Are Soldiers, The Knight from Olmedo,* and *Fuente ovejuna.* The best examples of his cloak-and-dagger plays are *The Gardener's Dog, Across the Bridge, Juana, The Lady Nit-Wit, The Girl with the Jug,* and *The King and the Farmer.* A collection of Vega's non-dramatic works in verse and prose fill 21 volumes and include pastoral romances, biographies of Spanish saints, long epic poems, and burlesques.

Luíz Camões (Luíz Camoëns) (1524/1525–1580) Portugal's national poet and author of the epic poem *The Lusiads,* which describes Vasco da Gama's discovery of the sea route to India. Born into an old, impoverished Portuguese aristocracy, Camões spent 17 years in India. He returned to Lisbon in 1570 and published *The Lusiads* in 1572. His nondramatic works include *Rimas,* a collection of poems (1595). He was also a great dramatist; his plays include *The Two Amphitryons* and *King Seleucus,* both comedies, and *Filodemo,* a morality play.

Miguel de Cervantes Saavedra (1547–1616) Spanish novelist, playwright and poet; creator of *Don Quixote;* and Spain's most important writer. As a youth, Cervantes joined the army and took part in the great naval battle of Lepanto against the Turks (1571), during which he received a wound that permanently crippled his left hand. En route to Spain he was captured by the Turks, sold into slavery, and ransomed five years later. The first part of *Don Quixote* was published in 1605 and the second part in 1615, and they were immediate successes. Originally conceived as a comic satire against the chivalric romances of the day, the novel describes realistically what befalls an elderly knight who sets out on his old horse, Rosinante, with his squire, Sancho Panza, to seek adventure. In the process he also finds love in the person of the peasant Dulcinea. The influence of the novel can be seen in the works of the classic 19th-century novelists, including Daniel Defoe, Henry Fielding, Sir Walter Scott, Charles Dickens, Gustave Flaubert, and Herman Melville. Cervantes also wrote some 20 to 30 plays, of which *The Traffic of Algiers, Eight New Comedies and Eight New Interludes,* and *Numantia* survive. Among his subsequent works are the 12 short stories of *Exemplary Tales,* as well as a romance, *The Labors of Pesiles and Sigismunds: A Northern Story.*

François Rabelais (1494–1553) French writer, author of the satirical classics *Pantagruel* (1532) and *Gargantua* (1534). Rabelais began his life as a Franciscan and later Benedictine monk but left the order to become a physician. His first success as a writer came with the publication of *Pantagruel,* which displays his genius as a storyteller, his profound sense of the comedy of language, and a mastery of the comic situation, monologue, dialogue, and action. His work was condemned as bawdy by civil and ecclesiastical authorities and was banned in France. *Pantagruel* was followed by *Pantagruel's Prognostication* (1532) and the *Third Book* (1546) and *Fourth Book* (1552) of *Gargantua.*

Desiderius Erasmus (1469–1536) Dutch humanist, the quintessential Renaissance scholar. He became an Augustinian monk and was ordained a priest in 1492. Later education in Paris turned him from scholastic theology to humanism, the learning or cultural impulse characterized by a revival of classical letters, a critical spirit, and a shift of emphasis from religious to secular concerns. He made four visits to England, where he lectured at the universities of Oxford and Cambridge and met Sir Thomas More, the chancellor of England; St. John Fisher, a professor at Cambridge University; and the theologian John Colet, who inspired him to study the Bible. He spent his later years visiting Italy, Belgium, Germany, and Switzerland, where he died. His greatest achievement was a Latin translation of the Greek New Testament. His secular publications include *Proverbs* (1500) and *The Praise of Folly* (1511).

Gil Vicente (1465–1536/1537) Portuguese playwright who wrote in both Spanish and Portuguese and who combined lyrical as well as satiric talents. From 1502 to 1536 he was the Portuguese poet laureate and wrote fervent patriotic verse, such as *Exhortation to War* (1513) and *Play of Fame* (1515) inspired by imperial campaigns. Vicente's 44 plays reflect the upheaval, squalor, and splendor of the era of great maritime explorations. Twelve of the plays were written in Spanish, 14 in Portuguese, and the remaining in both languages. His major plays included *Jupiter's Court* (1521), *The Forge of Love* (1524), *The Temple of Apollo* (1526), and *Summary of the History of God, The Ship of Love, The Coat of Arms of the City of Coimbra,* and *The Carriers* (all 1527). His last four plays show him at the peak of his powers: *The Pilgrimage of the Aggrieved* (1533), *Forest of Deceits* (1536), *Triumph of Winter* (1529) and *Amadís de Gaula* (1532–33).

Michel Eyquem de Montaigne (1533–1592) French courtier and the author of *Essais (Essays),* which established a new literary form. He began work on *Essays* in 1571; the first edition came out in 1580, and a second edition, in 1588. The

first edition consisted of two books of 57 and 37 chapters, each chapter, or essay, varying greatly in length. The second edition included a third book. *Essays* is considered one of the most captivating and intimate self-portraits in literature. In a world corrupted by violence and hypocrisy, Montaigne sought understanding through self-examination. The title of the book was revealing because it is roughly translated from the French as "attempts," implying trial and error and tentative exploration. The essays move freely from one topic to another and cover diverse and disparate subjects such as friendship, solitude, politics, sleep, fear, death, sadness, and moderation.

Christopher Marlowe (1564–1593) English poet and playwright. Marlowe's output was prodigious considering his short life—he died at 29, reportedly in a tavern brawl—and a writing career that spanned only six years. He created some of the finest plays of the Elizabethan era. He wrote the first, *Tamburlaine the Great* (published in 1590) while he was a student at Cambridge. His other plays include *The Jew of Malta* (1589), *Dr. Faustus* (1592), *Edward II* (1592), and *The Massacre at Paris* (1593), which were all published posthumously. His poem, the much praised *Hero and Leander,* was left incomplete at his death. *Dido, Queen of Carthage,* an unfinished play, was completed by Thomas Nashe in 1594.

Pierre de Ronsard (1524–1585) French poet. A student of the classics, Ronsard formed, with a group of fellow students, the literary group that came to be called the Pléiade, in emulation of the seven ancient Greek poets of Alexandria. The aim of the group was to elevate the French language to the level of the classical tongues as a medium of literary expression. *Odes,* Ronsard's first collection of poems, was based on the *Odes* of Horace. In *Les Amours* he used the Italian canzona, a medieval Italian lyric poem in stanzaic form, as a model. In *Bocages* and *Meslanges* (both 1554), two of his most exquisite poems, he found inspiration in the Greek poet Anacreon. *Continuation des Amours* and *Nouvelle Continuation des Amours* mined the same vein. In 1555 he began to write a series of long poems published as *Hymnes,* based on the style of the Greek poet Callimachus. In *Meslanges,* he criticized the Western colonization of the New World, whose native people he described as ideal and noble savages worthy of admiration. During the Wars of Religion in France, Ronsard, an extreme Royalist and Catholic, used his pen to attack the Protestants in *Discourse on the Miseries of These Times* (1562). As the unofficial poet laureate of France, he undertook but did not complete a national epic called *La Françiade,* an imitation of Virgil's *Aeneid.* The collected edition of his works, published in 1578, contained many new works including "Elegy Against the Woodcutters of Gatine," *Les Amours de Marie,* and *Sonnets pour Hélène.* His last verse collection, *Les Derniers Vers,* was published posthumously.

Key World Events of the Sixteenth Century

1500   Pedro Alvares Cabral claims Brazil for Portugal
1501   First African slaves are supplied to the Spanish on Hispaniola
1517   Martin Luther nails his Ninety-five Theses to the church door at Wittemberg
1519   Charles V becomes Holy Roman Emperor
1521   Luther is excommunicated at the Diet of Worms, marking the beginning of the Protestant Reformation. Portuguese navigator Ferdinand Magellan's expedition sails around the world, the first circumnavigation of the globe. Spanish conquistador Hernán Cortés and 600 soldiers overthrow the Aztec Empire
1526   Bābur overthrows the Lodī dynasty at the Battle of Panipet and establishes the Mogul dynasty in India
1529   Henry VIII of England seeks annulment of his marriage to Catherine of Aragon; denied his request, he repudiates papal supremacy and establishes himself as head of the Church of England
1532   The first Portuguese colony in Brazil is founded at São Vicente
1533   Francisco Pizarro conquers Peru and destroys the Inca Empire
1536   John Calvin published the *Institutes of Christian Religion,* the bedrock of Calvinism
1540   Ignatius Loyola founds the Jesuit Order, also known as the Society of Jesus
1541   Hernando de Soto discovers the Mississippi River
1543   Nicholas Copernicus lays the foundations of modern cosmology with his *On the Revolutions of the Heavenly Spheres*
1545   Council of Trent begins the Counter-Reformation
1558   England loses Calais, its last foothold on the Continent
1562   The Wars of Religion begin in France as the crown is drawn into a war with the Huguenots
1567   Netherlands revolt against Spain as William the Silent initiates an 80-year struggle for independence
1571   The Holy League, an alliance of Christian powers, defeats the Turks in a decisive naval battle at Lepanto
1588   English deal a blow to Spanish naval power by destroying the flotilla of warships known as the Armada
1598   Henry IV issues the Edict of Nantes, granting French Huguenots religious freedom and civil rights

1500

BIRTH
Wu Chengen, Chinese novelist

PUBLICATIONS
DUTCH
Adaagia Collection of proverbs by Desiderius Erasmus, humanist

ENGLISH
The Siege of Thebes Poem by John Lydgate

GERMAN
Liber de Arti Distellandi Tract by Hieronymous Brunschwig, naturalist

1501

BIRTH
Maurice Scève, French poet

DEATH
Mir Ali Shir Nava'i, Turkish poet and scholar

PUBLICATIONS
DUTCH
Enchiridion Militis Christianae Manual of Christian piety by Desiderius Erasmus

GERMAN
Ludus Dianae Allegorical verse drama by Conradus Celtis, German humanist

SCOTTISH
The Palice of Honour Poem by Gavin Douglas

1502

DEATH
Sogi, Japanese poet

PUBLICATIONS
LATIN
Amores Folk poem by Conradus Celtis, German writer

SPANISH
Comedy of Calisto and Melibea Novel by Fernando de Rojas

1503

BIRTH
Garcilaso de la Vega, Spanish poet

1504

PUBLICATIONS
ITALIAN
Arcadia Work in prose and poetry by Jacopo Sannazaro

PERSIAN
Anvare Soheyli (The Shining Star Canopus) Collection of verse fables by Hussain Vaeze Kashefi

1505

PUBLICATION
LATIN
Epitome Rerum Germanicarum German history by Jakob Wempfeling

1507

PUBLICATION
ITALIAN
Il libro della prima navigazione per oceano alle terre de'negri della Bassa Ethiopia Travel narrative by navigator Alvise da Cadamosto

1508

PUBLICATIONS
FRENCH
Annotations in Pandectas Prose tract by Guillaume Budé, scholar of philosophy and jurisprudence

ITALIAN
La Cassaria (The Coffer) Dramatic comedy by Ludovico Ariosto

SPANISH
Amadís de Gaula Romantic narrative by Garci Rodríguez de Montalvo

1509

BIRTH
John Calvin (Jean Cauvin), French Protestant reformer

PUBLICATIONS
ENGLISH
The Ship of Fools Translation of Sebastian Brant's *Das Narrenschiff* (1494) by Scottish-born Alexander Barclay

LATIN
The Praise of Folly Satire by Desiderius Erasmus, Dutch humanist and philosopher

1510

BIRTH
Lope de Rueda, Spanish playwright

PUBLICATION

ENGLISH
Everyman Translation of Peter Dorland van Diest's *Elckerlijk* (1495), a morality play

1511

PUBLICATION

BURMESE
Parayana Wuthtu Prose tract by Shin Thilawuntha, monk and poet

1512

PUBLICATION

SPANISH
Sea of Histories History by Fernán Pérez de Guzmán

1513

PUBLICATIONS

ENGLISH
The Troy Book Poem by John Lydgate

ITALIAN
La Calandria Comic play by Bernardo Dovizi, Cardinal Bibiena
The Prince Treatise on statecraft by Niccolò Machiavelli

PORTUGUESE
Auto de la sibila Casandra (Act of the Sibyl Cassandra) Religious drama by Gil Vicente

1515

PUBLICATIONS

ITALIAN
Sofonisma Tragedy by Giangiorgio Trissino

LATIN
Institutio Principis Christiani (The Education of a Christian Prince) Prose tract by Desiderius Erasmus, Dutch humanist and philosopher

SPANISH
Play of Fame Play by Gil Vicente

1516

PUBLICATIONS

ENGLISH
Magnyfycens Morality play by John Skelton
Utopia political essay by Sir Thomas More

ITALIAN
Orlando Furioso Poem by Ludovico Ariosto

LATIN
De Orbe Novo (The New World) Prose tract by Peter Martyr (Pietro Martire d'Anghiera)

PORTUGUESE
Auto de la Barca Morality play by Gil Vicente

1517

PUBLICATIONS

ENGLISH
The Tunnynge of Elynour Rummyng Comic poem by John Skelton

LATIN
Opus Maccaronicum Collection of satiric poems by Teofilo Folengo, Italian Benedictine monk

SPANISH
Propalladia (The First Fruits of Pallas) Collection of seven comedies by Bartolomé de Torres Naharro

1518

PUBLICATION

PORTUGUESE
Auto de la Barca de Purgatorio (The Ship of Purgatory) Morality play by Gil Vicente

1519

PUBLICATIONS

PORTUGUESE
Auto de la Barca de la Gloria (Act of the Ship of Glory) Morality play by Gil Vicente

TELUGU
Parijatapahanannamu Narrative poem by Timanna

1520

PUBLICATION

GERMAN
Address to the Nobility of the German Nation Polemical tract by Martin Luther, Protestant reformer

1521

PUBLICATIONS

ITALIAN
The Art of War by Niccolò Machiavelli

LATIN
Loci Communes Prose tract on the principles of the Reformation by Philip Melanchthon

1522

BIRTHS
Joachim du Bellay, French poet
Jacques Cujas, French jurist and legal writer

PUBLICATION

GERMAN
Schimpf und Ernst Collection of humorous short stories by Johann Pauli

1523

PUBLICATION

GERMAN
Die Wittenbergische Nachtigall Allegorical tale in verse by Hans Sachs, playwright

1524

BIRTH
Pierre de Ronsard, French poet

DEATH
Marko Marulić, Croatian poet and philosopher

1524/1525

BIRTH
Luíz Camões, Portuguese poet

1525

DEATH
Bartolomé de Torres Naharro, Spanish playwright

1526

BIRTH
Bâkî (Mahmud Abdülbâkî), Turkish poet

PUBLICATIONS

BURMESE
Kogan Pyo Collection of poems by Shin Maha Rahtathara

LATIN
De Partu Virginis Epic by Jacopo Sannazaro, Italian poet

SPANISH
The Temple of Apollo Play by Gil Vicente

1527

BIRTH
Luis de León, Spanish mystic and poet

PUBLICATIONS

LATIN
De Arte Poetica Tract on poetic theory by Marco Girolamo Vida

SPANISH
Summary of the History of God; The Ship of Love; The Coat of Arms of the City of Coimbra; The Carriers Plays by Gil Vicente

1528

BIRTH
Rémy Belleau, French poet

PUBLICATION

ITALIAN
Il Cortegiano (The Courtier) Prose dialogue by Baldassare Castiglione, humanist

1529

PUBLICATION

SPANISH
Triumph of Winter Play by Gil Vicente

1530

PUBLICATIONS

GERMAN
Das Schlaraffenland Collection of doggerel verse by Hans Sachs

ITALIAN
Sonetti e Canzoni Collection of verse by Jacopo Sannazaro

1532

BIRTHS
Jean-Antoine de Baïf, French poet
Étienne Jodelle, French playwright and poet

PUBLICATION

FRENCH
Pantagruel Bawdy satire by François Rabelais

1532–1533

PUBLICATION

SPANISH
Amadís de Gaula (Amadis of Gaul) Play by Gil Vicente

1533

BIRTH
Michel Eyquem de Montaigne, French essayist

DEATH
Ludovico Ariosto, Italian poet

PUBLICATION

SPANISH
The Pilgrimage of the Aggrieved Play by Gil Vicente

1534

BIRTHS
José de Anchieta, Portuguese Jesuit poet and playwright
Fernando de Herrera, Spanish lyric poet

PUBLICATION

FRENCH
Gargantua Satire by François Rabelais

1535

PUBLICATION

ENGLISH
Bible Translation by Miles Coverdale

1536

DEATHS
Desiderius Erasmus, Dutch humanist
Garcilaso de la Vega, Spanish poet
Gil Vicente, Portuguese playwright

PUBLICATION

SPANISH
Forest of Deceits Play by Gil Vicente

1541

PUBLICATION

ITALIAN
Orbecche Dramatic tragedy by Giambattista Cinzio Giraldi

1542

BIRTH
Saint John of the Cross (Juan de Yepes y Alvarez), Spanish mystic and poet

1543

BIRTH
Tulsīdās, Hindu religious poet

DEATH

Nicolaus Copernicus, Polish astronomer

PUBLICATION

LATIN

De Revolutionibus Orbium Coelestium (On the Revolution of the Spheres) Scientific treatise by Nicolaus Copernicus

LITERARY EVENT

Pope Paul III issues the *Index Librorum Prohibitorum,* a list of forbidden books, which predates the first official index of 1564

1544

BIRTHS

Ginés Pérez de Hita, Spanish writer
Torquato Tasso, Italian epic poet

DEATH

Clément Marot, French poet

PUBLICATION

FRENCH

Delie: Object of Highest Virtue Poetic cycle by Maurice Scève

1546

BIRTH

Johann Fischart, German satirist

PUBLICATION

ITALIAN

Orazia Tragic drama in verse by Pietro Aretino

1547

BIRTHS

Mateo Alemán, Spanish playwright
Miguel de Cervantes Saavedra, Spanish novelist, playwright, and poet

PUBLICATION

ITALIAN

L'Italia liberata dai Goti (The Deliverance of Italy from the Goths) Epic poem by Giangiorgio Trissino

1548

BIRTH

Giordano Bruno, Italian philosopher

PUBLICATION

SPANISH

Spiritual Exercises Religious writings by Ignatius of Loyola, founder of the Jesuit Order

1549

PUBLICATIONS

ENGLISH

The Whole Booke of Psalmes Collection of psalms translated from the Old Testament by poets Thomas Sternhold and John Hopkins

GERMAN

Grobianus Satire by Friedrich Dedekind

1550

BIRTHS

Juan de la Cueva, Spanish playwright and poet
Vicente Espinel, Spanish poet

PUBLICATIONS

FRENCH

Odes Poems by Pierre Ronsard

ITALIAN

The Lives of the Most Eminent Italian Architects, Painters and Sculptors by Giorgio Vasari, art historian

SWEDISH

Tobia Commedia (The Comedy of Tobias) Play by Olaus Petrie, statesman

1550–1553/1555

PUBLICATION

ITALIAN

Piacevoli notti (Facetious Nights) Collection of 74 stories by Giovanni Francesco Straparola

1552

BIRTHS
Théodore-Agrippa d'Aubigné, French poet
Paolo (Pietro) Sarpi, Italian philosopher
Edmund Spenser, English poet

PUBLICATIONS
FRENCH
Centuries Book of rhymed prophecies by Nostradamus (Michel de Nostredame), seer
Cléopâtre captive Play by Étienne Jodelle
Les Amours de P. de Ronsard Vandomoys, Ensemble de Bocages Collection of sonnets by Pierre de Ronsard

1553

DEATH
François Rabelais, French writer

1554

BIRTHS
Bálint Balassi, Hungarian lyric poet
John Lyle, English prose writer
Sir Walter Raleigh, English poet and adventurer
Sir Philip Sidney, English poet and scholar

PUBLICATIONS
FRENCH
Meslanges Poems by Pierre de Ronsard

ITALIAN
Le Novelle Collection of 214 short stories by Matteo Bandello

1555

BIRTHS
François de Malherbe, French poet
Luís de Sousa, Portuguese historian

PUBLICATION
FRENCH
Les Hymnes Collection of addresses and panegyrics by Pierre de Ronsard

1556

DEATHS
Pietro Aretino, Italian playwright and poet
Fuzûlî (Mehmed ibn Suleyman), Turkish poet

PUBLICATIONS
ENGLISH
The Spider and the Flie Verse allegory by John Heywood

SPANISH
Audi Filia (Listen, Son) Ascetic Christian text by Juan de Avila

1558

BIRTH
Thomas Kyd, English playwright

PUBLICATIONS
FRENCH
Regrets Melancholy satire by Joachim du Bellay

PERSIAN
Diviani Mataibat Collection of satires by Abdurrahman Mushfiqi

1559

PUBLICATION
SPANISH
La Diana Pastoral romance by Portuguese-born writer Jorge de Montemayor

1560

BIRTH
John Owen, Welsh poet

DEATHS
Joachim du Bellay, French poet
Maurice Scève, French poet

PUBLICATION
FRENCH
Songs and Sonnets Collected edition of the works of Pierre de Ronsard

1561

BIRTHS

Francis Bacon, English philosopher
Robert Southwell, English poet and Catholic martyr

1562

BIRTH

Lope de Vega, Spanish playwright

PUBLICATION

ITALIAN

Il Rinaldo Epic poem by Torquato Tasso

1563

PUBLICATIONS

ENGLISH

The Book of Martyrs Martyrology by John Foxe
A Mirrour for Magistrates Poetic work edited by George Ferrers
    and William Baldwin

1564

BIRTHS

Christopher Marlowe, English playwright
William Shakespeare, English playwright

1565

DEATH

Lope de Rueda, Spanish playwright

PUBLICATION

ITALIAN

Ecatommiti Collection of moral and love tales by Giambattisto
    Cinzio Giraldi

1566

PUBLICATIONS

ENGLISH

Ralph Roister Doister Play by Nicholas Udall

The Supposes Earliest prose comedy in English, translated from
    Ludovico Ariosto's *Gli Suppositi* by poet-playwright George
    Gascoigne

FRENCH

The Methods of History Historiography by Jean Bodin, philo-
    sopher

1567

BIRTHS

Thomas Campion, English poet
Thomas Nash, English playwright

1568

BIRTH

Tommaso Campanella, Italian philosopher

1569–1589

PUBLICATION

SPANISH

La Araucana Finest epic poem of the Spanish Golden Age of lit-
    erature by Alonso de Ercilla y Zúñiga

1570

BIRTHS

Firishtah, Indian Muslim historian
Thomas Middleton, English playwright

PUBLICATION

ITALIAN

The Four Books of Architecture Writings on architecture by the
    Renaissance architect Andrea Palladio

1571

BIRTHS

Thomas Dekker, English playwright
Ben Jonson, English playwright and poet
Matsunaga Teitoku, Japanese poet
Nef'i (Ömer), Turkish poet

PUBLICATION

ITALIAN
Light of Eyes Prose narrative by Azariah ben Moses dei Rossi, Jewish scholar and physician

1572

BIRTH
John Donne, English poet

PUBLICATION

PORTUGUESE
Os Lusíadas (The Lusitanians) National epic poem by Luíz de Camões

1573

BIRTH
Mathurin Régnier, French poet

DEATH
Étienne Jodelle, French playwright and poet

PUBLICATIONS

GERMAN
Der Flohatz Verse satire by Johann Fischart

LATIN
Austrias Poem by Guinean writer Juan Latino

1574

BIRTH
Thomas Heywood, English playwright

PUBLICATION

AWADHI
Rāmacaritmānas (Lake of the Acts of Rama) Epic religious poem by Tulsīdās, Hindu author

1575

BIRTH
Cyril Tourneur, English playwright

PUBLICATION

ITALIAN
Jerusalem Delivered Religious epic poem by poet and playwright Torquato Tasso

1577

DEATH
Rémy Belleau, French poet

PUBLICATION

ENGLISH
Chronicles First authoritative history of England, by Raphael Holinshed

1578

PUBLICATIONS

ENGLISH
Euphues: The Anatomy of Wit Prose romance by John Lyly

FRENCH
La Semaine (The Week) Religious epic poem by Guillaume de Salluste, seigneur du Bartas

1578

PUBLICATION

POLISH
The Dismissal of the Greek Envoys Poem by Jan Kochanowski

1579

BIRTHS
John Fletcher, English playwright
Luis Vélez de Guevara, Spanish playwright

PUBLICATION

ENGLISH
The Shepheard's Calendar Twelve eclogues, one for each month of the year, by Edmund Spenser

1580

BIRTHS
Francisco Gómez de Quevedo y Villegas, Spanish poet and satirist
John Webster, English playwright

DEATH
Luíz Camões, Portuguese poet

PUBLICATIONS

FRENCH
Essays by Michel de Montaigne, philosopher

ITALIAN
Aminta Pastoral drama by Torquato Tasso

POLISH
Threny Series of verse laments by Jan Kochanowski

1581

BIRTHS
Pieter Corneliszoon Hooft, Dutch historian, playwright, and poet
Juan Ruiz de Alarcón y Mendoza, Mexican-born Spanish playwright

1582

BIRTH
John Barclay, Scottish satirist

DEATHS
George Buchanan, Scottish poet
Wu Chengen, Chinese writer of fiction and poetry

LITERARY EVENT
Crusca Academy, for the study and "purification" of the Italian language, founded in Florence, Italy

PUBLICATIONS

ENGLISH
An Apologie for Poetrie Literary criticism by Philip Sidney
Diverse Voyages Touching the Discovery of America Travel narrative by Richard Hakluyt
New Testament translation by Roman Catholic scholars at Rheims and Douai

FRENCH
Bradamante Play by Robert Garnier

1583

BIRTHS
Hugo Grotius, Dutch jurist, humanist, and essayist
Philip Massinger, English playwright

PUBLICATIONS

FRENCH
Les Juives (The Jewish Women) Novel by Robert Garnier
Last Loves (Cleonice) Poems by Philippe Desportes

SPANISH
De los nombres de Cristo (The Names of Christ) Theological treatise by Fray Luis Ponce de León

1584

BIRTHS
Francis Beaumont, English playwright
Tirso de Molina (Gabriel Téllez), Spanish playwright

DEATH
Jan Kochanowski, Polish poet

PUBLICATION

ITALIAN
Spaccio della Bestia Trionfante (On the Infinite Universe and Worlds) Anti-Catholic work drawing heavily on Hermetic Gnosticism by Giordano Bruno

1585

BIRTHS
Uriel Acosta, Portuguese Jewish scholar
Francis Beaumont, English playwright
Gerbrand Adriaenszoon Bredero, Dutch poet and playwright
John Cotton, English clergyman and New England Puritan

DEATH
Pierre de Ronsard, French poet and critic

PUBLICATIONS

SPANISH
La Galatea Pastoral romance by Miguel de Cervantes Saavedra

TELUGU
Kalapurnodayamu Comedy of errors by Pimgali Suranna, Indian poet

1586

BIRTH
John Ford, English playwright

DEATH
Sir Philip Sydney, English poet

PUBLICATIONS

ENGLISH
Astrophel Pastoral elegy on the death of Philip Sidney by Edmund Spenser

ITALIAN

Annales Ecclesiastici Ecclesiastical history by Caesar Baronius

SPANISH

The First Part of the Angelica Poems by Barahond de Soto

1587

BIRTH

Joost van den Vondel, Dutch poet and dramatist

DEATH

Bach Van (Nguyen Bin Khiem), Vietnamese poet

PUBLICATION

POLISH

Victoria Deorum Poem by Sebastian Klonowic

1588

BIRTHS

Ivan Gundulić, Croatian poet and promoter of Slavic nationalism
Thomas Hobbes, English philosopher and essayist
Marin Mersenne, French philosopher

DEATHS

Abdurrahman Mushfiqi, Persian poet
Nawade I, Burmese poet

PUBLICATION

ENGLISH

Tres Thomae Roman Catholic prose tract by Thomas Stapleton

1589

BIRTHS

Honorat de Bueil, seigneur de Racan, French poet
Teimuraz I, Turko-Persian poet and monarch of Georgia

DEATH

Jean-Antoine de Baïf, French poet

PUBLICATIONS

ENGLISH

The Faerie Queene Epic poem by Edmund Spenser
Henry VI Play by William Shakespeare

FRENCH

Dialogues de Dom Frei Amador Arraiz Moral and religious tract by Amador Arrais

1590

BIRTHS

Uriel da Costa, Portuguese-born Dutch Jewish writer
Sara Copio Sullam, Italian Jewish poet

DEATHS

Jacques Cujas, French legal writer
Johann Fischart, German playwright
Guillaume de Salluste, seigneur du Bartas, French poet

PUBLICATIONS

ENGLISH

The Arcadia Prose romance by Philip Sidney
Rosalynde Prose romance by Thomas Lodge
Tamburlaine the Great Drama in blank verse by Christopher Marlowe

ITALIAN

Il pastor fido (The Faithful Shepherd) Pastoral tragicomedy by Giovanni Batista Guarini
Viaggio all'India Orientali Travel narrative of a journey from Aleppo to India by Gasparo Balbi

1591

BIRTHS

Joseph Solomon Delmedigo, Greek Jewish theologian, physician, and philosopher
Robert Herrick, English poet

DEATHS

Luis de León, Spanish mystic poet
Saint John of the Cross (Juan de Yepes y Alvarez), Spanish mystic poet

PUBLICATIONS

ENGLISH

Astrophel and Stella Sonnet sequence by Philip Sidney
The Comedy of Errors Play by William Shakespeare
Endimion, The Man in the Moone Allegorical prose play by John Lyly
Titus Andronicus Play by William Shakespeare

ITALIAN

Queen of Scotland Play by Federico della Valle

1592

BIRTHS

Johannes Amos Comenius, Czech Moravian churchman and educator
Pierre Gassendi, French philosopher and mathematician

DEATHS
Nahapet Khutchak, Armenian poet
Michel Eyquem de Montaigne, French essayist

PUBLICATIONS
CHINESE
Xiyou Ji (The Journey to the West) Travel narrative by Wu Chengen

ENGLISH
Midas Prose play by John Lyly
Richard III Tragedy by William Shakespeare
The Spanish Tragedie Play by Thomas Kyd

HEBREW
Zemah David (The Plant of David) History by David ben Solomon Gans

SPANISH
De Sacramento Matrimonii Prose tract by Jesuit Tomás Sánchez

1593

BIRTH
George Herbert, English metaphysical poet

DEATH
Christopher Marlowe, English poet and playwright

PUBLICATION
ENGLISH
The Taming of the Shrew Comedy by William Shakespeare

1594

DEATHS
Bálint Balassi, Hungarian lyric poet
Thomas Kyd, English playwright

PUBLICATIONS
ENGLISH
Dido, Queen of Carthage Play by Christopher Marlowe
Edward II Play by Christopher Marlowe, completed by Thomas Nashe
Love's Labour's Lost Play by William Shakespeare
The Rape of Lucrece Play by William Shakespeare
Shadow of the Night Poem by George Chapman
The Two Gentlemen of Verona Play by William Shakespeare

PORTUGUESE
Varias Rimas ao Bom Jesus Religious poems by Diego Bernardez

1595

BIRTHS
Thomas Carew, English poet
Jean Desmaret's de Saint-Sorlen, French critic
Bihari Lal, Hindi poet
Maciej Kazimierz Sarbiewski, Polish Jesuit poet

DEATHS
Robert Southwell, English poet and Catholic martyr
Torquato Tasso, Italian poet

PUBLICATIONS
ENGLISH
Amoretti Series of sonnets by Edmund Spenser
A Midsummer Night's Dream Comedy by William Shakespeare
Richard II Tragedy by William Shakespeare
Romeo and Juliet Tragedy by William Shakespeare

POLISH
The Boatmen Poem by Sebastian Klonowic

1596

BIRTHS
René Descartes, French philosopher
Constantijn Huygens, Dutch poet

PUBLICATIONS
ENGLISH
King John Play by William Shakespeare
The Merchant of Venice Play by William Shakespeare

1597

BIRTH
Vincent Voiture, French poet

DEATHS
José de Anchieta, Portuguese Jesuit poet and playwright
Fernando de Herrera, Spanish lyric poet

PUBLICATIONS
ENGLISH
Henry IV, Part I Play by William Shakespeare
Henry IV, Part II Play by William Shakespeare

1598

BIRTH
Georg Stiernhielm, Swedish poet

PUBLICATIONS
ENGLISH
The Blind Beggar of Alexandria Play by George Chapman
Every Man in His Humour Comedy by Ben Jonson
The Merry Wives of Windsor Play by William Shakespeare
Much Ado About Nothing Play by William Shakespeare

SPANISH
Arcadia Novel by Lope de Vega
La Dragontea Epic poem by Lope de Vega

1599

BIRTH
Meric Casaubon, Swiss-born English humanist

DEATH
Edmund Spenser, English poet

PUBLICATIONS
ENGLISH
As You Like It Play by William Shakespeare
Every Man Out of his Humour Play by Ben Jonson
Henry V Play by William Shakespeare
Julius Caesar Play by William Shakespeare

SPANISH
Guzmán de Alfarache Novel by novelist Mateo Alemán

THE SEVENTEENTH CENTURY

The 17th century was a period of turbulence, no less in literature than in politics, religion, and society. Massive shifts took place in a number of sectors at the same time, and new civilizations took shape under the fog of war. An intellectual upheaval resulted in a vast flow of new ideas in culture, metaphysics, politics, economics, and, above all, natural science. This is seen clearly in the expansion of Western culture into the most remote parts of the world. Europeans were exploring new continents, geographically as well as philosophically, and the existing non-Western cultures, especially the Islamic and Chinese, were subjected to immense pressures. Western Christendom, which had been thus far characterized by a unity of spirit and tradition, was being replaced, as Europe became more fragmented.

The spirit of the age was clearly reflected in the century's important literary works, all of which contained some degree of philosophy as writers tried to redefine the world around them. Four of the greatest literary works of the age were René Descartes's *Discourse on Method* (1647), Blaise Pascal's *Pensées* (1670), Francis Bacon's *Advancement of Learning* (1605), and Thomas Hobbes's *Leviathan* (1651), all of them weighted with serious reflections on the changing times. They were characterized by an effort to expand a skeptical, rationalistic mode of thought (formerly limited to science) to politics, religion, and society.

In Germany, Spain, and Italy, the result was baroque literature, an offshoot of baroque art, manifested in the works of Giambattista Marino in Italy, Luis de Góngora y Argote in Spain, and Martin Opitz in Germany. Baroque denoted a style marked by elaboration and ornament and the use of allegory, rhetoric, and daring artifice. In England, metaphysical poetry and Restoration drama were outstanding developments of the period. Metaphysical poetry was a highly intellectualized form of verse marked by bold and ingenious conceits, complex and subtle ideas, frequent use of paradox, and deliberate harshness or rigidity of expression. It was chiefly concerned with analysis of feeling. The term, first applied by John Dryden to John Donne, was expanded by Samuel Johnson to other poets like Richard Crashaw. The Restoration—so called because it represented the restoration to the English throne of the fun-loving Charles II after the austere Puritan Commonwealth—witnessed a resurgence of drama led by playwrights such as John Dryden. The golden age of French drama and letters included a galaxy of writers who continued the tradition of the Pléiade: Molière, Jean Racine, Pierre Corneille, Nicolas Boileau, and Jean de La Fontaine. In Holland three of the finest Dutch poets—Henric Spieghel, Daniël Heinsius, and Gerbrand Bredero—flourished during this period.

The greatest literary conflict in the 17th century was between the ancients and the moderns, or those who thought that literature should be modeled on Greek and Latin classics and those who favored vernacular and demotic expressions. The moderns eventually won, but their victory did not come until the 18th century.

Major Writers of the Seventeenth Century

Molière (Jean-Baptiste Poquelin) (1622–1673) French playwright considered the greatest of all French writers of comedy. His first success came in 1659 with *Les Précieuses ridicules (The Affected Young Ladies)*. Molière wrote little for publication; his plays were made for the stage. He never issued a collected or revised edition and never read proofs. Competition was the motto of his life, along with an unremitting struggle to maintain the interest and loyalty of his troupe's audiences and actors. His major plays were *The*

School for Wives (1663), *Tartuffe* (1669), *Le Misanthrope* (1667), *The Miser* (1669), *The Bourgeois Gentleman* (1671), *Don Juan* (1665), *The Blue Stockings* (1672), and his last play, *The Imaginary Invalid* (1674).

Pierre Corneille (1606–1684) French playwright, considered the father of French classical tragedy. His early plays included comedies and tragicomedies, such as *Mélite* (1630), *The Widow* (1632), *Clitandre* (1631), *The Royal Place* (1634), and *The Maidservant* (1634). He broke new ground with *Médée* (1635) and *Le Cid* (1637), the first classical tragedy of the French theater. A number of Roman tragedies followed: *Horace* (1641), *Cinna* (1643), and *Ployeucte* (1643), which together with *Le Cid* are known as the Classical Tetralogy. The Roman plays were followed by more tragedies: *The Death of Pompey* (1644), *Rodogune* (1645), *Theodore* (1646), and *Heraclius* (1647). In 1644 he turned again to comedy with *The Liar*. In his later years he continued to turn out a surprising number of comedies and tragedies, including *Don Sanche d'Aragon* (1650), *Andromède* (1650), *Nicomède* (1651), and *Pertharite* (1652). An interregnum of eight years followed, but after 1659 he produced one play a year. They included *The Golden Fleece* (1660), *Sertorius* (1662), *Othon* (1664), *Agésilas* (1666), *Attila* (1667), and *Pulchérie* (1672). His final play was the tragedy *Suréna* (1674).

Pedro Calderón de la Barca (1600–1681) Spanish dramatist and poet, second only to the 16th-century writer Lope de Vega in his influence on the Spanish theater. Calderón abandoned the ministry in 1623 and began to write plays. He returned to the church after 30 years and was ordained in 1651, but continued to write. Calderón's major secular plays were *The Painter of His Dishonor* (1645), *The Schism of England* (1627), *The Surgeon of His Honor* (1635), *Life Is a Dream* (1635), *The Mayor of Zalamea* (1640), and *The Daughter of the Air* (1653). Plays in which mythological themes predominate include *Echo and Narcissus* (1651), *The Statue of Prometheus* (1669), and *Wild Beasts Are Tamed by Love* (1669). Calderón also produced a large body of religious works, including *The Constant Prince* (1629), *The Wonder-Working Magician* (1637), *The Two Lovers of Heaven* (1636), and *The Female Joseph* (1640). Calderón was a prolific writer of *autos sacramentales* (morality plays), of which the best known are *The Lord's Vineyard* (1674), *The Merchant's Ship* (1674), *The New Shelter for the Poor* (1675), *The Greatest Day of Days* (1678), and *The Faithful Shepherd* (1678).

John Milton (1608–1674) One of the greatest poets in the English language and author of the epic *Paradise Lost* (1667), Milton was also a noted historian, scholar, pamphleteer, and Puritan partisan. He began writing poetry at college, composing "L'Allegro" and "Il Penseroso," later published in *Poems* (1645). He produced the masque *Comus* in 1634 (in which he dramatized the conflict of good and evil) and the elegy *Lycidas* in 1637. Milton was active in Oliver Cromwell's Commonwealth, serving as its chief propagandist. To this period belongs his defense of freedom speech, *Areopagitica* (1644). After the fall of the Commonwealth, Milton barely escaped with his life and then went blind. Defying his blindness, he wrote the great masterpiece with which his name will be ever associated: *Paradise Lost,* one of the supreme achievements of world literature because of its cosmic scope. He followed with the sequel, *Paradise Regained* (1671), which was published together with *Samson Agonistes.*

Blaise Pascal (1623–1662) French mathematician, philosopher, theologian, and physicist. As a scientist, Pascal invented the first digital calculator and the syringe and discovered Pascal's law of pressure and the principle of the hydraulic press. He is better known to posterity, however, as a religious thinker than as a scientist. A devout Roman Catholic, he was drawn to Jansenism, a pietist movement, and wrote the *Provincial Letters* in defense of his faith, followed by *Pensées*, a collection of apologetical notes on Christianity. Both were immediate successes, marked by a lapidary prose that introduced the modern era in French letters.

Chikamatsu Monzaemon (1653–1725) Japanese playwright, considered the greatest in Japanese theater. He is credited with more than 100 plays, most of which were written for the Bunraku, or puppet theater. The *Soga Heir* (1683) was the first work attributed to him. From 1684 to 1705 he wrote Kabuki plays (popular Japanese theater that blends realism and formalism through music, dance, and mime staged in spectacular costumes) but returned to Bunraku, working for Takemoto Gidayu's puppet theater. Chikamatsu wrote mostly historical romances and domestic tragedies. His most famous works are *The Battle of Coxinga* (1715) and *Double Suicide at Amijima* (1720).

Jean Racine (1639–1699) French playwright and master of classical tragedy, a rival of Molière and Pierre Corneille. His first dramatic success came in 1666, when the Hôtel de Bourgogne produced *Andromaque* with the playwright's mistress in the starring role. He followed this with his only comedy, *The Litigants* (1668). He returned to tragedy with *Britannicus* and *Berenice*, both set in imperial Rome. Four great tragedies established his dominance in the Paris theater: *Bajazet* (1672), *Mithridate* (1673), *Iphigénie en Aulide* (1674), and *Phèdre* (1677). The last was considered the most poetic of his tragedies. His last two plays were commissioned by Louis XIV's wife, Madame de Maintenon: *Esther* (1689) and *Athalie* (1691).

John Donne (1572–1631) English metaphysical poet. Born to devout Roman Catholic parents, John Donne began writing poetry as a student in London. His early writings include several secular poems, such as "Song" ("Go and catch a falling

star"), "A Valediction Forbidding Mourning," "The Bait," "The Canonization," "Elegy XX: To His Mistress Going to Bed," and "The Anniversary." Between 1603 and 1613 his first religious poems appeared in *The Holy Sonnets,* including "Death, Be Not Proud" and "Batter My Heart." In 1615 Donne accepted holy orders, and six years later he was installed as dean of St. Paul's Cathedral in London. As dean, he wrote the celebrated *Devotions upon Emergent Occasions,* which includes such passages as "No man is an island" and "Never send to know for whom the bell tolls; it tolls for thee."

Matsuo Bashō (Matsuo Munefusa) (1644–1694) The greatest of the Japanese haiku poets, Matsuo Bashō abandoned his samurai status in 1666 and devoted himself to poetry. In 1679 he wrote his first verse in a new style in which he attempted to go beyond dependence on form and allusion; he tried in the Zen fashion to illustrate the meaning of life in simple patterns and small objects. His finest work is the *renga,* or the linked verse, in which he excelled. In 1684 Bashō made the first of many journeys that figure prominently in his works. *The Narrow Road to the Deep North* (1694) describes his visit to northern Japan.

John Dryden (1631–1700) English poet and playwright so influential that the Restoration was for a time known as the Age of Dryden. When Charles II was restored to the English throne, Dryden wrote a number of laudatory poems, such as *Astrae Redux* (1660), *To His Sacred Majesty* (1661), and *Annus Mirabilis* (1667). The king named him poet laureate in 1668 and royal historiographer in 1670. When the London theaters reopened under the Restoration, Dryden produced a number of plays: *The Wild Gallant* (1663), *The Indian Queen* (1665), *The Indian Emperour* (1665), *Secret Love, or the Maiden Queen* (1667), *Tyrannick Love* (1669), *The Conquest of Granada by the Spaniards* (1670), *Marriage A-la-Mode* (1675), *Aureng-Zebe* (1675), and *All for Love* (1677). Dryden soon turned to verse satire with the publication of *Absalom and Achitophel* in 1681 and *Mac Flecknoe* in 1682. Dryden returned to the stage with the tragedy *Don Sebastian* (1690) and collaborated with Henry Purcell in *Amphitryon* (1690) and *King Arthur* (1691). With the failure of his tragicomedy *Love Triumphant* (1694) Dryden stopped writing for the theater, but he continued to translate the works of Latin authors. Besides his secular works, Dryden is known for his poem *The Hind and the Panther* (1687), an apology for the Roman Catholic Church, which he joined in 1685.

Key World Events of the Seventeenth Century

1600 Edo period begins in Japan as Tokugawa Ieyasu emerges victor at the Battle of Sekugahara

1603 Scottish and English crowns are united as James VI of Scotland ascends the English throne as James I

1605 French settlers found Port Royal, the first permanent European colony in Canada

1608 Virginia Company builds Jamestown in Virginia, the first English colony in North America. Telescope is invented by a Dutch lensmaker and improved by Galileo Galilei

1618 Thirty Years' War between Catholics and Protestants in the Holy Roman Empire begins with the Defenestration of Prague

1620 *Mayflower* lands at Plymouth Rock in Massachusetts and the Pilgrims found a Puritan commonwealth

1624 Dutch West Indian Company founds New Netherland, a colony on the Hudson River in what is now New York

1640 Portugal casts off Spanish rule as João II, duke of Bragança, declares himself John IV; Spain accepts Portuguese independence in 1668 after the Battle of Montesclaros

1642 Civil war begins in England between royalists and the Puritans, led by Oliver Cromwell

1644 Manchu rule begins in China following an invasion by Fulin

1648 Treaty of Westphalia ends the Thirty Years' War

1649 Charles I is executed at Whitehall following the triumph of the Puritans under Oliver Cromwell; the Commonwealth is established

1653 Commonwealth is superseded by the protectorate headed by Oliver Cromwell

1670 Hudson's Bay Company, the oldest joint-stock company in the world, is founded in Canada by English merchants seeking profits from the fur trade

1672 Royal African Company is founded to trade in slaves from West Africa

1685 Louis XIV revokes the Edict of Nantes in an effort to crush the Huguenots

1688 James II flees England as the Glorious Revolution places William of Orange on the English throne

1689 British Parliament passes the Toleration Act exempting Protestant Dissenters (but not Roman Catholics) from certain penal laws and guaranteeing them freedom of worship; it also passes the Bill of Rights, one of the fundamental instruments of the English constitution

1600

BIRTH
Pedro Calderón de la Barca, Spanish playwright and poet

DEATHS
Bâkî (Mahmud Abdülbâkî), Turkish poet
Giordano Bruno, Italian anti-Catholic philosopher

PUBLICATIONS

ENGLISH

Cynthia's Revels Comedy by Ben Jonson
Hamlet Play by William Shakespeare
The Shoemaker's Holiday Play by Thomas Dekker
Twelfth Night, or What You Will Play by William Shakespeare

POLISH

Judas Sack Poem by Sebastian Klonowic

1601

BIRTHS

Baltsar Gracián y Morales, Spanish Jesuit philosopher
Sā'ib of Tabriz, Persian poet
Tristan (François l'Hermite), French playwright and poet

DEATH

Thomas Nashe, English playwright

PUBLICATIONS

ENGLISH

Troilus and Cressida Play by William Shakespeare

PORTUGUESE

Brazilian

Prosopeya First national epic by Bento Teixeira Pinto

1603

PUBLICATION

ENGLISH

All's Well That Ends Well Play by William Shakespeare

1604

BIRTH

Manasseh ben Israel, Dutch-Jewish scholar

PUBLICATIONS

ENGLISH

The Malcontent Play by John Marston
Measure for Measure Play by William Shakespeare
The Passionate Shepheard Poem by Nicholas Breton
The Tragedy of Othello, Moor of Venice Play by William Shakespeare

The Tragical History of the Life and Death of Doctor Faustus Play by Christopher Marlowe

SPANISH

The Grandeur of Mexico Epic poem by Bernardo de Balbuena

1605

BIRTH

Sir Thomas Browne, English author

PUBLICATIONS

DUTCH

Grandida Play by Pieter Corneliszoon Hooft

ENGLISH

The Advancement of Learning Treatise by Francis Bacon
King Lear Play by William Shakespeare
Macbeth Play by William Shakespeare
The Tragedie of Philotas Masque by Samuel Daniel

SPANISH

Don Quijote de la Mancha, el ingenioso hidalgo (*Don Quixote*) Novel by Miguel de Cervantes Saavedra

1606

BIRTHS

Pierre Corneille, French playwright
Sir William D'Avenant, English poet and playwright

DEATH

John Lyle, English dramatist

PUBLICATIONS

ENGLISH

Antony and Cleopatra Play by William Shakespeare
If You Know Not Me, You Know Nobody Play by Thomas Heywood
The Queenes Arcadia Pastoral tragicomedy by Samuel Daniel
Volpone, or the Fox Play by Ben Jonson

1607

BIRTHS

Paul Gerhardt, German hymn writer
Georg Philipp Harsdörfer, German poet
Tukārām, Hindu Marathi poet
Francisco de Rojos Zorrilla, Spanish playwright

PUBLICATIONS

ENGLISH

Coriolanus Play by William Shakespeare
Holy Sonnets Poems by John Donne
Timon of Athens Play by William Shakespeare
A Woman Killed with Kindness Play by Thomas Heywood

1608

BIRTH

John Milton, English poet

PUBLICATIONS

ENGLISH

Pericles, Prince of Tyre Play by William Shakespeare
Philaster Play by Francis Beaumont and John Fletcher
The White Devil Play by John Webster

1609

BIRTHS

Paul Fleming, German lyric poet
Jean de Rotrou, French playwright
Sir John Suckling, English poet

PUBLICATIONS

ENGLISH

Appius and Virginia Tragic play by John Webster and Thomas Heywood
Cymbeline Play by William Shakespeare
Epicoene, or the Silent Woman Comedy by Ben Jonson
The Faerie Queene Poem by Edmund Spenser
Sonnets by William Shakespeare

1610

BIRTH

Paul Scarron, French poet

DEATHS

Juan de la Cueva, Spanish poet
Tomás Sánchez, Spanish Jesuit moralist

PUBLICATIONS

ENGLISH

The Alchemist Play by Ben Jonson
Winter's Tale Play by William Shakespeare

SPANISH

Peribanez Play by Lope de Vega

1611

LITERARY EVENTS

Authorized Version of the English Bible, also known as the King James Bible, is published
English translation of the *Iliad* by George Chapman

PUBLICATIONS

ENGLISH

An Anatomy of the World: The First Anniversary Elegiac lament by John Donne
Henry VIII Play by William Shakespeare
The Maid's Tragedy Tragedy by Francis Beaumont and John Fletcher
May Day Comedy by George Chapman
The Tempest Play by William Shakespeare

1612

BIRTHS

Anne Bradstreet, American poet
Samuel Butler, English poet
Richard Crashaw, English religious poet
Ku Chiang, Chinese scholar

DEATH

Giovanni Battista Guarini, Italian playwright

PUBLICATIONS

DUTCH

Teeuwis the Peasant Comedy by Samuel Coster

ENGLISH

Cupid's Revenge Play by Francis Beaumont and John Fletcher
The Progress of the Soul: The Second Anniversary Metaphysical poem by John Donne
The Widow's Tears Tragicomedy by George Chapman

1613

BIRTHS

Khushhal Khan Khatak, Afghan national poet
François de La Rochefoucauld, French writer of maxims

DEATHS

Natshinnaung, Burmese poet and monarch
Mathurin Régnier, French satirist

PUBLICATIONS

DUTCH

Geeraert van Velsen Play by Pieter Corneliszoon Hooft

ENGLISH

The Revenge of the Bussy D'Amboise Dramatic tragedy by George Chapman

SPANISH

Exemplary Stories Short stories by Miguel de Cervantes Saavedra
Fuente ovejuna Dramatic piece by Lope de Vega

1614

BIRTHS

Mateo Alemán, Spanish novelist
Hallgrimur Petursson, Icelandic hymn writer and poet

PUBLICATIONS

ENGLISH

Bartholomew Fair Dramatic comedy by Ben Jonson
The Duchess of Malfi Tragedy by John Webster
The History of the World History by Walter Raleigh
A Wife Poem by Thomas Overbury

1615

BIRTHS

Richard Baxter, English churchman and devotional writer
Dārā Shikōh, Indo-Persian mystic poet

DEATH

Nuruddin Muhammad Tahir Zuhuri, Indo-Persian poet

PUBLICATION

SPANISH

Pedro, the Artful Dodger Play by Miguel de Cervantes Saavedra

1616

DEATHS

Francis Beaumont, English playwright
Miguel de Cervantes Saavedra, Spanish novelist, playwright, and poet
Richard Hakluyt, English voyager
William Shakespeare, English playwright

PUBLICATIONS

ENGLISH

The Devil Is an Ass Comedy by Ben Jonson
The Forest Collection of short poems by Ben Jonson

FRENCH

Tragiques Poem in seven cantos by Théodore-Agrippa d'Aubigné

1617

PUBLICATIONS

DUTCH

Boeto Play by Dutch playwright Pieter Corneliszoon Hooft

FRENCH

Collected Works Theological treatises by John Calvin, Protestant reformer

1618

BIRTHS

Abraham Cowley, English poet
Richard Lovelace, English poet

DEATHS

Gerebrand Adriaanszoon Bredero, Dutch playwright
Sir Walter Raleigh, English poet and adventurer

PUBLICATIONS

CHINESE

Jin Ping Mei (The Plum in the Golden Vase) Novel, anonymous

ENGLISH

The Loyal Subject Play by John Fletcher
Pleasure Reconciled to Virtue Play by Ben Jonson

SPANISH

Life of Squire Marcos of Obregon Novel by Vicente Espinel
The Youth of the Cid Play by Guillén de Castro y Bellvis

1619

BIRTH

Savinien de Cyrano de Bergerac, French writer and adventurer

DEATH

Ginés Pérez de Hita, Spanish writer and soldier

PUBLICATIONS

FRENCH

La Bergeries Pastoral play in verse by Honorat du Bueil, seigneur de Racan

PORTUGUESE

Life of Archbishop Dominican Friar Bartolomeu dos Martires Biography by Luís de Sousa
Village Court Poems by Francisco Rodrigues Lobo

1620

BIRTH
Miklós Zrínyi, Hungarian poet

DEATHS
Thomas Campion, English poet
Firishtah, Indian Muslim historian

PUBLICATION

ENGLISH
Novum Organum Philosophical treatise by Francis Bacon

1621

BIRTHS
Jean de La Fontaine, French poet
Andrew Marvell, English metaphysical poet

PUBLICATIONS

ENGLISH
The Anatomy of Melancholy by Robert Burton
Women Beware Women Play by Thomas Middleton

1622

BIRTHS
Hans Jakob Christoffel von Grimmelshausen, German
    novelist
Molière (Jean-Baptiste Poquelin), French playwright
Henry Vaughan, Welsh poet

DEATHS
John Barclay, Scottish satirist
John Owen, Welsh poet

PUBLICATIONS

DUTCH
Exquisitely Foolish Satire by Constantijn Huygens
The Great Songbook Poems by Gerbrand Adriaenszoon Bredero

ENGLISH
The History of Henry VII Biography by Francis Bacon

ITALIAN
The Rape of the Bucket Mock heroic poem by Alessandro Tassoni

SPANISH
Gerardo, the Unfortunate Spaniard Romance by Gonzalo de
    Céspedes y Meneses

1623

BIRTH
Blaise Pascal, French scientist and theologian

DEATHS
Paolo (Pietro) Sarpi, Italian philosopher
Tulsidās, Hindu poet

LITERARY EVENT
First Folio of William Shakespeare is published

PUBLICATIONS

ENGLISH
The Devil's Law Case Tragicomedy by John Webster
The Duchess of Malfi Play by John Webster
The Cypresse Grove Meditations by Scottish poet William Drummond

LATIN
De Augmentis Scientiarum Treatise by English writer Francis
    Bacon

1624

BIRTHS
Angelus Silesius (Johannes Scheffler), German mystic writer
Arnold Geulincx, Belgian philosopher

DEATH
Vicente Espinel, Spanish poet

PUBLICATIONS

ENGLISH
Devotions Upon Emergent Occasions Devotions by John Donne
Rule a Wife and Have a Wife Comedy by John Fletcher

SPANISH
Bernardo; or the Victory at Roncesvilles Epic poem by Bernardo
    de Balbuena

1625

BIRTH
Wacław Potocki, Polish poet

DEATHS
John Fletcher, English playwright
Giambattista Marini, Italian poet
John Webster, English playwright

PUBLICATIONS

DUTCH
Palamedes, or Murdered Innocence Play by Joost van den Vondel
Ship's Talk Play by Constantijn Huygens

ENGLISH
"His Majesty's Escape at St. Andere" Poem by Edmund Waller
"On the Death of a Fair Infant Dying of a Cough" Elegy by John Milton
A Staple of News Comedy by Ben Jonson
The Woman's Prize, or the Tamer Tamed Play by John Fletcher

LATIN
The Law of War and Peace Legal work by Dutch scholar Hugo Grotius

TAMIL
Kantapuranam Poem of more than 10,000 stanzas by Kasiyappa Sivakariyar

1626

DEATHS
Francis Bacon, English philosopher
Cyril Tourneur, English playwright

PUBLICATION

ENGLISH
The New Atlantis Treatise on political philosophy by Francis Bacon

1627

DEATHS
Luis de Góngora y Argote, Spanish lyric poet
Thomas Middleton, English playwright

PUBLICATIONS

CROATIAN
Osman Epic poem by Ivan Gundulić

SPANISH
The Life of Buscon Picaresque novel by Francisco Gómez Quevedo y Villegas
Visions Satiric portraits by Francisco Gómez Quevedo y Villegas

1628

BIRTHS
John Bunyan, English allegorical writer
Charles Perrault, French poet

DEATH
François de Malherbe, French poet

PUBLICATIONS

ENGLISH
The Lover's Melancholy Play by John Ford
'Tis a Pity She's a Whore Play by John Ford

SPANISH
Truth Under Suspicion Comedy by Mexican-born playwright Juan Ruiz de Alarcón

1629

PUBLICATIONS

ENGLISH
The Roman Actor Play by Philip Massinger
"On the Morning of Christ's Nativity" Poem by John Milton

SPANISH
The Constant Prince Play by Pedro Calderón de la Barca
Phantom Lady Play by Pedro Calderón de la Barca

1630

DEATH
Théodore-Agrippa d'Aubigné, French poet

PUBLICATIONS

DANISH
Hexaemeron Religious poem by Anders Christiensen Arrebo, clergyman

DUTCH
Overijssel Songs and Poems Collection by Jacobus Revius

ENGLISH
"On Shakespeare" Poem by John Milton
The Honest Whore Play by Thomas Dekker

FRENCH
Melite, or the False Letters Comedy by Pierre Corneille
The Wood Nymph, or the Living Corpse Play by Jean Mairet

SPANISH
The Deceiver of Seville and the Stone Guest Drama by Tirso de Molina

1631

BIRTH
John Dryden, English poet and playwright

DEATH
John Donne, English poet

PUBLICATIONS
ENGLISH
Caesar and Pompey Dramatic tragedy by George Chapman
"Il Penseroso" Poem by John Milton

1632

BIRTHS
John Locke, English political philosopher
Jean Mabillon, French Benedictine monk and historian
Baruch Spinoza, Dutch Jewish philosopher

DEATHS
Thomas Dekker, English poet
Luís de Sousa, Portuguese historian

PUBLICATIONS
ENGLISH
Magnetic Lady, or Humours Reconciled Dramatic comedy by Ben Jonson
"L'Allegro" Poem by John Milton

LATIN
Roxana Tragedy by English poet and clergyman William Alabaster

1633

BIRTH
Samuel Pepys, English diarist

DEATH
George Herbert, English metaphysical poet

PUBLICATIONS
ENGLISH
Arcades Short dramatic piece by John Milton
The Holy Sonnets Poems by John Donne
The Jew of Malta Drama in blank verse by Christopher Marlowe
Poetical Blossomes Collection of poems by Abraham Cowley
"Song" ("Go and catch a falling star") Poem by John Donne
A Tale of a Tub Comedy by Ben Jonson
The Temple Collection of poems by George Herbert
A Valediction: Forbidding Mourning Poem by John Donne

FRENCH
Virginie Play by Jean Mairet

1634

DEATH
George Chapman, English playwright and poet

PUBLICATIONS
ENGLISH
Comus, A Masque Dramatic piece by John Milton

FRENCH
Sophonisbe Tragedy by Jean Mairet

LITERARY EVENT
Académie Française is founded in Paris

1635

BIRTH
Philippe Quinault, French playwright

DEATHS
Nef'i (Ömer), Turkish poet
Alessandro Tassoni, Italian poet
Lope de Vega, Spanish playwright

PUBLICATIONS
FRENCH
Mark Antony, or Cleopatra Play by Jean Mairet

GREEK
The Sacrifice of Abraham Mystery play by Vitzéntzos Kornáros

SPANISH
Life Is a Dream Metaphysical play by Pedro Calderón de la Barca
The Surgeon of His Honor Play by Pedro Calderón de la Barca

URDU
All Sentiments Poem by Indian writer Mulla Vajhi

1636

BIRTH
Nicolas Boileau, French poet and critic

PUBLICATIONS
ENGLISH
The Great Duke of Florence Romantic comedy by Philip Massinger

FRENCH
The Comic Illusion Comic drama by Pierre Corneille

SPANISH

Two Lovers of Heaven Play by Pedro Calderón de la Barca

1637

BIRTH
Mary White Rowlandson, English-born American writer

DEATH
Ben Jonson, English playwright

PUBLICATIONS

ENGLISH
Lycidas Poem by John Milton

FRENCH
Discours de la méthode Philosophical tract by René Descartes
Le Cid Tragicomedy by Pierre Corneille

SPANISH
The Wonder-Working Magician Religious drama by Pedro Calderón de la Barca

1638

BIRTH
Nicolas de Malebranche, French philosopher

DEATH
Ivan Gundulić, Croatian poet

PUBLICATIONS

DUTCH
Gysbreght von Aemstel Historical drama by Joost van den Vondel

ENGLISH
Barnabees Journal Rhymed verse (some in Latin) by Richard Brathwaite
The Goblins Comedy by Sir John Suckling
Love's Riddle Pastoral drama by Abraham Cowley

1639

BIRTHS
Increase Mather, American divine
Jean Racine, French playwright

DEATHS
Tommaso Campanella, Italian philosopher

Thomas Carew, English poet
John Ford, English playwright
Jean Ruiz de Alarcón y Mendoza, Spanish playwright

PUBLICATIONS

ENGLISH

American

An Almanac for New England for the Year 1639 First almanac published in the American colonies by William Pierce

British

The Tragedy of Chabot, Admiral of France Play by George Chapman

1640

BIRTHS
Aphra Behn, English poet, playwright, and novelist
Pu Songling, Chinese novelist and poet
William Wycherley, English playwright

DEATHS
Robert Burton, English writer
Uriel da Costa, Portuguese-born Dutch Jewish philosopher
Paul Fleming, German lyric poet
Philip Massinger, English playwright
Maciej Kazimierz Sarbiewski, Polish Jesuit poet

PUBLICATIONS

DUTCH
Joseph in Egypt Play by Joost van den Vondel

ENGLISH
Timber, or Discoveries Made Upon Men and Matter Miscellaneous reflections by Ben Jonson
Underwoods Minor poems by Ben Jonson

FRENCH
Cinna, or the Clemency of Augustus Dramatic tragedy by Pierre Corneille
Horace Tragedy by Pierre Corneille
Polyeucte Tragedy by Pierre Corneille

SPANISH
The Female Joseph Play by Pedro Calderón de la Barca
The Mayor of Zalamea Play by Pedro Calderón de la Barca

1641

DEATHS
Thomas Heywood, British playwright
Sara Copio Sullam, Italian Jewish poet

PUBLICATIONS

ENGLISH

The Cutter of Coleman Street Comedy by Abraham Cowley

FRENCH

Ibrahim, or the Illustrious Bassa Novel by Madeleine de Scudery

SPANISH

El diablo cojuelo Picaresque novel by Luis Vélez de Guevara

1642

BIRTHS

Ihara Saikaku, Japanese poet and novelist
Sir Isaac Newton, English scientist, mathematician, and philosopher

DEATH

Sir John Suckling, English poet and playwright

PUBLICATIONS

ENGLISH

The Cooper's Hell Poem by John Denham
De Cive Tract by Thomas Hobbes, philosopher
Religio Medici Journal of meditations by Thomas Browne

1643

LITERARY EVENT

Christiana Almanack First Norwegian printed book

1644

BIRTH

Matsuo Bashō (Matsuo Manefusa), Japanese poet

DEATH

Luis Vélez de Guevara, Spanish novelist and playwright

PUBLICATIONS

ENGLISH

American

The Bloody Tenet of Persecution for the Cause of Conscience Prose tract by Roger Williams, New England divine

British

Areopagitica: A Speech . . . for the Liberty of Unlicenced Printing to the Parliament of England Prose by John Milton

FRENCH

The Death of Pompey Play by Pierre Corneille
The Liar Play by Pierre Corneille
Rodogune Tragedy by Pierre Corneille

1645

BIRTHS

Jean de La Bruyère, French writer and translator
Carlos de Sigüenza y Góngora, Mexican chronicler and poet

DEATHS

Hugo Grotius, Dutch jurist
Francisco Gómez de Quevedo y Villegas, Spanish poet and satirist

PUBLICATIONS

ENGLISH

"Go, Lovely Rose" Poem by Edmund Waller

FRENCH

The Three Dorothys Comedy by Paul Scarron

SPANISH

The Painter of His Dishonor Play by Pedro Calderón de la Barca

1646

BIRTH

Gottfried Wilhelm Leibniz, German philosopher

PUBLICATIONS

ENGLISH

American

Milk for Babes, Drawn Out of the Breasts of Both Testaments Catechism by New England clergyman John Cotton

British

Brennoralt Tragedy by John Suckling
Fragmenta Aurea Collection of poems by John Suckling
Steps to the Temple Religious poem by Richard Crashaw

FRENCH

Le Véritable Saint Genest Dramatic tragedy by Jean de Rotrou

GERMAN

Leo Arminius Tragedy by Andreas Gryphius

1647

BIRTHS

Pierre Bayle, French philosopher
John Wilmot, earl of Rochester, English poet

DEATH

Pieter Corneliszoon Hooft, Dutch playwright and poet

PUBLICATIONS

ENGLISH

The Mistress Poetic cycle by Abraham Cowley
Noble Numbers; or, His Pious Pieces Collection of poems by
    Robert Herrick

1648

BIRTH

Petter Dass, Norwegian poet

DEATHS

Marin Mersenne, French philosopher
Tirso de Molina (Gabriel Téllez), Spanish playwright
Francisco de Rojas Zorrilla, Spanish playwright
Vincent Voiture, French poet

PUBLICATIONS

ENGLISH

Hesperides Collection of poems by Robert Herrick

FRENCH

Artemenes; or, the Grand Cyrus Novel by Madeleine de Scudéry
Le Roman comique Picaresque novel by Paul Scarron

1649

DEATHS

Richard Crashaw, English religious poet
Tukārām, Marathi poet

PUBLICATIONS

ENGLISH

"To Althea, from Prison" Poem by Richard Lovelace
"To Lucasta, Going to the Wars" Poem by Richard Lovelace
"Upon the Death of Lord Hastings" Poem by John Dryden

FRENCH

The Passions of the Soul Ethical treatise by René Descartes

GERMAN

Charles Stuart, or Majesty Murdered Tragic drama by Andreas
    Gryphius

1650

BIRTHS

Abdurrahman Mohammad, Afghan religious poet
Ahmade Khani, Kurdish poet
Jam Durak, Iranian (Baluchi) lyric poet

DEATHS

René Descartes, French philosopher
Jean de Rotrou, French playwright

PUBLICATIONS

ENGLISH

British

The Saints Everlasting Rest Tract by Presbyterian divine Richard
    Baxter

Welsh

The Glittering Flint Devotional verse by Henry Vaughan

FRENCH

Andromède Play by Pierre Corneille

1651

BIRTHS

Sor Juana Inés de la Cruz, Mexican poet and nun
François de Salignac de La Mothe-Fénelon, French mystic writer
    and Roman Catholic cleric

PUBLICATIONS

ENGLISH

The Leviathan Political treatise by Thomas Hobbes

FRENCH

Nicomède Play by Pierre Corneille

1652

BIRTH

Nahum Tate, Irish-born English poet and dramatist

DEATH

John Cotton, New England clergyman

PUBLICATIONS

ENGLISH

A Priest to the Temple Prose work by George Herbert

FRENCH

The Christian Socrates Religious dialogues by Jean-Louis Guez
    de Balzac

1653

BIRTH

Chikamatsu Monzaemon, Japanese playwright

PUBLICATIONS

ENGLISH

The Compleat Angler, or the Contemplative Man's Recreation Discourse on fishing by Izaak Walton
The Changeling Play by Thomas Middleton and William Rowley

FRENCH

The Blunderer Comedy by Molière

SPANISH

The Daughter of the Air Play by Pedro Calderón de la Barca

1654

DEATH

Matsunaga Teitoku, Japanese poet

PUBLICATIONS

CZECH

Orbis Sensualium Pictus First picture book for children by Johann Amos Commenius, educational reformer

DUTCH

Lucifer Play by Joost van den Vondel

FRENCH

Clélie: Histoire romaine Novel by Madeleine de Scudéry

SPANISH

Disdain Turned Against Disdain Dramatic comedy by Agustín Moreto y Cabaña

1655

BIRTHS

Johann Beer, German novelist
Jean François Regnard, French comic playwright

DEATHS

Savinien de Cyrano de Bergerac, French writer
Joseph Solomon Delmedigo, Jewish theologian, physician, and philosopher
Pierre Gassendi, French mathematician and philosopher
Daniel Heinsius, Dutch classical scholar
Tristan (François L'Hermite), French playwright and poet

1656

PUBLICATIONS

ENGLISH

Miscellanies Collection of poems by Abraham Cowley

FRENCH

Provincial Letters Prose pamphlets by Blaise Pascal

1657

DEATHS

Richard Lovelace, English Cavalier lyric poet
Manasseh ben Israel, Dutch-Jewish scholar and Talmudist

PUBLICATIONS

GERMAN

The Absurda Comica, or Master Peter Squentz Comic play by Andreas Gryphius
Cardenio und Celinde Tragedy by Andreas Gryphius
Carolus Stardus Tragedy by Andreas Gryphius
Catharina von Georgien Tragedy by Andreas Gryphius

1658

DEATHS

Baltasar Gracián y Morales, Spanish philosopher
George Philip Harsdörfer, German poet

PUBLICATIONS

ENGLISH

De Homine Tract by Thomas Hobbes
"Methought I Saw My Late Espoused Saint" Poem by John Milton

SWEDISH

Hercules Allegorical epic by Georg Stiernhielm

1659

DEATH

Dārā Shikōh, Indo-Persian scholar

PUBLICATIONS

DUTCH

Jephthah, or The Promised Sacrifice Tragedy by Joost van den Vondel

FRENCH

The Affected Ladies Play by Molière
The Amorous Quarrel Comedy by Molière

GERMAN

Papinianus Play by Andreas Gryphius

1660

BIRTH

Daniel Defoe, English novelist

DEATH

Paul Scarron, French cleric and writer

PUBLICATIONS

ENGLISH

Astrea Redux Poem by John Dryden

FRENCH

The Golden Fleece Tragedy by Pierre Corneille

1661

BIRTH

Florent Carton Dancourt, French playwright

PUBLICATIONS

FRENCH

The School for Husbands Comedy by Molière

SPANISH

Echo and Narcissus Play by Pedro Calderón de la Barca

1662

DEATH

Blaise Pascal, French philosopher

PUBLICATIONS

ENGLISH

The Day of Doom Poetic epic by American Puritan writer Michael Wigglesworth

FRENCH

The Princess of Montpensier Novel by Marie-Madeleine de La Fayette
The School for Wives Play by Molière
Sertorius Play by Pierre Corneille

1663

BIRTH

Cotton Mather, American Puritan divine

PUBLICATIONS

ENGLISH

Hudibras Burlesque poem by Samuel Butler
The Wild Gallant Play by John Dryden

GERMAN

Horribilicribrifax Satirical comedy by Andreas Gryphius

1664

BIRTHS

Matthew Prior, English poet
Sir John Vanbrugh, English playwright

DEATHS

Bihari Lal, Hindi poet
Andreas Gryphius, German lyric poet and playwright
Miklós Zrínyi, Hungarian poet

PUBLICATIONS

DUTCH

Adam in Exile Play by Joost van den Vondel

ENGLISH

American

Meditations Divine and Moral Collections of aphorisms by poet Anne Bradstreet

British

The Rival Ladies Play by John Dryden

FRENCH

The Forced Marriage Comedy-ballet by Molière
Othon Play by Pierre Corneille
Tartuffe Comedy by Molière
The Thebans, or the Enemy Brothers Tragedy by Jean Racine

1665

DEATH

Samuel Coster, Dutch playwright

PUBLICATIONS

ENGLISH

The Indian Emperour Heroic play by John Dryden
The Indian Queen Tragedy by John Dryden

FRENCH

Alexander the Great Tragedy by Jean Racine
Don Juan, or the Stone Guest Comedy in prose by Molière
Lives of Gallant Women Memoirs of Pierre de Bourdeille, seigneur de Brantôme
Maxims Collection of maxims by François de La Rochefocauld
Tales and Novels in Verse Humorous poetic tales by Jean de la Fontaine

1666

PUBLICATIONS

ENGLISH

Grace Abounding to the Chief of Sinners Autobiography by John Bunyan, religious allegorist

FRENCH

Agesilas Play by Pierre Corneille
La Misanthrope Comedy by Molière

GERMAN

The Chaste Joseph Novel by Hans Jakob Christoffel von Grimmelshausen, satirist

ICELANDIC

The Passion Hymns Poems by Hallgrimur Petursson

1667

BIRTH

Jonathan Swift, Irish-born English satirist

DEATH

Abraham Cowley, English poet

PUBLICATIONS

DUTCH

Noah Play by Joost van den Vondel

ENGLISH

Annus Mirabilis Poem by John Dryden
Paradise Lost Poetic epic by John Milton
Secret Love, or the Maiden Queen Tragicomedy by John Dryden

FRENCH

Andromaque Dramatic tragedy by Jean Racine
Attila Play by Pierre Corneille

1668

BIRTHS

Alain-René Lesage, French novelist
Giambattista Vico, Italian philosopher

DEATH

Sir William D'Avenant, English poet and playwright

PUBLICATIONS

FRENCH

Fables: Selected Fables in Verse Verse fables by Jean de La Fontaine

The Litigants Comedy by Jean Racine
The Miser Comic drama in prose by Molière

SWEDISH

Muses Poems by Georg Stiernhielm

1669

DEATHS

Arnold Geulincx, Belgian philosopher
Agustín Moreto y Cabaña, Spanish playwright

PUBLICATIONS

ENGLISH

Tyrannic Love, or the Royal Martyr Heroic play in rhymed couplets by John Dryden

FRENCH

Britannicus Dramatic tragedy by Jean Racine

GERMAN

Simplicissmus the Vagabond, that is the Life of a Strange Adventurer Named Melchio Sternfels von Fuchsheim Novel by Hans Jakob Christoffel von Grimmelshausen

SPANISH

Statue of Prometheus Play by Pedro Calderón de la Barca
Wild Beasts Are Tamed by Love Play by Pedro Calderón de la Barca

1670

BIRTH

William Congreve, English playwright

DEATHS

Johann Amos Comenius, Czech educational reformer
Honorat de Bueil, seigneur de Racan, French poet

PUBLICATIONS

ENGLISH

The Conquest of Grenada Play by John Dryden

FRENCH

Bérénice Play by Jean Racine
Pensées Meditations by Blaise Pascal
The Would-Be Gentleman Comedy-ballet in prose by Molière

1671

BIRTH

Colley Cibber, British playwright and poet

DEATH

Meric Casaubon, Swiss-born English humanist

PUBLICATIONS

ENGLISH

Love in a Wood Comedy of intrigue by William Wycherley
Paradise Regained Epic poem and sequel to *Paradise Lost* by John Milton
Samson Agonistes Tragedy by John Milton

FRENCH

The Cheats of Scapin Play by Molière
The Bourgeois Gentleman Play by Molière

1672

BIRTHS

Joseph Addison, English essayist
Ludovico Antonio Muratori, Italian historian
Sir Richard Steele, Irish-born English essayist

DEATHS

Anne Bradstreet, American poet
Georg Stiernhielm, Swedish poet

PUBLICATIONS

ENGLISH

Marriage A-la-Mode Play by John Dryden

FRENCH

Bajazet Play by Jean Racine
The Learned Ladies Play by Molière
Pulchérie Play by Pierre Corneille

1673

DEATH

Molière (Jean-Baptiste Poquelin), French playwright

PUBLICATIONS

ENGLISH

Amboyna Dramatic tragedy by John Dryden
The Gentleman Dancing Master Play by William Wycherley

FRENCH

The Imaginary Invalid Comedy by Molière
Mithridates Dramatic tragedy by Jean Racine

RUSSIAN

Life First Russian autobiography, by Avvakum Petrovich

1674

BIRTH

Prosper Jolyot, sieur de Crais-Billon (Crébillon), French playwright

DEATHS

Robert Herrick, English poet
John Milton, English poet
Hallgrimur Petursson, Icelandic hymn writer

PUBLICATIONS

DANISH

Spiritual Chorus Hymns by Thomas Kingo

FRENCH

The Art of Poetry Didactic and satirical poem by Nicolas Boileau
Iphigénie en Aulide Tragedy by Jean Racine
On the Search after Truth Treatise by Nicolas de Malebranche, philosopher

ITALIAN

Il Pentamerone Collection of 50 Neapolitan tales by folklorist Giambattista Basile

1675

BIRTHS

Arai Hakuseki, Japanese historian and writer
Francesco Scipione Maffei, Italian playwright
Louis de Rouvroy de Saint-Simon, French memoirist

PUBLICATIONS

ENGLISH

Aureng-Zebe Historical play by John Dryden
The Country Wife Play by William Wycherley

1676

DEATHS

Paul Gerhardt, German hymn writer
Jean Desmarets de Saint-Sorlen, French critic
Hans Jakob Christoffel von Grimmelshausen, German novelist

PUBLICATIONS

ENGLISH

American

A Looking-Glass for the Times Poem by Peter Folger

British

Don Carlos Play by Thomas Otway

1677

DEATHS
Baruch Spinoza, Dutch-Jewish philosopher
Angelus Silesius (Johannes Scheffler), German mystic writer
Sã'ib of Tabriz, Persian poet

PUBLICATIONS
ENGLISH
American

"Elegy Upon the Death of Reverend Mr. Thomas Shepard" Poem by Uriah Oakes

British

The Plain Dealer Play by William Wycherley
The Rover, or the Banished Cavaliers Play by Aphra Behn
The State of Innocence and Fall of Man Play by John Dryden

FRENCH
Phaedre Tragedy by Jean Racine

1678

BIRTH
George Farquhar, Irish playwright

DEATHS
Andrew Marvell, English poet
Mary White Rowlandson, American writer of North America's first Indian captivity narrative

PUBLICATIONS
ENGLISH
American

Poems Collection by Anne Bradstreet

British

Oroonoko, or the History of the Royal Slave Novel by Aphra Behn
The Pilgrim's Progress, from This World to That Which Is to Come Allegory by John Bunyan

FRENCH
La Princesse de Clèves Novel by Marie-Madeleine de La Fayette

1679

DEATHS
Thomas Hobbes, English philosopher
Joost van den Vondel, Dutch poet

PUBLICATIONS
CHINESE
Strange Stories from a Chinese Studio Collection of folk tales by Pu Songling

ENGLISH
Caius Marius Play by Thomas Otway
Fifty Comedies and Tragedies Plays by John Fletcher and Francis Beaumont
Troilus and Cressida Play by John Dryden

1680

BIRTH
Philippe Destouches, French playwright

DEATHS
Samuel Butler, English satirist
François de La Rouchefoucauld, French moral philosopher
Hayashi Shunsai, Japanese historian
John Wilmot, English poet

PUBLICATIONS
ENGLISH
The Orphan Play by Thomas Otway
The Soldier's Fortune Comedy by Thomas Otway

SPANISH
The Glories of Querétaro Chronicle of the Church of the Virgin of Guadalupe by Mexican historian Carlos de Sigüenza y Góngora

1681

BIRTH
Ahmed Nedim, Turkish poet

DEATHS
Pedro Calderón de la Barca, Spanish playwright
Gu Jiang, Chinese scholar and writer

PUBLICATIONS
ENGLISH
Absalom and Achitophel Poem by John Dryden
"The Garden" Poem by Andrew Marvell
The Spanish Fryar Verse Comedy by John Dryden
"To His Coy Mistress" Poem by Andrew Marvell

FRENCH
Discourse on Universal History Historical tract by Jacques-Bénigne Bossuet

1682

DEATH
Sir Thomas Browne, English writer

PUBLICATIONS
ENGLISH
The City Heiress Dramatic comedy by Aphra Behn
The Holy War Allegory by John Bunyan
Mac Flecknoe Satire by John Dryden
Religio Laici, or a Layman's Faith Doxography by John Dryden
Venice Preserved Play by Thomas Otway

JAPANESE
The Life of an Amorous Man Novel by Ihara Saikaku

1683

BIRTH
Edward Young, English poet

DEATH
Izaak Walton, English writer

PUBLICATIONS
ENGLISH
The Duke of Guise Play by John Dryden and Nathaniel Lee

FRENCH
Le Mercure galant Satirical comedy by Edme Boursault

GERMAN
Tales of Summer Novel by Johann Beer

JAPANESE
The Soga Heir Play by Chikamatsu Monzaemon

SPANISH
The Determination of a House Play by Sor Juana Inés de la Cruz, Mexican scholar and nun

1684

BIRTH
Baron Ludvig Holberg, Norwegian-Danish playwright, poet and essayist

DEATH
Pierre Corneille, French playwright

PUBLICATION
SPANISH
Occidental Paradise History by Carlos de Sigüenza y Góngora

1685

BIRTHS
George Berkeley, Irish philosopher
John Gay, English poet

PUBLICATIONS
ENGLISH
Albion and Albanius Opera by John Dryden
Of Divine Love Didactic poem by Edmund Waller
Threnodia Augustalis Pindaric ode by John Dryden

1686

DEATH
Jean Mairet, French playwright

PUBLICATIONS
ENGLISH
"Of the Last Verses Written in His Book" Poem by Edmund Waller

JAPANESE
Successful Kagekiyo Puppet play by Chikamatsu Monzaemon
Five Women Who Chose Love Novel by Ihara Saikaku
A Woman Who Devoted Her Entire Life to Love-Making Novel by Ihara Saikaku

1687

DEATHS
Constantijn Huygens, Dutch humanist and poet
Edmund Waller, English poet

PUBLICATIONS
ENGLISH
The Hind and the Panther Poem by John Dryden
Mathematical Principles of Natural Philosophy Tract by Isaac Newton
Song for St. Cecilia's Day Poem by John Dryden

FRENCH
Treatise on the Education of Girls Prose tract by François de la Mothe Fenelon

1688

BIRTHS

Alexander Pope, English poet
Pierre Carlet de Chamberlain de Marivaux, French playwright and novelist

DEATHS

John Bunyan, English allegorist
Philippe Quinault, French poet and playwright

PUBLICATIONS

ENGLISH

Britannia Rediviva Poem on the birth of a prince by John Dryden

FRENCH

The Character, or Manners of the Age with the Characters of Theophrastus Satire by moralist Jean de la Bruyère
Digression on Ancients and Moderns Tract by Bernard de Fontenelle

1689

BIRTHS

Alexis Piron, French playwright
Samuel Richardson, English novelist
Charles-Louis de Secondat, baron de La Brède et de Montesquieu, French philosopher

DEATHS

Khushhal Khan Khatak, Afghan national poet
Chu Yongshun, Chinese writer
Aphra Behn, English poet, playwright, and novelist

PUBLICATIONS

FRENCH

Esther Play by Jean Racine

SPANISH

Flood for the Muse's Springs Poems by Sor Juana Inés de la Cruz, Mexican scholar and nun

SWEDISH

Helicon's Flowers Poem by Lars Johansson

1690

LITERARY EVENT

Academy of Arcadia founded in Rome

PUBLICATIONS

ENGLISH

Amphitryon Comedy by John Dryden
Don Sebastian Tragicomedy by John Dryden
An Essay Concerning Human Understanding Philosophical tract by John Locke

SPANISH

The Divine Narcissus Play by Sor Juana Inés de la Cruz, Mexican scholar and nun
The Misadventures of Alonso Ramirez Chronicle by Mexican historian Carlos de Sigüenza y Góngora

1691

PUBLICATIONS

ENGLISH

King Arthur Play by John Dryden

FRENCH

Athalie Tragedy with chorus by Jean Racine

1692

BIRTHS

Carlo Innocenzo Frugoni, Italian poet
Pierre-Claude Nivelle de La Chaussée, French playwright

PUBLICATIONS

ENGLISH

"Eleanora: A Panegyrical Poem to the Memory of the Countess of Abingdon" Elegy by John Dryden
Incognita Novel by John Dryden

FRENCH

The Fashionable Bourgeois Ladies Comedy by Florent Carton Dancourt

SPANISH

Poems Collection by Sor Juana Inés de la Cruz, Mexican scholar and nun

1693

DEATHS

Marie-Madeleine de La Fayette, French novelist and biographer
Saikaku Ihara, Japanese novelist and poet

PUBLICATIONS

ENGLISH

American

The Wonders of the Invisible World Theological tract by cleric Cotton Mather

British

The Old Bachelor Dramatic comedy by John Dryden

1694

BIRTH
Voltaire (François-Marie Arouet), French philosopher and icon of the Enlightenment

DEATH
Matsuo Bashō (Matsuo Munefusa), Japanese poet

PUBLICATIONS

ENGLISH
British

The Double Dealer Comedy by William Congreve
Love Triumphant Last dramatic comedy by John Dryden

Irish

The Fatal Marriage Play by Thomas Southerne

FRENCH
La Sérénade Play by Jean-François Regnard

JAPANESE
The Narrow Road to the Deep North Travel narrative by poet Matsuo Bashō

1695

DEATHS
Sor Juana Inés de la Cruz, Mexican poet and nun
Jean de La Fontaine, French poet
Henry Vaughan, Welsh poet

PUBLICATION

ENGLISH
Love for Love Comedy by William Congreve

1696

DEATHS
Jean de la Bruyère, French prose writer
Anselm von Ziegler, German novelist
Wacław Potocki, Polish poet

PUBLICATION

FRENCH
The Gamester Dramatic farce by Jean-François Regnard

1697

BIRTH
Antoine-François Prévost d'Exiles (Abbé Prévost), French novelist, clergyman, and journalist

DEATH
Sirhindī Nāsir Alī, Persian poet

PUBLICATIONS

ENGLISH
"Alexander's Feast, or the Power of Music; An Ode in Honour of St. Cecilia's Day" Poem by John Dryden
The Mourning Bride Tragedy by William Congreve

FRENCH
Historical and Critical Dictionary Dictionary by philosopher Pierre Bayle
Mother Goose Tales Collection of fairy tales by Charles Perrault

1698

BIRTHS
Johann Jakob Bodmer, Swiss historian and poet
Pietro Metastasio, Italian poet

PUBLICATION

ENGLISH
Eleutheria Tract by American theologian Cotton Mather

1699

DEATH
Jean Racine, French playwright

PUBLICATIONS

ENGLISH
Fables, Ancient and Modern Verse by John Dryden

FRENCH
The Adventures of Telemachus Satire by cleric François de Salignac Fenelon

THE EIGHTEENTH CENTURY

The 18th century is known as the Age of Reason, a time when construction of the modern world atop the foundations laid in the previous two centuries began to assume its present shape. By this time, Europe had attained cultural and political supremacy; other countries and regions remained shadows in the background. Literature was becoming the forum of choice in which great issues were debated, won, or lost. The spread of literacy assured authors wide readership, and critical literary journals and associations began to make their appearance. Publishers began to establish themselves as commercial enterprises and to compete for books and authors. New genres were introduced, such as the psychological novel and sublime poetry, which goes beyond technical rules of prosody to produce works of great moral, emotional, and imaginative depth.

In England, the novel emerged as a major art form in the works of such popular writers as Henry Fielding, Daniel Defoe, Tobias Smollett, Samuel Richardson, and Laurence Sterne. In France, on the other hand, the consuming passion was philosophy and politics. The works of Voltaire, Jean-Jacques Rousseau, Denis Diderot, Jean d'Alembert, and others provided the kindling for the French Revolution at the end of the century. The great epoch in German literature also came in the late 18th century, when an outpouring of emotional grandeur led to the Sturm und Drang movement, characterized by a revolt against the sterile rationalism of the Enlightenment. Exponents of Sturm and Drang held that the basic truths of existence can be apprehended only through faith, emotion, instinct, impulse, and intuition. Associated with this movement were two of the great names in German literature, Johann Wolfgang von Goethe and Friedrich Schiller.

Major Writers of the Eighteenth Century

Johann Wolfgang von Goethe (1749–1832) German poet, novelist, playwright, and philosopher. He is the greatest figure in the German Romantic movement, and his influence has stretched beyond the century of his birth. In 1773 he gave the fledgling Sturm und Drang movement its first major drama, *Götz von Berlichingen,* and next year its first novel, *The Sorrows of Young Werther.* After 1775 he lived in Weimar and fell in love with Charlotte von Stein, who inspired some of his finest lyrics, such as "Erlking." Goethe next lived in Rome, and his plays *Iphigenie auf Tauris* (1787), *Egmont* (1788), *Faust, ein Fragment* (1790), and *Torquato Tasso* (1790); the poem *Roman Elegies* (1795); and the bildungsroman *Wilhelm Meister's Apprenticeship* all reflect this "Roman period." To his last years belongs his supreme achievement, the drama *Faust* (part I, 1808; part II, 1832).

Johann Christoph Friedrich von Schiller (1759–1805) Leading German playwright of the romantic movement. His first play, *The Robbers* (1781), a stirring protest against corruption in high places, brought him into conflict with the duke of Württemberg. Schiller fled to Thuringia, where he wrote the tragedy *Cabal and Love* (1784). His first major poetic drama, *Don Carlos* (1787), helped to establish blank verse (unrhymed verse, especially unrhymed iambic pentameter) as a new medium. The composer Ludwig van Beethoven used Schiller's hymn "Ode to Joy" for the choral movement of his Ninth Symphony. A chance meeting with Johann Wolfgang

von Goethe in 1794 led to an enduring friendship that left an imprint on German literature. Schiller was also a noted historian and his *History of the Thirty Years' War* (1791–93) provided him with the grist for his dramatic *Wallenstein* trilogy (1789–99). Schiller wrote four other plays: *Maria Stuart* (1800), *The Maid of Orleans* (1801), *The Bride of Messina* (1803), and *William Tell* (1804). Among his most popular works are the songs "Life and the Ideal," "The Walk," and "The Power of Song," and the ballads "The Glove," "The Diver," and "The Cranes of Ibycus." Schiller formulated his views on aesthetics in a series of essays: "Über Anmut und Würde" on moral grace, "Über das Erhabene" on the sublime, and "Über naive und sentimentalische Dichtung" on two types of poetic creativity.

Voltaire (François-Marie Arouet) (1694–1778) French author. Voltaire was a great writer less for his works than for the enormous influence he had on his contemporaries as an apologist for rationalism and as a crusader against bigotry and tyranny. His first attempt at literature was the epic poem *Henriade,* whose lampoons so offended the regency and the church that he was imprisoned in the Bastille and then exiled to England. Returning to France in 1728 or 1729, Voltaire tried his hand at history, producing *Charles XII* (1731) and *Le Siècle de Louis XIV* (1751), and at philosophy, with *Lettres philosophiques* (1754). In 1750 he accepted an invitation from Frederick II of Prussia to go to Berlin. Leaving Berlin in 1754, he settled in Switzerland. The work for which is best known is *Candide* (1759), a satire.

Jonathan Swift (1667–1745) The foremost prose satirist in the English language. His greatest satire was *Gulliver's Travels* (1726), a work designed, in his words, "to vex the world." The Irish still consider him one of their greatest sons and patriots. In 1695 he was ordained an Anglican priest in England. He returned to Ireland in 1699 as chaplain and secretary to the earl of Berkeley, a lord justice. To this period belongs his religious satire *A Tale of a Tub* (1704). In 1710 he returned to London as the chief political writer for the earl of Oxford. He changed parties to become a Tory, or conservative (because of Tory support for the established church against dissenters) and wrote *Journal to Stella,* a diary in the form of letters to his friend Esther Johnson, whom he called Stella, on the changing political landscape. His Tory support gained him the deanery of St. Patrick's Cathedral in Dublin. With the death of Queen Anne and the accession of George I in 1714, the Tories were ousted from power, and Swift withdrew from public life. His later writings include *Drapier's Letters* (1724–25) and *A Modest Proposal for Preventing the Children of Poor People In Ireland from Being a Burden to their Parents* (1729), a work of supreme irony.

Robert Burns (1759–1796) National poet of Scotland who wrote primarily in Scottish dialect. Unschooled, Burns nev-

ertheless was familiar with the works of Shakespeare and John Milton and the songs and folk tales of the Highlands. His first collection, *Poems, Chiefly in the Scottish Dialect* (1786), met with immediate success. Moving from the Highlands to Edinburgh, Burns helped James Johnson and George Thompson produce an anthology of Scottish songs. Among the songs for which Burns is best known are "Green Grow the Rashes, O"; "John Anderson, My Jo"; "Red, Red Rose"; "Wille Brew'd a Peck o'Maut"; "Ye Banks and Braes o' Bonnie Doon"; and "Auld Lang Syne."

William Blake (1757–1827) English poet, painter, and visionary artist whose mystical and original poems are among the earliest and most creative legacies of romanticism. His first volume of poetry, *Poetical Sketches by Mr. W.B.* (1783), was published when he was 26. In 1784 he started a print shop in London where he developed "illuminated printing," a special technique of relief etching in which each page of a book was printed in monochrome from an engraved plate containing both text and illustrations. An astonishing burst of creative activity followed when he produced *Songs of Innocence* and *The Book of Thel* (both 1789), *The French Revolution* (1791), *The Marriage of Heaven and Hell* and *Visions of the Daughters of Albion* (both 1793), and *Songs of Experience* (1794). After 1793 his poems appeared in a series of prophetic books: *America: A Prophecy* (1793); *Europe: A Prophecy* (1794); *The Book of Urizen* (1794); and *The Book of Ahania, The Book of Los,* and *The Song of Los* (all 1795). Blake's longest poem was his epic *Jerusalem* (written and etched between 1804 and 1820), which is the most richly decorated of his illuminated books. The only notable poem Blake wrote after *Jerusalem* was *The Everlasting Gospel,* a fragmentary and unfinished work on Jesus Christ. He continued to illustrate books until his death, and some of his best pictures appeared in editions of the Book of Job (1821) and Dante's *Divine Comedy* (1825).

Jean-Jacques Rousseau (1712–1778) French philosopher, writer, and political theorist. The turning point of his life was meeting with the encyclopedist Denis Diderot, who persuaded him to write two discourses that brought him fame: *Discourse on the Sciences and Arts* (1750) and *Discourse on the Origin of Inequality* (1755). In 1756 Rousseau began work on his two novels, *Julie; or, The New Eloise* (1761) and *Emile; or, On Education* (1762), both of which became enormously popular. However, it was with *Social Contract* (1762) that he secured his place in the European intellectual world by advancing ideas on the origins of social polity that were innovative at the time. Both the *Social Contract* and *Emile* were condemned by the Parlement of Paris, and Rousseau was forced to seek asylum in Switzerland (where he was born) and later move to England. He returned to France in 1767 and wrote his autobiography, *Confessions,* which was published posthumously in 1782 and 1789.

Gotthold Ephraim Lessing (1729–1781) German playwright, critic, and writer on philosophy and aesthetics. He created the first truly German drama free of foreign influences. At Leipzig, where he was a student of theology, he wrote a number of his early comedies, including *Damon; or, True Friendship* (1747), *The Old Maid* (1749), *The Jew* (1754), *The Misogynist* (1755), and *The Free Thinker* (1755). He moved to Berlin and resumed his theatrical work, producing a six-volume edition of his works that includes *Miss Sara Sampson* (1755), the first important domestic tragedy in German literature. In 1760 he went to Breslau where his first critical treatise on aesthetics, *Laocoon: An Essay on the Limits of Painting and Poetry* (1766) was published. He also produced a comic masterpiece, *Minna von Barnhelm; or, A Soldier's Fortune* (1767), which marks the beginning of classical German comedy. His last years were spent at Wolfenbüttel, where he wrote the tragedy *Emilia Galotti* (1772), the dramatic poem *Nathan the Wise* (1779), and his last work, *The Education of the Human Race* (1780).

Cao Xueqin (Cao Zhan) (1715–1763) Chinese writer, author of *Dream of the Red Chamber* (c. 1742), generally considered the greatest Chinese novel. It describes the decline of the Jia family and the ill-fated love between Baoyu and Lin Daiyu. Cao had written only 80 chapters of the work before his death, and it was completed by Gao E, an unknown writer.

Alexander Pope (1688–1744) English poet and satirist of the Augustan neoclassical period. His first major work was *An Essay on Criticism* (1711), about the art of writing. It was followed by his mock epic *The Rape of the Lock* (1714). Living in an age marked by bitter polemical debates on moral and political issues, Pope, as a Roman Catholic who supported Tory positions, left his former associates Joseph Addison and Richard Steele and joined the conservative Scriblerius Club. Pope embarked on *An Essay on Man* in 1733–34, which was designed as a prelude to an unfinished larger work. Among his later works were *An Epistle to Dr. Arbuthnot* (1735) and *The New Dunciad* (1742).

Key World Events of the Eighteenth Century

1703	Tsar Peter the Great founds St. Petersburg as the capital of Russia
1704	John Churchill, the duke of Marlborough, wins the Battle of Blenheim and inflicts a crushing defeat on the French in the War of the Spanish Succession
1707	Scotland and England sign the Act of Union, forming Great Britain
1713	Treaty of Utrecht ends War of the Spanish Succession; England gains the advantage in the contest for overseas empires
1738	John Wesley begins open-air preaching, marking the foundation of the Methodist Church
1763	Treaty of Paris ends Seven Years' War; France loses its North American territories
1770	James Cook of the Royal Navy sails into Botany Bay in Australia and hoists the Union Jack
1772	Russia, Prussia, and Austria carve up the Polish kingdom; two later partitions in 1793 and 1795 remove Poland from the map of Europe
1773	American colonists vent their anger against England by throwing cargoes of tea imported from the mother country into the Boston harbor, an incident later known as the Boston Tea Party
1776	American colonies declare their independence; Revolutionary War begins
1781	American War of Independence ends at Yorktown in a decisive victory for the rebels; two years later, in 1783, England formally recognizes U.S. independence
1787	U.S. Constitution is adopted
1789	Louis XVI summons the Estates-General, the first step in a series of acts that by midyear culminates in the French Revolution
1791	National Assembly in France drafts a new constitution
1793	Reign of Terror begins in Paris following the execution of Louis XVI
1795	Five-man executive council called the Directory is established by the Convention; Napoléon Bonaparte seizes power and is named commander in chief
1798	Napoléon is defeated in the Battle of the Nile by English admiral Horatio Nelson
1799	Napoléon overthrows the Directory

1700

BIRTH
James Thomson, Scottish poet

DEATHS
Johann Beer, German novelist and poet
John Dryden, English poet and playwright
Carlos de Sigüenza y Góngora, Mexican chronicler and poet

PUBLICATIONS
ENGLISH
British

The Way of the World Play by William Congreve

Irish

The Constant Couple; or a Trip to the Jubilee Play by George Farquhar

1701

BIRTHS

Johann Jakob Bretinger, German literary critic
Wu Jingzi, Chinese novelist and poet

DEATHS

Edmonde Boursault, French writer
Madeleine de Scudéry, French novelist and essayist

PUBLICATIONS

ENGLISH

The Christian Hero Essay by Sir Richard Steele
The Funeral; or, Grief A-la-Mode Play by Sir Richard Steele

JAPANESE

Hamkampu Historical chronicle by Arai Hakuseki

1702

BIRTHS

Ignacio de Luzán Claramunt de Suelves y Gurrea, Spanish essayist
Yokai Yagu, Japanese poet

DEATH

Christian Weise, German educator and playwright

PUBLICATION

ENGLISH

Magnalia Christi Americana Prose tract by American divine Cotton Mather

1703

BIRTHS

Henry Brooke, Irish novelist
Jonathan Edwards, American theologian

DEATHS

Charles Perrault, French poet
Samuel Pepys, English diarist

PUBLICATIONS

ENGLISH

The Lying Lover Comedy by Richard Steele

JAPANESE

The Love Suicide at Sonezaki Tragedy by Chikamatsu Monzaemon

1704

BIRTH

Charles Pinto Duclos, French moralist and essayist

DEATH

John Locke, English political philosopher

PUBLICATIONS

ENGLISH

The Battle of the Books Satire by Jonathan Swift
"The Campaign" Poem by Joseph Addison
A Tale of a Tub Prose satire by Jonathan Swift

FRENCH

The Amorous Follies Comedy of manners by Jean-François Regnard

1705

DEATH

Michael Wigglesworth, English-born American poet

PUBLICATIONS

DUTCH

The Grumbling Hive; or, Knaves Turned Honest Satire in verse by Bernard Mandeville

ENGLISH

The Careless Husband Comic drama by Colley Cibber
The Tender Husband Comedy by Richard Steele

FRENCH

Idoménée Dramatic tragedy by Prosper Jolyot (Crébillon)

1706

BIRTH

Benjamin Franklin, American statesman and writer

DEATHS

Pierre Bayle, French philosopher
John Evelyn, English diarist

PUBLICATION

ENGLISH

The Recruiting Officer Play by George Farquhar

1707

BIRTHS

Henry Fielding, English novelist
Carlo Goldoni, Italian playwright
Claude-Prosper Jolyot de Crébillon (Crébillon fils), French
    novelist
Moshe Hayyim Luzzatto, Italian Jewish poet and playwright

DEATHS

Petter Dass, Norwegian poet
George Farquhar, Irish playwright
Jean Mabillon, French Benedictine historian

PUBLICATIONS

ENGLISH

The Beaux's Stratagem Five-act comedy by Irish playwright
    George Farquhar

FRENCH

Atreus and Thyseus Dramatic tragedy by Prosper Jolyot
    (Crébillon)
Crispin, Rival of His Master Comedy by Alain-René Lesage
The Devil Upon Two Sticks Picaresque novel by Alain-René
    Lesage

1708

BIRTHS

Olof von Dalin, Swedish historian and poet
Albrecht von Haller, Swiss poet

PUBLICATIONS

ENGLISH

Wine Burlesque in verse by John Gay

FRENCH

Electra Tragedy by Prosper Jolyot (Crébillon)
The Residuary Legatee Verse comedy by Jean-François Regnard
The Universal Heir Play by Jean-François Regnard

1709

BIRTH

Samuel Johnson, English lexicographer and essayist

DEATH

Jean-François Regnard, French playwright

PUBLICATION

ENGLISH

Pastorals Collection of poems by Alexander Pope

1710

PUBLICATIONS

ENGLISH

Journal to Stella Series of letters by Irish-born satirist Jonathan
    Swift
Of the Principles of Human Knowledge Prose tract by Irish-born
    philosopher George Berkeley

FRENCH

Turcaret; or, The Financier Comedy by Alain-René Lesage

GERMAN

Theodicee Prose piece by philosopher Gottfried Wilhelm Leibniz

1711

BIRTH

David Hume, Scottish philosopher

DEATH

Nicolas Boileau, French critical writer

PUBLICATIONS

ENGLISH

Essay on Criticism Work in heroic couplets by poet Alexander
    Pope

FRENCH

Rhadamistus and Zenobia Dramatic tragedy by Prosper Jolyot
    (Crébillon)

1712

BIRTH

Jean-Jacques Rousseau, French philosopher

PUBLICATIONS

ENGLISH

The Messiah Sacred eclogue by Alexander Pope
The Rape of the Lock Mock epic poem by Alexander Pope

FRENCH

The Fair and Wise Father Play by Pierre Carlet de Marivaux

1713

BIRTHS

Denis Diderot, French novelist, dramatist, and critic
Laurence Sterne, English novelist

PUBLICATIONS

ENGLISH

Cato Dramatic tragedy by Joseph Addison
Ode for Music on St. Cecilia's Day Poem by Alexander Pope
Rural Sports Poem by John Gay
"To the Nightingale" Poem by Anne Finch
Windsor Forest Pastoral poem by Alexander Pope

1714

DEATH

Benjamin Tompson, American poet

PUBLICATIONS

ENGLISH

The Shepherd's Week Pastoral poems by John Gay
The Fable of the Bees; or Private Vices, Public Benefits Verse satire
   by Dutch-born Bernard Mandeville

1715

BIRTHS

Christian Furchegott Gellert, German poet and moralist
Ewald Christian von Kleist, German poet
Cao Xueqin, Chinese novelist

DEATHS

François de Salignac de La Mothe-Fénelon, French mystic writer
Nicolas de Malebranche, French philosopher
Pu Songling, Chinese short story writer
Nahum Tate, English poet and dramatist

PUBLICATIONS

ENGLISH

The Drummer Comic play by Joseph Addison
What D'Ye Call It Satirical farce by John Gay

FRENCH

Gil Blas Picaresque novel by Alain-René Lesage

1716

BIRTHS

Buson, Japanese Haiku poet
Thomas Gray, English poet

DEATHS

Gottfried Wilhelm Leibniz, German philosopher
William Wycherley, English playwright

PUBLICATION

JAPANESE

Ori-Taku-Shiba Autobiography by Arai Hakuseki

1717

BIRTH

Horace Walpole, English writer

PUBLICATION

ENGLISH

Eloisa to Abelard Satirical poem by Alexander Pope

1718

PUBLICATIONS

ENGLISH

Alma, or the Progress of the Mind Dialogue by Matthew Prior
Solomon on the Vanity of the World Long soliloquy by Matthew
   Prior

FRENCH

Oedipus Dramatic tragedy by Voltaire

1719

BIRTHS

Johann Wilhelm Ludwig Gleim, German poet
Michel-Jean Sedaine, French playwright and poet

DEATH

Joseph Addison, English essayist

PUBLICATIONS

DANISH

Pedar Paars Mock epic poem by Ludvig Holberg

ENGLISH

The Life and Adventures of Robinson Crusoe Novel by Daniel
   Defoe

1720

BIRTH

Carlo Gozzi, Italian playwright

PUBLICATIONS

ENGLISH

The Adventures of Captain Singleton Novel by Daniel Defoe
Memoirs of a Cavalier Novel by Daniel Defoe

JAPANESE
The Love Suicides at Amijimi Play by Chikamatsu Monzaemon

1721

BIRTHS
William Collins, English poet
Tobias George Smollett, Scottish novelist

DEATH
Matthew Prior, English poet

PUBLICATIONS
ENGLISH
The Revenge, a Tragedy Play by Edward Young

FRENCH
Persian Letters Novel by Charles-Louis de Secondat, baron de La Brède et de Montesquieu

JAPANESE
The Woman Killer and the Hell of Oil Play by Chikamatsu Monzaemon

1722

BIRTHS
Christopher Smart, English poet
Joseph Wharton, English poet
José de Santa Rita Durão, Brazilian poet

PUBLICATIONS
ENGLISH
The Conscious Lovers Dramatic comedy by Richard Steele
A Journal of the Plague Year Historical reconstruction by Daniel Defoe
Moll Flanders Novel by Daniel Defoe

1723

DEATHS
Claude Fleury, French church historian
Johann Christian Gunther, German poet
Increase Mather, American divine

PUBLICATIONS
DANISH
Jean de France Play by Ludvig Holberg
Jeppe of the Hill Play by Ludvig Holberg
The Political Tinker Play by Ludvig Holberg
The Weather Cock Play by Ludvig Holberg

FRENCH
Harlequin Brightened by Love Play by Pierre Carlet de Chamberlain de Marivaux
La Henriade Epic poem by Voltaire

1724

BIRTHS
Immanuel Kant, German philosopher
Friedrich Gottlieb Klopstock, German religious poet

PUBLICATIONS
ENGLISH
The Drapier's Letters Four epistolary essays by Jonathan Swift
Roxana; or, the Unfortunate Mistress Novel by Daniel Defoe

FRENCH
School for Mothers Play by Pierre Carlet de Chamberlain de Marivaux

1725

BIRTH
Giovanni Giacomo Casanova, Italian adventurer and cynic

DEATHS
Arai Hakuseki, Japanese essayist and historian
Chikamatsu Monzaemon, Japanese playwright
Florent Carton Dancourt, French playwright

PUBLICATIONS
ENGLISH
The Universal Passion; or, The Love of Fame Series of satires by Edward Young

FRENCH
Isle of Slaves Play by Pierre Carlet de Chamberlain de Marivaux

1726

BIRTH
Louise-Florence d'Épinay, French writer

DEATH
Sir John Vanbrugh, English playwright

PUBLICATIONS
ENGLISH
Irish
Gulliver's Travels Prose satire by Jonathan Swift

Scottish
"Winter" Poem (first section of *The Seasons*) by James Thomson

1727

DEATH
Sir Isaac Newton, English scientist and theologian

PUBLICATIONS
ENGLISH
British

Fables Collection of moral stories by John Gay

Scottish

"Summer" Poem (second part of *The Seasons*) by James Thomson

FRENCH
Annibal Play by Pierre Carlet de Chamberlain de Marivaux
Isle of Reason Play by Pierre Carlet de Chamberlain de Marivaux
The Married Philosopher Comic drama by Philippe Destouches

HEBREW
Tower of Victory Romantic allegorical play by Italian-Jewish poet Moshe Hayyim Luzzatto

1728

DEATH
Cotton Mather, American divine

PUBLICATIONS
ENGLISH
British

The Beggar's Opera Musical play by John Gay
The Dunciad Mock epic by Alexander Pope

Scottish

Cyclopaedia, or, an Universal Dictionary of Arts and Sciences by Ephraim Chambers, encyclopedist
"Spring" Poem (third part of *The Seasons*) by James Thomson

1729

BIRTHS
Edmund Burke, Irish-born English parliamentarian
Gotthold Ephraim Lessing, German playwright and freethinker
Moses Mendelssohn, German philosopher
Giuseppe Parini, Italian poet

DEATHS
William Congreve, English playwright
Richard Steele, English playwright and essayist

PUBLICATIONS
ENGLISH
British

Polly Musical by John Gay

Irish

A Modest Proposal Satire by Jonathan Swift

FRENCH
The New Colony Play by Pierre Carlet de Chamberlain de Marivaux

1730

BIRTHS
Oliver Goldsmith, Irish-born English poet, essayist, novelist, and playwright
Johann Georg Hamann, German philosopher and theologian

DEATH
Ahmed Nedim, Turkish poet

PUBLICATIONS
ENGLISH
British

Tom Thumb, A Tragedy Dramatic farce by Henry Fielding

Scottish

"Autumn" Poem (last part of *The Seasons*) by James Thomson

FRENCH
The Game of Love and Chance Prose comedy by Pierre Carlet de Chamberlain de Marivaux

1731

BIRTHS
William Cowper, English poet
Ramón de la Cruz, Spanish playwright
Girolamo Tiraboschi, Italian scholar

DEATH
Daniel Defoe, English novelist

PUBLICATIONS
DANISH
Erasmus Montanus Play by Ludvig Holberg
The Funny Man Play by Ludvig Holberg

FRENCH
The Life of Marianne Novel by Pierre Carlet de Chamberlain de Marivaux
Manon Lescaut Novel by Antoine-François Prévost d'Exiles (Abbé Prévost)

1732

BIRTH
Pierre-Augustin Caron de Beaumarchais, French playwright

DEATH
John Gay, English playwright and poet

PUBLICATIONS
FRENCH
The Conceited Count Moralistic comedy by Philippe Destouches
Zaire Dramatic tragedy by Voltaire

1733

BIRTH
Christoph Martin Wieland, German writer

DEATH
Bernard Mandeville, Dutch-born English satirist

PUBLICATIONS
ENGLISH
American
Poor Richard's Almanack Reference book by Benjamin Franklin

British
Essay on Man Philosophic essay in verse by Alexander Pope

FRENCH
The Death of Caesar Dramatic tragedy by Voltaire

1734

BIRTHS
Akinari Ueda, Japanese novelist
Vicente García de la Huerta, Spanish playwright and poet
Francisco Manuel de Nascimento, Portuguese poet
Sukurada Jisuke, Japanese playwright

PUBLICATIONS
ENGLISH
Liberty Poem by Scotsman James Thomson

FRENCH
Considerations of the Causes of the Grandeur and Decadence of the Romans Prose essay by philosopher Charles-Louis de Secondat, baron de La Brède et de Montesquieu
The Fortunate Peasant Novel by Pierre Carlet de Chamberlain de Marivaux

1735

BIRTHS
James Beattie, Scottish poet and essayist
Ignacy Krasicki, Polish poet

PUBLICATIONS
ENGLISH
Epistle to Several Persons Poem by Alexander Pope
An Epistle to Dr. Arbuthnot Poem by Alexander Pope

1736

PUBLICATIONS
ENGLISH
Pasquin Satirical comedy by Henry Fielding

FRENCH
The Game of Love and Chance Play by Pierre Carlet de Chamberlain de Marivaux

1737

BIRTHS
Jacques-Henri Bernardin de Saint-Pierre, French novelist
Edward Gibbon, English historian
Thomas Paine, English-born American pamphleteer and radical

PUBLICATIONS
ENGLISH
American
A Faithful Narrative of the Surprising Work of God Sermon by New England divine Jonathan Edwards

British
The First Epistle of the Second Book of Horace to Augustus Poem by Alexander Pope
The Historical Register for the Year 1736 Political satire by Henry Fielding

Scottish
Concordance to the Holy Scriptures by Alexander Cruden

FRENCH
False Confessions Comedy by Pierre Carlet de Chamberlain de Marivaux

1738

PUBLICATIONS
ENGLISH
London: A Poem Poem by Samuel Johnson

"One Thousand Seven Hundred Thirty Eight. A Dialogue Something Like Horace" Poem by Alexander Pope

FRENCH

The Poetry Craze Comedy by Alexis Piron

SWEDISH

The Envious Man Dramatic tragedy by Olof van Dalin

1739

BIRTHS

Christian Friedrich Daniel Schubert, German poet

PUBLICATION

ENGLISH

Edward and Eleanore Tragedy by Scotsman James Thomson

1740

BIRTHS

James Boswell, Scottish biographer
Matthias Claudius, German poet
Donatien-Alphonse-François de Sade (Marquis de Sade), French writer

PUBLICATIONS

ENGLISH

British

Pamela; or, Virtue Rewarded Novel by Samuel Richardson

Scottish

Alfred Dramatic masque by James Thomson and David Mallet

FRENCH

The Test Comedy in prose by Pierre Carlet de Chamberlain de Marivaux

SWEDISH

Tale of the Horse Prose work by historian and poet Olof von Dalin

1741

BIRTH

Pierre-Ambroise-François Choderlos de Laclos, French novelist

DEATH

Bernard de Montfaucon, French critic

PUBLICATIONS

ENGLISH

American

Sinners in the Hands of an Angry God Sermon by New England divine Jonathan Edwards

British

An Apology for the Life of Mrs Shamela Andrews Novel by Henry Fielding
Memoirs of Martinus Scriblerus Satirical piece by Alexander Pope and John Arbuthnot
Works Poems by Alexander Pope

1742

PUBLICATIONS

ENGLISH

The Complaint; or, Night Thoughts on Life, Death and Immortality Didactic poem by Edward Young
Joseph Andrews Novel by Henry Fielding
"Ode on a Distant Prospect of Eton College" Poem by Thomas Gray
"Ode on the Spring" Poem by Thomas Gray
"Ode to Adversity" Poem by Thomas Gray
Persian Eclogues Pastorals by William Collins

GERMAN

Odes and Songs Poems by Friedrich von Hagedorn

1743

BIRTHS

Gavrila Romanovich Derzhavin, Russian poet
Johannes Ewald, Danish lyric poet
Johann David Wyss, Swiss writer

PUBLICATIONS

ENGLISH

British

The Dunciad Satirical poem in four books by Alexander Pope
The Life of Jonathan Wild the Great Satirical novel by Henry Fielding

Scottish

The Grave Long poem in blank verse by Robert Blair

FRENCH

Mérope Dramatic tragedy by Voltaire

1744

BIRTH

Johann Gottfried von Herder, German critic and poet

DEATHS
Oliver Goldsmith, Irish-born English novelist, poet, and playwright
Alexander Pope, English poet
Giambattista Vico, Italian philosopher

PUBLICATIONS
ENGLISH
Sermons Sermons by Jonathan Swift

ITALIAN
The Annals of Italy History by Ludovico Antonio Muratori

1745

DEATH
Jonathan Swift, Irish-born English satirist and clergyman

PUBLICATION
ENGLISH
Tancred and Sigismunda Dramatic tragedy by Scottish poet James Thomson

1746

BIRTHS
Johann Wilhelm Heinse, German poet
Stephanie-Félicité Ducrest de Saint-Aubin, comtesse de Genlis, French novelist

PUBLICATIONS
ENGLISH
American

A Treatise Concerning Religious Affections Theological treatise by New England divine Jonathan Edwards

British

"Ode to Fancy" Poem by Joseph Wharton

Scottish

"The Tears of Scotland" Poem by Tobias George Smollett

FRENCH
Philosophical Thoughts Meditations by philosopher Denis Diderot

GERMAN
Fables and Stories Collection of stories by Christian Furchtegott Gellert

1747

BIRTHS
Gottfried August Burger, German lyric poet
György Bessenyei, Hungarian lyric poet

DEATHS
Alain-René Lesage, French novelist and playwright
Moshe Hayyim Luzzatto, Italian Jewish writer

PUBLICATIONS
ENGLISH
Clarissa Harlowe Epistolary novel by Samuel Richardson
Odes on Several Descriptive and Allegoric Subjects Collection of poems by William Collins

FRENCH
Zadig Philosophical tale by Voltaire

GERMAN
The Sick Woman Comedy by Christian Furchtegott

1748

BIRTHS
Adamantios Koraïs, Greek man of letters
Emmanuel-Joseph Sieyès, French pamphleteer
Christian zu Stolberg, German lyric poet

DEATH
James Thomson, Scottish poet

PUBLICATIONS
ENGLISH
British

Fanny Hill, Memoirs of a Woman of Pleasure Erotic novel by John Cleland

Scottish

The Adventures of Roderick Random Novel by Tobias Smollett
The Castle of Indolence Poem by James Thomson
Philosophical Essays Concerning Human Understanding Philosophical tract by David Hume

FRENCH
The Spirit of the Laws Political tract by Charles-Louis de Secondat, baron de La Brède et de Montesquieu

GERMAN
The Messiah Religious epic by Friedrich Klopstock

ITALIAN
The Crafty Widow Play by Carlo Goldoni

1749

BIRTHS
Vittorio Alfieri, Italian poet
Johann Wolfgang von Goethe, German poet
Lorenzo Da Ponte, Italian poet

PUBLICATIONS
ENGLISH
Irene Tragic drama by Samuel Johnson
Tom Jones, a Foundling Novel by Henry Fielding

GERMAN
The Spring Poem by Ewald Christian von Kleist

1750

BIRTH
Lenor de Almeida da Portugal, Portuguese poet

PUBLICATIONS
FRENCH
Discourse on the Sciences and the Arts Essay by Jean-Jacques
    Rousseau

ITALIAN
The Coffee-House Comedy by Carlo Goldoni
The Comic Theater Dramatic comedy by Carlo Goldoni

1751

BIRTHS
Johan Henrik Kellgren, Swedish poet
Jakob Michael Reinhold Lenz, German playwright
Richard Brinsley Sheridan, Irish-born English playwright
Johann Heinrich Voss, German poet

PUBLICATIONS
ENGLISH
British

Amelia Novel by Henry Fielding
"Elegy Written in a Country Churchyard" Poem by Thomas
    Gray

Scottish

The Adventures of Peregrine Pickle Novel by Tobias Smollett

FRENCH
Encyclopédie First volume by the Encyclopedists

1752

BIRTHS
Frances Burney, English novelist and diarist
Thomas Chatterton, English poet
Philip Freneau, American poet
Friedrich Maximilian von Klinger, German playwright and novelist

PUBLICATION
ITALIAN
Mine Hostess Play by Carlo Goldoni

1753

BIRTH
Phillis Wheatley, African-American poet

DEATH
George Berkeley, Irish philosopher and divine

PUBLICATIONS
ENGLISH
American

Freedom of the Will Theological treatise by New England the-
    ologian Jonathan Edwards

British

The History of Sir Charles Grandison Novel by Samuel Richardson

Scottish

The Adventures of Ferdinand, Count Fathom Novel by Tobias
    Smollett

ITALIAN
The Mistress of the Inn Play by Carlo Goldoni

1754

BIRTH
George Crabbe, English poet

DEATHS
Henry Fielding, English novelist
Baron Ludvig Holberg, Norwegian-Danish poet and playwright
Pierre-Claude Nivelle de La Chaussée, French playwright
Ignacio de Luzán Claramunt de Suelves y Gurrea, Spanish liter-
    ary critic
Wu Jingzi, Chinese novelist and poet

PUBLICATIONS
GERMAN
Daphnis Pastoral eclogue by Swiss writer Salomon Gessner

1755

BIRTH
Philibert-Louis Debucourt, French poet

DEATHS

Louis de Rouvroy, duc de Saint-Simon, French statesman
Francesco Scipione Maffei, Italian playwright
Charles-Louis de Secondat, baron de La Brède et de
    Montesquieu, French philosopher

PUBLICATIONS

ENGLISH

A Dictionary of the English Language by Samuel Johnson

FRENCH

The Maid of Orleans Mock epic poem by Voltaire

GERMAN

The Misogynist Play by Gotthold Ephrain Lessing
Miss Sara Sampson Domestic tragedy by Gotthold Ephraim
    Lessing

1756

BIRTH

Willem Bilderdijk, Dutch poet

PUBLICATION

ENGLISH

Lives of the Fathers, Martyrs and Other Principal Saints Hagiog-
    raphy by Alban Butler

1757

BIRTHS

William Blake, English poet
Julian Ursyn Niemcewicz, Polish playwright and novelist
Royall Tyler, American poet

DEATH

Colley Cibber, English poet and playwright

PUBLICATIONS

ENGLISH

"The Bard" Pindaric ode by Thomas Gray

FRENCH

The Natural Son; or, The Proofs of Virtue Play by Denis Diderot

1758

BIRTH

Noah Webster, American lexicographer

DEATH

Jonathan Edwards, American theologian

PUBLICATIONS

FRENCH

The Father of the Family Dramatic comedy by Denis
    Diderot

SPANISH

*History of the Famous Preacher Fray Gerundio of Campazas, alias
    Zotes* Satire by José Francisco de Isla

SWEDISH

The Death of Abel Biblical play and heroic prose poem by
    Salomon Gessner

1759

BIRTHS

William Beckford, English novelist
Robert Burns, Scottish poet
Ferenc Kazinczy, Hungarian man of letters
Johann Christoph Friedrich von Schiller, German playwright
    and poet
Mary Wollstonecraft (Godwin), English feminist writer

DEATHS

William Collins, English poet
Ewald Christian von Kleist, German poet

PUBLICATIONS

ENGLISH

Rasselas, Prince of Abyssinia Philosophical romance by Samuel
    Johnson
Tristram Shandy Novel by Laurence Sterne

FRENCH

Candide Satire by Voltaire

1760

BIRTH

Johann Peter Hebel, German poet

PUBLICATIONS

ENGLISH

Sir Launcelot Greaves Novel by Scotsman Tobias Smollett

ITALIAN

The Boors Play by Carlo Goldoni

1761

BIRTH
August Friedrich Ferdinand von Kotzebue, German playwright

DEATH
Samuel Richardson, English novelist

PUBLICATIONS
FRENCH
Aline, Queen of Golkonda Novel by Chevalier Stanislas-Jean de Boufflers
Julie; or, the New Heloise Epistolary novel by Jean-Jacques Rousseau
Rameau's Nephew Novel by Denis Diderot

1762

BIRTHS
André-Marie de Chénier, French poet
Johann Gottlieb Fichte, German philosopher

DEATH
Prosper Jolyot, sieur de Crais-Billon (Crébillon) French playwright

PUBLICATIONS
ENGLISH
Resignation Moral treatise by poet Edward Young

FRENCH
Emile; or, A Treatise on Education Treatise by Jean-Jacques Rousseau
The Social Contract Political philosophy by Jean-Jacques Rousseau

ITALIAN
The Squabbles at Chioggia Comedy by Carlo Goldoni

1763

BIRTHS
János Batsányi, Hungarian poet
Johann Paul Friedrich Richter, German poet

DEATHS
Cao Xueqin, Chinese novelist
Olof von Dalin, Swedish historian and poet
Pierre Carlet de Chamberlain de Marivaux, French playwright
Antoine-François Prévost d'Exiles (Abbé Prévost), French novelist
William Shenstone, English poet

PUBLICATIONS
ENGLISH
Temora Epic poem by Scottish writer James Macpherson

ITALIAN
Il Giorno Sequence of poems by Guiseppe Parini

1764

BIRTHS
Jens Baggesen, Danish poet and novelist
Marie-Joseph-Blaise Chénier, French satirist and dramatist
Ann Ward Radcliffe, English romantic novelist

PUBLICATIONS
CHINESE
The Dream of the Red Chamber Novel by Cao Xueqin

ENGLISH
The Castle of Otranto Novel by Horace Walpole
The Traveller; or, A Prospect of Society Poem by Oliver Goldsmith

FRENCH
Philosophical Dictionary Dictionary by Voltaire

1765

BIRTH
Nguyen Du, Vietnamese poet

DEATH
Edward Young, English poet

PUBLICATION
FRENCH
The Duel Five-act play by Michel-Jean Sedaine

1766

BIRTHS
Nikolay Mikhaylovich Karamzin, Russian historian and novelist
Madame de Staël (Anne-Louise-Germaine de Staël), French playwright and novelist

PUBLICATIONS
ENGLISH
The Vicar of Wakefield Novel by Oliver Goldsmith

GERMAN
Agathon Bildungsroman by Christoph Martin Wieland
Laocoön Treatise by Gotthold Ephraim Lessing

POLISH
Marriage by the Calendar Play by Franciszek Bohomolec

1767

BIRTHS
Benjamin Constant de Rebecque, French novelist
Maria Edgeworth, English novelist
August Wilhelm von Schlegel, German poet and critic
Takizawa Bakin, Japanese novelist

PUBLICATIONS
FRENCH
Eugénie Play by Pierre-Augustin Caron de Beaumarchais

GERMAN
Minna von Barnhelm; or, The Soldier's Fortune Comic drama by
Gotthold Ephraim Lessing

1768

BIRTHS
François-August-René de Chateaubriand, French writer
Friedrich Ernst Daniel Schleiermacher, German theologian
Friedrich Ludwig Zacharias Werner, German playwright

DEATHS
Carlo Innocenzo Frugoni, Italian poet
Laurence Sterne, English novelist

PUBLICATIONS
ENGLISH
"The Descent of Odin: An Ode" Poem by Thomas Gray
False Delicacy Play by Hugh Kelly
"The Fatal Sisters: An Ode" Poem by Thomas Gray
The Good Natur'd Man Comedy by Oliver Goldsmith
The Mysterious Mother Tragedy by Horace Walpole
A Sentimental Journey Through France and Italy Comic novel by
Laurence Sterne

FRENCH
The Unexpected Wager One-act comedy by Michel-Jean Sedaine

JAPANESE
Tales of the Rainy Moon Collection of stories by Akinari Ueda

1769

BIRTHS
Ernst Moritz Arndt, German poet
Ivan Andreyevich Krylov, Russian fabulist

DEATH
Christian Furchtegott Gellert, German poet

PUBLICATION
PORTUGUESE
O Uruguia Epic poem by Brazilian writer Basilio da Gama

1770

BIRTHS
Georg Wilhelm Friedrich Hegel, German philosopher
Christian Friedrich Holderlin, German poet
William Wordsworth, English poet

DEATH
Thomas Chatterton, English poet

PUBLICATIONS
DANISH
Ralf Krage Tragedy by Johannes Ewald

ENGLISH
The Deserted Village Poem by Oliver Goldsmith

FRENCH
The Two Friends; or, The Merchant of Lyons Play by Pierre-
Augustin Caron de Beaumarchais

1771

BIRTHS
Charles Brockden Brown, American writer
Népomucène Lemercier, French playwright
Sir Walter Scott, Scottish novelist

DEATHS
Thomas Gray, English poet
Tobias Smollett, Scottish novelist

PUBLICATIONS
ENGLISH
American
The Autobiography Memoirs of Benjamin Franklin

Scottish
The Expedition of Humphrey Clinker Epistolary novel by Tobias
Smollett
The Man of Feeling Novel by Henry Mackenzie
The Minstrel Poem by James Beattie

GERMAN
Odes Collection of lyrics by Friedrich Gottlieb Klopstock

The History of Lady Sophia Sternhelm Novel by Sophie van La Roche

ITALIAN

The Beneficent Grouch Comedy by Carlo Goldoni

RUSSIAN

Russian Epic Russian national epic by Mikhail Matveyevich Kheraskov

1772

BIRTHS

Samuel Taylor Coleridge, English romantic poet
Novalis (Friedrich Leopold von Hardenberg), German poet and novelist
Manuel José Quintana, Spanish poet
Friedrich von Schlegel, German philosopher

PUBLICATIONS

DANISH

Love Without Stockings Play by Johan Wessel

GERMAN

Emilia Galotti Tragedy by Gotthold Ephraim Lessing

HUNGARIAN

The Tragedy of Agis Historical drama by Gyorgy Bessenyei

1773

BIRTHS

Mihály Csokonai Vitéz, Hungarian poet
René-Charles Guilbert de Pixérécourt, French playwright
Johann Ludwig Tieck, German romantic poet
Wilhelm Heinrich Wackenroder, German writer

DEATH

Alexis Piron, French poet

PUBLICATIONS

DANISH

The Joys of Rungsted Lyric by Johannes Ewald

ENGLISH

She Stoops to Conquer Play by Oliver Goldsmith

GERMAN

"Lenore" Ballad by Gottfried August Burger
Gotz von Berlichingen Play by Johann Wolfgang von Goethe

1774

BIRTH

Robert Southey, English poet

DEATHS

Oliver Goldsmith, Irish-born English poet, playwright, and novelist
Albrecht von Haller, Swiss poet

PUBLICATIONS

DANISH

The Death of Balder Play by Johannes Ewald

GERMAN

The Sorrows of Young Werther Novel by Johann Wolfgang von Goethe
The Story of the Abderites Historical and satirical novel by Christopher Martin Wieland
The Tutor; or, the Advantages of Private Education Play by Jakob Michael Reinhold Lenz

1775

BIRTHS

Jane Austen, English novelist
Charles Lamb, English essayist
Walter Savage Landor, English poet and critic
Matthew Gregory "Monk" Lewis, English novelist
Friedrich Wilhelm Joseph Schelling, German philosopher

PUBLICATIONS

ENGLISH

The Duena Comic opera by Richard Brinsley Sheridan
A Journey to the Western Islands of Scotland Travel narrative by Samuel Johnson
The Rivals Play by Richard Brinsley Sheridan
St. Patrick's Day; or, The Scheming Lieutenant Comic opera by Richard Brinsley Sheridan

FRENCH

The Barber of Seville Comedy by Pierre-Augustin Caron de Beaumarchais

GERMAN

The Soldiers Tragicomedy by Jakob Michael Reinhold Lenz
The Twins Tragedy by Friedrich Maximilian von Klinger

1776

BIRTHS

Joseph von Gorres, German Roman Catholic writer
Ernest Theodor Wilhelm Hoffman, German folklorist

DEATHS
Johann Jakob Breitinger, Swiss-German critic
David Hume, Scottish philosopher

PUBLICATIONS
ENGLISH
American
Common Sense Political pamphlet by English-born Thomas Paine
British
The History of the Decline and Fall of the Roman Empire First tome in multivolume work by Edward Gibbon

GERMAN
Julius von Tarent Tragedy by Johann Anton Leisewitz
Sturm und Drang Dramatic fantasy by Friedrich Maximilian von Klinger

ITALIAN
Antigone Tragedy by Vittorio Alfieri

POLISH
The Adventures of Nicholas Try-All Novel by Ignacy Krasicki

1777

BIRTHS
Friedrich Heinrich Karl de la Motte Fouqué, German romantic poet
Heinrich von Kleist, German poet and playwright

DEATH
Claude-Prosper Jolyot de Crébillon (Crébillon fils), French novelist

PUBLICATIONS
ENGLISH
Poems Posthumously published collection of poems by Thomas Chatterton
The School for Scandal Play by Richard Brinsley Sheridan

1778

BIRTHS
Clemens Brentano, German poet
Ugo Foscolo, Italian poet
William Hazlitt, English essayist

DEATHS
Jean-Jacques Rousseau, French philosopher
Voltaire (François-Marie Arouet), French writer

PUBLICATIONS
ENGLISH
Evelina; or, A Young Lady's Entrance into the World Novel by Frances Burney

FRENCH
Irène Dramatic tragedy by Voltaire
Oedipus at the Home of Admetus Tragedy by Jean-François Ducis

GERMAN
Plastik Metaphysical tract by Johann Herder

SPANISH
Raquel Play by Vicente García de la Huerta

1779

BIRTHS
Francis Scott Key, American poet
Clement Clarke Moore, American poet and biblical scholar
Thomas Moore, Irish poet
Adam Gottlob Oehlenschlager, Danish poet and playwright

PUBLICATIONS
ENGLISH
The Critic Dramatic burlesque by Richard Brinsley Sheridan
The Lives of the English Poets Biographies by Samuel Johnson
Olney Hymns Collection of Congregational odes by William Cowper and John Newton

GERMAN
Nathan the Wise Play by Gotthold Ephraim Lessing

RUSSIAN
On the Death of Prince Meshchersky Ode by Gavrila Derzhavin

1780

BIRTHS
Pierre-Jean de Béranger, French poet
Charles Nodier, French writer of fairy tales

PUBLICATIONS
GERMAN
Oberon Poem by Christoph Martin Wieland
Songs for the People Collection of poems by Matthias Claudius

1781

BIRTHS
Ludwig Joachim von Arnim, German romantic novelist
Andrés Bello, Venezuelan poet
Adelbert Chamisso, German lyrical poet

DEATHS

Johannes Ewald, Danish poet and playwright
Gotthold Ephraim Lessing, German playwright

PUBLICATIONS

ENGLISH

The British Prison Ship Poem by American Philip Freneau

GERMAN

German

Critique of Pure Reason Philosophical tract by Immanuel Kant
The Robbers Play by Johann Christoph Friedrich von Schiller

Swiss

Leonard and Gertrude Novel by educator Johann Heinrich Pestalozzi

1782

BIRTH

Hughes-Félicité-Robert de Lamennais, French essayist

DEATH

Pietro Metastasio, Italian poet

PUBLICATIONS

ENGLISH

Cecilia, or Memoirs of an Heiress Novel by Frances Burkey
The Dunciad Poem by Alexander Pope
Poems Collection of poems by William Cowper

FRENCH

Confessions Autobiography (books I–VI) by Jean-Jacques Rousseau
Dangerous Liaisons Epistolary novel by Pierre-Ambroise-François Chaderlos de Laclos

GERMAN

"Erlking" Ballad by Johann Wolfgang von Goethe

PORTUGUESE

Caramuru Epic poem by Brazilian writer José de Santa Rita Durão

1783

BIRTHS

Washington Irving, American writer
Stendhal (Marie-Henri Beyle), French novelist

DEATHS

Johann Jakob Bodmer, Swiss poet
Buson, Japanese haiku poet

Charles Colle, French satiric poet
Yokai Yagu, Japanese poet

PUBLICATIONS

ENGLISH

The Village Poem by George Crabbe
Poetical Sketches Short poems by William Blake

GERMAN

Fiesco; or, The Conspiracy of Genoa Play by Johann Friedrich von Schiller

RUSSIAN

The Minor Play by Denis Ivanovich Fonvizin

1784

BIRTH

Henry Leigh Hunt, English poet

DEATHS

Denis Diderot, French intellectual
Samuel Johnson, English lexicographer
José de Santa Rita Durão, Brazilian poet
Phillis Wheatley, African-American poet

PUBLICATIONS

ENGLISH

The Task Poem by William Cowper

FRENCH

The Marriage of Figaro; or, The Madness of a Day Comedy by Pierre-Augustin Caron de Beaumarchais

GERMAN

Cabal and Love Play by Johann Friedrich von Schiller

RUSSIAN

Ode to the Deity Poem by Gavrila Romanovich Derzhavin

1785

BIRTHS

Bettina von Arnim, German writer
Thomas De Quincey, English writer
Jakob Grimm, German folklorist
Alessandro Manzoni, Italian novelist
Thomas Love Peacock, English novelist

PUBLICATIONS

ENGLISH

Journal of a Tour of the Hebrides, with Samuel Johnson Travel narrative by James Boswell

FRENCH

The 120 Days of Sodom Pornographic novel by Marquis de Sade

RUSSIAN

Vladimir Reborn Play by Mikhail Kheraskov

1786

BIRTH

Wilhelm Karl Grimm, German folklorist

PUBLICATIONS

ENGLISH

American

Poems Collection of poems by Philip Freneau

British

Vathek Fantasy by William Beckford

Scottish

Poems, Chiefly in the Scottish Dialect Poems by Robert Burns

1787

BIRTHS

Francisco de Paula Martínez de la Rosa, Spanish playwright
Johann Ludwig Uhland, German lyric poet

DEATH

Vicente García de la Huerta, Spanish playwright, poet, and critic

PUBLICATIONS

ENGLISH

The Contrast First American comic play by Royall Tyler

GERMAN

Don Carlos, Infant of Spain Tragic historical play by Johann Friedrich von Schiller

1788

BIRTHS

George Gordon Byron (Lord Byron), English poet
Joseph Eichendorff, German romantic poet
Arthur Schopenhauer, German philosopher

DEATH

Johann Georg Hamann, German philosopher and theologian

PUBLICATIONS

FRENCH

Paul et Virginie Sentimental French idyll by Jacques-Henri Bernardin de Saint-Pierre

GERMAN

Critique of Practical Reason Philosophical treatise by Immanuel Kant
Egmont Dramatic tragedy by Johann Wolfgang von Goethe
Iphigenie auf Tauris Play by Johann Wolfgang von Goethe

1789

BIRTH

James Fenimore Cooper, American novelist

PUBLICATIONS

ENGLISH

The Book of Thel Poetic allegory by William Blake
Songs of Innocence Poems by William Blake

FRENCH

Charles IX; or, La Sainte-Barthelemy Play by Marie-Joseph Chénier
Confessions Autobiography (books VII–XII) by Jean-Jacques Rousseau

GERMAN

The Stranger Play by August Kotzebue

1790

BIRTHS

Carsten Hauch, Danish poet, playwright, and novelist
Marie-Louis-Alphonse de Prat de Lamartine, French poet

DEATH

Benjamin Franklin, American statesman and writer

PUBLICATIONS

ENGLISH

Reflections on the Revolution in France Treatise by parliamentarian Edmund Burke

GERMAN

Torquato Tasso Dramatic tragedy by Johann Wolfgang von Goethe
The Indian Exiles Play by August Kotzebue

RUSSIAN

Letters of a Russian Traveler Travel narrative by Nikolay Mikhaylovich Karamzin

SWEDISH

Fredmans Epistlar Songs by Carl Michael Bellmann

1791

BIRTHS

Sergey Timofeyevich Aksakov, Russian novelist
Franz Grillparzer, Austrian playwright
Johann Ludvig Heiberg, Danish dramatic poet
Karl Theodor Korner, German lyric poet
Angel de Saavedra, Spanish poet and playwright
Augustin-Eugène Scribe, French playwright

DEATH

Christian Friedrich Daniel Schubert, German poet

PUBLICATIONS

ENGLISH

American

The Rights of Man Political treatise by Thomas Paine

British

The Mysteries of Udolpho Novel by Ann Radcliffe

Scottish

The Life of Samuel Johnson Biography by James Boswell
Tam O'Shanter Poem by Robert Burns

FRENCH

Henry VIII Dramatic tragedy by Marie-Joseph Chénier
Justine Erotic novel by Marquis de Sade

1792

BIRTHS

Frederick Marryat, English naval novelist
Percy Bysshe Shelley, English romantic poet

DEATH

Jakob Michael Reinhold Lenz, German playwright and poet

PUBLICATIONS

ENGLISH

A Vindication of the Rights of Woman Feminist manifesto by Mary Wollstonecraft

PORTUGUESE

Marilia de Dirceau Love lyrics by Tomas Antonion Gonzaga

RUSSIAN

"Little Liza" Short story by Nikolai Mikhailovich Karamzin

1793

BIRTHS

Carl Jonas Love Almqvist, Swedish writer
Jean-François-Casimir Delavigne, French playwright
Aleksander Fredro, Polish playwright

DEATH

Carlo Goldoni, Italian playwright

PUBLICATIONS

ENGLISH

The Marriage of Heaven and Hell Poetic satire by William Blake
"An Evening Walk" Poem by William Wordsworth

GERMAN

The Invisible Lodge Novel by Jean Paul Friedrich Richter

SPANISH

Moroccan Letters Commentary by José de Cadalso y Vázquez

1794

BIRTHS

William Cullen Bryant, American poet
Leopold Zunz, German-Jewish scholar

DEATHS

Gottfried August Burger, German lyric poet
André-Marie de Chénier, French poet
Ramón de la Cruz, Spanish playwright
Edward Gibbon, English historian

PUBLICATIONS

ENGLISH

American

The Age of Reason Treatise by Thomas Paine

British

The First Book of Urizen Series of poems by William Blake
Songs of Experience Collection of poems by William Blake

FRENCH

Agamemnon Play by Népomucène Lemercier

GERMAN

Hesperus Romantic novel by Jean Paul Friedrich Richter

RUSSIAN

The Waterfall Poems by Gavrila Derzhavin

1795

BIRTHS
Thomas Carlyle, Scottish essayist and historian
Aleksandr Sergeyevich Griboyedov, Russian playwright
John Keats, English romantic poet
Leopold von Ranke, German historian
Jacques-Nicolas-Augustin Thierry, French historian

DEATHS
Carl Michael Bellmann, Swedish poet
James Boswell, Scottish biographer
Johan Henrik Kellgren, Swedish poet

PUBLICATIONS
ENGLISH
The Book of Ahania Series of poems by William Blake
The Book of Los Series of poems by William Blake
The Borderers Verse drama by William Wordsworth
"The Eolian Harp" Poem by William Blake
"The Song of Los" Poem by William Blake

FRENCH
Abufar Tragedy by Jean-François Ducis

GERMAN
Luise Epic idyll by Johann Heinrich Voss
Roman Elegies Lyric poems by Johann Wolfgang von Goethe
Wilhelm Meister's Apprenticeship Bildungsroman by Johann Wolfgang von Goethe

1796

BIRTHS
Abdullah bin Abdul Kader, Malay writer
Manuel Bretón de los Herreros, Spanish playwright
Fernán Caballero (Cecilia Böhl de Faber), Spanish novelist
Karl Leberecht Immermann, German playwright
Charles Auguste von Platen, German lyric poet

DEATHS
Robert Burns, Scottish poet
James Macpherson, Scottish poet

PUBLICATIONS
ENGLISH
Memoirs Autobiography by historian Edward Gibbon
The Monk Gothic novel by Matthew Gregory Lewis
The Parent's Assistant Collection of didactic stories for children by Maria Edgeworth

GERMAN
The Flower, Fruit and Thorn Pieces Novel by Jean Paul Friedrich Richter

Life of Quintus Fixelin, Extracted from 15 Letter Boxes Novel by Jean Paul Friedrich Richter

SWEDISH
The Merry Festival Poems by Anna Maria Lenngren

1797

BIRTHS
Annette Elisabeth Droste-Hülshoff, German poet
Jeremias Gotthelf, Swiss writer
Heinrich Heine, German poet
Mary Wollstonecraft Shelley, English novelist
Alfred Victor Vigny, French romantic writer

DEATHS
Edmund Burke, English parliamentarian
Michel-Jean Sedaine, French poet and playwright
Horace Walpole, English writer
Mary Wollstonecraft (Godwin), English feminist writer

PUBLICATIONS
ENGLISH
American

The Algerine Captive; or, The Life and Adventures of Dr. Updike Underhill Picaresque novel by Royall Tyler

British

The Four Zoas: The Torment of Love and Jealousy in the Death and Judgment of Albion Symbolic poem by William Blake
The Italian Gothic novel by Ann Radcliffe
Osorio Tragedy by Samuel Taylor Coleridge

GERMAN
Hermann and Dorothea Epic idyll by Johann Wolfgang von Goethe
Hyperion Novel by Johann Christian Friedrich Holderlin

SWEDISH
The Boys Poems by Anna Maria Lenngren

1798

BIRTHS
Willibald Alexis (Georg Wilhelm Heinrich Haring), German novelist and playwright
John Banim, Irish novelist
Auguste Comte, French philosopher
Giacomo Leopardi, Italian poet
Jules Michelet, French historian
Adam Mickiewicz, Polish poet
Dhionísios Solomos, Greek poet

DEATHS

Giovanni Giacomo Casanova, Italian adventurer and cynic
Wilhelm Heinrich Wackenroder, German Romantic writer

PUBLICATIONS

ENGLISH

American

Wieland; or, The Transformation Epistolary Gothic novel by Charles Brockden Brown

British

The Castle Spectre Melodrama by Matthew Gregory Lewis
Gebir Epic poem by Walter Savage Landor
"Lines Composed a Few Miles Above Tintern Abbey" Poem by William Wordsworth
Lyrical Ballads Collection of poems by William Wordsworth and Samuel Taylor Coleridge
"The Old Familiar Faces" Poem by Charles Lamb
"The Rime of the Ancient Mariner" Poem by Samuel Taylor Coleridge
The Tale of Rosamund Gray and Old Blind Margaret Tragic story by Charles Lamb

GERMAN

Wallenstein's Camp Play by Johann Christoph Friedrich von Schiller

SWEDISH

The Empire of Stupidity Poems by Alberto Lista

1799

BIRTHS

Amos Bronson Alcott, American philosopher and poet
Honoré de Balzac, French novelist

João Baptista de Silva Leitão de Almeida Garrett, Portuguese poet and novelist
Thomas Hood, English poet
Aleksandr Sergeyvich Pushkin, Russian poet

DEATHS

Pierre-Augustin Caron de Beaumarchais, French playwright
Giuseppe Parini, Italian poet

PUBLICATIONS

ENGLISH

American

Arthur Merwyn Novel by Charles Brockden Brown
Edgar Huntley Novel by Charles Brockden Brown
Ormond Novel by Charles Brockden Brown

British

The Castaway Poem by William Cowper
"Lucy Gray, or, Solitude" Poem by William Wordsworth
Pizarro Tragedy by Richard Brinsley Sheridan
The Prelude, or, Growth of a Poet's Mind Autobiographical poem by William Wordsworth

Scottish

"Holy Willie's Prayer" Satire by Robert Burns
The Jolly Beggars: A Cantata Comic opera in three parts by Robert Burns

GERMAN

Heinrich von Otterdingen Philosophical romance by Novalis
Lucinde Romance by Johann Christoph Friedrich von Schiller
The Piccolomini Dramatic piece by Johann Christoph Friedrich von Schiller
Wallenstein's Death Play (part of trilogy) by Johann Christoph Friedrich von Schiller

HUNGARIAN

Dorottya Play by Mihály Csokonai Vitéz

THE NINETEENTH CENTURY

If all the centuries were ranked as literary eras, the 19th century would rank at the top, outranking even the 20th, for its level and quality of literary activity. It was also first time that nations such as the United States and Russia began to contribute to the literary canon and a global literary village began to take shape. Translations, increased literacy, and cheaper printing processes made authors from every language and country accessible to readers throughout the world; literary traditions and genres flowed across national boundaries, and the influence of certain great authors could be felt worldwide.

The 19th century was the formative era for many modern literary and artistic movements, including romanticism, impressionism, symbolism, and realism. Romanticism was the predominant literary movement of the early 19th century. Many characteristics of romanticism sprang from philosophical sources that had assumed the role of surrogate religion. One such philosophical source was Jean-Jacques Rousseau, whose emphasis on the individual and the power of inspiration and nature influenced William Wordsworth in England, Johann Christian Friedrich Holderlin and Ludwig Tieck in Germany, and Jacques-Henri Bernardin de Saint-Pierre in France. Romanticism was also a reaction against the 18th-century rationalism of such philosophers as Georg Wilhelm Friedrich Hegel and David Hume. Even beyond literature, romanticism was manifest in the works of such Christian writers as Søren Kierkegaard, founder of modern existentialism. The cardinal tenets of romanticism were self-knowledge, subjectivity, inspiration, and a love of nature, however imperfectly defined. The central role of inspiration in the creative process made the romantic poet a visionary and seer, unbound by rules. Poetry was freed from its 18th-century preoccupation with social context, and the poet was answerable only to ultimate truth. Two classic examples of the romantic poet as visionary were John Keats, who died in his early 20s, and George Gordon Byron, better known as Lord Byron, whose life was seared by recklessness.

In the early and middle 19th century, the Romantic style was evident in poetry throughout Europe—in the work of José de Espronceda y Delgado in Spain, Ugo Foscolo and Giacomo Leopardi in Italy, Aleksandr Pushkin and Mikhail Lermontov in Russia, and Adam Bernard Mickiewicz in Poland. In the nascent United States, the romantic thread ran through the adventure stories of James Fenimore Cooper, the poetry of Walt Whitman and Henry Wadsworth Longfellow, and the transcendentalism of Ralph Waldo Emerson and Henry David Thoreau. Transcendentalism was an idealistic and somewhat utopian system of thought based on a belief in the essential unity of all humanity, the innate goodness of human beings, and the supremacy of experience over logic. It represented the first flowering of American literary genius, but the impetus of romanticism began to wane after the 19th century, especially after World War I.

Arguably, the first postromantic poet was Heinrich Heine in Germany, followed by Nikolaus Lenau (Nikolaus Franz Niembsch von Strehlenau) in Austria; nonetheless, postromanticism became fully developed in France by the Parnassians. Originating with Théophile Gautier, Parnassianism was in some ways an offshoot of romanticism rather than a reaction against it. By concentrating on the purely formal and aesthetic elements of poetry, it shaped the direction of literary sensibility. Its most illustrious representative was Charles-Pierre Baudelaire, who tried make *decadence* a respectable word. Two other postromantic movements were impressionism and symbolism. Paul Verlaine, foremost of the impressionists, borrowed idioms from painting, sculpture, and music to evoke subjective and sensory impressions of events and people. Symbolism, a selective use of words and images to evoke tenuous moods and meanings, was perfected by Stéphane Mallarmé and Arthur Rimbaud.

Realism, the fourth literary movement of the 19th century, assumed two forms. In the hands of Jane Austen, Benjamin Constant, Stendhal (Marie-Henri Beyle), Gustave Flaubert, Guy de Maupassant, Giovanni Verga, Émile Zola, and Honoré de Balzac, it became a detailed and verbally scrupulous examination—or "autopsy," as Zola called it—of individual human actions and emotions. But for the greatest of the century's writers, such as Fyodor Dostoyevsky, Charles Dickens, Thomas Hardy, Nikolay Gogol, and Anton Chekhov, it was driven by a larger social and philosophical purpose. For them, literature was not art for art's sake, but was driven by a goal and a mission.

Major Writers of the Nineteenth Century

Fyodor Mikhaylovich Dostoyevsky (1821–1881) Russian writer who helped develop the psychological novel as one of the dominant forms of literature. His works were also precursors of the existentialist novel in which the subject is not only the physical human person, but also the human spirit and soul. As a Christian, Dostoyevsky combined profound spiritual insights into the human condition with an uncanny ability to explore the darkest recesses of the human mind. His four great masterpieces are *The Brothers Karamazov* (1879–80), *Crime and Punishment* (1866), *The Idiot* (1868–69), and *The Possessed* (1872). Hounded by debtors and beset by gambling losses, Dostoyevsky wrote furiously throughout his life as a means to bringing in income and turned out more than 40 books, including *The Double* (1846), *Poor Folk* (1846), *House of the Dead* (1860–62), *The Friend of the Family* (1859), *The Insulted and the Injured* (1861), and *Notes from Underground* (1864).

Charles Dickens (1812–1870) English novelist, the greatest of the Victorian era. Dickens possessed an inexhaustible power to create unforgettable characters, an acute ear for characteristic speech patterns, a strong narrative impulse, an inventive prose style, compassion for the poor, and a strong antipathy to social evils. In his early life Dickens encountered misfortune: His father was thrown into debtors' prison and Charles had to drop out of school to work in a factory. Images of prison and destitution recur in many of Dickens's novels. Almost all of his works are well known and popular, beginning with *Pickwick Papers* (1837) and ending with the unfinished *The Mystery of Edwin Drood* (1870). In between he wrote *Oliver Twist* (1838), *Nicholas Nickleby* (1839), *The Old Curiosity Shop* (1841), *Barnaby Rudge* (1841), *Martin Chuzzlewit* (1844), *A Christmas Carol* (1843, familiar throughout the world in its stage, film, and television versions), *The Cricket on the Hearth* (1846), *David Copperfield* (1850), *Bleak House* (1853), *Hard Times* (1854), *Little Dorrit* (1857), *Great Expectations* (1861), *Our Mutual Friend* (1865), and *A Tale of Two Cities* (1859).

Leo Nikolayevich Tolstoy, Count (1828–1910) Russian novelist, author of two of the world's greatest novels, *War and Peace* (1865–69) and *Anna Karenina* (1875–77). His novella *The Death of Ivan Ilyich* (1886) is considered a masterpiece of psychological realism. Tolstoy was the son of a Russian noble family with somewhat quirky socialist and religious convictions, and his personal life was marked by deep inner turmoil. He established his reputation with *The Cossacks* in 1863 and went on to write the two novels with which his name will be forever associated. In *Confession* (1884) he presented an account of his spiritual crisis: He eventually turned to a form of Christian anarchism and devoted the rest of his life to promoting social reform and nonviolence. In *What Is Art?* (1898), he tried to give art a moral and religious function. He wrote one more full-length novel, *Resurrection* (1899), with an implied Christian message of hope for a scarred humanity, and one more play, *The Power of Darkness* (1888).

Aleksandr Sergeyevich Pushkin (1799–1837) Russian national poet and founder of modern Russian literature. Born into a noble family (his mother was descended from a black Abyssinian), Pushkin began his literary career in 1814. While at the Imperial Lyceum at Tsarkoye Selo he completed his first major work, the romantic poem *Ruslan and Ludmila* (1820). Exiled from St. Petersburg for his "Ode to Liberty" (1820), he began his "southern cycle" of romantic narrative poems: *The Prisoner of the Caucasus* (1820–21), *The Robber Brothers* (1821–22), and *The Fountain of Bakhchsaray* (1823). In 1823 he began work on his masterpiece, *Eugene Onegin*, on which he continued to work until 1831. Moving to Pskov, he wrote ballads and stories based on Russian history, such as "The Bridegroom" (1825), and "The Gypsies" (1824), the poem "Count Nulin" (1827), and his great historical tragedy, *Boris Godunov* (1831). Czar Nicholas I allowed Pushkin to return to Moscow, where he abandoned his revolutionary fervor and took up Russian history, the theme of *The Stanzas* (1826), *The Negro of Peter the Great* (1827), the historical poem "Poltava" (1829), and "The Bronze Horseman" (1837). The Moscow period also produced the poem "To My Friends" (1828); *Egyptian Nights* (1835); the short story "The Queen of Spades" (1834); four tragedies, *The Covetous Knight* (1836), *Mozart and Salieri* (1831), *The Stone Guest* (1839), and *Feast in the Time of Plague* (1832); five short prose tales collected in *Tales of the Late Ivan Petrovich Belkin* (1831); the comic poem "A Small House in Kolomna"; and many lyrics. In 1831 Pushkin settled in St. Petersburg, where he began a series of historical studies and novels, including *The History of the Village of Goryukhina* (1837), the novels *Captain's Daughter* (1836) and *Dubrovsky* (1841), and *A History of Pugachov* (1834) on the Pugachov Rebellion.

Honoré de Balzac (1799–1850) French writer whose monumental work *The Human Comedy* is one of the greatest realist

novels in literature. His writing career began in 1829 when he produced his first successful novels, *Les Chouans* and *The Physiology of Marriage,* followed by *Scenes from Private Life* in 1830. From 1832 to 1835 he produced more than 20 works, including *The Country Doctor* (1833), *Eugenie Grandet* (1833), *The Illustrious Gaudissart* (1833), and *Le Père Goriot* (1835). He also published three sets of *Droll Stories.* Between 1836 and 1839 he wrote the *Antiques Cabinet* (1839), the first two parts of *Lost Illusions* (1837–43), and *The Firm of Nucingen* (1838). In 1840 he began work on one of the most massive literary projects ever embarked on by an author: *The Human Comedy,* a Dantesque survey of human society that eventually included about 90 novels. In the last decade of his life, Balzac produced many more masterpieces such as *A Shady Business* (1841), *The Black Sheep* (1841–42), *Harlot, High and Low* (1843–47), *Cousin Bette* (1846), and *Cousin Pons* (1847).

Henry James (1843–1916) American novelist. A naturalized British subject from 1915, he focused on Anglo-American culture and was a pioneer of realism in the United States. The relative innocence of the New World in conflict with the corruption and wisdom of the Old World is the principal theme of his novels. His major novels include *Roderick Hudson* (1876), *The American* (1877), *Daisy Miller* (1879), *Washington Square* (1880), *The Portrait of a Lady* (1881), *The Bostonians* (1886), *The Princess Cassmassima* (1886), *The Tragic Muse* (1890), *The Spoils of Poynton* (1897), *What Maisie Knew* (1897), *The Turn of the Screw* (1898), *The Awkward Age* (1899), *The Wings of the Dove* (1902), *The Ambassadors* (1903), and *The Golden Bowl* (1904).

Giacomo Leopardi (1798–1837) Italian lyric poet, often called the Prince of Pessimists. Beset by physical problems all his life, Leopardi poured out his bitterness in poems such as "Approach of Death" (1816, published 1835). Some of his saddest lyrics were inspired by his frustrated loves and the death from tuberculosis of Terese Fattorini, subject of "A Silvia." His poems were collected in *Canzoni* (1824), *Operette Morali* (1827), *I Canti* (1831), and *Ginestra* (1836). His finest lyrics are called *Idilli.*

Søren Aabye Kierkegaard (1813–1855) Danish philosopher and founder of existentialism. Nearly all of his works were published under pen names suited to the particular work. His first work, *Either/Or* (1843), offered an alternative to an aesthetic or moral view of life arising from a person's conscious decision. *Fear and Trembling* and *Repetition* (both 1843) dealt with faith and the idea of sacrifice, showing clearly the Christianization of Kierkegaard's ideas. *Philosophical Fragments* and *The Concept of Dread* (both 1844) defined his idea of freedom as central to existence, the first shot across the bow at Hegelianism, the dominant rationalistic philosophy of the time. In 1845 Kierkegaard published *Stages on Life's Way,* his most mature achievement. In it he adds a third, religious di-

mension to life's aesthetic and moral dimensions. As Kierkegaard's outlook on life became increasingly somber, he initiated a full-scale attack of Hegel in *Concluding Unscientific Postscript.* In it he summarized his philosophy that subjectivity is truth; Kierkegaard attacked Hegel's attempt to systematize existence, declaring that such a system can never be constructed since existence is incomplete and constantly changing. These tenets have become the foundation of modern existentialism. He waged his last battle against the established church in the works *Edifying Discourses on Diverse Spirits* (1847), *Works of Love* (1847), *Christian Discourses* (1848), *The Sickness Unto Death* (1849), and *Training in Christianity* (1850).

Nikolay Vasilyevich Gogol (1809–1852) Russian writer whose novel *Dead Souls* and short story "The Overcoat" (both 1842) are among the best-loved classics of Russian literature and the foundations of 19th-century Russian realism. His first story collections, *Mirgorod* and *Arabesques,* appeared in 1835 and included two of his best stories, "Taras Bulba" and "Diary of a Mad Man." He developed a friendship with Aleksandr Pushkin, who suggested to him the themes of *Dead Souls* and *The Government Inspector* (1836). The publication of his collected works in 1842 made Gogol one of the most popular writers in Russia. His creative powers began to fail, however, and when his later works were rejected, he was crushed and slid into madness. He fell under the spell of a fanatical priest and died of starvation.

Jane Austen (1775–1817) English novelist. Between 1811 and 1817 she published six of the most widely read novels in the English language: *Sense and Sensibility* (1811), *Pride and Prejudice* (1813), *Mansfield Park* (1814), *Emma* (1815), *Persuasion* (1817), and *Northanger Abbey* (1817). Her novels are essentially domestic romances but are remarkably modern in their characterization, wit, and realism.

Edgar Allan Poe (1809–1849) American short story writer, poet, and critic noted for his macabre fiction and considered the father of the detective story. Poe published his first book, *Tamerlane and Other Poems* (1827), at age 18. "A MS. Found a Bottle" was his first short story. In 1839 the first collection of his stories, *Tales of the Grotesque and Arabesque,* appeared, and six years later his poem "The Raven" gained national attention. Thereafter most of his stories and poems focused on the eerie and the mysterious, such as the short stories "Ulalume," "The Fall of the House of Usher," "The Masque of the Red Death," "The Premature Burial," "The Black Cat," "The Cask of Amontillado," "The Tell-Tale Heart," "Ligeia," and "The Pit and the Pendulum." At the same time, he wrote many stories that displayed analytic powers, as in "The Gold Bug"; detective stories, such as "The Murders in the Rue Morgue"; and science fiction. Poe's genius was recognized not only in the United States but also in Europe, especially France.

Gustave Flaubert (1821–1880) French novelist, author of the celebrated *Madame Bovary* (1857). He began to work on that novel in 1851 after a tour of the Middle East and completed it in five years. When the book was published, he was immediately brought to trial on charges of obscenity and narrowly escaped conviction. He then began work on *Salammbô,* a novel about ancient Carthage. In 1869 he published his third major novel, *Sentimental Education. The Temptation of Saint Anthony* followed in 1874. Critics rate his *Three Tales* (1877), containing the stories "A Simple Heart," "The Legend of Saint Julian the Hospitaller," and "Herodias," as his masterpiece, although it is less well known than his other works. He also wrote a number of plays, but none of them were well received.

William Wordsworth (1770–1850) English poet whose *Lyrical Ballads* (1798, written with Samuel Taylor Coleridge) helped launch the English romantic movement. In 1843 he succeeded Robert Southey as poet laureate of England. His verse collections included *The Prelude* (1850), *Poems, in Two Volumes* (1807), *Poems Chiefly of Early and Late Years* (1842), *Yarrow Revisited and Other Poems* (1835), *Sonnets* (1838), and *The Borderers, A Tragedy* (1842). His most memorable poems have found a permanent home in English literature. They include "Tintern Abbey," "Lucy," "Matthew," "The Brothers," "Michael," "The River Duddon," and "Ode: Intimations of Immortality."

Anton Pavlovich Chekhov (1860–1904) Russian playwright and short story writer. Chekhov's plays are among those most often performed around the world, in an array of languages. *Uncle Vanya* (1897), a drama in four acts and a study in aimlessness and hopelessness, is only one of the many masterpieces that are his legacies to the theater. Also popular are *Three Sisters* (1901), *The Cherry Orchard* (1904), *The Bear* (1888), *The Proposal* (1889), *The Seagull* (1904), *The Wedding* (1889), and *The Anniversary* (1891). *Three Sisters* is a drama in four acts in which the characters are stifled in their dreary provincial lives and alternate between boredom and yearning. *The Cherry Orchard* is a play in four acts that chronicles the decline of the charming Renavskaya family. *The Seagull* is a drama in four acts that deals with lost opportunities and the clash of generations. Chekhov was also a master of the short story. Most of his great stories were written at his country estate in the village of Melikhovo. His Melikhovo stories include "Neighbors" (1892), "Ward Number Six" (1892), "The Black Monk" (1894), "The Murder" (1895), "Ariadne" (1895), and "The Peasants" (1897).

Charles-Pierre Baudelaire (1821–1867) One of the greatest French poets of his era. In 1844 he had a liaison with a black woman who inspired his first cycle of erotic poems, *The Black Venus.* At this time he also composed many of the poems that later formed part of *The Flowers of Evil,* his sole collection published in his lifetime. His mature period began with his discovery of Edgar Allan Poe, whose work he translated into French. In 1852 he took up with a white woman, who was the inspiration of his cycle called *The White Venus.* Two years later, an affair with a Parisian actress led to *The Green-Eyed Venus.* In 1857 he published *The Flowers of Evil,* which resulted in his prosecution for obscenity and blasphemy; his name became a byword for depravity. The remaining years of his life were darkened by growing failure and despair, and he slipped into a financial morass and physical crisis from which he never recovered.

Mark Twain (Samuel Langhorne Clemens) (1835–1910) One of the best known American writers, Twain led an adventurous life and based many of his novels and stories on personal experiences. He worked as a printer, steamboat pilot, miner, and journalist, and his pseudonym was borrowed from a riverman's term for water two fathoms deep. His first story, "The Celebrated Jumping Frog of Calaveras County," was an immediate success. In 1866 he went on a world tour, and his reports were collected and published as *Innocents Abroad* (1869). Similarly, *Roughing It* (1872) was a chronicle of his journeys in the Pacific Islands. Encouraged by his reception, Twain wrote a series of popular novels: *Tom Sawyer* (1876), *A Tramp Abroad* (1880), *The Prince and the Pauper* (1881), *Life on the Mississippi* (1883), and *Huckleberry Finn* (1884). In 1889 he published *A Connecticut Yankee in King Arthur's Court,* an imaginary travel account. After nearly going bankrupt from imprudent financial undertakings, Twain rebounded with the publication of *The Tragedy of Pudd'nhead Wilson* (1894). His last work was *The Man That Corrupted Hadleyburg* (1900).

August Strindberg (1849–1912) Swedish playwright who pioneered expressionist drama, in which subconscious thoughts, emotions, and inner struggles of the playwright are presented through a wide variety of nonnaturalistic techniques, including abstraction, distortion, exaggeration, primitivism, fantasy, and symbolism. Through his plays and stories he became the acknowledged voice of modern Sweden. Throughout life he was tormented by religious doubt, personal setbacks, and professional insecurities, and these were reflected in his works. Among his plays the most popular and significant were *Master Olof* (1872), a historical drama on the Swedish Reformation; *Lucky Peter's Travels* (1881), *The New Kingdom* (1882), *Comrades* (1888), *The Father* (1887), *Miss Julie* (1888), *The Pariah* (1889), *The Creditors* (1890), *The Saga of the Folkings* (1899), *Gustav Vasa* (1899), *The Dance of Death* (1901), *A Dream Play* (1902), and *The Ghost Sonata* (1907). *The Great Highway* (1909) was a symbolic presentation of his own life. In between plays, Strindberg wrote novels and stories. The first novel was *The Red Room* (1879); the first collection of his short stories,

Married (1884–85), led to prosecution for blasphemy. His most creative phase was the last decade of the century, when he produced the novels *The People of Hemso* (1887) and *By the Open Sea* (1890). Bitterness after parting from his third wife in 1904 colors the grotesquely satirical novel *Black Banners* (1907). His last collections of short stories were *Fair Haven and Foul Strand* (1902) and *Tales* (1903). Strindberg's religious crises are reflected in *Inferno* (1898) and *To Damascus* (1898–1904). He wrote two autobiographies: *The Son of a Servant* (1886–87) and *Alone* (1903).

Percy Bysshe Shelley (1792–1822) English romantic poet whose life was brief yet one of the most productive in the annals of poetry. He issued his first major poem, *Queen Mab,* in 1813, when he was barely 21. During a summer in Geneva he composed "Hymn to Intellectual Beauty," and *Mont Blanc.* Traveling to Italy in 1818, he began to concentrate on his poetic impulses. He began *Julian and Maddalo* (1819) and published *Prometheus Unbound* (1820) with some of his finest short poems including "Ode to Liberty," "Ode to the West Wind," "The Cloud," and "To a Skylark." He moved to Pisa, Italy, in 1820 and wrote three works: *Epipsychidion,* a fable; "Adonais" (1821) on the untimely death of John Keats; and the verse drama *Hellas,* celebrating Greek Revolution against Turkish rule. He was working on *The Triumph of Life,* a poetic narrative, when he drowned at sea at age 30.

George Gordon Byron (Lord Byron) (1788–1824) English romantic poet whose bohemian life was reflected in his unconventional poetry. In 1812 he published the first two cantos of *Childe Harold's Pilgrimage* and found himself suddenly famous. The poem relates the adventures of a young knight who, disillusioned with his pursuit of pleasure, seeks distraction by going on a solitary pilgrimage. It exposed the disconnect between romantic idealism and the reality of resulting melancholy and disillusionment. Even as he conducted numerous affairs and his marriage ended in divorce, he continued to write furiously, turning out *The Giaour* (1813), *The Bride of Abydos* (1813), *The Corsair* (1814), and *Lara* (1814). Public indignation against his immorality forced him to self-exile in Europe, first in Geneva, where he wrote *The Prisoner of Chillon* (1816) and *Manfred* (1817), and then to Rome, where he wrote *Beppo* and his greatest poem, *Don Juan* (1819–24). Enamored of Teresa, Countess Guiccioli, he followed her to Ravenna, where he wrote *The Prophecy of Dante* and the poetic dramas *Marino Faliero, Sardanapalus, The Two Foscari,* and *Cain* (all published in 1821). In 1823 Byron joined the Greek struggle for independence from the Turkish barbarians. He left for Missolonghi, where he died at age 36.

Walter Scott, Sir (1771–1832) Scottish novelist whose historical novels portrayed the panorama of Scotland's history. He was a born storyteller and wrote in a rich and ornate literary style. His first full-length narrative poem, *The Lay of the Last Minstrel* (1805), reflected his interest in the border ballads of his native country. It was followed by *Marmion* (1808), *The Lady of the Lake* (1810), *Rokeby* (1813), and *Lord of the Isles* (1815). In 1814 he published his first novel, *The Waverley,* the story of the Jacobite Rebellion of 1745. With its success, he embarked on a series of historical novels that included *Guy Mannering* (1815), *The Antiquary* (1816), *The Black Dwarf* (1816), *Old Mortality* (1816), *Rob Roy* (1817), *The Heart of Midlothian* (1818), *The Bride of Lammermoor* (1819), and *A Legend of Montrose* (1819). Scott then turned to British history with *Ivanhoe* (1819), *The Monastery* (1820), *The Abbot* (1820), *Kenilworth* (1821), *The Pirate* (1822), *The Fortunes of Niger* (1822), and *Quentin Durward* (1823). His last novels included *Redgauntlet* (1824) and *The Talisman* (1825).

Alfred, Lord Tennyson (1809–1892) English poet, the most important of the Victorian poets. Tennyson established his reputation with *Poems, Chiefly Lyrical* (1830), which included "Mariana." A second volume followed in 1832 that included the famous "Lady of Shallott" and "The Lotos-Eaters." His grief over the sudden death of his friend Henry Hallam inspired him to write a series of poems that were collected in *In Memoriam.* To this period also belongs the brooding poem *Maud.* In 1842 he published the two-volume *Poems* that included "Ulysses," "Morte d'Arthur," "The Two Voices," "Locksley Hall," and "The Vision of Sin." In 1850, he was appointed poet laureate and in 1854 wrote "Charge of the Light Brigade." The *Idylls of the King* (1859) and *Enoch Arden* (1864) were great successes. In 1886 he published a new volume of poetry in which he bemoaned the decline of culture. During his later years he published two more volumes: *Demeter and Other Poems* (1889) and *The Death of Oneone, Akbar's Dream and Other Poems* (1892).

Natsume Sōseki (Natsume Kinosuke) (1867–1916) Outstanding Japanese novelist of the Meiji era and the first Japanese practitioner of the realist novel. He was a teacher by profession and wrote novels on the side. He established his reputation with three novels: *I Am Cat* (1905–6), *Botchan: Master Darling* (1906), and *The Three-Cornered World* (1906). In 1907 he gave up teaching and devoted himself entirely to writing. During the remaining years of his life he wrote *The Gate* (1910), *The Wayfarer* (1912–13), *Kokoro* (1914), and *Grass on the Wayside* (1915).

Heinrich Heine (1797–1856) German poet. Heine's parents were Jewish, but he converted to Protestantism. During his lifetime he published three volumes of lyrical verse. Of these the third, *Romanzero,* is the best, and saddest, filled with heartrending laments on the human condition, inspired by his failing health and finances. His first collection, *The Book of Songs* (1827) was, on the other hand, youthful and passionate; his second volume, *New Poems* (1844), redolent of his new-

found sense of social engagement. Between volumes he wrote a number of travel narratives, an autobiography, social and political criticism, and literary polemics that were widely imitated. He wrote three works on native land, all of them negative, about German reactionary policies, and they were banned in Germany.

Arthur Rimbaud (1854–1891) French symbolist poet and adventurer. Symbolists expressed individual experiences through subtle and suggestive use of metaphorical language. Many expressed a morbid interest in the bizarre. Rimbaud was a restless spirit who even as a youth wanted to shock the bourgeois with his wild conduct. He expressed a disgust with life and sought to become a poet so that he could, in his words, "become an instrument for the voice of the eternal": He believed that the poet was a seer who must disregard the conventional concept of individual personality and become the voice of the infinite. Rimbaud sent the poet Paul Verlaine (1844–1896) specimens of his poetry, among them the sonnet "Voyelles." Verlaine was so impressed that he invited Rimbaud to come to Paris and live with him. Rimbaud's response was "The Drunken Boat," a poem of astonishing verbal virtuosity. He soon became involved in a sexual relationship with Verlaine. In 1872 Verlaine abandoned his wife and left France with Rimbaud for London. Back in France the following year, Verlaine shot and wounded Rimbaud. During his time with Verlaine, Rimbaud wrote two of his best known works: *Illuminations* (1886) and *A Season in Hell* (1873). Rimbaud traveled to Africa (1875–76), where he fell ill. Returning to France, he died in Marseille after his leg was amputated.

Henrik Johan Ibsen (1828–1906) Norwegian playwright who revived the European theater in the 19th and early 20th centuries. Ibsen's first play, *Catilina* (1850), embodies themes that would preoccupy him all his life, such as a rebellious hero and a destructive mistress. He worked first at Bergen and then at the Norwegian Theater in Christiania, producing such plays as *Love's Comedy* (1862) and *The Pretenders* (1863). When the Norwegian Theater failed in 1864 he left Norway and for the next 27 years lived abroad. During this period he wrote *Brand* (1866), *Peer Gynt* (1867), *Pillars of Society* (1877), *A Doll's House* (1879), *Ghosts* (1881), *An Enemy of the People* (1882), *The Wild Duck* (1884), *Rosmersholm* (1886), *The Lady from the Sea* (1888), and *Hedda Gabler* (1890). Ibsen returned to Norway in 1891. Thereafter he wrote *The Master Builder* (1892), *Little Eyolf* (1894), *John Gabriel Borkman* (1896), and *When We Dead Awaken* (1899).

Key World Events of the Nineteenth Century

1801	Ireland joins Great Britain, forming the United Kingdom
1803	U.S. president Thomas Jefferson purchases Louisiana from France for $27 million
1804	Haiti gains independence from France and becomes the first republic in the New World outside the United States
1805	Horatio Nelson inflicts crippling defeat on France at Trafalgar but dies in battle. Napoléon, in a stunning victory, defeats Russia and Austria at Austerlitz
1807	Slave trade is abolished in the British Empire
1812	Napoléon's Grand Army is destroyed in Russia
1814	Napoléon is defeated at the Battle of Leipzig; Napoléon abdicates and is exiled to the island of Elba in the Mediterranean. The Congress of Vienna redraws the map of Europe and restores the Bourbon monarchy in France
1815	Napoléon returns to Paris, assembles an army, but is defeated for the last time at Waterloo; he is exiled to the island of St. Helena in the South Atlantic
1816	Joseph Nipce, French physicist, produces the first photograph on metal
1817	José Francisco de San Martín and Simón Bolívar begin liberation of South America from Spanish rule
1818	Greeks begin their war of independence against Turkish oppressors
1819	U.S. president James Monroe proclaims the Monroe Doctrine asserting the country's authority in the Western Hemisphere
1832	Whigs led by Lord Grey pass the Great Reform Act, laying the foundation of modern democracy in Great Britain by enlarging the electorate
1833	Great Britain abolishes slavery throughout its empire
1835	Boers, the original Dutch settlers in South Africa, escape British control by setting out on the Great Trek from Cape Town across the Orange River into northern Natal
1845	Potato famine depopulates Ireland. United States annexes Texas
1848	Karl Marx and Friedrich Engels publish *The Communist Manifesto*
1850	Taiping rebellion led by Hong Xiuquan, a visionary, breaks out in China but is crushed with the aid of Western powers
1854	Commodore Matthew Perry forces the Tokugawa shogunate in Japan to open doors to Western merchants and ships
1856	Henry Bessemer invents the steel converter
1857	U.S. Supreme Court finds against Dred Scott, a slave, and thus legitimizes slavery in the United States
1858	The Indian Mutiny (also known as the Sepoy Rebellion) breaks out in Bengal; although suppressed, it leads to the end of the rule of the East India Company and the British takeover of the Indian territories
1859	Charles Darwin publishes *On the Origin of Species*
1860	Abraham Lincoln is elected president of the United States by a narrow margin
1861	U.S. Civil War breaks out as the South secedes from the Union; the Confederacy attacks Fort Sumter. Victor Emmanuel II becomes king of a united Italy in the aftermath of the military successes of the Risorgimento. Tsar Alexander II abolishes serfdom

1863	Lincoln issues the Emancipation Proclamation, abolishing slavery
1864	First Communist International is founded in London; the opening address is delivered by Karl Marx, who becomes its first president
1865	U.S. Civil War ends as the Confederacy surrenders at Appomattox
1866	Gregor Mendel, an Austrian monk, discovers genetics
1867	Austro-Hungarian monarchy is established with Franz Joseph as emperor; it lasts until 1918
1868	Meiji Restoration ends shogun power in Japan and launches the country on a course of rapid modernization
1869	Pope Pius IX holds the First Vatican Council, which promulgates the Doctrine of Papal Infallibility. Suez Canal is built by Ferdinand de Lesseps, a French engineer
1876	Alexander Graham Bell invents the telephone
1882	British occupation of Egypt signals the beginning of the European scramble for Africa; within a few decades all of Africa, with the exception of Ethiopia, will come under European rule
1885	Karl Benz invents the automobile
1894	Japan launches its imperialist plan to dominate Asia by making war on China. Muslim Ottomans massacre millions of Armenians and other Christians in a campaign of extermination that lasts until the mid-1920s
1895	The Lumière brothers invent photography. Guglielmo Marconi invents the radio. Wilhelm Roentgen invents X rays
1898	In the Spanish-American War, the United States gains Philippines and Cuba and establishes itself as a new imperial power
1899	Boer War breaks out in South Africa between the Boers and the British; within two years the Boers are forced to capitulate

1800

BIRTHS

Yevgeny Abramovich Baratynsky, Russian poet
Antonio Feliciano Castilho, Portuguese poet
Thomas Babington Macaulay, English essayist and historian
France Prešeren, Slovene poet
Mihály Vörösmarty, Hungarian poet
Nasif Yasiji, Arab-Lebanese Christian scholar

DEATH

William Cowper, English poet

PUBLICATIONS

ENGLISH

Castle Rackrent Novel by Maria Edgeworth
"Michael" Pastoral poem by William Wordsworth

GERMAN

Hymns to the Night Prose poems by Novalis
Titan Novel by Johann Paul Richter
Maria Stuart Play by Johann Christoph Friedrich von Schiller

1801

BIRTHS

William Barnes, English poet
Christian Dietrich Grabbe, German playwright
Johann Nestroy, Austrian playwright
John Henry Newman, English essayist and Catholic cardinal

DEATHS

Ignacy Krasicki, Polish poet
Novalis (Friedrich Leopold von Hardenberg), German poet

PUBLICATIONS

ENGLISH

American

Clara Howard Love story by Charles Brockden Brown
Jane Talbot Novel by Charles Brockden Brown

British

Belinda Novel by Maria Edgeworth
Thalaba the Destroyer Long poem by Robert Southey

Irish

Poetical Works by Thomas Moore

FRENCH

Atala Novel by François-Auguste-René de Chateaubriand
The Genius of Christianity Commentary by François-Auguste-René de Chateaubriand

GERMAN

The Two Klingsbergs Play by August von Kotzebue
The Maid of Orleans Tragedy by Johann Christoph Friedrich von Schiller

JAPANESE

Diary of My Father's Death Poems by Kobayashi Issa

1802

BIRTHS

Alexander Dumas père, French novelist
Victor-Marie Hugo, French novelist
Nikolaus Lenau (Nikolaus Franz Niembsch von Strehlenau), Austrian poet

LITERARY EVENT

The Edinburgh Review, influential British quarterly journal, is founded

PUBLICATIONS

DANISH

Poems by Adam Gottlob Oehlenschläger
The Golden Horns Poems by Adam Gottlob Oehlenschläger

ENGLISH

British

"Dejection: An Ode" Poem by Samuel Taylor Coleridge
John Woodvil Tragedy by Charles Lamb
"My Heart Leaps Up When I Behold" Poem by William Wordsworth
"Ode: Intimations of Immortality from Recollections of Early Childhood" Poem by William Wordsworth
"Resolution and Independence" Poem by William Wordsworth

Scottish

Minstrelsy of the Scottish Border Three-volume collection by Sir Walter Scott

FRENCH

Delphine Epistolary novel by Madame de Staël

GERMAN

Henry of Ofterdingen Romance by Novalis

ITALIAN

The Last Letters of Jaccopo Ortis Novel by Ugo Foscolo

1803

BIRTHS

Thomas Lowell Beddoes, English poet
George Borrow, English travel writer
Ralph Waldo Emerson, American essayist and poet
Friedrich Reinhold Kreutzwald, Estonian poet and compiler of the national epic *Kalevipoeg*
Edward George Bulwer-Lytton, English novelist
Prosper Mérimée, French novelist
Robert Smith Surtees, English comic novelist
Fyodor Ivanovich Tyutchev, Russian poet

DEATHS

Vittorio Alfieri, Italian poet
James Beattie, Scottish poet
Johann Wilhelm Ludwig Gleim, German poet
Johann Wilhelm Heinse, German poet
Johann Gottfried von Herder, German poet and critic
Friedrich Gottlieb Klopstock, German religious poet
Pierre-Ambroise-François Choderlos de Laclos, French novelist
François de Saint-Lambert, French poet

PUBLICATIONS

GERMAN

The Bride of Messina Play by Johann Christoph Friedrich von Schiller
The Feud of the Schroffensteins Play by Heinrich von Kleist
The Sons of the Valley Religious play by Zacharias Werner

1804

BIRTHS

Ludwig Andreas Feuerbach, German philosopher
Francesco Domenico Guerrazzi, Italian novelist
Nathaniel Hawthorne, American novelist
Eduard Morike, German poet
Johan Ludvig Runeberg, Finnish-Swedish poet
Charles-Augustin Saint-Beuve, French literary critic
George Sand (Amandine-Aurore-Lucie Dudevant), French novelist
Eugène Sue, French novelist

DEATH

Immanuel Kant, German philosopher

PUBLICATIONS

ENGLISH

British

"I Wandered Lonely as a Cloud" Poem by William Wordsworth
"Ode to Duty" Poem by William Wordsworth
Popular Tales Collection of stories by Maria Edgeworth
"She Was a Phantom of Delight" Poem by William Wordsworth

FRENCH

Memoirs of a Father Autobiography by Jean-François Marmontel

GERMAN

William Tell Verse drama by Johann Christoph Friedrich von Schiller

1805

BIRTHS

Hans Christian Andersen, Danish writer of children's stories
Esteban Echeverría, Argentine poet
Adalbert Stifter, Austrian novelist
Alexis-Charles-Henri Clérel de Tocqueville, French historian and commentator

DEATHS

Mihály Csokonai Vitéz, Hungarian poet
Johann Christoph Friedrich von Schiller, German playwright and poet

PUBLICATIONS

ENGLISH

British

Madoc Romantic poem by Robert Southey
"The Solitary Reaper" Poem by William Wordsworth

Scottish

The Lay of the Last Minstrel Poem in six cantos by Sir Walter Scott

FRENCH
René Novel by François-Auguste-René de Chateaubriand

1806

BIRTHS

Elizabeth Barrett Browning, English poet
André-Henri-Constant van Hasselt, Belgian poet
Heinrich Laube, German playwright
Sakurada Jisuke, Japanese playwright
John Stuart Mill, English philosopher

DEATH

Carlo Gozzi, Italian satirist and playwright

PUBLICATION

GERMAN
The Cross on the Baltic Sea Play by Zacharias Werner

1807

BIRTHS

Jonas Hallgrimsson, Icelandic poet
Henry Wadsworth Longfellow, American poet
John Greenleaf Whittier, American poet

PUBLICATIONS

DANISH
Hakon Jarl Tragedy by Adam Gottlob Oehlenschläger

ENGLISH
American

Salmagundi, or The Whim-Whams and Opinions of Launcelot Langstaff, Esq., and Others Collection of satirical poems by Washington Irving

British

The Family Shakespeare Expurgated version of Shakespeare's plays by censor Thomas Bowdler
Hours of Idleness Poems by Lord Byron
Letters of Espriella Prose piece by Robert Southey
Palmerin of England Chivalric romance by Robert Southey
The Parish Register Poem by George Crabbe
Poems in Two Volumes Collection by William Wordsworth
Sir Eustace Grey Long poem by George Crabbe
Tales from Shakespeare Tales retold in prose by Charles and Mary Lamb
"The World Is Too Much With Us" Poem by William Wordsworth

FRENCH
Corinne Romantic novel by Madame de Staël

GERMAN
Martin Luther; or The Consecration of Strength Play by Zacharias Werner

ITALIAN
Of Sepulchres Poem by Ugo Foscolo

1808

BIRTHS

Jules-Amédée Barbey d'Aurevilly, French novelist
José de Espronceda y Delgado, Spanish poet
Jean-Baptiste-Alphonse Karr, French novelist
Abraham Mapu, Lithuanian Jewish novelist
Gérard de Nerval (Gérard Labrunie), French writer
Henrik Arnold Wergeland, Norwegian poet

PUBLICATIONS

ENGLISH
British

The Adventures of Ulysses Recreation of Homeric epic by Charles Lamb

Scottish

Marmion, a Tale of Flodden Field Poem in six cantos by Sir Walter Scott

GERMAN
Attila, King of the Huns Play by Zacharias Werner
The Broken Pitcher Play by Heinrich von Kleist
Cathy from Heilbronn; or, The Trial by Fire Play by Heinrich von Kleist
Faust Part I of the dramatic tragedy by Johann Wolfgang von Goethe
The Marquis of O Novella by Heinrich von Kleist
Penthesilia Play by Heinrich von Kleist
Robert Guiskard Unfinished drama by Heinrich von Kleist

RUSSIAN
Lyudmila Ballad by Vasily Andreyvich Zhukovsky

1809

BIRTHS

Petrus Borel (Joseph-Pierre Borel), French poet, novelist, and critic
Charles Darwin, English naturalist
Edward FitzGerald, English translator and poet
Nikolay Vasilyevich Gogol, Russian novelist and playwright
Heinrich Hoffmann, German writer
Oliver Wendell Holmes, American physician, poet, and essayist
Edgar Allan Poe, American poet, short story writer, essayist, and pioneer of the detective story

Juliusz Słowacki, Polish romantic poet
Alfred, Lord Tennyson, English poet

DEATH
Thomas Paine, English-born American pamphleteer

PUBLICATIONS

ENGLISH

American

Collected Poems by Philip Freneau
A History of New York Satirical history by Washington Irving

British

Mrs. Leicester's School Collection of stories by Charles and Mary
  Lamb

FRENCH

Christophe Colomb Comedy by Népomucène Lemercier
The Martyrs Prose epic by François-Auguste-René de
  Chateaubriand

GERMAN

Army Chaplain Schmelzle's Journey Novel by Jean Paul Friedrich
  Richter
Dr. Katzenberger's Journey to the Spa Novel by Jean Paul
  Friedrich Richter

1810

BIRTHS
Margaret Fuller, American transcendentalist and woman of
  letters
Elizabeth Gaskell, English novelist
Maurice de Guérin, French poet
Karel Hynek Mácha, Czech lyric poet
Alfred de Musset, French poet
Alexandros Rizos Rangabe, Greek scholar and playwright

DEATH
Charles Brockden Brown, American novelist

PUBLICATIONS

DUTCH
The Destruction of the First World Epic poem by Willem
  Bilderdijk

ENGLISH
British

The Borough Epistolary poem by George Crabbe

Scottish

The Lady of the Lake Poem in six cantos by Sir Walter Scott

GERMAN
Katherine of Heilbronn Play by Heinrich von Kleist
The Twenty-fourth of February Play by Zacharias Werner

1811

BIRTHS
Théophile Gautier, French poet and novelist
Vissarion Grigoryevich Belinsky, Russian critic
Karl Ferdinand Gutzkow, German playwright
Jules Sandeau, French novelist
Harriet Beecher Stowe, American novelist
William Makepeace Thackeray, English novelist

DEATHS
György Bessenyei, Hungarian lyric poet
Marie-Joseph-Blaise Chénier, French satirist and dramatist
Heinrich von Kleist, German playwright and poet

PUBLICATIONS

ENGLISH
British

Sense and Sensibility Novel by Jane Austen

GERMAN
The Battle of Herman Play by Heinrich von Kleist
The Prince of Homburg Play by Heinrich von Kleist
Undine Novel by Friedrich de la Motte Fouqué

HUNGARIAN
The Tartars in Hungary Play by Károly Kisfaludy
Thorns and Flowers Epigrams by Ferenc Kacinczy

1812

BIRTHS
Robert Browning, English poet
Hendrik Conscience, Flemish novelist
Charles Dickens, English novelist
Ivan Alexandrovich Goncharov, Russian novelist
Zygmunt Krasinski, Polish romantic poet
Josef Ignacy Kraszewski, Polish novelist and poet
Edward Lear, English writer of light verse

PUBLICATIONS

ENGLISH
British

The Absentee Novel by Maria Edgeworth
Childe Harold's Pilgrimage Long poem by Lord Byron
Count Julian Verse tragedy by Walter Savage Landor

GERMAN
Grimm's Fairy Tales Collection by folklorists Jakob and Wilhelm
  Grimm

1813

BIRTHS
Georg Büchner, German poet
Friedrich Hebbel, German playwright
Søren Aabye Kierkegaard, Danish existential philosopher
Otto Ludwig, German playwright and novelist

DEATHS
Karl Theodor Korner, German lyric poet
Christoph Martin Wieland, German novelist

PUBLICATIONS
ENGLISH
British

The Bride of Abydon Verse tale by Lord Byron
The Giaour Verse tale by Lord Byron
The Life of Horatio Nelson Biography by Robert Southey
Pride and Prejudice Novel by Jane Austen
Queen Mab Poem by Percy Bysshe Shelley

Irish

The Twopenny Post Bag Collection of satiric poems by Thomas Moore

Scottish

The Bridal of Triermain Poem by Sir Walter Scott
Rokeby Poem in six cantos by Sir Walter Scott

GERMAN
German

Peter Schlemihl Humorous story by French-born writer Aldelbert von Chamisso

Swiss

The Swiss Family Robinson Children's classic story by Johann David Wyss

ITALIAN
Inni Sacri Collection of romantic poems by Alessandro Manzoni

1814

BIRTHS
Gertrudis Gómez de Avellaneda, Cuban-Spanish poet and playwright
Joseph Sheridan Le Fanu, Irish novelist
Michael Yurevich Lermontov, Russian novelist
Charles Reade, English novelist
Taras Shevchenko, Ukrainian poet

DEATHS
Jacques-Henri Bernardin de Saint-Pierre, French novelist
Johann Gottlieb Fichte, German philosopher
Donatien-Alphonse-François de Sade (Marquis de Sade), French writer

PUBLICATIONS
ENGLISH
American

"The Star-Spangled Banner" Poem (and later the U.S. national anthem) by Francis Scott Key

British

The Corsair Poem in heroic couplets by Lord Byron
The Excursion Philosophical poem by Robert Southey
Lara Poem in heroic couplets by Lord Byron
Mansfield Park Novel by Jane Austen
Patronage Novel by Maria Edgeworth
Roderick, the Last of the Goths Poem by Robert Southey
To Byron Sonnet by John Keats

Scottish

Waverely Novel by Sir Walter Scott

FRENCH
The Dog of Montargis; or, The Forest of Bundy Melodrama by René-Charles Guilbert de Pixérécourt

GERMAN
Tales of Hoffman Gothic tales by fabulist E. T. W. Hoffman

JAPANESE
Satomi and the Eight Dogs Novel by Bakin Takizawa

1815

BIRTHS
Franz Emanuel Geibel, German poet
Richard Henry Dana, American novelist
Anthony Trollope, English novelist

DEATH
Matthias Claudius, German poet

PUBLICATIONS
ENGLISH
British

Emma Novel by Jane Austen

Scottish

Guy Mannering Novel by Sir Walter Scott
Lord of the Isles Poem in six cantos by Sir Walter Scott

FRENCH
Songs Collection by Pierre-Jean de Béranger

GERMAN
The Devil's Elixir Collection of tales by E. T. W. Hoffman
Songs Collection by lyricist Johann Ludwig Uhland

HUNGARIAN
Bánk bán Play by József Katona

RUSSIAN
The Newlyweds Play by Aleksandr Sergeyevich Griboyedov

SPANISH
Mexican

The Itching Parrot Picaresque satire by José Joaquín Fernández de Lizardi

1816

BIRTHS
Charlotte Brontë, English novelist
Gustav Freytag, German novelist
Kawatake Mokuami, Japanese playwright

DEATHS
Gavrila Romanovich Derzhavin, Russian poet
Richard Brinsley Sheridan, Irish playwright

PUBLICATIONS
ENGLISH
British

Alastor; or, The Spirit of Solitude Romantic poem by Percy Bysshe Shelley
"Christabel" Unfinished poem by Samuel Taylor Coleridge
"The Dream" Visionary romantic poem in blank verse by Lord Byron
The Headlong Hall Novel by Thomas Love Peacock
"Hymn to Intellectual Beauty" Romantic poem by Percy Bysshe Shelley
"Kubla Khan" Romantic poem by Samuel Taylor Coleridge
Mont Blanc Poem by Percy Bysshe Shelley
"On First Looking into Chapman's Homer" Sonnet by John Keats
"Parisi'na" Poem by Lord Byron
"The Prisoner of Chillon" Poem by Lord Byron
"The Siege of Corinth" Poem by Lord Byron
The Story of Rimini Poetical work by Leigh Hunt

Scottish

The Antiquary Novel by Sir Walter Scott
The Black Dwarf Novel by Sir Walter Scott
Old Mortality Novel by Sir Walter Scott

FRENCH
Adolphe Novel by Benjamin Constant de Rebecque

GERMAN
Songs of the Fatherland Collection by Johann Ludvig Ihland

ITALIAN
Songs Collection by Giacomo Leopardi

RUSSIAN
The History of Russia History by Nikolai Karamzin

1817

BIRTHS
János Arany, Hungarian poet
Theodor Woldsen Storm, German poet
Henry David Thoreau, American essayist
José Zorilla y Moral, Spanish poet and playwright

DEATHS
Jane Austen, English novelist
Madame de Staël (Anne-Louise-Germaine Necker de Staël), French playwright and novelist

LITERARY EVENT
Blackwood's Magazine is founded in Edinburgh, Scotland

PUBLICATIONS
ENGLISH
American

"Thanatopsis" Poem in blank verse by William Cullen Bryant

British

Biographia Literaria Essays by Samuel Taylor Coleridge
"The Lament of Tasso" Poem by Lord Byron
Manfred Dramatic poem by Lord Byron
Melincourt; or, Sir Oran Haut-ton Novel by Thomas Love Peacock
Northanger Abbey Novel by Jane Austen
Ormond Novel by Maria Edgeworth
Persuasion Novel by Jane Austen
Sanditon Novel by Jane Austen
Zapolya Dramatic poem by Samuel Taylor Coleridge

Irish

Lalla Rookh Poem by Thomas Moore

Scottish

Harold the Dauntless Novel by Sir Walter Scott
Rob Roy Novel by Sir Walter Scott

GERMAN
Austrian

The Ancestors Play by Franz Grillparzer

German

Strange Stories Collection of tales by E. T. W. Hoffman

HUNGARIAN
The Suitors Play by Karoly Kisfaludy

1818

BIRTHS

Emily Brontë, English poet and novelist
Charles-Marie-René Leconte de Lisle, French Parnassian poet
Karl Marx, German political philosopher
Ivan Sergeyvich Turgenev, Russian novelist
Aasmund Olafsson Vinje, Norwegian poet

DEATHS

Matthew Gregory "Monk" Lewis, English Gothic novelist
Johann David Wyss, Swiss writer

PUBLICATIONS

ENGLISH

American

"To a Water Fowl" Poem by William Cullen Bryant

British

Beppo Poem in mock heroic style by Lord Byron
Endymion Poem in four books by John Keats
Frankenstein; or, the Modern Prometheus Novel by Mary Wollstonecraft Shelley
The Fudge Family in Paris Satirical verse by Thomas Moore
Nightmare Abbey Novel by Thomas Love Peacock
"Ozymandias" Sonnet by Percy Bysshe Shelley

Scottish

The Heart of Midlothian Novel by Sir Walter Scott

GERMAN

Sappho Tragedy in verse by Austrian playwright Franz Grillparzer

GREEK

Metai Poems by Kristijonas Donelaitis

1819

BIRTHS

Arthur Hugh Clough, English poet
George Eliot (Mary Ann Evans), English novelist
Theodor Fontane, German poet
Julia Ward Howe, American poet and suffragist
Gottfried Keller, Swiss poet and novelist
Charles Kingsley, English poet and novelist
James Russell Lowell, American poet and essayist
Herman Melville, American novelist
Francisco Manuel do Nascimento, Portuguese poet
John Ruskin, English essayist and art critic
Philip Schaff, Swiss-born American theologian and historian
Walt Whitman, American poet

DEATH

August Friedrich Ferdinand von Kotzebue, German playwright

PUBLICATIONS

DANISH

The Gods of the North Poetic epic by Adam Gottlob Oehlenschläger

ENGLISH

American

"The Legend of Sleepy Hollow" Short story by Washington Irving
The Sketch Book Collection of short stories by Washington Irving

British

The Cenci Dramatic tragedy by Percy Bysshe Shelley
Don Juan Epic satire by Lord Byron
"The Eve of St. Agnes" Poem by John Keats
"La Belle Dame sans Merci" Ballad by John Keats
Lamia Allegorical poem by John Keats
Mazeppa Poem by Lord Byron
"Ode on a Grecian Urn" Poem by John Keats
"Ode on Indolence" Poem by John Keats
"Ode on Melancholy" Poem by John Keats
"Ode to a Nightingale" Poem by John Keats
"Ode to Autumn" Poem by John Keats
"Ode to Psyche" Poem by John Keats
"Ode to the West Wind" Poem by Percy Bysshe Shelley
The Waggoner Fanciful poetic tale by William Wordsworth

Scottish

The Bride of Lammermoor Novel by Sir Walter Scott
Ivanhoe Novel by Sir Walter Scott
A Legend of Montrose Novel by Sir Walter Scott

GERMAN

The Serapion Brothers Collection of gothic tales by E. T. W. Hoffman
West Eastern Divan Collection of lyrics by Johann Wolfgang von Goethe
The World as Will and Idea Philosophical treatise by Arthur Schopenhauer

JAPANESE

The Year of My Life Poetic diary by Kobayashi Issa

1820

BIRTHS

Émile Augier, French playwright
Dion Boucicault, Irish-born American poet
Anne Brontë, English novelist
Afanasy Afanasyevich Fet, Russian poet
Multatuli (Eduard Douwes Dekker), Dutch writer

DEATH
Nguyen Du, Vietnamese poet

PUBLICATIONS
DUTCH
The Destruction of the First Creation Unfinished epic by Willem Bilderdijk

ENGLISH
American

Precaution Novel by James Fenimore Cooper

British

Hyperion Incomplete epic poem by John Keats
"Ode to Liberty" Poem by Percy Bysshe Shelley
Prometheus Unbound Dramatic poem by Percy Bysshe Shelley
"The Skylark" Poem by Percy Bysshe Shelley
"The Sensitive Plan" Poem by Percy Bysshe Shelley

Irish

Melmoth the Wanderer Gothic romance by Charles Robert Maturin

Scottish

The Abbot Novel by Sir Walter Scott
The Monastery Historical novel and sequel to *The Abbot* by Sir Walter Scott

FRENCH
Poetic Meditations Collection of poems by Alphonse de Lamartine

HUNGARIAN
Irene Play by Károly Kisfaludy

ITALIAN
The Count of Carmagnola Historical tragedy in verse by Alessandro Manzoni

RUSSIAN
"Ode to Liberty" Poem by Aleksandr Pushkin
The Prisoner of the Caucasus Poems by Aleksandr Pushkin
Ruslan and Lyudmila Poem by Aleksandr Pushkin

1821

BIRTHS
Vasile Alecsandri, Romanian lyric poet and playwright
Henri Frédéric Amiel, Swiss diarist
Charles-Pierre Baudelaire, French poet
Richard Burton, English orientalist and adventurer
Fyodor Mikhaylovich Dostoyevsky, Russian novelist
Gustave Flaubert, French novelist
Nikolay Alexseyevich Nekrasov, Russian lyrical poet
Cyprian Kamil Norwid, Polish poet
Aleksey Pisemsky, Russian novelist and playwright

DEATHS
John Keats, English poet
Christian zu Stolberg, German lyric poet

PUBLICATIONS
ENGLISH
American

Poems Collection by William Cullen Bryant
The Spy: A Tale of the Neutral Ground Novel by James Fenimore Cooper

British

"Adonais: An Elegy on the Death of John Keats" Poem by Percy Bysshe Shelley
Cain: A Mystery Dramatic tragedy in verse by Lord Byron
Confessions of an Opium Eater Autobiographical narrative by Thomas De Quincey
Epipsychidion Poem by Percy Bysshe Shelley
Marino Faliero Doge of Venice Historical tragedy by Lord Byron
Sardanapalus Dramatic tragedy by Lord Byron
Table Talk; or, Original Essays on Men and Manners Collection of essays by William Hazlitt
The Two Foscara Historical tragedy by Lord Byron

Scottish

Kenilworth Novel by Sir Walter Scott

GERMAN
Austrian

The Golden Fleece Trilogy of short dramatic pieces by Franz Grillparzer

German

Fredegonde and Brunehaut Tragedy by Népomucène Lemercier
Gedichte Collection by Heinrich Heine
Tom-Cat Murr Novel by E. T. W. Hoffman
The Warrior's Battle Play by Heinrich von Kleist
Wilhelm Meister's Travels Part II Fictional narrative by Johann Wolfgang von Goethe

ITALIAN
The Fifth of May Poem by Alessandro Manzoni

RUSSIAN
The Robber Brothers Poems by Aleksandr Pushkin

1822

BIRTHS
Matthew Arnold, English poet and critic
Edmond de Goncourt, French novelist
Janko Král', Slovak poet

DEATHS
Ernst Theodor Wilhelm Hoffman, German folklorist
Percy Bysshe Shelley, English romantic poet

PUBLICATIONS

ENGLISH

American

A Visit from St. Nicholas ("'Twas the Night Before Christmas")
    Poem by Clement C. Moore

British

The Ghost of Abel Short dramatic dialogue by William Blake
Heaven and Earth Play by Lord Byron
Hellas Lyrical drama by Percy Bysshe Shelley
Maid Marian Novel by Thomas Love Peacock
Memorials of a Tour on the Continent Collection of poems by
    William Wordsworth
Werner Dramatic tragedy by Lord Byron

Scottish

The Fortunes of Nigel Novel by Sir Walter Scott

FRENCH

On Love Psychological discourse by Stendhal
Poems Collection of romantic verse by Alfred de Vigny

POLISH

Austrian

Husband and Wife Play by Aleksander Fredro

Polish

Poetry Poems by Adam Bernard Mickiewicz

RUSSIAN

Woe from Wit Play by Aleksandr Griboyedov

1823

BIRTHS

Théodore de Banville, French Parnassian poet
Imre Madách, Hungarian poet
Alexander Ostrovsky, Russian playwright
Coventry Patmore, English poet
Sándor Petőfi, Hungarian poet
Charlotte Yonge, English religious and historical fiction writer

DEATHS

Ann Ward Radcliffe, English gothic novelist
Friedrich Ludwig Zacharias Werner, German romantic playwright

PUBLICATIONS

DUTCH

Objections to the Spirit of the Age Treatise by Isaäc da Costa,
    philosopher

ENGLISH

American

The Pilot Historical sea novel by James Fenimore Cooper
The Pioneers; or, The Sources of the Susquehanna Frontier Novel
    by James Fenimore Cooper

British

The Essays of Elia Collection of essays by Charles Lamb
The Island Poem by Lord Byron
*Valperga; or, The Life and Adventures of Castruccio, Prince of
    Lucca* Novel by Mary Wollstonecraft Shelley

Irish

Loves of the Angels Long poem by Thomas Moore

Scottish

Peveril of the Peak Novel by Sir Walter Scott
Quentin Durward Novel by Sir Walter Scott
St. Ronan's Well Novel by Sir Walter Scott

GERMAN

Lyrisches Intermezzo Collection of Lyrics by Heinrich Heine

GREEK

"Hymn to Liberty" Poem by Dhionísios Solomos

POLISH

Forefather's Eve Play in verse by Adam Bernard Mickiewicz
Grazyna Narrative poem by Adam Bernard Mickiewicz

RUSSIAN

The Fountain of Bakhchisaray Poems by Aleksandr Pushkin

1824

BIRTHS

Victor Balaguer, Catalan historian
Wilkie Collins, English novelist
Michael Madhusudan Datta, Bengali poet
Alexandre Dumas fils, French novelist

DEATH

George Gordon Byron (Lord Byron), English poet

PUBLICATIONS

ENGLISH

American

The Chestnut Tree Long poem by Royall Tyler
Tales of a Traveler Collection of stories by Washington Irving

British

The Adventures of Hajji Baba of Isphahan Satire by James Morier
The Deformed Transformed Unfinished play by Lord Byron
Imaginary Conversations Dialogues by Walter Savage Landor
William Meister's Apprenticeship Translation of Goethe's work of
    the same name by Thomas Carlyle

Scottish

Redgauntlet Novel by Sir Walter Scott

ITALIAN

Canzoni Poems by Giacomo Leopardi

RUSSIAN

"The Gypsies" Ballad by Aleksandr Pushkin

1825

BIRTHS

Richard Doddridge Blackmore, English novelist
Camilo Castelo Branco, Portuguese novelist
Thomas Henry Huxley, English essayist and biologist
Mór Jókai, Hungarian novelist
Conrad Ferdinand Meyer, Swiss poet and novelist

DEATH

Jean Paul Friedrich Richter, German novelist

PUBLICATIONS

ENGLISH

British

Diary Journal by Samuel Pepys
The Spirit of the Age Short essays by William Hazlitt
The Tale of Paraguay Long poem by Robert Southey

Irish

Tales of the O'Hara Family Short stories by John Banim

Scottish

The Talisman Novel by Sir Walter Scott

GERMAN

King Ottocar: His Rise and Fall Historical tragedy by Austrian playwright Franz Grillparzer

HUNGARIAN

Zalán futása National epic poem by Mihály Vörösmarty

POLISH

Crimean Sonnets Collection of poems by Adam Bernard Mickiewicz

RUSSIAN

Boris Godunov Dramatic tragedy by Aleksandr Pushkin
The Bridegroom Ballad by Aleksandr Pushkin

SPANISH

Cuban

"Niagara" Poem by José María Heredia

SWEDISH

Frithjofs Saga Epic ballad collection by Esias Tegner

1826

BIRTHS

Aleksandr Nikolayevich Afanasyev, Russian historian and folklorist
Walter Bagehot, English essayist and scholar

Carlo Collodi (Carlo Lorenzini), Italian journalist
Mikhail Evgrafovich Saltykov-Shchedrin (N. Shchedrin), Russian novelist
Josef Viktor von Scheffel, German poet and novelist

DEATHS

Jens Baggesen, Danish poet
Johann Peter Hebel, German poet
Nikolay Mikhaylovich Karamzin, Russian historian
Royall Tyler, American playwright, novelist, and poet
Johann Heinrich Voss, German poet

PUBLICATIONS

ENGLISH

American

The Last of the Mohicans Novel by James Fenimore Cooper

British

The Last Man Novel by Mary Wollstonecraft Shelley
The Plain Speaker Essays by William Hazlitt

Scottish

Woodstock; or, The Cavalier: A Tale of the Year 1651 Novel by Sir Walter Scott

FRENCH

Cinq-Mars Historical novel by Alfred-Victor de Vigny

GERMAN

The Fateful Prong Play by August Platen
Pictures of Travel Collection of travel sketches by poet Heinrich Heine

ITALIAN

The Betrothed Novel by Alessandro Manzoni
Memoirs of Casanova Autobiography by Giovanni Casanova
Versi Poems by Giacomo Leopardi

RUSSIAN

Stanzas Poems by Alexander Pushkin

SPANISH

Venezuelan

Silvas americanas Poem by Andrés Bello

1827

BIRTHS

Charles de Coster, Belgian poet
Octave Crémazie, French-Canadian poet
Johanna Spyri, Swiss writer of children's tales
Lew Wallace, American novelist

DEATHS

William Blake, English poet
José Joaquín Fernández de Lizardi, Mexican poet and playwright
Ugo Foscolo, Italian poet
William Hauff, German novelist

PUBLICATIONS

ENGLISH

American

The Prairie Novel by James Fenimore Cooper
The Red Rover Novel by James Fenimore Cooper
Tamerlane and Other Poems Collection by Edgar Allan Poe

British

Falkland Novel by Edward G. E. Bulwer-Lytton
"On an Infant Dying as Soon as It Is Born" Elegy by Charles Lamb
On Murder as One of the Fine Arts Essay by Thomas de Quincey

Irish

The Epicurean Novel by Thomas Moore

Scottish

The Highland Widow Short novel by Sir Walter Scott
The Surgeon's Daughter Novel by Sir Walter Scott
The Two Drovers Short story by Sir Walter Scott

FRENCH

Cromwell Drama in verse by Victor Hugo
Marriage for Money Play by Eugène Scribe

GERMAN

Buch der Leider Collection of popular verse by Heinrich Heine

GREEK

"The Free Besieged" Poem by Dhionísios Solomos

RUSSIAN

The Negro of Peter the Great Poem by Aleksandr Pushkin
"Count Nulin" Poem by Aleksandr Pushkin

SWEDISH

Lycksalighetens Poems by Per Daniel Amadeus Atterbom

1828

BIRTHS

Edmond François Valentin About, French writer
Henrik Johan Ibsen, Norwegian playwright
George Meredith, English novelist
Dante Gabriel Rossetti, English poet
Viktor Rydberg, Swedish writer
Count Leo Nikolayevich Tolstoy, Russian novelist
Jules Verne, French novelist

LITERARY EVENT

The Athenaeum is founded in London

PUBLICATIONS

ENGLISH

American

An American Dictionary of the English Language Dictionary by Noah Webster
Fanshawe Novel by Nathaniel Hawthorne

British

Pelham; or, The Adventures of a Gentleman Novel by Edward G. E. Bulwer-Lytton

Scottish

St. Valentine's Day; or, The Fair Maid of Perth Novel by Sir Walter Scott

POLISH

Konrad Wallenrod Narrative poem by Adam Bernard Mickiewicz

RUSSIAN

To My Friends Poem by Aleksandr Pushkin

1829

BIRTHS

José de Alencar, Brazilian novelist
William Michael Rossetti, English writer
Manuel Tamayo y Baus, Spanish playwright

DEATHS

Aleksandr Sergeyevich Griboyedov, Russian playwright
Karl Wilhelm Friedrich von Schlegel, German romantic philosopher

PUBLICATIONS

ENGLISH

American

Al Aaraaf Allegorical poem by Edgar Allan Poe

British

All for Love; or, A Sinner Well Saved Poem by Robert Southey
Deveroux Novel by Edward G. E. Bulwer-Lytton
The Disowned Novel by Edward G. E. Bulwer-Lytton
The Dream of Eugene Aram Poem by Thomas Hood
The Misfortunes of Elphin Satirical novel by Thomas Love Peacock
Timbuctoo Poem by Alfred, Lord Tennyson

Scottish

Anne of Geierstein; or, The Maiden of the Mist Novel by Sir Walter Scott

FRENCH

Les Chouans Novel by Honoré de Balzac
Life and Poetry of Joseph Delorme Poem by Charles-Augustin Saint-Beuve
Marion de Lorme Verse drama by Victor Hugo

GERMAN

Don Juan and Faust Tragedy by Christian Dietrich Grabbe
Kaiser Friedrich Barbarossa Dramatic tragedy by Christian
Dietrich Grabbe
The Romantic Oedipus Play by August Platen

NORWEGIAN

Poems, First Cycle Collection by Henrik Wergeland

RUSSIAN

"Poltava" Poem by Aleksandr Pushkin

1830

BIRTHS

Alberto Blest Gana, Chilean novelist
João de Deus, Portuguese lyric poet
Emily Dickinson, American poet
Guido Gazelle, Flemish poet
Jules Alfred Huot de Goncourt, French novelist and diarist
Judah Leon Gordon, Russian Jewish novelist and poet
Paul Heyse, German playwright and novelist
Frédéric Mistral, French Provençal poet
Christina Rossetti, English poet

DEATHS

Benjamin Constant de Rebecque, French writer
William Hazlitt, English writer
Stephanie-Félicité Ducrest de Saint-Aubin, comtesse de Genlis,
French novelist

PUBLICATIONS

ENGLISH

American

"Old Ironsides" Poem by Oliver Wendell Holmes
The Water Witch Novel by James Fenimore Cooper

British

Album Verses Collection of lyrics by Charles Lamb
"Mariana" Poem by Alfred, Lord Tennyson
Paul Clifford Novel by Edward G. E. Bulwer-Lytton
Poems, Chiefly Lyrical Collection by Alfred, Lord Tennyson

Scottish

Auchindrane; or, The Ayurshire Tragedy Play by Sir Walter Scott

FRENCH

Hernani Play by Victor Hugo
The Red and the Black Novel by Stendhal
Scenes from Private Life Short stories by Honoré de Balzac

GERMAN

Austrian

The Last Knight Poems by playwright Anastasius Grun

NORWEGIAN

Creation, Man and Messiah Verse drama by Henrik Wergeland

1831

BIRTHS

Nikolai Semenovich Leskov, Russian short-story writer
Wilhelm Raabe, German novelist
Victorien Sardou, French playwright

DEATHS

Ludwig Joachim von Arnim, German writer of popular tales
Willem Bilderdijk, Dutch poet
Georg Wilhelm Friedrich Hegel, German philosopher
Ferenc Kazinczy, Hungarian man of letters
Friedrich Maximilian von Klinger, German playwright

PUBLICATIONS

ENGLISH

American

The Bravo Novel by James Fenimore Cooper
Legends of New England in Prose and Verse Collection of poems
by John Greenleaf Whittier
Moll Pitcher Poetical narrative by John Greenleaf Whittier
Poems Collection by Edgar Allan Poe

British

The Adventures of a Younger Son Autobiographical novel by
Edward John Trelawny
Crotchet Castle Novel by Thomas Love Peacock

Scottish

Castle Dangerous Novel by Sir Walter Scott
Count Robert of Paris Novel by Sir Walter Scott

FRENCH

Autumn Leaves Collection of poems by Victor Hugo
Le Peau de chagrin Novel by Honoré de Balzac
Nôtre-Dame de Paris Novel by Victor Hugo
The Wild Ass's Skin Novel by Honoré de Balzac

GERMAN

Austrian

The Waves of the Sea and Love Tragedy by Franz Grillparzer

German

Napoleon, or the Hundred Days Historical drama by Christian
Friedrich Grabbe

ITALIAN

I Canti Collection of lyrics by Giacomo Leopardi

RUSSIAN

Boris Godunov Historical tragedy by Aleksandr Pushkin
Mozart and Salieri Tragedy by Aleksandr Pushkin
Tales of the Late Ivan Petrovich Belkin Stories by Aleksandr
Pushkin

1832

BIRTHS
Louisa May Alcott, American writer of children's literature
Bjørnstjerne Martinius Bjørnson, Norwegian novelist, poet, and
   playwright
Wilhem Busch, German writer
Lewis Carroll (Charles Lutwidge Dodgson), English fabulist
José Echegaray y Eizaguirre, Spanish playwright
Juan Montalvo, Ecuadorean essayist
Sir Leslie Stephen, English critic and cultural historian

DEATHS
George Crabbe, English poet
Philibert-Louis Debucourt, French poet
Philip Freneau, American poet
Johann Wolfgang von Goethe, German poet
Sir Walter Scott, Scottish novelist

PUBLICATIONS

ENGLISH
American
The Alhambra Spanish sketchbook by Washington Irving
The Heidenmauer; or, The Benedictines Novel by James Fenimore
   Cooper
My Kinsman, Major Molineaux Novel by Nathaniel Hawthorne
"Roger Malvin's Burial" Short story by Nathaniel Hawthorne

British
Eugene Aram Novel by Edward G. E. Bulwer-Lytton
Klosterheim Prose romance by Thomas De Quincey
"The Lady of Shalott" Poem by Alfred, Lord Tennyson
"Locksley Hall" Poem by Alfred, Lord Tennyson
"The Lotos-Eaters" Poem by Alfred, Lord Tennyson

Canadian
Wacousta Romantic novel by John Richardson

FINNISH
The Moose Hunters Poem by Johan Runeberg

FRENCH
Droll Stories Short stories by Honoré de Balzac
Indiana Novel by George Sand
Louis XI Play by Casimir Delavigne

GERMAN
Faust, Part II Epic drama by Johann Wolfgang von Goethe
Gedichte Melancholy verse by Nikolaus Lenau
Hemingard of the Oak Burial Mounds Novel by Aernoat Drost
Painter Nolten Novel by Eduard Morike

RUSSIAN
The Angel Romantic piece by Mikhail Lermontov
On the Death of Goethe Poem by Yevgeny Baratynsky
Feast in the Time of the Plague Tragedy by Aleksandr Pushkin

SPANISH
Argentine
Elvira Poem by Esteban Echeverría

Spanish
Ode to the Fatherland Poem by Buenaventura Carles Aribau

1833

BIRTH
Antonio de Alarcón, Spanish writer

DEATH
Adamantios Koraïs, Greek man of letters

PUBLICATIONS
ENGLISH
American
The Headman; or, The Abbaye des Vignerons Novel by James Fen-
   imore Cooper
Martin Faber Novel by William Gimore Simms
"A MS. Found in a Bottle" Short story by Edgar Allan Poe

British
Godolphin Historical novel by Edward G. E. Bulwer-Lytton
"Lead, Kindly Light" Hymn by John Cardinal Newman
Miscellaneous Poems Collection by Elizabeth Barrett Browning
"Oneone" Poem by Alfred, Lord Tennyson
Pauline Poem by Robert Browning
Sartor Resartus Essays by Thomas Carlyle

FRENCH
André del Sarto Prose drama by Alfred de Musset
Bertrand and Raton; or, The Art of Conspiracy Satirical play by
   Eugène Scribe
The Country Doctor Novel (part of *The Human Comedy*) by
   Honoré de Balzac
Eugénie Grandet Novel by Honoré de Balzac
The Follies of Marianne Play by Alfred de Musset
Lélia Novel by George Sand
The Tears Poems by Marceline Desbordes Valmore

GERMAN
Austrian
The Evil Spirit Lumpazivagabundus, or the Roguish Frio Dramatic
   farce by Johann Nestroy

German
The League of Cambrai Play by August Platen
The Wooers Romantic comedy by Joseph von Eichendorff

GREEK
"The Cretan" Poem by Dhionísios Solomos

NORWEGIAN
The Spaniard Poem by Henrik Wergeland

POLISH
Forefather's Eve Play by Adam Bernard Mickiewicz
Maiden's Vows Play by Aleksander Fredro

RUSSIAN
Eugene Onegin Novel in verse by Aleksandr Pushkin
A Small House in Kolomna Poem by Aleksandr Pushkin

1834

BIRTHS
Estanislao del Campo, Argentine poet
Julius Sophus Felix Dahn, German novelist
William Morris, English poet and designer
Jan Neruda, Czech poet and playwright
James Thomson, Scottish poet and essayist

DEATHS
Samuel Taylor Coleridge, English poet
Charles Lamb, English essayist
Friedrich Ernst Daniel Schleiermacher, German theologian

PUBLICATIONS

ENGLISH
American

Guy Rivers Novel by William Gilmore Simms

British

The Last Days of Pompeii Novel by Edward G. E. Bulwer-Lytton

FRENCH
Belgian

Primevères Collection of poems by André van Hasselt

French

Claude Gueux Novel by Victor Hugo
Lorenzaccio Historical prose tragedy by Alfred de Musset
Old Goriot Novel (part of *The Human Comedy*) by Honoré de Balzac

GERMAN
Austrian

A Dream Is Life Play by Franz Grillparzer

German

The Abbasids Epic fairy tale by August Platen
The Hessian Messenger Prose tract by Georg Buchner

POLISH
Master Thaddeus Epic poem by Adam Mickiewicz
Vengeance Play by Aleksander Fredro

RUSSIAN
"The Queen of Spades" Short story by Aleksandr Pushkin

SLOVENE
Garland of Sonnets Poetic collection by France Preseren

SPANISH
Sancho Saldana Novel by José Espronceda y Delgado

SWEDISH
The Queen's Diadem Historical novel by Carl Jonas Love Almqvist

1835

BIRTHS
Samuel Butler, English writer
Giosuè Carducci, Italian poet
Émile Gaboriau, French writer of detective fiction
Raffi (Hakob Melig-Hakobian), Armenian novelist
Leopold von Sacher-Masoch, Austrian novelist
Mendele Mokher Sefarim (Sholem Jacob Abramovich), Russian Yiddish writer
Mark Twain (Samuel Langhorne Clemens), American writer

DEATH
August von Platen, German poet

PUBLICATIONS

CZECH
Gypsies Novel by Karl Hynek Macha

DANISH
Fairy Tales Collection by fabulist Hans Christian Andersen

ENGLISH
American

The Monikens Novel by James Fenimore Cooper
The Partisan Novel by William Gilmore Simms
Politian, A Tragedy Drama in blank verse by Edgar Allan Poe
The Yemassee Novel by William Gilmore Simms
"Young Goodman Brown" Short story by Nathaniel Hawthorne

British

Captain Sword and Captain Pen Poem by Leigh Hunt
The Newcomes Novel by William Makepeace Thackeray
Paracelsus Dramatic poem by Robert Browning
Rienzi; or, The Last of the Tribunes Historical novel by Edward G. E. Bulwer-Lytton

FINNISH
Kalevala Epic poem completed in 1849 by Elias Lönnrot

FRENCH
The Candlestick Comic drama by Alfred de Musset
Chatterton Play by Alfred-Victor de Vigny
Democracy in America Political discourse by Alexis Charles de Tocqueville
Mademoiselle de Maupin Novel by Théophile Gautier

GERMAN
Danton's Death Four-act tragedy by Georg Buchner
Hannibal Dramatic tragedy by Christian Dietrich Grabbe
Wally the Doubter Novel by Karl Gutzkow

ITALIAN
Approach of Death Poem by Giacomo Leopardi

POLISH
Horsztynski Unfinished dramatic tragedy by Juliusz Słowacki
The Undivine Comedy Play by Count Zygmunt Krasiński

RUSSIAN
Arabesques Collection of short stories by Nikolai Gogol
"Diary of a Madman" Short story by Nikolai Gogol
Egyptian Nights Collection of poems by Aleksandr Pushkin
Mirgorod Collection of stories by Nikolai Gogol
"Taras Bulba" Story by Nikolai Gogol

SPANISH
Don Alvaro; or, The Power of Fate Play by Angel de Saavedra

1836

BIRTHS
Thomas Bailey Aldrich, American poet
Gustavo Adolfo Bécquer, Spanish lyric poet
Sir William Schwenck Gilbert, English playwright
Bret Harte, American writer
José Duarte Ramalho Ortigão, Portuguese essayist

DEATHS
Christian Dietrich Grabbe, German playwright
Karel Hynek Mácha, Czech poet
Claude-Jean Rouget de Lisle, French poet
Emmanuel-Joseph Sieyès, French pamphleteer

PUBLICATIONS
CZECH
May Epic poem by Karel Hynek Mácha

ENGLISH
American
Mellichampe, a Legend of the Santee Novel by William Gilmore
   Simms
Mogg Megone Poetic narrative on American Indians by John
   Greenleaf Whittier
Nature Essay by Ralph Waldo Emerson
Poems Collection by Oliver Wendell Holmes

British
Mr. Midshipman Easy Novel by Frederick Marryat
Pericles and Aspasia Long prose piece by critic Walter Savage Landor
The Posthumous Papers of the Pickwick Club Novel by Charles
   Dickens
Sketches by Boz Short tales by Charles Dickens

FINNISH
Hanna Collection of poems by Johan Runeberg

FRENCH
Confession of a Child of the Century Autobiographical novel
   Alfred de Musset
It Isn't Necessary to Promise Anything Play by Alfred de Musset

GERMAN
The Descendants Satirical novel by Karl Leberecht Immermann
Leonce and Lena Fairy tale comedy by Georg Buchner

POLISH
Iridion Play by Count Zygmunt Krasiński

RUSSIAN
The Captain's Daughter Historical novel by Aleksandr Pushkin
The Covetous Knight Tragedy by Aleksandr Pushkin
The Inspector General Five-act comedy by Nikolai Gogol

SLOVENE
Baptism by the Slavica Epic poem by France Preseren

SPANISH
The Troubadour Play by Antonio García Gutiérrez

1837

BIRTHS
Georg Moritz Ebens, German novelist
William Dean Howells, American critic
Algernon Charles Swinburne, English poet
Rosalía de Castro, Galician novelist

DEATHS
Georg Buchner, German playwright
Giacomo Leopardi, Italian poet
Aleksandr Sergeyevich Pushkin, Russian poet

PUBLICATIONS
ENGLISH
American
"Dr. Heidegger's Experiment" Story by Nathaniel Hawthorne
Twice-Told Tales Collection by Nathaniel Hawthorne

British
Ernest Maltravers Novel by Edward G. E. Bulwer-Lytton
Oliver Twist Novel by Charles Dickens
Strafford Dramatic tragedy by Robert Browning
The Yellow-Plush Correspondence Novel by William Makepeace
   Thackeray

Scottish
History of the French Revolution History by Thomas Carlyle

FRENCH

The Clique Play by Eugène Scribe
Lost Illusions Novel by Honoré de Balzac
Mauprat Novel by George Sand
The October Night Lyric by Alfred de Musset
Village Priest Novel by Honoré de Balzac

GERMAN

Austrian

Savonarola Religious epic by Nikolaus Lenau

German

Castle Durant Novella by Baron Joseph Eichendorff
Wozzek Poetic drama by Georg Buchner

Swiss

Mirror of the Peasants Novel by Jeremias Gotthelf

HUNGARIAN

The Call Patriotic lyric by Mihaly Vörösmarty

PORTUGUESE

Obras Completas Poems by Antonio Feliciano de Castilho

RUSSIAN

"The Bronze Horseman" Poem by Aleksandr Pushkin
"Death of a Poet" Poem (on the death of Aleksandr Pushkin) by Mikhail Lermontov

SPANISH

Argentine

"The Captive" Poem by Esteban Echeverría

Spanish

The Lovers of Teruel Play by Juan Eugenio Hartzenbusch

1838

BIRTHS

Henry Brooks Adams, American historian
Akhilléfs Paráskhos, Greek poet
George Otto Trevelyan, English historian
Auguste de Villiers de L'Isle-Adam, French writer

DEATHS

Adelbert von Chamisso, French lyric poet
Lorenzo Da Ponte, Italian poet

PUBLICATIONS

ENGLISH

American

Home As Found Novel by James Fenimore Cooper
"Ligeia" Short story by Edgar Allan Poe

The Narrative of Arthur Gordon Pym, of Nantucket Novel by Edgar Allan Poe
Richard Hardis; or, The Avenger of Blood Novel by William Gilmore Simms

British

The Lady of Lyons Play by Edward G. E. Bulwer-Lytton
Nicholas Nickleby Novel by Charles Dickens
Richelieu; or, The Conspiracy Historical play in blank verse by Edward G. E. Bulwer-Lytton
The Seraphim and Other Poems Collection of poems by Elizabeth Barrett Browning

FLEMISH

The Lion of Flanders Novel by Hendrik Conscience

FRENCH

Ruy Blas Verse rhapsody by Victor Hugo

GERMAN

German

Munchausen Novel by Karl Leberecht Immermann
Poems Collection by Annette Elisabeth von Droste-Hülshoff

Swiss

The Joys and Sorrows of a Schoolmaster Novel by Jeremias Gotthelf

1839

BIRTHS

Ludwig Anzengruber, Austrian playwright
Julio Dinis, Portuguese poet and playwright
Joaquim Maria Machado de Assis, Brazilian novelist
Ouida (Marie Louise de la Ramée), English novelist
Walter Horatio Pater, English essayist
Sully Prudhomme (René-François-Armand Prudhomme), French poet

DEATHS

José María Heredia, Cuban lyric poet
Maurice de Guérin, French poet
Leonor de Almeida de Portugal, Portuguese poet

PUBLICATIONS

ENGLISH

American

The Damsel of Darien Historical novel by William Gilmore Simms
"The Fall of the House of Usher" Short horror story by Edgar Allan Poe
Hyperion Prose romance by Henry Wadsworth Longfellow
Voices of the Night Collection of poems by Henry Wadsworth Longfellow

British

Andrea of Hungary, Fra Rupert, and Giovanna of Naples Dramatic tragedy by Walter Savage Landor

Catherine Novel by William Makepeace Thackeray
Deerbrook Novel by Harriet Martineau

FRENCH
The Charterhouse of Parma Novel by Stendhal
A Harlot of High and Low Novel by Honoré de Balzac
Poor Flowers Poems by Marcelina Desbordes-Valmore
Spiridion Novel by George Sand

GERMAN
Richard Savage Novel by Karl Gutzkow

RUSSIAN
The Stone Guest Tragedy in blank verse by Aleksandr Pushkin

SPANISH
The Student of Salamanca Poems by José Espronceda y Delgado

1840

BIRTHS
Wilfrid Blunt, English writer
Alphonse Daudet, French writer
Henry Austin Dobson, English poet
Thomas Hardy, English novelist
Namik Kemal, Turkish poet and prose writer
John Addington Symonds, English historian and poet
Giovanni Verga, Italian novelist
Émile-Édouard-Charles-Antoine Zola, French novelist

DEATHS
Frances Burney, English novelist and diarist
Karl Leberecht Immermann, German playwright and novelist
Népomucène Lemercier, French writer

LITERARY EVENT
The Dial, an American quarterly journal, is founded by Margaret Fuller

PUBLICATIONS
DUTCH
The Count of Talavera Novel by Jacob van Lennep

ENGLISH
American
Mercedes of Castile Novel by James Fenimore Cooper
Orphic Sayings Collection of aphorisms by Amos Bronson Alcott
The Pathfinder Novel by James Fenimore Cooper
Tales of the Grotesque and Arabesque Collection of short stories by Edgar Allan Poe
Two Years Before the Mast Novel by Richard Henry Dana

British
A Legend of Florence Play by Leigh Hunt
Money Comic play by Edward G. E. Bulwer-Lytton

The Old Curiosity Shop Novel by Charles Dickens
A Shabby Genteel Story Romantic tale by William Makepeace Thackeray
Sordello Poem by Robert Browning

Canadian
The Canadian Brothers Novel by John Richardson

FRENCH
Colomba Novel by Prosper Mérimée
The Glass of Water; or, Causes and Effects Play by Eugène Scribe
Marianna Novel by Jules Sandeau
Port-Royal Critical lectures by critic Charles-Augustin Saint-Beuve
Seven Strings of the Lyre Novel by George Sand

GERMAN
German
Judith Play by Friedrich Hebbel

Swiss
Needs of the Poor Novel by Jeremias Gotthelf

NORWEGIAN
Jan Van Huysum's Flowerpiece Narrative poem by Henrik Wergeland

RUSSIAN
A Hero of Our Times Novel by Mikhail Lermontov
The Novice Novel by Mikhail Lermontov

SPANISH
The Shoemaker and the King Play by José Zorrilla y Moral

1841

BIRTHS
William Henry Hudson, English novelist
Catule Mendes, French novelist and playwright

DEATHS
Mikhail Yurevich Lermontov, Russian romantic poet and novelist
Julian Ursyn Niemcewicz, Polish playwright and novelist

PUBLICATIONS
ENGLISH
American
Ballads and Other Poems Collection of poems by Henry Wadsworth Longfellow
The Deerslayer Frontier novel by James Fenimore Cooper
Essays Collection by Ralph Waldo Emerson
"The Murders in the Rue Morgue" Short story by Edgar Allan Poe
"The Wreck of the Hesperus" Poem by Henry Wadsworth Longfellow
A Year's Life, and Other Poems Collection of poems by James Russell Lowell

British

Barnaby Rudge Historical novel by Charles Dickens
The Great Hoggarty Diamond Novel by William Makepeace Thackeray
London Assurance Play by Dion Boucicault
"Miss Kilmansegg and Her Precious Leg, a Golden Legend" Poem by Thomas Hood
Pippa Passes Dramatic poem by Robert Browning

Scottish

On Heroes, Hero-Worship and the Heroic in History Historical discourse by Thomas Carlyle

GERMAN

Austrian

The Lass from the Suburbs; or, Honesty Is the Best Policy Comedy by Johann Nestroy

German

Countess Faustine Novel by Ida Hahn-Hahn
The Essence of Christianity Theological essay by Ludwig Feuerbach

Swiss

Uli the Farmhand Novel of village life by Jeremias Gotthelf

POLISH

Beniowski Poem by Juliusz Słowacki

RUSSIAN

The Demon Novel by Mikhail Lermontov

SPANISH

Cuban

Poems Collection by Gertrudis Gómez de Avellaneda

1842

BIRTHS

Ambrose Bierce, American writer
Georg Morris Brandes, Danish literary critic
François Coppée, French poet
Sidney Lanier, American poet
Stéphane Mallarmé, French poet
Karl May, German author of children's tales
Antero de Quental, Portuguese poet

DEATHS

John Banim, Irish poet
Clemens Brentano, German poet
José de Espronceda y Delgado, Spanish poet
Arnold Hermann Ludwig Heeren, German historian
Stendhal (Marie-Henri Beyle), French novelist

PUBLICATIONS

ENGLISH

American

Beauchampe Novel by William Gilmore Simms
"The Masque of the Red Death" Short story by Edgar Allan Poe
Poems on Slavery Collection of eight lyrics by Henry Wadsworth Longfellow
The Two Admirals Novel by James Fenimore Cooper
Wing-and-Wing Historical novel by James Fenimore Cooper

British

American Notes Travel narrative by Charles Dickens
The Bible in Spain Travel narrative by George Barrow
Dramatic Lyrics Collection by Robert Browning
The Fitzboodle Papers Novel by William Makepeace Thackeray
Lays of Ancient Rome Ballads by Thomas Babington Macaulay
"Locksley Hall" Poem by Alfred, Lord Tennyson
"Morte d'Arthur" Long Poem by Alfred, Lord Tennyson
"My Last Duchess" Poem by Robert Browning
"The Pied Piper of Hamelin" Poem by Robert Browning
Poems, Chiefly of Early and Late Years Collection by William Wordsworth
"Ulysses" Poem (dramatic monologue) by Alfred, Lord Tennyson
Zanoni Supernatural tale by Edward G. E. Bulwer-Lytton

FRENCH

Gaspard of the Night Prose poem by Louis Bertrand
The Mysteries of Paris Novel on Parisian slum life by Eugène Sue

GERMAN

Austrian

He Intends to Have a Fling Comedy by Johann Nestroy
The Albigensians Poetic epic by Nikolaus Lenau

German

The Jew's Birch Tree Novella by Annette Elisabeth von Droste-Hülshoff
Maria Magdalena Play by Friedrich Hebbel

HUNGARIAN

Versek Poems by Sándor Petófi

JAPANESE

Nanso Satomi Hakken Novel by Bakin Takizawa

NORWEGIAN

The Jew Poem by Henrik Wergeland

RUSSIAN

Dead Souls Novel by Nikolai Gogol
"The Overcoat" Short story by Nikolai Gogol

SPANISH

The Shoemaker and the King, Part II Play by José Zorrila y Moral

1843

BIRTHS

Edward Dowden, Irish critic
Henry James, American novelist
Benito Pérez Galdós, Spanish novelist and playwright
Peter Rosegger, Austrian poet and novelist
Bertha Kinsky von Suttner, Austrian writer
Carmen Sylva (Princess Elizabeth of Wied, later Queen Elizabeth of Romania), Romanian poet

DEATHS

Jean-François-Casimir Delavigne, French poet and playwright
Friedrich Heinrich Karl de la Motte Fouqué, German romantic novelist
Jacob Friedrich Fries, German philosopher
Johann Christian Friedrich Holderlin, German poet
Francis Scott Key, American poet
Robert Southey, English poet
Noah Webster, American lexicographer

PUBLICATIONS

DANISH

Either/Or Philosophical treatise by existentialist Søren Aabye Kierkegaard
Fear and Trembling Philosophical treatise by Søren Aabye Kierkegaard

ENGLISH

American

"The Gold Bug" Short story by Edgar Allan Poe
Lays of My Home and Other Poems Collection of poems by John Greenleaf Whittier
Le Mouchoir Short novel by James Fenimore Cooper
"The Pit and the Pendulum" Horror story by Edgar Allan Poe
The Spanish Student Poetic drama by Henry Wadsworth Longfellow
"The Tell-Tale Heart" Short story by Edgar Allan Poe
Wyandotte Novel of the Revolutionary War by James Fenimore Cooper

British

A Blot in the 'Scutcheon Tragic drama in blank verse by Robert Browning
A Christmas Carol Christmas story by Charles Dickens
Essays, Critical and Historical Collection of essays by Thomas Babington Macaulay
The Last of the Barons Historical novel by Edward G. E. Bulwer-Lytton
The Life and Adventures of Martin Chuzzlewit Novel by Charles Dickens
"The Song of the Shirt" Poem by Thomas Hood

Scottish

Past and Present Essays by Thomas Carlyle

FRENCH

Bouquets and Prayers Poems by Marcélie Desbordes-Valmore

GERMAN

Atta Troll Poem by Heinrich Heine
Black Forest Village Stories Collection by Berthold Auerbach
Schiller's Homeland Years Novel by Hermann Kurz

POLISH

The Moment Before Dawn Poem by Count Zygmuńt Krasiňski

1844

BIRTHS

Robert Bridges, English poet
Anatole France (Jacques-Anatole Thibault), French novelist
Gerard Manley Hopkins, British poet
Detlov von Liliencorn, German poet and novelist
Friedrich Wilhelm Nietzsche, German philosopher
Paul Verlaine, French poet

DEATHS

Ivan Andreyevich Krylov, Russian fabulist
Charles Nodier, French writer
René-Charles Guilbert de Pixérécourt, French playwright
Yevgeny Abramovich Baratynsky, Russian poet

PUBLICATIONS

DANISH

Philosophical Fragments Meditations by existentialist Søren Aabye Kierkegaard

ENGLISH

American

Afloat and Ashore Novel by James Fenimore Cooper
Miles Wallingford Novel by James Fenimore Cooper
Poems Collection by James Russell Lowell
"The Premature Burial" Short story by Edgar Allan Poe
"Rappaccini's Daughter" Short story by Nathaniel Hawthorne
The White-Footed Deer and Other Poems Collection by William Cullen Bryant

British

"Abou Ben Adhem" Poem by Leigh Hunt
The Chimes Christmas story by Charles Dickens
Coningsby Novel by Benjamin Disraeli
The Luck of Barry Lyndon, a Romance of the Last Century by Fitzboodle Novel by William Makepeace Thackeray
Poems Collection of poems by Elizabeth Barrett Browning

FINNISH

Kung Fjalar Unrhymed verse romance by Johan Runeberg

FRENCH

The Count of Monte Cristo Novel by Alexander Dumas père
The Three Musketeers Novel by Alexander Dumas père
The Wandering Jew Novel by Eugène Sue

GERMAN

Austrian

Collected Poems Collection of poems by Nikolaus Lenau
Man Full of Nothing Comedy by Nikolaus Nestroy

German

Germany, A Winter's Tale Collection of poems by Heinrich Heine
New Poems Collection by Heinrich Heine

NORWEGIAN

The English Pilot Narrative poem by Henrik Wergeland

SLOVAK

Recruit Poems by Janko Král'
Song Without a Name Poems by Janko Král'

SPANISH

Don Juan Tenorio Verse drama by José Zorrilla y Moral

1845

BIRTHS

George Edward Bateman Saintsbury, English literary critic
Carl Spitteler, Swiss poet
Jacinto Verdaguer, Catalan national poet

DEATHS

János Batsányi, Hungarian poet
Jonas Hallgrimsson, Icelandic poet
Thomas Hood, English poet
August Wilhelm von Schlegel, German poet and critic
Henrik Arnold Wergeland, Norwegian poet and playwright

PUBLICATIONS

DANISH

King Rene's Daughter Play by Henrik Hertz

ENGLISH

American

The Belfry of Bruges and Other Poems Collection by Henry Wadsworth Longfellow
Bigelow Papers Essays by critic James Russell Lowell
The Chainbearer Novel by James Fenimore Cooper
Helen Halsey; or, The Swamp State of Conelachita Border romance by William Gilmore Simms
"The Purloined Letter" Detective story by Edgar Allan Poe
The Raven and Other Poems Collection by Edgar Allan Poe
Satanstoe Novel by James Fenimore Cooper
The Stranger in Lowell Collection of essays by John Greenleaf Whittier
Tales Collection of short stories by Edgar Allan Poe
Women in the Nineteenth Century Feminist treatise by Margaret Fuller

British

Jeames's Diary Humorous narrative by William Makepeace Thackeray

FRENCH

Carmen Novel (later the basis for George Bizet's opera) by Prosper Mérimée
Les Paysans Novel by Honoré de Balzac
Twenty Years After Novel by Alexander Dumas père

GERMAN

Slovenly Peter Children's stories by Heinrich Hoffmann

HUNGARIAN

Janos the Hero Epic poem by Sándor Petófi

SLOVAK

The Eagle Poems by Janko Král'

1846

BIRTHS

Léon Bloy, French Catholic critic
Svatopluk Cech, Czech poet and novelist
Edmondo De Amicis, Italian novelist
Holger Henrik Herdoldt Drachmann, Danish poet
José Maria Eça de Quierós, Portuguese novelist
Rudolf Christoph Eucken, German philosopher
Henryk Sienkiewicz, Polish novelist

PUBLICATIONS

DANISH

Fairy Tale of My Life Autobiography by storyteller Hans Christian Andersen

ENGLISH

American

"The Cask of Amontillado" Short story by Edgar Allan Poe
Mosses from an Old Manse Short-story collection by Nathaniel Hawthorne
The Redskins Novel by James Fenimore Cooper
Typee Novel by Herman Melville

British

Bells and Pomegranates Collection of poems by Robert Browning
Book of Nonsense Limericks by Edward Lear
The Cricket on the Hearth Christmas story by Charles Dickens
Poems Collection by English writers Anne, Charlotte, and Emily Brontë

FRENCH

Cousin Bette Novel (part of *The Human Comedy*) by Honoré de Balzac
The Devil's Pool Novel by George Sand

GERMAN

Beyond Good and Evil Philosophical treatise by Friedrich Nietzsche
Otto the Marksman Epic poem by Gottfried Kinkel
The Valentine Dramatic comedy by Gustav Freytag

RUSSIAN
Poor Folk Novel by Fyodor Dostoyevsky
The Double Novel by Fyodor Dostoyevsky

1847

BIRTHS
Recaizade Mahmud Ekrem Bey, Turkish novelist
Jens Peter Jacobsen, Danish writer
Kálmán Mikszáth, Hungarian novelist
Bram Stoker, Anglo-Irish writer

PUBLICATIONS
ENGLISH
American

Evangeline, a Tale of Acadie Long narrative poem by Henry
    Wadsworth Longfellow
Omoo, A Narrative of Adventures on the South Seas Novel by
    Herman Melville
"Ulalume" Poem by Edgar Allan Poe

British

Agnes Grey Novel by Anne Brontë
The Children of the New Forest Children's novel by Frederick
    Marryat
Dombey and Son Novel by Charles Dickens
Jane Eyre Novel by Charlotte Brontë
The Macdermots of Ballycloran Novel by Anthony Trollope
The Princess, a Medley Poem by Alfred, Lord Tennyson
Vanity Fair Novel by William Makepeace Thackeray
Wuthering Heights Novel by Emily Brontë

FRENCH
Cousin Pons Novel (part of *The Human Comedy*) by Honoré de
    Balzac

GERMAN
Shock-Headed Peter Children's story by Heinrich Hoffmann

HUNGARIAN
Hungary in 1514 Novel by József Eötvös
Toldi Collection of poems by János Arany

1848

BIRTHS
Jean Aicard, Provençal poet
Khristo Botev, Bulgarian poet
Joris-Karl Huysmans, French novelist

DEATHS
Victor Grigoryevich Belinsky, Russian critic
Emily Brontë, English novelist

François-August-René de Chateaubriand, French writer
Annette Elisabeth Droste-Hulshöff, German poet and novelist
Joseph von Gorres, German Catholic writer
Frederick Marryat, English novelist
Takizawa Bakin, Japanese novelist

PUBLICATIONS
ENGLISH
American

The Bigelow Papers Satiric miscellany in prose and verse by James
    Russell Lowell
The Corsican Brothers Melodrama by Irish-born Dion
    Boucicault
The Crater Novel by James Fenimore Cooper
Eureka Prose poem by Edgar Allan Poe
Jack Tier Historical novel by James Fenimore Cooper
The Oak Openings; or, The Bee Hunter Novel by James Fenimore
    Cooper
The Sea Lions Historical novel by James Fenimore Cooper
The Vision of Sir Launfal Verse parable on the Holy Grail by
    James Russell Lowell

British

The Bothie of Tober-na-Voulich Poem by Arthur Hugh Clough
Harold, the Last of the Saxon Kings Historical novel by Edward G.
    E. Bulwer-Lytton
The Haunted Man and the Ghost's Bargain Christmas story by
    Charles Dickens
The History of Pendennis Fictionalized autobiography by
    William Makepeace Thackeray
The Kellys and the O'Kellys Novel by Anthony Trollope
Mary Barton, a Tale of Manchester Life Novel by Elizabeth
    Gaskell
The Saint's Tragedy Poetic drama on Elizabeth of Hungary by
    Charles Kingsley
The Tenant of Wildfell Hall Novel by Anne Brontë
Yeast Novel by Charles Kingsley

FRENCH
The Adventuress Verse drama by Émile Augier
The Country Waif Novel by George Sand
The Lady of the Camelias Novel by Alexander Dumas fils
Scenes of Bohemian Life Sketches (the basis of Puccini's opera *La
    Bohème*) by Henri Murger

HUNGARIAN
Rise, Magyar Poem by Sándor Petófi

1849

BIRTHS
Frances Hodgson Burnett, English-born American writer of
    children's stories
Sir Edmund Gosse, English poet and critic
William Ernest Henley, English poet and playwright
Alexander Kielland, Norwegian poet and playwright

James Whitcomb Riley, American poet
August Strindberg, Swedish playwright and novelist

DEATHS
Thomas Lowell Beddoes, English poet
Anne Brontë, English novelist
Maria Edgeworth, Irish novelist
Sándor Petőfi, Hungarian poet
Edgar Allan Poe, American poet, short story writer, essayist, and
  pioneer of the detective story
France Prešeren, Slovene poet
Juliusz Słowacki, Polish poet

PUBLICATIONS
ENGLISH
American

"Annabel Lee" Poem by Edgar Allan Poe
"Bells" Poem by Edgar Allan Poe
Kavanagh Novel by Henry Wadsworth Longfellow
Mardi Novel by Herman Melville
Poems Collection of poems by John Greenleaf Whittier
Redburn Novel by Herman Melville
The Seaside and the Fireside Collection of poems by Henry
  Wadsworth Longfellow

British

"The Ballad of Bouillabaisse" Poem by William Makepeace
  Thackeray
David Copperfield Novel by Charles Dickens
King Arthur Poem on Arthurian legends by Edward G. E.
  Bulwer-Lytton
The Seven Lamps of Architecture Treatise on architecture by John
  Ruskin
Shirley Novel by Charlotte Brontë
The Strayed Reveller Poem by Matthew Arnold

FRENCH
Adrienne Lecouvreur Tragedy by Eugène Scribe and Ernest
  Legouvé
Little Fadette Novel by George Sand
Memoirs Autobiography of François-August-René de
  Chateaubriand

GERMAN
Herod and Marianne Play by Friedrich Hebbel

GREEK
The Shark Poems by Dhionísios Solomos

HUNGARIAN
Toldi's Lane Epic poem by János Arany

MALAY
Abdullah's Story Novel by Abdullah bin Abdul Kadir

SPANISH
The Seagull Novel by Fernán Caballero

1850

BIRTHS
Edward Bellamy, American writer
Mikhail Eminescu, Romanian poet
Eugene Field, American poet
Lafcadio Hearn, American writer
Abílio Manuel Guerra Junqueiro, Portuguese poet
Pierre Loti (Louis-Marie-Julien Viaud), French novelist
Guy de Maupassant, French novelist
Robert Louis Stevenson, Scottish novelist
Ivan Vazov, Bulgarian poet and playwright

DEATHS
Honoré de Balzac, French novelist
Margaret Fuller, American Transcendentalist writer
Nikolaus Lenau (Nikolaus Franz Niembsch von Strehlenau),
  Austrian poet
Adam Gottlob Oehlenschläger, Danish poet and playwright
Gustav Schwab, German writer
William Wordsworth, English romantic poet

LITERARY EVENT
Harper's New Monthly, precursor to *Harper's Magazine,* is
  founded in New York

PUBLICATIONS
ENGLISH
American

The Scarlet Letter Novel by Nathaniel Hawthorne
Songs of Labor Poems by John Greenleaf Whittier
The Ways of the Hour Novel by James Fenimore Cooper
White Jacket; or, The World in a Man-of-War Novel by Herman
  Melville

British

Alton Locke, Tailor and Poet Novel by Charles Kingsley
Antonina; or, The Fall of Rome Novel by Wilkie Collins
Autobiography Narrative by Leigh Hunt
"The Blessed Damozel" Poem by Dante Gabriel Rossetti
Christmas Eve and Easter Day Poems by Robert Browning
Death's Jest-Book; or, The Fool's Tragedy Poem by Thomas Lovell
  Beddoes
"In Memoriam, A. H. H." Poem in memory of Arthur Henry
  Hallam by Alfred, Lord Tennyson
The Moorland Cottage Novella by Elizabeth Gaskell
The Prelude Poems by William Wordsworth
Rebecca and Rowenna: A Romance Upon Romance Novel by
  William Makepeace Thackeray
Sonnets from the Portuguese Poems by Elizabeth Barrett
  Browning

FLEMISH
Blind Rose Novel by Hendrik Conscience
The Conscript Novel by Hendrik Conscience
Wooden Clara Novel by Hendrik Conscience

FRENCH
Black Tulip Novel by Alexander Dumas père

ICELANDIC
Lad and Lass Novel by Jon Thoroddsen

NORWEGIAN
Catilina Play by Henrik Ibsen

RUSSIAN
From Another Shore Novel by Aleksandr Ivanovich Herzen
A Month in the Country Dramatic comedy by Ivan Sergeyevich Turgenev

1851

BIRTHS
Eduardo Acevedo Díaz, Uruguayan novelist
Rosario de Acuña, Spanish poet and playwright
Kate Chopin, American novelist
Arne Garborg, Norwegian novelist

DEATHS
James Fenimore Cooper, American novelist
Esteban Echeverría, Argentine poet
Mary Wollstonecraft Shelley, English novelist

PUBLICATIONS
ENGLISH
American

Dame de Pique Play by Dion Boucicault
The House of the Seven Gables Novel by Nathaniel Hawthorne
Katherine Walton Novel by William Gilmore Simms
Moby-Dick; or, The Whale Novel by Herman Melville
The Snow Image, and Other Tales Short stories by Nathaniel Hawthorne
Uncle Tom's Cabin Novel by Harriet Beecher Stowe

British

Cranford Novel by Elizabeth Gaskell
Lavengro Novel by George Borrow
Poems Collection by George Meredith
The Stones of Venice Architectural criticism by John Ruskin

FLEMISH
The Poor Gentleman Novel by Hendrik Conscience

FRENCH
An Italian Straw Hat Comedy by Eugène-Marin Labiche
Sacs et Parchemins Novel that became the play *Le Gendre de Monsieur Poirier* by Jules Sandeau

GERMAN
Austrian

Don Juan Novel by Nikolaus Lenau

German

The Green Henry Autobiographical novel by Gottfried Keller
Romanzero Collection of poems by Heinrich Heine

PORTUGUESE
Brazilian

Last Poems Collection by Brazilian poet Antônio Gonçalves Dias

1852

BIRTHS
Leopoldo Alas y Ureña, Spanish writer
Paul Bourget, French Catholic novelist
Ion Luca Caragiale, Romanian playwright
Lady Isabella Augusta Gregory, Irish playwright
George Augustus Moore, Irish novelist
Emilia de Pardo Bazán, Spanish novelist and feminist
Isaac Leib Peretz, Yiddish poet, playwright, and writer of short stories
Abdulhak Hamit Tarhan, Turkish poet and playwright

DEATHS
Nikolay Vasilyevich Gogol, Russian novelist
Thomas Moore, Irish poet and novelist
John Richardson, Canadian novelist

PUBLICATIONS
ENGLISH
American

The Blithedale Romance Novel by Nathaniel Hawthorne
Pierre; or, The Ambiguities Novel by Herman Melville

British

Bleak House Novel by Charles Dickens
Empedocles on Etna and Other Poems Collection by Matthew Arnold
The History of Henry Esmond Historical novel by William Makepeace Thackeray
Polonius Collection of aphorisms by Edward FitzGerald
Sohrab and Rustim Epic poem by Matthew Arnold

FRENCH
Contes et Faceties Collection of fantastic short tales by Gérard de Nerval
Enamels and Cameos Collection of poems by Théophile Gautier
Le Misanthrope et Lauvergnat Play by Eugène-Marin Labiche

GERMAN
Austrian

Kampi; or, The Millionairess and the Seamstress Comedy by Johan Nestroy

German

Agnes Bernauer Play by Christian Friedrich Hebbel
The Journalists Political play by Gustav Freytag
Poems Collection by Theodore Storm

NORWEGIAN
Norwegian Folk Tales Collection by Peter Christen Asbjørnsen and Jørgen Moe

RUSSIAN

A Sportsman's Sketches Collection of tales by Ivan Sergeyevich Turgenev

1853

BIRTHS

René Bazin, French Catholic writer
Sir Thomas Henry Hall Caine, English novelist
José Martí, Cuban poet
Stephan Gudmundson Stephansson, Iceland-born Canadian poet

DEATH

Ludwig Tieck, German romantic poet

PUBLICATIONS

ENGLISH

American

"Bartleby the Scrivener" Short story by Herman Melville
The Chapel of the Hermits, and Other Poems Collection by John Greenleaf Whittier
The Sword and the Distaff Revolutionary romance by William Gilmore Simms
Tanglewood Tales Collection of children's stories by Nathaniel Hawthorne
Vasconselos Novel of Mexican history by William Gilmore Simms

British

Balder Dead Narrative poem by Matthew Arnold
Christie Johnstone Romantic novel by Charles Reade
The Heir of Redclyffe Novel by Charlotte Yonge
Hypatia; or, New Foes with an Old Face Historical novel by Charles Kingsley
Imaginary Conversations of Greeks and Romans Prose work by Walter Savage Landor
My Novel; or, Varieties in English Life Novel by Edward G. E. Bulwer-Lytton
The Newcomes Novel by William Makepeace Thackeray
Peg Woffington Novel by Charles Reade
Poems Collection by Matthew Arnold
Ruth Novel by Elizabeth Gaskell
"The Scholar-Gipsy" Pastoral poem by Matthew Arnold
Villette Novel by Charlotte Brontë

FRENCH

The Punishments Poems by Victor Hugo

HUNGARIAN

A Hungarian Nabob Novel by Mór Jókai

PORTUGUESE

Brazilian

Memoirs of a Militia Sergeant Novel by Manuel Antonio de Almeida

ROMANIAN

Doine si Lacrimioare Lyrical poems by Vasile Alecsandri

RUSSIAN

Poverty Is No Disgrace Play by Aleksandr Ostrovsky

1854

BIRTHS

William Henry Drummond, Canadian poet
Arthur Rimbaud, French poet
Oscar Wilde, Irish novelist, dramatist, and poet

DEATHS

Jeremias Gotthelf, Swiss writer
João Baptiste de Silva Leitão de Almeida Garrett, Portuguese poet
Hughes-Félicité-Robert de Lamennais, French essayist
Abdullah bin Abdul Kadir, Malay writer

LITERARY EVENT

Felibrige, an association to promote the Provençal language, is founded by seven poets, including Frédéric Mistral

PUBLICATIONS

ENGLISH

American

The Encantadas Collection of stories by Herman Melville
Passion Flowers Poems by New England poet Julia Ward Howe
The Scout; or, The Black Riders of Congaree Novel by William Gilmore Simms
Walden; or, Life in the Woods Essays by Henry David Thoreau

British

Angel in the House Novel by Coventry Patmore
"Charge of the Light Brigade" Poem by Alfred, Lord Tennyson
Hard Times Novel by Charles Dickens
"Ode on the Death of the Duke of Wellington" Poem by Alfred, Lord Tennyson

FRENCH

The Chimeras Sonnets by Gérard de Nerval
Girls of Fire Fantastic tales by Gérard de Nerval

HUNGARIAN

Toldi's Evening Epic poem by János Arany

SPANISH

The Lady Play by Manuel Tamayo y Baus

1855

BIRTHS

Arthur Wing Pinero, English playwright
Georges Rodenbach, Belgian symbolist poet

Olive Schreiner, South African novelist
Émile Verhaeren, Belgian poet
Juan Zorrilla de San Martín, Uruguayan poet

DEATHS

Charlotte Brontë, English novelist
Søren Aabye Kierkegaard, Danish existentialist philosopher
Adam Bernard Mickiewicz, Polish poet
Gérard de Nerval (Gérard Labrunie), French symbolist writer
Mihály Vörösmarty, Hungarian poet

PUBLICATIONS

ENGLISH

American

The Age of Fable Collection by Thomas Bulfinch
Benito Cereno Novel by Herman Melville
The Forayers; or, The Raid of the Dog Days Novel by William Gilmore Simms
"I Sing the Body Electric" Poem by Walt Whitman
Israel Potter: His Fifty-five Years of Exile Novel by Herman Melville
Leaves of Grass Collection of poems by Walt Whitman
The Song of Hiawatha Verse narrative by Henry Wadsworth Longfellow
"Song of Myself" Poem by Walt Whitman

British

"Andrea del Sarto" Poem by Robert Browning
Bishop Blougram's Apology Long poem by Robert Browning
"Fra Lippo Lippi" Poem by Robert Browning
The Lances of Lynwood Novel by Charlotte Yonge
Little Dorritt Novel by Charles Dickens
Maud Melodramatic poem by Alfred, Lord Tennyson
Men and Women Collection of poems by Robert Browning
North and South Novel by Elizabeth Gaskell
Poems, Second Series Collection by Matthew Arnold
The Warden Novel (first in the Barsetshire series) by Anthony Trollope
Westward Ho! Novel by Charles Kingsley

FRENCH

Le Demi-Monde Play about the underworld by Alexander Dumas fils

GERMAN

Austrian

Catilina Play by Ferdinand Kurnberger

German

Agnes Bernauer Play by Friedrich Hebbel
Debit and Credit Novel by Gustav Freytag
The Proprietor of the Sun Inn Novel by Hermann Kurz
Robert und Guiscard Poem by Baron Joseph Eichendorff

RUSSIAN

A Month in the Country Play by Ivan Sergeyevich Turgenev

SPANISH

The Madness of Love Play by Manuel Tamayo y Baus

1856

BIRTHS

L. Frank Baum, American writer
Ivan Franko, Ukrainian writer
Sigmund Freud, Austrian psychologist
H. Rider Haggard, English novelist
Frank Harris, Irish-born American novelist and journalist
Vassily Vasilyevich Rozanov, Russian writer
George Bernard Shaw, Irish playwright

DEATHS

Heinrich Heine, German poet
Sándor Petófi, Hungarian poet
Jacques-Nicolas-Augustin Thierry, French historian

PUBLICATIONS

ENGLISH

American

Charlemont Border romance by William Gilmore Simms
Dred: A Tale of the Great Dismal Swamp Novel by Harriet Beecher Stowe
Eutaw Romantic novel of the American Revolution by William Gilmore Simms
The Panorama and Other Poems Collection by John Greenleaf Whittier
The Rise of the Dutch Republic History by John Lothrop Motley
"Song of the Open Road" Poem by Walt Whitman

British

Callista Novel by John Henry Cardinal Newman
The Daisy Chain Novel by Charlotte Yonge
The Espousals Long poem by Coventry Patmore
It Is Never Too Late to Mend Novel by Charles Reade
The Shaving of Shagpat; an Arabian Entertainment Burlesque fantasy by George Meredith

FRENCH

Les Contemplations Collection of poems by Victor Hugo
Madame Bovary Novel by Gustave Flaubert

GERMAN

German

Gyges and His Ring Play by Friedrich Hebbel
Mozart's Journey from Vienna to Prague Novella by Eduard Morike

Swiss

Die Leute von Seldwyla Collection of short stories by Gottfried Keller

RUSSIAN

The Diary of a Superfluous Man Short story by Ivan Turgenev
Rudin Novel by Ivan Turgenev
A Russian Schoolboy Novel by Sergei Timofeyvoch Aksakov

1857

BIRTHS

Aluizio Azevedo, Brazilian novelist
E. C. Bentley, English man of letters
Hermann Bang, Danish novelist
Joseph Conrad (Józef Teodor Konrad Korzeniowski), Polish-born English novelist
George Gissing, English novelist
Karl Adolf Gjellerup, Danish novelist
Gunnar Heiberg, Norwegian playwright
Henrik Pontoppidan, Danish novelist
Hermann Sudermann, German playwright and novelist

DEATHS

Auguste Comte, French philosopher
Joseph Eichendorff, German romantic poet
Alfred de Musset, French romantic poet
Dhionísios Solomos, Greek poet
Eugène Sue, French novelist

PUBLICATIONS

ENGLISH

American

The Confidence Man Novel by Herman Melville
The Piazza Sketches by Herman Melville
Poems Collection by Francis Scott Key
The Poor of New York Play by Dion Boucicault
"Santa Filomena" Poetic tribute to Florence Nightingale by Henry Wadsworth Longfellow

British

Aurora Leigh Blank verse by Elizabeth Barrett Browning
Barchester Towers Novel (second in the Barsetshire series) by Anthony Trollope
Farina, a Legend of Cologne Novel by George Meredith
"Janet's Repentance" Sketch (part of *Scenes of Clerical Life*) by George Eliot
"Mr. Gilfil's Love-Story" Sketch (part of *Scenes of Clerical Life*) by George Eliot
The Professor Novel by Charlotte Brontë
The Romany Rye Fictionalized autobiography by George Borrow
"The Sad Fortune of the Rev. Amos Barton" Sketch (part of *Scenes of Clerical Life*) by George Eliot
Tom Brown's Schooldays Novel by Thomas Hughes
Two Years Ago Novel by Charles Kingsley
The Virginians Novel by William Makepeace Thackeray

ESTONIAN

Kalevipoeg National epic poem by Friedrich Reinhold Kreutzwald

FRENCH

The Flowers of Evil Poems by Charles-Pierre Baudelaire

GERMAN

Austrian

Der Nachsommer Novel by Adalbert Stifter

ITALIAN

Rime Collection of poems by Giosuè Carducci

NORWEGIAN

Between the Battles Play by Bjørnstjerne Martinius Bjørnson

PORTUGUESE

Brazilian

O Guaranai Novel by José de Alencar

1858

BIRTHS

Eugène Brieux, French playwright
Alfred Doblin, German novelist
Rémy de Gourmont, French novelist, playwright, and critic
Thorsteinn Erlingsson, Icelandic poet
Selma Lagerlöf, Swedish novelist

LITERARY EVENT

The *Atlantic* magazine is founded

PUBLICATIONS

BENGALI

Sarmistha Play by Indian writer Michael Madhusudhan Datta

ENGLISH

American

The Age of Chivalry Arthurian and Welsh legends by Thomas Bulfinch
The Autocrat of the Breakfast-Table Essays, in the form of fictional conversations, by Oliver Wendell Holmes
The Courtship of Miles Standish Story in verse by Henry Wadsworth Longfellow

British

The Defense of Guenevere and Other Poems Collection by William Morris
Doctor Thorne Novel (third in the Barsetshire series) by Anthony Trollope
Merope, a Tragedy Play by Matthew Arnold
My Lady Ludlow Novel by Elizabeth Gaskell
Our American Cousin Comedic play by Tom Taylor
The Three Clerks Novel by Anthony Trollope

FRENCH

The Romance of a Poor Young Man Epistolary novel by Octave Feuillet
Women in Love Poems by Alphonse Daudet

LITHUANIAN

The Forest of Anyksciai Poem by Antanas Baranauskas

RUSSIAN

Childhood Years of Grandson Bagrov Novel by Sergey Timofeyvich Aksakov
A Thousand Souls Novel by Aleksey Pisemsky

Cuban

Baltasar Play by Gertrudis Gómez de Avellaneda

The Friend of the Family Novel by Fyodor Dostoyevsky
Oblomov Satirical novel by Ivan Aleksandrovich Goncharov
The Thunderstorm Play by Aleksandr Ostrovsky

1859

BIRTHS

Sholem Aleichem (Sholem Yakov Rabinowitz), Russian Jewish novelist
Henri Bergson, French philosopher
Cyriel Buysse, Flemish novelist and playwright
Sir Arthur Conan Doyle, English novelist
Kenneth Grahame, English writer of children's stories
Knut Hamsun, Norwegian novelist
Verner von Heidenstam, Swedish lyric poet
Alfred Edward Housman, English poet
Kostis Palamas, Greek lyric poet
Francis Thompson, English poet
Tsubouchi Shōyō, Japanese playwright and novelist

DEATHS

Bettina von Arnim, German writer
Petrus Borel, French poet, novelist, and critic
Thomas De Quincey, English essayist
Wilhelm Carl Grimm, Danish writer of children's stories
Henry Hallam, English historian
Leigh Hunt, English poet and essayist
Washington Irving, American writer
Thomas Babington Macaulay, English historian
Sergey Timofeyevich Aksakov, Russian novelist

PUBLICATIONS

ENGLISH

American

The Octoroon; or, Life in Louisiana Play by Dion Boucicault

British

Adam Bede Novel by George Eliot
Idylls of the King Poems by Alfred, Lord Tennyson
"On Liberty" Essay by political philosopher John Stuart Mill
On the Origin of Species by Means of Natural Selection Scientific manifesto by Charles Darwin
The Ordeal of Richard Feverel Novel by George Meredith
Rubaiyat of Omar Khayyam Translation of 12th-century Persian classic by Edward FitzGerald
A Tale of Two Cities Novel by Charles Dickens

FRENCH

Elle et Lui Autobiographical narrative by George Sand
Mireio: A Provençal Poem Pastoral poem by Frédéric Mistral

ITALIAN

The Life of Savonarola Biography by Pasquale Villari

RUSSIAN

A Bitter Lot Play by Aleksey Pisemsky

1860

BIRTHS

Mirza Sadeq Khan Amiri, Persian poet
Sir James M. Barrie, Scottish novelist and playwright
Anton Pavlovich Chekhov, Russian novelist
Simon Dubnow, Russian Jewish historian
Gustaf Fröding, Swedish lyric poet
Simeon Samuel Frug, Russian Jewish poet
Egzi'abeher Gabra, Ethiopian poet
Hannibal Hamlin Garland, American novelist
Salvatore di Giacomo, Italian poet
Jan Kasprowicz, Polish poet
Jules Laforgue, French poet
Togolok Moldo, Kirghiz poet
John Henderson Soga, South African poet and hymn writer
Mankayi Enoch Sontonga, South African poet
Owen Wister, American novelist

DEATHS

Ernst Moritz Arndt, German poet
Johann Ludvig Heiberg, Norwegian poet, playwright, historian, and critic
Arthur Schopenhauer, German philosopher

PUBLICATIONS

BENGALI

Tilottamsambhab Narrative poem by Michael Madhusudan Datta

ENGLISH

American

The Colleen Bawn Play by Dion Boucicault
The Conduct of Life Essays by Ralph Waldo Emerson
Home Ballads and Other Poems Verse collection by John Greenleaf Whittier
The Marble Faun Novel by Nathaniel Hawthorne
M'liss Novella by Bret Harte
"Out of the Cradle Endlessly Rocking" Poem by Walt Whitman

British

Evan Harrington Novel by George Meredith
Great Expectations Novel by Charles Dickens
The Mill on the Floss Novel by George Eliot
Tithonus Dramatic monologue by Alfred, Lord Tennyson
The Woman in White Novel by Wilkie Collins

Canadian

The Season Ticket Collection of sketches by Thomas Chandler Haliburton

DUTCH
Max Havelaar Novel by Multatuli (Eduard Douwes Dekker)

FINNISH
Kullervo Tragedy by Aleksis Kivi

FRENCH
Le Voyage de Monsieur Perrichon Play by Eugène-Marin Labiche
A Scrap of Paper Light comedy by Victorien Sardou

HUNGARIAN
The Tragedy of Man Verse drama by Imre Madách

NORWEGIAN
Brand Dramatic poem by Henrik Ibsen
The Happy Boy Tale by Bjørnstjerne Martinius Bjørnson

RUSSIAN
On the Eve Novel by Ivan Turgenev

SPANISH
Chilean
Arithmetic in Love Novel by Alberto Blest Gana

1861

BIRTHS
Juhani Aho, Finnish novelist and short-story writer
Gastón Fernando Deligne, Puerto Rican poet
David Frishman, German Hebrew essayist and novelist
Vazha Pshavela (Luka Razikashvili), Georgian poet
José Rizal, Filipino writer
Italo Svevo (Ettore Schmitz), Italian novelist
Sir Rabindranath Tagore, Indian poet
Uchimura Kanzo, Japanese critic
Alfred North Whitehead, British philosopher
Jurji Zaydan, Lebanese novelist and essayist
Grigor Zohrap, Armenian writer

DEATHS
Elizabeth Barrett Browning, English poet
Arthur Hugh Clough, English poet
Nikolai Alexandrovich Dobrolyubov, Russian essayist and poet
Francisco de Paula Martínez de la Rosa, Spanish playwright
Friedrich Karl von Savigny, German prose writer
Augustin-Eugène Scribe, French playwright and librettist
Taras Shevchenko, Ukrainian poet

PUBLICATIONS
BENGALI
Brajangana Cycle of lyrics by Indian writer Michael Madhusudan Datta
Meghnadbadh Epic poem by Michael Madhusudan Datta

DANISH
Valdemar Afterdag Ballad cycle by Carsten Hauch

ENGLISH
American
Incidents in the Life of a Slave Girl Written by Herself Autobiography by Harriet Jacobs

British
The Cloister and the Hearth Novel by Charles Reade
On Translating Homer Essays by Matthew Arnold
Orley Farm Novel by Anthony Trollope
Silas Marner Novel by George Eliot

FRENCH
The Bluff Play by Eugène-Marin Labiche

GERMAN
In the Castle Novella by Theodore Storm

NORWEGIAN
Travel Memoirs from the Summer of 1860 Essays and poems by Asamund Olavsson Vinje

RUSSIAN
The House of the Dead Novel by Fyodor Dostoyevsky
The Insulted and the Injured Novel by Fyodor Dostoyevsky

SLOVAK
The Gleam of a Clear Dawn Approached Poems by Janko Král'

1862

BIRTHS
Paul Adam, French symbolist writer
G. Venkata Appa Rao, Telugu poet and playwright
Maurice Barres, French novelist
Georges Feydeau, French playwright
Gerhart Hauptmann, German playwright
O. Henry (William Sydney Porter), American short-story writer
Maurice Maeterlinck, Belgian playwright and poet
Maironis (Jonas Mačiulis), Lithuanian poet
Mori Ōgai (Mori Rintarō), Japanese novelist
Sir Gilbert Parker, Canadian writer
Eden Philpotts, English novelist
Mirza Alakbar Sabir, Azerbaijani satirical poet
Arthur Schnitzler, Austrian Jewish playwright
Edith Wharton, American novelist

DEATHS
Francisco Martínez de la Rosa, Spanish playwright and poet
Johann Nestroy, Austrian playwright
Henry David Thoreau, American essayist
Johann Ludwig Uhland, German lyric poet

PUBLICATIONS
BENGALI
Birangana Epistolary poems by Indian writer Michael Madhusudan Datta

DUTCH

Ideas Collection of comments by Multatuli (Eduard Douwes Dekker)

ENGLISH

Goblin Market Poem by Christina Rossetti
Modern Love Fifty connected poems by George Meredith
The Small House in Allington Novel by Anthony Trollope
The Victories of Love Poem by Coventry Patmore

FLEMISH

The Land of Gold Novel by Hendrik Conscience

FRENCH

Dominique Novel by Eugène Fromentin
Isis Symbolist novel by Philippe-Auguste Villiers de L'Isle Adam
Les Misérables Novel by Victor Hugo
Salammbô Historical novel by Gustave Flaubert

GERMAN

Die Niebelungen Dramatic trilogy by Friedrich Hebbel

NORWEGIAN

Sigurd Slembe Historical play by Bjørnstjerne Martinius Bjørnson

RUSSIAN

Fathers and Sons Novel by Ivan Turgenev
The House of the Dead Novel by Fyodor Dostoyevsky

SPANISH

Chilean

Martín Rivas Novel by Alberto Blest Gana

Spanish

The Real Play by Manuel Tamayo y Baus

1863

BIRTHS

Shloime Ansky (Solomon Seinwil Rapoport), Russian Yiddish writer
Hermann Bahr, Austrian playwright
Constantine Cavafy, Greek poet
Louis Couperus, Dutch poet and novelist
Gabriele D'Annunzio, Italian poet
Richard Dehmel, German poet
Ferenc Herczeg, Hungarian playwright and novelist
Q. (Sir Arthur Thomas Quiller-Couch), English poet, novelist, and anthologist
George Santayana, Spanish-born American philosopher

DEATHS

Jakob Ludwig Carl Grimm, German folklorist
Christian Friedrich Hebbel, German playwright
William Makepeace Thackeray, English novelist
Alfred-Victor de Vigny, French poet

PUBLICATIONS

ENGLISH

American

Our Old Home Series of sketches by Nathaniel Hawthorne
"Paul Revere's Ride" Poem by Henry Wadsworth Longfellow
Tales of a Wayside Inn Narrative poem by Henry Wadsworth Longfellow

British

Romola Novel by George Eliot
The Water Babies Children's tale by Charles Kingsley

Irish

The House by the Churchyard Horror story by Joseph Sheridan Le Fanu

FRENCH

Belgian

Les Quatre incarnations du Christ Epic poem by André van Hasselt

French

Captain Fracasse Novel by Théophile Gautier

RUSSIAN

The Cossacks Novel by Leo Tolstoy
The Stormy Sea Novel by Aleksy Pisemsky

SPANISH

Galician Songs Poems by Rosalía de Castro
Quarrels of Honor Play by Manuel Tamayo y Baus

YIDDISH

Fathers and Sons Novel by Mendele Moker Sefarim

1864

BIRTHS

Hari Narayan Apti, Indian novelist
Einar Benediktsson, Icelandic poet
Caetano da Costa Alegre, black Portuguese poet
Richard Harding Davis, American novelist
Francis Viele Griffin, American-born French symbolist poet
Huseyin Rahmi Gurpinar, Turkish novelist
Herman Heijermans, Dutch playwright
Erik Axel Karlfeldt, Swedish poet
Sheikh Abdul Hasan Mahammed, Somali poet
Henri de Régnier, French poet
Jules Renard, French poet, diarist, and novelist
Shimei Futabatei, Japanese novelist
Miguel de Unamuno, Spanish philosopher
Frank Wedekind, German playwright
Israel Zangwill, English novelist and playwright
Stefan Zeromski, Polish poet and novelist

DEATHS

Nathaniel Hawthorne, American novelist
Walter Savage Landor, English poet and essayist

Imre Madách, Hungarian playwright and poet
Robert Smith Surtees, English comic novelist

PUBLICATIONS

ENGLISH

American

In Wartime and Other Poems Collection by John Greenleaf Whittier
The Maine Woods Autobiography by Henry David Thoreau

British

Apologia Pro Vita Sua Autobiography by John Henry Cardinal Newman
Dramatis Personae Collection of poems by Robert Browning
Emilia in England (later published as *Sandra Belloni*) Novel by George Meredith
Enoch Arden Poem by Alfred, Lord Tennyson
Our Mutual Friend Novel by Charles Dickens
Rabbi Ben Ezra Dramatic monologue by Robert Browning
Wives and Daughters Novel by Elizabeth Gaskell

Irish

Uncle Silas Horror story by Joseph Sheridan Le Fanu

FINNISH

Shoemakers of the Hearth Play by Aleksis Kivi

FRENCH

A Journey to the Center of the Earth Science fiction by Jules Verne
Le Chevalier des touches Novel by Jules-Amédée Barbey d'Aurevilly
Renée Mauperin Novel by Edmond and Jules de Goncourt

GERMAN

The Lost Manuscript Novel by Gustav Freytag

NORWEGIAN

The Pretenders Historical play by Henrik Ibsen

RUSSIAN

Notes from Underground Novel by Fyodor Dostoyevsky
Nowhere to Go Novel by Nikolay Leskov
War and Peace Epic novel by Leo Tolstoy

YIDDISH

"The Little Man" Short story by Mendele Mokher Sefarim

1865

BIRTHS

Micah Joseph Berdyczewski, Ukrainian Hebrew essayist
Sophus Niels Christen Claussen, Danish poet
Laurence Housman, English playwright
Rudyard Kipling, Indian-born English novelist
Dmitry Sergeyevich Merezhkovsky, Russian novelist, poet, and playwright

Emmuska Orczy, Hungarian-born English novelist
Rainis (Jānis Pliekšāns), Latvian poet and playwright
José Asunción Silva, Colombian novelist
Arthur Symons, Welsh-born English poet
Albert Verwey, Dutch poet
William Butler Yeats, Irish poet and playwright

DEATHS

Andrés Bello, Venezuelan poet
Frederika Bremer, Swedish novelist
Elizabeth Gaskell, English novelist
Thomas Chandler Haliburton, Canadian essayist
Otto Ludwig, German playwright
Angel de Saavedra, Spanish poet and playwright

PUBLICATIONS

BENGALI

The Chieftain's Daughter Novel by Bankim Chandra Chatterjee

ENGLISH

American

"The Celebrated Jumping Frog of Calaveras County" Story by Mark Twain
"Drum-Taps" Poem by Walt Whitman
Hans Brinker; or, the Silver Skates Children's story by Mary Mapes Dodge
"O Captain! My Captain!" Poem on the assassination of Abraham Lincoln by Walt Whitman
"When Lilacs Last in the Dooryard Bloom'd" Elegy by Walt Whitman

British

Alice's Adventures in Wonderland Children's fantasy by Lewis Carroll
Atlanta in Calydon Verse drama by Algernon Charles Swinburne
Our Mutual Friend Novel by Charles Dickens
Strathmore Novel by Ouida

FRENCH

From the Earth to the Moon Science fiction novel by Jules Verne
A Married Priest Novel by Jules-Amédée Barbey d'Aurevilly

GERMAN

Deep Shadows Poems by Theodor Storm

HEBREW

Ashmat Shomeron Novel by Abraham Mapu

PORTUGUESE

Brazilian

Iracema Novel by José de Alencar

Portuguese

Odes Modernas Collection of poems by Azores-born poet Antero de Quental

"Lady Macbeth of the Mtsensk District" Story by Nikolay Leskov
The Magic Ring Novel by Jewish writer Mendele Moker Sefarim

1866

BIRTHS
Jeppe Aakjaer, Danish poet and novelist
George Ade, American playwright
Carlos Arniches, Spanish playwright
Jacinto Benavente y Martínez, Spanish playwright
Joseph Ephraim Casely-Hayford, Ghanian novelist
Benedetto Croce, Italian philosopher
Euclides da Cunha, Brazilian historian and poet
Heinrich Federer, Swiss novelist
Hakob Hakobian, Armenian poet
Vyacheslav Ivanovich Ivanov, Romanian philosopher
Keshavasut (Krishnaji Kesav Damle), Marathi poet
U Lat, Burmese novelist
Sigbjørn Obstfelder, Norwegian poet
Pencho Petkov Slaveykov, Bulgarian poet
Beatrix Potter, English children's writer
Romain Rolland, French novelist
Joseph Lincoln Steffens, American journalist
Halid Ziya Usakligil, Turkish novelist
Ramón María del Valle-Inclán, Spanish novelist
Herbert George Wells, English novelist

DEATHS
Carl Jonas Love Almqvist, Swedish writer
Thomas Love Peacock, English novelist
Friedrich Ruckert, German poet

PUBLICATIONS
ENGLISH
American

Snow-Bound Poem by John Greenleaf Whittier

Australian

Ahasuerus in Rome Novel by Robert Hamerling

British

Felix Holt the Radical Novel by George Eliot
Hereward the Wake Novel by Charles Kingsley
The Last Chronicle of Barset Novel (in the Barsetshire series) by
    Anthony Trollope
Poems and Ballads Verse collection by Algernon Charles Swinburne
The Prince's Progress Allegorical poem by Christina Rossetti
"Thyrsis" Poem by Matthew Arnold
The Widow Lerouge Novel by Emile Gaboriau

FINNISH
Land of the Heather Poems by Aleksis Kivi

FRENCH
The Broken Verse Poem by Sully Prudhomme

Chandos Novel by Ouida
Trials Poem by Sully Prudhomme

NORWEGIAN
Brand Play by Henrik Ibsen

RUSSIAN
Crime and Punishment Novel by Fyodor Dostoyevsky
Who Can Be Happy and Free in Russia? Poem by Nikolay
    Nekrasov

SPANISH
Argentine

Fausto Poem by Estanislao del Campo

1867

BIRTHS
AE (George William Russell), Irish poet and essayist
Sayyid Shaykh bin Sayyid Ahmad al-Hadi, Malay novelist
Shio Aragvispireli, Georgian short-fiction writer
Arnold Bennett, English novelist
Petr Bezrŭc (Vladimir Vasek), Czech poet
Vicente Blasco Ibáñez, Spanish novelist
Raul Brandão, Portuguese novelist
Rubén Darío, Nicaraguan poet
Ernest Christopher Dawson, English poet
Tevfik Fikret, Turkish poet
John Galsworthy, English novelist
Kōda Rohan (Kōda Shigeyuki), Japanese novelist and poet
Henry Archibald Hertzeberg Lawson, Australian poet and writer
    of short fiction
Masaoka Shiki, Japanese poet and writer of short fiction
Nar-Dos (Mikhayel Hivhannisian), Armenian poet and novelist
Natsume Sōseki (Natsume Kinosuke), Japanese novelist
Phan Boi Chau, Vietnamese poet
Tewfiq Piramerd, Kurdish poet
Luigi Pirandello, Italian playwright
Władysław Stanisław Reymont, Polish novelist
Mayer-André-Marcel Schwob, French biographer and essayist
Isaiah Shembe, Zulu poet and hymn writer
Laura Ingalls Wilder, American children's writer

DEATHS
Charles-Pierre Baudelaire, French symbolist poet
Abraham Mapu, Lithuanian Jewish novelist

PUBLICATIONS
DANISH
Ravnen Novel by Jewish writer Meir Aron Goldschmidt

ENGLISH
American

Condensed Novels and Other Papers Series of humorous sketches
    by Bret Harte

Ragged Dick Children's story by Horatio Alger
The Tent on the Beach and Other Poems Collected verse of John Greenleaf Whittier
Tiger-Lilies Novel by Sidney Lanier

British

The Life and Death of Jason Poem in heroic couplets by William Morris
New Poems Collection by Matthew Arnold
Phineas Finn Novel by Anthony Trollope
"A Song of Italy" Poem by Algernon Charles Swinburne
Under Two Flags Novel by Ouida

FINNISH
Fugitives Play by Aleksis Kivi

FRENCH
Belgian
The Legend of Thyl Ulenspiegel Prose epic in Old French by Charles de Coster

French
Calendau Poem by Frédéric Mistral
Le Reliquaire Collection of poems by François Coppée
Poèmes saturnines Collection of poems by Paul Verlaine
Thérèse Raquin (*The Devil's Compact*) Novel by Emile Zola

GERMAN
Das Kapital Political tract by Karl Marx and Friedrich Engels

NORWEGIAN
Peer Gynt Dramatic poem by Henrik Ibsen

PORTUGUESE
Pupils of the Dean Novel by Julio Dinis

RUSSIAN
Smoke Novel by Ivan Turgenev

SPANISH
Colombian
Maria: A South American Romance Novel by Jorge Isaacs

Spanish
A New Drama Play by Manuel Tamayo y Baus

1868

BIRTHS
Gabra Iyasus Afawark, Ethiopian poet and novelist
Paul Claudel, French Catholic poet and playwright
W. E. B. DuBois, African-American writer and civil rights leader
Stefan George, German poet
Maxim Gorky, Russian novelist
José Pereira da Graça Aranha, Brazilian novelist
Gaston Leroux, French novelist and playwright
Edgar Lee Masters, American poet

Gustav Meyrink, Austrian novelist
Edmond Rostand, French poet and playwright
Ahmad Shawqi, Egyptian poet and playwright

DEATH
Adalbert Stifter, Austrian writer of folk tales

LITERARY EVENT
Overland Monthly is founded by Bret Harte

PUBLICATIONS
ENGLISH
American
Little Women Novel by Louisa May Alcott
"The Luck of the Roaring Camp" Short story by Bret Harte

British
"Ave Atque Vale" Elegy by Algernon Charles Swinburne
Earthly Paradise Poem by William Morris
Lucretius Dramatic monologue by Alfred, Lord Tennyson
"The Moonstone" Pioneer detective story by Wilkie Collins
The Ring and the Book Twelve dramatic monologues by Robert Browning

FRENCH
The Lady of Maldoro Poem in six cantos by Comte de Lautreamont
Le Petit chose Novel by Alphonse Daudet

ITALIAN
Levia gravia Poems by Giosuè Carducci
The Military Life Novel by Edmondo De Amicis

PORTUGUESE
An English Family Novel by Julio Dinis
Wild Flowers Poems by João de Deus

RUSSIAN
The Idiot Novel by Fyodor Dostoyevsky

1869

BIRTHS
Laurence Binyon, English poet and playwright
Bo Hjalmar Bergman, Swedish lyric poet
André Gide, French novelist
Jalil Mammadguluzada, Azerbaijani prose writer and playwright
Edgar Lee Masters, American poet and novelist
Martin Anderson Nexo, Danish novelist
Ozaki Kōyō (Ozaki Tokutarō), Japanese novelist, poet, and essayist
Edwin Arlington Robinson, American poet
Hjalmar Erik Soderberg, Swedish novelist
Suleyman of Stal, Dagestani poet
Booth Tarkington, American novelist and playwright
Stanisław Wyspianski, Polish poet and playwright
Mehmed Emin Yurdakul, Turkish poet

DEATHS

Marie-Louis-Alphonse de Prat de Lamartine, French romantic poet

Charles-Augustine Saint-Beuve, French critic, essayist, and novelist

PUBLICATIONS

ENGLISH

American

Among the Hills Poems by John Greenleaf Whittier

The Innocents Abroad Travel narrative by Mark Twain

"The Outcasts of Poker Flat" Short story by Bret Harte

"The Story of a Bad Boy" Children's story by Thomas Bailey Aldrich

Under the Willows and Other Poems Collected verse by James Russell Lowell

Australian

Leaves from Australian Forests Collection of poems by Henry Kendall

British

Culture and Anarchy Essays by Matthew Arnold

"Dipsychus" Poem by Arthur Hugh Clough

He Knew He Was Right Novel by Anthony Trollope

"The Holy Grail" Poem (seventh in the poetic cycle *The Idylls of the King*) by Alfred, Lord Tennyson

Lorna Doone Novel by Richard Doddridge Blackmore

FRENCH

Cain Poems by Charles-Marie-René Leconte de Lisle

Fêtes galantes Collection of poems by Paul Verlaine

Frou-Frou Light dramatic comedy by Ludovic Halevy and Henri Meilhac

"Herodias" Dramatic poem by Stéphane Mallarmé

Letters from My Mill Collection by Alphonse Daudet

Madame Gervaisais Novel by Edmond and Jules de Goncourt

Poems in Prose Collection by Charles Baudelaire

Sentimental Education Autobiographical novel by Gustave Flaubert

Solitude Poems by Sully Prudhomme

GERMAN

Austrian

The King of Zion Novel by Robert Hamerling

1870

BIRTHS

Hilaire Belloc, French-born English satirist and essayist

Solomon Bloomgarden, American scholar and poet

Christopher John Brennan, Australian poet

Ivan Alekseyevich Bunin, Russian novelist and poet

Hafiz Ibrahim, Egyptian poet

Aleksandr Ivanovich Kuprin, Russian poet

Amado Nervo, Mexican poet

Frank Norris (Benjamin Franklin Norris), American novelist

Tom Redcam (Thomas Henry MacDermot), Jamaican poet

Saki (Hector Hugh Munro), Burmese-born English short-story writer

Tran Te Xuong, Vietnamese poet

DEATHS

Gustavo Adolfo Bécquer, Spanish romantic poet

Charles Dickens, English novelist

Alexander Dumas père, French novelist

Jules de Goncourt, French novelist

Henrik Hertz, Danish poet and playwright

Aleksandr Ivanovich Herzen, Russian novelist

Comte de Lautreamont (Isidore-Lucien Ducasse), French poet

Prosper Merimée, French novelist

Charles-René de Montalembert, French historian

Aasmund Olafsson Vinje, Norwegian poet

PUBLICATIONS

ENGLISH

American

The Cathedral Long poem by James Russell Lowell

British

The Adventures of Harry Richmond Novel by George Meredith

The Grammar of Assent Theological treatise by John Henry Cardinal Newman

The Mystery of Edwin Drood Unfinished novel by Charles Dickens

Poems Collection by Dante Gabriel Rossetti

FINNISH

Seven Brothers Novel by Aleksis Kivi

FRENCH

Twenty Thousand Leagues Under the Sea Science fiction novel by Jules Verne

GERMAN

Austrian

The Priest of Kirchfield Play by Ludwig Anzengruber

NORWEGIAN

Arnjot Jelline Epic cycle by Bjørnstjerne Martinius Bjørnson

Poems and Songs Collected poetry of Bjørnstjerne Martinius Bjørnson

PORTUGUESE

Brazilian

Floating Foam Love lyrics by Antonio de Castro Alves

RUSSIAN

At Daggers Drawn Novel by Nikolay Leskov

The History of a Town Satirical and fictional history by Mikhail Evgrafovich Saltykov

A Lear of the Steppes Novel by Ivan Turgenev

The Precipice Novel by Ivan Goncharov

SPANISH

Mystical Poems and Songs Collection of verse by Catalan poet Mosen Jacinto Verdaguer

Reputable Men Play by Manuel Tamayo y Baus

1871

BIRTHS

Leonid Andreyev, Russian novelist and playwright
Winston Churchill, American novelist
Stephen Crane, American novelist
Grazia Deledda, Sardinian-born Italian novelist
Theodore Dreiser, American novelist
John Langalibalele Dube, Zulu novelist and collector of folk tales
Dan Karm, Maltese poet
Heinrich Mann, German novelist
Christian Morgenstern, German expressionist poet
Marcel Proust, French novelist
Stijn Streuvels (Frank Lateur), Flemish novelist
John Millington Synge, Irish playwright
Tokuda Shūsei, Japanese novelist
Tayama Katai, Japanese novelist
Lesia Ukrainka (Laryse Petrovina Kosack-Kvitka), Ukrainian poet and playwright
Paul Valéry, French poet

DEATHS

Aleksandr Nikolayevich Afanasyev, Russian folklorist
Willibald Alexis (Georg Wilhelm Heinrich Haring), German novelist
Julio Dinis, Portuguese poet, playwright, and novelist
Charles-Paul de Kock, French novelist and playwright
Nasif Yesiji, Arab-Lebanese Christian scholar

PUBLICATIONS

ENGLISH

American

Democratic Vistas Prose pamphlet by Walt Whitman
The Hoosier Schoolmaster Novel by Edward Eggleston
Little Men Novel by Louisa May Alcott
Passage to India Poem by Walt Whitman
Wake-Robin Essays on nature by John Burroughs

British

Balaustion's Adventure Poem by Robert Browning
The Descent of Man Tract on evolution by Charles Darwin
Desperate Remedies Novel by Thomas Hardy
"The Last Tournament" Poem (part of the *Idylls of the King*) by Alfred, Lord Tennyson
Middlemarch, a Study of Provincial Life Novel by George Eliot
"The Owl and the Pussycat" Nonsense poem by Edward Lear
Prince Hohenstiel-Schwangau Poetic monologue by Robert Browning
Songs Before Sunrise Collected verse by Algernon Charles Swinburne
Through the Looking Glass Children's novel by Lewis Carroll

FRENCH

"The Drunken Boat" Poem by Arthur Rimbaud
The Fortunes of the Rougon-Macquart Family Novel (first in a sequence of 20 completed in 1893) by Emile Zola

GERMAN

German

Master Arthur Novel by Wilhelm Raabe

Swiss

Hutten's Last Days Poem by Conrad Ferdinand Meyer

RUSSIAN

The Forest Dramatic comedy by Aleksandr Ostrovsky
Russian Woman Poem by Nikolay Alekseyevich Nekrasov

SPANISH

Argentine

The Abattoir Novel by Esteban Echeverría

Spanish

Rhymes Collected romantic verse by Gustavo Adolfo Bécquer

1872

BIRTHS

Pío Baroja, Basque writer
Max Beerbohm, English writer
Paul Laurence Dunbar, African-American poet
Hemachandra Gosawmi, Assamese historian and poet
Zane Grey, American novelist
Ichiyo Higuchi, Japanese novelist and poet
Krishnaji Prabhakar Khadilkar, Marathi playwright
Okamoto Kido, Japanese playwright
Bertrand Russell, English philosopher
José Enrique Rodó, Uruguayan essayist
Bhai Vir Singh, Punjabi poet and novelist

DEATHS

Ludwig Andreas Feuerbach, German philosopher
Théophile Gautier, French poet and novelist
Franz Grillparzer, Austrian playwright
Carsten Hauch, Danish poet, playwright, and novelist

PUBLICATIONS

DANISH

Mogens Story collection by Jens Peter Jacobsen

ENGLISH

American

The Pennsylvania Pilgrim and Other Poems Collection by John Greenleaf Whittier
Roughing It Autobiographical travel narrative by Mark Twain
Their Wedding Journey Novel by William Dean Howells

British

Erewhon Satirical utopian novel by Samuel Butler

Fifine at the Fair Dramatic poem by Robert Browning
"Gareth and Lynette" Poem (part of the *Idylls of the King*) by Alfred, Lord Tennyson
Under the Greenwood Tree Novel by Thomas Hardy

FRENCH

Around the World in Eighty Days Science fiction novel by Jules Verne
Les Illuminations Collection of prose and verse poems by Arthur Rimbaud

GERMAN

The Birth of Tragedy Metaphysical discourse by Friedrich Nietzsche
Main Currents in Nineteenth-Century Literature Criticism Scholarly work by Georg Brandes

NORWEGIAN

The Barque Future Novel by Jonas Lie

RUSSIAN

Cathedral Folk Novel by Nikolay Leskov
The Possessed Novel by Fyodor Dostoyevsky
Torrents of Spring Novel by Ivan Turgenev

SPANISH

Argentine

The Departure of Martin Fierro Epic poem by José Hernández

1873

BIRTHS

Azorín (José Martínez Ruiz), Spanish novelist, essayist, and critic
Mariano Azuela, Mexican novelist
Chaim Nachman Bialik, Ukrainian Jewish poet
Henri Barbusse, French novelist
Valery Yakovlevich Bryusov, Russian poet, novelist, and playwright
Willa Cather, American novelist
Colette (Sidonie-Gabrielle Colette), French novelist
Walter de la Mare, English poet and novelist
Ford Madox Ford (Ford Madox Hueffer), English essayist, poet, and novelist
Muhammad Iqbal, Urdu poet
Johannes Vilhelm Jensen, Danish novelist and poet
Kawahigashi Hekigoto, Japanese poet
N. Kumaran Asan, Malayalee poet
George Edward Moore, English philosopher and essayist
Charles Péguy, French Catholic poet and philosopher
Jakob Wasserman, German Jewish novelist and biographer

DEATHS

Manuel Bretón de los Herreros, Spanish playwright
Edward G. E. Bulwer-Lytton, English novelist
Michael Madhusudan Datta, Bengali poet
Emile Gaboriau, French detective novelist

Gertrudis Gómez de Avellaneda, Cuban poet and playwright
Francesco Domenico Guerrazzi, Italian writer
Joseph Sheridan Le Fanu, Irish novelist
Alessandro Manzoni, Italian novelist
John Stuart Mill, English political philosopher
Fyodor Ivanovich Tyutchev, Russian writer

PUBLICATIONS

BENGALI

The Poison Tree Novel by Indian writer Bankim Chandra Chatterjee

ENGLISH

American

A Chance Acquaintance Novel by William Dean Howells

British

The Eustace Diamonds Novel by Anthony Trollope
A Pair of Blue Eyes Novel by Thomas Hardy
Red Cotton Night-Cap Country Dramatic poem by Robert Browning

FRENCH

A Season in Hell Prose work by Arthur Rimbaud
The Wife of Claude Play by Alexandre Dumas père

GERMAN

The Ancestors Novel (part of cycle completed in 1881) by Gustav Freytag
Children of the World Novel by Paul Johann Heyse

HUNGARIAN

Man of Gold Novel by Mór Jókai

RUSSIAN

The Snow Maiden Play by Aleksandr Ostrovsky
Enchanted Wanderer Novel by Nikolay Leskov

SPANISH

Episodios nacionales First of a cycle of 46 novels (completed in 1912) by Benito Pérez Galdós

1874

BIRTHS

G. K. Chesterton, English essayist and novelist
Winston Churchill, English writer, historian, and statesman
Clarence Day, American writer
Robert Frost, American poet
Ellen Glasgow, American novelist
Drmit Gulia, Abkhazian poet
Hugo von Hofmannsthal, Austrian poet and playwright
Joseph Klausner, Lithuanian-born Israel historian and essayist
Karl Kraus, Austrian critic, playwright, and poet
Kyoshi Takahama, Japanese poet
Amy Lowell, American poet

Leopoldo Lugones, Argentine poet
Manuel Machado, Spanish poet and playwright
William Somerset Maugham, English novelist and playwright
Arthur van Schendel, Dutch novelist and short-story writer
Robert William Service, English-born Canadian poet
Gertrude Stein, American poet

DEATHS

André-Henri-Constant van Hasselt, Belgian poet
Jules Michelet, French historian
Fritz Reuter, German comic poet

PUBLICATIONS

BENGALI

The Two Rings Novel by Indian writer Bankim Chandra
    Chatterjee

ENGLISH

Australian

His Natural Life Novel by Marcus Clarke

British

Bothwell, A Tragedy Play by Algernon Charles Swinburne
Far from the Madding Crowd Novel by Thomas Hardy
Life of Christ Biography by Frederic William Farrar
Phineas Redux Novel by Anthony Trollope
Tiriel Symbolic poem by William Blake

Scottish

"The City of Dreadful Night" Long poem by James Thomson

FRENCH

Fromont the Younger and Risler the Elder Novel by Alphonse
    Daudet
The Mysterious Island Science fiction novel by Jules Verne
Ninety-Three Novel by Victor Hugo
Poèmes de Provence Collection by Jean Aicard
Songs Without Words Collection of verse by Paul Verlaine
The Temptation of Saint Anthony Short novel by Gustave
    Flaubert

PORTUGUESE

Death of Don Juan Poems by Abílio Manuel Guerra Junqueiro

SPANISH

Pepita Jiménez Novel by Juan Valera
The Three-Cornered Hat Novel by Pedro Antonio de Alarcón

1875

BIRTHS

Leo Baeck, German Jewish writer
John Buchan, Scottish novelist
Edgar Rice Burroughs, American novelist
Jean Charbonneau, French-Canadian poet
José Santos Chocano, Peruvian poet

Mehmed Ziya Gokalp, Turkish poet
Julio Herrera y Reissig, Uruguayan poet
Carl Jung, German psychologist
Antonio Machado, Spanish poet
Thomas Mann, German novelist
Samuel Edward Krune Mqhayi, Xhosa writer and poet
Rainer Maria Rilke, German lyric poet
Jakob Schaffner, Swiss novelist
Albert Schweitzer, Alsatian philosopher and theologian
Saul Tschernihowsky, Russian Jewish poet
Yonejiro Noguchi, Japanese poet
Edgar Wallace, English novelist and writer of suspense stories

DEATHS

Hans Christian Andersen, Danish writer of fairy tales
Antonio Feliciano Castilho, Portuguese poet
Charles Kingsley, English novelist
Eduard Friedrich Morike, German poet and playwright

PUBLICATIONS

ENGLISH

American

A Foregone Conclusion Novel by William Dean Howells
Roderick Hudson Novel by Henry James

British

Aristophanes' Apology Long poem in blank verse by Robert
    Browning
The Inn Album Dramatic poem by Robert Browning
Queen Mary Historical drama by Alfred, Lord Tennyson
The Way We Live Now Novel by Anthony Trollope
"The Wreck of the Deutschland" Poem by Gerard Manley
    Hopkins

NORWEGIAN

The Bankrupt Play by Bjørnstjerne Martinius Bjørnson
The Editor Play by Bjørnstjerne Martinius Bjørnson

RUSSIAN

Anna Karenina Novel by Leo Tolstoy

YIDDISH

The Travels and Adventures of Benjamin the Third Novel by Rus-
    sian Jewish writer Mendele Mokher Sefarim

1876

BIRTHS

Sherwood Anderson, American novelist
Henry Bernstein, French playwright
Olav Dunn, Norwegian novelist
Léon-Paul Fargue, French poet
Max Jacobs, French poet
Else Lasker-Schuler, German poet
Jack London (John Griffith Lond), American novelist
Mustafa Lufti al-Manfaluti, Egyptian writer

Filippo Tommaso Marinetti, Italian poet, novelist, and critic
Thomas Mokupo Mofolo, Basotho novelist
Abdulali Mustaghni, Afghan poet
Qi Rushan, Chinese playwright
Thakin Kopuijto Hmain, Burmese poet and playwright
O. E. Rölvaag, Norwegian-born American novelist
George Macaulay Trevelyan, English historian

DEATHS
Khristo Botev, Bulgarian poet
Aleksander Fredo, Polish playwright and novelist
Eugène-Samuel-Auguste Fromentin, French novelist
Janko Král', Slovak poet
George Sand (Amandine-Aurore-Lucie Dudevant), French novelist

PUBLICATIONS
ENGLISH
American

The Adventures of Tom Sawyer Novel by Mark Twain
The American Novel by Henry James
Clarel Poem by Herman Melville

British

Daniel Deronda Novel by George Eliot
Erectheus Drama in Greek form by Algernon Charles Swinburne
"The Growth of Love" Sonnet by Robert Bridges
Harold Historical drama by Alfred, Lord Tennyson
"The Hunting of the Snark" Poem by Lewis Carroll
The Prime Minister Novel by Anthony Trollope
The Story of Sigurd the Volsung and the Fall of the Niblungs Epic poem by William Morris

FRENCH
The Afternoon of a Faun Poem by Stéphane Mallarmé
Child's Songs Poems by Jean Aicard
Fru Marie Grubbe Historical novel by Jens Peter Jacobsen

PORTUGUESE
Loose Leaves Poems by João de Deus
Maternal Primer Poems by João de Deus
The Sin of Father Amaro Novel by José Maria de Eça de Quierós

RUSSIAN
The Golovlev Family Novel by Mikhail Evgrafovich Saltykov

SPANISH
Doña Perfecta Novel by Benito Pérez Galdós
Rienzi the Tribune Verse drama by Rosario de Acuña

1877

BIRTHS
Endre Ady, Hungarian poet
Derenik Demirtchian, Armenian poet and novelist
Herman Hesse, German novelist and poet
Sir Muhammad Iqbāl, Indian Muslim poet

Alfred Kubin, Austrian novelist, poet, and essayist
Aleksey Yaliseyevich Kulakoskiy, Yakut poet and philosopher
Mary Jane Mander, New Zealand novelist
Ullur Paramesvarayyar, Malayalee poet
Alexey Mikhailovich Remizov, Russian novelist
Raymond Roussel, French novelist
Hamzat Tsadasa, Dagestan poet
Peyo Yavorov, Bulgarian poet and playwright

DEATHS
José de Alençar, Brazilian novelist
Walter Bagehot, English political philosopher
Fernán Caballero (Cecilia Böhl de Faber), Spanish novelist
Johann Ludvig Runeberg, Swedish-Finnish poet

PUBLICATIONS
ENGLISH
British

Black Beauty Children's story by Anna Sewell
The Unknown Eros Collection of odes by Coventry Patmore
"The Windhover" Sonnet by Gerard Manley Hopkins

Canadian

The Golden Dog Novel by William Kirby

FRENCH
The Dram Shop Novel by Émile Zola
The Nabob Play by Alphonse Daudet

GERMAN
Aquis Submersus Historical novella by Theodor Storm

NORWEGIAN
The Pillars of Society Play by Henrik Ibsen

RUSSIAN
"The Dream of a Ridiculous Man" Short story by Fyodor Dostoyevsky
Virgin Soil Novel by Ivan Turgenev

SPANISH
La Atlántida Epic poem by Catalan writer Mosen Jacinto Verdaguer
Madman or Saint Play by José Echegaray y Eizaguirre

1878

BIRTHS
Mikhail Petrovich Artsybashev, Russian novelist and playwright
Sadruddin Ayni, Tajik poet
Massimo Bontempelli, Italian poet and novelist
Jean de Bosschere, Belgian novelist
Stanisław Brzozowski, Polish novelist, playwright, and critic
Martin Buber, Austrian Jewish philosopher

Hans Carossa, German poet and novelist
Alfred Doblin, German novelist and essayist
Edward Dunsany, Irish playwright
Herbert George de Lisser, Jamaican poet
Stephen Haweis, English poet
Sirek Walda Sellase Heruy, Ethiopian novelist
George Kaiser, German expressionist playwright
Eino Leino, Finnish poet, playwright, and novelist
John Masefield, English poet
Ferenc Molnár, Hungarian playwright and novelist
Horacio Quiroga, Uruguayan short-story writer, poet, and playwright
Charles-Ferdinand Remuz, Swiss novelist
Carl Sandburg, American poet
Upton Sinclair, American novelist
Takio Arishima, Japanese novelist
Anton Hansen Tammasaare, Estonian novelist
Robert Walser, Swiss novelist
Yosano Akiko, Japanese poet

DEATHS

William Cullen Bryant, American poet
Karl Ferdinand Gutzkow, German playwright
Nikolay Alekseyevich Nekrasov, Russian poet

PUBLICATIONS

ARMENIAN
Jalaleddin Novel by Hakob Maliq Hakobian Raffi

BENGALI
The Will of Krishnakunta Novel by Indian writer Bankim Chandra Chatterjee

CZECH
Stories from Mala Strava Collection of stories by Jan Neruda

ENGLISH
American
Daisy Miller Novel by Henry James

British
H.M.S. Pinafore Comic opera by W. S. Gilbert
"Pied Beauty" Sonnet by Gerard Manley Hopkins
Poems and Ballads Collected verse by Algernon Charles Swinburne
The Return of the Native Novel by Thomas Hardy

FRENCH
La Justice Poem by Sully Prudhomme

GERMAN
Before the Storm Novel by Theodore Fontane

PORTUGUESE
Cousin Basilio Novel by José Maria de Eça de Queirós

1879

BIRTHS
Alcides Arguedas, Bolivian novelist and historian
James Branch Cabell, American writer
Dorothy Canfield Fisher, American novelist and children's writer
E. M. Forster, English novelist
Uri Nissan Gnessin, Russian Jewish writer of short fiction
Vachel Lindsay, American poet
Masamune Hakucho, Japanese writer and critic
U Leti Pantita Maun Tyi, Burmese essayist and poet
Vallathol Narayana Menon, Malayalee poet
Lope K. Santos, Filipino novelist
Wallace Stevens, American poet
Herman Teirlinck, Flemish novelist, poet, short-story writer, playwright, and essayist

DEATHS
Charles de Coster, Belgian poet
Octave Crémazie, French-Canadian poet

PUBLICATIONS

ENGLISH
American
The Lady of the Aroostook Novel by William Dean Howells

British
The Egoist Novel by George Meredith
Hearts of Oak Play by Henry Arthur Jones
The Light of Asia Epic poem by Edwin Arnold
The Pirates of Penzance Comic opera by W. S. Gilbert
Travels with a Donkey in the Cevennes Travel narrative by Robert Louis Stevenson

FRENCH
Canadian
The Northern Flowers Poems by Louis-Honoré Fréchette
The Snow Birds Poems by Louis-Honoré Fréchette

French
Mémoires Autobiography (written 1729–38; published 1879–1928) of Duc de Saint-Simon

GERMAN
Austrian
Lottie, the Watchmaker Novel by Marie, Baroness von Ebner Eschenbach

German
Green Henry Novel by Gottfried Keller
Woyzeck Dramatic fragment by Georg Buchner

NORWEGIAN
A Doll's House Play by Henrik Ibsen

ROMANIAN
Mr. Leonida Play by Ion Luca Caragiale

RUSSIAN
The Brothers Karamazov Novel by Fyodor Dostoyevsky

SPANISH
Doña Luz Novel by Juan Valera

SWEDISH
The Red Room Novel by August Strindberg

1880

BIRTHS
Musa Abdul Illahi, Somali poet
Guillaume Apollinaire (Wilhelm Apollinaris de Kostrowitzki), Italian-born French poet
Tudor Arghezi, Romanian poet and novelist
Sholem Asch, Polish-born American novelist and playwright
Andrei Bely (Boris Nikolayevich Bugayev), Russian poet and novelist
Aleksandr Aleksandrovich Blok, Russian playwright
Radclyffe Hall, English novelist
Mikhail Javakhisvili, Georgian novelist
H. L. Mencken, American journalist, editor, and critic
Robert Musil, Austrian novelist
Alfred Noyes, English poet
Sean O'Casey, Irish playwright
Ramón Pérez de Ayala, Spanish novelist and poet
Prem Chand (Dhanpat Rai Srivastana), Indian novelist
Gershon Schoffman, German Jewish short-story writer and novelist
Jóhann Sigurjónsson, Icelandic playwright and poet
Oswald Spengler, German philosopher
Lytton Strachey, English biographer

DEATHS
Estanislao del Campo, Argentine poet
George Eliot (Mary Ann Evans), English novelist
Ludwig Andreas Feuerbach, German philosopher
Gustave Flaubert, French novelist
Tom Taylor, Scottish playwright

LITERARY EVENT
The *Dial* magazine is founded by Francis F. Browne

PUBLICATIONS
ARMENIAN
David Bele Novel by Hakob Malik Hakobian Raffi

DANISH
Niels Lynne Novel by Jens Jacobsen

ENGLISH
American
Ben-Hur: A Tale of the Christ Novel by Lew Wallace
A Tramp Abroad Travel narrative by Mark Twain

The Undiscovered Country Novel by William Dean Howells
Washington Square Novel by Henry James

British
Ballads and Other Poems Collection by Alfred, Lord Tennyson
The Duke's Children Novel by Anthony Trollope
Moths Novel by Ouida
Spring and Fall Collection of poems by Gerard Manley Hopkins
The Tragic Comedians Novel by George Meredith

FRENCH
"Ball of Fat" Short story by Guy de Maupassant
Nana Novel by Émile Zola
Pinto Tragedy by Népomucène Lemercier
Rarahu Novel by Pierre Loti

GERMAN
Swiss
Heidi Children's story by Johanna Spyri
The Saint Novella by Conrad Ferdiand Meyer

ITALIAN
Cavalleria rusticana Novella by Giovanni Verga

NORWEGIAN
Garman and Worse Novel by Alexander Lange Kielland

ROMANIAN
A Stormy Night Play by Ion Luca Caragiale

SPANISH
Ecuadorean
Catilinarians Collection of essays by Juan Montalvo

Spanish
The New Medley Collection of poems by Rosalía de Castro

1881

BIRTHS
George Bacovia (Gheorghe Vasilu), Romanian poet
Jacob Cohen, Russian-born Israeli poet
Roger-Martin du Gard, French novelist and playwright
Juan Ramón Jiménez, Spanish Andalusian poet
Mordecai Menahem Kaplan, Lithuanian-born American Jewish scholar and philosopher
Joel Lehtonen, Finnish novelist and short-story writer
Alfonso Henrique de Lima Barreto, Brazilian novelist and essayist
Emil Ludwig, German biographer
Lu Xun, Chinese critic
Gregorio Martínez Sierra, Spanish novelist and playwright
Giovanni Papini, Italian essayist and biographer
Stefan Zweig, Austrian biographer and novelist

DEATHS

Henri Frédéric Amiel, Swiss diarist
George Borrow, English travel writer
Thomas Carlyle, Scottish philosopher and historian
Marcus Andrew Hislop Clarke, Austrian novelist and playwright
Fyodor Mikhaylovich Dostoyevsky, Russian novelist
Sidney Lanier, African-American poet
Aleksey Pisemsky, Russian novelist and playwright
Edward John Trelawny, English writer and adventurer

PUBLICATIONS

DANISH

Clipped Wings Stories by Henrik Pontoppidan
Old and New Gods Poems by Holger Drachmann

ENGLISH

American

A Century of Dishonor Treatise on Native Americans by Helen Hunt Jackson
Dr. Breen's Practice Novel by William Dean Howells
The Portrait of a Lady Novel by Henry James
The Prince and the Pauper Novel by Mark Twain
Uncle Remus: His Songs and Sayings Collection of African-American lore, songs, and anecdotes by Joel Chandler Harris

British

Ayala's Angel Novel by Anthony Trollope
Ballads and Sonnets Collection by Dante Gabriel Rossetti
A Laodicean Novel by Thomas Hardy

Scottish

Virginibus Puerisque Essays by Robert Louis Stevenson

Welsh

Dreflan, Its People and Its Affairs Novel by Daniel Owen

FRENCH

Belgian

A Male Novel by Antoine Louis Camille Lemonnier

French

The Crime of Sylvestre Bonnard Novel by Anatole France
La Maison Tellier Collection of short stories by Guy de Maupassant

GERMAN

Swiss

Prometheus und Epimetheus Poem by Carl Spitteler

ITALIAN

The House by the Medlar Tree Novel by Giovanni Verga

NORWEGIAN

Ghosts Play by Henrik Ibsen
Working People Novel by Alexander Lange Kielland

PORTUGUESE

Brazilian

Epitaph for a Small Winner Novel by Joaquim Maria Machado de Assis
The Mulatto Novel by Aluizio Azevedo

RUSSIAN

The Tale of Cross-Eyed Lefty from Tula and the Steel Flea Novel by Nikolay Leskov

SPANISH

Argentine

Amalia: A Romance of the Argentine Novel by José Mármol

Spanish

The Disinherited Lady Novel by Benito Pérez Galdós

1882

BIRTHS

Mirza Abulkasim Quazvini Aref, Iranian poet
Subramanya C. Bharati, Tamil poet
Willem Ellschot, Flemish novelist
Leonhard Frank, German expressionist novelist and playwright
Jean Giraudoux, French poet and playwright
Susan Glaspell, American novelist
James Joyce, Irish novelist
Henri-René Lenormand, French playwright
Wyndham Lewis, English novelist
Vincus Kreve-McKevicius, Lithuanian poet, novelist, and playwright
Jacques Maritain, French Catholic philosopher
Sigrid Undset, Danish-born Norwegian novelist
Hendrik Willem Van Loon, Dutch-born American popular historian
Charles Vildrac, French poet, playwright, and essayist
P. G. Wodehouse, English comic novelist
Virginia Woolf, English novelist

DEATHS

János Arany, Hungarian poet
Richard Henry Dana Jr., American novelist
Charles Darwin, English biologist and author
Ralph Waldo Emerson, American transcendentalist author
Joseph-Arthur de Gobineau, French poet, writer of short fiction, and historian
Henry Kendall, Australian poet
Friedrich Reinhold Kreutzwald, Estonian poet
Henry Wadsworth Longfellow, American poet
Dante Gabriel Rossetti, English poet
James Thomson, English poet
Anthony Trollope, English novelist

PUBLICATIONS

ARMENIAN

The Golden Cockerell Novel by Hakob Malik Hakobian Raffi

BENGALI

Andanda Math (Temple of Bliss) Novel by Indian writer Bankim Chandra Bannerjee

DUTCH

The Country of Rembrandt History by Conrad Basken Huet

ENGLISH

American

In the Harbor Collection of poems by Henry Wadsworth
   Longfellow
A Modern Instance Novel by William Dean Howells
Specimen Days Collected verse by Walt Whitman

British

Marino Faliero, Doge of Venice Verse tragedy by Algernon Charles
   Swinburne
Tristram of Lyonesse Romantic poem by Algernon Charles
   Swinburne
Two on a Tower Novel by Thomas Hardy
The Silver King Play by Henry Arthur Jones

FRENCH

Canadian

Complete Works Collection of poems by Octave Crémazie

French

Down Stream Novel by Joris-Karl Huysmans
The Vultures Play by Henry Becque

GERMAN

The Joyful Wisdom Collection of essays and aphorisms by
   Friedrich Nietzsche
The Woman Taken in Adultery Novel by Theodore Fontane

NORWEGIAN

An Enemy of the People Play by Henrik Ibsen

SWEDISH

Poems Collection by Viktor Rydberg

UKRAINIAN

Boryslav Laughs Novel by Ivan Franko

1883

BIRTHS

Mihály Babits, Hungarian novelist and poet
Hjalmar Bergman, Swedish novelist and playwright
Robert Faesi, Swiss poet, playwright, and short-story writer
Fyodor Vasilyevich Gladkov, Russian novelist and playwright
Jaroslav Hašek, Czech novelist
T. E. Hulme, English critic and poet
Khalil Gibran, Lebanese-American poet and philosopher
Franz Kafka, Austrian Jewish novelist
John Maynard Keynes, English economist and writer
Sir Edward Montague Compton Mackenzie, English novelist
Naoya Shiga, Japanese novelist
Henry Masila Ndawo, Xhosa novelist and poet
José Ortega y Gassett, Spanish humanist and essayist
Pi Mounin, Burmese essayist and novelist
Katharine Susannah Prichard, Fijian-born Australian novelist

Alexey Nikolayevich Tolstoy, Russian novelist
Federigo Tozzi, Italian novelist and writer of short fiction
Hugo Wast, Argentine novelist and short-story writer
William Carlos Williams, American poet

DEATHS

Hendrik Conscience, Flemish novelist
Edward FitzGerald, English poet and translator
Karl Marx, German socialist and political philosopher
Cyprian Kamil Norwid, Polish poet and playwright
Jules Sandeau, French playwright and novelist
Ivan Sergeyevich Turgenev, Russian novelist

PUBLICATIONS

ARMENIAN

Sparks Novel by Hakob Malik Hakobian Raffi

CZECH

Plain Themes Collection of Poems by Jan Neruda

DANISH

Village Pictures Novel by Henrik Pontoppidan

ENGLISH

American

Life on the Mississippi Memoir by Mark Twain
"Little Orphan Annie" Poem by James Whitcomb Riley

British

Jocoseria Collection of poems by Robert Browning

Scottish

Treasure Island Novel by Robert Louis Stevenson

South African

The Story of a South African Farm Novel by Olive Schreiner

FRENCH

Belgian

The Flemish Collection of poems by Emile Verhaeren

French

Contes cruels Collection of short stories by Philippe-Auguste de
   L'Isle Adam

GERMAN

German

Thus Spake Zarathustra Philosophical discourse by Friedrich
   Nietzsche

Swiss

Extramundana Cosmic myths by Carl Spitteler

ITALIAN

Pinocchio: The Story of a Puppet Didactic story by Carlo Collodi

NORWEGIAN

Beyond Human Endurance Play by Bjørnstjerne Martinius
   Bjørnson

The Family at Gilje Novel by Jonas Lie
One of Life's Slaves Novel by Jonas Lie
Peasant Students Novel by Arne Garborg

ROMANIAN
The Evening Star Poem by Mikhail Eminescu

SPANISH
Martha and Mary Novel by Armando Palacio Valdés

UKRAINIAN
Zakhar Berkut Novel by Ivan Franko

1884

BIRTHS
Aleksandre Abasheli, Georgian poet and novelist
Gaddiel Robert Acquah, Ghana novelist and poet
Halide Edib Adivar, Turkish novelist
Johanna van Ammers-Küller, Dutch historian and novelist
Rafael Arévalo Martínez, Guatemalan novelist and short-story
   writer
Eduardo Barrios, Chilean writer
Yahya Kemal Beyatli, Turkish poet
George Duhamel, French novelist
Lion Feuchtwanger, German novelist
Abdurrauf Fitrat, Tajik-Uzbek novelist and satirist
Rómulo Gallegos, Venezuelan novelist
Ahmed Hasim, Turkish Symbolist poet
Jan van Nijlen, Flemish poet
Omar Seyfeddin, Turkish novelist
Angelos Sikelianós, Greek lyrical poet
Sri (B. M. Srikanthaya), Kannada poet
Su Manshu (Shu Jin), Chinese poet and novelist
Sir Hugh Walpole, New Zealand-born English novelist, play-
   wright, and critic
Yevgeny Ivanovich Zamyatin, Russian poet and playwright

DEATHS
Franz Emmanuel Geibel, German poet
Heinrich Laube, German playwright
Charles Reade, English novelist
Daniel Varuzhan, Armenian poet

LITERARY EVENT
First fascicle of the *Oxford English Dictionary* is published; last
   volume will not be printed until 1928

PUBLICATIONS
ENGLISH
American
The Adventures of Huckleberry Finn Novel by Mark Twain
The Lady or the Tiger? Collected short stories by Frank R.
   Stockton
Ramona Novel by Helen Hunt Jackson

British
Becket Dramatic tragedy by Alfred, Lord Tennyson
The Mikado Opera by W. S. Gilbert

Canadian
Old Spookses' Pass, Malcolm Katie and Other Poems Collection by
   Irish-born Isabella Valancy Crawford

FINNISH
The Railway Novel by Juhani Aho

FRENCH
French
Against the Grain Novel by Joris-Karl Huysmans
Jadis et Naguerre Collection of lyric poems by Paul Verlaine
L'Irréparable Novel by Paul Bourget
Nerto Epic poem by Frédéric Mistral
Sappho Novel by Alphonse Daudet
Vowels Collected sonnets by Arthur Rimbaud
Yesteryear and Yesterday Collected verse by Paul Verlaine

Swiss
Journal intime Diaries by Henri Frédéric Amiel

ITALIAN
Cavalleria rusticana Play by Giovanni Verga
The Intermezzo of Poems Collection of poems by Gabriele
   D'Annunzio

NORWEGIAN
The Wild Duck Tragicomedy by Henrik Ibsen
Aunt Virike Play by Gunnar Heiberg

POLISH
With Fire and Sword Historical novel by Henryk Sienkiewicz

ROMANIAN
A Lost Letter Play by Ion Luca Caragiale

SPANISH
Beside the River Sar Poems by Rosalía de Castro
The Regentess Novel by Leopoldo Alas

SWEDISH
Married Collection of short stories by August Strindberg

1885

BIRTHS
Muhammad Taqi Bahar, Persian poet
Dino Campana, Italian poet
Thomas Bertram Costain, American historical novelist
Isak Dinesen (Karen Christence Dinesen, Baroness Blixen), Dan-
   ish novelist
Ho Bieu Chanh (Ho Van Trung), Vietnamese novelist
Nikos Kazantzakis, Greek novelist

Velimir Vladimirovich Khlebnikov, Russian playwright, poet, and novelist
Kitahara Hakushu, Japanese poet
Dezsó Kosztolányi, Hungarian poet, novelist, and critic
Ring Lardner, American satirist
D. H. Lawrence, English novelist
Sinclair Lewis, American novelist
François Mauriac, French novelist and playwright
André Maurois (Emile Herzog), French novelist and biographer
Lekhnath Pandyal, Nepalese poet
Ezra Loomis Pound, American poet
Liviu Rebreanu, Romanian novelist and playwright
Jules Romains, French novelist, playwright, and poet
Sanatizade Kermani, Iranian novelist
Birger Sjöberg, Swedish poet
Vahan Terian (Ter-Grigorian), Armenian poet
Fritz von Unruh, German playwright, poet, and novelist
Anzia Yezierska, Russian-born American novelist

DEATHS
Edmund-François-Valentin About, French novelist
Rosalía de Castro, Galician novelist
Victor-Marie Hugo, French novelist
Susanna Strickland Moodie, English-born Canadian short-story writer

PUBLICATIONS
ARMENIAN
Samuel Novel by Hakob Malik Hakobian Raffi

ENGLISH
American
The Rise of Silas Lapham Novel by William Dean Howells

British
"Balin and Balan" Poem by Alfred, Lord Tennyson
Diana of the Crossways Novel by George Meredith
King Solomon's Mines Novel by Rider Haggard
Marius the Epicurean Philosophical romance by Walter Pater

Scottish
Child's Garden of Verses Collection of poems by Robert Louis Stevenson

Welsh
Autobiography of Rhys Lewis Novel by Daniel Owen

FRENCH
Axel Symbolist play by Philippe-Auguste de L'Isle-Adam
Bel ami Novel by Guy de Maupassant
Germinal Novel (part of *Les Rougon-Macquart* cycle) by Émile Zola
The Horla Short stories by Guy de Maupassant
Tomorrows Poems by Henri de Régnier
Woman of Paris Cynical comedy by Henry Becque

GERMAN
Austrian
Two Countesses Novel by Marie Baroness von Ebner-Eschenbach

RUSSIAN
Fables Collection of animal stories by Mikhail Saltykov
Makar's Dream Story by Vladimir Korolenko

SPANISH
Ecuadorean
Chapters Forgotten by Cervantes Comic piece by Juan Montalvo

1886

BIRTHS
Delmira Agustín, Uruguayan poet
Muhammad Taqi Bahar, Iranian poet and historian
Manuel Bandeira, Brazilian poet
Gottfried Benn, German poet and essayist
Herman Broch, Austrian playwright and novelist
Fernand Crommelynck, Belgian playwright
Nikolay Stepanovich Gumilyov, Russian poet
Ricardo Guiraldes, Argentine novelist
Maithilisharan Gupta, Hindi poet
Ishikawa Takuboku, Japanese poet
Alfred Joyce Kilmer, American poet
Hugh Lofting, American writer of children's books
Misak Metsarants, Armenian poet
Franz Rosenzweig, German Jewish religious writer
Siegfried Sassoon, English poet and novelist
Anempodist Ivanovich Sofronov, Yakut essayist and novelist
Wilbur Daniel Steele, American writer of short fiction
Gabdullah Takay, Turkish poet
Tanizaki Junichiro, Japanese novelist

DEATHS
Emily Dickinson, American poet
José Hernández, Argentine poet
Alexander Ostrovsky, Russian playwright
Leopold von Ranke, German historian
Josef Viktor von Scheffel, German poet and novelist
Leopold Zunz, German Jewish historian and scholar

PUBLICATIONS
ARMENIAN
The Tool Novel by Hakob Malik Hakobian Raffi

ENGLISH
American
The Bostonians Novel by Henry James
Indian Summer Novel by William Dean Howells
The Princess Casamassima Novel by Henry James

British
Demos Novel by George Gissing
Departmental Ditties Collection of mildly satiric verse by Rudyard Kipling
Little Lord Fauntleroy Play by Frances Hodgson Burnett
The Mayor of Castorbridge Novel by Thomas Hardy

Irish

Mosada Collected verse by William Butler Yeats

Scottish

Kidnapped Novel by Robert Louis Stevenson

The Strange Case of Dr. Jekyll and Mr. Hyde Novel by Robert Louis Stevenson

FRENCH

Belgian

The Monks Poems by Emile Verhaeren

The White Youthfulness Novel by Georges Rodenbach

French

The Fairy Council Collected verse by Jules Laforgue

Illuminations Prose poems by Arthur Rimbaud

The Imitation of Our Lady of the Moon Collected verse by Jules Laforgue

An Island Fisherman Novel by Pierre Loti

L'Eve Future Satiric novel by Philippe-Auguste Villiers de L'Isle Adam

GERMAN

Beyond Good and Evil: Prelude to a Philosophy of the Future Philosophical treatise by Friedrich Nietzsche

GREEK

Tragedy of My Country Poems by Kostis Palamas

ITALIAN

Heart of a Boy Series of sketches by Edmondo De Amicis

NORWEGIAN

Rosmersholm Play by Henrik Ibsen

POLISH

The Deluge Historical novel by Henryk Sienkiewicz

RUSSIAN

The Death of Ivan Ilyich Novella by Leo Tolstoy

SLOVAK

The Game-Keeper's Wife Novel by Hviezdoslav (Pal Orszagh)

SPANISH

Fortunata y Jacinta Four-volume novel by Benito Pérez Galdós

SWEDISH

The Son of a Servant Novel by August Strindberg

UKRAINIAN

Withered Leaves Collection of poems by Ivan Franko

1887

BIRTHS

Rupert Brooke, English poet

Blaise Cendrars (Frédéric Louis Sauser), Swiss-born French writer

Edna Ferber, American novelist

Martín Luis Guzmán, Mexican novelist

Robinson Jeffers, American poet

Pierre-Jean Jouve, French poet

Francis Ledwidge, Irish poet

René Maran, Martinique novelist

Marianne Moore, American poet

Samuel Eliot Morison, American historian

Salama Musa, Egyptian prose writer

Saint-John Perse (Marie-René-Auguste-Alexis Saint-Léger Léger), French poet

Edith Sitwell, English poet

Georg Trakl, Austrian poet

Alexander Woolcott, English writer

Arnold Zweig, German Jewish novelist

DEATHS

Isabella Valency Crawford, Canadian poet and novelist

Joseph Ignatius Kraszewski, Polish historical novelist

Jules Laforgue, French poet

Multatuli (Eduard Douwes Dekker), Dutch writer

PUBLICATIONS

DANISH

Children of Nature Collection of poems by Sophus Niels Christen Claussen

Stucco Novel by Hermann Bang

ENGLISH

American

The Minister's Charge; or, The Apprenticeship of Lemuel Barker Novel by William Dean Howells

British

Allan Quatermain Novel by H. Rider Haggard

Ballads and Poems of Tragic Life Collection of verse by George Meredith

The Deemster Novel by Hall Caine

She Novel by H. Rider Haggard

A Study in Scarlet Detective story by Arthur Conan Doyle

Woodlanders Novel by Thomas Hardy

FRENCH

Canadian

La Legende d'un Peuple Collected verse by Louis-Honoré Fréchette

French

La Tosca Play by Victorien Sardou

The Swans Collection of poems by American-born writer Francis Vielé-Griffin

GERMAN

Austrian

The Child of the Parish Novel by Maria, Baroness von Ebner Eschenbach

German

Dame Care Novel by Hermann Sudermann

JAPANESE
Ukigumo Novel by Shimei Futabatei

POLISH
Pan Michael Novel by Henryk Sienkiewicz

SPANISH
Mother Nature Novel by Emilia de Pardo Bazán
Noli Me Tangere Novel by Filipino writer José Rizal

SWEDISH
The Father Play by August Strindberg
Mrs. Marianne Novel by Victoria Benedictsson
The People of Hemso Novel by August Strindberg
Sensitiva Amorosa Collection of erotic sketches by Ola Hansson

1888

BIRTHS
Shmuel Yosef Agnon, Polish-born Israeli novelist
M. A. Aldanov (Mark Alexandrovich Landau), Russian novelist
Maxwell Anderson, American playwright
Dan Andersson, Swedish poet and novelist
Vicki Baum, Austrian novelist
Jean-Jacques Bernard, French playwright
George Bernanos, French Catholic novelist
Arthur Joyce Lunel Cary, Irish novelist
Raymond Chandler, American novelist
Nicolae Davidescu, Romanian poet and novelist
T. S. Eliot (Thomas Stearns Eliot), American-born English poet
Jacques Lacretelle, French novelist
Ghulam Ahmad Mahjur, Kashmiri Urdu poet
Katherine Mansfield, New Zealand novelist
Paul Morand, French novelist, poet, and essayist
Eugene Gladstone O'Neill, American playwright
Fernando Nogueira Pessoa, Portuguese poet and essayist
John Crowe Ransom, American poet and critic
Alan Seeger, American poet
Frans Eemil Sillanpaa, Finnish novelist
Tan Da (Nguyen Khac Hieu), Vietnamese poet
Giuseppe Ungaretti, Egyptian-born Italian poet

DEATHS
Louisa May Alcott, American novelist
Matthew Arnold, English poet and critic
Namik Kemal, Turkish poet
Eugene Labiche, French playwright
Raffi (Hakob Malik Hakobian), Armenian novelist
Theodor Storm, German poet and novelist

PUBLICATIONS
CZECH
F. L. Vek History by Alois Jirásek

ENGLISH
American
The Aspern Papers Novella by Henry James
Looking Backward Novel by Edward Bellamy

British
A Dream of John Ball Romantic fantasy by William Morris
"The Hound of Heaven" Poem by Francis Thompson
"The Man Who Would Be King" Story by Rudyard Kipling

FRENCH
Belgian
Les Débâcles Poems by Emile Verhaeren

French
"Amour" Poem by Paul Verlaine
The Cult of the Self Trilogy of novels by Maurice Barres
"Happiness" Poem by Sully Prudhomme

GERMAN
Austrian
Jakob der Letzte Novel by Peter Rosegger

German
Entanglements Novel by Theodore Fontane
Master Timpe Novel by Max Kretzen
The Rider on the White Horse Novella by Theodor Storm

NORWEGIAN
The Lady from the Sea Play by Henrik Ibsen

PORTUGUESE
The Maias Novel by José Maria Eça de Queirós

SPANISH
Nicaraguan
Blue Collection of poems by Rubén Darío

SWEDISH
Miss Julie One-act tragedy by August Strindberg
Pilgrimage and Wander Years Poems by Verner von Heidenstam

1889

BIRTHS
Conrad Aiken, American poet and novelist
Anna Akhmatova (Anna Andreyevna Gorenkjo), Russian poet
Hervey Allen, American novelist
Enid Bagnold, English novelist and playwright
Robert Charles Benchley, American humorist
Jean Cocteau, French playwright, novelist, and essayist
Maria Dabrowska, Polish writer and critic
Gunnar Gunnarsson, Icelandic novelist
Martin Heidegger, German philosopher
Yakup Kadri Karaosmanoglu, Turkish novelist and essayist
George Simon Kaufman, American playwright

Ibrahim al-Mazini, Egyptian novelist and poet
Claude McKay, Jamaican-born American poet
Sarah Gertrude Millin, South African novelist and writer of
    short stories
Gabriela Mistral (Lucila Godoy Alcayaga), Chilean poet
John Middleton Murry, English writer and critic
Pierre Reverdy, French poet and novelist
Alfonso Reyes, Mexican poet, short-story writer, and essayist
José Eustasio Rivera, Colombian poet and novelist
Marah Rusli, Indonesian novelist
Taha Hussain, Egyptian poet and prose writer
Vrindavanlal Varma, Indian Hindi novelist
Ben Ames Williams, American novelist and short-story writer

DEATHS

Ludwig Anzengruber, Austrian playwright and novelist
Emile Augier, French playwright
Jules-Amédee Barbey d'Aurevilly, French novelist
Robert Browning, English poet
Wilkie Collins, English novelist
Mikhail Eminescu, Romanian poet
Gerard Manley Hopkins, English poet
Juan Montalvo, Ecuadorean essayist
Mikhail Yefgrafovich Saltykov, Russian novelist and playwright
Auguste de Villiers de L'Isle-Adam, French playwright

PUBLICATIONS

DANISH

The Book of Songs Collection of poems by Holger Drachmann
Minna Novel by Karl Adolph Gjellerup
Tine Novel by Hermann Bang

DUTCH

Eline Vere Novel by Louis Marie Anne Couperus

ENGLISH

American

Annie Kilburn Novel by William Dean Howells
Chita: A Memory of Last Island Travel narrative by Lafcadio
    Hearn
A Connecticut Yankee in King Arthur's Court Fantasy by Mark
    Twain

British

Appreciations Prose collection by Walter Pater
Asolando Collection of poems by Robert Browning
"Crossing the Bar" Poem by Alfred, Lord Tennyson
Demeter and Other Poems Collection by Alfred, Lord Tennyson
The Profligate Play by Arthur Pinero
Sylvie and Bruno Children's story by Lewis Carroll
Three Men in a Boat Comic novel by Jerome K. Jerome

Canadian

Lake Lyrics and Other Poems Collection by William Wilfred
    Campbell

Irish

The Wanderings of Oisin Poems by William Butler Yeats

Scottish

The Master of Ballantrae Novel by Robert Louis Stevenson

FRENCH

Belgian

Hothouses Collection of poems by Maurice Maeterlinck

French

The Disciple Novel by Paul Bourget
The Joys Poems by American-born Francis Viélé-Griffin
Time and Freewill Philosophical treatise by Henri Bergson

GERMAN

Austrian

Lay Down Your Arms Novel by Bertha von Suttner

German

Before Dawn Play by Gerhart Hauptmann
Honor Dramatic work by Hermann Sudermann

Swiss

Butterflies Collection of lyrics by Carl Spitteler

ITALIAN

Mastro-don Gesualdo Novel by Giovanni Verga

JAPANESE

Amorous Confessions of Two Nuns Novel by Ozaki Kōyō
The Elegant Buddha Poetic tale by Kōda Rohan

NORWEGIAN

In God's Way Novel by Bjørnstjerne Martinius Bjørnson

SWEDISH

Pariah Play by August Strindberg

1890

BIRTHS

Iliya Abu Madi, Syrian-American poet
Oswald de Andrade, Brazilian poet, playwright, and novelist
Karel Čapek, Czech playwright
Agatha Christie, English novelist
Marc Connelly, American playwright
Walter Hasenclever, German playwright and poet
Paul Hazoume, Beninese novelist
Klabund (Alfred Henschke), German poet, novelist, and play-
    wright
Jigar Muradabadi, Urdu poet
Boris Pasternak, Russian lyric poet
Katherine Anne Porter, American short-story writer and novelist
Jean Rhys (Ella Gwendolyn Rees Williams), West Indian–born
    English novelist
B. Traven (Berwick Traven Torsvan), American-born German
    novelist

Franz Werfel, Czech-born Austrian Jewish poet and playwright
Stephan Zorian, Armenian novelist

DEATHS

Vasile Alecsandri, Romanian playwright and poet
Eduard von Bauernfeld, Austrian playwright
Dion Boucicault, Irish-born American playwright
Richard Burton, English explorer
Camilo Castelo Branco, Portuguese novelist
Carlo Collodi, Italian novelist
Caetano da Costa Alegre, Portuguese African poet
Gottfried Keller, Swiss novelist and poet
John Henry Newman, English essayist and Catholic cardinal

PUBLICATIONS

BENGALI

Mānasī Poems by Indian writer Rabindranath Tagore

DANISH

Clouds Novel by Henrik Pontappidan
Pledged Novel by Holger Drachmann

DUTCH

Verzen Collection of poems by Herman Gorter

ENGLISH

American

A Boy's Town Novel by William Dean Howells
A Hazard of New Fortunes Novel by William Dean Howells
Poems Collection by Emily Dickinson
The Tragic Muse Novel by Henry James

British

The Golden Bough Comparative study of beliefs and morals by
     James George Frazier
The Light That Failed Novel by Rudyard Kipling
News from Nowhere Novel by William Morris
The Picture of Dorian Gray Novel by Oscar Wilde
The Sign of Four Detective story starring Sherlock Holmes by
     Sir Arthur Conan Doyle

FRENCH

Belgian

The Black Torches Novel by Emile Verhaeren

French

Axel Dramatic prose poem by Auguste de Villiers de L'Isle Adam
Last Poems Collection by Jules Laforgue
The Life of Henry Brulard Unfinished novel by Stendhal
Queen Jane Historical tragedy by Frédéric Mistral
Thais Novel by Frédéric Mistral

GERMAN

Austrian

Inexpiable Novel by Maria, Baroness von Ebner-Eschenbach

German

The Coming of Peace Play by Gerhart Hauptmann

JAPANESE

The Perfumed Pillow Novel by Ozaki Kōyō

NORWEGIAN

Hedda Gabler Play by Henrik Ibsen
Hunger Novel by Knut Hamsun

ROMANIAN

The False Accusation Play by Ion Luca Caragiale

RUSSIAN

The Kreutzer Sonata Novel by Leo Tolstoy

SLOVAK

Ezo Vikolinsky Poems by Hviezdoslav

SPANISH

Cuban

Leaves in the Wind Poems by Julián del Casal

Spanish

His Only Sow Novel by Leopoldo Alas

SWEDISH

By the Open Sea Novel by August Strindberg
The Creditors Play by August Strindberg

1891

BIRTHS

Riccardo Bacchelli, Italian poet, playwright, and novelist
Mikhail Afanasevich Bulgakov, Russian novelist and play-
     wright
Ilya Ehrenburg, Russian novelist
Konstantine Gamsukhurdia, Georgian novelist
Sidney Coe Howard, American playwright
Hu Shi, Chinese scholar
Par Lagerkvist, Swedish poet, playwright and novelist
Osip Mandelstam, Russian poet
Henry Miller, American novelist
Kate Roberts, Welsh short-story writer
Nelly Sachs, German poet and playwright
Pedro Salinas, Spanish poet and playwright

DEATHS

Pedro Antonio de Alarcón, Spanish novelist and playwright
Theodore Faullain de Banville, French poet, playwright, and
     novelist
Ivan Alexandrovich Goncharov, Russian novelist
James Russell Lowell, American poet
Herman Melville, American novelist
Jan Neruda, Czech poet
Antero Tarquino de Quental, Portuguese poet
Arthur Rimbaud, French poet

PUBLICATIONS

CZECH
Between the Currents Novel by Alois Jirásek

ENGLISH

American

The Main Traveled Roads Collection of short stories by Hamlin Garland
"An Occurrence at Owl Creek Bridge" Short story by Ambrose Bierce
Tales of Soldier and Civilians Collection of short stories by Ambrose Bierce

British

The Adventures of Sherlock Holmes Collection of stories by Sir Arthur Conan Doyle
New Grub Street Novel by George Gissing
One of Our Conquerors Novel by George Meredith
Peter Ibbetson Novel by George du Maurier
Tess of the D'Urbervilles; A Pure Woman Novel by Thomas Hardy

Scottish

The Little Minister Novel by James M. Barrie

Welsh

The Trials of Enoc Huws Novel by Daniel Owen

FRENCH

Belgian

Along the Way Poems by Emile Verhaeren

French

Down There Novel by Joris-Karl Huysmans

GERMAN

Austrian

Yesterday Play by Hugo von Hofmansthal

German

Lonely Lives Play by Gerhart Hauptmann
Spring's Awakening Play by Frank Wedekind

JAPANESE
"The Five-Storied Pagoda" Short story by Kōda Rohan

NORWEGIAN
Tired Men Novel by Arne Garborg

PORTUGUESE

Brazilian

Philosopher or Dog? Novel by Joaquim Maria Machado de Assis

Portuguese

Hours Poems by Eugenio de Castro

SPANISH
El Filibusterismo Novel by Filipino José Rizal

SWEDISH
The Story of Gosta Berling Novel by Selma Lagerlöf

1892

BIRTHS
Ahmad Zaki Abu Shadi, Egyptian poet
Akutagawa Ryūnosuke, Japanese writer of short fiction
Richard Aldington, British poet and novelist
Ivo Andric, Yugoslav novelist
Djuna Barnes, American writer
Walter Benjamin, German critic
Ugo Betti, Italian playwright
Pearl S. Buck, American novelist
James M. Cain, American novelist
Ivy Compton-Burnett, English novelist
Bakary Diallo, Senegalese novelist
Janet Flanner, American novelist
Guo Moruo, Chinese writer
Léon Laleau, Haitian poet
Archibald MacLeish, American poet and playwright
Hugh McDiarmid (Christopher Murray Grieve), Scottish poet and critic
Endalkacaw Makonnen, Ethiopian novelist and playwright
Edna St. Vincent Millay, American poet
Muhammad Ali Jamalzadeh, Persian man of letters
Konstantin Georgievich Paustovsky, Russian novelist and playwright
Pham Quynh, Vietnamese scholar and translator
Elmer Rice (Elmer Reizenstein), American playwright
Satō Haruo, Japanese poet, novelist, and critic
Vita Sackville-West, English novelist and poet
W. Abraham Silva, Sinhalese novelist and short-story writer
Sir Francis Osbert Sitwell, English man of letters
Edith Irene Södergran, Russian-born Finnish-Swedish poet
Alfonsina Storni, Argentine poet
J. R. R. Tolkien, South African–born English novelist, poet, and writer of short fiction
Marina Ivanovna Tsvetayeva, Russian poet
Rusen Esref Unaydin, Turkish prose poet
Cesar Vallejo, Peruvian poet
Josef Weinheber, Austrian poet
Rebecca West, English novelist
Yoshikawa Eiji (Yoshikawa Hidetsugu), Japanese novelist

DEATHS
Afanasy Afanasyevich Fet, Russian poet
Judah Leon Gordon, Russian Jewish novelist and poet
Alexandros Rangabe, Greek scholar and playwright
Alfred, Lord Tennyson, English poet
Walt Whitman, American poet
John Greenleaf Whittier, American poet

PUBLICATIONS

DANISH
The Promised Land Novel by Henrik Pontoppidan

DUTCH

Ecstasy Novel by Louis Marie Anne Couperus

ENGLISH

American

The Monk and the Hangman's Daughter Medieval romance by
    Ambrose Bierce
Shore Acres Play by James A. Herne

British

Barrack-Room Ballads Collected verse of Rudyard Kipling
Lady Windermere's Fan Play by Oscar Wilde

Irish

The Countess Cathleen Historical play by William Butler Yeats

Scottish

The Beach of Falesa Long story by Robert Louis Stevenson

FRENCH

Belgian

Bruges, the Dead City Novel by Georges Rodenbach
Pelleas and Melissande Play by Maurice Maeterlinck

French

Autobiography of an Egotist Memoirs of Stendhal
Blanchette Play by Eugène Brieux
A False Saint Play by François de Curel

GERMAN

Austrian

The Death of Titian Play by Hugo von Hofmannsthal

German

The Weavers Play by German Gerhart Hauptmann

Swiss

Literary Parables Collection by Carl Spitteler

ITALIAN

The Intruder Novel by Gabriele D'Annunzio

MARATHI

Yasvantrav Khare Unfinished novel by Indian writer Hari Narayn
    Apte

NORWEGIAN

The Master Builder Play by Henrik Ibsen
Mysteries Novel by Knut Hamsun
Nameless Poem by Sigbjørn Obstfelder
Peace Novel by Arne Garborg

POLISH

Mr. Balcer in Brazil Story by Marja Konopnicka

PORTUGUESE

Alone Poems by Antonio Nobre

RUSSIAN

"Ward Number Six" Short story by Anton Chekhov

1893

BIRTHS

Faith Baldwin, American novelist
Martin à Beckett Boyd, Australian novelist
Frank A. Collymore, Barbadian poet
Pierre Drieu La Rochelle, French novelist and poet
Carlo Emilio Gadda, Italian novelist
Jorge Guillén, Spanish poet
Vicente Huidobro, Chilean poet
Nur Sultan Iskander, Indonesian novelist
Sergo Kldiashvili, Georgian poet
Miroslav Krleza, Yugoslav playwright and novelist
John Phillips Marquand, American novelist
Vladimir Mayakovsky, Russian poet, playwright, and essayist
Wilfred Owen, English poet
Dorothy Parker, American poet, short-story writer, and critic
I. A. Richards, English critic and poet
Dorothy Sayers, English writer
Viktor Borisovich Shklovsky, Russian critic and novelist
Ernst Toller, German Jewish playwright and novelist
Maria Pawlikowska-Jasnor Zewska, Polish poet
Zhiang Ziping, Chinese novelist

DEATHS

Kawatake Mokuami, Japanese playwright
Guy de Maupassant, French novelist and short story writer
Philip Shaff, Swiss-born American Presbyterian theologian and
    encyclopedist
John Addington Symonds, English poet and historian
Hippolyte-Adolphe Taine, French literary critic, historian, and
    essayist
José Zorrilla y Moral, Spanish playwright, poet, and novelist

PUBLICATIONS

BENGALI

The Golden Boat Stories by Indian writer Rabindranath Tagore

BULGARIAN

Under the Yoke Novel by Ivan Yazov

ENGLISH

American

Can Such Things Be? Collection of short stories by Ambrose
    Bierce
Maggie: A Girl of the Streets Novel by Stephen Crane
The World of Chance Autobiographical novel by William Dean
    Howells

British

"The Hound of Heaven" Poem by Francis Thompson
The Second Mrs. Tanqueray Play by Arthur Pinero

Irish

The Bog of Stars Historical novel by Standish O'Grady
Mrs. Warren's Profession Play by George Bernard Shaw
Salome Melodramatic play by Oscar Wilde

FRENCH
Belgian

The Moonstruck Countrysides Collected verse by Emile Verhaeren

The Right of the Strongest Novel by Cyril Buyesse

French

Bouborouche Farce by George Courteline
The Guest Play by François de Corel
Les Trophées Sonnets by Cuban-born José María de Heredia
Madame Devil-May-Care Play by Victorien Sardou and Emile Moreau
The Ride of Eldis Collected verse of Francis Vielé-Griffin
Théroigne de Méricourt Play by Paul-Ernest Hervieu

GERMAN
Austrian

Death and the Fool Play by Hugo von Hofmannsthal

German

The Beaver Coat Dramatic comedy by Gerhart Hauptmann
When Love Is Young Play by Max Halbe

HUNGARIAN
The Gyurkovics Girls Novel by Ferenc Herczeg

MARATHI
Mi Novel by Indian writer Hari Narayan Apte

PORTUGUESE
Brazilian

Missal Poems by João Cruze Sousa
Shields Poems by João Cruze Sousa

TAMIL
Kamalampal; or, The Fatal Rumor Novel by B. R. Rajam Iyer

1894

BIRTHS
Isaac Babel, Russian Jewish writer
Bibhutibhushan Bandyopadhyay, Bengali novelist
Louis-Ferdinand Céline (Louis-Ferdinand Destouches), French novelist and playwright
e. e. cummings, American poet
Dashiell Hammett, American novelist
Ben Hecht, American playwright
Aldous Huxley, English novelist
Jaroslav Iwaszkiewicz, Polish poet, novelist, playwright, and essayist
Berdi Kerbabayev, Turkmen novelist
John Ebenezer Clare McFarlane, Jamaican poet
Ngo Tat To, Vietnamese narrative writer and translator
Martinus Nijhoff, Dutch poet
Boris Pilnyak (Boris Andreyevich Vogau), Russian novelist
J. B. Priestley, English novelist

Abdullo Quodiriy, Uzbek novelist and satirist
Mahmud Taymur, Egyptian novelist
Dorothy Thompson, American journalist
James Thurber, American humorist
Kasimierz Wierzynski, Polish poet
Ye Shengtao, Chinese novelist

DEATHS
Bankim Chandra Chatterjee, Indian novelist
Oliver Wendell Holmes, American essayist, novelist, and poet
Charles-Marie-René Leconte de Lisle, French Parnassian poet
Walter Pater, English essayist and critic
Christina Rossetti, English poet
Robert Louis Stevenson, Scottish novelist

PUBLICATIONS
CZECH
Against All the World Novel by Alois Jirasell

DANISH
Night Guard Short novel by Henrik Pontoppidan

ENGLISH
American

Bayou Folk Collection of short stories by Kate Chopin
The Tragedy of Pudd'nhead Wilson Novel by Mark Twain
A Traveler from Altruria Novel by William Dean Howells

British

The Curse of Rebellious Susan Play by Henry Arthur Jones
Jude the Obscure Novel by Thomas Hardy
The Jungle Book Collection of stories from India by Rudyard Kipling
The King of Schnorrers Novel by Israel Zangwill
Lord Ormont and His Aminta Novel by George Meredith
The Maxman Novel by Hall Caine
The Memoirs of Sherlock Holmes Collection of detective stories by Sir Arthur Conan Doyle
The Prisoner of Zenda Novel by Anthony Hope
Trilby Novel by George du Maurier

Irish

Arms and the Man Comedy in three acts by George Bernard Shaw
Esther Waters Novel by George Moore
The Land of Heart's Desire Play in verse by William Butler Yeats

Scottish

Ballads and Songs Verse drama by John Davidson

FRENCH
The Book of Monelle Biographical study by Marcel Schwob
Carrot Top Novel by Jules Renard
The Half Virgins Novel by Marcel Prévost
Lucien Leuwen Autobiographical narrative by Stendhal

GERMAN
The Assumption of Hanneles Play by Gerhart Hauptmann

ITALIAN
The Triumph of Death Novel by Gabriele D'Annunzio

NORWEGIAN
The Balcony Play by Gunnar Heiberg
Little Eyolf Play by Henrik Ibsen
Pan Novel by Knut Hamsun

RUSSIAN
"The Black Monk" Short story by Anton Chekhov

SPANISH
Uruguayan
Solitude Novel by Eduardo Acevedo Díaz

SWEDISH
New Poems Collection by Gustaf Fröding

1895

BIRTHS
Corrado Alvaro, Italian novelist
Michael Arlen (Dikran Kouyoumdjian), Bulgarian-born English
    writer
Mikhail Bakhtin, Russian philosopher
Paul Éluard (Eugène Grindel), French poet
Omar Fakhuri, Lebanese essayist
Jean Giono, French novelist
Gilbert Gratiant, Martinique poet
Robert Graves, English poet and novelist
Juana de Ibarbourou, Uruguayan poet
Mohammad Ali Jamalzadeh, Iranian writer of short stories
David Jones, Welsh poet
Ernest Junger, German novelist and essayist
F. R. Leavis, English scholar and critic
Charles MacArthur, American playwright
Ezequiel Martínez Estrada, Argentine writer
Davith Stefansson, Icelandic poet
Titsian Tabisze, Georgian poet
Edmund Wilson, American critic
Sergey Aleksandrovich Yesenin, Russian poet
Mari Ziyada, Lebanese-born Egyptian critic and translator
Albin Zollinger, Swiss poet and novelist

DEATHS
Alexander Dumas fils, French playwright
Friedrich Engels, German political philosopher
Eugene Field, American poet
Gustav Freytag, German novelist and playwright
Jens Peter Jacobsen, Danish novelist and essayist
Nikolay Semyonovich Leskov, Russian novelist and short-story
    writer
José Martí, Cuban poet
Hugh Andrew Johnstone Munro, English scholar in Latin
Akhilléfs Paráskhos, Greek poet
Viktor Rydberg, Swedish writer

PUBLICATIONS

DANISH
The Old Adam Short novel by Henrik Pontoppidan

DUTCH
Song of Semblance and Substance Poem by Frederik Eeden

ENGLISH
American
The Red Badge of Courage Novel by Stephen Crane

British
The Amazing Marriage Novel by George Meredith
The Time Machine Novel by H. G. Wells

Irish
The Importance of Being Earnest Dramatic farce by Oscar Wilde

FRENCH
En Route Novel by Joris-Karl Huysman
The New Idol Play by François de Curel

GERMAN
Earth Spirit Play by Frank Wedekind
Effi Briest Novel by Theodor Fontane

JAPANESE
Growing Up Stories by Higuchi Ichiyo

NORWEGIAN
Pa St. Jorgen Novel by Amalie Bertha Skram

POLISH
Quo Vadis? Novel by Henryk Sienkiewicz

RUSSIAN
"Chelkash" Short story by Maxim Gorky

SPANISH
Juanita la Larga Novel by Juan Valera
Nazarín Novel by Benito Pérez Galdós

SWEDISH
Poems Collection by Verner von Heidenstam
Songs of Wilderness and Love Collection of poems by Andreas
    Karlfeldt

UKRAINIAN
Pillars of Society Novel by Ivan Franko

1896

BIRTHS
Antonin Artaud, French playwright and surrealist poet
Edmund Blunden, English poet and critic
André Breton, French poet and critic

Louis Bromfield, American novelist
A. J. Cronin, Scottish novelist
Heimito von Doderer, Austrian writer
John Dos Passos, American novelist
F. Scott Fitzgerald, American novelist
Jacob Glatstein, Yiddish poet and novelist
Vahe Haik (Vahe Tinchian), Armenian novelist and poet
Kostas Karyotakis, Greek poet
Guiseppe Tomasi di Lampedusa, Italian novelist
Mao Dun, Chinese novelist
Eugenio Montale, Italian poet
Henry de Montherlant, French novelist and playwright
Said Nafisi, Iranian novelist
Liam O'Flaherty, Irish novelist and short-story writer
Paul van Ostaijen, Belgian man of letters
Marjorie Kinnan Rawlings, American novelist
Manuel Rojas, Chilean novelist and short-story writer
Robert E. Sherwood, American playwright
Nikolay Semyonovich Tikhonov, Russian poet
Tristan Tzara (Samuel Rosenfeld), Romanian-born French poet
Josef Wittlin, Polish novelist, poet, and essayist
Xu Zhimo, Chinese poet
Rashid Yasami, Iranian historian
Yu Dafu, Chinese short-story writer
Carl Zuckmayer, German playwright and poet

DEATHS

João de Deus, Portuguese lyric poet
Edmond de Goncourt, French diarist, novelist, and playwright
Thomas Hughes, British novelist
Ichiyo Higachi, Japanese novelist
William Morris, English poet, essayist, printer, and designer
Coventry Patmore, British poet
José Rizal, Filipino poet
José Asunción Silva, Colombian poet
Harriet Beecher Stowe, American novelist and abolitionist
Paul Verlaine, French poet

PUBLICATIONS

BENGALI

Late Harvest Collection of stories by Indian writer Rabindranath Tagore

DANISH

High Song Short novel by Henrik Pontoppidan
Ida Brandt Novel by Hermann Bang

ENGLISH

American

The Country of the Pointed Firs Novel by Sarah Orne Jewett
Lyrics of Lowly Life Collection of verse by Paul Lawrence Dunbar
The Personal Recollections of Joan of Arc Romantic narrative by Mark Twain

British

The Island of Dr. Moreau Science fiction novel by H. G. Wells
Michael and His Lost Angel Play by Henry Arthur Jones
A Shropshire Lad Poetic cycle by A. E. Housman

To an Athlete Dying Young Poem by A. E. Housman
Verses Collection of poems by Ernest Dowson

Scottish

The Weir of Hermiston Novel by Robert Louis Stevenson

FRENCH

Belgian

The Sunlit Hours Collected verse of Emile Verhaeren

French

The Book of Masques Critical essays by Rémy de Gourmont
King Ubu Farce by Alfred Jarry
Matter and Memory Philosophical treatise by Henri Bergson

GERMAN

Austrian

Free Game Play by Arthur Schnitzler
Playing with Love Play by Arthur Schnitzler

ITALIAN

The Little World of the Past Novel by Antonio Fogazzaro
The Maidens of the Rocks Novel by Gabriele D'Annunzio

JAPANESE

Tears and Regrets Novel by Ozaki Kōyō

POLISH

The Comedienne Novel by Władysław Reymont

PORTUGUESE

Salome and Other Poems Collection by Eugenio de Castro

RUSSIAN

Christ and Antichrist Novel by Dmitry Sergeyevich Merezhkovsky
The Seagull Play by Anton Chekhov

SPANISH

Nicaraguan

Profane Hymns and Other Poems Collection by Rubén Darío

1897

BIRTHS

Mukhtar Auezov, Kazakh playwright
Georges Bataille, French novelist and poet
Władysław Broniewski, Polish poet
Nirod C. Chaudhuri, Indian historian and critic
Bernard De Voto, American novelist, historian, and critic
William Faulkner, American novelist
Valentin Petrovich Katayev, Russian poet and playwright
Alfred H. Mendes, Trinidadian novelist
Sacheverell Sitwell, English poet and art critic
Philippe Soupault, French poet, novelist, and critic
Yegishe Tcharents, Armenian poet

Thornton Wilder, American playwright and novelist
Nima Yushij, Iranian poet

DEATH
Alphonse Daudet, French novelist

PUBLICATIONS
ENGLISH
American

Children of the Night Collected verse by Edward Arlington Robinson
Desire's Baby Novel by Kate Chopin
Following the Equator Travel narrative by Mark Twain
The Landlord at Lion's Head Novel by William Dean Howells
A Night in Acadie Collection of stories by Kate Chopin
Richard Cory Collected verse by Edward Arlington Robinson
The Spoils of Poynton Novel by Henry James
What Maisie Knew Novel by Henry James

British

Captains Courageous Novel by Rudyard Kipling
The Invisible Man Novel by H. G. Wells
The Liars Play by Henry Arthur Jones
Liza of Lambeth Novel by W. Somerset Maugham
The Nigger of the "Narcissus" Novel by Joseph Conrad

Canadian

The Habitant and Other French-Canadian Poems Collection by Irish-born William Henry Drummond

Irish

Dracula Gothic horror story by Bram Stoker
The Flight of the Eagle Historical novel by Standish O'Grady

FINNISH
Panu Long novel by Juhani Aho

FRENCH
The Brightness of Life Collection of poems by Francis Vielé Griffin
Cyrano de Bergerac Play by Edmond Rostand
The Elm Tree in the Mall Novel by Anatole France
Games—Tough and Divine Collection of poems by Henri de Régnier
Joan of Arc Dramatic trilogy by Charles Péguy
The Lion's Meal Play by François de Curel
The Song of the Rhone Collection of poems by Frédéric Mistral
The Wicker Work Woman Novel by Anatole France
The Woman Who Was Poor Novel by Léon Bloy

GERMAN
Austrian

The Little Theater of the World Play by Hugo von Hofmannsthal
Madonna Dianora Play by Hugo von Hofmannsthal
Merry-Go-Round Play by Arthur Schnitzler
The White Fan Play by Hugo von Hofmannsthal

German

The Jews of Zirndorf Novel by Jakob Wasserman
The Year of the Soul Collection of poems by Stefan George

GREEK
The Graves Collected verse by Kostis Palamas
Iambs and Anapaests Collection of poems by Kostis Palamas

ICELANDIC
Stories and Poems Collected verse by Einar Benediktsson

JAPANESE
The Golden Demon Novel by Ozaki Kōyō

NORWEGIAN
In the Days of the Counselor Collection of short stories by Trygve Andersen
The People's Council Play by Gunnar Heiberg

POLISH
The Meeting Novel by Władysław Reymont

RUSSIAN
Uncle Vanya Play by Anton Chekhov

SPANISH
Argentine
Mountains of Gold Collection of poems by Leopoldo Lagones

Chilean
During the Reconquest Novel by Alberto Blest Gana

Spanish
Compassion Novel by Benito Pérez Galdós

SWEDISH
Inferno Autobiographical narrative by August Strindberg
The Miracles of Antichrist Novel by Selma Lagerlöf

TELUGU
Bride Price Social play by Indian writer Gurajtada Venkata Appa Rao

1898

BIRTHS
Vicente Aleixandre, Spanish poet
Damaso Alonso, Spanish poet
Stephen Vincent Benét, American poet and novelist
Bertolt Brecht, German poet and playwright
José Maria de Castro, Portuguese novelist
Rosa Chacel, Spanish novelist
Harindranath Chattopadhyay, Bengali prose writer and playwright
Malcolm Cowley, American critic
Federico García Lorca, Spanish poet and playwright

Michel de Ghelderode, Flemish poet and playwright
Tawfiq Husayn al-Hakim, Egyptian playwright and novelist
C. S. Lewis, English novelist and Christian apologist
Curzio Malaparte (Kurt Erich Suckert), Italian playwright, short-story writer, and novelist
Masuji Ibuse, Japanese novelist
Vilhelm Moberg, Swedish novelist
Luis Palés Matos, Puerto Rican poet and novelist
Erich Maria Remarque, German novelist
Tian Han, Chinese playwright
Simon Vesldijk, Dutch novelist
Yokomitsu Riichi, Japanese novelist
Alexander Raban Waugh, English novelist

DEATHS

Edward Bellamy, American writer
Lewis Carroll, English writer of children's stories
Georg Moritz Ebers, German novelist and Egyptologist
Theodor Fontane, German poet and novelist
Stephen Mallarmé, French poet
Conrad Ferdinand Meyer, Swiss poet and novelist
Georges Rodenbach, Belgian symbolist poet
Manuel Tamayo y Baus, Spanish playwright

LITERARY EVENT

American Academy of Arts and Letters is founded

PUBLICATIONS

DANISH

Lucky Peter First of eight-volume novel (completed in 1904) by Henrik Pontoppidan

ENGLISH

American

David Harum: A Story of American Life Novel by Edward Westcott
"The Open Boat" Short story by Stephen Crane
The Turn of the Screw Novel by Henry James

British

Children of the Mist Novel by Eden Phillpotts
Stories Toto Told Me Collected stories by Frederick Rolfe
Trelawney of the "Wells" Play by Sir Arthur Wang Pinero
The War of the Worlds Science fiction by H. G. Wells
Wessex Poems Collection by Thomas Hardy

Irish

Arms and the Man Play by George Bernard Shaw
The Ballad of Reading Gaol Poem by Oscar Wilde
Candida Play by George Bernard Shaw

FRENCH

"J'Accuse" Letter by Émile Zola
La Cathédrale Novel by Joris-Karl Huysmans
Phocas the Gardener Collection of poems by Francis Vielé-Griffin

GERMAN

German

Drayman Henschel Play by Gerhart Hauptmann

Swiss

Conrad der Leutnant Novel by Carl Spitteler

ITALIAN

The Children of Pleasure Novel by Gabriele D'Annunzio

NORWEGIAN

Victoria Novel by Knut Hamsun

POLISH

The Wild Rose Bush Collection of poems by Jan Kasprowicz

SPANISH

Mexican

Black Pearls Poems by Amado Nervo

SWEDISH

Fridolin's Songs Collection of poems by Andreas Karlfeldt
Splashes of Grail Poems by Gustav Fröding
Tales of a Manor Collection by Selka Lagerlöf
To Damascus Play by August Strindberg

1899

BIRTHS

Louis Adamic, Slovenian novelist
Marcel Arland, French novelist
Miguel Angel Asturias, Guatemalan novelist
Jacques Audiberti, French playwright, poet, and novelist
Aksel Bakunts (Aleksandr Tevosian), Armenian novelist
Jorge Luis Borges, Argentine novelist
Elizabeth Bowen, English novelist
Noël Coward, English playwright
Hart Crane, American poet
C. S. Forester, English historical novelist
Guido Gezelle, Flemish poet
Ernest Miller Hemingway, American novelist and short-story writer
Jaffar Jabbarly, Azerbaijani poet and playwright
Erich Kastner, German novelist, playwright, and poet
Kawabata Yasunari, Japanese novelist
R. Krishnamurthi, Tamil novelist
Jan Lechon, Polish poet
Dame Ngaio Marsh, New Zealand novelist
Hendrik Marsman, Dutch poet
Henri Michaux, Belgian-born French poet
Vladimir Vladimirovich Nabokov, Russian-born American novelist
Nazrul Islam, Bengali Muslim poet
Payrav (Otajon Sulaymoni), Tajik poet
Benjamin Peret, French poet and essayist
Allen Tate, American poet and critic
Theippam Maun Wa, Burmese playwright and novelist
Wen Yiduo, Chinese poet and critic
E. B. White, American essayist and novelist

DEATH

Guido Gezelle, Belgian poet

PUBLICATIONS

CZECH

Brotherhood Novel by Alois Jirasek

DANISH

The Holy Flame Poems by Holger Henrik Herholdt Drachmann
Willow Pipes Poems by Sophus Niels Christen Claussen

ENGLISH

American

Active Service Novel by Stephen Crane
The Awakening Novel by Kate Chopin
The Awkward Age Novel by Henry James
"The Man That Corrupted Hadleyburg" Short story by Mark Twain
The Man with the Hoe and Other Poems Collected verse by Edwin Markham
McTeague Novel by Frank Norris
Richard Carvel Novel by Winston Churchill
"The Yellow Wallpaper" Short story by Charlotte Perkins Gilman

FRENCH

Belgian

The Faces of Life Collection of poems by Emile Verhaeren

French

The Amethyst Ring Novel by Anatole France
The Dying Earth Novel by René Bazin
The Lady from Maxim's Humorous dramatic piece by Georges Feydeau

Les Stances Collection of poems by Greek-born Jean Moreas
Mademoiselle Cloque Novel by René Boylesve

GERMAN

Austrian

The Adventurer and the Singer Play by Hugo von Hofmannsthal
The Interpretation of Dreams Psychological treatise by Sigmund Freud
The Marriage of Sobeide Play by Hugo von Hofmannsthal

GREEK

The Beggar Novel by Andreas Karkavitsas

ITALIAN

In Praise of Sky, Sea, Earth and Heroes Poems by Gabriele D'Annunzio

NORWEGIAN

When We Dead Awaken Play by Henrik Ibsen

PORTUGUESE

Brazilian

Don Casamuro Novel by Joaquim Machado de Assis

Portuguese

Longings for Heaven Collection of poems by Eugenio de Castro

RUSSIAN

Resurrection Novel by Leo Tolstoy
"Twenty-Six Men and a Girl" Short story by Maxim Gorky

SWEDISH

Gustav Vasa Play by August Strindberg
The Saga of the Folkungs Play by August Strindberg

THE TWENTIETH CENTURY

The 20th century poses a special challenge to the literary historian. Narrow and sometimes shallow streams of national literatures merged into a virtual Amazon. One of the characteristics of the century was that, at least in literature, the word *national* became somewhat imprecise and outdated. Literary traditions overlapped; authors themselves were of mixed national heritage or were born in one country but wrote in the language of another; émigrés and expatriates became a large literary community within many Western countries.

Quantitatively, world literature has become so large that it defies any attempt to place it within neat categories. At the beginning of the 20th century approximately 4,000 literary works were published throughout the world in any one year. Only about 20 countries had a literary establishment of authors, editors, publishers, printers, and book reviewers. By the end of the century, according to the United Nations Educational, Scientific, and Cultural Organization (UNESCO), more than 130,000 literary works of all kinds and genres were published every year, and more than 110 countries had a fully developed literary establishment. Despite dire predictions about the death of print and the growing seductions of the electronic media, literature has become a colossus in its own right and is likely to remain so for the foreseeable future.

Qualitative changes also took place between the beginning of the 20th century and its end. One change was postcolonialism, a post–World War II phenomenon. More than 90 former colonial nations became independent between 1945 and 1990, but most of them retained the language of their former subjugators. Thus many writers in ex-French colonies of Africa continued to write in French, and many in the Indian subcontinent and former English colonies of Africa continued to write in English. As a result, the boundaries of Western literatures actually expanded even as the former imperial domains shrank. Some of the best writers in English are now found in India or Trinidad; some of the best in French, in Algeria or Senegal.

Another change in the 20th century was the gradual decline of European literature. Ruling political ideologies that dominated 20th-century Europe were antiliterary, particularly national socialism in Germany and communism in the Soviet Union and Eastern Europe. In addition, the growing Anglicization of world literature—as the lingua franca of the modern world, English is now in the same position as Latin was in the Middle Ages—led to a decline in other languages and even a slow death for some in Asia and Africa. According to *Ethnologue,* a record of the world's languages, more than 4,000 of the world's current 6,000 written languages will die out within the 21st century. Many unique literary traditions will die with them.

In literature, the early years of the 20th century were not markedly different from the late 19th century: Such authors as Joseph Conrad, Thomas Hardy, Henry James, and D. H. Lawrence, for example, employed conventional techniques and themes in their novels. The winds of change in themes, narrative techniques, and linguistic idioms began to blow with Marcel Proust's *Remembrance of Things Past* (1913), James Joyce's *Ulysses* (1922), André Gide's *Vatican Cellars* (1914), Franz Kafka's *The Trial* (published posthumously in 1925), and Thomas Mann's *Magic Mountain* (1924). A shift away from 19th-century styles and assumptions began with André Breton's *Manifesto of Surrealism* (1924), which called for spontaneity and a complete rupture with tradition. Surrealism reflected the influence of Sigmund Freud and his theories of the subconscious mind. In literature surrealism produced fantastic and incongruous imagery through unnatural juxtapositions and combinations. The uncertainty of the new century and the variety of attempts to give it some artistic coherence can be seen in Rainer Maria Rilke's *Sonnets to Orpheus* (1923), T. S. Eliot's *The Waste Land* (1922), and Luigi Pirandello's *Henry IV* (1922).

Since World War II, the cumulative pressures of disturbing social and political developments, along with the rise of technology, have changed the status of great literature in society.

Writers no longer carry the same authority they did in earlier centuries, nor do they have the commanding voice that made their forebears revered not merely as writers but as sages. Ironically, the rise of a global culture has helped to devalue literary tastes and traditions even as literacy and reading rates have risen. There are hosts of good, even brilliant middle-level writers, but few great ones at the top.

Major Writers of the Twentieth Century

James Joyce (1882–1941) Irish writer noted for his experimental prose and exploration of the human psyche in his classic works, such as *Ulysses* (1922) and *Finnegan's Wake* (1939). *Dubliners,* his first collection of stories, appeared in 1914. In 1916 he rewrote an earlier manuscript about his own life and published it as *A Portrait of the Artist as a Young Man.* The same year he also began working on *Ulysses,* but financial and physical problems slowed him down. Published in 1922 by Shakespeare & Company, an English-language bookshop in Paris, the novel immediately was accused of obscenity and faced censorship. He spent the last years of his life writing *Finnegan's Wake.* In both style and narrative form, Joyce pushed the boundaries more than any other author.

Franz Kafka (1883–1924) Czech-born writer in German whose metaphysically rich and symbolic novels explored the existential human condition. Each of his novels was a metaphor with which he tried to grasp essentially ungraspable truths. Kafka was born into a middle-class Jewish family in Prague, then part of the Austro-Hungarian Empire, but as an adolescent he declared himself an atheist and a socialist, and throughout life he was isolated from the Jewish community and its traditions. Only a few of his books were published during his lifetime. These included *Meditation* (1913), *The Judgment* (1916), *Metamorphosis* (1916), *In the Penal Colony* (1919), *A Country Doctor* (1919), and *A Hunger Artist* (1924). Misgivings about his work caused Kafka to request that his literary executor, Max Brod, destroy all his unpublished writings. Brod disregarded this request and published four of Kafka's greatest books: *The Trial* (1925), *The Castle* (1926), *Amerika* (1927), and a collection of shorter pieces, *The Great Wall of China* (1931).

Thomas Stearns Eliot (1888–1965) Anglo-American poet; winner of the Nobel Prize in literature in 1948. T. S. Eliot was born in St. Louis, Missouri, and studied at Harvard, but in 1914 he moved to England and became a British subject in 1927. His first important poem—and the first modernist masterpiece in English—was "The Love Song of J. Alfred Prufrock" (1917). In 1919 he published *Poems* containing "Gerontion," a meditative interior monologue in blank verse.

The Waste Land (1922) portrayed the shallowness of modern civilization devoid of its moral moorings. Between 1936 and 1942 he published *The Four Quartets.* Eliot also made his mark as a playwright. His best play was *Murder in the Cathedral* (1935) on the murder of Saint Thomas à Becket, but *Sweeney Agonistes* (1932) and *The Cocktail Party* (1950) also were well received. Eliot's critical works appear in *The Sacred Wood* (1920), *The Use of Poetry and the Use of Criticism* (1933), *The Idea of a Christian Society* (1939), and *Notes Toward the Definition of Culture* (1948).

William Butler Yeats (1865–1939) Irish poet and playwright; winner of the Nobel Prize in literature in 1923. Born into an Anglo-Irish Protestant family, Yeats lived in both Dublin and London. His early poems, collected in *Wanderings of Oisin and Other Poems* (1889), revealed his interest in Platonic, Neoplatonic, and alchemical traditions. His life changed in 1898 when he met Isabella Augusta, Lady Gregory, who shared his interest in the pagan folklore of Ireland. Together they founded the Irish Literary Theatre (later known as Abbey Theatre), which gave its first performance in Dublin in 1899 with Yeats's *The Countess of Cathleen.* Throughout his life he contributed many plays to the theater, including *The Land of Heart's Desire* (1894), *The Hour Glass* (1903), *The King's Threshold* (1904), *On Baile's Strand* (1905), and *Deirdre* (1907). Between 1909 and 1914 his plays and poems took on a new maturity, and his imagery became more sparse and resonant. From then until 1939, when his last verse collection, *Last Poems and Two Plays,* appeared, his inspiration never faltered, and he perfected his technique constantly. Notable among his poetry and plays of this period were *Responsibilities: Poems and a Play* (1914); *The Wild Swans at Coole* (1917); the poems "Sailing to Byzantium," "The Second Coming," and "Easter 1916"; and the collections *The Tower* (1928), *The Winding Stair* (1929), and *New Poems* (1938). Under the influence of the Japanese Nō drama, Yeats produced *Four Plays for Dancers* (1921) and *At the Hawk's Well* (1916).

Thomas Mann (1875–1955) German novelist; winner of the Nobel Prize in literature in 1929. He is noted for his finely crafted stories enriched by humor, irony, and parody and sustained by a many-layered narrative. His masterpieces were *Death in Venice* (1912), the somber story of a dying artist, and the long novel *The Magic Mountain* (1924), a bildungsroman recounting the formative years of Hans Castorp, an introspective engineer recuperating in a tuberculosis sanatorium in the Davos Mountains in Switzerland. His first novel, *Buddenbrooks* (1901), was followed by two novellas, *Tonio Kroger* and *Tristan* (both 1903). During the interwar years he wrote *Early Sorrow* (1926), *Mario and the Magician* (1930), and *Joseph and His Brothers* (1933), a tetralogy, as well as *The Beloved Returns* (1939). After World War II, he resumed his writing with *Doctor Faustus* (1947), *The Holy Sinner* (1951), *The Black Swan* (1953), and *Felix Krull* (1954).

George Bernard Shaw (1856–1950) Irish playwright; winner of the Nobel Prize in literature in 1925. Shaw was not only a great playwright but also a lively personality, a spellbinding orator, and a polemicist who loved to pick fights. A socialist, he used the theater as a forum for his ideas, and in plays he adopted an ironic comedic tone as the best means of prodding his audience to face unpleasant facts. His first play was the little-known *Widower's Houses* (1893), followed by *Mrs. Warren's Profession, Arms and the Man, Candida, The Man of Destiny,* and *You Never Can Tell* (all 1898). His great plays were produced in the first three decades of the new century: *Three Plays for Puritans, The Devil's Disciple, Caesar and Cleopatra,* and *Captain Brassbound's Conversion* (all 1901); *Man and Superman* (1903); *John Bull's Other Island* and *Major Barbara* (both 1907); *The Doctor's Dilemma* (1911); *Pygmalion* (1914); *Androcles and the Lion* (1916); and *Heartbreak House* (1919). The five linked plays under the collective title *Back to Methuselah* expounded his philosophy of creative evolution. His last two plays were *Saint Joan* (1924) and *The Apple Cart* (1930).

Ernest Miller Hemingway (1899–1961) American novelist and short-story writer; winner of the Nobel Prize in literature in 1954. His first important novel, *The Sun Also Rises,* appeared in 1926. Hemingway traveled widely and was an avid outdoorsman who engaged in skiing, hunting, fishing, and bullfighting, which provided the grist for many of his stories. Bullfighting was the subject for his nonfiction work *Death in the Afternoon* (1932) and an African safari for *Green Hills of Africa* (1935). His first best-seller was *A Farewell to Arms* (1929), followed by *To Have and Have Not* (1937). He chose to fight in the Spanish Civil War on the loyalist side and harvested these war experiences in the novel *For Whom the Bell Tolls* (1940) and in the short-story collection *The Fifth Column and the First Forty-Nine Stories* (1938), which included his some of his best, such as "The Short Happy Life of Francis Macomber" and "The Snows of Kilimanjaro." The former is the story of an African safari that interweaves courage, cowardice, and adultery; the latter is a stream-of-consciousness narrative about a novelist dying of gangrene poisoning while on an African safari. After seeing action in World War II, Hemingway returned to his adopted home in Cuba and in 1953 received the Pulitzer Prize for his short novel *The Old Man and the Sea* (1952). Hemingway was also a master of short fiction. Two of his most successful collections were *Men Without Women* (1927), which included the story "Hills Like White Elephants," and *Winner Take Nothing* (1933), which included the story "A Clean Well-Lighted Place." After Fidel Castro's revolution in 1959, Hemingway left Cuba the following year to settle in Idaho, where he committed suicide. His last book, *A Moveable Feast,* was published posthumously in 1964.

Eugene Gladstone O'Neill (1888–1953) American playwright; winner of the 1936 Nobel Prize in literature. His first full-length play was the Pulitzer Prize–winning *Beyond the Horizon* in 1920. During the next 25 years he completed 20 long plays and a number of shorter ones at the rate of almost one per year. Most of his plays were tragedies that reflected the tragedies of his own life: his bouts with alcoholism and attempts at suicide, the death of his older brother from alcoholism, and his parents' tormented relationship with each other and their children. The most celebrated of his plays are *Emperor Jones* (1921); *Anna Christie* (1922); *The Hairy Ape* (1923); *Bound East for Cardiff, In the Zone, The Long Voyage Home,* and *The Moon of the Caribbees* (all 1924); *Desire Under the Elms* (1925); *Mourning Becomes Electra* (1931); *The Great God Brown* (1926); *Strange Interlude* (1928); the comedy *Ah, Wilderness!* (1933); and *The Iceman Cometh* (1946). Two of his plays were produced posthumously: *Long Day's Journey into Night* (1956) and *A Moon for the Misbegotten* (1957). In many of his plays O'Neill used experimental techniques, such as expressionistic dialogue and spoken asides, that have since become commonplace.

Sir Rabindranath Tagore (1861–1941) Indian Bengali poet; winner of the Nobel Prize in literature in 1913. Tagore occupies a special position in the pantheon of Indian literature as the author of the finest lyrical poems in Bengali and also of the Indian national anthem, "Jana Gana Mana." He introduced many verse forms, such as the ode, to Bengali. His cadenced idioms had a sonorous ring when recited. He was also a gifted composer and set many of his poems to music. His best poems appear in *Gīt ̄añjalī* (1910), which brought him international fame, and *M ̄anasī,* his first collection in 1890. *A Bunch of Stories* was his first collection of short stories in 1912. He published several more collections: *The Golden Boat* (1893), *Late Harvest* (1896), *Dreams* (1900), and *Sacrifice* (1901). His only novel was *Gora* (1907–10). His complete works fill 26 volumes. Most of his works are available in the West only in translations, which do not fully convey the rich and many-layered nuances of his lapidary language.

Bertolt Brecht (1898–1956) German poet and playwright who made the theater a zone of ideological warfare. Until 1924 Brecht lived in Bavaria, where he wrote his first plays, *Baal* (1923) and *Drums in the Night* (1922), and produced his first professional play, *Edward II* (1924). Between 1924 and 1931 he lived in Berlin where he became a Marxist. In 1927 he published a collection of his poems and songs in *A Manual of Piety.* With composer Kurt Weill he wrote the operas *The Three-Penny Opera* (1928) and *The Rise and Fall of the City of Mahagonny* (1930). In 1933 he went into exile and was stripped of his German citizenship. From 1941 to 1947, when he left for the United States, he wrote some of his best plays: *Mother Courage and Her Children* (1941), *The Good Woman of Setzuan* (1943), *Life of Galileo* (1943), *Herr Puntila and His Man Mutti* (1943), and the *Caucasian Chalk Circle* (1948). In 1949 he returned to East Germany, where the

communist government treated him as a national hero. He outlined his theory of dramaturgy in *A Little Organum for the Theater* (1949).

Jorge Luis Borges (1899–1986) Argentine poet and short-story writer. His works created a dream world, an ironic version of the real one, with its own language and symbols. His first was *Fervor of Buenos Aires, Poems* (1923). He wrote a number of volumes of essays and poems and founded three literary journals. In the 1930s he began to create pure fiction, beginning with *A Universal History of Infamy* (1935). In 1938 he suffered a severe head wound that deprived him of his speech. The experience deepened his creativity, and during the next decade he produced his best fantastic stories, later collected in *The Aleph and Other Stories* (1933–69). In the 1950s he became totally blind. During this period his fiction took on the quality of a dream in which the distinction between reality and fantasy is erased. His works in the 1960s and 1970s, such as *The Dreamtigers* (1960), *The Book of Imaginary Beings* (1967), *Dr. Brodie's Report* (1970), and *The Book of Sand* (1975), are as much poetry as prose.

Luigi Pirandello (1867–1936) Italian playwright, novelist, and short-story writer; winner of the Nobel Prize in literature in 1934. Pirandello began writing early, publishing his first collection of verse, *Painful Joy,* in 1889. His early collections of stories, *Loves Without Love* (1894) and *The Jests of Life and Death* (1902–3), and his novels, *The Outcast* (1901) and *The Turn* (1902), prefigure the realism of his later works. With *The Late Mattia Pascal* (1904), he developed the psychological novel as his signature work. His other popular novels included *The Old and the Young* (1913) and *One, None and a Hundred Thousand* (1925–26). Pirandello first turned to the theater in 1898 with *The Vise.* By 1922 he had produced three great plays: *Right You Are—If You Think You Are* (1917), *Six Characters in Search of an Author* (1921), and *Henry IV* (1922). His other notable plays include *All for the Best* (1920), *To Clothe the Naked* (1923), *Each in His Own Way* (1924), and *Tonight We Improvise* (1930).

Graham Greene (1904–1991) English novelist and short-story writer whose stories explored the ambiguities of modern life. He was one of the most widely read novelists of the 20th century, largely because of his superb gifts as a storyteller, his fast-paced narrative, and his ability to endow suspense with a moral depth. He published his first book of verse, *Babbling April,* in 1925 and achieved modest success with his first novel, *The Man Within* (1929). He found his true voice with his fourth novel, *Orient Express* (1932), the first of his thrillers distinguished by their moral complexity and depth. Thereafter his novels flowed in quick succession: *This Gun for Hire* (1936), *Brighton Rock* (1938), *The Confidential Agent* (1939), *The Power and the Glory* (1940), *The Ministry of Fear* (1943), *The Heart of the Matter* (1948), *The*

Third Man (1949), *The End of the Affair* (1951), *The Quiet American* (1955), *Our Man in Havana* (1958), *A Burnt-Out Case* (1961), *The Comedians* (1966). *The Honorary Consul* (1973), *The Human Factor* (1978), *Monsignor Quixote* (1982), and *The Tenth Man* (1985). He summed up his life in two memoirs, *A Sort of Life* (1971) and *Ways of Escape* (1980). Many of his novels had distinctly religious themes in which sin and moral flaws played a prominent part. Almost all his major novels have been adapted into film.

Aleksandr Isayevich Solzhenitsyn (1918–) Russian novelist suffused with Christian orthodoxy and Slav nationalism; winner of the Nobel Prize in literature in 1974. He fought in World War II but was arrested in 1945 for writing a letter that criticized Joseph Stalin. He spent eight years in gulags (labor camps) and three more years in exile. He became famous overnight with the publication of his *One Day in the Life of Ivan Denisovich* (1962). Denied official imprimatur in the Soviet Union thereafter, Solzhenitsyn's works were published abroad. These included *The First Circle* (1968), *Cancer Ward* (1968), and *August 1914* (1971). When the first part of the *Gulag Archipelago* was published in 1973, Solzhenitsyn was arrested, charged with treason, and exiled. He spent the next 20 years in the United States working on *The Red Wheel* series, an epic history of the Russian Revolution. His Russian citizenship was restored after the fall of the Soviet Union; he returned to Russia in 1994.

Samuel Beckett (1906–1989) Irish-born French playwright; winner of the Nobel Prize in literature in 1989. Beckett was a contemporary of James Joyce and part of his circle. Before World War II Beckett wrote the novel *Murphy* (1938) and two volumes of poetry. After the war he settled in Paris and completed the novel *Watt* (1953); the prose trilogy *Molloy* (1951), *Malone Dies* (1951), and *The Unnamable* (1953), written in French; and the play for which he is best known, *Waiting for Godot* (1953), written in French and translated into English by Beckett. Many of his plays had few characters and minimal sets and were pared down to the barest essentials. Some were written in French and later translated in English. They were short and abstract playlets, or "dramaticules," as he called them. *Come and Go* (1967) had only 167 words; *Lessness* consisted of 60 sentences, each of which occurred twice; *Acts Without Words* were exactly that, and *Rockaby* lasted only 15 minutes. Although his subjects were somber and dealt with the angst and mystery of human existence, a comic strain ran through his works evoking pathos and laughter as he portrayed the futility of human actions and desires.

Joseph Conrad   (Józef Teodor Konrad Korzeniowski) (1857–1924) Polish-born English novelist and short-story writer. Most of Conrad's novels dealt with the sea, which for him became a metaphor of the human condition as he portrayed the struggle for survival in a hostile environment. Con-

rad's parents were exiled to Siberia from Poland by the czar. In 1878 Conrad signed on as a deckhand on a British freighter and served in the British navy for the next 16 years. His voyages provided the material for his novels *The Nigger of the "Narcissus"* (1897) and *Typhoon* (1902) and his short stories "The Shadow Line" and "Falk." A four-month command of a Congo river boat led to his enigmatic masterpiece, *The Heart of Darkness* (1902). By 1910, when he had settled in London, he had written his four major works: *Lord Jim* (1900), *Nostromo* (1904), *The Secret Agent* (1907), and *Under Western Eyes* (1911). His last novel was *Victory* (1915). He was a gifted storyteller with a love of adventure and exotic places, which he was able to convey to his readers in taut, austere prose.

Albert Camus (1913–1960) French novelist, essayist, and playwright; winner of the 1957 Nobel Prize in literature. In the 1930s Camus was part of a group of left-wing intellectuals of French-Algerian origin, and he began his career as a playwright. He wrote plays throughout his life, although many of them are now forgotten. They included *Cross Purposes* and *Caligula* (both 1944), *State of Siege* (1948), and *Just Assassins* (1950). Camus was a perceptive essayist who wrote lyrical meditations on the Algerian countryside and on the miserable living conditions of the Kabyle Muslims. However, it was as an existential philosopher that Camus made his mark on modern literature. As he moved into nihilism, his works were pervaded by a sense of the absurd. His themes moved between depicting human dignity and calling for an ill-defined rebellion against the system. He dealt with these issues in his novels *The Stranger* (1942), *The Plague* (1947), and *The Chute* (1956) and in his collections of essays *The Myth of Sisyphus* (1945) and *The Rebel* (1951).

Ezra Loomis Pound (1885–1972) American poet, often called a "poet's poet," because of his lasting influence on his contemporaries. Pound went to Europe in his early 20s and remained there until the end of World War II. He published his first book of poems, *A lume spento,* in Venice in 1908 and his second, *Personae,* in London, in 1909. By the end of World War I, Pound was already acknowledged as the high priest of modern poetry when he published two of his most important collections, *Quia Pauper Amavi* (1919), which contained "Homage to Sextus Propertius," and *Hugh Selwyn Mauberley* (1920). In 1920 he left England, first for Paris, then Rapallo, Italy, where he began publishing the *Cantos* (on which he continued to work throughout his life). He became an admirer of Benito Mussolini and during World War II openly sided with the Nazis. He was arrested by U.S. forces in 1945 and returned to the United States, where he was tried for treason but found mentally unfit and insane. *The Pisan Cantos* (1948) are among the most moving of his poems.

Rainer Maria Rilke (1875–1926) German poet, the most important in the early 20th century. He went to Paris in 1902 and during his Paris years developed a new style of lyrical poetry, the "object poem," which attempts to capture the plastic essence of a physical object. To do so he forced his language to extreme subtlety and refinement. His first poetic expression was a long three-part cycle of poems written between 1899 and 1903, *The Book of Hours* (1905). His *New Poems* (1907–8) represented a departure from conventional German poetry just as his work *The Notebook of Malte Laurid Brigge* (1910) did for prose. After *The Life of the Virgin Mary* (1913), Rilke published nothing until a burst of creativity in 1923, when he published his two greatest works: *Duino Elegies* and *Sonnets to Orpheus.*

Vladimir Vladimirovich Nabokov (1899–1977) Russian-born American novelist who wrote in both Russian and English. Nabokov began as a poet but shifted to prose, publishing his first novel, *Mary,* in 1926. His second novel, *King, Queen, Knave* (1928), was characterized by a highly idiosyncratic style that remained his signature for the rest of his life. His succeeding novels, all in Russian, were *The Defense* (1930), *Despair* (1936), and *Invitation to a Beheading* (1938). The novel *The Gift* (1937–38) revealed his gift of parody. His first novel in English was *The Real Life of Sebastian Knight* (1941), followed by *Bend Sinister* (1947), *Pale Fire* (1962), *Lolita* (1955), *Pnin* (1957), and *Ada* (1969). His autobiography, *Speak, Memory* (1951), is a literary classic in its own right.

Federico García Lorca (1898–1936) Spanish playwright and poet. The author of the collections *Book of Poems* (1921), *Songs* (1927), and *First Songs* (1936), Lorca found his true voice when he discovered the traditions of folk and gypsy music, which provided a new direction for his genius. *The Gypsy Ballads* (1928) and *Poem of the Cante Jondo* (1931) were inspired by this interest. His first successful play was the 1927 production of *Mariana Pineda,* a romantic verse drama. During 1929–30 he was in New York, and his American experience is recorded in *Poet in New York* (1940). Back in Spain in 1931 he wrote the poem *Divan of Tamarit* and the play *Bodas de sangre* (*Blood Wedding*), the first of a trilogy of folk dramas. The death of his friend Ignacio Sánchez Mejías was the occasion for his "Lament for the Death of a Bullfighter." Later he produced the second and third parts of the *Bodas de sangre* trilogy, *Yerma* and *La casa de Bernarda Alba.* In the Spanish Civil War, Lorca, who was a loyalist, was executed by the Nationalists.

Pablo Neruda (Neftalí Ricardo Reyes Basoalto) (1904–1973) Chilean poet; winner of the Nobel Prize in literature in 1971. His first successful work was *Twenty Love Poems and a Song of Despair* (1924). During the next decade he also wrote *Attempt of the Infinite Man* (1926), *Rings* (1926), and *The Enthusiastic Slingshooter* (1933). In 1927 he was named an honorary consul and served in several South Asian countries. During this period he wrote *Residence on Earth.* He returned

to Chile and thereafter until his death devoted as much time to politics as to literature. During this phase he produced his masterpiece, *General Song* (1950), one of Latin America's greatest epic poems.

Kawabata Yasunari (1899–1972) Japanese novelist; winner of the Nobel Prize in literature in 1968. Kawabata entered the world of literature with the semiautobiographical novel *The Izu Dancer* (1926). His best-known novels are *Snow Country* (1948), *Thousand Cranes* (1952), and *The Sound of the Mountain* (1952). Kawabata's narrative is characterized by a certain formlessness, abrupt transitions in imagery, and juxtaposition of the beautiful and ugly. His techniques are drawn from the linked verse, known as the rengi, in 15th-century Japanese poetry.

Lu Xun (Zhou Shuren) (1881–1936) The greatest figure in 20th-century Chinese literature, he gained fame with his first short story, "The Diary of a Madman." It was the first Western-style short story written wholly in Chinese. The short story remained his favorite literary genre, and he published a number of collections that combined humor and pathos, including *A Call to Arms* (1923), *Wandering* (1926), and *Old Tales Retold* (1936). Although best known for his short stories, Lu Xun was also a master of the prose essay. After the Communist takeover of mainland China in 1947, Lu Xun was hailed as a revolutionary hero and an exemplar of socialist realism.

Sigrid Undset (1882–1949) Norwegian novelist; winner of the Nobel Prize in literature in 1928. Her early novels deal with the position of middle-class women in society. These include *Images in a Mirror* (1917) and *Jenny* (1911). Her masterpiece is the trilogy *Kristin Lavransdatter* (1920–22), which is set in medieval times. In this work and in *The Master of Hestviken* (1925–27), religion plays a prominent role. Undset converted to Roman Catholicism in 1924, and her later novels have a strong spiritual element.

Key World Events of the Twentieth Century

1900	Chinese nationalists stage the Boxer Rebellion, supported by the reactionary dowager empress Cixi; more than 250 foreigners, mainly missionaries, are killed
1903	Wright brothers, Orville and Wilbur, fly the first power-driven, heavier-than-air plane, launching the age of aviation
1904	Japan, moving ahead with its imperialist designs, torpedoes the Russian fleet at Port Arthur (Lushun) in a surprise attack and win a decisive victory, the first by an Asian nation against a European power
1905	Striking workers march to the Winter Palace in St. Petersburg on Bloody Sunday but are met by troops who open fire, killing 500; the incident sparks a year-long revolution that is quelled only after Czar Nicholas issues the October Manifesto granting partial democracy
1908	Young Turks take over in Constantinople and oust Sultan Abdul Hamid. Austria-Hungary annexes Bosnia Herzegovina. King Leopold of Belgium relinquishes Congo, until then his personal fief, to the Belgian government
1911	Mexican rebels led by Pancho Villa and Emiliano Zapata help Francisco I. Madero overthrow the dictator Porfirio Díaz; ten years of turmoil follow until the restoration of order by General Alvaro Obregón in 1920
1912	Manchu dynasty is overthrown in China and a republican government is established under Yuan Shikai
1914	Archduke Francis Ferdinand is assassinated in Sarajevo, starting the cycle of events that lead to World War I. Panama Canal opens under the exclusive control of the United States
1916	Irish Republicans stage Easter uprising in Dublin but are overpowered by British troops
1917	United States enters the war after unrestricted submarine warfare by Germany ends American neutrality. Bolsheviks seize power in Russia, Czar Nicholas II abdicates; Red Guards stage coup; Vladimir Lenin is named leader of the Council of People's Commissars
1918	Allies impose the Treaty of Versailles on Germany; Treaty of Brest-Litovsk is rescinded to concede independence to Lithuania, Finland, Estonia, and Latvia, reconstitute Poland, and make Danzig a free city; the treaty of Saint-Germain forces Austria to cede Trieste, Istria, and Tyrol to Italy; Bohemia, Moravia, and Austrian Silesia to the new state of Czechoslovakia; Bukovina to Romania; and Bosnia-Herzegovina, Dalmatia, and Serbia to the new state of Yugoslavia
1919	League of Nations is established without U.S. participation
1922	Irish Free State is established as the Dail (Irish parliament) votes to accept a de facto partition of the island into a Catholic south and a Protestant north. Benito Mussolini, the Fascist leader, marches on Rome and seizes power
1926	John Logie Baird, a Scottish inventor, makes first television transmission
1927	Chinese nationalists (Kuomintang) take Shanghai and Nanking and establish effective government over all of China
1928	Alexander Fleming discovers penicillin
1929	New York stock market collapses as stock prices plunge. Leon Trotsky is expelled from the Soviet Union as Joseph Stalin wins a struggle for power
1931	Japan seizes Manchuria in defiance of the League of Nations

1932	Franklin D. Roosevelt is elected U.S. president and introduces the New Deal to salvage the economy
1933	Adolf Hitler is sworn in as German chancellor; German Reichstag is razed in a fire
1935	Italy invades Abyssinia; League of Nations fails to stop Fascist aggression. Mao Zedong ends the Long March at Yenan
1936	Civil war breaks out in Spain between the Falangists, led by General Francisco Franco, and the Republican government of Largo Caballero. Edward VIII of England abdicates and is succeeded by his brother as George VI
1938	Anschluss marks the unification of Germany and Austria
1939	Munich agreement between Germany and the Allies dismantles Czechoslovakia. Germany invades Poland; World War II begins as Great Britain and France declare war on Germany
1940	France falls to the Nazis
1941	Germany invades the Soviet Union; Japan bombs Pearl Harbor in surprise attack; United States and Great Britain declare war on Japan
1942	Lord Montgomery leads Allied victory at Al-Alamein, Egypt, thus turning back Axis march on Cairo
1943	German advance in the Soviet Union is halted at Stalingrad (Volgograd)
1944	The tide of war turns as Allies land at Normandy on D day and breach the Axis "Atlantic Wall"; Paris is liberated
1945	Berlin falls to the Allies; Germany surrenders; Hitler commits suicide. Nuclear bomb is dropped on Hiroshima and Nagasaki; Japan surrenders. Yalta and Potsdam conferences redraw the map of Europe and Asia; war crimes trials begin in Nuremberg; United Nations is founded
1947	United States launches the Marshall Plan to aid war-ravaged Europe. India and Pakistan gain independence from British rule
1948	Afrikaner Nationalist Party under Daniel Malan wins elections and initiates apartheid, or full segregation of races. The state of Israel is founded
1949	Communists drive the Kuomintang out of China and found the People's Republic
1950	North Korea invades South Korea, starting the Korean War
1953	Structure of DNA (deoxyribonucleic acid) is discovered by Francis Crick and James Watson
1954	French empire in Indochina collapses as Dien Bien Phu falls to the Viet Cong
1955	Rosa Parks is arrested for refusing to give up her seat to a white man on a bus in Montgomery, Alabama, starting the Alabama Bus Boycott in which Martin Luther King emerges as a national civil rights leader
1956	Gamal Abdel Nasser of Egypt nationalizes the Suez Canal. Soviet troops crush Hungarian reform movement
1957	Soviet Union launches *Sputnik I,* the first artificial satellite. European Economic Community is established at Rome with six members; it later will become
	the European Community (1967) and the European Union (1998)
1958	China takes the disastrous Great Leap Forward into chaos
1959	Fidel Castro overthrows dictator Fulgencio Batista in Cuba and seizes power
1960	The first oral contraceptive, Enovid-10, is marketed in the United States
1961	Bay of Pigs fails to topple Fidel Castro in Cuba. East Germany erects the Berlin Wall to stop emigration from the East to the West
1963	President John F. Kennedy is assassinated in Dallas; Lyndon B. Johnson becomes president
1964	United States escalates its involvement in Vietnam War
1966	Mao Zedong proclaims "cultural revolution" in China
1968	Soviet tanks crush the Prague Spring, a movement for the humanization of communism, led by Czech dissident Alexander Dubcek
1969	Astronaut Neil Armstrong takes "a giant step for mankind" as the first person to walk on the moon
1971	The first microchip is developed by Intel
1973	President Salvador Allende of Chile is ousted in a right-wing military coup led by Augusto Pinochet
1974	Turkey invades Cyprus and occupies one-third of the island. Watergate scandal forces Richard Nixon out of the White House, the first time a U.S. president resigns
1975	Portugal concedes independence to Mozambique and Angola. Khmer Rouge communist guerrillas capture Phnom Penh and seize power in Cambodia, beginning a campaign of genocide
1978	Israel and Egypt make peace at Camp David under U.S. auspices
1979	Ayatollah Khomeini returns to Iran from exile to lead a revolution that overthrows the shah. Soviet troops invade Afghanistan at the request of its communist government
1980	Iraq invades Iran. Solidarity trade union movement is launched in Poland, crystallizing opposition to the communist regime
1986	President Ferdinand Marcos is overthrown in the Philippines
1989	Berlin Wall is torn down as communism collapses in Eastern Europe
1990	Iraq occupies Kuwait, provoking the Gulf War
1991	Iraq is defeated in the Gulf War
1994	South Africa ends apartheid; Nelson Mandela is elected president in the nation's first free elections

1900

BIRTHS

Roberto Godofredo Christophersen Arlt, Argentine novelist
Aying (Qian Xingcun), Chinese critic and historian
Bing Zin, Chinese novelist and poet

Karin Boye, Swedish poet, novelist, and short-story writer
Reuben Tolakele Caluza, Zulu poet and lyricist
Robert Desnos, French poet and novelist
Gilberto Freyre, Brazilian novelist
Julian Green, French novelist
Muhammad Hejazi, Iranian novelist
Laura Z. Hobson, American novelist and short-story writer
Muhammas Mahdi al-Jawahiri, Iraqi poet
Eyvind Johnson, Swedish novelist
Aniceti Kitereza, Tanzanian novelist and folklorist
Maha Hswei, Burmese novelist
Guruprasad Mainali, Nepali writer of short fiction
Leopoldo Marechal, Argentine novelist and critic
Yoftahe Neguse, Ethiopian playwright and poet
Sean O'Faolain, Irish novelist
V. S. Pritchett, English novelist and short-story writer
Antoine de Saint-Exupéry, French writer of children's stories
Nathalie Sarraute, French novelist
George Seferis, Greek poet
Abraham Shlonsky, Ukrainian-born Israeli poet
Ignazio Silone, Italian novelist
Tu Mo (Ho Trong Hieu), Vietnamese poet
Thomas Clayton Wolfe, American novelist
Nairi Zarian (Hayastan Yeghiazarian), Armenian poet

DEATHS

R. D. Blackmore, English novelist
Stephen Crane, American novelist
Ernest Christopher Dawson, English poet
José Maria Eça de Queirós, Portuguese novelist
Friedrich Wilhelm Nietzsche, German philosopher
Sigbjørn Obstfelder, Norwegian poet and playwright
John Ruskin, English critic
Oscar Wilde, Irish novelist, dramatist, and poet

LITERARY EVENT

The Smart Set magazine is founded by William D'Alton Mann

PUBLICATIONS

BENGALI

Dreams Collection of stories by Indian writer Rabindranath
    Tagore

DANISH

The Fall of the King Biography by Johannes Jensen

DUTCH

The Deeps of Deliverance Novel by Frederik Eeden
The Good Hope Play by Herman Heijermans

ENGLISH

American

Contending Forces Novel by Pauline Hopkins
Sister Carrie Novel by Theodore Dreiser
The Son of the Wolf Collection of stories by Jack London
Whilomville Collection of stories by Stephen Crane
The Wonderful Wizard of Oz Children's story by L. Frank Baum

British

Lord Jim Novel by Joseph Conrad
Love and Mr. Lewisham Novel by H. G. Wells
Paola and Francesca Play by Stephen Phillips
Son of the Morning Novel by Eden Phillpotts

FRENCH

Clay Medals Poems by Henri de Régnier
The Eaglet Play by Edmond Rostand
The Winged Legend of Wieland the Blacksmith Poems by Francis
    Viélé-Griffin

HUNGARIAN

The Strange Marriage Novel by Kálmán Mikszáth

ITALIAN

The Flame of Life Play by Gabriele D'Annunzio
The Old Man of the Mountain Novel by Grazia Deledda

PORTUGUESE

Brazilian

Beacons Collection of poems by João de Cruze Sousa
Don Casmurro Novel by Joaquim Maria Machado de Assis

RUSSIAN

Third Vigil Collection of poems by Valery Yakovlevich Bryusov

SPANISH

The Castilian Soul Essays by Azorín (José Martínez Ruiz)
The Galley Slaves Play by Serafín and Joaquín Alvarez Quintero

UKRAINIAN

Crooked Paths Novel by Ivan Franko
From the Days of Sorrow Collection of poems by Ivan Franko

YIDDISH

Stories and Pictures Collection of stories by Polish Jewish writer
    Isaac Leib Peretz

1901

BIRTHS

Kjeld, Abell, Danish playwright
Dashti Ali, Iranian novelist
Gomar Bashirov, Tartar novelist
Nina Berberova, Russian émigré writer
Barbara Cartland, English romance novelist
Rolfus Reginald Raymond Dhlomo, Zulu novelist
Aleksandr Fadeyeyev, Russian novelist
Marieluise Fleisser, German playwright
Kristmann Gudmundsson, Icelandic novelist
Marie Luise Kaschnitz, German poet and novelist
André Malraux, French novelist and art historian

Murilo Mendes, Brazilian poet
Prince Modupe Paris, Guinean novelist
Julian Przybos, Polish poet
Salvatore Quasimodo, Italian poet
Jean-Joseph Rabearivelo, Malagasy poet
José Regio, Portuguese poet, novelist, and playwright
Laura Riding, American poet
G. Sankara Kurup, Malayalee poet
Jaroslav Seifert, Czech poet

DEATHS

Leopoldo Alas y Ureña, Spanish novelist and playwright
Victor Balaguer, Catalan historian
Johanna Spyri, Swiss writer of children's stories
Charlotte Mary Yonge, English novelist

LITERARY EVENT

PRIZES AND AWARDS
First Nobel Prize in literature: Sully Prudhomme (René-François-Armand Prudhomme), French poet

PUBLICATIONS

BENGALI
Sacrifice Collection of stories by Indian writer Rabindranath Tagore

ENGLISH
American

The Crisis Novel by Winston Churchill
Graustark Novel by George McCutcheon
The Octopus Novel by Frank Norris

Australian

Joe Wilson and His Mates Collection of short stories by Henry Lawson

British

The Hound of the Baskervilles Mystery novel by Arthur Conan Doyle
Kim Novel by Rudyard Kipling

Irish

Caesar and Cleopatra Play by George Bernard Shaw

FRENCH
Belgian

The Life of the Bee Meditations by Maurice Maeterlinck

French

Bubu du Montparnasse Novel by Charles-Louis Philippe
Daily Bread Novel by René Boylesve
Monsieur Bergeret in Paris Novel by Anatole France

GERMAN
Austrian

None But the Brave Novel by Arthur Schnitzler
Silberne Saiten Collection of poems by Stefan Zweig

German

Buddenbrooks Novel by Thomas Mann
The Marquis of Keith Play by Frank Wedekind

ITALIAN
The Outcast Novel by Luigi Pirandello

JAPANESE
Tangled Hair Collected verse by Yosano Akiko

POLISH
To a Dying World Collected verse by Jan Kasprowicz

RUSSIAN
The Romance of Leonardo da Vinci, the Forerunner Novel by Dmitry Sergeyevich Merezhkovsky
Three Sisters Play by Anton Chekhov

SWEDISH
The Dance of Death Play by August Strindberg
Easter Morality play by August Strindberg
Fridolin's Pleasure Garden Collection of poems by Andreas Karlfeldt
Jerusalem Novel by Selma Lagerlöf
Martin Birck's Youth Novel by Hjalmar Söderberg

1902

BIRTHS

Rafael Alberti, Spanish poet
Marcel Ayme, French novelist and playwright
Jorge Barbosa, Cape Verdean poet
Gwendolyn B. Bennet, African-American poet and short-story writer
Jaime Torres Bodet, Mexican poet and novelist
Johan Borgen, Norwegian novelist, short-story writer, and playwright
Luis Cernuda, Spanish poet
Tembot Charasha, Circassian novelist
Svimon Chikovani, Georgian poet
Nicolás Guillén, Cuban poet
Langston Hughes, African-American poet
Nazim Hikmet Ran, Turkish poet and playwright
Kota Sivarama Karanta, Kannada novelist
Kobayashi Hideo, Japanese critic
Halldor Laxness (Halldor Kiljan Gudyonsson), Icelandic novelist
Carlo Levi, Italian novelist
Ghabit Muzrepov, Kazakh novelist
Ogden Nash, American comic poet
Ramón Sender, Spanish-born American novelist
Stevie Smith (Florence Margaret Smith), English poet and novelist
Christina Stead, Australian novelist
John Ernst Steinbeck, American novelist
Ali Mahmud Taha, Egyptian poet

DEATHS

Samuel Butler, English novelist
Bret Harte, American novelist
Masaoka Shiki, Japanese poet
Benjamin Franklin Norris, American novelist
Jacinto Verdaguer, Catalan poet
Émile-Édouard-Charles-Antoine Zola, French novelist

LITERARY EVENTS

TLS (*Times Literary Supplement*) book review is founded in London

PRIZES AND AWARDS

Nobel Prize in literature: Theodor Mommsen, German historian

PUBLICATIONS

ENGLISH

American

The Call of the Wild Novel by Jack London
"A Deal in Wheat" Short story by Frank Norris
The Sport of the Gods Novel by Paul Laurence Dunbar
The Varieties of Religious Experience Lectures by William James
The Virginian Western novel by Owen Wister
The Wings of the Dove Novel by Henry James

British

Anna of the Five Towns Novel by Arnold Bennett
Heart of Darkness Novella by Joseph Conrad
Just So Stories Tales for children by Rudyard Kipling
"The Monkey's Paw" Short story by W. W. Jacobs
The Path to Rome Travel narrative by Hilaire Belloc
The Tale of Peter Rabbit Classic children's tale by Beatrix Potter

Irish

Cathleen ni Houlihan Play in verse by William Butler Yeats

Scottish

The Admirable Crichton Play by James M. Barrie

FRENCH

Belgian

The Little Man of God Novel by Camille Lemonnier
Monna Vanna Verse drama by the Maurice Maeterlinck
The Tumultuous Force Poem by Émile Verhaeren

French

The Immoralist Novel by André Gide

ITALIAN

After the Divorce Novel by Grazia Deledda
The Turn Novel by Luigi Pirandello

PORTUGUESE

Brazilian

Canaan Novel by José Pereira da Graça Aranha
Rebellion in the Backlands History by Euclides da Cunha

RUSSIAN

The Lower Depths Novel by Maxim Gorky
The Northern Symphony Prose poem by Andrei Bely

SPANISH

Spanish

Love and Pedagogy Novel by Miguel de Unamuno
Sonatas Four novelettes by Ramón María del Valle-Inclán
The Soul Poems by Manuel Machado

Uruguayan

The Matins of the Night Poems by Julio Herrera y Reissig

SWEDISH

A Dream Play Episodic play by August Strindberg
Fair Haven and Foul Strand Collection of stories by August Strindberg

1903

BIRTHS

Hans Christian Branner, Danish novelist
Erskine Caldwell, American novelist
Morley Edward Callaghan, Canadian novelist
Alejandro Casona, Spanish playwright
James Gould Cozzens, American novelist
Countee Cullen, African-American poet
Josef Czechowicz, Polish poet
Herbert Isaac Ernest Dhlomo, Zulu novelist, playwright, and poet
Sādeq Hedāyat, Iranian writer
Amado V. Hernandez, Filipino Tagalog novelist, playwright, and poet
Zora Neal Hurston, African-American writer
Jasimuddin, Bengali poet
Kobayashi Takiji, Japanese writer
Gurgen Mahari, Armenian poet and writer of short fiction
Eduardo Mallea, Argentine novelist
Alio Mirtskhulava, Georgian poet
Nguyen Cong Hoan, Vietnamese novelist and writer of short fiction
Anaïs Nin, French-born American novelist and diarist
George Orwell (Eric Arthur Blair), English novelist and essayist
Alan Paton, South African novelist
Raymond Queneau, French novelist, playwright, poet, and essayist
Raymond Radiguet, French novelist, playwright, and poet
Émile Roumer, Haitian poet and critic
Georges-Jacques-Christian Simenon, Belgian-born French writer of detective fiction
Bhagvaticharan Varma, Hindi novelist and poet
Evelyn Waugh, English novelist
Nathanael West (Nathan Weinstein), American novelist
Muhammad Yasmin, Indonesian poet and novelist
Yaspal, Hindi novelist and short fiction writer
Marguerite Yourcenar, Belgian-born Franco-American biographer, novelist, poet, and playwright

DEATHS

George Gissing, English novelist
William Ernest Henley, English poet
Eugenio María Hostos y Bonilla, Puerto Rican essayist and jour-
    nalist
Ozaki Kōyō (Ozaki Tokutarō), Japanese novelist and poet

LITERARY EVENTS

Prix Goncourt is established

PRIZES AND AWARDS

Nobel Prize in literature: Bjønstjerne Martinius Bjørnson,
    Norwegian poet, playwright, and novelist

PUBLICATIONS

ENGLISH

American

The Ambassadors Novel by Henry James
"The Beast in the Jungle" Short story by Henry James
The Land of Little Rain Novel by Mary Austin
The People of the Abyss Narrative sketches by Jack London
"Q.E.D." Short story by Gertrude Stein

Australian

Such Is Life Novel by Joseph Furphy

British

The Dynasts, an Epic Drama of the War with Napoleon Play by
    Thomas Hardy
The Private Papers of Henry Ryecroft Novel by George Gissing
Riders to the Sea Play by John Millington Synge
Typhoon Novel by Joseph Conrad
The Way of All Flesh Novel by Samuel Butler

Irish

In the Seven Woods Collection of poems by William Butler Yeats
In the Shadow of the Glen One-act play by John Millington Synge
Man and Superman Dramatic tragedy by George Bernard Shaw
Untitled Field Collection of short stories by George Moore

FINNISH

Whitsongs Poems by Eino Leino

FRENCH

Au Soleil de Juillet Novel by Paul Adam
The Child at the Balustrade Novel by René Boylesve
Donatienne Novel by René Bazin
The Lay Monk Novel by Joris-Karl Huysmans

GERMAN

Austrian

Elektra One-act verse drama by Hugo von Hofmannsthal

German

Tonio Kroger Novella by Thomas Mann
Tristan Novel by Thomas Mann
Two People Epic poem by Richard Dehmel

ITALIAN

Elias Portulu Novel by the Grazia Deledda

POLISH

The Hag Novel by Karol Irzykowski
Rotten Wood Novel by Wacław Berent

RUSSIAN

Pilot Stars Collection of poems by Vyacheslav Ivanov

SPANISH

Saturday Night Play by Jacinto Benavente y Martínez
Solitudes Poems by Antonio Machado

1904

BIRTHS

Bozorg Alavi, Persian writer
Osvaldo Alcantara (Baltasar Lopes de Silva), Cape Verdean
    novelist
Jonas Asitas, Lithuanian writer
Ba Jin (Li Feigan), Chinese novelist and short-story writer
Alejo Carpentier, Cuban novelist, poet, and playwright
Gladys May Casely-Hayford, Sierra Leonean poet
Cecil Day-Lewis, Irish-born English poet
Ding Ling, Chinese short-story writer
Richard Ghormley Eberhart, American poet
Elley (Seraphim Aramaanbys Kulaas'kar), Yakut poet
James Thomas Farrell, American novelist, critic, and writer of
    short stories
Witold Gombrowicz, Polish novelist, poet, and playwright
Graham Greene, English novelist and playwright
Moss Hart, American playwright
Hayashi Fumiko, Japanese novelist
Christopher Isherwood, English novelist
Andrzej Kusniewicz, Polish poet and novelist
Henry Martinson, Swedish novelist and poet
Nancy Mitford, English writer
Pablo Neruda (Neftalí Ricardo Reyes Basoalto), Chilean poet
Hamid Olimjon, Uzbek poet
K. V. Puttapu, Kannada poet
Isaac Bashevis Singer, Polish-born American novelist
Agustín Yáñez, Mexican novelist and short-story writer

DEATHS

Anton Pavlovich Chekhov, Russian novelist and playwright
Kate Chopin, American novelist
Lafcadio Hearn, American novelist
Mor Jakai, Hungarian novelist
Mankayi Enoch Sontonga, Xhosa poet

LITERARY EVENTS

Abbey Theatre is founded in Dublin
Prix Femme is established in Paris

PRIZES AND AWARDS

Nobel Prize in literature: Frédéric Mistral, French Provençal poet, and José Echegaray, Spanish playwright

PUBLICATIONS

DANISH

Children of Wrath: A Hired Man's Saga Novel by Jeppe Aakjaer

ENGLISH

American

The Fire Bringer Play by William Vaughan Moody
The Golden Bowl Novel by Henry James
Kwaiden Novel by Lafcadio Hearn
The Sea Wolf Novel by Jack London

British

Green Mansions Novel by W. H. Hudson
Hadrian the Seventh Autobiographical fantasy by Frederick Rolfe
The Napoleon of Notting Hill Novel by G. K. Chesterton
Nostromo Novel by Joseph Conrad
Reginald Collection of stories by Saki (H. H. Munro)
Shakespearean Tragedy Critical discourse by Andre Cecil Bradley

Irish

Spreading the News One-act play by Lady Augusta Gregory

Scottish

Peter Pan; or, The Boy Who Wouldn't Grow Up Dramatic fantasy by James Matthew Barrie

FINNISH

Simo the Bloodhound Collected verse of Eino Leino

FRENCH

Belgian

First Loves Collected verse by Émile Verhaeren

French

Jean Christophe Ten-volume novel (completed in 1912) by Romain Rolland
Le Théâtre de la Revolution Play by Romain Rolland

GERMAN

The Narrow Road to Happiness Autobiography by Paul Ernst
Pandora's Box Play by Frank Wedekind
Peter Camenzind Novel by Hermann Hesse

GREEK

Life Immovable Collected poems by Kostis Palamas

HUNGARIAN

Byzantium Play by Ferenc Herezeg

ITALIAN

Ashes Novel by Grazzia Deledda
The Daughter of Jorio Play by Gabriele D'Annunzio
The Late Mattia Pascal Novel by Luigi Pirandello

NORWEGIAN

The Tragedies of Love Play by Gunnar Heiberg

POLISH

Chlopi Forty-volume novel (completed in 1909) by Władysław Reymont

RUSSIAN

The Cherry Orchard Comic play by Anton Chekhov
Gold in Azure Collection of poems by Andrei Bely
The Seagull Play by Anton Chekhov
Translucency Poems by Vyacheslav Ivanov
Verses About the Lady Beautiful Collection of poems by Aleksandr Aleksandrovich Blok

SPANISH

Chilean

The Uprooted Novel by Alberto Blest Gana

Spanish

The Love That Passes Play by Serafín and Joaquín Alvarez Quintero
The Struggle for Life Trilogy of novels by Pío Baroja

UKRAINIAN

Fata Morgana Novel by Mikhaylo Kotsyubinsky

1905

BIRTHS

Gerrit Achterberg, Danish poet
Mulk Raj Anand, Indian novelist
H. E. Bates, English novelist
Herman Charles Bosman, South African writer
Elias Canetti, Bulgarian-born German novelist
Robert Guy Choquette, American-born French-Canadian writer and poet
Fumiko Enchi, Japanese novelist
Vasily Semenovich Grossman, Russian novelist, poet, and playwright
Yahya Haqqi, Egyptian essayist and novelist
Lillian Hellman, American playwright
Anandilal Jainendrakumar, Hindi novelist
Attila József, Hungarian poet and essayist
Patrick Kavanagh, Irish poet
Kesava Dev, Malayalee poet
Arthur Koestler, Hungarian novelist and critic
Stanley Kunitz, American poet
Emmanuel H. A. Made, Xulu poet, novelist, and biographer
Roger Mais, Jamaican poet, novelist, and playwright
Dehati Mohammad Masud, Iranian novelist
John O'Hara, American novelist
Anthony Powell, English novelist
Ayn Rand, Russian-born American novelist
Mary Renault (Mary Challans), English-born South African novelist
Kenneth Rexroth, American poet and critic

Jean-Paul Sartre, French philosopher, playwright, and novelist
Mikhail Aleksandrovich Sholokhov, Russian Cossack novelist
Charles Percy Snow, English scientist and novelist
Lionel Trilling, American critic
Erico Lopes Verissimo, Brazilian novelist and essayist
Robert Penn Warren, American novelist, poet, and critic
George Emlyn Williams, Welsh playwright

DEATHS
Keshavasut (Krishnaji Kesav Damle), Marathi poet
Mayer-André-Marcel Schwab, French writer of short fiction, biographer, essayist, and historian
Amalie Bertha Skram, Norwegian novelist, playwright, and writer of short fiction
Jules Verne, French science fiction novelist
Lew Wallace, American novelist

LITERARY EVENT
PRIZES AND AWARDS
Nobel Prize in literature: Henryk Sienkiewicz, Polish novelist

PUBLICATIONS
ENGLISH
American
"The Gift of the Magi" Short story by O. Henry (William Sidney Porter)
The House of Mirth Novel by Edith Wharton
The Life of Reason Five-volume philosophical treatise by George Santayana
"Paul's Case" Short story by Willa Cather
The Tree of Laughing Bells Collection of verse by Vachel Lindsay
The Troll Garden Short stories by Willa Cather

British
The Case-Book of Sherlock Holmes Detective stories by Arthur Conan Doyle
The Four Just Men Thriller by Edgar Wallace
Kipps Novel by H. G. Wells
The Return of Sherlock Holmes Detective stories by Arthur Conan Doyle
The Scarlet Pimpernel Novel by Hungarian-born novelist Baroness Emmuska Orczy
Where Angels Fear to Tread Novel by E. M. Forster

Irish
De Profundis Prose apologia by Oscar Wilde
"The Gods of Pegave" Short story by Edward Dunsany
Major Barbara Play by George Bernard Shaw

FINNISH
The Iron Gate Collected verse by Baron Barton Johan Sebastian Gripenberg
The Song of the Blood-Red Flower Novel by Johannes Linnankoski
Winter Night Collected verse of Eino Leino

FRENCH
The Whirlwind Play by Henry Bernstein

GERMAN
Austrian
The Countess of Charolais Play by Richard Beer-Hofmann
German
The Blue Angel Novel by Heinrich Mann
The Book of Hours Poems by Rainer Maria Rilke
The Prodigy Novel by Hermann Hesse

ITALIAN
The Gentle Language Novel by Edmondo De Amicis

JAPANESE
I Am a Cat Novel by Natsume Sōseki

SPANISH
Argentine
Twilights in the Garden Collected verse of Leopoldo Lugones
Spanish
Distant Gardens Collection of poems by Juan Ramón Jiménez
The Evil Doers of Good Play by Jacinto Benavente y Martínez

SWEDISH
Doctor Glas Novel by Hjalmar Söderberg

1906

BIRTHS
Said Faik Abasiyanik, Turkish short-story writer
Amma Achchygyya (Nijikulay Jogyorebis Muordinov), Yakut novelist, poet, and playwright
Sabahattin Ali, Turkish novelist
Jean Amrouche, Algerian poet
Samuel Beckett, Irish-born French playwright
John Betjeman, English poet laureate
Bhabhani Bhatacharya, Indian novelist
Dino Buzzati, Italian novelist and playwright
Brago Ismael Diop, Senegalese poet
William Empson, English poet and critic
Masud Farazad, Iranian poet
Archibald Campbell Jordan, South African poet and novelist
Malai Chuphinit, Thai novelist
Klaus Mann, German novelist, essayist, and playwright
R. K. Narayan, Indian novelist
Nhat Linh, Vietnamese novelist
Clifford Odets, American playwright
Puttumaipittan, Tamil novelist and poet
Henry Roth, American novelist
Leopold Sedar Senghor, Senegalese poet and statesman
Giorgios Theotokas, Greek poet
Benedict Wallet Bambatha Vilakazi, Zulu poet
Samad Vurghun, Azerbaijani poet
Vernon Phillips Watkins, Welsh poet and translator
Zhao Shuli, Chinese novelist and short-story writer

DEATHS
Paul Laurence Dunbar, African-American poet and novelist
Henrik Johan Ibsen, Norwegian playwright
Alexander Lange Kielland, Norwegian novelist and playwright
William Kirby, English-born Canadian novelist
José María de Pereda, Spanish novelist, poet, and playwright

LITERARY EVENT
PRIZES AND AWARDS
Nobel Prize in literature: Giosuè Carducci, Italian poet

PUBLICATIONS
ARMENIAN
Frights Collection of lyric poems by Daniel Varuzhan

DANISH
Denied a Country Novel by Hermann Bang
The Pilgrim Kamanita Novel by Karl Adolf Gjellerup

DUTCH
The Mountain of Light Novel by Louis Marie Anne Couperus

ENGLISH
American

Are You a Bromide? Humorous piece by Gelett Burgess
The Devil's Dictionary Satirical lexicography by Ambrose Bierce
The Education of Henry Adams Autobiography by Henry Adams
"The Furnished Room" Short story by O. Henry
The Jungle Novel by Upton Sinclair
White Fang Novel by Jack London

British

The Man of Property Novel (part of the *Forsyte Saga*) by John
    Galsworthy
Poems Collected verse of Walter de la Mare

Irish

The Doctor's Dilemma Play by George Bernard Shaw

Scottish

The Gentleman in Grey Play by Compton Mackenzie

FINNISH
Spring and the Untimely Return of Winter Novel by Juhani Aho

FRENCH
Belgian

The Manifest Splendor Collection of poems by Émile Verhaeren

French

Break at Noon Autobiography by Paul Claudel
The Claw Play by Henry Bernstein
Memoirs of Mistral Memoirs by Frédéric Mistral
The Winged Sandal Collection of poems by Henri de Régnier

GERMAN
German

And Pippa Dances Fairy tale play by Gerhart Hauptmann

The Quest for Historical Jesus Theological treatise by Albert
    Schweitzer

Swiss

Grass and Bell Poems by Carl Spitteler

HUNGARIAN
New Poems Collected verse of Endre Ady

ICELANDIC
Smooth Seas Collected verse of Einar Benediktsson

JAPANESE
Botchan: Master Darling Novel by Natsume Sōseki
Dream Flowers Collected verse of Yosano Akiko
The Three-Cornered World Novel by Natsume Sōseki

RUSSIAN
Mother Novel by Maxim Gorky
The River of Life Story by Aleksandr Kuprin

SPANISH
Peruvian

American Soul Collection of poems by José Santos Chocano

Spanish

Woman Triumphant Novel by Vicente Blasco Ibáñez

Uruguayan

Violet Poems Collection by Julio Herrera y Reissig

SWEDISH
Flora Och Pomona Collection of poems by Swedish poet Andreas
    Karlfeldt
Gertrud Play by Hjalmar Söderberg

TAGALOG
Rays and Sunrise Novel by Filipino writer Lope K. Santos

1907

BIRTHS
Wystan Hugh Auden, English poet and dramatist
Jacques Barzun, French-born American critic
Bernardes Brazdzionis, Lithuanian poet and writer of children's
    stories
Rachel Carson, American environmental writer
Daphne du Maurier, English novelist
Gunnar Ekelof, Swedish poet
Christopher Fry, English playwright
Rumer Godden, English novelist
Robert Anson Heinlein, American science fiction writer
Alec Derwent Hope, Australian poet and critic
Khalilullah Khalili, Afghan poet and historian
Helen Clark MacInnes, Scottish-born American novelist and
    playwright
Hugh MacLennan, Canadian novelist

Louis MacNeice, Irish-born poet
Bal Sitaram Mardhekar, Marathi poet
James Albert Michener, American novelist
Alberto Moravia, Italian novelist
U Nu, Burmese novelist and playwright
Jacques Roumain, Haitian poet
The Lu, Vietnamese poet
Miguel Torga, Portuguese poet
Zodji (U Thein Han), Burmese poet and playwright

DEATHS

Thomas Bailey Aldrich, American novelist and poet
Giosuè Carducci, Italian poet and scholar
William Henry Drummond, Canadian poet
Joris-Karl Huysmans, French novelist
Sully Prudhomme (René-François-Armand Prudhomme), French poet, philosopher, and essayist
Francis Thompson, English Catholic poet
Tran Te Xuong, Vietnamese poet
Stanisław Wyspianski, Polish playwright and poet

LITERARY EVENT

PRIZES AND AWARDS

Nobel Prize in literature: Rudyard Kipling, English writer

PUBLICATIONS

BENGALI

Gora Novel by Indian writer Rabindranath Tagore

DUTCH

A Lost Wanderer Novel by Arthur von Schendel
Voices Collected verse by Pieter Cornelis Boutens
A Wanderer in Love Novel by Arthur von Schendel

ENGLISH

American

The American Scene Novel by Henry James
The Iron Heel Novel by Jack London
"The Last Leaf" Short story by O. Henry

British

Fathers and Sons Autobiography by Edmund Gosse
The Longest Journey Autobiographical novel by E. M. Forster
The Secret Agent Novel by Joseph Conrad

Irish

Deirdre Heroic tragedy by William Butler Yeats
Major Barbara Play by George Bernard Shaw
The Playboy of the Western World Play by John Millington Synge
Wild Earth Poems by Padraic Colum

FRENCH

Creative Evolution Scientific thesis by Henri Bergson

GERMAN

Swiss

Two Little Misogynists Collection of stories by Carl Spitteler

GREEK

The Twelve Lays of the Gypsy Collected verse by Kostis Palamas

HEBREW

The God of Vengeance Play by Israeli writer Sholem Asch

HUNGARIAN

The Paul Street Boy Novel by Ferenc Molnár

ITALIAN

Saturday Sun Novel by Marino Moretti

RUSSIAN

Eros Collection of poems by Vyacheslav Ivanov
The Mask of Snow Collected verse of Aleksandr Aleksandrovich Blok
Sanine Novel by Mikhail Artsybashev

SPANISH

Spanish

The Bonds of Interest Comic play by Jacinto Benavente y Martínez
The Darkness at the Top Novel by Ramón Pérez de Ayala

Uruguayan

The White Book Collection of poems by Delmira Agustini

SWEDISH

Black Banners Novel by August Strindberg
The Ghost Sonata Fantasy by August Strindberg

1908

BIRTHS

Arthur Adamov, Franco-Russian playwright
Martín Adán (Rafael de la Fuente Benavides), Peruvian novelist
Sylvia Ashton-Warner, New Zealand poet and novelist
Nigel Balchin, English novelist
Agusti Batra, Catalan novelist
Simone de Beauvoir, French novelist and essayist
Paul Hamilton Engle, American poet
Ian Fleming, English novelist
Arthur Nuthall Fula, Afrikaans novelist and poet
Tommaso Landolfi, Italian novelist, playwright, and poet
Claude Levi-Strauss, Belgian anthropologist
Pashaogly Mir Jalal, Azerbaijani novelist and essayist
Armijn Pane, Indonesian playwright, short-story writer, and scholar
Teodor Parnicki, Polish historian and novelist
Cesare Pavese, Italian novelist and poet
Raja Rao, Indian novelist and short-story writer
Theodore Roethke, American poet
João Guimaraes Rosa, Brazilian short-story writer and novelist
William Saroyan, American novelist

Mark Schorer, American novelist and biographer
José García Villa, Filipino poet
Elio Vittorini, Sicilian novelist
Mika Waltari, Finnish novelist
Richard Wright, African-American novelist

DEATHS

Wilhelm Busch, German poet
Svatpluk Cech, Czech poet and novelist
François Coppée, French poet, novelist, and playwright
Edmondo De Amicis, Italian novelist
Holger Henrik Herholdt Drachmann, Danish poet
Joel Chandler Harris, American novelist
Bronson Crocker Howard, American playwright
Joaquim Maria Machado de Assis, Brazilian novelist
Misak Metsarants, Armenian poet
Ouida (Marie Louise de la Ramée), English novelist
Victorien Sardou, French playwright

LITERARY EVENT

PRIZES AND AWARDS

Nobel Prize in literature: Rudolf C. Eucken, German philosopher

PUBLICATIONS

AMHARIC

A Fictional Story Novel by Ethiopian writer Afawarq Gabra Iyasus

ARMENIAN

Dreams in the Twilight Collected verse of Vahan Terian

DANISH

The Long Journey Six-volume novel by Johannes Jensen

DUTCH

Breatijs Collected verse of Pieter Cornelis Boutens

ENGLISH

American

A lume spento Collected verse of Ezra Pound
The Circular Staircase Mystery novel by Mary Roberts Rinehart
The Iron Heel Novel by Jack London
"To Build a Fire" Short story by Jack London

British

Centuries of Meditations Poems by Thomas Traherne
The Man Who Was Thursday Novel by G. K. Chesterton
The Melting Pot Play by Israel Zangwill
The Old Wives' Tale Novel by Arnold Bennet
A Room with a View Novel by E. M. Forster
Tono-Bungoy Novel by H. G. Wells

Scottish

The Wind in the Willows Children's novel by Kenneth Grahame

FINNISH

Black Sonnets Poems by Baron Bartel Johan Sebastian
Frost Poems by Eino Leino
The Fugitives Novel by Johannes Linnankoski

FRENCH

Belgian

The Blue Bird Play by Maurice Maeterlinck

French

Israel Play by Henry Bernstein
Penguin Island Novel by Anatole France
The Unanimous Life Collected verse of Jules Romains

GERMAN

Austrian

The Road to the Open Novel by Arthur Schnitzler

German

Caspar Hauser Novel by Jakob Wasserman
The Songs of Songs Novel by Hermann Sudermann

Swiss

Saint Francis of Assisi Novel by Heinrich Federer
The Zurich Idyll Collection of poems by Robert Faesi

HUNGARIAN

The Noszty Boy and Mary Toth Novel by Kálmán Mikzáth

JAPANESE

The Bed Novel by Tayama Katai

OSSETIAN

Writings of a Prisoner Verse cycle by Georgian writer Taomaq Gaediaty

RUSSIAN

The Fiery Angel Novel by Valery Bryusov
Pavel Play by Dmitry Sergeyevich Mereazhkovsky
Verik Collected stories by Jewish writer Sholem Aleichem

SPANISH

Argentine

The Glory of Don Ramiro Novel by Enrique Rodriguez Larreta

Peruvian

Let There Be Light Collection of poems by José Santos Chocano

Spanish

Blood and Sand Novel by Vicente Blasco Ibáñez
Pure Elegies Collection of poems by Juan Ramón Jiménez

1909

BIRTHS

James Agee, American poet
Nelson Algren, American novelist

Eric Ambler, English novelist
Jerzy Andrzejewski, Polish novelist
Bian Zhilin, Chinese poet
María Luisa Bombal, Chilean novelist, short-story writer, and composer
Paul Bowles, American novelist, short-story writer, and composer
Jean Brierre, Haitian poet
John Wood Campbell Jr., American writer of science fiction
Cao Yu, Chinese playwright
Dazai Osamu (Tsushima Shuji), Japanese novelist
Peter De Vries, American satirical novelist
Laxmiprasad Devkota, Nepalese poet and playwright
Resat Enis, Turkish novelist
D. O. Fogunwa, Nigerian novelist
Jean Genet, French novelist and dramatist
John Glassco, Canadian poet and novelist
Miguel Hernández, Spanish poet and playwright
Maun Htin, Burmese playwright and novelist
Mahti Hussain, Azerbaijani novelist and playwright
Jalol Ikromi, Tajik novelist and playwright
Eugene Ionesco, French-Romanian playwright
Elia Kazan, Greek-born American playwright, novelist, and film director
José Lezama Lima, Cuban poet, novelist, and essayist
Erik Lindegren, Swedish poet
Clarence Malcolm Lowry, English novelist
Edgar Mittelholzer, Guyanese novelist, playwright, and poet
Manuel Mujica Lainez, Argentine novelist
Vladimir Neff, Czech novelist
Elder James Olson, American poet and literary critic
André Pieyre de Mandiargues, French novelist, poet, and playwright
Rachel de Queiroz, Brazilian novelist
Oscar Bento Ribas, Angolan novelist, poet, and playwright
Shabaan Robert, Tanzanian Swahili poet, novelist, and biographer
Abul-Qasim ash-Shabbi, Tunisian poet and critic
Stephen Spender, English poet and critic
Wallace Stegner, American novelist
Thach Lam, Vietnamese novelist
Simone Weil, French philosopher, playwright, and poet
Eudora Welty, American novelist
Komil Yashin, Uzbek poet, playwright, and critic

DEATHS
Euclides da Cunha, Brazilian novelist
Sarah Orne Jewett, American novelist
Detlev von Liliencron, German poet, playwright, and novelist
Cesare Lombroso, Italian criminologist
Catule Mendes, French poet
George Meredith, English novelist and poet
Shimei Futabatei, Japanese novelist
John Millington Synge, Irish playwright and poet
Algernon Charles Swinburne, English poet and playwright

LITERARY EVENTS
Apollon monthly is founded by Sergey Makovsky
La Nouvelle Revue Française is founded in Paris

PRIZES AND AWARDS
Nobel Prize in literature: Selma Lagerlöf, Swedish novelist

PUBLICATIONS
ARMENIAN
New Morning Collection of lyrics by Hakob Hakobian

ENGLISH
American
Martin Eden Autobiographical novel by Jack London
Personae Collection of poems by Ezra Pound

British
Ann Veronica Novel by H. G. Wells
The Silver Box Social drama by John Galsworthy

Irish
The Glittering Gate Play by Edward Dunsany

FRENCH
Belgian
The Bluebird Play by Maurice Maeterlinck

French
Joined Hands Collected verse by François Mauriac
Saint Matoral Collected verse of Max Jacob
Strait Is the Gate Novel by André Gide

GERMAN
Austrian
The Other Side Novel by Alfred Kubin

German
Wupper River Play by Else Lasker-Schuler

Swiss
Jakob von Gunten Novel by Robert Walser

GREEK
The Light-Shadowed Poem by Angelos Sikelianós

HUNGARIAN
Liliom Play by Ferenc Molnár

MALAYALAM
Fallen Flower Poem by Indian writer N. Kumaran Asan

NORWEGIAN
Poems Collection by Olaf Bull

PORTUGUESE
Brazilian
Memoirs of the Notary Public Isaias Caminha Novel by Alfonso Henriques de Lima Barreto

RUSSIAN

Ashes Collection of verses by Andrei Bely
Urn Collection of verses by Andrei Bely
Yama: The Pit Novel by Aleksandr Kuprin

SPANISH

Argentine

Sentimental Lunar Almanac Collected verse by Leopoldo Lugones

Spanish

The Evil Poem Collection of poems by Manuel Machado
Zalacaín el aventurero Novel by Pío Baroja

SWEDISH

The Great Highway Play by August Strindberg

1910

BIRTHS

Jean Anouilh, French playwright and novelist
Vaikam Muhammad Bashir, Malayalee novelist
Kemal Bilbasar, Turkish novelist
Daniel Olorunfami Fagunwa, Yoruba novelist
Jean Genet, French playwright, novelist, and poet
Julien Gracq (Louis Poirier), French novelist, poet, and playwright
Abdullah Habibi, Afghan poet
Bernard Kangro, Estonian poet
U Luhtu Hla, Burmese novelist
Nicholas John Turney Monsarrat, English novelist
Wright Morris, American novelist
Gul Khan Nasir, Baluchi poet and essayist
Qian Zhongshu, Chinese scholar and writer
Gwendolyn Ringwood, American-born Canadian playwright, poet, and novelist
Razul Rza, Azerbaijani poet, playwright, and novelist
Abdoulaye Sadji, Senegalese novelist
Fakhroddin Shadman, Iranian essayist and novelist
Srirangam Srinivasa Rao, Telugu poet
Kemal Tahir, Turkish novelist
Cahit Sitki Taranci, Turkish poet

DEATHS

Bjørnstjerne Martinius Bjørnson, Norwegian poet, playwright, and novelist
Julio Herrera y Reissig, Uruguayan poet
Julia Ward Howe, American poet and social reformer
William James, American philosopher and psychologist
Kálmán Mikszáth, Hungarian novelist
William Vaughan Moody, American poet and playwright
Jean Moreas (Johannes Papadiamantopulos), Greek-born French symbolist poet, playwright, and novelist
O. Henry (William Sidney Porter), American writer of short stories
Wilhelm Raabe, German novelist
Jules Renard, French diarist, poet, and novelist
Count Leo Nikolayevich Tolstoy, Russian novelist
Mark Twain (Samuel Langhorne Clemens), American novelist

LITERARY EVENT

PRIZES AND AWARDS
Nobel Prize in literature: Paul L. Heyse, German writer

PUBLICATIONS

BENGALI

Gītāñjalī Collected verse of Indian writer Rabindranath Tagore

ENGLISH

American

Burning Daylight Novel by Jack London
The Finer Grain Collection of short stories by Henry James
"Miniver Cheevy" Poem by Edwin Arlington Robinson
"The Ransom of Red Chief" Short story by O. Henry (William Sidney Porter)
The Spirit of Romance Literary criticism by Ezra Pound
The Town Down the River Collected verse by Edwin Arlington Robinson

British

Ballads and Poems Collection of verse by John Masefield
The Dynasts Epic drama by Thomas Hardy
Howards End Novel by E. M. Forster
Justice Play by John Galsworthy
Principia Mathematica Mathematical treatise by philosophers Bertrand Russell and Alfred North Whitehead
Reginald in Russia Collection of stories by Saki (H. H. Munro)
When His Hour Came Novel by Elinor Glyn

Irish

Deirdre of the Sorrows Unfinished tragic drama by John Millington Synge
The Green Hamlet and Other Poems Collection by William Butler Yeats

Scottish

The Twelve-Pound Note Play by James M. Barrie

FRENCH

Five Great Odes Poems by Paul Claudel
Impressions of Africa Novel by Raymond Roussel
The Phantom of the Opera Novel by Gaston Leroux
The Vagabond Novel by Colette

GERMAN

Austrian

Christina's Journey Home Play by Hugo von Hofmannsthal

German

The Fool in Christ, Emanuel Quint Novel by Gerhart Hauptmann
The Northern Lights Epic poem by Theodore Daubla
The Notebook of Matte Laurids Brigge Novel in journal form by Rainer Maria Rilke

Swiss

The Olympic Spring Collection of poems by Carl Spitteler

GREEK
The King's Flute Collected verse of Kostis Palamas

HUNGARIAN
The Black City Historical novel by Kálmán Mikszáth
The Complaint of a Poor Little Child Cycle of poems by Dezsó Kostolányi

JAPANESE
The Gate Novel by Natsume Sōseki
A Handful of Sand Collected verse of Ishikawa Takuboku

MARATHI
The Slaying of Kicak Play by Krishnaji Prabhakar Khadilkar

RUSSIAN
Evening Album Collection of poems by Marina Tsvetayeva
The Village Novel by Ivan Alekseyevich Bunin

SPANISH
Spanish
Adam in Paradise Philosophical treatise by José Ortega y Gasset
AMDG Autobiographical novel by Ramón Pérez de Ayala

Uruguayan
Morning Songs Collected verse by Delmira Agustini

SWEDISH
His Grace's Will Novel by Hjalmar Bergman

YIDDISH
The Golden Chain Mystical play by Polish Jewish writer Isaac Leib Peretz

1911

BIRTHS
Jacques Bahelele, Kikongo novelist
Hervé Bazin, French novelist and short-story writer
Elizabeth Bishop, American poet
Stanisław Brzozoski, Polish novelist and playwright
Hortense Calisher, American novelist and short-story writer
Jean-Raphael-Marie-Noël Cayrol, French poet
Odysseus Elytis, Greek poet, essayist, and translator
Max Rudolf Frisch, Swiss novelist and playwright
William Golding, English novelist
Albert Gomes, Trinidadian poet and novelist
Mirza Ibrahimov, Azerbaijani poet
Umashankar Joshi, Gujarati poet
Naguib Mahfouz, Egyptian novelist
Asrar-ul-haq Majaz, Urdu lyric poet
Achdiat Karta Mihardja, Indonesian novelist
Czeslaw Milosz, Lithuanian-born Polish poet
Flann O'Brien (Brian O'Nuallain), Irish novelist
Dennis Chukude Osadebay, West Nigerian poet
Gabriel Preil, Russian Hebrew poet

Terence Rattigan, English playwright
Ernesto Sábato, Argentine novelist
Nuqui Bienvenido Santos, Filipino novelist
Ousmane Diop Soce, Senegalese novelist and poet
K. Surangkhanag (Kanha Khiengsiri), Thai novelist
Mirzo Turzunzoda, Tajik poet and playwright
Sotim Ulughzoda, Tajik novelist and playwright
Tennessee Williams (Thomas Lanier Williams), American playwright

DEATHS
Wilhelm Dilthey, German philosopher
Gustaf Fröding, Swedish lyrical poet
Sir William Schwenck Gilbert, English lyricist
Alexandros Papadiamantis, Greek novelist
Mirza al-Akbar Sabir, Azerbaijani poet
Friedrich Spielhagen, German novelist

LITERARY EVENT
PRIZES AND AWARDS
Nobel Prize in literature: Maurice Maeterlinck, Belgian playwright

PUBLICATIONS

ARMENIAN
Abdulala Mahari Epic poem by Avetikh Isahakian

ENGLISH
American
The Cruise of the Snark Novel by Jack London
Ethan Frome Novel by Edith Wharton
Jennie Gerhardt Novel by Theodore Dreiser
The Making of Americans Novel by Gertrude Stein

British
The Chronicle of Clovis Collected stories of Saki (H. H. Munro)
The Country of the Blind Collection of short stories by H. G. Wells
The New Machiavelli Novel by H. G. Wells
The Secret Garden Children's story by Frances Hodgson Burnett
"Tobermory" Short story by Saki (H. H. Munro)
Under Western Eyes Novel by Joseph Conrad
Zuleika Dobson Novel by Max Beerbohm

Ghanaian
Ethiopia Unbound Novel by Joseph Ephraim Casely Hayford

Irish
The Doctor's Dilemma Play by George Bernard Shaw
The Gods of the Mountain Play by Edward Dunsany

FINNISH
Juha Romantic novel by Juhari Aho

FRENCH
Belgian
The Evening Hours Collected verse of Émile Verhaeren

French

The Christian Georgics Saga by Francis Jammes
Death of a Nobody Novel by Jules Romains
Eloges, and Other Poems Collection by Saint-John Perse
The Hostage Play by Paul Claudel
The Yoke of Pity Novel by Julien Breda

GERMAN
Austrian

Everyman One-act morality play in verse by Hugo von Hofmannsthal

German

My Life Autobiography by Richard Wagner
The Plants Play by Jewish playwright Carl Sternheim

Swiss

Lachweill Stories Novel by Heinrich Federer
Mountains and Men Novel by Heinrich Federer

ICELANDIC
Eyvind of the Hills Play by Johann Sigurjonsson

ITALIAN
The Colloquies Collected verse of Guido Gozzano

JAPANESE
Memories Poems by Kitahara Hakushu
The Wild Goose Novel by Mori Ōgai

NORWEGIAN
Jenny Novel by Sigrid Undset

POLISH
Alone Among Men Novel by Stanisław Brzozowski

RUSSIAN
Cor Ardens Collection of poems by Vyacheslav Ivanov

SPANISH
Peruvian

Symbolism Collected verse of José María Eguren

Spanish

Firmly Rooted Novel by Orsy Rovira

1912

BIRTHS
Ahmed Ali, Urdu novelist
Jorge Amado, Brazilian novelist
Said Aql, Lebanese poet, playwright, and novelist
Pierre Boule, French novelist
Roussan Camile, Haitian poet
José Luis Cano, Spanish poet

John Cheever, American novelist
Leon Gontran Damas, Guyanese poet
Lawrence George Durrell, English poet and novelist
William Everson, American poet
Northrop Frye, Canadian literary critic
Nikos Gatsos, Greek poet
Eugene Ionesco, Romanian-born French playwright and novelist
John Robin Jenkins, Scottish novelist
Pamela Hansford Johnson, English novelist
Abbé Alexis Kagame, Rwandan poet and historian
Qiyamuddin Khadir, Afghan poet
Nagib Mahfuz, Egyptian novelist and playwright
Sadat Hasan Manto, Urdu playwright and essayist
Mary McCarthy, American essayist and novelist
Mirsaid Mirshakar, Tajik poet and playwright
Istvan Orkeny, Hungarian playwright
William Sansom, English novelist
May Sarton, American poet, novelist, and essayist
Siddhicaran Srestha, Nepalese poet
Erwin Strithmatter, German novelist
Tungelbay Sydykbekov, Kirghiz poet
Barbara Tuchman, American historian
Mu Varadaracan, Tamil playwright and novelist
Vu Trong Phung, Vietnamese playwright and novelist
Patrick White, English-born Australian novelist
Terence de Vere White, Irish novelist and biographer

DEATHS
Hermann Bang, Danish novelist
Ion Luca Caragiale, Romanian playwright
Joseph Furphy, Australian novelist and poet
Ishikawa Takuboku, Japanese poet
Pencho Petkov Slaveykov, Bulgarian poet
Bram Stoker, Anglo-Irish novelist
August Strindberg, Swedish playwright and novelist

LITERARY EVENT
PRIZES AND AWARDS
Nobel Prize in literature: Gerhart Hauptmann, German playwright

PUBLICATIONS

ARMENIAN
Verses Collected verses by Vahan Terian

BENGALI
A Bunch of Stories Collected stories of Indian writer Rabindranath Tagore

CHINESE
The Lone Swan Autobiographical novel by Chinese poet Su Manshu

CZECH
The Good Soldier Schweik Novel by Jaroslav Hašek

DANISH
The Realm of the Dead Novel cycle by Henrik Pontoppidan

ENGLISH

American

The Autobiography of an Ex-Colored Man Novel by James Weldon Johnson

A Dome of Many-Colored Glass Collected verse by Amy Lowell

The Financier Novel by Theodore Dreiser

Flagons and Apples Collection of verse by Robinson Jeffers

The Promised Land Autobiography of Russian-born Mary Antin

Rhymes to Be Traded for Bread Collected verse by Vachel Lindsay

Riders of the Purple Sage Western novel by Zane Grey

British

The Matador of the Five Towns Collection of short stories by Arnold Bennett

FRENCH

Belgian

Wheat in Motion Collected verse by Émile Verhaeren

French

The Gods Are Athirst Novel by Anatole France

Le mystère des saints innocents Collected verse of Charles Péguy

Swann's Way Novel (part of *Remembrance of Things Past*) by Marcel Proust

The Tidings Brought to Mary Poetic drama by Paul Claudel

GERMAN

German

Ariadne and Naxos Play by Paul Ernst

Death in Venice Short novel by Thomas Mann

Morgue and Other Poems Collected verse of Gottfried Benn

My Heart Autobiographical novel by Else Lasker-Schuler

Swiss

The Theory of Psychoanalysis Psychological treatise by Carl Jung

GREEK

The Murderess Novel by Alexandros Papadiamantis

HINDI

Bharatbharati Epic poem by Indian writer Maithilisharan Gupta

ICELANDIC

The Borg Family Papers Novel by Gunnar Gunnarsson

ITALIAN

A Man—Finished Autobiography by Giovanni Papini

JAPANESE

The Wayfarer Novel by Natsume Sōseki

NORWEGIAN

I Will Defend My Country Play by Gunnar Heiberg

ROMANIAN

The Fairy at the Bottom of the Lake Novel by Nicolae Davidescu

RUSSIAN

Evening Collection of poems by Anna Akhmatova

Foreign Sky Collected verse of Nikolay Gumilyov

Solitary Thoughts Collection of maxims by Vasily Rozanov

The Sweet Secret Poems by Vyacheslav Ivanov

SPANISH

The Fox's Paw Novel by Ramón Pérez de Ayala

Malvaloca Play by Serafín and Joaquín Alvarez Quintero

Plains of Castile Collection of poems by Antonio Machado

Singing from the Depths Collection of poems by Manuel Machado

SWEDISH

The Serious Game Novel by Hjalmar Söderberg

Workers, a Story of Hatred Novel by Martin Koch

TAMIL

Kuyil's Song Poem by Indian poet Subramanya C. Bharati

Panchali's Vow Poem by Subramanya C. Bharati

TURKISH

Haluk's Notebook Collection of poems for children by Tevfik Fikret

1913

BIRTHS

Grigol Abashidze, Georgian poet

Raphael Ernest Grail Glikpo Armattoe, Ghanaian poet and historian

Marguerite Taos Amrouche, Algerian writer

George Granville Barker, English poet

Abdurrauf Benawa, Afghan poet

Albert Camus, French novelist, essayist, and playwright

Aimé Fernand Césaire, Martinique poet and playwright

Robertson Davies, Canadian poet, novelist, and playwright

Gyorgy Faludy, Hungarian-born Canadian poet, novelist, and biographer

Mouloud Feraoun, Algerian Kabyle novelist

Gertrud Fussenegger, German novelist

Robert Earl Hayden, American poet

Stefan Heym (Hellmuth Flieg), German novelist and poet

William Inge, American playwright

George Benson Johnston, Canadian poet

Kersti Merilaas, Estonian poet

Sripad Narayan Pendse, Marathi novelist

Jean-Jacques Rabemanajara, Malagasy poet and playwright

Victor Stafford Reid, Jamaican novelist and playwright

Delmore Schwartz, American poet and critic

Vittoorino Sereni, Italian poet

Karl Jay Shapiro, American poet, novelist, and critic

Irwin Shaw, American playwright and novelist

Claude Simon, French novelist

Douglas Stewart, Australian poet and playwright

Ronald Stuart Thomas, Welsh poet and essayist

Igor Torkar (Boris Fakin), Slovene novelist
Sandor Weores, Hungarian poet
Angus Frank Johnstone Wilson, English novelist

DEATHS

Aluizio Azevedo, Brazilian novelist
Gastón Fernando Deligne, Dominican poet and novelist
Edward Dowden, Irish scholar and critic
Uri Nissan Gnessin, Russian-Jewish writer of short fiction
Antoine-Louis-Camille Lemonnier, Belgian novelist
Abdulla Tukay, Tatar poet
Lesya Ukrainka (Laryse Petrivna Kosach Kvittka), Ukrainian poet and playwright

LITERARY EVENT

PRIZES AND AWARDS
Nobel Prize in literature: Rabindranath Tagore, Indian poet

PUBLICATIONS

ENGLISH

American

A Boy's Will Collection of verse by Robert Frost
The Custom of the Country Novel by Edith Wharton
General William Booth Enters into Heaven and Other Poems Collection by Vachel Lindsay
Mont-Saint-Michel and Chartres Meditative cultural essays by Henry Adams
O Pioneers! Novel by Willa Cather
Trees Collected verse of Joyce Kilmer

British

Chance Novel by Joseph Conrad
The Fugitive Play by John Galsworthy
The Lodger Mystery novel by Mary Adelaide Lowndes
Sons and Lovers Autobiographical novel by D. H. Lawrence
Widecombe Fair Novel by Eden Phillpotts
The Woman Thou Gavest Me Novel by Hall Caine

Irish

Pygmalion Play by George Bernard Shaw

South African

Don't Forget Novel by Daniel Malherbe

FRENCH

Alcools Collection of poems by Guillaume Apollinaire
The Boys in the Back Room Novel by Jules Romains
Ève Collected verse of Charles Péguy
The Last Domain Novel by Alain Fournier
Music Hall Sidelights Commentaries by Colette
The Tragedies of Faith Play by Romain Rolland
Young Man in Chains Novel by François Mauriac

GERMAN

Austrian

The Secret Play by Henry Bernstein
Totem and Taboo Treatise on psychiatry by Sigmund Freud

German

The Life of Virgin Mary Collected verse of Rainer Maria Rilke
The Tunnel Novel by Bernhard Kellerman

Swiss

Sixtus and Sesto Novel by Heinrich Federer

ICELANDIC

Waves Collection of poems by Einar Benediktsson

ITALIAN

The Old and the Young Novel by Luigi Pirandello

JAPANESE

Paulownia Blossom Collection of poems by Kitahara Hakushu

NORWEGIAN

The Catafalque Play by Gunnar Heiberg

RUSSIAN

Altar of Victory Novel by Valery Bryusov
My Childhood Autobiography by Maxim Gorky

SPANISH

The Passion Flower Play by Jacinto Benavente y Martínez
The Tragic Sense of Life Philosophical treatise by Miguel de Unamuno
Trotters and Dancers Novel by Ramón Pérez de Ayala

SWEDISH

The Timber Valley: A Story of Culture Novel by Martin Koch

1914

BIRTHS

Khwaja Ahmad Abbas, Urdu novelist
Aziz Ahmed, Urdu novelist
Aida Tsunao, Japanese poet
John Berryman, American poet
Adolfo Bioy Casares, Argentine writer
William Burroughs, American novelist
Krishan Chander, Urdu writer
Julio Cortázar, Belgian-born Argentine novelist
Marguerite Duras, Indochinese-born French novelist and playwright
Ralph Ellison, African-American novelist
Romain Gary, French novelist
John Hersey, American novelist
Randall Jarrell, American poet, critic, and novelist
Orhan Veli Kanik, Turkish poet
Orhan Kemal (Mehmet Rasit Kemali Ogutcu), Turkish poet and novelist
Kinoshita Junji, Japanese playwright
Kunnumpuzha Krishna Pillai, Malayalee poet
Paul Lomami-Tshibamba, Congolese novelist
Mario Luzi, Italian poet

Bernard Malamud, American novelist
Claude Mauriac, French novelist
Foteh Niyazi, Tajik poet
Nicanor Parra, Chilean poet
Octavio Paz, Mexican poet, playwright, and essayist
Jose Revueltas, Mexican novelist and short-story writer
Oktay Rifat, Turkish poet
Emmanuel Robles, French Algerian novelist
Budd Schulberg, American novelist
Hovhannes Shiraz, Armenian poet
Thakazhi Sivasankaran Pillai, Malayalee poet and writer of short fiction
William Stafford, American poet
Thein Pe Myint, Burmese novelist
Dylan Thomas, Welsh poet
Yoshiko Shibaki, Japanese novelist

DEATHS
Ambrose Bierce, American satirist
Delmira Agustini, Uruguayan poet
Recaizade Mahmud Ekrem Bey, Turkish novelist
Thorsteinn Erlingsson, Icelandic poet
Egzi'abekar Gabra, Ethiopian poet
Paul Johann Ludwig von Heyse, German novelist and playwright
Frédéric Mistral, French Provençal poet
Christian Morgenstern, German poet
Charles Péguy, French Catholic poet and philosopher
Bertha Suttner, Austrian novelist
George Trakl, Austrian poet
Peyo Yavorov, Bulgarian poet and playwright

LITERARY EVENT
The Little Review, avant-garde literary magazine, is founded by Margaret Anderson

PUBLICATIONS
ARABIC
Egyptian
Zaynab Novel by Muhammad Husayn Haykal

Lebanese
A Tear and a Smile Mystical essays by Khalil Gibran

ENGLISH
American
Chicago Collected verse of Carl Sandburg
The Congo and Other Poems Collection of verse by Vachel Lindsay
"The Death of a Hired Man" Narrative poem by Robert Frost
"Mending Wall" Poem by Robert Frost
North of Boston Collection of poems by Robert Frost
On Trial Play by Elmer Rice
Penrod Novel by Booth Tarkington
Sword Blades and Poppy Seed Poems by Amy Lowell
Tarzan of the Apes Novel by Edgar Rice Burroughs
Tender Buttons Essay by Gertrude Stein
The Titan Novel by Theodore Dreiser

Australian
Poems 1913 Collection by Christopher John Brennan

British
Art Discourse by Clive Bell
Beasts and Super Beasts Collection of stories by Saki (H. H. Munro)
"The Open Window" Short story by Saki

Irish
"The Dead" Short story by James Joyce
Dubliners Collection of short stories by James Joyce
Responsibilities, Poems and a Play Collection by William Butler Yeats

FRENCH
The Stuff of Youth Novel by François Mauriac

GERMAN
Austrian
In the Penal Colony Novel by Czech-born Franz Kafka

German
The Prince of Thebes Collection of short stories by Else Lasker-Schuler

HINDI
"The Beloved's Exile" Poem by Indian writer Ayodhyasimha Upadhyay Hariaudh
Past Lucknow Historical study by Indian writer Abdul-Halim Sharar

ITALIAN
Lyric Poems Collected verse of Riccardo Bacchelli
Orphic Songs Collection of lyrics by Dino Campana

JAPANESE
Kokoro Novel by Natsume Sōseki

RUSSIAN
Peterburg Prose poem by Andrei Bely
Rosary Collection of verses by Anna Akhmatova

SPANISH
Meditations on Quixote Philosophical treatise by José Ortega y Gasset
Mist Novel by Miguel de Unamuno

YIDDISH
Der Dibuk (The Dybbuk) Play by Russian Jewish writer Shloime Ansky (Solomon Seinwil Rapporport)

1915

BIRTHS
Lars Sven Ahlin, Swedish novelist

Roland Barthes, French critic
Rajinder Singh Bedi, Urdu novelist and playwright
René Belance, Haitian poet
Saul Bellow, Canadian-born American novelist
Rupert Brooke, English poet
A. Emile Disengomoko, Congolese novelist, poet, and essayist
Adonias Filho, Brazilian novelist, critic, and essayist
Takla Hawaryat Germacaw, Ethiopian novelist and playwright
Alfred Hauge, Norwegian poet and novelist
Kypros Hrysanthis, Greek-Cypriot poet and essayist
Mikael Kabbada, Ethiopian playwright and poet
Alfred Kazin, American critic
P. C. Kuttikrishnan, Malayalee novelist
Roland Glyn Mathias, Welsh poet, novelist, and essayist
Thomas Merton, American monk, mystic, and writer
Arthur Miller, American playwright
Noma Hiroshi, Japanese novelist
Eric M. Rauch, Trinidadian poet, playwright, and essayist
Jean Stafford, American novelist
Lee Vroman, Dutch poet, playwright, and novelist
Herman Wouk, American novelist

DEATHS

Tevfik Fikret, Turkish poet
Rémy de Gourmont, French critic, playwright, poet, and novelist
José Duarte Ramalho Ortigão, Portuguese essayist
Isaac Leib Peretz, Polish Jewish novelist
Daniel Varuzhan, Armenian poet
Grigor Zohrap, Armenian novelist

LITERARY EVENT

PRIZES AND AWARDS
Nobel Prize in literature: Romain Rolland, French novelist

PUBLICATIONS

CZECH
Darkness Novel by Alois Jirásek

ENGLISH
American

America's Coming of Age Literary criticism by Van Wyck Brooks
The Cantos Poetry Collection by Ezra Pound
The Genius Novel by Theodore Dreiser
"The Road Not Taken" Poem by Robert Frost
Song of the Lark Novel by Willa Cather
Spoon River Anthology Collection of poems by Edgar Lee Masters

Australian

The Pioneers Novel by Fijian-born Katharine Susannah Prichard

British

The Good Soldier: A Tale of Passion Novel by Ford Maddox Ford
"The Love Song of J. Alfred Prufrock" Poem by T. S. Eliot
1914 Collection of poems by Rupert Brooke

Of Human Bondage Novel by W. Somerset Maugham
Painted Roofs First volume in what would become 11-part novel *Pilgrimage* (completed in 1938) by Dorothy M. Richardson
The Rainbow Novel by D. H. Lawrence
"The Soldier" Poem by Rupert Brooke
The Valley of Fear Mystery story by Sir Arthur Conan Doyle
The Voyage Out Novel by Virginia Woolf

Scottish

The Thirty-Nine Steps Mystery novel by John Buchan

FRENCH
Belgian

Belgium's Agony Collection of poems by Émile Verhaeren

French

"You Are Men" Poem by Pierre-Jean Jouve

GERMAN
Austrian

Der Golem Novel by Gustav Meyrink
The Metamorphosis Novel by Czech-born writer Franz Kafka

German

The Three Leaps of Wang-Lun Novel by Alfred Doblin

JAPANESE
Michikusa Novel by Natsume Sōseki
"Rashomon" Short story by Akutagawa Ryūnosuke

RUSSIAN
A Cloud in Trousers Long poem by Vladimir Mayakovsky

SLOVAK
Blood-Red Sonnets Poems by Hviezdoslav

SPANISH
Chilean

The Love-Crazed Boy Novel by Eduardo Barrios

SWEDISH
New Poems Collection by Verner von Heidenstam

URDU
Secrets of the Self Long poem by Indian writer Muhammad Iqbāl

1916

BIRTHS

Giorgio Bassani, Italian novelist
Kazimierz Brandys, Polish novelist and essayist
Antonio Buero Vallejo, Spanish playwright
Camilo José Cela, Spanish novelist
Alice Childress, African-American novelist
Sadiq Chubak, Iranian author
John Ciardi, American poet and critic

Bernard Binlin Dadie, Ivorien novelist, playwright, and poet

Roald Dahl, Welsh writer of children's books

Charles Edward Eaton, American poet

Vergilio Ferreira, Portuguese novelist

Natalie Ginzburg, Italian novelist

Elizabeth Hardwick, American novelist and short-story writer

Ernest von Heerden, South African poet

Anne Hébert, French-Canadian poet

Wolfgang Hildesheimer, German playwright, novelist, and essayist

Yoshie Hotta, Japanese novelist

Revaz Margiani, Georgian poet

Amritlal Nagar, Hindi novelist

Hubert Ogunde, Nigerian playwright

Walker Percy, American novelist

La Sa Ramamitram, Tamil novelist

Samar Sen, Bengali poet

Haldun Taner, Turkish novelist and playwright

Yves Theriault, French-Canadian novelist

Peter Ulrich Weiss, German-born Swedish playwright, novelist, and essayist

Morris West, Australian novelist

DEATHS

Sholem Aleichem (Sholem Yakov Rabinowitz), Russian Jewish writer

Rubén Darío, Nicaraguan poet

Richard Harding Davis, American novelist

José Echegaray y Eizaguirre, Spanish playwright

Simeon Samuel Frug, Russian Jewish poet

Henry James, American novelist

Jack London (John Griffith London), American novelist

Natsume Sōseki (Natsume Kinosuke), Japanese novelist

James Whitcomb Riley, American poet

Saki (H. H. Munro), English novelist and short-story writer

Alan Seeger, American poet

Henryk Sienkiewicz, Polish novelist

Carmen Sylva (Princess Elizabeth of Wied, later Queen Elizabeth of Romania), Romanian poet

Émile Verhaeren, Belgian poet

LITERARY EVENT

PRIZES AND AWARDS

Nobel Prize in literature: Verner von Heidenstam, Swedish lyric poet

PUBLICATIONS

DUTCH

Spring Moon Collected verse by Pieter Cornelis Boutens

ENGLISH

American

Chicago Poems Collection by Carl Sandburg

Collected Poems Collection by Alan Seeger

Lustra Collection of poems by Ezra Pound

The Man Against the Sky Poems by Edwin Arlington Robinson

Mountain Interval Collection of poems by Robert Frost

Seventeen Novel by Booth Tarkington

British

Over the Brazier Collection of poems by Robert Bridges

The Spirit of Man Anthology of poems and prose edited by Robert Graves

Irish

Androcles and the Lion Play by George Bernard Shaw

The Brook Kerith Novel by George Moore

Easter 1916 Collected verse of William Butler Yeats

Portrait of the Artist as a Young Man Autobiographical novel by James Joyce

FINNISH

Dikter Collected verse by Swedish-born Edith Irene Södergran

FRENCH

Under Fire Novel by Henri Barbusse

GERMAN

Austrian

The Acension Novel by Hermann Bahr

The Judgment Long story by Czech-born writer Franz Kafka

German

From Morn to Midnight Play by Georg Kaiser

HEBREW

Mottke the Thief Novel by Sholem Asch

JAPANESE

Hekigoto Kushu Collected verse of Hekigoto Kawahigashi

Notes of a Student Examinee Novel by Kumne Maso

NORWEGIAN

The Great Hunger Novel by Johan Bojer

POLISH

Book of the Poor Collected verse of Jan Kasprowicz

RUSSIAN

The Gentleman from San Francisco Collected stories of Ivan Alekseyevich Bunin

He Who Gets Slapped Novel by Leonid Andreyev

SPANISH

Peruvian

The Ballad of the Figures Collected verse by José María Eguren

Spanish

The Four Horsemen of the Apocalypse Novel by Vicente Blasco Ibáñez

Spiritual Sonnets Poems by Juan Ramón Jiménez

SWEDISH

God's Beautiful World, a Story of Right and Wrong Novel by Martin Koch

1917

BIRTHS

José María Arguedas, Peruvian novelist
Louis Auchincloss, American novelist
Geraldo Bessa Victor, Angolan poet
Heinrich Böll, German novelist and playwright
Gwendolyn Brooks, African-American poet
Anthony Burgess, English novelist
Carlo Cassola, Italian novelist
Arthur C. Clarke, English-born Sri Lankan science fiction writer
George Robert Acworth Conquest, English poet, historian, and critic
Sumner Locke Elliott, Australian novelist and playwright
Leslie Fiedler, American Jewish literary critic
Hans Bague Jassin, Indonesian essayist and critic
al-Bashir Khurayyif, Tunisian novelist
Robert Lowell Jr., American poet
Djanetjo Ma Ma Lei, Burmese novelist
James Philip McAuley, Australian poet and critic
Carson McCullers, American novelist
Nam Cao (Tran Huu Tri), Vietnamese novelist
Joaquin Nicodemus, Filipino poet and essayist
Augusto Roa Bastos, Paraguayan novelist and short-story writer
Peter Taylor, American novelist, playwright, and short-story writer
Toshio Timao, Japanese novelist
Xuan Dieu, Vietnamese poet

DEATHS

Mirza Sadeq Khan Amiri, Persian poet
Léon Bloy, French novelist
Ivan Franko, Ukrainian writer
T. E. Hulme, English poet and critic
Francis Ledwidge, Irish poet
José Enrique Rodó, Uruguayan philosopher and essayist
Mendele Mokher Sefarim (Sholem Jacob Abramovich), Russian Jewish writer

LITERARY EVENTS

Pulitzer Prize is founded in New York

PRIZES AND AWARDS

Nobel Prize in literature: Karl A. Gjellerup, Danish poet, and Henrik Pontoppidan, Danish novelist

Pulitzer Prizes

Biography *Julia Ward Howe* by Laura E. Richards and Maude Howe Elliott
History *With Americans of Past and Present Days* by J. J. Jusserand

PUBLICATIONS

ENGLISH

American

The Chinese Nightingale and Other Poems Collected verse of Vachel Lindsay
The Cream of the Jest Novel by James Branch Cabell
Merlin Dramatic narrative in blank verse by Edwin Arlington Robinson
Renascence and Other Poems Collection of poems by Edna St. Vincent Millay
The Three Black Pennys Novel by Joseph Hergesheimer
To the Finland Station Essays by Edmund Wilson

British

The Loom of Youth Novel by Alec Waugh
Prufrock and Other Observations Collection of verse by T. S. Eliot

Irish

"The Wild Swans at Coole" Poem by William Butler Yeats

Scottish

Dear Brutus Play by J. M. Barrie
South Wind Satirical novel by Norman Douglas

FRENCH

Belgian

The Closed Door Collection of poems by Jean de Bosschere

French

Dance of the Dead Collected verse of Pierre-Jean Jouve
The Dice Box Collection of poems by Max Jacob
The Young Fate Poem by Paul Valery

GERMAN

German

Flesh Collected verse of Gottfried Benn
Gas Trilogy (completed in 1920) by Georg Kaiser
The Poor Novel by Heinrich Mann

Swiss

From the Surge Collected poems of Robert Faesi

GREEK

Prologue to Life Poems by Angelos Sikelianós

ITALIAN

Right You Are—If You Think You Are Play by Luigi Pirandello

JAPANESE

Descendants of Cain Novel by Takeo Arishima

NORWEGIAN

The Growth of the Soil Novel by Knut Hamsun
Images in a Mirror Novel by Sigrid Undset

SPANISH

Argentine

The Book of Landscapes Collected verse of Leopoldo Lugones

Mexican

Los caciques Novel by Mariano Azuela

Spanish

Abel Sánchez Novel by Miguel de Unamuno

Diary of a Poet Recently Married Journal by Juan Ramón Jiménez

Platero and I Series of prose poems by Juan Ramón Jiménez

SWEDISH

Plays of Marionettes Play by Bo Hjalmar Bergman

1918

BIRTHS

Muhammad Said Abdulla, Tanzanian Swahili writer
Timothy Mofolorunso Aluko, Nigerian novelist
Maragret Avison, Canadian poet
William Bronk, American poet
George Campbell, Jamaican playwright and poet
Yusuf al-Khal, Lebanese Christian poet
Madeleine L'Engle, American novelist
Elsa Morante, Italian novelist and poet
Nguyen Hong, Vietnamese novelist
Manuel de Pedrolo, Catalan novelist, playwright, and poet
Juan Rulfo, Mexican novelist
Srirat Sathawanapat, Thai novelist
Bert Schierbeek, Dutch novelist
Aleksandr Isayevich Solzhenitsyn, Russian novelist
Muriel Spark, Scottish novelist, playwright, and poet

DEATHS

Henry Brooks Adams, American historian
Guillaume Apollinaire, French poet
Alfred Joyce Kilmer, American poet
John McCrae, Canadian poet
Wilfred Owen, English poet
Peter Rosegger, Austrian poet and novelist
Edmond Rostand, French poet and playwright
Su Manshu (Su Jin) Chinese poet and novelist
Frank Wedekind, German playwright

LITERARY EVENT

PRIZES AND AWARDS

Pulitzer Prizes

Biography *Benjamin Franklin, Self-Revealed* by William Cabell Bruce
Drama *Why Marry?* by Jesse Lynch Williams
History *A History of the Civil War* by James Ford Rhodes
Novel *His Family* by Ernest Poole
Poetry *Love Songs* by Sara Teasdale

PUBLICATIONS

ARMENIAN

Sad People Collection of stories by Stephen Zorian

ENGLISH

American

The Education of Henry Adams Autobiography of Henry Adams

The Madman Collection of meditations by Lebanese writer Khalil Gibran

The Magnificent Ambersons Novel by Booth Tarkington

My Ántonia Novel by Willa Cather

British

Eminent Victorians Biographical sketches by Lytton Strachey

Poems Collection of poems by Gerard Manley Hopkins, edited by Robert Graves

"The Wreck of the Deutschland" Poem by Gerard Manley Hopkins

Irish

Last Songs Collection of poems by Francis Ledwidge

New Zealand

Prelude Short story by Katherine Mansfield

FRENCH

Belgian

The Burgomaster of Stilmonde Play by Maurice Maeterlinck

French

Calligrammes Poems by Guillaume Apollinaire

Crusts Play by Paul Claudel

The Silence of Colonel Bramble Collection of stories and sketches by André Maurois

GERMAN

Blackie the Fool Novel by Klabund (Alfred Henschke)

The Decline of the West Magisterial survey of Western civilization by Oswald Spengler

The Heretic of Soana Novel by Gerhart Hauptmann

Man Is Good Collection of short stories by Leonhard Frank

The Patrioteer Novel by Heinrich Mann

Reflections of a Nonpolitical Man Collection of essays by Thomas Mann

The World of Drama Five-volume theatrical criticism by Alfred Kerr

HEBREW

Under Moses Novel by Sholem Asch

JAPANESE

The Tiger Novel by Kume Masao

NORWEGIAN

The People of Juvik Novel by Olav Dunn

PERSIAN

Mysteries of Selflessness Poem by Muhammad Iqbāl

RUSSIAN

December the Fourteenth Novel by Dmitri Mereazhkovsky

The Pyre Collected poems by Nikolay Gumilyov

The Twelve Ballad by Aleksandr Aleksandrovich Blok

SPANISH

Argentine

Sweet Injury Collected verse by Alfonsina Storni

Chilean

A Down-and-Outer Novel by Eduardo Barrios

Mexican

Las moscas Novel by Mariano Azuela

SWEDISH

Flora Och Bellona Collected verse of Adreas Karlfeldt
The September Lyre Collection of poems by Edith Södergran

YAKUT

Game of Life Play by A. I. Sofronov

1919

BIRTHS

Peter Lee Abrahams, South African novelist
Joan Brossa, Catalan poet
Paul De Man, Belgian-born scholar and literary critic
Gevorg Emin (Karlen Karapetian), Armenian poet
Emyr Owen Humphreys, Welsh novelist, playwright, and poet
Noni Helen Nontando Jabavu, Xhosa novelist
Shirley Jackson, American novelist and short-story writer
Benedict Kiely, Irish novelist
Kuroda Saburo, Japanese poet
Doris Lessing, Persian-born Rhodesian-English novelist
Primo Levi, Italian Jewish novelist
Ezekiel Mphahlele, South African essayist and short-story writer
Subhas Mukopadhyaya, Bengali poet
Iris Murdoch, Irish-born English novelist
Abdurrahman Pazhwak, Afghan poet, novelist, and playwright
Frederick Pohl, American writer of science fiction
Sadiqullah Rishtin, Afghan writer
J. D. Salinger, American novelist
Yoshioka Minoru, Japanese poet

DEATHS

Endre Ady, Hungarian poet
Leonid Andreyev, Russian novelist and playwright
Hari Narayan Apte, Marathi novelist
L. Frank Baum, American novelist
Karl Adolf Gjellerup, Danish novelist
Amado Nervo, Mexican poet
Ricardo Palma, Peruvian novelist, playwright, poet, essayist, and writer of short fiction
William Michael Rossetti, English poet and essayist
Vasily Vasilyevich Rozanov, Russian essayist
Jóhann Sigurjónsson, Icelandic playwright and poet
Narayan Vama Tilak, Marathi Christian poet

LITERARY EVENT

PRIZES AND AWARDS

Nobel Prize in literature: Carl F. G. Spitteler, Swiss poet and novelist

Pulitzer Prizes

Autobiography   *The Education of Henry Adams* by Henry Adams
Novel   *The Magnificent Ambersons* by Booth Tarkington
Poetry   *Corn Huskers* by Carl Sandburg and *Old Road to Paradise* by Margaret Widdemer

PUBLICATIONS

ARABIC

The Procession Long ode by Lebanese-born writer Khalil Gibran

ENGLISH

American

The American Language Lexicographical classic by H. L. Mencken
"Homage to Sextus Propertius" Poem by Ezra Pound
Java Head Novel by Joseph Hergesheimer
Jurgen Novel by James Branch Cabell
Poems Collection by T. S. Eliot
Ten Days That Shook the World Political reportage on the Russian Revolution by John Reed
Winesburg, Ohio Collection of stories by Sherwood Anderson

British

The Moon and Sixpence Novel by W. Somerset Maugham
Night and Day Novel by Virginia Woolf
War Poems Collection of poems by Siegfried Sassoon

Irish

Heartbreak House Play by George Bernard Shaw
The Only Jealousy of Emer Verse play by William Butler Yeats

FINNISH

Meek Heritage Novel by Franz Eemil Sillanpää
Weedpatch Novel by Joel Lehtonen

FRENCH

La Défense de Tartuffe Collected verse of Max Jacob
Within a Budding Grove Novel (part of *Remembrance of Things Past*) by Marcel Proust

GERMAN

Austrian

A Country Doctor Collected short stories of Franz Kafka
In the Penal Colony Long story by Franz Kafka
Demian Novel by Hermann Hesse
The Psychological Outlook on Life Philosophical treatise by Karl Jaspers
The World's Illusion Novel by Jacob Wasserman

Swiss

The Epistle to the Romans Theological treatise by Karl Barth

HUNGARIAN
The Gates of Life Novel by Ferenc Herczeg

HEBREW
The Bridal Canopy Novel by Shmuel Yosef Agnon
Kidesh Halem Novel by Sholem Asch

ITALIAN
Gay Shipwrecks Collection of poems by Giuseppe Ungaretti
Ghisola Novel by Federigo Tozzi

JAPANESE
Heretics Collected poems of Kitahara Hakushu

MALAYALAM
Sita's Story Poem by N. Kumaran Asan

SPANISH
Argentine
Without Remedy Collected verse of Alfonsina Storni

Spanish
Stone and Sky Collected verse of Juan Ramón Jiménez

Uruguayan
Tongues of Diamond Collection of poems by Juana de Ibarourou

SWEDISH
Gaudy Observations Collection of poems by Edith Södergran
God's Orchid Comic novel by Hjalmar Bergman
The Rose Altar Collection of poems by Edith Södergran

1920

BIRTHS
Imam Abubakar, Hausa writer of short fiction
Jalal Ali Ahmed, Iranian novelist
Isaac Asimov, American writer
Ayukawa Nobuo, Japanese poet
Mallam Amadou Hampate Ba, Malian scholar and storyteller
Mario Benedetti, Uruguayan novelist
Jens Bjorneboe, Norwegian poet, playwright, and poet
Ray Bradbury, American science fiction writer
Edward Ricardo Braithwaite, Guyanan novelist
Charles Bukowski, American novelist and poet
João Cabral de Melo Neto, Brazilian poet and critic
Andrée Chedid, Egyptian-born French playwright, poet, and novelist
Miguel Delibes, Spanish novelist and journalist
Mohammad Dib, Algerian novelist
Dennis Joseph Enright, English poet
Lawrence Ferlinghetti, American Beat poet
Hazhar (Abdurrahman Sharafkandi), Kurdish poet
Abdurrahman al-Khamisi, Egyptian poet and novelist
Alex La Guma, South African novelist
Benjamin Letholoa Leshoai, South African novelist and playwright

Albert Memmi, French-Tunisian novelist
Howard Nemerov, American poet
Djabril Tamsir Niane, Malian storyteller
Joan Perucho, Catalan poet, novelist, and critic
Abdur Rahman ash-Sharqawi, Egyptian playwright and novelist
Harvey Swados, American novelist and critic
To Hoai (Nguyen Sen), Vietnamese novelist
To Huu (Nguyen Kim Thanh), Vietnamese poet
Amos Tutuola, Nigerian novelist

DEATHS
Paul Adam, French symbolist novelist
Dan Andersson, Swedish poet and novelist
Shloime Ansky (Solomon Samuel Rappoport), Russian Jewish playwright
Richard Dehmel, German poet
Alberto Blest Gana, Chilean novelist
William Dean Howells, American novelist and critic
Sheikh Abdille Hasan Mohammad, Somali oral poet
Varthanes Papazian, Armenian novelist
Benito Pérez Galdós, Spanish novelist, playwright, and essayist
Omar Seyfettin, Kazakh poet
Olive Shreiner, South African novelist
Vahan Terian, Armenian poet
Federigo Tozzi, Italian novelist and poet

LITERARY EVENT
PRIZES AND AWARDS
Nobel Prize in literature: Knut Hamsun, Norwegian novelist

Pulitzer Prizes

Biography *The Life of John Marshall* by Albert J. Beveridge
Drama *Beyond the Horizon* by Eugene O'Neill
History *The War with Mexico* by Justin H. Smith

PUBLICATIONS
ARABIC
Spirits Rebellious Mystical essays by Lebanese writer Khalil Gibran

CZECH
The Good Soldier Schweik Novel by Jaroslav Hašek
R.U.R. Play by Karel Čapek

DANISH
Pirate Dreams Collected poems of Tom Kristensen

ENGLISH
American
The Age of Innocence Novel by Edith Wharton
Beyond the Horizon Play by Eugene O'Neill
The Emperor Jones Play by Eugene O'Neill
A Few Figs from Thistles Poetry collection by Edna St. Vincent Millay
The Forerunner Mystical meditations by Lebanese-born Khalil Gibran
Hugh Selwyn Mauberley Poem by Ezra Pound
Main Street Novel by Sinclair Lewis

This Side of Paradise Novel by F. Scott Fitzgerald
Youth and the Bright Medusa Collected short stories by Willa Cather

British

In Chancery Novel by John Galsworthy
The Mysterious Affair at Styles First mystery novel by Agatha Christie
The Outline of History Popular world history by H. G. Wells
Poems Collection of verse (including "Gerontion" and "Sweeney Among the Nightingales") by T. S. Eliot
The Sacred Wood Collection of critical essays by T. S. Eliot
The Story of Dr. Dolittle Children's story by Hugh Lofting
Women in Love Novel by D. H. Lawrence

Irish

"The Second Coming" Poem by William Butler Yeats
Michael Robartes and the Dancer Collected poems by William Butler Yeats

Jamaican

San Gloria Verse drama by Tom Redcam

New Zealand

Bliss, and Other Stories Collection of short stories by Katherine Mansfield
The Story of a New Zealand River Novel by Jane Mander

Scottish

Columbine Play by Compton Mackenzie

FRENCH

Belgian

The Magnificent Cuckold Play by Fernand Crommelynck

French

Cheri Novel by Colette
The Failures Play by Henri-René Lenormand
The Guermantes Way Novel (part of *Remembrance of Things Past*) by Marcel Proust
If It Die Novel by André Gide
The Imitation of the Father Play by Paul Claudel
Life and Adventures of Salavin Five-volume novel cycle by Georges Duhamel
The Simoom Play by Henri-René Lenormand

GERMAN

Gas II Third play in trilogy by Georg Kaiser
Man and the Masses Play by Ernst Toller
Parricide Expressionist play by Arnolt Bronnen
Wallenstein Historical novel by Alfred Doblin

ITALIAN

All for the Best Play by Luigi Pirandello
The Intense Life Novel by Massimo Bontempelli
The Mother Novel by Grazzia Deledda
Three Crosses Novel by Federigo Tozzi

NORWEGIAN

Kristin Lavransdatter Volume I of *The Bridal Wreath Trilogy* by Sigrid Undset

POLISH

Downstream Novel by Sigfrid Siwertz
The Meadow Poem by Bolesław Leśmian
The Scarlet Poem Collection by Jan Lechon

RUSSIAN

The Dybbuk Play by Jewish playwright S. Ansky

SPANISH

Argentine

Languor Collected poems of Alfonsina Storni

SWEDISH

The Eternal Smile Novel by Par Lagerkvist
The Shadow of the Future Collection of poems by Edith Södergran

1921

BIRTHS

George Mackay Brown, Scottish poet, novelist, and playwright
Hayden Carruth, American poet
Dobrica Cosic, Serbian novelist
Necati Cumali, Turkish novelist
Friedrich Durrenmatt, German playwright
Cyprian Odiatu Duaka Ekwensi, Nigerian novelist
Ida Fink, Polish Jewish novelist
Margherita Guidacci, Italian poet
Lars Gyllensten, Swedish novelist
Alex Palmer Haley, African-American novelist
Theodore Wilson Harris, Guyanan novelist, poet, and critic
Idrus, Indonesian novelist and playwright
Ti Janakiraman, Tamil novelist and playwright
James Jones, American novelist
Fodeba Keita, Guinean poet and playwright
Carmen Laforet, Spanish novelist
Stanisław Lem, Polish novelist, playwright, and essayist
Eeva-Liisa Manner, Finnish poet and playwright
Gabriel Imomotimi Gbaingbain Okara, Nigerian poet and novelist
Janos Oilinszky, Hungarian poet
Ziya Qarzada, Afghan poet
Amrit Ray, Hindi novelist
Leonardo Sciascia, Sicilian novelist
Francisco José de Vasques Teneiro, Portuguese poet and novelist
Richard Wilbur, American poet

DEATHS

Juhani Aho, Finnish novelist and short-story writer
François-Victor-Jean Aicard, Provençal poet
Micah Joseph Berdyczewski, Polish Jewish novelist, philosopher, and essayist
Subramanya C. Bharati, Tamil poet
Aleksandr Aleksandrovich Blok, Russian poet
Henry Austin Dobson, English poet and essayist
George Feydeau, French playwright

Nikolay Stepanovich Gumilyov, Russian poet
Vladimir Korolenko, Russian novelist
U Lat, Burmese novelist
Emilia de Pardo Bazán, Spanish novelist and critic
Ivan Vazov, Bulgarian poet, novelist, and playwright

LITERARY EVENTS
PEN (Poets, Playwrights, Editors, Essayists, Novelists), an international writers' association, is founded in London

PRIZES AND AWARDS
Nobel Prize in literature:　Anatole France, French novelist

Pulitzer Prizes

Autobiography　*The Americanization of Edward Bok* by Edward Bok
Drama　*Miss Lulu Bett* by Zona Gale
History　*The Victory at Sea* by William Snowden Sims
Novel　*The Age of Innocence* by Edith Wharton

PUBLICATIONS
ENGLISH
American

Alice Adams Novel by Booth Tarkington
The Emperor Jones Play by Eugene O'Neill
"Mr. Flood's Party" Poem by Edwin Arlington Robinson
The Negro Speaks of Rivers Poetry collection by Langston Hughes
Poems Collected verse of Marianne Moore
Second April Collected verse of Edna St. Vincent Millay
Three Soldiers Novel by John Dos Passos

British

The Circle Novel by W. Somerset Maugham
Crome Yellow Novel by Aldous Huxley
Queen Victoria Biography by Lytton Strachey
To Let Novel by John Galsworthy

Irish

Back to Methuselah Play by George Bernard Shaw

FRENCH
Cities of the Plain Novel (part of *Remembrance of Things Past*) by Marcel Proust
La Laboratoire central Collected verse of Max Jacob
The Sulky Fire Play by Jean-Jacques Bernard

GERMAN
Austrian

The Difficult Man Play by Hugo von Hoffmannsthal
Tractatus Logico Philosophicus Philosophical treatise by Ludwig Wittgenstein

German

The Ninth of November Novel by Bernhard Kellerman
The Wonder Rabbi of Barcelona Collected short stories by Else Lasker-Schuler

ITALIAN
Life of Christ Biography of Giovanni Papini

Six Characters in Search of an Author Philosophical play by Luigi Pirandello
The Voice of God Novel by Marino Moretti

NORWEGIAN
The Last of the Vikings Novel by Johan Bojer

PERSIAN
There Was Once—Or Was There? Six short stories by Mohammad Ali Jamalzadeh

POLISH
The Republic of Babin Collected verse by Jan Lechon
The Water Hen Play by Stanisław Ignacy Witkiewicz

RUSSIAN
The Night Search Poem by Velimir Khlebnikov
Nikita's Childhood Autobiographical novel by Aleksey Tolstoy
Partisans Story by Vsevolod Ivanov
The Pillar of Fire Collection of poems by Nikolay Gumilyov
The Road to Calvary Epic communist novel by Alexey Tolstoy
Winter Sonnets Collection of poems by Vyacheslav Ivanov

SPANISH
Colombian

The Promised Land Novel by José Eustasio Rivera

Spanish

Belarmino and Apolonio Novel by Ramón Pérez de Ayala

Uruguayan

"Anaconda" Short story by Horacio Quiroga

1922

BIRTHS
Concha Alos, Spanish novelist
Kingsley Amis, English novelist
Jorge Andrade, Brazilian playwright
Alan Ansen, American poet
Chairil Anwar, Indonesian poet and essayist
Brendan Behan, Irish playwright
Vance Bye Bourjaily, American novelist
John Gerard Braine, English novelist
Donald Alfred Davie, American poet and critic
Mavis Gallant, Canadian novelist
Arpad Goncz, Hungarian playwright
Jack Kerouac, American Beat novelist
Kihara Koichi, Japanese poet
Philip Larkin, English poet
Alistair MacLean, Scottish novelist and poet
Antonio Agostinka Neto, Angolan poet and statesman
Pier Paolo Pasolini, Italian poet and novelist
Vasco Popa, Serbian poet
Alain Robbe-Grillet, French novelist and essayist

Stanlake J. T. Samkange, Zimbabwean novelist
Kurt Vonnegut Jr., American novelist

DEATHS
Wilfrid Scawen Blunt, English poet
David Fishman, German Jewish critic, poet, and writer of short
fiction
William Henry Hudson, English novelist
Velimir Vladimirovich Khlebnikhov, Russian novelist, poet, and
playwright
Henry Archibald Hertzburg Lawson, Australian short-fiction
writer and poet
Alfonso Henrique de Lima Barreto, Brazilian novelist
Mori Ōgai (Mori Rintarō), Japanese novelist
Marcel Proust, French novelist
Giovanni Verga, Italian novelist

LITERARY EVENTS
The Criterion, British literary review, is founded
Newbery Medal is established

PRIZES AND AWARDS
Nobel Prize in literature: Jacinto Benavente y Martínez, Spanish playwright

Pulitzer Prizes
Biography *A Daughter of the Middle Border* by Hamlin
Garland
Drama *Anna Christie* by Eugene O'Neill
History *The History of New England* by James Truslow Adams
Novel *Alice Adams* by Booth Tarkington
Poetry *Collected Poems* by Edwin Arlington Robinson

PUBLICATIONS
ARABIC
The Broken Wings Mystical meditations by Lebanese-born writer
Kahlil Gibran

DANISH
The Peacock Feather Collected verse of Tom Kristensen

DUTCH
The House of Joy Novel by Jo van Ammers-Kuller
The Slow Motion Picture Play by Herman Teirlinck

ENGLISH
American
Anna Christie Play by Eugene O'Neill
Babbitt Novel by Sinclair Lewis
The Beautiful and Damned Novel by F. Scott Fitzgerald
A Critical Fable Collected verse of Amy Lowell
"The Diamond as Big as the Ritz" Short story by F. Scott
Fitzgerald
The Hairy Ape Expressionist play by Eugene O'Neill
One of Ours Novel by Willa Cather
Rootabaga Stories Children's stories by Carl Sandburg
Tales of the Jazz Age Collected stories by F. Scott Fitzgerald

British
Aaron's Rod Novel by D. H. Lawrence
East of Suez Play by W. Somerset Maugham
The Forsyte Saga Trilogy by John Galsworthy (consisting of *The
Man of Property* [1906], *In Chancery* [1920], and *To Let*
[1921]) published as a single volume
Jacob's Room Novel by Virginia Woolf
The Judge Novel by Rebecca West
The Waste Land Poem by T. S. Eliot

Irish
Ulysses Novel by James Joyce

New Zealand
The Garden Party and Other Stories Collection by Katherine
Mansfield

FINNISH
A Cripple in Love Novel by Joel Lehtonen

FRENCH
Aimée Novel by Jacques Rivière
The Dream Eater Play by Henri-René Lenormand
The Enchanted Soul Seven-volume novel cycle by Romain
Rolland
The Graveyard by the Sea Collected verse of Paul Valery
The Kiss to the Leper Novel by François Mauriac
Open All Night Collection of short stories by Paul Morand
The World of the Thibaults Novel by Roger Martin du Gard

GERMAN
Austrian
The Great Salzburg Theater of the World Play by Hugo von
Hofmannsthal
The Last Days of Humanity Play by Karl Kram

German
Drums in the Night Play by Bertolt Brecht
Siddhartha Novel by Herman Hesse
Sonnets to Orpheus Collected verse of Rainer Maria Rilke

GREEK
Slaves in Their Chains Novel by Konstantinos Theotokis

HINDI
Love Retreat Novel by Prem Chand

INDONESIAN
Sitti Nurbaja Novel by Marah Rusli

ITALIAN
Henry IV Play by Luigi Pirandello

JAPANESE
The Shipwreck Novel by Kume Masao

POLISH
The Book of Day and the Book of Night Collection of poems by
Jaroslaw Iwaszkiewicz

PORTUGUESE

Brazilian

Hallucinated City Collected verse of Mario de Andrade

Portuguese

The Crime of Batista the Student Collection of short stories by Rui Ribeiro Couto

RUSSIAN

"Armored Train 14-69" Story by Vsvolod Ivanov
Colored Winds Stories by Vsvolod Ivanov
The Extraordinary Adventures of Julio Jurenito and His Disciples Novel by Ilya Ehrenburg
The Naked Year Novel by Boris Pilnyak
Tsar-Maiden Fairy tale in verse by Marina Tsvetayeva
Verses to Blok Collection of poems by Marina Tsvetayeva

SPANISH

Chilean

Brother Asno Novel by Eduardo Barrios
Desolation Poems by Gabriela Mistral

Mexican

The Delirious Heart Collection verse of Jaime Torres Bodet

Uruguayan

Wild Root Collection of poems by Juana de Ibarourou

SWEDISH

Frida's Book Collected verse by Birger Sjöberg

TURKISH

Palace to Let Novel by Yakup Kadri Karamosmanoglu

1923

BIRTHS

Daniel Abse, Welsh poet
Eugenio de Andrade, Portuguese poet
Brendan Behan, Irish playwright
Mia Berner, Swiss biographer
Yves Bonnefoy, French poet and essayist
Carlos Bousoño, Spanish poet and critic
Italo Calvino, Italian novelist and essayist
Paddy Chayefsky, American playwright
Stig Halvard Dagerman, Swedish novelist, playwright, and poet
James Dickey, American poet Novelist
Shusaku Endo, Japanese novelist
Nadine Gordimer, South African novelist
Joseph Heller, American novelist and playwright
Sherif Hetata, Egyptian novelist
Elizabeth Jane Howard, English novelist
Elizabeth Jolley, English-born Australian novelist and playwright
Hugh Kenner, Canadian literary critic
Denise Levertov, English-born American poet
Sara Lidman, Swedish novelist

Norman Mailer, American novelist
Nazik al-Malaika, Iraqi poet
William Modisane, South African novelist and poet
Alvaro Mutis, Colombian poet
John Ormond, Welsh poet
James Amos Purdy, American novelist
Nazir Qabbani, Syrian poet
Samuel Selvon, Trinidadian poet and playwright
Ousmane Sembene, Senegalese novelist
Muhammad Ishlaq Shamin, Baluchi Urdu poet
Tamura Ryuichi, Japanese poet

DEATHS

Rosario de Acuña, Spanish poet and playwright
Maurice Barres, French novelist
Louis Couperus, Dutch novelist
Jaroslav Hašek, Czech novelist
Abílio Manuel Guerra Junqueiro, Portuguese poet
Pierre Loti (Louis-Marie-Julien Viaud), French novelist
Katherine Mansfield (Katherine Mansfield Beauchamp), New Zealand short-story writer
Raymond Radiguet, French novelist, poet, and playwright
Edith Irene Södergran, Russian-born Finnish-Swedish poet
Takio Arishima, Japanese novelist
Hovhannes Thumanian, Armenian novelist, poet, and essayist

LITERARY EVENTS

Adelphi, a literary magazine, is founded in London by John Middleton Murray

PRIZES AND AWARDS

Nobel Prize in literature: William Butler Yeats, Irish playwright and poet

Pulitzer Prizes

Biography *Life and Letters of Walter H. Page* by Burton J. Hendrick
Drama *Icebound* by Owen Davis
History *The Supreme Court in United States History* by James Truslow Adams
Novel *One of Ours* by Willa Cather
Poetry *The Ballad of the Harp-Weaver; A Few Figs from Thistles; Eight Sonnets in American Poetry, 1922. A Miscellany* by Edna St. Vincent Millay

PUBLICATIONS

AMHARIC

Vain Entertainment Allegorical play by Ethiopian writer Yoftahe Neguse

CHINESE

Call to Arms Stories by Lu Xun
Red Candle Collected verse of Wen Ito

CZECH

The Camel Through the Needle's Eye Comedy by Frantisek Langer

ENGLISH

American

The Adding Machine Play by Elmer Rice
Harmonium Collection of poems by Wallace Stevens
A Lost Lady Novel by Willa Cather
New Hampshire Long satirical poem by Robert Frost
The Prophet Mystical meditation by Lebanese-born Khalil Gibran
Spring and All Collection of poems by William Carlos Williams
"Stopping by Woods on a Snowy Evening" Poem by Robert Frost

British

Antic Hay Novel by Aldous Huxley
The End of the House of Alard Novel by Sheila Kaye-Smith
Kangaroo Novel by D. H. Lawrence
Riceyman Steps Novel by Arnold Bennett

Irish

"Leda and the Swan" Sonnet by William Butler Yeats
Saint Joan Play by George Bernard Shaw
The Shadow of a Gunman Play by Sean O'Casey
Thy Neighbor's Wife Novel by Liam O'Flaherty

FRENCH

The Captive Novel (part of *Remembrance of Things Past*) by Marcel Proust
The Devil in the Flesh Novel by Raymond Radiguet
Genitrix Novel by François Mauriac
Knock; or, The Triumph of Medicine Play by Jules Romains
The Ripening Seed Novel by Colette
The Royal Domain Collected verse of Francis Viélé-Griffin

GERMAN

Bambi Novel by Felix Salten
The Decay and Restoration of Civilization Treatise on "reverence for life" by philosopher and medical missionary Albert Schweitzer
Duino Elegies Ten poems by Rainer Maria Rilke
I and Thou Theological treatise by Martin Buber

ITALIAN

Barrier to the Northwest Play by Massimo Bontempelli
To Clothe the Naked Play by Luigi Pirandello

MALAYALAM

A Tragic State Poem by Indian writer N. Kumaran Asan

RUSSIAN

The Thinker Tetralogy by M. A. Aldanov
The Glittering World Novel by Aleksandr Grin (Stepanovich Grinevsky)

SPANISH

Mexican

The Days Collection of poems by Jaime Torres Bodet
The House Collection of poems by Jaime Torres Bodet

Spanish

Honeymoon, Bittermoon Novel by Ramón Pérez de Ayala
The Labors of Urbano and Simona Novel by Ramón Pérez de Ayala
The Modern Theme Critical treatise by José Ortega y Gasset

1924

BIRTHS

Abe Kobo (Abe Kimifusa), Japanese novelist and playwright
Sheikh Kaluta bin Amri Abedi, Tanzanian Swahili poet
Jamaluddin Abro, Sindhi novelist
Claribel Alegría, Nicaraguan poet and essayist
Yehuda Amichai, German-born Israeli poet
James Baldwin, African-American novelist
Dennis Brutus, Zimbabwean poet and essayist
Truman Capote, American novelist
Iordan Chimet, Romanian poet and novelist
Humberto Constantini, Argentine poet, playwright, and novelist
José Donoso, Chilean novelist
Janet Frame, New Zealand novelist and poet
William H. Gass, American novelist and critic
Zbigniew Herbert, Polish poet, essayist, and novelist
Alfred Hutchinson, South African novelist and biographer
Osman Lins, Brazilian novelist and short-story writer
Kamala Markandaya (Kamala Purnaiya Taylor), Indian novelist
Lisel Mueller, German-born American poet and critic
Abioseh Nicol (Nicol Davidson), Sierra Leonean poet and short-story writer
Bernardo Santareno (António Martinho do Rosário), Portuguese poet and playwright
Efua Theodora Sutherland, Ghanaian playwright
Leon Uris, American novelist
Zahrat (Zareh Yaldizchian), Armenian poet

DEATHS

Eduardo Acevedo Díaz, Uruguayan novelist
Valery Yakovlevich Bryusov, Russian poet
Frances Hodgson Burnett, English children's writer
Joseph Conrad (Józef Teodor Konrad Korzeniowski), Polish-born English novelist
Anatole France (Jacques Anatole Thibault), French writer
Arne Gabourg, Norwegian novelist and poet
Mehmed Ziya Gokalp, Turkish poet, novelist, and essayist
Herman Heijermans, Dutch playwright, essayist, and novelist
Franz Kafka, Austrian Jewish novelist
N. Kumaran Asan, Malayalee poet
Mustafa Lufti al-Manfaluti, Egyptian novelist and essayist
Iraj Mirza, Persian poet
Carl Friedrich Georg Spitteler, Swiss poet and novelist

LITERARY EVENTS

American Mercury is founded by H. L. Mencken and Jean Nathan

PRIZES AND AWARDS

Nobel Prize in literature   Władysław Stanisław Reymont, Polish novelist

Pulitzer Prizes

Biography   *From Immigrant to Inventor* by Michael Idvorsky Pupin
Drama   *Hell-Bent for Heaven* by Hatcher Hughes

History *The American Revolution—A Constitutional Interpretation* by Charles Howard McIlwain
Novel *The Able McLaughlins* by Margaret Wilson
Poetry *New Hampshire: A Poem with Notes and Grace Notes* by Robert Frost

PUBLICATIONS
DUTCH
I Serve Play by Herman Teirlinck
Forms Collected verse by Martinus Nijhoff

ENGLISH
American
Balisand Novel by Joseph Hergesheimer
Beggar on Horseback Play by George S. Kaufman and Marc Connelly
Billy Budd, Foretopman Novel by Herman Melville
Chills and Fever Verse collection by John Crowe Ransom
Desire Under the Elms Tragic play by Eugene O'Neill
The Green Bay Tree Novel by Louis Bromfield
How to Write Short Stories Collection of stories by Ring Lardner
The Man Who Died Twice Poem by Edwin Arlington Robinson
Observations Collection of poems by Marianne Moore
So Big Novel by Edna Ferber
Tamar and Other Poems Collected verse by Robinson Jeffers
They Knew What They Wanted Play by Sidney Howard
What Price Glory? Play by Maxwell Anderson and Lawrence Stallings

British
Beau Geste Novel by Percival Christopher Wren
The Green Hat Novel by Michael Arlen
A Passage to India Novel by E. M. Forster
Precious Bane Novel by Mary Webb
Some Do Not Novel (part of *Parade's End*) by Ford Maddox Ford
The White Monkey Novel by John Galsworthy

Irish
The Black Soul Novel by Liam O'Flaherty
Juno and the Paycock Play by Sean O'Casey

South African
God's Stepchildren Novel by Sarah Gertrude Millin

FRENCH
Anabasis Collected verse of Saint-John Perse
The Durandeau Brothers Novel by Philippe Soupault
Man and His Phantoms Play by Henri-René Lenormand
The Springtime of Others Play by Jean-Jacques Bernard

GEORGIAN
Kvachi Kvachantiradze Novel by Mikheil Javakhishvili

GERMAN
Austrian
Fraulein Else Novella by Arthur Schnitzler
The Gallery of Mirrors Play by Henry Bernstein
A Hunger Artist Four stories by Franz Kafka

German
The Magic Mountain Novel by Thomas Mann

HINDI
Arena Novel by Prem Chand

ICELANDIC
Icelandic Loves Collection of stories by Kristmann Gudmundsson

ITALIAN
Each in His Own Way Play by Luigi Pirandello

JAPANESE
Naomi Novel by Tanizaki Junichiro

LATVIAN
The Sons of Jacob Play by Janis Rainis

NORWEGIAN
The Ship Sails On Novel by Nordahl Brun Grieg

POLISH
Silver and Black Collection of poems by Jan Lechon

PORTUGUESE
Brazilian
Sentimental Memoirs of João Miramar Novel by Oswald de Andrade

RUSSIAN
Ariadne Poetical tragedy by Marina Tsvetayeva
The Badgers Novel by Leonid Leonov
The Iron Flood Novel by Alexander Serafimovic

SPANISH
Chilean
Tenderness Collected verse of Gabriela Mistral
Twenty Love Poems and a Song of Despair Collected verse of Pablo Neruda
Colombian
The Vortex Novel by José Eustasio Rivera
Peruvian
The Vengeance of the Condor Novel by Ventura García Calderón
Spanish
New Songs Collection of poems by Antonio Machado

URDU
Bang-e-Dara Collection of verse by Muhammad Iqbāl

1925

BIRTHS
Garnik Addarian, Armenian poet
Ali Mohammad Afghani, Iranian novelist

Thea Beatrice May Astley, Australian novelist
Eddy J. Bruma, Surinamese playwright, poet, and novelist
Ernesto Cardenal, Nicaraguan poet
Jan Rynveld Carew, Guyanan novelist, playwright, and poet
Raz Dizzy, Jamaican poet and essayist
Tankred Dorst, German playwright and novelist
José Durand, Peruvian novelist and essayist
Frantz Fanon, Martinique essayist
Khalil Hawi, Lebanese poet
Donald Justice, American poet
Maxine Kumin, American poet and children's writer
Clarice Lispector, Ukrainian-born Brazilian novelist
Lars Lundqvist, Swedish poet
Jon Mirande, French-Basque poet and novelist
Mishima Yukio, Japanese novelist
Flannery O'Connor, American short-story writer and novelist
Kerima Polotan-Tuvera, Filipino novelist
Mohan Rakes, Hindi novelist
Ru Zhijuan, Chinese novelist
William Styron, American novelist
Yuri Valentinovich Trifonov, Russian novelist
Pramudya Ananta Tur, Indonesian novelist
Gore Vidal, American novelist, playwright, and critic
John Barrington Wain, English poet, critic, and novelist
Dieter Wellershof, German playwright, novelist, and essayist

DEATHS

Henry Rider Haggard, English novelist
Amy Lowell, American poet
Władysław Stanisław Reymont, Polish novelist
Sergei Aleksandrovich Yesenin, Russian poet
Stefan Zeromski, Polish poet and novelist

LITERARY EVENTS

Prix Renaudot is established in Paris

PRIZES AND AWARDS

Nobel Prize in literature: George Bernard Shaw, Irish playwright

Pulitzer Prizes

Biography   *Barrett Wendell and His Letter* by M. A. DeWolfe Howe
Drama   *They Knew What They Wanted* by Sidney Howard
History   *A History of the American Frontier* by Frederic L. Paxson
Novel   *So Big* by Edna Ferber
Poetry   *The Man Who Died Twice* by Edwin Arlington Robinson

PUBLICATIONS

AMHARIC
The New World Novel by Sirek Walda Sellase Heruy

BASOTHO
Charles: An Historical Romance Novel by Thomas Mokopu Mofolo

CZECH
Over the Waves of TSF Collected Poems of Jaroslav Seifert

DANISH
Heroics Collected verse of Sophus Niels Christian Claussen

DUTCH
The Man Without a Body Play by Hernan Teirlinck
The Rebel Generation Novel by Jo van Ammers-Kuller

ENGLISH

American

An American Tragedy Novel by Theodore Dreiser
Arrowsmith Novel by Sinclair Lewis
Barren Ground Novel by Ellen Glasgow
Collected Poems of H. D. Collected verse of Hilda Dolittle
Color Collected verse by Countee Cullen
XLI Poems Collected verse of e. e. cummings
The Great Gatsby Novel by F. Scott Fitzgerald
In the American Grain Critical Essays by William Carlos Williams
Manhattan Transfer Novel by John Dos Passos
Porgy Novel by Du Bose Heyward
Possession Novel by Louis Bromfield
The Professor's House Novel by Willa Cather
Roan Stallion, Tamar and Other Poems Collection by Robinson Jeffers
"Yet I Do Marvel" Sonnet by Countee Cullen

British

The Clayhanger Family Novel by Arnold Bennett
The Common Reader Collection of essays by Virginia Woolf
Mrs. Dalloway Novel by Virginia Woolf
Hay Fever Comedic Play by Noël Coward
"The Hollow Men" Poem by T. S. Eliot
No More Parades Novel (part of *Parade's End*) by Ford Madox Ford
Pastors and Masters Novel by Ivy Compton-Burnett

Irish

The Informer Novel by Liam O'Flaherty
The Shadow of a Gunman Play by Sean O'Casey
A Vision Philosophical discourse by William Butler Yeats

South African

The Little Karoo Collection of stories by Pauline Urmson Smith

FINNISH
The Flutist's Happiness Poem by Rabbe Enckell

FRENCH
The Coward Play by Henri-René Lenormand
The Journal of Jules Renard Autobiography of Jules Renard
Mysterious Weddings Collected verse of Pierre-Jean Jouve
On the Track of God Novel by Jacques Rivière
Paulina 1880 Prose work by Pierre-Jean Jouve
Simulacrum Poem by Michel Julien Leiris
The Sweet Cheat Gone Novel (part of *Remembrance of Things Past*) by Marcel Proust
Terror on the Mountain Novel by Charles-Ferdinand Ramuz

GERMAN

Austrian

The Tower Play by Hugo von Hofmannsthal
The Trial Unfinished novel by Franz Kafka

German

The Chief Novel by Heinrich Mann
The Happy Vineyard Play by Carl Zuckmayer
Jew Suss Novel by Lion Feuchtwanger
Mein Kampf Autobiography by Adolf Hitler

Swiss

Pope and Emperor in the Village Novel by Heinrich Federer

HUNGARIAN

The Bridge Play by Ferenc Herczeg

ITALIAN

Cuttlefish Bones Collected verse of Eugenio Montale
One, None, and a Hundred Thousand Novel by Luigi Pirandello
Our Goddess Play by Massimo Bontempelli

NORWEGIAN

The Master of Hestviken Novel by Sigrid Undset

POLISH

The Madman and the Nun Play by Stanisław Ignacy Witkiewicz

RUSSIAN

The Artamonov Business Novel by Maxim Gorky
Bread Givers Novel by Anzia Yezierska
Cement Proletarian novel by Fyodor Gladkhov
The Heart of a Dog Novel by Mikhail Bulgakov
Mitya's Love Novel by Ivan Bunin

SPANISH

Argentine

Ocher Collected verse by Alfonsina Storni

Guatemalan

The Office of Peace on Orolandia Novel by Martín Arévalo

Spanish

Human Verses Collection of poems by Gerardo Diego

SWEDISH

Guest of Reality Autobiographical novel by Par Lagerkvist
Swedenhielms Comedy by Hjalmar Bergman

TURKISH

The Forbidden Love Novel by Halid Ziya Usakligil

1926

BIRTHS

Archie Randolph Ammons, American poet
Paul Anderson, American science fiction writer

Ingeborg Bachmann, Austrian novelist, short-story writer, and poet
Abdul Wahhab al-Bayati, Egyptian poet
Paul Blackburn, American poet
Robert Bly, American poet
Michel Butor, French novelist
Driss Chraibi, Moroccan novelist
Robert White Creeley, American poet
René Depestre, Haitian poet, essayist, and novelist
James Patrick Donleavy, Irish-American playwright and novelist
Alda de Espirito Santo, São Tomé poet
John Robert Fowles, English novelist and poet
Memet Fuat, Turkish critic and novelist
Allen Ginsberg, American Beat poet
Kanai Choku, Japanese poet
Zareh Khrakhuni (Artho Tchiumpiushian), Armenian poet
Tadeusz Konwicki, Polish novelist
John Knowles, American novelist
Jean Margaret Wemyss Laurence, Canadian novelist
James Merrill, American poet
Alfonso Sastre, Spanish playwright
Peter Shaffer, English playwright
William DeWitt Snodgrass, American poet
Ludwik Vaculik, Czech novelist

DEATHS

Shio Aragvispireli, Georgian novelist
Rudolf Christoph Eucken, German philosopher
Jan Kasprowicz, Polish poet
Aleksey Yeliseyevich Kulakovskiy, Yakut poet and scholar
Eino Leino (Armas Eino Leopold Lonnbohm), Finnish poet, playwright, and novelist
Jean Richepin, Algerian-born French poet, novelist, and playwright
Rainer Maria Rilke, German poet, playwright, and novelist
Abdul-halim Sharar, Urdu novelist and historian
Israel Zangwill, English Jewish novelist and playwright

LITERARY EVENT

PRIZES AND AWARDS

Nobel Prize in literature: Grazia Deledda, Italian novelist

Pulitzer Prizes

Biography *The Life of Sir William Osler* by Harvey Cushing
Drama *Craig's Wife* by George Kelley
History *A History of the United States* by Edward Channing
Novel *Arrowsmith* by Sinclair Lewis
Poetry *What's O'Clock* by Amy Lowell

PUBLICATIONS

CHINESE

Wandering Collection of stories by Lu Xun

CZECH

The Nightingale Sings Out of Tune Collected verse of Jaroslav Seifert

ENGLISH

American

Dream Variation Collected verse of Langston Hughes
Early Autumn Novel by Louis Bromfield
The Great God Brown Play by Eugene O'Neill
Her Son's Wife Novel by Dorothy Canfield Fisher
The Love Nest and Other Stories Collection of stories by Ring Lardner
"Ode to the Confederate Dead" Poem by Allen Tate
Show Boat Novel by Edna Ferber
The Silver Cord Play by Sidney Howard
Soldiers' Pay Novel by William Faulkner
The Sun Also Rises Novel by Ernest Hemingway
The Weary Blues Collected verse of Langston Hughes
White Buildings Collection of poems by Hart Crane
White Wings Play by Philip Barry

British

A Man Could Stand Up Novel (part of *Parade's End*) by Ford Madox Ford
The Murder of Roger Ackroyd Mystery novel by Agatha Christie
The Plumed Serpent Novel by D. H. Lawrence
The Seven Pillars of Wisdom Autobiography by T. E. Lawrence
A Silver Spoon Novel (part of *Forsyte Saga*) by John Galsworthy
Sweeney Agonistes Poetic drama by T. S. Eliot
Winnie the Pooh Children's story by A. A. Milne

Canadian

"The Cachalot" Poem by E. J. Pratt

Irish

The Plough and the Stars Play by Sean O'Casey
The Silver Tassel Play by Sean O'Casey

ESTONIAN

Truth and Justice Novel by Anton Hamsen Tannasaare

FRENCH

Avarice House Novel by Julien Green
The Bullfighters Novel by Henri de Montherlant
Capital of Sorrow Collected verse of Paul Éluard
The Counterfeiters Novel by André Gide
Good Will Novel by Senegalese writer Bakary Diallo
The Last of Cheri Novel by Colette
New Weddings Collected verse by Pierre-Jean Jouve
Orpheus Play by Jean Cocteau
Star of Satan Novel by Georges Bernanos
The Unquiet Spirit Play by Jean-Jacques Bernard

GERMAN

Austrian

The Castle Novel by Franz Kafka

German

Carl and Anna Novel by Leonhard Frank
The Death Ship Novel by B. Traven

HUNGARIAN

Wonder Maid Novel by Deszo Kostolanyi

ITALIAN

Man in the Labyrinth Novel by Corrado Alvaro

JAPANESE

The Passion Philosophical treatise by Saneatsu Mushanokoji
The Secret Record of Naruto Novel by Yoshikawa Eiji

LITHUANIAN

Voices of Spring Collected verse of Maironis
One Hundred Springs Collected verse of Kazys Binkis

ROMANIAN

Yellow Sparks Verse collection by George Bacovia

RUSSIAN

Roman Sonnets Collection of poems by Vyacheslav Ivanov
The Embezzler Novel by Valentin Katayev

SPANISH

Argentine

The Angel of the Shadow Novel by Leopoldo Lugones
Days Like Arrows Novel by Leopoldo Marechal
Don Segundo Sombra Novel by Ricardo Güiraldes
The Rabid Toy Novel by Roberto Arlt

Spanish

Tiger Juan Novel by Ramón Pérez de Ayala
The Healer of His Honor Novel by Ramón Pérez de Ayala

Uruguayan

Los desterrados Collection of short stories by Horacio Quiroga

YIDDISH

Judge Not Novel by Sholem Asch

1927

BIRTHS

John Ashbery, American poet
Carlos Germán Belli, Peruvian poet
Juan Benet, Spanish novelist
François Billetdoux, French playwright
Günter Grass, German novelist, poet, playwright, and essayist
Malek Haddad, Algerian poet and novelist
Yusuf Idris, Egyptian novelist and playwright
Ivar Ivask, Estonian-born American poet and critic
Bertene Juvener, Guyanese novelist, playwright, and essayist
George Lamming, Barbadian poet, novelist, and critic
Venkatesh Digamber Madgulkar, Marathi novelist
Harry Kurt Victor Mulisch, Dutch novelist, poet, and essayist
Richard Murphy, Irish poet and essayist
Nayantara Pandit Sahgal, Indian novelist
Rafael Sánchez Ferlosio, Italian-born Spanish novelist
Neil Simon, American playwright
Ariano Vilar Suassuna, Brazilian playwright, novelist, and playwright
Charles Tomlinson, English poet

DEATHS

Akutagawa Ryūnosuke, Japanese novelist, poet, and essayist
Mikhail Petrovich Artsybashev, Russian novelist, playwright, and essayist
Solomon Bloomgarden, American Jewish scholar
Georg Morris Cohen Brandes, Danish literary historian and critic
Stephen Gudmundson Stephansson, Canadian poet
Ricardo Güiraldes, Argentine novelist
Maximilan Harden, German essayist
Gaston Leroux, French novelist and playwright
Matilde Serao, Greek-born Italian novelist

LITERARY EVENTS

Bagutta Prize is established in Italy
Prairie Schooner is founded by Lowry Charles Wimberly

PRIZES AND AWARDS

Nobel Prize in literature: Henri Bergson, French philosopher

Pulitzer Prizes

Biography *Whitman* by Emory Holloway
Drama *In Abraham's Bosom* by Paul E. Green
History *Pickney's Treaty* by Samuel Flagg Bemis
Novel *Early Autumn* by Louis Bromfield
Poetry *Fiddler's Farewell* by Leonora Speyer

PUBLICATIONS

ARABIC

Today and Tomorrow Collection of prose pieces by Egyptian writer Salama Musa

DUTCH

Paradise Regained Collected poems of Henrik Marsman

ENGLISH

American

Archy and Mehitabel Collected verses by Don Marquis
The Bridge of San Luis Rey Novel by Thornton Wilder
Death Comes for the Archbishop Novel by Willa Cather
Elmer Gantry Novel by Sinclair Lewis
Giants in the Earth Novel by Norwegian-born O. E. Rolvaag
God's Trombones Sermons in verse by James Weldon Johnson
A Good Woman Novel by Louis Bromfield
"Hills Like White Elephants" Short story by Ernest Hemingway
Main Currents in American Thought Intellectual history by Vernon Louis Parrington
Men Without Women Collection of 14 stories by Ernest Hemingway
Oil! Novel by Upton Sinclair
Paris Bound Play by Philip Barry
The Second Man Play by Samuel Nathaniel Behrman
Tristram Long poem by Edwin Arlington Robinson
U.S.A. Novel by John Dos Passos
We Autobiographical narrative by aviator Charles Lindbergh
The Women at Point Sur Long narrative poem by Robinson Jeffers

British

Aspects of the Novel Critical thesis by E. M. Forster
To the Lighthouse Novel by Virginia Woolf

Irish

"Sailing to Byzantium" Poem by William Butler Yeats

FRENCH

The Closed Garden Novel by Julien Green
The Deserted World Prose work by Pierre-Jean Jouve
The Horsehair Glove Collection of maxims by Pierre Reverdy
The Negro Novel by Philippe Soupault
Oedipus Rex Dramatic adaptation of the myth by Jean Cocteau
Opéra: Oeuvres Poétiques Verse collection by Jean Cocteau
Thérèse Desqueyroux Novel by François Mauriac
The Treason of the Intellectuals Treatise by Julien Bende

GERMAN

Austrian

Amerika Novel by Franz Kafka

German

Being and Time Seminal philosophical treatise by Martin Heidegger
The Case of Sergeant Grischa Novel by Arnold Zweig
Der Steppenwolf Novel by Hermann Hesse
The Treasure of Sierra Madre Novel by B. Traven

GREEK

Delphic Utterance Collected verse of Angelos Sikelianós

HUNGARIAN

The Children of Death Novel by Mihaly Babits

ICELANDIC

The Great Weaver from Kashmir Novel by Halldor Laxness

NORWEGIAN

Sinners in Summertime Novel by Sigurd Hoel

ROMANIAN

Suitable Words Collection of poems by Tudor Arghezi

RUSSIAN

Phaedra Poetical tragedy by Marina Tsvetayeva
The Rout Novel by Alexander Fadeyev
The Thief Novel by Leonid Leonov

SPANISH

The Court of Miracles Novel by Ramón María del Valle-Inclán
The Iberian Circle Nine-volume novel cycle by Ramón María del Valle-Inclán

SWEDISH

The Horn of Autumn Collection of poems by Andreas Karlfeldt
Lacemaker Lekholm Has an Idea Novel by Gustaf Hellström
The Triumph over Life Prose monologue by Par Lagerkvist

TAJIK
The Mountain Village Novel by Sadruddin Ayni

YIDDISH
Chaim Lederer's Return Novel by Sholem Asch

1928

BIRTHS
Edward Albee, American playwright
Maya Angelou (Marguerrite Johnson), African-American poet
Chingiz Aytmatov, Kirghiz novelist
Shawqi Baghdadi, Syrian novelist
Uwe Berger, German poet
Osborne Henry Kwesi Brew, Ghanaian poet and short-story writer
Edip Cansever, Turkish poet
Don Coles, Canadian poet and critic
Raymond Federman, French-born American novelist, poet, and critic
Carlos Fuentes, Mexican novelist, playwright, and critic
Gabriel García Márquez, Colombian novelist and critic
Edouard Glissant, Martinique poet
Thomas Kinsella, Irish poet and translator
Camara Laye, Guinean novelist
Veijo Meri, Finnish novelist, poet, and playwright
Cynthia Ozick, American novelist
Hermann Schurrer, German poet
André Schwarz-Bart, French novelist
Manuel Scorza, Peruvian poet and novelist
Anne Sexton, American poet
Alan Sillitoe, British novelist and critic
Awang Usman (Tongkat Warrant), Malay poet and novelist
Paul de Wispelaere, Flemish novelist, essayist, and critic

DEATHS
Heinrich Federer, Swiss novelist
Vicente Blasco Ibáñez, Spanish novelist
Edmund Gosse, English novelist and scholar
Hemachandra Goswami, Assamese poet and literary historian
Thomas Hardy, English novelist and poet
Kostas Karyotakis, Greek poet
Klabund (Alfred Henschke), German poet
Paul van Ostaijen, Belgian man of letters
José Eustasio Rivera, Colombian novelist and poet
Hermann Sudermann, German playwright and novelist
Italo Svevo (Ettore Schmitz), Italian novelist

LITERARY EVENT
PRIZES AND AWARDS
Nobel Prize in literature: Sigrid Undset, Norwegian novelist

Pulitzer Prizes

Biography *The American Orchestra and Theodore Thomas* by Charles Edward Russell
Drama *Strange Interlude* by Eugene O'Neill
History *Main Currents in American Thought* by Vernon Louis Parrington
Novel *The Bridge of San Luis Rey* by Thornton Wilder
Poetry *Tristram* by Edwin Arlington Robinson

PUBLICATIONS
ENGLISH
American
The Buck in the Snow Poetry collection by Edna St. Vincent Millay
Cawdor Collected verse by Robinson Jeffers
The Front Page Play by Charles MacArthur and Ben Hecht
Holiday Play by Philip Barry
Home to Harlem Novel by Claude McKay
John Brown's Body Long poem by Stephen Vincent Benét
Peder Victorious Novel by Norwegian-born O. E. Rolvaag
Strange Interlude Play by Eugene O'Neill
West-Running Brook Collection of poems by Robert Frost

Australian
The Montforts Novel by Martin à Beckett Boyd

British
All the Conspirators Novel by Christopher Isherwood
Decline and Fall Novel by Evelyn Waugh
Elizabeth and Essex Biography by Lytton Strachey
Lady Chatterley's Lover Novel by D. H. Lawrence
The Memoirs of a Fox-Hunting Man Memoirs (completed in 1936) by novelist Siegfried Sassoon
Orlando Biographical fantasy by Virginia Woolf
Point Counter Point Novel by Aldous Huxley
The Swan Song Novel by John Galsworthy
Undertones of War Autobiographical work by Edmund Blunden
The Well of Loneliness Novel by Radclyffe Hall

Irish
The Tower Collection of verse by William Butler Yeats

FRENCH
Last Nights of Paris Novel by Philippe Soupault
Nadja Surrealist novel by André Breton
Siegfried Play by Jean Giraudoux
Time Regained Novel (part of *Remembrance of Things Past*) by Marcel Proust

GEORGIAN
From Footpath to Railway Line Novel by Niko Lortkipanidze

GERMAN
German
The Maurizius Case Novel by Jakob Wasserman
The Phantom Lover Play by Georg Kaiser
The Three-Penny Opera Musical opera by Bertolt Brecht

Swiss
The Burning Bush Collection of poems by Robert Faesi

HINDI
Embezzlement Novel by Prem Chand

JAPANESE

Some Prefer Nettles Autobiographical novel by Tanizaki Junichiro

PORTUGUESE

Brazilian

Macunaima Novel by Mario de Andrade

Portuguese

Emigrants Novel by José Maria Ferreira de Castro

RUSSIAN

King, Queen, Knave Novel by Vladimir Nabokov
After Russia Collected verse of Marina Tsvetayeva

SPANISH

Colombian

The Marchioness of Yolombo Novel by Tomás Cairasquilla

Mexican

The Eagle and the Serpent Memoirs of Martín Luis Guzmán

Spanish

Canticle Collection of poems by Jorge Guillén
Gipsy Ballads Verse collection by Federico García Lorca
Hurrah to the Hilt Novel by Ramón María del Valle-Inclán
Toward Heaven and the Altars Play by Jacinto Benavente y Martínez

SWEDISH

Glowing Embers Collection of poems by Artur Lundkvist

TURKISH

The Song of Those Who Drink the Sun Collection of poems by Nazim Hikmet Ram

ZULU

An African Tragedy Novel by Rolfus Reginald Raymond Dhlomo

1929

BIRTHS

Yuz Aleshkovsky, Russian novelist
Alfred Alvarez, English writer
Brigid Brophy, English novelist
Guillermo Cabrera Infante, Cuban writer
Haroldo de Campos, Brazilian poet
Gérard Chenet, Haitian playwright and poet
Hans Magnus Enzensberger, German poet, essayist, and playwright
Brian Friel, Irish playwright and novelist
Ursula K. Le Guin, American writer of science fiction
Thom Gunn, English poet
Fazil Abdulovich Iskander, Abkhazian poet and novelist
Yacine Kateb, Algerian playwright and poet
Milan Kundera, Czech novelist, poet, and playwright
Ephraim Alfred Shadrack Lesoro, South African poet, playwright, and novelist

Paule Marshall, Barbadian-born American novelist
John Patrick Montague, American-born Irish poet and writer of short fiction
John Munonye, Nigerian novelist
John James Osborne, English playwright
Milorad Pavic, Yugoslav poet and novelist
Chaim Potok, Polish Jewish novelist
A. K. Ramanujan, Indian poet
Adrienne Rich, American poet and critic
Badr Shakir as-Sayyab, Iraqi poet
Gilbert Sorrentino, American novelist, poet, and critic
George Steiner, Austrian-American literary critic
Rajendra Yadav, Hindi novelist and translator

DEATHS

William Bliss Carman, Canadian poet
Gunnar Heiberg, Norwegian playwright
Hugo von Hofmannsthal, Austrian poet, playwright, novelist, and essayist
Arno Holz, German essayist and critic
Hamza Hakimzoda Niyoziy, Uzbek poet and playwright
Janis Rainis (Janis Plieksans), Latvian poet, playwright, and translator
Franz Rosenzweig, German Jewish translator
Birgen Sjöberg, Swedish poet

LITERARY EVENT

PRIZES AND AWARDS

Nobel Prize in literature: Thomas Mann, German novelist

Pulitzer Prizes

Biography *The Training of an American—The Earlier Life and Letters of Walter H. Page* by Burton J. Hendrick
Drama *Street Scene* by Elmer L. Rice
History *The Organization and Administration of the Union Army, 1861–1865* by Fred Albert Shannon
Novel *Scarlet Sister Mary* by Julie Peterkin
Poetry *John Brown's Body* by Stephen Vincent Benét

PUBLICATIONS

BENGALI

Song of the Road (Pather Panchali) Novel by Indian writer Bibhutibhushan Bandyopadhyay

CHINESE

The Dream of the Red Chamber Novel by Cao Zhan

CIRCASSIAN

Attack Novel by Tembot Charasha

CZECH

Tales from Two Pockets Collected stories of Karel Čapek

ENGLISH

American

Cavender's House Poems by Edwin Arlington Robinson
Dodsworth Novel by Sinclair Lewis
A Farewell to Arms Novel by Ernest Hemingway

Look Homeward, Angel Autobiographical novel by Thomas Wolfe
Meteor Play by Samuel Nathaniel Behrman
Sartosis Novel by William Faulkner
The Sound and the Fury Novel by William Faulkner
Street Scene Play by Elmer Rice

Australian

Coonardoo: The Well in the Shadow Novel by Fijian-born Katharine Susannah Prichard

British

Brothers and Sisters Novel by Dame Ivy Compton-Burnett
Death of a Hero Novel by Richard Aldington
Goodbye to All That Autobiography of Robert Graves
The Good Companions Novel by J. B. Priestley
A High Wind in Jamaica Novel by Richard Hughes
Journey's End Play by R. C. Sheriff
The Man Within Novel by Graham Greene
A Room of One's Own Essay by Virginia Woolf
The Testament of Beauty Long poem in four books by Robert Bridges

FRENCH

Children of the Game Novel by Jean Cocteau
The Dark Journey Novel by Julien Green
Glass Puddles Poems by Pierre Reverdy
The Holy Terrors Novel by Jean Cocteau
Le Sacrifice imperial Collection of poems by Max Jacob
L'Ordre Novel by Marcel Arland
The Satin Slipper Play by Paul Claudel
Southern Mail Novel by Antoine de Saint-Exupéry

GERMAN

Austrian

Grand Hotel Novel by Vicki Baum

German

All Quiet on the Western Front Novel by Erich Maria Remarque
Berlin Alexanderplatz Novel by Alfred Doblin
Calendar Histories Novel by Oskar Maria Graf

INDONESIAN

Indonesia, Land of My Birth Collection of poems by Muhammad Yamin

ITALIAN

Time of Indifference Novel by Alberto Moravia

MALAY

Princess Nur al-Ain Novel by Sayyid al-Hadi

RUSSIAN

Peter the Great Novel by Alexey Tolstoy

SPANISH

Argentine

Ode for Man and Woman Collected verse of Leopoldo Marechal
The Seven Madmen Novel by Roberto Arlt

Chilean

Portrait of a Paladin Novel by Vicente Huidobro

Mexican

The Shadow of the Leader Novel by Martín Luis Guzmán

Spanish

Concerning the Angels Collection of poems by Rafael Alberti
The Revolt of the Masses Philosophical treatise by José Ortega y Gasset

SWEDISH

Ghost Ship Collection of poems by Harry Martinson
The Seven Seas Novel by Harry Martinson
The Story of San Michael Semiautobiographical narrative by Alex Munthe

XHOSA

U-Don Jade Novel by Samuel Edward Krune Loliwe Mqhayi

1930

BIRTHS

Albert Chinualumogu Achebe, Nigerian Ibo novelist, poet, and essayist
Adonis (Ali Ahmed Said), Syrian poet
John Arden, British playwright
J. G. Ballard, English writer of science fiction
John Simmons Barth, American novelist
Edward Kamau Brathwaite, Barbadian poet, critic, and historian
Elaine Feinstein, English novelist, poet, and translator
Roy Fisher, English poet
Lorraine Hansberry, African-American poet
Ted Hughes, English poet
Iijima Koichi, Japanese poet and critic
Kaiko Takeshi, Japanese novelist
Duro Lapido, Yoruba playwright
François Mallet-Joris, Belgian novelist
Condetto Nenekhaly-Camara, Guinean poet and playwright
Christopher Robin Nicole, Guyanese novelist
Yambo Ouologuem, Malian poet and novelist
Cosmo George Leopoldt Pieterse, South African poet and playwright
Harold Pinter, English poet and playwright
Roberto Fernando Retamar, Cuban poet
Paavo Rintala, Finnish novelist
James David Rubadiri, Tanzanian novelist and poet
Ali Ahmed Said, Lebanese poet
Carlo Sgorlon, Italian critic and novelist
Jon Silkin, English poet and critic
Bernard Slade, Canadian playwright
Derek Walcott, West Indian poet and playwright

DEATHS

Jeppe Aakjaer, Danish poet and novelist
Robert Seymour Bridges, British poet, and critic
Joseph Ephraim Casely-Hayford, Ghanaian novelist and essayist

Sir Arthur Conan Doyle, English novelist
Alois Jirásek, Czech novelist
D. H. Lawrence, English novelist, poet and critic
Vladimir Vladimirovich Mayakovsky, Russian poet, playwright, and essayist
Tayama Katai, Japanese novelist
Uchimura Kanzo, Japanese critic

LITERARY EVENT

PRIZES AND AWARDS
Nobel Prize in literature: Sinclair Lewis, American novelist

Pulitzer Prizes

Biography   *The Raven* by Marquis James
Drama   *The Green Pastures* by Marc Connelly
History   *The War of Independence* by Claude H. Van Tyne
Novel   *Laughing Boy* by Oliver LaForge
Poetry   *Selected Poems* by Conrad Aiken

PUBLICATIONS

ARMENIAN
The Rock of Rushan Epic poem by Nairi Zarian

CHINESE
The Canker Novella by Mao Dun

DANISH
Havoc Novel by Tom Kristensen
The Virgin of Skalholt Historical novel by Gudmundur Kamban

DUTCH
The Johanna Maria Novel by Arthur van Schendel

ENGLISH
American

As I Lay Dying Novel by William Faulkner
The Bridge Epic poem by Hart Crane
Flowering Judas Collection of stories by Katherine Anne Porter
The 42nd Parallel Novel by John Dos Passos
The Great Meadow Novel by Elizabeth Madix Roberts
The Green Pastures Play by Marc Connelly
Laments for the Living Series of prose sketches by Dorothy Parker
The Maltese Falcon Novel by Dashiell Hammett
The Proof Collection of poems by Yvor Winters

Australian

The Fortunes of Richard Mahoney by Henry Handel Richardson

British

Angel Pavement Novel by J. B. Priestley
Ash Wednesday Series of poems by T. S. Eliot
Cakes and Ale Novel by W. Somerset Maugham
The Edwardian Novel by V. Sackville-West
Imperial Palace Novel by Arnold Bennett
Last and First Men Classic science fiction story by Olaf Stapledon
Private Lives Play by Noël Coward
Seven Types of Ambiguity: A Study of Its Effects on English Verse Literary criticism by William Empson
Vile Bodies Novel by Evelyn Waugh

FRENCH
French

Chronique des Pasquier Ten-volume novel cycle by Georges Duhamel
Immaculate Conception Surrealist novel by André Breton
The Satin Slipper Verse drama by Paul Claudel
Sido Memoirs of Colette

Haitian

"La Drama de Marchaterre" Poem by Jean Fernand Brierre

GERMAN
Austrian

Civilization and Its Discontents Psychological treatise by Sigmund Freud
The Man Without Qualities Multivolume novel by Robert Musil

German

Tales from the Vienna Woods Play by Odon Horvath
Italian Night Play by Odon Horvath
Narcissus and Goldmund Novel by Hermann Hesse
The Rise and Fall of the City of Mahoganny Opera by Bertolt Brecht

ICELANDIC
Cross Hollows Collected verse of Einar Benediktsson
Poems Collection by Davith Stefansson

ITALIAN
Revolt in Aspromonte Novel by Corrado Alvaro
Tonight We Improvise Play by Luigi Pirandello
Waters and Land Poem by Salvatore Quasimodo

POLISH
A Day Lie Every Day Collected verse of Josef Czechowicz

PORTUGUESE
Brazilian

Libertinism Poem by Manuel Bandeira

Portuguese

The Jungle Novel by José Maria Ferreira de Castro

ROMANIAN
Black Gate Novel by Tudor Arghezi
Wooden Icons Novel by Tudor Arghezi

RUSSIAN
The Defense Novel by Vladimir Nabokov
The Master and Margarita Novel by Mikhail Bulgakov
The Road to Nowhere Novel by Aleksandr Grin

SPANISH
Guatemalan

Legends of Guatemala Description of the Mayas by Miguel Angel Asturias

Mexican

Exile Collection of poems by Jaime Torres Bodet

Uruguayan

The Rise of the Winds Poem by Juana de Ibarbourou

SWEDISH

Black City Poems by Artur Lundkvist
Memories of My Childhood Autobiographical novel by Selma Lagerlöf

1931

BIRTHS

Donald Barthelme, American novelist
Thomas Bernhard, Austrian novelist
Augusto de Campos, Brazilian poet
Tamaz Chiladze, Georgian novelist
Sven Delblanc, Swiss novelist
E. L. Doctorow, American novelist
Nawal El Saadawi, Egyptian writer
Muhammad Miftah al-Fayturi, Egyptian poet and playwright
Jurg F. Federspeil, Swiss novelist, poet, playwright, and essayist
Juan Goytisolo, Spanish novelist
Paavo Haavikko, Finnish poet and novelist
Rolf Hochhuth, German playwright
Gert Hoffmann, German novelist
Ivan Klima, Czech novelist and playwright
Ivan Lalic, Serbian poet
John le Carré (David John Moore Cornwell), English spy novelist
Deirdre Levinson, Welsh-born American novelist
Taghi Modarressi, Iranian novelist
Toni Morrison (Chloe Anthony Wofford), African-American novelist
Flora Nwapa, Nigerian novelist
J. P. Okot p'Bitek, Ugandan novelist, poet, and essayist
Mordecai Richler, Canadian Jewish novelist and essayist
Richard Rive, South African novelist and poet
Savako Ariyoshi, Japanese novelist and playwright
Jovan Strezovski, Macedonian poet and novelist
Cemal Surya, Turkish poet and critic
Zakaria Tamer, Syrian novelist
Tanikawa Shuntaro, Japanese poet
Tomas Gosta Transtromer, Swedish poet and critic
Uoka Makoto, Japanese poet
Tchicaya Gerard-Felix U'Tam'si, Congolese poet
Fay Weldon, English novelist and playwright
Janwillem van de Wetering, Dutch novelist and children's story writer

DEATHS

Enoch Arnold Bennett, English novelist and playwright
Hjalmar Bergman, Swedish novelist and playwright
Thomas Henry Hall Caine, English novelist
Sophus Niels Christen Claussen, Danish poet
Taomaq Gaediaty, Ossetian poet, journalist, and literary critic
Khalil Gibran, Lebanese-American poet
José Pereira da Graça Aranha, Brazilian novelist

Erik Axel Karlfeldt, Swedish poet
Vachel Lindsay, American poet
Mysost Qamberdiaty, Ossetian poet
O. E. Rolvaag, Norwegian-born American novelist
Arthur Schnitzler, Austrian playwright and novelist
Xu Zhimo, Chinese poet
Juan Zorrilla de San Martín, Uruguayan poet

LITERARY EVENT

PRIZES AND AWARDS

Nobel Prize in literature: Erik A. Karlfeldt, Swedish poet

Pulitzer Prizes

Biography *Charles W. Eliot* by Henry James
Drama *Alison's House* Susan Glaspell
History *The Coming of the War, 1914* by Claude H. van Tyne
Novel *Years of Grace* by Margaret Ayer Barnes
Poetry *Collected Poems* by Robert Frost

PUBLICATIONS

ARABIC

Ibrahim the Writer Autobiographical novel by Egyptian writer Ibrahim al-Mazini

ENGLISH

American

Axel's Castle Social and literary criticism by Edmund Wilson
Brief Moment Play by Samuel Nathaniel Behrman
Counselor-at-Law Play by Elmer Rice
Fatal Interview Sonnet sequence by Edna St. Vincent Millay
The Good Earth Novel by Pearl S. Buck
The Journey, and Other Poems Collection by Yvor Winters
Many Thousands Gone Collected stories of John Peale Bishop
Mourning Becomes Electra Play by Eugene O'Neill
Mule Bone Play by Zora Neale Hurston and Langston Hughes
Of Time and the River Novel by Thomas Wolfe
Sanctuary Novel by William Faulkner
Shadows on the Rock Novel by Willa Cather
S.S. San Pedro Novel by James Gould Cozzens
Their Father's God Novel by Norwegian-born O. E. Rolvaag

British

Afternoon Men Novel by Anthony Powell
All Passion Spent Novel by V. Sackville-West
Collected Poems Collection by Laurence Binyon
Hatter's Castle Novel by A. J. Cronin
The History of Susan Spray, Female Preacher Novel by Sheila Kaye-Smith
The Waves Experimental novel by Virginia Woolf

Scottish

The Lost Cause Play by Sir Edward Montague Compton Mackenzie

FINNISH

The Maid Silja Novel by Frans Eemil Sillanpää

FRENCH

Approximate Man, and Other Writings Epic poem by Romanian-born Tristan Tzara
The Great Fear of the Well-Possessed Novel by George Bernanos
The Sex Fable Play by Edouard Bourdet

GERMAN

Austrian

Flight into Darkness Novel by Arthur Schnitzler
Radetzky March Novel by Joseph Roth

German

The Anarchist Novel (part of *The Sleepwalkers*) by Hermann Broch
The Captain of Kopenick Comedy by Carl Zuckmayer
The Romantic Novel (part of the trilogy *The Sleepwalkers*) by Hermann Broch

GREEK

The Turning Point Collection of poems by George Seferis

ICELANDIC

Salka Valka Novel by Halldor Laxness

NORWEGIAN

One Day in October Novel by Sigurd Hoel

RUSSIAN

Odessa Tales Collection of short stories by Isaac Babel

SESOTHO

Chaka Historical novel by Bantu writer Thomas Mokopu Mofolo

SPANISH

Argentine

The Flame Throwers Novel by Roberto Arlt

Peruvian

Color of Blood Novel by Ventura García Calderón

Spanish

Way of the Cross Collection of poems by Gerardo Diego

TAJIK

"The Bloody Throne" Poem by Payrav

1932

BIRTHS

Michael Anthony, Trinidadian novelist
Aharon Appelfeld, Romanian-born Israeli novelist
Mongo Beti (Alexandre Biyidi), Cameroonian novelist
Hedi Bouraoui, Tunisian poet
Robert Coover, American novelist and short-story writer
John Gregory Dunne, American novelist

Umberto Eco, Italian novelist
Sheila Fugard, English-born South African novelist and poet
Geoffrey Hill, British poet
Luce Irigaray, French philosopher
Kamaleswar, Hindi writer
Christopher John Koch, Australian novelist and scriptwriter
Samuel Asare Konadu, Ghanian novelist
Benjamin Matip, Cameroonian novelist, poet, and playwright
V. S. Naipaul, Trinidadian novelist
Julia O'Faolin, English-born Irish novelist
A. Turan Oflazoglu, Turkish playwright
Christopher Okigbo, Nigerian poet
Lenrie Peters, Gambian novelist and poet
Sylvia Plath, American poet
Manuel Puig, Argentine novelist
Jacques Ruband, French novelist and mathematician
Arvo Salo, Finnish playwright and poet
C. K. Stead, New Zealand poet
John Updike, American novelist
Vladimir Nikolaevich Voinovich, Russian novelist, poet, playwright, and essayist

DEATHS

René Bazin, French novelist
Christopher John Brennan, Australian poet, critic, and philosopher
Eugène Brieux, French playwright
Cyriel Buysse, Flemish novelist and playwright
Dino Campana, Italian poet
Hart Crane, American poet
Kenneth Grahame, English children's writer
Lady Isabella Augusta Gregory, Irish poet and playwright
Hafiz Ibrahim, Egyptian poet
Maironis (Jonas Mačiulis), Lithuanian poet
Jalil Mammadguluzada, Azerbaijani novelist and playwright
Gustav Meyrink, Austrian novelist and playwright
Sir Gilbert Parker, Canadian novelist
Ahmed Shawqi, Egyptian poet and playwright
Lytton Strachey, English biographer and essayist
Edgar Wallace, English writer of suspense stories

LITERARY EVENT

PRIZES AND AWARDS

Nobel Prize in literature: John Galsworthy, English novelist

Pulitzer Prizes

Biography *Theodore Roosevelt* by Henry F. Pringle
Drama *Of Thee I Sing* by George S. Kaufman, Morrie Ryskind, and Ira Gershwin
History *My Experiences in the World War* by John J. Pershing
Novel *The Good Earth* by Pearl S. Buck
Poetry *The Flowering Stone* by George Dillon

PUBLICATIONS

ARABIC

An Egyptian Childhood Autobiography by Egyptian writer Taha Hussain

CROATIAN

The Clembaj Family Play by Miroslav Krleza
The Return of Philip Latinowicz Play by Miroslav Krleza

DANISH

The World Play by Kaj Munk

ENGLISH

American

The Animal Kingdom Play by Philip Barry
Black Elk Speaks Oral biography by John Neihardt
Conquistador Long poem by Archibald MacLeish
Death in the Afternoon Novel by Ernest Hemingway
Dinner at Eight Play by George S. Kaufman and Edna Ferber
Guys and Dolls Collection of short stories by Damon Runyon
Light in August Novel by William Faulkner
"The Mediterranean" Poem by Allen Tate
Mutiny on the Bounty Historical novel by Charles Nordhoff and James Norman Hall
1919 Novel by John Dos Passos
The Thin Man Novel by Dashiell Hammett
Thurso's Landing and Other Poems Verse collection by Robinson Jeffers
Tobacco Road Novel by Erskine Caldwell
Twentieth Century Comedy by Ben Hecht
Young Lonigan: A Boyhood in Chicago Streets Novel by James T. Farrell

British

Black Mischief Novel by Evelyn Waugh
Brave New World Novel by Aldous Huxley
Cold Comfort Farm Novel by Stella Gibbons
The Memorial Novel by Christopher Isherwood
The Orators Verse collection by W. H. Auden
Orient Express Novel by Graham Greene

Irish

Skerret Novel by Liam O'Flaherty
Words for Music, Perhaps, and Other Poems Verse collection by William Butler Yeats

Scottish

Scots Unbound and Other Poems Verse collection by Hugh MacDiarmid

FINNISH

The Way of a Man Novel by Frans Eemil Sillanpää

FRENCH

Journey to the End of the Night Novel by Louis-Ferdinand Céline
Men of Goodwill Epic novel of 27 volumes (completed in 1946) by Jules Romains
Sabine Novel (first in the series *High Bridges*) by Jacques Lacretelle
The Strange River Novel by American-born Julien Green
The Two Sources of Morality and Religion Philosophical treatise by Henri Bergson
Viper's Tangle Novel by François Mauriac

GERMAN

Giganten Novel by Alfred Doblin
The Jewish War Novel by Lion Feuchtwanger
Little Man, What Now? Novel by Hans Fallada
The Realist Novel (part of the trilogy *The Sleepwalkers*) by Hermann Broch
St. Joan of the Stockyards Play by Bertolt Brecht

GREEK

The Cistern Poem by George Seferis

ITALIAN

The House of the Customs Officer and Other Poems Collection by Eugenio Montale
Sunken Oboe Collection of poems by Salvatore Quasimodo

POLISH

A Ballad from Beyond Collection by Josef Czechowicz
Jealousy and Medicine Novel by Michal Choromanski
Kordian and the Churl Novel by Leon Kruczkowski
Night and Day Epic narrative by Maria Dabrowska

PORTUGUESE

Brazilian

João Miguel Novel by Rachel de Queiroz
Plantation Boy Semiautobiographical novel (part of the Sugar Cane series) by José Lins de Rego

ROMANIAN

The Uprising Novel by Liviu Rebreanu

SPANISH

Argentine

False Love Novel by Roberto Arlt

Spanish

Poetry in Prose and Verse Collection by Juan Ramón Jiménez

SWEDISH

Bobinack Novel by Eyvind Johnson
The Diary of Selma Lagerlöf Autobiography by Selma Lagerlöf

URDU

The Song of Eternity Poem by Muhammad Iqbāl

1933

BIRTHS

Beryl Bainbridge, English novelist
Michel del Castillo, Spanish-born French novelist
Augustin Sonde Coulibaly, Burkinabe poet and novelist
Marian Engel, Canadian novelist
Ernest J. Gaines, African-American novelist
John Gardner, American novelist
Jerzy Grotowski, Polish playwright and producer
Sulistyautami Iesmaniasita, Javanese poet and novelist

Jerzy Nicodem Kosinski, Polish-born Russian-American novelist
Penelope Lively, English novelist
Ian McDonald, Trinidadian novelist and poet
Abdul Rahman Mounif, Saudi Arabian novelist
Cees Nooteboom, Dutch poet, novelist, poet, and playwright
Philip Roth, American novelist
Ahmed Shahnon, Malay novelist
James Stewart Alexander Simmons, Irish poet, playwright, and essayist
Susan Sontag, American essayist and novelist
Edwin Thumboo, Singaporean poet and critic
Stephen Vizinczey, Hungarian-born Canadian novelist, essayist, and playwright
Andrei Andreyevich Voznesesnky, Russian poet
Yevgeny Alexandrovich Yevtushenko, Russian poet, novelist, playwright, and essayist

DEATHS

Constantine Cavafy, Egyptian-born Greek poet
John Galsworthy, English novelist and playwright
Stefan George, German poet
Ahmet Hasim, Turkish poet
Kobayashi Takiji, Japanese writer
Ring Lardner, American satirist
George Augustus Moore, Anglo-Irish novelist
Nar-Dos (Mikhayel Hovhannesian), Armenian novelist
Payrav (Otajon Sulaymoni), Afghan Tajik poet
Tom Redcam (Thomas Henry MacDermot), Jamaican poet and novelist
Raymond Roussel, French novelist and playwright
George Edward Bateman Saintsbury, English critic and literary historian
Sara Teasdale, American poet

LITERARY EVENTS

Partisan Review, a literary quarterly, is founded

PRIZES AND AWARDS

Nobel Prize in literature: Ivan Alekseyevich Bunin, Russian novelist

Pulitzer Prizes

Biography *Grover Cleveland* by Allan Nevis
Drama *Both Your Houses* by Maxwell Anderson
History *The Significance of Sections in American History* by Frederick J. Turner
Novel *The Store* by T. S. Stribling
Poetry *Conquistador* by Archibald MacLeish

PUBLICATIONS

ARABIC

People of the Cave Novel by Egyptian writer Tawfiq al-Hakim
The Return of the Spirit Novel by Tawfiq al-Hakim

CHINESE

Leaves of Three Autumns Collected verse of Bian Zhilin

CZECH

Hordubal Novel by Karel Čapek

ENGLISH

American

Ah, Wilderness Play by Eugene O'Neill
The Autobiography of Alice B. Toklas Autobiographical narrative by Gertrude Stein
Both Your Houses Prose satire by Maxwell Anderson
Collected Poems Poems by Hart Crane
A Draft of XXX Cantos Verse collection by Ezra Pound
The Fault of Angels Novel by Paul Horgan
God's Little Acre Novel by Erskine Caldwell
The Last Adam Novel by James Gould Cozzens
Lost Horizon Novel by James Hilton
Miss Lonelyhearts Novel by Nathanael West
My Life and Hard Times Humorous stories by James Thurber
Poems 1924–1933 Collection by Archibald MacLeish
Winner Take Nothing Novel by Ernest Hemingway

British

An American Visitor Novel by Joyce Cary
Design for Living Play by Noël Coward
Down and Out in Paris and London Autobiographical piece by George Orwell
The Magnetic Mountain Poems by Irish-born poet Cecil Day-Lewis
Marlborough: His Life and Times Multivolume historical biography by Winston S. Churchill
Mount Zion Collected verse of John Betjeman
Murder on the Orient Express Mystery novel by Agatha Christie
The Pilgrim's Regress Christian apologetics by C. S. Lewis
The Shape of Things to Come Futuristic scenario by H. G. Wells

Irish

Within the Gates Play by Sean O'Casey

FINNISH

The Struggle of the Spirits Novel by Joel Lehtonen

FRENCH

The Cat Novel by Colette
The Frontenac Mystery Novel by François Mauriac
The Green Mare Novel by Marcel Aymé
Man's Estate Novel by André Malraux
Pasquier Chronicle Novel by Georges Duhamel

GERMAN

German

The Forty Days of Musa Dagh Novel by Franz Werfel
Joseph and His Brethren Biblical tetralogy by Thomas Mann
The Oppermanns Novel by Lion Feuchtwanger
Schlageter Play by Hans Johst
The Stranger from the Seine Novel by Hungarian-born Edmund Josef von Harvath

Swiss

Poems Collection by Albin Zollinger

ICELANDIC
The Fair World Poem by Tomas Gudmundsson
Independent People Novel by Halldor Laxness

ITALIAN
The Feeling of Time Collection of poems by Giuseppe Ungaretti
The Landslide Play by Ugo Betti
Scent of Eucalyptus Collection of poems by Salvatore Quasimodo

NORWEGIAN
Road to the World's End Novel by Sigurd Hoel

PORTUGUESE
"The Deceived Wives' Club" Short story by Rui Roberto Couto

SPANISH

Argentine
The Hunchbacks Collection of short stories by Roberto Arlt
X-Ray of the Pampa Psychological study by Ezequiel Martínez Estrada

Chilean
Residence on Earth Poem by Pablo Neruda

Mexican
Savage Moon Collection of poems by Octavio Paz

Spanish
Blood Wedding Folk tragedy by Federico García Lorca
My Voice Because of You Verse sequence by Pedro Salinas
Saint Manuel, the Good Martyr Novel by Miguel de Unamuno

SWEDISH
The Hangman Play by Par Lagerkvist
Rain at Daybreak Novel by Eyvind Johnson

1934

BIRTHS
Fleur Adcock, New Zealand born English poet
Elechi Amadi, Nigerian novelist
Mario Antonio, Angolan poet and writer of short stories
Imamu Amiri Baraka (LeRoi Jones), African-American poet, playwright, and novelist
Leonard Cohen, Canadian poet, novelist, and playwright
Joan Didion, American novelist and essayist
Forugh Farrokhzad, Iranian poet
Alastair Gray, Scottish novelist
Ikeda Masuo, Japanese novelist
T. Jayakantan, Tamil novelist
Uwe Johnson, German novelist and essayist
José Louzeiro, Brazilian novelist
N. Scott Momaday, Native American poet and novelist
Adolf Muschg, Swiss novelist, playwright, and critic
John Francisco Rechy, American novelist
Wole Soyinka (Akinwande Oluwole Soyinka), Nigerian poet, playwright, novelist, and critic

DEATHS
Sayyd Sheikh bin Sayyid Ahmad al-Hadi, Malay novelist
Mirza Abulkasim Qazvini Aref, Iranian poet
Hermann Bahr, Austrian playwright
Andrei Bely (Boris Nikolaevich Bugayev), Russian poet and novelist
Chaim Nachman Bialik, Ukrainian Jewish poet, writer of short stories, and essayist
José Santos Chocano, Peruvian poet
Jafar Jabbarly, Azerbaijani poet, novelist, and playwright
Joel Lehtonen, Finnish novelist and short-story writer
Abdulali Mustaghni, Afghan poet
Sir Arthur Wing Pinero, English playwright
Joachim Ringelnatz (Hans Botticher), German poet and novelist
Abul-Kasim ash-Shabbi, Tunisian poet and critic
Jakob Wasserman, German Jewish novelist

LITERARY EVENT

PRIZES AND AWARDS
Nobel Prize in literature: Luigi Pirandello, Italian playwright

Pulitzer Prizes

Biography   *John Hay* by Tyler Dennett
Drama   *Men in White* by Sidney Kingsley
History   *The People's Choice* by Herbert Agar
Novel   *Lamb in His Bosom* Caroline Hillyer
Poetry   *Collected Verse* by Robert Hillyer

PUBLICATIONS

CZECH
Meteor Novel by Karel Čapek
An Ordinary Life Novel by Karel Čapek

DANISH
Seven Gothic Tales Collected stories of Isak Dinesen
Windswept Dawn Novel by William Heinesen

DUTCH
Back to Ina Damman Novel by Simon Vestdijk
New Poems Collected verse of Martinus Nijhoff

ENGLISH

American
Amaranth Poem by Edwin Arlington Robinson
Appointment in Samarra Novel by John O'Hara
Call It Sleep Novel by Henry Roth
The Castaway Novella by James Gould Cozzens
The Children's Hour Play by Lillian Hellman
The Daring Young Man on the Flying Trapeze Novel by William Saroyan
The Postman Always Rings Twice Novel by James M. Cain
Tender Is the Night Novel by F. Scott Fitzgerald
Tropic of Cancer Sexually explicit autobiographical novel by Henry Miller
Yellow Jack Play by Sidney Howard
The Young Manhood of Studs Lonigan Novel (second in trilogy) by James T. Farrell

Wine from These Grapes Poetry collection by Edna St. Vincent Millay

British

Burmese Days Autobiographical novel by George Orwell
Goodbye, Mr. Chips Novel by James Hilton
A Handful of Dust Novel by Evelyn Waugh
I, Claudius Historical novel by Robert Graves
The Quest for Corvo Novel by Frederick Rolfe
The Search Novel by C. P. Snow
A Study of History Magisterial history of the world by Arnold Toynbee
Victoria Regina Play by Laurence Housman

Canadian

Such Is My Beloved Novel by Morley Callaghan

Irish

The House of Titans and Other Poems Collection by AE

Scottish

Stony Limits Collection of meditative poems by Hugh MacDiarmid

Welsh

18 Poems Collected verse by Dylan Thomas

FINNISH

People in the Summer Night Novel by Frans Eemil Sillanpää

FRENCH

Algerian

Cinders Collected verse by Jean Amrouche

French

The Bells of Basel Novel by Louis Aragon
The Difficult Times Play by Edouard Bourdet
The Dreamer Novel by Julien Green
The Duo Novel by Colette
The Dying Novel by Philippe Soupault
Heliogobalus, or the Crowned Antichrist Play by Antonin Artaud
The Infernal Machine Tragic play by Jean Cocteau
The Public Rose Poem by Paul Éluard
The Song of the World Novel by Jean Giono

GERMAN

Austrian

Nobleness and Extinction Poem by Josef Weinheber
The Triumph and Tragedy of Erasmus Rotterdamus Biographical sketch by Stefan Zweig

German

Babylonian Wandering Novel by Alfred Doblin
Kerkhoven's Third Existence Novel by Jakob Wasserman

ICELANDIC

White Nights Autobiographical novel by Kristmann Gudmundsson

PERSIAN

The Suitcase Collection of six short stories by Bozorg Alavi

PORTUGUESE

Brazilian

São Bernardo Novel by Graciliano Ramos

Portuguese

Message Collection of poems by Fernando Pessoa

RUSSIAN

And Quiet Flows the Don Novel by Mikhail Sholokhov

SPANISH

Argentine

The World of Seven Wells Collected verse of Alfonsino Storni

Peruvian

First Gold of the Indies Poems by José Santos Chocano

Spanish

Yerma Play by Federico García Lorca

SWEDISH

The Rivers Run Toward the Sea Collection of poems by Artur Lundkvist

1935

BIRTHS

Ahmed Abralmuti Hijazi, Egyptian poet and critic
Kofi Awoonor, Ghanaian poet, novelist, and playwright
Peter Bichsel, Swiss novelist and short-story writer
George Bowring, Canadian poet, novelist, and essayist
Dollar Brand, South African poet
Richard Brautigan, American novelist and poet
Ed Bullins, African-American playwright
John Pepper Clark, Nigerian poet, playwright, and critic
Zulfikar Ghose, Pakistani-American novelist, poet, and essayist
Rodney Hall, English-born Australian novelist, poet, and biographer
Ramón Hernández, Spanish novelist
Thomas Michael Keneally, Australian novelist, playwright, and essayist
Ken Kesey, American novelist
William Patrick Kinsella, Canadian novelist
Earl Lovelace, Trinidadian novelist, playwright, and poet
Thomas Bernard Murphy, Irish playwright
Lewis Nkosi, South African playwright, novelist, and essayist
Kenzaburo Oe, Japanese novelist
Fernando del Paso, Mexican novelist
E. Annie Proulx, American novelist
François Sagan (François Quoirez), French novelist
Thomas William Shapcott, Australian poet, novelist, and critic
Julian Randolph Stow, Australian novelist, poet, and writer of children's books
Mats Traat, Estonian novelist and poet

Luandino Vieira (José Vieira Mateus de Graça), Angolan poet and short-story writer

DEATHS

AE (George William Russell), Irish poet and playwright
Henri Barbusse, French novelist
Paul Bourget, French novelist and critic
Clarence Day, American writer
Fernando António Nogueira Pessoa, Portuguese poet
Edwin Arlington Robinson, American poet
Isaiah Shembe, Zulu poet and hymn writer
Anempodist Ivanovich Sofronov, Yakut playwright
Mahmud Tarzi, Afghan novelist, poet, and essayist
Tsoubouchi Shōyō, Japanese novelist and critic

LITERARY EVENT

PRIZES AND AWARDS

Pulitzer Prizes

Biography   *R. E. Lee* by Douglas S. Freeman
Drama   *The Old Maid* by Zoe Akins
History   *The Colonial Period of American History* by Charles Mclean Andrews
Novel   *Now in November* by Josephine Winslow Johnson
Poetry   *Bright Ambush* by Audrey Wurdemann

PUBLICATIONS

DUTCH

The House in Haarlem Novel by Arthur van Schendel

ENGLISH

American

The Bear Novella by William Faulkner
Butterfield 8 Novel by John O'Hara
The Green Hills of Africa Travel narrative by Ernest Hemingway
The House of Earth Novel by Pearl S. Buck
The Idea of Order at Key West Poem by Wallace Stevens
It Can't Happen Here Novel by Sinclair Lewis
Judgment Day Novel (third in the Studs Lonigan trilogy) by James T. Farrell
The Last Puritan Satirical novel by George Santayana
Life with Father Autobiographical sketch by Clarence Day
Little House on the Prairie Autobiographical children's novel by Laura Ingalls Wilder
Of Time and the River Novel by Thomas Wolfe
The Petrified Forest Play by Robert Emmet Sherwood
Pylon Novel by William Faulkner
Theory of Flight Collected verse of Muriel Rukeyser
Tortilla Flat Novel by John Steinbeck
Waiting for Lefty Play by Clifford Odets
Winterset Verse drama by Maxwell Anderson

British

The African Queen Novel by Cecil Scott Forester
The House in Paris Novel by Elizabeth Bowen
Murder in the Cathedral Verse play by T. S. Eliot
National Velvet Novel by Enid Bagnold
The Stars Look Down Novel by A. J. Cronin

This Bed Thy Centre Novel by Pamela Hansford Johnson
Twenty Thousand Streets Under the Sky Novel by Patrick Hamilton

Canadian

They Shall Inherit the Earth Novel by Morley Callaghan

INDIAN

Untouchable Novel by Mulk Raj Anand

FRENCH

French

The Crucial Scene Prose work by Pierre-Jean Jouve
Days of Contempt Novel by André Malraux
Sweat of Blood Collected verse by Pierre-Jean Jouve
Tiger at the Gates Dramatic tragedy by Jean Giraudoux

Senegalese

Karim, roman Sénégalais Novel by Ousmane Soce Diop

GERMAN

Auto-da-Fé Novel by Bulgarian-born English writer Elias Canetti
The Sons Novel by Lion Feuchtwanger

GREEK

Mythistorema (Myth-History) Collected poems of George Seferis

HINDI

Kamayani Epic poem by Jaysankar Prasad

JAPANESE

Before the Dawn Novel by Toson Shimazaki
Musashi Historical novel by Yoshikawa Eiji

NORWEGIAN

Our Power and Our Glory Play by Nordahl Brun Grieg

POLISH

Peacock's Feathers Novel by Leon Kruczkowski

PORTUGUESE

Brazilian

Calunga Novel by Jorge de Lima
Time and Eternity Collected verse of Murilo Mendes

Cape Verdean

Arquipalago Collection of verse by Jorge Barbosa

SPANISH

Colombian

Long Ago Novel by Tomás Corrasquilla

Spanish

Destruction or Love Poems by Vicente Aleixandre
"Lament for the Death of a Bullfighter" Poem by Federico García Lorca
Mr. Witt Among the Rebels Novel by Ramón Sender

SWEDISH
Flowering Nettle Novel by Henry Martinson

TURKISH
The Clown and His Daughter Novel by Halide Edib Adivar

UZBEK
Obid Ketman Novel by Abdullo Qodiriy

YIDDISH
Satan in Goray Novella by Polish-born novelist Isaac Bashevis Singer

1936

BIRTHS
Assisa Ajebar, Algerian novelist
Nikolai Baturin, Estonian novelist and poet
A. S. Byatt, English novelist
Don DeLillo, American novelist
André Dubus, American novelist
Henryk Grynberg, Polish poet and novelist
Vaclav Havel, Czech playwright
Jean Ikelle-Matiba, Cameroonian novelist, essayist, and poet
Ismail Kadare, Albanian novelist and poet
William McIlvanney, Scottish novelist and poet
Larry McMurtry, American novelist
Charles Nokan, Ivorien novelist, playwright, and poet
Nkem Nwankwo, Nigerian poet and playwright
Marge Piercy, American novelist
Georges Perec, French novelist
Sahle Berhane Mariam Sellasie, Ethiopian novelist
Mario Vargas Llosa, Peruvian novelist, playwright, and critic

DEATHS
G. K. Chesterton, English novelist, poet, and essayist
Grazia Cosima Deledda, Italian novelist and playwright
Federico García Lorca, Spanish lyric poet and playwright
Maxim Gorky (Aleksey Maximovich Pyeshkhov), Russian novelist, playwright, and essayist
Alfred Edward Housman, English poet
Rudyard Kipling, English poet and novelist
Dezsó Kosztolányi, Hungarian poet and novelist
Karl Kraus, Austrian poet and playwright
Lu Xun, Chinese novelist
Luigi Pirandello, Italian playwright, novelist, and poet
Prem Chand (Dhanpat Rai Srivastana), Indian novelist and playwright
Henri de Régnier, French poet
Oswald Spengler, German philosopher
Joseph Lincoln Steffens, American writer and muckraker
Miguel de Unamuno, Spanish philosopher, poet, essayist, and novelist
Ramón María del Valle-Inclan, Spanish poet and novelist

LITERARY EVENT
PRIZES AND AWARDS
Nobel Prize in literature: Eugene O'Neill, American playwright

Pulitzer Prizes
Biography *The Thought and Character of William James* by Ralph Barton Perry
Drama *Idiot's Delight* by Robert E. Sherwood
History *The Constitutional History of the United States* by Andrew C. McLaughlin
Novel *Honey in the Horn* by Harold L. Davis
Poetry *Strange Holiness* by Robert P. Tristram Coffin

PUBLICATIONS
BURMESE
Modern Monk Novel by Thein Pe Myint

CHINESE
Old Tales Retold Collected stories by Lu Xun
The Sunrise Play by Cao Yu

DANISH
I See a Wondrous Land Historical novel by Gunmundur Kamban

DUTCH
Mr. Visser's Journey Through Hell Novel by Simon Vestdijk

ENGLISH
American

Absalom, Absalom! Novel by William Faulkner
The Big Money Novel by John Dos Passos
Black Spring Autobiographical narrative by Henry Miller
Black Thunder Novel by Arna Bontemps
Double Indemnity Novel by James M. Cain
The Flowering of New England Literary history by Van Wyck Brooks
A Further Range Collection of verse by Robert Frost
Gone with the Wind Novel by Margaret Mitchell
House of Incest Novel by Anaïs Nin
In Dubious Battle Novel by John Steinbeck
My Ten Years in a Quandary and How They Grew Humorous pieces by Robert Benchley
Nightwood Novel by Djuna Barnes
"Ode to the Confederate Dead" Poem by Allen Tate
The People, Yes Collected verse of Carl Sandburg
Public Speech: Poems Collected verse of Archibald MacLeish
"The Sea of Grass" Short story by Conrad Richter
The Story Happy Life of Francis Macomber Novel by Ernest Hemingway
You Can't Take It With You Play by George S. Kaufman and Moss Hart

British

African Witch Novel by Joyce Cary
The Allegory of Love Prose tract by C. S. Lewis
The Ascent of F6 Play by W. H. Auden and Christopher Isherwood

Burnt Norton Poem (first of *The Four Quartets*) by T. S. Eliot
Eyeless in Gaza Autobiographical novel by Aldous Huxley
A General Theory of Employment, Interest and Money Classic economic thesis by John Maynard Keynes
A Gun for Sale Novel by Graham Greene
Journey Without Maps Autobiography of Graham Greene
Keep the the Apisdistra Flying Novel by George Orwell
On This Island Collected verse of W. H. Auden
Still Life Play by Noël Coward

Indian

Coolie Novel by Mulk Raj Anand

Irish

Bird Alone Novel by Sean O'Faolain

South African

The Miller Novel by Daniel Malherbe

FRENCH

Death on the Installment Plan Novel by Louis-Ferdinand Céline
Diary of a Country Priest Novel by Georges Bernanos
The Fertile Eyes Poem by Paul Éluard
The Girls Tetralogy by Henry de Montherlant
House of Incest Novel by Anaïs Nin
Midnight Novel by American-born Julien Green
Pity for Women Novel by Henry de Montherlant
Traveler Without Luggage Play by Jean Anouilh

GERMAN

Austrian

Belated Crown Poems by Josef Weinheber

German

The Rebellion of the Hanged Novel by B. Traven

Swiss

Starlit Early Morning Poems by Albin Zollinger

GREEK

Argo Novel by Yorgos Theotokos

HINDI

The Gift of a Cow Novel by Prem Chand

HUNGARIAN

People of Puszta Novel by Gyula Illyes

ITALIAN

Erato e Apollion Collected verse by Salvatore Quasimodo

POLISH

Salt of the Earth Novel by Josef Wittli
The Stranger Novel by Maria Kuncewicz

PORTUGUESE

Brazilian

Morning Star Collected verse of Manuel Bandeira

PUNJABI

Green Leaves Collection of verse by Sikh poet Mohan Singh

SPANISH

Argentine

History of Eternity Collection of essays by Jorge Luis Borges

Spanish

The House of Bernarda Alba Tragedy by Federico García Lorca
The Never Ending Lightning Poems by Miguel Hernández

SWEDISH

The Man Without a Soul Play by Par Lagerkvist
The Way Out Autobiographical novel by Henry Martinson

TURKISH

The Epic of Sheikh Badruddin Poem by Nazim Hikmet Ram
The Samovar Novel by Abasiyanik

YIDDISH

The Brothers Ashkenazi Novel by Polish-born American writer Israel Singer

1937

BIRTHS
Layla Ba'albakki, Lebanese novelist
Paul Bailey, English novelist
Yitzhak Ben-Ner, Israeli novelist
Hélène Cixous, French feminist critic and novelist
Maryse Condé, Guadeloupean novelist, playwright, and critic
Cameron Duodo, Ghanaian novelist, poet, and journalist
Furui Yoshikichi, Japanese novelist
Girish Karnad, Kannada playwright
Vitauts Ludens, Latvian poet
Patrick McGinley, Irish novelist
Nelida Pinon, Brazilian novelist
Thomas Pynchon, American novelist
Henrik Stangerup, Danish novelist
Tom Stoppard, Czech-born English playwright
Hannelies Taschau, German novelist

DEATHS
Sir James M. Barrie, Scottish playwright and novelist
John Drinkwater, English poet, playwright, and critic
Hakigoto Kawahigashi, Japanese poet
Hakob Hakobian, Armenian poet
Paolo Iashvili, Georgian poet
Mikheil Javakhisvili, Georgian novelist
Attila József, Hungarian poet and essayist
Boris Pilnyak (Boris Andreyevich Vogau), Russian novelist
Horacio Quiroga, Uruguayan short-story writer, essayist, poet, and playwright
Suleyman of Stal, Dagestani poet
Titsian Tabidze, Georgian poet

Abdülhak Hâmit Tarhan, Turkish poet and playwright
Yeghishe Tcharents, Armenian poet
Francis Vielé-Griffin, American-born French symbolist poet
Edith Wharton, American novelist
Yevgeny Zamyatin, Russian novelist and playwright

LITERARY EVENT

PRIZES AND AWARDS

Nobel Prize in literature: Roger Martin du Gard, French novelist and playwright

Pulitzer Prizes

Biography *Hamilton Fish* by Allan Nevins
Drama *You Can't Take It With You* by Moss Hart and George S. Kaufman
History *The Flowering of New England* by Van Wyck Brooks
Novel *Gone with the Wind* by Margaret Mitchell
Poetry *A Further Range* by Robert Frost

PUBLICATIONS

DANISH

Out of Africa Memoirs of Isak Dinesen

ENGLISH

American

"The Devil and Daniel Webster" Short story by Stephen Vincent Benét
The Education of Hyman Kaplan Humorous sketches by Hyman Kaplan
Golden Boy Play by Clifford Odets
The Late George Apley Novel by J. P. Marquand
The Man with the Blue Guitar Poem by Wallace Stevens
Noon Wine Long story by Katherine Anne Porter
Northwest Passage Novel by Kenneth Roberts
Of Mice and Men Novel by John Steinbeck
The Red Pony Collection of stories by John Steinbeck
Their Eyes Were Watching God Novel by Zora Neale Hurston
To Have and Have Not Novel by Ernest Hemingway

British

Blasting and Bombardiering Novel by Wyndham Lewis
"Calamiterror" Poem by George Barker
The Citadel Novel by A. J. Cronin
Death on the Nile Mystery novel by Agatha Christie
The Hobbit Novel by J. R. R. Tolkien
I Have Been There Before Play by J. B. Priestley
In Parenthesis Verse collection by David Jones
Revenge for Love Novel by Wyndham Lewis
The Road to Wigan Pier Travel narrative by George Orwell
Sally Bowles Novel by Christopher Isherwood
Time and the Conways Play by J. B. Priestley
The Years Novel by Virginia Woolf

Irish

Famine Novel by Liam O'Flaherty

South African

Turning Wheels Novel by Stuart Cloete

FRENCH

Algerian

Secret Star Collected verse by Jean Amrouche

French

Days of Hope Novel by André Malraux
The Demon of Good Novel by Henry de Montherlant

ICELANDIC

World Light Novel by Halldor Laxness

ITALIAN

People in Time Novel by Massimo Bontempelli

KIRGHIZ

Up the Mountains Novel by Tungelbay Sydykbekov

PERSIAN

The Blind Owl Novel by Sādeq Hedāyat

POLISH

Ferdydurke Novel by Witold Gombrowicz

PORTUGUESE

Brazilian

The Rocky Road Novel by Rachel de Queiroz

RUSSIAN

The Gift Novel by Vladimir Nabokov

SPANISH

Argentine

Five Southern Poets Poems by Leopoldo Marechal

Mexican

Beneath Your Clear Shadow and Other Poems Collected verse of Octavio Paz
Crypt Collection of poems by Jaime Torres Bodet
They Shall Not Pass Collected verse of Octavio Paz

THAI

The Prostitute Novel by K. Surangkhanang

YAKUT

Tales Collection of short stories by Amma Achchygyya

1938

BIRTHS

Frederick Forsyth, English novelist
John Guare, American playwright
Daniel Katz, Finnish novelist and humorist
Taban Lo Liyong, Ugandan novelist and poet
Lya Luft, Brazilian novelist
Dom Moraes, Indian Goan poet

Leslie Allan Murray, Australian poet and critic
Ngugi wa Thiong'o (James Thiong'o Ngugi), Kenyan novelist and playwright
Joyce Carol Oates, American novelist and critic
Alexander Petrov, Yugoslav poet and critic
Ishmael Reed, American poet and critic
Charles Simic, Yugoslavian-born American poet

DEATHS

Lascelles Abercrombie, English poet, playwright, and essayist
Karel Čapek, Czech playwright, novelist, and essayist
Gabriele D'Annunzio, Italian poet, novelist, and playwright
Sirek Walda Sellase Heruy, Ethiopian novelist and biographer
Edmund Husserl, Austrian philosopher
Sir Muhammad Iqbāl, Indian Muslim poet
Aleksandr Ivanovich Kuprin, Russian novelist
Leopoldo Lugones, Argentine poet, short-story writer, and historian
Osip Emilyevich Mandelstam, Russian poet
Alfonsina Storni, Argentine poet
Cesar Vallejo, Peruvian poet
Owen Wister, American novelist
Thomas Wolfe, American novelist

LITERARY EVENT

PRIZES AND AWARDS
Nobel Prize in literature: Pearl S. Buck, American novelist

Pulitzer Prizes

Biography *Andrew Jackson* by Marquis James and *Pedlar's Progress* by Odell Shepherd
Drama *Our Town* by Thornton Wilder
History *The Road to Reunion, 1856–1900* by Paul Herman Buck
Novel *The Late George Apley* by J. P. Marquand
Poetry *Cold Morning Sky* by Maria Zaturenska

PUBLICATIONS

ARABIC
Sarāh Novel by Egyptian writer Abbās Mahmud al-'Aqqād

CZECH
Honeymoon Ride Collected verse by Jaroslav Seifert
Switch off the Light Collected verse by Jaroslav Seifert

DUTCH
Gedlichten, 1904–1938 Collected verse of Jan van Nijlen

ENGLISH
American
Abe Lincoln in Illinois Play by Robert Emmet Sherwood
Anthem Novel by Russian-born Ayn Rand
The Buccaneers Novel by Edith Wharton
The Fifth Column and the First Forty-Nine Stories Collection of short stories by Ernest Hemingway
Guide to Kulchur Critical discourse by Ezra Pound
Our Town Play by Thornton Wilder
"The Snows of Kilimanjaro" Short story by Ernest Hemingway

Uncle Tom's Children Collection of four short stories by Richard Wright
The Unvanquished Novel by William Faulkner
U.S. 1 Poems by Muriel Rukeyser
The Yearling Novel by Marjorie Kinnan Rawlings

British
Brighton Rock Novel by Graham Greene
The Death of the Heart Novel by Elizabeth Bowen
Homage to Catalonia Autobiographical narrative by George Orwell
In Hazard Novel by Richard Hughes
Out of the Silent Planet Science fiction by C. S. Lewis
Rebecca Novel by Daphne du Maurier
Scoop Novel by Evelyn Waugh
When We Are Married Play by J. B. Priestley

Indian
Kanthapura Novel by Raja Rao

Irish
Autumn Journal Long verse essay by Louis MacNeice
Murphy Novel by Samuel Beckett

FRENCH
The Castle of Argol Novel by Julien Gracq
The Children of the Earth Novel by Raymond Queneau
The Diary of My Times Autobiographical narrative by Georges Bernanos
Nausea Novel by Jean-Paul Sartre

GERMAN
Austrian
Beware of Pity Novel by Stefan Zweig
Between Gods and Demons Poems by Josef Weinheber
The Capuchin Tomb Novel by Joseph Roth

German
The Blue Band Novel by Bernhard Kellerman
The Gardener of Toulouse Play by Georg Kaiser

HEBREW
A Guest for the Night Novel by Shmuel Yosef Halevi Czaczkes Agnon

ITALIAN
The Mill on the Po Trilogy by Riccardo Bacchelli
Poesie Collection of poems by Salvatore Quasimodo

PORTUGUESE
Brazilian
The Seamless Tunic Collected verse of Jorge de Lima

RUSSIAN
Invitation to a Beheading Novel by Vladimir Nabokov

SPANISH
Argentine
Mask and Trefoil Collected verse of Alfonsina Storni

Chilean

Destruction Collected verse of Gabriela Mistral

Guatemalan

The World of the Maharachias Novel by Martín Arévalo

Mexican

The Useless Life of Pito Perez Picaresque novel by José Rubén Romero

YORUBAN

The Forest of a Thousand Daemons Novel by Daniel Fagunwa

1939

BIRTHS

Ayi Kwei Armah, Ghanaian novelist
Margaret Atwood, Canadian novelist
Alan Ayckbourn, English playwright
Toni Cade Bambara, American novelist
Marie-Claire Blais, French-Canadian novelist and poet
Margaret Drabble, English novelist
Alfredo Bryce Echenique, Peruvian novelist
Gus Edwards, West Indian–born American playwright
Seamus Heaney, Irish poet
Amos Oz, Israeli novelist
José Emilio Pacheco, Mexican novelist, critic, and poet
Peter K. Palangyo, Tanzanian novelist
Dennis C. Scott, Jamaican playwright and poet
Frederick James Wah, Canadian poet
Yoshimasu Gozo, Japanese poet

DEATHS

Josef Czechowicz, Polish poet
Olav Dunn, Norwegian novelist
Henry Havelock Ellis, English sexologist and writer
Ford Madox Ford (Ford Madox Heuffer), English novelist, poet, and critic
Sigmund Freud, Austrian psychiatrist
Zane Grey, American western writer
Sidney Coe Howard, American playwright
U Leti Panita Maun Tyi, Burmese novelist, poet, and playwright
Antonio Machado, Spanish poet and playwright
Okamoto Kido, Japanese playwright
Bylatyan Oloksuoyebis Oyuunuskay (Platon Alekseyevich Sleptsov), Yakut poet
Abdullah Qodiriy, Uzbek satirist and novelist
Tan Da (Nguyen Khac Hieu), Vietnamese poet, playwright, and novelist
Ernst Toller, German playwright
Va Trong Phung, Vietnamese playwright and novelist
William Butler Yeats, Irish playwright and poet

LITERARY EVENTS

Kenyon Review, a literary journal, is founded by John Crowe Ransom

PRIZES AND AWARDS

Nobel Prize in literature:　Frans E. Sillanpää, Finnish novelist

Pulitzer Prizes

Biography　*Benjamin Franklin* by Carl van Doren
Drama　*Abe Lincoln in Illinois* by Robert E. Sherwood
History　*A History of American Magazines* by Frank Luther Mott
Novel　*The Yearling* by Marjorie Kinnan Rawlings
Poetry　*Selected Poems* by John Gould Fletcher

PUBLICATIONS

DANISH

The Melody That Got Lost Play by Kjeld Abell

ENGLISH

American

American Blues Group of one-act plays by Tennessee Williams
The Big Sleep Detective novel by Raymond Chandler
The Colossus of Maroussi Novel by Henry Miller
The Day of the Locust Novel by Nathanael West
"The Devil and Daniel Webster" Short story by Stephen Vincent Benét
Drums at Dusk Novel by Arna Bontemps
The Grapes of Wrath Novel by John Steinbeck
Key Largo Play by Maxwell Anderson
The Little Foxes Play by Lillian Hellman
The Man Who Came to Dinner Dramatic farce by Moss Hart and George S. Kaufman
Night Rider Novel by Robert Penn Warren
Pale Horse, Pale Rider Collection of three short stories by Katherine Anne Porter
The Philadelphia Story Comedy of manners by playwright Philip Barry
The Time of Your Life Play by William Saroyan
Tropic of Capricorn Fictional medley by Henry Miller
The Web and the Rock Novel by Thomas Wolfe
Wickford Point Novel by J. P. Marquand

British

After Many a Summer Dies the Swan Social criticism by Aldous Huxley
The Berlin Stories Novel by Christopher Isherwood
Black Narcissus Novel by Rumer Godden
A Coffin for Demetrios Crime novel by Eric Ambler
Coming Up for Air Novel by George Orwell
The Confidential Agent Novel by Graham Greene
The Family Reunion Verse drama by T. S. Eliot
Goodbye to Berlin Novel by Christopher Isherwood
Good Morning, Good Night Novel by West Indian–born novelist Jean Rhys
The Idea of a Christian Society Essay by T. S. Eliot
Still Centre Poetry collection by Stephen Spender

Canadian

Still Stands the House Folk drama by American-born Gwendolyn Ringwood

Irish

Finnegan's Wake Novel by James Joyce
Last Poems and Two Plays Final volume of poetry by William Butler Yeats
Mister Johnson Novel by Joyce Cary

South African

Flowering Rifle: A Poem from the Battlefields of Spain Long satirical poem by Roy Campbell

Welsh

How Green Was My Valley Novel by Richard Llewellyn
The Map of Love Collection of poems by Dylan Thomas

FRENCH

The Lepers Novel by Henry de Montherlant
The Unknown Sea Novel by François Mauriac
Wind, Sand and Stars Memoir by Antoine de Saint-Exupéry

GERMAN

Swiss

Autumn Tranquility Collection of poems by Albin Zollinger
The Great Restlessness Collection of poems by Albin Zollinger

HUNGARIAN

The Gladiators Novel by Arthur Koestler

ITALIAN

The Occasions Collection of poems by Eugenio Montale

JAPANESE

Love and Death Humanistic treatise by Mushanakoji Saneatsu

PORTUGUESE

Brazilian

Journey Poetry collection by Cecilia Meireles
The Obscure Woman Novel by Jorge de Lima
The Three Marias Novel by Rachel de Queiroz

RUSSIAN

The Fifth Seal Novel by Mark Aldanov
Man Collection of poems by Vyacheslav Ivanov

SPANISH

Peruvian

Human Poems Collection by Cesar Vallejo

Spanish

The Man Who Lurks Collected verse of Miguel Hernández

URDU

Defeat Autobiographical novel by Krishan Chander

VIETNAMESE

When the Light Is Out Novel by Ngo Tat To

YIDDISH

The Nazarene Novel by Polish-born American Sholem Asch

1940

BIRTHS

Joseph Wilfred Arbuquah, Ghanaian novelist
Russell Banks, American novelist
Arlindo Barbeitos, Angolan poet
Peter Benchley, American novelist
Joseph Brodsky, Russian-American poet
Jean-Marie Clezio, French novelist
Razmik Davoyan, Armenian poet
Nabile Fares, Kabylian poet
Maxine Hong Kingston, Chinese-American novelist
David McFadden, Canadian poet and novelist
Nguyen Mong-Giac, Vietnamese-American writer
Sheikh A. Nado, Senegalese poet and playwright
Olawale Rotimi, Yoruba playwright and scholar

DEATHS

Isaac Babel, Russian short-story writer and dramatist
Einar Benediktsson, Icelandic poet
Walter Benjamin, German literary critic
John Buchan, Scottish novelist
Mikhail Afanasevich Bulgakov, Russian novelist, playwright, and essayist
F. Scott Fitzgerald, American novelist
Hannibal Hamlin Garland, American novelist
Han Mac Tu (Nguyen Trong Tri), Vietnamese poet
Walter Hasenclever, German poet and playwright
Werner von Heidenstam, Swedish poet
Selma Lagerlöf, Swedish novelist
Hendrik Marsman, Dutch poet
Phan Boi Chau, Vietnamese poet
Pi Mounin, Burmese novelist
Anein ar-Rayhani, Lebanese poet, novelist, and essayist
Anton Hansen Tammasaare, Estonian novelist
Nathanael West (Nathan Wallenstein Weinstein), American novelist

LITERARY EVENTS

The Bell, Irish literary magazine, is founded

PRIZES AND AWARDS

Pulitzer Prizes

Biography   *Woodrow Wilson: Life and Letters* by Ray Stannard Baker
Drama   *The Time of Your Life* by William Saroyan
History   *Abraham Lincoln: The War Years* by Carl Sandburg
Novel   *The Grapes of Wrath* by John Steinbeck
Poetry   *Collected Poems* by Mark Van Doren

PUBLICATIONS

ARABIC

Iraqi

Doctor Ibrahim Novel by Dhun-Nun Ayyub

Syrian

Thickets Collection of poems by Ilya Abu Madi

BENGALI
Pedestrian Collection of poems by Subhas Mukhopadhyay

CHINESE
Torrent Trilogy by Ba Jin

CZECH
Bozena Nemcova's Fan Collected verse of Jaroslav Seifert
Dressed in Light Collected verse of Jaroslav Seifert

ENGLISH
American
Fables for Our Time Collected stories of James Thurber
Farewell, My Lovely Novel by Raymond Chandler
For Whom the Bell Tolls Novel by Ernest Hemingway
The Hamlet Novel by William Faulkner
The Heart Is a Lonely Hunter Novel by Carson McCullers
My Name Is Aram Collected short stories of Armenian-born
    William Saroyan
Native Son Novel by Richard Wright
The Ox-Bow Incident by Walter van Tilberg Clark
Sapphira and the Slave Girl Novel by Willa Cather
There Shall Be No Night Political play by Robert Emmet
    Sherwood
To the Finland Station Prose essay by Edmund Wilson
The Trees Novel by Conrad Richter
World's End Novel by Upton Sinclair

Australian
The Man Who Loved Children Novel by Christina Stead

British
Another Time Poetry collection by W. H. Auden
East Coker Poems (second of *The Four Quartets*) by T. S. Eliot
The Gathering Storm Collection of verse by William Empson
The Near and the Far Tetralogy by L. H. Myers
The Power and the Glory Novel by Graham Greene
The Problem of Pain Theological perspectives by C. S. Lewis
"September 1, 1939" Poem by W. H. Auden
Strangers and Brothers Eleven-volume novel sequence by C. P.
    Snow
Too Dear for My Possessing Novel by Pamela Hansford Johnson

Canadian
Brebeuf and His Brethren Collected verse of E. J. Pratt

Irish
Come Back to Erin Novel by Sean O'Faolain
People Dust Comic fantasy by Sean O'Casey
The Stars Turn Red Play by Sean O'Casey

South African
The Wrath of the Ancestral Spirits Novel by Archibald Campbell
    Jordan

Welsh
Portrait of the Artist as a Young Dog Collection of semiautobio-
    graphical short stories by Dylan Thomas

FRENCH
French
The Iliad; or, The Poem of Force Critical discourse by Simone
    Weil
Haitian
Rhythms of My Heart Collection of poems by René Balance

GERMAN
Alain and Elise Play by Georg Kaiser

GREEK
Book of Exercises Collected verse of George Seferis
Logbook I Collected verse of George Seferis

HUNGARIAN
Darkness at Noon Novel by Arthur Koestler

ITALIAN
The Seed Beneath the Snow Novel by Ignazio Silone
The Tartar Steppes Novel by Dino Buzzati

PORTUGUESE
Cathedral Square Collection of short stories by Rui Ribeiro
    Couto

SPANISH
Argentine
The Centaur Collected verse of Leopoldo Marechal
The Invention of Morel Novel by Adolfo Bioy Casares
Sonnets to Sophia Collected verse of Leopoldo Marechal
Spanish
Angeles de Compostela Collection of poems by Gerardo Diego

TURKISH
The Devil Within Novel by Sabahattin Ali

TURKMEN
Determined Step Novel by Berdi Kerbabayev

1941

BIRTHS
C. Lindsay Barrett, Jamaican novelist, poet, and playwright
Rachid Boudjedra, Algerian novelist
Reuben Mauro Machado, Brazilian novelist
R. Anthony McNeil, Jamaican poet
Sergio Sant'Anna, Brazilian poet, playwright, and novelist
Stanislaw Stratiev, Bulgarian novelist
Paul Theroux, American travel writer
Larry Woiwode, American novelist

DEATHS
Sherwood Anderson, American novelist
Mihály Babits, Hungarian poet and novelist

Henri Bergson, French philosopher
Karin Boye, Swedish poet and novelist
Simon Dubnow, Russian Jewish historian
James George Frazer, Scottish social anthropologist
Ayodhyasimha Upadhyay Hariaudh, Hindi poet and novelist
James Joyce, Irish writer
George Lyman Kittredge, American literary scholar
Dmitry Sergeyevich Merezhkovsky, Russian novelist, critic, and playwright
Elizabeth Madox Roberts, American novelist and poet
Hjalmar Erik Fredrik Söderberg, Swedish novelist
John Henderson Soga, South African hymn writer, poet, and translator
Sir Rabindranath Tagore, Indian Bengali poet, novelist, and philosopher
Ibrahim Taqan, Palestinian Arab poet
Marina Ivanovna Tsvetayeva, Russian poet
Sir Hugh Walpole, English novelist, playwright, and critic
Virginia Woolf, English novelist
Mari Ziyada, Arab critic and essayist
Albin Zollinger, Swiss poet and novelist

LITERARY EVENT
PRIZES AND AWARDS

Pulitzer Prizes

Biography *Jonathan Edwards* by Ola Elizabeth Winslow
Drama *There Shall Be No Night* by Robert E. Sherwood
History *The Atlantic Migration, 1607–1860* by Marcus Lee Hansen
Poetry *Sunderland Capture* by Leonard Bacon

PUBLICATIONS

AMHARIC
Good Example Novel by Takla Hawaryat Germasaw
The Voice of Blood Play by Endalkacaw Makonnen

DANISH
Jonatan's Journey Novel by Martin Hansen

ENGLISH

American

The American Renaissance Literary and historical study by F. O. Matthiessen
Be Angry at the Sun Poems by Robinson Jeffers
A Curtain of Green Collection of short stories by Eudora Welty
The Dust Which Is God Autobiographical novel in verse William Rose Benét
H. M. Pulham, Esq. Novel by J. P. Marquand
The Last Tycoon Unfinished novel by F. Scott Fitzgerald
Let Us Now Praise Famous Men Sketches of the rural poor by James Agee
Mildred Pierce Novel by James M. Cain
The New Criticism Literary discourse by John Crowe Ransom
Random Harvest Novel by James Hilton
The Real Life of Sebastian Knight Novel by Vladimir Nabokov
Reflections in a Golden Eye Gothic novel by Carson McCullers
Shenandoah Verse play by Delmore Schwartz

Watch on the Rhine Play by Lillian Hellman
"Why I Live at the P.O." Short story by Eudora Welty
The Wound and the Bow Literary criticism by Edmund Wilson

British

Blithe Spirit Play by Noël Coward
The Double Man Long poem by W. H. Auden
Dry Salvages Poem (third of *The Four Quartets*) by T. S. Eliot
Herself Surprised Novel by Joyce Cary
The Screwtape Letters Epistolary novel by C. S. Lewis

Scottish

The Monarch of the Glen Novel by Compton Mackenzie

Welsh

Ballad of the Mari Lwyd, and Other Poems Collection by Vernon Watkins

FRENCH
Heartbreak Poem by Louis Aragon
The Pure and the Impure Novel by Colette
A Woman of the Pharisees Novel by François Mauriac

GERMAN

Austrian

The Song of Berndotte Novel by Czech-born Jewish writer Franz Werfel

German

Mother Courage and Her Children Play by Bertolt Brecht

ICELANDIC
The Golden Gate Play by Davíd Stefánsson

ITALIAN
Revolution of the Sun Novel by Massimo Bontempelli
The Widow Fiorvanti Novel by Marino Moretti

RUSSIAN
The Fall of Paris Novel by Ilya Ehrenburg

SPANISH

Argentine

All Green Shall Perish Novel by Eduardo Mallea

Peruvian

Broad and Alien Is the World Novel on Peruvian Indians by Ciro Alegría

Spanish

Between the Coronation and the Sword Poems by Rafael Alberti
The Incredible Play Play by Jacinto Benavente y Martínez
The Lark of Truth Collection of poems by Gerardo Diego

TAJIK
Gulru Historical novel by Rahim Jalil

ZULU
The Valley of a Thousand Hills Collection of verse by Herbert Isaac Ernest Dhlomo

1942

BIRTHS

Isabel Allende, Chilean novelist and playwright
Ataol Behramoglu, Turkish poet
Ana Blandiana, Romanian lyric poet
Ariel Dorfman, Argentine-born Chilean poet and novelist
Douglas Eaglesham Dunn, Scottish poet
Peter Handke, Austrian playwright, novelist, essayist, and poet
Janette Turner Hospital, Australian-born Canadian novelist
John Irving, American novelist
Erica Jong, American poet and novelist
Garrison Keillor, American satirist
Ali Podrimja, Albanian poet
Paul Eerik Rummo, Estonian poet and playwright
Anthony Rudolf, English poet and playwright

DEATHS

Roberto Godofredo Christopherson Arlt, Argentine novelist and essayist
Miguel Hernández, Spanish poet and playwright
Kitahara Hakushu, Japanese poet
Robert Musil, Austrian novelist
Theippam Maum Wa, Burmese novelist, playwright, and critic
Yosano Akiko, Japanese poet
Stefan Zweig, Austrian novelist, playwright, and essayist

LITERARY EVENT

PRIZES AND AWARDS

Pulitzer Prizes

Biography   *Crusader in Crinoline* by Forrest Wilson
History   *Reveille in Washington* by Margaret Leech
Novel   *In This Our Life* by Ellen Glasgow
Poetry   *The Dust Which Is God* by William Rose Benét

PUBLICATIONS

DANISH

Winter's Tales Collection of short stories by Isak Dinesen
The Story of Borge Novel by Hans Christian Branner

DUTCH

Zero Hour Poem by Martinus Nijhoff

ENGLISH

American

Assignment in Brittany Novel by Scottish-born Helen MacInnes
Blood for a Stranger Collection of poems by Randall Jarrell
The Company She Keeps Novel by Mary McCarthy
Dragon Seed Novel by Pearl S. Buck
Dragon's Teeth Novel by Upton Sinclair
Dust Tracks on a Road Autobiography of Zora Neale Hurston
Go Down, Moses Collection of seven short stories by William Faulkner
The Just and the Unjust Novel by James Gould Cozzens
The Moon Is Down Short novel by John Steinbeck
On Native Grounds Literary criticism by Alfred Kazin

The Robber Bridegroom Novel by Eudora Welty
The Skin of Our Teeth Play by Thornton Wilder
A Witness Tree Collected verse of Robert Frost

British

Black Lamb and Grey Falcon Travel narrative by Rebecca West
The Keys of the Kingdom Novel by A. J. Cronin
Little Gidding Poem (last of *The Four Quartets*) by T. S. Eliot
Street Songs Collection of verse by Edith Sitwell
To Be a Pilgrim Novel by Joyce Cary
West with the Night Memoirs of aviator Beryl Markham

Irish

The Great Hunger Poem by Patrick Kavanagh
Red Roses for Me Play by Sean O'Casey

FRENCH

Antigone Dramatic tragedy by Jean Anouilh
The Exile and Other Poems Collected verse of Saint-John Perse
The Myth of Sisyphus Philosophical essay by Albert Camus
The Stranger Novel by Albert Camus

GERMAN

Austrian

The Royal Game Novella by Stefan Zweig

ITALIAN

And Suddenly It's Evening Collection of poems by Salvatore Quasimodo

PERSIAN

The Mad House Novel by Mohammad Ali Jamalzadeh

POLISH

Invincible Song Collection of poems by Czeslaw Milosz

PORTUGUESE

Brazilian

The Violent Land Novel by Jorge Amado

Portuguese

The Prince with Donkey Ears Novel by José Regio

São Tomean

The Island of the Holy Name Collection of verse by Francisco José de Vasques Tenreiro

SPANISH

Spanish

The Family of Pascal Duarte Novel by Camilo José Cela

Uruguayan

No Man's Land Novel by Juan Carlos Onetti

SWEDISH

The Seven Deadly Sins Collection of poems by Karin Maria Boge

TAJIK

The Golden Qishalq Poem by Mirsaid Mirshakar

1943

BIRTHS

Reinaldo Arenas, Cuban novelist
Peter Carey, Australian novelist
Nikki Giovanni, African-American poet
Louise Gluck, American poet
Marion Patrick Jones, Trinidadian novelist
Michael Ondaatje, Sri Lankan–born Canadian novelist, poet, and playwright
Justo Jorge Padrón, Spanish poet
Sam Shepard (Samuel Shepard Rogers), American playwright and novelist
Sasha Sokalov, Russian novelist
Steve Tesich, Yugoslav-born American playwright and novelist
José Luis de Tomás García, Spanish novelist

DEATHS

Carlos Arniches, Spanish playwright
Stephen Vincent Benét, American novelist and poet
Laurence Binyon, English poet and playwright
Radclyffe Hall, English novelist
Abdul Rahim bin Salim Kajai, Malay journalist
Kostis Palamas, Greek poet
Henrik Pontoppidan, Danish novelist and playwright
Beatrix Potter, English writer of children's stories
Shimazaki Tōson, Japanese novelist
Tokuda Shūsei, Japanese novelist
Saul Tschernichowsky, Russian-born Israeli poet
Simone Weil, French philosopher, playwright, and poet
Alexander Woolcott, American critic

LITERARY EVENT

PRIZES AND AWARDS

Pulitzer Prizes

Biography   *Admiral of the Ocean Sea* by Samuel Eliot Morison
Drama   *The Skin of Our Teeth* by Thornton Wilder
History   *Paul Revere and the World He Lived In* by Esther Forbes
Novel   *Dragon's Teeth* by Upton Sinclair
Poetry   *A Witness Tree* by Robert Frost

PUBLICATIONS

ARMENIAN

The Companions of Vardan Historical novel by Derenik Demirtchian

BURMESE

Man Is Insane Play by U Nu

DANISH

En Route to Myself Memoirs of Henrik Pontoppidan
Poems, 1901–43 Collected verse of Johannes Jensen

ENGLISH

American

The Big Rock Candy Mountain Novel by Wallace Stegner
A Certain Measure Collection of essays by Ellen Glasgow

The Fountainhead Novel by Ayn Rand
At Heaven's Gate Novel by Robert Penn Warren
The Human Comedy Novel by William Saroyan
A Moon for the Misbegotten Play by Eugene O'Neill
Number One Novel by John Dos Passos
Seasons of the Soul Collected verse of Allen Tate
The Trespassers Novel by Laura Z. Hobson
Two Serious Ladies Novel by Jane Bowles
The Way Some People Live Collection of short stories by John Cheever
Western Star Epic poem by Stephen Vincent Benét
The Wide Net Collection of short stories by Eudora Welty

British

Mere Christianity Apologetics by C. S. Lewis
The Ministry of Fear Novel by Graham Greene
None But the Lonely Heart Novel by Richard Llewellyn
A Poet's Notebook Miscellaneous prose collection by Edith Sitwell
Prelandra Science fiction by C. S. Lewis
The Small Black Room Novel by Nigel Balchin
Word Over All Collection of poems by Cecil Day-Lewis

Indian

The Will of the People Play by Bharati Sarabhai

FRENCH

Congolese

Where Shall I Go? Novel by A. Emile Disengomoko

French

Being and Nothingness Philosophical discourse by Jean-Paul Sartre
The Fable and the Flesh Novel by Marcel Aymé
Le Vin est tiré Novel by Robert Desnos
The Little Prince Children's fable by Antoine de Saint-Exupéry
Pierrot Novel by Raymond Queneau
The Wakeful State Collected verse of Robert Desnos

GERMAN

The Good Woman of Setzuan Play by Bertolt Brecht
Magister Ludi (The Glass Bead Game) Novel by Hermann Hesse

HUNGARIAN

Arrival and Departure Novel by Arthur Koestler

ICELANDIC

Iceland's Bell Trilogy by Halldor Laxness

ITALIAN

Land's End Collection of poems by Eugenio Montale

JAPANESE

The Makioka Sisters Novel by Tanizaki Junichiro

PORTUGUESE

Angolan

To the Sound of the Marimbas Poems by Geraldo Bessa Victor

Brazilian
Dead Fire Novel by José Lins de Rego

SPANISH
Mexican
Human Mourning Novel by José Revueltas

SWEDISH
Charcoal Burner's Ballad and Other Poems Collection by Dan Andersson

1944

BIRTHS
Eavan Boland, Irish poet and critic
Paul Durcan, Irish poet
Florence Onye Buchi Emecheta, Nigerian novelist
Kjartan Flagstad, Norwegian novelist
Merle Hodge, Trinidadian novelist
Christopher David Tully Hope, South African novelist, poet, and essayist
Witi Tame Ihimaera, New Zealand Maori novelist
Taher Ben Jelloum, Moroccan poet, novelist, and playwright
Maxime N'Debeka, Congolese poet and playwright
Izmet Ozel, Turkish poet
Botho Strauss, German playwright, poet, and novelist
Alice Walker, African-American novelist, poet, and essayist

DEATHS
George Ade, American novelist and playwright
Herbert George De Lisser, Jamaican novelist
Jean Giraudoux, French playwright and novelist
Huseyin Rahmi Gurpinar, Turkish novelist
Max Jacobs, French poet
Musal Jalil, Tatar poet
Niko Lotkipanidze, Georgian novelist, poet, and playwright
Filippo Tommaso Marinetti, Italian poet, novelist, and critic
Kaj Munk, Danish playwright
Hamid Olimjon, Uzbek poet and critic
Q. (Sir Arthur Thomas Quiller-Couch), English essayist, poet, and novelist
Liviu Rebreanu, Romanian novelist, playwright, and novelist
Roman Rolland, French novelist
Jacques Roumain, Haitian poet, novelist, and essayist
Antoine de Saint-Exupéry, French novelist
Jakob Schaffner, Swiss novelist
Ida M. Tarbell, American social historian and muckraker
Mehmed Emin Yurdakul, Turkish poet

LITERARY EVENT
PRIZES AND AWARDS
Nobel Prize in literature: Johannes V. Jensen, Danish novelist

Pulitzer Prizes

Biography *The American Leonardo: The Life of Samuel F. B. Morse* by Carlton Mabee

History *The Growth of American Thought* by Merle Curti
Novel *Journey in the Dark* by Martin Flavin
Poetry *Western Star* by Stephen Vincent Benét

PUBLICATIONS
ARABIC
Egyptian
The Lamp of Umm Hashim Novel by Yahya Haqqi

Lebanese
Kadmus Play by Said Aql

ENGLISH
American
Anna and the King of Siam Novel by Margaret Landon
A Bell for Adano Novel by John Hersey
Boston Adventure Novel by Jean Stafford
The Dangling Man Novel by Saul Bellow
Delta Wedding Novel by Eudora Welty
The Glass Menagerie Play by Tennessee Williams
Harvey Play by Mary Chase
The Leaning Tower Collection of stories by Katherine Anne Porter
The Man Who Had All the Luck Play by Arthur Miller
Passport to the War Collected verse of Stanley Kunitz
V-Letter and Other Poems Verse collection by Karl Shapiro
Yankee from Olympus Biography of Oliver Wendell Holmes by Catherine Drinker Bowen

British
Fair Stood the Wind for France Novel by H. E. Bates
Fireman Flower and Other Stories Collected stories of William Sansom
Green Song Collected verse of Edith Sitwell
The Green Years Novel by A. J. Cronin
The Horse's Mouth Novel by Joyce Cary
Left Hand, Right Hand Autobiography of Osbert Sitwell
The Razor's Edge Novel by W. Somerset Maugham
The Shrimp and the Anemone Novel by L. P. Hartley

FRENCH
French
Caligula Play by Albert Camus
Country Collected verse of Robert Desnos
Gigi Novel by Colette
No Exit Play by Jean-Paul Sartre
Our Lady of Flowers Novel by Jean Genet
The Virgin of Paris Collected verse of Pierre-Jean Jouve

Haitian
Masters of the Dew Novel by Jacques Roumain

ITALIAN
Agostino Novella by Alberto Moravia
Kaputt Novel by Curzio Malaperte
Two Adolescents Novel by Alberto Moravia

MALAYALAM
Childhood Friend Novel by Vaikam Mohammad Bashir

PORTUGUESE

Brazilian

Near to the Savage Heart Novel by Clarice Lispector

RUSSIAN

Evening Light Collection of poems by Vyacheslav Ivanon
Chariot of Wrath Novel by Leonid Leonov

SPANISH

"Children of Wrath" Poem by Damaso Alonso
"Dark Message" Poem by Damaso Alonso
The Lady of the Dawn Play by Alejandro Casona

SWEDISH

The Dwarf Novel by Par Lagerkvist

YAKUT

Springtime Novel by Amma Achchygyya

1945

BIRTHS

John Banville, Irish writer
Luiz Berto, Brazilian novelist
Annie Dillard, American poet and essayist
Nuruddin Farah, Somali novelist
Isaac Goldemberg, Peruvian novelist and poet
Shivadhar Srinivasa Naipaul, Trinidadian novelist
Gyorgy Petri, Hungarian poet
Josep-Lluis Segui, Catalan poet, playwright, and novelist
August Wilson, African-American playwright
Adam Zagajewski, Polish poet

DEATHS

Robert Benchley, American humorist
Ernst Cassirer, German philosopher
Robert Desnos, French poet
Theodore Dreiser, American novelist
Pierre Drieu La Rochelle, French novelist, poet, and essayist
Ellen Glasgow, American novelist
Georg Kaiser, German playwright
Else Lasker-Schuler, German poet
Samuel Edward Krune Loliwe Mqhayi, Xhosa poet
Maria Pawlikowska-Jasnorzewska, Polish poet
Pham Quynh, Vietnamese literary scholar and translator
Arthur Symons, English poet and critic
Alexey Nikolayevich Tolstoy, Soviet novelist
Halid Ziya Usakligil, Turkish novelist
Paul Valéry, French poet
Josef Weinheber, Austrian poet
Franz Werfel, Austrian novelist and playwright
Ya Dafu, Chinese short-story writer

LITERARY EVENT

PRIZES AND AWARDS

Nobel Prize in literature: Gabriela Mistral (Lucila Godoy Alcayaga), Chilean poet

Pulitzer Prizes

Biography *George Bancroft: Brahmin Rebel* by Russell Blaine Nye
Drama *Harvey* by Mary Chase
History *Unfinished Business* by Stephen Bonsal
Novel *A Bell for Adano* by John Hersey
Poetry *V-Letter and Other Poems* by Karl Shapiro

PUBLICATIONS

CZECH

The Helmet of Clay Collected verse of Jaroslav Seifert

DANISH

Lucky Kristoffer Novel by Martin Hansen

ENGLISH

American

The Air Conditioned Nightmare Criticism by Henry Miller
Black Boy Autobiography of Richard Wright
Cannery Row Novel by John Steinbeck
Cass Timberlane Novel by Sinclair Lewis
The Crack-Up Novel by F. Scott Fitzgerald
Essay on Rime Long poem on the art of poetry by Karl Shapiro
The Glass Menagerie Play by Tennessee Williams
A Grammar of Motives Literary criticism by Kenneth Little
If He Hollers, Let Him Go Novel by Chester Himes
Little Friend, Little Friend Collected verse of Randall Jarrell
A Street in Bronzeville Verse collection by Gwendolyn Brooks
Stuart Little Children's story by E. B. White

British

Animal Farm Novel by George Orwell
Brideshead Revisited Novel by Evelyn Waugh
For the Time Being Poems by W. H. Auden
Mine Own Executioner Novel by Nigel Balchin
The North Ship Collection of poems by Philip Larkin
The Pursuit of Love Novel by Nancy Mitford
Songs of the Cold Collection of poems by Edith Sitwell
That Hideous Strength Science fiction by C. S. Lewis
XX Poems Collected verse of Philip Larkin
The Way to the Tomb Play by Robert Duncan

Indian

The English Teacher Novel by R. K. Narayan

FINNISH

The Egyptian Novel by Mika Waltari

FRENCH

The Mad Woman of Chaillot Play by Jean Giraudoux
The Roads to Freedom Novel by Jean-Paul Sartre
Seuls Demeurent Collected verse of René Char

GERMAN

Austrian

The Death of Virgil Novel by Hermann Broch

GREEK
Heroic and Elegiac Song for the Lost Second Lieutenant of the Albanian Campaign Poem by Odysseus Elytis

ICELANDIC
Mother Iceland Novel by Guthmundur Hagalin

ITALIAN
Christ Stopped at Eboli Novel by Carlo Levi
The Naked Streets Novel by Vasco Pratolini

POLISH
Rescue Collection of poems by Czesław Milosz

SPANISH
Memoirs of Leticia Valle Novel by Rosa Chacel
Voices of My Song Collection of poems by Juan Ramón Jiménez

SWEDISH
My Death Is My Own Novel by Lars Ahlin
The Long Ships Novel by Frans Gunnar Bengtisson
Pippi Longstocking Children's story by Astrid Lindgren
The Snake First novel by Stig Dagerman
Trade Winds Collection of poems by Henry Martinson

URDU
Flight Novel by Aziz Ahmed

YIDDISH
The Family Moskat Novel by Polish-born American writer Isaac Bashevis Singer
"Gimpel the Fool" Short story by Isaac Bashevis Singer

1946

BIRTHS
Octavio Armand, Cuban novelist and poet
Andrei Codrescu, Romanian-born American poet
Andrea Dworkin, American novelist and feminist writer
Aleksander Kaletski, Russian novelist
Franz Xavier Kroetz, German playwright
Nakagami Kenji, Japanese novelist
Montserrat Roig, Catalan novelist
Irini Spanidou, Greek-born American novelist

DEATHS
Alcides Arguedas, Bolivian novelist and historian
Countee Cullen, African-American poet
Omar Fakhuri, Lebanese essayist
Harley Granville-Barker, English playwright and critic
Gerhart Hauptmann, German novelist, poet, and playwright
John Maynard Keynes, English economist
Damon Runyon, American novelist
Arthur von Schendel, Dutch novelist and short-story writer
Sri (B. M. Srikanthayya), Kannada translator and critic
Gertrude Stein, American novelist, critic, and poet

Booth Tarkington, American playwright and novelist
Herbert George Wells, English social historian, science fiction writer, novelist, and essayist
Wen Yiduo, Chinese poet, essayist, and critic

LITERARY EVENT
PRIZES AND AWARDS
Nobel Prize in literature: Herman Hesse, German novelist

Pulitzer Prizes

Biography   *Son of the Wilderness* by Linie Marsh Wolfe
Drama   *The State of the Union* by Russell Crouse and Howard Lindsay
History   *The Age of Jackson* by Arthur M. Schlesinger Jr.

PUBLICATIONS
DUTCH
Cryptogamen Anthology of poems by Gerrit Achterberg

ENGLISH
American

All the King's Men Novel by Robert Penn Warren
Another Part of the Forest Play by Lillian Hellman
The Bulwark Novel by Theodore Dreiser
The Call Novel by Norwegian-born Alfred Hauge
Delta Wedding Novel by Eudora Welty
The Iceman Cometh Play by Eugene O'Neill
Lord Weary's Castle Poetry collection by Robert Lowell
The Member of the Wedding Novel by Carson McCullers
Memoirs of Hecate County Collection of short stories by Edmund Wilson
North and South Poetry collection by Elizabeth Bishop
Paterson Long poem by William Carlos Williams
"The Quaker Graveyard in Nantucket" Poem by Robert Lowell
The Street Novel by Ann Petry

British

The Berlin Stories Novel by Chistopher Isherwood
Bright Day Novel by J. B. Priestley
The Inspector Calls Play by J. B. Priestley
Jill Autobiographical novel by Philip Larkin
Lord Hornblower Sea novel by C. S. Forester
A Phoenix Too Frequent Verse play by Chistopher Isherwood
The Purple Plain Novel by H. E. Bates
The River Novel by Rumer Godden
The Scarlet Tree Autobiography by Osbert Sitwell
Still Life Play by Noël Coward

South African

Mine Boy Novel by Peter Lee Abrahams

Welsh

The Dark Philosophers Novel by Gwyn Thomas
Deaths and Entrances Poetry collection by Dylan Thomas
"Fern Hill" Poem by Dylan Thomas

FINNISH
The Breath of Copper Collected verse of Robbe Enckell

FRENCH

All Men Are Mortals Novel by Simone de Beauvoir
Aurora Novel by Michel-Julien Leiris
The Eagle Has Two Heads Play by Jean Cocteau
For and Against Autobiographical novel by Jacques Lacretelle
Leaves of Hypnos Poetry collection by René Char
Malatesta Play by Henry de Montherlant
Quoat-Quoat Play by Jacques Audiberti
The Transient Hour Novel by Marcel Aymé
Winds Collection of poems by Saint-John Perse

GERMAN

The Devil's General Play by Carl Zuckmayer
Stalingrad Documentary novel by Theodore Plievier

GREEK

Zorba the Greek Novel by Nikos Kazantzakis

HINDI

Lakshmibai, Queen of Jhansi Historical novel by Vrindavanlal Varma

JAPANESE

Dark Painting Novel by Hiroshi Noma

KAZAKH

Abay's Road Biographical novel by Mukhtar Auezov

PERSIAN

The Custodian of the Divan Novel by Mohammad Ali Jamalzadeh

PORTUGUESE

Brazilian

Sagarana Collected stories of João Guimares Rosa

RUSSIAN

The Road to Calvary Trilogy of novels by Alexey Nikolayevich Tolstoy

SPANISH

Guatemalan

The President Novel by Miguel Asturias

Spanish

Springtime of Death Collection of poems by Carlos Bousoño

SWEDISH

The Island of the Doomed Novel by Stig Dagerman
Return to Ithaca Novel by Eyvind Johnson

URDU

Fire Novel by Aziz Ahmed

1947

BIRTHS

Paul Auster, American novelist, essayist, and poet
Patrick Grainville, French novelist

Reto Hanny, Swiss novelist
Evan X. Hyde, Belizean poet, playwright, and novelist
David Mamet, American playwright
Roy Patursson, Danish poet
Evelin E. Sullivan, German novelist
Roy E. Walker, Canadian playwright

DEATHS

Gabra Iyasus Afawark, Ethiopian Amharic novelist and poet
Willa Cather, American novelist
Winston Churchill, American novelist
Hans Fallada (Rudolf Ditzen), German novelist
Léon-Paul Fargue, French poet and essayist
Abdalrauf Fitrat, Tajik-Uzbek novelist and playwright
Ricarda Huch, German poet, novelist, and critic
Khai Hung (Tran Khanh Du), Vietnamese novelist
Kōda Rohan (Kōda Shigeyuki), Japanese novelist
Hugh Lofting, American writer of children's books
Manuel Machado, Spanish playwright and poet
Gregorio Martínez Sierra, Spanish playwright, novelist, and poet
Noguchi Yonejiro, Japanese poet and critic
Charles Bernard Nordhoff, English-born American novelist
Baroness Emmuska Orczy, Hungarian-born English novelist
Charles Ferdinand Ramuz, Swiss novelist
Benedict Wallet Bambatha Vilakazi, Zulu poet and novelist
Alfred North Whitehead, English philosopher
Yokomitsu Riichi, Japanese novelist
Zhang Ziping, Chinese novelist

LITERARY EVENTS

Strega, an Italian literary prize, is established
Epoch, a literary journal, is founded in Ithaca, New York

PRIZES AND AWARDS

Nobel Prize in literature: André Gide, French novelist

Pulitzer Prizes

Autobiography   *The Autobiography of William Allen White* by William Allen White
History   *Scientists Against Time* by James Phinney Baxter III
Novel   *All the King's Men* by Robert Penn Warren
Poetry   *Lord Weary's Castle* by Robert Lowell

PUBLICATIONS

ARABIC

Midaq Alley Novel by Egyptian writer Naguib Mahfouz

BURMESE

The Peasant Nga Ba Novel by Maun Htin

DUTCH

The Dew Trapper Collected verse of Jan van Nijlen

ENGLISH

American

All My Sons Play by Arthur Miller
The Beautiful Changes and Other Poems Collection by Richard Wilbur
Bend Sinister Novel by Vladimir Nabokov

The Circus in the Attic Collection of short stories by Robert Penn Warren

Gentleman's Agreement Novel by Laura Z. Hobson

The Harder They Fall Novel by Budd Schulberg

In Defense of Reason Literary criticism by Yvor Winters

I, the Jury Detective novel by Mickey Spillane

Joan of Lorraine Play by Maxwell Anderson

The Mother of Us All Opera libretto by Gertrude Stein

The Neon Wilderness Collection of short stories by Nelson Algren

The Pearl Novel by John Steinbeck

Steeple Bush Collected verse of Robert Frost

A Streetcar Named Desire Play by Tennessee Williams

Tales of the South Pacific Novel by James Michener

Trial of a Poet and Other Poems Collection by Karl Shapiro

The Victim Novel by Saul Bellow

The Wayward Bus Novel by John Steinbeck

British

The Age of Anxiety: A Baroque Eclogue Poetry collection by W. H. Auden

An Avenue of Stone Novel by Pamela Hansford Johnson

Collected Poems Collection by Siegfried Sassoon

The Dark Tower Play by Louis MacNiece

A Girl in Winter Novel by Philip Larkin

Great Morning Autobiography by Osbert Sitwell

Poems of Dedication Collection by Stephen Spender

The Volcano Novel by Malcolm Lowry

Scottish

Whiskey Galore Novel by Compton Mackenzie

FRENCH

Gravity and Grace Philosophical treatise by Simone Weil

If I Were You Novel by Julien Green

I Will Live the Love of Others Novel by Jean-Raphael-Marie-Noël Cayrol

The Maids Play by Jean Genet

The Master of Santiago Play by Henry de Montherlant

The Plague Novel by Albert Camus

Querrelle of Brest Novel by Jean Genet

The Taut Rope Novel by Claude Simon

GREEK

Thrush Collected verse of George Seferis

GERMAN

German

Dance of Death and Poems of the Times Collected verse of Marie Louise Kaschnitz

The Diary of a Young Girl Diary of German Jewish Holocaust victim Anne Frank

Doctor Faustus Novel by Thomas Mann

Swiss

The Chinese Wall Play by Max Frisch

Santa Cruz Play by Max Frisch

ITALIAN

Day After Day Collection of poems by Salvatore Quasimodo

The Dry Heart Novella by Natalie Ginzburg

Gothic Notebook Poem by Mario Luzi

Grief Collection of poems by Giuseppe Ungaretti

If This Is a Man Autobiography of Primo Levi

The Path to the Nest of Spiders Novel by Italo Calvino

A Tale of Poor Lovers Novel by Vasco Pratolini

Two Brothers Novel by Vasco Pratolini

The Woman of Rome Novel by Alberto Moravia

JAPANESE

A Red Moon in Her Face Novel by Hiroshi Noma

The Setting Sun Novel by Dazai Osamu

PERSIAN

The Story of the Water Channel Novel by Mohammad Ali Jamalzadeh

PORTUGUESE

Brazilian

Black Poems Collected verse of Jorge de Lima

Portuguese

Benilde, or the Virgin Mother Play by José Regio

SPANISH

Chilean

The Heights of Machu Picchu Collected verse of Pablo Neruda

Spanish

Animal at Bottom Poem by Juan Ramón Jiménez

TAJIK

Tajik Vengeance Prose collection by Foteh Niyazi

URDU

Shapes Collection of erotic quatrains by Firaq Gorakhpuri

YAKUT

The Fortune of Yakutsk Ballad by Elley

1948

BIRTHS

Kathy Acker, American novelist

Aldo Busi, Italian novelist

Katherine Govier, Canadian novelist

Bodo Kirchoff, German novelist

Erika Ritter, Canadian playwright and essayist

Leslie Marmon Silko, American novelist and poet

Alan Sillitoe, English novelist

George Szirtes, English-Hungarian poet and critic

Takahashi Michitsuna, Japanese novelist

DEATHS

Sabahattin Ali, Turkish novelist

Antonin Artaud, French playwright and poet

George Bernanos, French Catholic novelist
Dazai Osamu (Tsushima Shuji), Japanese novelist
Susan Glaspell, American novelist and playwright
Vicente Huidobro, Chilean poet, novelist, and playwright
Alfred Kerr (Alfred Kempner), German poet and critic
Krishnaji Prabhakar Khadilkar, Marathi playwright
Emil Ludwig, German biographer
Dehati Mohammad Mas'ud, Iranian novelist
Claude McKay, Jamaican poet, novelist, and critic
Thomas Mokopu Mofolo, Bosotho novelist
Kunnumpuzha Krishna Pillai, Malayalee poet
Puttamiputtan, Tamil novelist, essayist, and poet

LITERARY EVENTS
Bollingen Prize is established

PRIZES AND AWARDS
Nobel Prize in literature: T. S. Eliot, American-born English poet

Pulitzer Prizes

Biography   *Forgotten First Citizen: John Bigelow* by Margaret Clapp
Drama   *A Streetcar Named Desire* by Tennessee Williams
Fiction   *Tales of the South Pacific* by James Michener
History   *Across the Wide Missouri* by Bernard DeVoto
Poetry   *The Age of Anxiety* by W. H. Auden

PUBLICATIONS
AMHARIC
Hannibal Play by Mikael Kabbada

ARABIC
The Hand, the Earth and the Water Novel by Iraqi writer Dhun-Nun Ayyub

CHINESE
Rickshaw Boy Novel by Lao She

ENGLISH
American
Anne of the Thousand Days Play by Maxwell Anderson
The Circus in the Attic Collected verse of Robert Penn Warren
The Dispossessed Collection of verse by John Berryman
Guard of Honor Novel by James Gould Cozzens
"Homage to Mistress Bradstreet" Poem by John Berryman
The Ides of March Novel by Thornton Wilder
Intruder in the Dust Novel by William Faulkner
The Lost Son, and Other Poems Collection by Theodore Roethke
"The Lottery" Short story by Shirley Jackson
The Naked and the Dead Novel by Norman Mailer
Other Voices, Other Rooms Novel by Truman Capote
The Pisan Cantos Collection by Ezra Pound
Remembrance Rock Novel by Carl Sandburg
A Russian Journal Travel narrative by John Steinbeck
Seven Storey Mountain Autobiography of Catholic monk Thomas Merton
The Sheltering Sky Novel by Paul Bowles

Summer and Smoke Play by Tennessee Williams
The World Is a Wedding and Other Stories Collected short stories by Delmore Schwartz
The Year Has No Spring Novel by Norwegian-born Alfred Hauge
The Young Lions Novel by Irwin Shaw

British
The Browning Version Play by Terence Rattigan
Collected Poems Collected verse by Robert Graves
The Great Tradition Literary perspectives by F. R. Leavis
The Heart of the Matter Novel by Graham Greene
The Jacaranda Tree Novel by H. E. Bates
The Lady's Not for Burning Play by Christopher Fry
Laughter in the Next Room Autobiography by Osbert Sitwell
The Loved One Novel by Evelyn Waugh
Notes Toward the Definition of Culture Cultural criticism by T. S. Eliot
A Summer to Decide Novel by Pamela Hansford Johnson
The White Goddess Scholarly reflections by Robert Graves

South African
Cry, the Beloved Country Novel by Alan Paton

FRENCH
Algerian
Nedjma, Poem or Knife Poem by Kateb Yacine

Cameroonian
Mission Accomplished Novel by Mongo Beti

Congolese
The Crocodile Novel by Paul Lomami-Tshibamba

French
The Book Beside Me Collection of maxims by Pierre Reverdy
City Heights Novel by Emmanuel Robles
Dirty Hands Play by Jean-Paul Sartre
Montserrat Play by Emmanuel Robles
Portrait of a Man Unknown Novel by Nathalie Sarraute
Viper in the Fist Autobiography of Hervé Bazin

Martiniquan
Credo des sang-mélé ou je veux chanter la France Collection of verse and essays by Gilbert Gratiant

GERMAN
Austrian
Herod's Children Novel by Jewish writer Ilse Aichinger

German
The Caucasian Chalk Circle Play by Bertolt Brecht
The Dance of Death Novel by Bernhard Kellerman
The Sand for the Urns Verse by Romanian poet Paul Celan
Static Poems Collection by Gottfried Benn

HEBREW
The Day Before Yesterday Novel by Israeli writer Shmuel Yosef Halevi Czaczkes Agnon

ITALIAN
Disobedience Novel by Alberto Moravia

JAPANESE

The Road Sign at the End of the Street Novel by Abe Kobo
Snow Country Novel by Kawabata Yasunari
Thousand Cranes Novel by Kawabata Yasunari

KIKONGO

Kinzoni and His Grandson Makundu Novel by Congolese writer Jacques N. Bahelele

PERSIAN

Fairy Good Fortune Poem by Abolqasem Lahuti

POLISH

Ashes and Diamonds Novel by Jerszy Andrzejewski
Between the Wars Epic novel by Kazimierz Brandys

SERBO-CROATIAN

The Bridge on the Drina Novel by Yugoslav writer Ivo Andrič

SPANISH

Argentine

Adán Buenosayres Novel by Leopoldo Marechal
The Tunnel Novel by Ernesto Sábato

Chilean

Grand Gentleman and a Big Rascal Novel by Eduardo Barrios

Spanish

Nothing Novel by Carmen Laforet

SWEDISH

A Burnt Child Novel by Stig Dagerman
The Condemned Play by Stig Dagerman
The Road Novel by Harry Martinson

1949

BIRTHS

Peter Ackroyd, English novelist
Jamaica Kincaid, Antiguan-born American novelist
Haruki Murakami, Japanese novelist
Mary Robinson, American novelist
Patrick Suskind, German novelist and playwright

DEATHS

William Harvey Allen, American novelist
Chairil Anwar, Indonesian poet
Bao Dai (Zhao Zhenkai), Chinese poet
Ali ad-Duaji, Tunisian novelist and playwright
Vilhelm Ekelund, Swedish poet
Vyacheslav Ivanovich Ivanov, Russian poet and philosopher
Maurice Maeterlinck, Belgian novelist
Mary Jane Mander, New Zealand novelist and essayist
Klaus Mann, German playwright

Ibrahim al-Mazini, Egyptian novelist, poet, and critic
Margaret Mitchell, American novelist
Khalil Mutran, Egyptian poet
Henry Masila Ndawo, Xhosa novelist, poet, and collector of folk tales
Yoftahe Neguse, Ethiopian Amharic playwright and poet
Ullur Parameswarayyar, Malayalee poet and scholar
Ali Mahmud Taha, Egyptian poet
Sigrid Undset, Danish-born Norwegian novelist

LITERARY EVENT

PRIZES AND AWARDS

Nobel Prize in literature: William Faulkner, American novelist

Pulitzer Prizes

Biography *Roosevelt and Hopkins* by Robert E. Sherwood
Drama *Death of a Salesman* by Arthur Miller
Fiction *Guard of Honor* by James Gould Cozzens
History *The Disruption of American Democracy* by Roy Franklin Nichols
Poetry *Terror and Decorum* by Peter Viereck

PUBLICATIONS

DUTCH

In a Dark Wood Wandering Historical novel by Hella Haasse

ENGLISH

American

Annie Allen Collected verse of Gwendolyn Brooks
A Cycle of the West Five poems by John Neihardt
Death of a Salesman Play by Arthur Miller
Detective Story Play by Sidney Kingsley
The Golden Apples Collected stories of Eudora Welty
The Grand Design Novel by John Dos Passos
The Hero with a Thousand Faces Study of mythological themes by Joseph Campbell
The Man with the Golden Arm Novel by Nelson Algren
The Oasis Novel by Mary McCarthy
Point of No Return Novel by J. P. Marquand
A Rage to Live Novel by John O'Hara
The Story of a Staircase Play by Antonio Buero Vallejo
The Waterfall and the Bonfire Novel by Norwegian-born writer Alfred Hauge

British

The Boat Novel by L. P. Hartley
The Cocktail Party Verse drama by T. S. Eliot
The Heart of the Day Novel by Elizabeth Bowen
Love in a Cold Climate Novel by Nancy Mitford
1984 Novel by George Orwell
"Responsibility: The Pilots Who Destroyed Germany, Spring 1945" Poem by Stephen Spender
Stratton Play by Robert Duncan
The Third Man Novel by Graham Greene

Irish

Cock-a-Doodle-Dandy Dramatic comedy by Sean O'Casey

Welsh

All Things Betray Thee Novel by Gwyn Thomas

FINNISH

The Wanderer Novel by Mika Waltari

FRENCH

Deathwatch Play by Jean Genet
The Desert of Love Novel by François Mauriac
Dialogues des Carmelites Play by George Bernanos
Head Against the Wall Novel by Hervé Bazin
The Need for Roots Philosophical treatise by Simone Weil
The Second Sex Feminist manifesto by Simone de Beauvoir
The Thief's Journal Autobiography by Jean Genet

GERMAN

German

Barbera Blomberg Play by Carl Zuckmayer
Mother Courage and Her Children Play by Bertolt Brecht
The Train Was on Time Novel by Heinrich Böll

Swiss

When the War Was Over Play by Max Frisch

INDONESIAN

Atheist Novel by Achdiat Karta Mihardja
Gelenging Tekad Collection of verse by Ilham Notodijo
"Me" Poem by Chairil Anwar

ITALIAN

The Skin Novel by Curzio Malaparte

JAPANESE

The Bullfight Novel by Inoue Yasushi
Confessions of a Mask Novel by Yukio Mishima
The Cutter and Captain Shigemoto's Mother Novel by Tanizaki Junichiro
Ring of Youth Novel by Hiroshi Noma
Thousand Cranes Novel by Kawabata Yasunari
Twilight Crane Play by Kinoshita Junji

RUSSIAN

The Easing of Fate Collection of stories by Nina Berberova

SPANISH

Cuban

The Kingdom of This World Novel by Alejo Carpentier

Guatemalan

Men of Maize Novel by Miguel Angel Asturias

Mexican

Freedom Under Parole Collection of poems by Octavio Paz

Spanish

Words in the Sand Play by Antonio Buero Vallejo

SWEDISH

The Emigrants Four-volume epic novel by Wilhelm Moburg
Let Man Live Play by Par Lagerkvist
Modern Myths Novel by Lars Gyllensten
Snow Legend Collection of poems by Werner Aspenstrom

1950

BIRTHS

Hedin M. Klein, Danish poet
Medbh McGuckian, Irish poet
Timothy Mo, Hong Kong–born English novelist and critic
Tidor Rosic, Serbian novelist
Stella Voyatzoglou, Greek novelist

DEATHS

Bibhutibhushan Bandyopadhyay, Bengali novelist and essayist
William Rose Benét, American poet and novelist
Edgar Rice Burroughs, American novelist
Henry Courts-Mahler, German novelist
Johannes Vilhelm Jensen, Danish novelist and poet
Orhan Veli Kanik, Turkish poet
Heinrich Mann, German novelist
Edgar Lee Masters, American poet
Francis Otto Matthiessen, American critic and intellectual historian
Edna St. Vincent Millay, American poet
George Orwell (Eric Arthur Blair), English novelist
Cesare Pavese, Italian poet and novelist
Tawfiq Piramerd, Kurdish poet
George Bernard Shaw, Irish playwright

LITERARY EVENT

PRIZES AND AWARDS

Nobel Prize in literature: George Bernard Shaw, Irish playwright

Pulitzer Prizes

Biography *John Quincy Adams and the Foundations of American Foreign Policy* by Samuel Flagg Bemis
Drama *South Pacific* by Richard Rodgers, Oscar Hammerstein II, and Joshua Logan
Fiction *The Way West* by A. B. Guthrie Jr.
History *Art and Life in America* by Oliver W. Larkin
Poetry *Annie Allen* by Gwendolyn Brooks

PUBLICATIONS

DANISH

"Babette's Feast" Short story by Isak Dinesen
The Liar Novel by Martin Hansen
The Lost Musicians Novel by William Heinesen

ENGLISH

American

Across the River and Into the Trees Novel by Ernest Hemingway
Auroras of Autumn Collected verse of Wallace Stevens

Cast a Cold Eye Collection of criticism by Mary McCarthy
Ceremony and Other Poems Collected verse of Richard Wilbur
Come Back, Little Sheba Play by William Inge
Complete Poems Collected verse of Carl Sandburg
The God That Failed Novel by Richard Wright
Joe Hill Biographical novel by Wallace Stegner
The Martian Chronicles Science fiction novel by Ray Bradbury
A Rhetoric of Motives Critical perspectives by Kenneth Burke
The Town Novel by Conrad Richter
The Town and the City Novel by Jack Kerouac
The Wall Novel by John Hersey
A Woman of Means Novella by Peter Taylor
World Enough and Time Novel by Robert Penn Warren

British

The Beautiful Visit Novel by Elizabeth Jane Howard
The Boy with a Cart Verse play by Christopher Fry
The Grass Is Singing Novel by Doris Lessing
Noble Essences Autobiography by Osbert Sitwell
Parade's End Complete tetralogy by Ford Madox Ford
Venus Observed Play by Christopher Fry

Guyanan

Morning at the Office Novel by Edgar Mittelholzer

FRENCH
Canadian

The Torrent Novel by Anne Hébert
The Outlander Novel by Germaine Guèvremont

French

The Bald Soprano Play in two scenes by Eugène Ionesco
Ode Collected verse of Pierre-Jean Jouve
Waiting for God Devotional meditations by Simone Weil

GERMAN

Adam, Where Art Thou? Novel by Heinrich Böll
Music of the Future Poems by Marie Luise Kaschnitz

GREEK

Freedom or Death Novel by Nikos Kazantzakis

ITALIAN

Crime on Goat Island Play by Ugo Betti
The Promised Land Collection of poems by Giuseppe Ungaretti

JAPANESE

Thirst for Love Novel by Yukio Mishima

LITHUANIAN

The Temptation Satirical novel by Vincas Kreve-Mickievicius

PORTUGUESE
Brazilian

The Dog Without Feathers Collection of poems by João Cabral de Melo Neto

SPANISH
Chilean

General Song Epic poem by Pablo Neruda

Guatemalan

The Cyclone Novel by Miguel Angel Asturias

Mexican

The Labyrinth of Solidad Cultural history by Octavio Paz

Spanish

In the Burning Darkness Play by Antonio Buero Vallejo

Uruguayan

A Brief Life Novel by Juan Carlos Onetti
Lost Collection of poems by Juana de Ibarbourou

SWEDISH

Barabbas Novel by Par Lagerkvist

1951

BIRTHS

Nedim Gursel, Turkish novelist
Drazen Mazur, Croatian poet
Guy Vanderhaeghe, Canadian novelist

DEATHS

Louis Adamic, Slovenian novelist
Muhammad Taqi Bahar, Persian poet
Herman Charles Bosman, South African writer
James Bridie (Osborne Henry Mavor), Scottish playwright
Hermann Broch, Austrian novelist and playwright
Fumiko Hayashi, Japanese novelist, essayist, and poet
André Gide, French novelist
James Norman Hall, American novelist
Sādeq Hedāyat, Iranian novelist and playwright
Henri-René Lenormand, French playwright
Sinclair Lewis, American novelist
Nam Cao (Tran Huu Tri), Vietnamese novelist
Pedro Salinas, Spanish poet, novelist, and playwright
Angelos Sikelianós, Greek lyric poet
Hamzat Tsadasa, Dagestani poet
Ludwig Josef Johan Wittgenstein, Austrian philosopher
Rashid Yasami, Iranian historian and poet

LITERARY EVENTS

Drum, South African literary magazine, is founded in Johannesburg

PRIZES AND AWARDS

Nobel Prize in literature: Par Fabian Lagerkvist, Swedish novelist, playwright, and poet

Pulitzer Prizes

Biography   *John C. Calhoun: American Portrait* by Margaret Louise Coit
Fiction   *The Town* by Conrad Richter
History   *The Old Northwest, Pioneer Period, 1815–1840* by R. Carlyle Buley
Poetry   *Complete Poems* by Carl Sandburg

PUBLICATIONS

ARABIC

The Beginning and the End Novel by Egyptian writer Naguib Mahfouz

DUTCH

Yesterday Novel by Maria Dermont

ENGLISH

American

The Ballad of the Sad Café Novella and short stories by Carson McCullers
The Caine Mutiny Novel by Herman Wouk
The Catcher in the Rye Novel by J. D. Salinger
Chosen Country Novel by John Dos Passos
Collected Poems Collection by Marianne Moore
Foundation Science fiction novel by Isaac Asimov
From Here to Eternity Novel by James Jones
The Grass Harp Novel by Truman Capote
The Green Hills of Earth Science fiction novel by Robert Heinlein
Harlem Collected verse of Langston Hughes
The Illustrated Man Collection of science fiction stories by Ray Bradbury
In the Absence of Angels Collected short stories of Hortense Calisher
Lie Down in Darkness Novel by William Styron
Melville Godwin U.S.A. Novel by John P. Marquand
Montage of a Dream Deferred Poetry collection by Langston Hughes
Praise to the End! Collection of verse by Theodore Roethke
Requiem for a Nun Novel by William Faulkner
The Rose Tattoo Play by Tennessee Williams
The Seven-League Crutches Collection of verse by Randall Jarrell
Speak, Memory Autobiography by Russian-born Vladimir Nabokov

British

The Blessing Novel by Nancy Mitford
The Cruel Sea Novel by Nicholas Montserrat
A Dance to the Beginning of Time Twelve-volume novel cycle by Anthony Burgess
The End of the Affair Novel by Graham Greene
The Masters Novel by C. P. Snow
Our Lady's Tumbler Play by Ronald Duncan
A Question of Upbringing Novel (part of *Dance to the Music of Time*) by Anthony Powell
A Sleep of Prisoners Verse play by Christopher Fry

Canadian

The Loved and the Lost Novel by Morley Callaghan
Salterton Trilogy Novel cycle by Robertson Davies

Indian

The Autobiography of an Unknown Indian Autobiography of Nirad C. Chaudhuri

South African

Wild Conquest Novel by Peter Abrahams

FRENCH

Belgian

The Illusionist Novel by François Mallet-Joris

French

The City Whose Prince Is a Child Play by Henry de Montherlant
The Devil and the Good Lord Play by Jean-Paul Sartre
The Lesson Play by Romanian-born Eugène Ionesco
Memoirs of Hadrian Historical novel by Marguerite Yourcenar
Molloy Novel by Irish-born Samuel Beckett
The Rebel Essay by Albert Camus
Sea Marks Collection of poems by Saint-John Perse

GERMAN

The Holy Sinner Novel by Thomas Mann

INDONESIAN

The Paralyzed Novel by Pramudya Ananta Tur

ITALIAN

The Conformist Novel by Alberto Moravia
The Indian Hut Collected verse of Attilio Bertolucci
The Queen and the Rebels Play by Ugo Betti

JAPANESE

Fires on the Plain Novel by Shohei Ooka
Floating Cloud Novel by Hayashi Fumiko
Ascension of the Frog Play by Kinoshita Junji

KANNADA

A Child of the Kudiyas Novel by Kota Sivarama Karanta

SERBIAN

Far Away Is the Sun Novel by Dobrica Casic

SPANISH

Chilean

Born Guilty Novel by Manuel Rojas

Mexican

Eagle or Sun Collection of poems by Octavio Paz

Spanish

The Hive Novel by Camilo José Cela

SWEDISH

A Mystery Play of the Sufferings of Israel Play by German-born writer Nelly Sachs

1952

BIRTHS

Antoine Laurent, French novelist
Ryu Murakami, Japanese novelist
Vikram Seth, Indian novelist
Mara Zalite, Latvian poet

DEATHS
Mariano Azuela, Mexican novelist
Benedetto Croce, Italian historian and philosopher
John Dewey, American educational philosopher
Paul Éluard (Eugène Grindel), French poet
Knut Hamsun, Norwegian novelist
Ghulam Ahmad Mahjur, Kashmiri Urdu poet
Ferenc Molnár, Hungarian playwright
George Santayana, American philosopher, novelist, poet, and
    critic

LITERARY EVENT
PRIZES AND AWARDS
Nobel Prize in literature: François-Charles Mauriac, French
    novelist

Pulitzer Prizes

Biography   *Charles Evans Hughes* by Merlo J. Pusey
Drama   *The Shrike* by Joseph Kramm
Fiction   *The Caine Mutiny* by Herman Wouk
History   *The Uprooted* by Oscar Handlin
Poetry   *Collected Poems* by Marianne Moore

PUBLICATIONS
BALUCHI
Call Collected verse of Gul Khan Nasir

DANISH
Serpent and Bull Novel by Martin Hansen

DUTCH
The Scarlet City Novel by Hella Haasse

ENGLISH
American
The Catherine Wheel Novel by Jean Stafford
Charlotte's Web Children's story by E. B. White
"The Dragon and the Unicorn" Poem by Kenneth Rexroth
East of Eden Novel by John Steinbeck
Foundation and Empire Science fiction novel by Isaac Asimov
Giant Novel by Edna Ferber
The Groves of Academe Novel by Mary McCarthy
Invisible Man Novel by Ralph Ellison
Let It Come Down Novel by Paul Bowles
A Moon for the Misbegotten Play by Eugene O'Neill
The Natural Novel by Bernard Malamud
No, But I Saw the Movie Novel by Peter De Vries
The Old Man and the Sea Novella by Ernest Hemingway
Player Piano Novel by Kurt Vonnegut Jr.
The Silver Chalice Biblical novel by Thomas B. Costain
Wise Blood Novel by Flannery O'Connor

British
A Buyer's Market Novel (part of *Dance to the Music of Time*) by
    Anthony Powell
Hemlock and After Novel by Angus Wilson
Martha Quest Novel by Doris Lessing
Men at Arms Novel by Evelyn Waugh

The Mousetrap Mystery play by Agatha Christie
Sword of Honor Trilogy by Evelyn Waugh

Indian
Two Women Play by Bharati Sarabhai

Irish
A Prisoner of Grace Novel by Joyce Cary
Ten Burnt Offerings Collection of poems by Louis MacNeice

Nigerian
Africa Sings Collection of verse by Dennis Chukude Osadebay

South African
Stranger to Europe Collected verse of Guy Butler

Trinidadian
A Brighter Sun Novel by Samuel Selvon

Welsh
Collected Poems, 1934–1952 Collection by Dylan Thomas
In Country Sleep Collection of poems by Dylan Thomas

FINNISH
The Dark Angel Novel by Mika Waltari

FRENCH
Algerian
The Big House Novel by Mohammad Dib
Forgotten Hill Novel by Mouloud Mammeri

French
The Bridge Over the River Kwai Novel by Pierre Boulle
The Chairs Play by Eugène Ionesco
Constance Novel by Hervé Bazin
Dawn on Our Darkness Novel by Emmanuel Robles
The Horseman on the Roof Novel by Jean Giono
Language Collected verse of Pierre-Jean Jouve
The Waltz of the Toreadors Play by Jean Anouilh

GERMAN
Heart on the Left Autobiographical novel by Leonhard Franks
Poppy and Memory Collected verse of Paul Celan

ITALIAN
All Our Yesterdays Novella by Natalie Ginzburg
The Cloven Viscount Fantasy by Italo Calvino
A Cry and Landscapes Collected verse of Giuseppe Ungaretti
First Fruits of the Desert Collected verse of Mario Luzi
A Handful of Black Berries Novel by Ignazio Siolne

JAPANESE
The Sound of the Mountains Novel by Yasunari Kawabata
Zone of Emptiness Novel by Hiroshi Noma

KANNADA
The Road We Have Walked Collection of verse by Indian writer
    Gopalakrishna Adiga

PERSIAN
Her Eyes Novel by Bozorg Alavi

PORTUGUESE

Brazilian

The Invention of Orpheus Collected verse of Jorge de Lima

SWEDISH

Litany Collection of poems by Werner Aspenstrom

1953

BIRTHS

Adonis Fostieris, Greek poet
Rod Jones, Australian novelist

DEATHS

Bheeromal Mehrchand Advani, Sindhi playwright and critic
Raphael Ernest Grail Glikpo Armattoe, Ghanaian poet and historian
Hilaire Belloc, French-born English Catholic playwright and critic
Henry Bernstein, French playwright
Ugo Betti, Italian playwright and poet
Jean de Bosschere, Belgian poet, novelist, and critic
Ivan Alekseyevich Bunin, Russian novelist
Douglas Southall Freeman, American historian and biographer
Mudaliar Tiruvarur V. Kalyanisundaram, Tamil essayist and philosopher
Maha Hswei, Burmese novelist and essayist
Richard von Mises, Austrian philosopher
Martinus Nijhoff, Dutch poet
Eugene Gladstone O'Neill, American playwright
Marjorie Kinnan Rawlings, American novelist
Dylan Thomas, Welsh poet
Ben Ames Williams, American novelist

LITERARY EVENTS

Paris Review is founded by George Plimpton

PRIZES AND AWARDS

Nobel Prize in literature: Winston S. Churchill, English statesman and writer

Pulitzer Prizes

Biography *Edmund Pendleton, 1721–1803* by David J. Mays
Drama *Picnic* by William Inge
Fiction *The Old Man and the Sea* by Ernest Hemingway
History *The Era of Good Feelings* by George Dangerfield
Poetry *Collected Poems, 1917–1952* by Archibald MacLeish

PUBLICATIONS

BURMESE

Pauper Tyetko Novel by Banmo Tin Aun

ENGLISH

American

The Adventures of Augie March Novel by Canadian-born writer Saul Bellow

The Bridges at Toko-Ri Novel by James A. Michener
Brother to Dragons: A Tale in Verse and Voices Poetry and fiction by Robert Penn Warren
The Buried Lake Collected verse of Allen Tate
Camino Real Play by Tennessee Williams
Collected Poems Collection by Conrad Aiken
The Crucible Play by Arthur Miller
Fahrenheit 451 Science fiction novel by Ray Bradbury
Go Tell It on the Mountain Novel by James Baldwin
The Land of Silence Collected verse by May Sarton
Marty Play by Paddy Chayefsky
The Mirror and the Lamp: Romantic Theory and Critical Tradition Literary criticism by Mayer Howard Abrams
Nine Stories Collection by J. D. Salinger
The Outsider Autobiographical novel by Richard Wright
Picnic Play by William Inge
Poems, 1940–1953 Collection by Karl Shapiro
Second Foundation Science fiction novel by Isaac Asimov
The Solid Gold Cadillac Play by George S. Kaufman and Howard Teichman
The Southpaw Novel by Mark Harris
Tea and Sympathy Play by Robert Anderson
Teahouse of the August Moon Play by John Patrick
The Waking: Poems, 1933–1953 Collection by Theodore Roethke

British

Casino Royale James Bond mystery by Ian Fleming
Childhood's End Science fiction novel by English-born Sri Lankan writer Arthur Clarke
Except the Lord Novel by Irish-born Joyce Cary
The Go-Between Novel by L. P. Hartley
Hurry on Down Novel by John Wain
An Italian Visit Collected verse by Cecil Day-Lewis
Poems Collected verse by Elizabeth Jennings
The Second Curtain Novel by Roy Fuller
The Three Voices of Poetry Literary criticism by T. S. Eliot
Witness for the Prosecution Mystery story by Agatha Christie

Dominican

The Orchid House Novel by Phyllis Shand Allfrey

Irish

Watt Novel by Samuel Beckett

Nigerian

The Palm-Wine Drinkard Novel by Amos Tutuola

South African

The Dam Play by Guy Butler
The Dream and the Desert Collected short stories by Uys Krige
The Lying Days Novel by Nadine Gordimer

FINNISH

On Windy Nights Collected verse of Paavo Haavikko

FRENCH

French

The Erasers Novel by Alain Robbe-Grillet
The Lark Play by Jean Anouilh

The Lesson One-act play by Romanian-born writer Eugène Ionesco
Martereau Novel by Nathalie Sarraute
The Unnamable Novel by Irish-born writer Samuel Beckett
Waiting for Godot Play by Irish-born writer Samuel Beckett

Tunisian

The Pillar of Salt Novel by Albert Memmi

GERMAN

Acquainted with the Night Novel by Heinrich Böll
The Black Swan Novel by Thomas Mann
The Spell Novel by Herman Broch

HINDI

Seed Novel by Indian writer Amrit Ray

ITALIAN

The Faithful Lover Novel by Massimo Bontempelli

SERBIAN

"Bark" Poem by Vasko Popa

SPANISH

Cuban

The Lost Steps Social commentary by Alejo Carpentier

Spanish

The Cypresses Believe in God Novel by José María Gironella
Requiem for a Spanish Peasant Novel by Ramón Sender

SWEDISH

Cinnamoncandy Novel by Lars Ahlin

1954

BIRTHS

Carlo Ernest Geble, Irish novelist

DEATHS

Aleksandre Abasheli, Georgian poet
Said Faik Abasiyanik, Turkish novelist and poet
Oswald de Andrade, Brazilian poet, playwright, and novelist
Sadruddin Ayni, Tajik poet, novelist, and essayist
Jacinto Benavente y Martínez, Spanish playwright
Edmund Kerchever Chambers, English Shakespearean scholar
Colette (Sidonie-Gabrielle Colette), French novelist
Stig Halvard Dagerman, Swedish novelist, playwright, poet, and essayist
Nicolae Davidescu, Romanian novelist and poet
Ferenc Herczeg, Hungarian novelist and playwright
Vincas Kreve-Mickevicus, Lithuanian poet, novelist, and playwright
Martin Anderson Nexo, Danish novelist
Ngo Tat To, Vietnamese novelist

LITERARY EVENT

PRIZES AND AWARDS

Nobel Prize in literature: Ernest Hemingway, American novelist

Pulitzer Prizes

Autobiography *The Spirit of St. Louis* by Charles A. Lindbergh
Drama *The Teahouse of the August Moon* by John Patrick
History *A Stillness at Appomattox* by Bruce Catton
Poetry *The Waking* by Theodor Roethke

PUBLICATIONS

ARABIC

Egyptian

The Cheapest Night Collection of short stories by Yusuf Idris
The Earth Play by Abdur Rahman ash-Sharqawi

Iraqi

Broken Pitchers Collected verse by Adbul Wahhab al-Bayati

DANISH

The Last Lantern Collected verse by Tom Kristensen

ENGLISH

American

The Bachelor Party Play by Paddy Chayefsky
Collected Poems Collection by Wallace Stevens
The Dancing Bears Collection of poems by W. S. Merwin
The Enormous Radio and Other Stories Collection by John Cheever
A Fable Novel by William Faulkner
Hungerfield and Other Poems Collection by Robinson Jeffers
The Matchmaker Play by Thornton Wilder
Messiah Novel by Gore Vidal
The Ponder Heart Novel by Eudora Welty
The Second Tree from the Corner Miscellaneous essays by E. B. White
The Tunnel of Love Novel by Peter De Vries

British

Collected Poems Collection by C. S. Lewis
The Confidential Clerk Dramatic farce in verse by T. S. Eliot
The Dark Is Light Enough Verse play by Christopher Fry
The Death of Satan Play by Ronald Duncan
The Fellowship of the Ring Novel (first in the trilogy *The Lord of the Rings*) by J. R. R. Tolkien
Fighting Terms Verse collection by Thom Gunn
The Holy Stone Collected verse of Thomas Blackburn
Lord of the Flies Novel by William Golding
Lucky Jim Novel by Kingsley Amis
The New Men Novel by C. P. Snow
A Proper Marriage Novel (part of *The Children of Violence*) by Doris Lessing
Separate Tables Two one-act plays by Terence Rattigan

Canadian

The Acrobat Novel by Mordecai Richler
In the Midst of My Fever Collected verse by Irving Layton

Indian

Nectar in a Sieve Novel by Kamala Markandaya

Irish

The Quare Fellow Play by Brendan Behan
Under the Net First novel by Iris Murdoch

Nigerian

People of the City Novel by Cyprian Ekwensi

Welsh

A Child's Christmas in Wales Semiautobiographical story by
    Dylan Thomas
Under Milk Wood Verse drama by Dylan Thomas

FRENCH

French

All in a Night Novel by Jean-Raphael-Marie-Noël Cayrol
Bonjour Tristesse Novel by François Sagan
The Crowning of Spring Novel by Claude Simon
The Executioner Novel by Pierre Boulle
The Mandarins Novel by Simone de Beauvoir
Port Royal Play by Henry de Montherlant

Guinean

The Radiance of the King Novel by Camara Laye

Moroccan

The Simple Past Novel by Driss Chraibi

GERMAN

German

The Confessions of Felix Krull Picaresque novel by Thomas Mann

Swiss

I'm Not Stiller Novel by Max Frisch

GREEK

The Greek Passion Novel by Nikos Kazantzakis

ITALIAN

Ruin Novel by Beppe Fenoglio

JAPANESE

Forbidden Colors Novel by Yukio Mishima
The Sound of Waves Novel by Yukio Mishima

MALAYALAM

Ummachi Novel by P. C. Kuttikrishnan

PORTUGUESE

The Sibyl Novel by Maria Agustine Besse Luis

SERBIAN

Roots Novel by Dobrica Cosic

SPANISH

Argentine

The Dream of Heroes Novel by Adolfo Bioy Casares

Chilean

Poems and Antipoems Collected verse of Nicanor Parra
The Wine Press Poetry collection by Gabriela Mistral

Guatemalan

The Green Pope Novel by Miguel Angel Asturias

Mexican

Frontiers Collected verse of Jaime Torres Bodet

Spanish

The Brightness and the Blood Novel by Ignacio Aldecoa
History of the Heart Collected poems by Vicente Aleixandre
The Young Assassin Novel by Juan Goytisolo

SWEDISH

The Dogs Collection of poems by Werner Aspenstrom

TAJIK

Fire of Rose Collection of verse by Jigar Muradabadi
Loyalty Novel by Foteh Niyazi
The Morning of Our Lives Semiautobiographical novel by Sotim
    Ulughzoda

1955

BIRTHS
Thomas Bohme, German poet
Julio Llamazares, Spanish novelist, essayist, and poet
Julio Cesar Monteiro Martins, Brazilian novelist
Irina Ratushinskaya, Russian poet

DEATHS
Ahmad Zaki Abu Shadi, Egyptian poet and opera librettist
James Agee, American novelist
Paul Claudel, French playwright and poet
Bernard De Voto, American literary critic and novelist
Albert Einstein, German-American scientist
Roger Mais, Jamaican novelist, poet, and playwright
Asrar-ul-haq Majaz, Urdu lyrical poet
Thomas Mann, German novelist
Sadat Hasan Manto, Urdu novelist and playwright
José Ortega y Gasset, Spanish philosopher
Theodore Plievier, German novelist
Robert Emmet Sherwood, American playwright
Wallace Stevens, American poet

LITERARY EVENT
PRIZES AND AWARDS
Nobel Prize in literature: Halldor Laxness (Halldor Kiljan
    Gudyonsson), Icelandic novelist

Pulitzer Prizes

Biography   *The Taft Story* by William S. White
Drama   *Cat on a Hot Tin Roof* by Tennessee Williams
Fiction   *A Fable* by William Faulkner

History *Great River: The Rio Grande in North American History* by Paul Horgan
Poetry *Collected Poems* by Wallace Stevens

PUBLICATIONS

AMHARIC

I Went Abroad Novel by Ethiopian writer Giyorgis Walda Yohannes Walda

DUTCH

The Man in the Mirror Novel by Herman Teirlinck
The Ten Thousand Things Novel by Maria Dermont

ENGLISH

American

Andersonville Historical novel by MacKinley Kantor
A Band of Angels Novel by Robert Penn Warren
The Black Prince, and Other Stories Collection by Shirley Ann Grau
The Bride of the Innisfallen Collected stories of Eudora Welty
Bus Stop Play by William Inge
The Catered Affair Play by Paddy Chayefsky
Cat on a Hot Tin Roof Play by Tennessee Williams
A Charmed Life Novel by Mary McCarthy
The Deer Park Novel by Norman Mailer
The Diamond Cutters and Other Poems Collected verse of Adrienne Rich
The Ginger Man Novel by Irish-American writer J. P. Donleavy
A Good Man Is Hard to Find Collection of short stories by Flannery O'Connor
Lolita Novel by Vladimir Nabokov
Marjorie Morningstar Novel by Herman Wouk
The Matchmaker Novel by Thornton Wilder
No One Knows the Day Novel by Norwegian-born Alfred Hauge
Notes of a Native Son Essays by James Baldwin
The Opposing Self Nine essays by Lionel Trilling
Poems: North and South—A Cold Spring Collection by Elizabeth Bishop
The Recognition Novel by William Gaddis
Sincerely, Willis Wayde Novel by J. P. Marquand
The Spider's House Novel by Paul Bowles
Ten North Frederick Novel by John O'Hara
A View from the Bridge Play by Arthur Miller

Australian

The Tree of Man Novel by Patrick White

British

Amrita Novel by German-born English writer Ruth Prawer Jhabvala
The Chalk Garden Play by Enid Bagnold
Collected Poems, 1928–1953 Collection by Stephen Spender
Earthlight Science fiction novel by English-born Sri Lankan writer Arthur Clarke
The Inheritor Novel by William Golding
The Less Deceived Poetry collection by Philip Larkin
Officers and Gentlemen Novel by Evelyn Waugh
The Quiet American Novel by Graham Greene

The Shield of Achilles Collection of verse by W. H. Auden
Surprised by Joy: The Shape of My Early Life Autobiography by C. S. Lewis
That Uncertain Feeling Novel by Kingsley Amis
The Two Towers Novel (second in *The Lord of the Rings* trilogy) by J. R. R. Tolkien
A Way of Looking Collected verse by Elizabeth Jennings

Canadian

The Cold Green Element Poetry collection by Irving Layton
Son of a Smaller Hero Autobiographical novel by Mordecai Richler

Indian

Waiting for the Mahatma Novel by R. K. Narayan

Irish

The Lonely Passion of Judith Hearne Novel by Brian Moore
Not Honour More Novel by Joyce Cary

FINNISH

Birthplace Collected verse by Paavo Haavikko
The Etruscan Novel by Mika Waltari

FRENCH

Algerian

The Sleep of the Just Novel by Mouloud Mammeri

Armenian

Le Ping-Pong Play by Arthur Adamov

French

The Balcony Satiric play by Jean Genet
Nekrassov Play by Jean-Paul Sartre
The New Tenant Play by Romanian-born Eugène Ionesco
The Transgressor Novel by American-born Julien Green
The Voyeur Novel by Alain Robbe-Grillet
A World on the Wane Prose tract by Belgian-born anthropologist Claude Lévi-Strauss

Tunisian

Agar Novel by Albert Memmi
Strangers Novel by writer Albert Memmi

GREEK

The Last Temptation of Christ Novel by Nikos Kazantzakis

HAUSA

Shaihu Umar Novel by Nigerian statesman Abubakar Tafawa Balewa

ICELANDIC

Book of Seven Days Collected verse of Johannes Jonasson

ITALIAN

Bread and Wine Novel by Ignazio Silone

JAPANESE

White Man, Yellow Man Novel by Shusaku Endo

POLISH
The Issa Valley Novel by Czesław Milosz
The Morning Star Collection of stories by Maria Dabrowska

PORTUGUESE
Brazilian

The Moratorium Play by Jorge Andrade
Two Waters Collected verse of João Cabral de Melo Neto

SPANISH
Children of Chaos Novel by Juan Goytisolo

1956

BIRTH
Amitav Ghosh, Indian novelist

DEATHS
Corrado Alvaro, Italian novelist
Michael Arlen, Bulgarian-born English writer
Leo Baeck, German Jewish scholar
Pío Baroja, Basque novelist
Max Beerbohm, English writer
Gottfried Benn, German poet
E. C. Bentley, English man of letters
Bertolt Brecht, German playwright and poet
Louis Bromfield, American novelist
Hans Carossa, German poet and novelist
Ali Akbar Dekhoda, Iranian poet
Walter De la Mare, English poet and novelist
Derenik Demirtchian, Armenian novelist, poet, and playwright
Herbert Isaac Ernest Dhlomo, Zulu novelist, poet, and playwright
Aleksander Fadeyev, Russian novelist
Resat Nuri Guntekin, Turkish novelist and playwright
Ha Jin, Chinese-born American poet and novelist
Muhammad Husayn Haykal, Egyptian novelist and journalist
Jan Lechon, Polish poet
Charles MacArthur, American playwright
Bal Sitaram Mardhekar, Marathi poet
H. L. Mencken, American essayist, editor, and journalist
John Middleton Murry, English writer and critic
Giovanni Papini, Italian biographer, novelist, and poet
David Shimonowitz, Israeli poet
Cahit Sitki Taranci, Turkish poet
Samad Vurghun, Azerbaijani poet and playwright
Robert Walser, Swiss novelist, essayist, and poet

LITERARY EVENT
PRIZES AND AWARDS
Nobel Prize in literature: Juan Ramón Jiménez, Spanish poet and playwright

Pulitzer Prizes
Biography *Benjamin Henry Latrobe* by Talbot Faulkner Hamlin

Drama *Diary of Anne Frank* by Albert Hackett and Frances Goodrich
Fiction *Andersonville* by MacKinlay Kantor
History *The Age of Reform* by Richard Hofstadter
Poetry *Poems: North and South—A Cold Spring* by Elizabeth Bishop

PUBLICATIONS
AFRIKAANS
With Pleasure, Dear Sirs Novel by Arthur Nuthall Fula

ARABIC
Egyptian

Baina al-Qasraym Novel by Naguib Mahfouz
The Cairo Trilogy Novel by Naguib Mahfouz

Iraqi

Glory to Children and Olives Collection of verse by Abdul Wahhab al-Bayati

BURMESE
The Earth Is Laughing Collection of short stories by Khin Hnin Ju

CZECH
Silesian Songs Collected verse of Petre Bezruc

ENGLISH
American

At Play in the Fields of the Lord Novel by Peter Matthiessen
Band of Angels Novel by Robert Penn Warren
Bang the Drum Slowly Novel by Mark Harris
Compulsion Novel by Meyer Levin
Double Star Science fiction novel by Robert Heinlein
The Fixer Novel by Bernard Malamud
The Floating Opera Novel by John Barth
Giovanni's Room Novel by James Baldwin
Homage to Mistress Bradstreet Poetry collection by John Berryman
Howl, and Other Poems Collection by Beat poet Allen Ginsberg
The Last Hurrah Novel by Edwin O'Connor
The Lion and the Throne Biography of Sir Edward Coke by Catherine Drinker Bowen
Long Day's Journey into Night Autobiographical play by Eugene O'Neill
Seize the Day Novella by Saul Bellow
The Things of This World Verse collection by Richard Wilbur
A Walk on the Wild Side Novel by Nelson Algren

Australian

Summer of the Seventh Doll Play by Ray Lawler

British

The Last of the Wine Historical novel by Mary Renault
The Long View Novel by Elizabeth Jane Howard
The Nature of Passion Novel by German-born Ruth Prawer Jhabvala

The Outsider Philosophical discourse by Colin Wilson
Pincher Martin Novel by William Golding
The Return of the King Novel (final in the trilogy *The Lord of the Rings*) by J. R. R. Tolkien
A Thing of Beauty Novel by A. J. Cronin
The Towers of Trebizond Novel by Rose Macaulay

Guyanese

Black Label Poem by Leon Gontran Damas

Indian

Siddhartha: Man of Peace Historical play by Harindranath Chattopadhyay

Irish

Poems Collected verse by Thomas Kinsella

South African

The Dove Returns Play by Guy Butler

FINNISH

The Journey Collected verse of Eeva Liisa Manner

FRENCH

Cameroonian

Africa, We Do Not Pay Attention to You Novel by Benjamin Matep

French

The Balcony Play by Jean Genet
The Fall Novel by Albert Camus
Passing Time Novel by Michel Butor

GERMAN

Austrian

The Demons Novel by Heimito von Doderer

Swiss

The Visit: A Tragi-Comedy Play by Friedrich Durrenmatt

HINDI

The Drop and the Sea Novel by Indian writer Amritlal Nagar

INDONESIAN

Guerrilla Family Novel by Pramudya Ananda Tur

ITALIAN

Five Stories of Ferrara Novella by Giorgio Bassani
The Leopard Novel by Giuseppe Lampedusa
The Secret of Luca Novel by Ignazio Silone
The Storm and Other Poems Collected verse of Eugenio Montale

JAPANESE

The Key Novel by Tanizaki Junichiro
The Temple of the Golden Pavilion Novel by Mishima Yukio

MALAYALAM

Shrimps Novel by Thakazhi Sivasankara Pillai

PORTUGUESE

Brazilian

The Devil to Pay in the Backlands Epic novel by João Guimares Rosa
A Knife All Blade Collected verse by João Cabral de Melo Neto

POLISH

Hot Ashes Collection of poems by Mieczyslaw Jastrun
The Marshes Novel by Tadeusz Konwicki

SERBIAN

Field of No Rest Collected verse of Vasko Popa

SPANISH

Spanish

Landscape with Figures Collection of poems by Gerardo Diego
With the East Wind Novel by Ignacio Aldecoa

Uruguayan

Office Poems Collection by Mario Benedetti

1957

BIRTH

Emmanuel Carrère, French writer

DEATHS

Iliya Abu Madi, Lebanese poet
M. A. Aldanov (Mark Aleksandrovich Landau), Russian novelist, essayist, and biographer
Sholem Asch, Polish-born Israeli novelist
George Bacovia (Gheorghe Vasiliu), Romanian poet
Arthur Joyce Lunel Cary, Irish-born English novelist, essayist, and poet
Alfred Doblin, German novelist
Edward Dunsany, Irish playwright
Avetikh Isahakian, Armenian poet
Nikos Kazantzakis, Greek poet and novelist
Giuseppe Tomasi di Lampedusa, Italian novelist
Wyndham Lewis, English novelist
Clarence Malcolm Lowry, English novelist
Curzio Malaparte, Italian novelist
Gabriela Mistral (Lucila Godoy Alcáyaga), Chilean poet
Alexey Mikhailovich Remizov, Russian folklorist, novelist, playwright, and essayist
Dorothy L. Sayers, English writer
W. Abraham Silva, Sinhalese novelist
John William Van Druten, English-born American playwright and novelist
Bhai Vir Singh, Punjabi novelist and poet
Laura Ingalls Wilder, American children's writer

LITERARY EVENT

PRIZES AND AWARDS

Nobel Prize in literature: Albert Camus, French novelist and existentialist

Pulitzer Prizes

Biography *Profiles in Courage* by John F. Kennedy
Drama *Long Day's Journey into Night* by Eugene O'Neill
History *Russia Leaves the War: Soviet-American Relations, 1917–1920* by George F. Kennan
Poetry *Things of This World* by Richard Wilbur

PUBLICATIONS

ARABIC

Decline; or, Your Love Has Destroyed Me Autobiographical novel by Tunisian writer Al-Bashir Khurayyif

DUTCH

Too Late for This World Collected verse by Jan van Nijlen

ENGLISH

American

The Assistant Novel by Bernard Malamud
Atlas Shrugged Novel by Ayn Rand
By Love Possessed Novel by James Gould Cozzens
The Cat in the Hat Children's story by Dr. Seuss (Theodor Seuss Geisel)
A Citizen of the Galaxy Science fiction novel by Robert Heinlein
Dandelion Wine Science fiction novel by Ray Bradbury
The Dark at the Top of the Stairs Play by William Inge
A Death in the Family Novel by James Agee
The Door into Summer Science fiction novel by Robert Heinlein
Here and Now Collection of verse by Denise Levertov
Memoirs of a Catholic Childhood Memoir by Mary McCarthy
On the Road Novel by Beat writer Jack Kerouac
Pnin Novel by Vladimir Nabokov
Promises: Poems, 1954–1956 Collected verse by Robert Penn Warren
Some Came Running Novel by James Jones
The Town Novel by William Faulkner
The Wapshot Chronicle Novel by John Cheever
Words for the Wind Collected verse by Theodore Roethke

Australian

On the Beach Novel by English-born writer Nevil Shute
Voss Novel by Patrick White

British

The Dumb Waiter Play by Harold Pinter
The Entertainer Play by John Osborne
From Russia with Love James Bond spy novel by Ian Fleming
The Hawk in the Rain Collection of poems by Ted Hughes
Justine Novel (first of *The Alexandria Quartet*) by Lawrence Durrell
Look Back in Anger Play by John Osborne
On Poetry and Poets Collection of 16 essays by T. S. Eliot
The Ordeal of Gilbert Pinfold Novel by Evelyn Waugh
Room at the Top Novel by John Braine
The Sandcastle Novel by Iris Murdoch
The Sense of Movement Collected verse by Thom Gunn

Canadian

The Apprenticeship of Daddy Kravitz Novel by Mordecai Richler

A Choice of Enemies Novel by Mordecai Richler
Selected Poems Collected verse by Dorothy Livesay

Irish

Visitations Collection of lyrical poems by Louis MacNeice

Scottish

The Comforters Novel by Muriel Spark

FINNISH

The Manila Rope Novel by Veijo Meri

FRENCH

French

A Child of Our Time Autobiographical novel by Spanish-born writer Michel del Castillo
Endgame Play by Irish-born writer Samuel Beckett
Jealousy Novel by Alain Robbe-Grillet
Mythologies Collection of essays by Roland Barth
The Straw Man Novel by Jean Giono
The Wind Novel by Claude Simon

Guinean

I Was a Savage Autobiography by Prince Modupe Paris

GERMAN

Japhthah and His Daughters Novel by Lion Feuchtwanger

ICELANDIC

The Fish Can Sing Novel by Halldor Laxness

ITALIAN

Arturo's Island Novel by Elsa Morante
The Baron in the Trees Fantasy by Italo Calvino
Honor of Truth Collected verse by Mario Luzi
Two Women Novel by Alberto Moravia

JAPANESE

The Sea and Poison Novel by Shusaku Endo

NORWEGIAN

The Birds Novel by Tajei Vesaas

PASHTO

An Armful of Blossoms Collection of short stories by Pakistani novelist Abdul Karim

RUSSIAN

Doctor Zhivago Novel by Boris Pasternak
The Swan's Camp Collection of poems by Marina Tsvetayeva

SPANISH

Chilean

Coronation Novel by José Donoso

Mexican

Without Truce Collection of poems by Jaime Torres Bodet
Sun Stone Collection of poems by Octavio Paz

Spanish
Clamor Collection of poems by Jorge Guillén

SWEDISH
Night in the Market Tent Novel by Lars Ahlin

YIDDISH
Gimpel the Fool Collection of short stories by Isaac Bashevis Singer

1958

BIRTH
Ulf Eriksson, Swedish poet and novelist

DEATHS
Johannes R. Becher, German poet
Yahya Kemal Beyatli, Turkish poet
Petr Bezrůc (Vladimir Vasek), Czech poet
James Branch Cabell, American writer
Lion Feuchtwanger, German novelist
Jacob Fichman, Russian-born Israeli poet and critic
Dorothy Canfield Fisher, American novelist and short-story writer
Fyodor Vasilyevich Gladkov, Russian novelist, playwright, and essayist
Ho Biu Chanh (Ho Van Trung), Vietnamese novelist
Juan Ramón Jiménez, Spanish poet
Joseph Klausner, Lithuanian-born Israeli scholar and essayist
Emilie Rose Macaulay, English novelist and travel writer
Roger Martin du Gard, French novelist and playwright
George Edward Moore, English philosopher and essayist
Samala Musa, Egyptian essayist
Vallathol Narayana Menon, Malayalee poet
George Jean Nathan, American playwright
Alfred Noyes, English poet and biographer
Robert William Service, English-born Canadian poet and novelist
Abd al-Rahman Shukri, Egyptian poet

LITERARY EVENT
PRIZES AND AWARDS
Nobel Prize in literature: Boris Pasternak, Russian poet and novelist

Pulitzer Prizes
Biography *George Washington* by Douglas S. Freeman
Drama *Look Homeward, Angel* by Ketti Frings
Fiction *A Death in the Family* by James Agee
History *Banks and Politics in America* by Bray Hammond
Poetry *Promises: Poems, 1954–1956* by Robert Penn Warren

PUBLICATIONS
ARABIC
I Live Novel by Lebanese Shiite writer Layla Ba'albakki

ENGLISH
American

Breakfast at Tiffany's Novella by Truman Capote
A Coney Island of the Mind Collected verse by Lawrence Ferlinghetti
The Dharma Bums Novel by Jack Kerouac
The End of the Road Novel by John Barth
Exodus Novel by Leon Uris
From the Terrace Novel by John O'Hara
The Hard Blue Sky Novel by Shirley Ann Grau
In Time Like Air Collected verse by May Sarton
J.B. Verse play based on the Book of Job by Archibald MacLeish
The Magic Barrel Collection of short stories by Bernard Malamud
Methuselah's Children Science fiction novel by Robert Heinlein
The Pistol Novel by James Jones
Poems of a Jew Collected verse on the Holocaust by Karl Shapiro
The Subterraneans Novel by Jack Kerouac
Suddenly Last Summer Play by Tennessee Williams
The Sundial Novel by Shirley Jackson
The Ugly American Novel by William J. Lederer and Leon Burdick
Women on Gallows Hill Novel by Norwegian-born Alfred Hauge

British

Balthazar Novel (second of *The Alexandria Quartet*) by Lawrence Durrell
The Birthday Party Play by Harold Pinter
Brave New World Revisited Treatise on freedom by Aldous Huxley
The Catalyst Play by Ronald Duncan
Collected Poems Collected verse by John Betjeman
The Conscience of the Rich Novel by C. P. Snow
The Contenders Novel by John Wain
Epitaph for George Dillon Play by John Osborne and Anthony Creighton
The King Must Die Historical novel set in ancient Greece by Mary Renault
Mountolive Novel (third of *The Alexandria Quartet*) by Lawrence Durrell
The Once and Future King Quartet of novels by T. H. White
Our Man in Havana Novel by Graham Greene
A Painter of Our Time Novel by John Berger
A Ripple from the Storm Novel (part of the *Children of Violence*) by Doris Lessing
Saturday Night and Sunday Morning Novel by Alan Sillitoe

Indian

The Guide Novel by R. K. Narayan

Irish

Another September Collection of verse by Thomas Kinsella
Borstal Boy Autobiography by Brendan Behan
The Hostage Play by Brendan Behan
Krapp's Last Tape Play by Samuel Beckett

Nigerian

Things Fall Apart Novel by Chinua Achebe

Scottish

Momento Mori Novel by Muriel Spark

Welsh

Poetry for Supper Collection of verse by Ronald Stuart Thomas

FINNISH

Leaves, Pages Collected verse by Paavo Haavikko

FRENCH

Algerian

Last Impression Novel by Malek Haddad

Canadian

The Silent Rooms Novel by Anne Hébert

French

The Blacks Play by Jean Genet
The Grass Novel by Claude Simon
Memoirs of a Dutiful Daughter Autobiography by Simone de Beauvoir
Moderato Cantabile Novel by Marguerite Duras
Night Semiautobiography by Romanian-born American writer Elie Wiesel

GERMAN

Swiss

The Firebugs Play by Max Frisch

HINDI

The Lying Truth Novel by Yospal

INDONESIAN

Evening Verses from Gunung Gamping Collection of short stories by Javanese Christian poet and novelist Sukistyautami Iesmaniasita

ITALIAN

The Incomparable Earth Collected verse by Salvatore Quasimodo
Sixty Tales Collection of short stories by Dino Buzzati
The Three Slaves of Julius Caesar Historical novel by Riccardo Bacchelli

JAPANESE

Pluck the Bird and Destroy the Offspring Novel by Kenzaburo Oe
Proud Are the Dead Collection of short stories by Kenzaburo Oe

PERSIAN

The Headmaster Novella by Jalal Ali Ahmed
Pele-Mele Collection of short character sketches by Ali Akbar Dehkhoda

PORTUGUESE

Brazilian

Gabriela, Clove and Cinnamon Novel by Jorge Amado
Quarry of the Soul Play by Jorge Andrade

SPANISH

Chilean

Better Than Wine Novel by Manuel Rojas

Mexican

Where the Air Is Clear Novel by Carlos Fuentes

Peruvian

Deep River Autobiographical novel by José Maria Arguedas

Spanish

Death as a World of Life Novel by Francisco Ayala
The Disinherited Novel by Michel de Castillo
A Dreamer for the Nation Historical novel by Antonio Buero Vallejo

SWEDISH

The Rain Bird Novel by Sara Lidman
Secrets on the Way Collection of poems by Tomas Transtromer

TAJIK

I Am Guilty Psychological novel by Jalol Ikromi

1959

DEATHS

Maxwell Anderson, American playwright
Johan Bojer, Norwegian novelist
Raymond Chandler, American writer of suspense novels
Laxmiprasad Devkota, Nepali poet, novelist, and playwright
Laurence Housman, English novelist and essayist
Hans Henny Jahnn, German novelist
Alfred Kubin, Austrian novelist, poet, and essayist
Takahama Kyoshi, Japanese poet
Abolqasem Lahuti, Tajik poet and librettist
Edwin Muir, Scottish poet, novelist, and translator
Luis Palés Matos, Puerto Rican poet and novelist
Benjamin Peret, French poet, essayist, and novelist
Alfonso Reyes, Mexican poet and short-story writer
Zalman Schaiur, Russian novelist and poet
Galaktion Tabidze, Georgian poet
Ruben Esref Unaydin, Turkish essayist and prose poet

LITERARY EVENT

PRIZES AND AWARDS

Nobel Prize in literature: Salvatore Quasimodo, Italian poet

Pulitzer Prizes

Biography   *Woodrow Wilson, American Prophet* by Arthur Walworth
Drama   *J.B.* by Archibald MacLeish
Fiction   *The Travels of Jamie McPheeters* by Robert Lewis Taylor
History   *The Republican Era, 1869–1901* by Leonard D. White
Poetry   *Selected Poems, 1928–1958* by Stanley Kunitz

PUBLICATIONS

ARABIC

Guilt Novella by Egyptian writer Yusuf Idris

ARMENIAN

The Never Silent Bells Long poem by Paruir Sevak

ENGLISH

American

American Dream One-act play by Edward Albee
The Cave Novel by Robert Penn Warren
The Crow and the Heart Collection of verse by Hayden Carruth

The Elements of Style Classic manual on English usage by William Strunk Jr. and E. B. White
Flower, Fist and Bestial Wail Verse collection by Charles Bukowski
Goodbye, Columbus Novella and five short stories by Philip Roth
Hawaii Novel by James A. Michener
The Heart's Needle Collected verse by W. D. Snodgrass
Henderson the Rain King Novel by Saul Bellow
The House of Intellect Philosophical inquiry by French-born critic Jacques Barzun
Ko; or, A Season on Earth Epic poem by Kenneth Koch
Life Studies Collected verse by Robert Lowell
Malcolm Novel by James Purdy
The Mansion Novel by William Faulkner
Mexico City Blues Collection of verse by Beat writer Jack Kerouac
The Naked Lunch Novel by William S. Burroughs
The Poorhouse Fair First novel by John Updike
A Raisin in the Sun Play by Lorraine Hansberry
The Sandbox Play by Edward Albee
A Separate Peace Novel by John Knowles
Sirens of Titan Novel by Kurt Vonnegut Jr.
Skunk Hour Collected verse by Robert Lowell
Starship Troopers Science fiction novel by Robert Heinlein
A Stillness at Appomattox History of the Civil War by Bruce Catton
Sweet Bird of Youth Play by Tennessee Williams
The Tenth Man Play by Paddy Chayefsky
With Eyes at the Back of Our Heads Collection of verse by Denise Levertov
The Zoo Story One-act play by Edward Albee

Australian

The Devil's Advocate Novel by Morris West

Barbadian

Christopher First novel by Geoffrey Drayton

British

The Affair Novel by C. P. Snow
Birthday Party Play by Harold Pinter
The Dumb Waiter One-act play by Harold Pinter
The Edge of Day Autobiography by Laurie Lee
Free Fall Novel by William Golding
Goldfinger Spy novel by Ian Fleming
The Loneliness of the Long Distance Runner Collected short stories by Alan Sillitoe
The Ripple from the Storm Novel by Doris Lessing
The Sea Change Novel by Elizabeth Jane Howard
Two Cultures and the Scientific Revolution Intellectual inquiry by C. P. Snow
The Unspeakable Skipton Novel by Pamela Hansford Johnson

South African

Down Second Avenue Autobiographical novel by Ezekiel Mphahlele

FINNISH

The Secret of the Kingdom Novel by Mika Waltari
Winter Palace Collected verse by Paavo Haaviko

FRENCH

French

Becket, or the Honor of God Play by Jean Anouilh
Cities of the Interior Five-volume novel cycle by Anaïs Nin
Foreign Bodies Novel by Jean-Raphael-Marie-Noël Cayrol
In the Labyrinth Novel by Natalie Sarraute
The Last of the Just Novel by André Schwarz-Bart
Rhinoceros Play by Romanian-born writer Eugène Ionesco
Zazie in the Metro Satiric novel by Raymond Queneau

Ivorien

A Negro in Paris Novel by Bernard Binlin Dadie

GERMAN

Billiards at Half-Past Nine Novel by Heinrich Böll
The Tin Drum Novel by Günter Grass

GREEK

Worthy It Is Collected verse by Odysseus Elytis

HINDI

Forgotten Pictures Novel by Indian writer Bhagvaticharan Varma

ITALIAN

The Nonexistent Knight Fantasy by Italo Calvino

JAPANESE

Tan-Huang Novel by Inoue Yasushi
Volcano Novel by Shusaku Endo

POLISH

Female and Male Collection of stories by Michal Choromanski
Genesis Collection of poems by Mieczysław Jastrun

SPANISH

Cuban

La Paloma de vuelo popular: Elegias Collection of verse by Nicolás Guillén

Mexican

The Good Conscience Novel by Carlos Fuentes

Uruguayan

Montevideanos Collection of short stories by Mario Benedetti

THAI

Tomorrow Will Be Another Sunrise Novel by Srirat Sathapanawat

URDU

River of Fire Novel by Qurratu'l'ain Haidar

YIDDISH

The Magician of Lublin Novel by Polish-born American Jewish novelist Isaac Bashevis Singer

1960

DEATHS

Albert Camus, French novelist, essayist, and playwright
Vicki Baum, Austrian novelist
Massimo Bontempelli, Italian poet and novelist
Josef Ciger-Hronsky, Czech novelist
Jacob Cohen, Russian-born Israeli poet
Willem Elsschot, Flemish novelist and poet
Drmit Gulia, Abkhazian poet, playwright, and novelist
Zora Neale Hurston, African-American writer
John Philips Marquand, American novelist
Jigar Muradabadi, Urdu lyrical poet
Sir Lewis Bernstein Namier, Polish-born English historian
Boris Pasternak, Russian novelist
Eden Philpotts, English novelist
Pierre Reverdy, French poet and novelist
Richard Wright, African-American novelist
Nima Yushij, Iranian poet

LITERARY EVENT
PRIZES AND AWARDS
Nobel Prize in literature: Saint-John Perse (Marie-René-Auguste-Alexis Saint-Léger Léger), French poet

Pulitzer Prizes

Biography *John Paul Jones* by Samuel Eliot Morison
Drama *Fiorello!* by Jerome Weidman, George Abbott, Jerry Bock, and Sheldon Harnick
Fiction *Advise and Consent* by Allen Drury
History *In the Days of McKinley* by Margaret Leech
Poetry *Heart's Needle* by W. D. Snodgrass

PUBLICATIONS
ARABIC
The Monster Gods Novel by Lebanese Shiite novelist Layla Ba'albakki

CZECH
Between Three Borders Sketches of Slovakia by Ivan Klima

ENGLISH
American

The Bean Eaters Collected verse by Gwendolyn Brooks
The Colossus Poetry collection by Sylvia Plath
A Distant Trumpet Novel by Paul Horgan
Generation Without Farewell Novel by Kay Boyle
The House of Five Talents Novel by Louis Auchincloss
Lives of the Poets Biographical sketches by Louis Untermeyer
Love and Death in the American Novel Literary criticism by Leslie Fiedler
The Nephew Novel by James Purdy
Rabbit, Run Novel by John Updike
The Rise and Fall of the Third Reich History by William L. Shirer
The Rosy Crucifixion: Nexus Third volume of autobiography by Henry Miller
The Sot-Weed Factor Novel by John Barth

To Kill a Mockingbird Novel by Harper Lee
Tristessa Novel by Beat writer Jack Kerouac
The Violent Bear It Away Novel by Flannery O'Connor
Welcome to Hard Times Novel by E. L. Doctorow
West of Your City Collected verse by William Stafford
What a Kingdom It Was Collected verse of Galway Kinnell
The Woman at the Washington Zoo: Poems and Translations Collected verse by Randall Jarrell

British

The Balkan Trilogy Novel by Olivia Manning
Call for the Dead Thriller by John Le Carré
The Caretaker Play by Harold Pinter
Casanova's Chinese Restaurant Novel by Anthony Powell
Clea Concluding volume of *The Alexandria Quartet* by Lawrence Durrell
The Doctor Is Sick Novel by Anthony Burgess
Five-Finger Exercise Play by Peter Shaffer
Homage to Clio Collection of poems by W. H. Auden
A Kind of Loving Novel by Stan Barstow
Summoned by Bells Autobiography by John Betjeman
This Sporting Life Novel by David Story

Canadian

Rivers Among Rocks Collected verse by Ralph Gustafson

Indian

The Serpent and the Rope Novel by Raja Rao
A Silence of Desire Novel by Kamala Markandaya
The Whole Sky Novel by Rajendra Yadav

Irish

The Country Girls Trilogy Novel by Edna O'Brien
The Luck of Ginger Coffey Novel by Brian Moore

Nigerian

No Longer at Ease Novel by Chinua Achebe
The Trials of Brother Jero Play by Wole Soyinka

South African

Road to Ghana Autobiography by Alfred Hutchinson

Virgin Island

The King's Mandate Play in blank verse by Jose Antonio Jarvis

FINNISH
Incidents 1918 Novel by Veijo Meri
Orphic Hymns Collected verse by Eeva Liisa Manner

FRENCH
Belgian

The Favorite Historical novel by Françoise Mallet-Joris

Beninese

The Endless Trip Novel by Olympe Bhely Quenum
Snares Without End Novel by Olympe Bhely Quenum

French

Chronique Collected verse by Saint-John Perse
Degrees Novel by Michel Butor

The Flanders Road Novel by Claude Simon
In the Name of the Son Novel by Hervé Bazin
Nothing Important Ever Dies Novel by Romain Gary

Senegalese

God's Bits of Wood Novel by Ousmane Sembene

GERMAN
Party in Autumn Play by Tankred Dorst

ICELANDIC
Paradise Regained Novel by Halldor Laxness

ITALIAN
The Empty Canvas Novel by Alberto Moravia
An Old Man's Notebook Poem by Giuseppe Ungaretti

PORTUGUESE
Love Poems Collection of poems by Mario Antonio

SPANISH
Argentine

The Doer Prose poem by Jorge Luis Borges

Chilean

Shining Tip Novel by Manuel Rojas

Guatemalan

The Eyes of the Interred Novel by Miguel Angel Asturias

Nicaraguan

Zero Hour and Other Documentary Poems Collection by Ernesto Cardenal

Paraguayan

Son of Man Novel by Angusto Roa Bastos

Spanish

The Ladies-in-Waiting Historical play by Antonio Buero Vallejo
Without Reason Novel by Rosa Chacel

Uruguayan

The Truce Novel by Mario Benedetti

SWAHILI
The Home of the Spirits of the Ancestors Novel by Tanzanian writer Muhammad Said Abdulla

SWEDISH
The Days of His Grace Novel by Eyvind Johnson
The Death of Socrates Historical novel by Lars Gyllensten
A Molna Elegy Meditations by Gunnar Ekelof

1961

DEATHS
Kjeld Abell, Danish playwright
Mukhtar Auezov, Kazakh novelist and playwright

Roussan Camille, Haitian poet
Blaise Cendrars (Frédéric Louis Sauser), Swiss-born French writer
Louis-Ferdinand Céline (Louis-Ferdinand Destouches), French novelist, essayist, and playwright
Elmer Diktonius, Finnish novelist and poet
Leonhard Frank, German novelist and playwright
Dashiell Hammett, American novelist
Moss Hart, American playwright
Ernest Miller Hemingway, American novelist
Carl Gustav Jung, Swiss psychiatrist
Abdul Karim, Pushto novelist
Dan Karm, Maltese poet
George S. Kaufman, American playwright
Nirala, Hindi poet and novelist
Orixie (Nicolas Ormaetxea), Basque novelist and poet
Oscar Bento Ribas, Angolan novelist, playwright, and poet
Abdoulaye Sadji, Senegalese novelist
Dorothy Thompson, American writer and humorist
James Thurber, American humorist and writer

LITERARY EVENT
PRIZES AND AWARDS
Nobel Prize in literature: Ivo Andric, Yugoslav poet, essayist, and novelist

Pulitzer Prizes

Biography *Charles Sumner and the Coming of the Civil War* by David Donald
Drama *All the Way Home* by Tad Mosel
Fiction *To Kill a Mockingbird* by Harper Lee
History *Between War and Peace: The Potsdam Conference* by Herbert Feis
Poetry *Times Three: Selected Verse from Three Decades* by Phyllis McGinley

PUBLICATIONS
ARABIC
Egyptian

The Thief and the Dogs Novel by Naguib Mahfouz

Lebanese

The Flute and the Wind Collection of verse by Khalil Hawi

Sudanese

Time of Migration Northwards Novel by Al-Tayyib Salih

Tunisian

Barq al-Layl Novel by Al-Bashir Khurayyif

ENGLISH
American

The American Dream Play by Edward Albee
Catch-22 Novel by Joseph Heller
Clock Without Hands Novel by Carson McCullers
Eight Men Collected short stories by Richard Wright
Franny and Zooey Short stories by J. D. Salinger
Gideon Play by Paddy Chayefsky
Hombre Novel by Elmore Leonard

Horseman, Pass By Novel by Larry McMurtry
The House on Coliseum Street Novel by Shirley Ann Grau
Imitations Poetry collection by Robert Lowell
Kaddish and Other Poems Collected verse by Beat poet Allen Ginsberg
Lime Twig Novel by John Hawke
Midcentury Novel by John Dos Passos
Mila 18 Novel by Leon Uris
The Misfits Play by Arthur Miller
Mother Night Novel by Kurt Vonnegut Jr.
The Moviegoer Novel by Walker Percy
The Night of the Iguana Play by Tennessee Williams
Nobody Knows My Name Collection of essays by James Baldwin
Seduction of the Minotaur Novel by Anaïs Nin
A Shooting Star Novel by Wallace Stegner
Stranger in a Strange Land Science fiction novel by Robert A. Heinlein
The Winter of Our Discontent Novel by John Steinbeck

Australian

Riders in the Chariot Novel by Patrick White

British

A Burnt Out Case Novel by Graham Greene
A Fall of Moondust Science fiction novel by Arthur C. Clarke
A Foxglove Saga Novel by Auberon Waugh
Luther Play by John Osborne
Marnie Crime novel by Winston Graham
A Severed Head Novel by Iris Murdoch
Song for a Birth or a Death Collected verse by Elizabeth Jennings
Thunderball Spy novel by Ian Fleming
Unconditional Surrender Novel (part of *Sword of Honor*) by Evelyn Waugh

Canadian

A Passion in Rome Novel by Morley Callaghan
The Singing Flesh Collected verse by Irving Layton

Indian

The Man Eaters of Malgudi Novel by R. K. Narayan

Irish

Happy Days Play by Samuel Beckett
Solstices Collection of lyrical verse by Louis MacNeice

Nigerian

Jagua Nana Novel by Cyprian Odiatu Duaka Ekwensi
Song of a Goat Play by John Pepper Clark

Scottish

The Prime of Miss Jean Brodie Novel by Muriel Spark

Trinidadian

A House for Mr. Biswas Novel by Indian-born V. S. Naipaul

FRENCH

Madness and Civilization Philosophical inquiry by Michel Foucault
The Screens Play by Jean Genet
Vesuvius Novel by Emmanuel Robles

GEORGIAN

Wandering Through Three Times Play by Grigol Abashidze

GERMAN

German

Cat and Mouse Novel by Günter Grass

Swiss

Andorra Play by Max Frisch
Count Oederland Play by Max Frisch

GREEK

The Game of Madness and Prudence Play by Yogos Theotokos

ITALIAN

In the Magna Poem by Mario Luzi

JAPANESE

Diary of a Mad Old Man Novel by Tanizaki Junichiro
Okinawa Play by Kinoshita Junji

PERSIAN

The Husband of Ahu Khanom Novel by Ali Mohammad

POLISH

Return from the Stars Novel by Stanisław Lem

PORTUGUESE

Brazilian

The Apple in the Dark Novel by Clarice Lispector

RUSSIAN

Babi Yar Collection of poems by Yevgeny Yevtushenko

SERBIAN

Divisions Novel by Dobrica Cosic

SPANISH

Argentine

On Heroes and Tombs Novel by Ernesto Sábato

Peruvian

Oh Cybernetic Fairy Collection of poems by Carlos Germán Belli
The Sixth One Novel by José María Arguedas

Spanish

One Million Dead Novel by José María Gironelda

Uruguayan

The Shipyard Novel by Juan Carlos Onetti

TAJIK

The Lazy Steppe Long poem by Mirsaid Mirshakar

YIDDISH

The Agunah Novel by Lithuanian writer Chaim Grade
Spinoza of Market Street Short stories by Polish-born American writer Isaac Bashevis Singer

1962

BIRTH
Pia Juul, Danish poet

DEATHS
Gerrit Achterberg, Dutch poet
Richard Aldington, American poet
Jean Amrouche, Algerian poet
Georges Bataille, French novelist
Władysław Broniewski, Polish poet
e. e. cummings, American poet
Isak Dinesen (Baroness Karen Blixen), Danish novelist and adventurer
William Faulkner, American novelist
Mouloud Feraoun, Kabyle novelist
Michel de Ghelderode, Belgian playwright
Abdullah Goran, Kurdish poet
Herman Hesse, German novelist
Hu Shi, Chinese scholar
Robinson Jeffers, American poet
John Ebenezer Clare MacFarlane, Jamaican poet and essayist
Masamune Hakucho, Japanese novelist and critic
Ramon Pérez de Ayala, Spanish novelist, essayist, and poet
Qi Rushan, Chinese playwright
Shaaban Robert, Swahili poet, novelist, and essayist
Vita Sackville-West, English poet and novelist
George Macaulay Trevelyan, English historian
Hugo Wast, Argentine novelist and short-story writer
Muhammad Yamin, Indonesian poet, novelist, and historian
Yoshikawa, Eiji (Yoshikawa Hidetsugu), Japanese novelist

LITERARY EVENT
PRIZES AND AWARDS
Nobel Prize in literature: John Steinbeck, American novelist

Pulitzer Prizes

Drama *How to Succeed in Business Without Really Trying* by Frank Loesser and Abe Burrows
Fiction *The Edge of Sadness* by Edwin O'Connor
History *The Triumphant Empire, Thunder Clouds in the West* Lawrence H. Gibson
Nonfiction *The Making of the President, 1960* by Theodore H. White
Poetry *Poems* by Alan Dugan

PUBLICATIONS
ARABIC
Egyptian
Sin Novella by Yusuf Idris

Tunisian
The Mountain of Broom Novel by Mourad Bourbane

ENGLISH
American
All My Pretty Ones Poetry collection by Anne Sexton
Drowning with Others Collection of poems by James Dickey

For Love: Poems, 1959–1960 Collection by Robert Creeley
The Guns of August History of World War I by Barbara Tuchman
In Another Country Novel by James Baldwin
In the Clearing Collected verse of Robert Frost
Long Live Man Verse collection by Gregory Corso
Mountain Standard Time Trilogy of novels by Paul Horgan
One Flew Over the Cuckoo's Nest Novel by Ken Kesey
Pale Fire Novel by Vladimir Nabokov
Patriotic Gore Literary criticism by Edmund Wilson
Pictures from Brueghel Poetry collection by William Carlos Williams
Pigeon Feathers Short-story collection by John Updike
Plays for Bleecker Street Collected plays by Thornton Wilder
Portrait in Brownstone Novel by Louis Auchincloss
The Reivers: A Reminiscence Novel by William Faulkner
Ship of Fools Novel by Katherine Anne Porter
Something Wicked This Way Comes Science fiction novel by Ray Bradbury
Stern Novel by Bruce Jay Friedman
The Thin Red Line Novel by James Jones
Travels with Charley in Search of America Travel narrative by John Steinbeck
Who's Afraid of Virginia Woolf? Play by Edward Albee
A Wrinkle in Time Children's novel by Madeleine L'Engle

British

The Bull from the Sea Historical novel by Mary Renault
A Clockwork Orange Futuristic novel by Anthony Burgess
The Golden Notebook Novel by Doris Lessing
Hothouse Science fiction novel by Brian Aldiss
The Ipcress File Spy novel by Len Deighton
The Kindly Ones Novel (part of *Dance to the Music of Time*) by Anthony Powell
Life at the Top Novel by John Braine
The Pumpkin Eater Novel by Penelope Martin
Strike the Father Dead Novel by John Wain
Under the Volcano Novel by Malcolm Lowry

Canadian

My Happy Days in Hell Autobiography by Hungarian-born poet George Faludy

Irish

Downstream Collected verse by Thomas Kinsella

South African

The Sniper Play by Uys Krige

FRENCH
French

The Afternoon of Monsieur Andesmas Novel by Marguerite Duras
Birds Poems by St.-John Perse
Exit the King Play by Romanian-born Eugène Ionesco
The Palace Novel by Claude Simon
The Savage Mind Anthropological perspectives by Claude Lévi-Strauss
Snapshots Novel by Alain Robbe-Grillet
Totemism Anthropological treatise by Claude Lévi-Strauss
Watered Silk Collected verse by Pierre-Jean Jouvet

Ivorien

Wild Blew the Wind First novel by Charles Nokan

Moroccan

An Unclaimed Inheritance Novel by Driss Chraibi

GERMAN

German

The Night of the Generals Novel by Hans Hellmut Kirst
The Third Book About Achim Novel by Uwe Johnson
Your Silence, My Voice Collected verse of Marie Luise Kaschnitz

Swiss

The Physicists Play by Friedrich Durrenmatt

HUNGARIAN

Escape from Solitude Collected verse by Sandor Csoori

ITALIAN

The Garden of the Finzi-Continis Novel by Giorgio Massano
Harmony and Pastels Collection of poems by Eugenio Montale
It's a Hard Life Novel by Luciano Biancardi
Satura Collection of poems by Eugenio Montale

JAPANESE

The Woman in the Dunes Novel by Abe Kobe

POLISH

The Barbarian in the Garden Collection of essays by Zbigniew Herbert

RUSSIAN

One Day in the Life of Ivan Denisovich Novel by Aleksandr Solzhenitsyn

SPANISH

Argentine

Bomarzo Novel by Manuel Mujica Lainez

Chilean

Verses of the Salon Collected verse of Nicanor Parra

Cuban

Explosion in a Cathedral Novel by Alejo Carpentier

Spanish

The Bottom of the Glass Novel by Francisco Ayala
The Concert at Saint Ovide Play by Antonio Buero Vallejo
In a Vast Domain Poems by Vicente Aleixandre

TAJIK

Daughter of Fire Three-part novel by Jalol Ikromi

URDU

A Solid Sheet Novel by Rajinder Singh Bedi

YIDDISH

The Slave Novella by Polish-born American writer Isaac Bashevis Singer

1963

DEATHS

Eduardo Barrios, Chilean writer
Van Wyck Brooks, American intellectual historian
Luis Cernuda, Spanish poet
Jean-Maurice-Eugène-Clement Cocteau, French novelist
W. E. B. DuBois, African-American writer and civil rights leader
D. O. Fagunwa, Nigerian novelist
Robert Frost, American poet
Ramón Gómez de la Cerna, Spanish novelist, playwright, and biographer
Nazim Hikmet Ran, Turkish poet, playwright, and novelist
Aldous Huxley, English novelist
Jose Antonio Jarvis, Virgin Islands poet, playwright, and historian
Oliver La Farge, American novelist and anthropologist
C. S. Lewis, English writer and scholar
Louis MacNeice, Irish poet and classicist
Kovalam Madhava Panikkar, Indian historian, poet, and playwright
Endalkacaw Makonnen, Ethiopian Amharic novelist and playwright
Malai Chuphinit, Thai novelist
Nhat Linh (Nguyen Tuong Tam), Vietnamese novelist
Clifford Odets, American playwright
Sylvia Plath, American poet
John Cowper Powys, English poet, novelist, and essayist
Theodore Roethke, American poet
Lope K. Santos, Filipino poet and novelist
Ahmad Lufti as-Sayyid, Egyptian philosopher and essayist
Francisco José de Vasquez Tenreiro, São Tomean poet and novelist
Tristan Tzara (Samuel Rosenfeld), Romanian-born French poet, playwright, and essayist
William Carlos Williams, American poet

LITERARY EVENT

PRIZES AND AWARDS

Nobel Prize in literature: George Seferis, Greek poet

Pulitzer Prizes

Biography *Henry James* by Leon Edel
Fiction *The Reivers* by William Faulkner
History *Washington, Village and Capital, 1800–1878* by Constance McLaughlin Green
Nonfiction *The Guns of August* by Barbara W. Tuchman
Poetry *Pictures from Breughel* by William Carlos Williams

PUBLICATIONS

ALBANIAN

The General of the Dead Army Novel by Ismail Kadare

DUTCH

A Thread in the Dark Play by Hella Haasse

ENGLISH

American

Barefoot in the Park Play by Neil Simon
The Bell Jar Collection of poems by Sylvia Plath
Cat's Cradle Novel by Kurt Vonnegut Jr.
The Centaur Novel by John Updike
The Fire Next Time Epistolary essays on the condition of African Americans by James Baldwin
The Group Novel by Mary McCarthy
Idiots First Collection of short stories by Bernard Malamud
Leaving Cheyenne Novel by Larry McMurtry
The Moving Target Collection of verse by W. S. Merwin
Raise High the Roof Beam, Carpenters/Seymour: An Introduction Collection of two novellas by J. D. Salinger
Silent Spring Environmental classic by Rachel Carson
A Singular Man Novel by Irish-American writer J. P. Donleavy
Snapshots of a Daughter in Law: Poems, 1954–1962 Poetry collection by Adrienne Rich
V Novel by Thomas Pynchon
Visions of Gerard Novel by Beat writer Jack Kerouac

Australian

Careful, He Might Hear You Novel by Sumner Locke Elliott

British

The Collector Novel by John Fowles
The Girls of Slender Means Novel by Muriel Spark
Inside Mr. Enderby Novel by Anthony Burgess
The Spy Who Came in from the Cold Novel by John le Carré
Tom Jones Play by John Osborne

Canadian

The Incomparable Atuk Novel by Mordecai Richler

Nigerian

The Lion and the Jewel Play by Wole Soyinka
The Strong Bread Play by Wole Soyinka
The Swamp Dwellers Play by Wole Soyinka

South African

Blame Me on History Autobiographical novel by Walter Modisane

Trinidadian

The Games Were Coming Novel by Michael Anthony

FINNISH
Woman in the Mirror Novel by Veijo Meri

FLEMISH
To Become an Island Novel by Paul de Wispelacre

FRENCH

Belgian

A Letter to Myself Autobiography by François Mallet-Joris

Cameroonian

This Particular Africa Novel by Jean Ikelle-Matiba

French

The Chill of the Sun Novel by Jean-Raphael-Marie-Noël Cayrol
Exit the King Play by Romanian-born Eugène Ionesco

For a New Novel Collection of literary essays by Alain Robbe-Grillet
Golden Fruits Novel by Nathalie Sarraute
The Interrogation Novel by Jean-Marie Le Clezio
Planet of the Apes Novel by Pierre Boulle
A Stroll in the Air Play by Romanian-born Eugène Ionesco

Martinican

The Tragedy of King Christophe Play by Aimé Césaire

GERMAN

Austrian

The Waterfalls of Slunj Novel by Heimito von Doderer

German

The Clown Novel by Heinrich Böll
The Deputy Play by Rolf Hochhuth
Dog Years Novel by Günter Grass

HEBREW
In the Wilderness Novel by Aharon Appelfeld

ITALIAN
The Reawakening Autobiography by Jewish writer Primo Levi

KIRGHIZ
Tales of Mountains and Steppes Collection of short stories by Chingiz Aytmatov

POLISH
A Dreambook of Our Time Novel by Tadeusz Konwicki

PORTUGUESE

Brazilian

Evening Star Collected verse of Manuel Bandeira

RUSSIAN
Oranges from Morocco Novel by Vasily Pavlovich Aksyonov

SPANISH

Argentine

Hopscotch Novel by Julio Cortázar

Peruvian

The Time of the Hero Novel by Mario Vargas Llosa

SWEDISH
The Cassock Novel by Sven Delblanc
The Testament of Cain Novel by Lars Gyllensten

XHOSA
The Ochre People: Scenes from a South African Life Autobiographical novel by Noni Helen Nontando Jabavu

1964

DEATHS

Sheikh Kaluta bin Amri Abedi, Swahili poet
Halide Edib Adivar, Turkish novelist and essayist

Abbas Mahmud al-Aqqad, Egyptian novelist and poet
Konrad Bayer, Austrian poet and novelist
Brendan Behan, Irish playwright
Rachel Carson, American environmentalist
Vasily Semenovich Grossman, Russian novelist, playwright, and poet
Maithilisharan Gupta, Indian poet
Ben Hecht, American playwright
Thakin Koujto Hmain, Burmese poet, playwright, novelist, and historian
Ezequiel Martínez Estrada, Argentine writer
Sean O'Casey, Irish playwright
Flannery O'Connor, American novelist
Sato Haruo, Japanese poet and novelist
Badr Shakir as-Sayyab, Iraqi poet
Frans Eemil Sillanpää, Finnish novelist
Dame Edith Sitwell, English poet and critic
Davith Stefansson, Icelandic poet

LITERARY EVENT
PRIZES AND AWARDS
Caldecott Medal: *Where the Wild Things Are* by Maurice Sendak
Newbery Medal: *It's Like This, Cat* by Emily Nelville
Nobel Prize in literature: Jean-Paul Sartre, French novelist and socialist philosopher

Pulitzer Prizes

Biography *John Keats* by Walter Jackson Bate
History *Puritan Village: The Formation of a New England Town* by Sumner Chilton Powell
Nonfiction *Anti-Intellectualism in American Life* by Richard Hofstadter
Poetry *At the End of the Open Road* by Louis Simpson

PUBLICATIONS
ARMENIAN
"Caravans Are Still Marching" Poem by Silva Kaputikian

CZECH
The Castle Play by Ivan Klima

DANISH
The Good Hope Novel by William Heineson

ENGLISH
American

After the Fall Play by Arthur Miller
The Brigadier and the Golf Widow Collected stories by John Cheever
Cabot Wright Begins Novel by James Purdy
Collages Novel by Anaïs Nin
Come Back, Dr. Caligari Collection of short stories by Donald Barthelme
The Dead Lecturer Collected verse by Amiri Baraka (LeRoi Jones)
Desert of the Heart Novel by Jane Rule
Dutchman Play by Amiri Baraka (LeRoi Jones)

The Far Field Collection of verse by Theodore Roethke
Flood Novel by Robert Penn Warren
Flower Herding on Mount Monadnock Collected verse by Galway Kinnell
For the Union Dead Collection of poems by Robert Lowell
Helmets Collected verse by James Dickey
Herzog Novel by Saul Bellow
Julian Novel about Julian the Apostate by Gore Vidal
The Keepers of the House Novel by Shirley Ann Grau
Last Exit to Brooklyn Novel by Hubert Selby Jr.
More Stately Mansions Play by Eugene O'Neill
A Moveable Feast Memoir by Ernest Hemingway
Nova Express Novel by William S. Burroughs
The Passion of Joseph D. Play by Paddy Chayefsky
The Rector of Justin Novel by Louis Auchincloss
The Second Skin Novel by John Hawkes
77 Dream Songs Collection of poems by John Berryman
The Sign in Sidney Brustein's Window Play by Lorraine Hansberry
Shadow and Act Collection of essays by Ralph Ellison
The Slave Play by Amiri Baraka (LeRoi Jones)
"The Swimmer" Short story by John Cheever
The Toilet One-act play by Amiri Baraka (LeRoi Jones)
The Wapshot Scandal Novel by John Cheever

Australian

Captain Quiros Long poem by James Philip McAuley

British

African Stories Collection by Doris Lessing
Alms for Oblivion Novel cycle (completed in 1980) by Simon Raven
The Eve of Saint Venus Novel by Anthony Burgess
The Italian Girl Novel by Iris Murdoch
A Moment in Time Novel by H. E. Bates
The Royal Hunt of the Sun Play by Peter Shaffer
A Single Man Novel by Christopher Isherwood
The Spire Novel by William Golding
The Valley of Bones Novel by Anthony Powell

Ghanaian

Rediscovery and Other Poems Collection by Kofi Awoonor

Guyanese

Moscow Not My Mecca Novel by Jan Rynveld Carew

Irish

Philadelphia, Here I Come Play by Brian Friel

Kenyan

Weep Not Child Novel by Ngugi wa Thiong'o

Nigerian

The Voice Novel by Gabriel Imomotimi Gbaingbain Okara

South African

The Emergency Novel by Richard Rive
The Rhythm of Violence Play by Lewis Nkosi
The Two Lamps Play by Uys Krige

FINNISH
The Roman Novel by Mika Waltari
Thus Changed the Seasons Collected verse by Eeva Liisa Manner

FRENCH
Critical Essays Collection by Roland Barthes
The Eiffel Tower and Other Mythologies Collection of essays by Roland Barthes
The Ravishing of Lol V. Stein Novel by Marguerite Duras
The Raw and the Cooked Anthropological studies (part of *Mythologiques*) by Claude Lévi-Strauss

GERMAN
German
Dramen Play by Bulgarian-born English writer Elias Canetti
The Persecution and Assassination of Jean-Paul Marat, as Performed by the Inmates of the Asylum of Charenton Under the Direction of the Marquis de Sade Play by German-Swedish writer Peter Weiss

Swiss
A Wilderness of Mirrors Novel by Max Frisch

HINDI
The House of People Epic poem by Sumitranandan Pant

PORTUGUESE
Brazilian
The Passion According to G. H. Novel by Clarice Lispector

ROMANIAN
First Person Plural Collected verse by Ana Blandina

RUSSIAN
Forever Flowering Novel by Vasily Grossman
The Story of a Life Six-volume autobiography by Konstantin Paustovsky

SPANISH
Chilean
Shadows Against the Wall Novel by Manuel Rojas

Nicaraguan
The Psalms of Struggle and Liberation Collection of poems by Ernesto Cardenal

Peruvian
Foot on the Neck Collected verse by Carlos Germán Belli

Spanish
Bonfires Novel by Concha Alos
Reality and Desire Collection of poems by Luis Cernuda

TURKISH
Destan About Ali of Kesan Play by Haldun Taner

URDU
The Ocean of Night Novel by Ahmed Ali

YORUBAN
Yorubus, You Must Think Political play by Nigerian writer Hubert Ogunde

1965

BIRTH
Toni Pascal, Catalan novelist

DEATHS
Jacques Audiberti, French playwright, poet, novelist, and essayist
R. P. Blackmur, American poet
Martin Buber, Austrian Jewish philosopher
Reuben Tolakele Caluza, Zulu poet
Alejandro Cazona, Spanish playwright, poet, and essayist
Thomas Bertram Costain, American historical novelist
Maria Dabrowska, Polish writer
A. Emile Disengomoko, Kikongo novelist, poet, and essayist
T. S. Eliot, American-born English poet
Josef Grishashvili, Georgian poet and literary historian
Lorraine Hansberry, African-American playwright
Mahti Hussain, Azerbaijani novelist, playwright, and historian
Bashir al-Ibrahimi, Algerian philosopher and essayist
Shirley Jackson, American novelist and short-story writer
Randall Jarrell, American poet
Mohammad Mandur, Egyptian essayist and literary critic
W. Somerset Maugham, English novelist
Edgar Mittelholzer, Guyanan novelist, playwright, and poet
Jan van Nijlen, Flemish poet
Lekhnath Pandyal, Nepalese poet and novelist
Albert Schweitzer, German theologian, humanitarian, and writer
Georgi Shalberashvili, Georgian poet, novelist, and playwright
Tanizaki Junichiro, Japanese novelist
Paul Johannes Tillich, German-born American theologian

LITERARY EVENT
PRIZES AND AWARDS
Caldecott Medal: *May I Bring a Friend?* by Beatrice Schenk de Regniers
Newbery Medal: *Shadow of a Bull* by Maia Wojciechowska
Nobel Prize in literature: Mikhail Aleksandrovich Sholokhov, Russian novelist

Pulitzer Prizes
Biography *Henry Adams* by Ernest Samuels
Drama *The Subject Was Roses* by Frank D. Gilroy
Fiction *The Keepers of the House* by Shirley Ann Grau
History *The Greenback Era* by Irwin Unger
Nonfiction *O Strange New World* by Howard Mumford Jones
Poetry *77 Dream Songs* by John Berryman

PUBLICATIONS
ALBANIAN
The Monster Novel by Ismail Kadare

ARABIC

The Tragedy of Al-Hallaj Play by Egyptian writer Salah Abdassabur

The Thief Novel by Egyptian writer Naguib Mahfouz

CZECH

Closely Watched Trains Novel by Bohaamil Hrahal

The Memorandum Play by Vaclav Havel

ENGLISH

American

An American Dream Novel by Normal Mailer

Ariel Collected verse by Sylvia Plath

The Autobiography of Malcolm X Autobiography by African-American leader Malcolm X with Alex Haley

Beyond Culture Cultural perspectives by Lionel Trilling

Buckdancer's Choice Collected verse by James Dickey

Collected Stories Collection by Katherine Anne Porter

Dune Science fiction novel by Frank Herbert

The Effect of Gamma Rays on Man-in-the-Moon Marigolds Play by Paul Zindel

Everything That Rises Must Converge Short story collection by Flannery O'Connor

God Bless You, Mr. Rosewater Novel by Kurt Vonnegut Jr.

Incident at Vichy One-act play by Arthur Miller

The Lost World: New Poems Collection by Randall Jarrell

Mrs. Stevens Hears the Mermaids Singing Novel by May Sarton

The Odd Couple Play by Neil Simon

Of the Farm Novel by John Updike

The Painted Bird Semiautobiographical novel by Polish-born writer Jerzy Kosinski

The Source Novel by James A. Michener

Tiny Alice Play by Edward Albee

Australian

The Cave and the Spring: Essays on Poetry Essays by Alec Derwent Hope

The Shoes of the Fisherman Novel by Morris West

British

After Julius Novel by Elizabeth Jane Howard

Cork Street, Next to Hatter's Novel by Pamela Hansford Johnson

The Hollow Hill and Other Poems, 1960–1964 Collection by Kathleen Raine

The Homecoming Play by Harold Pinter

Landlocked Novel by Doris Lessing

Lost Empires Novel by J. B. Priestley

A Patriot for Me Play by John Osborne

The Room and Other Poems Collection by Cecil Day-Lewis

Canadian

In Praise of Older Women: Amorous Recollections of Andras Vajada Novel by Hungarian-born Stephen Vicinczy

Ethiopian

Oda Oak Oracle Novel by Tsegaye Gabre-Madhin

Nigerian

The Interpreters Novel by Wole Soyinka

The Road Play by Wole Soyinka

Scottish

The Mandelbaum Gate Novel by Muriel Spark

South African

The Beginners Novel by Jewish novelist Dan Jacobson

Trinidadian

The Year in San Fernando Novel by Michael Anthony

FINNISH

Private Jokinen's Marriage Leave Play by Veijo Meri

FLEMISH

My Living Shadow Novel by Paul de Wispelaere

FRENCH

The Blue Flowers Novel by Raymond Queneau

The Bond Novel by Jacques Borel

The Civil War Play by Henry de Montherlant

Fever Novel by Jean-Marie Le Clezio

HEBREW

Where the Jackals Howl and Other Stories Collection by Israeli writer Amos Oz

ITALIAN

Emergency Exit Novel by Ignazio Silone

From the Bottom of the Field Collected verse by Mario Luzi

An Italian Story Collection of three novellas by Vasco Pratolini

JAPANESE

The Sea of Fertility Novel by Yukio Mishima

MALAY

Burnt to a Cinder Novel by Ahmad Shahnon

NORWEGIAN

New Stories, Frydenberg Collection of short stories by Johan Borgen

PORTUGUESE

Brazilian

Whole Life Star Poetry collection by Manuel Bandeira

RUSSIAN

Verses and Poems Collection by Joseph Brodsky

SPANISH

Argentine

The Banquet of Severo Arcangelo Novel by Leopoldo Marechal

Cuban

Three Trapped Tigers Novel by Guillermo Cabrera Infante

Uruguayan

Thanks for the Fire Novel by Mario Benedetti

TAMIL

Mother Came Novel by Ti Janakiraman

Son Novel by La Sa Ramamitram

1966

DEATHS

Tafawa Balewa Abubakar, Nigerian novelist
Anna Akhmatova (Anna Andreyevna Gorenko), Russian poet
Johanna van Ammers-Küller, Dutch novelist
Hans Christian Banner, Danish novelist and playwright
André Breton, French surrealist poet and critic
Heimito von Doderer, Austrian novelist
Georges Duhamel, French poet, playwright, and novelist
Ghafur Ghulam Uzbek, novelist, poet, and critic
C. S. Forester, English historical novelist
Lao She, Chinese novelist
Georgi Leonidze, Georgian poet
Said Nafisi, Iranian novelist and critic
Flann O'Brien (Brian O'Nuallain), Irish novelist
Delmore Schwartz, American poet, novelist, and critic
Georgios Theotokas, Greek poet
Ello Vittorini, Italian novelist
Arthur David Waley, English scholar and translator
Evelyn Waugh, English novelist

LITERARY EVENT

PRIZES AND AWARDS

Caldecott Medal: *Always Room for One More* by Sorche Nic Leodhas
Newbery Award: *I, Juan de Pareja* by Elizabeth Borton de Treviño
Nobel Prize in literature: Shmuel Yosef Agnon, Israeli novelist, and Nelly Sachs, German poet and translator

Pulitzer Prizes

Biography *A Thousand Days* by Arthur Schlesinger Jr.
Fiction *Collected Stories* by Katherine Anne Porter
History *Life of the Mind in America* by Perry Miller
Nonfiction *Wondering Through Winter* by Edwin Way Teale
Poetry *Selected Poems* by Richard Eberhart

PUBLICATIONS

ACHOLI

Song of Lawino Poetic novel by Ugandan writer Okot p'Bitek

ENGLISH

American

Against Interpretation Collected essays of Susan Sontag
The Crying of Lot 49 Novel by Thomas Pynchon
A Delicate Balance Play by Edward Albee
Fantastic Voyage Science fiction novel by Isaac Asimov
The Fixer Novel by Bernard Malamud
Giles Goat-Boy Novel by John Barth
In Cold Blood "Nonfiction novel" by Truman Capote
Live or Die Poetry collection by Anne Sexton
The Moon Is a Harsh Mistress Science fiction novel by Robert Heinlein
A Private Mythology Poetry collection by May Sarton
The Saddest Summer of Samuel S. Novel by Irish-American writer J. P. Donleavy

The Star-Spangled Girl Play by Neil Simon
Trust Novel by Cynthia Ozick
Up Above the World Novel by Paul Bowles
The Woman at the Washington Zoo Poetry collection by Randall Jarrell

Australian

Collected Poetry Collected verse by A. D. Hope
This Island Now Novel by South African–born writer Peter Abrahams
Letters to Live Poets Poetry collection by Bruce Beaver
The Solid Mandala Novel by Patrick White
Tai-Pan Novel by James Clavell

British

A Bond Honored Play by John Osborne
Collected Shorter Poems Collection by W. H. Auden
The Comedians Novel by Graham Greene
High and Low Collected verse by John Betjeman
A House in Order Novel by Nigel Denis
The Jewel in the Crown First volume in the *The Raj Quartet* by Paul Scott
Rosencrantz and Gildenstern Are Dead Play by Tom Stoppard
The Soldier's Art Novel (part of *A Dance to the Music of Time*) by Anthony Powell
The Time of Angels Novel by Iris Murdoch
Wide Sargasso Sea Novel by Jean Rhys

Cameroonian

A Few Nights and Days Novel by Mbella Sonne Dipoko

Canadian

The Dumbfounding Collected verse by Margaret Avison

Irish

Death of a Naturalist Collected verse by Seamus Heaney

South African

The Wall of Death Play by Uys Krige

Zimbabwean

On Trial for My Country Novel by Stanlake Samkange

FINNISH

The Colonel's Driver Novella by Veijo Meri

FRENCH

Education by Stone Poetry collection by Jean-Raphael-Marie-Noël Cayrol
The Flood Novel by Jean-Marie Le Clezio
From Honey to Ashes Anthropological study (second volume of *Mythologiques*) by Claude Lévi-Strauss
Midday Midnight Novel by Jean-Raphael-Marie-Noël Cayrol
The Order of Things: An Archeology of Human Science Philosophical inquiry by Michel Foucault

GEORGIAN

The Goatibex Constellation Novel by Fazil Iskander

GERMAN

German

Offending the Audience Play by Peter Handke
The Plebeians Rehearse the Uprising Play by Günter Grass
The Unicorn Novel by Martin Walser

Swiss

The Meteor Play by Friedrich Durrenmatt

ITALIAN

To Give and to Have and Other Poems Collection by Salvator
  Quasimodo
The Offender Collected verse by Eugenio Montale
Xenia Collected verse by Eugenio Montale

JAPANESE

Silence Novel by Shusaku Endo

NORWEGIAN

Moment of Freedom Novel by Jens Bjorneboe

PORTUGUESE

Brazilian

Nine, Novena Novel by Osman Lins

RUSSIAN

Babi Yar Novel by Anatoly Kuznetsov
"A Jew from Lublin" Poem by Jacob Glatstein
The Master and Margarita Novel by Mikhail Bulgakov

SPANISH

Chilean

Hell Has No Limits Novel by José Donoso
This Sunday Novel by José Donoso

Cuban

Paraíso Novel by José Lezama Lima

Mexican

The Masked Days Collected stories of Carlos Fuentes

Peruvian

Through the Woods Below Poetry collection by Carlos Germán
  Belli

Spanish

Peace After the War Novel by José María Gironella

SWEDISH

Echoes and Traces Collection of poems by Tomas Transtromer
Lotus in Hades Novel by Lars Gyllensten

TURKISH

Human Landscapes Collection of poems by Nazim Hikmet Ran

YIDDISH

In My Father's Court Memoir by Polish-born American writer
  Isaac Bashevis Singer

1967

DEATHS

Turdor Arghezi, Romanian poet and novelist
Marcel Aymé, French novelist and playwright
Azorín (José Martínez Ruiz), Spanish essayist and novelist
Bo Hjalmar Bergman, Swedish lyrical poet
Jean Charbonneau, French-Canadian poet
Ilya Grigoryyevich Ehrenburg, Russian novelist
Forugh Farrokhhzad, Iranian poet
Langston Hughes, American poet, playwright, novelist, and essayist
Patrick Kavanagh, Irish poet
John Edward Masefield, English poet
André Maurois, French novelist
Carson McCullers, American novelist
Christopher Okigbo, Nigerian poet
Dorothy Parker, American short-story writer, poet, and critic
Elmer Rice (Elmer Leopold Reizenstein), American playwright
João Guimaraes Rosa, Brazilian novelist and short-story writer
Carl Sandburg, American poet and biographer
Siegfried Sassoon, English poet, novelist, and biographer
Herman Teirlink, Flemish poet, novelist, and playwright
Alice B. Toklas, American writer
Jean Toomer, American novelist
Vernon Phillips Watkins, English poet
Stephen Zorian, Armenian novelist and translator

LITERARY EVENT

PRIZES AND AWARDS

Caldecott Medal: *Sam, Bangs and Moonshine* by Evaline Ness
Newbery Medal: *Up a Road Slowly* by Irene Hunt
Nobel Prize in literature: Miguel Angel Asturias, Guatemalan
  novelist and poet

Pulitzer Prizes

Biography *Mr. Clemens and Mark Twain* by Justin Kaplan
Drama *A Delicate Balance* by Edward Albee
Fiction *The Fixer* by Bernard Malamud
History *Exploration and Empire: The Explorer and the Scientist
  in the Winning of the American West* by William H. Goetzmann
Nonfiction *The Problem of Slavery in Western Culture* by David
  Brion Davis
Poetry *Live or Die* by Anne Sexton

PUBLICATIONS

ARABIC

Miramar Novel by Egyptian writer Naguib Mahfouz

CZECH

Halley's Comet Collected verse of Jaroslav Seifert
The Joke Novel by Milan Kundera

ENGLISH

American

Berryman's Sonnets Collected verse by John Berryman
The Chosen Novel by Chaim Potok

The Confessions of Nat Turner Novel by William Styron
The Eighth Day Novel by Thornton Wilder
A Garden of Earthly Delights Novel by Joyce Carol Oates
Language and Silence: Essays on Language, Literature and the In-human Collection by George Steiner
Mystery Novel by Norwegian-born Alfred Hauge
Near the Ocean Collected verse by Robert Lowell
Night Light Collection of verse by Donald Justice
The Panther and the Lash: Poems of Our Times Poetry collection by Langston Hughes
Snow White Novel by Donald Barthelme
Trout Fishing in America Novel by Richard Brautigan
Washington, D.C. Novel by William Styron
When She Was Good Novel by Philip Roth

Australian

Bring Larks and Heroes Novel by Thomas Keneally

Barbadian

Rights of Passage Collection of verse by Edward Kamau Brathwaite

British

Autobiography, 1872–1914 Autobiography of philosopher Bertrand Russell
Collected Poems Collected verse by Elizabeth Jennings
Pilgrimage Novel (last in series) by Dorothy M. Richardson
The Pyramid Novel by William Golding
Tigers Collection of poems by Fleur Adcock
Touch Poetry collection by Thom Gunn
A Weekend with Claud Novel by Beryl Bainbridge

Cameroonian

Agatha Moudio's Sons Novel by Francis Bebey

Ghanaian

Edufa Play by Efua Theodora Sutherland
The Gab Boys Novel by Cameron Duodo

Indian

The Vendor of Sweets Novel by R. K. Narayan

Malawian

No Bride Price Novel by David Rubadiri

Nigerian

The Concubine Novel by Elechi Amadi
Efuru Novel by Flora Nwapa
Kongi's Harvest Play by Wole Soyinka
Man of the People Novel by Chinua Achebe

South African

The Orphan of the Desert Collected short stories by Uys Krige
The Stone Country Novel by Alex La Guma

Trinidadian

Green Days by the River Novel by Michael Anthony

FRENCH

French

Beloved Earth Novel by Jean-Marie Le Clezio
Elementary Structures of Kinship Anthropological studies by Claude Lévi-Strauss

Histoire Novel by Claude Simon
I Still Hear It Novel by Jean-Raphael-Marie-Noël Cayrol
The Margin Novel by André Pieyre de Mandiargues
Speech and Phenomena Philosophical study of Edmund Husserl by Jacques Derrida

Senegalese

The Exile of Albouri Play by Cheik A. Nadao

GERMAN

Austrian

Derangement Novel by Thomas Bernhard

German

Soldiers Play by Rolf Hochhuth

ITALIAN

Death of the Seasons Collected verse by Giuseppe Ungaretti

JAPANESE

The Silent Cry Novel by Kenzaburo Oe

MALAY

The Minister Novel by Ahmed Shahnon

POLISH

The Ascension Novel by Tadeusz Konwicki
Upstairs, Downstairs Novel by Michal Choromanski

PORTUGUESE

Brazilian

The Road Back Play by Jorge Andrade

RUSSIAN

The Holy Well Novel by Valentin Katayev

SPANISH

Argentine

The Book of Imaginary Beings Prose poem by Jorge Luis Borges

Colombian

No One Writes to the Colonel and Other Stories Collection by Gabriel García Márquez
One Hundred Years of Solitude Novel by Gabriel García Márquez

Mexican

A Change of Skin Novel by Carlos Fuentes
White Collection of poems by Octavio Paz

Peruvian

The Cubs, and Other Stories Novel by Mario Vargas Llosa

Spanish

The Architect and the Emperor of Assyria Play by Fernando Arrabal
The Basement Window Play by Antonio Buero Vallejo
Return to Region Novel by Juan Benet

Guide to the Underworld Collection of poems by Gunnar Ekelof

YIDDISH
The Manor Novel by Polish-born American writer Isaac Bashevis Singer

1968

DEATHS

Manuel Bandeira, Brazilian poet
Max Brod, German Jewish novelist, playwright, poet, and critic
Gunnar Ekelof, Swedish poet
Edna Ferber, American novelist
Han Tian, Chinese playwright
Stephen Haweis, English-born Dominican poet
Archibald Campbell Jordan, South African novelist
Eric Lindegren, Swedish poet
Thomas Merton, American monk and writer
Sarah Gertrude Millin, South African novelist, biographer, and essayist
Oybek, Uzbek poet and novelist
Konstantin Georgievich Paustovsky, Russian novelist and playwright
Salvatore Quasimodo, Italian poet
Sir Herbert Edward Read, English editor, poet, and critic
Conrad Michael Richter, American novelist
Marah Rusli, Indonesian novelist
Upton Beall Sinclair, American novelist
John Ernst Steinbeck, American novelist
Yvor Winters, American poet and critic
Arnold Zweig, German novelist and playwright

LITERARY EVENTS

Booker Prize, awarded to best novel in British Commonwealth, is established in London

PRIZES AND AWARDS

Caldecott Medal: *Drummer Hoff* by Barbara Emberley
Newbery Medal: *From the Mixed-Up Files of Mrs. Basil E. Frankweiler* by E. L. Konigsburg
Nobel Prize in literature: Yasunari Kawabata, Japanese novelist

Pulitzer Prizes

Biography *Memoirs, 1925–1950* by George F. Kennan
Fiction *The Confessions of Nat Turner* by William Styron
History *The Ideological Origins of the American Revolution* by Bernard Bailyn
Nonfiction *Rousseau and Revolution* by Will Durant
Poetry *The Hard Hours* by Anthony Hecht

PUBLICATIONS

ALBANIAN

The Wedding Novel by Ismail Kadare

ENGLISH

American

Airplane Dreams: Compositions from Journals Volume of verse by Allen Ginsberg
Black Feeling, Black Talk Collection of poems by Nikki Giovanni
Cleng Peerson Novel by Norwegian-born Alfred Hauge
Couples Novel by John Updike
Desert Solitaire Environmental meditations by Edward Abbey
House Made of Dawn Novel by Native American novelist N. Scott Momaday
In the Mecca Collection of poetry by Gwendolyn Brooks
The Legend of Svein and Maria Novel by Norwegian-born writer Alfred Hauge
The Light Around the Body Prose poems by Robert Bly
Lost in the Funhouse Collection of 14 stories by John Barth
Loving Hands at Home Novel by Diane Johnson
Miami and the Siege of Chicago Report on the 1968 Democratic national convention by Norman Mailer
Mosby's Memoirs and Other Stories Collection of short stories by Saul Bellow
Myra Breckinridge Novel by Gore Vidal
Plaza Suite Play by Neil Simon
The Price Play by Arthur Miller
Rescue the Dead Poem by David Ignatov
The Residual Years: Poems 1934–1948 Collected verse by William Everson
Slouching Toward Bethlehem Collected essays by Joan Didion
Steps Novel by Polish-born writer Jerzy Kosinski
Tell Me How Long the Train's Been Gone Novel by James Baldwin
The Universal Baseball Association, Inc., J. Henry Waugh, Prop. Novel by Robert Coover
A Wizard of Earthsea First volume of the science fiction series *The Earthsea Trilogy* by Ursula K. Le Guin

British

Another Part of the Wood Novel by Beryl Bainbridge
The Day of the Scorpions Novel (second volume of *The Raj Quartet*) by Paul Scott
Enderby Outside Novel by Anthony Burgess
Landscape Play by Harold Pinter
The Military Philosopher Novel (part of *A Dance to the Music of Time*) by Anthony Powell
The Nice and the Good Novel by Iris Murdoch

Canadian

Cocksure Novel by Mordecai Richler

Ghanaian

The Torrent Novel by Joseph Wilfred Abruquah
The Beautyful Ones Are Not Yet Born Novel by Ayi Kwei Armah

Tanzanian

Dying in the Sun Novel by Peter Palangyo

FINNISH

The Family Novel by Veijo Meri

1969

FRENCH

French

The Abyss Novel by Marguerite Yourcenar
The Black Rose Novel by Henry de Montherlant
The Flight of Icarus Novel by Raymond Queneau
The Origin of Table Manners Anthropological study (third volume of *Mythologiques*) by Claude Lévi-Strauss

Guyanan

Bozambo's Revenge: Colonialism Inside Out Novel by Bertene Juminer

Haitian

The Tragic Engagement Play by Gerard Chenet

Malian

The Wages of Violence Novel by Yambo Ouologuem

GERMAN

Austrian

A Party for Boris Play by Thomas Bernhard

German

Kaspar Play by Peter Handke
Toller Play by Tankred Dorst
Vietnam Discourse Play by Peter Weiss

HEBREW

My Michael Novel by Amos Oz

ICELANDIC

Christianity at a Glacier Novel by Halldor Laxness

ITALIAN

The Heron Novel by Giorgio Bassani

KURDISH

Dimdim Novel by Arabe Shamo

POLISH

To Get to the Heart of the Matter Novel by Michal Choromanski

RUSSIAN

Cancer Ward Novel by Aleksandr Solzhenitsyn
The First Circle Novel by Aleksandr Solzhenitsyn

SERBIAN

Secondary Heaven Poem by Vasko Popa

SPANISH

Argentine

Betrayed by Rita Hayworth Novel by Manuel Puig

Spanish

Poems of Consummation Collection of poems by Vicente Aleixandre

SWAHILI

The Well of Giningi Novel by Tanzanian writer Muhammed Said Abdulla

DEATHS

Jalal Al-e Ahmad, Iranian philosopher and essayist
José María Arguedas, Peruvian novelist
Sufi Abdukhaqq Khan Betab, Afghan Dari poet
Dame Ivy Compton-Burnett, English writer
Rómulo Gallegos, Venezuelan novelist
Witold Gombrowicz, Polish novelist, playwright, and essayist
Karl Jaspers, German existentialist philosopher
Jack Kerouac, American Beat writer
Gurgen Mahari, American poet and novelist
Katharine Susannah Prichard, Fijian-born Australian novelist, poet, and playwright
José Regio, Portuguese poet, playwright, and novelist
Sir Osbert Sitwell, English man of letters
Stijn Streuvels (Frank Lateur), Flemish novelist
B. Traven (Berwick Traven Torsvan), American-born German novelist
Vrindavanlal Varma, Hindi novelist
Kazimierz Wierzynski, Polish poet
Nairi Zavian (Hayastan Yeghiazarian), Armenian poet

LITERARY EVENT

PRIZES AND AWARDS

Booker Prize: *Something to Answer For* by P. H. Newby
Caldecott Medal: *The Fool of the World and the Flying Ship* by Arthur Ransome
Newbery Medal: *The High King* by Lloyd Alexander
Nobel Prize in literature: Samuel Beckett, Irish playwright and poet in English and French

Pulitzer Prizes

Biography *The Man from New York: John Quinn and His Friends* by B. L. Reid
Drama *The Great White Hope* by Howard Sackler
Fiction *House Made of Dawn* by N. Scott Momaday
History *Origins of the Fifth Amendment* by Leonard W. Levy
Nonfiction *The Armies of the Night* by Norman Mailer
Poetry *Of Being Numerous* by George Oppen

PUBLICATIONS

CZECH

The Jury Novel by Ivan Klima

ENGLISH

American

Ada Novel by Vladimir Nabokov
The Andromeda Strain Novel by Michael Crichton
Audubon: A Vision Poetry collection by Robert Lowell
Bullet Park Novel by John Cheever
The Chosen Place, the Timeless People Novel by Paule Marshall
The Complete Poems Collected verse by Randall Jarrell
The Dream Songs Collected verse by John Berryman
The Last of the Red Hot Lovers Play by Neil Simon
The Left Hand of Darkness Science fiction novel by Ursula K. Le Guin

Love Poems Collection of verse by Anne Sexton
The New Yorkers Novel by Hortense Calisher
Notebook, 1967–1968 Collection of verse by Robert Lowell
Pictures of Fidelman Novel by Bernard Malamud
Pieces Collection of poems by Robert Creely
Portnoy's Complaint Novel by Philip Roth
Pricksongs and Descants Collection of short stories by Robert Coover
Slaughter House-Five; or, The Children's Crusade by Kurt Vonnegut Jr.
Styles of Radical Will Collection of essays by Susan Sontag
Them Novel by Joyce Carol Oates
To Be Young, Gifted and Black Autobiography by Lorraine Hansberry
Untitled Subjects Poetry collection by Richard Howard
The Way to Rainy Mountain Novel by Native American writer N. Scott Momaday
What I'm Going to Do, I Think Novel by Larry Woiwode
Yellow Black Radio Broke Down Novel by Ishmael Reed

British

Animals Arrival Collected verse by Elizabeth Jennings
Bruno's Dream Novel by Irish Murdoch
A Clip of Steel Autobiographical novel by Thomas Blackburn
The Four-Gated City Novel by Doris Lessing
The French Lieutenant's Woman Novel by John Fowles
The Green Man Novel by Kingsley Amis
In This House of Brede Novel by Rumer Godden
In Transit Novel by Brigid Brophy
Mary, Queen of Scots Biography by Antonia Fraser
Silence Play by Harold Pinter
Something in Disguise Novel by Elizabeth Jane Howard

Canadian

Ixion's Wheel Collected verse by Ralph Gustafsom
Rules of Chaos; or, Why Tomorrow Doesn't Work Collected essays by Hungarian-born writer Stephen Vizinczey

Ethiopian

The Afersata Novel by Sahle Berhane Marian Selassie

Irish

Door into the Dark Collection of poems by Seamus Heaney

Nigerian

The Great Ponds Novel by Elechi Amadi
Poems from Prison Collection by Wole Soyinka

Saint Lucian

Nor Any Country Novel by Garth St. Omer

Trinidadian

The Humming Bird Tree Novel by Ian McDonald

FRENCH

French

The Archeology of Knowledge Epistemological inquiry by Michel Foucault
The Battle of Pharsalus Novel by Claude Simon
Destroy, She Said Novel by Marguerite Duras

Tunisian

The Scorpion or the Imaginary Confession Novel by Albert Memmi

GERMAN

Local Anesthetic Novel by Günter Grass
The Ward Wants to Be a Guardian Play by Peter Handke

ITALIAN

The Last Summer Collection of poems by Marino Moretti

JAPANESE

Teach Us to Outgrow Our Madness Novel by Kenzaburo Oe

MALAY

Premier Novel by Ahmad Shahnon

NORWEGIAN

The Gunpowder Tower Novel by Jens Bjornboe

RUSSIAN

The White Guard Novel by Mikhail Bulgakov

SPANISH

Argentine

Diary of the War of the Pig Novel by Adolfo Bioy Casares

Chilean

Big Work Collected verse by Nicanor Parra

Mexican

Tree Between the Walls Novel by José Emilio Pacheco

Spanish

And They Put Handcuffs on the Flowers Play by Fernando Arrabal
A Meditation Novel by Juan Benet
San Camilo, 1936 Novel by Camilo José Cela

YIDDISH

The Estate Novel by Polish-born American writer Isaac Bashevis Singer

1970

DEATHS

Arthur Adamov, Russian-French avant-garde playwright
Shmuel Yosef Agnon, Polish-born Israeli novelist
Nigel Balchin, English novelist
Louise Bogan, American poet and critic
Fernand Crommelynck, Flemish playwright
Joseph Wood Crutch, American scholar and critic
John Dos Passos, American novelist
Edward Morgan Forster, English novelist and critic
Erle Stanley Gardner, American detective writer
Jean Giono, French novelist
Amado V. Hernandez, Filipino poet and playwright

Orhan Kemal (Kemal Sadik Giogceli), Turkish novelist, poet, and essayist

Francis Parkinson Keyes, American novelist

Leopoldo Marechal, Argentine novelist

François Mauriac, French novelist, essayist, and playwright

Mishima Yukio (Kimitake Hiraoka), Japanese playwright, novelist, and essayist

John O'Hara, American novelist

Arminjn Pane, Indonesian playwright, novelist, and poet

Julis Przybos, Polish poet

Erich Maria Remarque, German-born American novelist

Bertrand Russell, English philosopher

Nelly Sachs, German poet and translator

Wilbur Daniel Steele, American novelist and playwright

Giuseppe Ungaretti, Italian poet

Fritz von Unruh, German playwright, poet, and novelist

Anzia Yezierska, Russian-born American novelist and critic

Zhao Shuli, Chinese novelist and short-story writer

LITERARY EVENT
PRIZES AND AWARDS
Booker Prize: *The Elected Member* by Bernice Rubens

Caldecott Medal: *Sylvester and the Magic Pebble* by William Steig

Newbery Medal: *Sounder* by William H. Armstrong

Nobel Prize in literature: Aleksandr Isayevich Solzhenitsyn, Russian novelist

Pulitzer Prizes

Biography *Huey Long* by T. Harry Williams

Drama *No Place to Be Somebody* by Charles Gordone

Fiction *Collected Stories* by Jean Stafford

History *Present at the Creation: My Years in the State Department* by Dean Acheson

Nonfiction *Gandhi's Truth: On the Origins of Militant Nonviolence* by Erik H. Erikson

Poetry *Untitled Subjects* by Richard Howard

PUBLICATIONS
ARABIC
The Fellah Novel by Egyptian writer Abdur-Rahman ash-Sharqawi

ARMENIAN
Twentieth Century Volume of verse by Gevorg Emin

ENGLISH
American

The Abduction Novel by Maxine Kumin

Bech: A Book Novel by John Updike

Being There Novel by Jerzy Kosinski

The Bluest Eye Novel by Toni Morrison

Cantos No. 1–117, 120 Collected verse by Ezra Pound

The Carriers of Ladders Collection of verse by W. S. Merwin

City Life Collection of short stories by Donald Barthelme

I Know Why the Caged Bird Sings Autobiographical work by Maya Angelou

Islands in the Stream Novel by Ernest Hemingway

I Will Fear No Evil Science fiction novel by Robert Heinlein

Jeremy's Vision First volume in the trilogy *Sleepers in Moon-Crowned Valleys* by James Purdy

Losing Battles Novel by Eudora Welty

Lucidites Poetry collection by Elizabeth Jennings

Mr. Sammler's Planet Novel by Saul Bellow

Of a Fire on the Moon Account of the *Apollo II* by Norman Mailer

Play It As It Lays Novel by Joan Didion

The Trumpet of the Swan Children's story by E. B. White

British

Crow: From the Life and Songs of the Crow Poetry collection by Ted Hughes

The Triple Echo Novel by H. E. Bates

The Whispering Roots Collected verse by Cecil Day-Lewis

A Yard of the Sun Play by Christopher Fry

Canadian

The Collected Works of Billy the Kidd: Left-Handed Poems Poetry collection by Michael Ondaatje

The Fifth Business First volume in *The Deptford Trilogy* by Robertson Davies

Irish

Lessness Short work, "neither play nor novel, neither poetry nor prose" by Samuel Beckett

Three Lovers Novel by Julia O'Faolain

Nigerian

Casualties: Poems, 1966–1968 Collection of verse by John Pepper Clark

Chief of the Honorable Minister Novel by Timothy Mofolorunso Aluko

Oil Man of Obanje Novel by John Munonye

Scottish

The Driver's Seat Novel by Muriel Spark

South African

The Rape of Tamar Novel by Dan Jacobson

Take Root or Die Play by Guy Butler

Trinidadian

Crick Crack Monkey Novel by Merle Hodge

FLEMISH
A Day on the Ground Novel by Paul de Wispelaere

Paul Against Paul Novel by Paul de Wispelaere

FRENCH
Belgian

The Paper House Autobiography by Françoise Mallet-Joris

Canadian

Kamouraska Novel by Anne Hébert

French

Italian Spring Novel by Emmanuel Robles

The Killing Game Play by Romanian-born Eugène Ionesco

War Novel by Jean-Marie Le Clezio

Guinean

The African Continent Play by Condetto Nenekhaly-Camara

GERMAN
Austrian

The Lime Works Novel by Thomas Bernhard

German

Anniversaries: From the Life of Gesine Cresspahl Four-volume novel (completed in 1984) by Uwe Johnson
Zettel's Dream Novel by Arno Schmidt
The Goalee's Anxiety at the Penalty Kick Novel by Peter Handke

Swiss

Portrait of a Planet Play by Friedrich Durrenmatt

ICELANDIC

Waxing Moon and Waning Moon Collected verse by Johannes Joansson

JAPANESE

The Judgment Play by Kinoshita Junji
The Doctor's Wife Novel by Sawako Ariyoshi

RUSSIAN

A Halt in the Wasteland Collected verse of Joseph Brodsky

SPANISH
Argentine

Dr. Brodie's Report Novel by Jorge Luis Borges

Chilean

The Obscene Bird of Night Novel by José Donoso

Peruvian

Sestinas and Other Poems Collected verse of Carlos Germán Belli

SWEDISH

The Memorial Novel by Sven Delblanc

ZULU

Zulu Poems Collection by Mazisi Raymond Kunene

1971

DEATHS

Jorge Barbosa, Cape Verdean poet
Paul Blackburn, American poet
John Wood Campbell Jr., American science fiction writer
Walter Van Tilburg Clark, American novelist
Jacob Glatstein, Polish-born poet, novelist, and critic
György Lukács, Hungarian literary critic, social theorist, and philosopher
Guruprasad Mainali, Nepalese novelist
Ogden Nash, American poet
Gershon Schoffman, German-born Hebrew novelist

George Seferis (Giorgios Sefiriadis), Greek poet
Paruir Sevak, Armenian poet
Fakhroddin Shadman, Iranian novelist and essayist
Shiga Naoya, Japanese novelist
Stevie Smith (Florence Margaret Smith), English novelist and poet
Simon Vestdijk, Dutch novelist and poet
Charles Vildrac, French poet and playwright

LITERARY EVENTS

The literary magazine *Antaeus* is founded by Paul Bowles and Samuel Halperin
Whitbread Book of the Year Award is established in United Kingdom

PRIZES AND AWARDS

Booker Prize: *In a Free State* by V. S. Naipaul
Caldecott Medal: *A Story a Story* by Gail E. Haley
Newbery Medal: *Summer of the Swans* by Betsy Byars
Nobel Prize in literature: Pablo Neruda (Neftalí Ricardo Reyes Basoalto), Chilean poet

Pulitzer Prizes

Biography *Robert Frost: The Years of Triumph, 1915–1938* by Lawrence Thompson
Drama *The Effect of Gamma Rays on Man-in-the-Moon Marigolds* by Paul Zindel
History *Roosevelt, the Soldier of Freedom* by James MacGregor Burns
Nonfiction *The Rising Sun* by John Toland
Poetry *The Carrier of Ladders* by William S. Merwin

PUBLICATIONS

DANISH
Severe Passions Novel by Sven Holm

ENGLISH
American

Angle of Repose Novel by Wallace Stegner
The Autobiography of Miss Jane Pittman Novel by Ernest J. Gaines
Birds of America Novel by Mary McCarthy
The Blood Oranges Novel by John Hawkes
The Book of Daniel Novel by E. L. Doctorow
The Book of Nightmares Collected verse by Galway Kinnell
Burning Novel by Diane Johnson
Collected Poems Collection by James Wright
The Condor Passes Novel by Shirley Ann Grau
Crossing the Water Collected verse by Sylvia Plath
The House of Blue Leaves Play by John Guare
The Last Picture Show Novel by Larry McMurtry
Love in the Ruins Novel by Walker Percy
Meet Me in the Green Glen Novel by Robert Penn Warren
The Onion Eaters Novel by J. P. Donleavy
Our Gang Novel by Philip Roth
The Prisoner of Second Avenue Play by Neil Simon
Scratch Verse play by Archibald MacLeish
The Swimmers and Other Selected Poems Poetry collection by Allen Tate

The Tenants Novel by Bernard Malamud
The Testing Tree Poetry collection by Stanley Kunitz
To Stay Alive Collection of poems by Denise Levertov
Transformations Collected verse by Anne Sexton
The Wild Boys Novel by William S. Burroughs
The Will to Change: Poems, 1968–1970 Poetry collection by Adrienne Rich

Belizean

North Amerikkan Blues Collected verse of Evan X. Hyde

British

An Accidental Man Novel by Iris Murdoch
Amana Gras Collected verse of Jon Silkin
Books Do Furnish a Room Novel (part of *A Dance to the Music of Time*) by Anthony Powell
Briefing for a Descent into Hell Novel by Doris Lessing
Butley Play by Simon Gray
The Day of the Jackal Suspense thriller by Frederick Forsyth
The High Tide in the Garden Collected verse by Fleur Adcock
Maurice Novel by E. M. Forster
Mercian Hymns Collected verse by Geoffrey Hill
Moly Collected verse by Thom Gunn
Old Times Play by Harold Pinter
Vermilion Sands Science fiction short stories by J. G. Ballard

Canadian

St. Urbain's Horseman Novel by Mordecai Richler

Ghanaian

This Earth, My Brother Novel by Kofi Awoonor

Nigerian

Madmen and Scientists Play by Wole Soyinka

Saint Lucian

The Dream on Monkey Mountain Play by Derek Walcott

FRENCH

Belgian

Blindness and Insight: Essays in the Rhetoric of Contemporary Criticism Essays on literary deconstruction by Paul de Man

French

The Other One Novel by American-born writer Julien Green

GERMAN

Austrian

Malina Lyrical novel by Ingeborg Bachmann

German

Group Portrait with Lady Novel by Heinrich Böll
The Ride Across Lake Constance Play by Peter Handke

GREEK

The Sovereign Sun Collection of poems by Odysseus Elytis

HUNGARIAN

Selected Poems Collection of poems by Gyula Illyes

KANNADA

Hayavadana Play by Girish Karnad

RUSSIAN

August 1914 Novel (part of *The Red Wheel*) by Aleksandr Solzhenitsyn

SPANISH

Mexican

East Slope Collection of poems by Octavio Paz

1972

DEATHS

August Arnist, Ethiopian literary critic and scholar
Martin Boyd, Australian novelist
Jean-Jacques Bernard, French playwright
John Berryman, American poet
Dino Buzzati, Italian novelist and playwright
Cecil Day-Lewis, Irish-born English poet
Robert Faesi, Swiss poet, playwright, and short-story writer
Alfred Hutchinson, South African playwright and novelist
Kawabata Yasunari, Japanese novelist
Compton Mackenzie, English novelist
Jacques Maritain, French philosopher and essayist
Jon Mirande, Basque poet and novelist
Henry de Montherlant, French novelist and playwright
Marianne Moore, American poet
Kenneth Patchen, American poet
Ezra Loomis Pound, American poet
Jules Romains (Louis Farigoule), French novelist
Edmund Wilson, American critic

LITERARY EVENT

PRIZES AND AWARDS

Booker Prize: *G* by John Berger
Caldecott Medal: *One Fine Day* by Nonny Hagrogian
Newbery Medal: *Mrs. Frisby and the Rats of NIMH* by Robert C. O'Brien
Nobel Prize in literature: Heinrich Boll, German novelist

Pulitzer Prizes

Biography *Eleanor and Franklin* by Joseph P. Lash
Fiction *Angle of Repose* by Wallace Stegner
History *Neither Black Nor White* by Carl N. Degler
Nonfiction *Stilwell and the American Experience in China, 1911–45* by Barbara W. Tuchman
Poetry *Collected Poems* by James Wright

PUBLICATIONS

CZECH

A Summer Affair Novel by Ivan Klima

ENGLISH

American

Bless Me Ultima Novel by Rudolfo A. Anaya
Book of Folly Poetry collection by Anne Sexton
The Breast Novel by Philip Roth
Chimera Collection of short stories by John Barth
A Day Book Collection of verse and prose by Robert Creeley
End Zone Novel by Don DeLillo
Gorilla, My Love Short stories by Toni Cade Bambara
Grendel Novel by John Gardner
Museums and Women and Other Stories Collection of stories by John Updike
The Optimist's Daughter Novel by Eudora Welty
The Sunlight Dialogues Novel by John Gardner
The Sunshine Boys Play by Neil Simon
The Tooth of Crime Play by Sam Shepard
Winter Trees Collection of poems by Sylvia Plath
The Word for World's Forest Science fiction novel by Ursula K. Le Guin

Australian

The Chant of Jimmie Blacksmith Novel by Thomas Keneally

British

Collected Poems Collection by Donald Davie
Harriet Said Novel by Beryl Bainbridge
Odd Girl Out Novel by Elizabeth Jane Howard
The Odessa File Thriller by Frederick Forsyth
Pasmore Novel by David Storey
Raw Material Novel by Alan Sillitoe
Relationships Collected verse by Elizabeth Jennings

Canadian

The Manticore Second volume in *The Deptford Trilogy* by Robertson Davies

Irish

The Captains and Kings Novel by Jennifer Johnston
The Rough Field Lengthy poem by American-born writer John Montague
"Wintering Out" Poem by Seamus Heaney

Nigerian

Jero's Metamorphosis Play by Wole Soyinka
Ovonramwen Nogbaisi Play by Olawale Rotimi

FRENCH

Dissemination Philosophical inquiry by Jacques Derrida
Margins of Philosophy Philosophical inquiry by Jacques Derrida

GERMAN

Request Concert Play by Franz Xavier Kroetz
A Sorrow Beyond Dreams Novel by Peter Handke
Vorgeschichten oder schone Gegend Probstein Novel by Helga Schutz

ITALIAN

Invisible Cities Novel by Italo Calvino

SERBIAN

Earth Erect Collection of poems by Vasko Popa
This Land, This Time Four-volume novel by Dobrica Cosic

SPANISH

A Winter Journey Novel by Juan Benet

YIDDISH

Enemies: A Love Story Novel by Polish-born American writer Isaac Bashevis Singer

1973

DEATHS

Conrad Aiken, American poet
Jonas Aistis, Lithuanian poet
Wystan Hugh Auden, English poet
Ingeborg Bachmann, Austrian novelist and poet
Arna Bontemps, American novelist, essayist, and historian
Catherine Drinker Bowen, American biographer
Pearl S. Buck, American novelist
Sir Noël Coward, English playwright
Carlo Emilio Gadda, Italian novelist
William Inge, American playwright
Alessandro Manzoni, Italian novelist
Gabriel Marcel, French Catholic philosopher
Jacques Maritain, French Catholic philosopher
Nancy Mitford, English writer
Vilhem Moberg, Swedish novelist
Pablo Neruda (Neftalí Ricardo Reyes Basoalto), Chilean poet
Manuel Rojas, Chilean novelist
Avraham Shlonsky, Ukrainian-born Israeli poet
Taha Hussain, Egyptian critic and essayist
Kemal Tahir, Turkish novelist
J. R. R. Tolkien, South African–born English novelist

LITERARY EVENT

PRIZES AND AWARDS

Booker Prize: *The Siege of Krishnapur* by J. G. Farrell
Caldecott Medal: *The Funny Little Women* by Lafcadio Hearn
Newbery Medal: *Julie of the Wolves* by Jean Craighead George
Nobel Prize in literature: Patrick White (Victor Martindale), Australian novelist

Pulitzer Prizes

Biography *Luce and His Empire* by W. A. Swanberg
Drama *That Championship Season* by Jason Miller
Fiction *The Optimist's Daughter* by Eudora Welty
History *People of Paradox: An Inquiry Concerning the Origins of American Civilization* by Michael Kammen
Nonfiction *Fire in the Lake: The Vietnamese and the Americans in Vietnam* by Frances Fitzgerald and *Children of Crisis* by Robert Coles
Poetry *Up Country* by Maxine Kumin

PUBLICATIONS

ARABIC

Harrouda Bildungsroman by Moroccan writer Tahar Ben Jelloun

ENGLISH

American

Breakfast of Champions; or, Goodbye Blue Monday Novel by Kurt Vonnegut Jr.
Burr Novel by Gore Vidal
Departures Collected verse by Donald Justice
The Dogs Bark: Public People and Private Places Prose miscellany by Truman Capote
The Dolphin Sonnet sequence by Robert Lowell
Do with Me What You Will Novel by Joyce Carol Oates
Exterminator! Novel by William S. Burroughs
A Fairy Tale of New York Novel by J. P. Donleavy
Gravity's Rainbow Novel by Thomas Pynchon
The Great American Novel Novel by Philip Roth
A Hero Ain't Nothing But a Sandwich Novel by Alice Childress
In Love and Trouble Collection of short stories by Alice Walker
Sleepers Joining Hands Collection of prose and verse by Robert Bly
Sula Novel by Toni Morrison
Theophilus North Novel by Thornton Wilder
A Wind in the Door Novel by Madeleine L'Engle

Australian

The Eye of the Storm Novel by Patrick White

British

The Black Prince Novel by Iris Murdoch
Crash Science fiction novel by J. G. Ballard
Equus Play by Peter Shaffer
Frankenstein Unbound Novel by Brian Aldiss
The Honorary Counsel Novel by Graham Greene
Prancing Novelist Critical biography of the novelist Ronald Firbank (1886–1926) by Brigid Brophy
Rendezvous with Rama Science fiction novel by Arthur C. Clarke
The Riverside Villas Murder Novel by Kingsley Amis
The Summer Before the Dark Novel by Doris Lessing
Temporary Kings Novel (part of *A Dance to the Music of Time*) by Anthony Powell

Canadian

The Pegnitz Junction Novella by Mavis Gallant

Ghanaian

Two Thousand Seasons Novel by Ayi Kwei Armah

Guyanese

Son of Guyana Autobiography by Arnold Apple

Indian

Two Virgins Novel by Kamala Markandaya

Irish

The Good Fight Collected verse by Thomas Kinsella
New Poems Collected verse by Thomas Kinsella

Jamaican

The Pond Collection of verse by Mervyn Morris

Nigerian

Season of Anomy Novel by Wole Soyinka

Trinidadian

Pan Beat First novel by Marion Patrick Jones

Saint Lucian

Another Life Collected verse by Derek Walcott

FINNISH

Poems from a Voyage Across the Sound Collected verse of Paavo Haavikko

FRENCH

Belgian

The Underground Game Novel by Françoise Mallet-Joris

French

The Giants Novel by Jean-Marie Le Clezio
A Hell of a Mess Play by Eugène Ionesco
Intervalle Novel by Michel Butor
Triptych Novel by Claude Simon

GERMAN

The Human Province Commentary by Bulgarian-born English writer Elias Canetti

HEBREW

Touch the Water, Touch the Wind Novel by Israeli writer Amos Oz

ITALIAN

The Castle of Crossed Destinies Novel by Italo Calvino

JAPANESE

Box Man Novel by Abe Kobo

MAORI

Tangi Novel by New Zealand writer Witi Ihimaera

NORWEGIAN

The Silence Novel by Jens Bjorneboe

PORTUGUESE

Brazilian

Living Water Novel by Clarice Lispector

RUSSIAN

The Gulag Archipelago Novel by Aleksandr Solzhenitsyn

SPANISH

Chilean

Persona Non Grata Memoir by Jorge Edwards

Colombian

Araucaima Mansion Novel by Alvaro Mutis

Uruguayan

Death and the Little Girl Novel by Juan Carlos Onetti

SWEDISH

The Cave in the Desert Novel by Lars Gyllensten
The Night of the Tribades Play by Per Olav Enquist
Stone Bird Novel by Sven Delblanc

1974

DEATHS

Miguel Angel Asturius, Guatemalan novelist and poet
H. E. Bates, English novelist
Edmund Charles Blunden, English poet, scholar, and critic
Jaime Torres Bodet, Mexican poet and novelist
José Maria Ferreira de Castro, Portuguese novelist
Marieluise Fleisser, German Bavarian playwright
David Michael Jones, English poet
Yakup Kadri Karaosmanoglu, Turkish man of letters
Marie Luise Kaschnitz, German poet and novelist
Erich Kastner, German novelist, poet, and playwright
Par Fabian Lagerkvist, Swedish playwright, poet, and novelist
John Crowe Ransom, American poet and critic
Erich M. Roach, Trinidadian poet, playwright, and critic
Anne Sexton, American poet

LITERARY EVENT
PRIZES AND AWARDS
Booker Prize: *Holiday* by Stanley Middleton
Caldecott Medal: *Duffy and the Devil* by Harve Zemach
Newbery Medal: *The Slave Dancer* by Paula Fox
Nobel Prize in literature: Eyvind Johnson, Swedish novelist, and Harry Martinson, Swedish poet and novelist

Pulitzer Prizes

Biography *O'Neill, Son and Artist* by Louis Sheaffer
History *The Americans: Democratic Experience* by Daniel J. Boorstein
Nonfiction *The Dance of Death* by Ernest Becker
Poetry *The Dolphin* by Robert Lowell

PUBLICATIONS
ENGLISH
American

The Avenue Bearing the Initial of Christ into the New World: Poems, 1946–1964 Collected verse by Galway Kinnell
Centennial Novel by James Michener
The Coat Without a Seam Collected verse by Stanley Kunitz
Death, Sleep and the Traveler Novel by John Hawkes
The Dispossessed Science fiction novel by Ursula K. Le Guin
Fifty-Two Pickup Crime novel by Elmore Leonard
Gather Together in My Name Autobiograpy by Maya Angelou
If Beale Street Could Talk Novel by James Baldwin
Killer Angels Historical novel by Michael Joseph Shaara Jr.
The Last Days of Louisiana Red Novel by Ishmel Reed

My Life as a Man Novel by Philip Roth
Look at the Harlequins! Novel by Vladimir Nabokov
The Memory of Old Jack Novel by Wendell Berry
Pilgrim at Tinker Creek Essays on nature by Anne Dillard
The Shadow Knows Novel by Diane Johnson
The Terrible Threshold Collected verse by Stanley Kunitz
Turtle Island Collected verse and prose by Gary Sherman Snyder

British

The Clockwork Testament Novel (final volume in the *Enderby Trilogy*) by Anthony Burgess
Concrete Island Science fiction novel by J. G. Ballard
The Dogs of War Thriller by Frederick Forsyth
Ending Up Novel by Kingsley Amis
Hers Novel by Alfred Alvarez
High Windows Collected verse by Philip Larkin
Lord Rochester's Monkey, Being the Life of John Wilmot, Earl of Rochester Biography by Graham Greene
The Memoirs of a Survivor Novel by Doris Lessing
A Nip in the Air Collected verse by John Betjeman
The Sacred and Profane Love Machine Novel by Iris Murdoch
Samuel Johnson Biographical and critical study by John Wain
The Scenic Route Collected verse by Fleur Adcock
The Sleeping Lord and Other Fragments Collection of short stories by David Jones

Irish

How Many Miles to Babylon? Novel by Jennifer Johnston

Nigerian

Death and the King's Horseman Play by Wole Soyinka

Scottish

The Abbess of Crewe Novel by Muriel Spark

South African

The Conservationist Novel by Nadine Gordimer

FRENCH
Not I Short play by Irish-born writer Samuel Beckett
Retable, Reverie Two-part novel by Chantal Chawaf

GERMAN
Austrian

The Force of Habit Play by Thomas Bernhard
The Hunting Party Play by Thomas Bernhard

German

The Lost Honor of Katherine Blum Novel by Heinrich Böll

GREEK
"The Stepchildren" Poem by Odysseus Elytis

ITALIAN
History: A Novel Novel by Elsa Morante

JAPANESE
When I Whistle Novel by Shusaku Endo

NORWEGIAN
The Ferry Crossing Novel by Edvard Hoem

POLISH
Pan Cogito Collected poems by Zbigniew Herbert

RUSSIAN
Pryasliny: A Saga of Peasant Life Novel by Fedor Aleksandrovich Abramov

SPANISH
Cuban

Reasons of State Novel by Alejo Carpentier

Mexican

Vicious Circle Play by José Agustín

Paraguayan

I, the Supreme Novel by Augusto Roa Bastos

Spanish

"Dialogue of Insight" Poem by Vicente Aleixandre

Uruguayan

Time to Embrace Novel by Juan Carlos Onetti

SWEDISH
Baltics Collected verse by Tomas Transtromer
Winter Lair Novel by Sven Delblanc

1975

DEATHS
Ivo Andric, Yugoslav poet, novelist, and essayist
Rafael Arévalo Martínez, Guatemalan novelist and short-story writer
Mikhail Bakhtin, Russian philosopher
Gunnar Gunnarsson, Icelandic novelist
Julian Sorrell Huxley, English poet, essayist, and biologist
Carlo Levi, Italian Jewish novelist
Erico Lopes Verissimo, Brazilian novelist
Murilo Mendes, Brazilian poet
Pier Paolo Pasolini, Italian poet, novelist, film director
Saint-John Perse (Marie-René-Auguste-Alexis Saint-Léger Léger), French poet
Jean Stafford, American novelist
Rex Stout, English novelist
Arnold Joseph Toynbee, English historian
Lionel Trilling, American literary critic
P. G. Wodehouse, English comic novelist
Thornton Wilder, American playwright and novelist

LITERARY EVENT
PRIZES AND AWARDS
Booker Prize: *The Conservationist* by Nadine Gordimer and *Heat and Dust* by Ruth Prawer Jhabvala
Caldecott Medal: *Arrow to the Sun* by Gerald McDermott

Newbery Medal: *M. C. Higgins the Great* by Virginia Hamilton
Nobel Prize in literature: Eugenio Montale, Italian poet and essayist

Pulitzer Prizes
Biography *The Power Broker: Robert Moses and the Fall of New York* by Robert A. Caro
Drama *Seascape* by Edward Albee
History *Jefferson and His Time* by Dumas Malone
Nonfiction *The Pilgrim at Tinker Creek* by Annie Dillard
Poetry *Turtle Island* by Gary Snyder

PUBLICATIONS
ENGLISH
American

Around the Bedroom Wall: A Family Album Novel by Larry Woiwode
The Assassins Novel by Joyce Carol Oates
A Chorus Line Musical play by James Kirkwood
The Collected Stories Collection by Hortense Calisher
Consenting Adult Novel by Laura Z. Hobson
The Dead Father Novel by Donald Barthelme
Far Tortuga Novel by Peter Matthiessen
The Freeing of the Dust Collection of verse by Denise Levertov
The Great Railway Bazaar Travel narrative by Paul Theroux
The Great Train Robbery Novel by Michael Crichton
Humboldt's Gift Novel by Saul Bellow
Looking for Mr. Goodbar Novel by Judith Rossner
The Monkey Wrench Gang Play by Edward Abbey
A Month of Sundays Novel by John Updike
Or Else: Poem Collected verse by Robert Penn Warren
Ragtime Novel by E. L. Doctorow
Seascape Play by Edward Albee
Self-Portrait in a Convex Mirror Collection of verse by John Ashbery
Terms of Endearment Novel by Larry McMurtry

Australian

Shogun Novel by James Clavell

British

Hearing Secret Harmonies Final volume of *A Dance to the Music of Time* by Anthony Powell
Heat and Dust Novel by German-born Anglo-American writer Ruth Prawer Jhabvala
High Rise Science fiction novel by J. G. Ballard
No Man's Land Play by Harold Pinter
Otherwise Engaged Novel by Simon Gray
Reflections on the Newgate Calendar Historical study of executions by Reyner Heppenstall
A Word Child Novel by Iris Murdoch

Canadian

American Buffalo Two-act play by David Mamet
The World of Wonders Final volume in *The Deptford Trilogy* by Robertson Davies

Guyanese

Song of the Sugarcanes Novel by Sheikh M. Sadik

Irish

North Collected poems by Seamus Heaney
Women in the Wall Novel by Julia O'Faolain

Scottish

Docherty Novel by William McIlvanney

FRENCH
Canadian

Children of the Black Sabbath Novel by Anne Hébert

French

Roland Barthes Autobiography by Roland Barthes

GERMAN
Austrian

Correction Novel by Thomas Bernhard

Swiss

Montauk Novel by Max Frisch

ITALIAN

The Periodic Table Collection of short stories by Primo Levi

PORTUGUESE
Brazilian

Os Tambores de São Luis Novel by Josue Montello

RUSSIAN

The Life and Extraordinary Adventures of Private Ivan Chonkin Novel by Vladimir Voinovich

SERBIAN

Wolf's Salt Collected poems by Vasko Popa

SPANISH
Argentine

The Book of Sand Collection of short stories by Jorge Luis Borges

Colombian

The Autumn of the Patriarch Novel by Gabriel García Márquez

SWEDISH

The Castrati Novel by Sven Delblanc

1976

DEATHS

Marguerite Taos Amrouche, Algerian writer
Jens Bjorneboe, Norwegian novelist, poet, and playwright
Dame Agatha Christie, English writer of detective fiction
Martín Luis Guzmán, Mexican novelist
Martin Heidegger, German existentialist philosopher
Eyvind Johnson, Swedish novelist
Pierre-Jean Jouve, French poet, novelist, essayist, and playwright

Alexander Lernet-Holenia, Austrian novelist
José Lezama Lima, Cuban poet and novelist
André Malraux, French novelist and cultural historian
James Philip McAuley, Australian poet and critic
Paul Morand, French novelist
Samuel Eliot Morison, American historian
Raymond Queneau, French novelist, poet, playwright, and essayist
José Revueltas, Mexican novelist and short-story writer
William Sansom, English novelist
Josef Wifflin, Polish essayist, novelist, and poet

LITERARY EVENT
PRIZES AND AWARDS
Booker Prize: *Saville* by David Storey
Caldecott Medal: *Why Mosquitoes Buzz in People's Ears* Retold by Verna Aardema
Newbery Medal: *The Grey King* by Susan Cooper
Nobel Prize in literature: Saul Bellow, American novelist

Pulitzer Prizes

Biography   *Edith Wharton: A Biography* by R. W. B. Lewis
Drama   *A Chorus Line* by Michael Bennet, James Kirkwood, Nicholas Dante, Marvin Hamlisch, and Edward Kleban
Fiction   *Humboldt's Gift* by Saul Bellow
History   *Larry of Santa Fe* by Paul Horgan
Nonfiction   *Why Survive? Being Old in America* by Robert N. Butler
Poetry   *Self-Portrait in a Convex Mirror* by John Ashbery

PUBLICATIONS
DANISH
The Tower at the End of the World Novel by William Heinesen

FLEMISH
A Day on the Ground Novel by Paul de Wispelaere

ENGLISH
American

Adult Bookstore Collected verse by Karl Shapiro
Bloodshed and Three Novellas Collected short stories of Cynthia Ozick
California Suite Play by Neil Simon
Childworld Novel by Joyce Carol Oates
The Coup Novel by John Updike
The Devil Finds Work Essay by James Baldwin
1876 Novel by Gore Vidal
The Franchiser Novel by Stanley Elkin
Geography III Poetry collection by Elizabeth Bishop
The Gin Game Play by D. L. Coburn
Heart of Aztlan Novel by Rudolfo A. Anaya
Marry Me: A Romance Novel by John Updike
Meridian Novel by Alice Walker
New and Collected Poems Collection by Archibald MacLeish
October Light Novel by John Gardner
Ratner's Star Novel by Don DeLillo
Roots: The Saga of an American Family Autobiographical narrative by Alex Haley

Singin' and Swingin' and Gettin' Merry Like Christmas Autobiographical narrative by Maya Angelou
The Spectator Bird Novel by Wallace Stegner
Speedboat Novel by Renata Adler
Swag Crime novel by Elmore Leonard
Travesty Novel by John Hawkes
The Western Approaches: Poems, 1973–1975 Collected poems by Howard Nemerov
Will You Please Be Quiet, Please? Collected stories of Raymond Carver
The Zodiac Collected verse by James Dickey

Australian

Shabbytown Calendar Collection of poems by Thomas William Shapcott

British

Dirty Linen Play by Tom Stoppard
Henry and Cato Novel by Iris Murdoch
Sadler's Birthday Novel by Rose Tremain
Saville Novel by David Storey
Sleep It Off Lady Collection of short stories by Jean Rhys
A Stitch in Time Children's story by Penelope Lively

Irish

Doctor Copernicus Historical novel by John Banville

South African

A Season in Paradise Novel by Jan Blom Breytenbach

Saint Lucian

Sea Grapes Collection of poems by Derek Walcott

FRENCH

Belgian

Allegra Novel by Françoise Mallet-Joris

French

Rules of the Game Autobiography by Michel-Julien Leiris
Topography of a Phantom City Novel by Alain Robbe-Grillet

Moroccan

Chronicle of Loneliness Novel by Tahar Ben Jelloun

GERMAN

The Left-Handed Woman Novel by Peter Handke

JAPANESE

Almost Transparent Blue Novella by Ryu Murakami
Pinch Runner's Record Novel by Kenzaburo Oe
The Promontory Novella by Kenji Nakagami

PORTUGUESE

Brazilian

The Queen of the Grecian Jails Novel by Osman Lins

SPANISH

Argentine

Kiss of the Spider Woman Novel by Manuel Puig

Spanish

The Maravillas District Novel by Rosa Chacel

SWEDISH

The Town Gate Novel by Sven Delblanc

1977

DEATHS

Aying, Chinese historian and critic
James M. Cain, American novelist
Edward Dahlberg, American novelist and poet
William Alexander Gerhardie, English critic, novelist, and biographer
James Jones, American novelist
MacKinlay Kantor, American novelist
Clarice Lispector, Ukrainian-born Brazilian novelist
Robert Lowell Jr., American poet
Vladimir Vladimirovich Nabokov, Russian-born American novelist
Anaïs Nin, French-born American novelist and critic
Sir Terence Rattigan, English playwright
Mark Schorer, American literary scholar and critic
Louis Untermeyer, American poet and literary critic
Yates Wheatley, English novelist
Henry Williamson, English novelist
Cecil Blanche Fitzgerald Woodham-Smith, English historian
Carl Zuckmayer, German playwright

LITERARY EVENT

PRIZES AND AWARDS

Booker Prize: *Staying On* by Paul Scott
Caldecott Medal: *Ashanti to Zulu* by Margaret Musgrove
Newbery Medal: *Roll of Thunder, Hear My Cry* by Mildred D. Taylor
Nobel Prize in literature: Vicente Aleixandre, Spanish poet

Pulitzer Prizes

Biography   *A Prince of Our Disorder: The Life of T. E. Lawrence* by John E. Mack
Drama   *The Shadow Box* by Michael Cristofer
History   *The Impending Crisis* by David M. Potter
Nonfiction   *Beautiful Swimmers* by William W. Warner
Poetry   *Divine Comedies* by James Merrill

PUBLICATIONS

ALBANIAN

The Great Winter Novel by Ismail Kadare

ENGLISH

American

Adultery and Other Choices Collected stories by André Dubus
A Book of Common Prayer Novel by Joan Didion
Chapter Two Play by Neil Simon
The Collected Poems Collection by Howard Nemerov

The Compass Flower Collected verse by W. S. Merwin
Day by Day Collection of autobiographical verse by Robert Lowell
The Destinies of Darcy Dancer, Gentleman Novel by Irish-American writer J. P. Donleavy
Duplications Epic poem by Kenneth Koch
Evidence of Love Novel by Shirley Ann Grau
Falconer Novel by John Cheever
How to Save Your Own Life Novel by Erica Jong
A Life in the Theater Play by David Mamet
The Public Burning Novel by Robert Coover
A Place to Come To Novel by Robert Penn Warren
The Professor of Desire Novel by Philip Roth
Song of Solomon Novel by Toni Morrison
True Confessions Novel by John Gregory Dunne

British

The Danger Tree Novel by Olivia Manning
Daniel Martin Novel by John Fowles
Every Good Day Deserves Favor Play by Tom Stoppard
The Honorable Schoolboy Spy novel by John le Carré
Inquiry Time Novel by Beryl Bainbridge
Samuel Johnson Biography by Walter Jackson Bate
The Silmarillion Novel by J. R. R. Tolkien
Some Unease and Angels Collection of essays and poems by Elaine Feinstein
Staying On Last novel by Paul Mark Scott

Canadian

Close to the Sun Again Novel by Morley Callaghan

Guyanese

De Silva Novel by Theodore Wilson Harris

Indian

Golden Honeycomb Novel by Kamala Markandaya

Irish

Shadows on Our Skin Novel by Jennifer Johnston

Scottish

Implements in their Places Collection of verse by William Sydney Graham

South African

The Confessions of Josef Baisz Novel by Dan Jacobson
From the Heart of the Country Novel by J. M. Coetzee

Welsh

The Way of If Collected poems by R. S. Thomas

FRENCH

French

The Living and Their Shadows Antinovel by Jacques Lacretelle

Tunisian

The Desert Novel by Albert Memmi

GERMAN

Mozart Biography by Wolfgang Hildesheimer
The Flounder Novel by Günter Grass

ITALIAN

Candido: or a Dream Dreamed in Sicily Novel by Leonardo Sciascia

JAPANESE

The Dirge of the Meridian Play by Kinoshita Junji

NORWEGIAN

Portland Valley Novel by Kjartan Flogstad

PORTUGUESE

Brazilian

The Hour of the Star Novel by Clarice Lispector

SPANISH

Peruvian

Aunt Julia and the Scriptwriter Comic autobiographical novel by Mario Vargas Llosa

1978

DEATHS

James Gould Cozzens, American novelist
Gontran Damas, Guyanese poet, novelist, and essayist
Janet Flanner, American journalist and novelist
Albert Gomes, Trinidadian poet and novelist
Guo Maruo, Chinese writer
F. R. Leavis, English literary critic
Osman Lins, Brazilian novelist
Hugh MacDiarmid (Christopher Murray Grieve), Scottish poet and essayist
Harry Martinson, Swedish poet and novelist
Margaret Mead, American anthropologist
Paul Mark Scott, English novelist
Ignacio Silone, Italian novelist
Sylvia Townsend Warner, English biographer and novelist

LITERARY EVENT

PRIZES AND AWARDS

Booker Prize: *The Sea, the Sea* by Iris Murdoch
Caldecott Medal: *Noah's Ark* by Peter Spier
Newbery Medal: *Bridge to Terabithia* by Katherine Peterson
Nobel Prize in literature: Isaac Bashevis Singer, Polish-born American novelist

Pulitzer Prizes

Biography *Samuel Johnson* by W. Jackson Bate
Drama *The Gin Game* by Donald L. Coburn
Fiction *Elbow Room* by James Alan McPherson
History *The Visible Hand: The Managerial Revolution in American Business* by Alfred D. Chandler Jr.
Nonfiction *The Dragons of Eden* by Carl Sagan
Poetry *Collected Poems* by Howard Nemerov

PUBLICATIONS

ENGLISH

American

Blood Ties Novel by Mary Lee Settle
Brothers, I Love You All Collected verse by Hayden Carruth
Buried Child Play by Sam Shepard
Chesapeake Novel by James A. Michener
A Distant Mirror: The Calamitious Fourteenth Century History by Barbara Tuchman
Final Payments Novel by Mary Gordon
Hello: A Journal Poetry collection by Robert Creeley
Hello, Darkness: The Collected Poems of L. E. Sussman Collection by L. E. Sussman
The Lincoln Relics Collected verse by Stanley Kunitz
Lying Low Novel by Diane Johnson
The Retrieval System Collected verse by Maxine Kumin
Samuel Johnson Biography by Jackson Bate
Son of the Morning Novel by Joyce Carol Oates
The Stories of John Cheever Collection by John Cheever
A Swiftly Tilting Planet Novel by Madeleine L'Engle
The Switch Novel by Elmore Leonard
The Veritable Years Collected verse by William Everson
The World According to Garp Novel by John Irving

British

The Battle Lost and Won Novel by Olivia Manning
Betrayal Play by Harold Pinter
Collected Stories Collection by Doris Lessing
The Human Factor Novel by Graham Greene
The Jake's Thing Novel by Kingsley Amis
Letters to Sister Benedicta Novel by Rose Tremain
Night and Day Play by Tom Stoppard
Russian Thinkers Collection of biographical essays by Isaiah Berlin
The Sea, the Sea Novel by Iris Murdoch
The Singapore Grip Novel by James Gordon Farrell
The Virgin in the Garden Novel by A. S. Byatt

Canadian

The Splits Play by Erika Ritter
Tribute Play by Bernard Slade

Irish

Lovers of Their Time Novel by William Trevor

New Zealand

Plumb Novel by Maurice Green

Nigerian

The Slave Novel by Elechi Amadi

Scottish

A Would-Be Saint Novel by John Robin Jenkins

South African

Stubborn Hope: New Poems and Selections from China Poems and Strains Collection by Dennis Brutus

Welsh

Frequencies Poetry by R. S. Thomas

FRENCH

A Regicide Novel by Alain Robbe-Grillet

GEORGIAN

Sandro of Chegem Novel by Fazil Iskander

GREEK

Maria Nefeli Long poem by Odysseus Elytis

ITALIAN

At the Fire of Controversy Collection of poems by Mario Luzi

JAPANESE

The Sky of September Novel by Michitsuna Takahashi
To the Aegean Sea Novella by Masuo Ikeda

POLISH

Bells in Winter Collection of poems by Czesław Milosz

RUSSIAN

The First Circle Novel by Aleksandr Solzhenitsyn
The Old Man Novel by Yuri Trifonov

SPANISH

Mexican

The Hydra Head Novel by Carlos Fuentes

SWEDISH

The March of the Musicians Novel by Per Olov Enquist

YIDDISH

Shosha Novel by Polish-born American writer Isaac Bashevis Singer

1979

DEATHS

Elizabeth Bishop, American poet
Johan Borgen, Norwegian novelist, playwright, and essayist
James Gordon Farrell, English novelist
James T. Farrell, American novelist
Juana de Ibarbourou, Uruguyan poet
Tommaso Landolfi, Italian novelist, poet, and playwright
Nicholas John Turney Monsarrat, English novelist
S. J. Perelman, American humorist
Jean Rhys (Ella Gwendolen Rees Williams), Dominica-born English novelist
I. A. Richards, English literary critic and scholar
Allen Tate, American poet and critic
Nikolay Semyonovich Tikhonov, Russian poet
Mika Waltari, Finnish novelist
Antonia White, English novelist

LITERARY EVENT

PRIZES AND AWARDS

Booker Prize: *Offshore* by Penelope Fitzgerald
Caldecott Medal: *The Girl Who Loved Wild Horses* by Paul Goble

Newbery Medal: *The Westing Game* by Ellen Raskin
Nobel Prize in literature: Odysseus Elytis, Greek poet

Pulitzer Prizes

Biography *Days of Sorrow and Pain: Leo Baeck and the Berlin Jews* by Leonard Baker
Drama *Buried Child* by Sam Shephard
Fiction *The Stories of John Cheever* by John Cheever
History *The Dred Scott Case* by Don E. Fehrenbacher
Nonfiction *On Human Nature* by Edward O. Wilson
Poetry *Now and Then: Poems, 1976–78* by Robert Penn Warren

PUBLICATIONS

CZECH

The Book of Laughter and Forgetting Novel by Milan Kundera

ENGLISH

American

Ashes and 7 Years from Somewhere Collected verse by Philip Levine
Birdy Novel by William Wharton
The Burning Mystery of Anna in 1951 Prose poem by Kenneth Koch
Cannibals and Missionaries Novel by Mary McCarthy
Crimes of the Heart Play by Beth Henley
The Drowning Season Novel by Alice Hoffman
The Executioner's Song Novel by Norman Mailer
The Ghost Writer Novel by Philip Roth
Jailbird Novel by Kurt Vonnegut Jr.
Legends of the Fall Three novellas by Jim Harrison
The Living End Novel by Stanley Elkin
Mulligan Stew Novel by Gilbert Sorrentino
The Old Patagonian Express: By Train Through the Americas Travel account by Paul Theroux
The Passion Artist Novel by John Hawkes
The Poems of Stanley Kunitz Collected verse by Stanley Kunitz
Rushes Novel by John Rechy
Schultz Novel by Irish-American writer J. P. Donleavy
Sophie's Choice Novel by William Styron
Talley's Folly Play by Lanford Wilson
Too Far to Go: The Maples Stories Short-story collection by John Updike
The White Album Novel by Joan Didion
The Year of the French Novel by Thomas Flanagan

Australian

The Confederates Novel by Thomas Keneally
The Twyborn Affair Novel by Patrick White

British

Amadeus Play by Peter Schaffer
Canopus in Argus: Archives Cycle of novels by Doris Lessing
The Flute Player Novel by D. M. Thomas
The Fountains of Paradise Science fiction novel by Arthur C. Clarke
The Inner Harbor Collected verse by Fleur Adcock
Lies and Secrets Collected verse by John Fuller
The Mangan Inheritance Novel by Brian Moore

Moments of Grace Collected verse by Elizabeth Jennings
Pig Earth Collection of poems, stories, and essays by John Berger
Remains of Elmet Collected verse, prose narrative, and photographs by Ted Hughes
Territorial Rights Novel by Muriel Spark

Irish

Field Work Collected verse of Seamus Heaney
The Old Jest Novel by Jennifer Johnston
One and Other Poems Collected verse by Thomas Kinsella

Nigerian

The Joys of Motherhood Novel by Florence Onye Buchi Emecheta

Saint Lucian

The Star-Apple Kingdom Collected verse by Derek Walcott

Trinidadian

A Bend in the River Novel by V. S. Naipaul
North of South: An African Journey Narrative by V. S. Naipaul

South African

Burger's Daughter Novel by Nadine Gordimer
Collected Poems Collected verse of E. T. Prince

FLEMISH

Between Garden and World Novel by Paul de Wispelaere

FRENCH

Algerian

1,001 Years of Nostalgia Novel by Rachid Boudjedra

Belgian

King Dickie Novel by Françoise Mallet-Joris

French

Le Rendez-vous Novel by Alain Robbe-Grillet

GERMAN

German

The Sinking of the Titanic Poem of 36 cantos by Hans Magnus Enzensberger
The Meeting at Telgte Novel by Günter Grass

Swiss

Yet Another Wish Novel by Adolf Muschg

HEBREW

Autumn Music Collected verse by Israeli poet Gabriel Preil
Badenheim 1939 Novel by Romanian-born Israeli writer Aharon Appelfeld

ITALIAN

If on a Winter's Night a Traveler Novel by Italo Calvino

JAPANESE

Coeval Games Novel by Kenzaburo Oe
Hear the Wind Novel by Haruki Murakami

1980

DEATHS

Roland Barthes, French critic
María Luisa Bomba, Chilean novelist and short-story writer
Alejo Carpentier, Cuban novelist
Marc Connelly, American playwright
Romain Gary, French novelist
Robert Hayden, American poet
Jaroslaw Iwaszkiewicz, Polish poet, novelist, and playwright
Camara Laye, Guinean novelist
Olivia Manning, English novelist
David Mercer, English playwright
Henry Miller, American novelist and playwright
Katherine Anne Porter, American short-story writer and novelist
Muriel Rukeyser, American poet
Bernardo Santareno (António Martinho do Rosário), Portuguese playwright
Jean-Paul Sartre, French novelist
C. P. Snow, English novelist
Benjamin Travers, English novelist and playwright
Kenneth Tynan, English dramatic critic
Giuseppe Ungaretti, Italian poet
Agustín Yáñez, Mexican novelist and short-story writer

LITERARY EVENT

PRIZES AND AWARDS

Booker Prize: *Rites of Passage* by William Golding
Caldecott Medal: *Ox-Cart Man* by Donald Hall
Newbery Medal: *A Gathering of Days* by Joan W. Blos
Nobel Prize in literature: Czesław Milosz, Polish poet and novelist

Pulitzer Prizes

Biography *The Rise of Theodore Roosevelt* by Edmund Morris
Drama *Talley's Folly* by Lanford Wilson
Fiction *The Executioner's Song* by Norman Mailer
History *Been in the Storm So Long* by Leon F. Litwack
Nonfiction *Godel, Escher, Bach: An Eternal Golden Braid* by Douglas R. Hofstadter
Poetry *Selected Poems* by Ronald Justice

PUBLICATIONS

CHINESE

Leaden Wings Novel by Zhang Jie

DUTCH

Rituals Novel by Cees Nooteboom

ENGLISH

American

Angel Landing Novel by Alice Hoffman
Bellefleur Novel by Joyce Carol Oates
Collected Stories Collection by Eudora Welty
Division Street Play by Steve Tesich
Falling in Place Novel by Ann Beattie

Fanny: Being the True History of the Adventures of Fanny Hackabout-Jones Novel by Erica Jong
How German Is It? Novel of postwar Germany by Walter Abish
I Ought to Be in Pictures Play by Neil Simon
Loon Lake Novel by E. L. Doctorow
Music for Chameleons: New Writings Miscellaneous collection by Truman Capote
The Number of the Beast Science fiction novel by Robert A. Heinlein
Peace Breaks Out Novel (companion to *A Separate Peace*) by John Knowles
The Second Coming Novel by Walker Percy
Sunrise Collected verse by Frederick Seidel
The Transit of Venus Novel by Shirley Hazard
Vida Novel by Marge Piercy

British

Earthly Powers Novel by Anthony Burgess
How Far You Can Go? Novel by David Lodge
The Illusionists Collection of poems by John Fuller
The Reign of Sparrows Collected verse by Roy Fuller
Rites of Passage Novel by William Golding
Setting the World on Fire Novel by Angus Wilson
Smiley's People Spy novel by John le Carré
The Sum of Things Novel by Olivia Manning
Victorian Voices Collected verse by Anthony Thwaite

Indian

Light of Day Novel by Anita Desai

Irish

Constantly Singing Poetry collection by James Simmons
In Her Own Image Poetry collection by Eavan Boland
No Country for Young Men Novel by English-born writer Julia O'Faolain
Translations Play by Brian Friel

Malaysian

No Man's Grove Collected verse by Shirley Lim

South African

A Soldier's Embrace Collected short stories by Nadine Gordimer
Waiting for the Barbarians Novel by J. M. Coetzee

FRENCH

Desert Novel by Jean-Marie Le Clezio

INDONESIAN

A Child of All Nations Novel by Pramudya Ananta Tur
This Earth of Mankind Novel by Pramudya Ananta Tur

ITALIAN

The Name of the Rose Novel by Umberto Eco

JAPANESE

The Samurai Novel by Shusaku Endo

RUSSIAN

The Burn Novel by Vasily Pavlovich Aksyonov

SPANISH

Mexican

Distant Relations Novel by Carlos Fuentes
Signals from the Flames Novel by José Emilio Pacheco

1981

DEATHS

Nelson Algren, American novelist
Enid Bagnold, English novelist
Gwendolyn B. Bennett, African-American poet and essayist
Paddy Chayefsky, American playwright
A. J. Cronin, Scottish novelist
David Garnett, English novelist and critic
John Glassco, Canadian poet and novelist
Pamela Hansford Johnson, English novelist
Abbé Alexis Kagame, Rwandan poet and historian
Miroslav Krleza, Croatian novelist
Mao Dun, Chinese novelist
Eugenio Montale, Italian poet and critic
János Pilinszky, Hungarian poet
William Saroyan, Armenian-American playwright and novelist
Yaakov Shabtai, Israeli novelist and playwright
Yuri Valentinovich Trifonov, Russian novelist
Alec Waugh, English novelist
Dame Frances Amelia Yates, English literary scholar

LITERARY EVENT

PRIZES AND AWARDS

Booker Prize: *Midnight's Children* by Salman Rushdie
Caldecott Medal: *Fables* by Arnold Lobel
Newbery Medal: *Jacob Have I Loved* by Katherine Paterson
Nobel Prize in literature: Elias Canetti, Bulgarian-born German novelist
PEN/Faulkner Award: *How German Is It?* by Walter Abish

Pulitzer Prizes

Biography *Peter the Great: His Life and World* by Robert K. Massie
Drama *Crimes of the Heart* by Beth Henley
Fiction *A Confederacy of Dunces* by John Kennedy Toole
History *American Education: The National Experience, 1783–1876* by Lawrence A. Cremin
Nonfiction *Fin-de-Siècle Vienna: Politics and Culture* by Carl E. Schorske
Poetry *The Morning of the Poem* by James Schuyler

PUBLICATIONS

ALBANIAN

The Palace of Dreams Novel by Ismail Kadare

CZECH

Jacques and His Master Play by Milan Kundera

DUTCH

A Song of Truth and Semblance Novel by Cees Noteboom

ENGLISH

American

A Coast of Trees Collected verse by A. R. Ammons
Creation Novel by Gore Vidal
The Heart of a Woman Autobiographical narrative by Maya Angelou
The Hotel New Hampshire Novel by John Irving
The Medusa and the Snail Essays on science by Lewis Thomas
Midnight Mass Novel by Paul Bowles
The Need to Hold Still Poetry collection by Lisel Muller
Plains Song Novel by Wright Morris
Poppa John Novel by Larry Woiwode
Rabbit Is Rich Novel by John Updike
A Soldier's Play Novel by Charles Fuller
Tar Baby Novel by Toni Morrison
True West Novel by David Shepard
Weep Not for Me Play by Gus Edwards
Zuckerman Unbound Novel by Philip Roth

Australian

Flaws in the Glass: A Self-Portrait Autobiography by Patrick White

British

Church Poems Collection by John Betjeman
The Cupboard Novel by Rose Tremain
Restoration Play by Edward Bond
The White Hotel Novel by D. M. Thomas

Canadian

The Chinese Insomniacs Collected verse by Josephine Jacobsen
Europe and Other Bad News Poetry collection by Irving Layton
The Rebel Angel Novel by Robertson Davies

Indian

Midnight's Children Novel by Salman Rushdie

Irish

The Christmas Tree Novel by Jennifer Johnston

Saint Lucian

The Fortunate Traveler Poems by Derek Walcott

Scottish

Lanark: A Life in Four Books First novel by Alasdair Gray

South African

July's People Novel by Nadine Gordimer

Welsh

Between Here and Now Poetry collection by R. S. Thomas

FRENCH

Djinn Novel by Alain Robbe-Grillet
Venice in Winter Novel by Emmanuel Robles

HUNGARIAN

Wings of Knives and Nails Collected poems by Sandor Csoori

JAPANESE

Hiroshima Novel by Minoru Oda

The Island of Crimea Novel by Vasily Pavlovich Aksyonov

SPANISH
Colombian

The Chronicle of a Death Foretold Novel by Gabriel García Márquez

1982

DEATHS

Djuna Barnes, American writer
Agusti Bartra, Catalan novelist and playwright
John Cheever, American novelist
Babette Deutsch, American poet and essayist
Resat Enis, Turkish novelist
John Gardner, American novelist
Geoffrey Langdon Hughes, English scholar
Richard Franklin Hugo, American poet and essayist
Eduardo Mallea, Argentine novelist
Archibald MacLeish, American poet
Dame Ngaio Marsh, New Zealand novelist
Georges Perec, French novelist
Ayn Rand, Russian-born American novelist
Kenneth Rexroth, American poet
Edgell Rickword, English poet and critic
Ramón Sender, Spanish-born American novelist, playwright, and poet
Frank Swinnerton, English novelist
Peter Ulrich Weiss, German-born Swedish playwright, novelist, and essayist

LITERARY EVENT
PRIZES AND AWARDS
Booker Prize: *Schindler's Ark* by Thomas Keneally
Caldecott Medal: *Jumanji* by Chris Van Allsburg
Newbery Medal: *A Visit to William Blake's Inn: Poems for Innocent and Inexperienced Travelers* by Nancy Willard
Nobel Prize in literature: Gabriel García Márquez, Colombian novelist
PEN/Faulkner Award: *The Chaneysville Incident* by David Bradley

Pulitzer Prizes

Biography   *Grant: A Biography* by William S. McFeeley
Drama   *A Soldier's Play* by Charles Fuller
Fiction   *Rabbit Is Rich* by John Updike
History   *Mary Chestnut's Civil War* edited by C. Van Woodward
Nonfiction   *The Soul of a New Machine* by Tracy Kidder
Poetry   *The Collected Poems* by Sylvia Plath

PUBLICATIONS
ALBANIAN
Broken April Novel by Ismail Kadare

CHINESE
The Wreath at the Foot of the Mountain Novel by Li Cunbao

DUTCH
The Assault Novel by Harry Mulisch

ENGLISH
American

Antarctic Traveler Poetry collection by Katha Pollitt
Bech Is Back Novel by John Updike
Bronx Primitive: Portraits in a Childhood Memoir by Kate Simon
The Burning House Collection of short stories by Ann Beattie
Cadillac Jack Novel by Larry McMurtry
Circles in the Water: Selected Poems Collected verse of Marge Piercy
The Color Purple Novel by Alice Walker
The Dean's December Novel by Saul Bellow
Dutch Shea, Jr. Novel by John Gregory Dunne
Friday Science fiction novel by Robert Heinlein
George Mills Novel by Stanley Elkin
God's Grace Novel by Bernard Malamud
Growing Up Autobiography by journalist Russell Baker
Life Supports: New and Collected Poems Collection by William Bronk
'Night, Mother Play by Marsha Norman
Oh What a Paradise It Seems Novel by John Cheever
Our Ground Time Here Will Be Brief Poetry collection by Maxine Kumin
Selected Poems Collected verse of Galway Kinnell
So Long, See You Tomorrow Novel by William Maxwell
The Terrible Twos Novel by Ishmael Reed
Virginie: Her Two Lives Novel by John Hawkes
The Women of Brewster Place Novel by Gloria Naylor

Australian

Schindler's Ark Novel by Thomas Keneally

British

Another Country Play by Julian Mitchell
An Englishman Abroad Screenplay by Alan Bennett
Getting It Right Novel by Elizabeth Jane Howard
Mantissa Novel by John Fowles
Monsignor Quixote Novel by Graham Greene
The Noël Coward Diaries Memoirs of Noël Coward
The Occasion of Poetry: Essays in Criticism and Autobiography Collection by Thom Gunn
The Real Thing Play by Tom Stoppard
The Survivors Novel by Elaine Feinstein
2010 Odyssey Two Science fiction novel by Arthur C. Clarke
Uncollected Poems Collection by John Betjeman

Canadian

Man Descending Collection of short stories by Guy Vanderhaeghe
The Prinzhorn Collection Collected verse by Dean Coles
Shoeless Joe Novel by William Patrick Kinsella

Irish

The Obedient Wife Novel by Julia O'Faolain

Trinidadian

The Wine of Astonishment Novel by Earl Lovelace

FLEMISH
I Have No Home Now Novel by Paul de Wispelaere

FRENCH
Canadian

In the Shadow of the Wind Novel by Anne Hébert

French

The Ear of the Other Philosophical inquiry by Jacques Derrida

GERMAN
German

The Spectacle at the Tower Novel by Gert Hoffmann

Swiss

The Ballad of Typhoid Mary Novel by Jurg F. Federspiel
Bluebeard: A Tale Short novel by Max Frisch

ITALIAN
If Not Now, When? Novel by Primo Levi

JAPANESE
Tomorrow Novel by Mitusaki Inoue
A Wild Sheep Chase Novel by Haruki Murakami

NORWEGIAN
Lillelord Trilogy of novels by Johan Bergen

RUSSIAN
A Dove in Santiago: A Novella in Verse Poem by Yevgeny Yevtushenko

SPANISH
Chilean

The House of the Spirits First novel by Isabel Allende

Cuban

Farewell to the Sea: A Novel of Cuba First novel by Reinaldo Arenas
Heroes Are Grazing in My Garden Novel by Herberto Padilla

Mexican

Deserted Cities Novel by José Agustín

Nicaraguan

Flowers from the Volcano Collected poems by Claribel Alegría

Spanish

The Dream of Sarajevo Novel by Carlos Rojas

YIDDISH
Collected Stories Collection by Polish-born American writer Isaac Bashevis Singer

1983

DEATHS
Fedor Aleksandrovich Abramov, Russian novelist
Jerzy Andrzejewski, Polish novelist

Paul De Man, Belgian literary critic
Owen Dodson, African-American poet and playwright
Kristmann Gudmundsson, Icelandic novelist
Eric Hoffer, American folk philosopher
Frances Hooker Horowitz, English poet
Mordecai Menahem Kaplan, Lithuanian-born American Jewish philosopher and scholar
Kobayashi Hideo, Japanese critic
Arthur Koestler, Hungarian-born English novelist, essayist, and philosopher
Ross MacDonald, American mystery writer
Vladimir Neff, Czech novelist
Mary Renault, English novelist
Merce Rodoreda, Catalan novelist
Manuel Scorza, Peruvian novelist and poet
Vittorio Sereni, Italian poet
Christina Stead, Australian novelist
Yves Theriault, French-Canadian novelist
Dame Rebecca West, Irish-born English novelist
Tennessee Williams, American playwright

LITERARY EVENT
PRIZES AND AWARDS
Booker Prize: *Life and Times of Michael K.* J. M. Coetzee
Caldecott Medal: *Shadow* by Blaise Cendrars
Newbery Medal: *Dicey's Song* by Cynthia Voigt
Nobel Prize in literature: William Gerald Golding, English novelist
PEN/Faulkner Award: *Seaview* by Toby Olson

Pulitzer Prizes

Biography *Growing Up* by Russell Baker
Drama *'Night Mother* by Marsha Norman
Fiction *The Color Purple* by Alice Walker
History *The Transformation of Virginia 1740–1790* by Rhys L. Isaac
Nonfiction *Is There No Place on Earth for Me?* by Susan Sheehan
Poetry *Selected Poems* by Galway Kinnell

PUBLICATIONS
ENGLISH
American

American Primitive Poetry collection by Mary Oliver
The Anatomy Lesson Novel (final volume of the Zuckerman trilogy) by Philip Roth
Ancient Evenings Fantasy by Norman Mailer
The Cannibal Galaxy Novel by Cynthia Ozick
Changing Light at Sandover Poetry collection by James Merrill
Country Music: Selected Early Poems by Charles Wright
Duluth Novel by Gore Vidal
Fool for Love Play by Sam Shepard
Ironweed Novel by William Kennedy
Moon Deluxe Collected short stories of Frederick Barthelme
Praisesong for the Widow Novel by Paule Marshall
Shaker, Why Don't You Sing? Poetry collection by Maya Angelou
Stick Crime novel by Elmore Leonard

Australian

Miss Peabody's Inheritance Novel by Elizabeth Jolley
Mr. Scobie's Riddle Novel by Elizabeth Jolley

British

Act of Darkness Novel by Swiss-born writer Francis King
The End of the World Novel by Anthony Burgess
Flying to Nowhere Novel by John Fuller
The Little Drummer Girl Thriller by John le Carré
Londoners Novel by Maureen Duffy
Mystery of the Charity of Charles Péguy Poem by Geoffrey Hill
A Personal History Autobiographical narrative by historian A. J. P. Taylor
Rates of Exchange Novel by Malcolm Stanley Bradbury

Indian

Shalimar Novel by Kamala Markandaya
A Tiger for Malgudi Novel by R. K. Narayan

Irish

The Dead Kingdom Poetic cycle by American-born John Montague

New Zealand

The Bone People Novel by Keri Hulme

South African

Life and Times of Michael K. Novel by J. M. Coetzee

Welsh

Burning Brambles: Selected Poems, 1944–1979 Collected verse of Roland Glyn Mathias

FRENCH

Belgian

The Angel's Wink Novel by Françoise Mallet-Joris

GERMAN

Winner Takes All Novel by Dieter Wellershof

HEBREW

Tzili: the Story of a Life Novel by Aharon Appelfeld

HUNGARIAN

Memory of Snow Collected verse by Sandor Csoori

ITALIAN

All the Poems Collected verse by Giorgio Caproni

JAPANESE

Rise Up, O Young Men of the New Age Collection of short stories by Kenzaburo Oe

PORTUGUESE

Brazilian

The Friar Collected verse of José Cabral de Melo Neto

SPANISH

Chilean

Widows Novel by Ariel Dorfman

Spanish

Mazurka for Two Dead People Novel by Camilo José Cela

YIDDISH

The Penitent Novel by Polish-born American writer Isaac Bashevis Singer

1984

DEATHS

Jorge Andrade, Brazilian playwright
Vicente Aleixandre, Spanish poet
Sylvia Ashton-Warner, New Zealand poet and novelist
Justin Brooks Atkinson, American drama critic
John Betjeman, English poet
Truman Capote, American writer
Julio Cortázar, Belgian-born Argentine novelist
William Empson, English literary critic
Jorge Guillén, Spanish poet and essayist
Lillian Hellman, American playwright
Uwe Johnson, German novelist
William Denis Johnston, Irish playwright and critic
Richmond Alexander Lattimore, American literary scholar, poet, and translator
Henri Michaux, Belgian-born French poet
Manuel Mujica Lainez, Argentine writer
Liam O'Flaherty, Irish novelist
John Boynton Priestley, English novelist, poet, and playwright
Gwendolyn Ringwood, American-born Canadian playwright, novelist, poet, and essayist
Savako Arevalo, Japanese novelist and playwright
Irwin Shaw, American novelist and playwright
Viktor Borisovich Shklovsky, Russian novelist
Mikhail Aleksandrovich Sholokhov, Russian novelist
Jesse Hilton Stuart, American poet and novelist

LITERARY EVENT

PRIZES AND AWARDS

Booker Prize: *Hotel du Lac* by Anita Brookner
Caldecott Medal: *The Glorious Flight: Across the Channel with Louis Bleriot* by Alice Provensen and Martin Provensen
Newbery Medal: *Dear Mr. Henshaw* by Beverly Cleary
Nobel Prize in literature: Jaroslav Seifert, Czech poet
PEN/Faulkner Award: *Sent for You Yesterday* by John Edgar Wideman

Pulitzer Prizes

Biography *Booker T. Washington* by Louis R. Harlan
Drama *Glengarry Glen Ross* by David Mamet
Fiction *Ironweed* by William Kennedy
Nonfiction *Social Transformation of American Medicine* by Paul Starr
Poetry *American Primitive* by Mary Oliver

PUBLICATIONS

ARABIC

The Moon of Shiraz Collection of verse by Iraqi poet Abdul Wahhab al-Bayyati

CZECH

The Unbearable Lightness of Being Novel by Milan Kundera

DUTCH

In the Dutch Mountains Novel by Cees Noteboom

ENGLISH

American

At the Bottom of the River Collected short stories of West Indian–born Jamaica Kincaid
Collected Poems, 1947–1980 Collection by Allen Ginsberg
Democracy Novel by Joan Didion
Fly Away Home Novel by Marge Piercy
Foreign Affairs Novel by Alison Lurie
Glengarry Glen Ross Play by David Mamet
Ground Work Collected verse by Robert Edward Duncan
Horses Make a Landscape Look More Beautiful Poetry collection by Alice Walker
Jacklight Poetry by Native American writer Louise Erdrich
The Legend of La Llorona Novel by Rudolfo Anaya
The Life and Times of Cotton Mather Biography by Kenneth Silverman
The Long Night of Francisco Santis Novel by Humberto Constantini
Ma Rainey's Black Bottom Play by August Wilson
Modus Vivendi Novel by Deirdre Levinson
Second Marriage Novel by Frederick Barthelme
Selected Poems Collection by Kenneth Rexroth
A Slow Fuse Collected verse by Theodore Weiss
Sunday in the Park with George Play by Stephen Joshua Sondheim and James Elliot Lapine
Tough Guys Don't Dance Novel by Norman Mailer
The Witches of Eastwick Novel by John Updike
Yin: New Poems Collected verse by Carolyn Ashley Kizer

Australian

The People's Other World Collected verse of Leslie Allan Murray
The Suburbs of Hell Novel by Randolph Stow

British

Empire of the Sun Novel by J. G. Ballard
Hotel du Lac Novel by Anita Brookner
The Paper Men Novel by William Golding
Small World Novel by David Lodge
Squaring the Circle Play by Tom Stoppard

Canadian

Book of Mercy Collected verse by Leonard Cohen
Criminals in Love Play by George F. Walker

Filipino

Po-on Novel by F. Sionil Jose

Indian

The Grand Man Epic poem by S. S. Bhoosnurmath

Irish

Collected Poems Collection by Michael Hartnett
Jumping the Train Tracks with Angela Collection of verse by Paul Durcan
The Railway Station Man Novel by Jennifer Johnston
Station Island Collected verse of Seamus Heaney
Venus and the Rain Collected verse by Medbh McGuckian

Nigerian

The Last Imam Novel by Ibrahim Tahir

Saint Lucian

Midsummer Song sequence of 54 poems by Derek Walcott

Scottish

The Only Problem Novel by Muriel Spark
Time in a Red Coat Novel by George Mackay Brown

South African

Kruger's Alp Novel by Christopher Hope

ESTONIAN

Return, Pinus Succinifera Collected verse by Jaan Kaplinski

FINNISH

Shining Solitude Collected verse by Risto Ahti

FRENCH

Egyptian

The Queen's Defeat Play by André Chedid

GERMAN

Der Himmel des Humoristen Novel by Lithuanian-born writer Viktoras Pivonas
Our Conquest Novel by Gert Hoffmann
The Wandering Jew Novel by Stefan Heym

HEBREW

Bridal Veil Novel by Israeli writer Moshe Shamir

HUNGARIAN

Restless Early Summer Collected verse by Gyorgy Gomori

ITALIAN

The Bedroom Poem by Attilio Bertolucci
Ipotesi d'Amore Collected verse by Annalisa Cima
La Città e la Casa Epistolary novel by Natalia Ginzburg

NORWEGIAN

Baldershawn Novel by Terje Stigen

POLISH

God's Face Miscellany of stories, essays, dialogues, and diaries by Jan Drzezdzon

PORTUGUESE

De Vitor ao Xadres Collected short stories by Antonio Torrado

RUSSIAN

Ardobiola Novel by Yevgeny Yevtushenko

SPANISH

Chilean

Of Love and Shadows Novel by Isabel Allende

Spanish

Acropolis Novel by Rosa Chacel
Crónica sentimental en rojo Murder mystery by Francisco González Ledesma

VIETNAMESE

A Tired Horse Trots On Collection of short stories by Nguyen Mong Giac

1985

DEATHS

Martín Adán (Rafael de la Fuente Benavides), Peruvian novelist and poet
Riccardo Bacchelli, Italian poet, playwright, and novelist
Heinrich Böll, German novelist, playwright, and essayist
Janet Taylor Caldwell, English novelist
Italo Calvino, Italian novelist and essayist
Nikos Gatsos, Greek poet and playwright
Robert Rank Graves, English poet, novelist, and critic
Jacques de Lacretelle, French novelist
Susan Katherina Langer, American philosopher and essayist
Philip Larkin, English poet
Helen Clark MacInnes, Scottish-born American novelist and playwright
Elsa Morante, Italian novelist and poet
Shivadhar Srinivasa Naipaul, Trinidadian novelist and essayist
Kate Roberts, Welsh short-story writer
Douglas Stewart, Australian poet and playwright
Elwyn Brooks White, American essayist, poet, and writer of non-fiction and children's books

LITERARY EVENT

PRIZES AND AWARDS

Booker Prize: *The Bone People* by Keri Hulme
Caldecott Medal: *Saint George and the Dragon* by Margaret Hodges
Newbery Medal: *The Hero and the Crown* by Robin McKinley
Nobel Prize in literature: Claude Simon, French novelist
PEN/Faulkner Award: *The Barracks Thief* by Tobias Wolff

Pulitzer Prizes

Biography *The Life and Times of Cotton Mather* by Kenneth Silverman
Drama *Sunday in the Park with George* by Stephen Sondheim and James Lapine
Fiction *Foreign Affairs* by Alison Lurie
History *Prophets of Regulation* by Thomas K. McCraw
Nonfiction *The Good War* by Studs Terkel
Poetry *Yin* by Caroline Kizer

PUBLICATIONS

AFRIKAANS

Citations About a Revolution Novel by South African writer Jeanette Ferreira

ARABIC

To the East of the Mediterranean Novel by Jordanian writer Abdul Rahman Mounif

CROATIAN

Quiet Fires Collection of poems by Slavko Mihalic

CZECH

My First Loves Collection of short stories by Ivan Klima
The Confession of Mr. K. Novel by Willem Brackman

DUTCH

The Damned Fathers Novel by Monica von Paemel

ENGLISH

American

Always Coming Home Science fiction novel by Ursula K. Le Guin
Annie John Novel by West Indian-born writer Jamaica Kincaid
The Cider House Rules Novel by John Irving
The Dangerous Summer Autobiographical narrative by Ernest Hemingway
Death Is a Lonely Business Science fiction novel by Ray Bradbury
Fences Play by August Wilson
The Flying Change Poetry collection by Henry Splawn Taylor
Fortune's Daughter Novel by Alice Hoffman
Galapagos Novel by Kurt Vonnegut Jr.
Healing Song for the Inner Ear Collected verse by Michael S. Harper
Lake Wobegon Days Novel by Garrison Kellor
Later the Same Day Collection of short stories by Grace Paley
Late Settings Poetry collection by James Merrill
Lonesome Dove Novel by Larry McMurtry
The Magic Kingdom Novel by Stanley Elkin
New and Selected Poems Collected verse by Robert Penn Warren
"The Old Forest" Short story by Peter Taylor
One Writer's Beginnings Memoir by Eudora Welty
Seeing Through the Sun Poetry collection by Native American writer Linda Hogan
Selected Poems, 1970–1983 Poetry collection by Native American writer Lance Henson
Smiles on Washington Square Novel by French-born writer Raymond Federman
Still Life Novel by A. S. Byatt
This Is Not a Letter and Other Poems Collection by Kay Boyle
The Triumph of Achilles Collected verse of Louise Gluck
White Noise Novel by Don DeLillo
World's Fair Novel by E. L. Doctorow

Australian

Foxybaby Novel by Elizabeth Jolley

British

Cousin Rosamund Novel by Rebecca West
The Good Terrorist Novel by Doris Lessing

Heleconia Winter Novel by Brian Aldiss
A Maggot Novel by John Fowles
Quinx; or, The Ripper's Tale Novel by Lawrence Durrell
Rough Crossing Play by Tom Stoppard
The Tenement Novel by Ian Crichton Smith
The Tenth Man Novel by Graham Greene

Canadian

Borderline Novel by Janette Turner Hospital
The Handmaid's Tale Novel by Margaret Atwood
Home Truths Collection of short stories by Mavis Gallant
Selected Poems, 1933–1980 Collected verse by Hungarian-born poet George Faludy
Waiting for Saskatchewan Collected verse by Frederick James Wah
What's Bred in the Bone Novel by Robertson Davies

Indian

Plans for Departure Novel by Nayantara Sahgal

Irish

The Price of Stone and Earlier Poems Collection of 50 sonnets by Richard Murphy
Station Island Collected verse of Seamus Heaney

Scottish

The Fall of Kelvin Walker: A Fable in the Sixties Novel by Alasdair Gray
The Stories of Muriel Spark Collection by Muriel Spark

ESTONIAN

Blowing Sand/A Winter Journey Collected verse of Bernard Kangro

FRENCH

Belgian

Laura's Daughter Novel by Françoise Mallet-Joris

French

De Guerre lasse Novel by François Sagan
The Gold Seeker Novel by Jean-Marie Le Clezio
An Obscure Man Novel by Marguerite Yourcenar

Moroccan

L'Enfant de sable Novel by Tahar Ben Jelloun

GERMAN

Austrian

Illywhacker Novel by Peter Carey
The Death of the Tenant Farmer, Ignaz Hajek Novel by Josef Haslinger

German

Frauen vor Flusblandschaft Novel by Heinrich Böll
The Parable of the Blind Novel by Gert Hoffmann

GREEK

The Hotel and the House and Other Pieces Collection of short stories by Anestis Evangelou
The Old Man with the Kites Novel by Yannis Ritsos

HUNGARIAN

They Think So Collected verse by Gyorgy Petri

INDONESIAN

Footsteps Novel by Pramudya Ananta Tur

ITALIAN

For the Baptism of Our Fragments Collected verse of Mario Luzi

JAPANESE

Passover/A Guest Who Came from Afar Two novellas by Kometani Fumiko

NORWEGIAN

The Bird and the White Table Cloth Novel by Aase Foss Abrahamsen
Injustice Novel by Carl-Martin Borgen
On the Brink Collected verse of Kurt Nervesen

PORTUGUESE

Brazilian

Rough and Ride Collected verse of João Cabral de Melo Neto
Inhabited Heart Collected verse Eugenio de Andrade
O Que Agora Me Inquieta Novel by Carlos Coutinho

RUSSIAN

The Anti-Soviet Soviet Union Collection of essays by Vladimir Voinovich
The Craft Novel by Sergei Dovlatov
Metro: A Novel of the Moscow Underground Novel by Alexander Kaletski

SPANISH

Argentine

Los conjurados Collected verse by Jorge Luis Borges

Chilean

Ardiente paciencia Novel by Antonio Skarmeta

Colombian

Love in the Time of Cholera Novel by Gabriel García Márquez

Mexican

1492: Life and Times of Juan Cabezon de Castilla Historical novel by Homero Aridjis
The Old Gringo Novel by Carlos Fuentes

Peruvian

Play by Play Novel by Isaac Goldemberg
The Real Life of Alejandro Mayta Novel by Mario Vargas Llosa

Spanish

El Griego Novel on El Greco by Jesús Fernández Santos
La otra orilla de la droga Novel by José Luis de Tomás García
Luna de Lobos Novel by Julio Llamazares

SWEDISH

Korn Collection of verse by Lars Lundqvist
Maria Alone Novel by Sven Delblanc

Songs from the Wings of Sorrow Poetry collection by Elisabeth Rynell

VIETNAMESE
Ivory and Opium Novel by Bach Mai

YIDDISH
The Image, and Other Stories Collection by Polish-born American writer Isaac Bashevis Singer

1986

DEATHS
Marcel Arland, French novelist
Simone de Beauvoir, French philosopher, feminist, novelist, and essayist
Jorge Luis Borges, Argentine novelist, poet, and translator
John Gerard Braine, English novelist
Sid Chaplain, English novelist
John Anthony Ciardi, American poet and critic
Ding Ling, Chinese short-story writer and novelist
Fumiko Enchi, Japanese novelist
Hans J. Frohlich, German novelist
Jean Genet, French playwright, novelist, and poet
Alfred Hauge, Norwegian-born American novelist
Laura Zametkin Hobson, American novelist
Christopher Isherwood, English novelist and poet
Valentin Petrovich Katayev, Russian novelist, playwright, and poet
Bernard Malamud, American novelist
Kersti Merilaas, Estonian poet
Juan Rulfo, Mexican novelist
Jaroslav Seifert, Czech poet

LITERARY EVENT
PRIZES AND AWARDS
Booker Prize: *The Old Devils* by Kingsley Amis
Caldecott Medal: *The Polar Express* by Chris Van Allsburg
Newbery Medal: *Sarah, Plain and Tall* by Patricia MacLachlan
Nobel Prize in literature: Wole Soynika, Nigerian novelist, poet, and playwright
PEN/Faulkner Award: *The Old Forest and Other Stories* by Peter Taylor

Pulitzer Prizes
Biography   *Louise Bogan: A Portrait* by Elizabeth Frank
Fiction   *Lonesome Dove* by Larry McMurtry
History   *. . . The Heavens and the Earth: A Political History of the Space Age* by Walter A. McDougall
Nonfiction   *Move Your Shadow* by Joseph Lelyweld and *Common Ground: A Turbulent Decade in the Lives of Three American Families* by J. Anthony Lukas
Poetry   *The Flying Change* by Henry Taylor

PUBLICATIONS
ENGLISH
American
All God's Children Need Traveling Shoes Autobiographical narrative by Maya Angelou

Carpenter's Gothic Novel by William Gaddis
The Complete Prose Collected essays by Marianne Moore
The Garden of Eden Novel by Ernest Hemingway
God's Snake Novel by Irini Spanidou
Joe Turner's Come and Gone Play by August Wilson
Kate Vaiden Novel by Reynolds Price
Many Waters Novel by Madeleine L'Engle
Marya: A Life Novel by Joyce Carol Oates
The Progress of Love Novel by Alice Munro
Roger's Version Novel by John Updike
A Summons to Memphis Novel by Peter Hillsman Taylor
Thomas and Beulah Poetry collection by Rita Dove
Wild Gratitude Collected verse by Edward Hirsch

Australian
Heart of the Country Novel by Greg Matthews
Memoirs of Many in One Novel by Patrick White
The Well Novel by Elizabeth Jolley

Barbadian
Roots Cultural history by Edward Kamau Brathwaite

British
A Chorus of Disapproval Play by Alan Ayckbourn
Gabriel's Lament Novel by Paul Bailey
Insular Passion Novel by Timothy Mo
The Old Devils Novel by Kingsley Amis
The Photographer in Winter Collected verse by Hungarian-born poet George Szirtes

Indian
The Circle of Reason Novel by Amitav Ghosh
The Golden Gate Verse novel by Vikram Seth

Irish
Mefisto Novel by John Banville
Bailegangaire Play by Thomas Murphy

New Zealand
The Incident Book Collected verse by Fleur Adcock
The Matriarch Novel by Maori writer Witi Ihimaera

Saint Lucian
Collected Poems, 1948–1984 Collected verse by Derek Walcott

Scottish
The Avoiding and Other Poems Collection by Aonghas MacNeacail

South African
Bopha Play by Percy Mtwa
Mating Birds Novel by Lewis Nkosi

Welsh
"Experimenting with an Amen" Poem by R. S. Thomas

FLEMISH
Letters from Nowhere Novel by Paul de Wispelaere

FRENCH
Canadian

Une belle journée d'avance Novel by Robert Lalonde

French

L'enfant roi Novel by Dominique Rolin

Guadeloupean

Moi, Tituba, sorcière noire de Salem Fictionalized biography of Tituba, a slave, by Maryse Condé

GERMAN
Field of Violets Novel by Gert Hoffman
The Rat Novel by Günter Grass
Tanzstunde Miscellaneous short fiction and travel pieces by Wolfgang Trampe

GREEK
"The Little Mariner" Poem by Odysseus Elytis

HEBREW
Selected Poetry Collected verse by German-born poet Yehuda Amichai
Smile of the Lamb Novel by David Grossman
To the Land of the Cattails Novel by Romanian-born writer Aharon Appelfeld

ITALIAN
The Damned and the Saved Autobiography by Primo Levi
In Purissimo Azzurro Collected verse by Elio Fiore
La Lettrice de Isasca Poetry collection by Agistino Richelmy

JAPANESE
Scandal Novel by Shusaku Endo

PERSIAN
The Book About Absent People Novel by Taghi Modarressi

PORTUGUESE
Brazilian

The Night of the Mad Cock Collected stories by Ariosto Augusto de Oliveiro

RUSSIAN
Kangaroo Novel by Yuz Aleshkovsky
Less Than One Collected verse by Joseph Brodsky

SPANISH
Cuban

Holy Smoke Novel by Guillermo Cabrera Infante

Spanish

The Men Cry Alone Novel by José María Gironella

1987

DEATHS

Jean-Marie-Lucien-Pierre Anouilh, French playwright and novelist

James Baldwin, African-American novelist, playwright, and essayist
James Alonzo Bishop, American biographer
John Braine, English novelist
Erskine Caldwell, American novelist
Humberto Constantini, Argentine novelist, playwright, and poet
Gilberto Freyre, Brazilian novelist
Tawfiq Husayn al-Hakim, Egyptian playwright
Jean Margaret Wemyss Laurence, Canadian novelist and essayist
Primo Levi, Italian Jewish scientist, novelist, poet, and essayist
Alistair MacLean, Scottish novelist and poet
Truman Nelson, American novelist and essayist
Lasgush Poradeci, Albanian poet
George Emlyn Williams, Welsh playwright
Marguerite Yourcenar, Belgian-born French novelist, poet, and essayist

LITERARY EVENT
PRIZES AND AWARDS
Booker Prize: *Moon Tiger* by Penelope Lively
Caldecott Medal: *Hey, Al* by Arthur Yorinks
Newbery Medal: *The Whipping Boy* by Sid Fleischman
Nobel Prize in literature: Joseph Brodsky, Russian-American poet
PEN/Faulkner Award: *Soldiers in Hiding* by Richard Wiley

Pulitzer Prizes

Biography *Bearing the Cross: Martin Luther King, Jr., and the Southern Christian Leadership Conference* by David J. Garrow
Drama *Fences* by August Wilson
Fiction *A Summons to Memphis* by Peter Taylor
History *Voyages to the West: A Passage in the Peopling of America on the Eve of the Revolution* by Bernard Bailyn
Nonfiction *Arab and Jew* by David K. Shipler
Poetry *Thomas and Beulah* by Rita Dove

PUBLICATIONS
DANISH
Engel Novel by Klaus Rifbjerg
Under Mausolaeet Collected verse of Henrik Nordbrandt

DUTCH
The Child with the Clown Doll Novel by Paula Gomes

ENGLISH
American

Alnilam Novel by James Dickey
Another Song for America Collection of verse by Native American poet Lance Hensen
Beloved Novel by Toni Morrison
Between Two Rivers: Selected Poems, 1956–1984 Collected verse by Native American poet Maurice Kenny
The Bonfire of the Vanities Novel by Tom Wolfe
The Closing of the American Mind Intellectual thesis by Allan David Bloom
The Counterlife Novel by Philip Roth

Driving Miss Daisy Play by Alfred Uhry
Flesh and Blood Collected verse by C. K. Williams
From Princeton One Afternoon: Collected Poems, 1950–1986 Collected verse by Theodore Weiss
Ground Work II: In the Dark Collected verse by Robert Duncan
Illumination Night Novel by Alice Hoffman
Kadisz Novel by Polish-born writer Henryk Grynberg
The Messiah of Stockholm Novel by Cynthia Ozick
More Die of Heartbreak Novel by Saul Bellow
New and Selected Poems Collected verse by William Morris Meredith
New and Selected Poems, 1940–1986 Collected verse by Karl Shapiro
The New York Trilogy (*City of Glass, Ghosts,* and *The Locked Room*) Mystery novel cycle by Paul Auster
Next: Two Poems Poetry collection by Lucille Clifton
Paco's Story Novel by Larry Heinemann
The Piano Lesson Play by August Wilson
The Prince of Tides Novel by Pat Conroy
The Red, White and Blue Novel by John Gregory Dunne
Sabbaths Collected poems by Wendell Berry
Sumerian Vistas Collected verse by A. R. Ammons
The Thanatos Syndrome Novel by Walker Percy
World's End Novel by T. Coraghessan Boyle
You Must Remember This Novel by Joyce Carol Oates

Australian

Captivity Captive Epic novel by Rodney Hall
Julia Paradise Novel by Rod Jones
The Playmaker Novel by Thomas Keneally
Songlines Descriptive narrative on Aborigines by Bruce Chatwin
Travel Dice Collected verse by Thomas Shappcott
Waiting for Childhood Novel by Sumner Locke Elliott

British

The Book and Brotherhood Novel by Iris Murdoch
Close Quarters Novel by William Golding
The Radiant Way Novel by Margaret Drabble

Canadian

Caprice Novel by George Bowring
In the Skin of a Lion Novel by Sri Lankan-born Michael Ondaatje

Indian

Avadheshwari Novel by Shankar Mokashi Punekar

Irish

Chat Show Novel by Terence de Vere White
The Fool's Sanctuary Novel by Jennifer Johnston
The Haw Lantern Collected verse of Seamus Heaney

New Zealand

Driving into the Storm: Selected Poems Collection by Ian Wedde

Nigerian

Anthills of the Savannah Novel by Chinua Achebe
The Flights Novel by William Conton
Minted Coins Collected verse by Okinba Launko

Saint Lucian

The Arkansas Treatment Collection of poems by Derek Walcott

South African

Black Swan Novel by Christopher Hope
Cape Town Theatrical Props Novel by Wilma Stockenstrom
Her Story Novel by Dan Jacobson
A Sport of Nature Novel by Nadine Gordimer

Sri Lankan

Trial by Terror: Sri Lankan Poems Collection by Jean Arasanayagam

FINNISH

Animalia Collected verse by Eva Kilpi
Anti Kepler's Laws Comic novel by Daniel Katz

FRENCH

French

Cuisine Novella Novel by Antoine Laurent
The Distant Lands Novel by American-born writer Julien Green
Etincelles dans les tenebres Novel by Chinese writer Dai Houying
L'arbre de rêve Novel by Dennis Quiring
L'heritage de Tante Carlotta Novel by Paula Jacques
Le regard de Vincent Novel by Anne Philippe
Psyche: Inventions of the Other Philosophical discourse by Jacques Derrida

Guadeloupean

Ton beau capitain Novel by Simone Schwarze-Bart

GERMAN

Absence Novel by Peter Handke
Alan Turing Novel by Rolf Hochhuth
Die Tochter Novel by Christiane Grosz
Uber Berge Kam Ich Collected verse by Lothar Walsdorf

GREEK

Achillea's Fiancé Novel by Alki Zei

HEBREW

Black Box Novel by Israeli writer Amos Oz

HUNGARIAN

Grazing into the Well Collected verse of Sandor Weores

ICELANDIC

Days with Monks Combination diary and set of reminiscences by Halldor Laxness
Flying Blind Novel by Omar P. Halldorrsson
Gunnladar Saga Novel by Svava Jacobsdottir
Urdargaldur Collected verse by Porsteinn fra Hamri

ITALIAN

La lunga notte Novel by Emilio Tadini
Quando Dio usci chiesa: Vita e fede in un borgio istriano del cinquecento Collected short stories of Fulvio Tomizza

JAPANESE

Norwegian Wood Novel in two volumes by Haruki Murakami
The Snow Dance Novel by Yoshiko Shibaki

KRIOLU

The Water's Eye Novel by Cape Verdean writer Manuel Veiga

LATVIAN

In My Own Home Collected verse by Vitants Ludens

LITHUANIAN

Anapus Gaiso Eilerasciati Collected verse by Jonas Juskaitis

NORWEGIAN

Katedralen Novel by Terje Stigen

PORTUGUESE

Brazilian

A Doce de Caetana Novel by Nelida Pinon

RUSSIAN

The Block Novel by Chingiz Aitmatov
The Heart of a Dog Satire by Mikhail Bulgakov
Uraniia Collected verse by Joseph Brodsky

SERBIAN

A Goat Who Wouldn't Be Mounted Collection of short stories by Tidor Rosic
Half Brothers Novel by Yugoslav writer Jovan Radulovic

SPANISH

Colombian

Los felinos del canciller Novel by Rafael Humberto Moreno-Dorani

Mexican

Christopher Unborn Novel by Carlos Fuentes
News from Empire Novel by Fernando del Paso

Peruvian

The Good Move Collected poems of Carlos Germán Belli
The Story Teller Novel by Mario Vargas Llosa

SWEDISH

Magic Lantern Memoir by Ingmar Bergman
Groucho in Green Collection of short stories by Eva Mattsson

1988

DEATHS

Raymond Carver, American novelist, poet, and essayist
Carlo Cassola, Italian novelist
Edward Chodorov, American playwright
Robert Heinlein, American science fiction writer
Teodor Parnicki, Polish historian and novelist
Alan Stewart Paton, South African novelist
Miguel Piñero, Puerto Rican poet and playwright
Michael Joseph Shaara Jr., American novelist

LITERARY EVENT

PRIZES AND AWARDS

Booker Prize: *Oscar and Lucinda* by Peter Carey
Caldecott Medal: *Owl Moon* by Jane Yolen
Newbery Medal: *Lincoln: A Photobiography* by Russell Freedman
Nobel Prize in literature: Naguib Mahfouz, Egyptian novelist
PEN/Faulkner Award: *World's End* by T. Coraghessan Boyle

Pulitzer Prizes

Biography *Look Homeward: A Life of Thomas Wolfe* by David Herber Donald
Drama *Driving Miss Daisy* by Alfred Uhry
Fiction *Beloved* by Toni Morrison
History *The Launching of American Modern Science, 1846–1876* by Robert V. Bruce
Nonfiction *The Making of the Atomic Bomb* by Richard Rhodes
Poetry *Partial Accounts: New and Selected Poems* by William Meredith

PUBLICATIONS

ALBANIAN

Happy Ending Collected verse by Ali Podrimja

CATALAN

With Women's Names Collection of short stories by Joseph Palau i Fabre

CHINESE

The August Sleepwalker Novel by Bei Dao

ENGLISH

American

AIDS and Its Metaphors Essay by Susan Sontag
American Appetites Novel by Joyce Carol Oates
The Bean Trees Novel by Barbara Kingsolver
Born Brothers Novel by Larry Woiwode
Breathing Lessons Novel by Anne Tyler
Call at Corazon Novel by Paul Bowles
Can't Quit You, Baby Novel by Ellen Douglas
Contact Highs: Selected Poems, 1957–1987 Collection by Alan Ansen
Danger Memory! Two Plays One-act plays by Arthur Miller
The Heidi Chronicles Play by Wendy Wasserstein
Libra Novel by Don De Lillo
The Middle Man and Other Stories Novel by Indian-born writer Bharati Mukherjee
New and Collected Poems Collection by Richard Wilbur
The One Day Poetry collection by Donald Hall
Stories in an Almost Classical Mode Collection by Harold Brodkey
The Tenants of Time Novel by Thomas Flanagan
Where I'm Calling From: New and Selected Stories Collected stories by Raymond Carver
A Writer's America: Landscape in Literature Autobiography and critical essay by Alfred Kazin

The Younger Son First volume of autobiographical trilogy by Karl Shapiro
Zone Journals Collected verse by Charles Wright

Australian

Kisses of the Enemy Novel by English-born Rodney Hall
The Sugar Mother Novel by Elizabeth Jolley

British

Any Old Iron Novel by Anthony Burgess
Collected Poems Collection by John Keith Stubbs
A Far Cry from Kensington Novel by Muriel Spark
The Fifth Child Novel by Doris Lessing

Canadian

Cat's Eye Novel by Margaret Atwood
The Lyre of Orpheus Novel by Robertson Davies

Indian

Mister Bahram Play by Gieve Patel
The Satanic Verses Novel by Salman Rushdie

Irish

Blood and Family Poems by Thomas Kinsella

Pakistani

Ice Candy Man Novel by Bapsi Sidhwa
Inland and Other Poems Collected verse of Alamgir Hashimi

South African

The Essential Gesture Collection of essays by Nadine Gordimer

FRENCH

Belgian

The Sadness of the Kite Novel by Françoise Mallet-Joris

Canadian

The First Garden Novel by Anne Hébert

Egyptian

Worlds, Mirrors, Magics Collection of short stories by André Chedid

French

Remise de peine Novel by Patrick Modiano

Tunisian

The Pharaoh Novel by Albert Memmi

GERMAN

Before the Rainy Season Novel by Gert Hoffman
The Exile Novel by Richard Wagner

HEBREW

The Immortal Bartfuss Novel by Romanian-born Israeli writer Aharon Appelfeld

INDONESIAN

House of Glass Novel by Pramudya Ananta Tur

ITALIAN

The Marriage of Cadmus and Harmony Novel by Roberto Calasso

LATVIAN

The Very Same Day Fictional narrative in prose and verse by Margita Gutmane

RUSSIAN

White Robes Novel by Vladimir Dudintsev

SERBIAN

Dictionary of the Khazars Novel by Milorad Pavic

SPANISH

Peruvian

In Praise of the Stepmother Novel by Mario Vargas Llosa
In the Remaining Terrestrial Time Poem by Carlos Germán Belli

Spanish

Christ Versus Arizona Novel by Camilo José Cela
The City of Marvels Novel by Eduardo Mendoza
The Elusiveness of Truth Novel by José Ferrater Mora
Fábula de fuentes Collection of poems by Rafael Juárez
Natural Sciences Novel by Rosa Chacel

YIDDISH

The Death of Methuselah and Other Stories Collection by Polish-born American writer Isaac Bashevis Singer

1989

DEATHS

Donald Barthelme, American novelist
Samuel Beckett, Irish-born French playwright
Thomas Bernhard, Austrian novelist
Raymond Carver, American novelist
Malcolm Cowley, American critic and poet
Birago Ismael Diop, Senegalese poet
Daphne du Maurier, English novelist
Nicolás Guillén, Cuban poet
Yacine Kateb, Algerian poet and playwright
Owen Lattimore, American scholar
Mary McCarthy, American novelist
Andrei Sakharov, Russian writer and activist
Lopes de Silva, Cape Verdean novelist and short-story writer
Georges Simenon, Belgian-born French detective novelist
Irving Stone, American novelist
Barbara Tuchman, American historian
Robert Penn Warren, American poet

LITERARY EVENT

PRIZES AND AWARDS

Booker Prize: *The Remains of the Day* by Kazuo Ishiguro
Caldecott Medal: *Song and Dance Man* by Karen Ackerman
Newbery Medal: *Joyful Noise: Poems for Two Voices* by Paul Fleischman
Nobel Prize in literature: Camilio José Cela, Spanish writer
PEN/Faulkner Award: *Dusk* by James Salter

Pulitzer Prizes

Biography *Oscar Wilde* by Richard Ellman
Drama *The Heidi Chronicles* by Wendy Wasserstein
Fiction *Breathing Lessons* by Anne Tyler
History *The Battle Cry of Freedom: The Civil War Era* by James M. McPherson and *Parting the Waters: America in the King Years, 1954–1963* by Taylor Branch
Nonfiction *A Bright Shining Lie: John Paul Vann and America in Vietnam* by Neil Sheehan
Poetry *New and Collected Poems* by Richard Wilbur

PUBLICATIONS

CHINESE
The Piano Tuner Novel by Cheng Nai Shen

DUTCH
In a Dark Wood Wandering Novel by Hella S. Haase
Last Call Novel by Harry Mulisch

ENGLISH
American
After You've Gone Collection of short stories by Alice Adams
The Ancient Child Novel by Native American writer N. Scott Momaday
Any Woman's Blues Novel by Erica Jong
The Bellarosa Connection Novella by Saul Bellow
Billy Bathgate Novel by E. L. Doctorow
Hence Novel by Brad Leithauser
If the River Was Whiskey Collection of short stories by T. Coraghessan Boyle
John Dollar Novel by Marianne Wiggins
Journey Novel by James A. Michener
The Joy Luck Club Novel by Amy Tan
Just Looking: Essays on Art Collection by John Updike
The Killing Man Novel by Mickey Spillane
Love, Action, Laughter and Other Sad Tales Collection of 16 stories by Budd Schulberg
Nemesis Futuristic novel by Isaac Asimov
The Outmost Dream Collection of essays and reviews by William Maxwell
The People and Uncollected Stories Unfinished novel and collected stories by Bernard Malamud
A Prayer for Owen Meany Novel by John Irving
Rummies Comic novel by Peter Benchley
The Shawl Novel by Cynthia Ozik
Some Freaks Collection of essays by David Mamet
Spartina Novel by John Casey
The Temple of My Familiar Novel by Alice Walker
Time's Power Poetry collection by Adrienne Rich
Transparent Gestures Collected poems of Rodney Jones
We Are Still Married Collection of essays, stories, letters, and poems by Garrison Keillor
The Writing Life Collection of essays by Annie Dillard

Australian
My Father's Moon Novel by Elizabeth Jolley

British
At Home and Abroad Collection of travel essays by V. S. Pritchett
Citizens: A Chronicle of the French Revolution Historical study by Simon Schama
Collected Poems Collection by Philip Larkin
Fire Down Below Novel by William Golding
Incline Our Hearts Novel by A. N. Wilson
A Natural Curiosity Novel by Margaret Drabble
The Remains of the Day Novel by Japanese-born writer Kazuo Ishiguro
The Russia House Spy thriller by John le Carré
The Warrior Queens Historical study by Antonia Fraser

Canadian
In Transit Collection of short stories by Mavis Gallant

Nigerian
Isara: A Voyage Round Essay Memoir by Wole Soyinka
Stars of the New Curfew Collection of short stories by Ben Okri

South African
Memory of Snow and of Dust Novel by Breyten Breytenbach

Trinidadian
A Casual Brutality Novel by Neil Bissoondath

FRENCH
The Acacia Novel by Claude Simon

GERMAN
Show Your Tongue Journal narrative by Günter Grass

HEBREW
For Every Sin Novel by Romanian-born Israeli writer Aharon Appelfeld
Katerina Novel by Aharon Appelfeld
See Under: Love Novel by Israeli writer David Grossman

HUNGARIAN
Barbarian Prayer Collected verse of Sandor Csoori

ITALIAN
Private Renaissance Novel by Maria Bellonci

PERSIAN
The Blindfold Horse: Memories of a Persian Childhood Autobiographical narrative by Shusha Guppy
The Pilgrim's Rules of Etiquette Novel by Taghi Modarressi

RUSSIAN
Children of the Arbat Novel by Anatoly Rybakov
The Courtyard Novel by Arkady Lvov

SPANISH
Colombian
The General in His Labyrinth Novel by Gabriel García Márquez

Peruvian
An Invincible Memory Novel by João Ubaldo Ribeiro
The Storyteller Novel by Mario Vargas Llosa

1990

DEATHS

Coelho Pinto de Andrade, Angolan poet, writer, and statesman
Richard Bevan Braithwaite, English philosopher
Morley Edward Callaghan, Canadian novelist and short-story writer
Jack Conroy, American novelist
Roald Dahl, Welsh author of children's books
Lawrence Durrell, English novelist
Friedrich Durrenmatt, Swiss novelist, playwright, and essayist
Feng Youlan, Chinese philosopher
Rosamund Nina Lehmann, English novelist
Michel Julien Leiris, French novelist
Ivar Lo-Johansson, Swedish novelist
John Hugh MacLennan, Canadian novelist and essayist
Alberto Moravia, Italian novelist
Malcolm Muggeridge, English journalist and Christian apologist
Lewis Mumford, American social philosopher
Walker Percy, American novelist
Manuel Puig, Argentine novelist
Yannis Ritsos, Greek poet
Adolf Rudnicki, Polish novelist
Anya Seton, American historical novelist and biographer
Philippe Soupault, French poet and novelist
Irving Wallace, American fiction writer
Patrick White, Australian novelist

LITERARY EVENT

PRIZES AND AWARDS

Booker Prize: *Possession* by A. S. Byatt
Caldecott Medal: *Lon Po Po* by Ed Young
Newbery Medal: *Number the Stars* by Lois Lowry
Nobel Prize in literature: Octavio Paz, Mexican poet and essayist
PEN/Faulkner Award: *Billy Bathgate* by E. L. Doctorow

Pulitzer Prizes

Biography *Machiavelli in Hell* by Sebastian de Grazia
Drama *The Piano Lesson* by August Wilson
Fiction *The Mambo Kings Play Songs of Love* by Oscar Hijuelos
History *In Our Image: America's Empire in the Philippines* by Stanley Karnow
Nonfiction *And Their Children After Them* by Dale Maharidge and Michael Williamson
Poetry *The World Doesn't End* by Charles Simic

PUBLICATIONS

ALBANIAN

Dossier H Novel by Ismail Kadare

BASQUE

Obabakoak Montage of 27 interconnected narratives by Spanish writer Bernardo Atxaga (Jose Irazu Garmendia)
Poemas híbridos Bilingual (Basque-Spanish) collection of verse by Bernardo Atxaga

CHINESE

Red Sorghum Novel by Mo Yan
The Sobbing Lancang River Novel by Zhu Lin

CZECH

How the Heart Is Torn Apart Poetry collection by Karel Siktanc
Immortality Novel by Milan Kundera
Love and Litter Novel by Ivan Klima
My Cheerful Mornings Novel by Ivan Klima

ENGLISH

American

Above the River Collected verse by James Wright
Animal Dreams Novel by Barbara Kingsolver
Because It Is Bitter and Because It Is My Heart Novel by Joyce Carol Oates
The Book of J Critical work by Harold Bloom on translation of the Bible
The Coast of Chicago Collection of stories by Stuart Dybek
Deception Novel by Philip Roth
Don Juan in the Village Novel by Jane DeLynn
Entered from the Sun Third volume in the Elizabethan trilogy by George Garrett
Iron John: A Book About Men Nonfiction by Robert Bly
The Light Possessed Novel by Alan Cheuse
The Mambo Kings Play Songs of Love Novel by Oscar Hijuelos
Middle Passage Novel about slavery by Charles Johnson
Old Soldier Novel by Vance Bourjaily
Philadelphia Fire Novel by John Edgar Wideman
Powers of Congress Collection of poems by Alice Fulton
Rabbit at Rest Final volume in the Rabbit trilogy by John Updike
Selected Poems Collection by Randall Jarrell
She Drove Without Stopping Novel by Jaime Gordon
They Want Bone Poetry collection by Robert Pinsky
Vineland Novel by Thomas Pynchon
When One Has Lived a Long Time Alone Poetry collection by Galway Kinnell
Wildlife Novel by Richard Ford
The World Doesn't End Collection of poems by Charles Simic
The World of the Ten Thousand Things: Poems, 1980–1990 Collection by Charles Wright

British

An Awfully Big Adventure Novel by Beryl Bainbridge
The Dwarfs Play by Harold Pinter
The Folks That Live on the Hill Novel by Kingsley Amis
The Gate of Angels Novel by Penelope Fitzgerald
Last Loves Play By Alan Sillitoe
The Light Years Novel by Elizabeth Jane Howard
Possession Novel by A. S. Byatt

Canadian

Friend of My Youth Collection of stories by Alice Munro
Property and Value Eighth novel in the 12-novel cycle *The New Age* by Hugh Hood
Roses Are Difficult Here Novel by W. O. Mitchell
Solomon Gursky Was Here Novel by Mordecai Richler
The Wild Blue Yonder Novel by Audrey Thomas

Indian

The World of Nagaraj Novel by R. K. Narayan

Irish

Amongst Women Novel by John McGahern
The Circus Animals Novel by James Plunkett
Lies of Silence Novel by Brian Moore
Selected Poems Collected verse by Derek Mahon
The South Novel by Colin Toibin

Saint Lucian

Omeros Epic poem by Derek Walcott

Scottish

Collected Poems Collected verse by Norman MacCaig
Symposium Novel by Muriel Spark

South African

My Son's Story Novel by Nadine Gordimer

FRENCH

French

La declaration Novel by Lydie Salvayre
L'homme ignore Novel by Olivier Targowla
Les champs d'honneur Novel by Jean Rouaud
Les frères romance Novel by Jean Colombier
Les quartières d'hiver Novel by Jean-Noel Pancrazi
Nous sommes eternels Novel by Pierrette Fleutiaux
On vient chercher Monsieur Jean Memoirs of Jean Tardieu
Parôle de singe Novel by Patrick Cahuzac
Silsie Novel Novel by Marie Redonnet

Senegalese

Poetical Works Collected writings of Leopold Senghor

GERMAN

Bodenloser Sstz Poetry collection by Volker Braun
Die Frau in den Kissen Novel by Brigitte Kronauer
Emanuel Novel by Jurg Laederach
Herzwand Autobiography by Peter Hartling
Lanzen im Eis Poetry collection by Unrich Schacht
Ludwig muss sterben Novel by Thomas Hettche
Mein Stuck Zeit Autobiography by Jurij Brezan
Raabe Baikal Memoirs by Thomas Strittmatter
Rebus Novel by Peter Rosei
Versuch uber die Jukebox Novel by Peter Handke

HEBREW

Adon Menuha Collection of poems by Avot Yeshurun
Ahayat David Novel by Yoram Kanuik
Avishag Novel by David Schutz
haLaila shebo Meta haTsiyonut Novel by Aharon Almog
Leil Zikharon Novel by Israel Ha'meiri
Likro la 'Atalefim Novel by Hanna Bat Shahar
Mar Mani Novel by A. B. Yehoshua
Sogrim et ha Yam Novella by Judith Katzir
Uvatzfifut Collected verse by Hamutal Bar-Yosef

HUNGARIAN

It Exists Somewhere Collection of poems by Gyorgy Petri
Naplo Collected verse by Miklos Radnoti

ITALIAN

Carossa Novel by Claudio Marabini
La chimera Historical novel by Sebastiano Vassalli
Due di due Novel by Andrea De Carlo
La lunga de vita Marianna Ucria Historical novel by Dacia Maraini
La via del ritorno Novel by Enrico Palandri
Serena Cruz Novel by Natalia Ginzburg

JAPANESE

Mirage of Fire Novel by Hideo Takubo
Requiem Novel by Kyoko Hayashi
Tower of Ecological Treatment Science fiction novel by Kenzaburo Oe

NORWEGIAN

Alte Kameraden Thriller by Fredrik Skagen
Efter ar og dag Memoirs by Tore Hamsun
Karjana Novel by Johannes Heggland
Tresjoereren Johannes Novel by Terje Stigen
Vinterhagen Play by Bjorg Vik

POLISH

Carnival and Lent Novel by Marek Nowakowski
Elegy for an Exit Collected verse by Zbigniew Herbert
Term of Office Novel by Jan Josef Sczepanski

PORTUGUESE

Brazilian

Boca do Inferno Novel by Ana Miranda
Brida Novel by Paulo Coelho
Calçada de Verao Collection of poems by Flora Figueiredo

Portuguese

Conquistador Novel by Almeida Faria
Fora de Horas Novel by Paulo de Costilho
History of the Siege of Lisbon Historical novel by José Saramago

RUSSIAN

The Beauty of Life Novella sequence by Yevgeny Popov
The Island of Crimea Novel by Vasily Aksyonov
The Day Lasts More Than a Hundred Years Novel by Chingiz Aytmatov
Face to Face Novella by Chingiz Aytmatov
A Russian Beauty Novel by Victor Yerofeyev

SERBIAN

Landscape Painted with Tea Novel by Milorad Pavic
The Sinner Last volume in the trilogy of novels by Dobrica Cosic
A Time of Evil Trilogy by Dobrica Cosic

SPANISH

Argentine

El Hombre que llegó a un pueblo Novel by Hector Tizón
El viajero de Agartha Novel by Abel Posse
La astucia de la razón Novel by José Pablo Feinmann

Chilean

Match Ball Novel by Antonio Skarmeta

Colombian

Por el sendero de los ángeles caídos Novel by Andrés Hoyos
Sinfonía desde el Nuevo Mundo Novel by Germán Espinosa
Summa de Magroll el Gaviero Collected poems by Alvaro Mutis

Cuban

Cocuyo Novel by Severo Sardy

Mexican

Constancia y otras novelas para vírgenes Novel by Carlos Fuentes
La campana Novel by Carlos Fuentes
La insólita historia de la santa de Cabora Novel by Brianda Domecq

Spanish

El manuscrito carmesí Historical novel by Antonio Gala
La soledad era esto Novel by Juan José Millas
La vieja sirena Epic historical novel by José Luis Sampedro

Venezuelan

La carujada Novel by Denzil Romero

SWEDISH

Forberedelser for wintersasongen Collection of poems by Lars Gustafsson
For levande och doda Collection of poems by Tomas Transtromer
I vantan pa pendeltaget Collection of poems by Karl Vennberg
Lydia i lampans sken Collected verse Ylva Eggehorn
Sorgen per capita Collected verse by Ernst Brunner

1991

DEATHS

George Granville Barker, English poet
François Billetdoux, French playwright
Manning Hope Clark, Australian historian
Max Rudolph Frisch, Swiss novelist and playwright
Northrop Frye, Canadian literary critic
Roy Broadbent Fuller, English poet and novelist
Natalia Ginzburg, Italian novelist
Graham Greene, English novelist
A. B. Guthrie Jr., American writer
William Heinesen, Danish Faeroese novelist
Wolfgang Hildesheimer, German novelist
Yusuf Idris, Egyptian playwright and novelist
Inoue Yasushi, Japanese novelist
Antonio Jacinto, Angolan poet
Jerzy Nikodem Kosinski, Polish-born American novelist
Artur Nils Lundkvist, Swedish novelist
Howard Nemerov, American poet
Noma Hiroshi, Japanese novelist
Sean O'Faolain (John Francis Whelan), Irish short-story writer
Vasko Popa, Serbian poet
Vasco Pratolini, Italian novelist

Laura Riding, American poet, critic, and writer
Dr. Seuss (Theodore Seuss Geisel), American writer of children's stories
Isaac Bashevis Singer, Polish-born American Jewish writer
Sir Angus Frank Johnstone Wilson, English novelist and literary critic
Frank Garvin Yerby, American novelist

LITERARY EVENT
PRIZES AND AWARDS
Booker Prize: *The Famished Road* by Ben Okri
Caldecott Medal: *Black and White* by David Macaulay
Newbery Medal: *Maniac Magee* by Jerry Spinelli
Nobel Prize in literature: Nadine Gordimer, South African novelist
PEN/Faulkner Award: *Philadelphia Fire* by Jerome Edgar Wideman

Pulitzer Prizes

Biography   *Jackson Pollock: An American Saga* by Stephen Naifeh and Gregory White Smith
Drama   *Lost in Yonkers* by Neil Simon
Fiction   *Rabbit at Rest* by John Updike
History   *A Midwife's Tale: The Life of Martha Ballard Based on Her Diary, 1785–1812* by Laurel Thatcher Ulrich
Nonfiction   *The Ants* by Bert Holldobler and Edward O. Wilson
Poetry   *Near Changes* by Mona van Duyn

PUBLICATIONS
BULGARIAN
Blind Dog Novella by Boris Hristow
Night Diary Collected verse by Blaga Dimitrova
Transit Collected verse by Blaga Dimitrova

CHINESE
Rice Novel by Su Tong
Mount Taibai Collection of short stories by Jia Pingwa

CZECH
Alone Against the Night Lyrical diary by dissident writer Dominik Tatarka

DANISH
Broder Jacob Novel on the Reformation by Henrik Stangerup
Dodningeuret Novel by Vibeke Gronfeldt
Fortoellinger om natten Novel by Peter Hoeg
Fru Astrid Grib Novel by Thit Jensen
Skyggen i dit sted Novel by Jens Christian Grondahl

ENGLISH
American

Almanac of the Dead Novel by Native American writer Leslie Marmon Silko
An Atlas of the Difficult World, Poems, 1988–1991 Collection by Adrienne Rich
Bitter Angel Collected verse by Amy Gerstler
Brotherly Love Novel by Pete Dexter
Harlot's Ghost Novel by Norman Mailer

Heat and Other Stories Collection by Joyce Carol Oates
Joe Novel by Larry Brown
The Kitchen God's Wife Novel by Amy Tan
Living Wills Collected verse by Cynthia Macdonald
Lost in Yonkers Play by Neil Simon
Mao II Novel by Don DeLillo
Mating Novel by Norman Rush
More Shapes Than One Collection of short stories by Fred Chapell
The Runaway Soul Novel by Harold Brodkey
Set for Life Novel by Judith Freeman
Skating in the Dark Novel by David Michael Kaplan
The Sweet Hereafter Novel by Russell Banks
A Thousand Acres Novel by Jane Smiley
What Work Is Collected verse by Philip Levine

British

The Famished Road Novel by Ben Okri
The Kindness of Women Autobiographical novel by J. G. Ballard
Marking Time Novel by Elizabeth Jane Howard
On Reading Turgenev Novel by William Trevor
The Redundancy of Courage Novel by Timothy Mo
Time's Arrow Novel by Kingsley Amis

Canadian

Fall from Grace Novel by L. R. Wright
The Invention of Truth Novel by Elizabeth Brewster
Isobars Collection of short stories by Janette Turner Hospital
Isolation Booth Novel by Hugh Hood
Murther & Walking Spirits Novel by Robertson Davies
Shadows in the Grass Collected verse by Ralph Gustafson
Something Happened Here Collection of short stories by Norman Levine
Such a Long Journey Novel by Indian-born writer Rohinton Mistry
Those Were the Mermaid Days Poetry collection by Patricia Young

Irish

The Invisible Worm Novel by Jennifer Johnston
Madonna and Other Poems Collection by Thomas Kinsella
The Van Novel by Roddy Doyle

South African

Hidden in the Heart Novel by Dan Jacobson

FRENCH

Belgian

Divine Novel by Françoise Mallet-Joris

French

The Daughters of Calvary Novel by Pierre Combescot
Deborah et les anges dissipés Novel by Paula Jacques
La dérive des sentiments Novel by Yves Simon
Odeur d'encre, odeur d'îles Novel by Vincent Jacq
Onitsha Novel by Jean-Marie Le Clezio
The Separation Novel by Dan Franck
Sous l'étoile du chien Novel by Bernard Puech
Un long Dimanche de fiancailles Novel by Sebastien Japrisot

GERMAN

Blaubarts Schatten Novel by Ulla Hahn
Kopfjager Novel by Uwe Timm
Lenins Hirn Novel by Tilman Spengler
Zukunftsmusik Collected verse by Hans Magnus Enzensberger

HEBREW

Ad haSof Novel by Moshe Shamir
Christus shel haDagim Novel by Yoel Hoffmann
Elef Levavot Novel by Dan Tsalka
Hamatzav baShlishi Novel by Amos Oz
Li viti Ota baDerekh leVeita Novel by Amalia Kahana-Carmon
Mesilat Barzel Novel by Aharon Appelfeld
Panim baA'nan Novel by Yoseel Birstein
Sefer haMeforash Novel by Avraham Heffner
Tanim shel Mora Collected verse by Rachel Gil

ITALIAN

Cantare nel buio Novel by Maria Corti
Il doppio regno Novel by Paola Capriolo
L'angelo nero Collection of short stories by Antonio Tabucchi
La palude definitiva Philosophical novel by Giorgio Manganelli
La strada per Roma Novel by Paolo Volponi
Res amissa Collection of lyrics by Giorgio Caproni
Verso Paola Long short story by Francesca Sanvitale

JAPANESE

Fantastic Gallery Novel by Yumiko Kurahashi
Moon in Shanghai Play by Hisashi Inoue
The Strange Story of Mammy Hunt Novel by Taeko Kohno

NORWEGIAN

Et virkelig liv Novel by Odd Koppenvag
Lyhamar Novel by Johannes Heggland
Poplene pa St. Hanshaugen Novel by Bjorg Vik
Salme ved reisens slutt Novel by Erik Fosnes Hansen
Seierherrene Novel by Roy Jacobsen
Til verdens ende Historical novel by Knut Faldbakken

PORTUGUESE

Brazilian

Agosto Novel by Rubem Fonseca
Amor que faz o mundo girar Novel by Ary Quintella
O baile de mascaras Play by Mauro Rasi

Portuguese

A quintas das virtudes Novel by Mario Caludio
Romantic Sonnets Collected verse by Natalia Correia
Um beijo dado mais tarde Novel by Maria Gabriela Llansol

ROMANIAN

The Levant Long epic poem by Mircea Cartarescu

RUSSIAN

Long Is Our Way Novel by Vladimir Makanin
Manhole Novel by Vladimir Makanin

SERBIAN

Chanticleer's Morsel Collected verse by Aleksandar Popovic
The Coming Out Book Collected verse by Mario Susko

SPANISH

Chilean

La vaca sagrada Novel by Diamela Eltit
Los años de la serpiente Novel by Antonio Ostornol

Colombian

El gran jaguar Novel by Bernardo Valderrama Andrade
El mensajero Novel by Fernando Vallejo
El rumor del astracán Novel by Azriel Bibliowicz
La otra selva Novel by Boris Salazar
Urbes luminosas Novel by Eduardo García Aguilar

Mexican

A la salud de la serpiente Narrative by Gustavo Sainz
Guerra en el paraíso Novel by Carlos Montemayor
La guerra de Galio Novel by Hector Aguilar Camín

Paraguayan

Los hochos de Zacarías Novel by Guillermo Morón

Spanish

Agenda Collected verse by José Hierro
Casi una leyenda Collected poems by Claudio Rodríguez
El caballero de Sajonia Historical novel by Juan Benet
El jinete polaco Novel by Antonio Muñoz Molina
El laberinto griego Novel (sixteenth in the cycle *Pepe Carvalho*) by Manuel Vázquez Montalbán
El metro de platino iridiado Philosophical novel by Alvaro Pombo
Galindez Novel by Manuel Vázquez Montalbán
The Knight of Saxony Novel by Juan Benet
La tierra prometida Novel by José María Guelbenzu
Los reinos combatientes Novel set in ancient China by Alvaro Pombo

SWEDISH

Det florentinska vildsvinet Novel by Lars Ahlin
Det himmselska gastabudet Novel by Lars Gyllensten
En kakelsattares eftermiddag Allegorical fable by Lars Gustafsson
Fuskaren Novel by P. G. Evander
Kapten Nemos Novel by P. O. Enquist
Tradet Collected verse by Goran Sonnevi

1992

DEATHS

Isaac Asimov, American science fiction writer
Kay Boyle, American novelist
Angela Carter, English novelist
Pietro di Donato, Italian-born American writer
M. F. K. Fisher, American writer on food
Alex Haley, African-American writer
George Mann MacBeth, Scottish-born English poet
Bill Naughton, Irish-born English playwright
Mary Norton, English writer of children's books
Elder James Olson, American poet, playwright, and critic
Rosemary Sutcliffe, English writer of children's books

LITERARY EVENT

PRIZES AND AWARDS

Booker Prize: *The English Patient* by Michael Ondaatje and *Sacred Hunger* by Barry Unsworth
Caldecott Medal: *Tuesday* by David Wiesner
Newbery Medal: *Shiloh* by Phyllis Reynolds Naylor
Nobel Prize in literature: Derek Walcott, Saint Lucian poet
PEN/Faulkner Award: *Mao II* by Don DeLillo

Pulitzer Prizes

Biography *Fortunate Son: The Healing of a Vietnam Vet* by Lewis B. Puller Jr.
Drama *The Kentucky Cycle* by Robert Schenkkan
Fiction *A Thousand Acres* by Jane Smiley
History *The Fate of Liberty: Abraham Lincoln and Civil Liberties* by Mark E. Neely Jr.
Nonfiction *The Prize: The Epic Quest for Oil* by Daniel Yergin
Poetry *Selected Poems* by James Tate

PUBLICATIONS

CHINESE

Rainbow Novel by Mao Dun

CROATIAN

Fording the Stream of Consciousness Novel by Dubravka Ugresic

CZECH

Colette Novel by Arnost Lustig
The End of the Patriarchate Novel by Frantisek Pavlicek

DANISH

Sidste sommer Novel on Danish Resistance in World War II by Tage Skou-Hansen
20 Digte Collected verse by Peter Lavgesen

ENGLISH

American

All the Pretty Horses Novel by Cormac McCarthy
Bailey's Café Novel by Gloria Naylor
Campo Santo Poetry collection by Susan Wood
Collected Poems, 1946–1991 by Hayden Carruth
A Dream of Mind Poetry collection by C. K. Williams
Heaven and Earth Collected verse by Albert Goldbarth
Jazz Novel by Toni Morrison
New and Selected Poems Collected verse by Mary Oliver
Outerbridge Reach Novel by Robert Stone
Possessing the Secret of Joy Novel by Alice Walker
Rum Punch Crime novel by Elmore Leonard
Turtle Moon Novel by Alice Hoffman
Very Old Bones Novel (part of the *Albany Cycle*) by William Kennedy
Violence Novel by Richard Bausch
The Volcano Lover Historical novel by Susan Sontag
Waiting to Exhale Novel by Terry McMillan
The Whole Motion Collection of poems by James Dickey
Young Men and Fire Philosophical reporting by Norman Maclean

British

Black Dogs Novel by Ian McEwan
Daughters of the House Novel by Michele Roberts
The Death of the Author Novel by Gilbert Adair
Dr. Criminale Novel by Malcolm Bradbury
Feast Days Collection of poems by John Burnside
Rain-Charm for the Duchy Poetry collection by Ted Hughes
Sacred Hunger Novel by Barry Unsworth

Canadian

The Chrome Suite Novel by Sandra Birdsell
The English Patient Novel by Michael Ondaatje
The Girl with the Botticelli Face Novel by W. D. Valgardson
The Last Magician Novel by Janette Turner Hospital

Nigerian

From Zia, with Love Novel by Wole Soyinka

Scottish

Curriculum Vitae Novel by Muriel Spark

South African

Serenity House Novel by Christopher Hope

FRENCH

Canadian

The Child Bordered with Dreams Novel by Anne Hébert

French

Aden Novel by Anne-Marie Garat
La démence du boxeur Lyrical novel by François Weyergans
The Lover Novel by Marguerite Duras
Tlacuilo Novel by Michel Rio

Martinican

Texaco Bilingual novel in French and Creole by Patrick Chamoiseau

GERMAN

German

The Call of the Toad Novel by Günter Grass
Die Braut im Park Novel by Roswitha Quadflieg
Der Fuchs war damals schon der Jager Novel by Herta Muller
Selige Zeiten, bruchige Welt Novel by Robert Menasse
Unstete Leute Novel by Christina Viragh

Swiss

Der Antiquar Novel by Hansjorg Schertenlieb

HEBREW

Mikdamot Novel by S. Yizhar
Post Mortem Novel by Yoram Kaniuk
Yoman shel Zug Me'ohav Novel by Yonat Sened and Alexander Sened
Yom haOr shel Anat Novel by Aharon Megged

HUNGARIAN

Kozma Play by Mihaly Kornis

ITALIAN

I giardini della favorita Novel by Dominico Campana

Il sole e innocenti Novel by Claudio Camarca
La casa a nord-est Novel by Sergio Maldini
Nottetempo, casa per casa Novel by Vincenzo Consolo
Marco e Mattio Novel by Sebastiano Vassalli

JAPANESE

Ask the Flowers Novel by Jakucho Setouchi
Floating Bridge Novel by Kunie Iwahashi

NORWEGIAN

Det Stutte livet Novel by Johannes Heggland
Kastanjetid Minimalist novel by Terje Larsen
Lykkens sonn Historical novel by Herbjorg Wassmo
Nattsol Collected poems by Stein Mehren
Trollbyen Novel by Karsten Alnaes
Villa Europa Novel by Ketil Bjornstad

PORTUGUESE

Brazilian

The Best Poems Poetry collection by Haroldo de Campos
Canteiros de saturno Novel by Ana Maria Machado
Eu, tiradentes Novel on the Mineiran conspiracy by Pascoal Motta
No coração do Brasil Black comedy by Miguel Falabella
Sonhos tropicais Novel by Moacyr Scliar
Uma historia de familia Novel by Silviano Santiago

Portuguese

Litoral Poetic novel by Wanda Ramos
O Evangelho segundo Jesus Cristo Novel by José Saramago
Partes de Africa Novel by Helder Macedo

ROMANIAN

Hands Behind My Back: Selected Poems Collected verse by Marin Sorescu

RUSSIAN

Fear Novel by Anatoly Rybakov
The Last Bow Novel by Viktor Astafyev
The Settlement of Centaurs Novel by Anatoly Kim

SERBIAN

An Ancient Book Poetry collection by Miodrag Pavlovic
Bread and Fear Novel by Milisav Savic
Eagle Nests Poetry collection by Veljko P. Bojic
Fear of the Bell Novel by Radoslav Bratic
17-57 Poems Collection by Veljko P. Bojic

SPANISH

Chilean

The Garden Next Door Novel by José Donoso

Colombian

Doce cuentos peregrinos Collection of short stories by Gabriel García Márquez

Honduran

The Ships Novel by Roberto Quesada

Mexican

The Buried Mirror Essays on Hispanic culture by Carlos Fuentes
Tinísima Historical novel by Elena Poniatowska

Spanish

Corazón tan blanco Novel by Javier Marías
El año del deluvio Novel by Eduardo Mendoza
El nido de los sueños Novel by Rosa Montero
La prueba del laberinto Novel by Fernando Sánchez Drago
Nubosidad variable Novel by Carmen Martín Gaite

SWEDISH

Dess ande kysst Collected poems by Arne Johnsson
Edith Novel about Finnish-Swedish poet Edith Sodergran by Ernst Brunner
Eftertradaren Novel by PerAgne Erkelius
Exterminate the Brutes Novel by Sven Lindqvist
Man i min alder Novel by Stig Claesson
Nar vagen vander Collected verse by Kjell Espmark
Tre borgerliga kvartetter Play by Lars Noren

1993

DEATHS

Abe Kobo, Japanese novelist
Juan Benet Goita, Spanish novelist
Nina Nikolayevna Berberova, Russian novelist
Anthony Burgess, English novelist
Kenneth Burke, English literary critic and philosopher
Peter De Vries, American comic writer
Penelope Ann Douglass Gilliatt, English writer and critic
Sir William Gerald Golding, English novelist
James Leo Herlihy, American novelist and playwright
John Richard Hersey, English novelist
Eleanor Alice Hibbert (Victoria Holt, Jean Plaidy), English novelist
Albert Habib Hourani, Arab English historian
Irving Howe, American literary critic
Ibuse Masuji, Japanese novelist
Mohammad Aziz Lahhabi, Moroccan writer and philosopher
Oodgeroo Noonuccal (Kath Walker, Kathleen Jean Mary Ruska), Australian Aborigine poet and writer
Gabriel Preil, American poet
Wallace Stegner, American novelist

LITERARY EVENT
PRIZES AND AWARDS
Booker Prize: *Paddy Clarke Ha Ha Ha* by Roddy Doyle
Caldecott Medal: *Mirette on the High Wire* by Emily Arnold McCully
Newbery Medal: *Missing May* by Cynthia Rylant
Nobel Prize in literature: Toni Morrison, African-American novelist
PEN/Faulkner Award: *Postcards* by E. Annie Proulx

Pulitzer Prizes

Biography *Truman* by David McCullogh
Drama *Angels in America—Millennium Approaches* by Tony Kushner
Fiction *A Good Scent from a Strange Mountain* by Robert Olen Butler
History *The Radicalism of the American Revolution* by Gordon S. Wood
Nonfiction *Lincoln at Gettysburg* by Garry Wills
Poetry *The Wild Iris* by Louise Gluck

PUBLICATIONS
BULGARIAN
Here I Am, in Perfect Leaf Today Collected verse of Petya Dubarova

CHINESE
Black Snow Novel by Liu Heng
Old River Daydreams Novel by Liu Heng
Old Sites Novel by Li Rui
A Season for Falling in Love Novel by Wang Meng

CZECH
Glorious Lousy Years Novel by Michael Viewegh

DANISH
Byen og verden Novel by Peer Hultberg
Den tolvte ritter Novel by Ib Michael
Der var engang Picaresque novel by Knud Holten
Dyr Novel by Juliane Preisler
Transparence Novel by Suzanne Broger

ENGLISH
American

Across the Bridge: Stories Collection by Mark Gallant
Balkan Ghosts: A Journey Through History Travel account by Robert D. Kaplan
Body and Soul Novel by Frank Conroy
Collected Early Poems, 1950–1970 Collection by Adrienne Rich
Collected Poems, 1930–1993 Collection by May Sarton
The Collected Stories Collection by William Trevor
Consider This, Señora Novel by Harriet Doerr
Garbage Collected verse by A. R. Ammons
A Good Scent from a Strange Mountain Novel by Robert Olen Butler
Gospel Novel by Wilton Barnhardt
A Lesson Before Dying Novel by Ernest J. Gaines
My Alexandria Collected verse by Mark Doty
One Dark Body Novel by Charlotte Watson Sherman
Operation Shylock Novel by Philip Roth
Pigs in Heaven Novel by Barbara Kingsolver
Postcards Novel by E. Annie Proulx
Rebel Powers Novel by Richard Bausch
Save Me, Joe Louis Novel by Madison Smartt Bell
Shadow Play Novel by Charles Baxter
The Shipping News Novel by E. Annie Proulx
Streets of Laredo Novel by Larry McMurtry
The Train Home Novel by Susan Richards Shreve

Australian

Remembering Babylon Novel by David Malouf

British

The Blue Afternoon Novel by William Boyd
Crossing the River Novel by West Indian-born writer Caryl Phillips
A Dead Man in Deptford Novel by Anthony Burgess
A Family Romance Novel by Anita Brookner
No Other Life Novel by Irish-born writer Brian Moore
Scar Tissue Novel by Canadian-born writer Michael Ignatieff
These Enchanted Woods Comedy of morals by Alan Massie
Under the Frog Black comedy by Hungarian-born writer Tibor Fischer
The Vicar of Sorrows Novel by A. N. Wilson

Canadian

Across the Bridge Collection of short stories by Mavis Gallant
Away Novel by Jane Urquhart
Be Sure to Close Your Eyes Ninth volume of a New Age novel cycle by Hugh Hood
The Bookseller Novel by Matt Cohen
Graven Images Novel by Audrey Thomas
Head Hunter Novel by Timothy Findley
In a Glass House Novel by Nino Ricci
The Robber Bride Novel by Margaret Atwood
The Stone Diaries Novel by Carol Shields
Stranger Music: Selected Poems and Songs Collection by Leonard Cohen

Indian

A Suitable Boy Novel by Vikram Seth

Irish

Paddy Clarke Ha Ha Ha Comic novel by Roddy Doyle

FRENCH

French

Les corps celestes Novel by Nicolas Brehal
L'espace anterieur Novel by Jean-Loup Trassard
L'invention du monde Novel by Olivier Rolin
L'oeil du silence Novel by Marc Lambron
Sa femme Short novel by Emmanuele Bernheim

Lebanese

La Rocher de Tanios Novel by Amin Maalouf

GERMAN

Bitte nicht sterben Novel by Gabriele Wohmann
Das Gluck Novel by Gert Hoffmann
Der Rote Ritter Novel by Adolf Muschg
Die Hortensien der frau von Roselius Novel by Ludwig Harig
Die Passionfrucht Novel by Hermann Peter Piwitt
Die velorene Geschichte Novel by Otto F. Walter
Dorf unterm Wind Novel by Johannes Schenk
Ich Kafkaesque novel by Wolfgang Hilbig
Landschaft mit Dornen Novel by Uwe Saeger
Melodien Novel by Helmut Krausser
Papas Koffer Novel by Gerhard Kopf

HEBREW

Abyss Novel by Aharon Appelfeld
Gladiator, or a Note on the Military Police Novel by Amnon Navot
Hot Hot Dogs Collection of stories by Nathan Shaham
Shining Lights Novel by S. Yizhar

HUNGARIAN

In the Draft Collection of pieces by Ivan Mandy
One-Minute Letters Collection of letters, stories, and fairy tales by Istvan Orkeny
The Prisoner of Urga Novel by Laszlo Krasznahorkai

ITALIAN

Fuochi Novel by Franco Ferrucci
Il cardillo addolorato Novel by Anna Maria Ortese
Il silenzio Novel by Gina Lagorio
La città del dottor Malagui Novel by Roberto Pazzi
Mezzi di transporto Novel by Elisabetta Rasy
Ninfa plebea Novel by Dominico Rea
Vendita galline Km 2 Novel by Aldo Busi

JAPANESE

Deep River Novel by Shusaku Endo
The Downfall of Macias Giri Novel by Natsuki Ikezawa
Woman in Her Prime Novel by Saichi Maruya
Unworldly Collection of poems by Shuntaro Tanigawa

MACEDONIAN

A Gate in the Cloud Collected verse by Sande Stojcevski

NORWEGIAN

Avlosning Novel by Tor Ulven
Engelen din, Robinson Novel by Edvard Hoem
Forforeren Novel by Jan Kjaerstad
Julie Novel by Anne Karin Elstad
Ormens ar Novel by Knut Faldbakken
Siste dikt Poetry collection by Ernst Orvil
Utsikt til paradiset Novel by Ingvar Ambjornsen

POLISH

Silence Novel by Julian Stryjkowski

PORTUGUESE

Brazilian

Armarinho de miudezas Collected verse by Waly Salamao
Madrugada Novel by Edla van Steen
Panteros Novel by Decio Pignatari
Perversas familias Historical novel by Luis Antonio de Assis Brasil
Sangue na floresta Novel by Antonio Olinto

Portuguese

A barragem Novel by Julio Moreira
O ultimo cais Novel by Helena Marques
The Year of the Death of Ricardo Reis Novel by José Saramago

RUSSIAN

Lines of Fate Novel by Mark Kharitonov
November 1916 Novel (part of *The Red Wheel*) by Aleksandr Solzhenitsyn
The Time: Night Novel by Lyudmila Petrushevskaya

SERBIAN
The Inner Side of the Wind Novel by Milorad Pavic

SPANISH
Argentine
Santo oficio de la memoria Novel by Mempo Giardinelli

Chilean
Fantasmas de carne y hueso Novel by Jorge Edwards

Colombian
Los ojos del basilisco Novel by Germán Espinosa
Una lección de abismo Novel by Ricardo Cano Gaviria

Mexican
El gran lector Novel by Ignacio Solares
El naranjo, o los círculos del tiempo Novel by Carlos Fuentes

Peruvian
La violencia del tiempo Three-volume novel by Miguel Gutiérrez
Lituma en los Andes Novel by Mario Vargas Llosa

Spanish
Días contados Novel by Juan Madrid
El embrujo de Shanghai Novel by Juan Marse
El jardín de las dudas Epistolary novel by Fernando Savater
La pasión turca Novel by Antonio Gala
Mar al fondo Collection of stories by José Luis Sampedro
Mientras la tierra gira Collection of stories by José Luis Sampedro
Real sitio Final volume of the trilogy *Los círculos del tiempo* by José Luis Sampedro

Venezuelan
Pieles de leopardo Novel by Humberto Mata
Yo soy la rumba Novel by Angel Gustavo Infante

SWEDISH
Agnar Memoirs by Sven Delblanc
Fungi Novel by Agneta Pleijel
Historien med hunden Novel by Lars Gustafsson
Infor nedrakningen Memoirs by Jan Myrdal
Minnena ser mig Memoirs of Tomas Transtromer
Min salig bror Jean Hendrich Epistolary novel by Carina Burman
Mitt namn skall vara Stig Dagerman Biography by Bjorn Ranelid
Pigan i Arras Novel by Stewe Claeson
Unter tiden Memoirs of Goran Turnstrom
Vattenorgel Novel by Lars Andersson

1994

DEATHS
Robert Albert Bloch, American novelist
Piere-François-Marie-Louis Boulle, French novelist
Charles Bukowski, American novelist, poet, and screenwriter
Elias Canetti, Bulgarian-born English novelist and playwright

Rosa Clotilde Cecilia María del Carmen Chacel, Spanish novelist and poet
Alice Childress, American playwright and novelist
James Clavell, English-born American novelist
Reginald John Clemo, English poet
Peter Hebblethwaite, English Catholic writer and Vaticanologist
Eugène Ionesco, Romanian-born French playwright
Leonid Maksimovich Leonov, Russian novelist and playwright
Juan Carlos Onetti, Uruguayan novelist
John James Osborne, English playwright
Sir Karl Raimund Popper, Austrian-born English philosopher
Dennis Christopher George Potter, English playwright
Robert Ivanovich Rozhdestvensky, Russian poet
Samuel Dickson Selvon, Trinidadian-born Canadian author
J. I. M. Stewart, English novelist and literary critic
Yoshiyuki Junnosuke, Japanese novelist

LITERARY EVENT
PRIZES AND AWARDS
Booker Prize: *How Late It Was, How Late* by James Kelman
Caldecott Medal: *Grandfather's Journey* by Allen Say
Newbery Medal: *The Giver* by Lois Lowry
Nobel Prize in literature: Kenzaburo Oe, Japanese novelist
PEN/Faulkner Award: *Operation Shylock* by Philip Roth

Pulitzer Prizes
Biography *W. E. B. Du Bois: Biography of a Race, 1868–1919* by David Levering Lewis
Drama *Three Tall Women* by Edward Albee
Fiction *The Shipping News* by E. Annie Proulx
Nonfiction *Lenin's Tomb: The Last Days of the Soviet Empire* by David Remnick
Poetry *Neon Vernacular* by Yusef Komunyakaa

PUBLICATIONS
ARABIC
Why Did You Leave the Horse Alone? Collected verse by Palestinian poet Mahmud Darwish

BULGARIAN
Life That Strives to Be a Poem Collected verse by Elisaveta Bagravana

CHINESE
Living Novel by Yu Hua
Love and Longing in Hong Kong Short novel by Wang Anyi
On the Margins Novel by Go Fei
The Red Room Tavern Novel by Ye Zhaoyan
Venice Diary Novel by A. Cheng

CZECH
Alexander in the Streetcar Collection of short stories by Pavel Reznicek
Cape of Good Hopelessness Novel by Lubmir Martinek
One Ship—Laura Blair Poetic parable by Ivan Divis
The Year of the Frog Novel by Martin M. Simecka

DANISH

Borderliners Nonfiction work on private schooling by Peter Hoeg
Elskede ukendte Novel by Kirsten Thorup
Her i noerheden Novel by Martha Christensen

DUTCH

Terug uit Irkoetsk Historical novel by Theun de Vries

ENGLISH

American

The Afterlife and Other Stories Collection by John Updike
The Angel of History Poetry collection by Carolyn Forché
Closing Time Novel by Joseph Heller
Conquest: Montezuma, Cortes and the Fall of Old Mexico History by Hugh Thomas
The Crossing Novel by Cormac McCarthy
A Fool of His Own Novel by William Gaddis
A Frolic of His Own Novel by William Gaddis
Like Most Revelations Poetry collection by Richard Howard
Mercy of a Rude Stream Novel by Henry Roth
Neon Vernacular Collected verse by Yusef Komunyakaa
Rare and Endangered Species Collection of short stories by Richard Bausch
Rider Collected verse by Mark Rudman
Roadwalker Novel by Shirley Ann Grau
Shelter Novel by Jayne Anne Phillips
The Simple Truth Poetry collection by Philip Levine
Snow Falling on Cedars Novel by David Guterson
A Son of the Circus Novel by John Irving
Three Tall Women Play by Edward Albee
The Waterworks Novel by E. L. Doctorow
What I Lived For Novel by Joyce Carol Oates
Without a Hero Collection of short stories by T. Coraghessan Boyle
Worship Company of Fletchers Collected poems by James Tate

Australian

Coda Novel by Thea Astley
Jacko: The Great Intruder Novel by Thomas Keneally
The Unusual Life of Tristan Smith Novel by Peter Carey

British

Knowledge of Angels Novel by Jill Paton Walsh
Theory of War Novel by Joan Brady
You Can't Do Both Novel by Kingsley Amis

Canadian

The Cunning Man Novel by Robertson Davies
A Discovery of Strangers Historical novel by Rudy Wiebe
Eriksdottir: A Tale of Dreams and Luck Novel by Joan Clark
Kitchen Music Novel by Charles Foran
Open Secrets Collection of short stories by Alice Munro
A Sudden Brightness Novel by Alice Boisonneau

New Zealand

Deep River Talk Collected verse by Maori poet Hone Tuwhare

Scottish

How Late It Was, How Late Novel by James Kelman

South African

Feather Fall Collected verse by Laurens van der Post
The Master of Petersburg Novel by J. M. Coetzee
None to Accompany Me Novel by Nadine Gordimer
On the Contrary Novel by Andre Brink

Sri Lankan

Reef Novel by Romesh Gunasekara

Trinidadian

A Way in the World Novel by V. S. Naipaul

FRENCH

Canadian

L'ecureuil noir Novel by Daniel Poliquin
Un ange cornu avec des ailes de tole Novel by Michel Tremblay
Va Savoir Novel by Rejean Ducharme

French

Comme des anges Novel by Frederic Boyer
Comme ton père Novel by Guillaume Le Touze
De coeur et de l'affection Novel by Jacques Teboul
Immobile dans le courant de fleuve Novel by Yves Berger
La fille de gobernator Novel by Paule Constant
Port-Soudan Novel by Olivier Rolin
Un aller simple Novel by Didier van Cauwelaert

GERMAN

Das rote Schiff Novel by Andreas Mand
Mein Hund, meine Sau, mein Leben Novel by Arnold Stadler
Waldernacht Novel by Ralf Rothmann

HEBREW

Alleles Novel by Avraham Heffner
As a Few Days Novel by Meir Shalev
Clouds Novel by Dan Tsalka
Don't Pronounce It Night Novel by Amos Oz
Laish Novel by Aharon Appelfeld
Return from India Novel by A. B. Yehoshua
The Zigzag Child Novel by David Grossman

ITALIAN

Arcodamore Novel by Andrea De Carlo
Attesa sul mare Novel by Francesco Biamonti
Il catino di zinco Novel by Margaret Mazzantini
Oceano mare Novel by Alessandro Baricco
Progetto Burlamacchi Novel by Francesca Duranti
Sostiene Pereira Novel by Antonio Tabucchi
Va' dove ti porta il cuore Novel by Susanna Tamaro

JAPANESE

Rainbow Promontory Biographical novel by Takashi Tsuji (Seiji Tsutsumi)

NORWEGIAN

Barnevakt Novel by Ketil Bjornstad
Elsi Lund Novel by Bjorg Vik
Omrade aldrifastlagt Collected verse by Sigmund Mjelve

Solformokelson Novel by Rolf Enger
Thranes metode Collection of stories by Oystein Lonn

POLISH

Word after Word Collected verse of Tadeusz Rzewicz

PORTUGUESE

A poeira levada pelo vento Collected verse by Joaquim Manuel Magalhaes
Na tua face Novel by Vergilio Ferreira

RUSSIAN

The Closed Down Theater Novel by Bulat Okudzhava
The Curly-Haired Lieutenant Novel by Irina Muraveva
The Dust and Ashes Novel by Anatoly Rybakov
Tell Me, Mom Novel by Lyudmila Petrushevskaya

SERBIAN

In the Line of Fire Collected verse by Vasa Mihailovic
On Roads and Through Space Collected verse by Sava Jankovic
A Premeditated Murder Novel by Slobodan Selenic

SPANISH

Colombian

Asuntos de un hidalgo disoluto Novel by Hector Abad Faciolince

Mexican

Diana: The Goddess Who Hunts Alone Novel by Carlos Fuentes
Duerme Novel by Carmen Bullosa
El infierno es un decir Collected poems by Francisco Hernández
El señor de los mil días Novel by Homero Aridjis
El silencio de la luna Collected verse by José Emilio Pacheco
Pasado presente Roman à clef by Juan García Ponce
Rasero Novel by Francisco Robelledo

Spanish

Azul Novel by Rosa Regas
Caballeros de fortuna Novel by Luis Landero
El asesinato, el perdedor Novel by Camilio José Cela
La cruz de San Andrés Novel by Camilio José Cela
La reina de las nieves Novel by Carmen Martín Gaite
Mañana en la batalla piensa Novel by Javier Marías

SWEDISH

Anna, Hanna och Johanna Novel by Marianne Frederiksson
Hemligheter kring vatten Novel by Kerstin Ekman
Synden Novel by Bjorn Ranelid
Under i september Novel by Klas Ostergren

TURKISH

Night Novel by Bilge Karasu

1995

DEATHS

Sir Kingsley Amis, English novelist
Earle Birney, Canadian poet

Robert Oxton Bolt, English playwright
Brigid Brophy, English novelist
Eileen Chang, Chinese novelist
Robert Close, Australian novelist
Donald Alfred Davie, English poet and critic
Robertson Davies, Canadian novelist
Michael Andreas Helmuth Ende, German writer of children's stories
Walter Braden Finney, American novelist
Charles Gordone, African-American playwright
Ralph Barker Gustafson, Canadian poet
Albert Hackett, American playwright
Patrick John, American playwright
Sidney Kingsley, American playwright
Vladimir Yemelyanovich Maksimov, Russian novelist
James Merrill, American poet
Aziz Nesin, Turkish satirist
Ellis Peters (Edith Mary Pargeter), English novelist
Emmanuel François Robles, Algerian-born French novelist and playwright
Henry Roth, American novelist
Andrew Salkey, Jamaican novelist
Kenule Beeson Saro-Wiwa, Nigerian playwright
May Sarton, Belgian-born American poet
Sir Stephen Spender, English poet and critic
Sony Labou Tansi, Congolese writer
Miguel Torga, Portuguese poet and diarist
Elleston Trevor, English writer of thriller novels
Calder Willingham, American novelist and screenwriter
George Woodcock, Canadian poet, critic, historian, and playwright
Marguerite Young, American novelist
Roger Zelazny, American science fiction writer

LITERARY EVENT

PRIZES AND AWARDS

Booker Prize: *The Ghost Road* by Pat Barker
Caldecott Medal: *Smoky Night* by Eve Bunting
Newbery Medal: *Walk Two Moons* by Sharon Creech
Nobel Prize in literature: Seamus Heaney, Irish poet
PEN/Faulkner Award: *Snow Falling on Cedars* by David Guterson

Pulitzer Prizes

Biography *Harriet Beecher Stowe: A Life* by Joan D. Hedrick
Drama *The Young Man from Atlanta* by Horton Foote
Fiction *The Stone Diaries* by Carol Shields
History *No Ordinary Time: Franklin and Eleanor Roosevelt: The Home Front in World War II* by Doris Kearns Goodwin
Nonfiction *The Beak of the Finch: A Story of Evolution in Our Time* by Jonathan Weiner
Poetry *The Simple Truth* by Philip Levine

PUBLICATIONS

ARABIC

Egyptian

Love in Exile Novel by Baha' Tahir

Lebanese

Dear Mr. Kawabata Novel by Rashid ad-Daif

Tunisian

The Slave Merchant Novel by Salah ad-Din Bujah

CHINESE

Pallid Night Novel by Jia Pingwa
To Live Novel by Yu Hua

CZECH

Deaths by Seconds Novel by Antonin Brousek

DANISH

Brev til manen Final volume in the trilogy *Vanillepigen* by Ib Michael

ENGLISH

American

All Rivers Run to the Sea Autobiography by Elie Wiesel
Broken Country Collected verse by Joseph Brodsky
Dark Fields of the Republic Poetry collection by Adrienne Rich
Independence Day Novel by Richard Ford
Landscape and Memory Historical narrative by Simon Schama
Mrs. Ted Bliss Novel by Stanley Elkin
Oswald's Tale Novel by Norman Mailer
Palimpsest Memoir by Gore Vidal
Passing Through: Later Poems, New and Selected Collected verse by Stanley Kunitz
Pillars of Hercules: A Grand Tour of the Mediterranean Travel narrative by Paul Theroux
Sabbath's Theater Novel by Philip Roth
A Scattering of Salts Poetry collection by James Merrill
The Stories of Vladimir Nabokov Collected stories, edited by Dmitri Nabokov
The Tiger in the Grass Autobiographical novel by Harriet Doerr
Time and Money Collected verse by William Matthews

Australian

Cry of the Rain Bird Novel by Patricia Bird
The Riders Novel by Tim Winton
A River Town Novel by Thomas Keneally

British

The Ghost Road Novel by Pat Barker
In Every Face I Meet Novel by South African-born writer Justin Cartwright

Canadian

Dead Men's Watches Novel by Hugh Hood
A Gift of Rags Novel by Abraham Boyarsky
Morning in the Burned House Collected verse by Margaret Atwood
Mother Love Novel by L. R. Wright
Other Women Novel by Evelyn Lau
The Rain Ascends Novel by Joy Kogawa
The Roaring Girl Collection of short stories by Greg Hollingshed

Indian

The Moor's Last Sigh Novel by Salman Rushdie

Nigerian

The Beatification of Area Boy Play by Wole Soyinka

FRENCH

Canadian

La demarche du crabe Novel by Monique LaRue
L'ingratitude Novel by Chinese-born writer Ying Chen
Noces de sable Novel by Rachel Leclerc

French

Blesse, ronce noire Novel by Claude-Louis Combet
C'est tout Novel by Marguerite Duras
C'etait toute une vie Novel by François Bon
Ici Tropisms by Nathalie Sarraute
La classe de neige Novel by Emmanuel Carrère
La folle allure Novel by Christian Bobin
La langue maternelle Autobiographical novel by Vassilis Alexakis
Lambeaux Novel by Charles Juliet
La pas si lent de l'amour Autobiographical work by Hector Bianciotti
Le testament français Novel by Russian émigré André Makine

GERMAN

Abschied von den Feinden Novel by Reinhard Jirgl
Morbus Kitahara Novel by Christoph Ransmayr
Unbekannt verzogen Novel by Michael Schulte

ITALIAN

Jack Frusciante e uscito dal gruppo Novel by Enrico Bruzzi
Passaggio in ombra Novel by Mariateresa Di Lascia
Sostiene Pereira Novel by Antonio Tabucchi
Staccando l'ombra da terra Novel by Daniele del Giudice

JAPANESE

The Chronicle of the Screw Turning Bird Novel by Haruki Murakami
The Glorious Life of Saigyo Novel by Kunio Tsuji
Radiation Collected verse by Sachiko Yoshihara

MACEDONIAN

Alexander and Death Historical novel by Slobadan Mickovic
All the Faces of Death Collection of short stories by Petre M. Andreevski
Pole Vault Collection of short stories by Dragi Mihajlovski
Providence Collected verse by Ante Popovski

NORWEGIAN

Allegretto Novel by Terje Stigen
Forskjellig Collected verse by Oyvind Berg
Fugledansen Novel by Ingvar Ambjornsen
Jordparadiset Varherres nedfallsfrukt Novel by Johannes Heggland
Lystreise Novel by Tove Nilsen
Omvei til Venus Novel by Torgeir Schgerven
Som dine dagerer Novel by Karin Elstad
Trylleflojten Novel by Sissel Lange-Nielsen

POLISH

Afterimages: Young Men from Those Years Memoirs by Marek
    Nowakowski
Three Times Novel by Dariusz Bitner

PORTUGUESE

Brazilian

A ultima quimera Biographical novel about the Brazilian poet
    Augusto dos Anjos by Ana Miranda
Perola Play by Mauro Rasi

Portuguese

Meditaçao sobre ruinas Collected verse by Nuno Judice
Mulheres de sombra Novel by Sofia Ferreira
Un deus passeando pela brisa da tarde Historical novel by Mario
    de Carvalho

RUSSIAN

A General and His Army Novel by Gyorgy Vladimov
The Odyssey Novel by Yevgeny Fyodorov
An Official Tale Novel by Oleg Pavlov

SERBIAN

Albion Albion Novel by Nikola Moravcevic
The Dead Spot Play by Aleksandar Popovic
Farewell, Liars Play by Aleksandar Popovic
The Rose Garden Play by Aleksandar Popovic
Turning Point Novel by Sava Jankovic

SPANISH

Argentine

Diario de Andrés Fava Short novel by Julio Cortázar

Colombian

Cartas cruzadas Novel by Darío Jaramillo Agudelo
Of Love and Other Demons Novel by Gabriel García Márquez

Cuban

Delito por bailar el chachacha Fictional memoirs by Guillermo
    Cabrera Infante

Spanish

El Crimen del cine Oriente Novel by Javier Tomeo
El sentimiento Novel by María Guelbenzu
La mirada del otro Novel by Fernando Delgado
Más allá del jardín Novel by Antonio Gala
Telepenia de Celia Cecilia Villalobo Novel by Alvaro Pombo

Venezuelan

Viejo Autobiographical novel by Adrián González León

SWEDISH

Hatet Novel by Kjell Espmark
Hummelhonung Novel by Togny Lindgren
Ljuset ur Skuggornas varld Novel by Lars Gyllensten
Rymdvarktaren Novel by Peter Nilson
Varddjuret Novel by Marie Hermanson

TURKISH

Bosphorus Fortress Novel by Nedim Gursel
Ruined Mountains Novel by Yunus Nadi

1996

DEATHS

Ai Qing, Chinese poet
Hervé Bazin, French novelist
'Abd al-Hamid Benhadugah, Algerian writer
Erma Bombeck, American humorist
Harold Brodkey (Aaron Roy Weintraub), American short-story
    writer and novelist
Joseph Brodsky, Russian-born American poet
George Mackay Brown, Scottish novelist
Gesualdo Bufalino, Italian novelist
Cao Yu, Chinese playwright
Marcia Gluck Davenport, American novelist
Geoffrey Dearmer, English poet
José Donoso, Chilean novelist and short-story writer
Marguerite Duras, Indochinese-born French novelist
Odysseus Elytis, Greek poet
Shusaku Endo, Japanese Christian novelist
Vergilio Ferreira, Brazilian novelist and essayist
Emile Habibi, Israeli Arab novelist
Buland al-Haidari, Iraqi Kurdish poet
Heidiji Hojo, Japanese playwright
Molly Keane, also wrote as M. J. Farrell (Mary Nesta Skrine),
    Anglo-Irish novelist
Ivan V. Lalic, Serbian poet
Mary Lavin, American-born Irish poet
Norman Alexander McCaig, Scottish poet
Sorley Maclean, Scottish Gaelic poet
Augustine A. Mandino, American writer and motivational
    speaker
Claude Mauriac, French antinovelist and memoirist
Gaston Miron, French-Canadian poet
Jessica Mitford, English-born American writer
David Mourao-Ferreira, Portuguese novelist
Laurens van der Post, South African writer
Alfred A. Poulin Jr., American poet
Sinclair Ross, Canadian novelist
Julian Stryjkowski, Polish Jewish novelist
Efua Theodora Sutherland, Ghanaian playwright, poet, and chil-
    dren's author
P. L. Travers (Helen Lyndon Goff), Australian-born English
    writer of children's books
Diana Trilling, American social and literary critic
Uno Chiyo, Japanese novelist
José María Valverde, Spanish poet and scholar

LITERARY EVENT

PRIZES AND AWARDS

Booker Prize: *Last Orders* by Graham Swift
Caldecott Medal: *Officer Buckle and Gloria* by Peggy
    Rathmann
Newbery Medal: *The Midwife's Apprentice* by Karen
    Cushman
Nobel Prize in literature: Wisława Szymborska, Polish poet
PEN/Faulkner Award: *Independence Day* by Richard Ford

Pulitzer Prizes

Biography   *God, a Biography* by Jack Miles
Drama   *Rent* by Jonathan Larson
Fiction   *Independence Day* by Richard Ford
History   *William Cooper's Town: Power and Persuasion on the Frontier of the Early American Republic* by Alan Taylor
Nonfiction   *The Haunted Land: Facing Europe's Ghosts After Communism* by Tina Rosenberg
Poetry   *The Dream of the United Field* by Jorie Graham

PUBLICATIONS

CHINESE

Ma Qiao Dictionary Novel by Han Shaogong
The Way of Living in the World Novel by Zhou Meiseng

CZECH

The Excursion Participants Novel by Michael Viewegh

DANISH

Bang Biographical novel by Dorrit Willumsen
Det skabtes vaklen Arabesker Novel by Soren Ulrik Thomsen
Rejsen med Emma Novel by Hanne Marie Svendsen
Tavshed i oktober Novel by Jens Christian Grondahl

ENGLISH

American

After Rain Novel by William Trevor
Angela's Ashes: A Memoir Autobiography by Frank McCourt
Atticus Novel by Ron Hansen
The Collected Stories of Mavis Gallant Collection by Mavis Gallant
The Dream of the Unified Field Collected verse by Jorie Graham
The Giant's House Novel by Elizabeth McCracken
Good Evening Mr. and Mrs. America and All the Ships at Sea Novel by Richard Bausch
The Here and Now Novel by Robert Cohen
The King of Babylon Shall Not Come Against You Novel by George Garrett
The Last Hotel for Women Novel by Vicki Covington
The Last Thing He Wanted Novel by Joan Didion
Mountains and Rivers Without End Poetic cycle by Gary Snyder
Reader's Block Novel by David Markson
Scrambled Eggs and Whiskey: Poems, 1991–1995 Collection by Hayden Carruth
Ship Fever and Other Stories Collection by Andrea Barrett
Sun Under Wood Collected verse by Robert Hass
The Visiting Physician Novel by Susan Richards Shreve
We Were the Mulvaneys Novel by Joyce Carol Oates
Women in Their Beds Novel by Gina Berriault

Australian

Billy Sunday Novel by Rod Jones
Remembering Babylon Novel by David Malouf
Vanishing Point Novel by Morris West

British

Behind the Scenes at the Museum Novel by Kate Atkinson
Cross Channel Novel by Julian Barnes
Every Man for Himself Novel by Beryl Bainbridge

Last Orders Novel by Graham Swift
Love, Again Novel by Doris Lessing
The Orchard on Fire Novel by Shena Mackay
A Spell in Winter Novel by Helen Dumore
The Tailor of Panama Spy novel by John le Carré
The Yellow Admiral Novel (18th in the Aubrey Matruin seafaring series) by Patrick O'Brian

Canadian

Alias Grace Novel by Margaret Atwood
Angel Walk Novel by Katherine Govier
The Cure for Death by Lightning Novel by Gail Anderson-Dargatz
A Fine Balance Novel by Indian-born writer Robinton Mistry
Fugitive Pieces Novel by Ann Michaels

Irish

Gunpowder Collected verse by Bernard O'Donoghue
Reading in the Dark Novel by Seamus Deane
The Spirit Level Collected verse by Seamus Heaney
The Woman Who Walked into Doors Novel by Roddy Doyle

New Zealand

New and Collected Poems, 1941–1995 Collection by Allen Curnow

FRENCH

French

À la frontière Collected verse by Michel Butor
Du plus loin de l'oubli Novel by Patrick Modano
Eclats de sel Novel by Sylvie Germain
La grande beune Novel by Pierre Michon
Le chasseur zero Novel by Pascale Roze
Le roi du bois Novel by Pierre Michon
L'organization Novel by Jean Rolin
Orlanda Novel by Jacqueline Harpma
Un silence d'environ une demi-heure Fictionalized autobiography by Boris Schreiber
Weekend de chasse a la mère Novel by Geneviève Brisac

Lebanese

Way of Migration Novel by Alexandre Najjar

GERMAN

Animal triste Novel by Monika Maron
Bodenlos Collected verse by Sarah Kirsch
Die Sache mit Randow Novel by Klaus Schelsinger
Medea: Stimmen Novel by Christa Wolf

HEBREW

The Deserter Novel by Dorit Abush
The Heart of Tel Aviv Novel by Nathan Shaham
My Skin Novel by Ori Dromer

ITALIAN

Alonso e i visonari Novel by Anna Maria Ortese
Canone inverso Novel by Paolo Maurensig
Diletta Constanza Biographical novel by Fausta Garavini
Fontano da casa Novel by Franco Ferrucci

Giaconda a dama con la luna Novel by Giuliana Morandini
Il bacio della Medusa Novel by Melania Mazzucco
Incerti di viaggio Novel by Roberto Pazzi
La terra è di tutti Novel by Ferdinando Camon
Seta Novel by Alessandro Baricco
Suicidi dovuti Novel by Aldo Busi

JAPANESE

St. Godhard Railway and Other Stories Collection by Yoko Tawada
Burnt Metropolis Novel by Otohiko Kaga
Endless Fiesta Novel by Takashi Tsuji
Poems of Haikai Tsuji Collection by Masao Tsuji

NORWEGIAN

Drift Novel by Ketil Bjornstad
En annen vei Novel by Finn Carling
Nar jeg ser deg Novel by Knut Faldbakken
Skammen Family saga by Bergjlot Hobaek Haff

POLISH

Ajol and Laor Collection of short stories by Stanisław Czycz
The Great Pause Collected verse by Urszula Koziol

PORTUGUESE

Brazilian

O buraco ne parede Novel by Rubem Fonseca
Farewell Collected verse by Carlos Drummond
Nao es tu, Brasil Novel by Marcelo Rubens Paiva

Portuguese

A casa da cabeça de cavalo Novel by Teolinda Gersao
Blindness Novel by José Saramago

RUSSIAN

Country of Origin Collection of short stories by Dmitry Bakin
A Stamp Album Novel by Andrey Sergeyev

SERBIAN

Bottomless Novel by Svetlana Velmar-Jankovic

SPANISH

Argentine

El cielo dividido Novel by Reina Roffe
El farmer Novel by Andrés Rivera
La madriguera Novel by Tununa Mercado

Colombian

Chapolas negras Novel by Fernando Vallejo
News of a Kidnapping Nonfiction work by Gabriel García Márquez

Mexican

Look for My Obituary and First Love Two novellas by Elena Garro
The Crystal Frontier Novel by Carlos Fuentes

Spanish

El amargo don de la belleza Novel by Terenci Moix
La cruz en la espada Novel by Nestor Luján

La piel del tambor Novel by Arturo Pérez Reverte
Las visiones de Lucrecia Novel by José María Merino
Lo raro es vivir Novel by Carmen Martín Gaite

SWEDISH

Gor mig levande Novel by Kerstin Ekman
Lifsens rot Novel by Sara Lidman
Mozarts tredje hjarna Collected verse by Goran Sonnevi
Paradis Collection of short stories by Ulf Eriksson
Sammanhang Prose poems by Birgitta Trotzig
Skimmer Novel by Goran Tunstrom
Sorgegondolen Collected poems by Tomas Transtromer

TURKISH

Dangerous Tales Novel by Ahmet Altan

1997

DEATHS

Gastón Baquero y Díaz, Cuban poet
William Burroughs, American Beat novelist
Antonio Callado, Brazilian novelist
James Dickey, American poet
Leon Edel, American biographer and critic
Brendan Gill, American writer
Allen Ginsberg, American Beat poet
Marguerite Henry, American writer of children's stories
Bohumil Hrabal, Czech writer
Elspeth Huxley, English writer
Mohammad Ali Jamalzadeh, Iranian novelist
Muhammad Mahdo al-Jawahiri, Iraqi poet
James Kruss, German writer of children's stories
Laurie Lee, English poet and prose writer
Denise Levertov, English-born American poet
Dulce María Loynaz, Cuban poet
William Procter Matthews III, American poet
Judith Merrill (Josephine Juliet Grossman), American-born Canadian science fiction writer
James Michener, American novelist
Bulat Shalvocih Okudzhava, Russian poet
Sir Victor Sawdon Pritchett, English writer
Harold Robbins, American novelist
Leo Rosten, Polish-born American Jewish writer
Andrey Donatovich Sinyavsky, Russian novelist and dissident
Robin Skelton, Canadian poet
Helen Foster Snow, American writer
Vladimir Alekseyevich Soloukhin, Russian novelist
Amos Tutuola, Nigerian novelist
Sadallah Wannus, Syrian playwright

LITERARY EVENT

PRIZES AND AWARDS

Booker Prize: *The God of Small Things* by Arundhati Roy
Caldecott Medal: *Golem* by David Wisniewski
Newbery Medal: *The View from Saturday* by E. L. Konigsburg

Nobel Prize in literature: Dario Fo, Italian playwright
PEN/Faulkner Award: *Women in Their Beds* by Gina Berriault

Pulitzer Prizes

Autobiography *Angela's Ashes* by Frank McCourt
Fiction *Martin Dressler: The Tale of an American Dreamer* by Steven Milhauser
History *Original Meanings: Politics and Ideas in the Making of the Constitution* by Jack N. Rakove
Nonfiction *Ashes to Ashes: America's Hundred Year Cigarette War, the Public Health and the Unabashed Triumph of Philip Morris* by Richard Kluger
Poetry *Alive Together: New and Selected Poems* by Lisel Mueller

PUBLICATIONS

CHINESE

Outstanding Talent—Yang Du Biographical novel by Tang Haoming and Zhu Shucheng
War and People Multivolume account of the war against Japan by Wang Huo
The Way of Living in the World Novel by Zhou Meisen
White Deer Plains Novel by Cheng Zhongshi

CZECH

Cat's Lives Historical novel by Eda Kriseova

DANISH

Mea Culpa Novel by Anne Holt
Men Jorden star til evig tid Novel by Pyrds Helle
Nar fisken fanger solen Novel by Mette Winge
Prins Novel by Ib Michaels
Skumring e Praha Novel by Finn Carling
Svart due Novel by Sissel Lie
Thomas Ripenseren Novel by Anne Marie Ejrnaes
Veien tlil Dhaka Novel by Ketil Bjornstad
Verden forswinner Novel by Liv Koltzow

DUTCH

Het bureau Novel by J. J. Voskuil
Het hof van barmhartigheid Novel by A. F. Th. Van der Heijden
Hertog van Egypte Novel by Margriet de Moor
Tydverdryf/Pastime Collected verse by Elisabeth Eybers

ENGLISH

American

The Actual Novella by Saul Bellow
The Aguero Sisters Novel by Cuban-born writer Cristina Garcia
American Pastoral Novel by Philip Roth
Cold Mountain Novel by Charles Frazier
Echo House Novel by Ward Just
Effort at Speech: New and Selected Poems Collection by William Meredith
Girls Novel by Frederick Busch
Jesus Saves Novel by Darcy Steinke
Lost Man's River Novel by Peter Matthiessen
Man Crazy Novel by Joyce Carol Oates
Martin Dressler Novel by Stephen Millhauser
Mason & Dixon Novel by Thomas Pynchon

The Puttermesser Papers Novel by Cynthia Ozick
Timequake Novel by Kurt Vonnegut Jr.
Toward the End of Time Futuristic novel by John Updike
Underworld Novel by Don De Lillo
West Wind Poetry collection by Mary Oliver
Women with Men Three novellas by Richard Ford

Australian

Caesar: Let the Dice Fly Novel on ancient Rome by Colleen McCullough
The Essence of the Thing Novel by Madeleine St. John
Jack Maggas Novel by Peter Carey

British

Down by the River Novel by Edna O'Brien
Every Man for Himself Novel by Beryl Bainbridge
Grace Notes Novel by Bernard MacLaverty
Quarantine Novel by Jim Crace
The Reader Short novel by Bernhard Schlink
The Way I Found Her Novel by Rose Tremain

Canadian

Barney's Version Novel by Mordecai Richler
Evening Light Novel by Harold Horwood
Larry's Party Novel by Carol Shields
On Glassy Wings: Poems New and Selected Collection by Anne Szumigalski
The Time Being Novel by Mary Meigs
Time Capsule: New and Selected Poems Collection by Pat Lowther
The Underpainter Novel by Jane Urquhart

Indian

The God of Small Things Novel by Arundhati Roy

New Zealand

Straw into Gold Selected new poems by C. K. Stead

Nigerian

Dangerous Love Novel by Ben Okri

FLEMISH

De geruchten Novel by Hugo Claus

FRENCH

Canadian

Cristoforo Historical novel by Willie Thomas

French

Amour noir Novel by Dominique Noguez
Casimir mene la grande Novel by Jean de Ormesson
The Diving Bell and the Butterfly Memoir by Jean-Dominique Bauby
La bataille Novel by Patrick Rambaud
L'Abyssin Novel by Jean-Christophe Rufin
La morseure Novel by Patrick Villemin
Les sept noms du peintre Novel by Philippe Le Guillou
Les voleurs de beauté Novel by Pascal Bruckner
Poisson d'or Novel by Jean-Marie Gustave Le Clezio
Un an Novel by Jean Echenoz
Un gachis Novel by Emmanuel Darley

Moroccan

La nuit de lerreur Novel by Tahar ben Jelloun

GERMAN

In einer dunken Nacht ging ich aus meinem stillen Haus Novel by Peter Handke
Von allem Anfang an Novel by Christoph Hein

HEBREW

The Ice Mine Novel by Aharon Appelfeld
A Night in Santa Paulina Novel by Yitzhak Orpaz
Voyage to the End of the Millennium Novel by A. B. Yehoshua
Winnie Mandela's Football Team Novel by Dalia Rabikovitz

ITALIAN

Anima mundi Novel by Susanna Tamaro
Dolce per se Novel by Dacia Maraini
Il caso Courrier Novel by Marta Morazzoni
Microcosmi Novel by Claudio Magris
Posillipo Novel by Elisabetta Rasy
Separazione Collection of short stories by Francesca Sanvitale
Sogni mancini Novel by Francesca Duranti

JAPANESE

Beautiful Days Novel by Nobuo Kojima
Missing Forever Collected poems by Kosuke Shibusawa
Paradise Lost Novel by Jun'ichi Watanabe

NORWEGIAN

Ibsens Italia Novel by Atle Naess
Kjoerlighetsdikt Collection of love poems by Stein Mehren

POLISH

Ash and Honey Collected verse by Artur Szlosarek
A Little Side-Road Dog Collection of essays by Czesław Milosz

PORTUGUESE

Brazilian

Alcacer Quibir Historical novel by Antonio Olinto
Lealdade Novel by Marcio Souza

Portuguese

De profundis valsa lenta Autobiographical novel by José Cardoso Pires
A God Strolling in the Cool of the Evening Novel by Mario de Carvalho
O monhe das cobras Collected verse by Rui Knopfli
Outrora agora Novel by Augusto Abelaira

RUSSIAN

Boris and Gleb Mythological novel by Yuri Buyda
The Cage Novel by Anatoly Azolsky
The East-West Wind Collected verse by Yelena Shvarts
Hilarion and the Dwarf Novella by Vladimir Gubin
The Ox of Frankfurt Collected short stories by Oleg Yuryev

SERBIAN

Looney Tunes Novel by Svetislav Basara
Lure Novel by David Albahari
The Sky Collected verse by Miroslav Maksimovic

SPANISH

Argentine

La muerte como efecto secundario Novel by Ana María Shua
Nuestra señora de la noche Novel by Marco Denevi

Cuban

Te di la vida entera Novel by Zoé Valdés

Mexican

Mal de amores Novel by Angeles Mastretta

Nicaraguan

El pacto Novel by Milagros Palma

Peruvian

Los cuadernos de don Rigoberto Novel by Mario Vargas Llosa

Spanish

Olvidado Rey Gudu Allegorical folk epic by Ana María Matute
La tempestad Novel by Juan Manuel de Prada
Los años indecisos Autobiographical reminiscences by Gonzalo Torrente Ballester
La forja de un ladrón Novel by Francisco Umbral
El pequeño heredero Novel by Gustavo Martín Garzo
La hija del caníbal Novel by Rosa Montero
Plenilunio Novel by Antonio Muñoz Molina
La mirada del alma Novel by Luis Mateo Díez
Limpieza de sangre Novel by Arturo Pérez Reverte
Quien Metanarrative Bilingual Spanish-English novel by Carlos Canique

SWEDISH

Den hogsta kasten Collection of poems by Carina Rydberg
Fageljagarna Poetic magnum opus by Lennart Sjogren
Israpport Novel by Werner Aspenstrom
Svindel Novel by Per Holmer

TURKISH

Look, the Euphrates Is Flowing Bloody First novel of a trilogy by Yashar Kemal

1998

DEATHS

Eric Ambler, English writer of thrillers
Cleveland Amory, American writer
Henry Steele Commager, American historian
Catherine Cookson, English writer
Marco Denevi, Argentine journalist and writer
Geoffrey Piers Henry Dutton, Australian writer
Walter Dumond Edmonds, American writer of historical novels
William Gaddis, American novelist
Elena Garro, Mexican poet, novelist, and writer of short stories
Rumer Godden, English novelist
James Goldman, American novelist and playwright
Julian Green, French novelist
Zbigniew Herbert, Polish, poet, essayist, and playwright

Ted Hughes, English poet
Hammond Innes, English novelist
Ernst Junger, German novelist and essayist
Halldor Laxness (Halldor Killjan Gudyonsson), Icelandic novelist
Hermann Lenz, German novelist
Janet Lewis, American poet and writer of children's stories
Robert Morasco, American playwright
W. O. Mitchell, Canadian novelist and playwright
Wright Morris, American novelist
Mya Than Tint, Burmese novelist and translator
Thomas Narcejac, French writer of crime novels
Anna Maria Ortese, Italian novelist
Octavio Paz, Mexican novelist
José Augusto Neves Cardoso, Portuguese writer of allegorical novels
Nizar Qabbani, Syrian poet
Gregor von Rezzori d'Arezzo, Austrian writer
Anatoly Naumovich Rybakov, Russian novelist
Iain Crichton Smith, Scottish poet, novelist, and playwright
Robert Geoffrey Trease, English writer of children's historical stories
Jerome Weidman, American novelist
Dorothy West, African-American novelist

LITERARY EVENT

PRIZES AND AWARDS
Booker Prize: *Amsterdam* by Ian McEwan
Caldecott Medal: *Rapunzel* by Paul O. Zelinsky
Newbery Medal: *Out of the Dust* by Karen Hesse
Nobel Prize in literature: José Saramago, Portuguese novelist
PEN/Faulkner Award: *The Bear Comes Home* by Rafi Zabor

Pulitzer Prizes

Autobiography *Personal History* by Katherine Graham
Drama *How I Learned to Drive* by Paula Vogel
Fiction *American Pastoral* by Philip Roth
History *Summer for the Gods: The Scopes Trial and America's Continuing Debate over Science and Religion* by Edward J. Larson
Nonfiction *Guns, Germs and Steel: The Fates of Human Societies* by Jared Diamond
Poetry *Black Zodiac* by Charles Wright

PUBLICATIONS

BULGARIAN
Sitting Duck Novel by Yordan Radichkov

CHINESE
The Centennial Sea-Wolf Novel by Wang Jiabing
Father Murdering Novel by Zeng Weihao
Hometown Noodles and Flower Novel by Liu Zhenyun
Silver City Novel by Li Rui
Toward Chaos Novel by Cong Weixi

CZECH
Identity Novel by Milan Kundera
Passion Novel by Ivan Hercikova

The Ultimate Intimacy Novel by Ivan Klima
Very Happy Marriage Collection of 13 psychological stories by Hans Belohradska

DANISH
Jeg har hort et stierneskud Travelogue and cultural philosophy by Carsten Jensen
Lucca Novel by Jens Christian Grondahl
Prioritaire Novel by Iselin C. Hermann
Slangen i Sydney Novel by Michael Larsen
Udsigten Novel by Christina Hesselholdt

DUTCH
Plankton Novel (third in the *Het Bureau* series) by J. J. Voskuil

ENGLISH
American

Bech at Bay Novel by John Updike
Charming Billy Novel by Alice McDermott
Cities of the Plain Last volume of *The Border Trilogy* by Cormac McCarthy
Cloudsplitter Novel by Russell Banks
Damascus Gate Novel by Robert Stone
Dreamer Historical-biographical novel on Martin Luther King Jr. by Charles Johnson
Esperanza's Box of Saints Novel by Mexican writer María Amparo Escandón
The Fall of a Sparrow Novel by Robert Hellenga
For Kings and Planets Novel by Ethan Canin
A Man in Full Novel by Tom Wolfe
Paradise Novel by Toni Morrison
Riven Rock Novel by T. Coraghessan Boyle
The Road Home Novel by Jim Harrison
This Time: New and Selected Poems Collection by Gerald Stern
A Widow for One Year Novel by John Irving
¡Yo! Novel by Dominican-born writer Julia Alvarez

Barbadian

Magical Realism Novel by Kamau Brathwaite

British

Amsterdam Short novel by Ian McEwan
Birthday Letters Poetry collection by Ted Hughes
Casanova Novel by Andrew Miller
Collected Poems, 1948–1998 Collection by D. J. Enright
Harry Potter and the Sorcerer's Stone Children's novel by J. K. Rowling
The Industry of Souls Novel by Martin Booth
Master Georgie Novel by Beryl Bainbridge
Pleasured Novel by Philip Hensher
Pieces of Light Novel by Adam Thorpe
Spider Web: A Novel Novel by Penelope Lively

Canadian

The Electrical Field Novel by Japanese-born writer Kerri Sakamoto
Freedom's Just Another Word Novel by Dakota Hamilton
Girlfriend in a Coma Novel by Douglas Coupland
The Healer Novel by Greg Hollingshead

The Love of a Good Woman Collection of short stories by Alice Munro
A Recipe for Bees Novel by Gail Anderson Dargatz
Strange Heaven Novel by Lynn Coady

Irish

Breakfast on Pluto Novel by Patrick McCabe
Opened Ground: Poems, 1956–1996 Collected verse by Seamus Heaney

Nigerian

Infinite Riches Novel by Ben Okri

Somalian

Secrets Novel by Nuruddin Farah

South African

The House Gun Novel by Nadine Gordimer

Sri Lankan

The Sandglass Novel by Romesh Gunasekara

FRENCH

Canadian

La petite fille qui aimait trop les allumettes Novel by Gaetan Soucy

French

Confidence pour confidence Novel by Paule Constant
La conversation Novel by Lorette Nobecourt
La maladie de Sachs Novel by Martin Winkler
La manuscrit de Port-Ebène Novel by Dominique Bona
La naissance des fantomes Novel by Marie Darrieussecq
Le cant silencieux des chouettes Novel by Albert Bensoussan
Le dit de Tianyi Novel by François Cheng
Le loup Mongol Lyric epic of Genghis Khan by Homeric
Le monde retrouve de Louis-François Pinagot Novel by Alan Corbin
Les particules élémentaires Novel by Michael Houellebecq
Perou Novel by Michel Braudeau
Un été memorable Novel by Jean Perol

GERMAN

Austrian

Vermutengen uber die Liebe in einem fremden Haus Novel by Ulrike Langle

German

Ein springender Brunnen Novel by Martin Walser
Pargfrider Novel by Stefan Heym
Simple Stories Collection by Inge Schulze

HEBREW

The Conversion Novel by Aharon Appelfeld
The Crime of Writing Novel by Hayim Lapid
In the Desert of a Lodging Place Novel by Yonat Sened and Alexander Sened
The Iron Tracks Novel by Aharon Appelfeld
Kneller's Happy Campers Novel by Etgar Keret
Lovely Malcomia Novel by S. Yizhar

Restoring Former Loves Novel by Yehoshua Kenaz
The Same Sea Novel by Amos Oz

ITALIAN

Adriatico Novel by Raffaele Nigro
Sentieri sotto la neve Collection of short stories by Mario Rigonia Stern
Uffizio delle tenebre Novel by Fausta Garavini

JAPANESE

At 0 A.M. in Buenos Aires Novel by Shu Fujisawa
Double Suicides Committed at Forty-Eight Waterfalls in Akame Novel by Chokitsu Kurumatani
"A Fiddler Crab" Short story by Kiyoko Murata
Germanium Nights Novel by Mangetsu Hanamura
A Mountain of Fire Roman-fleuve by Yuko Tshushima

MACEDONIAN

History of a Black Love Novel by Slobadan Mickovic

NORWEGIAN

Beretninger om beskyttelse Novel by Erik Fosnes Hansen
Hutchinsons effekt Novel by Geir Pollen
Kron og mynt Novel by Kjartan Flogstad
Noveller i samling Collection of short stories by Liv Koltzow
Tvillingfeber Novel by Britt Billdoen

PERSIAN

Seventy Tombstones Poetry collection by Yodallah Ryya'i

POLISH

Always a Fragment Autobiographical pieces by Tadeusz Rozewicz
Black Seasons Reminiscences by Maichal Glowisnki
Dance of Death: A Baroque Poem Collected verse by Tadeusz Rozewicz
Surgical Precision Literary miscellany by Stanisław Baranczak

PORTUGUESE

Brazilian

Achados e perdidos Novel by Luiz Alfredo Garcia-Roza
A dança final Play by Plinio Marcos
Jantando com Melvin Novel by Marcelo Coelho
Trilhos e quintais Novel by Carmen L. Oliveira

Portuguese

All the Names Novel by José Saramago
Pedro e Paula Novel by Helder Macedo

RUSSIAN

Adventures of an Iron and a Boot Novel by Lyudmila Petrushevskaya
Dream of a Tree Novel by Dmitry Bakin
The Escort Angel Novel by Viktor Pelevin
A Foreign Letter Novel by Aleksandr Morozov
The New Sweet Style Novel by Vasily Aksyonov
Solo on a Burning Trumpet Collected verse by Yelena Shvarts
Wake for a Red Bitch Autobiographical novel by Inga Petkavich

SERBIAN
Early Sorrows Novel by Danilo Kis

SLOVAK
Wonderful Night in Paris Collected verse of Marian Grupac

SPANISH
Cuban
Sonetos Collected verse by Carilda Oliver Labra

Mexican
Quien como Dios Novel by Eladia González

Peruvian
The Notebooks of Don Rigoberto Intellectual disquisition by Mario Vargas Llosa

Spanish
El hereje Novel by Miguel Delibes
O Cesar o nada Novel by Manuel Vásquez Montalbán
Irse de casa Novel by Carmen Martín Gaite
El dios dormido Novel by Fanny Rubio
El lapiz del carpintero Novel by Manuel Rivas
Pequeñas infamias Novel by Carmen Posada
Beatriz y los cuerpos celestes Novel by Lucía Etxebarria
Cuaderno de Nueva York Collected verse by José Hierro

Uruguayan
Patas arriba Fictionalized news stories by Eduardo Galeano

SWEDISH
Eldflugorna Collected verse by Folke Isakson
Och jag grep arorna och rodde Novel by Birgitta Lillpers
Sena sagor Novel by P. C. Jersild
Suject Angot Novel by Christine Angot

TURKISH
Call Me Crimson Novel by Yashar Kemal

1999

DEATHS
Rafael Alberti, Spanish poet and playwright
Germán Arciniegas Angueyra, Colombian historian, novelist, and essayist
Abdul Wahhab al-Bayati, Iraqi poet
Adolfo Bioy Casares, Argentine writer
Paul Bowles, American writer
João Cabral de Melo Neto, Brazilian poet
Nirad Chandra Chaudhuri, Indian novelist
Andre Dubus, American short-story writer
Clifton Fadiman, American critic and literary arbiter
Ricardo Garibay, Mexican writer
Joseph Heller, American writer
George Vincent Higgins, American crime writer
Dmitry Sergeyevich Likachev, Russian literary historian and intellectual

Naomi Mitchison, English writer of historical fiction
Brian Moore, Irish-born Canadian novelist
Penelope Mortimer, English novelist
Dame Iris Murdoch, English author and philosopher
Olga Orozco, Argentine poet
Thakazhi Sivasankara Pillai, Malayalee novelist
Mario Puzo, American novelist
Qian Zhongshu, Chinese scholar and writer
Nathalie Sarraute, French novelist
Gonzalo Torrente Ballester, Spanish literary critic and novelist
Morris West, Australian novelist

LITERARY EVENT
PRIZES AND AWARDS
Booker Prize: *Disgrace* by J. M. Coetzee
Caldecott Medal: *Snowflakes Bentley* by Mary Azarian
Newbery Medal: *Holes* by Louis Sachar
Nobel Prize in literature: Günter Grass, German novelist
PEN/Faulkner Award: *The Hours* by Michael Cunningham

Pulitzer Prizes
Biography *Lindbergh* by A. Scott Berg
Drama *Wit* by Margaret Edelson
Fiction *The Hours* by Michael Cunningham
History *Gotham: A History of New York City to 1898* by Edwin G. Burrows and Mike Wallace
Nonfiction *Annals of the Former World* by John McPhee
Poetry *Blizzard of One* by Mark Strand

PUBLICATIONS
BULGARIAN
The Gangster War Novel by Donka Petrunova
The Highway Collected short stories and novels by Yordan Radichkov
A Lassie Was Cracking Hazelnuts Novel by Konstantin Terziev
A Natural Novel Novel by Georgi Gospodinov

CROATIAN
The Museum of Unconditional Surrender Combination diary, memoir, notebook, and novel by Dubravka Ugresic

CZECH
Departure from the Castle Fictional diary by Jaroslav Putik
Grandmothers Novel by Petr Sabach
Night Tango: A Novel of One Summer of the End of the Century Novel by Jiri Kratochvil

DANISH
Ars Vivendi eller de syv Jevermater Collected verse by Georg Johannesen
Det gronne oje Novel by Katrine Marie Guldager
Dvoergenes dans Novel by Anne Marie Lon
Hjertelyd Novel by Jens Christian Grondahl
Hovedstolen Novel by Christina Hesselholdt
Om natten i Jerusalem Novel by Birgithe Kosovic
Tusindfodt Collected verse by Pia Tadrup
Zenobias liv Interwoven stories by Klovedal Reich

DUTCH

De Passievrucht Novel by Karel Glastra van Loon
De procedure Novel by Harry Mulisch
De verbeelding Novel by Herman Franke
The Discovery of Heaven Novel by Harry Mulisch
Hier is de tijd Collected verse by Esther Jansma

ENGLISH

American

Bone by Bone Concluding novel of the Everglades trilogy by Peter Matthiessen
The Book of Kings Novel by James Thackara
Broke Heart Blues Novel by Joyce Carol Oates
Close Range Collection of short stories by E. Annie Proulx
A Crime in the Neighborhood Novel by Suzanne Berne
East of the Mountains Novel by David Guterson
Empress of the Splendid Season Novel by Oscar Hijuelos
Gardens in the Dunes Novel by Leslie Marmon Silko
The Hours Novel by Michael Cunningham
Juneteenth Unfinished novel by Ralph Ellison
Midnight Salvage Poetry collection by Adrienne Rich
Plainsong Novel by Kent Haruf
Someone to Watch Over Me Collection of short stories by Richard Bausch
Vice Collected verse by Ai

Australian

Fredy Neptune Epic novel in verse by Lee Murray

British

Being Dead Novel by Jim Crace
Harry Potter and the Chamber of Secrets Children's novel by J. K. Rowling
Ingenious Pain Novel by Andrew Miller
Music and Silence Historical novel set in Denmark by Rose Tremain
Skellig Children's story by David Almond

Canadian

Almost Spring Collected verse by Nelson Ball
Elizabeth and After Novel by Matt Cohen
Gloria Novel by Keith Maillard
A Good House Novel by Bonnie Burnard
Human Bodies: New and Collected Poems, 1987–1999 Collected verse by Marilyn Bowering
The Island in Winter Collected verse by Terence Young
The Mark of the Angel Novel by Nancy Huston

Egyptian

The Map of Love Novel by Ahdaf Soueif

Indian

An Equal Music Novel by Vikram Seth
The Ground Beneath Her Feet Novel by Salman Rushdie

South African

Country of My Skull Novel by Antjie Krog
Disgrace Novel by J. M. Coetzee

FRENCH

Cameroonian

Amours sauvages Novel by Calixthe Beyala

Canadian

Am I Disturbing You? Novel by Anne Hébert
Gros mots Novel by Rejean Decharme

French

Anchise Novel by Maryline Desbiolles
Anielka Novel by François Taillandier
Clemence Picot Novel by Regis Jauffret
The Crime of Olga Arbyelina Novel by Russian-born writer André Makine
Des anges mineurs Novel by Antoine Volodine
Hilda Novel by Marie Ndiaye
La conference de Cintegabelle Novel by Lydie Salvayre
Le m'en vais Novel by Jean Echenoz
L'enfant léopard Novel by Daniel Picouly
L'oeuvre postume de Thomas Pilaster Novel by Eric Chevillard
L'offrande sauvage Novel by Jean-Pierre Milavanoff
Les idées heureuses Novel by Sebastien Lapaque
Le soleil des mourants Novel by Jean-Claude Izzo
Mon grand appartement Novel by Christian Oster
O.D.C. Novel by Clelie Aster
Pendant la chaleur du jour Novel by Hugues Pradier

GERMAN

Am kurzeren Ende der Sonnenallee Novel by Thomas Brussig
Anschlag Novel by Gert Neumann
Cherubin Hammer und Cherubin Hammer Novel by Peter Bichsel
Die Buchhandlerin Novel by Irene Bohme
Die Flaterrzunge Novel by Christian Delius
Eduards Heimkehr Novel by Peter Schneider
Er oder ich Novel by Sten Nadolny
My Century Novel by Günter Grass
Nach den Satiren Collected verse by Durs Grunbein
Pawels Briefe Novel by Monika Maron

HEBREW

Discovering Elijah Novel by S. Yizhar
Early Grace Novel by Eyal Megged
Four Mothers Novel by Shifra Horn
Our Weddings Novel by Dorit Rabinyan
The Pure Element of Time Novel by Hai'm Be'er
A Room Novel by Yuval Shimoni
Taking the Trend Novel by Orly Castel-Blum

ITALIAN

Dal silenzio delle campagne Collected verse by Ferdinando Comon
I cieli di vetro Novel by Guido Conti
L'età perfetta Novel by Roberto Cotroneo
L'impresa senza Novel by Paolo Barbaro
Lo sapsimo de Palermo Novel by Vincenzo Consolo
Lune Novel by Piero Meldini
Ocean Sea Novel by Alessandro Baricco

JAPANESE

Fly, Kylin Novel by Noboru Tsujihara
Hashish Gang Novel by Kunio Ogawa
Lights Thinning Tree Novel by Nobuko Takagi
The Never-Setting Sun Novel by Toyoko Yamazaki
Solar Eclipse Novel by Keiichiro Hirano
South of the Border, West of the Sun Novel by Haruki Murakami
The Sputnik Sweetheart Novel by Haruki Murakami

NORWEGIAN

Aske Novel by Toril Brekke
Bikubens song Novel by Frode Grytten
Elsk meg i morgen Novel by Ingvar Ambjornsen
Grenser Novel by Roy Jacobsen
Kan hende ved en bredd Short novel by Finn Carling
Maren Gripes nodwendige ritualer Novel by Oystein Lonn
Oppdageren Novel by Jan Kjaerstad

POLISH

Day Home, Night Home Novel by Olga Tokarczuk

PORTUGUESE

Brazilian

A confraria des espadas Novel by Rubem Fonseca
Manuscritos de Felipa Novel by Adelia Prado
Noturnos: contos Collection of short stories by Ana Miranda

Portuguese

As contadoras de historias Novel by Fernanda Botelho
A paixao Novel by Almeida Faria
Ferias de verao Novel by Julio Moreira

RUSSIAN

The Clay Machine Gun Novel by Viktor Pelevin
A Collective Notebook Novel by Aleksandr Morozov
Freedom Novel by Michael Butov
A Love Interest Novel by Anatoly Nayman
The Returnee Novel by Vladimir Maramzin
The River Last novel in a trilogy by Oleg Yermakov
An Unpleasant Man Novel by Anatoly Nayman

SERBIAN

Land, Land in Sight Collected verse by Doko Stojicic

SPANISH

Argentine

El décimo infierno Novel by Mempo Giardinelli
El evangelio según Van Hutten Novel by Abelardo Castillo

Chilean

Daughter of Fortune Novel by Isabel Allende

Colombian

El río del tiempo Novel by Fernando Vallejo

Cuban

Querido primer novio Novel by Zoé Valdés

Mexican

Estrellita marinera Novel by Laura Esquivel
Las soldaderas Novel by Elena Poniatowska

Ninguna eternidad como la mía Novel by Angeles Mastretta
Treinta años Novel by Carmen Boullosa
Tríptico del carnaval Trilogy by Sergio Pitol
The Years with Laura Diaz Novel by Carlos Fuentes

Peruvian

La amigdalitis de Tarzán Novel by Alfredo Bryce Echenique

Spanish

Atlas de geografía humana Novel by Almudena Grandes
El sol de Breda Novel by Arturo Pérez Reverte
La cuadratura del círculo Novel by Alvaro Pombo
Las historias de Marta y Fernando Novel by Gustavo Martín Garzo
Las moras agraces Novel by Carmen Jodra Davo
Madera de boi Novel by Camilo José Cela
Melocotones helados Novel by Espido Freire
Son de mar Novel by Manuel Vincent

Uruguayan

Buzón de tiempo Novel by Mario Benedetti

SWEDISH

Amorina Novel by Bengt Anderberg
Det bla skapet och andra berattelser Novel by Inger Alfven
Drivvd fran Arkadien Novel by Niklas Radstrom
En lampa som gor morker Novel by Per Odensten
Livlakarens besok Novel by Per Olov Enquist
Oskuldens minut Novel by Sara Lidman
Palatsbarnen Novel by Bjorn Collarp
Poetens liv Novel by Ellen Mattson
Rummet innanfor Collected verse by Ingrid Arvidsson
Vallmobadet Novel by Ernst Brunner
Vargskinnet Novel by Kerstin Ekman

2000

DEATHS

Yehuda Amichai, Israeli poet
Attilio Bertolucci, Italian poet, critic, and translator
Edgar Bowers, American poet
Sir Malcolm Bradbury, English critic and writer
Kazimierz Brandys, Polish novelist and essayist
Gwendolyn Brooks, African-American novelist
Antonio Buero Vallejo, Spanish playwright
Dame Barbara Cartland, English writer of romance novels
Barbara Cooney, American children's writer
Robert Cormier, American children's writer
Frederic Charles Antoine Dard, French writer of detective stories
L. Sprague de Camp, American writer of science fiction and fantasy
Penelope Fitzgerald, English novelist and biographer
Hushang Golshiri, Iranian writer and political activist
Gustav Herling Grudzinski, Polish novelist and essayist
Anne Hébert, French-Canadian novelist, poet, and playwright
A. D. Hope, Australian poet
Ali Sardar Jafri, Urdu poet

Ernst Jandl, Austrian poet
Carmen Martín Gaite, Spanish social-realist novelist
Pedro Mir, Dominican poet
N. Richard Nash, American playwright
Patrick O'Brian, English novelist and biographer
Herberto Padilla, Cuban poet
Anthony Dymoke Powell, English novelist
Alfred Wellington Purdy, Canadian poet
Ola Rotimi, Nigerian playwright
Ahmad Shamlu, Iranian poet
Karl Shapiro, American poet and critic
Goran Tunstrom, Swedish poet, novelist, and playwright
José Angel Valente, Spanish poet
A. E. van Vogt, American writer of science fiction
Judith Wright, American poet and writer
Xie Bingying, Chinese writer

LITERARY EVENT
PRIZES AND AWARDS
Booker Prize: *The Blind Assassin* by Margaret Atwood
Caldecott Medal: *Joseph Had a Little Overcoat* by Simms Taback
Newbery Medal: *Bud, Not Buddy* by Christopher Paul Curtis
Nobel Prize in literature: Gao Xingjian, Chinese writer
PEN/Faulkner Award: *Waiting* by Ha Jin

Pulitzer Prizes

Biography *Vera* by Stacy Schiff
Drama *Dinner with Friends* by Donald Margulies
Fiction *Interpreter of Maladies* by Jhumpa Lahiri
History *Freedom from Fear: American People in Depression and War, 1929–1945* by David M. Kennedy
Nonfiction *Embracing Defeat: Japan in the Wake of World War II* by John W. Dower
Poetry *Repair* by C. K. Williams

PUBLICATIONS
ARABIC
In Search of Walid Massoud Novel by Palestinian writer Jabra Ibrahim Jabra

BULGARIAN
Wake Me Yesterday Poetry collection by Kalin Donkov

CHINESE
Caisangzi Novel by Ye Guangcen
The Carnival Season Novel by Wang Meng
The Republic of Wine Novel by Mo Yan

CROATIAN
An Angel Offsides Novel by Zoran Feric
Note About the Author Novel by Julijana Matanovic

DANISH
Det rigtige Novel by Vibeke Gronfeldt
Drommebroer Collected poems by Henrik Nordbrandt
Genspejlet Novel by Svend Age Madsen
Mellen himlen og verden Historical novel by Anne Marie Tetevide

Nattens rygrad Novel by Arthur Krasilnikoff
Rejse for en fremmed Collected verse by Naja Marie Aidt
Trio Novel by Cecilie Lassen

DUTCH
Publieke werken Novel by Thomas Rosenboom

ENGLISH
American
Daughter Mine Novel by Herbert Gold
Embracing Defeat Poetry collection by C. K. Williams
The Feast of Love Novel by Charles Baxter
Gertrude and Claudius Retelling of Shakespeare's *Hamlet* by John Updike
The Heartsong of Charging Elk Historical novel by James Welch
The Human Stain Novel by Philip Roth
In the Name of Salomé Novel by Dominican-born writer Julia Alvarez
Jersey Rain Collected verse by Robert Pinsky
Licks of Love Story collection by John Updike
The Married Man Novel by Edmund White
Motherkind Novel by Jayne Anne Phillips
Nowhere Else on Earth Historical novel on the Civil War by Josephine Humphreys
Plum and Jaggers Novel by Susan Richards Shreve
Waiting Novel by Chinese-born writer Ha Jin
What Remains Fictional memoir by Nicholas Delbanco

Australian
Dark Palace Novel by Frank Moorhouse
Dream Stuff Collection of short stories by David Malouf
Drylands Novel by Thea Astley
Morgan's Run Novel by Colleen McCullough
Too Many Men Novel by Lily Brett

British
Harry Potter and the Prisoner of Azkaban Children's novel by J. K. Rowling
How the Dead Live Novel by Will Self
The Looking Glass Novel by Michele Roberts
Precious Thing Novel by Kristin Kenway
Unknown Pleasures Novel by Jason Cowley
When I Lived in Modern Times Novel by Linda Grant
When We Were Orphans Novel by Japanese-born writer Kazuo Ishiguro
White Teeth Novel by Zadie Smith
Wide Open Novel by Nicola Barker

Canadian
Anil's Ghost Novel by Michael Ondaatje
The Blind Assassin Novel by Margaret Atwood
Burridge Unbound Novel by Alan Cumyn
Cargo of Orchids Novel by Susan Musgrave
Mercy Among Children Novel by David Adams
The Rules of Engagement Novel by Catherine Bush
The Shadow Boxer Novel by Steven Heighten
A Student of Weather Novel by Elizabeth Hay
The Trade Novel by Fred Stenson

New Zealand

Talking About O'Dwyer Novel by C. K. Stead

Saint Lucian

Tiepolo's Hound Book-length poem by Derek Walcott

South African

The Rights of Desire Meditations by Andre Brink

FRENCH

Canadian

Un vent se lève qui eparpille Novel by Jean-Marc Dalpe

French

Dans ces bras-la Novel by Camille Laurens
Diabolus in musica Novel by Yan Apperry
Ingrid Caven Novel by Jean-Jacques Schuhl
Les aubes Novel by Linda Le
Les reveries de la femme sauvage Autobiographical fiction by Hélène Cixous
Ma vie folle Autobiographical fiction by Richard Morgieve
Porte disparu Autobiographical fiction by Fernando Arrabal
Terrasse à Rome Novel by Pascal Quignard

Ivorien

Allah n'est pas oblige Novel by Ahmadou Kourouma

GERMAN

Austrian

Das Vaterspiel Novel by Josef Haslinger

German

Das Provisorium Novel by Wolfgang Hilbig
Die Liebeswunsch Novel by Dieter Wellershof
Hampels Fluchten Picaresque novel by Michael Kumpfmuller
Liebesfluchten Novel by Bernhard Schlink
Teufelsbruck Novel by Brigitte Kronauer

HEBREW

A Journey into Winter Novel by Aharon Appelfeld
Love After All Novel by Mira Magen
Persephone Remembers Novel by Aharon Megged
Sarah, Sarah Novel by Ronit Matalon
Someone to Run With Novel by David Grossman

HUNGARIAN

Stonedial Novel by Gyorgy Konrad

ITALIAN

Di vento e di fuoco Novel by Giorgio Pressburger
La casa di ghiaccio Twenty Russian tales by Serena Vitale
La forza del passato Novel by Sandro Veronesi
Nati due volte Novel by Giuseppe Pontiggia
Nel momento Novel by Andrea de Carlo
Vaniglia e cioccolato Novel by Sveva Casati Modignani
Via Gemito Novel by Domenico Starnone

JAPANESE

Dream of Yudotei Enmoku Novel by Noboru Tsujihara
Giving Life Novel by Shun Medoruma

House in the Shadow Novel by Korean-born writer Gengetsu
Life Novel by Korean-born writer Miri Yu
My Grandpa Novel by Yasutaka Tsutsui
Naked Feet and Seashell Novel by Taku Miki
Promise in Summer Novel by Chuya Fujino
Rain Afterwards Rain? Novel by Keiko Iwasaka
Symbiotic Worm Novel by Ryu Murakami

NORWEGIAN

Aftensang Novel by Gunnar Staalesen
Brodrene Henrikson Novel by Cecilie Enger
I kjolvannet Novel by Per Petterson
Oppdageren Novel by Jan Kjaerstad

PORTUGUESE

Exortaçao aos crocodilos Novel by Antonio Lobo Antunes
Insania Novel by Heli Correia

RUSSIAN

Buddha's Little Finger Novel by Viktor Pelevin
Description Collected verse by Arkady Dragomoshchenko
A Person Not to Be Trusted Novel by Vladislav Otroshenko
Summary Novel by Sergey Gandlevsky
The Taking of Ismail Novel by Mikhail Shishkin
Whither Gone? And Where's the Window? Collected verse by Viktor Sosnora

SERBIAN

Druid from Sindidun Novel by Vladislav Bajac
How Much Is Belgrade Collection of 15 stories by Moma Dimic
Mexico War diary by Vladmir Arsenijevic

SLOVENE

Circles on the Water Novel by Peter Semolic

SPANISH

Argentine

El Sueño del señor Novel by Carlos Gamerro
Guerra conyugal Novel by Edgardo Russo
La resistencia Novel by Ernesto Sábato
Se esconde tras los ojos Novel by Pablo Toledo

Chilean

El sueño de la historia Novel by Jorge Edwards
Javiera Carrera, madre de la patria Novel by Virginia Vidal
Otro baile en Paris Novel by Enrique Lafourcade
Portrait in Sepia Novel by Isabel Allende

Mexican

Amphitryon Novel by Ignacio Padilla
The Five Suns of Mexico Novel by Carlos Fuentes
Viaje a los olivos Novel by Gerardo Cham

Peruvian

La fiesta del chivo Novel by Mario Vargas Llosa

Spanish

Carajicomedia Novel by Juan Goytisolo
Diario de 360° Novel in diary form by Luis Goytisolo

El alquimista impaciente Novel by Lorenzo Silva
El amante lesbiano Novel by José Luis Sampedro
La caída de Madrid Novel by Rafael Chirbes
La novia de Matisse Novelistic allegory by Manuel Vicent
La ruina del cielo Novel by Luis Mateo Díez

La sombra del angel Novel by Marina Mayoral
Las palabras de la vida Seventeen autobiographical and fictional
    sketches by Luis Mateo Díez
Los melomanos Novel by Alvaro del Amo
Mientras vivimos Novel by Maruja Torres

BIBLIOGRAPHY

Allibone, Samuel. *A Critical Dictionary of English Literature and British and American Authors.* 3 vols. Philadelphia, 1872.

Beaty, Jerome, and J. Paul Hunter. *New Worlds of Literature.* New York: W. W. Norton, 1989.

Becka, Jiri, ed. *Dictionary of Oriental Literatures.* 3 vols. New York: Basic Books, 1975.

Bruccoli, Matthew J., and Richard Lyman. *Dictionary of Literary Biography.* Detroit: Gale, 1978– .

Burt, Daniel S. *The Literary 100.* New York: Facts On File, 2001.

Colby, Vineta, ed. *World Authors.* New York: H. W. Wilson, 1985– .

Diagram Group, eds. *Who Wrote What When?* New York: Diagram Group, 1999.

Drabble, Margaret, ed. *The Oxford Companion to English Literature.* New York: Oxford University Press, 1985.

Garside, Peter. *Encyclopedia of Literature Criticism.* New York: Routledge, 1993.

Gassner, John, and Edward Quinn, eds. *The Reader's Encyclopedia of World Drama.* New York: Ty Crowell, 1969.

Hart, James D. *The Oxford Companion to World Literature.* New York: Oxford University Press, 1983.

Henderson, H. *Reference Guide to World Literature.* Detroit: Gale, 1995.

Kunitz, Stanley J., and Vineta Colby, eds. *European Authors, 1000–1900.* New York: H. W. Wilson, 1967.

Kunitz, Stanley J., and Howard Haycraft, eds. *Twentieth Century Authors.* New York: H. W. Wilson, 1942.

Lambdin, Laura, and Robert T. Lambdin. *Encyclopedia of Medieval Literature.* Westport, Conn.: Greenwood, 2000.

Lawall, Sarah N., ed. *Norton Anthology of World Masterpieces.* New York: W. W. Norton, 1998.

The Literary Almanac. Kansas City: Fine Communications, 1997.

Magill, Frank N., ed. *Magill's Survey of World Literature.* Tarrytown, N.Y.: Marshall Cavendish, 1992.

———. *Masterpieces of Women's Literature.* New York: Harper-Collins, 1996.

———. *Masterpieces of World Literature.* New York: HarperCollins, 1991.

Merriam-Webster Encyclopedia of Literature. Springfield, Mass.: Merriam-Webster, 1995.

MLA International Bibliography of Books and Articles on the Modern Languages and Literatures. Series. New York: Modern Language Association, 1989– .

Murphy, Bruce, ed. *Benet's Reader's Encyclopedia, Fourth Edition.* New York: HarperCollins, 1996.

O'Brien, Geoffrey, ed. *The Reader's Catalog.* New York: Reader's Catalog, 1989.

Rogal, Samuel G. *Calendar of Literary Facts.* Detroit: Gale, 1991.

———. *A Chronological Outline of American Literature.* Westport, Conn.: Greenwood, 1987.

———. *A Chronological Outline of British Literature.* Westport, Conn.: Greenwood, 1980.

Sader, Marion. *The Reader's Adviser: A Laymen's Guide to Literature.* 6 vols. Westport, Conn.: Greenwood, 1994.

Serafin, Stephen. *Encyclopedia of World Literature in the 20th Century.* 4 vols. Detroit: Gale, 1998.

Seymour-Smith, Martin. *Funk & Wagnall's Guide to Modern World Literature.* New York: Funk & Wagnall, 1973.

Snick, Gerard J. *Something About the Author.* Series. Detroit: Gale, 1978– .

Spiller, Robert E. *Literary History of the United States.* New York: Macmillan, 1963.

Steinberg, S. H. *Cassell's Encyclopedia of World Literature.* 2 vols. New York: Funk & Wagnall, 1954.

Strouf, Judie L. H. *Literature Lover's Book of Lists.* Paramus, N.J.: Prentice Hall, 1998.

Trosky, Susan, ed. *Contemporary Authors.* Series. Detroit: Gale, 1985– .

Wakeman, John, ed. *World Authors 1950–1995.* 9 vols. New York: H. W. Wilson, 1980– .

TITLE INDEX

Entries in the index are filed word for word.

17-57 Poems (Bojic) 278
18 Poems (Thomas) 199
20 Digte (Lavgesen) 277
XX Poems (Larkin) 212
XLI Poems (cummings) 186
The 42nd Parallel (Dos Passos) 193
77 Dream Songs (Berryman) 238, 239
The 120 Days of Sodom (Sade) 85
1,001 Years of Nostalgia (Boudjedra) 258
1492: Life and Times of Juan Cabezon de Castilla (Aridjis) 266
1876 (Vidal) 254
1914 (Brooke) 174
1919 (Dos Passos) 196
1984 (Orwell) 217
2010 Odyssey Two (Clarke) 261

A
À la frontière (Butor) 286
A la salud de la serpiente (Sainz) 277
A lume spento (Pound) 155, 166
Aaron's Rod (Lawrence) 182
The Abattoir (Echeverría) 128
Abay's Road (Auezov) 214
The Abbasids (Platen) 108
The Abbess of Crewe (Spark) 252
The Abbot (Scott) 93, 102
The Abduction (Kumin) 247
Abdullah's Story (Abdullah) 116
Abe Lincoln in Illinois (Sherwood) 204, 205
Abel Sánchez (Unamuno) 176
Abhijñanasakuntala (Kālidāsa) 14, 15
The Able McLaughlins (Wilson) 185
"Abou Ben Adhem" (Hunt) 113
Above the River (Wright) 273
Abraham Lincoln: The War Years (Sandburg) 206
Absalom, Absalom! (Faulkner) 201
Absalom and Achitophel (Dryden) 49, 63

Abschied von den Feinden (Jirgl) 284
Absence (Handke) 269
The Absentee (Edgeworth) 98
The Absurda Comica, or Master Peter Squentz (Gryphius) 59
Abudulala Mahari (Isahakian) 169
Abufar (Ducis) 87
Abyss (Appelfeld) 280
The Abyss (Yourcenar) 245
L'Abyssin (Rufin) 288
The Acacia (Simon) 272
An Accidental Man (Murdoch) 249
An Account of My Hut (Kamo Chomei) 23
Achados e perdidos (Garcia-Roza) 291
Acharnians (Aristophanes) 3
Achillea's Fiancé (Zei) 269
Acquainted with the Night (Böll) 223
The Acrobat (Richler) 223
Acropolis (Chacel) 265
Across the Bridge (Vega) 32
Across the Bridge: Stories (Gallant) 279, 280
Across the River and into the Trees (Hemingway) 218
Across the Wide Missouri (DeVoto) 216
Act of Darkness (King) 263
Active Service (Crane) 149
Acts Without Words (Beckett) 154
The Actual (Bellow) 288
Ad haSof (Shamir) 276
Ada (Nabokov) 155, 245
Adaagia (Erasmus) 34
Adam, Where Art Thou? (Böll) 219
Adam Bede (Eliot) 121
Adam in Exile (Vondel) 60
Adam in Paradise (Ortega y Gasset) 169
Adán Buenosayres (Marechal) 217
The Adding Machine (Rice) 184
Address to the Nobility of the German Nation (Luther) 36
Aden (Garat) 278
The Admirable Crichton (Barrie) 160

Admiral of the Ocean Sea (Morison) 210
Adolphe (Constant) 100
Adon Menuha (Yeshurun) 274
"Adonais" (Shelley) 93, 102
Adriatico (Nigro) 291
Adrienne Lecouvreur (Scribe and Legouvé) 116
Adult Bookstore (Shapiro) 254
Adultery and Other Choices (Dubus) 255
The Advancement of Learning (Bacon) 50
The Adventurer and the Singer (Hofmannsthal) 149
The Adventures of a Younger Son (Trelawny) 106
Adventures of an Iron and a Boot (Petrushevskaya) 291
The Adventures of Augie March (Bellow) 222
The Adventures of Captain Singleton (Defoe) 72
The Adventures of Ferdinand, Count Fathom (Smollett) 78
The Adventures of Hajji Baba of Isphahan (Morier) 103
The Adventures of Harry Richmond (Meredith) 127
The Adventures of Huckleberry Finn (Twain) 92, 136
The Adventures of Nicholas Try-All (Krasicki) 83
The Adventures of Peregrine Pickle (Smollett) 78
The Adventures of Roderick Random (Smollett) 77
The Adventures of Sherlock Holmes (Doyle) 142
The Adventures of Telemachus (Fénelon) 66
The Adventures of Tom Sawyer (Twain) 92, 131
The Adventures of Ulysses (Lamb) 97
The Adventuress (Augier) 115

Advise and Consent (Drury) 232
Aeneid (Virgil) 4, 11
Afensang (Staalesen) 296
The Afersata (Selassie) 246
The Affair (Snow) 231
The Affected Young Ladies (Molière) 47, 59
Afloat and Ashore (Cooper) 113
Africa, We Do Not Pay Attention to You (Matep) 227
Africa (Petrarch) 14
Africa Sings (Osadebay) 221
The African Continent (Nenekhaly-Camara) 248
The African Queen (Forester) 200
African Stories (Lessing) 238
An African Tragedy (Dhlomo) 191
African Witch (Cary) 201
After Julius (Howard) 240
After Many a Summer Dies the Swan (Huxley) 205
After Rain (Trevor) 286
After Russia (Tsvetayeva) 191
After the Divorce (Deledda) 160
After the Fall (Miller) 238
After You've Gone (Adams) 272
Afterimages: Young Men from Those Years (Nowakowski) 285
The Afterlife and Other Stories (Updike) 282
Afternoon Men (Powell) 194
The Afternoon of a Faun (Mallarmé) 131
Against Interpretation (Sontag) 241
Against the Grain (Huysmans) 136
Against the Wall (Jirásek) 144
Agamemnon (Lemercier) 86
Agar (Memmi) 225
Agatha Moudio's Sons (Bebey) 243
Agathon (Wieland) 80
The Age of Anxiety (Auden) 215, 216
The Age of Chivalry (Bulfinch) 120
The Age of Fable (Bulfinch) 119
The Age of Innocence (Wharton) 179, 181

The Age of Jackson (Schlesinger) 213
The Age of Reason (Paine) 86
The Age of Reform (Hofstadter) 226
Agenda (Hierro) 277
Agésilas (Corneille) 48, 61
Agnar (Delblanc) 281
Agnes Bernauer (Hebbel) 117, 119
Agnes Grey (Brontë) 115
Agostino (Moravia) 211
Agosto (Fonseca) 276
The Aguero Sisters (Garcia) 288
The Agunah (Grade) 234
Ah, Wilderness! (O'Neill) 153, 197
Ahasuerus in Rome (Hamerling) 125
Ahayat David (Kanuik) 274
AIDS and Its Metaphors (Sontag) 270
Aimée (Rivière) 182
The Air Conditioned Nightmare
   (Miller) 212
*Airplane Dreams: Compositions from
   Journals* (Ginsberg) 244
Ajax (Sophocles) 3
Ajol and Laor (Czycz) 287
Aklake Mohseni (Kashefi) 29
Al Aaraaf (Poe) 105
Alain and Elise (Kaiser) 207
Alan Turing (Hochhuth) 269
Alastor; or, The Spirit of Solitude (Shel-
   ley) 100
Albany Cycle (Kennedy) 277
The Albigensians (Lenau) 112
Albion Albion (Moravcevic) 285
Albion and Albanius (Dryden) 64
Album Verses (Lamb) 106
Alcacer Quibir (Olinto) 289
The Alchemist (Jonson) 51
Alcibiades (Plato) 3
Alcools (Apollinaire) 172
The Aleph and Other Stories (Borges)
   154
Alexander and Death (Mickovic) 284
Alexander in the Streetcar (Reznicek)
   281
Alexander the Great (Racine) 60
"Alexander's Feast, or the Power of
   Music; An Ode in Honour of St. Ce-
   cilia's Day" (Dryden) 66, 71
The Alexandria Quartet (Durrell) 228,
   229, 232
Alfred (Thomson and Mallet) 76
*The Algerine Captive; or, The Life and
   Adventures of Dr. Updike Underhill*
   (Tyler) 87
The Alhambra (Irving) 107
Alias Grace (Atwood) 286
Alice Adams (Tarkington) 181, 182
Alice's Adventures in Wonderland
   (Carroll) 124
Aline, Queen of Golkonda (Boufflers)
   80
Alison's House (Glaspell) 194
*Alive Together: New and Selected
   Poems* (Mueller) 288
All Citizens Are Soldiers (Vega) 32
All for Love, or, A Sinner Well Saved
   (Southey) 105
All for Love (Dryden) 49
All for the Best (Pirandello) 180
*All God's Children Need Traveling
   Shoes* (Angelou) 267
All Green Shall Perish (Mallea) 208
All in a Night (Cayrol) 224
All Men Are Mortals (Beauvoir) 214
All My Pretty Ones (Sexton) 235
All My Sons (Miller) 214
All Our Yesterdays (Ginzburg) 221

All Passion Spent (Sackville-West) 194
All Quiet on the Western Front (Re-
   marque) 192
All Rivers Run to the Sea (Wiesel) 284
All Sentiments (Mulla Vajhi) 55
All the Conspirators (Isherwood) 190
All the Faces of Death (Andreevski)
   284
All the King's Men (Warren) 213, 214
All the Names (Saramago) 291
All the Poems (Caproni) 263
All the Pretty Horses (McCarthy) 277
All the Way Home (Mosel) 233
All Things Betray (Thomas) 218
Allah n'est pas oblige (Kourouma) 296
Allan Quatermain (Haggard) 138
The Allegory of Love (Lewis) 201
Allegra (Mallet-Joris) 255
Allegretto (Stigen) 284
"L'Allegro" (Milton) 48, 55
Alleles (Heffner) 282
Un aller simple (Cauwelaert) 282
All's Well That Ends Well (Shake-
   speare) 50
Alma, or the Progress of the Mind
   (Prior) 72
*An Almanac for New England for the
   Year 1639* (Pierce) 56
Almanac of the Dead (Silko) 275
Almost Spring (Ball) 293
Almost Transparent Blue (Ryu) 255
Alms for Oblivion (Raven) 238
Anilam (Dickey) 268
Alone (Nobre) 143
Alone (Strindberg) 93
Alone Against the Night (Tatarka) 275
Alone Among Men (Brzozoski) 170
Along the Way (Verhaeren) 142
Alonso e i visionari (Ortese) 286
El alquimista impaciente (Silva) 297
Altar of Victory (Bryusov) 172
Alte Kameraden (Skagen) 274
Alton Locke, Tailor and Poet (Kingsley)
   116
Always a Fragment (Rozewicz) 291
Always Coming Home (Le Guin) 265
Always Room for One More (Leodhas)
   241
Am I Disturbing You? (Hébert) 293
Am kurzeren Ende der Sonnenallee
   (Brussig) 293
Amadeus (Shaffer) 258
Amadís de Gaula (Montalvo) 34
Amadís de Gaula (Vicente) 34
Amalia: A Romance of the Argentine
   (Mármol) 134
Amana Gras (Silkin) 249
El amante lesbiano (Sampedro) 297
Amaranth (Robinson) 198
El amargo don de la belleza (Moix) 287
The Amazing Marriage (Meredith) 145
The Ambassadors (James) 91, 161
Amboyna (Dryden) 62
AMDG (Pérez de Ayala) 169
Amelia (Fielding) 78
America: A Prophecy (Blake) 68
The American (James) 91, 131
American Appetites (Oates) 270
American Blues (Williams) 205
American Buffalo (Mamet) 253
*An American Dictionary of the English
   Language* (Webster) 105
American Dream (Albee) 230, 233
An American Dream (Mailer) 240
*American Education: The National Ex-
   perience, 1783–1876* (Cremin) 260

The American Language (Mencken)
   178
*The American Leonardo: The Life of
   Samuel F. B. Morse* (Mabee) 211
American Notes (Dickens) 112
*The American Orchestra and Theodore
   Thomas* (Russell) 190
American Pastoral (Roth) 288, 290
American Primitive (Oliver) 262, 263
The American Renaissance
   (Matthiessen) 208
*The American Revolution—A Consti-
   tutional Interpretation* (McIlwain)
   185
The American Scene (James) 165
American Soul (Chocano) 164
An American Tragedy (Dreiser) 186
An American Visitor (Cary) 197
The Americanization of Edward Bok
   (Bok) 181
The Americans: Democratic Experience
   (Boorstein) 252
America's Coming of Age (Brooks)
   174
Amerika (Kafka) 152, 189
The Amethyst Ring (France) 149
Ameto's Story of the Nymphs (Boccac-
   cio) 14
La amigdalitis de Tarzán (Bryce
   Echenique) 294
Aminta (Tasso) 42
Among the Hills (Whittier) 127
Amongst Women (McGahern) 274
Amor que faz o mundo girar (Quin-
   tella) 276
Amores (Ovid) 4
Amores Folk (Celtis) 34
Amoretti (Spenser) 44
Amorina (Anderberg) 294
Amorous Confessions of Two Nuns
   (Koyo) 140
The Amorous Follies (Regnard) 70
The Amorous Quarrel (Molière) 59
The Amorous Vision (Boccaccio) 14
"Amour" (Verlaine) 139
Amour noir (Noguez) 288
Les Amours (Ronsard) 33
Les Amours de Marie (Ronsard) 33
*Les Amours de P. de Ronsard Vando-
   moys, Ensemble de Bocages* (Ron-
   sard) 39
Amours sauvages (Beyala) 293
Amphitryon (Dryden) 49, 65
Amphitryon (Padilla) 296
Amrita (Jhabvala) 225
Amsterdam (McEwan) 290
Un an (Echenoz) 288
Anabasis (Perce) 185
Anabasis (Xenophon) 2
"Anaconda" (Quiroga) 181
Anapus Gaiso Eilerasciati (Juskaitis)
   270
The Anatomy Lesson (Roth) 262
The Anatomy of Melancholy (Burton)
   53
*An Anatomy of the World: The First
   Anniversary* (Donne) 51
The Ancestors (Freytag) 129
The Ancestors (Grillparzer) 100
Anchise (Desbiolles) 293
An Ancient Book (Pavlovic) 278
The Ancient Child (Momaday) 272
Ancient Evenings (Mailer) 262
And Pippa Dances (Hauptmann) 164
And Quiet Flows the Don (Sholokhov)
   199

And Suddenly It's Evening (Quasi-
   modo) 209
And Their Children After Them (Ma-
   haridge, Williamson) 273
And They Put Handcuffs on the Flowers
   (Arrabel) 246
Andanda Math (Bannerjee) 134
Andersonville (Kantor) 225, 226
Andorra (Frisch) 234
André del Sarto (Musset) 107
"Andrea del Sarto" (Browning) 119
*Andrea of Hungary, Fra Rupert, and
   Giovanna of Naples* (Landor) 110
Andrew Jackson (James) 204
Androcles and the Lion (Shaw) 153,
   175
Andromaque (Racine) 48, 61
The Andromeda Strain (Chrichton)
   245
Andromède (Corneille) 48, 58
Un ange cornu ave des ailes de tole
   (Tremblay) 282
The Angel (Lermontov) 107
Angel in the House (Patmore) 118
Angel Landing (Hoffman) 259
The Angel of History (Forché) 282
The Angel of the Shadow (Lugones)
   188
An Angel Offsides (Feric) 295
Angel Pavement (Priestley) 193
Angel Walk (Govier) 286
Angela's Ashes: A Memoir (McCourt)
   286, 288
Angeles de Compostela (Diego) 207
L'angelo nero (Tabucchi) 276
*Angels in America—Millennium Ap-
   proaches* (Kushner) 279
The Angel's Wink (Mallet-Joris) 263
Anger (Menander) 3
Angle of Repose (Stegner) 248, 249
Anielka (Taillandier) 293
Anil's Ghost (Ondaatje) 295
Anima mundi (Tamaro) 289
Animal at Bottom (Jiménez) 215
Animal Dreams (Kingsolver) 273
Animal Farm (Orwell) 212
The Animal Kingdom (Barry) 196
Animal triste (Maron) 286
Animalia (Kilpi) 269
Animals Arrival (Jennings) 246
Ann Veronica (Wells) 167
Anna, Hanna, och Johanna (Frederiks-
   son) 283
Anna and the King of Siam (Landon)
   211
Anna Christie (O'Neill) 153, 182
Anna Karenina (Tolstoy) 90, 130
Anna of the Five Towns (Bennett) 160
"Annabel Lee" (Poe) 116
Annales (Tacitus) 5
Annales Ecclesiastici (Baronius) 42
The Annals of Italy (Muratori) 77
Annals of the Former World (McPhee)
   292
*Anne of Geierstein; or, The Maiden of
   the Mist* (Scott) 105
Anne of the Thousand Days (Ander-
   son) 216
En annen vei (Carling) 287
Annibal (Marivaux) 73
Annie Allen (Brooks) 217, 218
Annie John (Kincaid) 265
Annie Kilburn (Howells) 140
*Anniversaries: From the Life of Gesine
   Cresspahl* (Johnson) 248
The Anniversary (Chekhov) 92

"The Anniversary" (Donne) 49
Annotations in Pandectas (Budé) 34
Annus Mirabilis (Dryden) 49, 61
El año del deluvio (Mendoza) 279
Los años de la serpiente (Ostornol) 277
Los años indecisos (Torrente Ballester) 289
Another Country (Mitchell) 261
Another Life (Walcott) 251
Another Part of the Forest (Hellman) 213
Another Part of the Wood (Bainbridge) 244
Another September (Kinsella) 229
Another Song for America (Hensen) 268
Another Time (Auden) 207
Anschlag (Neumann) 293
Antartic Traveler (Pollitt) 261
Anthem (Rand) 204
Anthills of the Savannah (Achebe) 269
Anti Kepler's Laws (Katz) 269
Antic Hay (Huxley) 184
The Antichrist (Broch) 195
Antigone (Alfieri) 83
Antigone (Anouilh) 209
Antigone (Sophocles) 3
Anti-Intellectualism in American Life (Hofstadter) 238
Der Antiquar (Schertenlieb) 278
The Antiquary (Scott) 93, 100
Antiques Cabinet (Balzac) 91
The Anti-Soviet Soviet Union (Voinovich) 266
Antonina; or, The Fall of Rome (Collins) 116
Antony and Cleopatra (Shakespeare) 50
The Ants (Holldobler, Wilson) 275
Anvare Soheyli (Kashefi) 34
Any Old Iron (Burgess) 271
Any Woman's Blues (Jong) 272
Apologia Pro Vita Sua (Newman) 124
An Apologie for Poetrie (Sidney) 42
An Apology for the Life of Mrs Shamela Andrews (Fielding) 76
Apology (Plato) 3
Appius and Virginia (Webster, Heywood) 51
The Apple Cart (Shaw) 153
The Apple in the Dark (Lispector) 234
Appointment in Samarra (O'Hara) 198
Appreciations (Pater) 140
The Apprenticeship of Duddy Kravitz (Richler) 228
"Approach of Death" (Leopardi) 91, 109
Approximate Man, and Other Writings (Tzara) 195
Aquis Submersus (Storm) 131
Arab and Jew (Shipler) 268
Arabesques (Gogol) 91, 109
Araucaima Mansion (Mutis) 251
La Araucana (Ercilla y Zúñiga) 40
L'arbre de rêve (Quiring) 269
Arcades (Milton) 55
Arcadia (Sannazaro) 34
The Arcadia (Sidney) 43
Arcadia (Vega) 45
The Archeology of Knowledge (Foucault) 246
The Architect and the Emperor of Assyria (Arrabel) 243

Arcodamore (De Carlo) 282
Ardiente paciencia (Skarmeta) 266
Ardobiola (Yevtushenko) 265
Are You a Bromide? (Burgess) 164
Arena (Prem) 185
Areopagitica (Milton) 48, 57
Argo (Theotokos) 202
"Ariadne" (Chekhov) 92
Ariadne (Tsvetayeva) 185
Ariadne and Naxos (Ernst) 171
Ariel (Plath) 240
Aristophanes' Apology (Browning) 130
Arithmetic in Love (Blest Gana) 122
The Arkansas Treatment (Walcott) 269
Armarinho de miudezas (Salamao) 280
An Armful of Blossoms (Karim) 228
The Armies of the Night (Mailer) 245
"Armored Train 14-69" (Ivanov) 183
Arms and the Man (Shaw) 144, 148, 153
Army Chaplain Schmelzle's Journey (Richter) 98
Arnjot Jelline (Bjørnson) 127
Around the Bedroom Wall: A Family Album (Woiwode) 253
Around the World in Eighty Days (Verne) 129
Arquipalago (Barbosa) 200
Arrival and Departure (Koestler) 210
Arrow to the Sun (McDermott) 253
Arrowsmith (Lewis) 186, 187
Ars amatoria (Ovid) 4, 11
Ars poetica (Horace) 4, 11
Ars Vivendi eller de syv Jevermater (Johannesen) 292
Art (Bell) 173
Art and Life in America (Larkin) 218
The Art of Poetry (Boileau) 62
The Art of War (Machiavelli) 36
The Artamonov Business (Gorky) 187
Artemenes; or, the Grand Cyrus (Scudéry) 58
Arthur Merwyn (Brown) 88
Arturo's Island (Morante) 228
As a Few Days (Shalev) 282
As I Lay Dying (Faulkner) 193
As You Like It (Shakespeare) 45
The Ascension (Bahr) 175
The Ascension (Konwicki) 237
Ascension of the Frog (Juji) 220
The Ascent of F6 (Auden, Isherwood) 201
El asesinato, el perdedor (Cela) 283
Ash and Honey (Szlosarek) 289
Ash Wednesday (Eliot) 193
Ashanti to Zulu (Musgrove) 255
Ashes (Bely) 168
Ashes (Deledda) 162
Ashes and 7 Years from Somewhere (Levine) 258
Ashes and Diamonds (Andrzejewski) 217
Ashes to Ashes: America's Hundred Year Cigarette War, the Public Health and the Unabashed Triumph of Philip Morris (Kluger) 288
Ashmat Shomeron (Mapu) 124
Ask the Flowers (Jakucho) 278
Aske (Brekke) 294
Asolando (Browning) 140
Aspects of the Novel (Forster) 189
The Aspern Papers (James) 139
The Assassins (Oates) 253
The Assault (Mulisch) 261

Assignment in Brittany (MacInnes) 209
The Assistant (Malamud) 228
The Assumption of Hanneles (Hauptmann) 144
Astadhyayi (Panini) 1
Astraea Redux (Dryden) 49, 60
Astrophel (Spenser) 42
Astrophel and Stella (Sidney) 43
La astucia de la razón (Feinmann) 274
Asuntos de un hidalgo disoluto (Abad Faciolince) 283
At Daggers Drawn (Leskov) 127
At Heaven's Gate (Warren) 210
At Home and Abroad (Pritchett) 272
At Play in the Fields of the Lord (Matthiessen) 226
At the Bottom of the River (Kincaid) 264
At the End of the Open Road (Simpson) 238
At the Fire of Controversy (Luzi) 257
At the Hawk's Well (Yeats) 152
At 0 A.M. in Buenos Aires (Shu) 291
Atala (Chateaubriand) 95
Athalie (Racine) 48, 65
Atheist (Mihardja) 218
Atlanta in Calydon (Swinburne) 124
The Atlantic Migration, 1607–1860 (Hansen) 208
La Atlántida (Verdaguer) 131
Atlas de geografia humana (Grandes) 294
An Atlas of the Difficult World, Poems, 1988–1991 (Rich) 275
Atlas Shrugged (Rand) 228
Atreus and Thyseus (Crébillon) 70
Atta Troll (Heine) 113
Attack (Charasha) 191
Attempt of the Infinite Man (Neruda) 155
Attesa sul mare (Biamonti) 282
Atticus (Hansen) 286
Attila (Corneille) 48, 61
Attila, King of the Huns (Werner) 97
Au Soleil de Juillet (Adam) 161
Les aubes (Le) 296
Auchindrane; or, The Ayurshire Tragedy (Scott) 106
Audi Filia (Juan de Avila) 39
Audubon: A Vision (Lowell) 245
August 1914 (Solzhenitsyn) 154, 249
The August Sleepwalker (Bei) 270
"Auld Lang Syne" (Burns) 68
Aunt Julia and the Scriptwriter (Vargas Llosa) 256
Aunt Virike (Heiberg) 136
Aureng-Zebe (Dryden) 49, 62
Aurora (Leiris) 214
Aurora Leigh (Browning) 120
Auroras of Autumn (Stevens) 218
Austrias (Latino) 41
Auto de la Barca (Vicente) 35
Auto de la Barca de la Gloria (Vicente) 35
Auto de la Barca de Purgatorio (Vicente) 35
Auto de la sibila Casandra (Vicente) 35
The Autobiography (Franklin) 81
Autobiography (Hunt) 116
Autobiography, 1872–1914 (Russell) 243
The Autobiography of Alice B. Toklas (Stein) 197
Autobiography of an Egotist (Stendhal) 143

The Autobiography of an Ex-Colored Man (Johnson) 171
The Autobiography of an Unknown Indian (Chadhuri) 220
The Autobiography of Malcolm X (Malcolm X) 240
The Autobiography of Miss Jane Pittman (Gaines) 248
Autobiography of Rhys Lewis (Owen) 137
The Autobiography of William Allen White (White) 214
The Autocrat of the Breakfast-Table (Holmes) 120
Auto-da-Fé (Canetti) 200
"Autumn" (Thomson) 74
Autumn Journal (MacNeice) 204
Autumn Leaves (Hugo) 106
Autumn Music (Preil) 258
The Autumn of the Patriarch (García Márquez) 254
Autumn Tranquility (Zollinger) 206
Avadheshwari (Punekar) 269
Avarice House (Green) 188
"Ave Atque Vale" (Swinburne) 126
The Avenue Bearing the Initial of Christ into the New World: Poems, 1946–1964 (Kinnell) 252
An Avenue of Stone (Johnson) 215
Avishag (Schutz) 274
Avlosning (Ulven) 280
The Avoiding and Other Poems (MacNeacail) 267
The Awakening (Chopin) 149
An Awfully Big Adventure (Bainbridge) 273
The Awkward Age (James) 91, 149
Axel (Villiers de L'Isle-Adam) 137, 141
Axel's Castle (Wilson) 194
Ayala's Angel (Trollope) 134
Azul (Regas) 283

B

Baal (Brecht) 153
Babbitt (Lewis) 182
Babbling April (Greene) 154
"Babette's Feast" (Dinesen) 218
Babi Yar (Kuznetsov) 242
Babi Year (Yevtushenko) 234
Babu du Montparnasse (Philippe) 159
Babylonian Wandering (Doblin) 199
Babylonians (Aristophanes) 3
Bacchae (Euripides) 2, 8
The Bachelor Party (Chayefsky) 223
Il bacio della Medusa (Mazzucco) 287
Back to Ina Damman (Vestdijk) 198
Back to Methuselah (Shaw) 153, 181
Badenheim 1939 (Appelfeld) 258
The Badgers (Leonov) 185
O baile de mascaras (Rasi) 276
Bailegangaire (Murphy) 267
Bailey's Café (Naylor) 277
Baina al-Qasraym (Mahfouz) 226
"The Bait" (Donne) 49
Bajazet (Racine) 48, 62
Balaustion's Adventure (Browning) 128
The Balcony (Genet) 225, 227
The Balcony (Heiberg) 145
The Bald Soprano (Ionesco) 219
Balder Dead (Arnold) 118
Baldershawn (Stigen) 264
"Balin and Balan" (Tennyson) 137
Balisand (Hergesheimer) 185
Balkan Ghosts (Kaplan) 279

The Balkan Trilogy (Manning) 232

"Ball of Fat" (Maupassant) 133

A Ballad from Beyond (Czechowicz) 196

"The Ballad of Bouillabaisse" (Thackeray) 116

The Ballad of Reading Gaol (Wilde) 148

The Ballad of the Figures (Eguren) 175

The Ballad of the Harp-Weaver (Millay) 183

Ballad of the Mari Lwyd and Other Poems (Watkins) 208

The Ballad of the Sad Café (McCullers) 220

The Ballad of Typhoid Mary (Federspiel) 262

Ballads and Other Poems (Longfellow) 111

Ballads and Other Poems (Tennyson) 133

Ballads and Poems (Masefield) 168

Ballads and Poems of Tragic Life (Meredith) 138

Ballads and Songs (Davidson) 144

Ballads and Sonnets (Rossetti) 134

Baltasar (Gómez de Avellaneda) 121

Balthazar (Durrell) 229

Baltics (Transtromer) 253

Bambi (Salten) 184

Band of Angels (Warren) 225, 226

Bang (Willumsen) 286

Bang the Drum Slowly (Harris) 226

Bang-e Dara (Iqbal) 185

Bánk bán (Katona) 100

The Bankrupt (Bjørnson) 130

Banks and Politics in America (Hammond) 229

Banquet (Dante) 14

The Banquet of Severo Arcangelo (Marechal) 240

Baptism by the Slavica (Preseren) 109

Barabbas (Lagerkvist) 219

The Barbarian in the Garden (Herbert) 236

Barbarian Prayer (Csoori) 272

The Barber of Seville (Beaumarchais) 82

Barbera Blomberg (Zuckmayer) 218

Barchester Towers (Trollope) 120

"The Bard" (Gray) 79

Barefoot in the Park (Simon) 237

"Bark" (Popa) 223

Barnabees Journal (Brathwaite) 56

Barnaby Rudge (Dickens) 90, 112

Barnevakt (Bjornstad) 282

Barney's Version (Richler) 288

The Baron in the Trees (Calvino) 228

Barq al-Layl (Khurayyif) 233

The Barque Future (Lie) 129

Barrack-Room Ballads (Kipling) 143

The Barracks Thief (Wolff) 265

A barragem (Moreira) 280

Barren Ground (Glasgow) 186

Barrett Wendell and His Letter (Howe) 186

Barrier to the Northwest (Bontempelli) 184

Bartholomew Fair (Jonson) 52

"Bartleby the Scrivener" (Melville) 118

The Basement Window (Buero Vallejo) 243

La bataille (Rambaud) 288

"Batter My Heart" (Donne) 49

The Battle Cry of Freedom: The Civil War Era (McPherson) 272

The Battle Lost and Won (Manning) 257

The Battle of Coxinga (Chikamatsu) 48

The Battle of Herman (Kleist) 98

The Battle of Pharsalus (Simon) 246

The Battle of the Books (Swift) 70

Bayou Folk (Chopin) 144

Be Angry at the Sun (Jeffers) 208

Be Sure to Close Your Eyes (Hood) 280

The Beach of Falesa (Stevenson) 143

Beacons (Cruze Sousa) 158

The Beak of the Finch: A Story of Evolution in Our Time (Weiner) 283

The Bean Eaters (Brooks) 232

The Bean Trees (Kingsolver) 270

The Bear (Chekhov) 92

The Bear (Faulkner) 200

The Bear Comes Home (Zabor) 290

Bearing the Cross: Martin Luther King, Jr., and the Southern Christian Leadership Conference (Garrow) 268

"The Beast of the Jungle" (James) 161

Beasts and Super Beasts (Saki) 173

The Beatification of Area Boy (Soyinka) 284

Beatriz y los cuerpos celestes (Etxebarria) 292

Beau Geste (Wren) 185

Beauchampe (Simms) 112

The Beautiful and Damned (Fitzgerald) 182

The Beautiful Changes and Other Poems (Wilbur) 214

Beautiful Days (Nobuo) 289

The Beautiful Ones Are Not Yet Born (Armah) 244

Beautiful Swimmers (Warner) 255

The Beautiful Visit (Howard) 219

The Beauty of Life (Popov) 274

The Beaux's Stratagem (Farquhar) 71

The Beaver Coat (Hauptmann) 144

Because It Is Bitter and Because It Is My Heart (Oates) 273

Bech: A Book (Updike) 247

Bech at Bay (Updike) 290

Bech Is Back (Updike) 261

Becket, or the Honor of God (Anouilh) 231

Becket (Tennyson) 136

The Bed (Tayama) 166

The Bedroom (Bertolucci) 264

Been in the Storm So Long (Litwack) 259

Before Dawn (Hauptmann) 140

Before the Dawn (Toson) 200

Before the Rainy Season (Hoffmann) 271

Before the Storm (Fontane) 132

The Beggar (Karkavitsas) 149

Beggar on Horseback (Kaufman) 185

The Beggar's Opera (Gay) 74

The Beginners (Jacobson) 240

The Beginning and the End (Mahfouz) 220

Behind the Scenes at the Museum (Atkinson) 286

Um beijo dado mais tarde (Ilansol) 276

Being and Nothingness (Sartre) 210

Being and Time (Heidegger) 189

Being Dead (Crace) 293

Being There (Kosinski) 247

Bel ami (Maupassant) 137

Belarmino and Apolonio (Pérez de Ayala) 181

Belated Crown (Weinheber) 202

The Belfry of Bruges and Other Poems (Longfellow) 114

Belgium's Agony (Verhaeren) 174

Belinda (Edgeworth) 95

A Bell for Adano (Hersey) 211, 212

The Bell Jar (Plath) 237

The Bellarosa Connection (Bellow) 272

"La Belle Dame sans Merci" (Keats) 101

Une belle journée d'avance (Lalonde) 268

Bellefleur (Oates) 259

"Bells" (Poe) 116

Bells and Pomegranates (Browning) 114

Bells in Winter (Milosz) 257

The Bells of Basel (Aragon) 199

Bellus Helveticum (Pirkheimer) 30

Beloved (Morrison) 268, 270

The Beloved Returns (Mann) 152

"The Beloved's Exile" (Upadhyay Hariaudh) 173

A Bend in the River (Naipaul) 258

Bend Sinister (Nabokov) 155, 214

Beneath Your Clear Shadow and Other Poems (Paz) 203

The Beneficent Grouch (Goldoni) 82

Ben-Hur: A Tale of the Christ (Wallace) 133

Benilde, or the Virgin Mother (Regio) 215

Beniowski (Słowacki) 112

Benito Cereno (Melville) 119

Benjamin Franklin, Self-Revealed (Bruce) 177

Benjamin Franklin (Van Doren) 205

Benjamin Henry Latrobe (Hamlin) 226

Beowulf 13, 19

Beppo (Byron) 93, 101

Bérénice (Racine) 48, 61

Beretninger om beskyttelse (Hansen) 291

La Bergeries (Racan) 52

Berlin Alexanderplatz (Doblin) 192

The Berlin Stories (Isherwood) 205, 213

Bernardo; or the Victory at Roncesvilles (Balbuena) 53

Berryman's Sonnets (Berryman) 242

Bertrand and Raton; or, The Art of Conspiracy (Scribe) 107

Beside the River Sar (Castro) 136

The Best Poems (Campos) 278

Betrayal (Pinter) 257

Betrayed by Rita Hayworth (Puig) 245

The Betrothed (Manzoni) 104

Better Than Wine (Rojas) 230

Between Gods and Demons (Weinheber) 204

Between Here and Now (Thomas) 260

Between the Battles (Bjørnson) 120

Between the Coronation and the Sword (Alberti) 208

Between the Currents (Jirásek) 142

Between the Wars (Brandys) 217

Between Three Borders (Klima) 232

Between Two Rivers: Selected Poems, 1956–1984 (Kenny) 268

Between War and Peace: The Potsdam Conference (Feis) 233

Beware of Pity (Zweig) 204

Beyond Culture (Trilling) 240

Beyond Good and Evil (Nietzsche) 114, 138

Beyond Human Endurance (Bjørnson) 135

Beyond the Horizon (O'Neill) 153, 179

Bharatbharati (Gupta) 171

Bhuridat Lingagyi (Rahtathara) 28

Bhuridat Zatpaung Pyo (Rahtathara) 29

Bible 1
   Coverdale translation 37
   King James version 51

The Bible in Spain (Barrow) 112

The Big House (Dib) 221

The Big Money (Dos Passos) 201

The Big Rock Candy Mountain (Stegner) 210

The Big Sleep (Chandler) 205

Big Work (Parra) 246

The Bigelow Papers (Lowell) 114, 115

Bikubers song (Grytten) 294

Billiards at Half-Past Nine (Böll) 231

Billy Bathgate (Doctorow) 272, 273

Billy Budd, Foretopman (Melville) 185

Billy Sunday (Jones) 286

Biographia Literaria (Coleridge) 100

Birangana (Datta) 122

Bird Alone (O'Faolain) 202

The Bird and the White Table Cloth (Abrahamsen) 266

Birds (Aristophanes) 3

The Birds (Vesaas) 228

Birds of America (McCarthy) 248

Birdy (Wharton) 258

The Birth of Tragedy (Nietzsche) 129

Birthday Letters (Hughes) 290

Birthday Party (Pinter) 229, 231

Birthplace (Haavikko) 225

Bishop Blougram's Apology (Browning) 119

Bitte nicht sterben (Wohmann) 280

Bitter Angel (Gerstler) 275

A Bitter Lot (Pisemsky) 121

Det bla skapet och andra berattelser (Alfven) 294

Black and White (Macaulay) 275

Black Banners (Strindberg) 93, 165

Black Beauty (Sewell) 131

Black Box (Oz) 269

Black Boy (Wright) 212

"The Black Cat" (Poe) 91

Black City (Lundkvist) 194

The Black City (Mikszáth) 169

Black Dogs (McEwan) 278

The Black Dwarf (Scott) 93, 100

Black Elk Speaks (Neihardt) 196

Black Feeling, Black Talk (Giovanni) 244

Black Forest Village Stories (Auerbach) 113

Black Gate (Arghezi) 193

Black Label (Damas) 227

Black Lamb and Grey Falcon (West) 209

Black Mischief (Waugh) 196

"The Black Monk" (Chekhov) 92, 145

Black Narcissus (Godden) 205

Black Pearls (Nervo) 148

Black Poems (Lima) 215

The Black Prince (Murdoch) 251

The Black Prince, and Other Stories (Grau) 225

The Black Rose (Montherlant) 245

Black Seasons (Glowinski) 291

The Black Sheep (Balzac) 91

Black Snow (Liu) 279

Black Sonnets (Sebastian) 166

The Black Soul (O'Flaherty) 185

Black Spring (Miller) 201
Black Swan (Hope) 269
The Black Swan (Mann) 152, 223
Black Thunder (Bontemps) 201
The Black Torches (Verhaeren) 141
Black Tulip (Dumas) 117
The Black Venus (Baudelaire) 92
Black Zodiac (Wright) 290
Blackie the Fool (Klabund) 177
The Blacks (Genet) 230
Blame Me on History (Modisane) 237
Blanchette (Brieux) 143
Blasting and Bombardiering (Waugh) 203
Blaubarts Shatten (Hahn) 276
Bleak House (Dickens) 90, 117
Bless Me Ultima (Anaya) 250
Blesse, ronce noire (Combet) 284
"The Blessed Damozel" (Rossetti) 116
The Blessing (Mitford) 220
The Blind Assassin (Atwood) 295
The Blind Beggar of Alexandria (Chapman) 45
Blind Dog (Hristow) 275
The Blind Owl (Hedāyat) 203
Blind Rose (Conscience) 116
The Blindfold Horse: Memories of a Persian Childhood (Guppy) 272
Blindness (Saramago) 287
Blindness and Insight: Essays in the Rhetoric of Contemporary Criticism (De Man) 249
Bliss, and Other Stories (Mansfield) 180
Blithe Spirit (Coward) 208
The Blithedale Romance (Hawthorne) 117
Blizzard of One (Strand) 292
The Block (Aitmatov) 270
Blood and Family (Kinsella) 271
Blood and Sand (Blasco Ibáñez) 166
Blood for a Stranger (Jarrell) 209
The Blood Oranges (Hawke) 248
Blood Ties (Settle) 257
Blood Wedding (García Lorca) 155, 198
Blood-Red Sonnets (Hviezdoslav) 174
Bloodshed and Three Novellas (Ozick) 254
The Bloody Tenet of Persecution for the Cause of Conscience (Williams) 57
"The Bloody Throne" (Payrav) 194
A Blot in the 'Scutcheon (Browning) 113
Blowing Sand/A Winter Journey (Kangro) 266
Blue (Darío) 139
The Blue Afternoon (Boyd) 280
The Blue Angel (Mann) 163
The Blue Band (Kellerman) 204
The Blue Bird (Maeterlinck) 166
The Blue Flowers (Queneau) 240
The Blue Stockings (Molière) 48
Bluebeard: A Tale (Frisch) 262
The Bluebird (Maeterlinck) 167
The Bluest Eye (Morrison) 247
The Bluff (Labiche) 122
The Blunderer (Molière) 59
The Boat (Hartley) 217
The Boatmen (Klonowic) 44
Bobinack (Johnson) 196
Boca do Inferno (Miranda) 274
Bocages (Ronsard) 33
Bodas de sangre (García Lorca) 155, 198
Bodenlos (Kirsch) 286
Bodenloser Sstz (Braun) 274

Body and Soul (Conroy) 279
Boeto (Hooft) 52
The Bog of Stars (O'Grady) 143
Bomarzo (Mujica Lainez) 236
The Bond (Borel) 240
A Bond Honored (Osborne) 241
The Bonds of Interest (Benavente y Martínez) 165
Bone by Bone (Matthiessen) 293
The Bone People (Hulme) 263, 265
The Bonfire of Vanities (Wolfe) 268
Bonfires (Alos) 239
Bonjour Tristesse (Sagan) 224
The Book About Absent People (Modarressi) 268
The Book and Brotherhood (Murdoch) 269
The Book Beside Me (Reverdy) 216
The Book of Ahania (Blake) 68, 87
A Book of Common Prayer (Didion) 255
The Book of Daniel (Doctorow) 248
The Book of Day and the Book of Night (Iwaszkiewicz) 182
Book of Exercises (Seferis) 207
Book of Folly (Sexton) 250
The Book of Good Love (Ruiz) 25
The Book of Hours (Rilke) 155, 163
The Book of Imaginary Beings (Borges) 154, 243
The Book of J (Bloom) 273
The Book of Kings (Thackara) 293
The Book of Landscapes (Lugones) 176
The Book of Laughter and Forgetting (Kundera) 258
The Book of Los (Blake) 68, 87
Book of Margery Kempe (Kempe) 27
The Book of Martyrs (Foxe) 40
The Book of Masques (Gourmont) 146
Book of Mercy (Cohen) 264
The Book of Monelle (Schwob) 144
The Book of Nightmares (Kinnell) 248
Book of Nonsense (Lear) 114
Book of Poems (García Lorca) 155
The Book of Sand (Borges) 154, 254
Book of Seven Days (Johannes) 225
The Book of Songs (Drachmann) 140
The Book of Songs (Heine) 93
Book of the City of Ladies (Christine de Pisan) 26
Book of the Duchess (Chaucer) 14
Book of the Poor (Kasprowicz) 175
The Book of Thel (Blake) 68, 85
The Book of Urizen (Blake) 68, 86
Booker T. Washington (Harlan) 263
Books Do Furnish a Room (Powell) 249
Books on Matters to Be Remembered (Petrarch) 14, 25
The Bookseller (Cohen) 280
The Boors (Goldoni) 79
Bopha (Mtwa) 267
The Border Trilogy (McCarthy) 290
The Borderers (Wordsworth) 87, 92
Borderline (Hospital) 266
Borderliners (Hoeg) 282
The Borg Family Papers (Gunnarsson) 171
Boris and Gleb (Buyda) 289
Boris Godunov (Pushkin) 90, 104, 106
Born Brothers (Woiwode) 270
Born Guilty (Rojas) 220
The Borough (Crabbe) 98
Borstal Boy (Behan) 229
Boryslav Laughs (Franko) 135
Bosphorus Fortress (Gursel) 285
Boston Adventure (Stafford) 211

The Bostonians (James) 91, 137
Botchan: Master Darling (Natsume) 93, 164
Both Your Houses (Anderson) 197
The Bothie of Tober-na-Voulich (Clough) 115
Bothwell, A Tragedy (Swinburne) 130
The Bottom of the Glass (Ayala) 236
Bottomless (Velmar-Jankovic) 287
Bouborouche (Courteline) 144
The Bouge of Court (Skelton) 29
Bound East for Cardiff (O'Neill) 153
Bouquets and Prayers (Desbordes-Valmore) 113
The Bourgeois Gentleman (Molière) 48, 62
Box Man (Abe) 251
The Boy with a Cart (Fry) 219
The Boys (Lenngren) 87
The Boys in the Back Room (Romains) 172
A Boy's Town (Howells) 141
A Boy's Will (Frost) 172
Bozambo's Revenge: Colonialism Inside Out (Juminer) 245
Bozena Nemcova's Fan (Seifert) 207
Bradamante (Garnier) 42
Brajangana (Datta) 122
Brand (Ibsen) 94, 122, 125
Die Braut im Park (Quadflieg) 278
Brave New World (Huxley) 196
Brave New World Revisited (Huxley) 229
The Bravo (Cooper) 106
Bread and Fear (Savic) 278
Bread and Wine (Silone) 225
Bread Givers (Yezierska) 187
Break at Noon (Claudel) 164
Breakfast at Tiffany's (Capote) 229
Breakfast of Champions: or, Goodby Blue Monday (Vonnegut) 251
Breakfast on Pluto (McCabe) 291
The Breast (Roth) 250
The Breath of Copper (Enckell) 213
Breathing Lessons (Tyler) 270, 272
Breatijs (Boutens) 166
Brebeuf and His Brethren (Pratt) 207
Brennoralt (Suckling) 57
Brev til manen (Michael) 284
Brida (Coelho) 274
The Bridal Canopy (Agnon) 179
The Bridal of Triermain (Scott) 99
Bridal Veil (Shamir) 264
The Bride of Abydos (Byron) 93, 99
The Bride of Innisfallen (Welty) 225
The Bride of Lammermoor (Scott) 93, 101
The Bride of Messina (Schiller) 68, 96
Bride Price (Appa) 147
"The Bridegroom" (Pushkin) 90, 104
Brideshead Revisited (Waugh) 212
The Bridge (Crane) 193
The Bridge (Herczeg) 187
The Bridge of San Luis Rey (Wilder) 189, 190
The Bridge on the Drina (Andric) 217
The Bridge Over the River Kwai (Boulle) 221
Bridge to Terabithia (Peterson) 256
The Bridges at Toko-Ri (Michener) 222
A Brief Life (Onetti) 219
Brief Moment (Behrman) 194
Briefing for a Descent into Hell (Lessing) 249
The Brigadier and the Golf Widow (Cheever) 238

Bright Ambush (Wurdemann) 200
Bright Day (Priestley) 213
A Bright Shining Lie: John Paul Vann and America in Vietnam (Sheehand) 272
A Brighter Sun (Selvon) 221
The Brightness and the Blood (Aldecoa) 224
The Brightness of Life (Viélé-Griffin) 147
Brighton Rock (Greene) 154, 204
Bring Larks and Heroes (Keneally) 243
Britannia Rediviva (Dryden) 65
Britannicus (Racine) 48, 61
The British Prison Ship (Freneau) 84
Broad and Alien Is the World (Alegría) 208
Brodrene Henrikson (Enger) 296
Broke Heart Blues (Oates) 293
Broken April (Kadare) 261
Broken Country (Brodsky) 284
The Broken Pitcher (Kleist) 97
Broken Pitchers (al-Bayati) 223
The Broken Verse (Prudhomme) 125
The Broken Wings (Gibran) 182
Bronx Primitive: Portaits in a Childhood (Simon) 261
"The Bronze Horseman" (Pushkin) 90, 110
The Brook Kerith (Moore) 175
Brother Asno (Barrios) 183
Brother to Dragons: A Tale in Verse and Voices (Warren) 222
Brotherhood (Jirásek) 149
Brotherly Love (Dexter) 275
Brothers and Sisters (Compton-Burnett) 192
The Brothers Ashkenazi (Singer) 202
The Brothers Karamazov (Dostoyevsky) 90, 133
The Brothers (Terence) 5
"The Brothers" (Wordsworth) 92
Brothers, I Love You All (Carruth) 257
The Browning Version (Rattigan) 216
The Bruce (Barbour) 26
Bruges, the Dead City (Rodenbach) 143
Bruno's Dream (Murdoch) 246
Brutus (Cicero) 4
The Buccaneers (Wharton) 204
Buch der Leider (Heine) 105
Die Buchhandlerin (Bohme) 293
The Buck in the Snow (Millay) 190
Buckdancer's Choice (Dickey) 240
Bucolic Song (Petrarch) 14, 25
Bucolicum carmen (Boccaccio) 14
Bud, Not Buddy (Curtis) 295
Budda's Little Finger (Pelevin) 296
Buddenbrooks (Mann) 152, 159
The Bull from the Sea (Renault) 235
Bullet Park (Cheever) 245
The Bullfight (Inoue) 218
The Bullfighters (Montherlant) 188
The Bulwark (Dreiser) 213
O buraco ne parede (Fonseca) 287
Het bureau (Voskuil) 288, 290
Burger's Daughter (Gordimer) 258
The Burgomaster of Stilmonde (Maeterlinck) 177
Buried Child (Sheperd) 257, 258
The Buried Lake (Tate) 222
The Buried Mirror (Fuentes) 279
Burmese Days (Orwell) 199
The Burn (Aksyonov) 259
Burning (Johnson) 248
Burning Brambles: Selected Poems, 1944–1979 (Mathias) 263

The Burning Bush (Faesi) 190
Burning Daylight (London) 168
The Burning House (Beattie) 261
The Burning Mystery of Anna in 1951 (Koch) 258
A Burnt Child (Dagerman) 217
Burnt Metropolis (Otohiko) 287
Burnt Norton (Eliot) 202
Burnt to a Cinder (Shahnon) 240
A Burnt-Out Case (Greene) 154, 234
Burr (Vidal) 251
Burridge Unbound (Cumyn) 295
Bus Stop (Inge) 225
Butley (Gray) 249
Butterfield 8 (O'Hara) 200
Butterflies (Spitteler) 140
A Buyer's Market (Powell) 221
Buzón de tiempo (Benedetti) 294
By Love Possessed (Cozzens) 228
By the Open Sea (Strindberg) 141
Byen og verden (Hultberg) 279
Byzantium (Herczeg) 162

C

Cabal and Love (Schiller) 67, 84
El caballero de Sajonia (Benet) 277
Caballeros de fortuna (Landero) 283
Cabot Wright Begins (Purdy) 238
"The Cachalot" (Pratt) 188
Los caciques (Azuela) 176
Cadillac Jack (McMurtry) 261
Caesar: Let the Dice Fly (McCullough) 288
Caesar and Cleopatra (Shaw) 153, 159
Caesar and Pompey (Chapman) 55
The Cage (Azolsky) 289
La caída de Madrid (Chirbes) 297
Cain (Byron) 93, 102
Cain (Leconte de Lisle) 127
The Caine Mutiny (Wouk) 220, 221
The Cairo Trilogy (Mahfouz) 226
Caisangzi (Ye) 295
Caius Marius (Otway) 63
Cakes and Ale (Maugham) 193
"Calamiterror" (Barker) 203
La Calandria (Dovizi) 35
Calçada de Verao (Figueiredo) 274
Calendar Histories (Graf) 192
Calendau (Mistral) 126
California Suite (Simon) 254
Caligula (Camus) 155, 211
Call at Corazon (Bowles) 270
Call for the Dead (Le Carré) 232
Call It Sleep (Roth) 198
Call Me Crimson (Kemal) 292
The Call of the Toad (Grass) 278
The Call of the Wild (London) 160
Call to Arms (Lu) 156, 183
The Call (Hauge) 213
Call (Nasir) 221
The Call (Vörösmarty) 110
Calligrammes (Apollinaire) 177
Callista (Newman) 119
Calunga (Lima) 200
The Camel Through the Needle's Eye (Langer) 183
Camino Real (Williams) 222
"The Campaign" (Addison) 70
La campana (Fuentes) 275
Campo Santo (Wood) 277
Can Such Things Be? (Bierce) 143
Canaan (Graça Aranha) 160
The Canadian Brothers (Richardson) 111
Cancer Ward (Solzhenitsyn) 154, 245
Cancionero (Encino) 29

Candida (Shaw) 148, 153
Candide (Voltaire) 68, 79
Candido: or a Dream Dreamed in Sicily (Sciascia) 256
The Candlestick (Musset) 108
The Canker (Mao) 193
Cannery Row (Steinbeck) 212
The Cannibal Galaxy (Ozick) 262
Cannibals and Missionaries (McCarthy) 258
Canone inverso (Maurensig) 286
"The Canonization" (Donne) 49
Canopus in Argus: Archives (Lessing) 258
Can't Quit You, Baby (Douglas) 270
Le cant silencieux des chouettes (Bensoussan) 291
Cantare ne buio (Corti) 276
Canteiros de saturno (Machado) 278
The Canterbury Tales (Chaucer) 14, 26
I Canti (Leopardi) 91, 106
Canticle (Guillén) 191
Cantos (Pound) 155, 174
Cantos No. 1–117, 120 (Pound) 247
Canzoni (Leopardi) 91, 103
Cape of Good Hopelessness (Martinek) 281
Cape Town Theatrical Props (Stockenstrom) 269
Capital of Sorrow (Éluard) 188
Capolas negras (Vallejo) 287
Caprice (Bowring) 269
Captain Broussard's Conversion (Shaw) 153
Captain Fracasse (Gautier) 123
The Captain of Kopenick (Zuckmayer) 195
Captain Quiros (McAuley) 238
Captain Sword and Captain Pen (Hunt) 108
The Captains and Kings (Johnston) 250
Captains Courageous (Kipling) 147
The Captain's Daughter (Pushkin) 90, 109
"The Captive" (Echeverría) 110
The Captive (Proust) 184
Captivity Captive (Hall) 269
The Capuchin Tomb (Roth) 204
Carajicomedia (Goytisolo) 296
Caramuru (Durão) 84
"Caravans Are Still Marching" (Kaputikian) 238
La cárcel de amor (San Pedro) 29
Cardenio und Celinde (Gryphius) 59
Il cardillo addolorato (Ortese) 280
Careful, He Might Hear You (Elliott) 237
The Careless Husband (Cibber) 70
The Caretaker (Pinter) 232
Cargo of Orchids (Musgrove) 295
Carl and Anna (Frank) 188
Carmen (Mérimée) 114
Carmina de Laudibus Estensium (Boiardo) 27
Carnival and Lent (Nowakowski) 274
The Carnival Season (Wang) 295
Carolus Stardus (Gryphius) 59
Carossa (Marabini) 274
Carpenter's Gothic (Gaddis) 267
The Carrier of Ladders (Merwin) 247, 248
The Carriers (Vicente) 36
Carrot Top (Renard) 144
Cartas cruzadas (Jaramillo Agudelo) 285

La carujada (Romero) 275
La casa a nort-est (Maldini) 278
A casa da cabeça de cavalo (Gersao) 287
La casa de Bernarda Alba (García Lorca) 155, 202
La casa di chiaccio (Vitale) 296
Casanova (Miller) 290
Casanova's Chinese Restaurant (Powell) 232
The Case Book of Sherlock Holmes (Doyle) 163
The Case of Sergeant Grischa (Zweig) 189
Casi una leyenda (Rodríguez) 277
Casimir mene la grande (Ormesson) 288
Casino Royale (Fleming) 222
"The Cask of Amontillado" (Poe) 91, 114
Caspar Hauser (Wasserman) 166
Cass Timberlane (Lewis) 212
La Cassaria (Ariosto) 34
The Cassock (Delblanc) 237
Cast a Cold Eye (McCarthy) 219
The Castaway (Cowper) 88
The Castaway (Cozzens) 198
The Castilian Soul (Martínez Ruiz) 158
Castle Dangerous (Scott) 106
Castle Durant (Eichendorff) 110
The Castle (Kafka) 152, 188
The Castle (Klima) 238
The Castle of Argol (Gracq) 204
The Castle of Crossed Destinies (Calvino) 251
The Castle of Indolence (Thomson) 77
The Castle of Otranto (Walpole) 80
Castle Rackrent (Edgeworth) 95
The Castle Spectre (Lewis) 88
The Castrati (Delblanc) 254
A Casual Brutality (Bissoondath) 272
Casualties: Poems, 1966–1968 (Clark) 247
The Cat (Colette) 197
Cat and Mouse (Grass) 234
The Cat in the Hat (Seuss) 228
Cat on a Hot Tin Roof (Williams) 224, 225
The Catafalque (Heiberg) 172
Catalina (Kurnberger) 119
The Catalyst (Duncan) 229
Catch-22 (Heller) 233
The Catcher in the Rye (Salinger) 220
The Catered Affair (Chayefsky) 225
Catharina von Georgien (Gryphius) 59
Cathedral Folk (Leskov) 129
The Cathedral (Lowell) 127
La Cathédrale (Huysmans) 148
Catherine (Thackeray) 111
The Catherine Wheel (Stafford) 221
Cathleen ni Houlihan (Yeats) 160
Cathy from Heilbronn; or, The Trial by Fire (Kleist) 97
Catilinarians (Montalvo) 133
Catilina (Ibsen) 94, 117
Cato (Addison) 72
Cat's Cradle (Vonnegut) 237
Cat's Eye (Atwood) 271
Cat's Lives (Kriseova) 288
The Caucasian Chalk Circle (Brecht) 153, 216
Causes (Callimachus) 4
Cavalleria rusticana (Verga) 133, 136
The Cave and the Spring: Essays on Poetry (Hope) 240

The Cave in the Desert (Gyllensten) 252
The Cave (Warren) 230
Cavender's House (Robinson) 191
Cawdor (Jeffers) 190
Cecilia, or Memoirs of an Heiress (Burkey) 84
"The Celebrated Jumping Frog of Calaveras County" (Twain) 92, 124
La Celestina (Rojas) 30
Cement (Gladkhov) 187
The Cenci (Shelley) 101
The Centaur (Marechal) 207
The Centaur (Updike) 237
Centennial (Michener) 252
The Centennial Sea-Wolf (Wang) 290
Centuries (Nostradamus) 39
Centuries of Meditations (Traherne) 166
A Century of Dishonor (Jackson) 134
Ceremony and Other Poems (Wilbur) 219
A Certain Measure (Glasgow) 210
C'est tout (Duras) 284
C'etait toute une vie (Bon) 284
Chaim Lederer's Return (Asch) 190
The Chainbearer (Cooper) 114
The Chairs (Ionesco) 221
Chaka (Mofolo) 195
The Chalk Garden (Bagnold) 225
Les champs d'honneur (Rouaud) 274
A Chance Acquaintance (Howells) 129
Chance (Conrad) 172
Chandos (Ouida) 125
The Chaneysville Incident (Bradley) 261
A Change of Skin (Fuentes) 243
The Changeling (Middleton, Rowley) 59
Changing Light at Sandover (Merrill) 262
La Chanson de Roland 13, 21
The Chant of Jimmie Blacksmith (Keneally) 250
Chanticleer's Morsel (Popovic) 276
The Chapel of the Hermits, and Other Poems (Whittier) 118
Chapter Two (Simon) 255
Chapters Forgotten by Cervantes (Montalvo) 137
Char Divan (Nava'i) 29
The Character, or Manners of the Age with the Characters of Theophrastus (La Bruyère) 65
Charcoal Burner's Ballad and Other Poems (Andersson) 211
"Charge of the Light Brigade" (Tennyson) 93, 118
Chariot of Wrath (Leonov) 212
Charlemont (Simms) 119
Charles Evans Hughes (Pusey) 221
Charles Stuart, or Majesty Murdered (Gryphius) 58
Charles Sumner and the Coming of the Civil War (Donald) 233
Charles W. Eliot (James) 194
Charles: An Historical Romance (Mofolo) 186
Charles IX; or, La Sainte-Barthelemy (Chénier) 85
Charles XII (Voltaire) 68
Charlotte's Web (White) 221
A Charmed Life (McCarthy) 225
Charmides (Plato) 3
Charming Billy (McDermott) 290
The Charterhouse of Parma (Stendhal) 111

La chasseur zero (Roze) 286

The Chaste Joseph (Grimmelshausen) 61

Chat Show (White) 269

Chatterton (Vigny) 108

The Cheapest Night (Idris) 223

The Cheats of Scapin (Molière) 62

"Chelkash" (Gorky) 145

Cheri (Colette) 180

The Cherry Orchard (Chekhov) 92, 162

Cherubin Hammer und Cherubin Hammer (Bichsel) 293

Chesapeake (Michener) 257

The Chestnut Tree (Tyler) 103

Le Chevalier des touches (Barbey d'Aurevilly) 124

Chicago (Sandburg) 173

Chicago Poems (Sandburg) 175

The Chief (Mann) 187

Chief of the Honorable Minister (Aluko) 247

The Chieftain's Daughter (Chatterjee) 124

The Child at the Balustrade (Boylesve) 161

The Child Bordered with Dreams (Hébert) 278

A Child of All Nations (Tur) 259

A Child of Our Time (Castillo) 228

A Child of the Kudiyas (Karanta) 220

The Child of the Parish (Ebner-Eschenbach) 138

Childe Harold's Pilgrimage (Byron) 93, 98

Childhood Friend (Bashir) 211

Childhood Years of Grandson Bagrov (Aksakov) 120

Childhood's End (Clarke) 222

Children of Chaos (Goytisolo) 226

Children of Crisis (Coles) 250

The Children of Death (Babits) 189

Children of Nature (Claussen) 138

The Children of Pleasure (D'Annunzio) 148

Children of the Arbat (Rybakov) 272

Children of the Black Sabbath (Hébert) 254

The Children of the Earth (Queneau) 204

Children of the Game (Cocteau) 192

Children of the Mist (Phillpotts) 148

The Children of the New Forest (Marryat) 115

Children of the Night (Robinson) 147

Children of the World (Heyse) 129

Children of Violence (Lessing) 223, 229

Children of Wrath: A Hired Man's Saga (Aakjaer) 148

"Children of Wrath" (Alonso) 212

The Children's Hour (Hellman) 198

A Child's Christmas in Wales (Thomas) 224

Child's Garden of Verses (Stevenson) 137

Child's Songs (Aicard) 131

Childworld (Oates) 254

The Chill of the Sun (Cayrol) 237

Chills and Fever (Ransom) 185

Chimera (Roth) 250

La chimera (Vassalli) 274

The Chimeras (Nerval) 118

The Chimes (Dickens) 113

The Chinese Insomniacs (Jacobsen) 260

The Chinese Nightingale and Other Poems (Lindsay) 176

The Chinese Wall (Frisch) 215

Chita: A Memory of Last Island (Hearn) 140

Chlopi (Reymont) 162

A Choice of Enemies (Richler) 228

A Chorus Line (Bennet, Kirkwood, Dante, Hamlisch, Kleban) 253, 254

A Chorus of Disapproval (Ayckbourn) 267

The Chosen (Potok) 242

Chosen Country (Dos Passos) 220

The Chosen Place, The Timeless People (Marshall) 245

Les Chouans (Balzac) 91, 105

Christ and Antichrist (Merezhkovsky) 146

Christ Stopped at Eboli (Levi) 213

"Christabel" (Coleridge) 100

Christian Discourses (Kierkegaard) 91

The Christian Georgics (Jammes) 170

The Christian Hero (Steele) 70

The Christian Socrates (Balzac) 58

Christiana Almanack 57

Christianity at a Glacier (Laxness) 245

Christie Johnstone (Reade) 118

Christina's Journey Home (Hofmannsthal) 168

A Christmas Carol (Dickens) 90, 113

Christmas Eve and Easter (Browning) 116

The Christmas Tree (Johnston) 260

Christophe Colomb (Lemercier) 98

Christopher (Drayton) 231

Christopher Unborn (Fuentes) 270

Christus shel haDagim (Hoffmann) 276

The Chrome Suite (Birdsell) 278

The Chronicle of a Death Foretold (García Márquez) 261

The Chronicle of Clovis (Saki) 169

Chronicle of Loneliness (Ben Jelloun) 255

The Chronicle of the Screw Turning Bird (Murakami) 284

Chronicles (Holinshed) 41

Chronique (Perse) 232

Chronique des Pasquier (Duhamel) 193

Church Poems (Betjeman) 260

The Chute (Camus) 155

Le Cid (Corneille) 48, 56

The Cider House Rules (Irving) 265

I cieli di vetro (Conti) 293

El cielo dividido (Roffe) 287

Cinders (Amrouche) 199

Cinna (Corneille) 48, 56

Cinnamoncandy (Ahlin) 223

Cinq-Mars (Vigny) 104

The Circle (Maugham) 181

The Circle of Reason (Ghosh) 267

Circles in the Water: Selected Poems (Piercy) 261

Circles on the Water (Semolic) 296

The Circular Staircase (Rinehart) 166

Los círculos del tiempo (Sampeda) 281

The Circus Animals (Plunkett) 274

The Circus in the Attic (Warren) 215, 216

The Cistern (Seferis) 196

The Citadel (Cronin) 203

Citations About a Revolution (Ferreira) 265

Cities of the Interior (Nin) 231

Cities of the Plain (McCarthy) 290

Cities of the Plain (Proust) 181

A Citizen of the Galaxy (Heinlein) 228

Citizens: A Chronicle of the French Revolution (Shama) 272

La città del dotor Malagui (Pazzi) 280

La Città e la Casa (Ginzburg) 264

City Heights (Robles) 216

The City Heiress (Behn) 64

City Life (Barthelme) 247

"The City of Dreadful Night" (Thomson) 130

City of Glass (Auster) 269

City of God (Augustine) 13, 18

The City of Marvels (Mendoza) 271

The City Whose Prince Is a Child (Montherlant) 220

The Civil War (Montherlant) 240

Civilization and Its Discontents (Freud) 193

Clamor (Guillén) 229

Clara Howard (Brown) 95

Clarel (Melville) 131

Clarissa Harlowe (Richardson) 77

La classe de neige (Carrère) 284

Claude Gueux (Hugo) 108

The Claw (Bernstein) 164

The Clay Machine Gun (Pelevin) 294

Clay Medals (Régnier) 158

The Clayhanger Family (Bennett) 186

Clea (Durrell) 232

"A Clean Well-Lighted Place" (Hemingway) 153

Clélie: Histoire romaine (Scudéry) 59

The Clembaj Family (Krleza) 196

Cleng Peerson (Hauge) 244

Cléopâtre captive (Jodelle) 39

A Clip of Steel (Blackburn) 246

Clipped Wings (Pontoppidan) 134

The Clique (Scribe) 110

Clitandre (Corneille) 48

Clock Without Hands (McCullers) 233

A Clockwork Orange (Burgess) 235

The Clockwork Testament (Burgess) 252

The Cloister and the Hearth (Reade) 122

Close Quarters (Golding) 269

Close Range (Proulx) 293

Close to the Sun Again (Callaghan) 256

The Closed Door (Bosschere) 176

The Closed Down Theater (Okudzhava) 283

The Closed Garden (Green) 189

Closely Watched Trains (Hrahbel) 240

The Closing of the American Mind (Bloom) 268

Closing Time (Heller) 282

"The Cloud" (Shelley) 93

A Cloud in Trousers (Mayakovsky) 174

Clouds (Aristophanes) 3, 7

Clouds (Pontoppidan) 141

Clouds (Tsalka) 282

Cloudsplitter (Banks) 290

The Cloven Viscount (Calvino) 221

The Clown (Böll) 237

The Clown and His Daughter (Adivar) 201

The Coast of Chicago (Dybek) 273

A Coast of Trees (Ammons) 260

The Coat of Arms of the City of Coimbra (Vicente) 36

The Coat Without a Seam (Kunitz) 252

Cock-a-Doodle-Dandy (O'Casey) 218

Cocksure (Richler) 244

The Cocktail Party (Eliot) 152

Cocuyo (Sardy) 275

Coda (Astley) 282

Coeval Games (Oe) 258

The Coffee-House (Goldoni) 78

A Coffin for Demetrios (Ambler) 205

Cold Comfort Farm (Gibbons) 196

The Cold Green Element (Layton) 225

Cold Morning Sky (Zaturenska) 204

Cold Mountain (Frazier) 288

Colette (Lustig) 277

Collages (Nin) 238

Collected Early Poems, 1950–1970 (Rich) 279

Collected Poems (Aiken) 222

Collected Poems (Betjeman) 229

Collected Poems (Binyon) 194

Collected Poems (Crane) 197

Collected Poems (Davie) 250

Collected Poems (Freneau) 98

Collected Poems (Frost) 194

Collected Poems (Graves) 216

Collected Poems (Hartnett) 264

Collected Poems (Jennings) 243

Collected Poems (Larkin) 272

Collected Poems (Lenau) 114

Collected Poems (Lewis) 223

Collected Poems (MacCaig) 274

Collected Poems (Moore) 220, 221

Collected Poems (Nemerov) 255, 256

Collected Poems (Plath) 261

Collected Poems (Prince) 258

Collected Poems (Robinson) 182

Collected Poems (Sassoon) 215

Collected Poems (Seeger) 175

Collected Poems (Stevens) 223, 225

Collected Poems (Stubbs) 271

Collected Poems (Van Doren) 206

Collected Poems (Wright) 248, 249

Collected Poems, 1917–1952 (MacLeish) 222

Collected Poems, 1928–1953 (Spender) 225

Collected Poems, 1930–1993 (Sarton) 279

Collected Poems, 1934–1952 (Thomas) 221

Collected Poems, 1946–1991 (Carruth) 277

Collected Poems, 1947–1980 (Ginsberg) 264

Collected Poems, 1948–1984 (Walcott) 267

Collected Poems, 1948–1998 (Enright) 290

Collected Poems of H.D. (Dolittle) 186

Collected Poetry (Hope) 241

Collected Shorter Poems (Auden) 241

Collected Stories (Calisher) 253

Collected Stories (Lessing) 257

Collected Stories (Porter) 240, 241

Collected Stories (Singer) 262

Collected Stories (Stafford) 247

Collected Stories (Trevor) 279

Collected Stories (Welty) 259

Collected Stories of Mavis Gallant (Gallant) 286

Collected Verse (Hillyer) 198

Collected Works (Calvin) 52

Collected Works of Billy the Kidd: Left-Handed Poems (Ondaatje) 247

A Collective Notebook (Morozov) 294

The Collector (Fowles) 237

The Colleen Bawn (Boucicault) 121

The Colloquies (Gozzano) 170
Colomba (Mérimée) 111
The Colonel's Daughter (Meri) 241
The Colonial Period of American History (Andrews) 200
Color (Cullen) 186
Color of Blood (Garcia Calderón) 195
The Color Purple (Walker) 261, 262
Colored Winds (Ivanov) 183
The Colossus (Plath) 232
The Colossus of Maroussi (Miller) 205
Columbine (Mackenzie) 180
Come and Go (Beckett) 154
Come Back, Dr. Caligari (Barthelme) 238
Come Back, Little Sheba (Inge) 219
Come Back to Erin (O'Faolain) 207
The Comedians (Greene) 154, 241
The Comedienne (Reymont) 146
Comedy of Calisto and Melibea (Rojas) 30, 34
The Comedy of Errors (Shakespeare) 31, 43
The Comforters (Spark) 228
The Comic Illusion (Corneille) 55
The Comic Theater (Goldoni) 78
The Coming of Peace (Hauptmann) 141
The Coming of the War, 1914 (Van Tyne) 194
The Coming Out Book (Susko) 276
Coming Up for Air (Orwell) 205
Comme des anges (Boyer) 282
Comme ton père (Le Touze) 282
Common Ground: A Turbulent Decade in the Lives of Three American Families (Lukas) 267
The Common Reader (Woolf) 186
Common Sense (Paine) 83
The Companions of Vardan (Demirtichian) 210
The Compass Flower (Merwin) 256
Compassion (Pérez Galdós) 147
The Complaint; or, Night Thoughts on Life, Death and Immortality (Young) 76
The Complaint of a Poor Little Child (Kosztolányi) 169
The Compleat Angler, or the Contemplative Man's Recreation (Walton) 59
The Complete Poems (Jarrell) 245
Complete Poems (Sandburg) 219
The Complete Prose (Moore) 267
Complete Works (Crémazie) 135
Compulsion (Levin) 226
Comrades (Strindberg) 92
Comus (Milton) 48, 55
The Conceited Count (Destouches) 75
The Concept of Dread (Kierkegaard) 91
Concerning Famous Women (Boccaccio) 14
Concerning the Angels (Alberti) 192
Concerning Vernacular Eloquence (Dante) 14
Concluding Unscientific Postscript (Kierkegaard) 91
Concordance to the Holy Scriptures (Cruden) 75
Concrete Island (Ballard) 252
The Concubine (Amadi) 243
The Condemned (Dagerman) 217
Condensed Novels and other Papers (Harte) 125
The Condor Passes (Grau) 248

The Conduct of Life (Emerson) 121
A Coney Island of the Mind (Ferlinghetti) 229
A Confederacy of Dunces (Toole) 260
The Confederates (Keneally) 258
La conference de Cintegabelle (Salvayre) 293
Confessio Amantis (Gower) 26
Confession (Tolstoy) 90
Confession of a Child of the Century (Musset) 109
Confessions (Rousseau) 68, 84, 85
Confessions of a Mask (Yukio) 218
Confessions of an Opium Eater (De Quincey) 102
The Confessions of Felix Krull (Mann) 224
The Confessions of Josef Baisz (Jacobson) 256
The Confessions of Mr. K. (Brackman) 265
The Confessions of Nat Turner (Styron) 243, 244
The Confidence Man (Melville) 120
Confidence pour confidence (Constant) 291
The Confidential Agent (Greene) 154, 205
The Confidential Clerk (Eliot) 223
The Conformist (Moravia) 220
A confraria das espadas (Fonseca) 294
The Congo and Other Poems (Lindsay) 173
Coningsby (Disraeli) 113
Los conjurados (Borges) 266
A Connecticut Yankee in King Arthur's Court (Twain) 92, 140
Conquest: Montezuma, Cortes and the Fall of Old Mexico (Thomas) 282
The Conquest of Granada by the Spaniards (Dryden) 49, 61
Conquistador (MacLeish) 196, 197
Conrad der Leutnant (Spitteler) 148
The Conscience of the Rich (Snow) 229
The Conscious Lovers (Steele) 73
The Conscript (Conscience) 116
Consenting Adult (Hobson) 253
The Conservationist (Gordimer) 252, 253
Consider This, Señora (Doerr) 279
Considerations of the Causes of the Grandeur and Decadence of the Romans (Montesquieu) 75
Constance (Bazin) 221
Constancia y otras novelas para vírgenes (Fuentes) 275
The Constant Couple; or a Trip to the Jubilee (Farquhar) 69
The Constant Prince (Calderón de la Barca) 48, 54
Constantly Singing (Simmons) 259
The Constitutional History of the United States (McLaughlin) 201
Contact Highs: Selected Poems, 1957–1987 (Ansen) 270
As contadoras de historias (Botelho) 294
The Contenders (Wain) 229
Contending Forces (Hopkins) 158
Contes cruels (Villiers de L'Isle-Adam) 135
Contes et Faceties (Nerval) 117
Continuation des Amours (Ronsard) 33
The Contrast (Tyler) 85
La conversation (Nobecourt) 291

The Conversion (Appelfeld) 291
Coolie (Anand) 202
Coonardoo: The Well in the Shadow (Prichard) 192
The Cooper's Hell (Denham) 57
Cor Ardens (Ivanov) 170
Corazón tan blanco (Marías) 279
Corinne (Staël) 97
Coriolanus (Shakespeare) 51
Cork Street, Next to Hatter's (Johnson) 240
Corn Huskers (Sandburg) 178
Coronation (Donoso) 228
Les corps celestes (Brehal) 280
Correction (Bernhard) 254
The Corsair (Byron) 93, 99
The Corsican Brothers (Boucicault) 115
Il Cortegiano (Castiglione) 36
The Cossacks (Tolstoy) 90, 123
Counselor-at-Law (Rice) 194
Count Julian (Landor) 98
"Count Nulin" (Pushkin) 90, 105
Count Oederland (Frisch) 234
The Count of Carmagnola (Manzoni) 102
The Count of Monte Cristo (Dumas père) 113
The Count of Talavera (Lennep) 111
Count Robert of Paris (Scott) 106
The Counterfeiters (Gide) 188
The Counterlife (Roth) 268
The Countess Cathleen (Yeats) 143, 152
Countess Faustine (Hahn-Hahn) 112
The Countess of Charolais (Beer-Hofmann) 163
Country (Desnos) 211
The Country Doctor (Balzac) 91, 107
A Country Doctor (Kafka) 152, 178
The Country Girls Trilogy (O'Brien) 232
Country Music: Selected Early Poems (Wright) 262
Country of My Skull (Krog) 293
Country of Origin (Bakin) 287
The Country of Rembrandt (Busken Huet) 134
The Country of the Blind (Wells) 169
The Country of the Pointed Firs (Jewett) 146
The Country Waif (Sand) 115
The Country Wife (Wycherley) 62
The Coup (Updike) 260
Couples (Updike) 244
The Court of Miracles (Valle-Inclán) 189
The Courtship of Miles Standish (Longfellow) 120
The Courtyard (Lvov) 272
Cousin Basilio (Eça de Queirós) 132
Cousin Bette (Balzac) 91, 114
Cousin Pons (Balzac) 91, 115
Cousin Rosamund (West) 265
The Covetous Knight (Pushkin) 90, 109
The Coward (Lenormand) 186
The Crack-Up (Fitzgerald) 212
The Craft (Dovlatov) 266
The Crafty Widow (Goldoni) 77
Craig's Wife (Kelly) 187
"The Cranes of Ibycus" (Schiller) 68
Cranford (Gaskell) 117
Crash (Ballard) 251
The Crater (Cooper) 115
Cratylus (Plato) 3

The Cream of the Jest (Cabell) 176
Creation (Vidal) 260
Creation, Man and Messiah (Wergeland) 106
Creative Evolution (Bergson) 165
The Creditors (Strindberg) 92, 141
Credo des san-mélé ou je veux chanter la France (Gratiant) 216
"The Cretan" (Solomos) 107
Crick Crack Monkey (Hodge) 247
The Cricket on the Hearth (Dickens) 90, 114
Crime and Punishment (Dostoyevsky) 90, 125
A Crime in the Neighborhood (Berne) 293
The Crime of Batista the Student (Ribeiro Couto) 183
The Crime of Olga Arbyelina (Makine) 293
The Crime of Sylvestre Bonnard (France) 134
The Crime of Writing (Lapid) 291
Crime on Goat Island (Betti) 219
Crimean Sonnetsi (Mickiewicz) 104
El crimen del cine Oriente (Tomeo) 285
Crimes of the Heart (Henley) 258
Criminals in Love (Walker) 264
A Cripple in Love (Lehtonen) 182
The Crisis (Churchill) 159
Crispin, Rival of His Master (Lesage) 71
Cristoforo (Thomas) 288
The Criterion (literary review) 182
Critias (Plato) 3
The Critic (Sheridan) 83
Critical Essays (Barthes) 239
A Critical Fable (Lowell) 182
Critique of Practical Reason (Kant) 85
Critique of Pure Reason (Kant) 84
Crito (Plato) 3
The Crocodile (Lomami-Tshibamba) 216
Crome Yellow (Huxley) 181
Cromwell (Hugo) 105
Crónica sentimental en rojo (Ledesma) 265
Crooked Paths (Franko) 158
Cross Channel (Barnes) 286
Cross Hollows (Einar) 193
The Cross on the Baltic Sea (Werner) 97
Cross Purposes (Camus) 155
The Crossing (McCarthy) 282
Crossing River (Phillips) 280
"Crossing the Bar" (Tennyson) 140
Crossing the Water (Plath) 248
Crotchet Castle (Peacock) 106
Crow: From the Life and Songs of the Crow (Hughes) 247
The Crow and the Heart (Carruth) 230
The Crowning of Spring (Simon) 224
The Crucial Scene (Jouve) 200
The Crucible (Miller) 222
The Cruel Sea (Montserrat) 220
The Cruise of the Snark (London) 169
Crusader in Crinoline (Wilson) 209
Crusts (Claudel) 177
La cruz en la espada (Luján) 287
Cry, the Beloved Country (Paton) 216
A Cry and Landscapes (Ungaretti) 221
Cry of the Rain Bird (Bird) 284
The Crying of Lot 49 (Pynchon) 241
Crypt (Torres Bodet) 203

Cryptogamen (Achterberg) 213
The Crystal Frontier (Fuentes) 287
Cuaderno de Nueva York (Hierro) 292
Los cuadernos de don Rigoberto (Vargas Llosa) 289
La cuadratura del círculo (Pombo) 294
The Cubs, and Other Stories (Vargas Llosa) 243
Cuisine Novella (Laurent) 269
The Cult of the Self (Barres) 139
Culture and Anarchy (Arnold) 127
The Cunning Man (Davies) 282
The Cupboard (Tremain) 260
Cupid's Revenge (Beaumont and Fletcher) 51
The Cure for Death by Lightning (Anderson-Dargat) 286
The Curly-Haired Lieutenant (Muraveva) 283
Curriculum Vitae (Spark) 278
The Curse of Rebellious Susan (Jones) 144
A Curtain of Green (Welty) 208
The Custodian of the Divan (Jamalzadeh) 214
The Custom of the Country (Wharton) 172
The Cutter and Captain Shigemoto's Mother (Tanizaki) 218
The Cutter of Coleman Street (Cowley) 57
Cuttlefish Bones (Montale) 187
A Cycle of the West (Neihardt) 217
The Cyclone (Asturias) 219
Cyclopaedia, or, an Universal Dictionary of Arts and Sciences (Chambers) 74
Cymbeline (Shakespeare) 51
Cynthia's Revels (Jonson) 50
The Cypresse Grove (Drummond) 53
The Cypresses Believe in God (Gironella) 223
Cyrano de Bergerac (Rostand) 147

D

Daily Bread (Boylesve) 159
The Daisy Chain (Yonge) 119
Daisy Miller (James) 91, 132
Dal silenzio delle campagne (Comon) 293
The Dam (Butler) 222
Damascus Gate (Stone) 290
Dame de Pique (Boucicault) 117
Dame (Sudermann) 138
The Dammed and the Saved (Levi) 268
Damon; or, True Friendship (Lessing) 69
The Damsel of Darien (Simms) 110
A dança final (Marcos) 291
The Dance of Death (Becker) 252
The Dance of Death (Kellerman) 216
The Dance of Death (Strindberg) 92, 159
Dance of Death: A Baroque Poem (Rozewicz) 291
Dance of Death and Poems of the Times (Kaschnitz) 215
Dance of the Dead (Jouve) 176
A Dance to the Beginning of Time (Burgess) 220
Dance to the Music of Time (Powell) 220, 221, 235, 241, 244, 249
The Dancing Bears (Merwin) 223
Dandelion Wine (Bradbury) 228

Danger Memory! Two Plays (Miller) 270
The Danger Tree (Manning) 256
Dangerous Liaisons (Laclos) 84
Dangerous Love (Okri) 288
The Dangerous Summer (Hemingway) 265
Dangerous Tales (Altan) 287
The Dangling Man (Bellow) 211
Daniel Deronda (Eliot) 131
Daniel Martin (Fowles) 256
Danish History (Saxo Grammaticus) 13
Dans ces bras-la (Laurens) 296
Danton's Death (Büchner) 109
Daphnis (Gessner) 78
The Daring Young Man on the Flying Trapeze (Saroyan) 198
The Dark Angel (Waltari) 221
The Dark at the Top of the Stairs (Inge) 228
Dark Fields of the Republic (Rich) 284
The Dark Is Light Enough (Fry) 223
The Dark Journey (Green) 192
Dark Painting (Hiroshi) 214
Dark Palace (Moorhouse) 295
The Dark Philosophers (Thomas) 213
The Dark Tower (MacNeice) 215
Darkness (Jirásek) 174
Darkness at Noon (Koestler) 207
The Darkness at the Top (Pérez de Ayala) 165
Daughter Mine (Gold) 295
Daughter of Fire (Ikromi) 236
Daughter of Fortune (Allende) 294
The Daughter of Jorio (D'Annunzio) 162
The Daughter of the Air (Calderón de la Barca) 48, 59
A Daughter of the Middle Border (Garland) 182
The Daughters of Calvary (Combescot) 276
Daughters of the House (Roberts) 278
David Bele (Raffi) 133
David Copperfield (Dickens) 90, 116
David Harum: A Story of American Life (Westcott) 148
Dawn on Our Darkness (Robles) 221
Day After Day (Quasimodo) 215
The Day Before Yesterday (Agnon) 216
A Day Book (Creeley) 250
Day by Day (Lowell) 256
Day Home, Night Home (Tokarczuk) 294
The Day Lasts More Than a Hundred Years (Aitmatov) 274
A Day Lie Every Day (Czechowicz) 193
The Day of Doom (Wigglesworth) 60
The Day of the Jackal (Forsyth) 249
The Day of the Locust (West) 205
The Day of the Scorpions (Scott) 244
A Day on the Ground (Wispelaere) 247, 254
The Days (Torres Bodet) 184
Days Like Arrows (Marechal) 188
Days of Contempt (Malraux) 200
The Days of His Grace (Johnson) 233
Days of Hope (Malraux) 203
Days of Sorrow and Pain: Leo Baeck and the Berlin Jews (Baker) 258
Days with Monks (Laxness) 269
De Arte Poetica (Vida) 36
De Augmentis Scientiarum (Bacon) 53

De beneficiis (Seneca) 5
De Cive (Hobbes) 57
De clementia (Seneca) 5
De coeur et de l'affection (Teboul) 282
De Guerre lasse (Sagan) 266
De Homine (Hobbes) 59
De ira (Seneca) 5
De los nombres de Cristo (León) 42
De oratore (Cicero) 4, 10
De Orbe Novo (Peter Martyr) 35
De otio (Seneca) 5
De Partu Virginis (Sannazaro) 36
De Profundis (Wilde) 163
De Revolutionibus Orbium Coelestium (Copernicus) 38
De Sacramento Matrimonii (Sánchez) 44
De Silva (Harris) 256
De tranquillitate animi (Seneca) 5
De Vitor ao Xadres (Torrado) 264
"The Dead" (Joyce) 173
The Dead Father (Barthelme) 253
Dead Fire (Rego) 211
The Dead Kingdom (Montague) 263
The Dead Lecturer (Baraka) 238
A Dead Man in Deptford (Burgess) 280
Dead Men's Watches (Hood) 284
Dead Souls (Gogol) 91, 112
The Dead Spot (Popovic) 285
"A Deal in Wheat" (Norris) 160
The Dean's December (Bellow) 261
Dear Brutus (Barrie) 176
Dear Mr. Henshaw (Cleary) 263
Dear Mr. Kawabata (ad-Daif) 284
"Death, Be Not Proud" (Donne) 49
Death, Sleep and the Traveler (Hawkes) 252
Death and the Fool (Hofmannsthal) 144
Death and the King's Horseman (Soyinka) 252
Death and the Little Girl (Onetti) 252
Death and the Ploughman (Johannes von Tepl) 26
Death as a World of Life (Ayala) 230
Death by Seconds (Brousek) 284
Death Comes to the Archbishop (Cather) 189
Death in the Afternoon (Hemingway) 153, 196
A Death in the Family (Agee) 228, 229
Death in Venice (Mann) 152, 171
Death Is a Lonely Business (Bradbury) 265
Death of a Hero (Aldington) 192
"The Death of a Hired Man" (Frost) 173
Death of a Naturalist (Heaney) 241
Death of a Nobody (Romains) 170
"Death of a Poet" (Lermontov) 110
Death of a Salesman (Miller) 217
The Death of Abel (Gessner) 79
The Death of Balder (Ewald) 82
The Death of Caesar (Voltaire) 75
The Death of Ivan Ilyich (Tolstoy) 90, 138
The Death of Methuselah and Other Stories (Singer) 271
The Death of Oneone, Akbar's Dream and Other Poems (Tennyson) 93
The Death of Pompey (Corneille) 48, 57
The Death of Satan (Duncan) 223
The Death of Socrates (Gyllensten) 233

The Death of the Author (Adair) 278
The Death of the Heart (Bowen) 204
Death of the Seasons (Ungaretti) 243
The Death of the Tenant Farmer, Ignaz Hajek (Haslinger) 266
The Death of Titian (Hofmannsthal) 143
The Death of Virgil (Broch) 212
Death on the Installment Plan (Céline) 202
Death on the Nile (Christie) 203
The Death Ship (Traven) 188
Deaths and Entrances (Thomas) 213
Death's Jest-Book; or, The Fool's Tragedy (Beddoes) 116
Deathwatch (Genet) 218
Les Débâcles (Verhaeren) 139
Debit and Credit (Freytag) 119
Deborah et les anges dissipés (Jacques) 276
Decameron (Boccaccio) 14, 25
The Decay and Restoration of Civilization (Schweitzer) 184
"The Deceived Wive's Club" (Ribeiro Couto) 198
The Deceiver of Seville and the Stone Guest (Tirso de Molina) 54
December the Fourteenth (Mereazhkovsky) 177
Deception (Roth) 273
El décimo infierno (Giardinelli) 294
La declaration (Salvayre) 274
Decline; or, Your Love Has Destroyed Me (Khurayyif) 228
Decline and Fall (Waugh) 190
The Decline of the West (Spengler) 177
The Deemster (Caine) 138
Deep River (Arguedas) 230
Deep River (Endo) 280
Deep River Talk (Tuwhare) 282
Deep Shadows (Storm) 124
The Deeps of Deliverance (Eeden) 158
The Deer Park (Mailer) 225
Deerbrook (Martineau) 111
The Deerslayer (Cooper) 111
Defeat (Chander) 206
The Defense (Nabokov) 155, 193
La Défense de Tartuffe (Jacob) 178
The Defense of Guenevere and Other Poems (Morris) 120
The Deformed Transformed (Byron) 103
Degrees (Butor) 232
Deirdra (Yeats) 152, 165
Deirdra of the sorrows (Synge) 168
"Dejection: An Ode" (Coleridge) 96
A Delicate Balance (Albee) 241, 242
Delie: Object of Highest Virtue (Scève) 38
The Delirious Heart (Torres Bodet) 183
Delito por bailar el chachacha (Cabrera Infante) 285
Delphic Utterance (Sikelianós) 189
Delphine (Staël) 96
Delta Wedding (Welty) 211, 213
The Deluge (Sienkiewicz) 138
La demarche du crabe (LaRue) 284
La démence du boxeur (Weyergans) 278
Demeter and Other Poems (Tennyson) 93, 140
Demian (Hesse) 178
Le Demi-Monde (Dumas) 119
Democracy (Didion) 264

Democracy in America (Tocqueville) 108

Democratic Vistas (Whitman) 128

The Demon (Lermontov) 112

The Demon of Good (Montherlant) 203

The Demons (Doderer) 227

Demos (Gissing) 137

Denied a Country (Bang) 164

Departmental Ditties (Kipling) 137

Departure from the Castle (Putik) 292

The Departure of Martin Fierro (Hernández) 129

Departures (Justice) 251

The Deptford Trilogy (Davies) 247, 250, 253

The Deputy (Hochhuth) 237

Derangement (Bernhard) 243

La dérive des sentiments (Simon) 276

Les Derniers Vers (Ronsard) 33

Des anges mineurs (Volodine) 293

The Descendants (Immermann) 109

Descendants of Cain (Arishima) 176

The Descent of Man (Darwin) 128

"The Descent of Odin: An Ode" (Gray) 81

Description (Dragomoshchenko) 296

Desert (Le Clezio) 259

The Desert (Memmi) 256

The Desert of Love (Mauriac) 218

Desert of the Heart (Rule) 238

Desert Solitaire (Abbey) 244

Deserted Cities (Agustín) 262

The Deserted Village (Goldsmith) 81

The Deserted World (Jouve) 189

The Deserter (Abush) 286

Design for Living (Coward) 197

Desire Under the Elms (O'Neill) 153, 185

Desire's Baby (Chopin) 147

Desolation (Mistral) 183

Despair (Nabokov) 155

Desperate Remedies (Hardy) 128

Dess ande kysst (Johnsson) 279

Destan About Ali of Kesan (Taner) 239

Los desterrados (Quiroga) 188

The Destinies of Darcy Dancer, Gentleman (Donleavy) 256

Destroy, She Said (Duras) 246

Destruction (Mistral) 205

The Destruction of the First Creation (Bilderdijk) 102

The Destruction of the First World (Bilderdijk) 98

Destruction or Love (Aleixandre) 200

Detective Story (Kingsley) 217

The Determination of a House (Cruz) 64

Determined Step (Kerbabayev) 207

Un deus passeando pela brisa da tarde (Carvalho) 285

Deveroux (Bulwer-Lytton) 105

"The Devil and Daniel Webster" (Benét) 203, 205

The Devil and the Good Lord (Sartre) 220

The Devil Finds Work (Baldwin) 254

The Devil in the Flesh (Radiguet) 184

The Devil Is an Ass (Jonson) 52

The Devil to Pay in the Backlands (Rosa) 227

The Devil Upon Two Sticks (Lesage) 71

The Devil Within (Ali) 207

The Devil's Advocate (West) 231

The Devil's Dictionary (Bierce) 164

The Devil's Disciple (Shaw) 153

The Devil's Elixir (Hoffman) 99

The Devil's General (Zuckmayer) 214

The Devil's Law Case (Webster) 53

The Devil's Pool (Sand) 114

Devotions upon Emergent Occasions (Donne) 49, 53

The Dew Trapper (Nijlen) 214

The Dharma Bums (Kerouac) 229

Di vento e di fuoco (Pressburger) 296

El diablo cojuelo (Vélez de Guevara) 57

Diabolus in musica (Apperry) 296

"Dialogue of Insight" (Aleixandre) 253

Dialogues de Dom Frei Amador Arraiz (Arrais) 43

Dialogues des Carmelites (Bernanos) 218

"The Diamond as Big as the Ritz" (Fitzgerald) 182

The Diamond Cutters and Other Poems (Rich) 225

Diana: The Goddess Who Hunts Alone (Fuentes) 283

La Diana (Montemayor) 39

Diana of the Crossways (Meredith) 137

Diana's Hunt (Boccaccio) 14

Diario de 360° (Goytisolo) 296

Diario de Andrés Fava (Cortázar) 285

Diary (Pepys) 104

Diary of a Country Priest (Bernanos) 202

Diary of a Mad Old Man (Tanizaki) 191

"Diary of a Madman" (Gogol) 91, 109

"The Diary of a Madman" (Lu) 156

Diary of a Poet Recently Married (Jiménez) 177

The Diary of a Superfluous Man (Turgenev) 119

The Diary of a Young Girl (Frank) 215

Diary of Anne Frank (Hackett, Goodrich) 215

Diary of My Father's Death (Issa) 95

The Diary of My Times (Bernanos) 204

The Diary of Selma Lagerlöf (Lagerlöf) 196

Diary of the War of the Pig (Bioy Casares) 246

Días contados (Madrid) 281

Der Dibuk (The Dybbuk) (Ansky) 173

The Dice Box (Jacob) 176

Dicey's Song (Voigt) 262

A Dictionary of the English Language (Johnson) 79

Dictionary of the Khazars (Pavic) 271

Dido, Queen of Carthage (Marlowe) 33, 44

The Difficult Man (Hofmannsthal) 181

The Difficult Times (Bourdet) 199

Digression on Ancients and Moderns (Fontenelle) 65

Dikter (Södergran) 175

Diletta Constanza (Garavini) 286

Dimdim (Shamo) 245

Dinner at Eight (Kaufman) 196

Dinner with Friends (Margulies) 295

El dios dormido (Rubio) 292

"Dipsychus" (Clough) 127

The Dirge of the Medidian (Kinoshita) 256

Dirty Linen (Stoppard) 255

The Discipline (Bourget) 140

Discours de la méthode (Descartes) 56

Discourse on the Miseries of These Times (Ronsard) 33

Discourse on the Origin of Inequality (Rousseau) 68

Discourse on the Sciences and the Arts (Rousseau) 68, 78

Discourse on Universal History (Bossuet) 63

Discovering Elijah (Yizhar) 293

The Discovery of Heaven (Mulisch) 293

A Discovery of Strangers (Wiebe) 282

Disdain Turned Against Disdain (Moreto y Cabaña) 59

Disgrace (Coetzee) 292, 293

The Disinherited (Castillo) 230

The Disinherited Lady (Pérez Galdós) 134

The Dismissal of the Greek Envoys (Kochanowski) 41

Disobedience (Moravia) 216

The Disowned (Bulwer-Lytton) 105

The Dispossessed (Le Guin) 252

The Disruption of American Democracy (Nichols) 217

Dissemination (Derrida) 250

Distant Gardens (Jiménez) 163

The Distant Lands (Green) 269

A Distant Mirror: The Calamitous Fourteenth Century (Tuchman) 257

Distant Relations (Fuentes) 260

A Distant Trumpet (Horgan) 232

Le dit de Tianyi (Cheng) 291

Divan of Tamarit (García Lorca) 155

Divan-e-Shams (Rūmī) 15

"The Diver" (Schiller) 68

Diverse Voyages Touching the Discovery of America (Hakluyt) 42

Diviani Mataibat (Mushfiqi) 39

Divine (Mallet-Joris) 276

Divine Comedies (Merrill) 255

Divine Comedy (Dante) 13, 14, 24

The Diving Bell and the Butterfly (Bauby) 288

Division Street (Tesich) 259

Divisions (Cosic) 234

Djinn (Robbe-Grillet) 260

Do With Me What You Will (Oates) 251

Dobrovsky (Pushkin) 90

Doce cuentos peregrinos (García Márquez) 278

A Doce de Caetana (Pinon) 270

Docherty (McIlvanney) 254

Doctor Copernicus (Banville) 255

Doctor Faustus (Mann) 152, 215

Doctor Glas (Söderberg) 163

Doctor Ibrahim (Ayyub) 206

The Doctor Is Sick (Burgess) 232

Doctor Thorne (Trollope) 120

Doctor Zhivago (Pasternak) 228

The Doctor's Dilemma (Shaw) 153, 164, 169

The Doctor's Wife (Sawako) 248

Dodningeuret (Gronfeldt) 275

Dodsworth (Lewis) 192

The Doer (Borges) 233

The Dog of Montargis; or, The Forest of Bundy (Pixérécourt) 99

The Dog Without Feathers (Melo Neto) 219

Dog Years (Grass) 237

The Dogs (Aspenstrom) 224

The Dogs Bar: Public People and Private Place (Capote) 251

The Dogs of War (Forsyth) 252

Doine si Lacrimioare (Alecsandri) 118

Dolce per se (Maraini) 289

A Doll's House (Ibsen) 94, 132

The Dolphin (Lowell) 251, 252

Dom Casmurro (Machado de Assis) 149, 158

Dombey and Son (Dickens) 115

A Dome of Many-Colored Glass (Lowell) 171

Dominique (Fromentin) 123

Don Alvaro; or, The Power of Fate (Saavedra) 109

Don Carlos (Otway) 62

Don Carlos (Schiller) 67, 85

Don Juan (Byron) 93, 101

Don Juan (Lenau) 117

Don Juan (Molière) 48, 60

Don Juan and Faust (Grabbe) 106

Don Juan in the VIllage (DeLynn) 273

Don Juan Tenorio (Zorrilla y Moral) 114

Don Quixote (Cervantes) 32, 50

Don Sanche d'Aragon (Corneille) 48

Don Sebastian (Dryden) 49

Don Segundo Sombra (Güiraldes) 188

Doña Luz (Valera) 133

Doña Perfecta (Pérez Galdós) 131

Donatienne (Bazin) 161

Don't Forget (Malherbe) 172

Don't Pronounce It Night (Oz) 282

The Door into Summer (Heinlein) 228

Door into the Dark (Heaney) 246

Il doppio regno (Capriolo) 276

Dorf uterm Wind (Schenk) 280

Dorottya (Csokonai) 88

Dossier H (Kadare) 273

The Double (Dostoyevsky) 90, 115

The Double Dealer (Congreve) 66

Double Indemnity (Cain) 201

The Double Man (Auden) 208

Double Star (Heinlein) 226

Double Suicide at Amijima (Chikamatsu) 48

Double Suicides Committed at Forty-Eight Waterfalls in Akame (Chokitsu) 291

A Dove in Santiago: A Novella in Verse (Yevtushenko) 262

The Dove Returns (Butler) 227

Down and Out in Paris and London (Orwell) 197

Down by the River (O'Brien) 288

Down Second Avenue (Mphahlele) 231

Down Stream (Huysmans) 135

Down There (Huysmans) 142

A Down-and-Outer (Barrios) 178

The Downfall of Macias Giri (Natsuki) 280

Downstream (Kinsella) 235

Downstream (Siwertz) 180

Dr. Breen's Practice (Howells) 134

Dr. Brodie's Report (Borges) 154, 248

Dr. Criminale (Bradbury) 278

Dr. Faustus (Marlowe) 33

"Dr. Heidegger's Experiment" (Hawthorne) 109

Dr. Katzenberger's Journey to the Spa (Richter) 98

Dracula (Stoker) 147

A Draft of XXX Cantos (Pound) 197

"The Dragon and the Unicorn" (Rexroth) 221
Dragon Seed (Buck) 209
The Dragons of Eden (Sagan) 256
Dragon's Teeth (Sinclair) 209, 210
La Dragontea (Vega) 45
The Dram Shop (Zola) 131
"La Drama de Marchaterre" (Brierre) 193
Dramatis Personae (Browning) 124
Dramen (Canetti) 239
Drapier's Letters (Swift) 68, 73
Drayman (Hauptmann) 148
"The Dream" (Byron) 100
The Dream and the Desert (Krige) 222
The Dream Eater (Lenormand) 182
Dream Flower (Yosano) 164
A Dream Is Life (Grillparzer) 108
"The Dream of a Ridiculous Man" (Dostoyevsky) 131
Dream of a Tree (Bakin) 291
The Dream of Eugene Aram (Hood) 105
The Dream of Heroes (Bioy Casares) 224
A Dream of John Ball (Morris) 139
A Dream of Mind (Williams) 277
The Dream of Sarajevo (Rojas) 262
Dream of the Red Chamber (Cao) 69, 80, 191
The Dream of the Unified Field (Graham) 286
Dream of Yudotei Enmoku (Noboru) 296
The Dream on Monkey Mountain (Walcott) 241
A Dream Play (Strindberg) 92, 160
The Dream Songs (Berryman) 245
Dream Stuff (Malouf) 295
Dream Variation (Hughes) 188
A Dreambook of Our Time (Konwicki) 237
Dreamer (Johnson) 290
The Dreamer (Green) 199
A Dreamer for the Nation (Buero Vallejo) 230
Dreams in Twilight (Terian) 166
Dreams (Tagore) 153, 158
The Dreamtigers (Borges) 154
Dred: A Tale of the Great Dismal Swamp (Stowe) 119
The Dred Scott Case (Fehrenbacher) 258
Dreflan, Its People and Its Affairs (Owen) 134
Dressed in Light (Seifert) 207
Drift (Bjornstad) 287
The Driver's Seat (Spark) 247
Driving into the Storm: Selected Poems (Wedde) 269
Driving Miss Daisy (Uhry) 269, 270
Drivvd fran Ardadien (Radstrom) 294
Droll Stories (Balzac) 91, 107
Drommebroer (Nordbrandt) 295
The Drop and the Sea (Nagar) 227
The Drowning Season (Hoffman) 258
Drowning with Others (Dickey) 235
Druid from Sindidun (Bajac) 296
The Drummer (Addison) 72
Drummer Hoff (Emberley) 244
Drums at Dusk (Bontemps) 205
Drums in the Night (Brecht) 153, 182
"Drum-Taps" (Whitman) 124
"The Drunken Boat" (Rimbaud) 94, 128
The Dry Heart (Ginzburg) 215

Dry Salvages (Eliot) 208
Drylands (Astley) 295
Du plus loin de l'oubli (Modano) 286
Dubliners (Joyce) 152, 173
The Duchess of Malfi (Webster) 52, 53
Due di due (De Carlo) 274
The Duel (Sedaine) 80
The Duena (Sheridan) 82
Duffy and the Devil (Zemach) 252
Duino Elegies (Rilke) 155, 184
The Duke of Guise (Dryden and Lee) 64
The Duke's Children (Trollope) 133
Duluth (Vidal) 262
The Dumb Waiter (Pinter) 228, 231
The Dumbfounding (Avison) 241
Dune (Herbert) 240
The Duo (Colette) 199
Duplications (Koch) 256
The Durandeau Brothers (Soupault) 185
During the Reconquest (Blest Gana) 147
Dusk (Salter) 271
The Dust and Ashes (Rybakov) 283
Dust Tracks on a Road (Hurston) 209
The Dust Which Is God (Benét) 208, 209
Dutch Shea, Jr. (Dunne) 261
Dutchman (Baraka) 238
Dvoergenes dans (Lon) 292
The Dwarf (Lagerkvist) 212
The Dwarfs (Pinter) 273
The Dybbuk (Ansky) 180
The Dying (Soupault) 199
The Dying Earth (Bazin) 149
Dying in the Sun (Palangyo) 244
The Dynasts, an Epic Drama of the War with Napoleon (Hardy) 161, 168
Dyr (Preisler) 279
Dyskolos (Menander) 3

E

Each in His Own Way (Pirandello) 154, 185
The Eagle (Král') 114
The Eagle and the Serpent (Guzmán) 191
The Eagle Has Two Heads (Cocteau) 214
Eagle Nests (Bojic) 278
Eagle or Sun (Paz) 220
The Eaglet (Rostand) 158
The Ear of the Other (Derrida) 262
Early Autumn (Bromfield) 188, 189
Early Grace (Megged) 293
Early Sorrow (Mann) 152
Early Sorrows (Kis) 292
The Earth (Sharqawi) 223
The Earth Is Laughing (Khin) 226
Earth Erect (Popa) 250
Earth Spirit (Wedekind) 145
Earthlight (Clarke) 225
Earthly Paradise (Morris) 126
Earthly Powers (Burgess) 259
The Earthsea Trilogy (Le Guin) 244
The Easing of Fate (Berberova) 218
East Coker (Eliot) 207
East of Eden (Steinbeck) 221
East of Suez (Maugham) 182
East of the Mountains (Guterson) 293
East Slope (Paz) 249
Easter (Strindberg) 159
"Easter 1916" (Yeats) 152, 175
The East-West Wind (Shvarts) 289

Ecatommiti (Giraldi) 40
Ecclesiastical History of the English Nation (Bede) 13, 14, 19
Echo and Narcissus (Calderón de la Barca) 48, 60
Echo House (Just) 288
Echoes and Traces (Transtromer) 242
Eclats de sel (Germain) 286
Eclogues (Virgil) 4
Ecstasy (Couperus) 143
L'ecureuil noir (Poliquin) 282
Edgar Huntley (Brown) 88
The Edge of Day (Lee) 231
The Edge of Sadness (O'Connor) 235
Edifying Discourses on Diverse Spirits (Kierkegaard) 91
The Edinburgh Review (literary magazine) 95
Edith (Brunner) 279
Edith Wharton: A Biography (Lewis) 254
The Editor (Bjørnson) 130
Edmund Pendleton, 1721–1803 (Mays) 222
Eduards Heimkehr (Schneider) 293
Education by Stone (Cayrol) 241
The Education of Henry Adams (Adams) 164, 177, 178
The Education of Hyman Kaplan (Kaplan) 203
The Education of the Human Race (Lessing) 69
Edufa (Sutherland) 243
Edward and Eleanore (Thomson) 76
Edward II (Brecht) 153
Edward II (Marlowe) 33, 44
The Edwardian (Sackville-West) 193
The Effect of Gamma Rays on Man-in-the-Moon Marigolds (Zindel) 240, 248
Effi Briest (Fontane) 145
Effort at Speech: New and Selected Poems (Meredith) 288
Efter ar og dag (Hamsun) 274
Eftertradaren (Erkelius) 279
Efuru (Nwapa) 243
Egmont (Goethe) 67, 85
The Egoist (Meredith) 132
The Egyptian (Waltari) 212
An Egyptian Childhood (Taha Hussain) 195
Egyptian Nights (Pushkin) 90, 109
The Eiffel Tower and Other Mythologies (Barthes) 239
Eight Men (Wright) 233
Eight New Comedies and Eight New Interludes (Cervantes) 32
Eight Sonnets in American Poetry, 1922. A Miscellany (Millay) 183
The Eighth Day (Wilder) 243
Either/Or (Kierkegaard) 91, 113
Elbow Room (McPherson) 256
Elckerlijk (Diest) 29, 35
Elder Edda 13
Eldflugorna (Isakson) 292
Eleanor and Franklin (Lash) 249
"Eleanora: A Panegyrical Poem to the Memory of the Countess of Abingdon" (Dryden) 65
The Elected Member (Rubens) 247
Electra (Crébillon) 71
Electra (Euripides) 2, 7
Electra (Sophocles) 3
The Electrical Field (Sakamoto) 290
Elef Levavot (Tsalka) 276
The Elegant Buddha (Rohan) 140

Elegy for an Exit (Herbert) 274
Elegy on Madonna Fiammetta (Boccaccio) 14
"Elegy Upon the Death of Reverend Mr. Thomas Shepard" (Oakes) 63
"Elegy Written in a Country Churchyard" (Gray) 78
"Elegy XX: To His Mistress Going to Bed" (Donne) 49
Elektra (Hofmannsthal) 161
The Elements of Style (Strunk, White) 231
Eleutheria (Mather) 66
Elias Portulu (Deledda) 161
Eline Vere (Couperus) 140
Elizabeth and After (Cohen) 293
Elizabeth and Essex (Strachey) 190
Elle et Lui (Sand) 121
The Elm Tree in the Mall (France) 147
Elmer Gantry (Lewis) 189
Eloges, and Other Poems (Perse) 170
Eloisa to Abelard (Pope) 72
Elsi Lund (Vik) 282
Elsk meg i morgen (Ambjornsen) 294
Elskede ukendte (Thorup) 282
The Elusiveness of Truth (Ferrater Mora) 271
Elvira (Echeverría) 107
Emanuel (Laederach) 274
Embezzlement (Prem) 190
The Embezzler (Katayev) 188
Embracing Defeat: Japan in the Wake of World War II (Dower) 295
Embracing Defeat (Williams) 295
El embrujo de Shanghai (Marse) 281
The Emergency (Rive) 238
Emergency Exit (Silone) 240
Emigrants (Ferreira de Castro) 191
The Emigrants (Moburg) 218
Emile; or, On Education (Rousseau) 68, 80
Emilia Galotti (Lessing) 69, 82
Emilia in England (Meredith) 124
Eminent Victorians (Strachey) 177
Emma (Austen) 91, 99
Empedocles on Etna and Other Poems (Arnold) 117
The Emperor Jones (O'Neill) 153, 179, 181
The Empire of Stupidity (Lista) 88
Empire of the Sun (Ballard) 264
Empress of the Splendid Season (Hijuelos) 293
The Empty Canvas (Moravia) 233
En Route (Huysmans) 145
En Route to Myself (Pontoppidan) 210
Enamels and Cameos (Gautier) 117
The Encantadas (Melville) 118
The Enchanted Soul (Rolland) 182
Enchanted Wanderer (Leskov) 129
Enchiridion Militis Christianae (Erasmus) 34
Encyclopédie (Encyclopedists) 78
The End of the Affair (Greene) 154, 220
The End of the House of Alard (Kaye-Smith) 184
The End of the Patriarchate (Pavlicek) 277
The End of the Road (Barth) 229
Enderby Outside (Burgess) 244
Enderby Trilogy (Burgess) 252
Endgame (Beckett) 228
Endimion, The Man in the Moone (Lyly) 43

Ending Up (Amis) 252
Endless Fiesta (Tsuji) 287
The Endless Trip (Quenum) 232
Endymion (Keats) 101
Eneit (Heinrich von Veldeke) 22
Enemies: A Love Story (Singer) 250
An Enemy of the People (Ibsen) 94, 135
L'Enfant de sable (Ben Jelloun) 266
L'enfant léopard (Picouly) 293
L'enfant roi (Rolin) 268
Engel (Rifbjerg) 268
Engelen din, Robinson (Hoem) 280
An English Family (Dinis) 126
The English Patient (Ondaatje) 277, 278
The English Pilot (Wergeland) 114
The English Teacher (Narayan) 212
An Englishman Abroad (Bennett) 261
Enoch Arden (Tennyson) 93, 124
The Enormous Radio and Other Stories (Cheever) 223
Entanglements (Fontane) 139
Entered from the Sun (Garrett) 273
The Entertainer (Osborne) 228
The Enthusiastic Slingshooter (Neruda) 155
The Envious Man (Dalin) 76
"The Eolian Harp" (Blake) 87
The Epic of Sheikh Badruddin (Hikmet Ran) 202
Epicoene, or the Silent Woman (Jonson) 51
The Epicurean (Moore) 105
Epinomis (Plato) 3
Epipsychidion (Shelley) 93, 102
Episodios nacionales (Pérez Galdós) 129
An Epistle to Dr. Arbuthnot (Pope) 69, 75
Epistle to Several Persons (Pope) 75
Epistle to the Heroines (Ovid) 4
The Epistle to the Romans (Barth) 178
Epistles (Horace) 4
Epitaph for a Small Winner (Machado de Assis) 134
Epitaph for George Dillon (Osborne, Creighton) 229
Epitome Rerum Germanicarum (Wempfeling) 34
Epodes (Horace) 4
An Equal Music (Seth) 293
Equus (Shaffer) 251
Er oder ich (Nadolny) 293
The Era of Good Feelings (Dangerfield) 222
The Erasers (Robbe-Grillet) 222
Erasmus Montanus (Holberg) 74
Erato e Apollion (Quasimodo) 202
Erectheus (Swinburne) 131
Erewhon (Butler) 128
Eriksdottir: A Tale of Dreams and Luck (Clark) 282
"Erlking" (Goethe) 67, 84
Ernest Maltravers (Bulwer-Lytton) 109
Eros (Ivanov) 165
Escape from Solitude (Csoori) 236
The Escort Angel (Pelevin) 291
L'espace anterieur (Trassard) 280
Esperanza's Box of Saints (Escandón) 290
The Espousals (Patmore) 119
Essais (Montaigne) 32–33, 42
An Essay on Criticism (Pope) 69, 71
An Essay on Man (Pope) 69, 75

Essay on Rime (Shapiro) 212
Essays (Emerson) 111
Essays, Critical and Historical (Macaulay) 113
The Essays of Elia (Lamb) 103
The Essence of Christianity (Feuerbach) 112
The Essence of the Thing (St. John) 288
The Essential Gesture (Gordimer) 271
The Estate (Singer) 246
Esther (Racine) 48, 65
Esther Waters (Moore) 144
Estrellita marinera (Esquivel) 294
L'età perfetta (Cotroneo) 293
Un été memorable (Perol) 291
The Eternal Smile (Lagerkvist) 180
Ethan Frome (Wharton) 169
Ethiopia Unbound (Hayford) 169
Etincelles dans les tenebres (Dai) 269
The Etruscan (Waltari) 225
Eu, tiradentes (Motta) 278
Eugene Aram (Bulwer-Lytton) 107
Eugene Onegin (Pushkin) 90, 108
Eugénie (Beaumarchais) 81
Eugénie Grandet (Balzac) 91, 107
The Eunuch (Terence) 5
Euphues: The Anatomy of Wit (Lyly) 41
Eureka (Poe) 115
Europe: A Prophecy (Blake) 68
Europe and Other Bad News (Layton) 260
The Eustace Diamonds (Trollope) 129
Eutaw (Simms) 119
Euthymdemus (Plato) 3
Euthyphoron (Plato) 3
Evan Harrington (Meredith) 121
O Evanelho segundo Jesus Cristo (Saramago) 278
Evangeline, a Tale of Acadie (Longfellow) 115
El evangelio según Van Hutten (Castillo) 294
Ève (Péguy) 172
L'Eve Future (Villiers de L'Isle-Adam) 138
The Eve of Saint Venus (Burgess) 238
"The Eve of St. Agnes" (Keats) 101
Evelina; or, A Young Lady's Entrance into the World (Burney) 83
Evening (Akhmatova) 171
Evening Album (Tsvetayeva) 169
The Evening Hours (Verhaeren) 169
Evening Light (Horwood) 288
Evening Light (Ivanov) 212
Evening Star (Bandeira) 237
The Evening Star (Eminescu) 136
Evening Verses from Gunung (Iesmaniasita) 230
"An Evening Walk" (Wordsworth) 86
The Everlasting Gospel (Blake) 68
Every Good Day Deserves Favor (Stoppard) 256
Every Man for Himself (Bainbridge) 286, 288
Every Man in His Humour (Jonson) 45
Every Man Out of His Humour (Jonson) 45
Everyman (English translation of *Elckerlijk*) 13, 35
Everyman (Hofmannsthal) 170
Everything That Rises Must Converge (O'Connor) 240
Evidence of Love (Grau) 256

The Evil Doers of Good (Benavente y Martínez) 163
The Evil Poem (Machado) 168
The Evil Spirit Lumpazivagabundus, or the Roguish Frio (Nestroy) 107
Except the Lord (Cary) 222
The Excursion (Southey) 99
The Excursion Participants (Viewegh) 286
The Executioner (Boulle) 224
The Executioner's Song (Mailer) 258, 259
Exemplary Tales (Cervantes) 32, 52
The Exhortation to War (Vicente) 32
Exile (Torres Bodet) 193
The Exile (Wagner) 271
The Exile and Other Poems (Perse) 209
Exit the King (Ionesco) 237
Exodus (Uris) 229
Exortaçao aos crocodilos (Lobo Antunes) 296
The Expedition of Humphrey Clinker (Smollett) 81
"Experimenting with an Amen" (Thomas) 267
Exploration and Empire: The Explorer and the Scientist in the Winning of the American West (Goetzmann) 242
Explosion in a Cathedral (Carpentier) 236
Exquisitely Foolish (Huygens) 53
Exterminate the Brutes (Lindqvist) 279
Exterminator! (Burroughs) 250
Extramundana (Spitteler) 135
The Extraordinary Adventures of Julio Jurenito and His Disciples (Ehrenburg) 183
The Eye of the Storm (White) 250
Eyeless in Gaza (Huxley) 202
The Eyes of the Interred (Asturias) 232
Eyvind of the Hills (Sigurjonsson) 170
Ezo Vikolinsky (Hviezdoslav) 141

F

F. L. Vek (Jirásek) 139
A Fable (Faulkner) 223, 224
The Fable and the Flesh (Aymé) 210
The Fable of the Bees; or Private Vices, Public Benefits (Mandeville) 72
Fables (Gay) 74
Fables (Lobell) 260
Fables (Saltykov-Shchedrin) 137
Fables, Ancient and Modern (Dryden) 66
Fables: Selected Fables in Verse (La Fontaine) 61
Fables and Stories (Gellert) 77
Fables for Our Time (Thurber) 207
Fábula de fuentes (Juárez) 271
The Faces of Life (Verhaeren) 149
The Faerie Queene (Spenser) 43, 51
Fageljagarna (Sjogren) 289
Fahrenheit 451 (Bradbury) 222
The Failures (Lenormand) 180
The Fair and Wise Father (Marivaux) 71
Fair Haven and Foul Strand (Strindberg) 93, 160
Fair Stood the Wind for France (Bates) 211
The Fair World (Tomas) 198
The Fairy at the Bottom of the Lake (Davidescu) 171

The Fairy Council (Laforgue) 138
Fairy Good Fortune (Lahuti) 217
Fairy Tale of My Life (Andersen) 114
A Fairy Tale of New York (Donleavy) 251
Fairy Tales (Andersen) 108
The Faithful Lover (Bontempelli) 223
A Faithful Narrative of the Suprising Work of God (Edwards) 75
The Faithful Shepherd (Calderón de la Barca) 48
Falconer (Cheever) 256
"Falk" (Conrad) 155
Falkland (Bulwer-Lytton) 105
The Fall (Camus) 227
Fall from Grace (Wright) 276
The Fall of a Sparrow (Hellenga) 290
The Fall of Kelvin Walker: A Fable in the Sixties (Gray) 266
A Fall of Moondust (Clarke) 234
The Fall of Paris (Ehrenburg) 208
The Fall of Princes (Lydgate) 29
"The Fall of the House of Usher" (Poe) 91, 110
The Fall of the King (Jensen) 158
Fallen Flower (Kumaran Asan) 167
Falling in Place (Beattie) 259
The False Accusation (Caragiale) 141
False Confessions (Marivaux) 75
False Delicacy (Kelly) 81
False Love (Arlt) 196
A False Saint (Curel) 143
The Family (Meri) 244
The Family at Gilje (Lie) 136
The Family Moskat (Singer) 213
The Family of Pascal Duarte (Cela) 209
The Family Reunion (Eliot) 205
A Family Romance (Brookner) 280
The Family Shakespeare (Bowdler) 97
Famine (O'Flaherty) 203
The Famished Road (Okri) 275, 276
Fanny: Being the True History of the Adventures of Fanny Hack-about-Jones (Jong) 259
Fanny Hill, Memoirs of a Woman of Pleasure (Cleland) 77
Fanshawe (Hawthorne) 105
Fantasmas de carne y hueso (Edwards) 281
Fantastic Gallery (Yumiko) 276
Fantastic Voyage (Asimov) 241
Far Away Is the Sun (Casic) 220
A Far Cry from Kensington (Spark) 271
The Far Field (Roethke) 238
Far from the Madding Crowd (Hardy) 130
Far Tortuga (Matthiesson) 253
Farewell (Drummond) 287
Farewell, Liars (Popovic) 285
Farewell, My Lovely (Chandler) 207
A Farewell to Arms (Hemingway) 153, 192
Farewell to the Sea: A Novel of Cuba (Arenas) 262
Farina, a Legend of Cologne (Meredith) 120
El farmer (Rivera) 287
The Fashionable Bourgeois Ladies (Dancourt) 65
Fata Morgana (Kotsyubinsky) 162
Fatal Interview (Millay) 194
The Fatal Marriage (Southerne) 66
"The Fatal Sisters: An Ode" (Gray) 81
The Fate of Liberty: Abraham Lincoln and Civil Liberties (Neely) 277

The Fateful Prong (Plater) 104
The Father (Strindberg) 92, 139
Father Murdering (Zeng) 290
The Father of the Family (Diderot) 79
Fathers and Sons (Gosse) 165
Fathers and Sons (Sefarim) 123
Fathers and Sons (Turgenev) 123
The Fault of Angels (Horgan) 197
Faust (Goethe) 67, 97, 107
Faust, ein Fragment (Goethe) 67
Fausto (Campo) 125
The Favorite (Mallet-Joris) 232
Fear (Rybakov) 278
Fear and Trembling (Kierkegaard) 91, 113
Fear of the Bell (Bratic) 278
Feast Days (Burnside) 278
Feast in the Time of Plague (Pushkin) 90, 107
The Feast of Love (Baxter) 295
Feather Fall (Post) 282
The Feeling of Time (Ungaretti) 198
Los felinos del canciller (Moreno-Dorani) 270
Felix Holt the Radical (Eliot) 125
Felix Krull (Mann) 152
The Fellah (Sharqawi) 247
The Fellowship of the Ring (Tolkien) 223
Female and Male (Choromanski) 231
The Female Joseph (Calderón de la Barca) 48, 56
Fences (Wilson) 265, 268
Ferdydurke (Gombrowicz) 203
Ferias de verao (Moreira) 294
"*Fern Hill*" (Thomas) 213
The Ferry (Hoem) 253
Fervor in Buenos Aires, Poems (Borges) 154
Fêtes galantes (Verlaine) 127
The Feud of the Schroffensteins (Kleist) 96
Fever (Le Clezio) 240
A Few Figs from Thistles (Millay) 179, 183
A Few Nights and Days (Dipoko) 241
A Fictional Story (Gabra Iyasus) 166
"*A Fiddler Crab*" (Kiyoko) 291
Field of Violets (Hoffmann) 268
Field Work (Heaney) 258
The Fiery Angel (Bryusov) 166
Fiesco; or, The Conspiracy of Genoa (Schiller) 84
La fiesta del chivo (Vargas Llosa) 296
Fifine at the Fair (Browning) 129
The Fifth Business (Davies) 247
The Fifth Child (Lessing) 271
The Fifth Column and the First Forty-Nine Stories (Hemingway) 153, 204
The Fifth of May (Manzoni) 102
The Fifth Seal (Aldanov) 206
Fifty Comedies and Tragedies (Fletcher, Beaumont) 63
Fifty-Two Pickup (Leonard) 252
Fighting Terms (Gunn) 223
El Filibusterismo (Rizal) 142
La fille du gobernator (Constant) 282
Filodemo (Camões) 32
Final Payments (Gordon) 257
The Financier (Dreiser) 171
Fin-de-Siècle Vienna: Politics and Culture (Schorske) 260
A Fine Balance (Mistry) 286
The Finer Grain (James) 168
Finnegan's Wake (Joyce) 152, 206
Fiorello! (Weidman, Abbott, Bock, Harnick) 232

Fire (Ahmed) 214
The Fire Bringer (Moody) 162
Fire Down Below (Golding) 272
Fire in the Lake: The Vietnamese and the Americans in Vietnam (Fitzgerald) 250
The Fire Next Time (Baldwin) 237
Fire of Rose (Muradabadi) 224
The Firebugs (Frisch) 230
Fireman Flower and Other Stories (Sansom) 211
Fires on the Plain (Shohei) 220
The Firm of Nucingen (Balzac) 91
Firmly Rooted (Rovira) 170
The First Circle (Solzhenitsyn) 154, 245, 257
The First Epistle of the Second Book of Horace to Augustus (Pope) 75
First Fruits of the Desert (Luzi) 221
The First Garden (Hébert) 271
First Gold of the Indies (Chocano) 199
First Loves (Verhaeren) 162
First Person Plural (Blandina) 239
First Songs (García Lorca) 155
The Fish Can Sing (Laxness) 228
The Fitzboodle Papers (Thackeray) 112
Five Great Odes (Claudel) 168
Five Southern Poets (Marechal) 203
Five Stories of Ferrara (Bassani) 227
The Five Suns of Mexico (Fuentes) 296
Five Women Who Chose Love (Ihara Saikaku) 64
Five-Finger Exercise (Shaffer) 232
"*The Five-Storied Pagoda*" (Rohan) 142
The Fixer (Malamud) 226, 241, 242
Flagons and Apples (Jeffers) 171
The Flame of Life (D'Annunzio) 158
The Flame Throwers (Arlt) 195
The Flanders Road (Simon) 233
Die Flaterrzunge (Delius) 293
Flaws in the Glass: A Self-Portrait (White) 260
The Flemish (Verhaeren) 135
Flesh (Benn) 176
Flesh and Blood (Williams) 269
Flight (Ahmed) 213
Flight into Darkness (Schnitzler) 195
The Flight of Icarus (Queneau) 245
The Flight of the Eagle (O'Grady) 147
The Flights (Conton) 269
Floating Bridge (Kunie) 278
Floating Cloud (Hayashi) 220
Floating Foam (Castro Alves) 127
The Floating Opera (Barth) 226
Der Flohatz (Fischart) 41
The Flood (Le Clezio) 241
Flood (Warren) 238
Flood for the Muse's Springs (Cruz) 65
Flora Och Bellona (Karlfeldt) 178
Flora Och Pomona (Karlfeldt) 164
Det florentisski vidsvinet (Ahlin) 277
The Flounder (Grass) 256
Flower, Fist and Bestial Wail (Bukowski) 231
The Flower, Fruit and Thorn Pieces (Richter) 87
Flower Herding on Mount Monadnock (Kinnell) 238
Flowering Judas (Porter) 193
Flowering Nettle (Martinson) 201
The Flowering of New England (Brooks) 201, 203
Flowering Rifle: A Poem from the Battlefields of Spain (Campbell) 206

The Flowering Stone (Dillon) 195
Flowers from the Volcano (Alegría) 262
The Flowers of Evil (Baudelaire) 92, 120
The Flute and the Wind (Hawi) 233
The Flutist's Happiness (Enckell) 186
Fly, Kylin (Noboru) 294
Fly Away Home (Piercy) 264
Flying Blind (Omar) 269
The Flying Change (Taylor) 265, 267
Flying to Nowhere (Fuller) 263
The Folks That Live on the Hill (Amis) 273
La folle allure (Bobin) 284
The Follies of Marianne (Musset) 107
Following the Equator (Twain) 147
Fontano da case (Ferrucci) 286
Fool for Love (Shepard) 262
The Fool in Christ, Emanuel Quint (Hauptmann) 168
The Fool of the World and the Flying Ship (Ransome) 245
The Fool's Sanctuary (Johnston) 269
Foot on the Neck (Belli) 239
Footsteps (Tur) 266
For a New Novel (Robbe-Grillet) 237
For and Against (Lacretelle) 214
For Every Sin (Appelfeld) 272
For Kings and Planets (Canin) 290
For levande och doda (Transtromer) 275
For Love: Poems, 1959–1960 (Creeley) 235
For the Baptism of Our Fragments (Luzi) 266
For the Time Being (Auden) 212
For the Union Dead (Lowell) 238
For Whom the Bell Tolls (Hemingway) 153, 207
The Forayers; or, The Raid of the Dog Days (Simms) 119
Forberedelser for wintersasongen (Gustafsson) 275
Forbidden Colors (Mishima) 224
The Forbidden Love (Usakligil) 187
The Force of Habit (Bernhard) 252
The Forced Marriage (Molière) 60
Fording the Stream of Consciousness (Ugresic) 277
Forefather's Eve (Mickiewicz) 103, 108
A Foregone Conclusion (Howells) 130
Foreign Affairs (Lurie) 264, 265
Foreign Bodies (Cayrol) 231
A Foreign Letter (Morozov) 291
Foreign Sky (Gumilyov) 171
The Forerunner (Gibran) 179
The Forest (Jonson) 52
The Forest (Ostrovsky) 128
The Forest of a Thousand Daemons (Fagunwa) 205
The Forest of Anyksciai (Baranauskas) 120
Forest of Deceits (Vicente) 37
Forever Flowering (Grossman) 239
Forforeren (Kjaerstad) 280
Forgotten First Citizen: John Bigelow (Clapp) 216
Forgotten Hill (Mammeri) 221
Forgotten Pictures (Varma) 231
La forja de un ladrón (Umbral) 289
Forms (Nijhoff) 185
Forskjellig (Berg) 284
Forsyte Saga (Galsworthy) 164, 182, 188

Fortoellinger om natten (Hoeg) 275
Fortunata y Jacinta (Pérez Galdós) 138
The Fortunate Peasant (Marivaux) 75
Fortunate Son: The Healing of a Vietnam Vet (Puller) 277
The Fortunate Traveler (Walcott) 260
The Fortune of Yakutsk (Elley) 215
Fortune's Daughter (Hoffman) 265
The Fortunes of Niger (Scott) 93, 103
The Fortunes of Richard Mahoney (Richardson) 193
The Fortunes of the Rougon-Macquart Family (Zola) 128
The Forty Days of Musa Dagh (Werfel) 197
La forza del passato (Veronesi) 296
Fouchi (Ferrucci) 280
Foundation (Asimov) 220
Foundation and Empire (Asimov) 221
The Fountain of Bakhchsaray (Pushkin) 90, 103
The Fountainhead (Rand) 210
The Four Books of Architecture (Palladio) 40
The Four Horsemen of the Apocalypse (Blasco Ibáñez) 175
The Four Just Men (Wallace) 163
Four Mothers (Horn) 293
Four Plays for Dancers (Yeats) 152
The Four Quartets (Eliot) 152
The Four Zoas: The Torment of Love and Jealousy in the Death and Judgment of Albion (Blake) 87
The Four-Gated City (Lessing) 246
A Foxglove Saga (Waugh) 234
The Fox's Paw (Pérez de Ayala) 171
Foxybaby (Jolley) 265
"*Fra Lippo Lippi*" (Browning) 119
Fragmenta Aurea (Suckling) 57
The Franchiser (Elkin) 254
La Françiade (Ronsard) 33
Frankenstein; or, the Modern Prometheus (Shelley) 101
Frankenstein Unbound (Aldiss) 251
Franny and Zooey (Salinger) 233
Die Frau in den Kissen (Kronauer) 274
Frauen vor Flusblandschaft (Böll) 266
Fraulein Else (Schnitzler) 185
Fredegonde and Brunehaut (Lemercier) 102
Fredmans Epistlar (Bellman) 86
Fredy Neptune (Murray) 293
"*The Free Besieged*" (Solomos) 105
Free Fall (Golding) 231
Free Game (Schnitzler) 146
The Free Thinker (Lessing) 69
Freedom (Butov) 289
Freedom from Fear: American People in Depression and War, 1929–1945 (Kennedy) 295
Freedom of the Will (Edwards) 78
Freedom or Death (Kazantzakis) 219
Freedom Under Parole (Paz) 218
Freedom's Just Another Word (Hamilton) 290
The Freeing of the Dust (Levertov) 253
The French Lieutenant's Woman (Fowles) 246
The French Revolution (Blake) 68
Frequencies (Thomas) 257
Les frères romance (Colombier) 274
The Friar (Melo Neto) 263
Frida's Book (Sjöberg) 183
Friday (Heinlein) 261

Fridolin's Pleasure Garden (Karlfeldt) 159
Fridolin's Songs (Karlfeldt) 148
Friend of My Youth (Munro) 273
The Friend of the Family (Dostoyevsky) 90, 121
Frights (Varuzhan) 164
Frithjofs Saga (Tegner) 104
Frogs (Aristophanes) 3
A Frolic of His Own (Gaddis) 282
From Another Shore (Herzen) 117
From Footpath to Railway Line (Lortkipanidze) 190
From Here to Eternity (Jones) 220
From Honey to Ashes (Lévi-Strauss) 241
From Immigrant to Inventor (Pupin) 184
From Morn to Midnight (Kaiser) 175
From Princeton One Afternoon: Collected Poems, 1950–1986 (Weiss) 269
From Russia with Love (Fleming) 228
From the Bottom of the Field (Luzi) 240
From the Days of Sorrow (Franko) 158
From the Earth to the Moon (Verne) 124
From the Heart of the Country (Coetzee) 256
From the Mixed-Up Files of Mrs. Basil E. Frankweiler (Konigsburg) 244
From the Surge (Faesi) 176
From the Terrace (O'Hara) 229
From Zia, with Love (Soyinka) 278
Fromont the Younger and Risler the Elder (Daudet) 130
The Front Page (MacArthur) 190
The Frontenac Mystery (Mauriac) 197
Frontiers (Torres Bodet) 224
Frost (Leino) 166
Frou-Frou (Meilhac and Halevy) 127
Fru Astrid Grib (Jensen) 275
Fru Marie Grubbe (Jacobsen) 131
Der Fuchs war damals schon der Jager (Muller) 278
The Fudge Family in Paris (Moore) 101
Fuente ovejuna (Vega) 32, 52
The Fugitive (Galsworthy) 172
Fugitive Pieces (Michaels) 286
Fugitives (Kivi) 126
The Fugitives (Linnankoski) 166
Fulgedansen (Ambjornsen) 284
The Funeral; or, Grief A-la-Mode (Steele) 70
Fungi (Pleijel) 281
The Funny Little Women (Hearn) 250
The Funny Man (Holberg) 74
"The Furnished Room" (Henry) 164
A Further Range (Frost) 201, 203
Fuskaren (Evander) 277

G

G (Berger) 249
The Gab Boys (Duodo) 243
Gabriela, Clove and Cinnamon (Amado) 230
Gabriel's Lament (Bailey) 267
Un gachis (Darley) 288
Galapagos (Vonnegut) 265
La Galatea (Cervantes) 42
Galician Songs (Castro) 123
Galindez (Vázquez Montalbán) 277
The Gallery of Mirrors (Bernstein) 185
The Galley Slaves (Alvarez Quintero) 158

Game of Life (Sofronov) 178
The Game of Love and Chance (Marivaux) 74, 75
The Game of Madness and Prudence (Theotokos) 234
The Game-Keeper's Wife (Hviezdoslav) 138
Games—Tough and Divine (Régnier) 147
The Games Were Coming (Anthony) 237
The Gamester (Regnard) 66
Gandhi's Truth: On the Origins of Militant Nonviolence (Erikson) 247
The Gangster War (Petrunova) 292
Garbage (Ammons) 279
"The Garden" (Marvell) 63
The Garden Next Door (Donoso) 278
A Garden of Earthly Delights (Oates) 243
The Garden of Eden (Hemingway) 267
The Garden of the Finzi-Cortinis (Massano) 236
The Garden Party and Other Stories (Mansfield) 182
The Gardener of Toulouse (Kaiser) 204
The Gardener's Dog (Vega) 32
Gardens in the Dunes (Silko) 293
"Gareth and Lynette" (Tennyson) 129
Gargantua (Rabelais) 32, 37
Garland of Sonnets (Preseren) 108
Garman and Worse (Kielland) 133
Gas (Kaiser) 176
Gas II (Kaiser) 180
Gaspard of the Night (Bertrand) 112
A Gate in the Cloud (Stojcevski) 280
The Gate (Natsume) 93, 169
The Gates of Angels (Fitzgerald) 273
The Gates of Life (Herczeg) 179
Gather Together in My Name (Angelou) 252
A Gathering of Days (Blos) 259
The Gathering Storm (Empson) 207
Gaudy Observations (Södergran) 179
Gay Shipwrecks (Ungaretti) 179
Gebir (Landor) 88
Gedichte (Heine) 102
Gedichte (Lenau) 107
Gedlichten, 1904–1938 (Nijlen) 204
Geeraert van Velsen (Hooft) 51
Gelenging Tekad (Notodijo) 218
Le Gendre de Monsieur Poirier (Sandeau, Augier) 117
A General and His Army (Vladimov) 285
The General in His Labyrinth (García Márquez) 272
The General of the Dead Army (Kadare) 236
General Song (Neruda) 156, 219
A General Theory of Employment, Interest and Money (Keynes) 202
General William Booth Enters into Heaven and Other Poems (Lindsay) 172
Generation Without Farewell (Boyle) 232
The Genius (Dreiser) 174
The Genius of Christianity (Chateaubriand) 95
Genspejlet (Madsen) 295
The Gentle Language (De Amicis) 163
The Gentleman Dancing Master (Wycherley) 62

The Gentleman from San Francisco (Bunin) 175
The Gentleman in Grey (Mackenzie) 164
Gentleman's Agreement (Hobson) 215
Gentrix (Mauriac) 184
Geography III (Bishop) 254
George Bancroft: Brahmin Refel (Nye) 212
George Mills (Elkin) 261
George Washington (Freeman) 229
Georgics (Virgil) 4
Gerardo, the Unfortunate Spaniard (Céspedes y Meneses) 53
Germania (Tacitus) 5
Germanium Nights (Mangetsu) 291
Germany, a Winter's Tale (Heine) 114
Germinal (Zola) 137
"Gerontion" (Eliot) 152
Gertrude and Claudius (Updike) 295
De geruchten (Claus) 288
Getting It Right (Howard) 261
Ghisola (Tozzi) 179
The Ghost of Abel (Blake) 103
The Ghost Road (Barker) 283, 284
Ghost Ship (Martinson) 192
The Ghost Sonata (Strindberg) 92, 165
The Ghost Writer (Roth) 258
Ghosts (Auster) 269
Ghosts (Ibsen) 94, 134
Giaconda a dama con la luna (Morandini) 287
Giant (Gerber) 221
The Giants (Le Clezio) 251
The Giant's House (McCracken) 286
Giants in the Earth (Rolvaag) 189
The Giaour (Byron) 93, 99
I giardini della favorita (Campana) 278
Gideon (Chayefsky) 233
The Gift (Nabokov) 155, 203
The Gift of a Cow (Prem) 202
A Gift of Rags (Boyarsky) 202
"The Gift of the Magi" (Henry) 163
Giganten (Doblin) 196
Gigi (Colette) 211
Gītāñjalī (Tagore) 153, 168
Gil Blas (Lesage) 72
Giles Goat-Boy (Barth) 241
Gilgamesh 1
"Gimpel the Fool" (Singer) 213
Gimpel the Fool (Singer) 229
The Gin Game (Coburn) 254, 256
Ginestra (Leopardi) 91
The Ginger Man (Donleavy) 225
Il Giorno (Parini) 80
Giovanni's Room (Baldwain) 226
Gipsy Ballads (García Lorca) 191
A Girl in Winter (Larkin) 215
The Girl Who Loved Wild Horses (Goble) 257
The Girl with the Botticelli Face (Valgardson) 278
The Girl with the Jug (Vega) 32
Girlfriend in a Coma (Coupland) 290
Girls (Busch) 288
The Girls (Montherlant) 202
Girls of Fire (Nerval) 118
The Girls of Slender Means (Spark) 237
The Giver (Lowry) 281
Giving Life (Shun) 296
Gladiator, or a Note on the Military Police (Navot) 280
The Gladiators (Koestler) 206

The Glass Menagerie (Williams) 211, 212
The Glass of Water; or, Causes and Effects (Scribe) 111
Glass Puddles (Reverdy) 192
The Gleam of a Clear Dawn Approached (Král') 122
Glengarry Glen Ross (Mamet) 263, 264
The Glittering Flint (Vaughan) 58
The Glittering Gate (Dunsany) 167
Gloria (Maillard) 293
The Glories of Querétaro (Sigüenza y Góngora) 63
The Glorious Flight: Across the Channel with Louis Bleriot (Provensen) 263
The Glorious Life of Saigyo (Kunio) 284
Glorious Lousy Years (Viewegh) 279
The Glory of Don Ramiro (Rodriguez Larreta) 166
Glory to the Children and Olives (al-Bayati) 226
"The Glove" (Schiller) 68
Glowing Embers (Lundkvist) 191
Das Gluck (Hoffmann) 280
"Go, Lovely Rose" (Waller) 57
Go Down, Moses (Faulkner) 209
Go Tell It on the Mountain (Baldwin) 222
The Goalee's Anxiety at the Penalty Kick (Handke) 248
A Goat Who Wouldn't Be Mounted (Rosic) 270
The Goatibex Constellation (Iskander) 241
The Go-Between (Hartley) 222
Goblin (Rossetti) 123
The Goblins (Suckling) 56
God, a Biography (Miles) 286
God Bless You, Mr. Rosewater (Vonnegut) 240
The God of Small Things (Roy) 287, 288
The God of the Mountain (Dunsany) 169
The God of Vengeance (Asch) 165
A God Strolling in the Cool of the Evening (Carvalho) 289
The God That Failed (Wright) 219
Gödel, Escher, Bach: An Eternal Golden Braid (Hofstadter) 259
Godolphin (Bulwer-Lytton) 107
The Gods Are Athirst (France) 171
God's Beautiful World (Koch) 175
God's Bits of Wood (Sembene) 233
God's Face (Drzezdzon) 264
God's Grace (Malamud) 261
God's Little Acre (Caldwell) 197
"The Gods of Pegave" (Dunsany) 163
The Gods of the North (Oehlenschlager) 101
God's Orchid (Bergman) 179
God's Snake (Spanidou) 267
God's Stepchildren (Millin) 185
God's Trombones (Johnson) 189
"The Gold Bug" (Poe) 91, 113
Gold in Azure (Bely) 162
The Gold Seeker (Le Clezio) 266
The Golden Apples (Welty) 217
The Golden Boat (Tagore) 143, 153
The Golden Bough (Frazier) 141
The Golden Bowl (James) 91, 162
Golden Boy (Odets) 203
The Golden Chain (Peretz) 169
The Golden Cockerell (Raffi) 134

The Golden Demon (Koyo) 147

The Golden Dog (Kirby) 131

The Golden Fleece (Corneille) 48, 60

The Golden Fleece (Grillparzer) 102

Golden Fruits (Sarraute) 237

The Golden Gate (Davíd) 208

The Golden Gate (Seth) 267

Golden Honeycomb (Markandaya) 256

The Golden Horns (Oehlenschläger) 96

Golden Legend (Jacobus de Voragine) 24

The Golden Notebook (Lessing) 235

The Golden Qishalq (Mirshakar) 209

Goldfinger (Fleming) 231

Der Golem (Meyrink) 174

Der Golem (Wisniewski) 287

The Golovlev Family (Saltykov-Shchedrin) 131

Gone With the Wind (Mitchell) 201, 203

The Good Companions (Priestley) 192

The Good Conscience (Fuentes) 231

The Good Earth (Buck) 194, 195

Good Evening Mr. and Mrs. America and All the Ships at Sea (Bausch) 286

Good Example (Germasaw) 208

The Good Flight (Kinsella) 251

The Good Hope (Heijermans) 158

The Good Hope (Heineson) 238

A Good House (Burnard) 293

A Good Man Is Hard to Find (O'Connor) 225

Good Morning, Good Night (Rhys) 205

The Good Move (Belli) 270

The Good Natur'd Man (Goldsmith) 81

A Good Scent from a Strange Mountain (Butler) 279

The Good Soldier: A Tale of Passion (Ford) 174

The Good Soldier Schweik (Hašek) 179

The Good Terrorist (Lessing) 265

The Good War (Terkel) 265

Good Will (Diallo) 188

A Good Woman (Bromfield) 189

The Good Woman of Setzuan (Brecht) 153, 210

Goodbye, Columbus (Roth) 231

Goodbye, Mr. Chips (Hilton) 199

Goodbye to All That (Graves) 192

Goodbye to Berlin (Isherwood) 205

Gor mig levande (Ekman) 287

Gora (Tagore) 153, 165

Gorgias (Plato) 3

Gorilla, My Love (Bambara) 250

Gospel (Barnhardt) 279

Gotham: A History of New York City to 1898 (Burrows, Wallace) 292

Gothic Notebook (Luzi) 215

Götz von Berlichingen (Goethe) 67, 82

The Government Inspector (Gogol) 91, 109

Grace Abounding to the Chief of Sinners (Bunyan) 61

Grace Notes (MacLaverty) 288

The Grammar of Assent (Newman) 127

A Grammar of Motives (Little) 212

El gran jaguar (Valderrama Andrade) 277

El gran lector (Solares) 281

The Grand Design (Dos Passos) 217

Grand Gentleman and a Big Rascal (Barrios) 217

Grand Hotel (Baum) 192

The Grand Man (Bhoosnurmath) 264

Le Grand Testament (Villon) 27

La grande beune (Michon) 286

The Grandeur of Mexico (Balbuena) 50

Grandfather's Journey (Say) 281

Grandida (Hooft) 50

Grandmothers (Sabach) 292

Grant: A Biography (McFeeley) 261

The Grapes of Wrath (Steinbeck) 205, 206

The Grass (Simon) 230

Grass and Bell (Spitteler) 164

The Grass Harp (Capote) 220

Grass on the Wayside (Natsume) 93

Graustark (McCutcheon) 159

The Grave (Blair) 76

Graven Images (Thomas) 280

The Graves (Palamas) 147

The Graveyard by the Sea (Valery) 182

Gravity and Grace (Weil) 215

Gravity's Rainbow (Pynchon) 250

Grazing into the Wall (Weöres) 269

Grazyna (Mickiewicz) 103

The Great American Novel (Roth) 250

The Great Duke of Florence (Massinger) 55

Great Expectations (Dickens) 90, 121

The Great Fear of the Well-Possessed (Bernanos) 195

The Great Gatsby (Fitzgerald) 186

The Great God Brown (O'Neill) 153, 188

The Great Highway (Strindberg) 92, 168

The Great Hoggarty Diamond (Thackeray) 112

The Great Hunger (Bojer) 175

The Great Hunger (Kavanagh) 209

The Great Meadow (Roberts) 193

Great Morning (Sitwell) 215

The Great Ponds (Amadi) 246

The Great Railway Bazaar (Theroux) 253

The Great Restlessness (Zollinger) 206

Great River: The Rio Grande in North American History (Horgan) 225

The Great Salzburg Theater of the World (Hofmannsthal) 182

The Great Songbook (Bredero) 53

The Great Tradition (Leavis) 216

The Great Train Robbery (Chrichton) 253

The Great Wall of China (Kafka) 152

The Great Weaver from Kashmir (Laxness) 189

The Great White Hope (Sackler) 245

The Great Winter (Kadare) 255

The Greatest Alcade (Vega) 32

The Greatest Day of Days (Calderón de la Barca) 48

The Greek Passion (Kazantzakis) 224

The Green Bay Tree (Bromfield) 185

Green Days by the River (Anthony) 243

"Green Grow the Rashes, O" (Burns) 68

The Green Hamlet and Other Poems (Yeats) 168

The Green Hat (Arlen) 185

Green Henry (Keller) 117, 132

Green Hills of Africa (Hemingway) 153, 200

The Green Hills of Earth (Heinlein) 220

Green Leaves (Singh) 202

The Green Man (Amis) 246

Green Mansions (Hudson) 162

The Green Mare (Aymé) 197

The Green Pastures (Connelly) 193

The Green Pope (Asturias) 224

Green Song (Sitwell) 211

The Green Years (Cronin) 211

The Greenback Era (Unger) 239

The Green-Eyed Venus (Baudelaire) 92

Grendel (Gardner) 250

Grenser (Jacobsen) 294

The Grey King (Cooper) 254

El griego (Fernández Santos) 266

Grief (Ungaretti) 215

Grimm's Fairy Tales (Grimm and Grimm) 98

Grobianus (Dedekind) 38

Det gronne oje (Guldager) 292

Gros mots (Decharme) 293

Groucho in Green (Mattsson) 270

The Ground Beneath Her Feet (Rushdie) 293

Ground Work (Duncan) 264

Ground Work III: In the Dark (Duncan) 269

The Group (McCarthy) 237

Group Portrait with Lady (Böll) 249

Grover Cleveland (Nevis) 197

The Groves of Academe (McCarthy) 221

Growing Up (Baker) 261, 262

Growing Up (Ichiyo) 145

The Growth of American Thought (Curti) 211

"The Growth of Love" (Bridges) 131

The Growth of the Soil (Hamsun) 176

The Grumbling Hive; or, Knaves Turned Honest (Mandeville) 70

O Guaranai (Alencar) 120

Guard of Honor (Cozzens) 216, 217

The Guermantes Way (Proust) 180

Guerra conyugal (Russo) 296

La guerra de Galico (Aguilar Camín) 277

Guerra en el paraíso (Montemayor) 277

Guerrilla Family (Tur) 227

The Guest (Corel) 144

A Guest for the Night (Agnon) 204

Guest of Reality (Lagerkvist) 187

The Guide (Narayan) 229

Guide to Kulchur (Pound) 204

Guide to the Underworld (Ekelof) 244

Guilt (Idris) 230

Gulag Archipelago (Solzhenitsyn) 154, 251

Gulliver's Travels (Swift) 68, 73

Gulru (Jalil) 208

A Gun for Sale (Greene) 202

Gunnladar Saga (Svava) 269

Gunpowder (O'Donoghue) 286

The Gunpowder Tower (Bjornboe) 246

Guns, Germs and Steel: The Fates of Human Societies (Diamond) 290

The Guns of August (Tuchman) 235, 236

Gustav Vasa (Strindberg) 92, 149

Guttilaya (Vetteve) 27

Guy Mannering (Scott) 93, 99

Guy Rivers (Simms) 108

Guys and Dolls (Runyan) 196

Guzmán de Alfarache (Alemán) 45

Gyges and His Ring (Hugo) 119

Gypsies (Macha) 108

"The Gypsies" (Pushkin) 90, 104

The Gypsy Ballads (García Lorca) 155

Gysbreght von Aemstel (Vondel) 56

The Gyurkovics Girls (Herczeg) 144

H

H. M. Pulham, Esq. (Marquand) 208

The Habitant and Other French-Canadian Poems (Drummond) 147

Hadrian the Seventh (Rolfe) 162

Haft Owrang (Jāmī) 27

The Hag (Irzykowski) 161

The Hairy Ape (O'Neill) 153, 182

Hakon Jarl (Oehlenschlager) 97

Half Brothers (Radulovic) 270

The Half Virgins (Prévost) 144

Halley's Comet (Seifert) 242

Hallucinated City (Andrade) 183

A Halt in the Wasteland (Brodsky) 248

Haluk's Notebook (Fikret) 171

Hamasah (Abū Tammām) 19

Hamatzav baShlishi (Oz) 276

Hamilton Fish (Nevins) 203

Hamkampu (Arai) 70

The Hamlet (Faulkner) 207

Hamlet (Shakespeare) 31, 50

Hampels Fluchten (Kumpfmuller) 296

The Hand, the Earth and the Water (Ayyub) 216

A Handful of Black Berries (Silone) 221

A Handful of Dust (Waugh) 199

A Handful of Sand (Ishikawa) 169

The Handmaid's Tale (Atwood) 266

Hands Behind My Back: Selected Poems (Sorescu) 278

The Hangman (Lagerkvist) 198

Hanna (Runeberg) 109

Hannibal (Grabbe) 109

Hannibal (Kabbada) 216

Hans Brinker; or, The Silver Skates (Dodge) 124

"Happiness" (Prudhomme) 139

The Happy Boy (Bjørnson) 122

Happy Days (Beckett) 234

Happy Ending (Podrimja) 270

The Happy Vineyard (Zuckmayer) 187

The Hard Blue Sky (Grau) 229

The Hard Hours (Hecht) 244

Hard Times (Dickens) 90, 118

The Harder They Fall (Schulberg) 215

Harlem (Hughes) 220

Harlequin Brightened by Love (Marivaux) 73

A Harlot High and Low (Balzac) 91, 111

Harlot's Ghost (Mailer) 275

Harmonium (Stevens) 184

Harmony and Pastels (Montale) 236

Harold, the Last of the Saxon Kings (Bulwer-Lytton) 115

Harold (Tennyson) 131

Harold the Dauntless (Scott) 100

Harper's New Monthly (precursor of Harper's Magazine) 116

Harriet Beecher Stowe: A Life (Hedrick) 283

Harriet Said (Bainbridge) 250

Harrouda (Ben Jelloun) 251

Harry Potter and Prisoner of Azkaban (Rowling) 295

Harry Potter and the Chamber of Secrets (Rowling) 293

Harry Potter and the Sorcerer's Stone (Rowling) 290

Harvey (Chase) 211, 212

Hashish Gang (Kunio) 294

Hatet (Espmark) 285

Hatter's Castle (Cronin) 194

The Haunted Land: Facing Europe's Ghosts After Communism (Rosenberg) 286

The Haunted Man and the Ghost's Bargain (Dickens) 115

Havoc (Kristensen) 193

The Haw Lantern (Heaney) 269

Hawaii (Michener) 231

The Hawk in the Rain (Hughes) 228

Hay Fever (Coward) 186

Hayavadana (Karnad) 249

A Hazard of New Fortunes (Howells) 141

He Intends to Have a Fling (Nestroy) 112

He Knew He Was Right (Trollope) 127

He Who Gets Slapped (Andreyev) 175

Head Against the Wall (Bazin) 218

Head Hunter (Findley) 280

The Headlong Hall (Peacock) 100

The Headman; or, The Abbaye des Vignerons (Cooper) 107

The Headmaster (Ahmed) 230

The Healer (Hollingshead) 290

The Healer of His Honor (Pérez de Ayala) 188

Healing Song for the Inner Ear (Harper) 265

Hear the Wind (Murakami) 258

Hearing Secret Harmonies (Powell) 253

The Heart Is a Lonely Hunter (McCullers) 207

Heart of a Boy (De Amicis) 138

The Heart of a Dog (Bulgakov) 187, 270

The Heart of a Woman (Angelou) 260

Heart of Aztlan (Anaya) 254

Heart of Darkness (Conrad) 155, 160

The Heart of Midlothian (Scott) 93, 101

The Heart of Tel Aviv (Shaham) 286

Heart of the Country (Matthews) 267

The Heart of the Day (Bowen) 217

The Heart of the Matter (Greene) 154, 216

Heart on the Left (Frank) 221

Heartbreak (Aragon) 208

Heartbreak House (Shaw) 153, 178

The Heart's Needle (Snodgrass) 231, 232

Hearts of Oak (Jones) 132

The Heartsong of Charging Elk (Welch) 295

Heat and Dust (Jhabvala) 253

Heat and Other Stories (Oates) 276

Heaven and Earth (Byron) 103

Heaven and Earth (Goldbarth) 277

The Heavens and the Earth: A Political History of the Space Age (McDougall) 267

Hecale (Callimachus) 4

Hedda Gabler (Ibsen) 94, 141

The Heidenmauer; or, The Benedictines (Cooper) 107

Heidi (Spyri) 133

The Heidi Chronicles (Wasserstein) 270, 272

The Heights of Machu Picchu (Neruda) 215

Heinrich von Otterdingen (Novalis) 88

The Heir of Redclyffe (Yonge) 118

Hekigoto Kushu (Kawahigashi) 175

Heleconia Winter (Aldiss) 266

Helen (Euripides) 7

Helen Halsey; or, The Swamp State of Conelachita (Simms) 114

Helicon's Flowers (Johansson) 65

Heliogobalus, or the Crowned Antichrist (Artaud) 199

Hell Has No Limits (Donoso) 242

A Hell of a Mess (Ionesco) 251

Hellas (Shelley) 93, 103

Hell-Bent for Heaven (Hughes) 184

Hello: A Journal (Creeley) 257

Hello, Darkness: The Collected Poems of L. E. Sussman (Sussman) 257

The Helmet of Clay (Seifert) 212

Helmets (Dickey) 238

Hemingard of the Oak Burial Mounds (Drost) 107

Hemligheter kring vatten (Ekman) 283

Hemlock and After (Wilson) 221

Hence (Leithauser) 272

Henderson the Rain King (Bellow) 231

Henno (Reuchlin) 29

La Henriade (Voltaire) 68, 73

Henry IV (Pirandello) 154, 182

Henry IV (Shakespeare) 31, 44

Henry V (Shakespeare) 45

Henry VI (Shakespeare) 31, 43

Henry VIII (Chénier) 86

Henry VIII (Shakespeare) 51

Henry Adams (Samuels) 239

Henry and Cato (Murdoch) 255

Henry James (Edel) 236

Henry of Ofterdingen (Novalis) 96

Heptamychos (Pherecydes) 2

Her Eyes (Alavi) 221

Her i noerheden (Christensen) 282

Her Son's Wife (Fisher) 188

Her Story (Jacobson) 269

Heraclius (Corneille) 48

Hercules (Stiernhielm) 59

The Here and Now (Cohen) 286

Here and Now (Levertov) 228

Here I Am, in Perfect Leaf Today (Dubarova) 279

El hereje (Delibes) 292

The Heretic of Soana (Hauptmann) 177

Heretics (Kitahara) 179

Hereward the Wake (Kingsley) 125

L'heritage de Tante Carlotta (Jacques) 269

Hermann and Dorothea (Goethe) 87

Hernani (Hugo) 106

A Hero Ain't Nothing but a Sandwich (Childress) 250

Hero and Leander (Marlowe) 33

The Hero and the Crown (McKinley) 265

A Hero of Our Times (Lermontov) 111

The Hero with a Thousand Faces (Campbell) 217

Herod and Marianne (Hebbel) 116

"Herodias" (Flaubert) 92

"Herodias" (Mallarmé) 127

Herod's Children (Aichinger) 216

Heroes Are Grazing in My Garden (Padilla) 262

Heroic and Elegiac Song for the Lost Second Lieutenant of the Albanian Campaign (Elytis) 213

Heroics (Claussen) 186

The Heron (Bassani) 245

Herr Puntila and His Man Mutti (Brecht) 153

Hers (Alvarez) 252

Herself Surprised (Cary) 208

Hertog van Egypte (Moor) 288

Herzog (Bellow) 238

Herzwand (Hartling) 274

Hesperides (Herrick) 58

Hesperus (Richter) 86

The Hessian Messenger (Büchner) 108

Hexaemeron (Arrebo) 54

Hey, Al (Yorinks) 268

Hidden in the Heart (Jacobson) 276

High and Low (Betjeman) 241

High Bridges (Lacretelle) 196

The High King (Alexander) 245

High Rise (Ballard) 253

High Song (Pontoppidan) 146

The High Tide in the Garden (Adcock) 249

A High Wind in Jamaica (Hughes) 192

High Windows (Larkin) 252

The Highland Widow (Scott) 105

The Highway (Radichkov) 292

La hija del caníbal (Montero) 289

Hilarion and the Dwarf (Gubin) 289

Hilda (Ndiaye) 293

"Hills Like White Elephants" (Hemingway) 153, 189

Der Himmel des Humoristen (Pivonas) 264

Det himmselska gastabudet (Gyllensten) 277

The Hind and the Panther (Dryden) 49, 64

Hipparchus (Plato) 3

Hippias Major (Plato) 3

Hippias Minor (Plato) 3

Hippolytus (Euripides) 2, 7

Hiroshima (Minoru) 260

His Grace's Will (Bergman) 169

"His Majesty's Escape at St. Andre" (Waller) 54

His Natural Life (Clarke) 130

His Only Sow (Alas) 141

Una historia de familia (Santiago) 278

Historiae (Tacitus) 5

Las historias de Marta y Fernando (Martín Garzo) 294

Historical and Critical Dictionary (Bayle) 66

The Historical Register for the Year 1736 (Fielding) 75

Historien med hunden (Gustafsson) 281

History (Herodotus) 3

History: A Novel (Morante) 252

History of a Black Love (Mickovic) 291

The History of a Town (Saltykov-Shchedrin) 127

History of Eternity (Borges) 202

The History of Henry Esmond (Thackeray) 117

The History of Henry VII (Bacon) 53

The History of Lady Sophia Sternhelm (La Roche) 82

The History of New England (Adams) 182

A History of New York (Irving) 98

The History of Pendennis (Thackeray) 115

A History of Pugachov (Pushkin) 90

The History of Russia (Karamzin) 100

The History of Sir Charles Grandison (Richardson) 78

The History of Susan Spray, Female Preacher (Kaye-Smith) 194

A History of the American Frontier (Paxson) 186

A History of the Civil War (Rhodes) 177

The History of the Decline and Fall of the Roman Empire (Gibbon) 83

History of the Destruction of Troy (Colonno) 24

History of the Famous Preacher Fray Gerundio de Campazas, alias Zotes (Isla) 79

History of the French Revolution (Carlyle) 109

History of the Heart (Aleixandre) 224

History of the Peloponnesian War (Thucydides) 3

History of the Thirty Years' War (Schiller) 68

A History of the United States (Channing) 187

The History of the Village of Gorykhina (Pushkin) 90

The History of the World (Raleigh) 52

The Hive (Cela) 220

Hjertelyd (Grondahl) 292

H.M.S. Pinafore (Gilbert) 132

The Hobbitt (Tolkien) 203

Los hochos de Zacarías (Morón) 277

Het hof van barmhartigheid (Heijden) 288

Den hogsta kasten (Rydberg) 289

Holes (Sachar) 292

Holiday (Barry) 190

Holiday (Middleton) 252

The Hollow Hill and Other Poems, 1960–1964 (Raine) 240

"The Hollow Men" (Eliot) 186

The Holy Flame (Drachmann) 149

"The Holy Grail" (Tennyson) 127

The Holy Sinner (Mann) 152, 220

Holy Smoke (Cabrera Infante) 268

The Holy Sonnets (Donne) 49, 51, 55

The Holy Stone (Blackburn) 223

The Holy Terrors (Cocteau) 192

The Holy War (Bunyan) 64

The Holy Well (Katayev) 243

"Holy Willie's Prayer" (Burns) 88

Homage to Catalonia (Orwell) 204

Homage to Clio (Auden) 232

"Homage to Mistress Bradstreet" (Berryman) 216

Homage to Mistress Bradstreet (Berryman) 226

"Homage to Sextus Propertius" (Pound) 155, 178

Hombre (Leonard) 233

El Hombre que llegó a un pueblo (Tizón) 274

Home As Found (Cooper) 110

Home Ballads and Other Poems (Whittier) 121

The Home of the Spirits of the Ancestors (Abdulla) 233

Home to Harlem (McKay) 190

Home Truths (Gallant) 266

The Homecoming (Pinter) 240

Hometown Noodles and Flower (Liu) 290

L'homme ignore (Targowla) 274

The Honest Whore (Dekker) 54

Honey in the Horn (Davis) 201

Honeymoon, Bittermoon (Pérez de Ayala) 184

Honeymoon Ride (Seifert) 204

Honor (Sudermann) 140

Honor of Truth (Luzi) 228

The Honorable Schoolboy (Le Carré) 256

The Honorary Consul (Greene) 154, 251

The Hoosier Schoolmaster (Eggleston) 128

Hopscotch (Cortázar) 237

Horace (Corneille) 48, 56

The Horla (Maupassant) 137

The Horn of Autumn (Karlfeldt) 189

Horribilicribrifax (Gryphius) 60

The Horsehair Glove (Reverdy) 189

Horseman, Pass By (McMurtry) 234

The Horseman on the Roof (Giono) 221

Horses Make a Landscape Look More Beautiful (Walker) 264

The Horse's Mouth (Cary) 211

Horsztynski (Słowacki) 109

The Hostage (Behan) 229

The Hostage (Claudel) 170

Hot Ashes (Jastrun) 227

Hot Hot Dogs (Shaham) 280

The Hotel and the House and Other Pieces (Evangelou) 266

Hotel du Lac (Brookner) 263, 264

The Hotel New Hampshire (Irving) 260

Hothouse (Aldiss) 235

Hothouses (Maeterlinck) 140

"The Hound of Heaven" (Thompson) 139, 143

The Hound of the Baskervilles (Doyle) 159

The Hour Glass (Yeats) 152

The Hour of the Star (Lispector) 256

Hours (Castro) 142

The Hours (Cunningham) 292, 293

Hours of Idleness (Byron) 97

The House (Torres Bodet) 184

The House by the Churchyard (Le Fanu) 123

The House by the Medlar (Verga) 134

A House for Mr. Biswas (Naipaul) 234

The House Gun (Gordimer) 291

The House in Haarlem (Schendel) 200

A House in Order (Denis) 241

The House in Paris (Bowen) 200

House in the Shadow (Gengetsu) 296

House Made of Dawn (Momaday) 244, 245

The House of Bernarda Alba (García Lorca) 155, 202

The House of Blue Leaves (Guare) 248

The House of Earth (Buck) 200

House of Fame (Chaucer) 14

The House of Five Talents (Auchincloss) 232

House of Glass (Tur) 271

House of Incest (Nin) 201, 202

The House of Intellect (Barzun) 231

The House of Joy (Ammers-Küller) 182

The House of Mirth (Wharton) 163

The House of People (Pant) 239

The House of the Customs Officer and Other Poems (Montale) 196

House of the Dead (Dostoyevsky) 90, 122, 123

The House of the Seven Gables (Hawthorne) 117

The House of the Spirits (Allende) 262

The House of Titans and Other Poems (AE) 199

The House on Coliseum Street (Grau) 234

Hovedstolen (Hesselholdt) 292

How Far Can You Go? (Lodge) 259

How German Is It? (Abish) 259, 260

How Green Was My Valley (Llewellyn) 206

How I Learned to Drive (Vogel) 290

How Late It Was, How Late (Kelman) 281, 282

How Many Miles to Babylon? (Johnston) 259

How Much Is Belgrade (Dimic) 296

How the Dead Live (Self) 295

How the Heart Is Torn Apart (Siktanc) 273

How to Save Your Life (Jong) 256

How to Succeed in Business Without Really Trying (Loesser, Burrows) 235

How to Write Short Stories (Lardner) 185

Howards End (Forster) 168

Howl, and Other Poems (Ginsberg) 226

Huckleberry Finn (Twain) 92, 136

Hudibras (Butler) 60

Huey Long (Williams) 247

Hugh Selwyn Mauberley (Pound) 155, 179

Human Bodies: New and Collected Poems, 1987–1999 (Bowering) 293

The Human Comedy (Balzac) 90–91

The Human Comedy (Saroyan) 210

The Human Factor (Greene) 154, 257

Human Landscapes (Hikmet Ran) 242

Human Mourning (Revueltas) 211

Human Poems (Vallejo) 206

The Human Province (Canetti) 251

The Human Stain (Roth) 295

Human Verses (Diego) 187

Humboldt's Gift (Bellow) 253, 254

Hummelhonung (Lindgren) 285

The Humming Bird Tree (McDonald) 246

The Hunchbacks (Arlt) 198

A Hungarian Nabob (Jókai) 118

Hungary in 1514 (Eötvös) 115

A Hunger Artist (Kafka) 152, 185

Hunger (Hamsun) 141

Hungerfield and Other Poems (Jeffers) 223

"The Hunting of the Snark" (Carroll) 131

The Hunting Party (Bernhard) 252

Hurrah to the Hilt (Valle-Inclán) 191

Hurry on Down (Wain) 222

Husband and Wife (Fredro) 103

The Husband of Ahu Khanom (Mohammad) 234

Hutchinsons effekt (Pollen) 291

Hutten's Last Days (Meyer) 128

The Hydra Head (Fuentes) 257

"Hymn to Intellectual Beauty" (Shelley) 93, 100

"Hymn to Liberty" (Solomos) 103

Hymnes (Ronsard) 33, 39

Hymns (Callimachus) 4

Hymns to the Night (Novalis) 95

Hypatia; or, New Foes with an Old Face (Kingsley) 118

Hyperion (Holderllin) 87

Hyperion (Keats) 102

Hyperion (Longfellow) 110

I

I, Claudius (Graves) 199

I, Juan de Pareja (Treviño) 241

I, the Jury (Spillane) 215

I, the Supreme (Roa Bastos) 253

I Am a Cat (Natsume) 93, 163

I Am Guilty (Ikromi) 230

I and Thou (Buber) 184

I Have Been There Before (Priestley) 203

I Have No Home Now (Wispelaere) 262

I knolvannet (Petterson) 296

I Know Why the Caged Bird Sings (Angelou) 247

I Live (Ba'albakki) 229

I Ought to Be in Pictures (Simon) 259

I See a Wondrous Land (Kamban) 201

I Serve (Teirlinck) 185

"I Sing the Body Electric" (Whitman) 119

I vantan pa pendeltaget (Vennberg) 275

"I Wandered Lonely as a Cloud" (Wordsworth) 96

I Was a Savage (Paris) 228

I Went Abroad (Walda) 225

I Will Defend My Country (Heiberg) 171

I Will Fear No Evil (Heinlein) 247

I Will Live the Love of Others (Cayrol) 215

Iambi (Callimachus) 4

Iambs and Anapaests (Palamas) 147

The Iberian Circle (Valle-Inclán) 189

Ibis (Callimachus) 4

Ibrahim, of the Illustrious Bassa (Scudéry) 57

Ibrahim the Writer (al-Mazini) 194

Ibsens Italia (Naess) 289

Ice Candy Man (Sidhwa) 271

The Ice Mine (Appelfeld) 289

Icebound (Davis) 183

Icelandic Loves (Gudmundsson) 185

Iceland's Bell (Laxness) 210

The Iceman Cometh (O'Neill) 153, 213

Ich (Hilbig) 280

Ici (Sarraute) 284

Ida Brandt (Bang) 146

The Idea of a Christian Society (Eliot) 152, 205

The Idea of Order at Key West (Stevens) 200

Ideas (Multatuli) 123

Les idées heureuses (Lapaque) 293

Identity (Kundera) 290

The Ideological Origins of the American Revolution (Bailyn) 244

The Ides of March (Wilder) 216

Idilli (Leopardi) 91

The Idiot (Dostoyevsky) 90, 126

Idiot's Delight (Sherwood) 201

Idiots First (Malamud) 237

Idoménée (Crébillon) 70

Idylls of the King (Tennyson) 93, 121

If Beale Street Could Talk (Baldwin) 252

If He Hollers, Let Him Go (Himes) 212

If I Were You (Green) 215

If It Die (Gide) 180

If Not Now, When? (Levi) 262

If on a Winter's Night a Traveler (Calvino) 258

If the River Was Whiskey (Boyle) 272

If This Is a Man (Levi) 215

If You Know Not Me, You Know Nobody (Heywood) 50

The Iliad; or, The Poem of Force (Weil) 207

Iliad (Homer) 2, 51

Illumination Night (Hoffman) 269

Les Illuminations (Rimbaud) 94, 129, 138

The Illusionist (Mallet-Joris) 220

The Illustrated Man (Bradbury) 220

The Illustrious Gaudissart (Balzac) 91

Illywhacker (Carey) 266

I'm Not Stiller (Frisch) 224

The Image, and Other Stories (Singer) 267

Images in a Mirror (Undset) 156, 176

Imaginary Conversations (Landor) 103, 118

The Imaginary Invalid (Molière) 48, 62

The Imitation of Our Lady of the Moon (Laforgue) 138

The Imitation of the Father (Claudel) 180

Imitations (Lowell) 234

Immaculate Conception (Breton) 193

Immobile dans le courant de fleuve (Berger) 282

The Immoralist (Gide) 160

The Immortal Bartfuss (Appelfeld) 271

Immortality (Kundera) 273

The Impending Crisis (Potter) 255

Imperial Palace (Bennett) 193

Implements in their Places (Graham) 256

The Importance of Being Earnest (Wilde) 145

L'impresa senza (Barbaro) 293

Impressions of Africa (Roussel) 168

In a Dark Wood Wandering (Haasse) 217, 272

In a Free State (Naipaul) 248

In a Glass House (Ricci) 280

In a Vast Domain (Aleixandre) 236

In Abraham's Bosom (Green) 189

In Another Country (Baldwin) 235

In Chancery (Galsworthy) 180, 182

In Cold Blood (Capote) 241

In Country Sleep (Thomas) 221

In Defense of Reason (Winters) 215

In Dubious Battle (Steinbeck) 201

In einer dunken Nacht gig ich aus meinen stillen Haus (Handke) 289

In Every Face I Meet (Cartwright) 284

In God's Way (Bjørnson) 140

In Hazard (Hughes) 204

In Her Own Image (Boland) 259

In Love and Trouble (Walker) 250

"In Memoriam, A.H.H." (Tennyson) 116

In Memoriam (Tennyson) 93

In My Father's Court (Singer) 242

In My Own Home (Ludens) 270

In Our Image: America's Empire in the Philippines (Karnow) 273

In Parenthesis (Jones) 203
In Praise of Older Women: Amorous Recollections of Andras Vajada (Vicinczy) 240
In Praise of Sky, Sea, Earth and Heroes (D'Annunzio) 149
In Praise of the Stepmother (Cela) 271
In Purissimo Azzurro (Fiore) 268
In Search of Walid Massoud (Jabra) 295
In the Absence of Angels (Calisher) 220
In the American Grain (Williams) 186
In the Burning Darkness (Buero Vallejo) 219
In the Castle (Storm) 122
In the Clearing (Frost) 235
In the Days of McKinley (Leech) 232
In the Days of the Counselor (Andersen) 147
In the Desert of a Lodging Place (Sened, Sened) 291
In the Draft (Mándy) 280
In the Dutch Mountains (Nooteboom) 264
In the Harbor (Longfellow) 135
In the Labyrinth (Sarraute) 231
In the Line of Fire (Mihailovic) 283
In the Magma (Luzi) 234
In the Mecca (Brooks) 244
In the Midst of My Fever (Layton) 223
In the Name of Salomé (Alvarez) 295
In the Name of the Son (Bazin) 233
In the Penal Colony (Kafka) 152, 173, 178
In the Seven Woods (Yeats) 161
In the Shadow of the Glen (Synge) 161
In the Shadow of the Wind (Hébert) 262
In the Skin of a Lion (Ondaatje) 269
In the Wilderness (Appelfeld) 237
In the Zone (O'Neill) 153
In This House of Brede (Godden) 246
In This Our Life (Glasgow) 209
In Time Like Air (Sarton) 229
In Transit (Brophy) 246
In Transit (Gallant) 272
In Wartime and Other Poems (Whittier) 124
Incerti di viaggio (Pazzi) 287
Incident at Vichy (Miller) 240
The Incident Book (Adcock) 267
Incidents (Meri) 232
Incidents in the Life of a Slave Girl Written by Herself (Jacobs) 122
Incline Our Hearts (Wilson) 272
Incognita (Dryden) 65
The Incomparable Atuk (Richler) 237
The Incomparable Earth (Quasimodo) 230
The Incredible Play (Benavente y Martínez) 208
Independence Day (Ford) 284, 285, 286
Independent People (Laxness) 198
Index Librorum Prohibitorum (Pope Paul III) 38
The Indian Emperour (Dryden) 49, 60
The Indian Exiles (Kotzebue) 85
The Indian Hut (Bertolucci) 220
The Indian Queen (Dryden) 49, 60
Indian Summer (Howells) 137
Indiana (Sand) 107
Indonesia, Land of My Birth (Yamin) 192
The Industry of Souls (Booth) 290
Inexpiable (Ebner-Eschenbach) 141

The Infernal Machine (Cocteau) 199
Inferno (Strindberg) 147
El infierno es un decir (Hernández) 283
Infinite Riches (Okri) 291
Infor nedrakningen (Myrdal) 281
The Informer (O'Flaherty) 186
Ingenious Pain (Miller) 293
L'ingratitude (Chen) 284
Ingrid Caven (Schuhl) 296
Inhabited Heart (Andrade) 266
The Inheritor (Golding) 225
Injustice (Borgen) 266
Inland and Other Poems (Hashimi) 271
The Inn Album (Browning) 130
The Inner Harbor (Adcock) 258
The Inner Side of the Wind (Pavic) 281
Inni Sacri (Manzoni) 99
The Innocents Abroad (Twain) 92, 127
Inquiry Time (Bainbridge) 256
Insania (Correia) 296
Inside Mr. Enderby (Burgess) 237
La insólita historia de la santa de Cabora (Domecq) 275
The Inspector Calls (Priestley) 213
The Inspector General (Gogol) 91, 109
Institutio Principis Christiani (Erasmus) 35
Insular Passion (Mo) 267
The Insulted and the Injured (Dostoyevsky) 90, 122
The Intense Life (Bontempelli) 180
The Intermezzo of Poems (D'Annunzio) 136
The Interpretation of Dreams (Freud) 149
Interpreter of Maladies (Lahiri) 295
The Interpreters (Soyinka) 240
The Interrogation (Le Clezio) 237
Intervalle (Butor) 251
The Intruder (D'Annunzio) 143
Intruder in the Dust (Faulkner) 216
L'invention du monde (Rolin) 280
The Invention of Morel (Bioy Casares) 207
The Invention of Orpheus (Lima) 222
The Invention of Truth (Brewster) 276
An Invincible Memory (Ubaldo Ribeiro) 272
Invisible Cities (Calvino) 250
The Invisible Lodge (Richter) 86
Invisible Man (Ellison) 221
The Invisible Man (Wells) 147
The Invisible Worm (Johnston) 276
Invitation to a Beheading (Nabokov) 155, 204
Ion (Euripides) 2, 7
The Ipcress File (Deighton) 235
Iphigenia at Aulis (Euripides) 2, 8
Iphigenie auf Tauris (Goethe) 67, 85
Iphigénie en Aulide (Racine) 48, 62
Ipotesi d'Amore (Cima) 264
Iracema (Alencar) 124
Irene (Johnson) 78
Irene (Kisfaludy) 102
Irène (Voltaire) 83
Iridion (Krasinski) 109
The Iron Flood (Serafimovic) 185
The Iron Gate (Gripenberg) 163
The Iron Heel (London) 165, 166
Iron John: A Book About Men (Bly) 273
The Iron Tracks (Appelfeld) 291
Ironweed (Kennedy) 262, 263

L'Irréparable (Bourget) 136
Irse de casa (Martín Gaite) 292
Is There No Place on Earth for Me? (Sheehan) 262
Isara: A Voyage Round Essay (Soyinka) 272
Isis (Villiers de L'Isle-Adam) 123
The Island (Byron) 103
An Island Fisherman (Loti) 138
The Island in Winter (Young) 293
The Island of Crimea (Aksyonov) 261, 274
The Island of Dr. Moreau (Wells) 146
The Island of the Doomed (Dagerman) 214
The Island of the Holy Name (Tenreiro) 209
Islands in the Stream (Hemingway) 247
Isle of Reason (Marivaux) 74
Isle of Slaves (Marivaux) 73
Isobars (Hospital) 276
Isolation Booth (Hood) 276
Israel (Bernstein) 166
Israel Potter: His Fifty-five Years of Exile (Melville) 119
Israpport (Aspenstrom) 289
The Issa Valley (Milosz) 226
It Can't Happen Here (Lewis) 200
It Exists Somewhere (Petri) 274
It Is Never Too Late to Mend (Reade) 119
It Isn't Necessary to Promise Anything (Musset) 109
L'Italia liberata dai Goti (Trissino) 38
The Italian (Radcliffe) 87
The Italian Girl (Murdoch) 238
Italian Night (Horvath) 193
Italian Spring (Robles) 247
An Italian Story (Pratolini) 240
An Italian Straw Hat (Labiche) 117
An Italian Visit (Day-Lewis) 222
The Itching Parrot (Fernández de Lizardi) 100
It's a Hard Life (Biancardi) 236
It's Like This, Cat (Nelville) 238
Ivanhoe (Scott) 93, 101
Ivory and Opium (Bach) 267
Iwein (Hartmann von Aue) 23
Ixion's Wheel (Gustafson) 246
The Izu Dancer (Kawabata) 156

J

The Jacaranda Tree (Bates) 216
"J'Accuse" (Zola) 148
Jack Frusciante e uscito dal gruppo (Bruzzi) 284
Jack Maggas (Carey) 288
Jack Tier (Cooper) 115
Jacklight (Erdrich) 264
Jacko: The Great Intruder (Keneally) 282
"The Jackpot" (Jackson) 216
Jackson Pollock: An American Saga (Naifeh, Smith) 275
Jacob Have I Loved (Paterson) 260
Jacob's Room (Woolf) 182
Jacques and His Master (Kundera) 260
Jadis et Naguerre (Verlaine) 136
Jagua Nana (Ekwensi) 234
Jailbird (Vonnegut) 258
The Jake's Thing (Amis) 257
Jakob der Letzte (Rosegger) 139
Jakob von Gunten (Walser) 167
Jalaleddin (Raffi) 132

Jan Van Huysum's Flowerpiece (Wergeland) 111
"Jana Gana Mana" (Tagore) 153
Jane Eyre (Brontë) 115
Jane Talbot (Brown) 95
"Janet's Repentance" (Eliot) 120
János the Hero (Petőfi) 114
Jantando com Melvin (Coelho) 291
Japhthah and His Daughters (Feuchtwanger) 228
El jardín de las dudas (Savatar) 281
Java Head (Hergesheimer) 178
Javiera Carrera, madre de la patria (Vidal) 296
Jazz (Morrison) 277
J.B. (MacLeish) 229, 230
Jealousy (Robbe-Grillet) 228
Jealousy and Medicine (Choromanski) 196
Jeame's Diary (Thackeray) 114
Jean Christophe (Rolland) 162
Jean de France (Holberg) 73
Jefferson and His Time (Malone) 253
Jeg har hort et stierneskud (Jensen) 290
Jennie Gerhardt (Dreiser) 169
Jenny (Undset) 156, 170
Jephthah, or The Promised Sacrifice (Vondel) 59
Jeppe of the Hill (Holberg) 73
Jeremy's Vision (Purdy) 247
Jero's Metmorphosis (Soyinka) 250
Jersey Rain (Pinsky) 295
Jerusalem (Blake) 100
Jerusalem (Lagerlöf) 159
Jerusalem Delivered (Tasso) 41
The Jests of Life and Death (Pirandello) 154
Jesus Saves (Steinke) 288
The Jew (Lessing) 69
The Jew (Wergeland) 112
"A Jew from Lublin" (Glatstein) 242
The Jew of Malta (Marlowe) 33, 55
Jew Suss (Feuchtwanger) 187
The Jewel in the Crown (Scott) 241
The Jewish War (Feuchtwanger) 196
The Jew's Birch Tree (Droste-Hülshoff) 112
The Jews of Zirndorf (Wasserman) 147
Jill (Larkin) 213
Jin Ping Mei (Anonymous) 52
El jinete polaco (Muñoz Molina) 277
Joan of Arc (Péguy) 147
Joan of Lorraine (Anderson) 215
João Miguel (Quieroz) 196
Jocoseria (Browning) 135
Joe (Brown) 276
Joe Hill (Stegner) 219
Joe Turner's Come and Gone (Wilson) 267
Joe Wilson and His Mates (Lawson) 159
The Johanna Maria (Schendel) 193
"John Anderson, My Jo" (Burns) 68
John Brown's Body (Benét) 190, 191
John Bull's Other Island (Shaw) 153
John C. Calhoun: American Portrait (Coit) 219
John Dollar (Wiggins) 272
John Gabriel Borkman (Ibsen) 94
John Jay (Dennett) 198
John Keats (Bate) 238
John Paul Jones (Morison) 232
John Quincy Adams and the Foundations of American Foreign Policy (Bemis) 218

John Woodvil (Lamb) 96
Joined Hands (Mauriac) 167
The Joke (Kundera) 242
The Jolly Beggars: A Cantata (Burns) 88
Jonatan's Journey (Hansen) 208
Jonathan Edwards (Winslow) 208
Jorparadiset Varherres nedfallsfrukt (Heggland) 284
Joseph and His Brothers (Mann) 152, 197
Joseph Andrews (Fielding) 76
Joseph Had a Little Overcoat (Taback) 295
Joseph in Egypt (Vondel) 56
Journal intime (Amiel) 136
Journal of a Tour of the Hebrides, with Samuel Johnson (Boswell) 84
The Journal of Jules Renard (Renard) 186
A Journal of the Plague Year (Defoe) 73
Journal to Stella (Swift) 68, 71
The Journalists (Freytag) 117
The Journey (Manner) 227
Journey (Meireles) 206
Journey (Michener) 272
The Journey, and Other Poems (Winters) 194
Journey in the Dark (Flavin) 211
A Journey into Winter (Appelfeld) 296
A Journey to the Center of the Earth (Verne) 124
Journey to the End of the Night (Céline) 196
A Journey to the Western Islands of Scotland (Johnson) 82
Journey Without Maps (Greene) 202
Journey's End (Sheriff) 192
The Joy Luck Club (Tan) 272
Joyful Noise: Poems for Two Voices (Fleischman) 271
The Joyful Wisdom (Nietzsche) 135
The Joys (Viélé-Griffin) 140
The Joys and Sorrows of a Schoolmaster (Gotthelf) 110
The Joys of Motherhood (Emecheta) 258
The Joys of Rungsted (Ewald) 82
Juana (Vega) 32
Juanita la Larga (Valera) 145
Judas Sack (Klonowic) 50
Jude the Obscure (Hardy) 144
The Judge (West) 182
Judge Not (Asch) 188
Judgment Day (Farrell) 200
The Judgment (Kafka) 152, 175
The Judgment (Kinoshita) 248
Judith (Hebbel) 111
Juha (Aho) 169
Les Juives (Garnier) 42
Julia Paradise (Jones) 269
Julian (Vidal) 238
Julian and Maddalo (Shelley) 93
Julie (Elstad) 280
Julie of the Wolves (George) 250
Julie; or, The New Eloise (Rousseau) 68, 80
Julius Caesar (Shakespeare) 31, 45
Julius von Tarent (Leisewitz) 83
Jumanji (Van Allsburg) 261
Jumping the Train Tracks with Angela (Durcan) 264
Juneteenth (Ellison) 293
The Jungle (Ferreira de Castro) 191
The Jungle (Sinclair) 164

The Jungle Book (Kipling) 144
Juno and the Paycock (O'Casey) 185
Jurgen (Cabell) 178
The Jury (Klima) 245
The Just and the Unjust (Cozzens) 209
Just Assassins (Camus) 155
Just Looking: Essays on Art (Updike) 272
Just So Stories (Kipling) 160
Justice (Galsworthy) 168
La Justice (Prudhomme) 132
Justine (Durrell) 228
Justine (Sade) 86

K

Kaddish and Other Poems (Ginsberg) 234
Kadisz (Grynberg) 269
Kadmus (Aql) 211
Kaiser Friedrich Barbarossa (Grabbe) 106
En kakelsattares eftermiddag (Gustafsson) 277
Kalapurnodayamu (Suranna) 42
Kalevala (Lönnrot) 108
Kalevipoeg (Kreutzwald) 96, 120
Kamalampal; or, The Fatal Rumor (Rajam Iyer) 144
Kamayani (Prasad) 200
Kamouraska (Hébert) 247
Kampi; or, The Millionairess and the Seamstress (Nestroy) 117
Kan hende ved en bredd (Carling) 294
Kangaroo (Aleshkovsky) 268
Kangaroo (Lawrence) 184
Kanhadade Prabandha (Padmanabhan) 27
Kantapuranam (Sivakariyar) 54
Kanthapura (Rao) 204
Das Kapital (Marx, Engels) 126
Kapten Nemos (Enquist) 277
Kaputt (Malaperte) 211
Karim, roman Sénégalais (Diop) 200
Karjana (Heggland) 274
Kaspar (Handke) 245
Kastanjetid (Larsen) 278
Kate Vaiden (Price) 267
Katedralen (Stigen) 270
Katerina (Appelfeld) 272
Katherine of Heilbronn (Kleist) 98
Katherine Walton (Simms) 117
Kavanagh (Longfellow) 116
Keep the Apisdistra Flying (Orwell) 202
The Keepers of the House (Grau) 238, 239
The Kellys and the O'Kellys (Trollope) 115
Kenilworth (Scott) 93, 102
The Kentucky Cycle (Schenkkan) 277
Kenyon Review (literary journal) 205
Kerkhoven's Third Existence (Wasserman) 199
The Key (Tanizaki) 191
Key Largo (Anderson) 205
The Keys of the Kingdom (Cronin) 209
Kidesh Halem (Asch) 179
Kidnapped (Stevenson) 138
Killer Angels (Shaara) 252
The Killing Game (Ionesco) 247
The Killing Man (Spillane) 272
Kim (Kipling) 159
A Kind of Loving (Barstow) 232
The Kindly Ones (Powell) 235
The Kindness of Women (Ballard) 276

The King (Vega) 32
The King and the Farmer (Vega) 32
King Arthur (Bulwer-Lytton) 116
King Arthur (Dryden) 49, 65
King Dickie (Mallet-Joris) 258
King John (Shakespeare) 44
King Lear (Shakespeare) 31, 50
The King Must Die (Renault) 229
The King of Babylon Shall Not Come Against You (Garrett) 286
The King of Schnorrers (Zangwill) 144
The King of Zion (Hamerling) 127
King Ottocar: His Rise and Fall (Grillparzer) 104
King, Queen, Knave (Nabokov) 155, 191
King Rene's Daughter (Hertz) 114
King Seleucus (Camões) 32
King Solomon's Mines (Haggard) 137
King Ubu (Jarry) 146
The Kingdom of This World (Carpentier) 218
The King's Flute (Palamas) 169
The King's Mandate (Jarvis) 232
The King's Threshold (Yeats) 152
Kinzoni and His Grandson Makundu (Bahele) 217
Kipps (Wells) 163
Kiss of the Spider Woman (Puig) 230
The Kiss to the Leper (Mauriac) 182
Kisses of the Enemy (Hall) 271
The Kitchen God's Wife (Tan) 276
Kitchen Music (Foran) 282
Kjoerlighetsdikt (Mehren) 289
Klosterheim (De Quincey) 107
Kneller's Happy Campers (Keret) 291
A Knife All Blade (Melo Neto) 227
The Knight from Olmedo (Vega) 32
The Knight of Saxony (Benet) 277
Knights (Aristophanes) 3
Knock; or, The Triumph of Medicine (Romains) 184
Knowledge of Angels (Walsh) 282
Ko; or, A Season on Earth (Koch) 231
Kogan Pyo (Rahtathara) 36
Kokinshu (Tsurayuki Ki) 20
Kokoro (Natsume) 93, 173
Kongi's Harvest (Soyinka) 243
Konrad Wallenrod (Mickiewicz) 105
Kopfjager (Timm) 276
Kordian and the Churl (Kruczkowski) 196
Korn (Lundqvist) 266
Kozma (Kornis) 278
Krapp's Last Tape (Beckett) 229
The Kreutzer Sonata (Tolstoy) 141
Kristin Lavransdatter (Undset) 156, 180
Kron og mynt (Flogstad) 291
Kruger's Alp (Hope) 264
"Kubla Khan" (Coleridge) 100
Kullervo (Kivi) 122
Kumarasambhava (Kālidāsa) 15
Kung Fjalar (Runeberg) 113
Kuyil's Song (Bharati) 171
Kvachi Kvachantiradze (Javakhishvili) 185
Kwaiden (Hearn) 162

L

El laberinto griego (Vázquez Montalbán) 277
La Laboratoire central (Jacob) 181
The Labors of Pesiles and Sigismunds: A Northern Story (Cervantes) 32
The Labors of Urbano and Simona (Pérez de Ayala) 184

Lacemaker Lekholm Has an Idea (Hellström) 189
Laches (Plato) 3
Lachweill Stories (Federer) 170
Lad and Lass (Thoroddsen) 117
The Ladies-in-Waiting (Buero Vallejo) 233
The Lady (Tamayo y Baus) 118
Lady Chatterley's Lover (Lawrence) 190
The Lady from Maxim's (Feydeau) 149
The Lady from the Sea (Ibsen) 94, 139
"Lady Macbeth of the Mtsensk District" (Leskov) 125
The Lady Nit-Wit (Vega) 32
The Lady of Lyons (Bulwer-Lytton) 110
The Lady of Maldoro (Lautréamont) 126
"The Lady of Shalott" (Tennyson) 93, 107
The Lady of the Aroostook (Howells) 132
The Lady of the Camelias (Dumas) 115
The Lady of the Dawn (Casona) 212
The Lady of the Lake (Scott) 93, 98
The Lady or the Tiger? (Stockton) 136
Lady Windermere's Fan (Wilde) 143
The Lady's Not for Burning (Fry) 216
haLaila shebo Meta ha Tsionut (Almog) 274
Laish (Appelfeld) 282
Lake Lyrics and Other Poems (Campbell) 140
Lake Wobegon Days (Keillor) 265
Lakshmibai, Queen of Jhansi (Varma) 214
Lalla Rookh (Moore) 100
Lamb in His Bosom (Hillyer) 198
Lambeaux (Juliet) 284
"Lament for the Death of a Bullfighter" (García Lorca) 155, 200
"The Lament of Tasso" (Byron) 100
Laments for the Living (Parker) 193
Lamia (Keats) 101
The Lamp of Umm Hashim (Haqqi) 211
En lampa som gor morker (Odensten) 294
The Lances of Lynwood (Yonge) 119
Land, Land in Sight (Stojicic) 294
The Land of Gold (Conscience) 123
The Land of Heart's Desire (Yeats) 144, 152
The Land of Little Rain (Austin) 161
The Land of Silence (Sarton) 222
Land of the Heather (Kivi) 125
Landlocked (Lessing) 240
The Landlord at Lion's Head (Howells) 147
Land's End (Montale) 210
Landscape (Pinter) 244
Landscape and Memory (Schama) 284
Landscape Painted with Tea (Pavic) 274
Landscape with Figures (Diego) 227
Landschaft mit Dornen (Saeger) 280
The Landslide (Betti) 198
Language (Jouve) 221
Language and Silence: Essays on Language, Literature and the Inhuman (Steiner) 243
La langue maternelle (Alexakis) 284
Languor (Storni) 180

Lanzen im Eis (Schacht) 274

Laocoon: An Essay on the Limits of Painting and Poetry (Lessing) 69, 80

A Laodicean (Hardy) 134

El lapiz del carpintero (Rivas) 292

Lara (Byron) 93, 99

The Lark (Anouilh) 222

The Lark of Truth (Diego) 208

Larry of Santa Fe (Horgan) 254

Larry's Party (Shields) 288

The Lass from the Suburbs; or, Honesty Is the Best Policy (Nestroy) 112

A Lassie Was Cracking Hazelnuts (Terziev) 292

The Last Adam (Cozzens) 197

Last and First Men (Stapledon) 193

The Last Bow (Astafyev) 278

Last Call (Mulisch) 272

The Last Chronicle of Barset (Trollope) 125

The Last Days of Humanity (Kram) 182

The Last Days of Louisiana Red (Reed) 252

The Last Days of Pompeii (Bulwer-Lytton) 108

The Last Domain (Fournier) 172

Last Exit to Brooklyn (Selby) 238

The Last Hotel for Women (Covington) 286

The Last Hurrah (O'Connor) 226

The Last Imam (Tahir) 264

Last Impression (Haddad) 230

The Last Knight (Grun) 106

The Last Lantern (Kristensen) 223

"The Last Leaf" (Henry) 165

Last Loves (Desportes) 42

Last Loves (Sillitoe) 273

The Last Magician (Hospital) 278

The Last Man (Shelley) 104

Last Nights of Paris (Soupault) 190

The Last of Cheri (Colette) 188

The Last of the Barons (Bulwer-Lytton) 108

The Last of the Just (Schwarz-Bart) 231

The Last of the Mohicans (Cooper) 104

The Last of the Red Hot Lovers (Simon) 245

The Last of the Vikings (Bojer) 181

The Last of the Wine (Renault) 226

Last Orders (Swift) 285, 286

The Last Picture Show (McMurtry) 248

Last Poems (Gonçalves Dias) 117

Last Poems (Laforgue) 141

Last Poems and Two Plays (Yeats) 152, 206

The Last Puritan (Santayana) 200

Last Songs (Ledwidge) 177

The Last Summer (Moretti) 246

The Last Tempatation of Christ (Kazantzakis) 225

The Last Thing He Wanted (Didion) 286

"The Last Tournament" (Tennyson) 128

The Last Tycoon (Fitzgerald) 208

The Late George Apley (Marquand) 203, 204

Late Harvest (Tagore) 146, 153

The Late Mattia Pascal (Pirandello) 154, 162

Later the Same Day (Paley) 265

Laughing Boy (LaForge) 193

Laughter in the Next Room (Sitwell) 216

The Launching of American Modern Science, 1846–1876 (Bruce) 270

Laura's Daughter (Mallet-Joris) 266

Lavengro (Borrow) 117

The Law of War and Peace (Grotius) 53

Lay Down Your Arms (Suttner) 140

The Lay Monk (Huysmans) 161

The Lay of the Last Minstrel (Scott) 93, 96

Lays of Ancient Rome (Macaulay) 112

Lays of My Home and Other Poems (Whittier) 113

The Lazy Steppe (Mirshakar) 234

"Lead, Kindly Light" (Newman) 107

Leaden Wings (Zhang) 259

The League of Cambrai (Platen) 107

Lealdade (Souza) 289

The Leaning Tower (Porter) 211

A Lear of the Steppes (Turgenev) 127

The Learned Ladies (Molière) 62

Leaves, Pages (Haavikko) 230

Leaves from Australian Forests (Kendall) 127

Leaves in the Wind (Casal) 141

Leaves of Grass (Whitman) 119

Leaves of Hypnos (Char) 214

Leaves of Three Autums (Bian) 197

Leaving Cheyenne (McMurtry) 237

Una lección de abismo (Cano Gaviria) 281

"Leda and the Swan" (Yeats) 184

Left Hand, Right Hand (Sitwell) 211

The Left Hand of Darkness (Le Guin) 245

The Left-Handed Woman (Handke) 255

A Legend of Florence (Hunt) 111

Legend of Good Women (Chaucer) 14

The Legend of La Llorona (Anaya) 264

A Legend of Montrose (Scott) 93, 101

"The Legend of Saint Julian the Hospitaller" (Flaubert) 92

"The Legend of Sleepy Hollow" (Irving) 101

The Legend of Svein and Maria (Hauge) 244

The Legend of Thyl Ulenspiegel (Coster) 126

La Legende d'un Peuple (Fréchette) 138

Legends of Guatemala (Asturias) 193

Legends of New England in Prose and Verse (Whittier) 106

Legends of the Fall (Harrison) 258

Leil Zikharon (Ha'meiri) 274

Lélia (Sand) 107

Lenins Hirn (Spengler) 276

Lenin's Tomb: The Last Days of the Soviet Empire (Remnick) 281

"Lenore" (Burger) 82

Leo Arminius (Gryphius) 57

Leon Po Po (Young) 273

Leonard and Gertrude (Pestalozzi) 84

Leonce and Lena (Büchner) 109

The Leopard (Lampedusa) 227

The Lepers (Montherlant) 206

The Less Deceived (Larkin) 225

Less Than One (Brodsky) 268

Lessness (Beckett) 154, 247

The Lesson (Ionesco) 220, 223

A Lesson Before Dying (Gaines) 279

Let It Come Down (Bowles) 221

Let Man Live (Lagerkvist) 218

Let There Be Light (Chocano) 166

Let Us Now Praise Famous Men (Agee) 208

A Letter to Myself (Mallet-Joris) 237

Letters from My Mill (Daudet) 127

Letters from Nowhere (Wispelaere) 267

Letters of a Russian Traveler (Karamzin) 85

Letters of Espriella (Southey) 97

Letters to Live Poets (Beaver) 241

Letters to Sister Benedicta (Tremain) 257

Lettres philosophiques (Voltaire) 68

La Lettrice de Isasca (Richelmy) 268

Die Leute von Seldwyla (Keller) 119

The Levant (Cartarescu) 276

Levia gravia (Carducci) 126

The Leviathan (Hobbes) 58

Li viti Ota baDerekh leVeita (Kahana-Carmon) 276

The Liar (Corneille) 48, 57

The Liar (Hansen) 218

The Liars (Jones) 147

Liber de Arti Distellandi (Hieronymous Brunschwig) 34

Libertinism (Bandeira) 193

Liberty (Thomson) 75

Libra (DeLillo) 270

Il libro della prima navigazione per oceano alle terre de'negri della Bassa Ethiopia (Cadamosto) 34

Licks of Love (Updike) 295

Lie Down in Darkness (Styron) 220

Lies and Secrets (Fuller) 258

Lies of Silence (Moore) 274

Lievesfluchter (Schlink) 296

Life (Miri) 296

Life (Petrovich) 62

The Life and Adventures of Martin Chuzzlewitartin Chuzzlewit (Dickens) 113

The Life and Adventures of Robinson Crusoe (Defoe) 72

Life and Adventures of Salavin (Duhamel) 180

The Life and Death of Jason (Morris) 126

The Life and Extraordinary Adventures of Private Ivan Chonkin (Voinovich) 254

Life and Letters of Walter H. Page (Hendrick) 183

Life and Poetry of Joseph Delorme (Saint-Beuve) 105

"Life and the Ideal" (Schiller) 68

The Life and Times of Cotton Mather (Silverman) 265

Life and Times of Michael K. (Coetzee) 262, 263

Life at the Top (Braine) 235

Life Immovable (Palamas) 162

A Life in the Theater (Mamet) 256

Life Is a Dream (Calderón de la Barca) 48, 55

The Life of an Amorous Man (Ihara Saikaku) 64

Life of Archbishop Dominican Friar Bartolomeu dos Martires (Sousa) 52

The Life of Buscon (Quevedo y Villegas) 54

Life of Christ (Farrar) 130

Life of Christ (Papini) 181

Life of Galileo (Brecht) 153

The Life of Henry Brulard (Stendhal) 141

The Life of Horatio Nelson (Southey) 99

The Life of John Marshall (Beveridge) 179

The Life of Jonathan Wild the Great (Fielding) 76

The Life of Julius Agricola (Tacitus) 5

The Life of Marianne (Marivaux) 74

Life of Quintus Fixelin, Extracted from 15 Letter Boxes (Richter) 87

The Life of Reason (Santayana) 163

The Life of Samuel Johnson (Boswell) 86

The Life of Sir William Osler (Cushing) 187

The Life of Solitude (Petrarch) 14, 25

Life of Squire Marcos of Obregon (Espinel) 52

The Life of the Bee (Maeterlinck) 159

Life of the Mind in America (Miller) 241

The Life of the Virgin Mary (Rilke) 155, 172

Life on the Mississippi (Twain) 92, 135

Life Studies (Lowell) 231

Life Supports; New and Collected Poems (Bronk) 261

Life That Strives to Be a Poem (Bagravana) 281

Life with Father (Day) 200

Lifsens rot (Lidman) 287

"Ligeia" (Poe) 91, 110

The Light Around the Body (Bly) 244

Light in August (Faulkner) 196

The Light of Asia (Arnold) 132

Light of Day (Desai) 259

Light of Eyes (Rossi) 41

The Light Possessed (Cheuse) 273

The Light That Failed (Kipling) 141

The Light Years (Howard) 273

Lights Thinning Tree (Nobuko) 294

The Light-Shadowed (Sikelianós) 167

Like Most Revelations (Howard) 282

Likro la 'Atalefim (Bat Shahar) 274

Liliom (Molnár) 167

Lillelord (Bergen) 262

Lime Twig (Hawkes) 234

The Lime Works (Bernhard) 248

Limpieza de sangre (Pérez Reverte) 289

Lincoln: A Photobiography (Freedman) 270

Lincoln at Gettysburg (Wills) 279

The Lincoln Relics (Kunitz) 257

Lindbergh (Berg) 292

"Lines Composed a Few Miles Above Tintern Abbey" (Wordsworth) 88, 92

Lines of Fate (Kharitonov) 280

The Lion and the Jewel (Soyinka) 237

The Lion and the Throne (Bowen) 226

The Lion of Flanders (Conscience) 110

The Lion's Meal (Curel) 147

Litany (Aspenstrom) 222

The Litigants (Racine) 48, 61

Litoral (Ramos) 278

Little Dorrit (Dickens) 90, 119

The Little Drummer Girl (Le Carré) 263

Little Eyolf (Ibsen) 94, 145

Little Fadette (Sand) 116

The Little Foxes (Hellman) 205

Little Friend, Little Friend (Jarrell) 212

Little Gidding (Eliot) 209

Little House on the Prairie (Wilder) 200

The Little Karoo (Smith) 186
"Little Liza" (Karamzin) 86
Little Lord Fauntleroy (Burnett) 137
"The Little Man" (Sefarim) 124
Little Man, What Now? (Fallada) 196
The Little Man of God (Lemonnier) 160
"The Little Mariner" (Elytis) 268
Little Men (Alcott) 128
The Little Minister (Barrie) 142
A Little Organum for the Theater (Brecht) 154
"Little Orphan Annie" (Riley) 135
The Little Prince (Saint-Exupéry) 210
A Little Side-Road Dog (Milosz) 289
The Little Theater of the World (Hofmannsthal) 147
Little Women (Alcott) 126
The Little World of the Past (Fogazzaro) 146
Lituma en los Andes (Vargas Llosa) 281
Live or Die (Sexton) 241, 242
Lives of Gallant Women (Brantôme) 60
The Lives of the English Poets (Johnson) 83
Lives of the Fathers, Martyrs and Other Principal Saints (Butler) 79
The Lives of the Most Eminent Italian Architects, Painters and Sculptors (Vasari) 38
Lives of the Poets (Untermeyer) 232
Living (Yu) 281
The Living and Their Shadows (Lacretelle) 256
The Living End (Elkin) 258
Living Water (Lispector) 251
Living Wills (Macdonald) 276
Livlakarens besok (Enquist) 294
Liza of Lambeth (Maugham) 147
Ljuset ur Skuggornas varld (Gyllensten) 285
Local Anesthetic (Grass) 246
Loci Communes (Melanchthon) 36
Lock of Berenice (Callimachus) 4
The Locked Room (Auster) 269
"Locksley Hall" (Tennyson) 93, 107, 112
The Lodger (Lowndes) 172
Logbook I (Seferis) 207
Lolita (Nabokov) 155, 225
London: A Poem (Johnson) 75
London Assurance (Boucicault) 112
Londoners (Duffy) 263
The Loneliness of the Long Distance Runner (Sillitoe) 231
Lonely Lives (Hauptmann) 142
The Lonely Passion of Judith Hearne (Moore) 225
Long Ago (Corrasquilla) 200
Long Day's Journey into Night (O'Neill) 153, 226, 228
Un long Dimanche de fiancailles (Japrisot) 276
Long Is Our Way (Makanin) 276
The Long Journey (Jensen) 166
Long Live Man (Corso) 235
The Long Ships (Bengtsson) 213
The Long View (Howard) 226
The Long Voyage Home (O'Neill) 153
The Longest Journey (Forster) 165
Longings for Heaven (Castro) 149
Look, the Euphrates Is Flowing Bloody (Kemal) 289

Look at the Harlequins! (Nabokov) 252
Look Back in Anger (Osborne) 228
Look for My Obituary and First Love (Garro) 287
Look Homeward: A Life of Thomas Wolfe (Donald) 270
Look Homeward, Angel (Frings) 229
Look Homeward, Angel (Wolfe) 192
Looking Backward (Bellamy) 139
Looking for Mr. Goodbar (Rossner) 253
The Looking Glass (Roberts) 295
A Looking-Glass for the Times (Folger) 62
The Loom of Youth (Waugh) 176
Loon Lake (Doctorow) 259
Looney Tunes (Basara) 289
Loose Leaves (Deus) 131
Lord Hornblower (Forester) 213
Lord Jim (Conrad) 155, 158
Lord of the Flies (Golding) 223
Lord of the Isles (Scott) 93, 99
The Lord of the Rings (Tolkien) 223, 225, 227
Lord Ormont and His Aminta (Meredith) 144
Lord Rochester's Monkey, Being the Life of John Wilmot, Earl of Rochester (Greene) 252
Lord Weary's Castle (Lowell) 213, 214
The Lord's Vineyard (Calderón de la Barca) 48
Lorenzaccio (Musset) 108
Lorna Doone (Blackmore) 127
Losing Battles (Welty) 247
Loss of Sons (Skallagrimsson) 20
Lost (Ibarbourou) 219
The Lost Cause (Mackenzie) 194
Lost Empires (Priestly) 240
The Lost Honor of Katerine Blum (Böll) 252
Lost Horizon (Hilton) 197
Lost Illusions (Balzac) 91, 110
Lost in the Funhouse (Barth) 244
Lost in Yonkers (Simon) 275, 276
A Lost Lady (Cather) 184
A Lost Letter (Caragiale) 136
Lost Man's River (Matthiessen) 288
The Lost Manuscript (Freytag) 124
The Lost Musicians (Heinesen) 218
The Lost Son, and Other Poems (Roethke) 216
The Lost Steps (Carpentier) 223
A Lost Wanderer (Schendel) 165
The Lost World: New Poems (Jarrell) 240
"The Lotos-Eaters" (Tennyson) 93, 107
Lottie, the Watchmaker (Ebner-Eschenbach) 132
Lotus in Hades (Gyllensten) 242
Louis XI (Delavigne) 107
Louise Bogan: A Portrait (Frank) 267
Le loup Mongol (Homeric) 291
Love, Action, Laughter and Other Sad Tales (Schulberg) 272
Love, Again (Lessing) 286
The Love Afflicted (Boccaccio) 14
Love After All (Magen) 296
Love and Death (Mushanakoji) 206
Love and Death in the American Novel (Fiedler) 232
Love and Litter (Klima) 273
Love and Longing in Hong Kong (Wang) 281

Love and Mr. Lewisham (Wells) 158
Love and Pedagogy (Unamuno) 160
Love for Love (Congreve) 66
Love in a Cold Climate (Mitford) 217
Love in a Wood (Wycherley) 62
Love in Exile (Baha'Tahir) 283
Love in the Ruins (Percy) 248
Love in the Time of Cholera (García Márquez) 266
A Love Interest (Nayman) 294
The Love Nest and Other Stories (Lardner) 188
The Love of a Good Woman (Munro) 291
Love Poems (Antonio) 233
Love Poems (Sexton) 246
Love Retreat (Prem) 182
"The Love Song of J. Alfred Prufrock" (Eliot) 152, 174
Love Songs (Teasdale) 177
Love Struck (Boccaccio) 14
The Love Suicide at Sonezaki (Chikamatsu) 70
The Love Suicides at Amijimi (Chikamatsu) 73
The Love That Passes (Alvarez Quintero) 162
Love Triumphant (Dryden) 49, 66
Love Without Stockings (Wessel) 82
The Love-Crazed Boy (Barrios) 174
The Loved and the Lost (Callaghan) 220
The Loved One (Waugh) 216
Lovely Malcomia (Yizhar) 291
The Lover (Duras) 278
Lovers (Plato) 3
The Lover's Melancholy (Ford) 54
The Lovers of Teruel (Hartzenbusch) 110
Lovers of Their Time (Trevor) 257
Love's Comedy (Ibsen) 94
Love's Labour's Lost (Shakespeare) 31, 44
Loves of the Angels (Moore) 103
Love's Riddle (Cowley) 56
Loves Without Love (Pirandello) 154
Loving Hands at Home (Johnson) 244
The Lower Depths (Gorky) 160
The Loyal Subject (Fletcher) 52
Loyalty (Niyazi) 224
Lucca (Grondahl) 290
Luce and His Empire (Swanberg) 250
Lucidities (Jennings) 247
Lucien Leuwen (Stendhal) 144
Lucifer (Vondel) 59
Lucinde (Schiller) 88
The Luck of Barry Lyndon, a Romance of the Last Century by Fitzboodle (Thackeray) 87
The Luck of Ginger Coffey (Moore) 232
"The Luck of the Roaring Camp" (Harte) 126
Lucky Jim (Amis) 223
Lucky Kristoffer (Hansen) 212
Lucky Peter (Pontoppidan) 148
Lucky Peter's Travels (Strindberg) 92
Lucrece (Shakespeare) 31, 44
Lucretius (Tennyson) 126
"Lucy" (Wordsworth) 92
"Lucy Gray, or Solitude" (Wordsworth) 88
Ludus Dianae (Celtis) 34
Ludwig muss sterben (Hettche) 274
Luise (Voss) 87
Luna de lobos (Llamazares) 266

Lune (Meldini) 293
La lunga de vita Marianna Ucria (Maraini) 274
La lunga notte (Tadini) 269
Lure (Albahari) 293
Os Lusíadas (Camões) 32, 41
Lustra (Pound) 175
Luther (Osborne) 234
Lycidas (Milton) 48, 56
Lycksalighetens (Atterbom) 105
Lydia i lampans sken (Eggehorn) 275
Lyhamar (Heggland) 276
The Lying Days (Gordimer) 222
The Lying Lover (Steele) 70
Lying Low (Johnson) 257
The Lying Truth (Yospal) 230
Lykkens sonn (Wassmo) 278
The Lyre of Orpheus (Davies) 271
Lyric Poems (Bacchelli) 173
Lyrical Ballads (Wordsworth, Coleridge) 88, 92
Lyrics of Lowly Life (Dunbar) 146
Lyrisches Intermezzo (Heine) 103
Lysis (Plato) 3
Lysistrata (Aristophanes) 3
Lystreise (Nilsen) 284
Lyudmila (Zhukovsky) 97

M

M. C. Higgins the Great (Hamilton) 253
Ma Qiao Dictionary (Han) 286
Ma Rainey's Black Bottom (Wilson) 264
Ma vie folle (Morgieve) 296
Mac Flecknoe (Dryden) 49, 64
Macbeth (Shakespeare) 31, 50
The Macdermots of Ballycloran (Trollope) 115
Machiavelli in Hell (de Grazia) 273
Macunaima (Andrade) 191
The Mad House (Jamalzadeh) 209
The Mad Woman of Chaillot (Giraudoux) 212
Madame Bovary (Flaubert) 92
Madame Devil-May-Care (Moreau, Sardou) 144
Madame Gervaisais (Goncourt and Goncourt) 127
Mademoiselle Cloque (Boylesve) 149
Mademoiselle de Maupin (Gautier) 108
Madera de boi (Cela) 294
The Madman (Gibran) 177
The Madman and the Nun (Witkiewicz) 187
Madman or Saint (Echegaray y Eizaguirre) 131
Madmen and Scientists (Soyinka) 241
Madness and Civilization (Foucault) 234
The Madness of Love (Tamayo y Baus) 119
Madoc (Southey) 96
Madonna and Other Poems (Kinsella) 276
Madonna Dianora (Hofmannsthal) 147
La madriguera (Mercado) 287
Madrugada (Steen) 280
Maggie: A Girl of the Streets (Crane) 143
A Maggot (Fowles) 266
The Magic Barrel (Malamud) 229
The Magic Kingdom (Elkin) 265
Magic Lantern (Bergman) 270

The Magic Mountain (Mann) 152, 185

The Magic Ring (Sefarim) 125

Magical Realism (Brathwaite) 290

The Magician of Lublin (Singer) 231

Magister Ludi (The Glass Bead Game) (Hesse) 210

Magnalia Christi Americana (Mather) 70

Magnetic Lady, or Humours Reconciled (Jonson) 55

The Magnetic Mountain (Day-Lewis) 197

The Magnificent Ambersons (Tarkington) 177, 178

The Magnificent Cuckold (Crommelynck) 180

Magnyfycens (Skelton) 35

The Maias (Eça de Queirós) 139

Maid Marian (Peacock) 103

The Maid of Orleans (Schiller) 68, 95

The Maid of Orleans (Voltaire) 79

The Maid Silja (Sillanpää) 195

The Maidens of the Rocks (D'Annunzio) 146

Maiden's Vows (Fredro) 108

The Maids (Genet) 215

The Maid's Tragedy (Beaumont, Fletcher) 51

The Maidservant (Corneille) 48

Main Currents in American Thought (Parrington) 189, 190

Main Currents in Nineteenth-Century Literature Criticism (Brandes) 129

Main Street (Lewis) 179

The Main Traveled Roads (Garland) 142

The Maine Woods (Thoreau) 124

La Maison Tellier (Maupassant) 134

Major Barbara (Shaw) 153, 163, 165

Makar's Dream (Korolenko) 137

The Making of Americans (Stein) 169

The Making of the Atomic Bomb (Rhodes) 270

The Making of the President, 1960 (White) 235

The Makioka Sisters (Tanizaki) 210

Mal de amores (Mastretta) 289

La maladie de Sachs (Winkler) 291

Malatesta (Montherlant) 214

Malavikagnimitra (Kālidāsa) 14

Malcolm (Purdy) 231

The Malcontent (Marston) 50

A Male (Lemonnier) 134

Malina (Bachmann) 249

Malone Dies (Beckett) 154

The Maltese Falcon (Hammett) 193

Malvaloca (Alvarez Quintero) 171

The Mambo Kings Play Songs of Love (Hijuelos) 273

Man (Ivanov) 206

The Man Against the Sky (Robinson) 175

Man and His Phantoms (Lenormand) 185

Man and Superman (Shaw) 153

Man and the Masses (Toller) 180

A Man Could Stand Up (Ford) 188

Man Crazy (Oates) 288

Man Descending (Vanderhaeghe) 261

The Man Eaters of Malgudi (Narayay) 234

The Man from New York: John Quinn and His Friends (Reid) 245

Man Full of Nothing (Nestroy) 114

Man i min alder (Claesson) 279

A Man in Full (Wolfe) 290

Man in the Labyrinth (Alvaro) 188

The Man in the Mirror (Teirlinck) 225

Man Is Good (Frank) 177

Man Is Insane (Nu) 210

The Man of Destiny (Shaw) 153

The Man of Feeling (Mackenzie) 81

Man of Gold (Jókai) 129

The Man of Property (Galsworthy) 164, 182

Man of the People (Achebe) 243

The Man She Hated (Menander) 3

The Man That Corrupted Hadleyburg (Twain) 92, 149

The Man Who Came to Dinner (Hart, Kaufman) 205

The Man Who Died Twice (Robinson) 185, 186

The Man Who Had All the Luck (Miller) 211

The Man Who Loved Children (Stead) 207

The Man Who Lurks (Hernández) 206

The Man Who Was Thursday (Chesterton) 166

"*The Man Who Would Be King*" (Kipling) 139

The Man with the Blue Guitar (Stevens) 203

The Man with the Golden Arm (Algren) 217

The Man with the Hoe and Other Poems (Markham) 149

The Man Within (Greene) 154, 192

The Man Without a Body (Teirlinck) 186

The Man Without a Soul (Lagerkvist) 202

The Man Without Qualities (Musil) 193

Mañana en la batalla piensa (Marías) 283

Mānasī (Tagore) 141, 153

The Mandarins (Beauvoir) 224

The Mandelbaum Gate (Spark) 240

A Man—Finished (Papini) 171

Manfred (Byron) 93, 100

Manhattan Transfer (Dos Passos) 186

Manhole (Makanin) 276

Maniac Magee (Spinelli) 275

The Manifest Splendor (Verhaeren) 164

The Manilla Rope (Meri) 228

Manon Lescaut (Prévost d'Exiles) 74

The Manor (Singer) 244

Man's Estate (Malraux) 197

Mansfield Park (Austen) 91, 99

The Mansion (Faulkner) 231

The Manticore (Davies) 250

Mantissa (Fowles) 261

A Manual of Piety (Brecht) 153

La manuscrit de Port-Ebène (Bona) 291

El manuscrito carmesí (Gala) 275

Manuscritos de Felipa (Prado) 294

Many Thousands Gone (Bishop) 194

Many Waters (L'Engle) 267

Mao II (DeLillo) 276, 277

The Map of Love (Soueif) 293

The Map of Love (Thomas) 206

Mar al fondo (Sampedro) 281

Mar Mani (Yehoshua) 274

The Maravillas District (Chacel) 230

The Marble Faun (Hawthorne) 121

The March of the Musicians (Enquist) 257

The Marchioness of Yolombo (Cairasquilla) 191

Marco e Mattio (Vassalli) 278

Mardi (Melville) 116

Maren Gripes nodwendige ritualer (Lonn) 294

Margins of Philosophy (Derrida) 250

Maria: A South American Romance (Isaacs) 126

Maria Alone (Delblanc) 266

Maria Magdalena (Hebbel) 112

Maria Nefeli (Elytis) 257

Maria Stuart (Schiller) 68, 95

Mariana Pineda (García Lorca) 155

"*Mariana*" (Tennyson) 93, 106

Marianna (Sandeau) 111

Marilia de Dirceau (Gonzaga) 86

Marino Faliero, Doge of Venice (Swinburne) 135

Marino Faliero (Byron) 93, 102

Mario and the Magician (Mann) 152

Marion de Lorme (Hugo) 105

Marius the Epicurean (Pater) 137

Marjorie Morningstar (Wouk) 225

Mark Antony, or Cleopatra (Mairet) 55

The Mark of the Angel (Huston) 293

Marlborough: His Life and Times (Churchill) 197

Marmion (Scott) 93, 97

Marnie (Graham) 234

The Marquis of Keith (Wedekind) 159

The Marquis of O (Kleist) 97

Marriage A-la-Mode (Dryden) 49, 62

Marriage by the Calendar (Bohomolec) 81

Marriage for Money (Scribe) 105

The Marriage of Cadmus and Harmony (Calasso) 271

The Marriage of Figaro; or, The Madness of a Day (Beaumarchais) 84

The Marriage of Heaven and Hell (Blake) 68, 86

The Marriage of Sobeide (Hofmannsthal) 149

Married (Strindberg) 93, 136

The Married Man (White) 295

The Married Philosopher (Destouches) 74

A Married Priest (Barbey d'Aurevilly) 124

Marry Me: A Romance (Updike) 254

The Marshes (Konwicki) 227

Martereau (Sarraute) 223

Martha and Mary (Palacio Valdés) 136

Martha Quest (Lessing) 221

The Martian Chronicles (Bradbury) 219

Martin Birck's Youth (Söderberg) 159

Martin Chuzzlewit (Dickens) 90

Martin Dressler: The Tale of an American Dreamer (Milhauser) 288

Martin Dressler (Millhauser) 288

Martin Eden (London) 167

Martin Faber (Simms) 107

Martin Luther; or The Consecration of Strength (Werner) 97

Martín Rivas (Blest Gana) 123

Marty (Chayefsky) 222

The Martyrs (Chateaubriand) 98

Mary (Nabokov) 155

Mary, Queen of Scots (Fraser) 246

Mary Barton, a Tale of Manchester Life (Gaskell) 115

Mary Chestnut's Civil War (Woodward) 261

Marya: A Life (Oates) 267

Más allá del jardín (Gala) 285

Mask and Trefoil (Storni) 204

The Mask of Snow (Blok) 165

The Masked Days (Fuentes) 242

Mason & Dixon (Pynchon) 288

"*The Masque of the Red Death*" (Poe) 91, 112

The Massacre at Paris (Marlowe) 33

The Master and Margarita (Bulgakov) 193, 242

Master Arthur (Raabe) 128

The Master Builder (Ibsen) 94, 143

Master Georgie (Bainbridge) 290

The Master of Ballantrae (Stevenson) 140

The Master of Hestviken (Undset) 156, 187

The Master of Persburg (Coetzee) 282

The Master of Santiago (Montherlant) 215

Master Olof (Strindberg) 92

Master Thaddeus (Mickiewicz) 108

Master Timpe (Kretzen) 139

The Masters (Snow) 220

Masters of the Dew (Roumains) 211

Mastro-don Gesualdo (Verga) 140

The Matador of the Five Towns (Bennett) 171

Match Ball (Skarmeta) 275

The Matchmaker (Wilder) 223, 225

Maternal Primer (Deus) 131

Mathematical Principles of Natural Philosophy (Newton) 64

Mating (Rush) 276

Mating Birds (Nkosi) 267

The Matins of the Night (Herrera y Reissig) 160

The Matriarch (Ihimaera) 267

Matter and Memory (Bergson) 146

"*Matthew*" (Wordsworth) 92

Maud (Tennyson) 93, 119

Mauprat (Sand) 110

Maurice (Forster) 249

The Maurizius Case (Wasserman) 190

Max Havelaar (Multatuli) 122

Maxims (La Rochefoucauld) 60

The Maxman (Caine) 144

May (Mácha) 109

May Day (Chapman) 51

May I Bring a Friend? (Regniers) 239

The Mayor of Castorbridge (Hardy) 137

The Mayor of Zalamea (Calderón de la Barca) 48, 56

Mazeppa (Byron) 101

Mazurka for Two Dead People (Cela) 263

McTeague (Norris) 149

"*Me*" (Anwar) 218

Mea Culpa (Holt) 288

The Meadow (Leśmian) 180

Measure for Measure (Shakespeare) 50

Medea (Euripides) 2, 7

Medea: Stimmen (Wolf) 286

Médée (Corneille) 48

Meditaçao sore reinas (Judice) 285

A Meditation (Benet) 246

Meditation (Kafka) 152

Meditations Divine and Moral (Bradstreet) 60

Meditations on Quixote (Ortega y Gasset) 173

"*The Mediterranean*" (Tate) 196

The Medusa and the Snail (Thomas) 260

Meek Heritage (Sillanpää) 178

Meet Me in the Green Glen (Warren) 248

The Meeting (Reymont) 147

Mefisto (Banville) 267

"Meghaduta" (Kālidāsa) 15

Meghnadbadh (Datta) 122

Mein Hund, meine Sau, mein Leben (Stadler) 282

Mein Kampf (Hitler) 187

Mein Stuck Zeit (Brezan) 274

Melincourt; or, Sir Oran Haut-ton (Peacock) 100

Mélite (Corneille) 48, 54

Mellen himlen og verden (Tetevide) 295

Mellichampe, a Legend of the Santee (Simms) 109

Melmoth the Wanderer (Maturin) 102

Melocotones helados (Freire) 294

Melodien (Krausser) 280

The Melody That Got Lost (Abell) 205

Los melomanos (Amo) 297

The Melting Pot (Zangwill) 166

Melville Godwin U.S.A. (Marquand) 220

The Member of the Wedding (McCullers) 213

Memento Mori (Heinrich von Melk) 22

Mémoires (Comines) 29

Mémoires (Saint-Simon) 132

Memoirs (Chateaubriand) 116

Memoirs (Gibbon) 87

Memoirs, 1925–1950 (Kennan) 244

Memoirs of a Catholic Childhood (McCarthy) 228

Memoirs of a Cavalier (Defoe) 72

Memoirs of a Dutiful Daughter (Beauvoir) 230

Memoirs of a Father (Marmontel) 96

Memoirs of a Fox-Hunting Man (Sassoon) 190

Memoirs of a Militia Sergeant (Almeida) 118

The Memoirs of a Survivor (Lessing) 252

Memoirs of Casanova (Casanova) 104

Memoirs of Hadrian (Yourcenar) 220

Memoirs of Hecate County (Wilson) 213

Memoirs of Leticia Valle (Chacel) 213

Memoirs of Many in One (White) 267

Memoirs of Martinus Scriblerus (Pope, Arbuthnot) 76

Memoirs of Mistral (Mistral) 164

The Memoirs of Sherlock Holmes (Doyle) 144

Memoirs of the Notary Public Isaias (Lima Barreto) 167

The Memorandum (Havel) 240

The Memorial (Delblanc) 248

The Memorial (Isherwood) 196

Memorials of a Tour on the Continent (Wordsworth) 103

Memories (Kitahara) 170

Memories of My Childhood (Lagerlöf) 194

The Memory of Old Jack (Berry) 252

Memory of Snow and of Dust (Breytenbach) 272

Memory of Snow (Csoori) 263

Men and Women (Browning) 119

Men at Arms (Waugh) 221

The Men Cry Alone (Gironella) 268

Men in White (Kingsley) 198

Men Jorden star til evig tid (Helle) 288

Men of Goodwill (Romains) 196

Men of Maize (Asturias) 218

Le m'en vais (Echenoz) 293

Men Without Women (Hemingway) 153, 189

"Mending Wall" (Frost) 173

Menexeums (Plato) 3

Meno (Plato) 3

El mensajero (Vallejo) 277

Mercedes of Castile (Cooper) 111

The Merchant of Venice (Shakespeare) 31, 44

The Merchant's Ship (Calderón de la Barca) 48

Mercian Hymns (Hill) 249

Le Mercure galant (Boursault) 64

Mercy Among Children (Adams) 295

Mercy of a Rude Stream (Roth) 282

Meridian (Walker) 254

Merlin (Robinson) 176

Mérope (Voltaire) 76

Merope, a Tragedy (Arnold) 120

The Merry Festival (Lenngren) 87

The Merry Wives of Windsor (Shakespeare) 45

Merry-Go-Round (Schnitzler) 147

Mesilat Barzel (Appelfeld) 276

Meslanges (Ronsard) 33, 39

Message (Pessoa) 199

The Messiah (Klopstock) 77

The Messiah (Pope) 71

Messiah (Vidal) 223

The Messiah of Stockholm (Ozick) 269

Metai (Donelaitis) 101

Metamorphoses (Ovid) 4

The Metamorphosis (Kafka) 152, 174

Meteor (Behrman) 192

Meteor (Čapek) 198

The Meteor (Durrenmatt) 242

The Methods of History (Bodin) 40

"Methought I Saw My Late Espoused Saint" (Milton) 59

Methuselah's Children (Heinlein) 229

Metrical Letters (Petrarch) 14, 25

Metro: A Novel of the Moscow Undergound (Kaletski) 266

El metro de platino iridiado (Pombo) 277

Mexico (Arsenijevic) 296

Mexico City Blues (Kerouac) 231

Mezza di transporto (Rasy) 280

Mi (Hari Narayan Apti) 144

Miami and the Seige of Chicago (Mailer) 244

"Michael" (Wordsworth) 92, 95

Michael and His Lost Angel (Jones) 146

Michael Robartes and the Dancer (Yeats) 180

Michikusa (Natsume) 174

Microcosmi (Magris) 289

Midaq Alley (Mahfouz) 214

Midas (Lyly) 45

Midcentury (Dos Passos) 234

Midday Midnight (Cayrol) 241

The Middle Man and Other Stories (Mukherjee) 270

Middle Passage (Johnson) 273

Middlemarch, a Study of Provincial Life (Eliot) 128

Midnight (Green) 202

Midnight Mass (Bowles) 260

Midnight Salvage (Rich) 293

Midnight's Children (Rushdie) 260

Midsummer (Walcott) 264

A Midsummer Night's Dream (Shakespeare) 31, 44

The Midwife's Apprentice (Cushman) 285

A Midwife's Tale: The Life of Martha Ballard, Based on Her Diary, 1785–1812 (Ulrich) 275

Mientras vivimos (Torres) 297

The Mikado (Gilbert) 136

Mikdamot (Yizhar) 278

Mila 18 (Uris) 234

Mildred Pierce (Cain) 208

Miles Wallingford (Cooper) 113

The Military Life (De Amicis) 126

The Military Philosopher (Powell) 244

Milk for Babies, Drawn Out of the Breasts of Both Testaments (Cotton) 57

The Mill on the Floss (Eliot) 121

The Mill on the Po (Bacchelli) 204

The Miller (Malherbe) 202

Min salig bror Jean Hendrich (Burman) 281

Mine Boy (Abrahams) 213

Mine Hostess (Goldoni) 78

Mine Own Executioner (Balchin) 212

The Minister (Shahnon) 243

The Minister's Charge; or, The Apprenticeship of Lemuel Barker (Howells) 138

The Ministry of Fear (Greene) 154, 210

"Miniver Cheevy" (Robinson) 168

Minna (Gjellerup) 140

Minna von Barnhelm; or, A Soldier's Fortune (Lessing) 69, 81

Minnena ser mig (Transtromer) 281

The Minor (Fonvizin) 84

The Minstrel (Beattie) 81

Minstrelsy of the Scottish Border (Scott) 96

Minted Coins (Launko) 269

The Miracles of Antichrist (Lagerlöf) 147

La mirada del alma (Díez) 289

La mirada del otro (Delgado) 285

Mirage of Fire (Hideo) 274

Miramar (Mahfouz) 242

Mireio: A Provençal Poem (Mistral) 121

Mirette on the High Wire (McCully) 279

Mirgorod (Gogol) 91, 109

The Mirror and the Lamp: Romantic Theory and Critical Tradition (Abrams) 222

Mirror of the Peasants (Gotthelf) 110

A Mirrour for Magistrates (Ferrers, Baldwin) 40

Misanthrope (Menander) 3

Le Misanthrope (Molière) 48, 61

Le Misanthrope et Lauvergnat (Labiche) 117

Miscellaneous Poems (Browning) 107

Miscellanies (Cowley) 59

The Miser (Molière) 48, 61

Les Misérables (Hugo) 123

The Misfits (Miller) 234

The Misfortunes of Elphin (Peacock) 105

The Misogynist (Lessing) 69, 79

Miss Julie (Strindberg) 92, 139

"Miss Kilmansegg and Her Precious Leg, a Golden Legend" (Hood) 112

Miss Lonelyhearts (West) 197

Miss Lulu Bett (Gale) 181

Miss Peabody's Inheritance (Jolley) 263

Miss Sara Sampson (Lessing) 69, 79

Missal (Cruz e Sousa) 144

Missing Forever (Kosuke) 289

Missing May (Rylant) 279

Mission Accomplished (Betti) 216

Mist (Unamuno) 173

Mister Bahram (Patel) 271

Mister Johnson (Cary) 206

The Mistress (Cowley) 58

The Mistress of the Inn (Goldoni) 78

Mithridate (Racine) 48, 62

Mitt namn skall vara Stig Dagerman (Ranelid) 281

Mitya's Love (Bunin) 187

Mizan al-Awzan (Nava'i) 29

M'liss (Harte) 121

Moby-Dick; or, The Whale (Melville) 117

Moderato Cantabile (Duras) 230

A Modern Instance (Howells) 135

Modern Love (Meredith) 123

Modern Monk (Thein) 201

Modern Myths (Gyllensten) 218

The Modern Theme (Ortega y Gasset) 184

A Modest Proposal (Swift) 68, 74

Modus Vivendi (Levinson) 264

Mogens (Jacobsen) 128

Mogg Megone (Whittier) 109

Moi, Tituba, sorcière noire de Salem (Condé) 268

Moll Flanders (Defoe) 73

Moll Pitcher (Whittier) 106

Molloy (Beckett) 154, 220

A Molna Elegy (Ekelof) 233

Moly (Gunn) 249

The Moment Before Dawn (Krasinski) 113

A Moment in Time (Bates) 238

Moment of Freedom (Bjorneboe) 242

Momento Mori (Spark) 229

Moments of Grace (Jennings) 258

Mon grand appartement (Oster) 293

The Monarch of the Glen (Mackenzie) 208

The Monastery (Scott) 93, 102

Le monde retrouve de Louis-François Pinagot (Corbin) 291

Money (Bulwer-Lytton) 111

O monhe das cobras (Knopfli) 289

The Monikens (Cooper) 108

The Monk (Lewis) 87

The Monk and the Hangman's Daughter (Bierce) 143

The Monkey Wrench Gang (Abbey) 253

"The Monkey's Paw" (Jacobs) 160

The Monks (Verhaeren) 138

Monna Vanna (Maeterlinck) 160

Monsieur Bergeret in Paris (France) 159

Monsignor Quixote (Greene) 154, 261

The Monster (Kadare) 239

The Monster Gods (Ba'albakki) 232

Mont Blanc (Shelley) 93, 100

Montage of a Dream Deferred (Hughes) 220

Montauk (Frisch) 254

Montevideanos (Benedetti) 231

The Montforts (Boyd) 190

A Month in the Country (Turgenev) 117, 119

A Month of Sundays (Updike) 253
Mont-Saint-Michel and Chartres (Adams) 172
The Moon and Sixpence (Maugham) 178
Moon Deluxe (Barthelme) 262
A Moon for the Misbegotten (O'Neill) 153, 210, 221
Moon in Shanghai (Hisashi) 276
The Moon Is a Harsh Mistress (Heinlein) 241
The Moon Is Down (Steinbeck) 209
The Moon of Shiraz (al-Bayati) 264
Moon Tiger (Lively) 268
"The Moonstone" (Collins) 126
The Moonstruck Countrysides (Verhaeren) 144
The Moorland Cottage (Gaskell) 116
The Moor's Last Sigh (Rushdie) 284
Moral Epistles (Seneca) 5
Las moras agraces (Jodra Davo) 294
The Moratorium (Andrade) 226
Morbus Kitahara (Ransmayr) 284
More Die of Heartbreak (Bellow) 269
More Shapes Than One (Chapell) 276
More Stately Mansions (O'Neill) 238
Morgan's Run (McCullough) 295
Morgue and Other Poems (Benn) 171
Morning at the Office (Mittelholzer) 219
Morning in the Burned House (Atwood) 284
The Morning of Our Lives (Ulughzoda) 224
The Morning of the Poem (Schuyler) 260
Morning Songs (Agustini) 169
Morning Star (Bandeira) 202
The Morning Star (Dabrowska) 226
Moroccan Letters (Cadalso y Vázquez) 86
La morseure (Villemin) 288
Le Morte d'Arthur (Malory) 28
"Morte d'Arthur" (Tennyson) 93, 112
Mosada (Yeats) 138
Mosby's Memoirs and Other Stories (Bellow) 244
Las moscas (Azuela) 178
Moscow Not My Mecca (Carew) 238
Mosses from an Old Manse (Hawthorne) 114
The Mother (Deledda) 180
Mother (Gorky) 164
Mother Came (Janakiraman) 240
Mother Courage and Her Children (Brecht) 153, 208, 218
Mother Goose Tales (Perrault) 66
Mother Iceland (Guthmundur) 213
The Mother-in-Law (Terence) 5
Mother Love (Wright) 284
Mother Nature (Pardo Bazán) 139
Mother Night (Vonnegut) 234
The Mother of Us All (Stein) 215
Motherkind (Phillips) 295
Moths (Ouida) 133
Mottke the Thief (Asch) 175
Le Mouchoir (Cooper) 113
Mount Taibai (Jia) 275
Mount Zion (Betjeman) 197
Mountain Interval (Frost) 175
The Mountain of Broom (Bourbane) 235
A Mountain of Fire (Yuko) 291
The Mountain of Light (Couperus) 164

Mountain Standard Time (Horgan) 235
The Mountain Village (Ayni) 190
Mountains and Men (Federer) 170
Mountains and Rivers Without End (Snyder) 286
Mountains of Gold (Lagones) 147
Mountolive (Durrell) 229
Mourning Becomes Electra (O'Neill) 153, 194
The Mourning Bride (Congreve) 66
The Mousetrap (Christie) 221
Move Your Shadow (Lelyveld) 267
A Moveable Feast (Hemingway) 153, 238
The Moviegoer (Percy) 234
The Moving Target (Merwin) 237
Mozart (Hildesheimer) 256
Mozart and Salieri (Pushkin) 90, 106
Mozart's Journey from Vienna to Prague (Morike) 119
Mozarts tredje hjarna (Sonnevi) 287
Mr. Balcer in Brazil (Konopnicka) 143
Mr. Clemens and Mark Twain (Kaplan) 242
"Mr. Flood's Party" (Robinson) 181
"Mr. Gilfil's Love-Story" (Eliot) 120
Mr. Leonida (Caragiale) 132
Mr. Midshipman Easy (Marryat) 109
Mr. Sammler's Planet (Bellow) 247
Mr. Scobie's Riddle (Jolley) 263
Mr. Visser's Journey Through Hell (Vestdijk) 201
Mr. Witt Among the Rebels (Sender) 200
Mrs. Dalloway (Woolf) 186
Mrs. Frisby and the Rats of NIMH (O'Brien) 249
Mrs. Leicester's School (Lamb and Lamb) 98
Mrs. Marianne (Benedictsson) 139
Mrs. Stevens Hears the Mermaids Singing (Sarton) 240
Mrs. Ted Bliss (Elkin) 284
Mrs. Warren's Profession (Shaw) 143, 153
"A MS. Found a Bottle" (Poe) 91, 107
Much Ado About Nothing (Shakespeare) 31, 45
La muerte como efecto secundario (Shua) 289
The Mulatto (Azevedo) 134
Mule Bone (Hurston) 194
Mulheres de sombra (Ferreira) 285
Mulligan Stew (Sorrentino) 258
Munchausen (Immermann) 110
"The Murder" (Chekhov) 92
Murder in the Cathedral (Eliot) 152, 200
The Murder of Roger Ackroyd (Christie) 188
Murder on the Orient Express (Christie) 197
The Murderess (Papadiamantis) 171
"The Murders in the Rue Morgue" (Poe) 91, 111
Murphy (Beckett) 154, 204
Murther & Walding Spirits (Davies) 276
Musashi (Yoshikawa) 200
Muses (Stiernhielm) 61
The Museum of Unconditional Surrender (Ugresic) 292
Museums and Women and Other Stories (Updike) 250

Music and Silence (Tremain) 293
Music for Chameleons: New Writings (Capote) 259
Music Hall Sidelights (Colette) 172
Music of the Future (Kaschnitz) 219
Mutiny on the Bounty (Nordhoff) 196
My Alexandria (Doty) 279
My Antonia (Cather) 177
My Century (Grass) 293
My Cheerful Mornings (Klima) 273
My Childhood (Gorky) 172
My Death Is My Own (Ahlin) 213
My Experiences in the World War (Pershing) 195
My Father's Moon (Jolley) 272
My First Loves (Klima) 265
My Grandpa (Yasutaka) 296
My Happy Days in Hell (Faludy) 235
My Heart (Lasker-Schuler) 171
"My Heart Leaps Up When I Behold" (Wordsworth) 96
My Kinsman, Major Molineaux (Hawthorne) 107
My Lady Ludlow (Gaskell) 120
"My Last Duchess" (Browning) 112
My Life (Wagner) 170
My Life and Hard Times (Thurber) 197
My Life as a Man (Roth) 252
My Living Shadow (Wispelaere) 240
My Michael (Oz) 245
My Name Is Aram (Saroyan) 207
My Novel; or, Varieties in English Life (Bulwer-Lytton) 118
My Skin (Dromer) 286
My Ten Years in a Quandary and How They Grew (Benchley) 201
My Voice Because of You (Salinas) 198
Myra Breckinridge (Vidal) 244
Le mystère des saints innocents (Péguy) 171
Mysteries (Hamsun) 143
The Mysteries of Paris (Sue) 112
Mysteries of Selfness (Iqbāl) 177
The Mysteries of Udolpho (Radcliffe) 86
The Mysterious Affair at Styles (Christie) 180
The Mysterious Island (Verne) 130
The Mysterious Mother (Walpole) 81
Mysterious Weddings (Jouve) 186
Mystery (Hauge) 243
The Mystery of Edwin Drood (Dickens) 90, 127
Mystery of the Charity of Charles Péguy (Hill) 263
A Mystery Play of the Sufferings of Israel (Sachs) 220
Mystical Poems and Songs (Verdaguer) 128
The Myth of Sisyphus (Camus) 155, 209
Mythistorema (Myth-History) (Seferis) 200
Mythologies (Barth) 228

N

Na tua face (Ferreira) 283
The Nabob (Daudet) 131
Nach den Satiren (Grunbein) 293
Der Nachsommer (Stifter) 120
Nadja (Breton) 190
Nahafat al-Uns (Jāmī) 28
La naissance des fantomes (Darrieussecq) 291
The Naked and the Dead (Mailer) 216

Naked Feet and Seashell (Taku) 296
The Naked Lunch (Burroughs) 231
The Naked Streets (Pratolini) 213
The Name of the Rose (Eco) 259
Nameless (Obstfelder) 143
Nana (Zola) 133
Nanso Satomi Hakken (Bakin) 112
Nao es tu, Brasil (Rubens Paiva) 287
Naomi (Tanizaki) 185
Napló (Radnóti) 274
Napoleon, or the Hundred Days (Grabbe) 106
The Napoleon of Notting Hill (Chesterton) 162
Nar fisken fanger solen (Winge) 288
Nar jeg ser deg (Faldbakken) 287
Nar vagen vander (Espmark) 279
El naranjo, o los círculos del tiempo (Fuentes) 281
Narcissus and Goldmund (Hesse) 193
The Narrative of Arthur Gordon Pym, of Nantucket (Poe) 110
Das Narrenschiff (Brant) 29
The Narrow Road to Happiness (Ernst) 162
The Narrow Road to the Deep North (Bashō) 49, 66
Nathan the Wise (Lessing) 69, 83
Nati due volte (Pontiggia) 296
National Velvet (Bagnold) 200
Native Son (Wright) 207
Nattens rygrad (Krasilnikoff) 295
Nattsol (Mehren) 278
The Natural (Malamud) 221
A Natural Curiosity (Drabble) 272
A Natural Novel (Gospodinov) 292
Natural Sciences (Chacel) 271
The Natural Son; or, The Proofs of Virtue (Diderot) 79
Nature (Emerson) 109
The Nature of Passion (Jhabvala) 226
Nausea (Sartre) 204
The Nazarene (Asch) 206
Nazarín (Pérez Galdós) 145
The Near and the Far (Myers) 207
Near Changes (van Duyn) 275
Near the Ocean (Lowell) 243
Near to the Savage Heart (Lispector) 212
Nectar in a Sieve (Markandaya) 224
Nedjma, Poem or Knife (Yacine) 216
The Need for Roots (Weil) 218
The Need to Hold Still (Muller) 260
Needs of the Poor (Gotthelf) 111
The Negro (Soupault) 189
A Negro in Paris (Dadie) 231
The Negro of Peter the Great (Pushkin) 90, 105
The Negro Speaks of Rivers (Hughes) 181
"Neighbors" (Chekhov) 92
Neither Black Nor White (Degler) 249
Nekrassov (Sartre) 225
Nel momento (Carlo) 296
Nemesis (Asimov) 272
Neon Vernacular (Komunyakaa) 281, 282
The Neon Wilderness (Algren) 215
The Nephew (Purdy) 232
Nerto (Mistral) 136
The Never Ending Lightning (Hernández) 202
The Never Silent Bells (Sevak) 230
Never-Setting Sun (Toyoko) 294
The New Age (Hood) 273

New and Collected Poems (MacLeish) 254
New and Collected Poems (Wilbur) 270, 272
New and Collected Poems, 1941–1995 (Curnow) 286
New and Selected Poems (Meredith) 269
New and Selected Poems (Oliver) 277
New and Selected Poems (Warren) 265
New and Selected Poems, 1940–1986 (Shapiro) 265
The New Atlantis (Bacon) 54
The New Colony (Marivaux) 74
The New Criticism (Ransom) 208
A New Drama (Tamayo y Baus) 126
The New Dunciad (Pope) 69, 74, 76, 84
New Grub Street (Gissing) 142
New Hampshire (Frost) 184, 185
The New Idol (Curel) 145
The New Kingdom (Strindberg) 92
The New Life (Dante) 14, 24
The New Machiavelli (Wells) 169
The New Medley (Castro) 133
The New Men (Snow) 223
New Morning (Hadobian) 167
New Poems (Ady) 164
New Poems (Arnold) 126
New Poems (Fröding) 145
New Poems (Heidenstam) 174
New Poems (Heine) 93, 114
New Poems (Kinsella) 251
New Poems (Nijhoff) 198
New Poems (Rilke) 155
New Poems (Yeats) 152
The New Shelter for the Poor (Calderón de la Barca) 48
New Songs (Machado) 185
New Stories, Frydenberg (Borgen) 240
The New Sweet Style (Aksyonov) 291
The New Tenant (Ionesco) 225
New Testament (translation) 42
New Weddings (Jouve) 188
The New World (Heruy) 186
The New York Trilogy (Auster) 269
The New Yorkers (Calisher) 246
The Newcomes (Thackeray) 108, 118
The Newlyweds (Griboyedov) 100
News from Empire (Paso) 270
News from Nowhere (Morris) 141
News of a Kidnapping (García Márquez) 287
Next: Two Poems (Clifton) 269
"Niagara" (Heredia) 104
The Nice and the Good (Murdoch) 244
Nicholas Nickleby (Dickens) 90, 110
Nicomède (Corneille) 48, 58
El nido de los sueños (Montero) 279
Die Niebelungen (Hebbel) 123
Niels Lynne (Jacobsen) 133
The Nigger of the "Narcissus" (Conrad) 147, 155
Night (Karasu) 283
Night (Wiesel) 230
'Night, Mother (Norman) 261, 262
Night and Day (Dabrowska) 196
Night and Day (Stoppard) 257
Night and Day (Woolf) 178
Night Diary (Dimitrova) 275
Night Guard (Pontoppidan) 144
A Night in Acadie (Chopin) 147
A Night in Santa Paulina (Orpaz) 289
Night in the Market Town (Ahlin) 229
Night Light (Justice) 243

The Night of the Generals (Kirst) 236
The Night of the Iguana (Williams) 234
The Night of the Mad Cock (Oliveiro) 268
The Night of the Tribades (Enquist) 252
Night Rider (Warren) 205
The Night Search (Khlebnikov) 181
Night Tango: A Novel of One Summer of the End of the Century (Kratochvil) 292
The Nightingale Sings Out of Tune (Siefert) 187
Nightmare Abbey (Peacock) 101
Nightwood (Barnes) 201
Nikita's Childhood (Tolstoy) 181
Nine, Novena (Lins) 242
Nine Stories (Salinger) 222
Ninety-Three (Hugo) 130
Ninfa plebea (Rea) 280
Ninguna eternidad como la mía (Mastretta) 294
The Ninth of November (Kellerman) 181
A Nip in the Air (Betjeman) 252
No, But I Saw the Movie (De Vries) 221
No Bride Price (Rubadiri) 243
No caração do Brasil (Falabella) 278
No Country for Young Men (O'Faolain) 259
No Exit (Sartre) 211
No Longer at Ease (Achebe) 232
No Man's Grove (Lim) 259
No Man's Land (Onetti) 209
No Man's Land (Pinter) 253
No More Parades (Ford) 186
No One Knows the Day (Hauge) 225
No One Writes to the Colonel and Other Stories (García Márquez) 243
No Ordinary Time: Franklin and Eleanor Roosevelt: The Home Front in World War II (Goodwin) 283
No Other Life (Moore) 280
No Place to Be Somebody (Gordone) 247
Noah (Vondel) 61
Noah's Ark (Spier) 256
Noble Essences (Sitwell) 219
Noble Numbers; or, His Pious Pieces (Herrick) 58
Nobleness and Extinction (Weinheber) 199
Nobody Knows My Name (Baldwin) 234
Noces de sable (Leclerc) 284
The Noël Coward Diaries (Coward) 261
Noli Me Tangere (Rizal) 139
Nomoi (Plato) 3
None but the Brave (Schnitzler) 159
None but the Lonely Heart (Llewellyn) 210
None to Accompany Me (Gordimer) 282
The Nonexistent Knight (Calvino) 231
Noon Wine (Porter) 203
Nor Any Country (St. Omer) 246
North (Heaney) 254
North Amerikkan Blues (Hyde) 249
North and South (Bishop) 213
North and South (Gaskell) 119
North of Boston (Frost) 173
North of South: An African Journey (Naipaul) 258

The North Ship (Larkin) 212
Northanger Abbey (Austen) 91, 100
The Northern Flowers (Fréchette) 132
The Northern Lights (Daubla) 168
The Northern Symphony (Bely) 160
Northwest Passage (Roberts) 203
Norwegian Folk Tales (Asbjørnsen, Moe) 117
Norwegian Wood (Murakami) 269
Nostromo (Conrad) 155, 162
The Noszty Boy and Mary Tóth (Mikszáth) 166
Not Honour More (Cary) 225
Not I (Beckett) 252
Note About the Author (Matanovic) 295
Notebook, 1967–1968 (Lowell) 246
The Notebook of Malte Laurids Brigge (Rilke) 155, 168
The Notebooks of Don Rigoberto (Vargas Llosa) 292
Notes from Underground (Dostoyevsky) 90, 124
Notes of a Native Son (Baldwin) 225
Notes of a Student Examinee (Maso) 175
Notes Toward the Definition of Culture (Eliot) 152, 216
Nothing (Laforet) 217
Nothing Important Ever Dies (Gary) 233
Nôtre-Dame de Paris (Hugo) 106
Nottetempo, casa per case (Consolo) 278
Noturnos: contos (Miranda) 294
Nous sommes eternels (Fleutiaux) 274
Nouvelle Continuation des Amours (Ronsard) 33
Nova Express (Burroughs) 238
Le Novelle (Bandello) 39
Noveller i samling (Koltzow) 291
November 1916 (Solzhenitsyn) 280
La novia de Matisse (Vincent) 297
The Novice (Lermontov) 111
Novum Organum (Bacon) 53
Now and Then: Poems, 1976–1978 (Warren) 258
Now in November (Johnson) 200
Nowhere Else on Earth (Humphreys) 295
Nowhere to Go (Leskov) 124
Nubosidad variable (Martín Gaite) 279
Nuestra señora de la noche (Denevi) 289
La nuit de lerreur (Ben Jelloun) 289
Numantia (Cervantes) 32
The Number of the Beast (Heinlein) 259
Number One (Dos Passos) 210
Number the Stars (Lowry) 273
The Nuremberg Chronicle (Schedel) 29

O

"O Captain! My Captain!" (Whitman) 124
O Cesar o nada (Vásquez Montalbán) 292
O Pioneers! (Cather) 172
O Strange New World (Jones) 239
The Oak Openings; or, The Bee Hunter (Cooper) 115
The Oasis (McCarthy) 217
Obabakoak (Atxaga) 273
The Obedient Wife (O'Faolain) 261

Oberon (Wieland) 83
Obid Ketman (Qodiriy) 201
Objections to the Spirit of the Age (Costa) 103
Oblomov (Goncharov) 121
Obras Completas (Castilho) 110
The Obscene Bird of Night (Donoso) 248
An Obscure Man (Yourcenar) 266
The Obscure Woman (Lima) 206
Observations (Moore) 185
The Occasion of Poetry: Essays in Criticism and Autobiography (Gunn) 261
The Occasions (Montale) 206
Occidental Paradise (Sigüenza y Góngora) 64
"An Occurrence at Owl Creek Bridge" (Bierce) 142
The Ocean of Night (Ali) 239
Ocean Sea (Baricco) 293
Och jag grep arorna och rodde (Lillpers) 292
La Ocher de Tanios (Maalouf) 280
Ocher (Storni) 187
The Ochre People: Scenes from a South African Life (Jabavu) 237
October Light (Gardner) 254
The October Night (Musset) 110
The Octopus (Norris) 159
The Octoroon; or, Life in Louisiana (Boucicault) 121
Oda Oark Oracle (Gabre-Madhin) 240
O.D.C. (Aster) 293
The Odd Couple (Simon) 240
Odd Girl Out (Howard) 250
Ode (Jouve) 219
"Ode: Intimations of Immortality" (Wordsworth) 92, 96
Ode for Man and Woman (Marechal) 192
"Ode on a Distant Prospect of Eton College" (Gray) 76
"Ode on a Grecian Urn" (Keats) 101
"Ode on Indolence" (Keats) 101
"Ode on Melancholy" (Keats) 101
"Ode on the Death of the Duke of Wellington" (Tennyson) 118
"Ode on the Spring" (Gray) 76
"Ode to a Nightingale" (Keats) 101
"Ode to Adversity" (Gray) 76
"Ode to Autumn" (Keats) 101
"Ode to Duty" (Wordsworth) 96
"Ode to Fancy" (Wharton) 77
"Ode to Joy" (Schiller) 67
"Ode to Liberty" (Pushkin) 90, 102
"Ode to Liberty" (Shelley) 93, 102
"Ode to Psyche" (Keats) 101
"Ode to the Confederate Dead" (Tate) 188, 201
Ode to the Deity (Derzhavin) 84
Ode to the Fatherland (Aribau) 107
"Ode to the West Wind" (Shelley) 93, 101
Odes (Horace) 4
Odes (Klopstock) 81
Odes (Ronsard) 33, 38
Odes and Songs (Hagedorn) 76
Odes Modernas (Quental) 124
Odes to Several Descriptive and Allegoric Subjects (Collins) 77
The Odessa File (Forsyth) 250
Odessa Tales (Babel) 195
Odeur d'encre, odeur d'îles (Jacq) 276
The Odyssey (Fyodorov) 285

Odyssey (Homer) 2

Oedipus (Voltaire) 72

Oedipus at Colonus (Sophocles) 3

Oedipus at the Home of Admetus (Ducis) 83

Oedipus Rex (Cocteau) 189

Oedipus Rex (Sophocles) 3

L'oeil du silence (Lambron) 280

L'oeuvre postume de Thomas Pilaster (Chevillard) 293

Of a Fire on the Moon (Mailer) 247

Of Being Numerous (Oppen) 245

Of Divine Love (Waller) 64

Of Human Bondage (Maugham) 174

Of Love and Other Demons (García Márquez) 285

Of Love and Shadows (Allende) 265

Of Mice and Men (Steinbeck) 203

Of Sepulchres (Foscolo) 97

"Of the Last Verses Written in His Book" (Waller) 64

Of the Principles of Human Knowledge (Berkeley) 71

Of Thee I Sing (Kaufman, Ryskind, Gershwin) 195

Of Time and the River (Wolfe) 194, 200

The Offender (Montale) 242

Offending the Audience (Handke) 242

The Office of Peace on Orolandia (Arévalo) 187

Office Poems (Benedetti) 227

Officer Buckle and Gloria (Rathmann) 285

Officers and Gentlemen (Waugh) 225

An Official Tale (Pavlov) 285

L'offrande sauvage (Milavanoff) 293

Offshore (Fitzgerald) 257

Oh Cybernetic Fairy (Belli) 234

Oh What a Paradise It Seems (Cheever) 261

Oil! (Sinclair) 189

Oil Man of Oanje (Munonye) 247

Los ojos del basilisco (Espinosa) 281

Okinawa (Kinoshita) 234

The Old Adam (Pontoppidan) 145

Old and New Gods (Drachmann) 134

The Old and the Young (Pirandello) 172

The Old Bachelor (Dryden) 65

The Old Curiosity Shop (Dickens) 90, 111

The Old Devils (Amis) 267

"The Old Familiar Faces" (Lamb) 88

"The Old Forest" (Taylor) 265

The Old Forest and Other Stories (Taylor) 267

Old Goriot (Balzac) 108

The Old Gringo (Fuentes) 266

"Old Ironsides" (Holmes) 106

The Old Jest (Johnston) 258

The Old Maid (Lessing) 69

The Old Main (Akins) 200

The Old Man (Trifonov) 257

The Old Man and the Sea (Hemingway) 153, 221, 222

The Old Man of the Mountain (Deladda) 158

The Old Man with the Kites (Ritsos) 266

An Old Man's Notebook (Ungaretti) 233

Old Mortality (Scott) 93, 100

The Old Northwest, Pioneer Period, 1815–1840 (Buley) 219

The Old Patagonian Express: By Train Through the Americas (Theroux) 258

Old River Daydreams (Liu) 279

Old Road to Paradise (Widdemer) 178

Old Sites (Li) 279

Old Soldier (Bourjaily) 273

Old Spookses' Pass, Malcolm Katie and Other Poems (Crawford) 136

Old Tales Retold (Lu) 156, 201

The Old Wives' Tale (Bennett) 166

Oliver Twist (Dickens) 90, 109

Olney Hymns (Cowper, Newton) 83

Olvidado Rey Gudu (Matute) 289

The Olympic Spring (Spitteler) 168

Om natten i Jerusalem (Kosovic) 292

Omeros (Walcott) 274

Omoo, a Narrative of Adventures on the South Seas (Melville) 115

Omrade aldrifastlagt (Mjelve) 282

Omvei til Venus (Schgerven) 284

"On an Infant Dying as Soon as It Is Born" (Lamb) 105

On Baile's Strand (Yeats) 152

On Duties (Cicero) 4

"On First Looking into Chapman's Homer" (Keats) 100

On Glassy Wings: New and Selected Poems (Lowther) 288

On Heroes, Hero-Worship and the Heroic in History (Carlyle) 112

On Heroes and Tombs (Sábato) 234

On Human Nature (Wilson) 258

On Illustrious Men (Petrarch) 14, 25

"On Liberty" (Mill) 121

On Love (Stendhal) 103

On Monarchy (Dante) 14

On Murder as One of the Fine Arts (De Quincey) 105

On Native Grounds (Kazin) 209

On Poetry and Poets (Eliot) 228

On Reading Turgenev (Trevor) 276

On Religious Idleness (Petrarch) 14, 25

On Roads and Through Space (Jankovic) 283

"On Shakespeare" (Milton) 54

On the Beach (Shute) 228

On the Brink (Nervesen) 266

On the Contrary (Brink) 282

"On the Death of a Fair Infant Dying of a Cough" (Milton) 54

On the Death of Goethe (Baratynsky) 107

On the Death of Prince Meshchersky (Derzhavin) 83

On the Different Conceptions of the Chief Good and Evil (Cicero) 4

On the Eve (Turgenev) 122

On the Farm (Updike) 240

On the Fates of Famous Men (Boccaccio) 14

On the Genealogy of the Gods of the Gentiles (Boccaccio) 14

"On the Morning of Christ's Nativity" (Milton) 54

On the Nature of Gods (Cicero) 4

On the Orator (Cicero) 4, 10

On the Origin of Species by Means of Natural Selection (Darwin) 121

On the Reckoning of Time (Bede) 14

On the Road (Kerouac) 228

On the Search after Truth (Malebranche) 62

On the State (Cicero) 4, 10

On the Track of God (Rivière) 186

On This Island (Auden) 202

On Time (Bede) 14

On Translating Homer (Arnold) 122

On Trial (Rice) 173

On Trial for My Country (Samkange) 241

On vient chercher Monsieur Jean (Tardieu) 274

On Windy Nights (Haavikko) 222

The Once and Future King (White) 229

One, None, and a Hundred Thousand (Pirandello) 154, 187

One and Other Poems (Kinsella) 258

One Dark Body (Sherman) 279

The One Day (Hall) 270

One Day in October (Hoel) 195

One Day in the Life of Ivan Denisovich (Solzhenitsyn) 154, 236

One Fine Day (Hagrogian) 249

One Flew Over the Cuckoo's Nest (Kesey) 235

One Hundred Springs (Binkis) 188

One Hundred Years of Solitude (García Márquez) 243

One Million Dead (Gironelda) 234

One of Life's Slaves (Lie) 136

One of Our Conquerors (Meredith) 142

One of Ours (Cather) 182, 183

One Ship—Laura Blair (Divis) 281

One the Margins (Go) 281

"One Thousand Seven Hundred Thirty Eight. A Dialogue Something Like Horace" (Pope) 76

One Writer's Beginnings (Welty) 265

O'Neill, Son and Artist (Shaeffer) 252

One-Minute Letters (Örkény) 280

"Oneone" (Tennyson) 107

The Onion Eaters (Donleavy) 241

Onitsha (Le Clezio) 276

The Only Jealousy of Emer (Yeats) 178

The Only Problem (Spark) 264

Open All Night (Morand) 182

"The Open Boat" (Crane) 148

Open Secrets (Munro) 282

"The Open Window" (Saki) 173

Opened Ground: Poems, 1956–1996 (Heaney) 291

Opéra: Oeuvres Poétiques (Cocteau) 189

Operation Shylock (Roth) 279, 281

Operette Morali (Leopardi) 91

The Opermanns (Feuchtwanger) 197

Oppdageren (Kjaerstad) 294, 296

The Opposing Self (Trilling) 225

The Optimist's Daughter (Welty) 250

Opus Maccaronicum (Folengo) 35

Or Else: Poem (Warren) 253

Oranges from Morocco (Aksyonov) 237

Orator (Cicero) 4

The Orators (Auden) 196

Orazia (Aretino) 38

Orbecche (Giraldi) 37

Orbis Sensualium Pictus (Commenius) 59

The Orchard (Sa'dī) 23

The Orchard on Fire (Mackay) 286

The Orchid House (Allfrey) 222

The Ordeal of Gilbert Pinfold (Waugh) 228

The Ordeal of Richard Feverel (Meredith) 121

The Order of Things: An Archeology of Human Science (Foucault) 241

An Ordinary Life (Čapek) 198

L'Ordre (Arland) 192

Oresteia (Aeschylus) 2, 6

Orestes (Euripides) 8

The Organization and Administration of the Union Army, 1861–1865 (Shannon) 191

L'organization (Rolin) 286

Orient Express (Greene) 154, 196

The Origin of Table Manners (Lévi-Strauss) 245

Original Meanings: Politics and Ideas in the Making of the Constitution (Rakove) 288

Origins of the Fifth Amendment (Levy) 245

Ori-Taku-Shiba (Arai) 72

Orlanda (Harpma) 286

Orlando (Woolf) 190

Orlando Furioso (Ariosto) 35

Orley Farm (Trollope) 122

Ormens ar (Faldbakken) 280

Ormond (Brown) 88

Ormond (Edgeworth) 100

Oroonoko, or the History of the Royal Slave (Behn) 63

The Orphan (Otway) 63

The Orphan of the Desert (Krige) 243

Orpheus (Cocteau) 188

Orpheus (Politian) 28

Orphic Hymns (Manner) 232

Orphic Sayings (Alcott) 111

Orphic Songs (Campana) 173

Os Tambores de São Luis (Montello) 254

Oscar and Lucinda (Carey) 270

Oscar Wilde (Ellman) 272

Oskuldens minut (Lidman) 294

Osman (Gundulić) 54

Osorio (Coleridge) 87

Oswald's Tale (Mailer) 284

The Other One (Green) 249

The Other Side (Kubin) 167

Other Voices, Other Rooms (Capote) 216

Other Women (Lau) 284

Otherwise Engaged (Gray) 253

Othon (Corneille) 48, 60

La otra orilla de la droga (Tomás García) 266

La otra selva (Salazar) 277

Otro baile en París (Lafourcade) 296

Otto the Marksman (Kinkel) 114

Our American Cousin (Taylor) 120

Our Conquest (Hoffmann) 264

Our Gang (Roth) 248

Our Goddess (Bontempelli) 187

Our Ground Time Here Will Be Brief (Kumin) 261

Our Lady of the Flowers (Genet) 211

Our Lady's Tumbler (Duncan) 220

Our Man in Havana (Greene) 154, 229

Our Mutual Friend (Dickens) 90, 124

Our Old Home (Hawthorne) 123

Our Power and Our Glory (Grieg) 200

Our Town (Wilder) 204

Our Wedding (Rabinyan) 293

Out of Africa (Dinesen) 203

"Out of the Cradle Endlessly Rocking" (Whitman) 121

Out of the Dust (Hesse) 290

Out of the Silent Planet (Lewis) 204

The Outcast (Pirandello) 154, 159

"The Outcasts of Poker Flat" (Harte) 127

Outerbridge Reach (Stone) 277

The Outlander (Guèvremont) 219

The Outline of History (Wells) 180

The Outmost Dream (Maxwell) 272
Outrora agora (Abelaira) 289
The Outsider (Wilson) 227
The Outsider (Wright) 222
Outstanding Talent—Yang Du (Tang, Zhu) 288
Over the Brazier (Bridges) 175
Over the Waves of TSF (Siefert) 186
"The Overcoat" (Gogol) 91, 112
Overijssel Songs and Poems (Revius) 54
Ovonramwen Nogbaisi (Rotimi) 250
"The Owl and the Pussycat" (Lear) 128
Owl Moon (Yolen) 270
The Ox of Frankfurt (Yuryev) 289
The Ox-Bow Incident (Clark) 207
Ox-Cart Man (Hall) 259
Oxford English Dictionary (first fascicle) 136
"Ozymandias" (Shelley) 101

P

Pa St. Jorgen (Skram) 145
Paco's Story (Heinemann) 269
El pacto (Palma) 289
Paddy Clarke Ha Ha Ha (Doyle) 279, 280
Painful Joy (Pirandello) 154
The Painted Bird (Kosinski) 240
Painted Roofs (Richardson) 174
Painter Nolten (Morike) 107
The Painter of His Dishonor (Calderón de la Barca) 48, 57
A Painter of Our Time (Berger) 229
A Pair of Blue Eyes (Hardy) 129
A paixao (Faria) 294
Las palabras de la vida (Díez) 297
The Palace of Dreams (Kadare) 260
Palace to Let (Karamosmanoglu) 183
Palamedes, or Murdered Innocence (Vondel) 54
Palatsbarnen (Collarp) 294
Pale Fire (Nabokov) 155, 235
Pale Horse, Pale Rider (Porter) 205
The Palice of Honour (Douglas) 34
Palimpsest (Vidal) 284
Pallid Night (Jia) 284
Palmerin of England (Southey) 97
The Palm-Wine Drinkard (Tutuola) 222
La paloma de vuelo popular: Elegias (Guillén) 231
La palude definitiva (Manganelli) 276
Pamela; or, Virtue Rewarded (Richardson) 76
Pan (Hamsun) 145
Pan Beat (Jones) 251
Pan Cogito (Herbert) 253
Pan Michael (Sienkiewicz) 139
Panchali's Vow (Bharati) 171
Pandora's Box (Wedekind) 162
Panim baA'nan (Birstein) 276
The Panorama and Other Poems (Whittier) 119
Pantagruel (Rabelais) 32, 37
Panteros (Pignatari) 280
The Panther and the Lash: Poems of Our Times (Hughes) 243
Panu (Aho) 147
Paola and Francesca (Phillips) 158
Papas Koffer (Kopf) 280
The Paper Men (Golding) 264
Papinianus (Gryphius) 59
The Parable of the Blind (Hoffmann) 266

Paracelsus (Browning) 108
Parade's End (Ford) 185, 186, 188, 219
Paradis (Eriksson) 287
Paradise (Morrison) 290
Paradise Lost (Jun'ichi) 289
Paradise Lost (Milton) 48, 61
Paradise Regained (Laxness) 233
Paradise Regained (Marsman) 189
Paradise Regained (Milton) 48, 62
Paraíso (Lima) 242
The Paralyzed (Tur) 220
Parayana Wuthtu (Shin) 35
The Parent's Assistant (Edgeworth) 87
Pargfrider (Heym) 291
The Pariah (Strindberg) 92, 140
Parijatapahanannamu (Timanna) 36
Paris Bound (Barry) 189
The Parish Register (Crabbe) 97
"Parisi'na" (Byron) 100
The Parlement of Foules (Chaucer) 14, 26
Parmedides (Plato) 3
Parôle de sige (Cahuzac) 274
Parricide (Bronnen) 180
Partes de Africa (Macedo) 278
Partial Accounts: New and Selected Poems (Meredith) 270
Les particules élémentaires (Houellebecq) 291
Parting the Waters: America in the King Years, 1954–1963 (Branch) 272
The Partisan (Simms) 108
Partisan Review (literary quarterly) 197
Partisans (Ivanov) 181
A Party for Boris (Bernhard) 245
Party in Autumn (Dorst) 233
La pas si lent de l'amour (Bianciotti) 284
Pasado presente (García Ponce) 283
La pasión turca (Gala) 281
Pasmore (Storey) 250
Pasquier Chronicle (Duhamel) 197
Pasquin (Fielding) 75
A Passage to India (Forster) 185
Passage to India (Whitman) 128
Passaggio in ombra (Di Lascia) 284
De Passievrucht (Loon) 293
Passing Through: Later Poems, New and Selected (Kunitz) 284
Passing Time (Butor) 227
Passion (Hercikova) 290
The Passion (Saneatsu) 188
The Passion According to G.H. (Lispector) 239
The Passion Artist (Hawkes) 258
The Passion Flower (Benavente y Martínez) 172
Passion Flowers (Howe) 118
The Passion Hymns (Petursson) 61
A Passion in Rome (Callaghan) 234
The Passion of Joseph D. (Chayefsky) 238
The Passionate Shepheard (Breton) 50
Die Passionfrucht (Piwitt) 280
The Passions of the Soul (Descartes) 58
Passover/A Guest Who Came from Afar (Kometani) 266
Passport to the War (Kunitz) 211
Past and Present (Carlyle) 113
Past Lucknow (Sharar) 173
Il pastor fido (Guarini) 43
Pastorals (Pope) 71
Pastors and Masters (Compton-Burnett) 186
Patas arriba (Galeano) 292

Paterson (Williams) 213
The Path to Rome (Belloc) 160
The Path to the Nest of Spiders (Calvino) 215
The Pathfinder (Cooper) 111
A Patriot for Me (Osborne) 240
The Patrioteer (Mann) 177
Patriotic Gore (Wilson) 235
Patronage (Edgeworth) 99
Paul Against Paul (Wispelaere) 247
Paul Clifford (Bulwer-Lytton) 106
Paul et Virginie (Bernardin de Saint-Pierre) 85
Paul Revere and the World He Lived In (Forbes) 210
"Paul Revere's Ride" (Longfellow) 123
The Paul Street Boy (Molnár) 165
Paulina (Jouve) 186
Pauling (Browning) 107
Paulownia Blossom (Kitahara) 172
"Paul's Short Case" (Cather) 163
Pauper Tyetko (Banmo) 222
Pavel (Merezhkovsky) 166
Pawels Briefe (Maron) 293
Les Paysans (Balzac) 114
Peace (Aristophanes) 3, 7
Peace (Garborg) 143
Peace After the War (Gironella) 242
Peace Breaks Out (Knowles) 259
The Peacock Feather (Kristensen) 182
Peacock's Feathers (Kruczkowski) 200
The Pearl (Steinbeck) 215
The Peasant Nga Ba (Maun) 214
Peasant Students (Garborg) 136
"The Peasants" (Chekhov) 92
Le Peau de chagrin (Balzac) 106
Pedar Paars (Holberg) 72
Peder Victorious (Rolvaag) 190
Pedestrian (Mukopadhyay) 207
Pedlar's Progress (Sheperd) 204
Pedro, the Artful Dodger (Cervantes) 52
Pedro e Paula (Macedo) 291
Peer Gynt (Ibsen) 94, 126
Peg Woffington (Reade) 118
The Pegnitz Junction (Gallant) 251
Pele-Mele (Dehkhoda) 230
Pelham; or, The Adventures of a Gentleman (Bulwer-Lytton) 105
Pelleas and Melissande (Maeterlinck) 143
Pendant la chaleur du jour (Pradier) 293
Penguin Island (France) 166
The Penitent (Singer) 263
The Pennsylvania Pilgrim and Other Poems (Whittier) 128
Penrod (Tarkington) 173
Pensées (Pascal) 48, 61
"Il Penseroso" (Milton) 48, 55
Il Pentamerone (Basile) 62
Penthesilia (Kleist) 97
The People, Yes (Sandburg) 201
The People and Uncollected Stories (Malamud) 272
People Dust (O'Casey) 207
People in Summer Night (Sillanpää) 199
People in Time (Bontempelli) 203
The People of Hemso (Strindberg) 93, 139
The People of Juvik (Dunn) 177
People of Paradox: An Inquiry Concerning the Origins of American Civilization (Kammen) 250

People of Puszta (Illyés) 202
The People of the Abyss (London) 161
People of the Cave (al-Hakim) 197
People of the City (Ekwensi) 224
The People's Choice (Agar) 198
The People's Council (Heiberg) 147
The People's Other World (Murray) 264
Pepe Carvalho (Vázquez Montalbán) 277
Pepita Jiménez (Valera) 130
Pequeñas infamias (Posada) 292
El pequeño heredero (Martín Garzo) 289
Le Père Goriot (Balzac) 91
The Perfumed Pillow (Koyo) 141
Peribanez and the Commander of Ocana (Vega) 32, 51
Pericles, Prince of Tyre (Shakespeare) 51
Pericles and Aspasia (Landor) 109
The Periodic Table (Levi) 254
Perola (Rasi) 285
Perou (Braudeau) 291
The Persecution and Assassination of Jean-Paul Marat, as Performed by the Inmates of the Asylum of Charenton Under the Direction of the Marquis de Sade (Weiss) 239
Persephone Remembers (Megged) 296
Persian Eclogues (Collins) 76
Persian Letters (Montesquieu) 73
Persians (Aeschylus) 2
A Person Not to Be Trusted (Otroshenko) 296
Persona Non Grata (Edwards) 251
Personae (Pound) 155, 167
Personal History (Graham) 290
A Personal History (Taylor) 263
The Personal Recollections of Joan of Arc (Twain) 146
Persuasion (Austen) 91, 100
Pertharite (Corneille) 48
Perversas familias (Assis Brasil) 280
Peter Camenzind (Hesse) 162
Peter Ibbetson (du Maurier) 142
Peter Pan; or, The Boy Who Wouldn't Grow Up (Barrie) 162
Peter Schlemihl (Chamisso) 99
Peter the Great (Tolstoy) 192
Peter the Great: His Life and World (Massie) 260
Petersburg (Bely) 173
Le Petit chose (Daudet) 126
Le Petit Testament (Villon) 27
La petite fille qui aimait trop les allumettes (Soucy) 291
Petrarch's Secret (Petrarch) 14
The Petrified Forest (Sherwood) 200
Peveril of the Peak (Scott) 103
Phaedo (Plato) 3
Phaedra (Tsvetaeva) 189
Phaedrus (Plato) 3
Phantom Lady (Calderón de la Barca) 54
The Phantom Lover (Kaiser) 190
The Phantom of the Opera (Leroux) 168
The Pharaoh (Memmi) 271
Pharsalia (Lucan) 5
Phèdre (Racine) 48, 63
Philadelphia, Here I Come (Friel) 238
Philadelphia Fire (Wideman) 273, 275
The Philadelphia Story (Barry) 205
Philaster (Beaumont, Fletcher) 51
Philebus (Plato) 3

Philoctetes (Sophocles) 3, 7
Philosopher or Dog? (Machado de Assis) 142
Philosophical Dictionary (Voltaire) 80
Philosophical Essays Concerning Human Understanding (Hume) 77
Philosophical Fragments (Kierkegaard) 91, 113
Philosophical Thoughts (Diderot) 77
Phineas Finn (Trollope) 126
Phineas Redux (Trollope) 130
Phocas the Gardener (Viélé-Griffin) 148
A Phoenix Too Frequent (Isherwood) 213
Phormio (Terence) 5
The Photographer in Winter (Szirtes) 267
The Physiology of Marriage (Balzac) 91
Piacevoli notti (Straparola) 38
The Piano Lesson (Wilson) 269, 273
The Piano Tuner (Cheng) 272
The Piazza (Melville) 120
The Piccolomini (Schiller) 88
Pickney's Treaty (Bemis) 189
Pickwick Papers (Dickens) 90, 109
Picnic (Inge) 222
The Picture of Dorian Gray (Wilde) 141
Pictures from Breughel (Williams) 235, 236
Pictures of Fidelman (Malamud) 246
Pictures of Travel (Heine) 104
Pieces (Creely) 246
Pieces of Light (Thorpe) 290
"Pied Beauty" (Hopkins) 132
"The Pied Piper of Hamelin" (Browning) 112
La piel del tambor (Pérez Reverte) 287
Pieles de leopardo (Mata) 281
Pierre; or, The Ambiguities (Melville) 117
Pierrot (Queneau) 210
Pig Earth (Berger) 258
Pigan i Arras (Claeson) 281
Pigeon Feathers (Updike) 235
Pigs in Heaven (Kingsolver) 279
Pilgrim at Tinker Creek (Dillard) 252
The Pilgrim at Tinker Creek (Dillard) 253
The Pilgrim Kamanita (Gjellerup) 164
Pilgrimage (Richardson) 174, 243
Pilgrimage and Wander (Heidenstam) 139
The Pilgrimage of the Aggrieved (Vicente) 37
The Pilgrim's Progress (Lewis) 197
The Pilgrim's Progress, from This World to What Which Is to Come (Bunyan) 63
The Pilgrim's Rules of Etiquette (Modarressi) 272
The Pillar of Fire (Gumilyov) 181
The Pillar of Salt (Memmi) 223
Pillars of Hercules: A Grand Tour of the Mediterranean (Theroux) 284
Pillars of Society (Franko) 145
Pillars of Society (Ibsen) 94, 131
The Pilot (Cooper) 103
Pilot Stars (Ivanov) 161
Pinch Runner's Record (Oe) 230
Pincher Martin (Golding) 227
Le Ping-Pong (Adamov) 255
Pinocchio: The Story of a Puppet (Collodi) 135

Pinto (Lemercier) 133
The Pioneers (Prichard) 174
The Pioneers; or, The Sources of the Susquehanna Frontier (Cooper) 103
Pippa Passes (Browning) 112
Pippi Longstocking (Lindgren) 213
The Pirate (Scott) 93
The Pirates of Penzance (Gilbert) 132
The Pisan Cantos (Pound) 155, 216
The Pistol (Jones) 229
"The Pit and the Pendulum" (Poe) 91, 113
Pity for Women (Montherlant) 202
Pizarro (Sheridan) 88
A Place to Come To (Warren) 256
The Plague (Camus) 155, 215
The Plain Dealer (Wycherley) 63
The Plain Speaker (Hazlitt) 104
Plain Themes (Neruda) 135
Plains of Castile (Machado) 171
Plains Song (Morris) 260
Plainsong (Haruf) 293
Planet of the Apes (Boulle) 237
Plankton (Voskuil) 290
Plans for Departure (Sahgal) 266
Plantation Boy (Rego) 196
The Plants (Sternheim) 170
Plastik (Herder) 83
Platero and I (Jiménez) 177
Play by Play (Goldemberg) 266
Play It As It Lays (Didion) 247
Play of Fame (Vicente) 32, 35
Play of St. Nicholas (Bodel) 23
The Playboy of the Western World (Synge) 165
Player Piano (Vonnegut) 221
Playing with Love (Schnitzler) 146
The Playmaker (Keneally) 269
Plays for Bleecker Street (Wilder) 235
Plays of Marionettes (Bergman) 177
Plaza Suite (Simon) 244
Pleasure Reconciled to Virtue (Jonson) 52
Pleasured (Hensher) 290
The Plebians Rehearse the Uprising (Grass) 242
Pledged (Drachmann) 141
Plenilunio (Muñoz Molina) 289
The Plough and the Stars (O'Casey) 188
Ployeucte (Corneille) 48
Pluck the Bird and Destroy the Offspring (Oe) 230
Plum and Jaggers (Shreve) 295
Plumb (Green) 257
The Plumed Serpent (Lawrence) 188
Pnin (Nabokov) 155, 228
A poeira levada pelo vento (Magalhaes) 283
A Poem of One Hundred Links Composed by Three Poets at Minase (Sogi) 28
Poem of the Cante Jondo (García Lorca) 155
Poemas híbridos (Atxaga) 273
Poèmes de Provence (Aicard) 130
Poèmes saturnines (Verlaine) 126
Poems (Arnold) 118
Poems (Bradstreet) 63
Poems (Brontë, Brontë, and Brontë) 114
Poems (Browning) 113
Poems (Bryant) 102
Poems (Bull) 167
Poems (Chatterton) 83
Poems (Cowper) 84

Poems (Cruz) 65
Poems (Davith) 193
Poems (de la Mare) 164
Poems (Dickinson) 141
Poems (Droste-Hülshoff) 110
Poems (Dugan) 235
Poems (Eliot) 152, 178, 180
Poems (Freneau) 85
Poems (Gómez de Avellaneda) 112
Poems (Graves, ed.) 177
Poems (Heidenstam) 145
Poems (Holmes) 109
Poems (Jennings) 222
Poems (Key) 120
Poems (Kinsella) 227
Poems (Lowell) 113
Poems (Meredith) 117
Poems (Milton) 48
Poems (Moore) 181
Poems (Oehlenschläger) 96
Poems (Poe) 106
Poems (Rossetti) 127
Poems (Rydberg) 135
Poems (Storm) 117
Poems (Tennyson) 93
Poems (Vigny) 103
Poems (Whittier) 116
Poems (Zollinger) 197
Poems, 1901–43 (Jensen) 210
Poems, 1913 (Brennan) 173
Poems, 1924–1933 (MacLeish) 197
Poems, 1940–1953 (Shapiro) 222
Poems, Chiefly in the Scottish Dialect (Burns) 68, 85
Poems, Chiefly Lyrical (Tennyson) 93, 106
Poems, Chiefly of Early and Late Years (Wordsworth) 92, 112
Poems, First Cycle (Wergeland) 106
Poems: North and South 226
Poems: North and South—A Cold Spring (Bishop) 225
Poems and Antipoems (Para) 224
Poems and Ballads (Swinburne) 125, 132
Poems and Songs (Bjørnson) 127
Poems from a Voyage Across the Sound (Haavikko) 251
Poems from Prison (Soyinka) 246
Poems in Prose (Baudelaire) 127
Poems in Two Volumes (Wordsworth) 97
Poems of a Jew (Shapiro) 229
Poems of Consummation (Aleixandre) 245
Poems of Dedication (Spender) 215
Poems of Haikai Tsuji (Masao) 287
Poems of Stanley Kunitz (Kunitz) 258
Poems on Slavery (Longfellow) 112
Poesie (Quasimodo) 204
Poet in New York (García Lorca) 155
Poetens liv (Mattson) 294
Poetic Edda 13
Poetic Meditations (Lamartine) 102
Poetical Blossoms (Cowley) 55
Poetical Sketches by Mr. W.B. (Blake) 68, 84
Poetical Works (Moore) 95
Poetical Works (Senghor) 274
Poetry (Mickiewicz) 103
The Poetry Craze (Piron) 76
Poetry for Supper (Thomas) 229
Poetry in Prose and Verse (Jiménez) 196
A Poet's Notebook (Sitwell) 210
Point Counter Point (Huxley) 190

Point of No Return (Marquand) 217
The Poison Tree (Chatterjee) 129
Poisson d'or (Le Clezio) 288
The Polar Express (Van Allsburg) 267
Pole Vault (Mihajlovski) 284
Politian, a Tragedy (Poe) 108
The Political Tinker (Holberg) 73
Polly (Gay) 74
Polonius (FitzGerald) 117
"Poltava" (Pushkin) 90, 106
Polyeucte (Corneille) 56
The Pond (Morris) 251
The Ponder Heart (Welty) 223
Po-on (Jose) 264
The Poor (Mann) 176
Poor Flowers (Desbordes-Valmore) 111
Poor Folk (Dostoyevsky) 90, 115
The Poor Gentleman (Conscience) 117
The Poor of New York (Boucicault) 120
Poor Richard's Almanack (Franklin) 75
The Poorhouse Fair (Updike) 231
Pope and Emperor in the Village (Federer) 187
Poplene pa St. Hanshaugen (Vik) 276
Poppa John (Woiwode) 260
Poppy and Memory (Celan) 221
Popular Tales (Edgeworth) 96
Por el sendero de los ángeles caídos (Hoyos) 275
Porgy (Heyward) 186
Port Royal (Montherlant) 224
Porte disparu (Arrabal) 296
Portland Valley (Flogstad) 256
Portnoy's Complaint (Roth) 246
Portrait in Brownstone (Auchincloss) 235
Portrait in Sepia (Allende) 296
The Portrait of a Lady (James) 91, 134
Portrait of a Man Unknown (Sarraute) 216
Portrait of a Paladin (Huidobro) 192
Portrait of a Planet (Durrenmatt) 248
Portrait of the Artist as a Young Dog (Thomas) 207
A Portrait of the Artist as a Young Man (Joyce) 152, 175
Port-Royal (Saint-Beuve) 111
Posillipo (Rasy) 289
The Possessed (Dostoyevsky) 90, 129
Possessing the Secret of Joy (Walker) 277
Possession (Bromfield) 186
Possession (Byatt) 273
Post Mortem (Kaniuk) 278
Postcards (Proulx) 279
The Posthumous Papers of the Pickwick Club (Dickens) 90, 109
The Postman Always Rings Twice (Cain) 198
Poverty Is No Disgrace (Ostrovsky) 118
The Power and the Glory (Greene) 154, 207
The Power Broker: Robert Moses and the Fall of New York (Caro) 253
The Power of Darkness (Tolstoy) 90
"The Power of Song" (Schiller) 68
Powers of Congress (Fulton) 273
The Prairie (Cooper) 105
The Praise of Folly (Erasmus) 32, 35
Praise to the End! (Roethke) 220
Praisesong for the Widow (Marshall) 262

Prancing Novelist (Brophy) 251

A Prayer for Owen Meany (Irving) 272

Precaution (Cooper) 102

Precious Bane (Webb) 185

Precious Thing (Kenway) 295

The Precipice (Goncharov) 127

Prelandra (Lewis) 210

The Prelude, or, Growth of a Poet's Mind (Wordsworth) 88, 116

Prelude (Mansfield) 177

The Prelude (Wordsworth) 92

"The Premature Burial" (Poe) 91, 113

A Premeditated Murder (Selenic) 283

Premier (Shahnon) 246

Present at the Creation: My Years in the State Department (Acheson) 247

The President (Asturias) 214

The Pretenders (Ibsen) 94, 124

The Price (Miller) 244

The Price of Stone and Earlier Poems (Murphy) 266

The Price of Thebes (Lasker-Schuler) 173

Pricksongs and Descants (Coover) 246

Pride and Prejudice (Austen) 91, 99

The Priest of Kirchfield (Anzengruber) 127

A Priest to the Temple (Herbert) 58

The Prime Minister (Trollope) 131

The Prime of Miss Jean Brodie (Spark) 234

Primevères (Hasselt) 108

The Prince (Machiavelli) 35

The Prince and the Pauper (Twain) 92, 134

Prince Hohensteil-Schwangau (Browning) 128

The Prince of Homburg (Kleist) 98

A Prince of Our Disorder: The Life of T. E. Lawrence (Mack) 255

The Prince of Tides (Conroy) 269

The Prince with Donkey Ears (Regio) 209

The Prince's Progress (Rossetti) 125

The Princess, a Medley (Tennyson) 115

The Princess Cassmassima (James) 91, 137

Princess Nur al-Nin (al-Hadi) 192

The Princess of Montpensier (La Fayette) 60

La Princesse de Clèves (La Fayette) 63

Principia Mathematica (Russell, Whitehead) 168

Prins (Michaels) 288

The Prinzhorn Collection (Coles) 261

Prioritaire (Hermann) 290

"The Prisoner of Chillon" (Byron) 93, 100

A Prisoner of Grace (Cary) 221

The Prisoner of Second Avenue (Simon) 248

The Prisoner of the Caucasus (Pushkin) 90, 102

The Prisoner of Urga (Krasznahorkai) 280

The Prisoner of Zenda (Hope) 144

Private Jokinen's Marriage Leave (Meri) 240

Private Lives (Coward) 193

A Private Mythology (Sarton) 241

The Private Papers of Henry Ryecroft (Gissing) 161

Private Renaissance (Bellonci) 272

The Prize: The Epic Quest for Oil (Yergin) 277

The Problem of Pain (Lewis) 207

The Problem of Slavery in Western Culture (Davis) 242

De procedure (Mulisch) 293

The Procession (Gibran) 178

The Prodigy (Hesse) 163

Profane Hymns and Other Poems (Darío) 146

The Professor (Brontë) 120

The Professor of Desire (Roth) 256

The Professor's House (Cather) 186

Profiles in Courage (Kennedy) 228

The Profligate (Pinero) 140

De profundis valsa lenta (Cardoso Pires) 289

Progetto Burlamacchi (Duranti) 282

The Progress of Love (Munro) 267

The Progresse of the Soul: The Second Anniversary (Donne) 51

Prologue to Life (Sikelianós) 176

Prometheus and Epimetheus (Spitteler) 134

Prometheus Unbound (Shelley) 93, 102

Promise in Summer (Chuya) 296

The Promised Land (Antin) 171

The Promised Land (Pontoppidan) 142

The Promised Land (Rivera) 181

The Promised Land (Ungaretti) 219

Promises: Poems, 1954–1956 (Warren) 228, 229

The Promontory (Kenji) 255

The Proof (Winters) 193

Propalladia (Torres Naharro) 35

A Proper Marriage (Lessing) 223

Property and Value (Hood) 273

The Prophecy of Dante (Byron) 93

The Prophet (Gibran) 184

Prophets of Regulation (McCraw) 265

The Proposal (Chekhov) 92

The Proprietor of the Sun Inn (Kurz) 119

Prose Edda 13

Prosopeya (Pinto) 50

The Prostitute (Surangkhanang) 203

Protagoras (Plato) 3

Proud Are the Dead (Oe) 230

Proverbs (Erasmus) 32, 34

Providence (Popovski) 284

Provincial Letters (Pascal) 48, 59

Das Provisorium (Hilbig) 296

La prueba del laberinto (Sánchez Drago) 279

Prufrock and Other Observations (Eliot) 176

Pryasliny: A Saga of Peasant Life (Abramov) 253

The Psalms of Struggle and Liberation (Cardenal) 239

Psyche: Inventions of the Other (Derrida) 269

The Psychological Outlook on Life (Jaspers) 178

The Public Burning (Coover) 256

The Public Rose (Éluard) 199

Public Speech: Poems (MacLeish) 201

Publieke werken (Rosenboom) 295

Pulchérie (Corneille) 48, 62

The Pumpkin Eater (Martin) 235

The Punishments (Hugo) 118

Pupils of the Dean (Dinis) 126

The Pure and the Impure (Colette) 208

Pure Elegies (Jiménez) 166

The Pure Element of Time (Be'er) 293

Puritan Village: The Formation of a New England Town (Powell) 238

"The Purloined Letter" (Poe) 114

The Purple Plain (Bates) 213

The Pursuit of Love (Mitford) 212

The Puttermesser Papers (Ozick) 288

Pygmalion (Shaw) 153, 172

Pylon (Faulkner) 200

The Pyramid (Golding) 243

The Pyre (Gumilyov) 177

Q

"Q.E.D." (Stein) 161

"The Quaker Graveyard in Nantucket" (Lowell) 213

Quando Dio usci chiesa: Vita e fede in un borgio istriano del cinquecento (Tomizza) 269

Quarantine (Crace) 288

The Quare Fellow (Behan) 224

Quarrels of Honor (Tamayo y Baus) 123

Quarry of the Soul (Andrade) 230

Les quartières d'hiver (Pancrazi) 274

Les Quatre incarnations du Christ (Hasselt) 123

O Que Agora Me Inquieta (Coutinho) 266

The Queen and the Rebels (Betti) 220

Queen Jane (Mistral) 141

Queen Mab (Shelley) 93, 99

Queen Mary (Tennyson) 130

Queen of Scotland (Della Valle) 43

"The Queen of Spades" (Pushkin) 90, 108

The Queen of the Grecian Jails (Lins) 230

Queen Victoria (Strachey) 181

The Queenes Arcadia (Daniel) 50

The Queen's Defeat (Chedid) 264

The Queen's Diadem (Almqvist) 108

Quentin Durward (Scott) 93, 103

Querido primer novio (Valdés) 294

Querrelle of Brest (Genet) 215

The Quest for Corvo (Rolfe) 199

The Quest for Historical Jesus (Schweitzer) 164

A Question of Upbringing (Powell) 220

Quia Pauper Amavi (Pound) 155

Quien como Dios (González) 292

Quien Metanarrative (Canique) 289

The Quiet American (Greene) 154, 225

Quiet Fires (Mihalic) 265

A quintas das virtudes (Caludio) 276

Quinx; or, The Ripper's Tale (Durrell) 266

Quo Vadis? (Sienkiewicz) 145

Quoat-Quoat (Audiberti) 214

R

R. E. Lee (Freeman) 200

Raabe Baikal (Strittmatter) 274

Rabbi Ben Ezra (Browning) 124

Rabbit, Run (Updike) 232

Rabbit at Rest (Updike) 273, 275

Rabbit Is Rich (Updike) 260

The Rabid Toy (Arlt) 188

Radetzky March (Roth) 195

The Radiance of the King (Laye) 224

The Radiant Way (Drabble) 269

Radiation (Sachiko) 284

The Radicalism of the American Revolution (Wood) 279

A Rage to Live (O'Hara) 217

Ragged Dick (Alger) 126

Raghuvamsa (Kālidāsa) 14–15

Ragtime (Doctorow) 253

The Railway (Aho) 136

The Railway Station Man (Johnston) 264

Rain Afterwards Rain? (Keiko) 296

The Rain Ascends (Kogawa) 284

Rain at Daybreak (Johnson) 198

The Rain Bird (Lidman) 230

The Rainbow (Lawrence) 174

Rainbow (Mao) 277

Rainbow Promontory (Tsuji) 282

Rain-Charm for the Duchy (Hughes) 278

Raise High the Roof Beam, Carpenters/Seymour: An Introduction (Salinger) 237

A Raisin in the Sun (Hansberry) 231

The Raj Quartet (Scott) 241, 244

Ralf Krage (Ewald) 81

Ralph Roister Doister (Udall) 40

Ramacaritmanas (Tulsīdās) 41

Rameau's Nephew (Diderot) 80

Ramona (Jackson) 136

Random Harvest (Hilton) 208

"The Ransom of Red Chief" (Henry) 168

The Rape of Lucrece (Shakespeare) 31, 44

The Rape of Tamar (Jacobson) 247

The Rape of the Bucket (Tassoni) 53

The Rape of the Lock (Pope) 69

"Rappaccini's Daughter" (Hawthorne) 113

Rapunzel (Zelinsky) 290

Raquel (García de la Huerta) 83

Rarahu (Loti) 133

Rare and Endangered Species (Bausch) 282

Lo raro es vivir (Martín Gaite) 287

Rasero (Robelledo) 283

"Rashomon" (Akutagawa) 174

Rasselas, Prince of Abyssinia (Johnson) 79

The Rat (Grass) 268

Rates of Exchange (Bradbury) 263

Ratner's Star (DeLillo) 254

The Raven (James) 193

"The Raven" (Poe) 91

The Raven and Other Poems (Poe) 114

The Ravishing of Lol V. Stein (Duras) 239

Ravnen (Goldsmith) 125

The Raw and the Cooked (Lévi-Strauss) 239

Raw Material (Sillitoe) 250

Rays and Sunrise (Santos) 164

The Razor's Edge (Maugham) 211

The Reader (Schlink) 288

Reader's Block (Markson) 286

Reading in the Dark (Deane) 286

The Real (Tamayo y Baus) 123

The Real Life of Alejandro Mayta (Vargas Llosa) 266

The Real Life of Sebastian Knight (Nabokov) 155, 208

Real sitio (Sampedro) 281

The Realist (Broch) 196

Reality and Desire (Cernuda) 239

Reasons of State (Carpentier) 253

The Reawakening (Levi) 237

Rebecca (du Maurier) 204

Rebecca and Rowenna: A Romance Upon Romance (Thackeray) 116

The Rebel (Camus) 155, 220
The Rebel Angel (Davies) 260
The Rebel Generation (Ammers-
   Küller) 186
Rebellion in the Backlands (Cunha)
   160
The Rebellion of the Hanged (Traven)
   202
Rebus (Rosei) 274
A Recipe for Bees (Dargatz) 291
The Recognition (Gaddis) 225
Recruit (Král') 114
The Recruiting Officer (Farquhar) 70
The Rector of Justin (Auchincloss) 238
"Red, Red Rose" (Burns) 68
The Red, White and Blue (Dunne) 269
The Red and the Black (Stendhal) 106
The Red Badge of Courage (Crane)
   145
Red Candle (Wen) 183
Red Cotton Night-Cap Country
   (Browning) 129
A Red Moon in Her Face (Hiroshi)
   215
The Red Pony (Steinbeck) 203
The Red Room (Strindberg) 92, 133
The Red Room Tavern (Ye) 281
Red Roses for Me (O'Casey) 209
The Red Rover (Cooper) 105
Red Sorghum (Mo) 273
The Red Wheel (Solzhenitsyn) 154,
   249, 280
Redburn (Melville) 116
Redgauntlet (Scott) 93, 103
Rediscovery and Other Poems
   (Awoonor) 238
The Redskins (Cooper) 114
The Redundancy of Courage (Mo) 276
Reef (Gunasekara) 282
Reflections in a Golden Eye (Mc-
   Cullers) 208
Reflections of a Nonpolitical Man
   (Mann) 177
Reflections on the Revolution in France
   (Burke) 85
Le regard de Vincent (Philippe) 269
The Regentess (Alas) 136
A Regicide (Robbe-Grillet) 257
Reginald (Saki) 162
Reginald in Russia (Saki) 168
Regrets (Bellay) 39
La reina de las nieves (Martín Gaite)
   283
Reinke de Vos (Alkmaar) 29
The Reivers (Faulkner) 235, 236
Rejse for en fremmed (Aidt) 295
Rejsen med Emma (Svendsen) 286
Relationships (Jennings) 250
Religio Laici, or a Layman's Faith
   (Dryden) 64
Religio Medici (Browne) 57
Le Reliquaire (Coppée) 126
Remains of Elmet (Hughes) 258
The Remains of the Day (Ishiguro)
   271, 272
Remedia amoris (Ovid) 4
Remembering Babylon (Malouf) 280,
   286
Remembrance of Things Past (Proust)
   171, 178, 180, 181, 184, 186, 190
Remembrance Rock (Sandburg) 216
Remise de peine (Modiano) 271
Renascence and Other Poems (Millay)
   176
Rendevous with Rama (Clarke) 251
Le Rendez-vous (Robbe-Grillet) 258

René (Chateaubriand) 97
Renée Mauperin (Goncourt and
   Goncourt) 124
Rent (Larson) 286
Repair (Williams) 295
Repetition (Kierkegaard) 91
Republic (Plato) 3
The Republic of Babin (Lechon) 181
The Republic of Wine (Mo) 295
The Republican Era, 1869–1901
   (White) 230
Reputable Men (Tamayo y Baus) 128
Request Concert (Kroetz) 250
Requiem (Kyoko) 274
Requiem for a Nun (Faulkner) 220
Requiem for a Spanish Peasant
   (Sender) 223
Res amissa (Caproni) 276
Rescue (Milosz) 213
Rescue the Dead (Ignatov) 244
Residence on Earth (Neruda) 155, 198
The Residual Years: Poems 1934–1948
   (Everson) 244
The Residuary Legatee (Regnard) 71
Resignation (Young) 80
La resistencia (Sábato) 296
"Resolution and Independence"
   (Wordsworth) 96
Responsibilities: Poems and a Play
   (Yeats) 152, 173
"Responsibility: The Pilots Who De-
   stroyed Germany, Spring 1945"
   (Spender) 217
Restless Early Summer (Gömöri) 264
Restoration (Bond) 260
Restoring Former Loves (Kenaz) 291
Resurrection (Tolstoy) 90, 149
Retable, Reverie (Chawaf) 252
The Retrieval System (Kumin) 257
Return, Pinus Succinifera (Kaplinski)
   264
Return from India (Yehoshua) 282
Return from the Stars (Lem) 234
The Return of Philip Latinowicz
   (Krleza) 196
The Return of Sherlock Holmes (Doyle)
   163
The Return of the King (Tolkien) 227
The Return of the Native (Hardy) 132
The Return of the Spirit (al-Hakim)
   197
Return to Ithaca (Johnson) 214
Return to Region (Benet) 243
The Returnee (Maramzin) 294
Reveille in Washington (Leech) 209
The Revenge, a Tragedy (Young) 73
Revenge for Love (Lewis) 203
The Revenge of the Bussy D'Amboise
   (Chapman) 52
Les reveries de la femme sauvage
   (Cixous) 296
Revolt in Aspromonte (Alvaro) 193
The Revolt of the Masses (Ortega y
   Gasset) 192
Revolution of the Sun (Bontempelli)
   208
Rhadamistus and Zenobia (Crébillon)
   71
A Rhetoric of Motives (Burke) 219
Rhinoceros (Ionesco) 231
Rhymes (Bécquer) 128
Rhymes to Be Traded for Bread (Lind-
   say) 171
The Rhythm of Violence (Nkosi) 238
Rhythms of My Heart (Balance) 207
Rice (Su) 275

Riceyman Steps (Bennett) 184
Richard Carvel (Churchill) 149
Richard Cory (Robinson) 147
Richard Hardis; or, The Avenger of
   Blood (Simms) 110
Richard II (Shakespeare) 31, 44
Richard III (Shakespeare) 31, 44
Richard Savage (Gutzkow) 111
Richelieu; or, The Conspiracy (Bulwer-
   Lytton) 110
Rickshaw Boy (Lao) 216
The Ride Across Lake Constance
   (Handke) 249
The Ride of Eldis (Viélé-Griffin) 144
The Rider on the White Horse (Storm)
   139
Rider (Rudman) 282
The Riders (Winton) 284
Riders in the Chariot (White) 234
Riders of the Purple Sage (Grey) 171
Riders to the Sea (Synge) 161
Rienzi; or, The Last of the Tribunes
   (Bulwer-Lytton) 108
Rienzi the Tribune (Acuña) 131
The Right of the Strongest (Buysse) 144
Right You Are—If You Think You Are
   (Pirandello) 154, 176
The Rights of Desire (Brink) 296
The Rights of Man (Paine) 86
Rights of Passage (Brathwaite) 243
Det rigtige (Gronfeldt) 295
Rig-Veda 1
Rimas (Camões) 32
Rime (Carducci) 120
"The Rime of the Ancient Mariner"
   (Coleridge) 88
Il Rinaldo (Tasso) 40
The Ring and the Book (Browning)
   126
Ring of Youth (Hiroshi) 218
Rings (Neruda) 155
El río del tiempo (Vallejo) 294
The Ripening Seed (Colette) 184
The Ripple from the Storm (Lessing)
   229, 231
Rise, Magyar (Petófi) 115
The Rise and Fall of the City of Ma-
   hoganny (Brecht) 153, 193
The Rise and Fall of the Third Reich
   (Shirer) 232
The Rise of Silas Lapham (Howells)
   137
The Rise of the Dutch Republic (Mot-
   ley) 119
The Rise of the Winds (Ibarbourou)
   194
The Rise of Theodore Roosevelt (Mor-
   ris) 259
Rise Up, O Young Men of the New Age
   (Oe) 263
The Rising Sun (Toland) 248
Rites of Passage (Golding) 259
Rituals (Nooteboom) 259
The Rival Ladies (Dryden) 60
The Rivals (Sheridan) 82
Riven Rock (Boyle) 290
"The River Duddon" (Wordsworth)
   92
The River (Godden) 213
The River (Yermakov) 294
River of Fire (Haidar) 231
The River of Life (Kuprin) 164
A River Town (Keneally) 284
Rivers Among Rocks (Gustafson) 232
The Rivers Run Toward the Sea (Lund-
   kvist) 199

The Riverside Willas Murder (Amis)
   251
The Road (Martinson) 217
The Road (Soyinka) 240
The Road Back (Andrade) 243
The Road Home (Harrison) 290
"The Road Not Taken" (Frost) 174
The Road Sign at the End of the Street
   (Abe) 217
The Road to Calvary (Tolstoy) 181, 214
Road to Ghana (Hutchinson) 232
The Road to Nowhere (Grin) 193
The Road to Reunion, 1856–1900
   (Buck) 204
The Road to the Open (Schnitzler) 166
Road to the World's End (Hoel) 198
The Road to Wigan Pier (Orwell) 203
The Road We Have Walked (Adiga)
   221
The Roads to Freedom (Sartre) 212
Roadwalker (Grau) 282
Roan Stallion, Tamar and Other Poems
   (Jeffers) 186
The Roaring Girl (Hollingshed) 284
Rob Roy (Scott) 93, 100
The Robber Bride (Atwood) 280
The Robber Bridegroom (Welty) 209
The Robber Brothers (Pushkin) 90,
   102
The Robbers (Schiller) 67, 84
Robert Frost: The Years of Triumph,
   1915–1938 (Thompson) 248
Robert Guiskard (Kleist) 97
Robert und Guiscard (Eichendorff)
   119
The Rock of Rushan (Zarian) 193
Rockaby (Beckett) 154
The Rocky Road (Quieroz) 203
Roderick, The Last of the Goths
   (Southey) 99
Roderick Hudson (James) 91, 130
Rodogune (Corneille) 48, 57
"Roger Malvin's Burial" (Hawthorne)
   107
Roger's Version (Updike) 267
Le roi du bois (Michon) 286
Rokeby (Scott) 93, 99
Roland Barthes (Barthes) 254
Roll of Thunder, Hear My Cry (Taylor)
   255
The Roman (Waltari) 239
The Roman Actor (Massinger) 54
Le Roman comique (Scarron) 58
Roman Elegies (Goethe) 67, 87
Roman Sonnets (Ivanov) 188
The Romance of a Poor Young Man
   (Feuillet) 120
The Romance of Leonardo da Vinci
   (Merezhkovsky) 159
The Romantic (Broch) 195
The Romantic Oedipus (Platen) 106
Romantic Sommets (Correia) 276
The Romany (Borrow) 120
Romanzero (Heine) 93, 117
Romeo and Juliet (Shakespeare) 31, 44
Romola (Eliot) 123
A Room (Shimoni) 293
The Room and Other Poems (Day-
   Lewis) 240
Room at the Top (Braine) 228
A Room of One's Own (Woolf) 192
A Room with a View (Forster) 166
Roosevelt, the Soldier of Freedom
   (Burns) 248
Roosevelt and Hopkins (Sherwood)
   217

Rootabaga Stories (Sandburg) 182
Roots (Brathwaite) 267
Roots (Cosic) 224
Roots: The Saga of an American Family (Haley) 254
Rosalynde (Lodge) 43
Rosary (Akhmatova) 173
The Rose Altar (Södergran) 179
The Rose Garden (Popovic) 285
The Rose Garden (Sa'dī) 24
The Rose Tattoo (Williams) 220
Rosencrantz and Guildenstern Are Dead (Stoppard) 241
Roses Are Difficult Here (Mitchell) 273
Rosmersholm (Ibsen) 94, 138
The Rosy Crucifixion: Nexus (Miller) 232
Der Rote Ritter (Muschg) 280
Das rote Schiff (Mand) 282
Rotten Wood (Berent) 161
Rough and Ride (Melo Neto) 266
Rough Crossing (Stoppard) 266
The Rough Field (Montague) 250
Roughing It (Twain) 92, 128
Rousseau and Revolution (Durant) 244
The Rout (Fadeyev) 189
The Rover, or the Banished Cavaliers (Behn) 63
Roxana (Alabaster) 55
Roxana; or, the Unfortunate Mistress (Defoe) 73
The Royal Domain (Viélé-Griffin) 184
The Royal Game (Zweig) 209
The Royal Hunt of the Sun (Shaffer) 238
The Royal Place (Corneille) 48
Rubaiyat of Omar Khayyam (Fitz-Gerald) 121
Rudin (Turgenev) 119
Ruin (Fenoglio) 224
La ruina del cielo (Díez) 297
Ruined Mountains (Nadi) 285
Rule a Wife and Have a Wife (Fletcher) 53
Rules of Chaos; or, Why Tomorrow Doesn't Work (Vizinczey) 246
The Rules of Engagement (Bush) 295
Rules of the Game (Leiris) 255
Rum Punch (Leonard) 277
Rummet innanfor (Arvidsson) 294
Rummies (Benchley) 272
El rumor del astracán (Bibliowicz) 277
The Runaway Soul (Brodkey) 276
R.U.R. (Čapek) 179
Rural Sports (Gay) 72
Rushes (Rechy) 258
Ruslan and Ludmila (Pushkin) 90, 102
The Russia House (Le Carré) 272
Russia Leaves the War: Soviet-American Relations, 1917–1920 (Kennan) 228
A Russian Beauty (Yerofeyev) 274
Russian Epic (Kheraskov) 82
A Russian Schoolboy (Aksakov) 119
Russian Thinkers (Berlin) 257
Russian Woman (Nekrasov) 128
Ruth (Gaskell) 118
Ruy Blas (Hugo) 110
Rymdvraktaren (Nilson) 285

S

Sa femme (Bernheim) 280
Sabbaths (Berry) 269
Sabbath's Theater (Roth) 284

Sabine (Lacretelle) 196
Die Sache mit Randow (Schelsinger) 286
The Sacred and Profane Love Machine (Murdoch) 252
Sacred Hunger (Unsworth) 277, 278
The Sacred Wood (Eliot) 152, 180
Sacrifice (Tagore) 153, 159
Le Sacrifice imperial (Jacob) 192
The Sacrifice of Abraham (Kornáros) 55
"The Sad Fortune of the Rev. Amos Barton" (Eliot) 120
Sad People (Zorian) 177
The Saddest Summer of Samuel S. (Donleavy) 241
Sadler's Birthday (Tremain) 255
The Sadness of the Kite (Mallet-Joris) 271
Saentieri sotto la neve (Stern) 291
The Saga of the Folkings (Strindberg) 92, 149
Sagarana (Guimares Rosa) 214
"Sailing to Byzantium" (Yeats) 152, 189
The Saint (Meyer) 133
Saint Francis of Assisi (Federer) 166
Saint George and the Dragon (Hodges) 265
Saint Joan (Shaw) 153, 184
Saint Manuel the Good Martyr (Unamuno) 198
Saint Matoral (Jacob) 167
The Saints Everlasting Rest (Baxter) 58
The Saint's Tragedy (Kingsley) 115
Salaman u Absal (Jāmī) 28
Salame ved reisens slutt (Hansen) 276
Salammbô (Flaubert) 92, 123
Salka Valka (Laxness) 195
Sally Bowles (Isherwood) 203
Salmagundi, or The Whim-Whams and Opinions of Launcelot Langstaff, Esq., and Others (Irving) 97
Salome (Wilde) 143
Salome and Other Poems (Castro) 146
Salt of the Earth (Wittli) 202
Salterton Trilogy (Davies) 220
Sam, Bangs and Moonshine (Ness) 242
The Same Sea (Oz) 291
Sammanhang (Trotzig) 287
Samson Agonistes (Milton) 48, 62
Samuel (Raffi) 137
Samuel Johnson (Bate) 256, 257
Samuel Johnson (Wain) 252
The Samurai (Endo) 259
San Camilo (Cela) 246
Sancho Saldana (Espronceda y Delgado) 108
Sanctuary (Faulkner) 194
The Sand for the Urns (Celan) 216
The Sandbox (Albee) 231
The Sandcastle (Murdoch) 228
The Sandglass (Gunasekara) 291
Sanditon (Austen) 100
Sandra Belloni (Meredith) 124
Sandro of Chegem (Iskander) 257
Sangue na floresta (Olinto) 280
Sanine (Artsybasheff) 165
Santa Cruz (Frisch) 215
"Santa Filomena" (Longfellow) 120
Santo oficio de la memoria (Giardinelli) 281
São Bernardo (Ramos) 199
Sapphira and the Slave Girl (Cather) 207

Sappho (Daudet) 136
Sappho (Grillparzer) 101
Lo sapsimo de Palermo (Consolo) 293
Sarāh (al-Aqqad) 204
Sarah, Plain and Tall (MacLachlan) 267
Sarah, Sarah (Matalon) 296
Sardanapalus (Byron) 93, 102
Sarmistha (Datta) 120
Sartor Resartus (Carlyle) 107
Sartosis (Faulkner) 192
Satan in Goray (Singer) 201
The Satanic Verses (Rushdie) 271
Satanstoe (Cooper) 114
The Satin Slipper (Claudel) 192, 193
Satires (Horace) 4
Satires (Juvenal) 4
Satomi and the Eight Dogs (Bakin) 99
Satura (Montale) 236
Saturday Night (Benavente y Martínez) 161
Saturday Night and Sunday Morning (Sillitoe) 229
Saturday Sun (Moretti) 165
Savage Moon (Paz) 198
Saville (Storey) 254, 255
Savonarola (Lenau) 110
Sayahatnameye Hateme Tai (Kashefi) 28
Scandal (Endo) 268
Scar Tissue (Ignatieff) 280
The Scarlet City (Haasse) 221
The Scarlet Letter (Hawthorne) 116
The Scarlet Pimpernel (Orczy) 163
The Scarlet Poem (Lechon) 180
Scarlet Sister Mary (Peterkin) 191
The Scarlet Tree (Sitwell) 213
A Scattering of Salts (Merrill) 284
Scenes from Private Life (Balzac) 91, 106
Scenes of Bohemian Life (Murger) 115
The Scenic Route (Adcock) 252
Scent of Eucalyptus (Quasimodo) 198
Schiller's Homeland Years (Kurz) 113
Schimpf und Ernst (Pauli) 36
Schindler's Ark (Keneally) 261
The Schism of England (Calderón de la Barca) 48
Schlageter (Johst) 197
Das Schlaraffenland (Sachs) 37
"The Scholar-Gipsy" (Arnold) 118
The School for Husbands (Molière) 60
School for Mothers (Marivaux) 73
The School for Scandal (Sheridan) 83
The School for Wives (Molière) 47–48, 60
Schultz (Donleavy) 258
Scientists Against Time (Baxter) 214
Scoop (Waugh) 204
The Scorpion or the Imaginary Confession (Memmi) 246
Scots Unbound and Other Poems (MacDiarmid) 196
The Scout; or, The Black Riders of Congaree (Simms) 118
Scrambled Eggs and Whiskey: Poems, 1991–1995 (Carruth) 286
A Scrap of Paper (Sardou) 122
Scratch (MacLeish) 248
The Screens (Genet) 234
The Screwtape Letters (Lewis) 208
Se esconde tras los ojos (Toledo) 296
The Sea, the Sea (Murdoch) 256, 257
The Sea and Poison (Endo) 228
The Sea Change (Howard) 231
Sea Grapes (Walcott) 255

The Sea Lions (Cooper) 115
Sea Marks (Perse) 220
The Sea of Fertility (Mishima) 240
"The Sea of Grass" (Richter) 201
Sea of Histories (Pérez de Guzmán) 35
The Sea Wolf (London) 162
The Seagull (Caballero) 116
The Seagull (Chekhov) 92, 146, 162
The Seamless Tunic (Lima) 204
The Search (Snow) 199
Seascape (Albee) 253
The Seaside and the Fireside (Longfellow) 116
A Season for Falling in Love (Wang) 279
A Season in Hell (Rimbaud) 94, 129
A Season in Paradise (Breytenbach) 255
Season of Anomy (Soyinka) 251
The Season Ticket (Haliburton) 121
The Seasons (Thomson) 74
Seasons of the Soul (Tate) 210
Seaview (Olson) 262
Second April (Millay) 181
The Second Coming (Percy) 259
"The Second Coming" (Yeats) 152, 180
The Second Curtain (Fuller) 222
Second Foundation (Asimov) 222
The Second Man (Behrman) 189
Second Marriage (Barthelme) 264
The Second Mrs. Tanqueray (Pinero) 143
The Second Sex (Beauvoir) 218
The Second Skin (Hawkes) 238
The Second Tree from the Corner (White) 223
Secondary Heaven (Popa) 245
The Secret (Bernstein) 172
The Secret Agent (Conrad) 155, 165
The Secret Garden (Burnett) 169
Secret Love, or the Maiden Queen (Dryden) 49, 61
The Secret Record of Naruto (Yoshikawa) 188
Secret Star (Amrouche) 203
Secrets (Farah) 291
Secrets of the Self (Iqbāl) 174
Secrets on the Way (Transtromer) 230
Secular Hymns (Horace) 4
Seduction of the Minotaur (Nin) 234
Seed (Ray) 223
The Seed Beneath the Snow (Silone) 207
Seeing Through the Sun (Hogan) 265
See Under: Love (Grossman) 272
Sefere haMeforash (Heffner) 276
Seierherrene (Jacobsen) 276
Seize the Day (Bellow) 226
Selected Poems (Aiken) 193
Selected Poems (Eberhart) 241
Selected Poems (Fletcher) 205
Selected Poems (Illyés) 249
Selected Poems (Jarrell) 273
Selected Poems (Justice) 259
Selected Poems (Kinnell) 261, 262
Selected Poems (Livesay) 228
Selected Poems (Mahon) 274
Selected Poems (Rexroth) 264
Selected Poems (Tate) 277
Selected Poems, 1928–1958 (Kunitz) 230
Selected Poems, 1933–1980 (Faludy) 266
Selected Poems, 1970–1983 (Henson) 265

Selected Poetry (Amichai) 268
Self-Portrait in a Convex Mirror (Ashbery) 253, 254
The Self-Tormentor (Terence) 5
Selige Zeiten, burchige Welt (Menasse) 278
La Semaine (du Bartas) 41
Sena sagor (Jersild) 292
El señor de los mil días (Aridjis) 283
Sense and Sensibility (Austen) 91, 98
The Sense of Movement (Gunn) 228
Sensitiva Amorosa (Hansson) 139
"The Sensitive Plan" (Shelley) 102
Sent for You Yesterday (Wideman) 263
Sentimental Education (Flaubert) 92, 127
A Sentimental Journey Through France and Italy (Sterne) 81
Sentimental Lunar Almanac (Lugones) 168
Sentimental Memoirs of João Miramar (Andrade) 185
El sentimiento (Guelbenzu) 285
A Separate Peace (Knowles) 231, 259
Separate Tables (Rattigan) 223
The Separation (Franck) 276
Separazione (Sanvitale) 289
Les sept noms du peintre (Le Guillou) 288
"September 1, 1939" (Auden) 207
The September Lyre (Södergran) 178
The Seraphim and Other Poems (Browning) 110
The Serapion Brothers (Hoffman) 101
Serena Cruz (Ginzburg) 274
La Sérénade (Regnard) 66
Serenity House (Hope) 278
Sergius (Reuchlin) 29
The Serious Game (Söderberg) 171
Sermons (Swift) 77
Serpent and Bull (Hansen) 221
The Serpent and the Rope (Rao) 232
Sertorius (Corneille) 48, 60
Sestinas and Other Poems (Belli) 248
Set for Life (Freeman) 276
Seta (Baricco) 287
The Setting Sun (Dazai) 215
Setting the World on Fire (Wilson) 259
The Settlement of Centaurs (Kim) 278
Seuls Demeurent (Char) 212
Seven Against Thebes (Aeschylus) 2
Seven Brothers (Kivi) 127
The Seven Deadly Sins (Boge) 209
Seven Gothic Tales (Dinesen) 198
The Seven Lamps of Architecture (Ruskin) 111
The Seven Madmen (Arlt) 192
The Seven Pillars of Wisdom (Lawrence) 188
The Seven Seas (Martinson) 192
Seven Storey Mountain (Merton) 216
Seven Strings of the Lyre (Sand) 111
Seven Types of Ambiguity: A Study of Its Effects on English Verse (Empson) 193
The Seven-League Crutches (Jarrell) 220
Seventeen (Tarkington) 175
Seventy Tombstones (Ryya'i) 291
Severe Passions (Holm) 248
A Severed Head (Murdoch) 234
The Sex Fable (Bourdet) 195
A Shabby Genteel Story (Thackeray) 111

Shabbytown Calendar (Shapcott) 255
Shadow (Cendrars) 262
Shadow and Act (Ellison) 238
The Shadow Box (Cristofer) 255
The Shadow Boxer (Heighten) 295
The Shadow Knows (Johnson) 252
"The Shadow Line" (Conrad) 155
Shadow of a Bull (Wojciechowska) 239
The Shadow of a Gunman (O'Casey) 184, 186
The Shadow of the Future (Södergran) 180
The Shadow of the Leader (Guzmán) 192
Shadow of the Night (Chapman) 44
Shadows Against the Wall (Rojas) 239
Shadows in the Grass (Gustafson) 276
Shadows on Our Skin (Johnston) 256
Shadows on the Rock (Cather) 194
A Shady Business (Balzac) 91
Shah-nameh (Firdawsī) 20
Shaihu Umar (Balewa) 225
Shaker, Why Don't You Sing? (Angelou) 262
Shakespearean Tragedy (Bradley) 162
Shalimar (Markandaya) 263
The Shape of Things to Come (Wells) 197
Shapes (Gorakhpuri) 215
The Shark (Solomos) 116
The Shaving of Shagpat, an Arabian Entertainment (Meredith) 119
The Shawl (Ozick) 272
She (Haggard) 138
She Drove Without Stopping (Gordon) 273
She Stoops to Conquer (Goldsmith) 82
"She Was a Phantom of Delight" (Wordsworth) 96
Shelter (Phillips) 282
The Sheltering Sky (Bowles) 216
Shenandoah (Schwartz) 208
The Shepheard's Calendar (Spenser) 41
The Shepherd's Week (Gay) 72
The Shield (Menander) 3
The Shield of Achilles (Auden) 225
Shields (Cruz e Sousa) 144
Shijing 1
Shiloh (Naylor) 277
Shining Lights (Yizhar) 280
Shining Solitude (Ahti) 264
Shining Tip (Rojas) 232
Ship Fever and Other Stories (Barrett) 286
The Ship of Fools (Barclay) 34
Ship of Fools (Porter) 235
The Ship of Love (Vicente) 36
The Ship Sails On (Grieg) 185
The Shipping News (Proulx) 281
The Ships (Quesada) 278
Ship's Talk (Huygens) 54
The Shipwreck (Kume) 182
The Shipyard (Onetti) 234
Shirley (Brontë) 116
Shock-Headed Peter (Hoffmann) 115
Shoeless Joe (Kinsella) 261
The Shoemaker and the King, Part II (Zorrilla y Moral) 112
The Shoemaker and the King, Part III (Zorrilla y Moral) 111
The Shoemaker's Holiday (Dekker) 50
Shoemakers of the Hearth (Kivi) 124
The Shoes of the Fisherman (West) 240

Shogun (Clavell) 253
A Shooting Star (Stegner) 234
Shore Acres (Herne) 143
A Short Bunch of Stories (Tagore) 153
"The Short Happy Life of Francis Macomber" (Hemingway) 153, 201
Shosha (Singer) 257
Show Boat (Ferber) 188
Show Your Tongue (Grass) 272
The Shrike (Kramm) 221
The Shrimp and the Anemone (Hartley) 211
Shrimps (Pillai) 227
A Shropshire Lad (Housman) 146
The Sibyl (Besse Luis) 224
Sic et Non (Abélard) 22
The Sick Woman (Furchtegott) 77
The Sickness Unto Death (Kierkegaard) 91
Siddhartha (Hesse) 182
Siddhartha: Man of Peace (Chattopadhyay) 227
Sido (Colette) 193
Sidste sommer (Skou-Hansen) 277
Le Siècle de Louis XIV (Voltaire) 68
"The Siege of Corinth" (Byron) 100
The Siege of Krishnapur (Farrell) 250
The Siege of Thebes (Lydgate) 34
Siegfried (Giraudoux) 190
The Sign in Sidney Brustein's Window (Hansberry) 238
The Sign of Four (Doyle) 141
Signals from the Flames (Pacheco) 260
The Significance of Sections in American History (Turner) 197
Sigurd Slembe (Bjørnson) 123
Silas Marner (Eliot) 122
Silberne Saiten (Zweig) 159
The Silence (Bjorneboe) 251
Silence (Endo) 242
Silence (Pinter) 246
Silence (Stryjkowski) 280
Un silence d'environ une demi-heure (Schreiber) 286
The Silence of Colonel Bramble (Maurois) 177
A Silence of Desire (Markandaya) 232
El silencio de la luna (Pacheco) 283
The Silent Cry (Oe) 230
The Silent Rooms (Hébert) 230
Silent Spring (Carson) 237
Il silenzio (Lagorio) 280
Silesian Songs (Bezruc) 226
The Silmarillion (Tolkien) 256
Silsie (Redonnet) 274
Silvas americanas (Bello) 104
Silver and Black (Lechon) 185
The Silver Box (Galsworthy) 167
The Silver Chalice (Costain) 221
Silver City (Li) 290
The Silver Cord (Howard) 188
The Silver King Play (Jones) 135
A Silver Spoon (Galsworthy) 188
The Silver Tassel (O'Casey) 188
"A Silvia" (Leopardi) 91
Simo the Bloodhound (Leino) 162
The Simoom (Lenormand) 180
"A Simple Heart" (Flaubert) 92
The Simple Past (Chraibi) 224
Simple Stories (Schulze) 291
The Simple Truth (Levine) 282, 283
Simplicissimus the Vagabond, that is the Life of a Strange Adventurer Named Melchio Sternfels von Fuchsheim (Grimmelshausen) 61
Simulacrum (Leiris) 186

Sin (Idris) 235
The Sin of Father Amaro (Eça de Queirós) 131
Sincerely, Willis Wayde (Marquand) 225
Sinfonía desde el Nuevo Mundo (Espinosa) 275
The Singapore Grip (Farrell) 257
Singin' and Swingin' and Gettin' Merry Like Christmas (Angelou) 255
The Singing Flesh (Layton) 234
Singing from the Depths (Machado) 171
A Single Man (Isherwood) 238
A Singular Man (Donleavy) 237
The Sinking of the Titanic (Enzensberger) 258
The Sinner (Cosic) 274
Sinners in Summertime (Hoel) 189
Sinners in the Hands of an Angry God (Edwards) 76
Sir Eustace Grey (Crabbe) 97
Sir Launcelot Greaves (Smollett) 79
Sirens of Titan (Vonnegut) 231
Siste dikt (Orvil) 280
Sister Carrie (Dreiser) 158
Sita's Story (Kumaran Asan) 179
Sitti Nurbaja (Rusli) 182
Sitting Duck (Radichkov) 290
Six Characters in Search of an Author (Pirandello) 154, 181
The Sixth One (Arguedas) 234
Sixtus and Sesto (Federer) 172
Sixty Tales (Buzzati) 230
Det skabtes vaklen Arabesker (Thomsen) 286
Skammen (Haff) 287
Skating in the Dark (Kaplan) 276
Skellig (Almond) 293
Skerret (O'Flaherty) 196
The Sketch Book (Irving) 101
Sketches by Boz (Dickens) 109
Skimmer (Tunstrom) 287
The Skin (Malaparte) 218
The Skin of Our Teeth (Wilder) 209, 210
Skumring e Praha (Carling) 288
Skunk Hour (Lowell) 231
The Sky (Maksimovic) 289
The Sky of September (Michitsuna) 257
Skyggen i dit sted (Grondahl) 275
"The Skylark" (Shelley) 102
Slangen i Sydney (Larsen) 290
Slaughterhouse Five; or, The Children's Crusade (Vonnegut) 246
The Slave (Amadi) 257
The Slave (Baraki) 238
The Slave (Singer) 236
The Slave Dancer (Fox) 252
The Slave Merchant (Bujah) 284
Slaves in Their Chains (Theotokis) 182
The Slaying of Kicak (Khadilkar) 169
Sleep It Off Lady (Rhys) 255
A Sleep of Prisoners (Fry) 220
The Sleep of the Just (Mammeri) 225
Sleepers in Moon-Crowded Valleys (Purdy) 247
Sleepers Joining Hands (Bly) 250
The Sleeping Lord and Other Fragments (Jones) 252
The Sleepwalkers (Broch) 195, 196
Slouching Toward Bethlehem (Didion) 244
Slovenly Peter (Hoffmann) 114
A Slow Fuse (Weiss) 264

The Slow Motion Picture (Teirlinck) 182

The Small Black Room (Balchin) 210

The Small House in Allington (Trollope) 123

"A Small House in Kolomna" (Pushkin) 90, 108

Small World (Lodge) 264

Smile of the Lamb (Grossman) 268

Smiles on Washington Square (Federman) 265

Smiley's People (Le Carré) 259

Smoke (Turgenev) 126

Smoky Night (Bunting) 283

Smooth Seas (Benediktsson) 164

The Snake (Dagerman) 213

Snapshots of a Daughter in Law Poems, 1954–1962 (Rich) 237

Snares Without End (Quenum) 232

The Sniper (Krige) 235

The Snow Birds (Fréchette) 132

Snow Country (Kawabata) 156, 217

The Snow Dance (Yoshiko) 269

Snow Falling on Cedars (Guterson) 282, 283

The Snow Image, and Other Tales (Hawthorne) 117

Snow Legend (Aspenstrom) 218

The Snow Maiden (Ostrovsky) 129

Snow White (Barthelme) 243

Snow-Bound (Whittier) 125

Snowflakes Bentley (Azarian) 292

"The Snows of Kilimanjaro" (Hemingway) 153, 204

So Big (Ferber) 185, 186

So Long, See You Tomorrow (Maxwell) 261

The Sobbing Lancang River (Zhu) 273

Social Contract (Rousseau) 68, 80

Social Transformation of American Medicine (Starr) 263

Sofonisma (Trissino) 35

Soga Heir (Chikamatsu) 48, 64

Sogni mancini (Duranti) 289

Sogrim et ha Yam (Katzir) 274

Sohrab and Rustim (Arnold) 117

El sol de Breda (Pérez Reverte) 294

Solar Eclipse (Heiichiro) 294

Las soldaderas (Poniatowska) 294

"The Soldier" (Brooke) 174

Soldiers (Hochhuth) 243

The Soldiers (Lenz) 82

The Soldier's Art (Powell) 241

A Soldier's Embrace (Gordimer) 259

The Soldier's Fortune (Otway) 63

Soldiers in Hiding (Wiley) 268

Soldier's Pay (Faulkner) 188

A Soldier's Play (Fuller) 260, 261

Il sole e innocenti (Camarca) 278

La soledad era esto (Millas) 275

Le soleil des mourants (Izzo) 293

Solformokelson (Enger) 283

The Solid Gold Cadillac (Kaufman, Teichman) 222

The Solid Mandala (White) 241

A Solid Sheet (Bedi) 236

"The Solitary Reaper" (Wordsworth) 96

Solitary Thoughts (Rozanov) 171

Solitude (Acevedo Díaz) 145

Solitude (Prudhomme) 127

Solitudes (Machado) 161

Solo on a Burning Trumpet (Shvarts) 217

Solomon Gursky Was Here (Richler) 273

Solomon on the Vanity of the World (Prior) 72

Solstices (MacNeice) 234

Som dine dagerer (Elstad) 284

La sombra del angel (Mayoral) 297

Some Came Running (Jones) 228

Some Do Not (Ford) 185

Some Freaks (Mamet) 272

Some Prefer Nettles (Tanizaki) 191

Some Unease and Angels (Feinstein) 256

Someone to Run With (Grossman) 296

Someone to Watch Over Me (Bausch) 293

Something Happened Here (Levine) 276

Something in Disguise (Howard) 246

Something to Answer For (Newby) 245

Something Wicked This Way Comes (Bradbury) 235

Son (Ramamitram) 240

Son de mar (Vincent) 294

The Son of a Servant (Strindberg) 93, 138

Son of a Smaller Hero (Richler) 225

Son of Guyana (Apple) 251

Son of Man (Roa Bastos) 233

A Son of the Circus (Irving) 282

Son of the Morning (Oates) 257

Son of the Morning (Phillpotts) 158

Son of the Wilderness (Wolfe) 213

The Son of the Wolf (London) 158

Sonatas (Valle-Inclán) 160

Sonetos (Oliver Labra) 292

Sonetti e Canzoni (Sannazaro) 37

"Song" (Donne) 48, 55

Song and Dance Man (Ackerman) 271

Song for a Birth or a Death (Jennings) 234

Song for St. Cecilia's Day (Dryden) 64

Song of a Goat (Clark) 234

The Song of Berndotte (Werfel) 208

The Song of Eternity (Iqbāl) 174

The Song of Hiawatha (Longfellow) 119

Song of Hildebrand 13

"A Song of Italy" (Swinburne) 126

Song of Lawino (p'Bitek) 241

"The Song of Los" (Blake) 68, 87

"Song of Myself" (Whitman) 119

Song of Roland 13, 21

Song of Semblance and Substance (Eeden) 145

Song of Solomon (Morrison) 256

The Song of the Blood-Red Flower (Linnankoski) 163

Song of the Lark (Cather) 174

"Song of the Open Road" (Whitman) 119

The Song of the Rhone (Mistral) 147

Song of the Road (Pather Panchali) (Bandyopadhyay) 199

"The Song of the Shirt" (Hood) 113

Song of the Sugarcanes (Sadik) 253

The Song of the World (Giono) 199

The Song of Those Who Drink the Sun (Hikmet Ran) 191

A Song of Truth and Semblance (Nooteboom) 260

Song Without a Name (Král') 114

Songlines (Chatwin) 269

Songs (Béranger) 99

Songs (García Lorca) 155

Songs (Leopardi) 100

Songs (Uhland) 99

Songs and Sonnets (Ronsard) 39

Songs Before Sunrise (Swinburne) 128

Songs for the People (Claudius) 83

Songs from the Wings of Sorrow (Rynell) 267

Songs of Experience (Blake) 68, 86

Songs of Innocence (Blake) 68, 85

Songs of Labor (Whittier) 116

The Songs of Songs (Sudermann) 166

Songs of the Cold (Sitwell) 212

Songs of the Fatherland (Ihland) 100

Songs of Wilderness and Love (Karlfeldt) 145

Songs Without Words (Verlaine) 130

Sonhos tropicais (Scliar) 278

Sonnets (Shakespeare) 51

Sonnets (Wordsworth) 92

Sonnets from the Portuguese (Browning) 116

Sonnets pour Hélène (Ronsard) 33

Sonnets to Orpheus (Rilke) 155, 182

Sonnets to Sophia (Marechal) 207

The Sons (Feuchtwanger) 200

Sons and Lovers (Lawrence) 172

The Sons of Jacob (Rainis) 185

The Sons of the Valley (Werner) 96

Sophie's Choice (Styron) 258

Sophist (Plato) 3

Sophonisbe (Mairet) 55

Sordello (Browning) 111

Sorgegondolen (Transtromer) 287

Sorgen per capita (Brunner) 275

A Sorrow Beyond Dreams (Handke) 250

The Sorrows of Young Werther (Goethe) 67, 82

A Sort of Life (Greene) 154

Sostiene Pereira (Tabucchi) 282, 284

The Sot-Weed Factor (Barth) 232

The Soul (Machado) 160

The Soul of a New Machine (Kidder) 261

The Sound and the Fury (Faulkner) 192

The Sound of the Mountain (Kawabata) 156, 221

The Sound of Waves (Mishima) 224

Sounder (Armstrong) 247

The Source (Michener) 240

Sous l'étoile du chien (Puech) 276

South of the Border, West of the Sun (Murakami) 294

South Pacific (Rogers, Hammerstein, Logan) 218

The South (Toibin) 274

South Wind (Douglas) 176

Southern Mail (Saint-Exupéry) 192

The Southpaw (Harris) 222

The Sovereign Sun (Elytis) 249

Spaccio della Bestia Trionfante (Bruno) 42

The Spaniard (Wergeland) 107

The Spanish Fryar (Dryden) 63

The Spanish Tragedie (Kyd) 44

Sparks (Raffi) 135

Spartina (Casey) 272

Speak, Memory (Nabokov) 155, 220

Specimen Days (Whitman) 135

The Spectacle at the Tower (Hoffmann) 262

The Spectator Bird (Stegner) 255

Speedboat (Adler) 255

The Spell (Broch) 223

A Spell in Winter (Dumore) 286

The Spider and the Flie (Heywood) 39

Spider Web: A Novel (Lively) 290

The Spider's House (Bowles) 225

Den Spieghel der Salicheit van Elckerlijk (Diest) 29, 35

Spinoza of Market Street (Singer) 234

The Spire (Golding) 238

Spiridion (Sand) 111

The Spirit Level (Heaney) 286

The Spirit of Man (Graves) 175

The Spirit of Romance (Pound) 168

The Spirit of St. Louis (Lindbergh) 223

The Spirit of the Age (Hazlitt) 104

The Spirit of the Laws (Montesquieu) 77

Spirits Rebellious (Gibran) 179

Spiritual Chorus (Kingo) 62

Spiritual Couplets (Rūmī) 15

Spiritual Exercises (Ignatius of Loyola) 38

Spiritual Sonnets (Jiménez) 175

Splashes of Grail (Fröding) 148

The Splits (Ritter) 257

The Spoils of Poynton (James) 91, 147

Spoon River Anthology (Masters) 174

A Sport of Nature (Gordimer) 269

The Sport of the Gods (Dunbar) 160

A Sportsman's Sketches (Turgenev) 118

Spreading the News (Gregory) 162

The Spring (Kleist) 78

"Spring" (Thomson) 74

Spring and All (Williams) 184

Spring and Fall (Hopkins) 133

Spring and the Untimely Return of Winter (Aho) 164

Spring Moon (Boutens) 175

Ein springender Brunnen (Walser) 291

Spring's Awakening (Wedekind) 142

Springtime (Achchygyya) 212

Springtime of Death (Bousoño) 214

The Springtime of Others (Bernard) 185

The Sputnik Sweetheart (Murakami) 294

The Spy: A Tale of the Neutral Ground (Cooper) 102

The Spy Who Came in from the Cold (Le Carré) 237

The Squabbles at Chioggia (Goldoni) 80

Squaring the Circle (Stoppard) 264

S.S. San Pedro (Cozzens) 194

St. Godhard Railway and Other Stories (Yoko) 287

St. Joan of the Stockyards (Brecht) 196

St. Patrick's Day; or, The Scheming Lieutenant (Sheridan) 82

St. Ronan's Well (Scott) 103

St. Urbain's Horseman (Richler) 249

St. Valentine's Day; or, The Fair Maid of Perth (Scott) 105

Staccando l'ombra da terra (del Giudice) 284

Stages on Life's Way (Kierkegaard) 91

Stalingrad (Plievier) 214

A Stamp Album (Sergeyev) 287

Les Stances (Moreas) 149

Stanzas (Pushkin) 90, 104

Stanzas Begun for the Tournament of the Magnificent Giuliano de Medici (Politian) 28

Stanzas for the Death of His Father (Manrique) 29

A Staple of News (Jonson) 54

Star of Satan (Bernanos) 188

The Star-Apple Kingdom (Walcott) 258

Starlit Early Morning (Zollinger) 202
The Stars Look Down (Cronin) 200
Stars of the New Curfew (Okri) 272
The Stars Turn Red (O'Casey) 207
Starship Troopers (Heinlein) 231
"The Star-Spangled Banner" (Key) 99
The Star-Spangled Girl (Simon) 241
The State of Innocence and Fall of Man (Dryden) 63
State of Siege (Camus) 155
The State of the Union (Crouse, Lindsay) 213
Statesman (Plato) 3
Static Poems (Benn) 216
Station Island (Heaney) 264, 266
The Statue of Prometheus (Calderón de la Barca) 48, 61
Staying On (Scott) 255, 256
Steeple Bush (Frost) 215
"The Stepchildren" (Elytis) 252
Steppenwolf (Hesse) 189
Steps (Kosinski) 244
Steps to the Temple (Crashaw) 57
Stern (Friedman) 235
Stick (Leonard) 262
Still Centre (Spender) 205
Still Life (Byatt) 265
Still Life (Coward) 202, 213
Still Stands the House (Ringwood) 205
A Stillness at Appomattox (Catton) 223, 231
Stilwell and the American Experience in China, 1911–45 (Tuchman) 249
A Stitch in Time (Lively) 255
Stone and Sky (Jiménez) 179
Stone Bird (Delblanc) 252
The Stone Country (La Guma) 243
The Stone Diaries (Shields) 280, 283
The Stone Guest (Pushkin) 90, 111
Stonedial (Konrád) 296
Stony Limits (MacDiarmid) 199
"Stopping by Woods on a Snowy Evening" (Frost) 184
The Store (Stribling) 197
Stories and Pictures (Peretz) 158
Stories and Poems (Benediktsson) 147
Stories from Mala Strava (Neruda) 132
Stories in an Almost Classical Mode (Brodkey) 270
The Stories of John Cheever (Cheever) 257, 258
The Stories of Muriel Spark (Spark) 266
The Stories of Venice (Ruskin) 117
The Stories of Vladimir Nabokov (Nabokov) 284
Stories Toto Told Me (Rolfe) 148
The Storm and Other Poems (Montale) 227
A Stormy Night (Caragiale) 133
The Stormy Sea (Pisemsky) 123
A Story—a Story (Haley) 248
"The Story of a Bad Boy" (Aldrich) 127
The Story of a Life (Paustovsky) 239
The Story of a New Zealand River (Mander) 180
The Story of a South African Farm (Schreiner) 135
The Story of a Staircase (Buero Vallejo) 217
The Story of Borge (Branner) 209
The Story of Dr. Dolittle (Lofting) 180
The Story of Gosta Berling (Lagerlöf) 142

The Story of Rimini (Hunt) 100
The Story of San Michael (Munthe) 192
The Story of Sigurd the Volsung and the Fall of the Niblungs (Morris) 131
The Story of the Abderites (Wieland) 82
The Story of the Water Channel (Jamalzadeh) 215
The Storyteller (Vargas Llosa) 270, 272
La strada per Roma (Volponi) 276
Strafford (Browning) 109
Strait Is the Gate (Gide) 167
The Strange Case of Dr. Jekyll and Mr. Hyde (Stevenson) 138
Strange Heaven (Coady) 291
Strange Holiness (Coffin) 201
Strange Interlude (O'Neill) 153, 190
The Strange Marriage (Mikszáth) 158
The Strange River (Green) 196
Strange Stories (Hoffman) 100
Strange Stories from a Chinese Studio (Pu) 63
The Strange Story of Mammy Hunt (Taeko) 276
The Stranger (Camus) 155, 209
The Stranger (Kotzebue) 85
The Stranger (Kuncewicz) 202
The Stranger from the Seine (Harvath) 197
Stranger in a Strange Land (Heinlein) 234
The Stranger in Lowell (Whittier) 114
Stranger Music: Selected Poems and Songs (Cohen) 280
Stranger to Europe (Butler) 221
Strangers (Memmi) 225
Strangers and Brothers (Snow) 207
Strathmore (Ouida) 124
Stratton (Duncan) 217
Straw into Gold (Stead) 288
The Straw Man (Giono) 228
The Strayed Reveller (Arnold) 116
A Street in Bronzeville (Brooks) 212
The Street (Petry) 213
Street Scene (Rice) 191, 192
Street Songs (Sitwell) 209
A Streetcar Named Desire (Williams) 215, 216
Streets of Laredo (McMurtry) 279
Strike the Father Dead (Wain) 235
A Stroll in the Air (Ionesco) 237
The Strong Bread (Soyinka) 237
The Struggle for Life (Baroja) 162
Stuart Little (White) 212
Stubborn Hope: New Poems and Selections from China Poems and Strains (Brutus) 257
Stucco (Bang) 138
The Student of Salamanca (Espronceda y Delgado) 111
A Student of Weather (Hay) 295
A Study (Doyle) 138
A Study of History (Toynbee) 199
The Stuff of Youth (Mauriac) 173
Sturm und Drang (Klinger) 83
Det Stutte livet (Heggland) 278
Styles of Radical Will (Sontag) 246
The Subject Was Roses (Gilroy) 239
The Subterraneans (Kerouac) 229
The Suburbs of Hell (Stow) 264
Successful Kagekiyo (Chikamatsu) 64
Such a Long Journey (Mistry) 276
Such Is Life (Furphy) 161
Such Is My Beloved (Callaghan) 199

A Sudden Brightness (Boisonneau) 282
Suddenly Last Summer (Williams) 229
El sueño de la historia (Edwards) 296
El sueño del señor (Gamerro) 296
The Sugar Mother (Jolley) 271
Suicidi dovuti (Busi) 287
A Suitable Boy (Seth) 280
Suitable Words (Arghezi) 189
The Suitcase (Alavi) 199
The Suitors (Kisfaludy) 100
Suject Angot (Angot) 292
Sula (Morrison) 250
The Sulky Fire (Bernard) 181
The Sum of Things (Manning) 259
Sumerian Vistas (Ammons) 269
Summa de Magroll el Gaviero (Mutis) 275
Summary (Gandlevsky) 296
Summary of the History of God (Vicente) 36
"Summer" (Thomson) 74
A Summer Affair (Klima) 249
Summer and Smoke (Williams) 216
The Summer Before the Dark (Lessing) 251
Summer for the Gods: The Scopes Trial and America's Continuing Debate over Science and Religion (Larson) 290
Summer of the Seventh Doll (Lawler) 226
Summer of the Swans (Byars) 248
A Summer to Decide (Johnson) 216
Summoned by Bells (Betjeman) 232
A Summons to Memphis (Taylor) 267, 268
The Sun Also Rises (Hemingway) 153, 188
Sun Stone (Paz) 228
Sun Under Wood (Hass) 286
Sunday in the Park with George (Sondheim, Lapine) 264, 265
Sunderland Capture (Bacon) 208
The Sundial (Jackson) 229
Sunken Oboe (Quasimodo) 196
The Sunlight Dialogues (Gardner) 250
The Sunlit Hours (Verhaeren) 146
The Sunrise (Cao) 201
Sunrise (Hazard) 259
The Sunshine Boys (SImon) 250
Suppliants (Aeschylus) 6
The Supposes (Gascoigne) 40
Gli Suppositi (Ariosto) 40
The Supreme Court in United States History (Adams) 183
Suréna (Corneille) 48
The Surgeon of His Honor (Calderón de la Barca) 48, 55
The Surgeon's Daughter (Scott) 105
Surgical Precision (Baranczak) 291
Surprised by Joy: The Shape of My Early Life (Lewis) 225
Svart due (Lie) 288
Svindel (Holmer) 289
Swag (Leonard) 255
The Swamp Dwellers (Soyinka) 237
The Swan Song (Galsworthy) 190
The Swan's Camp (Tsvetayeva) 228
The Swans (Viélé-Griffin) 138
Swan's Way (Proust) 171
Sweat of Blood (Jouve) 200
Swedenhielms (Bergman) 187
Sweeney Agonistes (Eliot) 152, 188
Sweet Bird of Youth (Williams) 231
The Sweet Cheat Gone (Proust) 186
The Sweet Hereafter (Banks) 276

Sweet Injury (Storni) 178
The Sweet Secret (Ivanov) 171
A Swiftly Tilting Planet (L'Engle) 257
The Swimmers and Other Selected Poems (Tate) 248
The Swiss Family Robinson (Wyss) 99
The Switch (Leonard) 257
Switch off the Light (Seifert) 204
The Sword and the Distaff (Simms) 118
Sword Blades and Poppy Seed (Lowell) 173
Sword of Honor (Waugh) 221, 234
Sylvester and the Magic Pebble (Steig) 247
Sylvie and Bruno (Carroll) 140
Symbiotic Worm (Ryu) 296
Symbolism (Eguren) 170
Symposium (Plato) 3
Symposium (Spark) 274
Synden (Ranelid) 283

T

Table Talk; or, Original Essays on Men and Manners (Hazlitt) 102
Tablets (Callimachus) 4
Tada uti Mawgun (Rahtathara) 29
The Taft Story (White) 224
The Tailor of Panama (Le Carré) 286
Tai-Pan (Clavell) 241
Tajik Vengeance (Niyazi) 215
Take Root or Die (Butler) 247
The Taking of Ismail (Shishkin) 296
Taking the Trend (Castel-Blum) 293
Tale from Two Pockets (Čapek) 191
A Tale of a Tub (Jonson) 55
A Tale of a Tub (Swift) 68, 70
The Tale of Cross-Eyed Lefty from Tula and the Steel Flea (Leskov) 134
The Tale of Paraguay (Southey) 104
The Tale of Peter Rabbit (Potter) 160
A Tale of Poor Lovers (Pratolini) 215
The Tale of Rosamund Gray and Old Blind Margaret (Lamb) 88
Tale of the Fiesole Nymph (Boccaccio) 14
Tale of the Horse (Dalin) 76
A Tale of Two Cities (Dickens) 90, 121
Tales (Achchygyya) 203
Tales (Poe) 114
Tales (Strindberg) 93
Tales and Novels in Verse (La Fontaine) 60
Tales from Shakespeare (Lamb and Lamb) 97
Tales from the Vienna Woods (Horvath) 193
Tales of a Manor (Lagerlöf) 148
Tales of a Traveler (Irving) 103
Tales of a Wayside Inn (Longfellow) 123
Tales of Hoffman (Hoffman) 99
Tales of Mountains and Steppes (Aytmatov) 237
Tales of Soldiers and Civilians (Bierce) 142
Tales of Summer (Beer) 64
Tales of the Genji (Murasaki Shikibu) 15
Tales of the Grotesque and Arabesque (Poe) 91, 111
Tales of the Jazz Age (Fitzgerald) 182
Tales of the Late Ivan Petrovich Belkin (Pushkin) 90, 106
Tales of the O'Hara Family (Banim) 104

Tales of the Rainy Moon (Ueda) 81
Tales of the South Pacific (Michener) 215, 216
The Talisman (Scott) 93, 104
Talking About O'Dwyer (Stead) 296
Talley's Folly (Wilson) 258, 259
Tam O'Shanter (Burns) 86
Tamar and Other Poems (Jeffers) 185
Tamburlaine the Great (Marlowe) 33, 43
Tamerlane and Other Poems (Poe) 91, 105
The Taming of the Shrew (Shakespeare) 31, 44
Tancred and Sigismunda (Thomson) 77
Tangi (Ihimaera) 251
Tangled Hair (Yosano) 159
Tan-Huang (Inoue) 231
Tanim shel Mora (Gil) 276
Tanzstunde (Trampe) 268
Tar Baby (Morrison) 260
"Taras Bulba" (Gogol) 91, 109
The Tartar Steppes (Buzzati) 207
The Tartars in Hungary (Kisfaludy) 98
Tartuffe (Molière) 48, 60
Tarzan of the Apes (Burroughs) 173
The Task (Cowper) 84
The Taut Rope (Simon) 215
Tavshed i oktober (Grondahl) 286
Tazkerat Osh-sho-Ara (Daulatshah) 28
Te de la vida entera (Valdés) 289
Tea and Sympathy (Anderson) 222
Teach Us to Outgrow Our Madness (Oe) 246
Teahouse of the August Moon (Patrick) 222
The Teahouse of the August Moon (Patrick) 223
A Tear and a Smile (Gibran) 173
The Tears (Valmore) 107
Tears and Regrets (Koyo) 146
"The Tears of Scotland" (Smollett) 77
Teeuwis the Peasant (Coster) 51
Telepenia de Celia Cecilia Villalobo (Pombo) 285
Tell Me, Mom (Petrusevskaya) 283
Tell Me How Long the Train's Been Gone (Baldwin) 244
"The Tell-Tale Heart" (Poe) 91, 113
Temora (Macpherson) 80
The Tempest (Shakespeare) 31, 51
La tempestad (Prada) 289
The Temple (Herbert) 55
The Temple of Apollo (Vicente) 36
The Temple of My Familiar (Walker) 272
The Temple of the Golden Pavilion (Mishima) 227
Temporary Kings (Powell) 251
The Temptation (Kreve) 219
The Temptation of Saint Anthony (Flaubert) 92, 130
Ten Burn Offerings (MacNeice) 221
Ten Days That Shook the World (Reed) 178
Ten North Frederick (O'Hara) 225
The Ten Thousand Things (Demont) 225
The Tenant of Wildfell Hall (Brontë) 115
The Tenants (Malamud) 249
The Tenants of Time (Flanagan) 270
Tender Buttons (Stein) 173

The Tender Husband (Steele) 70
Tender Is the Night (Fitzgerald) 198
Tenderness (Mistral) 185
The Tenement (Smith) 266
The Tent on the Beach and Other Poems (Whittier) 126
The Tenth Man (Chayefsky) 231
The Tenth Man (Greene) 154, 266
Term of Office (Sczepanski) 274
Terms of Endearment (McMurtry) 253
La terra è di tutti (Camon) 287
Terrasse à Rome (Quignard) 296
The Terrible Threshold (Kunitz) 252
The Terrible Twos (Reed) 261
Terror and Decorum (Viereck) 217
Terror on the Mountain (Ramuz) 186
Terug uit Irkoetsk (Vries) 282
Tess of the D'Urbervilles; A Pure Woman (Hardy) 142
The Test (Marivaux) 76
Le testament français (Makine) 284
The Testament of Beauty (Bridges) 192
The Testament of Cain (Gyllensten) 237
The Testing Tree (Kunitz) 249
Teufelsbruck (Kronauer) 296
Texaco (Chamoiseau) 278
Thais (Mistral) 141
Thalaba the Destroyer (Southey) 95
"Thanatopsis" (Bryant) 100
The Thanatos Syndrome (Percy) 269
Thanks for the Fire (Benedetti) 240
That Championship Season (Miller) 250
That Hideous Strength (Lewis) 212
That Uncertain Feeling (Amis) 225
Theaetetus (Plato) 3
Le Théâtre de la Revolution (Rolland) 162
The Thebans, or the Enemy Brothers (Racine) 60
Their Eyes Were Watching God (Hurston) 203
Their Father's God (Rolvaag) 194
Their Wedding Journey (Howells) 128
Them (Oates) 246
Theodicee (Leibniz) 71
Theodore (Corneille) 48
Theodore Roosevelt (Pringle) 195
Theophilus North (Wilder) 250
Theory of Flight (Rukeyser) 200
The Theory of Psychoanalysis (Jung) 171
Theory of War (Brady) 282
There Shall Be No Night (Sherwood) 207, 208
There Was Once—Or Was There? (Jamalzadeh) 181
Thérèse Desqueyroux (Mauriac) 189
Thérèse Raquin (Zola) 126
Théroigne de Méricourt (Hervieu) 144
These Enchanted Woods (Massie) 280
They Knew What They Wanted (Howard) 185, 186
They Shall Inherit the Earth (Callaghan) 200
They Shall Not Pass (Paz) 203
They Think So (Petri) 266
They Want Bone (Pinsky) 273
Thickets (Abu Madi) 206
The Thief (Leonov) 189
The Thief (Mahfouz) 240
The Thief and the Dogs (Mahfouz) 233

The Thief's Journal (Genet) 218
The Thin Man (Hammett) 196
The Thin Red Line (Jones) 235
A Thing of Beauty (Cronin) 227
Things Fall Apart (Achebe) 229
Things of This World (Wilbur) 226, 228
The Thinker (Aldanov) 184
The Third Book About Achim (Johnson) 236
The Third Man (Greene) 154, 217
Third Vigil (Bryusov) 158
Thirst for Love (Mishima) 219
The Thirty-Nine Steps (Buchan) 174
This Bed Thy Centre (Johnson) 200
This Earth, My Brother (Awoonor) 249
This Earth of Mankind (Tur) 259
This Gun for Hire (Greene) 154
This Is Not a Letter and Other Poems (Boyle) 265
This Island Now (Abrahams) 241
This Land, This Time (Cosic) 250
This Particular Africa (Ikelle-Matiba) 237
This Side of Paradise (Fitzgerald) 180
This Sporting Life (Story) 232
This Sunday (Donoso) 242
This Time: New and Selected Poems (Stern) 290
Thomas and Beulah (Dove) 267, 268
Thomas Ripenseren (Ejrnaes) 288
Thorns and Flowers (Kazinczy) 98
Those Were the Mermaid Days (Young) 276
The Thought and Character of William James (Perry) 201
A Thousand Acres (Smiley) 276, 277
Thousand Cranes (Kawabata) 156, 217, 218
A Thousand Days (Schlesinger) 241
A Thousand Souls (Pisemsky) 120
Thranes metode (Lonn) 283
A Thread in the Dark (Haasse) 236
The Three Black Pennys (Hergesheimer) 176
The Three Clerks (Trollope) 120
Three Crosses (Tozzi) 180
The Three Dorothys (Scarron) 57
The Three Leaps of Want-Lun (Doblin) 174
Three Lovers (O'Faolain) 247
The Three Marias (Quieroz) 206
Three Men in a Boat (Jerome) 140
The Three Musketeers (Dumas) 113
Three Plays for Puritans (Shaw) 153
Three Sisters (Chekhov) 92, 159
The Three Slaves of Julius Caesar (Bacchelli) 230
Three Soldiers (Dos Passos) 181
Three Tales (Flaubert) 92
Three Tall Women (Albee) 281, 282
Three Times (Bitner) 285
Three Trapped Tigers (Cabrera Infante) 240
The Three Voices of Poetry (Eliot) 222
The Three-Cornered Hat (Alarcón) 130
The Three-Cornered World (Natsume) 93, 164
The Three-Penny Opera (Brecht) 153, 190
Threnodia Augustalis (Dryden) 64
Threny (Kochanowski) 42
Through the Looking Glass (Carroll) 128
Through the Woods Below (Belli) 242

Thrush (Seferis) 215
Thunderball (Fleming) 234
The Thunderstorm (Ostrovsky) 121
Thurso's Landing and Other Poems (Jeffers) 196
Thus Changed the Seasons (Manner) 239
Thus Spake Zarathustra (Nietzsche) 135
Thy Neighbor's Wife (O'Flaherty) 184
Thyestes (Seneca) 5, 12
"Thyrsis" (Arnold) 125
The Tidings Brought to Mary (Claudel) 171
Tiepolo's Hound (Walcott) 296
La tierra promitida (Guelbenzu) 277
The Tiger (Kumne) 177
Tiger at the Gates (Giraudoux) 200
A Tiger for Malgudi (Narayan) 263
The Tiger in the Grass (Doerr) 284
Tiger Juan (Pérez de Ayala) 188
Tiger-Lilies (Lanier) 126
Tigers (Adcock) 243
Til verdes ende (Faldbakken) 276
Tilottamsambhab (Datta) 121
Timber, of Discoveries Made Upon Men and Matter (Jonson) 56
The Timber Valley: A Story of Culture (Koch) 172
Timbuctoo (Tennyson) 105
The Time: Night (Petrushevskaya) 280
Time and Eternity (Mendes) 200
Time and Freewill (Bergson) 140
Time and Money (Matthews) 284
Time and the Conways (Priestley) 203
Time in a Red Coat (Brown) 264
The Time Machine (Wells) 145
The Time of Angels (Murdoch) 241
A Time of Evil (Cosic) 274
Time of Indifference (Moravia) 192
Time of Migration Northwards (Salih) 233
The Time of the Hero (Vargas Llosa) 237
The Time of Your Life (Saroyan) 205, 206
Time Remembered (Proust) 190
Time to Embrace (Onetti) 253
Timeaus (Plato) 3
Timequake (Vonnegut) 288
Time's Arrow (Amis) 276
Time's Power (Rich) 272
Times Three: Selected Verse from Three Decades (McGinley) 233
Timon of Athens (Shakespeare) 51
The Tin Drum (Grass) 231
Tine (Bang) 142
Tinísima (Poniatowska) 279
Tiny Alice (Albee) 240
A Tired Horse Trots On (Nguyen) 265
Tired Men (Garborg) 142
Tiriel (Blake) 130
'Tis a Pity She's a Whore (Ford) 54
The Titan (Dreiser) 173
Titan (Richter) 95
Tithonus (Tennyson) 121
Titus Andronicus (Shakespeare) 43
Tlacuilo (Rio) 278
To a Dying World (Kasprowicz) 159
"To a Skylark" (Shelley) 93
"To a Water Fowl" (Bryant) 101
"To Althea, from Prison" (Lovelace) 58
To an Athlete Dying Young (Housman) 146

To Be a Pilgrim (Cary) 209
To Be Young, Gifted and Black (Hansberry) 246
To Become an Island (Wispelaere) 237
"To Build a Fire" (London) 166
To Byron (Keats) 99
To Clothe the Naked (Pirandello) 154, 184
To Damascus (Strindberg) 93, 148
To Get to the Heart of the Matter (Choromanski) 245
To Give and to Have and Other Poems (Quasimodo) 242
To Have and Have Not (Hemingway) 153, 203
"To His Coy Mistress" (Marvell) 63
To His Sacred Majesty (Dryden) 49
To Kill a Mockingbird (Lee) 232, 233
To Let (Galsworthy) 181, 182
To Live (Yu) 284
"To Lucasta, Going to the Wars" (Lovelace) 58
"To My Friends" (Pushkin) 90, 105
To Stay Alive (Levertov) 249
To the Aegean Sea (Masuo) 257
To the East of the Mediterranean (Mounif) 265
To the Finland Station (Wilson) 176, 207
To the Land of the Cattails (Appelfeld) 268
To the Lighthouse (Woolf) 189
"To the Nightingale" (Finch) 72
To the Sound of the Marimbas (Bessa Victor) 210
Tobacco Road (Caldwell) 196
"Tobermory" (Saki) 169
Tobia Commedia (Petrie) 38
Die Tochter (Grosz) 269
Today and Tomorrow (Musa) 189
Toldi (Arany) 115
Toldi's Evening (Arany) 118
Toldi's Lane (Arany) 116
Toller (Dorst) 245
Den tolvte ritter (Michael) 279
Tom Brown's Schooldays (Hughes) 120
Tom Jones (Osborne) 237
Tom Jones, a Foundling (Fielding) 78
Tom Sawyer (Twain) 92, 131
Tom Thumb, a Tragedy (Fielding) 74
Tom-Cat Murr (Hoffman) 102
Tomorrow (Mitusaki) 262
Tomorrow Will Be Another Sunrise (Sathapanawat) 231
Tomorrows (Régnier) 137
Ton beau capitain (Schwarze-Bart) 269
Tongues of Diamond (Ibarbourou) 179
Tonight We Improvise (Pirandello) 154, 193
Tonio Kroger (Mann) 152, 161
Tono-Bungoy (Wells) 166
Too Late for This World (Nijlen) 228
Too Many Men (Brett) 295
The Tool (Raffi) 137
The Tooth of Crime (Shepard) 250
Topography of a Phantom City (Robbe-Grillet) 255
Torquato Tasso (Goethe) 67, 85
The Torrent (Abruquah) 244
Torrent (Ba) 207
The Torrent (Herbert) 219
Torrents of Spring (Turgenev) 129
Tortilla Flat (Steinbeck) 200

La Tosca (Sardou) 138
Totem and Taboo (Freud) 172
Touch (Gunn) 243
Touch the Water, Touch the Wind (Oz) 251
Tough Guys Don't Dance (Mailer) 264
Toward Chaos (Cong) 290
Toward Heaven and the Altars (Benavente y Martínez) 191
Toward the End of Time (Updike) 288
The Tower (Hofmannsthal) 187
The Tower (Yeats) 152, 190
The Tower at the End of the World (Heinesen) 254
Tower of Ecological Treatment (Oe) 274
Tower of Victory (Luzzatto) 74
The Towers of Trebizond (Macaulay) 227
The Town (Faulkner) 228
The Town (Richter) 219
The Town and the City (Kerouac) 219
The Town Down the River (Robinson) 168
The Town Gate (Delblanc) 230
Trachiniae (Sophocles) 3
Tractatus Logico Philosophicus (Wittgenstein) 181
The Trade (Stenson) 295
Trade Winds (Martinson) 213
Tradet (Sonnevi) 277
The Traffic of Algiers (Cervantes) 32
The Tragedie of Philotas (Daniel) 50
The Tragedies of Faith (Rolland) 172
The Tragedies of Love (Gunnarsson) 162
The Tragedy of Agis (Bessenyei) 82
The Tragedy of Al-Hallaj (Abdassabur) 240
The Tragedy of Chabot, Admiral of France (Chapman) 56
The Tragedy of King Christophe (Césaire) 237
The Tragedy of Man (Madách) 122
Tragedy of My Country (Palamas) 138
The Tragedy of Othello, Moor of Venice (Shakespeare) 50
The Tragedy of Pudd'nhead Wilson (Twain) 92, 144
The Tragic Comedians (Meredith) 133
The Tragic Engagement (Chenet) 245
The Tragic Muse (James) 91, 141
The Tragic Sense of Life (Unamuno) 172
A Tragic State (Kumaran Asan) 184
The Tragical History of the Life and Death of Doctor Faustus (Marlowe) 50
Tragiques (Aubigné) 52
The Train Home (Shreve) 279
The Train Was on Time (Böll) 218
Training in Christianity (Kierkegaard) 91
The Training of an American—The Earlier Life and Letters of Walter H. Page (Hendrick) 191
A Tramp Abroad (Twain) 92, 133
The Transformation of Virginia 1740–1790 (Isaac) 262
Transformations (Sexton) 249
The Transgressor (Green) 225
The Transient Hour (Aymé) 214
Transit (Dimitrova) 275
Translations (Friel) 259
Translucency (Ivanov) 162
The Transmission of the Flower of Acting Style (Zeami Motokiyo) 15

Transparence (Broger) 279
Transparent Gestures (Jones) 272
Travel Dice (Shapcott) 269
Travel Memoirs from the Summer of 1860 (Vinje) 122
A Traveler from Altruria (Howells) 144
Traveler Without Luggage (Anouilh) 202
The Traveller; or, A Prospect of Society (Goldsmith) 80
The Travels and Adventures of Benjamin the Third (Sefarim) 130
The Travels of Jamie McPheeters (Taylor) 230
Travels with a Donkey in the Cevennes (Stevenson) 132
Travels with Charley in Search of America (Steinbeck) 235
Travesty (Hawkes) 255
Tre borgerliga kvartetter (Noren) 279
The Treason of the Intellectuals (Benda) 189
Treasure Island (Stevenson) 135
The Treasure of Sierra Madre (Traven) 189
A Treatise Concerning Religious Affections (Edwards) 77
Treatise on the Education of Girls (Fénelon) 64
Tree Between the Walls (Pacheco) 246
The Tree of Laughing Bells (Lindsay) 163
Trees (Kilmer) 172
The Trees (Richter) 207
Treinta años (Boullosa) 294
Trelawney of the "Wells" (Pinero) 148
Tres Thomae (Stapleton) 43
Tresjoereren Johannes (Stigen) 274
The Trespassers (Hobson) 210
The Trial (Kafka) 152, 187
Trial by Terror: Sri Lankan Poems (Arasanayagam) 269
Trial of a Poet and Other Poems (Shapiro) 215
Trials (Prudhomme) 125
The Trials of Brother Jero (Soyinka) 232
The Trials of Enoc Huws (Owen) 142
Tribute (Slade) 257
Trilby (Du Maurier) 144
Trilhos e quintais (Oliveira) 291
Trio (Lassen) 295
Tripitaka 1
The Triple Echo (Bates) 247
Tríptico del carnaval (Pitol) 294
Triptych (Simon) 251
Tristam of Lyonesse (Swinburne) 135
Tristan (Mann) 152, 161
Tristan und Isolde (Gottfried von Strassburg) 23
Tristessa (Kerouac) 232
Tristia (Ovid) 4
Tristram (Robinson) 189, 190
Tristram Shandy (Sterne) 79
The Triumph and Tragedy of Erasmus Rotterdamus (Zweig) 199
The Triumph of Achilles (Gluck) 265
The Triumph of Death (D'Annunzio) 145
The Triumph of Life (Shelley) 93
Triumph of Winter (Vicente) 37
The Triumph over Life (Lagerkvist) 189
The Triumphant Empire, Thunder Clouds in the West (Gibson) 235

Troilus and Creseyde (Chaucer) 14
Troilus and Cressida (Dryden) 63
Troilus and Cressida (Shakespeare) 50
Trojan Women (Euripides) 2, 7
The Troll Garden (Cather) 163
Trollbyen (Alnaes) 278
Les Trophées (Heredia) 144
Tropic of Cancer (Miller) 198
Tropic of Capricorn (Miller) 205
Trotters and Dancers (Pérez de Ayala) 172
The Troubadour (García Gutiérrez) 109
Trout Fishing in America (Brautigan) 243
The Troy Book (Lydgate) 35
The Truce (Benedetti) 233
True Confessions (Dunne) 256
True West (Shepard) 260
Truman (McCullogh) 279
The Trumpet of the Swan (White) 247
Trust (Ozick) 241
Truth and Justice (Tannasaare) 188
Truth Under Suspicion (Ruiz de Alarcón) 54
Tryllefløyten (Lange-Nielsen) 284
Tsar-Maiden (Tsvetayeva) 183
Tuesday (Wiesner) 277
The Tumultuous Force (Verhaeren) 160
The Tunnel (Kellerman) 172
The Tunnel (Sábato) 217
The Tunnel of Love (De Vries) 223
The Tunnynge of Elynour Rummyng (Skelton) 35
Turcaret; or, The Financier (Lesage) 71
The Turn (Pirandello) 154, 160
The Turn of the Screw (James) 91, 148
Turning Point (Jankovic) 285
The Turning Point (Seferis) 195
Turning Wheels (Cloete) 203
Turtle Island (Snyder) 252, 253
Turtle Moon (Hoffman) 277
The Tuscan Disputations (Cicero) 4
Tusindfodt (Tadrup) 292
The Tutor; or, the Advantages of Private Education (Lenz) 82
Tvillingfeber (Billdoen) 291
Twelfth Night, or What You Will (Shakespeare) 50
The Twelve (Blok) 177
The Twelve Lays of the Gypsy (Palamas) 165
The Twelve-Pound Note (Barrie) 168
Twentieth Century (Emin) 247
Twentieth Century (Hecht) 196
Twenty Love Poems and a Song of Despair (Neruda) 155, 185
Twenty Thousand Leagues Under the Sea (Verne) 127
Twenty Thousand Streets Under the Sky (Hamilton) 200
Twenty Years After (Dumas) 114
The Twenty-fourth of February (Werner) 98
"Twenty-Six Men and a Girl" (Gorky) 149
Twice-Told Tales (Hawthorne) 109
Twilight Crane (Kinoshita) 218
Twilight in the Garden (Lugones) 163
The Twins (Klinger) 82
The Two Admirals (Cooper) 112
Two Adolescents (Moravia) 211
The Two Amphitryons (Camões) 32
Two Brothers (Pratolini) 215

Two Countesses (Ebner-Eschenbach) 137

Two Cultures and the Scientific Revolution (Snow) 231

The Two Drovers (Scott) 105

The Two Foscari (Byron) 93, 102

The Two Friends; or, The Merchant of Lyons (Beaumarchais) 81

The Two Gentlemen of Verona (Shakespeare) 44

The Two Klingsbergs (Kotzebue) 95

The Two Lamps (Krige) 238

Two Little Misogynists (Spitteler) 165

The Two Lovers of Heaven (Calderón de la Barca) 48, 56

Two on a Tower (Hardy) 135

Two People (Dehmel) 161

Two Serious Ladies (Bowles) 210

The Two Sources of Morality and Religion (Bergson) 196

Two Thousand Seasons (Armah) 251

The Two Towers (Tolkien) 225

Two Virgins (Markandaya) 251

"The Two Voices"(Tennyson) 93

Two Waters (Melo Neto) 226

Two Women (Moravia) 228

Two Women (Sarabhai) 221

Two Years Ago (Kingsley) 120

Two Years Before the Mast (Dana) 111

The Twopenny Post Bag (Moore) 99

The Twyborn Affair (White) 258

Tydverdryf/Pastime (Eybers) 288

Typee (Melville) 114

Typhoon (Conrad) 155, 161

Tyrannick Love (Dryden) 49, 61

Tzili: The Story of a Life (Appelfeld) 263

U

Uber Berge Kam Ich (Walsdorf) 269

"Über das Erhabene" (Schiller) 68

"Über naive and sentimentalische Dichtung" (Schiller) 68

U-Don Jade (Mqhayi) 192

Uffizio delle tenebre (Garavini) 291

The Ugly American (Lederer, Burdick) 229

Ukigumo (Futabatei) 139

"Ulalume" (Poe) 91, 115

Uli the Farmhand (Gotthelf) 112

A ultima quimera (Miranda) 285

The Ultimate Intimacy (Klíma) 290

O ultimo cais (Marques) 280

Ulysses (Joyce) 152, 182

"Ulysses" (Tennyson) 93, 112

Ummachi (Kuttikrishnan) 224

The Unanimous Life (Romains) 166

The Unbearable Lightness of Being (Kundera) 264

Unbekannt verzogen (Schulte) 284

An Unclaimed Inheritance (Chraibi) 236

Uncle Remus: His Songs and Sayings (Harris) 134

Uncle Silas (Le Fanu) 124

Uncle Tom's Cabin (Stowe) 117

Uncle Tom's Children (Wright) 204

Uncle Vanya (Chekhov) 92, 147

Uncollected Poems (Betjeman) 261

Unconditional Surrender (Waugh) 234

Under Fire (Barbusse) 175

Under i september (Ostergren) 283

Under Mausolaeet (Nordbrandt) 268

Under Milk Wood (Thomas) 224

Under Moses (Asch) 177

Under the Frog (Fischer) 280

Under the Greenwood (Hardy) 129

Under the Net (Murdoch) 224

Under the Volcano (Lowry) 235

Under the Windows and Other Poems (Lowell) 127

Under the Yoke (Yazov) 143

Under Two Flags (Ouida) 126

Under Western Eyes (Conrad) 155, 169

The Underground Game (Mallet-Joris) 251

The Underpainter (Urquhart) 288

Undertones of War (Blunden) 190

Underworld (DeLillo) 288

Undine (Fouqué) 98

The Undiscovered Country (Howells) 133

The Undivine Comedy (Krasinski) 109

The Unexpected Wager (Sedaine) 81

Unfinished Business (Bonsal) 212

The Unicorn (Walser) 242

The Universal Baseball Association, Inc., J. Henry Waugh, Prop. (Coover) 244

The Universal Heir (Regnard) 71

A Universal History of Infamy (Borges) 154

The Universal Passion; or, The Love of Fame (Young) 73

The Unknown Eros (Patmore) 131

Unknown Pleasures (Cowley) 295

The Unknown Sea (Mauriac) 206

The Unnamable (Beckett) 154, 223

An Unpleasant Man (Nayman) 294

The Unquiet Spirit (Bernard) 188

The Unspeakable Skipton (Johnson) 231

Unstete Leute (Viragh) 278

Unter tiden (Turnstrom) 281

Untitled Field (Moore) 161

Untitled Subjects (Howard) 246, 247

Untouchable (Anand) 200

The Unusual Life of Tristan Smith (Carey) 282

The Unvanquished (Faulkner) 204

Unworldly (Shuntaro) 280

Up a Road Slowly (Hunt) 242

Up Above the World (Bowles) 241

Up Country (Kumin) 250

Up the Mountains (Sydykbekov) 203

"Upon the Death of Lord Hastings" (Dryden) 59

The Uprising (Rebrenu) 196

The Uprooted (Blest Gana) 162

The Uprooted (Handlin) 221

Upstairs, Downstairs (Choromanski) 243

Uraniia (Brodski) 270

Urbes luminosas (García Aguilar) 277

Urdargaldur (Porsteinn) 269

Urn (Bely) 168

O Uruguia (Gama) 81

U.S. 1 (Rukeyser) 204

U.S.A. (Dos Passos) 189

The Use of Poetry and the Use of Criticism (Eliot) 152

The Useless Life of Pito Perez (Romero) 205

Utopia (More) 35

Utsikt til paradiset (Ambjornsen) 280

Uvatzfifut (Bar-Yosef) 274

V

V (Pynchon) 237

Va' dove ti porta il cuore (Tamaro) 282

Va Savoir (Ducharme) 282

La vaca sagrada (Eltit) 277

The Vagabond (Colette) 168

Vain Entertainment (Neguse) 183

Valdemar Afterdag (Hauch) 122

"A Valediction Forbidding Mourning" (Donne) 49, 55

The Valentine (Freytag) 114

The Valley of a Thousand Hills (Dhlomo) 208

The Valley of Bones (Powell) 238

The Valley of Fear (Doyle) 174

Vallmobadet (Brunner) 294

Valperga; or, The Life and Adventures of Castruccio, Prince of Lucca (Shelley) 103

The Van (Doyle) 276

Vaniglia e cioccolato (Modignani) 296

Vanillepigen (Michael) 284

Vanishing Point (West) 286

Vanity Fair (Thackeray) 115

De var engang (Holten) 279

Varddjuret (Hermanson) 285

Vargskinnet (Ekman) 294

Varias Rimas ao Bom Jesus (Bernardez) 44

The Varieties of Religious Experience (James) 160

Vasconselos (Simms) 118

Das Vaterspiel (Haslinger) 296

Vathek (Beckford) 85

Vattenorgel (Andersson) 281

Veien tlil Dhaka (Bjornstad) 288

Vendita galline Km 2 (Busi) 280

The Vendor of Sweets (Narayan) 243

Vengeance (Fredro) 108

The Vengeance of the Condor (García Calderón) 185

Venice Diary (Cheng) 281

Venice in Winter (Robles) 260

Venice Preserved (Otway) 64

Un vent se léve qui eparpille (Dalpe) 296

Venus and Adonis (Shakespeare) 31

Venus and the Rain (McGuckian) 264

Venus Observed (Fry) 219

Vera (Schiff) 295

De verbeelding (Franke) 293

Verden forswinner (Koltzow) 288

Verik (Aleichem) 166

Le Véritable Saint Genest (Rotrou) 57

The Veritable Years (Everson) 257

Die verlorene Geschichte (Walter) 280

Vermilion Sands (Ballard) 249

Vermutengen uber die Liebe in einem fremden Haus (Langle) 291

Versek (Petöfi) 112

Verses (Dowson) 146

Verses About the Lady Beautiful (Blok) 162

Verses and Poems (Brodsky) 240

Verses of the Salon (Parra) 236

Verses to Blok (Tsvetayeva) 183

Versi (Leopardi) 104

Verso Paola (Sanvitale) 276

Versuch uber die Jukebox (Handke) 274

Very Happy Marriage (Belohradska) 290

Very Old Bones (Kennedy) 277

The Very Same Day (Gutmane) 271

Verzen (Gorter) 141

Vesuvius (Robles) 234

La via del ritorno (Palandri) 274

Via Gemito (Starnone) 296

Viaggio all'India Orientali (Balbi) 43

Viaje a los olivos (Cham) 296

El viajero de Agartha (Posse) 274

The Vicar of Sorrows (Wilson) 280

The Vicar of Wakefield (Goldsmith) 80

Vice (Ai) 293

Vicious Circle (Agustín) 253

The Victim (Bellow) 215

Victoria (Hamsun) 148

Victoria Deorum (Klonowic) 43

Victorian Voices (Thwaite) 259

The Victories of Love (Patmore) 123

The Victory at Sea (Sims) 181

Victory (Conrad) 155

Vida (Piercy) 259

La vieja sirena (Sampedro) 275

Viejo (González León) 285

Vietnam Discourse (Weiss) 245

The View from Saturday (Konigsburg) 287

A View from the Bridge (Miller) 225

Vikramorvasi (Kālidāsa) 14

Vile Bodies (Waugh) 193

Villa Europa (Bjornstad) 278

The Village (Bunin) 169

The Village (Crabbe) 84

Village Court (Rodrigues Lobo) 52

Village Pictures (Pontoppidan) 135

Village Priest (Balzac) 110

Villette (Brontë) 118

Le Vin est tiré (Desnos) 210

A Vindication of the Rights of Woman (Wollstonecraft) 86

Vineland (Pynchon) 273

Vinterhagen (Vik) 274

Violence (Bausch) 277

La violencia del tiempo (Gutiérrez) 281

The Violent Bear It Away (O'Connor) 232

The Violent Land (Amado) 209

Violet Poems (Herrera y Reissig) 164

Viper in the Fist (Bazin) 216

Viper's Tangle (Mauriac) 196

The Virgin in the Garden (Byatt) 257

The Virgin of Paris (Jouve) 211

The Virgin of Skalholt (Kamban) 193

Virgin Soil (Turgenev) 131

The Virginian (Wister) 160

The Virginians (Thackeray) 120

Virginibus Puerisque (Stevenson) 134

Virginie (Mairet) 55

Virginie: Her Two Lives (Hawkes) 261

Et virkelig liv (Koppenvag) 276

The Vise (Pirandello) 154

The Visible Hand: The Managerial Revolution in American Business (Chandler) 256

A Vision (Yeats) 186

"The Vision of Sin"(Tennyson) 93

The Vision of Sir Launfal (Lowell) 115

Las visiones de Lucrecia (María Merino) 287

Visions (Quevedo y Villegas) 54

Visions of Gerard (Kerouac) 237

Visions of the Daughters of Albion (Blake) 68

The Visit: A Tragi-Comedy (Durrenmatt) 227

A Visit from St. Nicholas (Moore) 103

A Visit to William Blake's Inn: Poems for Innocent and Inexperienced Travelers (Willard) 261

Visitations (MacNeice) 228

The Visiting Physician (Shreve) 286

Vladimir Reborn (Kheraskov) 85
V-Letter and Other Poems (Shapiro) 211, 212
The Voice (Okara) 238
The Voice of Blood (Makonnen) 208
The Voice of God (Moretti) 181
Voices (Boutens) 165
Voices of My Song (Jiménez) 213
Voices of Spring (Maironis) 188
Voices of the Night (Longfellow) 110
Volcano (Endo) 231
The Volcano (Lowery) 215
The Volcano Lover (Sontag) 277
Les voleurs de beauté (Bruckner) 288
Volpone, or the Fox (Jonson) 50
Von allem Anfang an (Hein) 289
Vorgeschichten oder schone Gegend Probstein (Schutz) 250
The Vortex (Rivera) 185
Voss (White) 228
Vowels (Rimbaud) 136
Le Voyage de Monsieur Perrichon (Labiche) 122
The Voyage Out (Woolf) 174
Voyage to the End of the Millennium (Yehoshua) 289
Voyages to the West: A Passage in the Peopling of America on the Eve of the Revolution (Bailyn) 268
"Voyelles" (Rimbaud) 94
The Voyeur (Robbe-Grillet) 225
The Vultures (Becque) 135

W

W. E. B. Du Bois: Biography of a Race, 1868–1919 (Lewis) 281
Wacousta (Richardson) 107
The Wages of Violence (Ouologuem) 245
The Waggoner (Wordsworth) 101
Waiting (Ha) 295
Waiting for Childhood (Elliott) 269
Waiting for God (Weil) 219
Waiting for Godot (Beckett) 154, 223
Waiting for Lefty (Odets) 200
Waiting for Saskatchewan (Wah) 266
Waiting for the Barbarians (Coetzee) 259
Waiting for the Mahatma (Naroyan) 225
Waiting to Exhale (McMillan) 277
Wake for a Red Bitch (Petkavich) 217
Wake Me Yesterday (Donkov) 295
The Wakeful State (Desnos) 210
Wake-Robin (Burroughs) 128
The Waking: Poems, 1933–1953 (Roethke) 222, 223
Walden; or, Life in the Woods (Thoreau) 118
Waldernacht (Rothmann) 282
"The Walk" (Schiller) 68
A Walk on the Wild Side (Algren) 226
Walk Two Moons (Creech) 283
The Wall (Hersey) 219
The Wall of Death (Krige) 241
Wallenstein (Doblin) 180
Wallenstein's Camp (Schiller) 88
Wallenstein's Death (Schiller) 88
Wally the Doubter (Gutzkow) 109
The Waltz of the Toreadors (Anouilh) 221
The Wanderer (Waltari) 218
A Wanderer in Love (Schendel) 165
Wandering (Lu) 156, 187
The Wandering Jew (Heym) 264

The Wandering Jew (Sue) 113
The Wandering of Oisin (Yeats) 140
Wandering Through Three Times (Abashidze) 234
Wanderings of Oisin and Other Poems (Yeats) 152
The Wapshot Chronicle (Cheever) 228, 238
War (Le Clezio) 247
War and Peace (Tolstoy) 90, 124
War and People (Wang) 288
The War of Independence (Van Tyne) 193
The War of the Worlds (Wells) 148
War Poems (Sassoon) 178
The War with Mexico (Smith) 179
"Ward Number Six" (Chekhov) 92, 143
The Ward Wants to Be a Guardian (Handke) 246
The Warden (Arnold) 119
The Warrior Queens (Fraser) 272
The Warrior's Battle (Kleist) 102
Washington, D.C. (Styron) 243
Washington, Village and Capital, 1800–1878 (Green) 236
Washington Square (James) 91, 133
Wasps (Aristophanes) 3
The Waste Land (Eliot) 152, 182
Watch on the Rhine (Hellman) 208
The Water Babies (Kingsley) 123
The Water Hen (Witkiewicz) 181
The Water Witch (Cooper) 106
The Waterfall and the Bonfire (Hauge) 217
The Waterfall (Derzhavin) 86
The Waterfalls of Slunj (Doderer) 237
Waters and Land (Quasimodo) 193
The Water's Eye (Veiga) 270
The Waterworks (Doctorow) 282
Watt (Beckett) 154, 222
The Waverley (Scott) 93, 99
Waves (Benediktsson) 172
The Waves (Woolf) 194
The Waves of the Sea and Love (Grillparzer) 106
Waxing Moon and Waning Moon (Johannes) 248
The Way I Found Her (Tremain) 288
A Way in the World (Naipaul) 282
The Way of a Man (Sillanpää) 196
The Way of All Flesh (Butler) 161
The Way of It (Thomas) 256
The Way of Living in the World (Zhou) 286, 288
A Way of Looking (Jennings) 225
Way of Migration (Najjar) 286
Way of the Cross (Diego) 195
The Way of the World (Congreve) 69
The Way Out (Martinson) 202
The Way Some People Live (Cheever) 210
The Way to Rainy Mountain (Momaday) 246
The Way to the Tomb (Duncan) 212
The Way We Live Now (Trollope) 130
The Way West (Guthrie) 218
The Wayfarer (Natsume) 93, 171
Ways of Escape (Greene) 154
The Ways of the Hour (Cooper) 116
The Wayward Bus (Steinbeck) 215
We (Lindbergh) 189
We Are Still Married (Keillor) 272
We Were the Mujlvaneys (Berriault) 286
Wealth (Aristophanes) 3

The Weary Blues (Hughes) 188
The Weather Cock (Holberg) 73
The Weavers (Hauptmann) 143
The Web and the Rock (Wolfe) 205
The Wedding (Chekhov) 92
The Wedding (Kadare) 244
Weedpatch (Lehtonen) 178
Weekend de chasse a la mère (Brisac) 286
A Weekend with Claud (Bainbridge) 243
Weep Not Child (Ngugi) 24
Weep Not for Me (Edwards) 260
The Weir of Hermiston (Stevenson) 146
Welcome to Hard Times (Doctorow) 232
The Well (Jolley) 267
The Well of Giningi (Abdulla) 245
The Well of Loneliness (Hall) 190
Werner (Byron) 103
Wessex Poems (Hardy) 148
West Eastern Divan (Goethe) 101
West of Your City (Stafford) 232
West Wind (Oliver) 288
West with the Night (Markham) 209
The Western Approaches: Poems, 1973–1975 (Nemerov) 255
Western Star (Benét) 210, 211
The Westing Game (Raskin) 258
West-Running Brook (Frost) 190
Westward Ho! (Kingsley) 119
What a Kingdom It Was (Kinnell) 232
What D'Ye Call It (Gay) 72
What I Lived For (Oates) 282
What I'm Going to Do, I Think (Woiwode) 246
What Is Art? (Tolstoy) 90
What Maisie Knew (James) 91, 147
What Price Glory? (Anderson) 185
What Remains (Delblanco) 295
What Work Is (Levine) 276
What's Bred in the Bone (Davies) 266
What's O'Clock (Lowell) 187
Wheat in Motion (Verhaeren) 171
When His Hour Came (Glyn) 168
When I Lived in Modern Times (Grant) 295
When I Whistle (Endo) 242
"When Lilacs Last in the Dooryard Bloom'd" (Whitman) 124
When Love Is Young (Halbe) 144
When One Has Lived a Long Time Alone (Kinnell) 273
When She Was Good (Roth) 243
When the Light Is Out (Ngo) 206
When the War Was Over (Frisch) 218
When We Are Married (Priestley) 204
When We Dead Awaken (Ibsen) 94, 149
When We Were Orphans (Ishiguro) 295
Where Angels Fear to Tread (Forster) 163
Where I'm Calling From: New and Selected Stories (Carver) 270
Where Shall I Go? (Disengomoko) 210
Where the Air Is Clear (Fuentes) 230
Where the Jackals Howl and Other Stories (Oz) 240
Where the Wild Things Are (Sendak) 238
Whilomville (Crane) 158
The Whipping Boy (Fleischman) 268

The Whirlwind (Bernstein) 163
Whiskey Galore (Mackenzie) 215
The Whispering Roots (Day-Lewis) 247
White (Paz) 243
The White Book (Agustini) 165
White Buildings (Crane) 188
White Deer Plains (Cheng) 288
The White Devil (Webster) 51
The White Fan (Hofmannsthal) 147
White Fang (London) 164
The White Goddess (Graves) 216
The White Guard (Bulgakov) 246
The White Hotel (Thomas) 260
White Jacket; or, The World in a Man-of-War (Melville) 116
White Man Yellow Man (Endo) 225
The White Monkey (Galsworthy) 185
White Nights (Gudmundsson) 199
White Robes (Dudintsev) 271
White Teeth (Smith) 295
White Wings (Barry) 188
The White Woman (Baudelaire) 92
The White Youthfulness (Rodenbach) 138
The White-Footed Deer and Other Poems (Bryant) 113
Whither Gone? And Where's the Window? (Sosnora) 296
Whitman (Holloway) 189
Whitsongs (Leino) 161
Who Can Be Happy and Free in Russia? (Nekrasov) 125
The Whole Booke of Psalmes (Sternhold, Hopkins) 38
Whole Life Star (Bandeira) 240
The Whole Motion (Dickey) 277
The Whole Sky (Yadav) 232
Who's Afraid of Virginia Woolf? (Albee) 235
Why Did You Leave the Horse Alone? (Darwish) 281
"Why I Live at the P.O." (Welty) 208
Why Marry? (Williams) 177
Why Mosquitoes Buzz in People's Ears (Aardema) 254
Why Survive? Being Old in America (Butler) 254
The Wicker Work Woman (France) 147
Wickford Point (Marquand) 205
The Wide Net (Welty) 210
Wide Open (Barker) 295
Wide Sargasso Sea (Rhys) 241
Widecombe Fair (Phillpotts) 172
The Widow (Corneille) 48
The Widow Fiorvanti (Moretti) 208
A Widow for One Year (Irving) 290
The Widow Lerouge (Gaboriau) 125
Widower's Houses (Shaw) 153
Widows (Dorfman) 263
The Widow's Tears (Chapman) 51
Wieland; or, The Transformation (Brown) 88
A Wife (Overbury) 52
The Wife of Claude (Dumas) 129
The Wild Ass's Skin (Balzac) 106
Wild Beasts Are Tamed by Love (Calderón de la Barca) 48, 61
Wild Blew the Wind (Nokan) 236
The Wild Blue Yonder (Thomas) 273
The Wild Boys (Burroughs) 249
Wild Conquest (Abrahams) 220
The Wild Duck (Ibsen) 94, 136
Wild Earth (Colum) 165
Wild Flowers (Deus) 126

The Wild Gallant (Dryden) 49, 60
The Wild Goose (Mori) 170
Wild Gratitude (Hirsch) 267
The Wild Iris (Gluck) 279
Wild Root (Ibarourou) 183
The Wild Rose Bush (Kasprowicz) 148
A Wild Sheep Chase (Murakami) 262
"The Wild Swans at Coole" (Yeats) 176
The Wild Swans at Coole (Yeats) 152
A Wilderness of Mirrors (Frisch) 239
Wildlife (Ford) 273
Wilhelm Meister's Apprenticeship (Goethe) 67, 87, 103
Wilhelm Meister's Apprenticeship (Carlyle) 103
Wilhelm Meister's Travels (Goethe) 102
The Will of Krishnakunta (Chatterjee) 132
The Will of the People (Sarabhai) 210
The Will to Change: Poems, 1968–1970 (Rich) 249
Will You Please Be Quiet, Please? (Carver) 255
"Wille Brew'd a Peck o'Maut" (Burns) 68
William Cooper's Town: Power and Persuasion on the Frontier of the Early American Republic (Taylor) 286
William Tell (Schiller) 68, 96
Willow Pipes (Claussen) 149
Wind, Sand and Stars (Saint-Exupéry) 206
The Wind (Simon) 228
A Wind in the Door (L'Engle) 250
Wind in the Pines (Zeami Motokiyo) 15
The Wind in the Willows (Grahame) 166
"The Windhover" (Hopkins) 131
The Winding Stair (Yeats) 152
Winds (Perse) 214
Windsor Forest (Pope) 72
Windswept Dawn (Heinesen) 198
Wine (Gay) 71
Wine from These Grapes (Millay) 199
The Wine of Astonishment (Lovelace) 261
The Wine Press (Mistral) 224
Winesburg, Ohio (Anderson) 178
Wing-and-Wing (Cooper) 112
The Winged Legend of Wieland the Blacksmith (Viélé-Griffin) 158
The Winged Sandal (Régnier) 164
Wings of Knives and Nails (Csoori) 260
The Wings of the Dove (James) 91, 160
Winner Take Nothing (Hemingway) 153, 197
Winner Takes All (Wellershof) 263
Winnie Mandela's Football Team (Rabikovitz) 289
Winnie the Pooh (Milne) 188
"Winter" (Thomson) 73
A Winter Journey (Benet) 250
Winter Lair (Delblanc) 253
Winter Night (Leino) 163
The Winter of Our Discontent (Steinbeck) 234
Winter Sonnets (Ivanov) 181
Winter Trees (Plath) 250
"Wintering Out" (Heaney) 250

The Winter's Tale (Shakespeare) 31, 51
Winter's Tales (Dinesen) 209
Winterset (Anderson) 200
Wise Blood (O'Connor) 221
Wit (Edelson) 292
The Witches of Eastwick (Updike) 264
With Eyes at the Back of Our Heads (Levertov) 231
With Fire and Sword (Sienkiewicz) 136
With Pleasure, Dear Sirs (Fula) 226
With the East Wind (Aldecoa) 227
With Women's Names (Palau i Fabre) 270
Withered Leaves (Franko) 138
Within a Budding Grove (Proust) 178
Within the Gates (O'Casey) 197
Without a Hero (Boyle) 282
Without Reason (Chacel) 233
Without Remedy (Storni) 179
Without Truce (Torres Bodet) 228
Witness for the Prosecution (Christie) 222
A Witness Tree (Frost) 209, 210
Die Wittenbergische Nachtigall (Sachs) 36
Wives and Daughters (Gaskell) 124
A Wizard of Earthsea (Le Guin) 244
Woe from Wit (Griboyedov) 103
Wolf's Salt (Popa) 254
The Woman at the Washington Zoo: Poems and Translations (Jarrell) 232, 241
Woman in Her Prime (Saichi) 280
The Woman in the Dunes (Abe) 236
Woman in the Mirror (Meri) 237
The Woman in White (Collins) 121
A Woman Killed with Kindness (Heywood) 51
The Woman Killer and the Hell of Oil (Chikamatsu) 73
The Woman of Andros (Terence) 5, 9
A Woman of Means (Taylor) 219
Woman of Paris (Becque) 137
The Woman of Rome (Moravia) 215
The Woman of Samos (Menander) 3
A Woman of the Pharisees (Mauriac) 208
The Woman Taken in Adultery (Fontane) 135
The Woman Thou Gavest Me (Caine) 172
Woman Triumphant (Blasco Ibáñez) 164
A Woman Who Devoted Her Entire Life to Love-Making (Ihara Saikaku) 64
The Woman Who Was Poor (Bloy) 147
The Woman's Prize, or the Tamer Tamed (Fletcher) 54
The Women at Point Sur (Jeffers) 189
Women at the Ecclesia (Aristophanes) 3
Women at the Thesmophoria (Aristophanes) 3
Women Beware Women (Middleton) 53
Women in Love (Daudet) 120
Women in Love (Lawrence) 180
Women in the Nineteenth Century (Fuller) 114
Women in the Wall (O'Faolain) 254
Women in Their Beds (Berriault) 288

The Women of Brewster Place (Naylor) 261
Women on Gallows Hill (Hauge) 229
The Women Who Walked into Doors (Doyle) 288
Women with Men (Ford) 288
Wonder Maid (Kosztolányi) 188
The Wonder Rabbi of Barcelona (Lasker-Schuler) 181
Wonderful Night in Paris (Grupac) 292
The Wonderful Wizard of Oz (Baum) 158
Wondering Through Winter (Teale) 241
The Wonders of the Invisible World (Mather) 65
The Wonder-Working Magician (Calderón de la Barca) 48, 56
The Wood Nymph, or the Living Corpse (Mairet) 55
Wooden Clara (Conscience) 116
Wooden Icons (Arghezi) 193
Woodlanders (Hardy) 138
Woodrow Wilson, American Prophet (Walworth) 230
Woodrow Wilson: Life and Letters (Baker) 206
Woodstock; or, The Cavalier: A Tale of The Year 1651 (Scott) 104
The Wooers (Eichendorff) 107
Word after Word (Rzewic) 283
A Word Child (Murdoch) 253
The Word for World's Forest (Le Guin) 250
Word over All (Day-Lewis) 210
Words for Music, Perhaps, and Other Poems (Yeats) 196
Words for the Wind (Roethke) 228
Words in the Sand (Buero Vallejo) 218
Workers, a Story of Hatred (Koch) 171
Working People (Kielland) 134
Works (Pope) 76
Works of Love (Kierkegaard) 91
The World (Munk) 196
The World According to Garp (Irving) 257
The World as Will and Idea (Schopenhauer) 101
The World Doesn't End (Simic) 273
World Enough and Time (Warren) 219
The World Is a Wedding and Other Stories (Schwartz) 216
"The World Is Too Much With Us" (Wordsworth) 97
World Light (Laxness) 203
The World of Chance (Howells) 143
The World of Drama (Kerr) 177
The World of Nagaraj (Narayan) 274
The World of Seven Wells (Storni) 199
The World of the Maharachias (Arévalo) 205
The World of the Ten Thousand Things: Poems, 1980–1990 (Wright) 273
The World of the Thibaults (Martin du Gard) 182
The World of Wonders (Davies) 253
A World on the Wane (Lévi-Strauss) 225
Worlds, Mirrors, Magics (Chedid) 271
World's End (Boyle) 269, 270
World's End (Sinclair) 207
World's Fair (Doctorow) 265

The World's Illusion (Wasserman) 178
Worship Company of Fletchers (Tate) 282
Worthy It Is (Elytis) 231
The Would-Be Gentleman (Molière) 61
A Would-Be Saint (Jenkins) 257
The Wound and the Bow (Wilson) 208
Woyzeck (Büchner) 110, 132
The Wrath of the Ancestral Spirits (Jordan) 207
The Wreath at the Foot of the Mountain (Li) 261
"The Wreck of the Deutschland" (Hopkins) 130, 177
"The Wreck of the Hesperus" (Longfellow) 111
A Wrinkle in Time (L'Engle) 235
A Writer's America: Landscape in Literature (Kazin) 270
The Writing Life (Dillard) 272
Writings of a Prisoner (Gaediaty) 166
Wupper River (Lasker-Schuler) 167
Wuthering Heights (Brontë) 115
Wyandotte (Cooper) 113

X

Xenia (Montale) 242
Xiyou Ji (Wu) 44
X-Ray of the Pampa (Martínez Estrada) 198

Y

Yama: The Pit (Kuprin) 168
Yankee from Olympus (Bowen) 211
A Yard of the Sun (Fry) 247
Yarrow Revisited and Other Poems (Wordsworth) 92
Yasvantrav Khare (Hari Narayan Apti) 143
"Ye Banks and Braes o'Bonnie Doon" (Burns) 68
The Year Has No Spring (Hauge) 216
The Year in San Fernando (Anthony) 240
The Year of My Life (Issa) 101
The Year of the Death of Ricardo Reis (Saramago) 280
The Year of the French (Flanagan) 258
The Year of the Frog (Simecka) 281
The Year of the Soul (George) 147
The Yearling (Rawlings) 204, 205
The Years (Woolf) 203
A Year's Life, and Other Poems (Lowell) 111
Years of Grace (Barnes) 194
The Years with Laura Diaz (Fuentes) 294
Yeast (Kingsley) 115
The Yellow Admiral (O'Brian) 286
Yellow Black Radio Broke Down (Reed) 246
Yellow Jack (Howard) 198
Yellow Sparks (Bacovia) 188
"The Yellow Wallpaper" (Gilman) 149
The Yellow-Plush Correspondence (Thackeray) 109
The Yemassee (Simms) 108
Yerma (García Lorca) 155, 199
Yesterday (Dermont) 220
Yesterday (Hofmansthal) 142
Yesteryear and Yesterday (Verlaine) 136
Yet Another Wish (Muschg) 258

"Yet I Do Marvel" (Cullen) 186
Yijing (Wenwang) 1
Yin: New Poems (Kizer) 264, 265
¡Yo! (Alvarez) 290
Yo soy la rumba (Infante) 281
The Yoke of Pity (Breda) 170
Yom haOr shel Anat (Megged) 278
Yoman shel Zug Me'ohav (Sened, Sened) 278
Yorubus, You Must Think (Ogunde) 239
"You Are Men" (Jouve) 174
You Can't Do Both (Amis) 282
You Can't Take It With You (Hart, Kaufman) 201, 203
You Must Remember This (Oates) 269
You Never Can Tell (Shaw) 153

The Young and the Old (Pirandello) 154
The Young Assassin (Goytisolo) 224
The Young Fate (Valery) 176
"Young Goodman Brown" (Hawthorne) 108
The Young Lions (Shaw) 216
Young Lonigan: A Boyhood in Chicago Streets (Farrell) 196
The Young Man from Atlanta (Foote) 283
Young Man in Chains (Mauriac) 172
The Young Manhood of Studs Lonigan (Farrell) 198
Young Men and Fire (Maclean) 277
Younger Edda 13
The Younger Son (Shapiro) 271

Your Silence, My Voice (Kaschnitz) 236
Youth and the Bright Medusa (Cather) 180
The Youth of the Cid (Castro y Bellvís) 52
Yusuf u Zulaikha (Jāmī) 28

Z

Zadig (Voltaire) 77
Zaire (Voltaire) 75
Zakhar Berkut (Franko) 136
Zalacaín el aventurero (Baroja) 168
Zalán futása (Vörösmarty) 104
Zanoni (Bulwer-Lytton) 112
Zapolya (Coleridge) 100
Zaynab (Haykal) 173
Zazie in the Metro (Queneau) 231

Zemah David (Gans) 44
Zenobias liv (Reich) 292
Zero Hour (Nijhoff) 209
Zero Hour and Other Documentary Poems (Cardenal) 232
Zettel's Dream (Schmidt) 248
The Zigzag Child (Grossman) 282
The Zodiac (Dickey) 255
Zone Journals (Wright) 271
Zone of Emptiness (Hiroshi) 221
The Zoo Story (Albee) 231
Zorba the Greek (Kazantzakis) 214
Zucherman Unbound (Roth) 260
Zukunftsmusik (Enzensberger) 276
Zuleika Dobson (Beerbohm) 169
Zulu Poems (Kunene) 248
The Zurich Idyll (Faesi) 166

Author Index

Entries in the index are filed word for word.

A

Aakjaer, Jeppe 125, 162, 192
Aardema, Verna 254
Abad Faciolince, Hector 283
Abasheli, Aleksandre 136, 223
Abashidze, Grigol 171, 234
Abasiyanik, Said Faik 163, 223
Abbas, Khwaja Ahmad 172
Abbey, Edward 244, 253
Abbott, George 232
Abdass-abur, Salah 240
Abdul Illahi, Musa 133
Abdülbâki, Mahmud *See* Bâki
Abdulla, Muhammad Said 177, 206, 233, 245
Abdullah bin Abdul Kadir 87, 116, 118
Abdurrahman Mohammad 58
Abdurrahman Sharafkandi *See* Hazhar
Abe Kobo (Abe Kimifusa) 184, 217, 236, 251, 279
Abedi, Sheikh Kaluta bin Amri 184, 237
Abelaira, Augusto 289
Abélard, Pierre 22
Abell, Kjeld 158, 205, 233
Abercrombie, Lascelles 204
Abish, Walter 259, 260
About, Edmond François Valentin 105, 137
Abrahams, Peter Lee 178, 213, 220, 241
Abrahamsen, Aase Foss 266
Abralmuti Hizazi, Ahmad 199
Abramov, Fedor Aleksandrovich 253, 262
Abramovich, Sholem Jacob *See* Sefarim, Mendele Mokher
Abrams, Mayer Howard 222
Abro, Jamaluddin 184
Abruquah, Joseph Wilfred 244

Abse, Daniel 183
Abu Madi, Iliya 140, 206, 227
Abu al-Majd Majdud ibn Adam *See* Sanā'ī
Abu Shadi, Ahmad Zaki 142, 224
Abū Tammām 19
Abubakar, Imam 179
Abudakar, Tafawa Balewa 241
Abush, Dorit 286
Accius, Lucius 9, 10
Acevedo Díaz, Eduardo 117, 145, 184
Achchygyya, Amma (Nijikulay Jogyorebis Muordinov) 163, 203, 212
Achebe, Albert Chinualumogu (Chinua) 192, 229, 232, 243, 269
Acheson, Dean 247
Achterberg, Gerritt 162, 213, 235
Acker, Kathy 215
Ackerman, Karen 271
Ackroyd, Peter 217
Acosta, Uriel 42
Acuña, Rosario de 117, 131, 183
Adair, Gilbert 278
Adam, Paul 122, 161, 179
Adamic, Louis 148, 219
Adamov, Arthur 165, 225, 246
Adams, Alice 272
Adams, David 295
Adams, Henry Brooks 110, 164, 172, 177, 178
Adams, James Truslow 182, 183
Adán, Martín (Rafael de la Fuente Benavides) 165, 265
Adcock, Fleur 198, 243, 249, 252, 258, 267
Addarian, Garnik 185
Addison, Joseph 62, 71, 72
Ade, George 125, 211
Adiga, Gopalakrishna 221
Adivar, Halide Ebid 201, 237
Adler, Renata 255
Adonis (Ali Ahmed Said) 192
Advani, Bheeromal Mehrchand 222
Ady, Endre 131, 164, 178

AE (George William Russell) 125, 199, 200
Aelian 17
Aeschylus 2, 6
Afanasyev, Viktor Grigoryevich 104, 128
Afawark, Gabra Iyasus 126, 214
Afghani, Ali Mohammad 185
Agar, Herbert 198
Agathon 7, 8
Agee, James 166, 208, 224, 228
Agnon, Shmuel Yosef 139, 179, 204, 216, 241, 246
Agruedas, Alcides 213
Aguilar Camín, Hector 277
Agustín, José 253, 262
Agustini, Delmira 137, 165, 169, 173
Ahlin, Lars Sven 173, 213, 223, 229, 277
Ahmad, Jalal Al-e 245
Ahmade Khani 58
Ahmed, Aziz 172, 213, 214
Ahmed, Jalal Ali 179, 230
Ahmedi, Taceddin 25, 26
Aho, Juhani 122, 136, 147, 164, 169, 180
Ahti, Risto 264
Ai 293
Ai Qing 285
Aicard, François-Victor-Jean 115, 130, 131, 180
Aichinger, Ilse 216
Aidt, Naja Marie 295
Aiken, Conrad 139, 193, 222, 250
Aistis, Jonas 250
Aitmatov, Chingiz 270, 274
Ajebar, Assisa 201
Akhmatova, Anna (Anna Andreyevna Gorenko) 139, 171, 173, 241
Akiko, Yosano 132
Akins, Zoe 200
Aksakov, Sergey Timofeyevich 86, 119, 120, 121
Aksyonov, Vasily Pavlovich 237, 259, 261, 274, 291

Akutagawa Ryūnosuke 142, 174, 189
Alabaster, William 55
Alarcón, Antonio de 107, 130, 141
Alas y Ureña, Leopoldo 117, 136, 141, 159
Alavi, Bozorg 161, 199
Alavi, Gopalakrishna 221
Albahari, David 289
Albee, Edward 190, 230, 231, 233, 235, 240, 241, 242, 253, 281, 282
Alberti, Rafael 159, 192, 208, 292
Alcaeus 6
Alcantar, Osvaldo (Baltasar Lopes de Silva) 161
Alcott, Amos Bronson 88, 111, 126
Alcott, Louisa May 107, 128, 139
Aldanov, M. A. 139, 184, 206, 227
Aldecoa, Ignacio 224, 227
Aldington, Richard 142, 192, 235
Aldiss, Brian 235, 251, 266
Aldrich, Thomas Bailey 109, 127, 165
Alecsandri, Vasile 102, 118, 141
Alegría, Claribel 184, 262
Alegría, Rafael 208
Aleichem, Sholem 166, 175
Aleixandre, Vicente 147, 200, 224, 236, 245, 253, 255, 263
Aleksandrovich, Mikhail 163
Alemán, Mateo 38, 45, 52
Alencar, José de 105, 120, 124, 131
Aleshkovsky, Yuz 191, 268
Alexakis, Vassilis 284
Alexander, Lloyd 245
Alexis, Willibald 87, 128
Alfieri, Vittorio 77, 83, 96
Alfven, Inger 294
Alger, Horatio 126
Algren, Nelson 166, 215, 217, 226, 260
Ali, Ahmed 170, 239
Ali, Dashti 158
Ali, Sabahattin 163, 207, 215
Alkmaar, Hinrek van 29
Allen, William Hervey 139, 217
Allende, Isabel 209, 262, 265, 294, 296

Allfrey, Phyllis Shand 222
Almeida, Manuel Antônio de 118
Almeida de Portugal, Leonor de 78, 110
Almog, Aharon 274
Almond, David 293
Almqvist, Carl Jonas Love 86, 108, 125
Alnaes, Karsten 278
Alonso, Damaso 147, 212
Alos, Concha 181, 239
Altan, Ahmet 287
Aluko, Timothy Mofolorunso 177, 247
Alvarez, Alfred 191, 252
Alvarez, Julia 290, 295
Alvarez Quintero, Serafín and Joaquín 158, 162, 171
Alvaro, Corrado 145, 188, 193, 226
Amadi, Elechi 198, 243, 246, 257
Amado, Jorge 209, 230
Ambjornsen, Ingvar 280, 284, 294
Ambler, Eric 167, 205, 289
Amichai, Yehuda 184, 268, 294
Amiel, Henri Frédéric 102, 134, 136
Amīr Khosrow 23, 25
Amiri, Mirza Sadeq Khan 121, 176
Amis, Kingsley 181, 223, 225, 246, 251, 252, 257, 267, 273, 276, 282, 283
Ammers-Küller, Johanna van 136, 182, 186, 241
Ammons, Archie Randolph 187, 260, 269, 279
Amo, Alvaro del 297
Amory, Cleveland 289
Amrouche, Jean 163, 199, 203, 235
Amrouche, Marguerite Taos 171, 254
Anand, Mulk Raj 162, 200, 202
Anaya, Rudolfo A. 250, 254, 264
Anchieta, José de 37, 44
Anderberg, Bengt 294
Andersen, Hans Christian 96, 108, 114, 130
Andersen, Tryggve 147
Anderson, Margaret 173
Anderson, Maxwell 139, 185, 197, 200, 205, 215, 216, 230
Anderson, Paul 187
Anderson, Robert 222
Anderson, Sherwood 130, 178, 207
Anderson-Dargat, Gail 286
Andersson, Dan 139, 179, 211
Andersson, Lars 281
Andrade, Coelho Pinto de 273
Andrade, Eugenio de 183, 266
Andrade, Jorge 181, 226, 230, 243, 263
Andrade, Mario de 183, 191
Andrade, Oswald de 140, 185, 223
Andreevski, Petre M. 284
Andrews, Charles McLean 200
Andreyev, Leonid 128, 175, 178
Andric, Ivo 142, 217, 233, 253
Andrzejewski, Jerzy 167, 217, 262
Angelou, Maya 190, 247, 252, 255, 260, 262, 267
Angot, Christine 292
Anouilh, Jean 168, 202, 209, 221, 222, 231, 268
Ansen, Alan 181, 270
Ansky, Shloime (Solomon Seinwil Rapoport) 123, 173, 179, 180
Anthony, Michael 195, 237, 240, 243
Antin, Mary 171
Antonio, Mario 198, 233

Anvarī (Awhad ad-Dīn ibn Vāhid ad-Dīn Muhammad Khāvarānī) 22
Anwar, Chairil 181, 217, 218
Anzengruber, Ludwig 110, 127, 140
Apollinaire, Guillaume 133, 172, 177
Apollonius of Rhodes 9
Appa, Gurajtada Venkata Rao 122, 147
Appelfeld, Aharon 195, 237, 258, 263, 268, 271, 272, 276, 280, 282, 289, 291, 296
Apperry, Yan 296
Apple, Arnold 251
Apte, Hari Narayan 123, 143, 144, 178
Aql, Said 211
al-Aqqad, Abbas Mahmud 204, 238
Aragon, Louis 199, 208
Aragvispireli, Shio 125, 187
Arai Hakuseki 62, 69, 73
Arany, János 100, 115, 116, 118, 134
Arasanayagam, Jean 269
Arbuah, Joseph Wilfred 206
Arbuthnot, John 76
Archilocus 6
Arciniegas Angueyra, Germán 292
Arden, John 192
Aree, James 229
Aref, Mirza Abulkasim Qazvini 134, 198
Arenas, Reinaldo 210, 262
Aretino, Pietro 29, 38, 39
Arévalo, Martín 187, 205
Arévalo Martínez, Rafael 136, 253
Arghezi, Tudor 133, 189, 193, 242
Arguedas, Alcides 132
Arguedas, José María 176, 230, 234, 245
Aribau, Buenaventura Carles 107
Aridjis, Homero 266, 283
Ariosto, Ludovico 28, 34, 35, 37, 40
Arishima Takeo 132, 176
Aristarchus 9, 10
Aristophanes 3, 7, 8
Aristotle 3, 8
Arland, Marcel 148, 192, 267
Arlen, Michael 145, 185, 226
Arlt, Roberto Godofredo Christophersen 157, 188, 192, 195, 196, 198, 209
Armah, Ayi Kwei 205, 244, 251
Armand, Octavio 213
Armattoe, Raphael Ernest Grail Glipko 171, 222
Armstrong, William H. 247
Arndt, Ernst Moritz 81, 121
Arniches, Carlos 125, 210
Arnim, Bettina von 84, 121
Arnim, Ludwig Joachim von 83, 106
Arnist, August 249
Arnold, Edwin 132
Arnold, Matthew 102, 116, 117, 118, 119, 120, 122, 125, 126, 127, 139
Arouet, François-Marie See Voltaire
Arrabal, Fernando 243, 246, 296
Arrais, Amador 43
Arrebo, Anders Christiensen 54
Arsenijevic, Vladimir 296
Artaud, Antonin 145, 199, 215
Artsybashev, Mikhail 131, 165, 189
Arvidsson, Ingrid 294
Asbjørnsen, Peter Christen 117
Asch, Sholem 133, 165, 175, 177, 179, 188, 190, 206, 227
Ashbery, John 188, 253, 254
Ashton-Warner, Sylvia 263

Asik Pasha 24, 25
Asimov, Isaac 179, 220, 221, 222, 241, 272, 277
Asitas, Jonas 161
Aspenstrom, Werner 218, 222, 224, 289
Assis Brasil, Luis Antonio de 280
Astafyev, Viktor 278
Aster, Clelie 293
Astley, Thea Beatrice May 186, 282, 295
Asturias, Miguel Angel 148, 193, 214, 218, 219, 224, 233, 242, 252
Asvaghosa 12, 17
Atkinson, Justin Brooks 263
Atkinson, Kate 286
'Attār, Farīd od-Dīn 22, 23
Atterbom, Per Daniel Amadeus 105
Atticus, Titus Pomponius 10
Atwood, Margaret 205, 266, 271, 280, 284, 286, 295
Atxaga, Bernardo (José Irazu Garmedia) 273
Aubigné, Théodore-Agrippa d' 39, 52, 54
Auchincloss, Louis 176, 232, 235, 238
Auden, Wystan Hugh 164, 196, 201, 202, 207, 208, 212, 215, 216, 225, 232, 241, 250
Audiberti, Jacques 148, 214, 239
Auerbach, Berthold 113
Auezov, Mukhtar 146, 214, 233
Augier, Émile 101, 115, 140
Augustine (St. Augustine) 13, 17, 18
Austen, Jane 82, 91, 98, 99, 100
Auster, Paul 214, 269
Austin, Mary 161
Avison, Margaret 177, 241
Awhad ad-Dīn ibn Vāhid ad-Dīn Muhammad Khāvarānī See Anvarī
Awoonor, Kofi 199, 238, 249
Ayala, Francisco 230, 236
Ayckbourn, Alan 205, 267
Aying (Qian Xingcun) 157, 255
Aymé, Marcel 159, 197, 210, 214, 242
Ayni, Sadruddin 131, 190, 223
Aytmatov, Chingiz 190, 237
Ayukawa Nobuo 174
Ayyub, Dhun-Nun 206, 216
Azarian, Mary 292
Azevedo, Aluizio 120, 134, 172
Azolsky, Anatoly 289
Azorín (José Martínez Ruiz) 129, 158, 242
Azquah, Gaddiel Robert 136
Azuela, Mariano 129, 176, 178, 221

B

Ba, Mallam Amadou Hampate 179
Ba Jin (Li Feigan) 161, 207
Ba'albakki, Layla 202, 229, 232
Babel, Isaac 144, 195, 206
Babits, Mihály 135, 189, 207
Bacchelli, Riccardo 141, 173, 204, 230, 265
Bach Mai 267
Bach Van 28, 43
Bachmann, Ingeborg 187, 249, 250
Bacon, Francis 40, 50, 53, 54
Bacon, Leonard 208
Bacovia, George (Gheorghe Vasiliu) 133, 188, 227
Baeck, Leo 130, 226
Bagehot, Walter 104, 131
Baggesen, Jens 80, 104
Baghdadi, Shawqi 190

Bagnold, Enid 139, 200, 225, 260
Bagravana, Elisaveta 281
Bahar, Muhammad Taqi 136, 137, 218, 219
Baha' Tahir 283
Bahelele, Jacques 169, 217
Bahr, Hermann 123, 175, 198
Baïf, Jean-Antoine de 37, 43
Bailey, Paul 202, 267
Bailyn, Bernard 244, 268
Bainbridge, Beryl 196, 243, 244, 250, 256, 273, 286, 288, 290
Bajac, Vladislav 296
Baker, Leonard 258
Baker, Ray Stannard 206
Baker, Russell 261, 262
Bakhtin, Mikhail 145, 253
Bâkî (Mahmud Adülbâki) 36, 49
Bakin, Dmitry 287, 291
Bakunts, Aksel 148
Balaguer, Victor 103, 159
Balance, René 207
Balassi, Bálint 39, 44
Balbi, Gasparo 43
Balbuena, Bernardo de 50, 53
Balchin, Nigel 165, 210, 212, 246
Baldwin, Faith 143
Baldwin, James 184, 222, 225, 226, 234, 235, 237, 244, 252, 254, 268
Baldwin, William 40
Balewa, Abubakar Tafawa 225
Ball, Nelson 293
Ballard, J. G. 192, 249, 251, 252, 253, 264, 276
Balzac, Honoré de 88, 90–91, 105, 106, 107, 110, 111, 114, 115, 116
Balzac, Jean-Louis Guez de 58
Bambara, Toni Cade 205, 250
Bandeira, Manuel 137, 193, 202, 237, 240, 244
Bandello, Matteo 39
Bandyopadhyay, Bibhutibhushan 144, 191, 218
Bang, Hermann 120, 138, 140, 146, 164
Banim, John 87, 104, 112
Banks, Russell 206, 276, 290
Banmo Tin Aun 222
Banner, Hans Christian 241
Bannerjee, Bankim Chandra 134
Banville, John 212, 255, 267
Banville, Théodore de 103, 141
Bao Dai (Zhao Zhenkai) 217
Baquero y Díaz, Gastón 287
Baraka, Imamu Amiri (LeRoi Jones) 198, 238
Baranauskas, Antanas 120
Baranczak, Stanisław 291
Baratynsky, Yevgeny Abramovich 95, 107, 113
Barbaro, Paolo 293
Barbeitos, Arlindo 206
Barbey d'Aurevilly, Jules-Amédée 97, 124, 140
Barbosa, Jorge 159, 200, 248
Barbour, John 26
Barbusse, Henri 129, 175, 200
Barclay, Alexander 34
Barclay, John 42, 53
Baricco, Alessandro 287, 293
Barker, George Granville 171, 203, 275
Barker, Nicola 295
Barker, Pat 283, 284
Barnes, Djuna 142, 201, 261
Barnes, Julian 286

Barnes, Margaret Ayer 194
Barnes, William 95
Barnhardt, Wilton 279
Baroja, Pío 128, 162, 168, 226
Baronius, Caesar 43
Barres, Maurice 122, 139, 183
Barrett, Andrea 286
Barrett, C. Lindsay 207
Barrie, James Matthew 121, 142, 160, 162, 168, 176, 202
Barrios, Eduardo 136, 174, 178, 183, 217, 236
Barrow, George 112
Barry, Philip 188, 189, 190, 196, 205
Barstow, Stan 232
Bartas, Guillaume de Salluste, seigneur du 41, 43
Barth, John Simmons 192, 226, 229, 232, 241, 244, 250
Barth, Karl 178
Barth, Roland 228
Barthelme, Donald 194, 238, 243, 247, 253, 262, 271
Barthelme, Frederick 264
Barthes, Roland 174, 239, 254, 259
Bartra, Agusti 261
Bar-Yosef, Hamutal 274
Barzun, Jacques 164, 231
Basara, Svetislav 289
Bashir, Vaikam Muhammad 168, 211
Bashirov, Gomar 158
Bashō See Matsuo Bashō
Basile, Giambattista 62
Bassani, Giorgio 174, 227, 245
Bat Shahar, Hanna 274
Bataille, Georges 146, 235
Bate, Walter Jackson 238, 256, 257
Bates, H. E. 162, 211, 213, 216, 238, 247, 252
Batra, Agusti 165
Batsányi, János 80, 114
Baturin, Nikolai 201
Bauby, Jean-Dominique 288
Baudelaire, Charles-Pierre 92, 102, 120, 125, 127
Bauernfeld, Eduard von 141
Baum, L. Frank 119, 158, 178
Baum, Vicki 139, 192, 232
Bausch, Richard 282, 286, 293
Baxter, Charles 295
Baxter, James Phinney, III 214
Baxter, Richard 52, 58
al-Bayati, Abdul Wahhab 187, 226, 264, 292
Bayer, Konrad 238
Bayle, Pierre 57, 66, 70
Bazin, Hervé 169, 216, 218, 221, 233, 285
Bazin, René 118, 149, 161, 195
Beattie, Ann 259, 261
Beattie, James 75, 81, 96
Beaumarchais, Pierre-Augustin Caron de 75, 81, 82, 84, 88
Beaumont, Francis 42, 51, 52, 63
Beauvoir, Simone de 165, 214, 218, 224, 230, 267
Beaver, Bruce 241
Bebey, Francis 243
Becher, Johannes R. 229
Becker, Ernest 252
Beckett, Samuel 154, 163, 204, 220, 222, 223, 228, 229, 234, 245, 247, 271
Beckford, William 79, 85
Becque, Henry 135, 137
Bécquer, Gustavo Adolfo 109, 127, 128

Beddoes, Thomas Lowell 96, 116
Bede, the Venerable 13, 14, 18, 19
Bedi, Rajinder Singh 174, 236
Be'er, Hai'm 293
Beer, Johann 59, 64, 69
Beerbohm, Max 128, 169, 226
Beer-Hofmann, Richard 163
Behan, Brendan 181, 183, 224, 229, 238
Behn, Aphra 56, 63, 64, 65
Behramoglu, Ataol 209
Behrman, Samuel Nathaniel 189, 192, 194
Bei Dao 270
Belance, René 174
Belinsky, Vissarion Grigoryevich 98, 115
Bell, Clive 173
Bellamy, Edward 116, 139, 148
Bellay, Joachim du 36, 39
Belleau, Rémy 36, 41
Belli, Carlos Germán 188, 234, 239, 242, 248, 270
Bellman, Carl Michael 86, 87
Bello, Andrés 83, 104, 124
Belloc, Hilaire 127, 160, 222
Bellonci, Maria 272
Bellow, Saul 174, 211, 215, 222, 226, 231, 238, 244, 247, 253, 254, 261, 269, 272, 288
Belohradska, Hans 290
Bely, Andrei 133, 160, 162, 168, 173, 198
Bemis, Samuel Flagg 189, 218
Ben Jelloun, Tahar 251, 255, 266, 289
Benavente y Martínez, Jacinto 125, 161, 163, 165, 172, 182, 191, 208, 223
Benawa, Abdurrauf 171
Benchley, Peter 206, 272
Benchley, Robert Charles 139, 201, 212
Benda, Julien 189
Benedetti, Mario 179, 227, 231, 233, 240, 294
Benedictsson, Victoria 139
Benediktsson, Einar 123, 147, 164, 172, 193, 206
Benet, Juan 188, 243, 246, 250, 277
Benét, Stephen Vincent 147, 190, 191, 203, 205, 210, 211
Benét, William Rose 208, 209, 218
Benet Goita, Juan 279
Bengtsson, Frans Gunnar 213
Benhadugah, 'Abd al-Hamid 285
Benjamin, Walter 142, 206
Benn, Gottfried 137, 171, 176, 216, 226
Ben-Ner, Yitzhak 202
Bennet, Gwendolyn B. 159
Bennet, Michael 254
Bennett, Alan 261
Bennett, Arnold 125, 160, 166, 171, 184, 186, 193, 194
Bennett, Gwendolyn B. 260
Bensoussan, Albert 291
Bentley, E. C. 120, 226
Béranger, Pierre-Jean de 83, 99
Beranos, George 216
Berberova, Nina Nikolayevna 158, 218, 279
Berdyczewski, Micah Joseph 124, 180
Berent, Wacław 161
Berg, A. Scott 292
Berg, Oyvind 284
Bergen, Johan 262
Berger, John 229, 249, 258

Berger, Uwe 190
Berger, Yves 282
Bergman, Bo Hjalmar 126, 177, 242
Bergman, Hjalmar Frederick Elgerus 135, 169, 179, 187, 194
Bergman, Ingmar 270
Bergson, Henri 121, 140, 146, 165, 189, 196, 208
Berkeley, George 64, 78
Berlin, Isaiah 257
Bernanos, Georges 139, 188, 195, 202, 204, 218
Bernard, Jean-Jacques 139, 181, 185, 188, 249
Bernardez, Diego 44
Bernardin de Saint-Pierre, Jacques-Henri 75, 85, 99
Berne, Suzanne 293
Berner, Mia 183
Bernhard, Thomas 194, 243, 245, 248, 252, 254, 271
Bernheim, Emmanuele 280
Bernstein, Henry 130, 163, 164, 166, 172, 185, 222
Berriault, Gina 286, 288
Berry, Wendell 252, 269
Berryman, John 172, 216, 226, 238, 239, 242, 245, 249
Berto, Luiz 212
Bertolucci, Attilio 220, 264, 294
Bertrand, Louis 112
Bessa Victor, Geraldo 176, 210
Besse Luis, Maria Agustine 224
Bessenyei, György 77, 82, 98
Betab, Sufi Abdukhaqq Khan 245
Beti, Mongo (Alexandre Biyidi) 195, 216
Betjeman, John 163, 197, 229, 232, 241, 252, 260, 261, 263
Betti, Ugo 142, 198, 219, 220, 222
Beveridge, Albert J. 179
Bey, Recaizade Mahmud Ekrem 173
Beyala, Calixthe 293
Beyatli, Yahya Kemal 136, 229
Beyle, Marie-Henri See Stendhal
Bezrǔc, Petr (Vladimir Vasek) 125, 226, 229
Bharati, Subramanya C. 134, 171, 180
Bhatacharya, Bhabhani 163
Bhoosnurmath, S. S. 264
Bialik, Chaim Nachman 129, 198
Biamonti, Alessandro 282
Bian Zhilin 167, 197
Biancardi, Luciano 236
Bianciotti, Hector 284
Bibliowicz, Azriel 277
Bichsel, Peter 199, 293
Bierce, Ambrose 112, 142, 143, 164, 173
Bihari Lal 44, 60
al-Bīrūnī 20, 21
Bilbasar, Kemal 168
Bilderdijk, Willem 79, 98, 102, 106
Billdoen, Britt 291
Billetdoux, François 188, 275
Bing Zin 157
Binkis, Kazys 188
Binyon, Laurence 126, 194, 210
Bioy Casares, Adolfo 172, 207, 224, 246, 292
Bird, Patricia 284
Birdsell, Sandra 278
Birney, Earle 283
Birstein, Yoseel 276
Bishop, Elizabeth 169, 213, 225, 226, 254, 257

Bishop, James Alonzo 268
Bishop, John Peale 194
Bissoondath, Neil 272
Bitner, Dariusz 285
Biyidi, Alexandre See Beti, Mongo
Bjorneboe, Jens 179, 242, 246, 251, 254
Bjørnson, Bjørnstjerne Martinius 107, 120, 122, 123, 127, 130, 161, 168
Bjornstad, Ketil 278, 282, 287, 288
Blackburn, Paul 187, 248
Blackburn, Thomas 223, 246
Blackmore, Richard Doddridge 104, 127, 158
Blackmur, R. P. 239
Blair, Eric Arthur See Orwell, George
Blair, Robert 76
Blais, Marie-Claire 205
Blake, William 68, 79, 84, 85, 86, 87, 103, 104, 130
Blandiana, Ana 209, 239
Blasco Ibáñez, Vicente 125, 164, 166, 175, 190
Blest Gana, Alberto 106, 122, 123, 147, 162, 179
Bloch, Robert Albert 281
Blok, Aleksandr Aleksandrovich 133, 162, 165, 177, 180
Bloom, Allan David 268
Bloom, Harold 273
Bloomgarden, Solomon 127, 189
Blos, Joan W. 259
Bloy, Léon 114, 147, 176
Blunden, Edmund 145, 190, 252
Blunt, Wilfrid 111, 182
Bly, Robert 187, 244, 250, 273
Bo Juyi 19
Bobin, Christian 284
Boccaccio, Giovanni 14, 24, 25
Bock, Jerry 232
Bodel, Jean 23
Bodin, Jean 40
Bodmer, Johann Jakob 66, 84
Bogan, Louise 246
Boge, Karin Maria 209
Bohme, Irene 293
Bohme, Thomas 224
Bohomolec, Franciszek 81
Boiardo, Matteo Maria 27
Boileau, Nicolas 55, 62, 71
Boisonneau, Alice 282
Bojer, Johan 175, 181, 230
Bojic, Veljko P. 278
Bok, Edward 181
Boland, Eavan 211, 259
Böll, Heinrich 176, 218, 219, 223, 231, 237, 249, 252, 265, 266
Bolt, Robert Oxton 283
Bombal, María Luisa 167, 259
Bombeck, Erma 285
Bon, François 284
Bona, Dominique 291
Bond, Edward 260
Bonnefoy, Yves 183
Bonsal, Stephen 212
Bontempelli, Massimo 131, 180, 184, 187, 203, 208, 223, 232
Bontemps, Arna 201, 205, 250
Boorstein, Daniel J. 252
Booth, Martin 290
Borel, Jacques 240
Borel, Petrus 97, 121
Borgen, Carl-Martin 266
Borgen, Johan 159, 240, 257
Borges, Jorge Luis 148, 154, 202, 233, 243, 248, 254, 266, 267
Borrow, George 96, 117, 120, 134

Bosman, Herman Charles 162, 219
Bosschere, Jean de 131, 176, 222
Bossuet, Jacques-Bénigne 63
Boswell, James 76, 84, 86, 87
Botelho, Fernanda 294
Botev, Khristo 115, 131
Botticher, Hans *See* Ringelnatz, Joachim
Boucicault, Dion 101, 112, 115, 117, 120, 121, 141
Boudjedra, Rachid 207, 258
Boufflers, Stanislas-Jean, chevalier de 80
Boulle, Pierre 221, 224, 237, 281
Boullosa, Carmen 294
Bouraoui, Hedi 195
Bourbane, Mourad 235
Bourdet, Edouard 195, 199
Bourget, Paul 117, 136, 140, 200
Bourjaily, Vance Bye 181, 273
Boursault, Edme 64, 70
Bousoño, Carlos 183, 214
Boutens, Pieter Cornelis 165, 166, 175
Bowdler, Thomas 97
Bowen, Catherine Drinker 211, 226, 250
Bowen, Elizabeth 148, 200, 204, 217
Bowering, Marilyn 293
Bowers, Edgar 294
Bowles, Jane 210
Bowles, Paul 167, 216, 221, 225, 241, 260, 270, 292
Bowring, George 269
Boyarsky, Abraham 284
Boyd, Martin à Beckett 143, 190, 249
Boyd, William 280
Boye, Karin 158, 208
Boyer, Frederic 282
Boyle, Kay 232, 265, 277
Boyle, T. Coraghessan 269, 270, 272, 282, 290
Boylesve, René 149, 159, 161
Brackman, Willem 265
Bradbury, Malcom Stanley 263, 278
Bradbury, Ray 179, 219, 220, 222, 228, 235, 265, 294
Bradley, Andre Cecil 162
Bradley, David 261
Bradstreet, Anne 51, 60, 62, 63
Brady, Joan 282
Braine, John Gerard 181, 228, 235, 267, 268
Braithwaite, Edward Ricardo 179
Braithwaite, Richard Bevan 273
Branch, Taylor 272
Brand, Dollar 199
Brandão, Raul 125
Brandes, Georg Morris 112, 129, 189
Brandys, Kazimierz 174, 217, 294
Branner, Hans Christian 160, 209
Brant, Sebastian 29
Brantôme, Pierre de Bourdeille, seigneur de 60
Brathwaite, Edward Kamau 192, 243, 267, 290
Brathwaite, Richard 56
Bratic, Radoslav 278
Braudeau, Michel 291
Braun, Volker 274
Brautigan, Richard 243
Brazdzionis, Bernardes 164
Brecht, Bertolt 147, 153–154, 182, 190, 193, 196, 208, 210, 216, 218, 226
Breda, Julien 170
Bredero, Gerbrand Adriaenszoon 42, 52, 53

Brehal, Nicolas 280
Breitinger, Johann Jakob 83
Brekke, Toril 294
Bremer, Frederika 124
Brennan, Christopher John 127, 173, 195
Brentano, Clemens 83, 112
Bretinger, Johann Jakob 70
Breton, André 145, 190, 193, 241
Bretón de los Herreros, Manuel 87, 129
Brett, Lily 295
Brew, Osborne Henry Kwesi 190
Brewster, Elizabeth 276
Breytenbach, Breyten 272
Breytenbach, Jan Blom 255
Brezan, Jurij 274
Bridges, Robert Seymour 113, 131, 175, 192
Bridie, James (Osborne Henry Mavor) 219
Brierre, Jean 167, 193
Brieux, Eugène 120, 143, 195
Brink, Andre 282, 296
Brisac, Geneviève 286
Broch, Hermann 137, 195, 196, 212, 219, 223
Brod, Max 244
Brodkey, Harold (Aaron Roy Weintraub) 270, 276, 285
Brodsky, Joseph 206, 240, 248, 268, 270, 284, 285
Broger, Suzanne 279
Bromfield, Louis 146, 185, 186, 188, 189, 226
Broniewski, Władysław 146, 235
Bronk, William 177, 261
Bronnen, Arnolt 180
Brontë, Anne 101, 114, 115, 116
Brontë, Charlotte 100, 114, 115, 116, 118, 119, 120
Brontë, Emily 101, 114, 115
Brooke, Henry 70
Brooke, Rupert 138, 174
Brookner, Anita 263, 264, 280
Brooks, Gwendolyn 176, 212, 217, 218, 232, 244, 294
Brooks, Van Wyck 174, 201, 203, 236
Brophy, Brigid 191, 246, 251, 283
Brossa, Joan 178
Brousek, Antonin 284
Brown, Charles Brockden 81, 88, 95, 98
Brown, George Mackay 180, 264, 285
Brown, Larry 276
Browne, Francis F. 133
Browne, Thomas 50, 57, 64
Browning, Elizabeth Barrett 97, 107, 110, 113, 116, 120, 122
Browning, Robert 98, 107, 108, 109, 111, 112, 113, 114, 116, 119, 124, 126, 128, 129, 130, 135, 140
Bruce, Robert V. 270
Bruce, William Cabell 177
Bruckner, Pascal 288
Bruma, Eddy J. 186
Brunner, Ernst 275, 279, 294
Bruno, Giordano 38, 42, 49
Brussig, Thomas 293
Brutus, Dennis 184, 257
Bruzzi, Enrico 284
Bryant, William Cullen 86, 100, 101, 102, 113, 132
Bryce Echenique, Alfredo 294
Bryusov, Valery Yakovlevich 129, 158, 166, 172, 184

Brzozowski, Stanisław 131, 169, 170
Buber, Martin 132, 184, 239
Buchan, John 130, 174, 206
Buchanan, George 42
Büchner, Georg 99, 108, 109, 110, 132
Buck, Paul Herman 204
Buck, Pearl S. 142, 194, 195, 200, 204, 209, 250
Buero Vallejo, Antonio 174, 218, 219, 230, 233, 243, 294
Bufalino, Gesauldo 285
Bujah, Salah ad-Din 284
Bukowski, Charles 179, 231, 281
Buley, R. Carlyle 219
Bulfinch, Thomas 119, 120
Bulgakov, Mikhail Afanasyevich 141, 187, 193, 206, 242, 246, 270
Bull, Olaf 167
Bullins, Ed 199
Bulwer-Lytton, Edward George 96, 105, 106, 107, 108, 109, 110, 111, 112, 113, 115, 116, 118, 129
Bunin, Ivan Alekseyevich 127, 169, 175, 187, 197, 222
Bunting, Eve 283
Bunyan, John 54, 61, 63, 64, 65
Burdick, Leon 229
Burger, Gottfried August 77, 82, 86
Burgess, Anthony 176, 220, 232, 235, 237, 238, 244, 252, 259, 271, 279, 280
Burgess, Gelett 164
Burke, Edmund 74, 85, 87
Burke, Kenneth 219, 279
Burkey, Frances 84
Burman, Carina 281
Burnard, Bonnie 293
Burnett, Frances Hodgson 115, 137, 169, 184
Burney, Frances 78, 83, 111
Burns, James MacGregor 248
Burns, Robert 68, 79, 85, 86, 87, 88
Burnside, John 278
Burroughs, Edgar Rice 130, 173, 218
Burroughs, John 128
Burroughs, William 172, 231, 238, 249, 250, 287
Burrows, Abe 235
Burrows, G. 292
Burton, Richard 102, 141
Burton, Robert 53, 56
Busch, Frederick 288
Busch, Wilhelm 107, 166
Bush, Catherine 295
Busi, Aldo 215, 280, 287
Busken Huet, Conrad 134
Buson 72, 84
Butler, Guy 221, 222, 227, 247
Butler, Robert N. 254
Butler, Robert Olen 279
Butler, Samuel 51, 60, 63, 79, 108, 128, 160, 161
Butor, Michel 187, 227, 232, 251, 286
Butov, Michael 294
Buyda, Yuri 289
Buysse, Cyriel 121, 144, 195
Buzzati, Dino 163, 207, 230, 249
Byars, Bersy 248
Byatt, A.S. 201, 257, 265, 273
Brutus, Dennis
Byron, George Gordon (Lord Byron) 85, 93, 97, 98, 99, 100, 101, 102, 103

C

Caballero, Fernán 87, 116, 131
Cabell, James Branch 132, 176, 178, 229

Cabral de Melo Neto, João 292
Cabrera Infante, Guillermo 191, 240, 268, 285
Cadalso y Vázquez, José de 86
Cadamosto, Alvise da 34
Cahuzac, Patrick 274
Cain, James M. 142, 198, 201, 208, 255
Caine, Thomas Henry Hall 118, 138, 144, 172, 194
Cairasquilla, Tomás 191
Calasso, Roberto 271
Calderón de la Barca, Pedro 48, 49, 54, 55, 56, 59, 60, 61, 63
Caldwell, Erskine 160, 196, 197, 268
Caldwell, Janet Taylor 265
Calisher, Hortense 169, 220, 246, 253
Callado, Antonio 287
Callaghan, Morley Edward 160, 199, 200, 220, 234, 256, 273
Callimachus 3–4, 8, 9
Caludio, Mario 276
Caluza, Reuben Tolakele 158, 239
Calvin, John 34, 52
Calvino, Italo 183, 215, 221, 228, 231, 250, 251, 258, 265
Camarca, Claudio 278
Camille, Roussan 233
Camões, Luíz 32, 36, 41
Camon, Ferdinando 287
Campana, Dino 136, 173, 195
Campana, Dominico 278
Campanella, Tommaso 40, 56
Campbell, George 177
Campbell, John Wood, Jr. 167, 248
Campbell, Joseph 217
Campbell, Roy 206
Campbell, William Wilfred 140
Campion, Thomas 40, 53
Campo, Estanislao del 108, 125, 133
Campos, Augusto de 194
Campos, Haroldo de 191, 278
Camus, Albert 155, 171, 209, 211, 215, 220, 227, 232
Canetti, Elias 162, 200, 251, 260, 281
Canin, Ethan 290
Canique, Carlos 289
Cano Gaviria, Ricardo 281
Cansever, Edip 190
Cao Xueqin 69, 72, 80, 191
Cao Yu 167, 201, 285
Cao Zhi 17
Čapek, Karel 140, 179, 191, 197, 198, 204
Capote, Truman 184, 216, 220, 229, 241, 251, 259, 263
Caproni, Giorgio 263, 276
Caragiale, Ion Luca 117, 132, 133, 136, 141
Cardenal, Ernesto 186, 233, 239
Cardoso Pires, José 289
Carducci, Giosuè 108, 120, 126, 164, 165
Carew, Jan Rynveld 186, 238
Carew, Thomas 44, 56
Carey, Peter 210, 266, 270, 282, 288
Carling, Finn 287, 288, 294
Carlo, Andrea de 296
Carlyle, Thomas 87, 103, 107, 109, 112, 113, 134
Carman, William Bliss 191
Carmen Chacel, Rosa Clotilde Celia María del 281
Caro, Robert A. 253
Carossa, Hans 132, 226
Carpentier, Alejo 161, 218, 223, 236, 253, 259

Carrère, Emmanuel 227, 284

Carroll, Lewis (Charles Lutwidge Dodgson) 107, 124, 128, 131, 140, 148

Carruth, Hayden 180, 230, 257, 277, 286

Carson, Rachel 164, 237, 238

Cartarescu, Mircea 276

Carter, Angela 277

Cartland, Barbara 158, 294

Cartwright, Justin 284

Carvalho, Mario de 285, 289

Carver, Raymond 255, 270, 271

Cary, (Arthur) Joyce Lunel 139, 197, 201, 206, 208, 209, 211, 221, 222, 225, 227

Casal, Julián del 141

Casanova, Giovanni Giacomo 73, 88, 104

Casaubon, Meric 45, 62

Casely-Hayford, Gladys May 161

Casely-Hayford, Joseph Ephraim 125, 192

Casey, John 272

Casic, Dobrica 220

Casona, Alejandro 160, 212

Cassirer, Ernst 212

Cassola, Carlo 176, 270

Castel-Blum, Orly 293

Castelo Branco, Camilo 104, 141

Castiglione, Baldassare 36

Castilho, António Feliciano 95, 110, 130

Castillo, Abelardo 294

Castillo, Michel del 196, 228, 230

Castro, Eugenio de 142, 146, 149

Castro, José Maria de 147

Castro, Rosalía de 109, 123, 133, 136, 137

Castro Alves, Antônio de 127

Castro y Bellvís, Guillén de 52

Cather, Willa 129, 163, 172, 174, 177, 180, 182, 183, 184, 186, 189, 194, 207, 214

Catton, Bruce 223, 231

Catullus 5, 10

Cauwelaert, Didier van 282

Cavafy, Constantine 123, 196

Cavalcanti, Guido 23, 24

Cayrol, Jean-Raphael-Marie-Noël 169, 215, 224, 231, 237, 241

Cazona, Alejandro 239

Cech, Svatopluk 114, 166

Cela, Camilo José 174, 209, 220, 246, 263, 271, 283, 294

Celan, Paul 216, 221

Céline, Louis-Ferdinand 144, 196, 202, 233

Celtis, Conradus 34

Cen Shen 19

Cendrars, Blaise (Frédéric Louis Sauser) 138, 233, 262

Cernuda, Luis 159, 236, 239

Cervantes Saavedra, Miguel de 32, 38, 42, 50, 52

Césaire, Aimé Fernand 171, 237

Céspedes y Meneses, Gonzalo de 53

Chacel, Rosa 147, 213, 230, 233, 265, 271

Challans, Mary See Renault, Mary

Cham, Gerardo 296

Chambers, Edmund Kercheve 223

Chambers, Ephraim 74

Chamisso, Adelbert von 83, 99, 110

Chamoiseau, Patrick 278

Chander, Krishan 172, 206

Chandler, Alfred D., Jr. 256

Chandler, Raymond 139, 205, 207, 230

Chang, Eileen 283

Channing, Edward 187

Chapell, Fred 276

Chaplain, Sid 267

Chapman, George 44, 45, 51, 52, 55, 56

Char, René 212, 214

Charasha, Tembot 159, 191

Charbonneau, Jean 130, 242

Chase, Mary 211, 212

Chateaubriand, François-Auguste-René de 81, 95, 97, 98, 115, 116

Chatterjee, Bankim Chandra 124, 129, 132, 144

Chatterton, Thomas 78, 81, 83

Chattopadhyay, Harindranath 147, 227

Chatwin, Bruce 269

Chaucer, Geoffrey 14, 25, 26

Chaudhuri, Nirod C. 146, 220, 292

Chawaf, Chantal 252

Chayefsky, Paddy 183, 222, 223, 225, 231, 233, 238, 260

Chedid, André 179, 264, 271

Cheever, John 210, 223, 228, 238, 245, 256, 257, 258, 261

Chekhov, Anton Pavlovich 92, 121, 143, 145, 146, 147, 159, 161, 162

Chen, Ying 284

Chenet, Gérard 191, 245

Cheng, A. 281

Cheng, François 291

Cheng Nai Shen 272

Cheng Zongshi 288

Chénier, André-Marie de 80, 86

Chénier, Marie-Joseph-Blaise de 80, 85, 86, 98

Chesterton, G. K. 129, 162, 166, 201

Cheuse, Alan 273

Chevillard, Eric 293

Chields, Carol 283

Chikamatsu Monzaemon 48, 58, 64, 70, 73

Chikovani, Svimon 159

Chiladze, Tamaz 194

Childress, Alice 174, 250, 281

Chimet, Iordan 184

Chirbes, Rafael 297

Chocano, José Santos 130, 164, 166, 198, 199

Chodorov, Edward 270

Chokitsu Kurumatani 291

Chopin, Kate 117, 144, 147, 149, 161

Choquette, Robert Guy 162

Choromanski, Michal 196, 231, 243, 245

Chraibi, Driss 187, 224, 236

Chrichton, Michael 245, 253

Christensen, Martha 282

Christie, Agatha 140, 180, 188, 197, 203, 221, 222, 254

Christine de Pisan 25, 26, 27

Chu Yongshun 65

Chubak, Sadiq 174

Churchill, Winston (American author) 128, 149

Churchill, Winston (English statesman) 129, 159, 197, 214, 222

Chuya Fujino 296

Ciardi, John 174, 267

Cibber, Colley 61, 70, 79

Cicero 4, 10

Ciger-Hronsky, Josef 232

Cima, Annalisa 264

Cixous, Hélène 202, 296

Claeson, Stewe 281

Claesson, Stig 279

Clapp, Margaret 216

Clark, Joan 282

Clark, John Pepper 199, 234, 247

Clark, Manning Hope 275

Clark, Walter Van Tilburg 207, 248

Clarke, Arthur C. 176, 222, 225, 234, 251, 261

Clarke, Marcus 130, 134

Claudel, Paul 126, 164, 168, 170, 171, 177, 180, 192, 193, 224

Claudian 18

Claudius, Matthias 76, 83, 99

Claus, Hugo 288

Claussen, Sophus 124, 138, 149, 186, 194

Clavell, James 241, 253, 281

Cleary, Beverly 263

Cleland, John 77

Clemens, Samuel Langhorne See Twain, Mark

Clemo, Reginald John 281

Clifton, Lucille 269

Cloete, Stuart 203

Close, Robert 283

Clough, Arthur Hugh 101, 115, 122, 127

Coady, Lynn 291

Coburn, Donald L. 254, 256

Cocteau, Jean 139, 188, 189, 192, 199, 214, 236

Codrescu, Andrei 213

Coelho, Marcelo 291

Coelho, Paulo 274

Coetzee, J. M. 256, 259, 262, 263, 282, 292, 293

Coffin, Robert P. Tristram 201

Cohen, Jacob 133, 232

Cohen, Leonard 198, 264, 280

Cohen, Matt 280, 293

Cohen, Robert 286

Coit, Margaret Louise 219

Coleridge, Samuel Taylor 82, 87, 88, 92, 96, 100, 108

Coles, Dean 261

Coles, Don 190

Coles, Robert 250

Colette (Sidonie-Gabrielle Colette) 129, 168, 172, 180, 184, 188, 193, 197, 199, 208, 211, 223

Collarp, Bjorn 294

Colle, Charles 84

Collins, Wilkie 103, 116, 121, 126, 140

Collins, William 73, 76, 77, 79

Collodi, Carlo 104, 135, 141

Collymore, Frank A. 143

Colombier, Jean 274

Colonno, Guido delle 24

Colum, Padraic 165

Combescot, Pierre 276

Combet, Claude-Louis 284

Comenius, Johannes Amos 43, 61

Comines, Philippe de 29

Commager, Henry Steele 289

Commenius, Johann Amos 59

Comon, Ferdinando 293

Compton-Burnett, Ivy 142, 186, 192, 245

Comte, Auguste 87, 120

Condé, Maryse 202, 268

Cong Weixi 290

Congreve, William 61, 66, 69, 74

Connelly, Marc 140, 185, 193, 259

Conquest, George Robert Acworth 176

Conrad, Joseph (Józef Teodor Konrad Korzeniowski) 120, 147, 154–155, 158, 160, 161, 162, 165, 169, 172, 184

Conroy, Frank 279

Conroy, Jack 273

Conroy, Pat 269

Conscience, Hendrik 98, 110, 116, 117, 123, 135

Consolo, Vincenzo 278, 293

Constant, Benjamin 81, 100, 106

Constant, Paule 282, 291

Constantini, Humberto 184, 268

Conti, Guido 293

Conton, William 269

Cookson, Catherine 289

Cooney, Barbara 294

Cooper, James Fenimore 85, 102, 103, 104, 105, 106, 107, 108, 110, 111, 112, 113, 114, 115, 116, 117

Cooper, Susan 254

Coover, Robert 195, 244, 246, 256

Copernicus, Nicolaus 38

Coppée, François 112, 126, 166

Corbin, Alan 291

Corel, François de 144

Cormier, Robert 294

Corneille, Pierre 48, 50, 54, 55, 56, 57, 58, 60, 61, 62, 64

Corrasquilla, Tomás 200

Correia, Heli 296

Correia, Natalia 276

Corso, Gregory 235

Cortázar, Julio 172, 237, 263, 285

Corti, Maria 276

Cosic, Dobrica 180, 224, 234, 250, 274

Costa, Isaäc da 103

Costa, Uriel da 43, 56

Costa Alegre, Caetano da 123, 141

Costain, Thomas Bertram 136, 221, 239

Coster, Charles de 104, 126, 132

Coster, Samuel 51, 60

Cotroneo, Roberto 293

Cotton, John 42, 57, 58

Coulibaly, Augustin Sonde 196

Couperus, Louis 123, 140, 143, 164, 183

Coupland, Douglas 290

Courteline, George 144

Courts-Mahler, Henry 218

Coutinho, Carlos 266

Coverdale, Miles 37

Covington, Vicki 286

Coward, Noël 148, 186, 193, 197, 202, 208, 213, 250, 261

Cowley, Abraham 52, 55, 56, 57, 58, 59, 61

Cowley, Jason 295

Cowley, Malcolm 147, 271

Cowper, William 74, 83, 84, 88, 95

Cozzens, James Gould 160, 194, 197, 198, 209, 216, 217, 228, 256

Crabbe, George 78, 84, 97, 98, 107

Crace, Jim 288, 293

Crane, Hart 148, 188, 193, 195, 197

Crane, Stephen 128, 143, 145, 148, 149, 158

Crashaw, Richard 51, 57, 58

Crawford, Isabella Valancy 136, 138

Crébillon See Jolyot, Prosper, sieur de Crais-Billon

Crébillon fils *See* Jolyot de Crébillon,
    Claude-Prosper
Creech, Sharon 283
Creeley, Robert 187, 235, 246, 250, 257
Creighton, Anthony 229
Crémazie, Octave 104, 132, 135
Cremin, Lawrence A. 260
Cristofer, Michael 255
Croce, Benedetto 125, 221
Crommelynck, Fernand 137, 180, 246
Cronin, A. J. 146, 194, 200, 203, 209,
    211, 227, 260
Crouse, Russell 213
Cruden, Alexander 75
Crutch, Joseph Wood 246
Cruz, Ramón de la 74, 86
Cruz, Sor Juana Inés de la 58, 64, 65,
    66
Cruz e Sousa, João da 144, 158
Csokonai Vitéz, Mihály 82, 88, 96
Csoóri, Sándor 236, 260, 263, 272
Cueva, Juan de la 38, 51
Cujas, Jacques 36, 43
Cullen, Countee 160, 186, 213
Cumali, Necati 180
cummings, e. e. 144, 186, 235
Cumyn, Alan 295
Cunha, Euclides da 125, 160, 167
Cunningham, Michael 292, 293
Curel, François de 143, 145, 147
Curnow, Allen 286
Curti, Merle 211
Curtis, Christopher Paul 295
Cushing, Harvey 187
Cushman, Karen 285
Cyrano de Bergerac, Savinien 52, 59
Czechowicz, Josef 160, 193, 196, 205
Czycz, Stanisław 287

D

Da Ponte, Lorenzo 77, 110
Dabrowska, Maria 139, 196, 226, 239
Dadie, Bernard Binlin 175, 231
Dagerman, Stig Halvard 183, 213,
    214, 217, 223
Dahl, Roald 175, 273
Dahlberg, Edward 255
Dahn, Julius Sophus Felix 108
Dai Houying 269
ad-Daif, Rashid 284
Dalin, Olof von 71, 76, 80
Dalpe, Jean-Marc 296
Damas, Gontran 256
Damas, Leon Gontran 227
Damle, Krishnaji Keshav *See*
    Keshavasut
Dana, Richard Henry 99, 111, 134
Dancourt, Florent Carton 60, 65, 73
Dangerfield, George 222
Daniel, Samuel 50
D'Annunzio, Gabriele 123, 136, 143,
    145, 146, 148, 149, 158, 162, 204
Dante, Nicholas 254
Dante Alighieri 14, 24
Dārā Shikōh 52, 59
Dard, Frederic Charles Antoine 294
Dargatz, Gail Anderson 291
Darío, Rubén 125, 139, 146, 175
Darley, Emmanuel 288
Darrieussecq, Albert 291
Darwin, Charles 97, 121, 128, 134
Darwish, Mahmud 281
Dass, Petter 58, 71
Datta, Michael Madhusudan 103,
    120, 121, 122, 129
Daubla, Theodore 168

Daudet, Alphonse 111, 120, 126, 127,
    130, 131, 136, 147
Daulatshah, Alaoddoule Bakhtishah
    Samarqandi 28
D'Avenant, William 50, 61
Davenport, Marcia Gluck 285
David, David Brio 242
Davidescu, Nicolae 139, 171, 223
Davidson, John 144
Davidson, Nicol *See* Nicol, Abioseh
Davie, Donald Alfred 181, 250, 283
Davies, Robertson 171, 220, 247, 250,
    253, 260, 266, 271, 276, 282, 283
Davis, Harold L. 201
Davis, Owen 183
Davis, Richard Harding 123, 175
Davoyan, Razmik 206
Dawson, Ernest Christopher 125, 158
Day, Clarence 129, 200
Day-Lewis, Cecil 161, 197, 210, 222,
    240, 247, 249
Dazai Osamu (Tsushima Shuji) 167,
    215, 216
De Amicis, Edmondo 114, 126, 138,
    163, 166
de Camp, L. Sprague 294
De Carlo, Andrea 274, 282
de Grazia, Sebastian 273
De la Mare, Walter 129, 164, 226
De Lisser, Herbert George 211
De Man, Paul 178, 249, 262
De Quincey, Thomas 84, 102, 105,
    107, 121
De Voto, Bernard 146, 224
De Vries, Peter 167, 221, 223, 279
Deane, Seamus 286
Dearmer, Geoffrey 285
Debucourt, Philibert-Louis 78, 107
Decharme, Rejean 293
Decimus Junius Juvenalis *See* Juvenal
Dedekind, Friedrich 38
Defoe, Daniel 60, 72, 73, 74
Degler, Carl N. 249
Dehkhoda, Ali Akabar 230
Dehmel, Richard 123, 161, 179
Deighton, Len 235
Dekhoda, Ali Akbar 226
Dekker, Eduard Douwes *See*
    Multatuli
Dekker, Thomas 40, 54, 55
del Giudice, Daniele 284
Delavigne, Jean-François-Casimir 86,
    107, 113
Delblanc, Sven 194, 230, 237, 248,
    252, 253, 254, 266, 281
Delblanco, Nicholas 295
Deledda, Grazia Cosima 128, 158,
    160, 161, 162, 180, 187, 201
Delgado, Fernando 285
Delibes, Miguel 179, 292
Deligne, Gastón Fernando 122, 172
DeLillo, Don 201, 254, 270, 276, 277,
    288
Delius, Christian 293
Della Valle, Federico 43
Delmedigo, Joseph Solomon 43, 59
DeLynn, Jane 273
Demirtichian, Derenik 131, 210, 226
Denevi, Marco 289
Denis, Nigel 241
Dennett, Tyler 198
Depestre, René 187
Dermont, Maria 220, 225
Derrida, Jacques 250, 262, 269
Derzhavin, Gavrila Romanovich 76,
    83, 84, 86, 100

Desai, Anita 259
Desbiolles, Mayline 293
Desbordes-Valmore, Marceline 111,
    113
Descartes, René 44, 56, 58
Desmarets de Saint-Sorlin, Jean 44, 62
Desnos, Robert 158, 210, 211, 212
Desportes, Philippe 42
Destouches, Philippe 63, 74, 75
Deus, João de 106, 126, 131, 146
Deutsch, Babette 261
Devkota, Laxmiprasad 167, 230
DeVoto, Bernard 216
Dewey, John 221
Dexter, Pete 275
Dhlomo, Herbert Isaac Ernest 160,
    208, 226
Dhlomo, Rolfus Reginald Raymond
    158, 191
Di Lascia, Mariateresa 284
Diallo, Bakary 142, 188
Diamond, Jared 290
Dib, Mohammad 179, 221
Dickens, Charles 90, 98, 109, 110,
    111, 112, 113, 114, 115, 116, 117,
    118, 119, 121, 124, 127
Dickey, James 183, 235, 238, 240, 255,
    268, 277, 287
Dickinson, Emily 106, 137, 141
Diderot, Denis 71, 77, 79, 80, 84
Didion, Joan 198, 244, 247, 255, 264,
    286
Diego, Gerardo 187, 195, 207, 208,
    227
Diest, Peter Dorland van 29, 35
Díez, Luis Mateo 289, 297
Diktonius, Elmer 233
Dillard, Annie 212, 252, 253, 272
Dillon, George 195
Dimic, Moma 296
Dimitrova, Blaga 275
Dinesen, Isak 136, 198, 203, 209, 218,
    235
Ding Ling 161, 267
Dinis, Julio 110, 126, 128
Diop, Brago Ismael 163, 271
Diop, Ousmane Soce 200
Dipoko, Mbella Sonn 241
Disengomoko, A. Emile 174, 210, 239
Disraeli, Benjamin 113
Ditzen, Rudolf *See* Fallada, Hans
Divis, Ivan 281
Dizzy, Raz 186
Dlithey, Wilhelm 169
Doblin, Alfred 120, 132, 174, 180,
    192, 196, 199, 227
Dobrolyubov, Nikolay Aleksan-
    drovich 122
Dobson, Henry Austin 111, 180
Doctorow, E. L. 194, 232, 248, 253,
    259, 265, 272, 273, 282
Doderer, Heimito von 146, 227, 237,
    241
Dodge, Mary Mapes 124
Dodgson, Charles Lutwidge *See*
    Carroll, Lewis
Dodson, Owen 262
Doerr, Harriet 279, 284
Dolittle, Hilda 186
Domecq, Brianda 275
Donald, David 233, 270
Donato, Pietro di 277
Donelaitis, Kristijonas 101
Donkov, Kalin 295
Donleavy, J. P. 187, 225, 237, 241,
    249, 251, 256, 258

Donne, John 41, 48–49, 51, 55
Donoso, José 184, 228, 242, 248, 278,
    285
Dorfman, Ariel 209, 263
Dorst, Tankred 186, 233, 245
Dos Passos, John 146, 181, 186, 189,
    193, 196, 201, 210, 217, 220, 234, 246
Dostoyevsky, Fyodor Mikhaylovich
    90, 102, 115, 121, 122, 123, 124, 125,
    126, 129, 131, 133, 134
Doty, Mark 279
Douglas, Ellen 270
Douglas, Gavin 34
Douglas, Norman 176
Dove, Rita 267, 268
Dovizi, Bernardo 35
Dovlatov, Sergei 266
Dowden, Edward 113, 172
Dower, John W. 295
Dowson, Ernest 146
Doyle, Arthur Conan 121, 138, 141,
    142, 144, 159, 163, 174, 193
Doyle, Roddy 276, 279, 280, 286
Drabble, Margaret 205, 269, 272
Drachmann, Holger Henrik Herholdt
    114, 134, 140, 141, 149, 166
Dragomoshchenko, Arkady 296
Drayton, Geoffrey 231
Dreiser, Theodore 128, 158, 169, 171,
    173, 174, 186, 212, 213
Drieu La Rochelle, Pierre 143, 212
Drinkwater, John 202
Dromer, Ori 286
Droste-Hülshoff, Annette Elisabeth
    87, 110, 112, 115
Drummond, Carlos 287
Drummond, William 53
Drummond, William Henry 118, 147,
    165
Drury, Allen 232
Dryden, John 49, 54, 58, 60, 61, 62,
    63, 64, 65, 66, 69
Drzezdzon, Jan 264
Du Bois, W. E. B. 126, 236
Du Fu (Tu Fu) 15, 19
du Maurier, Daphne 164, 204, 271
Du Maurier, George 142, 144
ad-Duaji, Ali 217
Dubarova, Petya 279
Dube, John Langalibalele 128
Dubnow, Simon 121, 208
Dubus, Andre 292
Dubus, André 25
Ducharme, Rejean 282
Ducis, Jean-François 83, 87
Duclos, Charles Pinto 70
Dudevant, Amandine-Aurore-Lucie
    See Sand, George
Dudintsev, Vladimir 271
Duffy, Maureen 263
Dugan, Alan 235
Duhamel, Georges 136, 180, 193, 197,
    241
Dumas, Alexandre, fils 103, 115, 119,
    145
Dumas, Alexandre, père 95, 113, 114,
    117, 127, 129
Dumore, Helen 286
Dunbar, Paul Laurence 128, 146, 160,
    164
Duncan, Robert 212, 217, 264, 269
Duncan, Ronald 220, 223, 229
Dunn, Douglas Eaglesham 209
Dunn, Olav 130, 177
Dunne, John Gregory 195, 256, 261,
    269

Dunsany, Edward 132, 163, 167, 169, 227
Duodo, Cameron 202, 243
Durak, Jam 58
Durand, José 186
Durant, Will 244
Duranti, Francesca 282, 289
Durão, José de Santa Rita 73, 84
Duras, Marguerite 172, 230, 239, 246, 278, 284, 285
Durcan, Paul 211, 264
Durrell, Lawrence 228, 229, 232, 266, 273
Durrenmatt, Friedrich 180, 227, 236, 242, 248, 273
Dutton, Geoffrey Piers Henry 289
Duyn, Mona van 275
Dworkin, Andrea 213
Dybek, Stuart 273

E

Eaton, Charles Edward 175
Ebens, Georg Moritz 109
Eberhart, Richard 241
Ebers, Georg Moritz 148
Ebner-Eschenbach, Marie, Baroness von 132, 137, 138, 141
Eça de Queirós, José Maria de 114, 131, 132, 139, 158
Echegaray y Eizaguirre, José 107, 131, 162, 175
Echenique, Alfredo Bryce 205
Echenoz, Jean 288, 293
Echeverría, Esteban 96, 107, 110, 117, 128
Eco, Umberto 195, 259
Edel, Leon 236, 287
Edelson, Margaret 292
Edgeworth, Maria 81, 87, 95, 96, 98, 99, 100, 116
Edib Advar, Halide 136
Edmonds, Walter Dumond 289
Edwards, Gus 205, 260
Edwards, Jonathan 70, 75, 76, 77, 78, 79
Edwards, Jorge 251, 281, 296
Eeden, Frederik 145, 158
Eggehorn, Ylva 275
Eggleston, Edward 128
Eguren, José María 170, 175
Ehrenburg, Ilya 141, 183, 208, 242
Eichendorff, Joseph 85, 107, 110, 119, 120
Einstein, Albert 224
Ejrnaes, Anne Marie 288
Ekelof, Gunnar 164, 233, 244
Ekelund, Vilhelm 217
Ekman, Kerstin 283, 287, 294
Ekrem, Recaizade Mahmud Bey 115
Ekwensi, Cyprian Odiatu Duaka 180, 224, 234
El Saadawi, Nawal 194
Eliot, George (Mary Ann Evans) 101, 120, 121, 122, 123, 125, 128, 131, 133
Eliot, Thomas Stearns (T. S.) 139, 152, 174, 176, 178, 180, 182, 186, 188, 193, 200, 202, 205, 207, 208, 209, 216, 222, 223, 228, 239
Elizabeth, queen of Romania (princess of Wied) See Sylva, Carmen
Elkin, Stanley 254, 258, 261, 265, 284
Elley (Seraphim Aramaanbys Kulaas'kar) 161, 215
Elliott, Maude Howe 176
Elliott, Sumner Locke 176, 237, 269

Ellis, Henry Havelock 205
Ellison, Ralph 172, 221, 238, 293
Ellman, Richard 272
Elsschot, Willem 134, 232
Elstad, Anne Karin 280, 284
Eltit, Diamela 277
Éluard, Paul (Eugène Grindel) 145, 188, 199, 202, 221
Elytis, Odysseus 169, 213, 231, 249, 257, 258, 268, 285
Emberley, Barbara 244
Emecheta, Florence Onye Buchi 211, 258
Emerson, Ralph Waldo 96, 109, 111, 121, 134
Emin, Gevorg (Karlen Karapetian) 178, 247
Eminescu, Mikhail 116, 136, 140
Empson, William 163, 193, 207, 263
Enchi, Fumiko 162
Encino, Juan del 29
Enckell, Rabbe 186, 213
Ende, Michael Andreas Helmuth 283
Endo, Shusaku 183, 225, 228, 242, 252, 259, 268, 280, 285
Engel, Marian 196
Engels, Friedrich 126, 145
Enger, Cecilie 296
Enger, Rolf 283
Engle, Paul Hamilton 165
Enheduanna 1
Enis, Resat 167, 261
Ennius, Quintus 9
Enquist, Per Olav 252, 257, 277, 294
Enright, Dennis Joseph 179, 290
Enzensberger, Hans Magnus 191, 258, 276
Eötvös, József 115
Ephorus 8
Épinay, Louise-Florence d' 73
Erasmus, Desiderius 28, 32, 34, 35, 37
Ercilla y Zúñiga, Alonso de 40
Erdrich, Louise 264
Erikson, Erik H. 247
Eriksson, Ulf 229, 287
Erkelius, PerAgne 279
Erlingsson, Thorsteinn 120, 173
Ernst, Paul 162, 171
Escandón, María Amparo 290
Espinel, Vicente 38, 52, 53
Espinosa, Germán 275, 281
Espirito Santo, Alda de 187
Espmark, Kjell 279, 285
Espronceda y Delgado, José de 97, 108, 111, 112
Esquivel, Laura 294
Etxebarria, Lucía 292
Eucken, Rudolf C. 114, 166, 187
Euripides 2–3, 6, 7, 8
Evander, P. G. 277
Evangelou, Anestis 266
Evans, Mary Ann See Eliot, George
Evelyn, John 70
Everson, William 244, 257
Ewald, Johannes 76, 81, 82, 84
Eybers, Elisabeth 288

F

Fadeyev, Alexander 158, 189, 226
Fadiman, Clifton 292
Faesi, Robert 135, 166, 176, 190, 249
Fagunwa, Daniel Olorunfami 168, 205, 236
Fakhuri, Omar 145, 213
Fakin, Boris See Torkar, Igor
Falabella, Miguel 278

Faldbakken, Knut 276, 280, 287
Fallada, Hans (Rudolf Ditzen) 196, 214
Faludy, Gyorgy 171, 235, 266
Fanon, Frantz 186
Farah, Nuruddin 212, 291
Farazad, Masud 163
Fares, Nabile 206
Fargue, Léon-Paul 130, 214
Faria, Almeida 294
Farigoule, Louis See Romains, Jules
Farquhar, George 63, 69, 71
Farrar, Frederic William 130
Farrell, James Gordon 250, 257
Farrell, James Thomas 161, 196, 198, 200, 257
Farrokhzad, Forugh 198, 242
Faulkner, William 146, 188, 192, 193, 194, 196, 200, 201, 204, 207, 209, 216, 217, 220, 223, 224, 228, 231, 235, 236
al-Fayturi, Muhammad Miftah 194
Federer, Heinrich 125, 166, 170, 172, 187, 190
Federman, Raymond 190, 265
Federspiel, Jurg F. 194, 262
Fehrenbacher, Don E. 258
Feinmann, José Pablo 274
Feinstein, Elaine 192, 256
Feis, Herbert 233
Fénelon, François de Salignac de La Mothe- 58, 64, 66, 72
Feng Youlan 273
Fenoglio, Beppe 224
Feraoun, Mouloud 171, 235
Ferber, Edna 138, 185, 186, 188, 196, 221, 244
Feric, Zoran 295
Ferlinghetti, Lawrence 179, 229
Fernández de Lizardi, José Joaquín 100, 104
Fernández Santos, Jesús 266
Ferrater Mora, José 271
Ferreira, Jeanette 265
Ferreira, Sofia 285
Ferreira, Vergilio 283, 285
Ferreira de Castro, José Maria 191, 193, 252
Ferreria, Vergilio 175
Ferrers, George 40
Ferrucci, Franco 280, 286
Fet, Afanasy Afanasyevich 101, 142
Feuchtwanger, Lion 136, 187, 196, 197, 200, 228, 229
Feuerbach, Ludwig Andreas 96, 112, 128, 133
Feuillet, Octave 120
Feydeau, Georges 122, 149, 180
Fichman, Jacob 229
Fichte, Johann Gottlieb 80, 99
Fiedler, Leslie 176, 232
Field, Eugene 116, 145
Fielding, Henry 71, 75, 76, 78
Figueiredo, Flora 274
Filho, Adonias 174
Finch, Anne 72
Findley, Timothy 280
Fink, Ida 180
Finney, Walter Braden 283
Fiore, Elio 268
Firbank, Ronald 251
Firdawsī 20, 21
Firishtah 40, 53
Fischart, Johann 38, 41, 43
Fischer, Tibor 280

Fisher, Dorothy Canfield 132, 188, 229
Fisher, M. F. K. 277
Fisher, Roy 192
Fishman, David 182
Fitrat, Abdalrauf 136, 214
Fitzgerald, F. Scott 146, 180, 182, 186, 198, 206, 208, 212
Fitzgerald, Frances 250
Fitzgerald, Penelope 257, 273, 294
FitzGerald, Edward 97, 117, 121, 135
Flagstad, Kjartan 211
Flanagan, Thomas 258, 270
Flanner, Janet 142, 256
Flaubert, Gustave 92, 102, 123, 127, 130, 133
Flavin, Martin 211
Fleischman, Paul 271
Fleischman, Sid 268
Fleisser, Marieluise 158, 252
Fleming, Ian 165, 222, 228, 231, 234
Fleming, Paul 51, 56
Fletcher, John 41, 51, 52, 53, 54, 63, 205
Fleury, Claude 73
Fleutiaux, Pierrette 274
Flieg, Hellmuth See Heym, Stefan
Flogstad, Kjartan 256, 291
Fo, Dario 288
Fogazzaro, Antonio 146
Fogunwa, D. O. 167
Folengo, Teofilo 35
Folger, Peter 62
Fonseca, Rubem 276, 287, 294
Fontane, Theodor 101, 132, 135, 139, 145, 148
Fontenelle, Bernard de 65
Fonvizin, Denis Ivanovich 84
Foote, Horton 283
Foran, Charles 282
Forbes, Esther 210
Forché, Carolyn 282
Ford, Ford Madox (Ford Madox Heuffer) 129, 174, 185, 186, 188, 205, 219
Ford, John 42, 54, 56
Ford, Richard 273, 284, 285, 286, 288
Forester, C. S. 148, 200, 213, 241
Forster, E. M. 132, 163, 165, 166, 168, 185, 189, 246, 249
Forsyth, Frederick 203, 249, 250, 252
Fortunatus, Venantius 18
Foscolo, Ugo 83, 96, 97, 104
Fostieris, Adonis 222
Foucault, Michel 234, 241, 246
Fouqué, Friedrich Heinrich Karl de La Motte 83, 98, 113
Fournier, Alain 172
Fowles, John Robert 187, 237, 246, 256, 261, 266
Fox, Paula 252
Foxe, John 40
Frame, Janet 184
France, Anatole 113, 134, 147, 149, 159, 166, 171, 181, 184
Franck, Dan 276
Frank, Anne 215
Frank, Elizabeth 267
Frank, Leonhard 134, 177, 188, 221, 233
Franke, Herman 293
Franklin, Benjamin 70, 75, 81, 85
Franko, Ivan 119, 135, 136, 138, 145, 158, 176
Fraser, Antonia 246, 272
Frazer, James George 208

Frazier, Charles 288
Frazier, Sir George James 141
Fréchette, Louis-Honoré 132, 138
Frederiksson, Marianne 283
Fredro, Aleksander 86, 103, 108, 131
Freedman, Russell 270
Freeman, Douglas Southall 200, 222, 229
Freeman, Judith 276
Freire, Espido 294
Freneau, Philip 78, 84, 85, 98, 107
Freud, Sigmund 119, 149, 172, 193, 205
Freyre, Gilberto 158, 268
Freytag, Gustav 100, 114, 117, 119, 124, 129, 145
Friedman, Bruce Jay 235
Friel, Brian 191, 238, 259
Fries, Jacob Friedrich 113
Frings, Ketti 229
Frisch, Max Rudolf 169, 215, 218, 224, 230, 234, 239, 254, 262, 275
Frishman, David 122
Fröding, Gustaf 121, 145, 148, 169
Frohlich, Hans J. 267
Froissart, Jean 25, 26
Fromentin, Eugène 123, 131
Frost, Robert 129, 172, 173, 174, 175, 184, 185, 190, 194, 201, 203, 209, 210, 215, 235, 236
Frug, Simeon Samuel 121, 175
Frugoni, Carlo Innocenzo 65, 81
Fry, Christopher 164, 216, 219, 220, 223, 247
Frye, Northrop 275
Fuat, Memet 187
Fuente Benavides, Rafael de la See Adán, Martín
Fuentes, Carlos 190, 231, 242, 243, 257, 260, 266, 270, 275, 279, 281, 283, 287, 294, 296
Fugard, Sheila 195
Fujiwara Sadaie 22, 23
Fula, Arthur Nuthall 165, 226
Fuller, Charles 260, 261
Fuller, John 258, 263
Fuller, Margaret 98, 111, 114, 116
Fuller, Roy Broadbent 222, 275
Fulton, Alice 273
Fumiko Enchi 267
Fumiko Hayashi 219
Furchtegott, Christian 77
Furphy, Joseph 161
Fussenegger, Gertrud 171
Futabatei Shimei 123, 139
Fuzûlî 29, 39
Fyodorov, Yevgeny 285

G

Gaboriau, Émile 108, 125, 129
Gabourg, Arne 184
Gabra, Egzi'abeher 121, 173
Gabra Iyasus, Afawarq 166
Gabre-Madhin, Tsegaye 240
Gadda, Carlo Emilio 143, 250
Gaddis, William 225, 267, 282, 289
Gaediaty, Taomaq 166, 194
Gaines, Ernest J. 196, 248, 279
Gaius Cornelius Tacitus See Tacitus
Gaius Valerius Catullus See Catullus
Gala, Antonio 275, 281, 285
Gale, Zona 181
Galeano, Eduardo 292
Gallant, Mark 279
Gallant, Mavis 181, 251, 266, 272, 280, 286

Gallegos, Rómulo 136, 245
Galsworthy, John 125, 164, 167, 168, 172, 180, 181, 182, 185, 188, 190, 195
Gama, Basílio da 81
Gamerro, Carlos 296
Gamsukhurdia, Konstantine 141
Gandlevsky, Sergey 296
Gans, David ben Solomon 44
Gao Xingjian 295
Garat, Anne-Marie 278
Garavini, Fausta 286, 291
Garborg, Arne 117, 136, 142, 143
Garcia, Cristina 288
García Aguilar, Eduardo 277
García Calderón, Ventura 185, 195
García de la Huerta, Vicente 83, 85
García Gutiérrez, Antonio 109
García Lorca, Federico 147, 155, 191, 198, 199, 200, 201, 202
García Márquez, Gabriel 190, 243, 254, 261, 266, 272, 278, 285, 287
García Ponce, Juan 283
García Villa, José 166
Garcia-Roza, Luiz Alfredo 291
Garcilaso de la Vega 34, 37
Gardner, Erle Stanley 246
Gardner, John 196, 250, 254, 261
Garibay, Ricardo 292
Garland, Hannibal Hamlin 121, 142, 182, 206
Garnett, David 260
Garnier, Robert 42
Garrett, George 273, 286
Garrett, João Baptista da Silva Leitão de 88, 118
Garro, Elena 287, 289
Garrow, David J. 268
Gary, Romain 172, 233, 259
Gascoigne, George 40
Gaskell, Elizabeth 98, 115, 116, 117, 118, 119, 120, 124
Gass, William H. 184
Gassendi, Pierre 43, 59
Gatsos, Nikos 265
Gautier, Théophile 98, 108, 117, 123, 128
Gay, John 64, 72, 74, 75
Gazelle, Guido 106
Geble, Carlo Ernest 223
Geibel, Franz Emanuel 99, 136
Geisel, Theodore Seuss See Dr. Seuss
Gellert, Christian Furchegott 72, 77, 81
Genet, Jean 167, 168, 211, 215, 218, 225, 227, 230, 234, 267
Gengetsu 296
George, Jean Craighead 250
George, Stefan 126, 147, 196
Gerhardie, William Alexander 255
Gerhardt, Paul 50, 62
Germacaw, Takla Hawaryat 174
Germain, Sylvie 286
Germasaw, Takla Hawaryat 208
Gersao, Teolinda 287
Gershwin, Ira 195
Gerstler, Amy 275
Gessner, Salomon 78, 79
Geulincx, Arnold 53, 61
Gezelle, Guido 148, 149
Ghafur Ghulam 241
Ghelderode, Michel de 148, 235
Ghormley Eberhart, Richard 161
Ghose, Zulfikar 199
Ghosh, Amitav 226, 267
Giacomo, Salvatore di 121

Giardinelli, Mempo 281, 294
Gibbon, Edward 75, 83, 86, 87
Gibbons, Stella 196
Gibran, Khalil 135, 173, 177, 178, 179, 182, 184, 194
Gibson, Lawrence H. 235
Gide, André 126, 160, 167, 180, 188, 214, 219
Gil, Rachel 276
Gilbert, William Schwenck 109, 132, 136, 169
Gill, Brendan 287
Gilliatt, Penelope 279
Gilman, Charlotte Perkins 149
Gilroy, Frank D. 239
Ginsberg, Allen 187, 226, 234, 244, 264, 287
Ginzburg, Natalia 175, 215, 221, 264, 274, 275
Giogceli, Kemal Sadik See Kemal, Orhan
Giono, Jean 145, 199, 221, 228, 246
Giovanni, Nikki 210, 244
Giraldi, Giambattista Cinzio 37, 40
Giraudoux, Jean 134, 190, 200, 211, 212
Gironella, José María 223, 234, 242, 268
Gissing, George 120, 137, 142, 161
Gjellerup, Karl Adolf 120, 140, 164, 176, 178
Gladkov, Fyodor Vasilyevich 135, 187, 229
Glasgow, Ellen 129, 186, 209, 210, 212
Glaspell, Susan 134, 194, 216
Glassco, John 167, 260
Glatstein, Jacob 146, 242, 248
Gleim, Johann Wilhelm Ludwig 72, 96
Glissant, Edouard 190
Glowisnki, Maichal 291
Gluck, Louise 210, 265, 279
Glyn, Elinor 168
Gnessin, Uri Nissan 132, 172
Go Fei 281
Gobineau, Joseph-Arthur, comte de 134
Goble, Paul 257
Godden, Rumer 164, 205, 213, 246, 289
Godoy Alcayaga, Lucila See Mistral, Gabriela
Goethe, Johann Wolfgang von 67, 77, 82, 84, 85, 87, 97, 101, 102, 103, 107
Goetzmann, William H. 242
Goff, Helen Lyndon See Travers, P. L.
Gogol, Nikolay Vasilyevich 91, 97, 109, 112, 117
Gökalp, Mehmed Ziya 130, 184
Gold, Herbert 295
Goldbarth, Albert 277
Goldemberg, Isaac 212, 266
Golding, William 169, 223, 225, 227, 231, 238, 243, 259, 262, 264, 269, 272, 279
Goldman, James 289
Goldoni, Carlo 71, 77, 78, 79, 80, 82, 86
Goldsmith, Meir Aron 125
Goldsmith, Oliver 74, 77, 80, 81, 82
Golshiri, Hushang 294
Gombrowicz, Witold 161, 203, 245
Gomes, Albert 169, 256
Gómez de Avellaneda, Gertrudis 99, 112, 121, 129
Gómez de la Cerna, Ramón 236

Gömöri, György 264
Gonçalves Dias, Antônio 117
Goncharov, Ivan Alexandrovich 98, 121, 127, 141
Goncourt, Edmond de 102, 124, 127, 146
Goncourt, Jules Alfred Huot de 106, 124, 127
Göncz, Árpád 181
Góngora y Argote, Luis de 54
Gonzaga, Tomas Antonion 86
González, Eladia 292
González León, Adrián 285
Goodrich, Frances 226
Goodwin, Doris Kearns 283
Gorakhpuri, Firaq 215
Goran, Abdullah 235
Gordimer, Nadine 183, 222, 252, 253, 258, 259, 269, 271, 274, 275, 282, 291
Gordon, Jaime 273
Gordon, Judah Leon 142
Gordon, Mary 257
Gordone, Charles 247, 283
Gorenko, Anna Andreyevna See Akhmatova, Anna
Gorky, Maxim (Aleksey Maximovich Pyeshkov) 126, 145, 149, 160, 164, 172, 187, 201
Gorres, Joseph von 82, 115
Gorter, Herman 141
Gosawmi, Hemachandra 128
Gospodinov, Georgi 292
Gosse, Edmund 115, 165, 190
Goswami, Hemachandra 190
Gottfried von Strassburg 23
Gotthelf, Jeremias 87, 110, 111, 112, 118
Gourmont, Rémy de 120, 146, 174
Govier, Katherine 215, 286
Gower, John 26
Goytisolo, Juan 194, 224, 226
Goytisolo, Luis 296
Gozzano, Guido 170
Gozzi, Carlo 72, 97
Grabbe, Christian Dietrich 95, 106, 106, 109
Graça Aranha, José Pereira da 126, 160, 194
Gracián, Baltasar y Morales 50, 59
Gracq, Julien (Louis Poirier) 168, 204
Grade, Chaim 234
Graf, Oskar Maria 192
Graham, Jorie 286
Graham, Katherine 290
Graham, William Sydney 256
Graham, Winston 234
Grahame, Kenneth 121, 166, 195
Grainville, Patrick 214
Grandes, Almudena 294
Grant, Linda 295
Granville-Barker, Harley 213
Grass, Günter 188, 231, 234, 237, 242, 246, 256, 268, 272, 278, 292, 293
Gratiant, Gilbert 145, 216
Grau, Shirley Ann 225, 229, 234, 238, 239, 248, 256, 282
Graves, Robert 145, 175, 177, 192, 199, 216, 265
Gray, Alastair 198, 266
Gray, Simon 249, 253
Gray, Thomas 72, 76, 78, 79, 81
Green, Constance McLaughlin 236
Green, Julian 158, 188, 189, 192, 196, 199, 202, 215, 225, 249, 269, 289
Green, Maurice 257

Green, Paul E. 189
Greene, Graham 154, 161, 192, 196, 202, 204, 205, 207, 210, 216, 217, 220, 225, 229, 234, 241, 251, 252, 257, 261, 266, 275
Gregory, Lady Isabella Augusta 117, 162, 195
Grey, Zane 128, 171, 205
Griboyedov, Aleksandr Sergeyevich 87, 100, 103, 105
Grieg, Nordahl Brun 185, 200
Grillparzer, Franz 86, 100, 101, 102, 104, 106, 108, 128
Grimm, Jakob 84, 98, 123
Grimm, Wilhelm Karl 85, 98, 121
Grimmelshausen, Hans Jacob Christoffel von 53, 61, 62
Grin, Aleksandr (Stepanovich Grinevsky) 184, 193
Grindel, Eugène See Éluard, Paul
Grinevsky, Stepanovich See Grin, Aleksandr
Gripenberg, Barton Johan Sebastian 163
Grishashvili, Josef 239
Grondahl, Jens Christian 275, 286, 290, 292
Gronfeldt, Vibeke 275, 295
Grossman, David 268, 272, 282, 296
Grossman, Josephine Juliet See Merrill, Judith
Grossman, Vasily Semenovich 162, 238, 239
Grosz, Christiane 269
Grotius, Hugo 42, 53, 57
Grotowski, Jerzy 196
Grudzinski, Gustav Herling 294
Grun, Anastasius 106
Grunbein, Durs 293
Grupac, Marian 292
Grynberg, Henryk 201, 269
Gryphius, Andreas 57, 58, 59, 60
Grytten, Frode 294
Gu Jiang 63
Guare, John 203, 248
Guarini, Giovanni Battista 43, 51
Gubin, Vladimir 289
Gudmundsson, Kristmann 158, 185, 199, 262
Gudmundsson, Tomas 198
Gudyonsson Halldor Kiljan See Laxness, Halldor
Guelbenzu, José María 277, 285
Guérin, Maurice de 98, 110
Guerrazzi, Francesco Domenico 96, 129
Guèvremont, Germaine 219
Guidacci, Margherita 180
Guillén, Jorge 143, 191, 229, 263
Guillén, Nicolás 159, 231, 271
Guimares Rosa, João 165, 214
Güiraldes, Ricardo 137, 188, 189
Guldager, Katrine Marie 292
Gulia, Drmit 129, 232
Gumilyov, Nikolay Stepanovich 137, 171, 177, 181
Gunasekara, Romesh 282, 291
Gundulić, Ivan 43, 54, 56
Gunn, Thom 223, 228, 243, 249, 261
Gunnarsson, Gunnar 139, 171, 253
Guntekin, Resat Nuri 226
Gunther, Johann Christian 73
Guo Maruo 256
Guppy, Shusha 272
Gupta, Maithilisharan 137, 171, 238
Gurpinar, Huseyin Rahmi 123, 211

Gursel, Nedim 219, 285
Gustafson, Ralph Barker 232, 246, 276, 283
Gustafsson, Lars 275, 277, 281
Guterson, David 282, 283, 293
Guthmundur Hagalin 213
Guthrie, A. B., Jr. 218, 275
Gutiérrez, Miguel 281
Gutmane, Margita 271
Gutzkow, Karl Ferdinand 98, 109, 111, 132
Guzmán, Martín Luis 138, 191, 192, 254
Gyllensten, Lars 180, 218, 233, 237, 242, 252, 277, 285

H

Ha Jin 226, 295
Haasse, Hella 217, 221, 236, 272
Haavikko, Paavo 194, 222, 225, 230, 251
Habibi, Abdullah 168
Habibi, Emile 285
Hackett, Albert 226, 283
Haddad, Malek 188, 230
al-Hadi, Sayyid 125, 192, 298
Häfez 24, 26
Haff, Bergjlot Hobaek 287
Hagedorn, Friedrich von 76
Haggard, H(enry) Rider 119, 137, 138, 186
Hagrogian, Nonny 249
Hahn, Ulla 276
Hahn-Hahn, Ida 112
Haidar, Qurratu'l'ain 231
al-Haidari, Buland 285
Haik, Vahe 146
Hakigoto Kawahigashi 202
al-Hakim, Tawfiq (Husayn) 148, 197, 268
Hakluyt, Richard 42, 52
Hakobian, Hakob 125, 167, 202
Halbe, Max 144
Halevy, Ludovic 127
Haley, Alex Palmer 180, 240, 254, 277
Haley, Gail E. 248
Haliburton, Thomas Chandler 121, 124
Hall, Donald 259, 270
Hall, James Norman 196, 219
Hall, Radclyffe 133, 190, 210
Hall, Rodney 199, 269, 271
Hallam, Henry 121
Halldorrsson, Omar P. 269
Haller, Albrecht von 71, 82
Hallgrimsson, Jonas 97, 114
Hamann, Johann Georg 74, 85
Ha'meiri, Israel 274
Hamerling, Robert 125, 127
Hamilton, Dakota 290
Hamilton, Patrick 200
Hamilton, Virginia 253
Hamlin, Talbot Faulkner 226
Hamlisch, Marvin 254
Hammerstein, Oscar 218
Hammett, Dashiell 144, 193, 196, 233
Hammond, Bray 229
Hamsun, Knut 121, 141, 143, 145, 148, 176, 179, 221
Hamsun, Tore 274
Han Mac Tu (Nguyen Trong Tri) 206
Han Shaogong 286
Han Tian 244
Han Yu 19
Handke, Peter 209, 242, 245, 246, 248, 249, 250, 255, 269, 274, 289

Handlin, Oscar 221
Hanny, Reto 214
Hansberry, Lorraine 192, 231, 238, 239, 246
Hansen, Erik Fosnes 276, 291
Hansen, Marcus Lee 208
Hansen, Martin 208, 212, 218, 221
Hansen, Ron 286
Hansson, Ola 139
Haqqi, Yahya 162, 211
Harden, Maximilan 189
Hardwick, Elizabeth 175
Hardy, Thomas 111, 128, 129, 130, 132, 134, 135, 137, 138, 142, 144, 148, 161, 168, 190
Hariaudh, Ayodhyasimha Upadjyay 208
Harlan, Louis R. 263
Harnick, Sheldon 232
Harper, Michael S. 265
Harpma, Jacqueline 286
Harris, Frank 119
Harris, Joel Chandler 134, 166
Harris, Mark 222, 226
Harris, Theodore Wilson 180, 256
Harrison, Jim 258, 290
Harsdörfer, Georg Philipp 50, 59
Hart, Moss 161, 201, 203, 205, 233
Harte, Bret 109, 121, 125, 126, 127, 160
Hartley, L. P. 211, 217, 222
Hartling, Peter 274
Hartmann von Aue 23
Hartnett, Michael 264
Hartzenbusch, Juan Eugenio 110
Haruf, Kent 293
Harvath, Edmund Josef von 197
Hašek, Jaroslav 135, 179, 183
Hasenclever, Walter 140, 206
Hashimi, Alamgir 271
Hasim, Ahmet 136, 197
Haslinger, Josef 266, 296
Hass, Robert 286
Hasselt, André-Henri-Constant van 97, 108, 123, 130
Hauch, Carsten 85, 122, 128
Hauff, William 104
Hauge, Alfred 174, 213, 216, 217, 225, 229, 243, 244, 267
Hauptmann, Gerhart 122, 140, 141, 142, 143, 144, 148, 164, 168, 177, 213
Havel, Vaclav 201, 240
Haweis, Stephen 132, 244
Hawi, Khalil 186, 233
Hawkes, John 234, 238, 248, 252, 255, 258, 261
Hawthorne, Nathaniel 96, 105, 107, 108, 109, 113, 114, 116, 117, 121, 123
Hay, Elizabeth 295
Hayashi Fumiko 161, 220
Hayashi Shunsai 63
Hayden, Robert Earl 171, 259
Hayford, Joseph Ephraim Casely 169
Haykal, Muhammad Husayn 173, 226
Hazard, Shirley 259
Hazhar (Abdurrahman Sharafkandi) 179
Hazlitt, William 83, 102, 104, 106
Hazoume, Paul 140
Heaney, Seamus 205, 241, 246, 250, 254, 258, 264, 266, 269, 283, 286, 291
Hearn, Lafcadio 116, 140, 161, 162, 250

Hebbel, Friedrich 99, 111, 112, 116, 117, 119, 123
Hebblethwaite, Peter 281
Hebel, Johann Peter 79, 104
Hébert, Anne 175, 219, 230, 247, 254, 271, 278, 293, 294
Hecht, Anthony 244
Hecht, Ben 144, 190, 196, 238
Hedāyat, Sādeq 160, 203, 219
Hedrick, Joan D. 283
Heerden, Ernst von 175
Heeren, Arnold Hermann Ludwig 112
Heffner, Avraham 276, 282
Hegel, Georg Wilhelm Friedrich 81, 106
Heggland, Johannes 274, 276, 278, 284
Heiberg, Gunnar 136, 145, 147, 162, 171, 172, 191
Heiberg, Johann Ludvig 86, 121
Heidegger, Martin 139, 189, 254
Heidenstam, Verner von 121, 139, 145, 174, 175, 206
Heidiji Hojo 285
Heighten, Steven 295
Heiichiro Hirano 294
Heijermans, Herman 123, 158, 184
Hein, Christoph 289
Heine, Heinrich 87, 93–94, 102, 103, 104, 105, 113, 114, 117, 119
Heinemann, Larry 269
Heinesen, William 198, 218, 238, 254, 275
Heinlein, Robert Anson 164, 220, 226, 228, 229, 231, 234, 241, 247, 259, 261, 270
Heinrich von Melk 22
Heinrich von Veldeke 22
Heinse, Johann Wilhelm 77, 96
Heinsius, Daniel 59
Hejazi, Muhammad 158
Helle, Pyrds 288
Hellenga, Robert 290
Heller, Joseph 183, 233, 282, 292
Hellman, Lillian 162, 198, 205, 208, 213, 263
Hellström, Gustaf 189
Hemingway, Ernest Miller 148, 153, 188, 189, 192, 196, 197, 200, 201, 203, 204, 207, 218, 221, 222, 223, 233, 238, 247, 265, 267
Hendrick, Burton J. 183, 191
Henley, Beth 258
Henley, William Ernest 115, 161
Henry, Marguerite 287
Henry, O. (William Sydney Porter) 122, 163, 164, 165, 168
Henschke, Alfred See Klabund
Hensen, Lance 268
Hensher, Philip 290
Henson, Lance 265
Herbert, Frank 240
Herbert, George 44, 55, 58
Herbert, Zbigniew 184, 236, 253, 274, 289
Hercikova, Ivan 290
Herczeg, Ferenc 123, 144, 162, 179, 187, 223
Herder, Johann Gottfried von 76, 83, 96
Heredia, José María de 104, 110, 144
Hergesheimer, Joseph 176, 178, 185
Herlihy, James Leo 279
Hermann, Iselin C. 290

Hermanson, Marie 285
Hernandez, Amado V. 160, 246
Hernández, Francisco 283
Hernández, José 129, 137
Hernández, Miguel 167, 202, 206, 209
Hernández, Ramón 199
Herne, James A. 143
Herodotus 3, 6, 7
Herrera, Fernando de 37, 44
Herrera y Reissig, Julio 130, 160, 164, 168
Herrick, Robert 43, 58, 62
Hersey, John Richard 172, 211, 212, 219, 279
Hertz, Henrik 114, 127
Heruy, Sirek Walda Sellase 132, 186, 204
Hervieu, Paul-Ernest 144
Herzen, Aleksandr Ivanovich 117, 127
Hesse, Hermann 131, 162, 163, 178, 182, 189, 193, 210, 213, 235
Hesse, Karen 290
Hesselholdt, Christina 290, 292
Hetata, Sherif 183
Hettche, Thomas 274
Heuffer, Ford Madox See Ford, Ford Madox
Heym, Stefan 171, 264, 291
Heyse, Paul (Johann Ludwig von) 106, 129, 168, 173
Heyward, Du Bose 186
Heywood, John 39
Heywood, Thomas 41, 50, 51, 56
Hibbert, Eleanor Alice (Victoria Holt, Jean Plaidy) 279
Hideo Takubo 274
Hieronymous Brunschwig 34
Hierro, José 277, 292
Higgins, George Vincent 292
Higuchi Ichiyo 128, 145, 146
Hijuelos, Oscar 273, 293
Hikmet Ran, Nazim 159, 191, 202, 236, 242
Hilbig, Wolfgang 280, 296
Hildegard 21, 22
Hildesheimer, Wolfgang 175, 256, 275
Hill, Geoffrey 195, 249, 263
Hillyer, Caroline 198
Hillyer, Robert 198
Hilton, James 197, 199, 208
Himes, Chester 212
Hiroshi Noma 174, 214, 215, 218, 221
Hirsch, Edward 267
Hisashi Inoue 276
Hisdai ibn Shaprut 20
Hitler, Adolf 187
Ho Biu Chanh (Ho Van Trung) 136, 229
Ho Trong Hieu See Tu Mo
Ho Van Trung See Ho Biu Chanh
Hobbes, Thomas 43, 57, 58, 59, 63
Hobson, Laura Z. 158, 210, 215, 253, 267
Hochhuth, Rolf 194, 237, 243, 269
Hodge, Merle 211, 247
Hodges, Margaret 265
Hoeg, Peter 275, 282
Hoel, Sigurd 189, 195, 198
Hoem, Edvard 253, 280
Hoffer, Eric 262
Hoffman, Alice 258, 259, 265, 269, 277
Hoffman, Ernest Theodor Wilhelm 82, 99, 100, 101, 102

Hoffmann, Gert 194, 262, 264, 266, 268, 271, 280
Hoffmann, Heinrich 97, 114, 115
Hoffmann, Yoel 276
Hofmannsthal, Hugo von 129, 142, 143, 144, 147, 149, 161, 168, 170, 181, 182, 187, 191
Hofstadter, Douglas R. 259
Hofstadter, Richard 226, 238
Hogan, Linda 265
Holberg, Ludvig 64, 72, 73, 74, 78
Holderlin, Christian Friedrich 81, 87, 113
Holinshed, Raphael 41
Holldobler, Bert 275
Hollingshead, Greg 284, 290
Holloway, Emory 189
Holm, Sven 248
Holmer, Per 289
Holmes, Oliver Wendell 97, 106, 109, 120, 144
Holt, Anne 288
Holt, Victoria See Hibbert, Eleanor Alice
Holten, Knud 279
Holz, Arno 191
Homer 2, 6
Homeric (French author) 291
Hood, Hugh 273, 276, 280, 284
Hood, Thomas 88, 105, 112, 113, 114
Hooft, Pieter Corneliszoon 42, 50, 51, 52, 58
Hope, Alec Derwent 164, 240, 241, 294
Hope, Anthony 144
Hope, Christopher David Tully 211, 264, 269, 278
Hopkins, Gerard Manley 113, 130, 131, 132, 133, 140, 177
Hopkins, John 38
Hopkins, Pauline 158
Horace 4, 10, 11
Horgan, Paul 197, 225, 232, 235, 254
Horn, Shifra 293
Horowitz, Frances Hooker 262
Horváth, Ödön 193
Horwood, Harold 288
Hospital, Janette Turner 209, 266, 276, 278
Hostos y Bonilla, Eugenio María 161
Hotta, Yoshie 175
Houellebecq, Michael 291
Hourani, Albert Habib 279
Housman, Alfred Edward 121, 146, 201
Housman, Laurence 124, 199, 230
Howard, Bronson Crocker 166
Howard, Elizabeth Jane 183, 219, 226, 231, 240, 246, 250, 261, 273
Howard, Richard 246, 247, 282
Howard, Sidney 141, 185, 186, 188, 198, 205
Howe, Irving 279
Howe, Julia Ward 101, 118, 168, 176
Howe, M. A. DeWolfe 186
Howells, William Dean 109, 128, 129, 130, 132, 133, 134, 135, 137, 138, 140, 141, 143, 144, 147, 179
Hoyos, Andrés 275
Hrabel, Bohumil 240, 287
Hristow, Boris 275
Hrysanthis, Kypros 174
Htin, Maun 167
Hu Shi 141, 235
Huch, Ricarda 214
Hudson, William Henry 111, 162, 182

Hughes, Geoffrey Langdon 261
Hughes, Hatcher 184
Hughes, Langston 159, 181, 188, 194, 220, 242, 243
Hughes, Richard 192, 204
Hughes, Ted 192, 228, 247, 258, 278, 290
Hughes, Thomas 120, 146
Hugo, Richard Franklin 261
Hugo, Victor-Marie 95, 105, 106, 108, 110, 118, 119, 123, 130, 137
Huidobro, Vicente 143, 192, 216
Hulme, Keri 263, 265
Hulme, T. E. 135, 176
Hultberg, Peer 279
Hume, David 71, 77, 83
Humphreys, Emyr Owen 178
Humphreys, Josephine 295
Hunt, Henry Leigh 84, 100, 108, 111, 113, 116, 121
Hunt, Irene 242
Hurston, Zora Neal 160, 194, 203, 209, 232
Hussain, Mahti 167, 239
Husserl, Edmund 204
Huston, Nancy 293
Hutchinson, Alfred 184, 232, 249
Huxley, Aldous 144, 181, 184, 190, 196, 202, 205, 229, 236
Huxley, Elspeth 287
Huxley, Julian Sorrell 253
Huxley, Thomas Henry 104
Huygens, Constantijn 44, 53, 54, 64
Huysmans, Joris-Karl 115, 135, 136, 142, 145, 148, 161, 165
Hviezdoslav (Pal Orszagh) 138, 141, 174
Hyde, Evan X. 214, 249

I

Iashvili, Paolo 202
Ibarbourou, Juana de 145, 179, 183, 194, 219, 257
Ibn Gabirol 21
Ibrahim, Hafiz 127, 195
al-Ibrahimi, Bashir 239
Ibrahimov, Mirza 169
Ibsen, Henrik Johan 94, 105, 117, 122, 124, 125, 126, 131, 132, 134, 135, 136, 138, 139, 141, 143, 145, 149, 164
Ibuse Masuji 279
Idris, Yusuf 188, 223, 230, 235, 275
Idrus 180
Iesmaniasita, Sulistyautami 196, 230
Ignatieff, Michael 280
Ignatius of Loyola 38
Ignatov, David 244
Ihara Saikaku 57, 64, 65
Ihimaera, Witi Tame 211, 251, 267
Ihland, Johann Ludvig 100
Iijima Koichi 192
Ikeda Masuo 198
Ikelle-Matiba, Jean 201, 237
Ikromi, Jalol 167, 230, 236
Ilansol, María Gabriela 276
Illyés, Gyula 202, 249
Immermann, Karl Leberecht 87, 109, 110, 111
Infante, Angel Gustavo 281
Inge, William 171, 219, 222, 225, 228, 250
Innes, Hammond 290
Inoue Yasushi 218, 231, 275
Ionesco, Eugène 167, 219, 220, 221, 223, 225, 231, 237, 247, 251, 281

Iqbāl, Muhammad 129, 131, 174, 177, 185, 196
Irazu Garmedia, José See Atxaga, Bernardo
Irigaray, Luce 195
Irving, John 209, 257, 260, 265, 272, 282, 290
Irving, Washington 84, 97, 98, 101, 103, 107, 121
Irzykowski, Karol 161
Isaac, Rhys L. 262
Isaacs, Jorge 126
Isahakian, Avetikh 169, 227
Isakson, Folke 292
Isherwood, Christopher 161, 190, 196, 201, 203, 205, 213, 238, 267
Ishiguro, Kazuo 271, 272, 295
Ishikawa Takuboku 137, 169
Iskander, Fazil Abdulovich 191, 241, 257
Iskander, Nur Sultan 143
Isla, José Francisco de 79
Ivanov, Vsvolod 181, 183
Ivanov, Vyacheslav Ivanovich 125, 161, 162, 165, 170, 171, 181, 188, 206, 212, 217
Ivask, Ivar 188
Iwaszkiewicz, Jaroslaw 144, 182, 259
Izzo, Jean-Claude 293

J

Jabavu, Noni Helen Nontando 178, 237
Jabbarly, Jaffar 148, 198
Jabra, Jabra Ibrahim 295
Jacinto, Antonio 275
Jackson, Helen Hunt 134, 136
Jackson, Shirley 178, 216, 229, 239
Jacob, Max 167, 176, 178, 181, 192
Jacobs, Harriet 122
Jacobs, Max 130, 211
Jacobs, W. W. 160
Jacobsen, Jens Peter 115, 128, 131, 133, 145
Jacobsen, Josephine 260
Jacobsen, Roy 276, 294
Jacobson, Dan 240, 247, 256, 269, 276
Jacobus de Voragine 24
Jacopone da Todi 23, 24
Jacq, Vincent 276
Jacques, Paula 269, 276
Jafri, Ali Sardar 294
Jahnn, Hans Henny 230
Jainendrakumar, Anandilal 162
Jakucho Setouchi 278
Jalil, Musal 211
Jalil, Rahim 208
Jamalzadeh, Mohammad Ali 142, 145, 181, 209, 214, 215, 287
James, Cyril Lionel Robert 158
James, Henry 91, 113, 130, 131, 132, 133, 134, 137, 139, 141, 147, 148, 149, 160, 161, 162, 165, 168, 175, 194
James, Marquis 193, 204
James, William 160, 168
Jāmī (Mowlānā Nūr od-Dīn 'Abd or-Rahmān ebn Ahmad) 26, 27, 28, 29
Jammes, Francis 170
Janakiraman, Ti 180, 240
Jandl, Ernst 295
Jankovic, Sava 283, 285
Japrisot, Sebastien 276
Jaramillo Agudelo, Darío 285
Jarīr (Jarīr ibn 'Atīyah ibn al-Khatfā) 18, 19

Jarrell, Randall 172, 209, 212, 220, 232, 239, 240, 241, 245, 273
Jarry, Alfred 146
Jarvis, José Antonio 232, 236
Jasimuddin 160
Jaspers, Karl 178, 245
Jassin, Hans Bague 176
Jastrun, Mieczyslaw 227
Javakhishvili, Mikheil 133, 185, 202
al-Jawahiri, Muhammad Mahdi 158, 287
Jayakantan, T. 198
Jeffers, Robinson 138, 171, 185, 186, 189, 190, 196, 208, 223, 235
Jelloum, Taher Ben 211
Jenkins, John Robin 257
Jennings, Elizabeth 222, 225, 234, 243, 246, 247, 250, 258
Jensen, Carsten 290
Jensen, Johannes Vilhelm 129, 158, 166, 210, 211, 218
Jensen, Thit 275
Jerome, Jerome K. 140
Jersild, P. C. 292
Jewett, Sarah Orne 146, 167
Jhabvala, Ruth Prawer 225, 226, 253
Jia Pingwa 275, 284
Jiménez, Juan Ramón 133, 163, 166, 175, 177, 179, 196, 213, 215, 226, 229
Jirásek, Alois 139, 142, 144, 149, 174, 193
Jirgl, Reinhard 284
Joansson, Johannes 248
Jodelle, Étienne 37, 39, 41
Jodra Davo, Carmen 294
Johannes von Tepl 26
Johannesen, Georg 292
Johansson, Lars 65
John, Patrick 283
John of the Cross, Saint 37, 43
Johnson, Charles 273, 290
Johnson, Diane 244, 248, 252, 257
Johnson, Eyvind 158, 196, 198, 214, 233, 252, 254
Johnson, James Weldon 171, 189
Johnson, Josephine Winslow 200
Johnson, Pamela Hansford 200, 207, 215, 216, 231, 240, 260
Johnson, Samuel 71, 78, 79, 82, 83, 84
Johnson, Uwe 198, 236, 248, 263
Johnsson, Arne 279
Johnston, George Benson 171
Johnston, Jennifer 250, 252, 256, 258, 260, 264, 269, 276
Johnston, William Denis 263
Johst, Hans 197
Jókai, Mór 104, 118, 129, 161
Jolley, Elizabeth 183, 263, 265, 267, 271, 272
Jolyot, Prosper, sieur de Crais-Billon (Crébillon) 62, 71, 80
Jolyot de Crébillon, Claude-Prosper (Crébillon fils) 71, 83
Jones, David Michael 145, 203, 252
Jones, Henry Arthur 132, 135, 144, 146, 147
Jones, Howard Mumford 239
Jones, James 180, 220, 228, 229, 235, 255
Jones, LeRoi See Baraka, Imamu Amiri
Jones, Marion Patrick 210, 251
Jones, Rod 222, 269, 286
Jones, Rodney 272

Jong, Erica 209, 256, 259, 272
Jonson, Ben 40, 45, 50, 51, 52, 54, 55, 56
Jordan, Archibald Campbell 163, 207, 244
Jose, R. Sionil 264
Joshi, Umashankar 169
Jouve, Pierre-Jean 138, 174, 176, 186, 188, 189, 200, 211, 219, 221, 254
Joyce, James 134, 152, 173, 175, 182, 206, 208
József, Attila 162, 202
Juan de Avila 39
Juárez, Rafael 271
Judah ha-Levi 21, 22
Judice, Nuno 285
Juliet, Charles 284
Juminer, Bertene 245
Jung, Carl Gustav 130, 171, 233
Junger, Ernest 145, 290
Jun'ichi Watanabe 289
Junqueiro, Abílio Manuel Guerra 116, 183
Juskaitis, Jonas 270
Jusserand, J. J. 176
Just, Ward 288
Justice, Donald 186, 243, 251
Justice, Ronald 259
Juul, Pia 235
Juvenal 4, 11, 17
Juvener, Bertene 188

K

Kabbada, Mikael 174, 216
Kadare, Ismail 201, 236, 239, 244, 255, 260, 261, 273
Kafka, Franz 135, 152, 173, 174, 175, 178, 184, 185, 188, 189
Kagame, Abbé Alexis 260
Kahana-Carmon, Amalia 276
Kaiko Takeshi 192
Kaiser, Georg 132, 175, 176, 180, 190, 204, 207, 212
Kajai, Abdul Rahim bin Salim 210
Kakinomoto Hitomaro 18
Kaletski, Aleksander 213, 266
Kālidāsa 14–15, 18
Kalyanisundaram, Mudaliar Tiruvarus V. 222
Kamaleswar 195
Kamban 23
Kamban, Gudmundur 193, 201
Kamban, Kavicakravarti 22
Kammen, Michael 250
Kamo Chomei 22, 23
Kanai Choku 187
Kanami 25, 26
Kangro, Bernard 168, 266
Kanha Khiengsiri See Surangkhanang, K.
Kanik, Orhan Veli 172, 218
Kaniuk, Yoram 278
Kant, Immanuel 73, 84, 85, 96
Kantor, MacKinlay 225, 226, 255
Kanuik, Yoram 274
Kaplan, David Michael 276
Kaplan, Hyman 203
Kaplan, Justin 242
Kaplan, Mordecai Menahem 133, 262
Kaplan, Robert D. 279
Kaplinski, Jaan 264
Kaputikian, Silva 238
Karamosmanoglu, Yakup Kadri 183
Karamzin, Nikolay Mikhaylovich 80, 85, 86, 100, 104
Karanta, Kota Sivarama 159, 220

Karaosmanoglu, Yakup Kadri 139, 252
Karapetian, Karlen See Emin, Gevorg
Karasu, Bilge 283
Karim, Abdul 228, 233
Karkavitsas, Andreas 149
Karlfeldt, Andreas 159, 164, 178, 189
Karlfeldt, Erik Axel 123, 145, 148, 194
Karm, Dan 128, 233
Karnad, Girish 202, 249
Karnow, Stanley 273
Karr, Jean-Baptiste-Alphonse 97
Karyotakis, Kostas 146, 190
Kaschefi, Hussain Vaeze 28, 29, 34
Kaschnitz, Marie Luise 158, 215, 219, 236, 252
Kasprowicz, Jan 121, 148, 159, 175, 187
Kastner, Erich 148, 252
Katayev, Valentin 146, 188, 243, 267
Kateb, Yacine 191, 271
Katona, József 100
Katz, Daniel 269
Katzir, Judith 274
Kaufman, George Simon 139, 185, 195, 196, 201, 203, 205, 222, 233
Kavanagh, Patrick 162, 209, 242
Kawabata Yasunari 148, 156, 217, 218, 221, 244, 249
Kawahigashi Hekigoto 129, 175
Kawatake Mokuami 100, 143
Kaye-Smith, Sheila 184, 194
Kazan, Elia 167
Kazantzakis, Nikos 136, 214, 219, 224, 225, 227
Kazin, Alfred 174, 209, 270
Kazinczy, Ferenc 79, 98, 106
Keane, Molly (M. J. Marrell) 285
Keats, John 87, 99, 100, 101, 102
Keiko Iwasaka 296
Keillor, Garrison 209, 265, 272
Keita, Fodeba 180
Keller, Gottfried 101, 117, 119, 132, 141
Kellerman, Bernhard 172, 181, 204, 216
Kellgren, Johan Henrik 78, 87
Kelly, George 187
Kelly, Hugh 81
Kelman, James 281, 282
Kemal, Namik 111, 139
Kemal, Orhan (Kemal Sadik Giogceli) 172, 247
Kemal, Yashar 289, 292
Kempe, Margery 25, 27
Kempner, Alfred See Kerr, Alfred
Kenaz, Yehoshua 291
Kendall, Henry 127, 134
Keneally, Thomas Michael 199, 243, 250, 258, 261, 269, 282, 284
Kenji Nakagami 255
Kennan, George F. 228, 244
Kennedy, David M. 295
Kennedy, John F. 228
Kennedy, William 262, 263, 277
Kenner, Hugh 183
Kenny, Maurice 268
Kenway, Kristin 295
Kerbabayev, Berdi 144, 207
Keret, Etgar 291
Kerouac, Jack 181, 219, 228, 229, 231, 232, 237, 245
Kerr, Alfred (Alfred Kempner) 177, 216
Kesava Dev 162
Kesey, Ken 199, 235

Keshavasut (Krishnaji Keshav Damle) 125, 163
Key, Francis Scott 83, 99, 113, 120
Keyes, Francis Parkinson 247
Keynes, John Maynard 135, 202, 213
Khadilkar, Krishnaji Prabhakar 128, 169, 216
Khai Hung (Tran Khanh Du) 214
al-Khal, Yusuf 177
Khalili, Khalilullah 164
al-Khamisi, Abdurrahman 179
Khāqānī 21, 22, 23
Kharitonov, Mark 280
Kheraskov, Mikhail Matveyevich 82, 85
Khin Hnin Ju 226
Khlebnikov, Velimir Vladimirovich 137, 181, 182
Khrakhumi, Zareh (Artho Tchiumpiushian) 187
Khurayyif, al-Bashir 176, 228, 233
Khushhal Khan Khatak 51, 65
Khutchak, Nahapet 44
Kidder, Tracy 261
Kielland, Alexander Lange 115, 133, 134, 164
Kiely, Benedict 178
Kierkegaard, Søren Aabye 91, 99, 113, 119
Kihara Koichi 181
Kilmer, Alfred Joyce 137, 172, 177
Kilpi, Eva 269
Kim, Anatoly 278
Kimitake Hiraoka See Mishima Yukio
Kincaid, Jamaica 217, 264, 265
King, Francis 263
Kingo, Thomas 62
Kingsley, Charles 101, 115, 116, 118, 119, 120, 123, 125, 130
Kingsley, Sidney 198, 217, 283
Kingsolver, Barbara 270, 273, 279
Kingston, Maxine Hong 206
Kinkel, Gottfried 114
Kinnell, Galway 232, 238, 248, 252, 261, 262, 273
Kinoshita Junji 172, 218, 220, 234, 248, 256
Kinsella, Thomas 190, 227, 229, 235, 251, 258, 271, 276
Kinsella, William Patrick 199, 261
Kipling, Rudyard 124, 137, 139, 141, 143, 144, 147, 159, 160, 165, 201
Kirby, William 131, 164
Kirchoff, Bodo 215
Kirsch, Sarah 286
Kirst, Hans Hellmut 236
Kis, Danilo 292
Kisfaludy, Károly 98, 100, 102
Kitahara Hakushu 137, 170, 172, 179, 209
Kitereza, Aniceti 158
Kittredge, George Lyman 208
Kivi, Aleksis 122, 124, 125, 126, 127
Kiyoko Murata 291
Kizer, Caroline 264, 265
Kjaerstad, Jan 280, 294, 296
Klabund (Alfred Henschke) 140, 177, 190
Klausner, Joseph 129, 229
Kldiashvili, Sergo 143
Kleban, Edward 254
Klein, Hedin M. 218
Kleist, Ewald Christian von 72, 78, 79
Kleist, Heinrich von 83, 96, 97, 98, 102

Klima, Ivan 194, 232, 238, 245, 249, 265, 273, 290
Klinger, Friedrich Maximilian von 78, 82, 83, 106
Klonowic, Sebastian 43, 44, 50
Klopstock, Friedrich Gottlieb 73, 77, 81, 96
Kluger, Richard 288
Knopfli, Rui 289
Knowles, John 187, 231, 259
Kobayashi Hideo 159, 160, 262
Kobayashi Issa 95, 101
Kobayashi Takiji 197
Koch, Christopher John 195
Koch, Kenneth 231, 256, 258
Koch, Martin 171, 172, 175
Kochanowski, Jan 41, 42
Kock, Charles-Paul de 128
Kōda Rohan (Kōda Shigeyuki) 125, 140, 142, 214
Koestler, Arthur 162, 206, 207, 210, 262
Kogawa, Joy 284
Koltzow, Liv 288, 291
Kometani Fumiko 266
Komunyakaa, Yusef 282
Konadu, Samuel Asare 195
Konigsburg, E. L. 244, 287
Konopnicka, Marja 143
Konrád, György 296
Konwicki, Tadeusz 187, 227, 237, 243
Kopf, Gerhard 280
Koppenvag, Odd 276
Koraïs, Adamántios 77, 107
Koretz, Franz Xavier 213
Kornáros, Vitzéntzos 55
Korner, Karl Theodor 86, 99
Kornis, Mihály 278
Korolenko, Vladimir 137, 181
Korzeniowski, Józef Teodor Konrad See Conrad, Joseph
Kosinski, Jerzy 197, 240, 244, 247, 275
Kosovic, Birgithe 292
Kosuke Shibusawa 289
Kosztolányi, Dezsó 137, 169, 188, 201
Kotsyubinsky, Mikhaylo 162
Kotzebue, August (Friedrich Ferdinand) von 80, 85, 95, 101
Kourouma, Ahmadou 296
Král', Janko 102, 114, 122, 131
Kram, Karl 182
Kramm, Joseph 221
Krasicki, Ignacy 75, 83, 95
Krasilnikoff, Arthur 295
Krasinski, Zygmunt 98, 109, 113
Kraszewski, Josef Ignacy 98, 138
Krasznahorkai, László 280
Kratochvil, Jiri 292
Kraus, Karl 129, 201
Krausser, Helmut 280
Kretzen, Max 139
Kreutzwald, Friedrich Reinhold 96, 120, 134
Kreve-Mickievicius, Vincas 134, 219, 223
Krige, Uys 222, 235, 238, 241, 243
Kriseova, Eda 288
Krishna Pillai, Kunnumpuzha 172
Krishnamurthi, R. 148
Kristensen, Tom 182, 193, 223
Krleza, Miroslav 143, 196, 260
Kroetz, Franz Xavier 250
Krog, Antjie 293
Kronauer, Brigitte 274, 296
Kruczkowski, Leon 196, 200

Kruss, James 287
Krylov, Ivan Andreyevich 81, 113
Ku Chiang 51
Kubin, Alfred 131, 167, 230
Kuitz, Stanley 230
Kulaas'kar, Seraphim Aramaanbys See Elley
Kulakoskiy, Aleksey Yaliseyevich 131, 187
Kumaran Asan, N. 129, 167, 179, 184
Kumin, Maxine 186, 247, 250, 257, 261
Kumne Maso 175, 177, 182
Kumpfmuller, Michael 296
Kuncewicz, Maria 202
Kundera, Milan 191, 242, 258, 260, 264, 273, 290
Kunene, Mazisi Raymond 248
Kunie Iwahashi 278
Kunio Ogawa 294
Kunio Tsuji 284
Kunitz, Stanley 162, 211, 249, 252, 257, 258, 284
Kuprin, Aleksandr Ivanovich 127, 164, 168, 204
Kurnberger, Ferdinand 119
Kuroda Saburo 178
Kurz, Hermann 113, 119
Kushner, Tony 279
Kusniewicz, Andrzej 161
Kuttikrishnan, P. C. 174, 224
Kuznetsov, Anatoly 242
Kvittka, Laryse Petrivna Kosach See Ukrainka, Lesya
Kyd, Thomas 39, 44
Kyoko Hayashi 274
Kyoshi Takahama 130, 230

L
La Bruyère, Jean de 57, 65, 66
La Chaussée, Pierre-Claude Nivelle de 65, 78
La Farge, Oliver 236
La Fayette, Marie-Madeleine de 60, 63, 65
La Fontaine, Jean de 53, 60, 61, 66
La Guma, Alex 179, 243
La Roche, Sophie von 82
La Rochefoucauld, François 51, 60, 63
Labiche, Eugène-Marin 117, 122, 139
Laclos, Pierre-Ambroise-François Choderlos de 76, 84, 96
Lacretelle, Jacques 139, 196, 214, 256, 265
Laederach, Jurg 274
Laforet, Carmen 180, 217
LaForge, Oliver 193
Laforgue, Jules 121, 138, 141
Lafourcade, Enrique 296
Lagerkvist, Par Fabian 141, 180, 187, 189, 198, 202, 212, 218, 219, 252
Lagerlöf, Selma 120, 142, 147, 148, 159, 167, 194, 196, 206
Lagones, Leopoldo 147
Lagorio, Gina 280
Lahhabi, Mohammad Aziz 279
Lahiri, Jhumpa 295
Lahuti, Abolqasem 217, 230
Laleau, Léon 142
Lalic, Ivan 194, 285
Lalonde, Robert 268
Lamartine, Marie-Louis-Alphonse de Prat de 85, 102, 127
Lamb, Charles 82, 88, 96, 97, 98, 103, 105, 106, 108
Lamb, Mary 97, 98

Lambron, Marc 280
Lamennais, Hugues-Félicité-Robert de 84, 118
Lamming, George 188
Lampedusa, Guiseppe Tomasi di 146, 227
Landero, Luis 283
Landolfi, Tommaso 165, 257
Landon, Margaret 211
Landor, Walter Savage 82, 88, 98, 103, 109, 110, 118, 123
Lange-Nielsen, Sissel 284
Langer, Frantisek 183
Langer, Susan Katherina 265
Langle, Ulrike 291
Lanier, Sidney 112, 126, 134
Lao She 216, 241
Lapaque, Sebastien 293
Lapid, Hayim 291
Lapido, Duro 192
Lapine, James 264, 265
Lardner, Ring 137, 185, 188, 197
Larkin, Oliver W. 218
Larkin, Philip 181, 212, 215, 225, 252, 265, 272
Larsen, Michael 290
Larsen, Terje 278
Larson, Edward J. 290
Larson, Jonathan 286
LaRue, Monique 284
Lash, Joseph P. 249
Lasker-Schuler, Else 130, 167, 171, 173, 181, 212
Lassen, Cecilie 295
Lat, U 125, 181
Lateur, Frank See Streuvels, Stijn
Latino, Juan 41
Lattimore, Owen 271
Lattimore, Richmond Alexander 263
Lau, Evelyn 284
Laube, Heinrich 97, 136
Launko, Okinba 269
Laurence, Jean Margaret Wemyss 187, 268
Laurens, Camille 296
Laurent, Antoine 220, 269
Lautréamont, Comte de (Isidore-Lucien Ducasse) 126, 127
Lavgesen, Peter 277
Lavin, Mary 285
Lawler, Ray 226
Lawrence, D. H. 137, 172, 174, 180, 182, 184, 188, 190, 193
Lawrence, T. E. 188
Lawson, Henry Hertzberg 125, 159, 182
Laxness, Halldor (Halldor Kiljan Gudyonsson) 159, 189, 195, 198, 203, 210, 224, 228, 233, 245, 269, 290
Laye, Camara 190, 224, 259
Layton, Irving 223, 225, 234, 260
Le, Linda 296
Le Carré, John 194, 232, 237, 256, 259, 263, 272, 286
Le Clezio, Jean-Marie 206, 237, 240, 241, 247, 251, 259, 266, 276, 288
Le Fanu, (Joseph) Sheridan 99, 123, 124, 129
Le Guillou, Philippe 288
Le Guin, Ursula K. 191, 244, 245, 250, 252, 265
Le Touze, Guillaume 282
Lear, Edward 98, 114, 128
Leavis, F. R. 145, 216, 256
Lechon, Jan 148, 180, 181, 185, 226

Leclerc, Rachel 284
Leconte de Lisle, Charles-Marie-René 101, 127, 144
Lederer, William J. 229
Ledesma, González 265
Ledwidge, Francis 138, 176, 177
Lee, Harper 232, 233
Lee, Laurie 231, 287
Lee, Nathaniel 64
Leech, Margaret 209, 232
Léger, Marie-René-Auguste-Aléxis Saint-Léger See Perse, Saint-John
Legouvé, Ernest 116
Lehmann, Rosamund Nina 273
Lehtonen, Joel 133, 178, 182, 198
Leibniz, Gottfried Wilhelm 57, 71, 72
Leino, Eino 132, 161, 162, 163, 166, 187
Leiris, Michel Julien 186, 214, 255, 273
Leisewitz, Johann Anton 83
Leithauser, Brad 272
Lekhnath Paudyal 137
Lelyweld, Joseph 267
Lem, Stanisław 180, 234
Lemercier, Népomucène 81, 86, 98, 102, 111, 133
Lemonnier, Antoine Louis Camille 134, 160, 172
Lenau, Nikolaus 95, 107, 110, 112, 114, 116, 117
L'Engle, Madeleine 177, 235, 250, 257, 267
Lennep, Jacob van 111
Lenngren, Anna Maria 87
Lenormand, Henri-René 134, 180, 182, 185, 186, 219
Lenz, Hermann 290
Lenz, Jakob Michael Reinhold 78, 82, 86
Leodhas, Sorche Nic 241
León, Luis de 36, 42, 43
Leonard, Elmore 233, 252, 255, 257, 262, 277
Leonidze, Georgi 241
Leonov, Leonid 185, 189, 212, 281
Leopardi, Giacomo 87, 91, 100, 103, 104, 106, 109
Lermontov, Mikhail Yuryevich 99, 107, 110, 111, 112
Lernet-Holenia, Alexander 254
Leroux, Gaston 126, 168, 189
Lesage, Alain-René 61, 71, 72, 77
Leshoai, Benjamin Letholoa 179
Leśmian, Bolesław 180
Leskov, Nikolai Semenovich 106, 124, 125, 127, 129, 134, 145
Lesoro, Ephraim Alfred Shadrack 191
Lessing, Doris 178, 219, 221, 223, 229, 231, 235, 238, 240, 246, 249, 251, 252, 257, 258, 265, 271, 286
Lessing, Gotthold Ephraim 69, 74, 79, 80, 81, 83, 84
Levertov, Denise 183, 228, 231, 249, 253, 287
Levi, Carlo 159, 213, 215, 253, 262
Levi, Primo 178, 237, 254, 268
Levin, Meyer 226
Levine, Norman 276
Levine, Philip 258, 276, 282, 283
Levinson, Deirdre 194, 264
Lévi-Strauss, Claude 165, 225, 239, 241, 245
Levy, Leonard W. 245
Lewis, C. S. 148, 197, 201, 204, 207, 208, 210, 212, 223, 225, 236

Lewis, David Levering 281
Lewis, Janet 290
Lewis, Matthew Gregory "Monk" 82, 87, 88, 101
Lewis, R. W. B. 254
Lewis, Sinclair 137, 179, 182, 186, 187, 189, 192, 193, 200, 212, 219
Lewis, Wyndham 134, 203, 227
Lezama Lima, José 167, 242, 254
Li Cunbao 261
Li Feigan See Ba Jin
Li Rui 279, 290
Lidman, Sara 183, 230, 287, 294
Lie, Jonas 129, 136
Lie, Sissel 288
Likachev, Dmitry Sergeyevich 292
Liliencron, Detlev von 113, 167
Lillpers, Birgitta 292
Lim, Shirley 259
Lima, Jorge de 200, 204, 206, 215, 222
Lima Barreto, Alfonso Henriques de 133, 167, 182
Lindbergh, Charles 189, 223
Lindegren, Erik 167, 244
Lindgren, Astric 213
Lindgren, Togny 285
Lindqvist, Sven 279
Lindsay, Howard 213
Lindsay, Vachel 132, 163, 171, 172, 173, 176, 194
Linnankoski, Johannes 163, 166
Lins, Osman 184, 230, 242, 256
Lispector, Clarice 186, 212, 234, 239, 251, 255, 256
Lisser, Herbert George de 132
Lista, Alberto 88
Little, Kenneth 212
Litwack, Leon F. 259
Liu Heng 279
Liu Zhenyun 290
Lively, Penelope 197, 255, 268, 290
Livesay, Dorothy 228
Livius Andronicus 9
Livy 10, 11
Liyong, Taban Lo 203
Llamazares, Julio 224, 266
Llewellyn, Richard 206, 210
Lobel, Arnold 260
Lobo Antunes, Antonio 296
Locke, John 55, 70
Lodge, David 259, 264
Lodge, Thomas 43
Loesser, Frank 235
Lofting, Hugh 137, 180, 214
Logan, Joshua 218
Lo-Johansson, Ivar 273
Lomami-Tshibamba, Paul 172, 216
Lombroso, Cesare 167
Lon, Anne Marie 292
London, Jack 130, 158, 160, 161, 162, 164, 165, 166, 167, 168, 169, 175
Longfellow, Henry Wadsworth 97, 110, 111, 112, 114, 115, 116, 119, 120, 123, 134, 135
Lonn, Oystein 283, 294
Lönnrot, Elias 108
Loon, Hendrik Willem Van 134
Loon, Karel Glastra van 293
Lopes de Silva, Baltasar See Alcantar, Osvaldo
Lopes Verissimo, Erico 163, 253
Lortkipanidze, Niko 190
Loti, Pierre (Louis-Marie-Julien Viaud) 116, 133, 138, 183
Lotkipanidze, Niko 211
Louzeiro, José 198

Lovelace, Earl 199, 261
Lovelace, Richard 52, 58, 59
Lowell, Amy 129, 171, 173, 182, 186, 187
Lowell, James Russell 101, 111, 113, 114, 115, 127, 141
Lowell, Robert, Jr. 176, 213, 214, 231, 234, 238, 243, 245, 246, 251, 252, 255, 256
Lowndes, Mary Adelaide 172
Lowry, Clarence Malcolm 167, 215, 227, 235
Lowry, Lois 273, 281
Lowther, Pat 288
Loynaz, Dulce María 287
Lu Ji 17
Lu Xun (Zhou Shuren) 133, 156, 183, 187, 201
Lu You 21, 23
Lucan 5, 11, 12
Lucian 17
Lucius Annaeus See Seneca
Ludens, Vitauts 202, 270
Ludwig, Emil 133, 216
Ludwig, Otto 99, 124
Luft, Lya 203
Lugones, Leopoldo 130, 163, 168, 176, 188, 204
Luhtu Hla, U 168
Luján, Nestor 287
Lukács, György 248
Lukas, J. Anthony 267
Lundkvist, Artur 191, 194, 199, 275
Lundqvist, Lars 186, 266
Lurie, Alison 264, 265
Lustig, Arnost 277
Luther, Martin 36
Luzán Claramunt de Suelves y Gurrea, Ignacio de 70, 78
Luzi, Mario 172, 215, 221, 228, 234, 240, 257, 266
Luzzatto, Moshe Hayyim 71, 74, 77
Lvov, Arkady 272
Lydgate, John 29, 35
Lyle, John 39, 43, 44, 50
Lyly, John 41

M
Ma Ma Lei, Djanetjo 176
Maalouf, Amin 280
al-Ma'arrī 20, 21
Mabee, Carlton 211
Mabillon, Jean 55, 71
MacArthur, Charles 145, 190, 226
Macaulay, David 275
Macaulay, Emilie Rose 229
Macaulay, Rose 227
Macaulay, Thomas Babington 95, 112, 113, 121
MacBeth, George Mann 277
MacCaig, Norman 274
MacDermot, Thomas Henry 197
MacDiarmid, Hugh 196, 199, 256
Macdonald, Cynthia 276
Macdonald, Ross 262
Macedo, Helder 278, 291
MacFarlane, John Ebenezer Clare 235
Mácha, Karel Hynek 98, 108, 109
Machado, Ana Maria 278
Machado, Antonio 130, 161, 171, 185, 205
Machado, Manuel 130, 160, 168, 171, 214
Machado, Reuben Mauro 207
Machado de Assis, Joaquim Maria 110, 134, 142, 149, 158, 166

Machiavelli, Niccolò 35, 36
MacInnes, Helen Clark 164, 209, 265
Mačiulis, Jonas See Maironis
Mack, John E. 255
Mackay, Shena 286
Mackenzie, Compton 164, 180, 194, 208, 215, 249
Mackenzie, Henry 81
Mackenzie, Sir Edward Montague Compton 135
MacLachlan, Patricia 267
MacLaverty, Bernard 288
MacLean, Alistair 181, 268
Maclean, Norman 277
MacLeish, Archibald 142, 196, 197, 201, 222, 229, 230, 248, 254, 261
MacLennan, Hugh 164
MacNeacail, Aonghas 267
MacNeice, Louis 165, 204, 215, 221, 228, 234, 236
Macpherson, James 80, 87
Madách, Imre 103, 122, 124
Made, Emmanuel H. A. 162
Madgulkar, Venkatesh Digamber 188
Madhava Panikkar, Kovalam 236
Madrid, Juan 281
Madsen, Svend Age 295
Maeterlinck, Maurice 122, 140, 143, 159, 160, 166, 167, 169, 177, 217
Maffei, Francesco Scipione 62, 79
Magalhaes, Joaquim Manuel 283
Magen, Mira 296
Magris, Claudio 289
Maha Hswei 158, 222
Mahammed, Sheikh Abdul Hasan 123
Mahari, Gurgen 160, 245
Maharidge, Dale 273
Mahfouz, Naguib 169, 214, 220, 226, 233, 240, 242, 270
Mahjur, Ghulam Ahmad 139, 221
Mahon, Derek 274
Mailer, Norman 183, 216, 225, 240, 244, 245, 247, 258, 259, 262, 264, 275, 284
Maillard, Keith 293
Mainali, Guruprasad 158, 248
Mairet, Jean 54, 55, 64
Maironis (Jonas Mačiulis) 122, 188, 195
Mais, Roger 162, 224
Majaz, Asrar-ul-haq 169, 224
Makanin, Vladimir 276
Makine, André 284, 293
Makonnen, Endalkacaw 142, 208, 236
Malai Chuphinit 163
al-Malaika Nazik 183
Malamud, Bernard 173, 221, 226, 229, 237, 241, 242, 246, 249, 261, 267, 272
Malaparte, Curzio 148, 211, 218, 227
Malcolm X 240
Maldini, Sergio 278
Malebranche, Nicolas de 56, 62
Malherbe, Daniel 172, 202
Malherbe, François de 39, 54
Mali Chuphinit 236
Mallarmé, Stéphane 112, 127, 131, 148
Mallea, Eduardo 160, 208, 261
Mallet, David 76
Mallet-Joris, Françoise 192, 220, 232, 237, 251, 255, 258, 263, 266, 271, 276
Malone, Dumas 253
Malory, Sir Thomas 28

Malouf, David 280, 286, 295
Malraux, André 158, 197, 200, 203, 254
Mamet, David 214, 253, 256, 263, 264, 272
Mammadguluzada, Jalil 126, 195
Mammeri, Mouloud 221, 225
Manasseh ben Israel 50, 59
Mand, Andreas 282
Mandelstam, Osip 141, 204
Mander, Mary Jane 131, 180, 217
Mandeville, Bernard 70, 72, 75
Mandino, Augustine A. 285
Mandur, Mohammad 239
Mándy, Iván 280
al-Manfaluti, Mustafa Lutfi 131, 184
Manganelli, Giorgio 276
Mangetsu Hanamura 291
Mann, Heinrich 128, 163, 176, 177, 187, 218
Mann, Klaus 163, 217
Mann, Thomas 130, 152, 159, 161, 171, 177, 185, 191, 197, 215, 220, 223, 224
Manner, Eeva-Liisa 180, 227, 232
Manning, Olivia 232, 256, 257, 259
Manrique, Jorge 29
Mansfield, Katherine 139, 177, 180, 182, 183
Manto, Sadat Hasan 224
Manzoni, Alessandro 84, 99, 102, 104, 129, 250
Mao Dun 146, 193, 260, 277
Mapu, Abraham 97, 124, 125
Marabini, Claudio 274
Maraini, Dacia 274, 289
Maramzin, Vladimir 294
Maran, René 138
Marcel, Gabriel 250
Marcos, Plinio 291
Marcus Tullius Cicero See Cicero
Mardhekar, Bal Sitaram 165, 226
Marechal, Leopoldo 158, 188, 192, 203, 207, 217, 240, 247
Margiani, Revaz 175
Margulies, Donald 295
Marías, Javier 279, 283
Marinetti, Filippo Tommaso 131, 211
Marini, Giambattista 53
Maritain, Jacques 134, 249, 250
Marivaux, Pierre Carlet de 65, 71, 74, 75, 76, 80
Markandaya, Kamala (Kamala Purnaiya Taylor) 184, 224, 232, 251, 256, 263
Markham, Beryl 209
Markham, Edwin 149
Markson, David 286
Marlowe, Christopher 33, 40, 43, 44
Mármol, José 134
Marmontel, Jean-François 96
Maron, Monika 286, 293
Marot, Clément 29, 38
Marquand, John Phillips 143, 203, 204, 205, 208, 217, 220, 225, 232
Marques, Helena 280
Marquis, Don 189
Marrell, M. J. See Keane, Molly
Marryat, Frederick 86, 109, 115
Marse, Juan 281
Marsh, Dame Ngaio 148, 261
Marshall, Paule 191, 245, 262
Marsman, Hendrik 148, 189, 206
Martí, José 118, 145
Martial 11, 16
Martin, Penelope 235

Martin du Gard, Roger 133, 182, 203, 229
Martín Gaite, Carmen 279, 283, 287, 292, 295
Martín Garzo, Gustavo 289, 294
Martindale, Victor See White, Patrick
Martineau, Harriet 111
Martinek, Lubmir 281
Martínez de la Rosa, Francisco de Paula 85, 122
Martínez Estrada, Ezequiel 145, 198, 238
Martínez Ruiz, José See Azorín
Martínez Sierra, Gregorio 133, 214
Martinson, Harry 161, 192, 201, 202, 213, 217, 252, 256
Marulić, Marko 27, 36
Marvell, Andrew 53, 63
Marx, Karl 101, 126, 135
Masamune Hakucho 132, 235
Masao Tsuji 287
Masaoka Shiki 125, 160
Masefield, John Edward 132, 168, 242
Massano, Giorgio 236
Massie, Alan 280
Massie, Robert K. 260
Massinger, Philip 42, 54, 55, 56
Masters, Edgar Lee 126, 174, 218
Mastretta, Angeles 289, 294
Mas'ud, Dehati Mohammad 162, 216
Masuji Ibuse 148
Masuo Ikeda 257
Mata, Humberto 281
Matalon, Ronit 296
Matanovic, Julijana 295
Matep, Benjamin 227
Mather, Cotton 65, 70, 74
Mather, Increase 56, 73
Mathias, Roland Glyn 174, 263
Mathiessen, F. O. 208
Matip, Benjamin 195
Matsunaga Teitoku 40, 59
Matsuō Bashō (Matsuo Munefusa) 49, 57, 66
Matthews, Greg 267
Matthews, William Proctor, III 284, 287
Matthiessen, Francis Otto 218
Matthiessen, Peter 226, 253, 288, 293
Mattson, Ellen 294
Mattsson, Eva 270
Maturin, Charles Robert 102
Matute, Ana María 289
Maugham, William Somerset 130, 147, 174, 178, 181, 182, 193, 211, 239
Maun Htin 214
Maun Tyi, U Leti Pantita 132, 205
Maupassant, Guy de 116, 133, 134, 137, 143
Maurensig, Paolo 286
Mauriac, Claude 173, 285
Mauriac, François 137, 167, 172, 173, 182, 184, 189, 196, 197, 206, 208, 218, 221, 247
Maurois, André 137, 177
Mavor, Osborne Henry See Bridie, James
Maxsimov, Vladimir Yemelyanovich 283
Maxwell, William 261, 272
May, Karl 112
Mayakovsky, Vladimir 143, 174, 193
Mayoral, Marina 297
Mays, David J. 222
al-Mazini, Ibrahim 140, 194, 217

Mazur, Drazen 219
Mazzucco, Melania 287
McAuley, James Philip 176, 238, 254
McCabe, Partick 291
McCaig, Norman Alexander 285
McCarthy, Cormac 277, 282, 290
McCarthy, Mary 217, 219, 221, 225, 228, 237, 248, 258, 271
McCourt, Frank 286, 288
McCracken, Elizabeth 286
McCrae, John 177
McCraw, Thomas K. 265
McCullers, Carson 176, 208, 213, 220, 233, 242
McCullogh, David 279
McCullough, Colleen 288, 295
McCully, Emily Arnold 279
McCutcheon, George 159
McDermott, Alice 290
McDermott, Gerald 253
McDiarmid, Hugh 142
McDonald, Ian 197, 246
McDougall, Walter A. 267
McEwan, Ian 278, 290
McFadden, David 206
McFarlane, John Ebenezer Clare 144
McFeeley, William S. 261
McGahern, John 274
McGinley, Patrick 202
McGinley, Phyllis 233
McGuckian, Medbh 218, 264
McIlvanney, William 201, 254
McIlwain, Charles Howard 185
McKay, Claude 140, 190, 216
McKinley, Robin 265
McLaughlin, Andrew C. 201
McMillan, Terry 277
McMurtry, Larry 201, 234, 237, 248, 253, 261, 265, 267, 279
McNeil, R. Anthony 207
McPhee, John 292
McPherson, James Alan 256
McPherson, James M. 272
Mead, Margaret 256
Megged, Aharon 278, 296
Megged, Eyal 293
Mehren, Stein 278, 289
Meilhac, Henri 127
Meireles, Cecilia 206
Melanchthon, Philip 36
Meldini, Piero 293
Melo Neto, João Cabral de 179, 219, 226, 227, 263, 266
Melville, Herman 101, 114, 115, 116, 117, 118, 119, 120, 131, 141, 185
Memmi, Albert 179, 223, 225, 246, 256, 271
Menander 3, 8, 9
Menasse, Robert 278
Mencken, H. L. 133, 178, 184, 226
Mendelssohn, Moses 74
Mendes, Alfred H. 146
Mendes, Catule 111, 167
Mendes, Murilo 159, 200, 253
Mendoza, Eduardo 271, 279
Menon, Vallathol Narayana 132, 229
Mercado, Tununa 287
Mercer, David 259
Mereazhkovsky, Dmitri 177
Meredith, George 105, 117, 119, 120, 121, 123, 124, 127, 132, 133, 137, 138, 142, 144, 145, 167
Meredith, William Morris 269, 270, 288
Merezhkovsky, Dmitry Sergeyevich 124, 146, 159, 166, 208

Meri, Veijo 190, 228, 232, 237, 240, 241, 244
Merilaas, Kersti 171, 267
Mérimée, Prosper 96, 111, 114, 127
Merino, José María 287
Merrill, James 187, 255, 262, 283, 284
Merrill, Judith (Josephine Juliet Grossman) 287
Mersenne, Marin 43, 58
Merton, Thomas 174, 216, 244
Merwin, William S. 223, 237, 247, 248, 256
Metastasio, Pietro 66, 84
Metsarants, Misak 137, 166
Meyer, Conrad Ferdinand 104, 128, 133, 148
Meyrink, Gustav 126, 174, 195
Michael, Ib 279, 284, 288
Michaels, Ann 286
Michaux, Henri 148, 263
Michelet, Jules 87, 130
Michener, James Albert 165, 215, 216, 222, 231, 240, 252, 257, 272, 287
Michitsuna Takahashi 257
Michon, Pierre 286
Mickiewicz, Adam 87, 103, 104, 105, 108, 119
Mickovic, Slobodan 284, 291
Middleton, John 140
Middleton, Stanley 252
Middleton, Thomas 40, 53, 54, 59
Mihailovic, Vasa 283
Mihajlovski, Dragi 284
Mihalic, Slavko 265
Mihardja, Achdiat Karta 169, 218
Mikszáth, Kálmán 115, 158, 166, 168, 169
Milavanoff, Jean-Pierre 293
Miles, Jack 286
Milhauser, Steven 288
Mill, John Stuart 97, 121, 129
Millas, Juan José 275
Millay, Edna St. Vincent 142, 176, 179, 181, 183, 190, 194, 199, 218
Miller, Andrew 290, 293
Miller, Arthur 174, 205, 211, 214, 217, 222, 225, 232, 234, 238, 240, 244, 270
Miller, Henry 141, 198, 201, 205, 212, 259
Miller, Jason 250
Miller, Perry 241
Millhauser, Stephen 288
Millin, Sarah Gertrude 140, 185, 244
Millington, John 128
Milne, A. A. 188
Milosz, Czeslaw 169, 213, 226, 257, 259, 289
Milton, John 48, 51, 54, 55, 57, 59, 61, 62
Minamoto Shitago 20
Minoru Oda 260
Mir, Pedro 295
Mir Jalal, Pashaogly 165
Miranda, Ana 274, 285, 294
Mirande, Jon 186, 249
Miri Yu 296
Miron, Gaston 285
Mirshakar, Mirsaid 209, 234
Mirtskhulava, Alio 160
Mirza, Iraj 184
Mises, Richard von 222
Mishima Yukio (Kimitake Hiraoka) 186, 218, 219, 224, 227, 240, 247
Mistral, Frédéric 106, 118, 121, 126, 136, 141, 147, 162, 164, 173

Mistral, Gabriela (Lucila Godoy Alcayaga) 140, 183, 185, 205, 212, 224, 227
Mistry, Robinton 276, 286
Mitchell, Julian 261
Mitchell, Margaret 201, 203, 217
Mitchell, W. O. 273, 290
Mitchison, Naomi 292
Mitford, Nancy 161, 212, 217, 220, 250, 285
Mittelholzer, Edgar 167, 219, 239
Mitusaki Inoue 262
Mjelve, Sigmund 282
Mo, Timothy 218, 267, 276
Mo Yan 273, 295
Moberg, Vilhelm 148, 218, 250
Modano, Patrick 286
Modarressi, Taghi 194, 268, 272
Modiano, Patrick 271
Modignani, Sveva Casati 296
Modisane, Walter 237
Modisane, William 183
Modupe Paris, Prince 159
Moe, Jørg 117
Mofolo, Thomas Mokopu 131, 186, 195, 216
Mohammad, Abdille Hasan, Sheikh 179
Mohammad, Ali 234
Moix, Terenci 287
Moldo, Togolok 121
Molière (Jean-Baptiste Poquelin) 47–48, 53, 59, 60, 61, 62
Molnár, Ferenc 132, 165, 167, 221
Momaday, N. Scott 198, 244, 245, 246, 272
Mommsen, Theodor 160
Mong-Giac, Nguyen 206
Monsarrat, Nicholas John Turney 168, 257
Montague, John Patrick 191, 250, 263
Montaigne, Michael Eyquem de 32–33, 37, 42, 44
Montale, Eugenio 146, 187, 196, 206, 210, 227, 236, 242, 253, 260
Montalembert, Charles-René de 127
Montalvo, Garci Rodríguez de 34
Montalvo, Juan 107, 133, 137, 140
Monteiro Martins, Julio Cesar 224
Montello, Josue 254
Montemayor, Carlos 277
Montemayor, Jorge de 39
Montero, Rosa 279, 289
Montesquieu, Charles-Louis de Secondat, baron de La Brède et de 65, 73, 75, 77, 79
Montfaucon, Bernard de 76
Montherlant, Henry de 146, 202, 203, 206, 214, 215, 220, 224, 240, 245, 249
Montserrat, Nicholas 220
Moodie, Susanna Strickland 137
Moody, William Vaughan 162, 168
Moor, Margriet de 288
Moore, Brian 225, 232, 274, 280, 292
Moore, Clement Clarke 83, 103
Moore, George Augustus 117, 144, 161, 175, 197
Moore, George Edward 129, 229
Moore, Marianne 138, 181, 185, 220, 221, 249, 267
Moore, Thomas 83, 95, 99, 100, 101, 103, 105, 117
Moorhouse, Frank 295
Moraes, Dom 203
Morand, Paul 139, 182, 254
Morandini, Giuliana 287

Morante, Elsa 177, 228, 252, 265
Morasco, Robert 290
Moravcevic, Nikola 285
Moravia, Alberto 165, 192, 211, 215, 216, 220, 228, 233, 273
More, Thomas 35
Moreas, Jean (Johannes Papadiamantopulos) 149, 168
Moreau, Emile 144
Moreira, Julio 280, 294
Moreno-Dorani, Rafeal Humberto 270
Moreto y Cabaña, Agustín 59, 61
Moretti, Marino 165, 181, 208, 246
Morgenstern, Christian 128, 173
Morgieve, Richard 296
Mori Ōgai (Mori Rintarō) 121, 170, 182
Morier, James 103
Morike, Eduard 96, 107, 119, 130
Morison, Samuel Eliot 138, 210, 232, 254
Morón, Guillermo 277
Morozov, Aleksandr 291, 294
Morris, Edmund 259
Morris, Mervyn 251
Morris, William 108, 120, 126, 131, 139, 141, 146
Morris, Wright 168, 260, 290
Morrison, Toni 194, 247, 250, 256, 260, 268, 270, 277, 279, 290
Mortimer, Penelope 292
Moruo, Guo 142
Mosel, Tad 233
Motley, John Lothrop 119
Mott, Frank Luther 205
Motta, Pascoal 278
Mounif, Abdul Rahman 197, 265
Mourao-Ferreira, David 285
Mowlanā Nūr od-Dīn 'Abd or-Rahmān ebn Ahmad See Jāmī
Mphahlele, Ezekiel 178, 231
Mqhayi, Samuel Edward Krune Loliwe 130, 192, 212
Mtwa, Percy 267
Mueller, Lisel 184, 288
Muggeridge, Malcolm 273
Muir, Edwin 230
Mujica Lainez, Manuel 167, 236, 263
Mukherjee, Bharati 270
Mukopadhyay, Subhas 178, 207
Mulisch, Harry Kurt Victor 188, 261, 272, 293
Mulla Vajhi 55
Muller, Herta 278
Muller, Lisel 260
Multatuli (Eduard Douwes Dekker) 101, 122, 123, 138
Mumford, Lewis 273
Munk, Kaj 196, 211
Munonye, John 191, 247
Muñoz Molina, Antonio 277, 289
Munro, Alice 267, 273, 282, 291
Munro, H. H. See Saki
Munro, Hugh Andrew Johnstone 145
Munthe, Alex 192
Muordinov, Nijikulay Jogyorebis See Achchygyya, Amma
Muradabadi, Jigar 140, 224, 232
Murakami, Haruki 217, 258, 262, 269, 284, 294
Murasaki Shikibu 15, 20, 21
Muratori, Ludovico Antonio 62, 77
Muraveva, Irina 283
Murdoch, Iris 178, 224, 228, 234, 238, 241, 244, 246, 249, 251, 252, 253, 255, 256, 257, 269, 292

Murger, Henri 115
Murphy, Richard 188, 266
Murphy, Thomas Bernard 199, 267
Murray, Lee 293
Murray, Leslie Allan 204, 264
Murry, John Middleton 183, 226
Musa, Salama 138, 189, 229
Muschg, Adolf 198, 258, 280
Musgrove, Margaret 255
Musgrove, Susan 295
Mushanakoji Saneatsu 206
Mushfiqi, Abdurrahman 39, 43
Musil, Robert 133, 193, 209
Musset, Alfred de 98, 107, 108, 109, 110
Mustaghni, Abdulali 131, 198
al-Mutanabbī 20
Mutis, Alvaro 183, 251, 275
Mutran, Khalil 217
Muzrepov, Ghabit 159
Mya Than Tint 290
Myers, L. H. 207
Myrdal, Jan 281

N
Nabokov, Dmitri 284
Nabokov, Vladimir Vladimirovich 148, 155, 191, 193, 203, 204, 208, 214, 220, 225, 228, 235, 245, 252, 255
Nadi, Yunus 285
Nado, Sheikh A. 206
Nadolny, Sten 293
Naess, Atle 289
Nafisi, Said 146, 241
Nagar, Amritlal 175, 227
Naifeh, Stephen 275
Naipaul, Shivadhar Srinivasa 212, 265
Naipaul, V. S. 195, 234, 248, 258
Najjar, Alexandre 286
Nakagami Kenji 213
Nam Cao (Tran Huu Tri) 176, 219
Namier, Lewis Bernstein 232
Narayan, R. K. 163, 212, 225, 229, 234, 243, 263, 274
Narcejac, Thomas 290
Nar-Dos 125, 197
Nascimento, Francisco Manuel do 75, 101
Nash, N. Richard 295
Nash, Ogden 159, 248
Nashe, Thomas 40, 50
Nasir, Gul Khan 168, 221
Nathan, Jean 184, 229
Natshinnaung 51
Natsuki Ikezawa 280
Natsume Sōseki (Natsume Kinosuke) 93, 125, 163, 164, 169, 171, 173, 174, 175
Naughton, Bill 277
Nava'i, Mir Ali Shir 27, 29, 34
Navot, Amnon 280
Nawade I 29, 43
Naylor, Gloria 261, 277
Naylor, Phyllis Reynolds 277
Nayman, Anatoly 294
Nazrul Islam 148
Ndawo, Henry Masila 135, 217
N'Debeka, Maxime 211
Ndiaye, Marie 293
Nedim, Ahmed 63, 74
Neely, Mark E., Jr. 277
Neff, Vladimir 167, 262
Nef'i 40, 55
Neguse, Yoftahe 158, 183, 217
Neihardt, John 196, 217

Nekrasov, Nikolay Alekseyevich 102, 125, 128, 132
Nelson, Truman 268
Nelville, Emily 238
Nemerov, Howard 179, 255, 256, 275
Nenekhaly-Camara, Condetto 192, 248
Neruda, Jan 108, 132, 135, 141
Neruda, Pablo (Neftalí Ricardo Reyes Basoalto) 155–156, 161, 185, 198, 215, 219, 248, 250
Nerval, Gérard de 97, 117, 118, 119
Nervesen, Kurt 266
Nervo, Amado 127, 148, 178
Nesimi, Seyid Imadeddin 26
Nesin, Aziz 283
Ness, Evaline 242
Nestroy, Johann 95, 107, 112, 114, 117, 121
Neto, Antonio Agostinka 181
Neumann, Gert 293
Neves Cardoso, José Augusto 290
Nevins, Allan 203
Nevis, Allan 197
Newby, P. H. 245
Newman, John Henry Cardinal 95, 107, 119, 124, 127, 141
Newton, Isaac 57, 64, 74
Newton, John 83
Nexo, Martin Anderson 126, 223
Nezāmī 22, 23
Ngo Tat To 206, 223
Ngugi wa Thiong'o (James Thiong'o Ngugi) 204, 223
Nguyen Cong Hoan 160
Nguyen Du 80, 102
Nguyen Hong 177
Nguyen Khac Hieu See Tan Da
Nguyen Kim Thanh See To Huu
Nguyen Mong Giac 265
Nguyen Sen See To Hoai
Nguyen Toung Tam See Nhat Linh
Nguyen Trong Tri See Han Mac Tu
Nhat Linh (Nguyen Toung Tam) 163, 236
Niane, Djabril Tamsir 179
Nichols, Roy Franklin 217
Nicodemus, Joaquin 176
Nicol, Abioseh (Nicol Davidson) 184
Nicole, Christopher Robin 192
Niemcewicz, Julian Ursyn 79, 111
Nietzsche, Friedrich Wilhelm 113, 114, 129, 135, 138, 158
Nigro, Raffaele 291
Nijhoff, Martinus 144, 185, 198, 209, 222
Nijlen, Jan van 136, 204, 214, 228, 239
Nilsen, Tove 284
Nilson, Peter 285
Nin, Anaïs 160, 201, 202, 231, 234, 238, 255
Nirala 233
Niyazi, Foteh 173, 215, 224
Niyoziy, Hamza Hakimzoda 191
Nkosi, Lewis 199, 238, 267
Nobecourt, Lorette 291
Noboru Tsujihara 294, 296
Nobre, Antonio 143
Nobuko Takagi 294
Nobuo Kojima 289
Nodier, Charles 83, 113
Noguchi Yonejiro 214
Noguez, Dominique 288
Nokan, Charles 201, 236
Noma Hiroshi 275

Noonuccal, Oodgero (Kath Walker, Kathleen Jean Mary Ruska) 279
Nooteboom, Cees 197, 259, 260, 264
Nordbrandt, Henrik 268, 295
Nordhoff, Charles Bernard 196, 214
Noren, Lars 279
Norman, Marsha 261, 262
Norris, Benjamin Franklin 160
Norris, Frank 127, 149, 159, 160
Norton, Mary 277
Norwid, Cyprian Kamil 102, 135
Nostradamus 39
Notodijo, Ilham 218
Novalis 82, 88, 95, 96
Nowakowski, Marek 274, 285
Noyes, Alfred 133, 229
Nu, U 165, 210
Nwandwo, Nkem 201
Nwapa, Flora 194, 243
Nye, Russell Blaine 212

O
Oakes, Uriah 63
Oates, Joyce Carol 204, 243, 246, 251, 253, 254, 257, 259, 267, 269, 270, 273, 276, 282, 288, 293
O'Brian, Patrick 286
O'Brien, Edna 232, 288
O'Brien, Flann (Brian O'Nuallain) 169, 241
O'Brien, Patrick 295
O'Brien, Robert C. 249
Obstfelder, Sigbjørn 125, 143, 158
O'Casey, Sean 133, 184, 185, 186, 188, 197, 207, 209, 218, 238
O'Connor, Edwin 226, 235
O'Connor, Flannery 186, 221, 225, 232, 238, 240
Odensten, Per 294
Odets, Clifford 163, 200, 203, 236
O'Donoghue, Bernard 286
Oe, Kenzaburo 199, 230, 243, 246, 255, 258, 263, 274, 281
Oehlenschläger, Adam Gottlob 83, 96, 97, 101, 116
O'Faolain, Julia 195, 254, 259, 261
O'Faolain, Sean (John Francis Whelan) 158, 202, 207, 247, 275
O'Flaherty, Liam 146, 184, 185, 186, 196, 203, 263
Oflazoglu, A. Turan 195
O'Grady, Standish 143, 147
Ogunde, Hubert 175, 239
O'Hara, John 162, 198, 200, 217, 225, 229, 247
Oilinszky, Janos 180
Okamoto Kido 205
Okara, Gabriel Imomotimi Gbaingbain 180, 238
Okigbo, Christopher 195, 242
Okri, Ben 272, 275, 276, 288, 291
Okudzhava, Bulat Shavocih 283, 287
Olimjon, Hamid 161, 211
Olinto, Antonio 280, 289
Oliveira, Carmen L. 291
Oliveiro, Ariosto Augusto de 268
Oliver, Mary 262, 263, 277, 288
Oliver Labra, Carilda 292
Oloksuoyebis Oyuunuskay, Bylatyan (Platon Aledseyevich Sleptsov) 205
Olson, Elder James 167, 277
Olson, Toby 262
Ondaatje, Michael 210, 247, 269, 277, 278, 295
O'Neill, Eugene Gladstone 139, 153, 179, 181, 182, 185, 188, 190, 194

O'Neill, Eugene Gladstone (contin-
ued) 197, 201, 210, 213, 221, 222,
226, 228, 238
Onetti, Juan Carlos 209, 219, 234,
252, 253, 281
O'Nuallain, Brian See O'Brien, Flann
Oodiriy, Abdullah 205
Oppen, George 245
Orczy, Emmuska 124, 163, 214
Orixie (Nicolas Ormaetxea) 233
Örkény, István 280
Ormaetxea, Nicolas See Orixie
Ormesson, Jean de 288
Ormond, John 183
Orozco, Olga 292
Orpaz, Yitzhak 289
Orszagh, Pal See Hviezdoslav
Ortega y Gasset, José 135, 169, 173,
184, 192, 224
Ortese, Anna Maria 286, 290
Ortese, Gina 280
Ortigão, José Duarte Ramalho 109, 174
Orvil, Ernst 280
Orwell, George (Eric Arthur Blair)
160, 197, 199, 202, 203, 204, 205,
212, 217, 218
Osadebay, Dennis Chukude 169, 221
Osborne, John James 191, 228, 229,
234, 237, 240, 241, 281
Ostaijen, Paul van 146, 190
Oster, Christian 293
Ostergren, Klas 283
Ostornol, Antonio 277
Ostrovsky, Aleksandr 103, 118, 121,
128, 129, 137
Otohiko Kaga 287
Otroshenko, Vladislav 296
Otway, Thomas 62, 63, 64
Ouida (Marie Louise de la Ramée)
110, 124, 125, 126, 133, 166
Ouologuem, Yambo 192, 245
Ouyang Xiu 20, 21
Overbury, Thomas 52
Ovid 4, 10, 11
Owen, Daniel 134, 137, 142
Owen, John 39, 53
Owen, Wilfred 143, 177
Oybek 244
Oz, Amos 205, 240, 245, 251, 269,
276, 282, 291
Ozaki Kōyō (Ozaki Tokutarō) 126,
140, 141, 146, 147, 161
Ozel, Izmet 211
Ozick, Cynthia 190, 241, 254, 262,
269, 272, 288

P
Pacheco, José Emilio 205, 246, 260,
283
Padilla, Herberto 262, 295
Padilla, Ignacio 296
Padmanabhan 27
Padrón, Justo Jorge 210
Paine, Thomas 75, 83, 86, 98
Palacio Valdés, Armando 136
Palamas, Kostis 121, 138, 147, 162,
165, 169, 210
Palandri, Enrico 274
Palangyo, Peter K. 205, 244
Palau i Fabre, Joseph 270
Palés Matos, Luis 148, 230
Paley, Grace 265
Palma, Milagros 289
Palma, Ricardo 178
Pancrazi, Jean-Noel 274
Pandyal, Lekhnath 239

Pane, Armijn 165, 247
Pant, Sumitranandan 239
Papadiamantis, Alexandros 169, 171
Papadiamantopulos, Johannes See
Moreas, Jean
Papazian, Varthanes 179
Papini, Giovanni 133, 171, 181, 226
Para, Nicanor 224
Paramesvarayyar, Ullur 131, 217
Paráskhos, Akhilléfs 110, 145
Pardo Bazán, Emilia de 117, 139, 181
Pargeter, Edith Mary See Peters, Ellis
Parini, Giuseppe 74, 80, 88
Paris, Prince Modupe 228
Parker, Dorothy 143, 193, 242
Parker, Gilbert 122, 195
Parnicki, Teodor 165, 270
Parra, Nicanor 173, 236, 246
Parrington, Vernon Louis 189, 190
Pascal, Blaise 48, 53, 59, 60, 61
Pascal, Toni 239
Paso, Fernando del 199, 270
Pasolini, Pier Paolo 181, 253
Pasternak, Boris 140, 228, 229, 232
Patchen, Kenneth 249
Patel, Gieve 271
Pater, Walter Horatio 110, 137, 140,
144
Paterson, Katherine 260
Patmore, Coventry 118, 119, 123,
131, 146
Paton, Alan Stewart 160, 216, 270
Patrick, John 222, 223
Patursson, Roy 214
Paul III (pope) 38
Pauli, Johann 36
Paulinus of Nola 17, 18
Paustovsky, Konstantin Georgievich
142, 239, 244
Pavese, Cesare 165, 218
Pavic, Milorad 191, 271, 274, 281
Pavlicek, Frantisek 277
Pavlov, Oleg 285
Pavlovic, Miodrag 278
Pawlikowska-Jasnorzewska, Maria
212
Paxson, Frederic L. 186
Payrav (Otajon Sulaymoni) 148, 194,
197
Paz, Octavio 173, 198, 203, 218, 220,
228, 243, 249, 273, 290
Pazhwak, Abdurrahman 178
Pazzi, Roberto 280, 287
p'Bitek, Okot J. P. 194, 241
Peacock, Thomas Love 84, 100, 101,
103, 105, 106, 125
Pedrolo, Manuel de 177
Péguy, Charles 129, 147, 171, 172,
173
Pelevin, Viktor 291, 294, 296
Pendse, Sripad Narayan 171
Pepys, Samuel 55, 70, 104
Percy, Walker 175, 234, 248, 259, 269,
273
Perec, Georges 201, 261
Pereda, José María de 164
Perelman, S. J. 257
Peret, Benjamin 148, 230
Peretz, Isaac Leib 117, 158, 169, 174
Pérez de Ayala, Ramón 133, 165, 169,
171, 172, 181, 184, 188, 235
Pérez de Guzmán, Fernán 35
Pérez de Hita, Ginés 38, 52
Pérez Galdós, Benito 113, 129, 131,
134, 138, 145, 147, 179
Pérez Reverte, Arturo 287, 289, 294

Perol, Jean 291
Perrault, Charles 54, 66, 70
Perry, Ralph Barton 201
Perse, Saint-John (Marie-René-
August-Aléxis Saint-Léger Léger)
138, 170, 185, 209, 214, 220, 232, 253
Pershing, John J. 195
Perucho, Joan 179
Pessoa, Fernando António Nogueira
139, 199, 200
Pestalozzi, Johann Heinrich 84
Peterkin, Julie 191
Peters, Ellis (Edith Mary Pargeter) 283
Peters, Lenrie 195
Peterson, Katherine 256
Petkavich, Inga 217
Petőfi, Sándor 103, 112, 114, 115,
116, 119
Petrarch (Francesco Petrarca) 14, 24,
25
Petri, György 212, 266, 274
Petrie, Olaus 38
Petrov, Alexander 204
Petrovich, Avvakum 62
Petrunova, Donka 292
Petrushevskaya, Lyudmila 280, 283,
291
Petry, Ann 213
Petterson, Per 296
Petursson, Hallgrimur 52, 61, 62
Pham Quynh 142, 212
Phan Boi Chau 125, 206
Pherecydes 2
Philippe, Anne 269
Philippe, Charles-Louis 159
Phillips, Caryl 280
Phillips, Jayne Anne 282, 295
Phillips, Stephen 158
Phillpotts, Eden 122, 148, 158, 172,
232
Pi Mounin 135, 206
Picouly, Daniel 293
Pierce, William 56
Piercy, Marge 201, 259, 261, 264
Pieterse, Cosmo George Leopoldt 192
Pieyre de Mandiargues, André 167
Pignatari, Decio 280
Pilinszky, János 260
Pillai, Kunnumpuzha Krishna 216
Pillai, Thakazhi Sivasankara 173, 227,
292
Pilnyak, Boris (Boris Andreyevich
Vogau) 144, 202
Pindar 2, 6, 7
Pinero, Arthur Wing 118, 140, 143,
148, 198
Piñero, Miguel 270
Pinon, Nelida 202, 270
Pinsky, Robert 273, 295
Pinter, Harold 192, 228, 229, 231,
232, 240, 244, 246, 249, 253, 257,
273
Pinto, Bento Teixeira 50
Piramerd, Tewfiq 125, 218
Pirandello, Luigi 125, 154, 159, 160,
162, 172, 176, 180, 181, 182, 184,
185, 187, 193, 198, 201
Pirkheimer, Willibald 30
Piron, Alexis 65, 76, 82
Pisemsky, Aleksey 102, 120, 121, 123,
134
Pitol, Sergio 294
Pivonas, Viktoras 264
Piwitt, Hermann Peter 280
Pixérécourt, René-Charles Guilbert de
82, 99, 113

Plaidy, Jean See Hibbert, Eleanor
Alice
Platen, Charles August von 87, 104,
106, 107, 108
Plath, Sylvia 195, 232, 236, 237, 240,
250, 261
Plato 3, 7, 8
Plautus 9
Pleijel, Agneta 281
Plieksans, Janis See Rainis
Plievier, Theodore 214, 224
Pliny the Elder 11, 12
Pliny the Younger 12, 16
Plunkett, James 274
Plutarch 11, 17
Podrimja, Ali 209, 270
Poe, Edgar Allan 91, 97, 105, 106,
107, 108, 110, 111, 112, 113, 114,
115, 116
Pohl, Frederick 178
Poirier, Louis See Gracq, Julien
Poliquin, Daniel 282
Politian 27, 28, 29
Pollen, Geir 291
Pollitt, Katha 261
Polotan-Tuvera, Kerima 186
Pombo, Alvaro 277, 285, 294
Poniatowska, Elena 279, 294
Pontiggia, Giuseppe 296
Pontoppidan, Henrik 120, 134, 135,
141, 142, 144, 145, 146, 148, 176, 210
Poole, Ernest 177
Popa, Vasko 181, 223, 245, 250, 254,
275
Pope, Alexander 65, 69, 72, 74, 76, 77
Popov, Yevgeny 274
Popovic, Aleksandar 276, 285
Popovski, Ante 284
Popper, Karl 281
Poquelin, Jean-Baptiste See Molière
Poradeci, Lasgush 268
Porsteinn fra Hamri 269
Porter, Katherine Anne 140, 193, 203,
205, 211, 235, 240, 241, 259
Porter, William Sydney See Henry, O.
Posada, Carmen 292
Posse, Abel 274
Post, Laurens van der 282, 285
Potocki, Wacław 53, 66
Potok, Chaim 191, 242
Potter, Beatrix 125, 160, 210
Potter, David M. 255
Potter, Dennis Christopher George
281
Poulin, Alfred A., Jr. 285
Pound, Ezra Loomis 137, 155, 166,
167, 168, 174, 175, 178, 179, 197,
204, 247, 249
Powell, Anthony Dymoke 162, 194,
220, 221, 232, 235, 238, 241, 244,
249, 251, 253, 295
Powell, Sumner Chilton 238
Powys, John Cowper 236
Prada, Juan Manuel de 289
Pradier, Hugues 293
Prado, Adelia 294
Prasad, Jaysankar 200
Pratolini, Vasco 213, 215, 240, 275
Pratt, E. J. 188, 207
Preil, Gabriel 169, 258, 279
Preisler, Juliane 279
Prem Chand (Dhanpat Rai Srivas-
tana) 133, 182, 185, 190, 201, 202
Preseren, France 95, 108, 109, 116
Pressburger, Giorgio 296
Prévost, Marcel 144

Prévost d'Exiles, Antoine-François 66, 74, 80
Price, Reynolds 267
Prichard, Katharine Susannah 135, 174, 192, 245
Priestley, J. B. 144, 192, 193, 203, 204, 213, 240, 263
Prince, E. T. 258
Pringle, Henry F. 195
Prior, Matthew 60, 73
Pritchett, V. S. 158, 272, 287
Propertius, Sextus 10, 11
Proulx, E. Annie 199, 279, 281, 293
Proust, Marcel 128, 171, 178, 180, 181, 182, 184, 186, 190
Provensen, Alice 263
Provensen, Martin 263
Prudentius (Aurelius Prudentius Clemens) 17, 18
Prudhomme, Sully (René-François-Armand) 110, 125, 127, 132, 139, 159, 165
Przybos, Julian 159, 247
Pshavela, Vazha 122
Pu Songling 56, 63, 72
Publius Ovidius Naso See Ovid
Publius Vergilius Maro See Virgil
Puech, Bernard 276
Puig, Manuel 195, 230, 273
Puller, Lewis B., Jr. 277
Punekar, Shankar Mokashi 269
Pupin, Michael Idvorsky 184
Purcell, Henry 49
Purdy, Alfred Wellington 295
Purdy, James Amos 183, 231, 232, 238, 247
Pusey, Mero J. 221
Pushkin, Aleksandr Sergeyvich 88, 90, 102, 103, 104, 105, 106, 107, 108, 109, 110, 111
Putik, Jaroslav 292
Puttapu, K. V. 161
Putumaippittan 163, 216
Puzo, Mario 292
Pyeshkov, Aleksey Maximovich See Gorky, Maxim
Pynchon, Thomas 202, 237, 241, 250, 273, 288

Q

Q. (Sir Arthur Thomas Quiller-Couch) 123, 211
Qabbani, Nizar 183, 290
Qamberdiaty, Mysost 194
Qarzada, Ziya 180
Qi Rushan 131, 235
Qian Xingcun See Aying
Qian Zhongshu 168, 292
Qodiriy, Abdullo 201
Qu Yuan 1, 8, 9
Quadflieg, Roswitha 278
Quasimodo, Salvatore 159, 193, 196, 198, 202, 204, 209, 215, 230, 242, 244
Queiroz, Rachel de 167, 196, 203, 206
Queneau, Raymond 160, 204, 210, 231, 240, 245, 254
Quental, Antero de 112, 124, 141
Quenum, Olympe Bhely 232
Quesada, Roberto 278
Quevedo y Villegas, Francisco Gómez de 41, 54, 57
Quignard, Pascal 296
Quiller-Couch, Sir Arthur Thomas See Q.
Quinault, Philippe 55, 65

Quintana, Manuel José 82
Quintella, Ary 276
Quintilian 11, 12
Quintus Horatius Flaccus See Horace
Quiring, Dennis 269
Quiroga, Horacio 132, 181, 188, 202
Quodiriy, Abdullo 144

R

Raabe, Wilhelm 106, 128, 168
Rabearivelo, Jean-Joseph 159
Rabelais, François 29, 32, 37, 39
Rabemanajara, Jean-Jacques 171
Rabikovitz, Dalia 289
Rabinyan, Dorit 293
Racan, Honorat de Bueil, seigneur de 43, 52, 61
Racine, Jean 48, 56, 60, 61, 62, 63, 65, 66
Radcliffe, Ann Ward 80, 86, 87, 103
Radichkov, Yordan 290, 292
Radiguet, Raymond 160, 183, 184
Radnóti, Miklós 274
Radstrom, Niklas 294
Radulovic, Jovan 270
Raffi, Hakob Maliq Hakobian 132, 133, 134, 135, 137, 139
Rahtathara, Shin Maha 28, 29, 36
Raine, Kathleen 240
Rainis (Janus Plieksans) 124, 185, 191
Rajam Iyer, B. R. 144
Rakes, Mohan 186
Rakove, Jack N. 288
Raleigh, Walter 39, 52
Ramamitram, La Sa 175, 240
Ramanujan, A. K. 191
Rambaud, Patrick 288
Ramée, Marie Louise de la See Ouida
Ramos, Graciliano 199
Ramos, Wanda 278
Ramuz, Charles-Ferdinand 186, 214
Rand, Ayn 162, 204, 210, 228, 261
Ranelid, Bjorn 281, 283
Rangabe, Alexandros Rizos 98, 142
Ranke, Leopold von 87, 137
Ransmayr, Christoph 284
Ransom, John Crowe 139, 185, 205, 208, 252
Ransome, Arthur 245
Rao, Raja 165, 204, 232
Rapoport, Solomon Seinwil See Ansky, Shloime
Rasi, Mauro 276, 285
Rasit Kemali Ogutcu, Mehmet 172
Raskin, Ellen 258
Rasy, Elisabetta 280, 289
Rathmann, Peggy 285
Rattigan, Terence 169, 216, 223, 255
Ratushinskaya, Irina 224
Rauch, Eric M. 174
Raven, Simon 238
Rawlings, Marjorie Kinnan 146, 204, 205, 222
Ray, Amrit 180, 223
ar-Rayhani, Anein 206
Rea, Dominico 280
Read, Herbert Edward 244
Reade, Charles 99, 118, 119, 122, 136
Rebreanu, Liviu 137, 196, 211
Rechy, John Francisco 198, 258
Redcam, Tom 127, 180, 197
Redonnet, Marie 274
Reed, Ishmael 204, 246, 252, 261
Reed, John 178
Rees Williams, Ella Gwendolen See Rhys, Jean

Regas, Rosa 283
Regio, José 159, 209, 215, 245
Regnard, Jean François 59, 66, 70, 71
Régnier, Henri de 123, 137, 147, 158, 164, 201
Régnier, Mathurin 41, 51
Regniers, Beatrice Schenk de 239
Rego, José Lins de 196, 211
Reich, Klovedal 292
Reid, B. L. 245
Reid, Victor Stafford 171
Reizenstein, Elmer Leopold See Rice, Elmer
Remarque, Erich Maria 148, 192, 247
Remizov, Aleksey Mikhaylovich 131, 227
Remnick, David 281
Remuz, Charles-Ferdinand 132
Renard, Jules 123, 144, 168, 186
Renault, Mary 162, 226, 229, 235, 262
Retamar, Roberto Fernando 192
Reuchlin, Johannes 29
Reuter, Fritz 130
Reverdy, Pierre 140, 189, 192, 216, 232
Revius, Jacobus 54
Revueltas, José 173, 211, 254
Rexroth, Kenneth 162, 221, 261, 264
Reyes, Alfonso 140, 230
Reyes Basoalto, Neftalí Ricardo See Neruda, Pablo
Reymont, Władysław Stanisław 125, 146, 147, 162, 184, 186
Reznicek, Pavel 281
Rezzori d'Arezzo, Gregor von 290
Rhodes, James Ford 177
Rhodes, Richard 270
Rhys, Jean (Ella Gwendolen Rees Williams) 140, 205, 241, 255, 257
Ribas, Oscar Bento 167, 233
Ribeiro Couto, Rui 183, 198
Ricci, Nino 280
Rice, Elmer (Elmer Leopold Reizenstein) 142, 173, 184, 191, 192, 194, 242
Rich, Adrienne 191, 225, 237, 249, 272, 275, 279, 284, 293
Richards, I. A. 143, 257
Richards, Laura E. 176
Richardson, Dorothy M. 174, 243
Richardson, Henry Handel 193
Richardson, John 107, 111, 117
Richardson, Samuel 65, 76, 77, 78, 80
Richelmy, Agistino 268
Richepin, Jean 187
Richler, Mordecai 194, 223, 225, 228, 237, 244, 249, 273, 288
Richter, Conrad Michael 201, 207, 219, 244
Richter, Johann Paul Friedrich 80, 86, 87, 95, 98, 104
Rickword, Edgell 261
Riding, Laura 159, 275
Rifat, Oktay 173
Rifbjerg, Klaus 268
Riichi, Yokomitsu 148
Riley, James Whitcomb 116, 135, 175
Rilke, Rainer Maria 130, 155, 163, 168, 172, 182, 184, 187
Rimbaud, Arthur 94, 118, 128, 129, 136, 138, 141
Rinehart, Mary Roberts 166
Ringelnatz, Joachim (Hans Botticher) 198
Ringwood, Gwendolyn 168, 205, 263
Rintala, Paavo 192

Rio, Michel 278
Rishtin, Sadiqullah 178
Ritsos, Yannis 266, 273
Ritter, Erika 215, 257
Rivas, Manuel 292
Rive, Richard 194, 238
Rivera, Andrés 287
Rivera, José Eustasio 140, 181, 185, 190
Rivière, Jacques 182, 186
Rizal, José 122, 139, 142, 146
Roa Bastos, Augusto 176, 233, 253
Roach, Erich M. 252
Robbe-Grillet, Alain 181, 222, 225, 228, 237, 255, 257, 258, 260
Robbins, Harold 287
Robelledo, Francisco 283
Robert, Shabaan 167, 235
Roberts, Elizabeth Madix 193, 208
Roberts, Kate 141, 265
Roberts, Kenneth 203
Roberts, Michele 278, 295
Robinson, Edwin Arlington 126, 147, 168, 175, 176, 181, 182, 185, 186, 189, 190, 191, 198, 200
Robinson, Mary 217
Robles, Emmanuel 173, 216, 221, 234, 247, 260, 283
Rodenbach, Georges 118, 138, 143, 148
Rodgers, Richard 218
Rodó, José Enrique 128, 176
Rodoreda, Merce 262
Rodrigues Lobo, Francisco 52
Rodríguez, Claudio 277
Rodriguez Larreta, Enrique 166
Roethke, Theodore 165, 216, 220, 222, 223, 228, 236, 238
Roffe, Reina 287
Roig, Montserrat 213
Rojas, Carlos 262
Rojas, Fernando de 30, 34
Rojas, Manuel 146, 220, 230, 233, 239, 250
Rojas Zorrilla, Francisco de 50, 58
Rolfe, Frederick 148, 162, 199
Rolin, Dominique 268
Rolin, Jean 286
Rolin, Olivier 280
Rolland, Romain 125, 162, 172, 174, 182, 211
Rölvaag, O. E. 131, 189, 190, 194
Romains, Jules (Louis Farigoule) 137, 166, 170, 172, 184, 196, 249
Romero, Denzil 275
Romero, José Rubén 205
Ronsard, Pierre de 33, 36, 38, 39, 42
Rosa, João Guimaraes 227, 242
Rosário, António Martinho do See Santareno, Bernardo
Rosegger, Peter 113, 139, 177
Rosei, Peter 274
Rosenberg, Tina 286
Rosenboom, Thomas 295
Rosenzweig, Franz 137, 191
Rosic, Tidor 218, 270
Ross, Sinclair 285
Rossetti, Christina 106, 123, 125, 144
Rossetti, Dante Gabriel 105, 116, 127, 134
Rossetti, William Michael 105, 178
Rossi, Azariah ben Moses dei 41
Rossner, Judith 253
Rostand, Edmond 126, 147, 158, 177
Rosten, Leo 287
Roth, Henry 163, 198, 282, 283

Roth, Joseph 195, 204
Roth, Philip 197, 231, 243, 246, 248, 250, 252, 256, 258, 260, 262, 268, 273, 279, 281, 284, 288, 290, 295
Rothmann, Ralf 282
Rotimi, Olawale (Ola) 206, 250, 295
Rotrou, Jean de 51, 57, 58
Rouaud, Jean 274
Rouget de Lisle, Claude-Joseph 109
Roumain, Jacques 165, 211
Roumer, Émile 160
Rousseau, Jean-Jacques 68, 71, 78, 80, 83
Roussel, Raymond 131, 168, 197
Rovira, Orsy 170
Rowlandson, Mary White 56, 63
Rowley, William 59
Rowling, J. K. 290, 293, 295
Roy, Arundhati 287, 288
Rozanov, Vasily Vasilyevich 119, 171, 178
Roze, Pascale 286
Rozewicz, Tadeusz 291
Rozhdestvensky, Robert Ivanovich 281
Ru Zhijuan 186
Rubadiri, James David 192, 243
Ruban, Jacques 195
Rubens, Bernice 247
Rubens Paiva, Marcelo 287
Rubio, Fanny 292
Ruckert, Friedrich 125
Rudman, Mark 282
Rudnicki, Adolf 273
Rudolf, Anthony 209
Rueda, Lope de 35, 40
Rufin, Jean-Christophe 288
Ruiz, Juan 24, 25
Ruiz de Alarcón y Mendoza, Juan 42, 54, 56
Rukeyser, Muriel 200, 204, 259
Rule, Jane 238
Rulfo, Juan 177, 267
Rummo, Paul Eerik 209
Rūdakī 20
Runeberg, Johan Ludvig 96, 109, 113, 131
ar-Rūmī, Jalāl ad-Dīn 15, 23, 24
Runyon, Damon 196, 213
Rush, Norman 276
Rushdie, Salman 260, 271, 284, 293
Ruska, Kathleen Jean Mary *See* Noonuccal, Oodgeroo
Ruskin, John 101, 116, 117, 158
Rusli, Marah 140, 182, 244
Russell, Bertrand 128, 168, 243, 247
Russell, Charles Edward 190
Russell, George William *See* AE
Russo, Edgardo 296
Rustaveli, Shota 22, 23
Rybakov, Anatoly Naumovich 272, 278, 283, 290
Rydberg, Carina 289
Rydberg, Viktor 105, 135, 145
Rylant, Cynthia 279
Rynell, Elisabeth 267
Ryskind, Morrie 195
Ryu Murakami 220, 255, 296
Ryya'i, Yodallah 291
Rza, Razul 168
Rzewic, Tadeusz 283

S

Saavedra, Angel de 86, 109, 124
Sabach, Petr 292
Sábato, Ernesto 169, 217, 234, 296
Sabir, Mirza al-Akbar 122, 169

Sachar, Louis 292
Sacher-Masoch, Leopold von 108
Sachiko Yashihara 284
Sachs, Hans 36
Sachs, Nelly 141, 220, 241, 247
Sackler, Howard 245
Sackville-West, Vita 142, 193, 194, 235
Sade, Donatien-Alphonse-François de (Marquis de Sade) 76, 85, 86, 99
Sa'dī 23, 24
Sadik, Sheikh M. 253
Sadji, Abdoulaye 168, 233
Saeger, Uwe 280
Sagan, Carl 256
Sagan, François 199, 224, 266
Sahgal, Nayantara Pandit 188, 266
Sā'ib of Tabriz 50, 63
Saichi Maruya 280
Said, Ali Ahmed *See* Adonis
Saigyo 21, 22
St. John, Madeleine 288
St. Omer, Garth 246
Saint-Aubin, Stephanie-Félicité Ducrest de 77, 106
Saint-Beuve, Charles-Augustin 96, 105, 111, 127
Saint-Exupéry, Antoine de 158, 192, 206, 210, 211
Saint-Lambert, François de 96
Saintsbury, George Edward Bateman 114, 197
Saint-Simon, Louis de Rouvroy de 62, 79, 132
Sainz, Gustavo 277
Sakamoto, Kerri 290
Sakharov, Andrei 271
Saki (H. H. Munro) 127, 162, 168, 169, 173, 175
Sakurada Jisuke 97
Salamao, Waly 280
Salazar, Boris 277
Salih, Al-Tayyib 233
Salinas, Pedro 141, 198, 219
Salinger, J.D. 178, 220, 222, 233, 237
Salkey, Andrew 283
Sallust 10
Salo, Arvo 195
Salten, Felix 184
Salter, James 271
Saltykov-Shchedrin, Mikhail Evgrafovich 104, 127, 131, 137, 140
Salvayre, Lydie 274, 293
Samkange, Stanlake J. T. 182, 241
Sampedro, José Luis 275, 281, 297
Samuels, Ernest 239
San Pedro, Diego 29
Sanā'ī (Abū al-Majd Majdud ibn Adam) 21, 22
Sanatizade Kermani 137
Sánchez, Tomás 44, 51
Sánchez Drago, Fernando 279
Sánchez Ferlosio, Rafael 188
Sand, George (Amandine-Aurore-Lucie Dudevant) 96, 107, 110, 111, 114, 115, 116, 121, 131
Sandburg, Carl 132, 173, 175, 178, 182, 201, 206, 216, 219, 242
Sandeau, Jules 98, 111, 117, 135
Saneatsu Mushanokoji 188
Sankara Kurup, G. 159
Sannazaro, Jacopo 34, 36
Sansom, William 211, 254
Sant'Anna, Sergio 207
Santareno, Bernardo (António Martinho do Rosário) 184, 259

Santayana, George 123, 163, 200, 221
Santiago, Silviano 278
Santillana, Iñigo López de Mendoza, marqués de 26, 27
Santos, Lope K. 132, 164, 236
Santos, Nuqui Bienvenido 169
Sanvitale, Francesca 276, 289
Sappho of Lesbos 4, 6
Sarabhai, Bharati 210, 221
Saramago, José 278, 280, 287, 290, 291
Sarbiewski, Maciej Kazimierz 44, 56
Sardou, Victorien 106, 122, 138, 144, 166
Sardy, Severo 275
Saro-Wiwa, Kenule Beeson 283
Saroyan, William 165, 198, 205, 206, 207, 210, 260
Sarpi, Paolo 39, 53
Sarraute, Nathalie 158, 216, 223, 231, 237, 284, 292
Sarton, May 222, 229, 240, 241, 279, 283
Sartre, Jean-Paul 163, 204, 210, 211, 212, 220, 225, 238, 259
Sassoon, Siegfried 137, 178, 190, 215, 242
Sastre, Alfonso 187
Sathapanawat, Sirat 177, 231
Satō Haruo 142, 238
Sauser, Frédéric Louis *See* Cendrars, Blaise
Savako Arevalo 263
Savatar, Fernando 281
Savic, Milisav 278
Savigny, Friedrich Karl von 122
Sawako Ariyoshi 194, 248
Saxo Grammaticus 13
Say, Allen 281
Sayers, Dorothy 143, 227
as-Sayyab, Badr Shakir 191, 238
as-Sayyid, Ahmad Lufti 236
Scarron, Paul 51, 57, 58, 60
Scève, Maurice 34, 38, 39
Schacht, Unrich 274
Schaff, Philip 101
Schaffner, Jakob 130, 211
Schaiur, Zalman 230
Schama, Simon 284
Schedel, Hartmann 29
Scheffel, Josef Viktor von 104, 137
Schelling, Friedrich Wilhelm Joseph 82
Schelsinger, Klaus 286
Schendel, Arthur van 130, 165, 193, 200, 213
Schenk, Johannes 280
Schenkkan, Robert 277
Schertenlieb, Hansjorg 278
Schgerven, Torgeir 284
Schierbeek, Bert 177
Schiff, Stacy 295
Schiller, Johann Christoph Friedrich von 67–68, 79, 84, 88, 95, 96
Schlegel, August Wilhelm von 81, 105, 114
Schlegel, Friedrich von 82
Schleiermacher, Friedrich Ernst Daniel 81, 108
Schlesinger, Arthur M., Jr. 213, 241
Schlink, Bernhard 288, 296
Schmidt, Arno 248
Schneider, Peter 293
Schnitzler, Arthur 122, 146, 147, 159, 166, 185, 194, 195
Schoffman, Gershon 133, 248

Schopenhauer, Arthur 85, 101, 121
Schorer, Mark 166, 255
Schorske, Carl E. 260
Schreiber, Boris 286
Schreiner, Olive 119, 135
Schubert, Christian Friedrich Daniel 76, 86
Schuhl, Jean-Jacques 296
Schulberg, Budd 173, 215, 272
Schulte, Michael 284
Schulze, Inge 291
Schurrer, Hermann 190
Schutz, David 274
Schutz, Helga 250
Schuyler, James 260
Schwab, Gustav 116
Schwab, Mayer-André-Marcel 163
Schwartz, Delmore 171, 208, 216, 241
Schwarz-Bart, André 190, 231
Schwarze-Bart, Simone 269
Schweitzer, Albert 130, 164, 184, 239
Schwob, Mayer-André-Marcel 125, 144
Sciascia, Leonardo 180, 256
Scliar, Moacyr 278
Scorza, Manuel 190, 262
Scott, Dennis C. 205
Scott, Paul 241, 244, 256
Scott, Walter 81, 93, 96, 97, 98, 99, 100, 101, 102, 103, 104, 105, 106, 107
Scribe, Augustin-Eugène 86, 105, 107, 110, 111, 116, 122
Scudéry, Madeleine de 57, 58, 59, 69
Sczepanski, Jan Josef 274
Sebastian, Bartel Johan 166
Sedaine, Michel-Jean 72, 80, 81, 87
Seeger, Alan 139, 175
Sefarim, Mendele Mokher 108, 123, 124, 125, 130, 176
Seferis, George (Giorgios Sefiriadis) 158, 195, 196, 200, 207, 215, 236, 248
Segui, Josep-Lluis 212
Seifert, Jaroslav 159, 207, 212, 242, 263, 267
Seiji Tsutsumi *See* Tsuji, Takashi
Selassie, Sahle Berhane Mariam 201, 246
Selby, Hubert, Jr. 238
Selenic, Slobodan 283
Self, Will 295
Selvon, Samuel 183, 221, 281
Sembene, Ousmane 183, 233
Semenon, Georges-Jacques-Christian 160
Semolic, Peter 296
Sen, Samar 175
Sendak, Maurice 238
Sender, Ramón 159, 200, 223, 261
Seneca 4–5, 11, 12
Sened, Alexander 278, 291
Sened, Yonat 278, 291
Senghor, Leopold Sedar 163
Serafimovic, Alexander 185
Serao, Matilde 189
Sereni, Vittoorino 171, 262
Sergeyev, Andrey 287
Service, Robert William 130, 229
Seth, Vikram 220, 267, 280, 293
Seton, Anya 273
Settle, Mary Lee 257
Seuss, Dr. (Theodore Seuss Geisel) 228, 275
Sevak, Paruir 230, 248
Sewell, Anna 131

Sexton, Anne 190, 235, 241, 242, 246, 249, 250, 252
Seyfeddin, Omer 136, 179
Sgorlon, Carlo 192
Shaara, Michael Joseph, Jr. 252, 270
ash-Shabbi, Abul-Qasim 167, 198
Shabtai, Yaakov 260
Shadman, Fakhroddin 168, 248
Shaff, Philip 143
Shaffer, Peter 187, 232, 238, 251, 258
Shaham, Nathan 280, 286
Shahnon, Ahmed 197, 240, 243, 246
Shakespeare, William 31, 40, 43, 44, 50, 51, 52, 53
Shalberashvili, Georgi 239
Shalev, Meir 282
Shama, Simon 272
Shamin, Muhammad Ishlaq 183
Shamir, Moshe 264, 276
Shamlu, Ahmad 295
Shamo, Arabe 245
Shannon, Fred Albert 191
Shapcott, Thomas William 199, 255, 269
Shapiro, Karl Jay 171, 211, 212, 215, 222, 229, 254, 269, 271, 295
Sharar, Abdul-Halim 173, 187
ash-Sharqawi, Abdur Rahman 179, 223, 247
Shaw, George Bernard 119, 143, 144, 148, 153, 159, 163, 164, 165, 169, 172, 175, 178, 181, 184, 186, 218
Shaw, Irwin 171, 216, 263
Shawqi, Ahmad 126, 195
Sheaffer, Louis 252
Sheehan, Neil 272
Sheehan, Susan 262
Shelley, Mary Wollstonecraft 87, 101, 103, 104, 117
Shelley, Percy Bysshe 86, 93, 99, 100, 101, 102, 103
Shembe, Isaiah 125, 200
Shenstone, William 80
Shepard, David 260
Shepard, Sam 210, 250, 257, 258, 262
Sheperd, Odell 204
Sheridan, Richard Brinsley 78, 82, 83, 88, 100
Sheriff, R. C. 192
Sherman, Charlotte Watson 279
Sherwood, Robert E. 146, 200, 201, 204, 205, 207, 208, 217, 224
Shevchenko, Taras 99, 122
Shibaki, Yoshiko 173
Shields, Carol 280, 283, 288
Shiga Naoya 135, 248
Shimazaki Tōson 210
Shimei Futabatei 167
Shimoni, Yuval 293
Shimonowitz, David 226
Shin Thilawuntha 35
Shipler, David K. 268
Shiraz, Hovhannes 173
Shirer, William L. 232
Shishkin, Mikhail 296
Shklovsky, Viktor Borisovich 143, 263
Shlonsky, Abraham 158, 250
Shohei Ooka 220
Sholem Aleichem 121
Sholokhov, Mikhail Aleksandrovich 199, 239, 263
Shreiner, Olive 179
Shreve, Susan Richards 279, 286, 295
Shu Fujisawa 291
Shua, Ana María 289
Shukri, Abd al-Rahman 229

Shun Medoruma 296
Shuntaro Tanagawa 280
Shute, Nevil 228
Shvarts, Yelena 217, 289
Sidhwa, Bapsi 271
Sidney, Philip 39, 42, 43
Siefert, Jaroslaw 186, 187, 204
Sienkiewicz, Henryk 114, 136, 138, 139, 145, 163, 175
Sieyès, Emmanuel-Joseph 77, 109
Sigüenza y Góngora, Carlos de 57, 63, 64, 69
Sigurjónsson, Jóhann 133, 170, 178
Sikelianós, Angelos 136, 167, 176, 189, 219
Siktanc, Karel 273
Silesius, Angelus 53, 63
Silkin, Jon 192, 249
Silko, Leslie Marmon 215, 275, 293
Sillanpää, Frans Eemil 139, 178, 195, 199, 205, 238
Sillitoe, Alan 190, 215, 229, 231, 250, 273
Silone, Ignazio 158, 207, 221, 225, 240, 256
Silva, José Asunción 124, 146
Silva, Lopes de 271
Silva, Lorenzo 297
Silva, W. Abraham 142, 227
Silverman, Kenneth 265
Simecka, Martin M. 281
Simenon, Georges 271
Simic, Charles 204, 273
Simmons, James Stewart Alexander 197, 259
Simms, William Gimore 107, 108, 109, 110, 112, 114, 117, 118, 119
Simon, Claude 171, 215, 224, 228, 230, 233, 246, 251, 265, 272
Simon, Kate 261
Simon, Neil 188, 237, 240, 241, 244, 245, 248, 250, 254, 255, 259, 275, 276
Simon, Yves 276
Simpson, Louis 238
Sims, William Snowden 181
Sinclair, Upton 132, 164, 189, 207, 209, 210, 244
Singer, Isaac Bashevis 161, 201, 202, 213, 229, 231, 234, 236, 242, 244, 246, 250, 256, 257, 262, 263, 267, 271, 275
Singh, Mohan 202
Sinyavsky, Andrey Donatovich 287
Sirhindī Nāsir Alī 66
Sitwell, (Francis) Osbert 142, 211, 213, 215, 216, 219, 245
Sitwell, Edith 138, 209, 210, 211, 212, 238
Sitwell, Sacheverell 146
Sivakariyar, Kasiyappa 54
Siwertz, Sigfrid 180
Sjöberg, Birger 137, 183, 191
Sjogren, Lennart 289
Skagen, Fredrik 274
Skallagrimsson, Egill 20
Skarmeta, Antonio 266, 275
Skelton, John 29, 35
Skelton, Robin 287
Skou-Hansen, Tage 277
Skram, Amalie Bertha 145, 163
Skrine, Mary Nesta See Keane, Molly
Slade, Bernard 192, 257
Slaveykov, Pencho Petkov 125
Sleptsov, Platon Aledseyevich See Oloksuoyebis Oyuunuskay, Bylatyan

Słowacki, Juliusz 98, 109, 112, 116
Smart, Christopher 73
Smiley, Jane 276, 277
Smith, Florence Margaret See Smith, Stevie
Smith, Gregory White 275
Smith, Iain Crichton 266, 290
Smith, Justin H. 179
Smith, Pauline Urmson 186
Smith, Stevie (Florence Margaret Smith) 159, 248
Smith, Zadie 295
Smollett, Tobias George 73, 77, 78, 79, 81
Snodgrass, William DeWitt 187, 231, 232
Snow, Charles Percy 163, 199, 207, 220, 223, 229, 231, 259
Snow, Helen Foster 287
Snyder, Gary 252, 253, 286
Soce, Ousmane Diop 169
Söderberg, Hjalmar Erik 126, 159, 163, 171, 208
Södergran, Edith Irene 142, 175, 178, 179, 180, 183
Sofronov, Anempodist Ivanovich 137, 178, 200
Soga, John Henderson 121
Sogi 26, 28, 34
Sokalov, Sasha 210
Solares, Ignacio 281
Solomos, Dhionísios 87, 103, 105, 107, 116, 120
Soloukhin, Vladimir Alekseyevich 287
Solzhenitsyn, Aleksandr Isayevich 154, 177, 236, 245, 247, 249, 251, 257, 280
Sondheim, Stephen 264, 265
Sonnevi, Goran 277, 287
Sontag, Susan 197, 241, 246, 270, 277
Sontonga, Mankayi Enoch 121, 161
Sophocles 3, 6, 7, 8
Sorescu, Marin 278
Sorrentino, Gilbert 191, 258
Sosnora, Viktor 296
Soucy, Gaetan 291
Soueif, Ahdaf 293
Soupault, Philippe 146, 185, 189, 190, 199, 273
Sousa, Luís de 39, 52, 55
Southerne, Thomas 66
Southey, Robert 82, 95, 96, 97, 99, 104, 105, 113
Southwell, Robert 40, 44
Souza, Marcio 289
Soyinka, Akinwande Oluwole (Wole) 198, 232, 237, 240, 241, 243, 246, 250, 251, 252, 267, 272, 278, 284
Spanidou, Irini 213, 267
Spark, Muriel 177, 228, 229, 234, 237, 240, 247, 252, 264, 271, 274, 278
Spender, Stephen 167, 205, 215, 217, 225, 283
Spengler, Oswald 133, 177, 201
Spengler, Tilman 276
Spenser, Edmund 39, 41, 42, 43, 44, 45
Speyer, Leonora 189
Spielhagen, Friedrich 169
Spier, Peter 256
Spillane, Mickey 215, 272
Spinelli, Jerry 275
Spinoza, Baruch 55, 63
Spitteler, Carl 114, 134, 135, 140, 143, 148, 164, 165, 168, 178, 184

Spyri, Johanna 104, 133, 159
Sri (B. M. Srikanthayya) 136, 213
Srirangam Srinivasa Rao 168
Srikanthayya, B. M. See Sri
Srivastana, Dhanpat Rai See Prem Chand
Staalesen, Gunnar 296
Staël, Anne-Louise-Germaine de 80, 96, 97, 100
Stafford, Jean 174, 211, 221, 247, 253
Stafford, William 173, 232
Stallings, Lawrence 185
Stangerup, Henrik 202, 275
Stapledon, Olaf 193
Starnone, Domenico 296
Starr, Paul 263
Statius, Publius Papinius 11, 12
Stead, C. K. 195, 288, 296
Stead, Christina 159, 207, 262
Steele, Richard 62, 70, 73, 74
Steele, Wilbur Daniel 137, 247
Steen, Edla van 208
Stefánsson, Davíd 145, 193, 208, 238
Steffens, Joseph Lincoln 125, 201
Stegner, Wallace 167, 210, 219, 234, 248, 249, 255, 279
Steig William 247
Stein, Gertrude 130, 161, 169, 173, 197, 213, 215
Steinbeck, John 159, 200, 201, 203, 205, 206, 209, 212, 215, 221, 234, 235, 244
Steiner, George 191, 243
Steinke, Darcy 288
Stendhal (Marie-Henri Beyle) 84, 103, 106, 111, 112, 141, 143, 144
Stenson, Fred 295
Stephansson, Stephan Gudmundson 118, 189
Stephen, Leslie 107
Stern, Gerald 290
Stern, Mario Rigonia 291
Sterne, Laurence 71, 79, 81
Sternheim, Carl 170
Sternhold, Thomas 38
Stevens, Wallace 132, 184, 200, 203, 218, 223, 224, 225
Stevenson, Robert Louis 116, 132, 134, 135, 137, 138, 140, 143, 144, 146
Steward, J. I. M. 281
Stewart, Douglas 171, 265
Stierhielm, Georg 44, 59, 61, 62
Stifter, Adalbert 96, 120, 126
Stigen, Terje 264, 270, 274, 284
Stockenstrom, Wilma 269
Stockton, Frank R. 136
Stojcevski, Sande 280
Stojicic, Doko 294
Stoker, Bram 115, 147
Stolberg, Christian zu 77, 102
Stone, Irving 271
Stone, Robert 277, 290
Stoppard, Tom 202, 241, 255, 256, 257, 264, 266
Storey, David 250, 254, 255
Storm, Theodor Woldsen 100, 117, 122, 124, 131, 139
Storni, Alfonsina 142, 178, 179, 180, 187, 199, 204
Story, David 232
Stout, Rex 253
Stow, Julian Randolph 199, 264
Stowe, Harriet Beecher 98, 117, 119, 146
Strachey, Lytton 133, 177, 181, 190, 195

Strand, Mark 292
Straparola, Giovanni Francesco 38
Strateiv, Stanislaw 207
Strauss, Botho 211
Streuvels, Stijn (Frank Lateur) 128, 245
Strezovski, Jovan 194
Stribling, T. S. 197
Strindberg, August 92–93, 116, 133, 136, 138, 139, 140, 141, 147, 148, 149, 159, 160, 165, 168
Strittmatter, Thomas 274
Strunk, William, Jr. 231
Stryjkowski, Julian 280, 285
Stuart, Jesse Hilton 263
Stubbs, John Keith 271
Styron, William 186, 220, 243, 244, 258
Su Dongpo 21
Su Manshu 136, 177
Su Tong 275
Suassuna, Ariono Vilar 188
Suckling, John 51, 56, 57
Sudermann, Hermann 120, 138, 140, 166, 190
Sue, Eugène 96, 112, 113, 120
Suetonius 12, 17
Sukurada Jisuke 75
Sulaymoni, Otajon See Payrav
Süleyman Çelebi 25, 26
Suleyman of Stal 126, 202
Sullam, Sara Copio 43, 56
Sullivan, Evelin E. 214
Surangkhanang, K. (Kanha Khiengsiri) 169, 203
Suranna, Pimgali 42
Surtees, Robert Smith 96, 124
Surya, Cemal 194
Suskind, Patrick 217
Susko, Mario 276
Sussman, L. E. 257
Sutcliffe, Rosemary 277
Sutherland, Efua Theodora 184, 243, 285
Suttner, Bertha Kinsky von 113, 140, 173
Svava Jacobsdottir 269
Svendsen, Hanne Marie 286
Svevo, Italo 122, 190
Swados, Harvey 179
Swanberg, W. A. 250
Swift, Graham 285, 286
Swift, Jonathan 61, 68, 70, 71, 73, 74, 77
Swinburne, Algernon Charles 109, 124, 125, 126, 128, 130, 131, 132, 135, 167
Swinnerton, Frank 261
Sydney, Philip 42
Sydykbekov, Tungelbay 203
Sylva, Carmen (Elizabeth, queen of Romania) 113, 175
Symonds, John Addington 111, 143
Symons, Arthur 124, 212
Synge, John Millington 161, 165, 167, 168
Szirtes, George 215, 267
Szlosarek, Artur 289
Szymborska, Wisława 285

T

Taback, Simms 295
Tabidze, Galaktion 230
Tabidze, Titsian 145, 202
Tabucchi, Antonio 276, 282, 284
Tacitus 5, 12, 17

Tadini, Emilio 269
Tadrup, Pia 292
Taeko Kohno 276
Tagore, Rabindranath 122, 141, 143, 146, 153, 158, 159, 165, 168, 172, 208
Taha, Ali Mahmud 159, 217
Taha Hussain 140, 195, 250
Tahir, Ibrahim 264
Tahir, Kemal 168, 250
Taillandier, François 293
Taine, Hippolyte-Adolphe 143
Takahashi Michitsuna 215
Takay, Gabdullah 137
Takio Arishima 183
Takizawa Bakin 81, 99, 112, 115
Taku Miki 296
Tamaro, Susanna 282, 289
Tamayo y Baus, Manuel 105, 118, 119, 123, 126, 128, 148
Tamer, Zakaria 194
Tammasaare, Anton Hansen 132, 206
Tamura Ryuichi 183
Tan, Amy 272, 276
Tan Da (Nguyen Khac Hieu) 139, 205
Taner, Haldun 175, 239
Tang Haoming 288
Tanikawa Shuntaro 194
Tanizaki Junichiro 137, 185, 191, 210, 218, 227, 234, 239
Tannasaare, Anton Hamsen 188
Tansi, Sony Labou 283
Tao Qian 17, 18
Taqan, Ibrhim 208
Taranci, Cahit Sitki 168, 226
Tarbell, Ida M. 211
Tardieu, Jean 274
Targowla, Olivier 274
Tarhan, Abdülhak Hâmit 117, 203
Tarkington, Booth 126, 173, 175, 177, 178, 181, 182, 213
Tarzi, Mahmud 200
Taschau, Hannelies 202
Tasso, Torquato 38, 40, 41, 42, 44
Tassoni, Alessandro 53, 55
Tatarka, Dominik 275
Tate, Allen 148, 188, 196, 201, 210, 222, 248, 257, 277, 282
Tate, Nahum 58, 72
Tayama Katai 128, 166
Taylor, A. J. P. 263
Taylor, Alan 286
Taylor, Henry 265, 267
Taylor, Kamala Purnaiya See Markandaya, Kamala
Taylor, Mildred D. 255
Taylor, Peter 176, 219, 265, 267, 268
Taylor, Robert Lewis 230
Taylor, Tom 120, 133
Taymur, Mahmud 144
Tcharents, Yegishe 146, 203
Tchiumpiushian, Artho See Khrakhumi, Zareh
Teale, Edwin Way 241
Teasdale, Sara 177, 197
Teboul, Jacques 282
Tegner, Esias 104
Teichman, Howard 222
Teimuraz I 43
Teirlinck, Herman 132, 182, 185, 186, 225, 242
Tennyson, Alfred, Lord 93, 98, 105, 106, 107, 112, 115, 116, 118, 119, 121, 124, 126, 127, 128, 129, 130, 131, 133, 136, 137, 140, 142
Tenreiro, Francisco José de Vasquez 209, 236

Terence 5, 9
Terian, Vahan 137, 166, 179
Terkel, Studs 265
Terziev, Konstantin 292
Tesich, Steve 210, 259
Tetevide, Anne Marie 295
Tevfik Fikret 125
Thach Lam 167
Thackara, James 293
Thackeray, William Makepeace 98, 108, 109, 111, 112, 113, 114, 115, 116, 117, 118, 120, 123
Thakin Kopuijto Hmain 131, 238
The Lu 165
Thein Han, U See Zodji
Thein Pe Myint 173, 201
Theippam Maum Wa 148, 209
Theocritus 4, 8, 9
Theotokás, Georgios 163, 202, 234, 241
Theotokis, Konstantinos 182
Theriault, Yves 175, 262
Theroux, Paul 207, 253, 258, 284
Thibault, Jacques-Anatole See France, Anatole
Thierry, Jacques-Nicolas-Augustin 87, 119
Thomas, Audrey 273, 280
Thomas, D. M. 260
Thomas, Dylan 173, 199, 206, 207, 213, 221, 222, 224
Thomas, Gwyn 213, 218
Thomas, Hugh 282
Thomas, Lewis 260
Thomas, Ronald Stuart 171, 229, 256, 257, 260, 267
Thomas, Willie 288
Thompson, Dorothy 144, 233
Thompson, Francis 121, 139, 143, 165
Thompson, Lawrence 248
Thomsen, Soren Ulrik 286
Thomson, James 69, 74, 75, 76, 77, 108, 130, 134
Thoreau, Henry David 100, 118, 122, 124
Thoroddsen, Jon 117
Thorpe, Adam 290
Thorup, Kirsten 282
Thucydides 3, 7, 8
Thumanian, Hovhannes 183
Thumboo, Edwin 197
Thurber, James 144, 197, 207, 233
Thwaite, Anthony 259
Tian Han 148
Tibullus 10, 11
Tieck, Johann Ludwig 82, 118
Tikhonov, Nikolay Semyonovich 146, 257
Tilak, Narayan Vama 178
Tillich, Paul Johannes 239
Timanna 36
Timao, Toshio 176
Timm, Uwe 276
Tiraboschi, Girolamo 74
Tirso de Molina 42, 54, 58
Tizón, Hector 274
To Hoai (Nguyen Sen) 179
To Huu (Nguyen Kim Thanh) 179
Tocqueville, Alexis-Charles-Henri Clérel de 96, 108
Toibin, Colin 274
Tokarczuk, Olga 294
Toklas, Alice B. 242
Tokuda Shūsei 128, 210
Toland, John 248
Toledo, Pablo 296

Tolkien, J. R. R. 142, 203, 223, 225, 227, 250, 256
Toller, Ernst 143, 180, 205
Tolstoy, Aleksey 181, 192, 212, 214
Tolstoy, Leo Nikolayevich 90, 105, 123, 124, 130, 135, 138, 141, 149, 168
Tomás García, José Luis de 210, 266
Tomeo, Javier 285
Tomizza, Fulvio 269
Tomlinson, Charles 188
Tompson, Benjamin 72
Toole, John Kennedy 260
Toomer, Jean 242
Torga, Miguel 165, 283
Torkar, Igor (Boris Fakin) 172
Torrado, Antonio 264
Torrente Ballester, Gonzalo 289, 292
Torres, Maruja 297
Torres Bodet, Jaime 159, 183, 184, 193, 203, 224, 228, 252
Torres Naharro, Bartolomé de 28, 35, 36
Torsvan, Berwick Traven See Traven, B.
Toson Shimazaki 200
Tourneur, Cyril 41, 54
Toynbee, Arnold 199, 253
Toyoko Yamazaki 294
Tozzi, Federigo 135, 179, 180
Traat, Mats 199
Traherne, Thomas 166
Trakl, Georg 138, 173
Trampe, Wolfgang 268
Tran Huu Tri See Nam Cao
Tran Khanh Du See Khai Hung
Tran Te Xuong 127, 165
Transtromer, Tomas Gosta 194, 230, 242, 253, 275, 281, 287
Trassard, Jean-Loup 280
Traven, B. (Berwick Traven Torsvan) 140, 188, 189, 202, 245
Travers, Benjamin 259
Travers, P. L. (Helen Lyndon Goff) 285
Trease, Robert Geoffrey 290
Trelawny, Edward John 106, 134
Tremain, Rose 255, 257, 260, 288, 293
Tremblay, Michel 282
Trevelyan, George Macaulay 131, 235
Trevelyan, George Otto 110
Treviño, Elizabeth Borton de 241
Trevor, Elleston 283
Trevor, William 257, 276, 279, 286
Trifonov, Yuri Valentinovich 186, 260
Trilling, Diana 285
Trilling, Lionel 163, 225, 240, 253
Trissino, Giangiorgio 35, 38
Tristan 50, 59
Trollope, Anthony 99, 115, 120, 122, 123, 125, 126, 127, 129, 130, 131, 133, 134
Trotzig, Birgitta 287
Tsadasa, Hamzat 131, 219
Tsalka, Dan 276, 282
Tschernichowsky, Saul 130, 210
Tsubouchi Shōyō 121, 200
Tsuji, Takashi (Seiji Tsutsumi) 282, 287
Tsunao, Aida 172
Tsurayuki Ki 20
Tsushima Shuji See Dazai Osamu
Tsvetayeva, Marina 142, 169, 183, 185, 189, 191, 208, 228
Tu Fu See Du Fu
Tu Mo (Ho Trong Hieu) 158

Tuchman, Barbara 235, 236, 249, 257, 271
Tukārām 50, 58
Tukay, Abdulla 172
Tulsīdās 37, 41, 53
Tunstrom, Goran 287, 295
Tur, Pramudya Ananta 186, 220, 227, 259, 266, 271
Turgenev, Ivan Sergeyevich 101, 117, 118, 119, 122, 123, 126, 127, 129, 131, 135
Turner, Frederick J. 197
Turnstrom, Goran 281
Turzunzoda, Mirzo 169
Tutuola, Amos 179, 222, 287
Tuwhare, Hone 282
Twain, Mark (Samuel Langhorne Clemens) 92, 108, 124, 127, 128, 131, 133, 134, 135, 136, 140, 144, 146, 147, 149, 168
Tyler, Anne 270, 272
Tyler, Royall 79, 85, 87, 103, 104
Tynan, Kenneth 259
Tyutchev, Fyodor Ivanovich 96, 129
Tzara, Tristan 146, 195, 236

U

Ubaldo Ribeiro, João 272
Uchimura Kanzo 122, 193
Ueda Akinari 75, 81
Ugresic, Dubravka 277, 292
Uhland, Johann Ludwig 85, 99, 122
Uhry, Alfred 269, 270
Ukrainka, Lesya (Laryse Petrivna Kosach Kvittka) 128, 172
Ulrich, Laurel Thatcher 275
Ulughzoda, Sotim 169, 224
Ulven, Tor 280
'Umar ibn Abī Rabī'ah 18, 19
Umbral, Francisco 289
Unamuno, Miguel de 123, 160, 172, 173, 176, 198, 201
Unaydin, Rusen Esref 142, 230
Undset, Sigrid 134, 156, 170, 176, 180, 187, 190, 217
Ungaretti, Giuseppe 139, 179, 198, 215, 219, 221, 233, 243, 247, 259
Unger, Irwin 239
Uno Chiyo 285
Unruh, Fritz von 137, 247
Unsworth, Barry 277, 278
Untermeyer, Louis 232, 255
Uoka Makoto 194
Upadhyay Hariaudh, Ayodhyasimha 173
Updike, John 195, 231, 232, 235, 237, 240, 244, 247, 250, 253, 254, 260, 261, 264, 267, 272, 273, 275, 282, 288, 290, 295
Uris, Leon 184, 229, 234
Urquhart, Jane 288
Usakligil, Halid Ziya 125, 187, 212
Usman, Awang (Tongkat Warrant) 190
U'Tam'si, Tchicaya Gerard-Felix 194

V

Va Trong Phung 205
Vaculik, Ludwik 187
Valderrama Andrade, Bernardo 277
Valdés, Zoé 289, 294
Valente, José Angel 295
Valera, Juan 130, 133, 145
Valéry, Paul 128, 176, 182, 212
Valgardson, W. D. 278
Valle-Inclán, Ramón María del 125, 160, 189, 191, 201

Vallejo, Cesar 142, 204, 206
Vallejo, Fernando 277, 287, 294
Valmore, Marceline Desbordes 107
Valverde, José María 285
Van Allsburg, Chris 261, 267
Van der Heijden, A. F. Th. 288
Van Doren, Carl 205
Van Doren, Mark 206
Van Druten, John William 227
Van Tyne, Claude H. 193, 194
Vanbrugh, John 60, 73
Vanderhaeghe, Guy 219, 261
Vargas Llosa, Mario 201, 237, 243, 256, 266, 270, 272, 281, 289, 292, 296
Varma, Bhagvaticharan 160, 231
Varma, Vrindavanlal 140, 214, 245
Varro, Marcus Terentius 10, 11
Varuzhan, Daniel 136, 164, 174
Vasari, Giorgio 38
Vasek, Vladimir See Bezrūc, Petr
Vasiliu, Gheorghe See Bacovia, George
Vasques Teneiro, Francisco José de 180
Vásquez Montalbán, Manuel 292
Vassalli, Sabastiano 274, 278
Vaughan, Henry 53, 58, 66
Vazov, Ivan 116, 181
Vázquez Montalbán, Manuel 277
Vega, Lope de 32, 40, 45, 55
Veiga, Manuel 270
Vélez de Guevara, Luis 41, 57
Velmar-Jankovic, Svetlana 287
Vennberg, Karl 275
Verdaguer, Jacinto 114, 128, 131, 160
Verga, Giovanni 111, 133, 134, 136, 140, 182
Vergil See Virgil
Verhaeren, Émile 119, 135, 138, 139, 141, 142, 144, 146, 149, 160, 162, 164, 169, 171, 174, 175
Verlaine, Paul 113, 126, 127, 130, 136, 139, 146
Verne, Jules 105, 124, 127, 129, 130, 163
Veronesi, Sandro 296
Verwey, Albert 124
Vesaas, Tajei 228
Vestdijk, Simon 148, 198, 201, 248
Vetteve 27
Viaud, Louis-Marie-Julien See Loti, Pierre
Vicente, Gil 27, 32, 35, 36, 37
Vicinczy, Stephen 240
Vico, Giambattista 61, 77
Vida, Marco Girolamo 36
Vidal, Gore 186, 223, 238, 244, 251, 254, 260, 262, 284
Vidal, Virginia 296
Vieira Mateus de Graça, José 200
Viélé-Griffin, Francis 123, 138, 140, 144, 147, 148, 158, 184, 203
Viereck, Peter 217
Viewegh, Michael 279, 286
Vigny, Alfred Victor 87, 103, 104, 108, 123
Vik, Bjorg 274, 276, 282
Vilakazi, Benedict Wallet Bambatha 163, 214
Vildrac, Charles 134, 248
Villemin, Patrick 288
Villiers de L'Isle-Adam, Auguste de 110, 123, 135, 137, 138, 140, 141
Villon, François 27
Vincent, Manuel 294, 297

Vinje, Aasmund Olafson 101, 122, 127
Vir Singh, Bhai 128, 227
Viragh, Christina 278
Virgil 4, 10, 11
Vitale, Serena 296
Vittorini, Elio 166, 241
Vizinczey, Stephen 197, 246
Vladimov, Gyorgy 285
Vogau, Boris Andreyevich See Pilnyak, Boris
Vogel, Paula 290
Voigt, Cynthia 262
Voinovich, Vladimir Nikolaevich 195, 254, 266
Voiture, Vincent 44, 58
Volodine, Antoine 293
Volponi, Paolo 276
Voltaire (François-Marie Arouet) 66, 68, 72, 73, 75, 76, 77, 79, 80, 83
Vondel, Joost van den 43, 54, 56, 59, 60, 61, 63
Vonnegut, Kurt, Jr. 182, 221, 231, 234, 237, 240, 246, 251, 258, 265, 288
Vörösmarty, Mihály 95, 104, 110, 119
Voskuil, J. J. 288, 290
Voss, Johann Heinrich 78, 87, 104
Voyatzoglou, Stella 218
Voznesesnky, Andrei Andreyevich 196
Vries, Theun de 282
Vroman, Lee 174
Vurghun, Samad 163, 226

W

Wackenroder, Wilhelm Heinrich 82, 88
Wagner, Richard 170, 271
Wah, Frederick James 205, 266
Wain, John Barrington 186, 222, 229, 235, 252
Walafrid Strabo 19
Walcott, Derek 192, 241, 251, 255, 258, 260, 264, 267, 269, 274, 277, 296
Walda, Giyorgis Walda Yohannes 225
Waley, Arthur David 241
Walker, Alice 211, 250, 254, 261, 262, 264, 272, 277
Walker, George F. 264
Walker, Kath See Noonuccal, Oodgero
Walker, Roy E. 214
Wallace, Edgar 130, 163, 195
Wallace, Irving 273
Wallace, Lew 104, 133, 163
Wallace, Mike 292
Waller, Edmund 57, 64
Walpole, Horace 72, 80, 81, 87
Walpole, Hugh 136, 208
Walsdorf, Lothar 269
Walser, Martin 242, 291
Walser, Robert 132, 167, 226
Walsh, Jill Paton 282
Waltari, Mika 166, 212, 218, 221, 225, 239, 257
Walter, Otto F. 280
Walton, Izaak 59, 64
Walworth, Arthur 230
Wang Anyi 281
Wang Huo 288
Wang Jiabing 290
Wang Meng 279, 295
Wang Shifu 23, 25
Wannus, Sadallah 287
Warner, Sylvia Townsend 256

Warner, William W. 255
Warrant, Tongkat See Usman, Awang
Warren, Robert Penn 163, 205, 210, 213, 214, 215, 216, 219, 222, 225, 226, 228, 229, 230, 238, 248, 253, 256, 258, 265, 271
Wasserman, Jakob 129, 147, 166, 178, 190, 198, 199
Wasserstein, Wendy 270, 272
Wassmo, Herbjorg 278
Wast, Hugo 135, 235
Watkins, Vernon Phillips 163, 208, 242
Waugh, Alec 176, 260
Waugh, Alexander Raban 148
Waugh, Auberon 234
Waugh, Evelyn 160, 190, 193, 196, 199, 204, 212, 216, 221, 225, 228, 234, 241
Webb, Mary 185
Webster, John 41, 51, 52, 53
Webster, Noah 79, 105, 113
Wedde, Ian 269
Wedekind, Frank 123, 142, 145, 159, 162, 177
Weidman, Jerome 232, 290
Weil, Simone 167, 207, 210, 215, 218, 219
Weiner, Jonathan 283
Weinheber, Josef 142, 199, 202, 204, 212
Weinstein, Nathan Wallenstein See West, Nathanael
Weintraub, Aaron Roy See Brodkey, Harold
Weise, Christian 70
Weiss, Peter Ulrich 175, 239, 245, 261
Weiss, Theodore 264, 269
Welch, James 295
Weldon, Fay 194
Wellershof, Dieter 186, 263
Wells, Herbert George 125, 145, 146, 147, 148, 158, 163, 166, 167, 169, 180, 197, 213
Welty, Eudora 167, 208, 209, 210, 211, 213, 217, 223, 225, 247, 250, 259, 265
Wempfeling, Jakob 34
Wen Ito 183
Wen Yiduo 148, 213
Wenwang 1
Weöres, Sándor 172, 269
Werfel, Franz 141, 197, 208, 212
Wergeland, Henrik Arnold 97, 106, 107, 111, 112, 114
Werner, Friedrich Ludwig Zacharias 81, 96, 97, 98, 103
Wessel, Johan 82
West, Dorothy 290
West, Morris 175, 231, 240, 286, 292
West, Nathanael (Nathan Wallenstein Weinstein) 160, 197, 205, 206
West, Rebecca 142, 182, 209, 262, 265
Westcott, Edward 148
Wetering, Janwillem van de 194
Weyergans, François 278
Wharton, Edith 122, 163, 169, 172, 179, 181, 203, 204
Wharton, Joseph 73, 77
Wharton, Willam 258
Wheatley, Phillis 78, 84
Wheatley, Yates 255
Whelan, John Francis See O'Faolain, Sean
White, Antonia 257
White, E. B. 148, 212, 221, 223, 231, 247, 265

White, Edmund 295
White, Leonard D. 230
White, Patrick (Victor Martindale) 228, 234, 241, 250, 258, 260, 267, 273
White, T. H. 229
White, Terence de Vere 269
White, Theodore H. 235
White, William Allen 214
White, William S. 224
Whitehead, Alfred North 122, 168, 214
Whitman, Walt 101, 119, 121, 124, 128, 135, 142
Whittier, John Greenleaf 97, 106, 109, 113, 114, 116, 118, 119, 121, 124, 125, 126, 127, 128, 142
Widdemer, Margaret 178
Wideman, John Edgar 263, 273, 275
Wiebe, Rudy 282
Wieland, Christoph Martin 75, 80, 82, 83, 99
Wierzynski, Kasimierz 144, 245
Wiesel, Elie 230, 284
Wiesner, David 277
Wifflin, Josef 254
Wiggins, Marianne 272
Wigglesworth, Michael 60, 70
Wilbur, Richard 180, 214, 219, 226, 228, 270, 272
Wilde, Oscar 118, 141, 143, 145, 148, 158, 163
Wilder, Laura Ingalls 125, 200, 227
Wilder, Thornton 147, 189, 190, 204, 209, 210, 216, 223, 225, 235, 243, 250, 253
Wiley, Richard 268
Willard, Nancy 261
Williams, Ben Ames 140, 222
Williams, C. K. 269, 277, 295
Williams, George Emlyn 163, 268
Williams, Jesse Lynch 177
Williams, Roger 57
Williams, T. Harry 247
Williams, Tennessee (Thomas Lanier) 169, 205, 211, 212, 215, 216, 220, 222, 224, 225, 229, 231, 234, 262
Williams, William Carlos 135, 184, 186, 213, 235, 236
Williamson, Henry 255
Williamson, Michael 273
Willingham, Calder 283
Wills, Garry 279
Willumsen, Dorrit 286
Wilmot, John 57, 63
Wilson, A. N. 272, 280
Wilson, Angus Frank Johnstone 172, 221, 259, 275
Wilson, August 212, 264, 265, 267, 268, 269, 273
Wilson, Colin 227
Wilson, Edmund 145, 176, 194, 207, 208, 213, 235, 249

Wilson, Edward O. 258, 275
Wilson, Forrest 209
Wilson, Lanford 258, 259
Wilson, Margaret 185
Winge, Mette 288
Winkler, Martin 291
Winslow, Ola Elizabeth 208
Winters, Yvor 193, 194, 215, 244
Winton, Tim 284
Wisniewski, David 287
Wispelaere, Paul de 190, 237, 240, 247, 254, 262, 267
Wister, Owen 121, 160, 204
Witkiewicz, Stanisław Ignacy 181, 187
Wittgenstein, Ludwig 181, 219
Wittlin, Józef 146, 202
Wodehouse, P.G. 134, 253
Wohmann, Gabriele 280
Woiwode, Larry 207, 246, 253, 260, 270
Wojciechowska, Maia 239
Wolf, Christa 286
Wolfe, Linie Marsh 213
Wolfe, Thomas Clayton 158, 192, 194, 200, 204, 205
Wolfe, Tom 268, 290
Wolff, Tobias 265
Wollstonecraft, Mary 79, 86, 87
Wood, Gordon S. 279
Wood, Susan 277
Woodcock, George 283
Woodham-Smith, Cecil Blanche Fitzgerald 255
Woodnah 255
Woodward, C. Van 261
Woolcott, Alexander 138, 210
Woolf, Virginia 134, 174, 178, 182, 186, 189, 190, 192, 194, 203, 208
Wordsworth, William 81, 86, 88, 92, 95, 96, 97, 101, 103, 112, 116
Wouk, Herman 174, 220, 221, 225
Wren, Percival Christopher 185
Wright, Charles 262, 271, 273, 290
Wright, James 248, 249, 273
Wright, Judith 295
Wright, L. R. 276, 284
Wright, Richard 166, 204, 207, 212, 219, 222, 232, 233
Wu Chengen 33, 42, 44
Wu Jingzi 70, 78
Wurdemann, Audrey 200
Wycherley, William 56, 62, 63, 72
Wyspianski, Stanisław 126, 165
Wyss, Johann David 76, 99, 101

X

Xenophanes 6
Xenophon 2, 7, 8
Xie Bingying 295
Xu Zhimo 146, 194
Xuan Dieu 176

Y

Ya Dafu 212
Yacine, Kateb 216
Yadav, Rajendra 191, 232
Yaldizchian, Zareh See Zahrat
Yamin, Muhammad 192, 235
Yáñez, Agustín 161, 259
Yasami, Rashid 146, 219
Yashin, Komil 167
Yasmin, Muhammad 160
Yaspal 160
Yasutaka Tsutsui 296
Yates, Frances Amelia, Dame 260
Yavorov, Peyo 131, 173
Yaziji, Nasif 95, 128
Yazov, Ivan 143
Ye Guangcen 295
Ye Shengtao 144
Ye Zhaoyzn 281
Yeats, William Butler 124, 138, 140, 143, 144, 152, 160, 161, 165, 168, 173, 175, 176, 178, 180, 183, 184, 186, 189, 190, 196, 205, 206
Yeghiazarian, Hayastan See Zavian, Nairi
Yehoshua, A. B. 274, 282, 289
Yerby, Frank Garvin 275
Yergin, Daniel 277
Yermakov, Oleg 294
Yerofeyev, Victor 274
Yesenin, Sergey Aleksandrovich 145
Yeshurun, Avot 274
Yevtushenko, Yevgeny Alexandrovic 196, 234, 262, 265
Yezierska, Anzia 137, 187, 247
Yizhar, S. 278, 280, 291, 293
Yokai Yagu 70, 84
Yoko Tawada 287
Yokomitsu Riichi 214
Yolen, Jane 270
Yonejiro Noguchi 130
Yonge, Charlotte Mary 103, 118, 119, 159
Yorinks, Arthur 268
Yosano Akiko 159, 164, 209
Yoshida Kenko 24, 25
Yoshikawa Eiji 142, 188, 200, 235
Yoshiko Shibaki 269
Yoshimaus Gozo 205
Yoshioka Minoru 178
Yoshiyuki Junnosuke 281
Yospal 230
Young, Ed 273
Young, Edward 64, 73, 76, 80
Young, Marguerite 283
Young, Patricia 276
Young, Terence 293
Yourcenar, Marguerite 160, 220, 245, 266, 268
Yu Dafu 146
Yu Hua 281, 284
Yuko Tshushima 291

Yumiko Kurahashi 276
Yurdakul, Mehmed Emin 126, 211
Yuryev, Oleg 289
Yushij, Nima 147, 232

Z

Zabor, Rafi 290
Zagajewski, Adam 212
Zahrat (Zareh Yaldizchian) 184
Zalite, Mara 220
Zamyatin, Yevgeny Ivanovich 136, 203
Zangwill, Israel 123, 144, 166, 187
Zarian, Nairi 158, 193
Zaturenska, Maria 204
Zavian, Nairi (Hayastan Yeghiazarian) 245
Zaydan, Jurji 122
Zeami Motokiyo 15, 25, 27
Zei, Alki 269
Zelazny, Roger 283
Zelinsky, Paul O. 290
Zemach, Harve 252
Zeng Weihao 290
Zeromski, Stefan 123, 186
Zewska, Maria Pawlikowska-Jasnor 143
Zhang Jie 259
Zhang Ziping 214
Zhao Shuli 163, 247
Zhao Zhenkai See Bao Dai
Zhou Meiseng 286, 288
Zhou Shuren See Lu Xun
Zhu Lin 273
Zhu Shucheng 288
Zhukovsky, Vasily Andreyvich 97
Ziegler, Anselm von 66
Zindel, Paul 240, 248
Ziping, Zhiang 143
Ziyada, Mari 145, 208
Zodji (U Thein Han) 165
Zohrap, Grigor 122, 174
Zola, Émile-Édouard-Charles-Antoine 111, 126, 128, 131, 133, 137, 148, 160
Zollinger, Albin 145, 197, 202, 206, 208
Zorian, Stephan 141, 177, 242
Zorrilla de San Martín, Juan 119, 194
Zorrilla y Moral, José 100, 111, 112, 114, 143
Zrínyi, Miklós 53, 60
Zuckmayer, Carl 146, 187, 195, 214, 218, 255
Zuhayr 18
Zuhuri, Nuruddin Muhammad Tahir 52
Zunz, Leopold 86, 137
Zweig, Arnold 189, 244
Zweig, Arthur 159
Zweig, Stefan 133, 138, 199, 204, 209

GENRE INDEX

Entries in the index are filed word for word.

A

allegory
The Book of Thel (Blake) 68, 85
The Holy War (Bunyan) 64
En kakelsattares eftermiddag (Gustafsson) 277
The Pilgrim's Progress, from This World to What Which Is to Come (Bunyan) 63
Salaman u Absal (Jāmī) 28

almanac
An Almanac for New England for the Year 1639 (Pierce) 56
Poor Richard's Almanack (Franklin) 75

anthropological study
From Honey to Ashes (Lévi-Strauss) 241
The Origin of Table Manners (Lévi-Strauss) 245
The Raw and the Cooked (Lévi-Strauss) 239

antinovel
Ici (Sarraute) 284
The Living and Their Shadows (Lacretelle) 256

aphorism
The Joyful Wisdom (Nietzsche) 135
Meditations Divine and Moral (Bradstreet) 60
Orphic Sayings (Alcott) 111
Polonius (FitzGerarld) 117

apologia
De Profundis (Wilde) 163

architecture
The Four Books of Architecture (Palladio) 40
The Stories of Venice (Ruskin) 117

autobiographical narrative
All God's Children Need Traveling Shoes (Angelou) 267

Always a Fragment (Rozewicz) 291
Los años indecisos (Torrente Ballester) 289
The Autobiography of Alice B. Toklas (Stein) 197
Black Spring (Miller) 201
The Blindfold Horse: Memories of a Persian Childhood (Guppy) 272
The Dangerous Summer (Hemingway) 265
The Diary of My Times (Bernanos) 204
Down and Out in Paris and London (Orwell) 197
The Heart of a Woman (Angelou) 260
Homage to Catalonia (Orwell) 204
I Know Why the Caged Bird Sings (Angelou) 247
Life with Father (Day) 200
Ma vie folle (Morgieve) 296
Night (Wiesel) 230
Las palabras de la vida (Diez) 297
La pas si lent de l'amour (Bianciotti) 284
A Personal History (Taylor) 263
Porte disparu (Arrabal) 296
Les reveries de la femme sauvage (Cixous) 296
Roots: The Saga of an American Family (Haley) 254
Un silence d'environ une demi-heure (Schreiber) 286
Singin' and Swingin' and Gettin' Merry Like Christmas (Angelou) 255
The Triumph and Tragedy of Erasmus Rotterdamus (Zweig) 199

autobiographical novel
AMDG (Pérez de Ayala) 169
Blame Me on History (Modisane) 237

A Child of Our Time (Castillo) 228
A Clip of Steel (Blackburn) 246
Decline; or, Your Love Has Destroyed Me (Khurayyif) 228
Defeat (Chander) 206
Down Second Avenue (Mphahlele) 231
The Dust Which Is God (Benét) 208
Eyeless in Gaza (Huxley) 202
For and Against (Lacretelle) 214
Guest of Reality (Lagerkvist) 187
Hadrian the Seventh (Rolfe) 162
Heart on the Left (Frank) 221
Ibrahim the Writer (al-Mazini) 194
Jill (Larkin) 213
The Kindness of Women (Ballard) 276
La langue maternelle (Alexakis) 284
The Longest Journey (Forster) 165
Martin Eden (London) 167
Memories of My Childhood (Lagerlöf) 194
The Morning of Our Lives (Ulughzoda) 224
My Heart (Lasker-Schuler) 171
Nikita's Childhood (Tolstoy) 181
The Outsider (Wright) 222
A Portrait of the Artist as a Young Man (Joyce) 152, 175
De profundis valsa lenta (Cardoso Pires) 289
Son of a Smaller Hero (Richler) 225
Sons and Lovers (Lawrence) 172
The Story of San Michael (Munthe) 192
The Tiger in the Grass (Doerr) 284
Viejo (González León) 285
Wake for a Red Bitch (Petkavich) 217

The Way Out (Martinson) 202
White Nights (Gudmundsson) 199

autobiography
The Adventures of a Younger Son (Trelawny) 106
Afterimages: Young Men from Those Years (Nowakowski) 285
Agnar (Delblanc) 281
All Rivers Run to the Sea (Wiesel) 284
Alone (Strindberg) 93
The Americanization of Edward Bok (Bok) 181
Angela's Ashes: A Memoir (McCourt) 286, 288
Apologia Pro Vita Sua (Newman) 124
The Autobiography (Franklin) 81
Autobiography (Hunt) 116
Autobiography, 1872–1914 (Russell) 143
Autobiography of an Egotist (Stendhal) 143
The Autobiography of an Unknown Indian (Chadhuri) 220
The Autobiography of Malcolm X (Malcolm X) 240
The Autobiography of William Allen White (White) 214
Black Boy (Wright) 212
Black Seasons (Glowisnki) 291
Book of Margery Kempe (Kempe) 27
Borstal Boy (Behan) 229
Break at Noon (Claudel) 164
Bronx Primitive: Portaits in a Childhood (Simon) 261
Confession of a Child of the Century (Musset) 109
Confessions (Rousseau) 68, 84, 85
Confessions of an Opium Eater (De Quincey) 102
The Dammed and the Saved (Levi) 268

autobiography *(continued)*
Days with Monks (Laxness) 269
Delito por bailar el chachacha (Cabrera Infante) 285
The Diary of Selma Lagerlöf (Lagerlöf) 196
The Diving Bell and the Butterfly (Bauby) 288
Dust Tracks on a Road (Hurston) 209
The Eagle and the Serpent (Guzmán) 191
The Edge of Day (Lee) 231
The Education of Henry Adams (Adams) 164
Efter ar og dag (Hamsun) 274
An Egyptian Childhood (Taha Hussain) 195
Elle et Lui (Sand) 121
En Route to Myself (Pontoppidan) 210
Fairy Tale of My Life (Andersen) 114
Fathers and Sons (Gosse) 165
Flaws in the Glass: A Self-Portrait (White) 260
Gather Together in My Name (Angelou) 252
Goodbye to All That (Graves) 192
Grace Abounding to the Chief of Sinners (Bunyan) 61
Great Morning (Sitwell) 215
Growing Up (Baker) 261
Herzwand (Hartling) 274
The History of Pendennis (Thackeray) 115
I Was a Savage (Paris) 228
If This Is a Man (Levi) 215
In My Father's Court (Singer) 242
Incidents in the Life of a Slave Girl Written by Herself (Jacobs) 122
Inferno (Strindberg) 93, 147
Infor nedrakningen (Myrdal) 281
Isara: A Voyage Round Essay (Soyinka) 272
The Journal of Jules Renard (Renard) 186
Journey Without Maps (Greene) 202
Laughter in the Next Room (Sitwell) 216
Left Hand, Right Hand (Sitwell) 211
A Letter to Myself (Mallet-Joris) 237
Life (Petrovich) 62
Lives of Gallant Women (Brantôme) 60
Lucien Leuwen (Stendhal) 144
Magic Lantern (Bergman) 270
The Maine Woods (Thoreau) 124
A Man—Finished (Papini) 171
Mein Kampf (Hitler) 187
Mein Stuck Zeit (Brezan) 274
Mémoires (Comines) 29
Mémoires (Saint-Simon) 132
Memoirs (Chateaubriand) 116
Memoirs (Gibbon) 87
Memoirs of a Catholic Childhood (McCarthy) 228
Memoirs of a Dutiful Daughter (Beauvoir) 230
Memoirs of a Father (Marmontel) 96
Memoirs of a Fox-Hunting Man (Sassoon) 190

Memoirs of Casanova (Casanova) 104
Memoirs of Mistral (Mistral) 164
Minnena ser mig (Transtromer) 281
A Moveable Feast (Hemingway) 238
The Museum of Unconditional Surrender (Ungresic) 292
My Childhood (Gorky) 172
My Happy Days in Hell (Faludy) 235
My Life (Wagner) 170
The Narrow Road to Happiness (Ernst) 162
Noble Essences (Sitwell) 219
The Noël Coward Diaries (Coward) 261
The Ochre People: Scenes from a South African Life (Jabavu) 237
On vient chercher Monsieur Jean (Tardieu) 274
One Writer's Beginnings (Welty) 265
Ori-Taku-Shiba (Arai) 72
Out of Africa (Dinesen) 203
Palimpsest (Vidal) 284
Persona Non Grata (Edwards) 251
Personal History (Graham) 290
Petrarch's Secret (Petrarch) 14
The Prelude, or, Growth of a Poet's Mind (Wordsworth) 88
The Promised Land (Antin) 171
Raabe Baikal (Strittmatter) 274
The Reawakening (Levi) 237
Road to Ghana (Hutchinson) 232
Roland Barthes (Barthes) 254
The Romany (Borrow) 120
The Rosy Crucifixion: Nexus (Miller) 232
Rules of the Game (Leiris) 255
The Scarlet Tree (Sitwell) 213
The Seven Pillars of Wisdom (Lawrence) 188
Seven Storey Mountain (Merton) 216
Sido (Colette) 193
The Son of a Servant (Strindberg) 93
Son of Guyana (Apple) 251
A Sort of Life (Greene) 154
Speak, Memory (Nabokov) 155, 220
The Spirit of St. Louis (Lindbergh) 223
The Story of a Life (Paustovsky) 239
Summoned by Bells (Betjeman) 232
Surprised by Joy: The Shape of My Early Life (Lewis) 225
The Thief's Journal (Genet) 218
To Be Young, Gifted and Black (Hansberry) 246
Undertones of War (Blunden) 190
Unter tiden (Turnstrom) 281
Viper in the Fist (Bazin) 216
Ways of Escape (Greene) 154
We (Lindbergh) 189
West with the Night (Markham) 209
What Remains (Delblanco) 295
Wind, Sand and Stars (Saint-Exupéry) 206
A Writer's American: Landscape in Literature (Kazin) 270
The Younger Son (Shapiro) 271

B

ballad
"The Ballad of Bouillabaisse" (Thackeray) 116
Ballad of the Mari Lwyd and Other Poems (Watkins) 208
Ballads and Other Poems (Longfellow) 111
Ballads and Other Poems (Tennyson) 133
Ballads and Poems of Tragic Life (Meredith) 138
Ballads and Songs (Davidson) 144
Ballads and Sonnets (Rossetti) 134
"La Belle Dame sans Merci" (Keats) 101
"The Bridegroom" (Pushkin) 90, 104
"Erkling" (Goethe) 67, 84
Frithjofs Saga (Tegner) 104
Home Ballads and Other Poems (Whittier) 121
Lays of Ancient Rome (Macaulay) 112
"Lenore" (Burger) 82
Lyudmila (Zhukovsky) 97
Poems and Ballads (Swinburne) 125, 132
The Twelve (Blok) 177
Valdemar Afterdag (Hauch) 122
biographical novel
Abay's Road (Auezov) 214
Diletta Constanza (Garavini) 286
Joe Hill (Stegner) 219
Lives of the Poets (Untermeyer) 232
Outstanding Talent—Yang Du (Tang, Zhu) 288
Rainbow Promontory (Tsuji) 282
A ultima quimera (Miranda) 285
biography
Admiral of the Ocean Sea (Morison) 210
The American Leonardo: The Life of Samuel F. B. Morse (Mabee) 211
The American Orchestra and Theodore Thomas (Russell) 190
Andrew Jackson (James) 204
Barrett Wendell and His Letter (Howe) 186
Bearing the Cross: Martin Luther King, Jr., and the Southern Christian Leadership Conference (Garrow) 268
Benjamin Franklin (Van Doren) 205
Benjamin Franklin, Self-Revealed (Bruce) 179
Benjamin Henry Latrobe (Hamlin) 226
Black Elk Speaks (Neihardt) 196
The Book of Monelle (Schwob) 144
Booker T. Washington (Harlan) 263
Charles Evans Hughes (Pusey) 221
Charles Sumner and the Coming of the Civil War (Donald) 233
Charles W. Eliot (James) 194
Concerning Famous Women (Boccaccio) 14
Crusader in Crinoline (Wilson) 209

A Daughter of the Middle Border (Garland) 182
Days of Sorrow and Pain: Leo Baech and the Berlin Jews (Baker) 258
Edith Wharton: A Biography (Lewis) 254
Edmund Pendleton, 1721–1803 (Mays) 222
Elizabeth and Essex (Strachey) 190
Eminent Victorians (Strachey) 177
The Fall of the King (Jensen) 158
Forgotten First Citizen: John Bigelow (Clapp) 216
Fortunate Son: The Healing of a Vietnam Vet (Puller) 277
From Immigrant to Inventor (Pupin) 184
George Bancroft: Brahmin Refel (Nye) 212
George Washington (Freeman) 229
God, a Biography (Miles) 286
Grant: A Biography (McFeeley) 261
Grover Cleveland (Nevis) 197
Hamilton Fish (Nevins) 203
Harriet Beecher Stowe: A Life (Hedrick) 283
Henry Adams (Samuels) 239
Henry James (Edel) 236
The History of Henry VII (Bacon) 53
Huey Long (Williams) 247
Jackson Pollock: An American Saga (Naifeh, Smith) 275
John C. Calhoun: American Portrait (Coit) 219
John Jay (Dennett) 198
John Keats (Bate) 238
John Paul Jones (Morison) 232
John Quincy Adams and the Foundations of American Foreign Policy (Bemis) 218
Jonathan Edwards (Winslow) 208
Life and Letters of Walter H. Page (Hendrick) 199
The Life and Times of Cotton Mather (Silverman) 265
Life of Archbishop Dominican Friar Bartolomeu dos Martires (Sousa) 52
Life of Christ (Farrar) 130
Life of Christ (Papini) 181
The Life of Horatio Nelson (Southey) 99
The Life of John Marshall (Beveridge) 179
The Life of Samuel Johnson (Boswell) 86
The Life of Sir William Osler (Cushing) 187
Lindbergh (Berg) 292
The Lion and the Throne (Bowen) 226
The Lives of the English Poets (Johnson) 83
Lord Rochester's Monkey, Being the Life of John Wilmot, Earl of Rochester (Greene) 252
Louise Bogan: A Portrait (Frank) 267
Luce and His Empire (Swanberg) 250

Machiavelli in Hell (de Grazia) 273

The Man from New York: John Quinn and His Friends (Reid) 245

Marlborough: His Life and Times (Churchill) 197

Mary, Queen of Scots (Fraser) 246

Memoirs, 1925–1950 (Kennan) 244

A Midwife's Tale: The Life of Martha Ballard, Based on Her Diary, 1785–1812 (Ulrich) 275

Mitt namn skall vara Stig Dagerman (Ranelid) 281

Moi, Tituba, sorcière noire de Salem (Condé) 268

Mozart (Hildesheimer) 256

Mr. Clemens and Mark Twain (Kaplan) 242

Nahafat al-Uns (Jāmī) 28

On Illustrious Men (Petrarch) 14, 25

On the Fates of Famous Men (Boccaccio) 14

O'Neill, Son and Artist (Shaeffer) 252

Orlando (Woolf) 190

Oscar Wilde (Ellman) 272

Pedlar's Progress (Sheperd) 204

Peter the Great: His Life and World (Massie) 260

The Power Broker: Robert Moses and the Fall of New York (Caro) 253

Prancing Novelist (Brophy) 251

A Prince of Our Disorder: The Life of T. E. Lawrence (Mack) 255

Profiles in Courage (Kennedy) 228

Queen Victoria (Strachey) 181

R. E. Lee (Freeman) 200

The Raven (James) 193

The Rise of Theodore Roosevelt (Morris) 259

Robert Frost: The Years of Triumph, 1915–1938 (Thompson) 248

Roosevelt and Hopkins (Sherwood) 217

Samuel Johnson (Bate) 256, 257

Samuel Johnson (Wain) 252

Son of the Wilderness (Wolfe) 213

The Taft Story (White) 224

Theodore Roosevelt (Pringle) 195

The Thought and Character of William James (Perry) 201

A Thousand Days (Schlesinger) 241

The Training of an American—The Earlier Life and Letters of Walter H. Page (Hendrick) 191

Truman (McCullogh) 279

Vera (Schiff) 295

W. E. B. Du Bois: Biography of a Race, 1868–1919 (Lewis) 281

Whitman (Holloway) 189

Woodrow Wilson, American Prophet (Walworth) 230

Woodrow Wilson: Life and Letters (Baker) 206

Yankee from Olympus (Bowen) 211

C

character sketch
Pele-Mele (Dehkhoda) 230

children's literature *See also* tale/story
The Cat in the Hat (Seuss) 228
Charlotte's Web (White) 221
Little House on the Prairie (Wilder) 200
The Little Prince (Saint-Exupéry) 210
Pippi Longstocking (Lindgren) 213
Peter Pan; or, The Boy Who Wouldn't Grow Up (Barrie) 162
Rootabaga Stories (Sandburg) 182
The Secret Garden (Burnett) 169
Skellig (Almond) 293
A Stitch in Time (Lively) 255
The Story of Dr. Dolittle (Lofting) 180
Stuart Little (White) 212
The Tale of Peter Rabbit (Potter) 160
The Trumpet of the Swan (White) 247
The Wind in the Willows (Grahame) 166
Winnie the Pooh (Milne) 188
The Wonderful Wizard of Oz (Baum) 158

comedy *See also* humorous piece
The Absurda Comica, or Master Peter Squentz (Gryphius) 59
The Amorous Follies (Regnard) 70
The Amorous Quarrel (Molière) 59
Amphitryon (Dryden) 49, 65
Arms and the Man (Shaw) 144, 148
As You Like It (Shakespeare) 45
Babylonians (Aristophanes) 3
The Barber of Seville (Beaumarchais) 82
Bartholomew Fair (Jonson) 52
The Beaux's Stratagem (Farquhar) 71
The Beaver Coat (Hauptmann) 144
The Beneficent Grouch (Goldoni) 82
The Blunderer (Molière) 59
La Calandria (Dovizi) 35
The Camel Through the Needle's Eye (Langer) 183
The Candlestick (Musset) 108
The Captain of Kopenick (Zuckmayer) 195
The Careless Husband (Cibber) 70
La Cassaria (Ariosto) 34
Chapters Forgotten by Cervantes (Montalvo) 137
Christophe Colomb (Lemercier) 98
The City Heiress (Behn) 64
Cock-a-Doodle-Dandy (O'Casey) 218
The Coffee-House (Goldoni) 78
The Comedy of Errors (Shakespeare) 31, 43
The Comic Theater (Goldoni) 78
The Conceited Count (Destouches) 75
The Conscious Lovers (Steele) 73
The Contrast (Tyler) 85
Crispin, Rival of His Master (Lesage) 71
The Critic (Sheridan) 83

The Cutter of Coleman Street (Cowley) 57
Cynthia's Revels (Jonson) 50
Damon; or, True Friendship (Lessing) 69
The Devil Is an Ass (Jonson) 52
Disdain Turned Against Disdain (Moreto y Cabaña) 59
Don Juan (Molière) 48, 60
The Double Dealer (Congreve) 66
The Drummer (Addison) 72
Epicoene, or the Silent Woman (Jonson) 51
Every Man in His Humour (Jonson) 45
False Confessions (Marivaux) 75
The Fashionable Bourgeois Ladies (Dancourt) 65
The Father of the Family (Diderot) 79
Fifty Comedies and Tragedies (Fletcher, Beaumont) 63
The Forced Marriage (Molière) 60
The Forest (Ostrovsky) 128
The Free Thinker (Lessing) 69
Frou-Frou (Meilhac and Halevy) 127
The Game of Love and Chance (Marivaux) 74, 75
The Goblins (Suckling) 56
The Golden Fleece (Corneille) 48, 60
The Good Natur'd Man (Goldsmith) 81
The Government Inspector (Gogol) 91, 109
The Great Duke of Florence (Massinger) 55
He Intends to Have a Fling (Nestroy) 112
Henno (Reuchlin) 29
Horribilicribrifax (Gryphius) 60
The Imaginary Invalid (Molière) 48, 62
The Inspector General (Gogol) 91, 109
An Italian Straw Hat (Labiche) 117
The Jew (Lessing) 69
Kalapurnodayamu (Suranna) 42
Kampi; or, The Millionairess and the Seamstress (Nestroy) 117
King Seleucus (Camões) 32
The Lass from the Suburbs; or, Honesty Is the Best Policy (Nestroy) 112
Leonce and Lena (Büchner) 109
The Liar (Corneille) 48, 57
The Litigants (Racine) 48, 61
Love for Love (Congreve) 66
Love in a Wood (Wycherley) 62
Love's Labour's Lost (Shakespeare) 31, 44
The Lying Lover (Steele) 70
Magnetic Lady, or Humours Reconciled (Jonson) 55
Man Full of Nothing (Nestroy) 114
The Marriage of Figaro; or, The Madness of a Day (Beaumarchais) 84
The Married Philosopher (Destouches) 74
May Day (Chapman) 51
The Merchant of Venice (Shakespeare) 31, 44

Le Mercure galant (Boursault) 64
The Merry Wives of Windsor (Shakespeare) 45
A Midsummer Night's Dream (Shakespeare) 31, 44
Minna von Barnhelm; or, A Soldier's Fortune (Lessing) 69, 81
The Miser (Molière) 48, 61
The Misogynist (Lessing) 69, 79
Money (Bulwer-Lytton) 111
Much Ado About Nothing (Shakespeare) 31, 45
The Old Bachelor (Dryden) 66
The Old Maid (Lessing) 69
Our American Cousin (Taylor) 120
Pasquin (Fielding) 75
Peace (Aristophanes) 3, 7
The Poetry Craze (Piron) 76
Propalladia (Torres Naharro) 35
The Residuary Legatee (Regnard) 71
Rule a Wife and Have a Wife (Fletcher) 53
The School for Husbands (Molière) 60
A Scrap of Paper (Sardou) 122
Sergius (Reuchlin) 29
The Sick Woman (Furchtegott) 77
The Soldier's Fortune (Otway) 63
The Spanish Fryar (Dryden) 63
The Squabbles at Chioggia (Goldoni) 80
A Staple of News (Jonson) 54
The Supposes (Gascoigne) 40
Gli Suppositi (Ariosto) 40
Swedenhielms (Bergman) 187
A Tale of a Tub (Jonson) 55
The Taming of the Shrew (Shakespeare) 31, 44
Tartuffe (Molière) 48, 60
Teeuwis the Peasant (Coster) 51
The Tender Husband (Steele) 70
The Test (Marivaux) 76
These Enchanted Woods (Massie) 280
The Three Dorothys (Scarron) 57
Truth Under Suspicion (Ruiz de Alarcón) 54
Turcaret; or, The Financier (Lesage) 71
Twentieth Century (Hecht) 196
The Two Amphitryons (Camões) 32
Under the Frog (Fischer) 280
The Unexpected Wager (Sedaine) 81
The Valentine (Freytag) 114
Woman of Paris (Becque) 137
The Wooers (Eichendorff) 107
The Would-Be Gentleman (Molière) 61

cosmographical work
Heptamychos (Pherecydes) 2

crime novel *See also* detective story; mystery novel
Fifty-Two Pickup (Leonard) 252
Marnie (Graham) 234
Stick (Leonard) 262
Swag (Leonard) 255

criticism *See* cultural criticism; literary criticism; social criticism; theatrical criticism

cultural criticism *See also* essay
Beyond Culture (Trilling) 240

cultural criticism (continued)
  The Closing of the American Mind
    (Bloom) 268
  Guide to Kulchur (Pound) 204
  Notes Toward the Definition of
    Culture (Eliot) 152, 216

D

detective story See also short story
  The Big Sleep (Chandler) 205
  The Case Book of Sherlock Holmes
    (Doyle) 163
  I, the Jury (Spillane) 215
  The Return of Sherlock Holmes
    (Doyle) 163
dialogue
  Alcibiades (Plato) 3
  Alma, or the Progress of the Mind
    (Prior) 72
  Apology (Plato) 3
  The Art of War (Machiavelli) 36
  Charmides (Plato) 3
  The Christian Socrates (Balzac) 58
  Il Cortegiano (Castiglione) 36
  Cratylus (Plato) 3
  Critias (Plato) 3
  Crito (Plato) 3
  Death and the Ploughman (Jo-
    hannes von Tepl) 26
  De los nombres de Cristo (León) 42
  Epinomis (Plato) 3
  Euthymdemus (Plato) 3
  Euthyphoron (Plato) 3
  The Ghost of Abel (Blake) 103
  Gorgias (Plato) 3
  Hipparchus (Plato) 3
  Hippias Major (Plato) 3
  Hippias Minor (Plato) 3
  Imaginary Conversations (Landor)
    103, 118
  Laches (Plato) 3
  Lovers (Plato) 3
  Lysis (Plato) 3
  Menexeums (Plato) 3
  Meno (Plato) 3
  Nomoi (Plato) 3
  Parmedides (Plato) 3
  Phaedo (Plato) 3
  Phaedrus (Plato) 3
  Philebus (Plato) 3
  Protagoras (Plato) 3
  Republic (Plato) 3
  Sophist (Plato) 3
  Spaccio della Bestia Trionfante
    (Bruno) 42
  Statesman (Plato) 3
  Symposium (Plato) 3
  Theaetetus (Plato) 3
  Timeaus (Plato) 3
diary
  An Account of My Hut (Kamo
    Chomei) 23
  Alone Against the Night (Tatarka)
    275
  Days with Monks (Laxness) 269
  Departure from the Castle (Putik)
    292
  Diary (Pepys) 104
  Diary of a Poet Recently Married
    (Jiménez) 177
  The Diary of a Young Girl (Frank)
    215
  God's Face (Drzezdzon) 264
  Journal intime (Amiel) 136
  Journal to Stella (Swift) 68, 71
  Mexico (Arsenijevic) 296

Religio Medici (Browne) 57
Show Your Tongue (Grass) 272
The Year of My Life (Issa) 101
dictionary
  An American Dictionary of the
    English Language (Webster)
    105
  A Dictionary of the English Lan-
    guage (Johnson) 79
  Historical and Critical Dictionary
    (Bayle) 66
  Oxford English Dictionary 136
  Philosophical Dictionary (Voltaire)
    80
doxography
  Religio Laici, or a Layman's Faith
    (Dryden) 64
drama See also play
  Abe Lincoln in Illinois (Sherwood)
    205
  Abhijñanasakuntala (Kālidāsa)
    14, 15
  Alison's House (Glaspell) 194
  All the Way Home (Mosel) 233
  Aminta (Tasso) 42
  Angels in America—Millennium
    Approaches (Kushner) 279
  Anna Christie (O'Neill) 182
  Auto de la sibila Casandra (Vi-
    cente) 35
  Beyond the Horizon (O'Neill) 179
  The Borderers (Wordsworth) 87
  Both Your Houses (Anderson)
    197
  Buried Child (Sheperd) 258
  Cat on a Hot Tin Roof (Williams)
    224
  A Chorus Line (Bennet, Kirk-
    wood, Dante, Hamlisch, Kle-
    ban) 254
  Craig's Wife (Kelly) 187
  Creation, Man and Messiah
    (Wergeland) 106
  Cromwell (Hugo) 105
  Death of a Salesman (Miller) 217
  The Deceiver of Seville and the
    Stone Guest (Tirso de Molina)
    54
  A Delicate Balance (Albee) 242
  Diary of Anne Frank (Hackett,
    Goodrich) 226
  Dinner with Friends (Margulies)
    295
  Driving Miss Daisy (Uhry) 270
  The Effect of Gamma Rays on
    Man-in-the-Moon Marigolds
    (Zindel) 248
  The Family Reunion (Eliot) 205
  Fences (Wilson) 268
  Fiorello! (Weidman, Abbott,
    Bock, Harnick) 232
  The Gin Game (Coburn) 256
  Glengarry Glen Ross (Mamet) 263
  The Great White Hope (Sackler)
    245
  The Green Pastures (Connelly)
    193
  Gysbreght von Aemstel (Vondel)
    56
  Harvey (Chase) 212
  The Heidi Chronicles (Wasser-
    stein) 272
  Hell-Bent for Heaven (Hughes)
    184
  How I Learned to Drive (Vogel)
    290

How to Succeed in Business With-
  out Really Trying (Loesser, Bur-
  rows) 235
Icebound (Davis) 183
Idiot's Delight (Sherwood) 201
In Abraham's Bosom (Green) 189
Interpreter of Maladies (Lahiri)
  295
J.B. (MacLeish) 230
Joan of Arc (Péguy) 147
The Kentucky Cycle (Schenkkan)
  277
Long Day's Journey into Night
  (O'Neill) 228
Look Homeward, Angel (Frings)
  229
Lost in Yonkers (Simon) 275
Love's Riddle (Cowley) 56
Malavikagnimitra (Kālidāsa) 14
The Man Who Came to Dinner
  (Hart, Kaufman) 205
Marion de Lorme (Hugo) 105
Men in White (Kingsley) 198
Miss Lulu Bett (Gale) 181
'Night, Mother (Norman) 262
No Place to Be Somebody (Gor-
  done) 247
Oedipus Rex (Cocteau) 189
Of Thee I Sing (Kaufman,
  Ryskind, Gershwin) 195
The Old Main (Akins) 200
Orpheus (Politian) 28
Our Town (Wilder) 204
The Piano Lesson (Wilson) 273
The Piccolomini (Schiller) 88
Picnic (Inge) 222
Play of St. Nicholas (Bodel) 23
Rent (Larson) 286
Robert Guiskard (Kleist) 97
San Gloria (Redcam) 180
Seascape (Albee) 253
The Shadow Box (Cristofer) 255
The Shrike (Kramm) 221
The Skin of Our Teeth (Wilder)
  210
A Soldier's Play (Fuller) 261
South Pacific (Rogers, Hammer-
  stein, Logan) 218
The State of the Union (Crouse,
  Lindsay) 213
Still Stands the House (Ringwood)
  205
Strange Interlude (O'Neill) 190
Street Scene (Rice) 191
A Streetcar Named Desire
  (Williams) 216
The Subject Was Roses (Gilroy)
  239
Sunday in the Park with George
  (Sondheim, Lapine) 265
Sweeney Agonistes (Eliot) 188
Talley's Folly (Wilson) 259
The Teahouse of the August Moon
  (Patrick) 223
That Championship Season
  (Miller) 250
There Shall Be No Night (Sher-
  wood) 208
They Knew What They Wanted
  (Howard) 186
Three Tall Women (Albee) 281
The Time of Your Life (Saroyan)
  206
The Tragedy of Agis (Bessenyei) 82
Under Milk Wood (Thomas) 224
Vikramorvasi (Kālidāsa) 14

Why Marry? (Williams) 177
Winterset (Anderson) 200
Wit (Edelson) 292
Woyzeck (Büchner) 110, 132
You Can't Take It With You (Hart,
  Kaufman) 203
The Young Man from Atlanta
  (Foote) 283
dramatic narrative
  Merlin (Robinson) 176

E

eclogue
  Daphnis (Gessner) 78
  The Messiah (Pope) 71
  The Shepheard's Calendar
    (Spenser) 41
economic thesis
  A General Theory of Employment,
    Interest and Money (Keynes)
    202
educational writing
  Proverbs (Erasmus) 32, 34
elegy
  Astrophel (Spenser) 42
  "Ave Atque Vale" (Swinburne)
    126
  "In Memoriam, A.H.H." (Ten-
    nyson) 116
  "On an Infant Dying as Soon as It
    Is Born" (Lamb) 105
  "On the Death of a Fair Infant
    Dying of a Cough" (Milton) 54
  La paloma de vuelo popular:
    Elegias (Guillén) 231
  Pure Elegies (Jiménez) 166
  Roman Elegies (Goethe) 67, 87
  "When Lilacs Last in the Door-
    yard Bloom'd" (Whitman) 124
encyclopedia
  Cyclopaedia, or, an Universal Dic-
    tionary of Arts and Sciences
    (Chambers) 74
  Encyclopédie 78
environmental writing
  Desert Solitaire (Abbey) 244
  Silent Spring (Carson) 237
epic
  Abudulala Mahari (Isahakian)
    169
  The Adventures of Ulysses (Lamb)
    97
  The Albigensians (Lenau) 112
  Amadís de Gaula (Montalvo) 34
  Approximate Man, and Other
    Writings (Tzara) 195
  La Araucana (Ercilla y Zúñiga) 40
  Arnjot Jelline (Bjørnson) 127
  La Atlántida (Verdaguer) 131
  Baptism by the Slavica (Preseren)
    109
  Beowulf 13, 19
  Bernardo; or the Victory at Ron-
    cesvilles (Balbuena) 53
  Bharatbharati (Gupta) 171
  The Bruce (Barbour) 26
  Bucolic Song (Petrarch) 14, 25
  Caramuru (Durão) 84
  La Chanson de Roland 13, 21
  The Day of Doom (Wigglesworth)
    60
  De Partu Virginis (Sannazaro) 36
  The Departure of Martin Fierro
    (Hernández) 129
  The Destruction of the First Cre-
    ation (Bilderdijk) 102

The Destruction of the First World (Bilderdijk) 98

Divine Comedy (Dante) 13, 14, 24

La Dragontea (Vega) 45

Duplications (Koch) 256

The Dynasts, an Epic Drama of the War with Napoleon (Hardy) 161, 168

Eneit (Heinrich von Veldeke) 22

The Faerie Queene (Spenser) 43, 51

Gebir (Landor) 88

General Song (Neruda) 156, 219

The Gods of the North (Oehlenschlager) 101

The Grand Man (Bhoosnurmath) 264

The Grandeur of Mexico (Balbuena) 50

La Henriade (Voltaire) 68, 73

Hercules (Stiernhielm) 59

The House of People (Pant) 239

Hyperion (Keats) 102

Iliad (Homer) 2, 51

L'Italia liberata dai Goti (Trissino) 38

Iwein (Hartmann von Aue) 23

János the Hero (Petófi) 114

Jerusalem Delivered (Tasso) 41

Kalevala (Lönnrot) 108

Kalevipoeg (Kreutzwald) 96, 120

Kamayani (Prasad) 200

Ko; or, A Season on Earth (Koch) 231

The Legend of Thyl Ulenspiegel (Coster) 126

The Light of Asia (Arnold) 132

Le loup Mongol (Homeric) 291

Os Lusíadas (Camões) 32, 41

The Maid of Orleans (Voltaire) 79

The Martyrs (Chateaubriand) 98

Master Thaddeus (Mickiewicz) 108

May (Mácha) 109

Meghnadbadh (Datta) 122

The Messiah (Klopstock) 77

Nerto (Mistral) 136

The New Dunciad (Pope) 69, 74, 76, 84

Night and Day (Dabrowska) 196

The Northern Lights (Daubla) 168

Odyssey (Homer) 2

Olvidado Rey Gudu (Matute) 289

Omeros (Walcott) 274

Osman (Gundulić) 54

Otto the Marksman (Kinkel) 114

Paradise Lost (Milton) 48, 61

Paradise Regained (Milton) 48, 62

Pedar Paars (Holberg) 72

Prosopeya (Pinto) 50

Les Quatre incarnations du (Hasselt) 123

Ramacaritmanas (Tulsīdās) 41

The Rape of the Lock (Pope) 69

Reinke de Vos (Alkmaar) 29

Il Rinaldo (Tasso) 40

Russian Epic (Kheraskov) 82

Savonarola (Lenau) 110

La Semaine (du Bartas) 41

Shah-nameh (Firdawsī) 20

Sohrab and Rustim (Arnold) 117

The Story of Sigurd the Volsung and the Fall of the Niblungs (Morris) 131

Temora (Macpherson) 80

Toldi (Arany) 115

Toldi's Evening (Arany) 118

Toldi's Lane (Arany) 116

Tristan und Isolde (Gottfried von Strassburg) 23

Two People (Dehmel) 161

O Uruguia (Gama) 81

Western Star (Benét) 210

Zalán futása (Vörösmarty) 104

epigram

Thorns and Flowers (Kazinczy) 98

epistolary essay

Drapier's Letters (Swift) 68, 73

The Fire Next Time (Baldwin) 237

epistolary novel

La Città e la Casa (Ginzburg) 264

Clarissa Harlowe (Richardson) 77

Dangerous Liaisons (Laclos) 84

The Expedition of Humphry Clinker (Smollett) 81

El jardín de las dudas (Savatar) 281

Julie; or, The New Eloise (Rousseau) 68, 80

Min salig bror Jean Hendrich (Burman) 281

Pamela; or, Virtue Rewarded (Richardson) 76

The Screwtape Letters (Lewis) 208

Wieland; or, The Transformation (Brown) 88

epistolary poem

Birangana (Datta) 122

The Borough (Crabbe) 98

essay *See also* critical essay; epistolary essay; treatise

The Sacred Wood (Eliot) 180

Against Interpretation (Sontag) 241

AIDS and Its Metaphors (Sontag) 270

The Anti-Soviet Soviet Union (Voinovich) 266

The Autocrat of the Breakfast-Table (Holmes) 120

Autumn Journal (MacNeice) 204

The Barbarian in the Garden (Herbert) 236

The Bigelow Papers (Lowell) 114, 115

Biographia Literaria (Coleridge) 100

The Book of Masques (Gourmont) 146

The Buried Mirror (Fuentes) 279

Catilinarians (Montalvo) 133

The Cave and the Spring: Essays on Poetry (Hope) 240

A Certain Measure (Glasgow) 210

The Christian Hero (Steele) 70

The Common Reader (Woolf) 186

The Complete Prose (Moore) 267

The Conduct of Life (Emerson) 121

Considerations of the Causes of the Grandeur and Decadence of the Romans (Montesquieu) 75

Credo des san-mélé ou je veux chanter la France (Gratiant) 216

Critical Essays (Barthes) 239

Culture and Anarchy (Arnold) 127

De beneficiis (Seneca) 5

De clementia (Seneca) 5

De ira (Seneca) 5

De otio (Seneca) 5

De tranquillitate animi (Seneca) 5

Democracy in America (Tocqueville) 108

The Devil Finds Work (Baldwin) 254

Discourse on the Origin of Inequality (Rousseau) 68

Discourse on the Sciences and the Arts (Rousseau) 68, 78

Drapier's Letters (Swift) 68, 73

The Eiffel Tower and Other Mythologies (Barthes) 239

Essais (Montaigne) 32–33, 42

Essays (Emerson) 111

Essays, Critical and Historical (Macaulay) 113

The Essays of Elia (Lamb) 103

The Essence of Christianity (Feuerbach) 112

The Essential Gesture (Gordimer) 271

For a New Novel (Robbe-Grillet) 237

God's Face (Drzezdzon) 264

The Golden Bough (Frazier) 141

History of Eternity (Borges) 202

The Idea of a Christian Society (Eliot) 152, 205

The Joyful Wisdom (Nietzsche) 135

Just Looking: Essays on Art (Updike) 272

Laocoon: An Essay on the Limits of Painting and Poetry (Lessing) 69, 80

Less Than One: Selected Essays (Brodsky) 267

A Little Side-Road Dog (Milosz) 289

Main Currents in Nineteenth-Century Literature Criticism (Brandes) 129

The Medusa and the Snail (Thomas) 260

Mont-Saint-Michel and Chartres (Adams) 172

Moral Epistles (Seneca) 5

The Myth of Sisyphus (Camus) 155, 209

Mythologies (Barth) 228

Nature (Emerson) 109

Nobody Knows My Name (Baldwin) 234

Notes of a Native Son (Baldwin) 225

The Occasion of Poetry: Essays in Criticism and Autobiography (Gunn) 261

"On Liberty" (Mill) 121

On Love (Stendhal) 103

On Murder as One of the Fine Arts (De Quincey) 105

On Poetry and Poets (Eliot) 228

On Translating Homer (Arnold) 122

The Opposing Self (Trilling) 225

The Outmost Dream (Maxwell) 272

Past and Present (Carlyle) 113

Patas arriba (Galeano) 292

The Physiology of Marriage (Balzac) 91

Pig Earth (Berger) 258

Pilgrim at Tinker Creek (Dillard) 252

The Plain Speaker (Hazlitt) 104

Port-Royal (Saint-Beuve) 111

The Rebel (Camus) 155, 220

Reflections of a Nonpolitical Man (Mann) 177

A Room of One's Own (Woolf) 192

Rules of Chaos; or, Why Tomorrow Doesn't Work (Vizinczey) 246

Russian Thinkers (Berlin) 257

Sartor Resartus (Carlyle) 107

The Second Tree from the Corner (White) 223

Shadow and Act (Ellison) 238

Slouching Toward Bethlehem (Didion) 244

Some Freaks (Mamet) 272

Some Unease and Angels (Feinstein) 256

The Spirit of the Age (Hazlitt) 104

Spirits Rebellious (Gibran) 179

The Stranger in Lowell (Whittier) 114

Styles of Radical Will (Sontag) 246

Table Talk; or, Original Essays on Men and Manners (Hazlitt) 102

A Tear and a Smile (Gibran) 173

Tender Buttons (Stein) 173

To the Finland Station (Wilson) 176

Travel Memoirs from the Summer of 1860 (Vinje) 122

"Über das Erhabene" (Schiller) 68

"Über naive und sentimentalische Dichtung" (Schiller) 68

Utopia (More) 35

Virginibus Puerisque (Stevenson) 134

Wake-Robin (Burroughs) 128

Walden; or, Life in the Woods (Thoreau) 118

We Are Still Married (Keillor) 272

What Is Art? (Tolstoy) 90

The Writing Life (Dillard) 272

F

fantasy

Ancient Evenings (Mailer) 262

The Baron in the Trees (Calvino) 228

The Cloven Viscount (Calvino) 221

The Earthsea Trilogy (Le Guin) 244

The Ghost Sonata (Strindberg) 92, 165

The Nonexistent Knight (Calvino) 231

People Dust (O'Casey) 207

farce

Bouborouche (Courteline) 144

The Evil Spirit Lumpazivagabundus, or the Roguish Frio (Nestroy) 107

The Gamester (Regnard) 66

The Importance of Being Earnest (Wilde) 145

King Ubu (Jarry) 146

Tom Thumb, A Tragedy (Fielding) 74

What D'Ye Call It (Gay) 72

G

grammar

Astadhyayi (Panini) 1

H

hagiography
Golden Legend (Jacobus de Voragine) 24
Lives of the Fathers, Martyrs and Other Principal Saints (Butler) 79
historical novel
1492: Life and Times of Juan Cabezon de Castilla (Aridjis) 266
Alexander and Death (Mickovic) 284
Andersonville (Kantor) 225, 226
August 1914 (Solzhenitsyn) 154, 249
The Black City (Mikszáth) 169
The Bull from the Sea (Renault) 235
El caballero de Sajonia (Benet) 277
Cat's Lives (Kriseova) 288
Cristoforo (Thomas) 288
The Death of Socrates (Gyllensten) 233
Un deus passeando pela brisa da tarde (Carvalho) 285
A Discovery of Strangers (Wiebe) 282
Dreamer (Johnson) 290
The Favorite (Mallet-Joris) 232
In a Dark Wood Wandering (Haasse) 217
Killer Angels (Shaara) 252
The King Must Die (Renault) 229
Lakshmibai, Queen of Jhansi (Varma) 214
The Last of the Wine (Renault) 226
La lunga de vita Marianna Ucria (Maraini) 274
Lykkens sonn (Wassmo) 278
El manuscrito carmesí (Gala) 275
Mellen himlen og verden (Tetevide) 295
Memoirs of Hadrian (Yourcenar) 220
Musashi (Yoshikawa) 200
November 1916 (Solzhenitsyn) 280
Nowhere Else on Earth (Humphreys) 295
Terug uit Irkoetsk (Vries) 282
The Three Slaves of Julius Caesar (Bacchelli) 230
Tinísima (Poniatowska) 279
La vieja sirena (Sampedro) 275
The Volcano Lover (Sontag) 277
history
Abraham Lincoln: The War Years (Sandburg) 206
Across the Wide Missouri (DeVoto) 216
The Age of Jackson (Schlesinger) 213
The Age of Reform (Hofstadter) 226
American Education: The National Experience, 1783–1876 (Cremin) 260
The American Renaissance (Matthiessen) 208
The American Revolution—A Constitutional Interpretation (McIlwain) 185
The Americans: Democratic Experience (Boorstein) 252

Anabasis (Xenophon) 2
Annales (Tacitus) 5
Annales Ecclesiastici (Baronius) 43
The Annals of Italy (Muratori) 77
Art and Life in America (Larkin) 218
The Atlantic Migration, 1607–1860 (Hansen) 208
Banks and Politics in America (Hammond) 229
The Battle Cry of Freedom: The Civil War Era (McPherson) 272
Been in the Storm So Long (Litwack) 259
Bellus Helveticum (Pirkheimer) 30
Between War and Peace: The Potsdam Conference (Feis) 233
Charles XII (Voltaire) 68
Chronicles (Holinshed) 41
Citizens: A Chronicle of the French Revolution (Shama) 272
The Colonial Period of American History (Andrews) 200
The Coming of the War, 1914 (Van Tyne) 194
Conquest: Montezuma, Cortes and the Fall of Old Mexico (Thomas) 282
The Constitutional History of the United States (McLaughlin) 201
The Country of Rembrandt (Busken Huet) 134
Danish History (Saxo Grammaticus) 13
The Decline of the West (Spengler) 177
Discourse on Universal History (Bossuet) 63
The Disruption of American Democracy (Nichols) 217
A Distant Mirror: The Calamitous Fourteenth Century (Tuchman) 257
The Dred Scott Case (Fehrenbacher) 258
Ecclesiastical History of the English Nation (Bede) 13, 14, 19
Epitome Rerum Germanicarum (Wempfeling) 34
The Era of Good Feelings (Dangerfield) 222
Exploration and Empire: The Explorer and the Scientist in the Winning of the American West (Goetzmann) 242
F. L. Vek (Jirásek) 139
The Fate of Liberty Abraham Lincoln and Civil Liberties (Neely) 277
Fire in the Lake: The Vietnamese and the Americans in Vietnam (Fitzgerald) 250
The Flowering of New England (Brooks) 201, 203
Freedom from Fear: American People in Depression and War, 1929–1945 (Kennedy) 295
Germania (Tacitus) 5
The Glories of Querétaro (Sigüenza y Góngora) 63
Gotham: A History of New York City to 1898 (Burrows, Wallace) 292

Great River: The Rio Grande in North American History (Horgan) 225
The Greenback Era (Unger) 239
The Growth of American Thought (Curti) 211
The Guns of August (Tuchman) 235
Hamkampu (Arai) 70
The Heavens and the Earth: A Political History of the Space Age (McDougall) 267
Historiae (Tacitus) 5
History (Herodotus) 3
A History of American Magazines (Mott) 205
The History of New England (Adams) 182
A History of New York (Irving) 98
A History of Pugachov (Pushkin) 90
The History of Russia (Karamzin) 100
A History of the American Frontier (Paxson) 186
A History of the Civil War (Rhodes) 177
The History of the Decline and Fall of the Roman Empire (Gibbon) 83
History of the French Revolution (Carlyle) 109
History of the Peloponnesian War (Thucydides) 3
History of the Thirty Years' War (Schiller) 68
A History of the United States (Channing) 187
The History of the Village of Gorykhina (Pushkin) 90
The History of the World (Raleigh) 52
The Ideological Origins of the American Revolution (Bailyn) 244
The Impending Crisis (Potter) 255
In Our Image: America's Empire in the Philippines (Karnow) 273
In the Days of McKinley (Leech) 232
Jefferson and His Time (Malone) 253
A Journal of the Plague Year (Defoe) 73
Landscape and Memory (Schama) 284
Larry of Santa Fe (Horgan) 254
The Launching of American Modern Science, 1846–1876 (Bruce) 270
The Life of Julius Agricola (Tacitus) 5
Life of the Mind in America (Miller) 241
The Lives of the Most Eminent Italian Architects, Painters and Sculptors (Vasari) 38
Main Currents in American Thought (Parrington) 189, 190
Mary Chestnut's Civil War (Woodward) 261
The Methods of History (Bodin) 40
My Experiences in the World War (Pershing) 195
Neither Black Nor White (Degler) 249

No Ordinary Time: Franklin and Eleanor Roosevelt: The Home Front in World War II (Goodwin) 283
The Nuremberg Chronicle (Schedel) 29
Occidental Paradise (Sigüenza y Góngora) 64
The Old Northwest, Pioneer Period, 1815–1840 (Buley) 219
On Heroes, Hero-Worship and the Heroic in History (Carlyle) 112
The Organization and Administration of the Union Army, 1861–1865 (Shannon) 191
Original Meanings: Politics and Ideas in the Making of the Constitution (Rakove) 288
Origins of the Fifth Amendment (Levy) 245
The Outline of History (Wells) 180
Parting the Waters: America in the King Years, 1954–1963 (Branch) 272
Past Lucknow (Sharar) 173
Paul Revere and the World He Lived In (Forbes) 210
People of Paradox: An Inquiry Concerning the Origins of American Civilization (Kammen) 250
The People's Choice (Agar) 198
Pickney's Treaty (Bemis) 189
Prophets of Regulation (McCraw) 265
Puritan Village: The Formation of a New England Town (Powell) 238
The Radicalism of the American Revolution (Wood) 279
Rebellion in the Backlands (Cunha) 160
The Republican Era, 1869–1901 (White) 230
Reveille in Washington (Leech) 209
The Rise and Fall of the Third Reich (Shirer) 232
The Rise of the Dutch Republic (Motley) 119
The Road to Reunion, 1856–1900 (Buck) 204
Roosevelt, the Soldier of Freedom (Burns) 248
Roots (Brathwaite) 267
Russia Leaves the War: Soviet-American Relations, 1917–1920 (Kennan) 228
Scientists Against Time (Baxter) 214
Sea of Histories (Pérez de Guzmán) 35
Le Siècle de Louis XIV (Voltaire) 68
The Significance of Sections in American History (Turner) 197
A Stillness at Appomattox (Catton) 223, 231
A Study of History (Toynbee) 199
Summer for the Gods: The Scopes Trial and America's Continuing Debate over Science and Religion (Larson) 290
The Supreme Court in United States History (Adams) 183

The Transformation of Virginia, 1740–1790 (Isaac) 262

The Triumphant Empire, Thunder Clouds in the West (Gibson) 235

Unfinished Business (Bonsal) 212

The Uprooted (Handlin) 221

The Victory at Sea (Sims) 181

The Visible Hand: The Managerial Revolution in American Business (Chandler) 256

Voyages to the West: A Passage in the Peopling of America on the Eve of the Revolution (Bailyn) 268

The War of Independence (Van Tyne) 193

The War with Mexico (Smith) 179

The Warrior Queens (Fraser) 272

Washington, Village and Capital, 1800–1878 (Green) 236

William Cooper's Town: Power and Persuasion on the Frontier of the Early American Republic (Taylor) 286

Zemah David (Gans) 44

humorous piece *See also* comedy

Are You a Bromide? (Burgess) 164

The Education of Hyman Kaplan (Kaplan) 203

My Ten Years in a Quandary and How They Grew (Benchley) 201

hymn

"Hymn to Intellectual Beauty" (Shelley) 93, 100

"Hymn to Liberty" (Solomos) 103

Hymnes (Ronsard) 33, 39

Hymns (Callimachus) 4

Hymns to the Night (Novalis) 95

"Lead, Kindly Light" (Newman) 107

Spiritual Chorus (Kingo) 62

J

journal *See* diary

L

lecture

The Varieties of Religious Experience (James) 160

letter *See also* epistolary essay; epistolary novel; epistolary poem

"J'Accuse" (Zola) 148

One-Minute Letters (Örkény) 280

limerick

Book of Nonsense (Lear) 114

literary criticism

The Air Conditioned Nightmare (Miller) 212

America's Coming of Age (Brooks) 174

An Apologie for Poetrie (Sidney) 42

Axel's Castle (Wilson) 194

Blindness and Insight: Essays in the Rhetoric of Contemporary Criticism (De Man) 249

The Book of J (Bloom) 273

For a New Novel (Robbe-Grillet) 237

A Grammar of Motives (Little) 212

The Great Tradition (Leavis) 216

Guide to Kulchur (Pound) 204

The Iliad; or, The Poem of Force (Weil) 207

In Defense of Reason (Winters) 215

Language and Silence: Essays on Language, Literature and the Inhuman (Steiner) 243

Love and Death in the American Novel (Fiedler) 232

The Mirror and the Lamp: Romantic Theory and Critical Tradition (Abrams) 222

The New Criticism (Ransom) 208

On Native Grounds (Kazin) 209

Patriotic Gore (Wilson) 235

The Sacred Wood (Eliot) 152

Seven Types of Ambiguity: A Study of Its Effects on English Verse (Empson) 193

Shakespearean Tragedy (Bradley) 162

The Spirit of Romance (Pound) 168

The Three Voices of Poetry (Eliot) 222

The Use of Poetry and the Use of Criticism (Eliot) 152

The Wound and the Bow (Wilson) 208

A Writer's American: Landscape in Literature (Kazin) 270

M

manifesto

On the Origin of Species by Means of Natural Selection (Darwin) 121

The Second Sex (Beauvoir) 218

A Vindication of the Rights of Woman (Wollstonecraft) 86

manual

The Elements of Style (Strunk, White) 231

The Transmission of the Flower of Acting Style (Zeami Motokiyo) 15

masque

Alfred (Thomson and Mallet) 76

Arcades (Milton) 55

Comus (Milton) 48, 55

The Tragedie of Philotas (Daniel) 50

mathematics

Principia Mathematica (Russell, Whitehead) 168

maxim

The Book Beside Me (Reverdy) 216

The Horsehair Glove (Reverdy) 189

Maxims (La Rochefoucauld) 60

Solitary Thoughts (Rozanov) 171

meditative writing

The Broken Wings (Gibran) 182

The Forerunner (Gibran) 179

The Life of the Bee (Maeterlinck) 159

The Madman (Gibran) 177

A Molna Elegy (Ekelof) 233

The Prophet (Gibran) 184

The Rights of Desire (Brink) 296

Waiting for God (Weil) 219

melodrama

The Castle Spectre (Lewis) 88

The Corsican Brothers (Boucicault) 115

The Dog of Montargis; or, The Forest of Bundy (Pixérécourt) 99

Salome (Wilde) 143

memoir *See* autobiography

monologue

Lucretius (Tennyson) 126

Prince Hohensteil-Schwangau (Browning) 128

Rabbi Ben Ezra (Browning) 124

The Ring and the Book (Browning) 126

Tithonus (Tennyson) 121

morality play

Auto de la Barca de la Gloria (Vicente) 35

Auto de la Barca do Purgatorio (Vicente) 35

Auto de la Barca (Vicente) 35

Everyman 13, 35

Filodemo (Camões) 32

Magnyfycens (Skelton) 35

mystery novel

Casino Royale (Fleming) 222

The Circular Staircase (Rinehart) 166

City of Glass (Auster) 269

Crónica sentimental en rojo (Ledesma) 265

Death on the Nile (Christie) 203

Ghosts (Auster) 269

The Hound of the Baskervilles (Doyle) 159

The Locked Room (Auster) 269

The Lodger (Lowndes) 172

The Murder of Roger Ackroyd (Christie) 188

Murder on the Orient Express (Christie) 197

The Mysterious Affair at Styles (Christie) 180

The New York Trilogy (Auster) 269

The Thirty-Nine Steps (Buchan) 174

The Valley of Fear (Doyle) 174

Witness for the Prosecution (Christie) 222

mythography

The Hero with a Thousand Faces (Campbell) 217

On the Genealogy of the Gods of the Gentiles (Boccaccio) 14

N

narrative *See* autobiographical narrative; dramatic narrative

narrative poem

"The Death of a Hired Man" (Frost) 173

narrative sketch

The People of the Abyss (London) 161

nonfiction *See also* biography; history; prose

And Their Children After Them (Maharidge, Williamson) 273

Annals of the Former World (McPhee) 292

Anti-Intellectualism in American Life (Hofstadter) 238

The Ants (Holldobler, Wilson) 275

The Armies of the Night (Mailer) 245

Ashes to Ashes: America's Hundred Year Cigarette War, the Public

Health and the Unabashed Triumph of Philip Morris (Kluger) 288

The Beak of the Finch: A Story of Evolution in Our Time (Weiner) 283

Beautiful Swimmers (Warner) 255

A Bright Shining Lie: John Paul Vann and America in Vietnam (Sheehand) 272

Brutus (Cicero) 4

Children of Crisis (Coles) 250

Common Ground: A Turbulent Decade in the Lives of Three American Families (Lukas) 267

The Dance of Death (Becker) 252

The Dragons of Eden (Sagan) 256

Embracing Defeat: Japan in the Wake of World War II (Dower) 295

Fin-de-Siècle Vienna: Politics and Culture (Schorske) 260

Gandhi's Truth: On the Origins of Militant Nonviolence (Erikson) 247

Gödel, Escher, Bach: An Eternal Golden Braid (Hofstadter) 259

The Good War (Terkel) 265

Guns, Germs and Steel: The Fates of Human Societies (Diamond) 290

The Guns of August (Tuchman) 236

The Haunted Land: Facing Europe's Ghosts After Communism (Rosenberg) 286

In the Draft (Mándy) 280

Is There No Place on Earth for Me? (Sheehan) 262

The Law of War and Peace (Grotius) 53

Lenin's Tomb: The Last Days of the Soviet Empire (Remnick) 281

The Life of Solitude (Petrarch) 14, 25

Lincoln at Gettysburg (Wills) 279

A Little Organum for the Theater (Brecht) 154

The Making of the Atomic Bomb (Rhodes) 270

The Making of the President, 1960 (White) 235

Move Your Shadow (Lelyveld) 267

O Strange New World (Jones) 239

On Duties (Cicero) 4

On Human Nature (Wilson) 258

On Religious Idleness (Petrarch) 14, 25

On the Different Conceptions of the Chief Good and Evil (Cicero) 4

On the Nature of Gods (Cicero) 4

On the Orator (Cicero) 4, 10

On the Origin of Species (Darwin) 121

Orator (Cicero) 4

The Pilgrim at Tinker Creek (Dillard) 253

Present at the Creation: My Years in the State Department (Acheson) 247

The Prize: The Epic Quest for Oil (Yergin) 277

The Problem of Slavery in Western Culture (Davis) 242

nonfiction (continued)
 The Rising Sun (Toland) 248
 Rousseau and Revolution (Durant)
  244
 The Second Sex (Beauvoir) 218
 Social Transformation of American
  Medicine (Starr) 263
 The Soul of a New Machine (Kid-
  der) 261
 Stilwell and the American Experi-
  ence in China, 1911–45 (Tuch-
  man) 249
 Ten Days That Shook the World
  (Reed) 178
 Tazkerat Osh-sho-Ara (Daulat-
  shah) 28
 The Tusculan Disputations (Ci-
  cero) 4
 A Vindication of the Rights of
  Women (Wollstonecraft) 86
 War and People (Wang) 288
 Why Survive? Being Old in Amer-
  ica (Butler) 254
 Wondering Through Winter
  (Teale) 241
 X-Ray of the Pampa (Martínez
  Estrada) 198
novel See also antinovel; autobiographical novel; biographical novel;
 crime novel; epistolary novel; fan-
 tasy; historical novel; mystery novel;
 novella; picaresque novel; roman à
 clef; roman-fleuve; science fiction;
 spy novel; thriller; tropism; western
 novel
 The 42nd Parallel (Dos Passos) 193
 The 120 Days of Sodom (Sade) 85
 1,001 Years of Nostalgia (Boudje-
  dra) 258
 1876 (Vidal) 254
 1919 (Dos Passos) 196
 1984 (Orwell) 217
 A la salud de la serpiente (Sainz)
  277
 Aaron's Rod (Lawrence) 182
 The Abattoir (Echeverría) 128
 The Abbess of Crewe (Spark) 252
 The Abbot (Scott) 93, 102
 The Abduction (Kumin) 247
 Abdullah's Story (Abdullah) 116
 Abel Sánchez (Unamuno) 176
 The Able McLaughlins (Wilson)
  185
 Absalom, Absalom! (Faulkner)
  201
 Abschied von den Feinden (Jirgl)
  284
 Absence (Handke) 269
 The Absentee (Edgeworth) 98
 Abyss (Appelfeld) 280
 The Abyss (Yourcenar) 245
 L'Abyssin (Rufin) 288
 The Acacia (Simon) 272
 An Accidental Man (Murdoch)
  249
 Achados e perdidos (Garcia-Roza)
  291
 Achillea's Fiancé (Zei) 269
 Acquainted with the Night (Böll)
  223
 The Acrobat (Richler) 223
 Acropolis (Chacel) 265
 Across the River and into the Trees
  (Hemingway) 218
 Act of Darkness (King) 263
 Active Service (Crane) 149

Ad haSof (Shamir) 276
Ada (Nabokov) 155, 245
Adam, Where Art Thou? (Böll)
 219
Adam Bede (Eliot) 121
Adán Buenosayres (Marechal)
 217
Aden (Garat) 278
Adolphe (Constant) 100
Adriatico (Nigro) 291
Adventures of an Iron and a Boot
 (Petrushevskaya) 291
The Adventures of Augie March
 (Bellow) 222
The Adventures of Captain Single-
 ton (Defoe) 72
The Adventures of Ferdinand,
 Count Fathom (Smollett) 78
The Adventures of Harry Rich-
 mond (Meredith) 127
The Adventures of Huckleberry
 Finn (Twain) 92, 136
The Adventures of Nicholas Try-All
 (Krasicki) 83
The Adventures of Peregrine Pickle
 (Smollett) 78
The Adventures of Roderick Ran-
 dom (Smollett) 77
The Adventures of Tom Sawyer
 (Twain) 92, 131
Advise and Consent (Drury) 232
Afensang (Staalesen) 296
Afloat and Ashore (Cooper) 113
Africa, We Do Not Pay Attention
 to You (Matep) 227
The African Queen (Forester) 200
An African Tragedy (Dhlomo)
 191
African Witch (Cary) 201
After Julius (Howard) 240
After Rain (Trevor) 286
After the Divorce (Deledda) 160
Afternoon Men (Powell) 194
Against the Grain (Huysmans)
 136
Against the Wall (Jirásek) 144
Agar (Memmi) 225
Agatha Moudio's Sons (Bebey) 243
Agathon (Wieland) 80
The Age of Innocence (Wharton)
 179, 181
Agnes Grey (Brontë) 115
Agosto (Fonseca) 276
The Aguero Sisters (Garcia) 288
The Agunah (Grade) 234
Ahasuerus in Rome (Hamerling)
 125
Ahayat David (Kanuk) 274
Aimée (Rivière) 182
Alan Turing (Hochhuth) 269
Albany Cycle (Kennedy) 277
Albion Albion (Moravcevic) 285
Alcacer Quibir (Olinto) 289
The Alexandria Quartet (Durrell)
 228, 229, 232
The Algerine Captive; or, The Life
 and Adventures of Dr. Updike
 Underhill (Tyler) 87
Alias Grace (Atwood) 286
Alice Adams (Tarkington) 181, 182
Alice's Adventures in Wonderland
 (Carroll) 124
Aline, Queen of Golkonda (Bouf-
 flers) 80
All Green Shall Perish (Mallea)
 208

All in a Night (Cayrol) 224
All Men Are Mortals (Beauvoir)
 214
All Passion Spent (Sackville-West)
 194
All Quiet on the Western Front
 (Remarque) 192
All the Conspirators (Isherwood)
 190
All the King's Men (Warren) 213,
 214
All the Names (Saramago) 291
All the Pretty Horses (McCarthy)
 277
All Things Betray (Thomas) 218
Allah n'est pas oblige (Kourouma)
 296
Allan Quatermain (Haggard) 138
Allegra (Mallet-Joris) 255
Allegretto (Stigen) 284
Alleles (Heffner) 282
Un aller simple (Cauwelaert) 282
Alms for Oblivion (Raven) 238
Alnilam (Dickey) 268
Alone Among Men (Brzozoski)
 170
Alonso e i visionari (Ortese) 286
El alquimista impaciente (Silva)
 297
Altar of Victory (Bryusov) 172
Alton Locke, Tailor and Poet
 (Kingsley) 116
Am I Disturbing You? (Hébert)
 293
Am kurzeren Ende der Sonnenallee
 (Brussig) 293
Amalia: A Romance of the Argen-
 tine (Mármol) 134
El amargo don de la belleza (Moix)
 287
The Amazing Marriage (Mered-
 ith) 145
The Ambassadors (James) 91, 161
Amelia (Fielding) 78
The American (James) 91, 131
American Appetites (Oates) 270
An American Dream (Mailer) 240
American Pastoral (Roth) 288,
 290
The American Scene (James) 165
An American Tragedy (Dreiser)
 186
An American Visitor (Cary) 197
Amerika (Kafka) 152, 189
The Amethyst Ring (France) 149
La amigdalitis de Tarzán (Bryce
 Echenique) 294
Amongst Women (McGahern)
 274
Amor que faz o mundo girar
 (Quintella) 276
Amorina (Anderberg) 294
Amorous Confessions of Two Nuns
 (Koyo) 140
Amour noir (Noguez) 288
Amours sauvages (Beyala) 293
Amphitryon (Padilla) 296
Amrita (Jhabvala) 225
Amsterdam (McEwan) 290
Un an (Echenoz) 288
The Anatomy Lesson (Roth) 262
The Ancestors (Freytag) 129
Anchise (Desbiolles) 293
The Ancient Child (Momaday) 272
And Quiet Flows the Don
 (Sholokhov) 199

Andanda Math (Bannerjee) 134
The Andromeda Strain (Chrich-
 ton) 245
Un ange cornu ave des ailes de tole
 (Tremblay) 282
Angel in the House (Patmore) 118
Angel Landing (Hoffman) 259
The Angel of the Shadow (Lu-
 gones) 188
An Angel Offsides (Feric) 295
Angel Pavement (Priestley) 193
Angel Walk (Govier) 286
The Angel's Wink (Mallet-Joris)
 263
Angle of Repose (Stegner) 248, 249
Anielka (Taillandier) 293
Anil's Ghost (Ondaatje) 295
Anima mundi (Tamaro) 289
Animal Dreams (Kingsolver) 273
Animal Farm (Orwell) 212
Animal triste (Maron) 286
Ann Veronica (Wells) 167
Anna, Hanna, och Johanna (Fred-
 eriksson) 283
Anna and the King of Siam (Lan-
 don) 211
Anna Karenina (Tolstoy) 90, 130
Anna of the Five Towns (Bennett)
 160
Anne of Geierstein; or, The Maiden
 of the Mist (Scott) 105
En annen vei (Carling) 287
Annie John (Kincaid) 265
Annie Kilburn (Howells) 140
Anniversaries: From the Life of Ge-
 sine Cresspahl (Johnson) 248
El año del deluvio (Mendoza) 279
Los años de la serpiente (Ostornol)
 277
Another Part of the Wood (Bain-
 bridge) 244
Anschlag (Neumann) 293
Anthem (Rand) 204
Anthills of the Savannah (Achebe)
 269
Anti Kepler's Laws (Katz) 269
Antic Hay (Huxley) 184
The Antichrist (Broch) 195
Der Antiquar (Schertenlieb) 278
The Antiquary (Scott) 93, 100
Antiques Cabinet (Balzac) 91
Antonina; or, The Fall of Rome
 (Collins) 116
Any Old Iron (Burgess) 271
Any Woman's Blues (Jong) 272
An Apology for the Life of Mrs
 Shamela Andrews (Fielding) 76
The Apple in the Dark (Lispector)
 234
Appointment in Samarra
 (O'Hara) 198
The Apprenticeship of Duddy
 Kravitz (Richler) 228
Araucaima Mansion (Mutis) 251
L'arbre de rêve (Quiring) 269
Arcadia (Vega) 45
Arcodamore (De Carlo) 282
Ardiente paciencia (Skarmeta)
 266
Ardobiola (Yevtushenko) 265
Arena (Prem) 185
Argo (Theotokos) 202
Arithmetic in Love (Blest Gana)
 122
Army Chaplain Schmelzle's Jour-
 ney (Richter) 98

Around the Bedroom Wall: A Family Album (Woiwode) 253
Arrival and Departure (Koestler) 210
Arrowsmith (Lewis) 186, 187
The Artamonov Business (Gorky) 187
Artemenes; or, the Grand Cyrus (Scudéry) 58
Arthur Merwyn (Brown) 88
Arturo's Island (Morante) 228
As a Few Days (Shalev) 282
As I Lay Dying (Faulkner) 193
The Ascension (Bahr) 175
The Ascension (Konwicki) 237
El asesinato, el perdedor (Cela) 283
Ashes (Deledda) 162
Ashes and Diamonds (Andrzejewski) 217
Ashmat Shomeron (Mapu) 124
Ask the Flowers (Jakucho) 278
Aske (Brekke) 294
The Assassins (Oates) 253
The Assault (Mulisch) 261
Assignment in Brittany (MacInnes) 209
The Assistant (Malamud) 228
La astucia de la razón (Feinmann) 274
Asuntos de un hidalgo disoluto (Abad Faciolince) 283
At Daggers Drawn (Leskov) 127
At Heaven's Gate (Warren) 210
At Play in the Fields of the Lord (Matthiessen) 226
At 0 A.M. in Buenos Aires (Shu) 291
Atala (Chateaubriand) 95
Atheist (Mihardja) 218
Atlas de geografía humana (Grandes) 294
Atlas Shrugged (Rand) 228
Attack (Charasha) 191
Attesa sul mare (Biamonti) 282
Atticus (Hansen) 286
Au Soleil de Juillet (Adam) 161
Les aubes (Le) 296
August 1914 (Solzhenitsyn) 154, 249
The August Sleepwalker (Bei) 270
Aurora (Leiris) 214
The Autobiography of an Ex-Colored Man (Johnson) 171
The Autobiography of Miss Jane Pittman (Gaines) 248
Autobiography of Rhys Lewis (Owen) 137
Auto-da-Fé (Canetti) 200
The Autumn of the Patriarch (García Márquez) 254
Avadheshwari (Punekar) 269
Avarice House (Green) 188
An Avenue of Stone (Johnson) 215
Avishag (Schutz) 274
Avlosning (Ulven) 280
The Awakening (Chopin) 149
An Awfully Big Adventure (Bainbridge) 273
The Awkward Age (James) 91, 149
Ayala's Angel (Trollope) 134
Azul (Regas) 283
Babbitt (Lewis) 182
Babi Yar (Kuznetsov) 242
Babu du Montparnasse (Philippe) 159

Babylonian Wandering (Doblin) 199
Il bacio della Medusa (Mazzucco) 287
Back to Ina Damman (Vestdijk) 198
Badenheim 1939 (Appelfeld) 258
The Badgers (Leonov) 185
Bailey's Café (Naylor) 277
Baina al-Qasraym (Mahfouz) 226
Baldershawn (Stigen) 264
Balisand (Hergesheimer) 185
The Ballad of Typhoid Mary (Federspiel) 262
Balthazar (Durrell) 229
Bambi (Salten) 184
Band of Angels (Warren) 225, 226
Bang (Willumsen) 286
Bang the Drum Slowly (Harris) 226
The Banquet of Severo Arcangelo (Marechal) 240
Barabbas (Lagerkvist) 219
Barchester Towers (Trollope) 120
Barnaby Rudge (Dickens) 90, 112
Barnevakt (Bjornstad) 282
Barney's Version (Richler) 288
Barq al-Layl (Khurayyif) 233
The Barque Future (Lie) 129
A barragem (Moreira) 280
Barren Ground (Glasgow) 186
La bataille (Rambaud) 288
The Battle Lost and Won (Manning) 257
The Battle of Pharsalus (Simon) 246
Be Sure to Close Your Eyes (Hood) 280
The Bean Trees (Kingsolver) 270
The Bear (Faulkner) 200
Beatriz y los cuerpos celestes (Etxebarria) 292
Beau Geste (Wren) 185
Beauchampe (Simms) 112
The Beautiful and Damned (Fitzgerald) 182
Beautiful Days (Nobuo) 289
The Beautiful Ones Are Not Yet Born (Armah) 244
The Beautiful Visit (Howard) 219
Because It Is Bitter and Because It Is My Heart (Oates) 273
Bech: A Book (Updike) 247
Bech at Bay (Updike) 290
Bech Is Back (Updike) 261
The Bed (Tayama) 166
Before the Dawn (Toson) 200
Before the Rainy Season (Hoffmann) 271
Before the Storm (Fontane) 132
The Beggar (Karkavitsas) 149
The Beginning and the End (Mahfouz) 220
Behind the Scenes at the Museum (Atkinson) 286
Um beijo dado mais tarde (Ilansol) 276
Being Dead (Crace) 293
Being There (Kosinski) 247
Bel ami (Maupassant) 137
Belarmino and Apolonio (Pérez de Ayala) 181
Belinda (Edgeworth) 95
A Bell for Adano (Hersey) 211, 212
Bellefleur (Oates) 259

The Bells of Basel (Aragon) 199
Beloved (Morrison) 268, 270
The Beloved Returns (Mann) 152
A Bend in the River (Naipaul) 258
Bend Sinister (Nabokov) 155, 214
Ben-Hur: A Tale of the Christ (Wallace) 133
Benito Cereno (Melville) 119
Beretninger om beskyttelse (Hansen) 291
Berlin Alexanderplatz (Doblin) 192
The Berlin Stories (Isherwood) 205, 213
Betrayed by Rita Hayworth (Puig) 245
The Betrothed (Manzoni) 104
Better Than Wine (Rojas) 230
Between the Currents (Jirásek) 142
Between the Wars (Brandys) 217
Beware of Pity (Zweig) 204
The Big House (Dib) 221
The Big Money (Dos Passos) 201
The Big Rock Candy Mountain (Stegner) 210
Bikubers song (Grytten) 294
Billiards at Half-Past Nine (Böll) 231
Billy Bathgate (Doctorow) 272
Billy Budd, Foretopman (Melville) 185
Billy Sunday (Jones) 286
Bird Alone (O'Faolain) 202
The Bird and the White Table Cloth (Abrahamsen) 266
The Birds (Vesaas) 231
Birds of America (McCarthy) 248
Birdy (Wharton) 258
Bitte nicht sterben (Wohmann) 280
Det bla skapet och andra berattelser (Alfven) 294
Black Banners (Strindberg) 93, 165
Black Beauty (Sewell) 131
Black Box (Oz) 269
Black Dogs (McEwan) 278
The Black Dwarf (Scott) 93, 100
Black Gate (Arghezi) 193
Black Mischief (Waugh) 196
Black Narcissus (Godden) 205
The Black Prince (Murdoch) 251
The Black Rose (Montherlant) 245
The Black Sheep (Balzac) 91
Black Snow (Liu) 279
The Black Soul (O'Flaherty) 185
Black Swan (Hope) 269
The Black Swan (Mann) 152, 223
Black Thunder (Bontemps) 201
The Black Torches (Verhaeren) 141
Black Tulip (Dumas) 116
Blackie the Fool (Klabund) 177
Blasting and Bombardiering (Waugh) 203
Blaubarts Shatten (Hahn) 276
Bleak House (Dickens) 90, 117
Bless Me Ultima (Anaya) 250
Blesse, ronce noire (Combet) 284
The Blessing (Mitford) 220
The Blind Assassin (Atwood) 295
The Blind Owl (Hedāyat) 203
Blind Rose (Conscience) 116
Blindness (Saramago) 287
The Blithedale Romance (Hawthorne) 117

The Block (Aitmatov) 270
Blood and Sand (Blasco Ibáñez) 166
The Blood Oranges (Hawkes) 248
Blood Ties (Settle) 257
Blowing Sand/A Winter Journey (Kangro) 266
The Blue Afternoon (Boyd) 280
The Blue Angel (Mann) 163
The Blue Band (Kellerman) 204
The Blue Flowers (Queneau) 240
Bluebeard: A Tale (Frisch) 262
The Bluest Eye (Morrison) 247
The Boat (Hartley) 217
Bobinack (Johnson) 196
Boca do Inferno (Miranda) 274
Body and Soul (Conroy) 279
The Bog of Stars (O'Grady) 143
Bomarzo (Mujica Lainez) 236
The Bond (Borel) 240
Bone by Bone (Matthiessen) 293
The Bone People (Hulme) 263
The Bonfire of Vanities (Wolfe) 268
Bonfires (Alos) 239
Bonjour Tristesse (Sagan) 224
The Book About Absent People (Modarressi) 268
The Book and Brotherhood (Murdoch) 269
A Book of Common Prayer (Didion) 255
The Book of Daniel (Doctorow) 248
The Book of Kings (Thackara) 293
The Book of Laughter and Forgetting (Kundera) 258
Books Do Furnish a Room (Powell) 249
The Bookseller (Cohen) 280
The Border Trilogy (McCarthy) 290
Borderline (Hospital) 266
The Borg Family Papers (Gunnarsson) 171
Boris and Gleb (Buyda) 289
Born Brothers (Woiwode) 270
Born Guilty (Rojas) 220
Bosphorus Fortress (Gursel) 285
Boston Adventure (Stafford) 211
The Bostonians (James) 91, 137
Botchan: Master Darling (Natsume) 93, 164
The Bottom of the Glass (Ayala) 236
Bottomless (Velmar-Jankovic) 287
Box Man (Abe) 251
The Boys in the Back Room (Romains) 172
A Boy's Town (Howells) 141
Bozambo's Revenge: Colonialism Inside Out (Juminer) 245
Die Braut im Park (Quadflieg) 278
Brave New World (Huxley) 196
Brave New World Revisited (Huxley) 229
The Bravo (Cooper) 106
Bread and Fear (Savic) 278
Bread and Wine (Silone) 225
Bread Givers (Yezierska) 187
Breakfast of Champions: or, Goodby Blue Monday (Vonnegut) 251
Breakfast on Pluto (McCabe) 291

novel *(continued)*

The Breast (Roth) 250
Breathing Lessons (Tyler) 272
Brev til manen (Michael) 284
Brida (Coelho) 274
The Bridal Canopy (Agnon) 179
Bridal Veil (Shamir) 264
The Bride of Lammermoor (Scott) 93, 101
Brideshead Revisited (Waugh) 212
The Bridge of San Luis Rey (Wilder) 189, 190
The Bridge on the Drina (Andric) 217
The Bridge Over the River Kwai (Boulle) 221
The Bridges at Toko-Ri (Michener) 222
A Brief Life (Onetti) 219
Briefing for a Descent into Hell (Lessing) 249
Bright Day (Priestley) 213
The Brightness and the Blood (Aldecoa) 224
Brighton Rock (Greene) 154, 204
Bring Larks and Heroes (Keneally) 243
Broad and Alien Is the World (Alegría) 208
Broder Jacob (Stangerup) 275
Brodrene Henrikson (Enger) 296
Broke Heart Blues (Oates) 293
Broken April (Kadare) 261
The Brook Kerith (Moore) 175
Brother Asno (Barrios) 183
Brother to Dragons: A Tale in Verse and Voices (Warren) 222
Brotherhood (Jirásek) 149
Brotherly Love (Dexter) 275
Brothers and Sisters (Compton-Burnett) 192
The Brothers Ashkenazi (Singer) 202
The Brothers Karamazov (Dostoyevsky) 90, 133
Bruges, the Dead City (Rodenbach) 143
Bruno's Dream (Murdoch) 246
The Buccaneers (Wharton) 204
Die Buchhandlerin (Bohme) 293
Budda's Little Finger (Pelevin) 296
Buddenbrooks (Mann) 152, 159
Bullet Park (Cheever) 245
The Bullfight (Inoue) 218
The Bullfighters (Montherlant) 188
The Bulwark (Dreiser) 213
O buraco ne parede (Fonseca) 287
Het bureau (Voskuil) 288, 290
Burger's Daughter (Gordimer) 258
Burmese Days (Orwell) 199
The Burn (Aksyonov) 259
Burning (Johnson) 248
Burning Daylight (London) 168
A Burnt Child (Dagerman) 217
Burnt Metropolis (Otohiko) 287
Burnt to a Cinder (Shahnon) 240
A Burnt-Out Case (Greene) 154, 234
Burr (Vidal) 251
Burridge Unbound (Cumyn) 295
Butterfield 8 (O'Hara) 200
A Buyer's Market (Powell) 221
Buzón de tiempo (Benedetti) 294

By Love Possessed (Cozzens) 228
By the Open Sea (Strindberg) 141
Byen og verden (Hultberg) 279
Caballeros de fortuna (Landero) 283
Cabot Wright Begins (Purdy) 238
Los caciques (Azuela) 176
Cadillac Jack (McMurtry) 261
Caesar: Let the Dice Fly (McCullough) 288
The Cage (Azolsky) 289
La caída de Madrid (Chirbes) 297
The Caine Mutiny (Wouk) 220, 221
The Cairo Trilogy (Mahfouz) 226
Caisangzi (Ye) 295
Cakes and Ale (Maugham) 193
Calendar Histories (Graf) 192
The Call (Hauge) 213
Call at Corazon (Bowles) 270
Call for the Dead (Le Carré) 232
Call It Sleep (Roth) 198
Call Me Crimson (Kemal) 292
The Call of the Toad (Grass) 278
The Call of the Wild (London) 160
Callista (Newman) 119
Calunga (Lima) 200
La campana (Fuentes) 275
Canaan (Graça Aranha) 160
The Canadian Brothers (Richardson) 111
Cancer Ward (Solzhenitsyn) 154, 245
Candido: or a Dream Dreamed in Sicily (Sciascia) 256
Cannery Row (Steinbeck) 212
The Cannibal Galaxy (Ozick) 262
Cannibals and Missionaries (McCarthy) 258
Canone inverso (Maurensig) 286
Canopus in Argus: Archives (Lessing) 258
Can't Quit You, Baby (Douglas) 270
Le cant silencieux des chouettes (Bensoussan) 291
Cantare ne buio (Corti) 276
Canteiros de saturno (Machado) 278
Cape of Good Hopelessness (Martinek) 281
Cape Town Theatrical Props (Stockenstrom) 269
Capolas negras (Vallejo) 287
Caprice (Bowring) 269
Captain Fracasse (Gautier) 123
The Captains and Kings (Johnston) 250
Captains Courageous (Kipling) 147
The Captain's Daughter (Pushkin) 90, 109
The Captive (Proust) 184
Captivity Captive (Hall) 269
The Capuchin Tomb (Roth) 204
Carajicomedia (Goytisolo) 296
"Caravans Are Still Marching" (Kaputikian) 238
Il cardillo addorlorato (Ortese) 280
Cargo of Orchids (Musgrove) 295
Carl and Anna (Frank) 188
Carmen (Mérimée) 114
Carnival and Lent (Nowakowski) 274
The Carnival Season (Wang) 295

Carossa (Marabini) 274
Carpenter's Gothic (Gaddis) 267
Carrot Top (Renard) 144
Cartas cruzadas (Jaramillo Agudelo) 285
La carujada (Romero) 275
A casa a nort-est (Maldini) 278
A casa da cabeça de cavalo (Gersao) 287
Casanova (Miller) 290
Casanova's Chinese Restaurant (Powell) 232
The Case of Sergeant Grischa (Zweig) 189
Casimir mene la grande (Ormesson) 288
Caspar Hauser (Wasserman) 166
Cass Timberlane (Lewis) 212
The Cassock (Delblanc) 237
Cast a Cold Eye (McCarthy) 219
Castle Dangerous (Scott) 106
The Castle (Kafka) 152, 188
The Castle of Argol (Gracq) 204
The Castle of Crossed Destinies (Calvino) 251
The Castle of Otranto (Walpole) 80
Castle Rackrent (Edgeworth) 95
The Castrati (Delblanc) 254
A Casual Brutality (Bissoondath) 272
The Cat (Colette) 197
Cat and Mouse (Grass) 234
Catch-22 (Heller) 233
The Catcher in the Rye (Salinger) 220
Cathedral Folk (Leskov) 129
La Cathédrale (Huysmans) 148
Catherine (Thackeray) 111
The Catherine Wheel (Stafford) 221
Cat's Cradle (Vonnegut) 237
Cat's Eye (Atwood) 271
The Cave (Warren) 230
The Cave in the Desert (Gyllensten) 252
Cecilia, or Memoirs of an Heiress (Burkey) 84
Cement (Gladkhov) 187
The Centaur (Updike) 237
Centennial (Michener) 252
The Centennial Sea-Wolf (Wang) 290
C'est tout (Duras) 284
C'etait toute une vie (Bon) 284
Chaim Lederer's Return (Asch) 190
The Chainbearer (Cooper) 114
Chaka (Mofolo) 195
Les champs d'honneur (Rouaud) 274
Chance (Conrad) 172
A Chance Acquaintance (Howells) 129
Chandos (Ouida) 125
A Change of Skin (Fuentes) 243
The Chant of Jimmie Blacksmith (Keneally) 250
Chariot of Wrath (Leonov) 212
Charlemont (Simms) 119
Charles: An Historical Romance (Mofolo) 186
A Charmed Life (McCarthy) 225
Charming Billy (McDermott) 290
The Charterhouse of Parma (Stendhal) 111

La chasseur zero (Roze) 286
The Chaste Joseph (Grimmelshausen) 61
Chat Show (White) 269
Cheri (Colette) 180
Cherubin Hammer und Cherubin Hammer (Bichsel) 293
Chesapeake (Michener) 257
Le Chevalier des touches (Barbey d'Aurevilly) 124
The Chief (Mann) 187
Chief of the Honorable Minister (Aluko) 247
The Chieftain's Daughter (Chatterjee) 124
The Child at the Balustrade (Boylesve) 161
The Child Bordered with Dreams (Hébert) 278
A Child of All Nations (Tur) 259
A Child of the Kudiyas (Karanta) 220
The Child of the Parish (Ebner-Eschenbach) 138
Childhood Friend (Bashir) 211
Childhood Years of Grandson Bagrov (Aksakov) 120
Children of Chaos (Goytisolo) 226
The Children of Death (Babits) 189
The Children of Pleasure (D'Annunzio) 148
Children of the Arbat (Rybakov) 272
Children of the Black Sabbath (Hébert) 254
The Children of the Earth (Queneau) 204
Children of the Game (Cocteau) 192
Children of the Mist (Phillpotts) 148
The Children of the New Forest (Marryat) 115
Children of the World (Heyse) 129
Children of Violence (Lessing) 223, 229
Children of Wrath: A Hired Man's Saga (Aakjaer) 162
Childworld (Oates) 254
The Chill of the Sun (Cayrol) 237
Chimera (Barth) 250
La chimera (Vassalli) 274
The Chimes (Dickens) 113
Chlopi (Reymont) 162
A Choice of Enemies (Richler) 228
Chosen Country (Dos Passos) 220
The Chosen Place, the Timeless People (Marshall) 245
Les Chouans (Balzac) 91, 105
Christ and Antichrist (Merezhkovsky) 146
Christ Stopped at Eboli (Levi) 213
Christianity at a Glacier (Laxness) 245
Christie Johnstone (Reade) 118
A Christmas Carol (Dickens) 90, 113
The Christmas Tree (Johnston) 260
Christopher (Drayton) 231
Christopher Unbound (Fuentes) 270
Christus shel haDagim (Hoffmann) 276

The Chrome Suite (Birdsell) 278

The Chronicle of a Death Foretold (García Márquez) 261

Chronicle of Loneliness (Ben Jelloun) 255

The Chronicle of the Screw Turning Bird (Murakami) 284

Chronique des Pasquier (Duhamel) 193

The Chute (Camus) 155

The Cider House Rules (Irving) 265

I cieli di vetro (Conti) 293

El cielo dividido (Roffe) 287

Cinnamoncandy (Ahlin) 223

Cinq-Mars (Vigny) 104

The Circle (Maugham) 181

The Circle of Reason (Ghosh) 267

Circles on the Water (Semolic) 296

Los círculos del tiempo (Sampeda) 281

The Circus Animals (Plunkett) 274

The Citadel (Cronin) 203

Citations About a Revolution (Ferreira) 265

Cities of the Interior (Nin) 231

Cities of the Plain (McCarthy) 290

Cities of the Plain (Proust) 181

La città del dotor Malaguì (Pazzi) 280

City Heights (Robles) 216

The City of Marvels (Mendoza) 271

Clara Howard (Brown) 95

La classe de neige (Carrère) 284

Claude Gueux (Hugo) 108

The Clay Machine Gun (Pelevin) 294

The Clayhanger Family (Bennett) 186

Clea (Durrell) 232

Clélie: Histoire romaine (Scudéry) 59

Cleng Peerson (Hauge) 244

Clock Without Hands (McCullers) 233

A Clockwork Orange (Burgess) 235

The Clockwork Testament (Burgess) 252

The Cloister and the Hearth (Reade) 122

Close Quarters (Golding) 269

Close to the Sun Again (Callaghan) 256

The Closed Down Theater (Okudzhava) 283

The Closed Garden (Green) 189

Closely Watched Trains (Hrahbel) 240

Closing Time (Heller) 282

Clouds (Pontoppidan) 141

Clouds (Tsalka) 282

Cloudsplitter (Banks) 290

The Clown (Böll) 237

The Clown and His Daughter (Adivar) 201

Cocksure (Richler) 244

Cocuyo (Sardy) 275

Coda (Astley) 282

Coeval Games (Oe) 258

A Coffin for Demetrios (Ambler) 205

Cold Comfort Farm (Gibbons) 196

Cold Mountain (Frazier) 288

Colette (Lustig) 277

Collages (Nin) 238

A Collective Notebook (Morozov) 294

The Collector (Fowles) 237

Colomba (Mérimée) 111

Color of Blood (García Calderón) 195

The Color Purple (Walker) 261, 262

The Colossus of Maroussi (Miller) 205

Come Back to Erin (O'Faolain) 207

The Comedians (Greene) 154, 241

The Comedienne (Reymont) 146

Comedy of Calisto and Melibea (Rojas) 34

The Comforters (Spark) 228

Coming Up for Air (Orwell) 205

Comme des anges (Boyer) 282

Comme ton père (Le Touze) 282

The Companions of Vardan (Demirtichian) 210

Compassion (Pérez Galdós) 147

Compulsion (Levin) 226

The Condor Passes (Grau) 248

A Confederacy of Dunces (Toole) 260

The Confederates (Keneally) 258

La conference de Cintegabelle (Salvayre) 293

Confessions of a Mask (Mishima) 218

The Confessions of Josef Baisz (Jacobson) 256

The Confessions of Mr. K. (Brackman) 265

The Confessions of Nat Turner (Styron) 243, 244

The Confidence Man (Melville) 120

Confidence pour confidence (Constant) 291

The Confidential Agent (Greene) 154, 205

The Conformist (Moravia) 220

A confraria das espadas (Fonseca) 294

Coningsby (Disraeli) 113

A Connecticut Yankee in King Arthur's Court (Twain) 92, 140

Conrad der Leutnant (Spitteler) 148

The Conscience of the Rich (Snow) 229

The Conscript (Conscience) 116

Consenting Adult (Hobson) 253

The Conservationist (Gordimer) 252

Consider This, Señora (Doerr) 279

Constance (Bazin) 221

Constancia y otras novelas para vírgenes (Fuentes) 275

As contadoras de historias (Botelho) 294

The Contenders (Wain) 229

Contending Forces (Hopkins) 158

La conversation (Nobecourt) 291

The Conversion (Appelfeld) 291

Coolie (Anand) 202

Coonardoo: The Well in the Shadow (Prichard) 192

Corazón tan blanco (Marías) 279

Corinne (Staël) 97

Cork Street, Next to Hatter's (Johnson) 240

Coronation (Donoso) 228

Les corps celestes (Brehal) 280

Correction (Bernhard) 254

The Cossacks (Tolstoy) 90, 123

The Count of Monte Cristo (Dumas père) 113

The Count of Talavera (Lennep) 111

Count Robert of Paris (Scott) 106

The Counterfeiters (Gide) 188

The Counterlife (Roth) 268

Countess Faustine (Hahn-Hahn) 112

The Country Doctor (Balzac) 91, 107

Country of My Skull (Krog) 293

The Country of the Pointed Firs (Jewett) 146

The Country Waif (Sand) 115

The Coup (Updike) 254

Couples (Updike) 244

The Court of Miracles (Valle-Inclán) 189

The Courtyard (Lvov) 272

Cousin Basilio (Eça de Queirós) 132

Cousin Bette (Balzac) 91, 114

Cousin Pons (Balzac) 91, 115

Cousin Rosamund (West) 265

The Crack-Up (Fitzgerald) 212

The Craft (Dovlatov) 266

Cranford (Gaskell) 117

The Crater (Cooper) 115

The Cream of the Jest (Cabell) 176

Creation (Vidal) 260

Crick Crack Monkey (Hodge) 247

Crime and Punishment (Dostoyevsky) 90, 125

A Crime in the Neighborhood (Berne) 293

The Crime of Olga Arbyelina (Makine) 293

The Crime of Sylvestre Bonnard (France) 134

The Crime of Writing (Lapid) 291

El Crimen del cine Oriente (Tomeo) 285

A Cripple in Love (Lehtonen) 182

The Crisis (Churchill) 159

The Crocodile (Lomami-Tshibamba) 216

Crome Yellow (Huxley) 181

Crooked Paths (Franko) 158

Cross Channel (Barnes) 286

The Crossing (McCarthy) 282

Crossing River (Phillips) 280

Crotchet Castle (Peacock) 106

The Crowning of Spring (Simon) 224

The Cruel Sea (Montserrat) 220

The Cruise of the Snark (London) 169

La cruz en la espada (Luján) 287

Cry, the Beloved Country (Paton) 216

Cry of the Rain Bird (Bird) 284

The Crying of Lot 49 (Pynchon) 241

The Crystal Frontier (Fuentes) 287

Los cuadernos de don Rigoberto (Vargas Llosa) 289

La cuadratura del círculo (Pombo) 294

The Cubs, and Other Stories (Vargas Llosa) 243

Cuisine Novella (Laurent) 269

The Cult of the Self (Barres) 139

The Cunning Man (Davies) 282

The Cupboard (Tremain) 260

The Cure for Death by Lightning (Anderson-Dargat) 286

The Curly-Haired Lieutenant (Muraveva) 283

Curriculum Vitae (Spark) 278

The Custodian of the Divan (Jamalzadeh) 214

The Custom of the Country (Wharton) 172

The Cutter and Captain Shigemoto's Mother (Tanizaki) 218

The Cyclone (Asturias) 219

The Cypresses Believe in God (Gironella) 223

Daily Bread (Boylesve) 159

The Daisy Chain (Yonge) 119

Daisy Miller (James) 91, 132

Damascus Gate (Stone) 290

Dame (Sudermann) 138

The Damsel of Darien (Simms) 110

The Dance of Death (Kellerman) 216

A Dance to the Beginning of Time (Burgess) 220

Dance to the Music of Time (Powell) 220, 221, 235, 241, 244, 249

The Danger Tree (Manning) 256

Dangerous Tales (Altan) 287

The Dangling Man (Bellow) 211

Daniel Deronda (Eliot) 131

Daniel Martin (Fowles) 256

Dans ces bras-la (Laurens) 296

The Daring Young Man on the Flying Trapeze (Saroyan) 198

The Dark Angel (Waltari) 221

The Dark Journey (Green) 192

Dark Painting (Hiroshi) 214

Dark Palace (Moorhouse) 295

The Dark Philosophers (Thomas) 213

Darkness (Jirásek) 174

Darkness at Noon (Koestler) 207

The Darkness at the Top (Pérez de Ayala) 165

Daughter Mine (Gold) 295

Daughter of Fire (Ikromi) 236

Daughter of Fortune (Allende) 294

The Daughters of Calvary (Combescot) 276

Daughters of the House (Roberts) 278

David Bele (Raffi) 133

David Copperfield (Dickens) 90, 116

David Harum: A Story of American Life (Westcott) 148

Dawn on Our Darkness (Robles) 221

The Day Before Yesterday (Agnon) 216

Day Home, Night Home (Tokarczuk) 294

The Day Lasts More Than a Hundred Years (Aitmatov) 274

novel *(continued)*

The Day of the Locust (West) 205
The Day of the Scorpions (Scott) 244
A Day on the Ground (Wispelaere) 247, 254
Days Like Arrows (Marechal) 188
Days of Contempt (Malraux) 200
The Days of His Grace (Johnson) 233
Days of Hope (Malraux) 203
De coeur et de l'affection (Teboul) 282
De Guerre lasse (Sagan) 266
De Silva (Harris) 256
The Dead Father (Barthelme) 253
Dead Fire (Rego) 211
A Dead Man in Deptford (Burgess) 280
Dead Men's Watches (Hood) 284
Dead Souls (Gogol) 91, 112
The Dean's December (Bellow) 261
Dear Mr. Kawabata (ad-Daif) 284
Death, Sleep and the Traveler (Hawkes) 252
Death and the Little Girl (Onetti) 252
Death as a World of Life (Ayala) 230
Death by Seconds (Brousek) 284
Death Comes to the Archbishop (Cather) 189
Death in the Afternoon (Hemingway) 153, 196
A Death in the Family (Agee) 228, 229
Death in Venice (Mann) 152, 171
Death of a Hero (Aldington) 192
Death of a Nobody (Romains) 170
The Death of the Author (Adair) 278
The Death of the Heart (Bowen) 204
The Death of the Tenant Farmer, Ignaz Hajek (Haslinger) 266
The Death of Virgil (Broch) 212
Death on the Installment Plan (Céline) 202
The Death Ship (Traven) 188
Debit and Credit (Freytag) 119
Deborah et les anges dissipés (Jacques) 276
December the Fourteenth (Mereazhkovsky) 177
Deception (Roth) 273
El décimo infierno (Giardinelli) 294
La declaration (Salvayre) 274
Decline and Fall (Waugh) 190
The Deemster (Caine) 138
Deep River (Arguedas) 230
Deep River (Endo) 280
The Deeps of Deliverance (Eeden) 158
The Deer Park (Mailer) 225
Deerbrook (Martineau) 111
The Deerslayer (Cooper) 111
The Defense (Nabokov) 155, 193
Degrees (Butor) 232
Delphine (Staël) 96
Delta Wedding (Welty) 211, 213
The Deluge (Sienkiewicz) 138

La demarche du crabe (LaRue) 284
La démence du boxeur (Weyergans) 278
Demian (Hesse) 178
Democracy (Didion) 264
The Demon (Lermontov) 112
The Demon of Good (Montherlant) 203
The Demons (Doderer) 227
Demos (Gissing) 137
Denied a Country (Bang) 164
The Deptford Trilogy (Davies) 247, 250, 253
Der Golem (Meyrink) 174
Derangement (Bernhard) 243
La dérive des sentiments (Simon) 276
Des anges mineurs (Volodine) 293
The Descendants (Immermann) 109
Descendants of Cain (Arishima) 176
Desert (Le Clezio) 259
The Desert (Memmi) 256
The Desert of Love (Mauriac) 218
Desert of the Heart (Rule) 238
Deserted Cities (Agustín) 262
The Deserter (Abush) 286
Desire's Baby (Chopin) 147
Despair (Nabokov) 155
Desperate Remedies (Hardy) 128
The Destinies of Darcy Dancer, Gentleman (Donleavy) 256
Destroy, She Said (Duras) 246
Determined Step (Kerbabayev) 207
Deveroux (Bulwer-Lytton) 105
The Devil in the Flesh (Radiguet) 184
The Devil to Pay in the Backlands (Rosa) 227
The Devil Upon Two Sticks (Lesage) 71
The Devil Within (Ali) 207
The Devil's Advocate (West) 231
The Devil's Pool (Sand) 114
The Dharma Bums (Kerouac) 229
Di vento e di fuoco (Pressburger) 296
El diablo cojuelo (Vélez de Guevara) 57
Diabolus in musica (Apperry) 296
Diana: The Goddess Who Hunts Alone (Fuentes) 283
Diana of the Crossways (Meredith) 137
Diario de 360° (Goytisolo) 296
Diario de Andrés Fava (Cortázar) 285
Diary of a Country Priest (Bernanos) 202
Diary of a Mad Old Man (Tanizaki) 234
Diary of the War of the Pig (Bioy Casares) 246
Días contados (Madrid) 281
Dictionary of the Khazars (Pavic) 271
Dimdim (Shamo) 245
El dios dormido (Rubio) 292
The Discipline (Bourget) 140
Discovering Elijah (Yizhar) 293
The Discovery of Heaven (Mulisch) 293

Disgrace (Coetzee) 293
The Disinherited (Castillo) 230
The Disinherited Lady (Pérez Galdós) 134
Disobedience (Moravia) 216
The Disowned (Bulwer-Lytton) 105
The Distant Lands (Green) 269
Distant Relations (Fuentes) 260
A Distant Trumpet (Horgan) 232
Le dit de Tianyi (Cheng) 291
Divine (Mallet-Joris) 276
Divisions (Cosic) 234
Djinn (Robbe-Grillet) 260
Do With Me What You Will (Oates) 251
Dobrovsky (Pushkin) 90
A Doce de Caetana (Pinon) 270
Docherty (McIlvanney) 254
Doctor Faustus (Mann) 152, 215
Doctor Glas (Söderberg) 163
Doctor Ibrahim (Ayyub) 206
The Doctor Is Sick (Burgess) 232
Doctor Thorne (Trollope) 120
Doctor Zhivago (Pasternak) 228
The Doctor's Wife (Sawako) 248
Dodningeuret (Gronfeldt) 275
Dodsworth (Lewis) 192
Dog Years (Grass) 237
Dolce per se (Maraini) 289
Dom Casmurro (Machado de Assis) 149, 158
Dombey and Son (Dickens) 115
Dominique (Fromentin) 123
Don Juan (Lenau) 117
Don Juan in the VIllage (DeLynn) 273
Don Quixote (Cervantes) 32, 50
Don Segundo Sombra (Güiraldes) 188
Doña Luz (Valera) 133
Doña Perfecta (Pérez Galdós) 131
Donatienne (Bazin) 161
Don't Forget (Malherbe) 172
Don't Pronounce It Night (Oz) 282
Il doppio regno (Capriolo) 276
Dorf uterm Wind (Schenk) 280
Dossier H (Kadare) 273
The Double (Dostoyevsky) 90, 115
Double Indemnity (Cain) 201
Double Suicides Committed at Forty-Eight Waterfalls in Akame (Chokitsu) 291
Down by the River (O'Brien) 288
Down Stream (Huysmans) 135
Down There (Huysmans) 142
A Down-and-Outer (Barrios) 178
The Downfall of Macias Giri (Natsuki) 280
Downstream (Siwertz) 180
Dr. Breen's Practice (Howells) 134
Dr. Brodie's Report (Borges) 154, 248
Dr. Criminale (Bradbury) 278
Dr. Katzenberger's Journey to the Spa (Richter) 98
Dracula (Stoker) 147
Dragon Seed (Buck) 209
Dragon's Teeth (Sinclair) 209, 210
The Dram Shop (Zola) 131
Dream of a Tree (Bakin) 291
The Dream of Heroes (Bioy Casares) 224
A Dream of John Ball (Morris) 139
Dream of the Red Chamber (Cao) 69, 80, 191

Dream of Yudotei Enmoku (Noboru) 296
A Dreambook of Our Time (Konwicki) 237
The Dreamer (Green) 199
A Dreamer for the Nation (Buero Vallejo) 230
Dred: A Tale of the Great Dismal Swamp (Stowe) 119
Dreflan, Its People and Its Affairs (Owen) 134
Drift (Bjornstad) 287
The Driver's Seat (Spark) 247
Drivvd fran Ardadien (Radstrom) 294
The Drop and the Sea (Nagar) 227
The Drowning Season (Hoffman) 258
Druid from Sindidun (Bajac) 296
Drums at Dusk (Bontemps) 205
Drylands (Astley) 295
Du plus loin de l'oubli (Modano) 286
Due di due (De Carlo) 274
The Duke's Children (Trollope) 133
Duluth (Vidal) 262
The Duo (Colette) 199
The Durandeau Brothers (Soupault) 185
During the Reconquest (Blest Gana) 147
The Dust and Ashes (Rybakov) 283
Dutch Shea, Jr. (Dunne) 261
Dvoergenes dans (Lon) 292
The Dwarf (Lagerkvist) 212
The Dying (Soupault) 199
The Dying Earth (Bazin) 149
Dying in the Sun (Palangyo) 244
Dyr (Preisler) 279
Early Autumn (Bromfield) 188, 189
Early Grace (Megged) 293
Early Sorrow (Mann) 152
Early Sorrows (Kis) 292
Earthly Powers (Burgess) 259
The Earthsea Trilogy (Le Guin) 244
East of Eden (Steinbeck) 221
East of the Mountains (Guterson) 293
Echo House (Just) 288
Eclats de sel (Germain) 286
Ecstasy (Couperus) 143
L'ecureuil noir (Poliquin) 282
Edgar Huntley (Brown) 88
The Edge of Sadness (O'Connor) 235
Edith (Brunner) 279
Eduards Heimkehr (Schneider) 293
The Edwardian (Sackville-West) 193
Effi Briest (Fontane) 145
Eftertradaren (Erkelius) 279
Efuru (Nwapa) 243
The Egoist (Meredith) 132
The Egyptian (Waltari) 212
The Eighth Day (Wilder) 243
The Electrical Field (Sakamoto) 290
Elef Levavot (Tsalka) 276
Elias Portulu (Deledda) 161
Eline Vere (Couperus) 140
The Elm Tree in the Mall (France) 147

Elmer Gantry (Lewis) 189

Eloges, and Other Poems (Perse) 170

Elsi Lund (Vik) 282

Elsk meg i morgen (Ambjornsen) 294

The Elusiveness of Truth (Ferrater Mora) 271

Emanuel (Laederach) 274

Embezzlement (Prem) 190

The Embezzler (Katayev) 188

El embrujo de Shanghai (Marse) 281

The Emergency (Rive) 238

Emergency Exit (Silone) 240

Emigrants (Ferreira de Castro) 191

The Emigrants (Moburg) 218

Emile; or, On Education (Rousseau) 68, 80

Emilia in England (Meredith) 124

Emma (Austen) 91, 99

Empire of the Sun (Ballard) 264

Empress of the Splendid Season (Hijuelos) 293

The Empty Canvas (Moravia) 233

En Route (Huysmans) 145

The Enchanted Soul (Rolland) 182

Enchanted Wanderer (Leskov) 129

The End of the Affair (Greene) 154, 220

The End of the House of Alard (Kaye-Smith) 184

The End of the Patriarchate (Pavlicek) 277

The End of the Road (Barth) 229

Enderby Outside (Burgess) 244

Enderby Trilogy (Burgess) 252

Ending Up (Amis) 252

Endless Fiesta (Tsuji) 287

The Endless Trip (Quenum) 232

Enemies: A Love Story (Singer) 250

L'Enfant de sable (Ben Jelloun) 266

L'enfant léopard (Picouly) 293

L'enfant roi (Rolin) 268

Engel (Rifbjerg) 268

Engelen din, Robinson (Hoem) 280

An English Family (Dinis) 126

The English Patient (Ondaatje) 278

The English Teacher (Narayan) 212

Entanglements (Fontane) 139

Entered from the Sun (Garrett) 273

The Epicurean (Moore) 105

Episodios nacionales (Pérez Galdós) 129

Epitaph for a Small Winner (Machado de Assis) 134

An Equal Music (Seth) 293

Er oder ich (Nadolny) 293

The Erasers (Robbe-Grillet) 222

Erewhon (Butler) 128

Eriksdottir: A Tale of Dreams and Luck (Clark) 282

Ernest Maltravers (Bulwer-Lytton) 109

The Escort Angel (Pelevin) 291

L'espace anterieur (Trassard) 280

Esperanza's Box of Saints (Escandón) 290

The Essence of the Thing (St. John) 288

The Estate (Singer) 246

Esther Waters (Moore) 144

Estrellita marinera (Esquivel) 294

L'età perfetta (Cotroneo) 293

Un été memorable (Perol) 291

The Eternal Smile (Lagerkvist) 180

Ethan Frome (Wharton) 169

Ethiopia Unbound (Hayford) 169

Etincelles dans les tenebres (Dai) 269

The Etruscan (Waltari) 225

Eu, tiradentes (Motta) 278

Eugene Aram (Bulwer-Lytton) 107

Eugenie Grandet (Balzac) 91, 107

The Eustace Diamonds (Trollope) 129

Eutaw (Simms) 119

Evan Harrington (Meredith) 121

O Evanelho segundo Jesus Cristo (Saramago) 278

El evangelio según Van Hutten (Castillo) 294

L'Eve Future (Villiers de L'Isle-Adam) 138

The Eve of Saint Venus (Burgess) 238

Evelina; or, A Young Lady's Entrance into the World (Burney) 83

Evening Light (Horwood) 288

Every Man for Himself (Bainbridge) 286, 288

Evidence of Love (Grau) 256

Except the Lord (Cary) 222

The Excursion Participants (Viewegh) 286

The Executioner (Boulle) 224

The Executioner's Song (Mailer) 258, 259

The Exile (Wagner) 271

Exodus (Uris) 229

Exortaçao aos crocodilos (Lobo Antunes) 296

Explosion in a Cathedral (Carpentier) 236

Exterminate the Brutes (Lindqvist) 279

Exterminator! (Burroughs) 250

The Extraordinary Adventures of Julio Jurenito and His Disciples (Ehrenburg) 183

The Eye of the Storm (White) 250

The Eyes of the Interred (Asturias) 232

A Fable (Faulkner) 223, 224

The Fable and the Flesh (Aymé) 210

Fair Stood the Wind for France (Bates) 211

The Fairy at the Bottom of the Lake (Davidescu) 171

A Fairy Tale of New York (Donleavy) 251

The Faithful Lover (Bontempelli) 223

Falconer (Cheever) 256

Falkland (Bulwer-Lytton) 105

The Fall (Camus) 227

Fall from Grace (Wright) 276

The Fall of a Sparrow (Hellenga) 290

The Fall of Kelvin Walker: A Fable in the Sixties (Gray) 266

The Fall of Paris (Ehrenburg) 208

Falling in Place (Beattie) 259

False Love (Arlt) 196

The Family (Meri) 244

The Family at Gilje (Lie) 136

The Family Moskat (Singer) 213

The Family of Pascal Duarte (Cela) 209

A Family Romance (Brookner) 280

Famine (O'Flaherty) 203

The Famished Road (Okri) 276

Fanny: Being the True History of the Adventures of Fanny Hack-about-Jones (Jong) 259

Fanny Hill, Memoirs of a Woman of Pleasure (Cleland) 77

Fanshawe (Hawthorne) 105

Fantasmas de carne y hueso (Edwards) 281

Fantastic Gallery (Yumiko) 276

Far Away Is the Sun (Casic) 220

A Far Cry from Kensington (Spark) 271

Far from the Madding Crowd (Hardy) 130

Far Tortuga (Matthiessen) 253

Farewell, My Lovely (Chandler) 207

A Farewell to Arms (Hemingway) 153, 192

Farewell to the Sea: A Novel of Cuba (Arenas) 262

Farina, a Legend of Cologne (Meredith) 120

El farmer (Rivera) 287

Fata Morgana (Kotsyubinsky) 162

Father Murdering (Zeng) 290

Fathers and Sons (Sefarim) 123

Fathers and Sons (Turgenev) 123

The Fault of Angels (Horgan) 197

Fear (Rybakov) 278

Fear of the Bell (Bratic) 278

The Feast of Love (Baxter) 295

Los felinos del canciller (Moreno-Dorani) 270

Felix Holt the Radical (Eliot) 125

Felix Krull (Mann) 152

The Fellah (Sharqawi) 247

The Fellowship of the Ring (Tolkien) 223

Ferdydurke (Gombrowicz) 203

Ferias de verao (Moreira) 294

The Ferry (Hoem) 253

Fever (Le Clezio) 240

A Few Nights and Days (Dipoko) 241

A Fictional Story (Gabra Iyasus) 166

Field of Violets (Hoffmann) 268

The Fiery Angel (Bryusov) 166

La fiesta del chivo (Vargas Llosa) 296

The Fifth Business (Davies) 247

The Fifth Child (Lessing) 271

The Fifth Seal (Aldanov) 206

El Filibusterismo (Rizal) 142

La fille du gobernator (Constant) 282

Final Payments (Gordon) 257

The Financier (Dreiser) 171

A Fine Balance (Mistry) 286

Finnegan's Wake (Joyce) 152, 206

Fire (Ahmed) 214

Fire Down Below (Golding) 272

Fires on the Plain (Shohei) 220

The Firm of Nucingen (Balzac) 91

Firmly Rooted (Rovira) 170

The First Circle (Solzhenitsyn) 154, 245, 257

The First Garden (Hébert) 271

The Fish Can Sing (Laxness) 228

The Fitzboodle Papers (Thackeray) 112

The Five Suns of Mexico (Fuentes) 296

Five Women Who Chose Love (Ihara Saikaku) 64

The Fixer (Malamud) 226, 241, 242

The Flame Throwers (Arlt) 195

The Flanders Road (Simon) 233

Die Flaterrzunge (Delius) 293

Flight (Ahmed) 213

Flight into Darkness (Schnitzler) 195

The Flight of Icarus (Queneau) 245

The Flight of the Eagle (O'Grady) 147

The Flights (Conton) 269

Floating Bridge (Kunie) 278

Floating Cloud (Hayashi) 220

The Floating Opera (Barth) 226

The Flood (Le Clezio) 241

Flood (Warren) 238

Det florentisski vidsvinet (Ahlin) 277

The Flounder (Grass) 256

The Flower, Fruit and Thorn Pieces (Richter) 87

Flowering Nettle (Martinson) 201

The Flute and the Wind (Hawi) 233

Fly, Kylin (Noboru) 294

Fly Away Home (Piercy) 264

Flying Blind (Omar) 269

Flying to Nowhere (Fuller) 263

The Folks That Live on the Hill (Amis) 273

La folle allure (Bobin) 284

Fontano da case (Ferrucci) 286

The Fool's Sanctuary (Johnston) 269

Footsteps (Tur) 266

For Every Sin (Appelfeld) 272

For Kings and Planets (Canin) 290

For Whom the Bell Tolls (Hemingway) 153, 207

The Forayers; or, The Raid of the Dog Days (Simms) 119

Forbidden Colors (Mishima) 224

The Forbidden Love (Usakligil) 187

Fording the Stream of Consciousness (Ugresic) 277

A Foregone Conclusion (Howells) 130

Foreign Affairs (Lurie) 264, 265

Foreign Bodies (Cayrol) 231

A Foreign Letter (Morozov) 291

The Forest of a Thousand Daemons (Fagunwa) 205

Forever Flowering (Grossman) 239

Forforeren (Kjaerstad) 280

Forgotten Hill (Mammeri) 221

Forgotten Pictures (Varma) 231

La forja de un ladrón (Umbral) 289

novel *(continued)*

Forsyte Saga (Galsworthy) 164, 182, 188

Fortoellinger om natten (Hoeg) 275

Fortunata y Jacinta (Pérez Galdós) 138

The Fortunate Peasant (Marivaux) 75

Fortune's Daughter (Hoffman) 265

The Fortunes of Niger (Scott) 93, 103

The Fortunes of Richard Mahoney (Richardson) 193

The Fortunes of the Rougon-Macquart Family (Zola) 128

The Forty Days of Musa Dagh (Werfel) 197

La forza del passato (Veronesi) 296

Fouchi (Ferrucci) 280

The Fountainhead (Rand) 210

The Four Horsemen of the Apocalypse (Blasco Ibáñez) 175

Four Mothers (Horn) 293

The Four-Gated City (Lessing) 246

A Foxglove Saga (Waugh) 234

The Fox's Paw (Pérez de Ayala) 171

Foxybaby (Jolley) 265

The Franchiser (Elkin) 254

Frankenstein; or, the Modern Prometheus (Shelley) 101

Frankenstein Unbound (Aldiss) 251

Die Frau in den Kissen (Kronauer) 274

Frauen vor Flusblandschaft (Böll) 266

Free Fall (Golding) 231

Freedom (Butov) 294

Freedom or Death (Kazantzakis) 219

Freedom Under Parole (Paz) 218

Freedom's Just Another Word (Hamilton) 290

The French Lieutenant's Woman (Fowles) 246

Les frères romance (Colombier) 274

The Friend of the Family (Dostoyevsky) 90, 121

A Frolic of His Own (Gaddis) 282

From Another Shore (Herzen) 117

From Footpath to Railway Line (Lortkipanidze) 190

From Here to Eternity (Jones) 220

From the Heart of the Country (Coetzee) 256

From the Terrace (O'Hara) 229

From Zia, with Love (Soyinka) 278

Fromont the Younger and Risler the Elder (Daudet) 130

The Frontenac Mystery (Mauriac) 197

Fru Astrid Grib (Jensen) 275

Fru Marie Grubbe (Jacobsen) 131

Der Fuchs war damals schon der Jäger (Muller) 278

Fugitive Pieces (Michaels) 286

The Fugitives (Linnankoski) 166

Fulgedansen (Ambjornsen) 284

Fungi (Pleijel) 281

Fuskaren (Evander) 277

The Gab Boys (Duodo) 243

Gabriela, Clove and Cinnamon (Amado) 230

Gabriel's Lament (Bailey) 267

Un gachis (Darley) 288

Galapagos (Vonnegut) 265

Galindez (Vázquez Montalbán) 277

The Game-Keeper's Wife (Hviezdoslav) 138

The Games Were Coming (Anthony) 237

The Gangster War (Petrunova) 292

The Garden Next Door (Donoso) 278

A Garden of Earthly Delights (Oates) 243

The Garden of Eden (Hemingway) 267

The Garden of the Finzi-Cortinis (Massano) 236

Gardens in the Dunes (Silko) 293

Garman and Worse (Kielland) 133

The Gate (Natsume) 93, 169

The Gates of Angels (Fitzgerald) 273

The Gates of Life (Herczeg) 179

A General and His Army (Vladimov) 285

The General in His Labyrinth (García Márquez) 272

The General of the Dead Army (Kadare) 236

Generation Without Farewell (Boyle) 232

The Genius (Dreiser) 174

Genspejlet (Madsen) 295

The Gentle Language (De Amicis) 163

Gentleman's Agreement (Hobson) 215

Gentrix (Mauriac) 184

George Mills (Elkin) 261

Germanium Nights (Mangetsu) 291

Germinal (Zola) 137

Gertrude and Claudius (Updike) 295

De geruchten (Claus) 288

Getting It Right (Howard) 261

Ghisola (Tozzi) 179

The Ghost Road (Barker) 284

The Ghost Writer (Roth) 258

Giaconda a dama con la luna (Morandini) 287

Giant (Gerber) 221

The Giant's House (McCracken) 286

The Giants (Le Clezio) 251

Giants in the Earth (Rolvaag) 189

I giardini della favorita (Campana) 278

The Gift (Nabokov) 155, 203

The Gift of a Cow (Prem) 202

A Gift of Rags (Boyarsky) 284

Giganten (Doblin) 196

Gigi (Colette) 211

Gil Blas (Lesage) 72

Giles Goat-Boy (Barth) 241

The Ginger Man (Donleavy) 225

Giovanni's Room (Baldwain) 226

A Girl in Winter (Larkin) 215

The Girl with the Botticelli Face (Valgardson) 278

Girlfriend in a Coma (Coupland) 290

Girls (Busch) 288

The Girls (Montherlant) 202

The Girls of Slender Means (Spark) 237

Giving Life (Shun) 296

Gladiator, or a Note on the Military Police (Navot) 280

The Gladiators (Koestler) 206

Gloria (Maillard) 293

The Glorious Life of Saigyo (Kunio) 284

Glorious Lousy Years (Viewegh) 279

The Glory of Don Ramiro (Rodriguez Larreta) 166

Das Gluck (Hoffmann) 280

Go Tell It on the Mountain (Baldwin) 222

The Goalee's Anxiety at the Penalty Kick (Handke) 248

The Goatibex Constellation (Iskander) 241

The Go-Between (Hartley) 222

God Bless You, Mr. Rosewater (Vonnegut) 240

The God of Small Things (Roy) 288

A God Strolling in the Cool of the Evening (Carvalho) 289

The God That Failed (Wright) 219

Godolphin (Bulwer-Lytton) 107

The Gods Are Athirst (France) 171

God's Beautiful World (Koch) 175

God's Bits of Wood (Sembene) 233

God's Grace (Malamud) 261

God's Little Acre (Caldwell) 197

God's Orchid (Bergman) 179

God's Snake (Spanidou) 267

God's Stepchildren (Millin) 185

The Gold Seeker (Le Clezio) 266

The Golden Bowl (James) 91, 162

The Golden Cockerell (Raffi) 134

The Golden Demon (Koyo) 147

The Golden Dog (Kirby) 131

Golden Fruits (Sarraute) 237

Golden Honeycomb (Markandaya) 256

The Golden Notebook (Lessing) 235

The Golovlev Family (Saltykov-Shchedrin) 131

Gone With the Wind (Mitchell) 201, 203

The Good Companions (Priestley) 192

The Good Conscience (Fuentes) 231

The Good Earth (Buck) 194, 195

Good Evening Mr. and Mrs. America and All the Ships at Sea (Bausch) 286

Good Example (Germasaw) 208

The Good Hope (Heineson) 238

A Good House (Burnard) 293

Good Morning, Good Night (Rhys) 205

A Good Scent from a Strange Mountain (Butler) 279

The Good Soldier: A Tale of Passion (Ford) 174

The Good Soldier Schweik (Hašek) 179

The Good Terrorist (Lessing) 265

Good Will (Diallo) 188

A Good Woman (Bromfield) 189

Goodbye, Mr. Chips (Hilton) 199

Goodbye to Berlin (Isherwood) 205

Gor mig levande (Ekman) 287

Gora (Tagore) 153, 165

Gospel (Barnhardt) 279

Grace Notes (MacLaverty) 288

El gran jaguar (Valderrama Andrade) 277

El gran lector (Solares) 281

The Grand Design (Dos Passos) 217

Grand Gentleman and a Big Rascal (Barrios) 217

Grand Hotel (Baum) 192

La grande beune (Michon) 286

Grandmothers (Sabach) 292

The Grapes of Wrath (Steinbeck) 205, 206

The Grass Harp (Capote) 220

The Grass Is Singing (Lessing) 219

Grass on the Wayside (Natsume) 93

The Grass (Simon) 230

Graustark (McCutcheon) 159

Graven Images (Thomas) 280

The Graveyard by the Sea (Valery) 182

Gravity's Rainbow (Pynchon) 250

The Great American Novel (Roth) 250

Great Expectations (Dickens) 90, 121

The Great Fear of the Well-Possessed (Bernanos) 195

The Great Gatsby (Fitzgerald) 186

The Great Hoggarty Diamond (Thackeray) 112

The Great Hunger (Bojer) 175

The Great Meadow (Roberts) 193

The Great Ponds (Amadi) 246

The Great Train Robbery (Chrichton) 253

The Great Weaver from Kashmir (Laxness) 189

The Great Winter (Kadare) 255

The Greek Passion (Kazantzakis) 224

The Green Bay Tree (Bromfield) 185

Green Days by the River (Anthony) 243

The Green Hat (Arlen) 185

Green Henry (Keller) 117, 132

Green Hills of Africa (Hemingway) 153, 200

The Green Man (Amis) 246

Green Mansions (Hudson) 162

The Green Mare (Aymé) 197

The Green Pope (Asturias) 224

The Green Years (Cronin) 211

Grendel (Gardner) 250

Grenser (Jacobsen) 294

El griego (Fernández Santos) 266

Det gronne oje (Guldager) 292

Gros mots (Decharme) 293

The Ground Beneath Her Feet (Rushdie) 293

The Group (McCarthy) 237

Group Portrait with Lady (Böll) 249

The Groves of Academe (McCarthy) 221

The Growth of the Soil (Hamsun) 176

O Guaranai (Alencar) 120

Guard of Honor (Cozzens) 216, 217

The Guermantes Way (Proust) 180

Guerra conyugal (Russo) 296

La guerra de Galico (Aguilar Camín) 277

Guerra en el paraíso (Montemayor) 277

Guerrilla Family (Tur) 227

A Guest for the Night (Agnon) 204

The Guide (Narayan) 229

Gulag Archipelago (Solzhenitsyn) 154, 251

Gulru (Jalil) 208

A Gun for Sale (Greene) 202

Gunnladar Saga (Svava) 269

The Gunpowder Tower (Bjornboe) 246

Guy Mannering (Scott) 93, 99

Guy Rivers (Simms) 108

Guzmán de Alfarache (Alemán) 45

Gypsies (Macha) 108

The Gyurkovics Girls (Herczeg) 144

H. M. Pulham, Esq. (Marquand) 208

The Hag (Irzykowski) 161

Half Brothers (Radulovic) 270

The Half Virgins (Prévost) 144

Hamatzav baShlishi (Oz) 276

The Hamlet (Faulkner) 207

The Hand, the Earth and the Water (Ayyub) 216

A Handful of Black Berries (Silone) 221

A Handful of Dust (Waugh) 199

The Handmaid's Tale (Atwood) 266

The Hard Blue Sky (Grau) 229

Hard Times (Dickens) 90, 118

The Harder They Fall (Schulberg) 215

A Harlot High and Low (Balzac) 91, 111

Harlot's Ghost (Mailer) 275

Harold, the Last of the Saxon Kings (Bulwer-Lytton) 115

Harold the Dauntless (Scott) 100

Harriet Said (Bainbridge) 250

Harrouda (Ben Jelloun) 251

Harry Potter and Prisoner of Azkaban (Rowling) 295

Harry Potter and the Chamber of Secrets (Rowling) 293

Harry Potter and the Sorcerer's Stone (Rowling) 290

Hashish Gang (Kunio) 294

Hatet (Espmark) 285

Hatter's Castle (Cronin) 194

The Haunted Man and the Ghost's Bargain (Dickens) 115

Havoc (Kristensen) 193

Hawaii (Michener) 231

A Hazard of New Fortunes (Howells) 141

He Knew He Was Right (Trollope) 127

He Who Gets Slapped (Andreyev) 175

Head Against the Wall (Bazin) 218

Head Hunter (Findley) 280

The Headlong Hall (Peacock) 100

The Headman; or, The Abbaye des Vignerons (Cooper) 107

The Healer (Hollingshead) 290

The Healer of His Honor (Pérez de Ayala) 188

Hear the Wind (Murakami) 258

Hearing Secret Harmonies (Powell) 253

The Heart Is a Lonely Hunter (McCullers) 207

The Heart of a Dog (Bulgakov) 187, 270

Heart of Aztlan (Anaya) 254

The Heart of Darkness (Conrad) 155

The Heart of Midlothian (Scott) 93, 101

The Heart of Tel Aviv (Shaham) 286

Heart of the Country (Matthews) 267

The Heart of the Day (Bowen) 217

The Heart of the Matter (Greene) 154

The Heartsong of Charging Elk (Welch) 295

Heat and Dust (Jhabvala) 253

The Heidenmauer; or, The Benedictines (Cooper) 107

Heinrich von Otterdingen (Novalis) 88

The Heir of Redclyffe (Yonge) 118

Heleconia Winter (Aldiss) 266

Helen Halsey; or, The Swamp State of Conelachita (Simms) 114

Hell Has No Limits (Donoso) 242

Hemingard of the Oak Burial Mounds (Drost) 107

Hemligheter kring vatten (Ekman) 283

Hemlock and After (Wilson) 221

Hence (Leithauser) 272

Henderson the Rain King (Bellow) 231

Henry and Cato (Murdoch) 255

Henry of Ofterdingen (Novalis) 96

Her Eyes (Alavi) 221

Her i noerheden (Christensen) 282

Her Son's Wife (Fisher) 188

Her Story (Jacobson) 269

The Here and Now (Cohen) 286

El hereje (Delibes) 292

The Heretic of Soana (Hauptmann) 177

Hereward the Wake (Kingsley) 125

L'heritage de Tante Carlotta (Jacques) 269

A Hero Ain't Nothing but a Sandwich (Childress) 250

A Hero of Our Times (Lermontov) 111

Herod's Children (Aichinger) 216

Heroes Are Grazing in My Garden (Padilla) 262

The Heron (Bassani) 245

Hers (Alvarez) 252

Herself Surprised (Cary) 208

Hertog van Egypte (Moor) 288

Herzog (Bellow) 238

Hesperus (Richter) 86

Hidden in the Heart (Jacobson) 276

High Bridges (Lacretelle) 196

A High Wind in Jamaica (Hughes) 192

The Highland Widow (Scott) 105

La hija del caníbal (Montero) 289

Hilda (Ndiaye) 293

Der Himmel des Humoristen (Pivonas) 264

Det himmelska gastabudet (Gyllensten) 277

Hiroshima (Minoru) 260

His Family (Poole) 177

His Grace's Will (Bergman) 169

His Natural Life (Clarke) 130

His Only Sow (Alas) 141

Una historia de familia (Santiago) 278

Las historias de Marta y Fernando (Martín Garzo) 294

Historien med hunden (Gustafsson) 281

History: A Novel (Morante) 252

The History of a Town (Saltykov-Shchedrin) 127

The History of Henry Esmond (Thackeray) 117

The History of Lady Sophia Sternhelm (La Roche) 82

The History of Sir Charles Grandison (Richardson) 78

The History of Susan Spray, Female Preacher (Kaye-Smith) 194

The Hive (Cela) 220

Hjertelyd (Grondahl) 292

The Hobbitt (Tolkien) 203

Los hochos de Zacarías (Morón) 277

Het hof van barmhartigheid (Heijden) 288

The Holy Sinner (Mann) 152, 220

Holy Smoke (Cabrera Infante) 268

The Holy Terrors (Cocteau) 192

The Holy Well (Katayev) 243

Hombre (Leonard) 233

El hombre que llegó a un pueblo (Tizón) 274

Home As Found (Cooper) 110

The Home of the Spirits of the Ancestors (Abdulla) 233

Home to Harlem (McKay) 190

Hometown Noodles and Flower (Liu) 290

L'homme ignore (Targowla) 274

Honey in the Horn (Davis) 201

Honeymoon, Bittermoon (Pérez de Ayala) 184

The Honorary Consul (Greene) 154, 251

The Hoosier Schoolmaster (Eggleston) 128

Hopscotch (Cortázar) 237

Hordubal (Čapek) 197

Horseman, Pass By (McMurtry) 234

The Horseman on the Roof (Giono) 221

The Horse's Mouth (Cary) 211

Hotel du Lac (Brookner) 264

The Hotel New Hampshire (Irving) 260

The Hour of the Star (Lispector) 256

The Hours (Cunningham) 292, 293

The House by the Medlar (Verga) 134

A House for Mr. Biswas (Naipaul) 234

The House in Haarlem (Schendel) 200

A House in Order (Denis) 241

House in the Shadow (Gengetsu) 296

House Made of Dawn (Momaday) 244, 245

The House of Earth (Buck) 200

The House of Five Talents (Auchincloss) 232

House of Glass (Tur) 271

House of Incest (Nin) 201, 202

The House of Mirth (Wharton) 163

House of the Dead (Dostoyevsky) 90, 122, 123

The House of the Seven Gables (Hawthorne) 117

The House of the Spirits (Allende) 262

The House on Coliseum Street (Grau) 234

Hovedstolen (Hesselholdt) 292

How Far Can You Go? (Lodge) 259

How German Is It? (Abish) 259

How Green Was My Valley (Llewellyn) 206

How Many Miles to Babylon? (Johnston) 252

How the Dead Live (Self) 295

How to Save Your Life (Jong) 256

Howards End (Forster) 168

Huckleberry Finn (Twain) 92, 136

The Human Comedy (Balzac) 90–91

The Human Comedy (Saroyan) 210

The Human Factor (Greene) 154, 257

Human Mourning (Revueltas) 211

The Human Stain (Roth) 295

Humboldt's Gift (Bellow) 253, 254

Hummelhonung (Lindgren) 285

The Humming Bird Tree (McDonald) 246

A Hungarian Nabob (Jókai) 118

Hungary in 1514 (Eötvös) 115

Hunger (Hamsun) 141

Hurrah to the Hilt (Valle-Inclán) 191

Hurry on Down (Wain) 222

The Husband of Ahu Khanom (Mohammad) 234

Hutchinsons effekt (Pollen) 291

The Hydra Head (Fuentes) 257

Hypatia; or, New Foes with an Old Face (Kingsley) 118

Hyperion (Holderllin) 87

Hyperion (Longfellow) 110

I, Claudius (Graves) 199

I, the Supreme (Roa Bastos) 253

I Am a Cat (Natsume) 93, 163

I Am Guilty (Ikromi) 230

I Have No Home Now (Wispelaere) 262

I knolvannet (Petterson) 296

novel *(continued)*

I Live (Ba'albakki) 229
I See a Wondrous Land (Kamban) 201
I Went Abroad (Walda) 225
I Will Live the Love of Others (Cayrol) 215
The Iberian Circle (Valle-Inclán) 189
Ibrahim, of the Illustrious Bassa (Scudéry) 57
Ibsens Italia (Naess) 289
Ice Candy Man (Sidhwa) 271
The Ice Mine (Appelfeld) 289
Iceland's Bell (Laxness) 210
Ich (Hilbig) 280
Ida Brandt (Bang) 146
Les idées heureuses (Lapaque) 293
Identity (Kundera) 290
The Ides of March (Wilder) 216
The Idiot (Dostoyevsky) 90, 126
If Beale Street Could Talk (Baldwin) 252
If He Hollers, Let Him Go (Himes) 212
If I Were You (Green) 215
If It Die (Gide) 180
If Not Now, When? (Levi) 262
If on a Winter's Night a Traveler (Calvino) 258
Illumination Night (Hoffman) 269
The Illusionist (Mallet-Joris) 220
The Illustrious Gaudissart (Balzac) 91
Illywhacker (Carey) 266
I'm Not Stiller (Frisch) 224
Images in a Mirror (Undset) 156, 176
Immaculate Conception (Breton) 193
Immobile dans le courant de fleuve (Berger) 282
The Immoralist (Gide) 160
The Immortal Bartfuss (Appelfeld) 271
Immortality (Kundera) 273
Imperial Palace (Bennett) 193
L'impresa senza (Barbaro) 293
Impressions of Africa (Roussel) 168
In a Dark Wood Wandering (Haasse) 272
In a Glass House (Ricci) 280
In Another Country (Baldwin) 235
In Chancery (Galsworthy) 180, 182
In Cold Blood (Capote) 241
In Dubious Battle (Steinbeck) 201
In einer dunken Nacht gig ich aus meinen stillen Haus (Handke) 289
In Every Face I Meet (Cartwright) 284
In God's Way (Bjørnson) 140
In Praise of Older Women: Amorous Recollections of Andras Vajada (Vicinczy) 240
In Praise of the Stepmother (Cela) 271
In Purissimo Azzurro (Fiore) 268
In Search of Walid Massoud (Jabra) 295
In the Desert of a Lodging Place (Sened, Sened) 291

In the Dutch Mountains (Nooteboom) 264
In the Labyrinth (Sarraute) 231
In the Name of Salomé (Alvarez) 295
In the Name of the Son (Bazin) 233
In the Penal Colony (Kafka) 173
In the Shadow of the Wind (Hébert) 262
In the Skin of a Lion (Ondaatje) 269
In the Wilderness (Appelfeld) 237
In This House of Brede (Godden) 246
In This Our Life (Glasgow) 209
In Transit (Brophy) 246
Incerti di viaggio (Pazzi) 287
Incidents (Meri) 232
Incline Our Hearts (Wilson) 272
Incognita (Dryden) 65
The Incomparable Atuk (Richler) 237
Independence Day (Ford) 284, 286
Independent People (Laxness) 198
Indian Summer (Howells) 137
Indiana (Sand) 107
The Industry of Souls (Booth) 290
Inexpiable (Ebner-Eschenbach) 141
Infinite Riches (Okri) 291
The Informer (O'Flaherty) 186
Ingenious Pain (Miller) 293
L'ingratitude (Chen) 284
Ingrid Caven (Schuhl) 296
The Inheritor (Golding) 225
Injustice (Borgen) 266
The Inner Side of the Wind (Pavic) 281
Inquiry Time (Bainbridge) 256
Insania (Correia) 296
Inside Mr. Enderby (Burgess) 237
La insólita historia de la santa de Cabora (Domecq) 275
Insular Passion (Mo) 267
The Insulted and the Injured (Dostoyevsky) 90, 122
The Intense Life (Bontempelli) 180
The Interpreters (Soyinka) 240
The Interrogation (Le Clezio) 237
The Intruder (D'Annunzio) 143
Intruder in the Dust (Faulkner) 216
L'invention du monde (Rolin) 280
The Invention of Morel (Bioy Casares) 207
The Invention of Truth (Brewster) 276
An Invincible Memory (Ubaldo Ribeiro) 272
Invisible Cities (Calvino) 250
The Invisible Lodge (Richter) 86
Invisible Man (Ellison) 221
The Invisible Worm (Johnston) 276
Invitation to a Beheading (Nabokov) 155, 204
Iracema (Alencar) 124
The Iron Flood (Serafimovic) 185
The Iron Heel (London) 165, 166
The Iron Tracks (Appelfeld) 291
Ironweed (Kennedy) 262, 263
L'Irréparable (Bourget) 136
Irse de casa (Martín Gaite) 292

Isis (Villiers de L'Isle-Adam) 123
An Island Fisherman (Loti) 138
The Island of Crimea (Aksyonov) 261, 274
The Island of the Doomed (Dagerman) 214
Islands in the Stream (Hemingway) 247
Isolation Booth (Hood) 276
Israel Potter: His Fifty-five Years of Exile (Melville) 119
Israpport (Aspenstrom) 289
The Issa Valley (Milosz) 226
It Can't Happen Here (Lewis) 200
It Is Never Too Late to Mend (Reade) 119
The Italian (Radcliffe) 87
The Italian Girl (Murdoch) 238
Italian Spring (Robles) 247
It's a Hard Life (Biancardi) 236
Ivanhoe (Scott) 93, 101
Ivory and Opium (Bach) 267
The Izu Dancer (Kawabata) 156
The Jacaranda Tree (Bates) 216
Jack Frusciante e uscito dal gruppo (Bruzzi) 284
Jack Maggas (Carey) 288
Jack Tier (Cooper) 115
Jacko: The Great Intruder (Keneally) 282
Jacob's Room (Woolf) 182
Jagua Nana (Ekwensi) 234
Jailbird (Vonnegut) 258
The Jake's Thing (Amis) 257
Jakob der Letzte (Rosegger) 139
Jakob von Gunten (Walser) 167
Jalaleddin (Raffi) 132
Jane Eyre (Brontë) 115
Jane Talbot (Brown) 95
Jantando com Melvin (Coelho) 291
Japhthah and His Daughters (Feuchtwanger) 228
Java Head (Hergesheimer) 178
Javiera Carrera, madre de la patria (Vidal) 296
Jazz (Morrison) 277
Jealousy and Medicine (Choromanski) 196
Jealousy (Robbe-Grillet) 228
Jeame's Diary (Thackeray) 114
Jean Christophe (Rolland) 162
Jennie Gerhardt (Dreiser) 169
Jenny (Undset) 156, 170
Jeremy's Vision (Purdy) 247
Jerusalem (Lagerlöf) 159
Jesus Saves (Steinke) 288
Jew Suss (Feuchtwanger) 187
The Jewel in the Crown (Scott) 241
The Jewish War (Feuchtwanger) 196
The Jews of Zirndorf (Wasserman) 147
Jin Ping Mei 52
El jinete polaco (Muñoz Molina) 277
João Miguel (Quieroz) 196
Joe (Brown) 276
The Johanna Maria (Schendel) 193
John Dollar (Wiggins) 272
The Joke (Kundera) 242
Jonatan's Journey (Hansen) 208
Jorparadiset Varherres nedfallsfrukt (Heggland) 284

Joseph and His Brothers (Mann) 152, 197
Joseph Andrews (Fielding) 76
Journey (Michener) 272
Journey in the Dark (Flavin) 211
A Journey into Winter (Appelfeld) 296
Journey to the End of the Night (Céline) 196
The Joy Luck Club (Tan) 272
The Joys and Sorrows of a Schoolmaster (Gotthelf) 110
The Joys of Motherhood (Emecheta) 258
Juanita la Larga (Valera) 145
Jude the Obscure (Hardy) 144
The Judge (West) 182
Judge Not (Asch) 188
Judgment Day (Farrell) 200
Juha (Aho) 169
Les Juives (Garnier) 42
Julia Paradise (Jones) 269
Julian (Vidal) 238
Julie (Elstad) 280
Juneteenth (Ellison) 293
The Jungle (Ferreira de Castro) 191
The Jungle (Sinclair) 164
Jurgen (Cabell) 178
The Jury (Klima) 245
The Just and the Unjust (Cozzens) 209
Justine (Durrell) 228
Justine (Sade) 86
Kadisz (Grynberg) 269
Kamalampal; or, The Fatal Rumor (Rajam Iyer) 144
Kamouraska (Hébert) 247
Kan hende ved em bredd (Carling) 294
Kangaroo (Aleshkovsky) 268
Kangaroo (Lawrence) 184
Kanthapura (Rao) 204
Kapten Nemos (Enquist) 277
Kaputt (Malaperte) 211
Karim, roman Sénégalais (Diop) 200
Karjana (Heggland) 274
Kastanjetid (Larsen) 278
Kate Vaiden (Price) 267
Katedralen (Stigen) 270
Katerina (Appelfeld) 272
Katherine Walton (Simms) 117
Kavanagh (Longfellow) 116
Keep the Apisdistra Flying (Orwell) 202
The Keepers of the House (Grau) 238, 239
The Kellys and the O'Kellys (Trollope) 115
Kenilworth (Scott) 93, 102
Kerkhoven's Third Existence (Wasserman) 199
The Key (Tanizaki) 218
The Keys of the Kingdom (Cronin) 209
Kidesh Halem (Asch) 179
Kidnapped (Stevenson) 138
The Killing Man (Spillane) 272
Kim (Kipling) 159
A Kind of Loving (Barstow) 232
The Kindly Ones (Powell) 235
King Dickie (Mallet-Joris) 258
The King of Babylon Shall Not Come Against You (Garrett) 286

The King of Schnorrers (Zangwill) 144

The King of Zion (Hamerling) 127

King, Queen, Knave (Nabokov) 155, 191

King Solomon's Mines (Haggard) 137

The Kingdom of This World (Carpentier) 218

Kinzoni and His Grandson Makundu (Bahele) 217

Kipps (Wells) 163

Kiss of the Spider Woman (Puig) 230

The Kiss to the Leper (Mauriac) 182

Kisses of the Enemy (Hall) 271

The Kitchen God's Wife (Tan) 276

Kitchen Music (Foran) 282

Kneller's Happy Campers (Keret) 291

The Knight of Saxony (Benet) 277

Knowledge of Angels (Walsh) 282

Kokoro (Natsume) 93, 173

Kongi's Harvest (Soyinka) 243

Kopfjager (Timm) 276

Kordian and the Churl (Kruczkowski) 196

The Kreutzer Sonata (Tolstoy) 141

Kristin Lavransdatter (Undset) 156, 180

Kron og mynt (Flogstad) 291

Kruger's Alp (Hope) 264

Kvachi Kvachantiradze (Javakhishvili) 185

Kwaiden (Hearn) 162

La cárcel de amor (San Pedro) 29

El laberinto griego (Vázquez Montalbán) 277

The Labors of Urbano and Simona (Pérez de Ayala) 184

Lacemaker Lekholm Has an Idea (Hellstrom) 189

Lachweill Stories (Federer) 170

Lad and Lass (Thoroddsen) 116

Lady Chatterley's Lover (Lawrence) 190

The Lady of the Aroostook (Howells) 132

The Lady of the Camelias (Dumas) 115

The Lady of the Lake (Scott) 98

haLaila shebo Meta ha Tsionut (Almog) 274

Laish (Appelfeld) 282

Lake Wobegon Days (Keillor) 265

Lamb in His Bosom (Hillyer) 198

Lambeaux (Juliet) 284

The Lamp of Umm Hashim (Haqqi) 211

En lampa som gor morker (Odensten) 294

The Lances of Lynwood (Yonge) 119

The Land of Gold (Conscience) 123

The Land of Little Rain (Austin) 161

Landlocked (Lessing) 240

The Landlord at Lion's Head (Howells) 147

Landscape Painted with Tea (Pavic) 274

Landschaft mit Dornen (Saeger) 280

A Laodicean (Hardy) 134

El lapiz del carpintero (Rivas) 292

Larry's Party (Shields) 288

A Lassie Was Cracking Hazelnuts (Terziev) 292

The Last Adam (Cozzens) 197

The Last Bow (Astafyev) 278

Last Call (Mulisch) 272

The Last Chronicle of Barset (Trollope) 125

The Last Days of Louisiana Red (Reed) 252

The Last Days of Pompeii (Bulwer-Lytton) 108

The Last Domain (Fournier) 172

Last Exit to Brooklyn (Selby) 238

The Last Hotel for Women (Covington) 286

The Last Hurrah (O'Connor) 226

The Last Imam (Tahir) 264

Last Impression (Haddad) 230

The Last Magician (Hospital) 278

The Last Man (Shelley) 104

Last Nights of Paris (Soupault) 190

The Last of Cheri (Colette) 188

The Last of the Barons (Bulwer-Lytton) 113

The Last of the Just (Schwarz-Bart) 231

The Last of the Mohicans (Cooper) 104

The Last of the Vikings (Bojer) 181

Last Orders (Swift) 286

The Last Picture Show (McMurtry) 248

The Last Puritan (Santayana) 200

The Last Tempatation of Christ (Kazantzakis) 225

The Last Thing He Wanted (Didion) 286

The Last Tycoon (Fitzgerald) 208

The Late George Apley (Marquand) 203, 204

The Late Mattia Pascal (Pirandello) 154, 162

Laughing Boy (LaForge) 193

Laura's Daughter (Mallet-Joris) 266

Lavengro (Borrow) 117

Lay Down Your Arms (Suttner) 140

The Lay Monk (Huysmans) 161

The Lay of the Last Minstrel (Scott) 96

Leaden Wings (Zhang) 259

Lealdade (Souza) 289

A Lear of the Steppes (Turgenev) 127

Leaving Cheyenne (McMurtry) 237

Una lección de abismo (Cano Gaviria) 281

The Left-Handed Woman (Handke) 255

The Legend of La Llorona (Anaya) 264

A Legend of Montrose (Scott) 93, 101

The Legend of Svein and Maria (Hauge) 244

Leil Zikharon (Ha'meiri) 274

Lélia (Sand) 107

Lenins Hirn (Spengler) 276

Leonard and Gertrude (Pestalozzi) 84

The Leopard (Lampedusa) 227

The Lepers (Montherlant) 206

A Lesson Before Dying (Gaines) 279

Let It Come Down (Bowles) 221

Letters from Nowhere (Wispelaere) 267

Letters to Sister Benedicta (Tremain) 257

Li viti Ota baDerekh leVeita (Kahana-Carmon) 276

The Liar (Hansen) 218

Libra (DeLillo) 270

Lie Down in Darkness (Styron) 220

Lies of Silence (Moore) 274

Lievesfluchter (Schlink) 296

Life (Miri) 296

The Life and Adventures of Martin Chuzzlewitartin Chuzzlewit (Dickens) 113

The Life and Adventures of Robinson Crusoe (Defoe) 72

Life and Adventures of Salavin (Duhamel) 180

The Life and Extraordinary Adventures of Private Ivan Chonkin (Voinovich) 254

Life and Times of Michael K. (Coetzee) 262, 263

Life at the Top (Braine) 235

The Life of an Amorous Man (Ihara Saikaku) 64

The Life of Buscon (Quevedo y Villegas) 54

The Life of Henry Brulard (Stendhal) 141

The Life of Jonathan Wild the Great (Fielding) 76

The Life of Marianne (Marivaux) 74

Life of Quintus Fixelin, Extracted from 15 Letter Boxes (Richter) 87

Life of Squire Marcos of Obregon (Espinel) 52

Life on the Mississippi (Twain) 92, 135

Lifsens rot (Lidman) 287

Light in August (Faulkner) 196

Light of Day (Desai) 259

The Light Possessed (Cheuse) 273

The Light That Failed (Kipling) 141

The Light Years (Howard) 273

Lights Thinning Tree (Nobuko) 294

Likro la 'Atalefim (Bat Shahar) 274

Lillelord (Bergen) 262

Lime Twig (Hawkes) 234

The Lime Works (Bernhard) 248

Limpieza de sangre (Pérez Reverte) 289

Lines of Fate (Kharitonov) 280

The Lion of Flanders (Conscience) 110

Litoral (Ramos) 278

Little Dorrit (Dickens) 90, 119

Little Fadette (Sand) 116

Little Man, What Now? (Fallada) 196

The Little Man of God (Lemonnier) 160

Little Men (Alcott) 128

The Little Minister (Barrie) 142

Little Women (Alcott) 126

The Little World of the Past (Fogazzaro) 146

Lituma en los Andes (Vargas Llosa) 281

The Living End (Elkin) 258

Living Water (Lispector) 251

Livlakarens besok (Enquist) 294

Liza of Lambeth (Maugham) 147

Ljuset ur Skuggornas varld (Gyllensten) 285

Local Anesthetic (Grass) 246

Lolita (Nabokov) 155, 225

Londoners (Duffy) 263

The Loneliness of the Long Distance Runner (Sillitoe) 231

The Lonely Passion of Judith Hearne (Moore) 225

Lonesome Dove (McMurtry) 265, 267

Long Ago (Corrasquilla) 200

Un long Dimanche de fiancailles (Japrisot) 276

Long Is Our Way (Makanin) 276

The Long Journey (Jensen) 166

The Long Ships (Bengtisson) 213

The Long View (Howard) 226

Look, the Euphrates Is Flowing Bloody (Kemal) 289

Look at the Harlequins! (Nabokov) 252

Look Homeward, Angel (Wolfe) 192

Looking for Mr. Goodbar (Rossner) 253

The Looking Glass (Roberts) 295

The Loom of Youth (Waugh) 176

Loon Lake (Doctorow) 259

Looney Tunes (Basara) 289

Lord Hornblower (Forester) 213

Lord Jim (Conrad) 155, 158

Lord of the Flies (Golding) 223

Lord of the Isles (Scott) 99

The Lord of the Rings (Tolkien) 223, 225, 227

Lord Ormont and His Aminta (Meredith) 144

Lorna Doone (Blackmore) 127

Losing Battles (Welty) 247

Lost Empires (Priestly) 240

The Lost Honor of Katerine Blum (Böll) 252

Lost Horizon (Hilton) 197

Lost Illusions (Balzac) 91, 110

A Lost Lady (Cather) 184

Lost Man's River (Matthiessen) 288

The Lost Manuscript (Freytag) 124

The Lost Musicians (Heinesen) 218

A Lost Wanderer (Schendel) 165

Lottie, the Watchmaker (Ebner-Eschenbach) 132

Lotus in Hades (Gyllensten) 242

Love, Again (Lessing) 286

Love After All (Magen) 296

Love and Litter (Klima) 273

Love and Mr. Lewisham (Wells) 158

Love and Pedagogy (Unamuno) 160

Love in a Cold Climate (Mitford) 217

Love in Exile (Baha'Tahir) 283

Love in the Ruins (Percy) 248

novel *(continued)*
　Love in the Time of Cholera (García Márquez) 266
　A Love Interest (Nayman) 294
　The Love of a Good Woman (Munro) 291
　Love Retreat (Prem) 182
　The Love-Crazed Boy (Barrios) 174
　The Loved and the Lost (Callaghan) 220
　The Loved One (Waugh) 216
　Lovely Malcomia (Yizhar) 291
　The Lover (Duras) 278
　Lovers of Their Time (Trevor) 257
　Loving Hands at Home (Johnson) 244
　The Lower Depths (Gorky) 160
　Loyalty (Niyazi) 224
　Lucca (Grondahl) 290
　Lucinde (Schiller) 88
　The Luck of Barry Lyndon, a Romance of the Last Century by Fitzboodle (Thackeray) 113
　The Luck of Ginger Coffey (Moore) 232
　Lucky Jim (Amis) 223
　Lucky Kristoffer (Hansen) 212
　Lucky Peter (Pontoppidan) 148
　Ludwig muss sterben (Hettche) 274
　Luna de Lobos (Llamazares) 266
　Lune (Meldini) 293
　La lunga notte (Tadini) 269
　Lure (Albahari) 289
　Lyhamar (Heggland) 276
　The Lying Days (Gordimer) 222
　Lying Low (Johnson) 257
　The Lying Truth (Yospal) 230
　The Lyre of Orpheus (Davies) 271
　Lystreise (Nilsen) 284
　Ma Qiao Dictionary (Han) 286
　The Macdermots of Ballycloran (Trollope) 115
　Macunaima (Andrade) 191
　The Mad House (Jamalzadeh) 209
　Madame Bovary (Flaubert) 92
　Madame Gervaisais (Goncourt and Goncourt) 127
　Mademoiselle Cloque (Boylesve) 149
　Mademoiselle de Maupin (Gautier) 108
　Madera de boi (Cela) 294
　La madriguera (Mercado) 287
　Madrugada (Steen) 280
　Maggie: A Girl of the Streets (Crane) 143
　A Maggot (Fowles) 266
　The Magic Kingdom (Elkin) 265
　The Magic Mountain (Mann) 152, 185
　The Magic Ring (Sefarim) 125
　Magical Realism (Brathwaite) 290
　The Magician of Lublin (Singer) 231
　Magister Ludi (The Glass Bead Game) (Hesse) 210
　The Maias (Eça de Queirós) 139
　Maid Marian (Peacock) 103
　The Maid Silja (Sillanpää) 195
　The Maidens of the Rocks (D'Annunzio) 146
　Main Street (Lewis) 179
　The Making of Americans (Stein) 169

　The Makioka Sisters (Tanizaki) 210
　Mal de amores (Mastretta) 289
　La maladie de Sachs (Winkler) 291
　Malcolm (Purdy) 231
　A Male (Lemonnier) 134
　Malina (Bachmann) 249
　Malone Dies (Beckett) 154
　The Maltese Falcon (Hammett) 193
　The Mambo Kings Play Songs of Love (Hijuelos) 273
　A Man Could Stand Up (Ford) 188
　Man Crazy (Oates) 288
　The Man Eaters of Malgudi (Narayay) 234
　Man i min alder (Claesson) 279
　A Man in Full (Wolfe) 290
　Man in the Labyrinth (Alvaro) 188
　The Man in the Mirror (Teirlinck) 225
　The Man of Feeling (Mackenzie) 81
　Man of Gold (Jókai) 129
　The Man of Property (Galsworthy) 164, 182
　Man of the People (Achebe) 243
　The Man Who Loved Children (Stead) 207
　The Man Who Was Thursday (Chesterton) 166
　The Man with the Golden Arm (Algren) 217
　The Man Within (Greene) 154, 192
　The Man Without Qualities (Musil) 193
　Mañana en la batalla piensa (Marías) 283
　The Mandarins (Beauvoir) 224
　The Mandelbaum Gate (Spark) 240
　Manhattan Transfer (Dos Passos) 186
　Manhole (Makanin) 276
　The Manilla Rope (Meri) 228
　Manon Lescaut (Prévost d'Exiles) 74
　The Manor (Singer) 244
　Man's Estate (Malraux) 197
　Mansfield Park (Austen) 91, 99
　The Mansion (Faulkner) 231
　The Manticore (Davies) 250
　Mantissa (Fowles) 261
　La manuscrit de Port-Ebène (Bona) 291
　Manuscritos de Felipa (Prado) 294
　Many Waters (L'Engle) 267
　Mao II (DeLillo) 276
　The Map of Love (Soueif) 293
　Mar Mani (Yehoshua) 274
　The Marble Faun (Hawthorne) 121
　The March of the Musicians (Enquist) 257
　The Marchioness of Yolombo (Cairasquilla) 191
　Marco e Mattio (Vassalli) 278
　Mardi (Melville) 116
　Maren Gripes nodwendige ritualer (Lonn) 294
　Maria: A South American Romance (Isaacs) 126

　Maria Alone (Delblanc) 266
　Marianna (Sandeau) 111
　Mario and the Magician (Mann) 152
　Marius the Epicurean (Pater) 137
　Marjorie Morningstar (Wouk) 225
　The Mark of the Angel (Huston) 293
　Marmion (Scott) 97
　The Marriage of Cadmus and Harmony (Calasso) 271
　The Married Man (White) 295
　A Married Priest (Barbey d'Aurevilly) 124
　Marry Me: A Romance (Updike) 254
　The Marshes (Konwicki) 227
　Martereau (Sarraute) 223
　Martha and Mary (Palacio Valdés) 136
　Martha Quest (Lessing) 221
　Martin Birck's Youth (Söderberg) 159
　Martin Chuzzlewit (Dickens) 90
　Martin Dressler (Millhauser) 288
　Martin Faber (Simms) 107
　Martín Rivas (Blest Gana) 123
　Mary (Nabokov) 155
　Mary Barton, a Tale of Manchester Life (Gaskell) 115
　Marya: A Life (Oates) 267
　Más allá del jardín (Gala) 285
　Mason & Dixon (Pynchon) 288
　The Master and Margarita (Bulgakov) 193, 242
　Master Arthur (Raabe) 128
　Master Georgie (Bainbridge) 290
　The Master of Ballantrae (Stevenson) 140
　The Master of Hestviken (Undset) 156, 187
　The Master of Persburg (Coetzee) 282
　Master Timpe (Kretzen) 139
　The Masters (Snow) 220
　Masters of the Dew (Roumains) 211
　Mastro-don Gesualdo (Verga) 140
　Match Ball (Skarmeta) 275
　The Matchmaker (Wilder) 225
　Mating (Rush) 276
　Mating Birds (Nkosi) 267
　The Matriarch (Ihimaera) 267
　Mauprat (Sand) 110
　Maurice (Forster) 249
　The Maurizius Case (Wasserman) 190
　Max Havelaar (Multatuli) 122
　The Maxman (Caine) 144
　The Mayor of Castorbridge (Hardy) 137
　Mazurka for Two Dead People (Cela) 263
　McTeague (Norris) 149
　Mea Culpa (Holt) 288
　Medea: Stimmen (Wolf) 286
　A Meditation (Benet) 246
　Meditation (Kafka) 152
　Meek Heritage (Sillanpää) 178
　Meet Me in the Green Glen (Warren) 248
　The Meeting (Reymont) 147
　Mefisto (Banville) 267
　Mein Hund, meine Sau, mein Leben (Stadler) 282

　Melincourt; or, Sir Oran Haut-ton (Peacock) 100
　Mellichampe, a Legend of the Santee (Simms) 109
　Melocotones helados (Freire) 294
　Melodien (Krausser) 280
　Los melomanos (Amo) 297
　Melville Godwin U.S.A. (Marquand) 220
　The Member of the Wedding (McCullers) 213
　Memoirs of a Cavalier (Defoe) 72
　Memoirs of a Militia Sergeant (Almeida) 118
　The Memoirs of a Survivor (Lessing) 252
　Memoirs of Leticia Valle (Chacel) 213
　Memoirs of Many in One (White) 267
　Memoirs of the Notary Public Isaias (Lima Barreto) 167
　The Memorial (Delblanc) 248
　The Memorial (Isherwood) 196
　The Memory of Old Jack (Berry) 252
　Memory of Snow and of Dust (Breytenbach) 272
　Men at Arms (Waugh) 221
　The Men Cry Alone (Gironella) 268
　Men Jorden star til evig tid (Helle) 288
　Men of Goodwill (Romains) 196
　Men of Maize (Asturias) 218
　Le m'en vais (Echenoz) 293
　El mensajero (Vallejo) 277
　Mercedes of Castile (Cooper) 111
　Mercy Among Children (Adams) 295
　Mercy of a Rude Stream (Roth) 282
　Meridian (Walker) 254
　Mesilat Barzel (Appelfeld) 276
　Messiah (Vidal) 223
　The Messiah of Stockholm (Ozick) 269
　The Metamorphosis (Kafka) 152, 174
　Meteor (Čapek) 198
　Metro: A Novel of the Moscow Undergound (Kaletski) 266
　El metro de platino iridiado (Pombo) 277
　Mezza di transporto (Rasy) 280
　Mi (Hari Narayan Apti) 144
　Michikusa (Natsume) 174
　Microcosmi (Magris) 289
　Midaq Alley (Mahfouz) 214
　Midcentury (Dos Passos) 234
　Midday Midnight (Cayrol) 241
　Middle Passage (Johnson) 273
　Middlemarch, a Study of Provincial Life (Eliot) 137
　Midnight (Green) 202
　Midnight Mass (Bowles) 260
　Midnight's Children (Rushdie) 260
　Mientras vivimos (Torres) 297
　Mikdamot (Yizhar) 278
　Mila 18 (Uris) 234
　Mildred Pierce (Cain) 208
　Miles Wallingford (Cooper) 113
　The Military Life (De Amicis) 126

The Military Philosopher (Powell) 244

The Mill on the Floss (Eliot) 121

The Mill on the Po (Bacchelli) 204

The Miller (Malherbe) 202

Mine Boy (Abrahams) 213

Mine Own Executioner (Balchin) 212

The Minister (Shahnon) 243

The Minister's Charge; or, The Apprenticeship of Lemuel Barker (Howells) 138

The Ministry of Fear (Greene) 154, 210

Minna (Gjellerup) 140

Minstrelsy of the Scottish Border (Scott) 96

The Miracles of Antichrist (Lagerlöf) 147

La mirada del alma (Díez) 289

La mirada del otro (Delgado) 285

Mirage of Fire (Hideo) 274

Miramar (Mahfouz) 242

Mirror of the Peasants (Gotthelf) 110

Les Misérables (Hugo) 123

The Misfortunes of Elphin (Peacock) 105

Miss Lonelyhearts (West) 197

Miss Peabody's Inheritance (Jolley) 263

Mission Accomplished (Betti) 216

Mist (Unamuno) 173

Mister Johnson (Cary) 206

Mitya's Love (Bunin) 187

Moby-Dick; or, The Whale (Melville) 117

Moderato Cantabile (Duras) 230

A Modern Instance (Howells) 135

Modern Monk (Thein) 201

Modern Myths (Gyllensten) 218

Modus Vivendi (Levinson) 264

Moll Flanders (Defoe) 73

Molloy (Beckett) 154, 220

A Moment in Time (Bates) 238

Moment of Freedom (Bjorneboe) 242

Momento Mori (Spark) 229

Mon grand appartement (Oster) 293

The Monarch of the Glen (Mackenzie) 208

The Monastery (Scott) 93, 102

Le monde retrouve de Louis-François Pinagot (Corbin) 291

The Monikens (Cooper) 108

The Monk (Lewis) 87

The Monk and the Hangman's Daughter (Bierce) 143

Monsieur Bergeret in Paris (France) 159

Monsignor Quixote (Greene) 154, 261

The Monster (Kadare) 239

The Monster Gods (Ba'albakki) 232

Montauk (Frisch) 254

The Montforts (Boyd) 190

A Month of Sundays (Updike) 253

The Moon and Sixpence (Maugham) 178

The Moon Is Down (Steinbeck) 209

The Moor's Last Sigh (Rushdie) 284

Las moras agraces (Jodra Davo) 294

Morbus Kitahara (Ransmayr) 284

More Die of Heartbreak (Bellow) 269

Morgan's Run (McCullough) 295

Morning at the Office (Mittelholzer) 219

La morseure (Villemin) 288

Las moscas (Azuela) 178

Moscow Not My Mecca (Carew) 238

The Mother (Deledda) 180

Mother (Gorky) 164

Mother Came (Janakiraman) 240

Mother Iceland (Guthmundur) 213

Mother Love (Wright) 284

Mother Nature (Pardo Bazán) 139

Mother Night (Vonnegut) 234

Motherkind (Phillips) 295

Moths (Ouida) 133

Mottke the Thief (Asch) 175

Le Mouchoir (Cooper) 113

The Mountain of Broom (Bourbane) 235

The Mountain of Light (Couperus) 164

Mountain Standard Time (Horgan) 235

The Mountain Village (Ayni) 190

Mountains and Men (Federer) 170

Mountolive (Durrell) 229

A Moveable Feast (Hemingway) 153

The Moviegoer (Percy) 234

Mozarts tredje hjarna (Sonnevi) 287

Mr. Midshipman Easy (Marryat) 109

Mr. Sammler's Planet (Bellow) 247

Mr. Scobie's Riddle (Jolley) 263

Mr. Visser's Journey Through Hell (Vestdijk) 201

Mr. Witt Among the Rebels (Sender) 200

Mrs. Dalloway (Woolf) 186

Mrs. Marianne (Benedictsson) 139

Mrs. Stevens Hears the Mermaids Singing (Sarton) 240

Mrs. Ted Bliss (Elkin) 284

La muerte como efecto secundario (Shua) 289

The Mulatto (Azevedo) 134

Mulheres de sombra (Ferreira) 285

Mulligan Stew (Sorrentino) 258

Munchausen (Immermann) 110

The Murderess (Papadiamantis) 171

Murphy (Beckett) 154, 204

Murther & Walding Spirits (Davies) 276

The Museum of Unconditional Surrender (Ugresic) 292

Music and Silence (Tremain) 293

Music Hall Sidelights (Colette) 172

Mutiny on the Bounty (Nordhoff) 196

My Antonia (Cather) 177

My Century (Grass) 293

My Cheerful Mornings (Klima) 273

My Death Is My Own (Ahlin) 213

My Father's Moon (Jolley) 272

My Grandpa (Yasutaka) 296

My Kinsman, Major Molineaux (Hawthorne) 107

My Lady Ludlow (Gaskell) 120

My Life as a Man (Roth) 252

My Living Shadow (Wispelaere) 240

My Michael (Oz) 245

My Novel; or, Varieties in English Life (Bulwer-Lytton) 118

My Skin (Dromer) 286

My Son's Story (Gordimer) 274

Myra Breckinridge (Vidal) 244

Mysteries (Hamsun) 143

The Mysteries of Paris (Sue) 112

The Mysteries of Udolpho (Radcliffe) 86

Mystery (Hauge) 243

The Mystery of Edwin Drood (Dickens) 90, 127

Na tua face (Ferreira) 283

Der Nachsommer (Stifter) 120

Nadja (Breton) 190

La naissance des fantomes (Darrieussecq) 291

The Naked and the Dead (Mailer) 216

Naked Feet and Seashell (Taku) 296

The Naked Lunch (Burroughs) 231

The Naked Streets (Pratolini) 213

The Name of the Rose (Eco) 259

Nana (Zola) 133

Nanso Satomi Hakken (Bakin) 112

Nao es tu, Brasil (Rubens Paiva) 287

Naomi (Tanizaki) 185

The Napoleon of Notting Hill (Chesterton) 162

Nar fisken fanger solen (Winge) 288

Nar jeg ser deg (Faldbakken) 287

El naranjo, o los círculos del tiempo (Fuentes) 281

Narcissus and Goldmund (Hesse) 193

The Narrative of Arthur Gordon Pym, of Nantucket (Poe) 110

Nati due volte (Pontiggia) 296

National Velvet (Bagnold) 200

Native Son (Wright) 207

The Natural (Malamud) 221

A Natural Curiosity (Drabble) 272

A Natural Novel (Gospodinov) 292

Natural Sciences (Chacel) 271

Nausea (Sartre) 204

The Nazarene (Asch) 206

Nazarín (Pérez Galdós) 145

The Near and the Far (Myers) 207

Near to the Savage Heart (Lispector) 212

Nectar in a Sieve (Markandaya) 224

Needs of the Poor (Gotthelf) 111

The Negro (Soupault) 189

A Negro in Paris (Dadie) 231

Nel momento (Carlo) 296

The Nephew (Purdy) 232

Never-Setting Sun (Toyoko) 294

The New Age (Hood) 273

New Grub Street (Gissing) 142

The New Machiavelli (Wells) 169

The New Men (Snow) 223

The New Sweet Style (Aksyonov) 291

The New World (Heruy) 186

The New Yorkers (Calisher) 246

The Newcomes (Thackeray) 108, 118

News from Empire (Paso) 270

News from Nowhere (Morris) 141

The Nice and the Good (Murdoch) 244

Nicholas Nickleby (Dickens) 90, 110

El nido de los sueños (Montero) 279

Niels Lynne (Jacobsen) 133

The Nigger of the "Narcissus" (Conrad) 147, 155

Night (Karasu) 283

Night and Day (Woolf) 178

Night Guard (Pontoppidan) 144

A Night in Santa Paulina (Orpaz) 289

Night in the Market Town (Ahlin) 229

The Night of the Generals (Kirst) 236

Night Rider (Warren) 205

Night Tango: A Novel of One Summer of the End of the Century (Kratochvil) 292

Nightwood (Barnes) 201

Nine, Novena (Lins) 242

Ninety-Three (Hugo) 130

Ninfa plebea (Rea) 280

Ninguna eternidad como la mía (Mastretta) 294

The Ninth of November (Kellerman) 181

No, But I Saw the Movie (De Vries) 221

No Country for Young Men (O'Faolain) 259

No Longer at Ease (Achebe) 232

No Man's Land (Onetti) 209

No More Parades (Ford) 186

No One Knows the Day (Hauge) 225

No Other Life (Moore) 280

Noces de sable (Leclerc) 284

Noli Me Tangere (Rizal) 139

None but the Brave (Schnitzler) 159

None but the Lonely Heart (Llewellyn) 210

None to Accompany Me (Gordimer) 282

Nor Any Country (St. Omer) 246

North and South (Gaskell) 119

Northanger Abbey (Austen) 91, 100

Northwest Passage (Roberts) 203

Norwegian Wood (Murakami) 269

Nostromo (Conrad) 155, 162

The Noszty Boy and Mary Tóth (Mikszáth) 166

Not Honour More (Cary) 225

Note About the Author (Matanovic) 295

novel *(continued)*

The Notebook of Malte Laurids Brigge (Rilke) 155, 168
Notes from Underground (Dostoyevsky) 90, 124
Notes of a Student Examinee (Maso) 175
Nothing (Laforet) 217
Nothing Important Ever Dies (Gary) 233
Nôtre-Dame de Paris (Hugo) 106
Nottetempo, casa per case (Consolo) 278
Nous sommes eternels (Fleutiaux) 274
Nova Express (Burroughs) 238
November 1916 (Solzhenitsyn) 280
La novia de Matisse (Vincent) 297
The Novice (Lermontov) 111
Now in November (Johnson) 200
Nowhere to Go (Leskov) 124
Nubosidad variable (Martín Gaite) 279
Nuestra señora de la noche (Denevi) 289
La nuit de lerreur (Ben Jelloun) 289
Number One (Dos Passos) 210
O Cesar o nada (Vásquez Montalbán) 292
O Pioneers! (Cather) 172
The Oak Openings; or, The Bee Hunter (Cooper) 115
The Oasis (McCarthy) 217
The Obedient Wife (O'Faolain) 261
Obid Ketman (Qodiriy) 201
Oblomov (Goncharov) 121
The Obscene Bird of Night (Donoso) 248
An Obscure Man (Yourcenar) 266
The Obscure Woman (Lima) 206
The Ocean of Night (Ali) 239
Ocean Sea (Baricco) 293
Och jag grep arorna och rodde (Lillpers) 292
La Ocher de Tanios (Maalouf) 280
October Light (Gardner) 254
The Octopus (Norris) 159
Oda Oark Oracle (Gabre-Madhin) 240
O.D.C. (Aster) 293
Odd Girl Out (Howard) 250
Odeur d'encre, odeur d'îles (Jacq) 276
The Odyssey (Fyodorov) 285
L'oeil du silence (Lambron) 280
L'oeuvre postume de Thomas Pilaster (Chevillard) 293
Of Human Bondage (Maugham) 174
Of Love and Other Demons (García Márquez) 285
Of Love and Shadows (Allende) 265
Of Mice and Men (Steinbeck) 203
Of Time and the River (Wolfe) 194, 200
The Office of Peace on Orolandia (Arévalo) 187
Officers and Gentlemen (Waugh) 225
An Official Tale (Pavlov) 285
L'offrande sauvage (Milavanoff) 293

Oh What a Paradise It Seems (Cheever) 261
Oil Man of Oanje (Munonye) 247
Oil! (Sinclair) 189
Los ojos del basilisco (Espinosa) 281
The Old and the Young (Pirandello) 172
The Old Curiosity Shop (Dickens) 90, 111
Old Goriot (Balzac) 108
The Old Gringo (Fuentes) 266
The Old Jest (Johnston) 258
The Old Man (Trifonov) 257
The Old Man of the Mountain (Deladda) 158
The Old Man with the Kites (Ritsos) 266
Old Mortality (Scott) 93, 100
Old River Daydreams (Liu) 279
Old Sites (Li) 279
Old Soldier (Bourjaily) 273
The Old Wives' Tale (Bennett) 166
Oliver Twist (Dickens) 90, 109
Om natten i Jerusalem (Kosovic) 292
Omoo, a Narrative of Adventures on the South Seas (Melville) 115
Omvei til Venus (Schgerven) 284
On Heroes and Tombs (Sábato) 234
On Reading Turgenev (Trevor) 276
On the Beach (Shute) 228
On the Eve (Turgenev) 122
On the Farm (Updike) 240
On the Road (Kerouac) 228
On the Track of God (Rivière) 186
On Trial for My Country (Samkange) 241
The Once and Future King (White) 229
One, None, and a Hundred Thousand (Pirandello) 154, 187
One Dark Body (Sherman) 279
One Day in October (Hoel) 195
One Day in the Life of Ivan Denisovich (Solzhenitsyn) 154, 236
One Flew Over the Cuckoo's Nest (Kesey) 235
One Hundred Years of Solitude (García Márquez) 243
One Million Dead (Gironelda) 234
One of Life's Slaves (Lie) 136
One of Our Conquerors (Meredith) 142
One of Ours (Cather) 182, 183
One the Margins (Go) 281
The Onion Eaters (Donleavy) 241
Onitsha (Le Clezio) 276
The Only Problem (Spark) 264
Open Secrets (Munro) 282
Operation Shylock (Roth) 279
The Opermanns (Feuchtwanger) 197
Oppdageren (Kjaerstad) 294, 296
The Optimist's Daughter (Welty) 250
Oranges from Morocco (Aksyonov) 237
The Orchard on Fire (Mackay) 286

The Orchid House (Allfrey) 222
The Ordeal of Gilbert Pinfold (Waugh) 228
The Ordeal of Richard Feverel (Meredith) 121
An Ordinary Life (Čapek) 198
L'Ordre (Arland) 192
L'organization (Rolin) 286
Orient Express (Greene) 154, 196
Orlanda (Harpma) 286
Orley Farm (Trollope) 122
Ormens ar (Faldbakken) 280
Ormond (Brown) 88
Ormond (Edgeworth) 100
Oroonoko, or the History of the Royal Slave (Behn) 63
Os Tambores de São Luis (Montello) 254
Oskuldens minut (Lidman) 294
Oswald's Tale (Mailer) 284
The Other One (Green) 249
The Other Side (Kubin) 167
Other Voices, Other Rooms (Capote) 216
Other Women (Lau) 284
Otherwise Engaged (Gray) 253
La otra orilla de la droga (Tomás García) 266
La otra selva (Salazar) 277
Otro baile en Paris (Lafourcade) 296
Our Conquest (Hoffmann) 264
Our Gang (Roth) 248
Our Lady of the Flowers (Genet) 211
Our Man in Havana (Greene) 154, 229
Our Mutual Friend (Dickens) 90, 124
Our Wedding (Rabinyan) 293
The Outcast (Pirandello) 154, 159
Outerbridge Reach (Stone) 277
The Outlander (Guèvremont) 219
Outrora agora (Abelaira) 289
The Ox-Bow Incident (Clark) 207
Pa St. Jorgen (Skram) 145
Paco's Story (Heinemann) 269
El pacto (Palma) 289
Paddy Clarke Ha Ha Ha (Doyle) 280
The Painted Bird (Kosinski) 240
Painted Roofs (Richardson) 174
Painter Nolten (Morike) 107
A Painter of Our Time (Berger) 229
A Pair of Blue Eyes (Hardy) 129
A paixao (Faria) 294
The Palace of Dreams (Kadare) 260
Palace to Let (Karamosmanoglu) 183
Palatsbarnen (Collarp) 294
Pale Fire (Nabokov) 155, 235
Pallid Night (Jia) 284
Palmerin of England (Southey) 97
The Palm-Wine Drinkard (Tutuola) 222
La palude definitiva (Manganelli) 276
Pan (Hamsun) 145
Pan Beat (Jones) 251
Pan Michael (Sienkiewicz) 139
Panim baA'nan (Birstein) 276
Panteros (Pignatari) 280
Panu (Aho) 147

Papas Koffer (Kopf) 280
The Paper Men (Golding) 264
The Parable of the Blind (Hoffmann) 266
Parade's End (Ford) 185, 186, 188, 219
Paradise (Morrison) 290
Paradise Lost (Jun'ichi) 289
Paradise Regained (Laxness) 233
Paraíso (Lima) 242
The Paralyzed (Tur) 220
Pargfrider (Heym) 291
Parôle de sige (Cahuzac) 274
Partes de Africa (Macedo) 278
Les particules élémentaires (Houellebecq) 291
The Partisan (Simms) 108
La pasión turca (Gala) 281
Pasmore (Storey) 250
Pasquier Chronicle (Duhamel) 197
A Passage to India (Forster) 185
Passaggio in ombra (Di Lascia) 284
De Passievrucht (Loon) 293
Passing Time (Butor) 227
Passion (Hercikova) 290
The Passion According to G.H. (Lispector) 239
The Passion Artist (Hawkes) 258
A Passion in Rome (Callaghan) 234
Die Passionfrucht (Piwitt) 280
Pastors and Masters (Compton-Burnett) 186
The Path to the Nest of Spiders (Calvino) 215
The Pathfinder (Cooper) 111
The Patrioteer (Mann) 177
Patronage (Edgeworth) 99
Paul Against Paul (Wispelaere) 247
Paul Clifford (Bulwer-Lytton) 106
Paul et Virginie (Bernardin de Saint-Pierre) 85
The Paul Street Boy (Molnár) 165
Pauper Tyetko (Banmo) 222
Pawels Briefe (Maron) 293
Les Paysans (Balzac) 114
Peace (Garborg) 143
Peace After the War (Gironella) 242
Peace Breaks Out (Knowles) 259
Peacock's Feathers (Kruczkowski) 200
The Pearl (Steinbeck) 215
The Peasant Nga Ba (Maun) 214
Peasant Students (Garborg) 136
Le Peau de chagrin (Balzac) 106
Peder Victorious (Rolvaag) 190
Pedro e Paula (Macedo) 291
Peg Woffington (Reade) 118
The Pegnitz Junction (Gallant) 251
Pelham; or, The Adventures of a Gentleman (Bulwer-Lytton) 105
Pendant la chaleur du jour (Pradier) 293
Penguin Island (France) 166
The Penitent (Singer) 263
Penrod (Tarkington) 173
People in Summer Night (Sillanpää) 199
People in Time (Bontempelli) 203

The People of Hemso (Strindberg) 93, 139
The People of Juvik (Dunn) 177
People of Puszta (Illyés) 202
People of the Cave (al-Hakim) 197
People of the City (Ekwensi) 224
Pepe Carvalho (Vázquez Montal-bán) 277
Pepita Jiménez (Valera) 130
Pequeñas infamias (Posada) 292
El pequeño heredero (Martín Garzo) 289
Le Père Goriot (Balzac) 91
The Perfumed Pillow (Koyo) 141
Perou (Braudeau) 291
Persephone Remembers (Megged) 296
Persian Letters (Montesquieu) 73
A Person Not to Be Trusted (Otroshenko) 296
The Personal Recollections of Joan of Arc (Twain) 146
Persuasion (Austen) 91, 100
Perversas familias (Assis Brasil) 280
Peter Camenzind (Hesse) 162
Peter Ibbetson (du Maurier) 142
Peter the Great (Tolstoy) 192
Le Petit chose (Daudet) 126
La petite fille qui aimait trop les allumettes (Soucy) 291
Peveril of the Peak (Scott) 103
The Phantom of the Opera (Leroux) 168
The Pharaoh (Memmi) 271
Philadelphia Fire (Wideman) 273
Philosopher or Dog? (Machado de Assis) 142
Phineas Finn (Trollope) 126
Phineas Redux (Trollope) 130
The Piano Tuner (Cheng) 272
Pickwick Papers (Dickens) 90, 109
The Picture of Dorian Gray (Wilde) 141
Pictures of Fidelman (Malamud) 246
Pieces of Light (Thorpe) 290
La piel del tambor (Pérez Reverte) 287
Pieles de leopardo (Mata) 281
Pierre; or, The Ambiguities (Melville) 117
Pierrot (Queneau) 210
Pigan i Arras (Claeson) 281
Pigs in Heaven (Kingsolver) 279
The Pilgrim Kamanita (Gjellerup) 164
Pilgrimage (Richardson) 174, 243
The Pilgrim's Rules of Etiquette (Modarressi) 272
The Pillar of Salt (Memmi) 223
Pillars of Society (Franko) 145
The Pilot (Cooper) 103
Pinch Runner's Record (Oe) 230
Pincher Martin (Golding) 227
The Pioneers; or, The Sources of the Susquehanna Frontier (Cooper) 103
The Pioneers (Prichard) 174
The Pirate (Scott) 93
The Pistol (Jones) 229
Pity for Women (Montherlant) 202
A Place to Come To (Warren) 256
The Plague (Camus) 155, 215

Plains Song (Morris) 260
Plainsong (Haruf) 293
Planet of the Apes (Boulle) 237
Plankton (Voskuil) 290
Plans for Departure (Sahgal) 266
Plantation Boy (Rego) 196
Play by Play (Goldemberg) 266
Play It As It Lays (Didion) 247
Player Piano (Vonnegut) 221
The Playmaker (Keneally) 269
Pleasured (Hensher) 290
Pledged (Drachmann) 141
Plenilunio (Muñoz Molina) 289
Pluck the Bird and Destroy the Off-spring (Oe) 230
Plum and Jaggers (Shreve) 295
Plumb (Green) 257
The Plumed Serpent (Lawrence) 188
Pnin (Nabokov) 155, 228
Poetens liv (Mattson) 294
Point Counter Point (Huxley) 190
Point of No Return (Marquand) 217
The Poison Tree (Chatterjee) 129
Poisson d'or (Le Clezio) 288
The Ponder Heart (Welty) 223
Po-on (Jose) 264
The Poor (Mann) 176
Poor Folk (Dostoyevsky) 90, 115
The Poor Gentleman (Conscience) 117
The Poorhouse Fair (Updike) 231
Pope and Emperor in the Village (Federer) 187
Poplene pa St. Hanshaugen (Vik) 276
Poppa John (Woiwode) 260
Por el sendero de los ágeles caídos (Hoyos) 275
Porgy (Heyward) 186
Portland Valley (Flogstad) 256
Portnoy's Complaint (Roth) 246
Portrait in Brownstone (Auchincloss) 235
Portrait in Sepia (Allende) 296
The Portrait of a Lady (James) 91, 134
Portrait of a Man Unknown (Sarraute) 216
Portrait of a Paladin (Huidobro) 192
Posillipo (Rasy) 289
The Possessed (Dostoyevsky) 90, 129
Possessing the Secret of Joy (Walker) 277
Possession (Bromfield) 186
Possession (Byatt) 273
Post Mortem (Kaniuk) 278
Postcards (Proulx) 279
The Posthumous Papers of the Pickwick Club (Dickens) 90, 109
The Postman Always Rings Twice (Cain) 198
The Power and the Glory (Greene) 154, 207
The Prairie (Cooper) 105
Praisesong for the Widow (Marshall) 262
A Prayer for Owen Meany (Irving) 272
Precaution (Cooper) 102
Precious Bane (Webb) 185
Precious Thing (Kenway) 295

The Precipice (Goncharov) 127
A Premeditated Murder (Selenic) 283
Premier (Shahnon) 246
Pride and Prejudice (Austen) 91, 99
The Prime Minister (Trollope) 131
The Prime of Miss Jean Brodie (Spark) 234
The Prince and the Pauper (Twain) 92, 134
The Prince of Tides (Conroy) 269
The Prince with Donkey Ears (Regio) 209
The Princess Cassmassima (James) 91, 137
Princess Nur al-Nin (al-Hadi) 192
The Princess of Montpensier (La Fayette) 60
La Princesse de Clèves (La Fayette) 63
Prins (Michaels) 288
Prioritaire (Hermann) 290
The Prisoner of Urga (Krasznahorkai) 280
The Prisoner of Zenda (Hope) 144
The Private Papers of Henry Ryecroft (Gissing) 161
Private Renaissance (Bellonci) 272
De procedure (Mulisch) 293
The Prodigy (Hesse) 163
The Professor (Brontë) 120
The Professor of Desire (Roth) 256
The Professor's House (Cather) 186
Progetto Burlamacchi (Duranti) 282
The Progress of Love (Munro) 267
Promise in Summer (Chuya) 296
The Promised Land (Pontoppidan) 142
The Promised Land (Rivera) 181
A Proper Marriage (Lessing) 223
Property and Value (Hood) 273
The Proprietor of the Sun Inn (Kurz) 119
The Prostitute (Surangkhanang) 203
Das Provisorium (Hilbig) 296
La prueba del laberinto (Sánchez Drago) 279
Pryasliny: A Saga of Peasant Life (Abramov) 253
The Public Burning (Coover) 256
Publieke werken (Rosenboom) 295
Pupils of the Dean (Dinis) 126
The Pure and the Impure (Colette) 208
The Pure Element of Time (Be'er) 293
The Purple Plain (Bates) 213
The Pursuit of Love (Mitford) 212
The Puttermesser Papers (Ozick) 288
Pylon (Faulkner) 200
The Pyramid (Golding) 243
Quarantine (Crace) 288
Les quartières d'hiver (Pancrazi) 274
O Que Agora Me Inquieta (Coutinho) 266
The Queen of the Grecian Jails (Lins) 230

The Queen's Diadem (Almqvist) 108
Quentin Durward (Scott) 93, 103
Querido primer novio (Valdés) 294
Querrelle of Brest (Genet) 215
The Quest for Corvo (Rolfe) 199
A Question of Upbringing (Powell) 220
Quien como Dios (González) 292
Quien Metanarrative (Canique) 289
The Quiet American (Greene) 154, 225
A quintas das virtudes (Caludio) 276
Quinx; or, The Ripper's Tale (Durrell) 266
Quo Vadis? (Sienkiewicz) 145
Rabbit, Run (Updike) 232
Rabbit at Rest (Updike) 273, 275
Rabbit Is Rich (Updike) 260
The Rabid Toy (Arlt) 188
The Radiance of the King (Laye) 224
The Radiant Way (Drabble) 269
A Rage to Live (O'Hara) 217
Ragtime (Doctorow) 253
The Railway (Aho) 136
The Railway Station Man (Johnston) 264
Rain Afterwards Rain? (Keiko) 296
Rain at Daybreak (Johnson) 198
The Rain Bird (Lidman) 230
The Rainbow (Lawrence) 174
Rainbow (Mao) 277
The Raj Quartet (Scott) 241, 244
Rameau's Nephew (Diderot) 80
Ramona (Jackson) 136
Random Harvest (Hilton) 208
The Rape of Tamar (Jacobson) 247
Rarahu (Loti) 133
Lo raro es vivir (Martín Gaite) 287
Rasero (Robelledo) 283
The Rat (Grass) 268
Rates of Exchange (Bradbury) 263
Ratner's Star (DeLillo) 254
The Ravishing of Lol V. Stein (Duras) 239
Ravnen (Goldsmith) 125
Raw Material (Sillitoe) 250
Rays and Sunrise (Santos) 164
The Razor's Edge (Maugham) 211
The Reader (Schlink) 288
Reader's Block (Markson) 286
Reading in the Dark (Deane) 286
The Real Life of Alejandro Mayta (Vargas Llosa) 266
The Real Life of Sebastian Knight (Nabokov) 155, 208
Real sitio (Sampedro) 281
The Realist (Broch) 196
Rebecca (du Maurier) 204
Rebecca and Rowenna: A Romance Upon Romance (Thackeray) 116
The Rebel Angel (Davies) 260
The Rebel Generation (Ammers-Küller) 186
The Rebellion of the Hanged (Traven) 202
Rebus (Rosei) 274
The Recognition (Gaddis) 225

novel *(continued)*

The Rector of Justin (Auchincloss) 238

The Red, White and Blue (Dunne) 269

The Red and the Black (Stendhal) 106

The Red Badge of Courage (Crane) 145

The Red Room (Strindberg) 92, 133

The Red Room Tavern (Ye) 281

The Red Rover (Cooper) 105

Red Sorghum (Mo) 273

The Red Wheel (Solzhenitsyn) 154, 249, 280

Redburn (Melville) 116

Redgauntlet (Scott) 93, 103

The Redskins (Cooper) 114

The Redundancy of Courage (Mo) 276

Reef (Gunasekara) 282

Reflections in a Golden Eye (McCullers) 208

Le regard de Vincent (Philippe) 269

The Regentess (Alas) 136

A Regicide (Robbe-Grillet) 257

La reina de las nieves (Martín Gaite) 283

The Reivers (Faulkner) 235, 236

Rejsen med Emma (Svendsen) 286

The Remains of the Day (Ishiguro) 272

Remembering Babylon (Malouf) 280, 286

Remembrance of Things Past (Proust) 171, 178, 180, 181, 184, 186, 190

Remembrance Rock (Sandburg) 216

Remise de peine (Modiano) 271

Le Rendez-vous (Robbe-Grillet) 258

René (Chateaubriand) 97

Renée Mauperin (Goncourt and Goncourt) 124

The Republic of Wine (Mo) 295

Requiem for a Nun (Faulkner) 220

Requiem for a Spanish Peasant (Sender) 223

Requiem (Kyoko) 274

La resistencia (Sábato) 296

Restoring Former Loves (Kenaz) 291

Resurrection (Tolstoy) 90, 149

Retable, Reverie (Chawaf) 252

Return from India (Yehoshua) 282

Return from the Stars (Lem) 234

The Return of the King (Tolkien) 227

The Return of the Native (Hardy) 132

The Return of the Spirit (al-Hakim) 197

Return to Ithaca (Johnson) 214

Return to Region (Benet) 243

The Returnee (Maramzin) 294

Revenge for Love (Lewis) 203

Revolt in Aspromonte (Alvaro) 193

Revolution of the Sun (Bontempelli) 208

Rice (Su) 275

Riceyman Steps (Bennett) 184

Richard Carvel (Churchill) 149

Richard Hardis; or, The Avenger of Blood (Simms) 110

Richard Savage (Gutzkow) 111

Rickshaw Boy (Lao) 216

The Riders (Winton) 284

Riders in the Chariot (White) 234

Rienzi; or, The Last of the Tribunes (Bulwer-Lytton) 108

The Right of the Strongest (Buysse) 144

Ring of Youth (Hiroshi) 218

El río del tiempo (Vallejo) 294

The Ripening Seed (Colette) 184

The Ripple from the Storm (Lessing) 229, 231

The Rise of Silas Lapham (Howells) 137

Rites of Passage (Golding) 259

Rituals (Nooteboom) 259

Riven Rock (Boyle) 290

The River (Godden) 213

The River (Yermakov) 294

River of Fire (Haidar) 231

A River Town (Keneally) 284

The Riverside Willas Murder (Amis) 251

The Road (Martinson) 217

The Road Home (Harrison) 290

The Road Sign at the End of the Street (Abe) 217

The Road to Calvary (Tolstoy) 181, 214

The Road to Nowhere (Grin) 193

The Road to the Open (Schnitzler) 166

Road to the World's End (Hoel) 198

The Roads to Freedom (Sartre) 212

Roadwalker (Grau) 282

Rob Roy (Scott) 93, 100

The Robber Bride (Atwood) 280

The Robber Bridegroom (Welty) 209

The Rocky Road (Quieroz) 203

Roderick Hudson (James) 91, 130

Roger's Version (Updike) 267

Le roi du bois (Michon) 286

Le Roman comique (Scarron) 58

The Roman (Waltari) 239

The Romance of a Poor Young Man (Feuillet) 120

The Romance of Leonardo da Vinci (Merezhkovsky) 159

The Romantic (Broch) 195

Romola (Eliot) 123

A Room (Shimoni) 293

Room at the Top (Braine) 228

A Room with a View (Forster) 166

Roots (Cosic) 224

Roses Are Difficult Here (Mitchell) 273

Der Rote Ritter (Muschg) 280

Das rote Schiff (Mand) 282

Rotten Wood (Berent) 161

The Rout (Fadeyev) 189

Roxana; or, the Unfortunate Mistress (Defoe) 73

Rudin (Turgenev) 119

Ruin (Fenoglio) 224

La ruina del cielo (Diez) 297

Ruined Mountains (Nadi) 285

The Rules of Engagement (Bush) 295

Rum Punch (Leonard) 277

Rummies (Benchley) 272

El rumor del astracán (Bibliowicz) 277

The Runaway Soul (Brodkey) 276

Rushes (Rechy) 258

A Russian Beauty (Yerofeyev) 274

A Russian Schoolboy (Aksakov) 119

Ruth (Gaskell) 118

Rymdvarktaren (Nilson) 285

Sa femme (Bernheim) 280

Sabbath's Theater (Roth) 284

Sabine (Lacretelle) 196

Die Sache mit Randow (Schelsinger) 286

The Sacred and Profane Love Machine (Murdoch) 252

Sacred Hunger (Unsworth) 277, 278

The Saddest Summer of Samuel S. (Donleavy) 241

Sadler's Birthday (Tremain) 255

The Sadness of the Kite (Mallet-Joris) 271

Saint Francis of Assisi (Federer) 166

Saint Manuel the Good Martyr (Unamuno) 198

Salame ved reisens slutt (Hansen) 276

Salammbô (Flaubert) 92, 123

Salka Valka (Laxness) 195

Sally Bowles (Isherwood) 203

Salt of the Earth (Wittli) 202

Salterton Trilogy (Davies) 220

The Same Sea (Oz) 291

The Samurai (Endo) 259

San Camilo (Cela) 246

Sancho Saldana (Espronceda y Delgado) 108

Sanctuary (Faulkner) 194

The Sandcastle (Murdoch) 228

The Sandglass (Gunasekara) 291

Sanditon (Austen) 100

Sandra Belloni (Meredith) 124

Sandro of Chegem (Iskander) 257

Sangue na floresta (Olinto) 280

Sanine (Artsybasheff) 165

Santo oficio de la memoria (Giardinelli) 281

São Bernardo (Ramos) 199

Sapphira and the Slave Girl (Cather) 207

Sappho (Daudet) 136

Lo sapsimo de Palermo (Consolo) 293

Sarāh (al-Aqqad) 204

Sarah, Sarah (Matalon) 296

Sartosis (Faulkner) 192

Satanstoe (Cooper) 114

Satomi and the Eight Dogs (Bakin) 99

Saturday Night and Sunday Morning (Sillitoe) 229

Saturday Sun (Moretti) 165

Saville (Storey) 255

Scandal (Endo) 268

Scar Tissue (Ignatieff) 280

The Scarlet City (Haasse) 221

The Scarlet Letter (Hawthorne) 116

The Scarlet Pimpernel (Orczy) 163

Scarlet Sister Mary (Peterkin) 191

Schiller's Homeland Years (Kurz) 113

Schindler's Ark (Keneally) 261

Schultz (Donleavy) 258

Scoop (Waugh) 204

The Scorpion or the Imaginary Confession (Memmi) 246

The Scout; or, The Black Riders of Congaree (Simms) 118

Se esconde tras los ojos (Toledo) 296

The Sea, the Sea (Murdoch) 257

The Sea and Poison (Endo) 228

The Sea Change (Howard) 231

The Sea Lions (Cooper) 115

The Sea of Fertility (Mishima) 240

The Sea Wolf (London) 162

The Seagull (Caballero) 116

The Search (Snow) 199

A Season for Falling in Love (Wang) 279

A Season in Paradise (Breytenbach) 255

Season of Anomy (Soyinka) 251

The Second Coming (Percy) 259

The Second Curtain (Fuller) 222

Second Marriage (Barthelme) 264

The Second Skin (Hawkes) 238

The Secret Agent (Conrad) 155, 165

The Secret Record of Naruto (Yoshikawa) 188

Secrets (Farah) 291

Seduction of the Minotaur (Nin) 234

Seed (Ray) 223

The Seed Beneath the Snow (Silone) 207

See Under: Love (Grossman) 272

Sefere haMeforash (Heffner) 276

Seierherrene (Jacobsen) 276

Selige Zeiten, burchige Welt (Menasse) 278

Sena sagor (Jersild) 292

El señor de los mil días (Aridjis) 283

Sense and Sensibility (Austen) 91, 98

Sentimental Education (Flaubert) 92, 127

A Sentimental Journey Through France and Italy (Sterne) 81

Sentimental Memoirs of João Miramar (Andrade) 185

A Separate Peace (Knowles) 231, 259

The Separation (Franck) 276

Separazione (Sanvitale) 289

Les sept noms du peintre (Le Guillou) 288

Serena Cruz (Ginzburg) 274

Serenity House (Hope) 278

The Serious Game (Söderberg) 171

Serpent and Bull (Hansen) 221

Set for Life (Freeman) 276

Seta (Baricco) 287

The Setting Sun (Dazai) 215

Setting the World on Fire (Wilson) 259

The Settlement of Centaurs (Kim) 278

Seven Brothers (Kivi) 127
The Seven Madmen (Arlt) 192
The Seven Seas (Martinson) 192
Seven Strings of the Lyre (Sand) 111
Seventeen (Tarkington) 175
Severe Passions (Holm) 248
A Severed Head (Murdoch) 234
The Shadow Boxer (Heighten) 295
The Shadow Knows (Johnson) 252
The Shadow of the Leader (Guzmán) 192
Shadows Against the Wall (Rojas) 239
Shadows on Our Skin (Johnston) 256
Shadows on the Rock (Cather) 194
A Shady Business (Balzac) 91
Shaihu Umar (Balewa) 225
Shalimar (Markandaya) 263
The Shape of Things to Come (Wells) 197
The Shawl (Ozick) 272
She (Haggard) 138
She Drove Without Stopping (Gordon) 273
Shelter (Phillips) 282
The Sheltering Sky (Bowles) 216
Shining Lights (Yizhar) 280
Shining Tip (Rojas) 232
Ship of Fools (Porter) 235
The Ship Sails On (Grieg) 185
The Shipping News (Proulx) 281
The Ships (Quesada) 278
The Shipwreck (Kume) 182
The Shipyard (Onetti) 234
Shirley (Brontë) 116
Shoeless Joe (Kinsella) 261
The Shoes of the Fisherman (West) 240
Shogun (Clavell) 253
A Shooting Star (Stegner) 234
Shosha (Singer) 257
Show Boat (Ferber) 188
The Shrimp and the Anemone (Hartley) 211
Shrimps (Pillai) 227
The Sibyl (Besse Luis) 224
Siddhartha (Hesse) 182
Sidste sommer (Skou-Hansen) 277
Signals from the Flames (Pacheco) 260
Silas Marner (Eliot) 122
The Silence (Bjorneboe) 251
Silence (Endo) 242
Silence (Stryjkowski) 280
A Silence of Desire (Markandaya) 232
The Silent Cry (Oe) 230
The Silent Rooms (Hébert) 230
Il silenzio (Lagorio) 280
The Silmarillion (Tolkien) 256
Silsie (Redonnet) 274
The Silver Chalice (Costain) 221
Silver City (Li) 290
A Silver Spoon (Galsworthy) 188
The Simple Past (Chraibi) 224
Simplicissimus the Vagabond, that is the Life of a Strange Adventurer Named Melchio Sternfels von Fuchsheim (Grimmelshausen) 61
The Sin of Father Amaro (Eça de Queirós) 131

Sincerely, Willis Wayde (Marquand) 225
Sinfonía desde el Nuevo Mundo (Espinosa) 275
The Singapore Grip (Farrell) 257
A Single Man (Isherwood) 238
A Singular Man (Donleavy) 237
The Sinner (Cosic) 274
Sinners in Summertime (Hoel) 189
Sir Launcelot Greaves (Smollett) 79
Sirens of Titan (Vonnegut) 231
Sister Carrie (Dreiser) 158
Sitti Nurbaja (Rusli) 182
Sitting Duck (Radichkov) 290
The Sixth One (Arguedas) 234
Sixtus and Sesto (Federer) 172
Det skabtes vaklen Arabesker (Thomsen) 286
Skammen (Haff) 287
Skating in the Dark (Kaplan) 276
Skerret (O'Flaherty) 196
Skimmer (Tunstrom) 287
The Skin (Malaparte) 218
Skumring e Praha (Carling) 288
The Sky of September (Michitsuna) 257
Skyggen i dit sted (Grondahl) 275
Slangen i Sydney (Larsen) 290
The Slave (Amadi) 257
The Slave Merchant (Bujah) 284
Slaves in Their Chains (Theotokis) 182
The Sleep of the Just (Mammeri) 225
Sleepers in Moon-Crowded Valleys (Purdy) 247
The Sleepwalkers (Broch) 195, 196
The Small Black Room (Balchin) 210
The Small House in Allington (Trollope) 123
Small World (Lodge) 264
Smile of the Lamb (Grossman) 268
Smiles on Washington Square (Federman) 265
Smoke (Turgenev) 126
The Snake (Dagerman) 213
Snares Without End (Quenum) 232
Snow Country (Kawabata) 156, 217
The Snow Dance (Yoshiko) 269
Snow Falling on Cedars (Guterson) 282
Snow White (Barthelme) 243
So Big (Ferber) 185, 186
So Long, See You Tomorrow (Maxwell) 261
The Sobbing Lancang River (Zhu) 273
Sogni mancini (Duranti) 289
El sol de Breda (Pérez Reverte) 294
Solar Eclipse (Heiichiro) 294
Las soldaderas (Poniatowska) 294
The Soldier's Art (Powell) 241
Soldier's Pay (Faulkner) 188
A Soldier's Play (Fuller) 260
Il sole e innocenti (Camarca) 278
La soledad era esto (Millas) 275
Le soleil des mourants (Izzo) 293
Solformokelson (Enger) 283

The Solid Mandala (White) 241
A Solid Sheet (Bedi) 236
Solitude (Acevedo Díaz) 145
Solomon Gursky Was Here (Richler) 273
Som dine dagerer (Elstad) 284
La sombra del angel (Mayoral) 297
Some Came Running (Jones) 228
Some Do Not (Ford) 185
Some Prefer Nettles (Tanizaki) 191
Someone to Run With (Grossman) 296
Something in Disguise (Howard) 246
Son (Ramamitram) 240
Son de mar (Vincent) 294
The Son of a Servant (Strindberg) 138
Son of Man (Roa Bastos) 233
A Son of the Circus (Irving) 282
Son of the Morning (Oates) 257
Son of the Morning (Phillpotts) 158
The Song of Berndotte (Werfel) 208
Song of Lawino (p'Bitek) 241
Song of Solomon (Morrison) 256
The Song of the Blood-Red Flower (Linnankoski) 163
Song of the Lark (Cather) 174
Song of the Road (Pather Panchali) (Bandyopadhyay) 191
Song of the Sugarcanes (Sadik) 253
The Song of the World (Giono) 199
A Song of Truth and Semblance (Nooteboom) 260
Sonhos tropicais (Scliar) 278
Sophie's Choice (Styron) 258
A Sorrow Beyond Dreams (Handke) 250
The Sorrows of Young Werther (Goethe) 67, 82
Sostiene Pereira (Tabucchi) 282, 284
The Sot-Weed Factor (Barth) 232
The Sound and the Fury (Faulkner) 192
The Sound of the Mountain (Kawabata) 156, 221
The Sound of Waves (Mishima) 224
The Source (Michener) 240
Sous l'étoile du chien (Puech) 276
The South (Toibin) 274
South of the Border, West of the Sun (Murakami) 294
South Wind (Douglas) 176
Southern Mail (Saint-Exupéry) 192
The Southpaw (Harris) 222
Sparks (Raffi) 135
Spartina (Casey) 272
The Spectacle at the Tower (Hoffmann) 262
The Spectator Bird (Stegner) 255
Speedboat (Adler) 255
The Spell (Broch) 223
A Spell in Winter (Dumore) 286
Spider Web: A Novel (Lively) 290
The Spider's House (Bowles) 225
The Spire (Golding) 238

Spiridion (Sand) 111
The Spoils of Poynton (James) 91, 147
A Sport of Nature (Gordimer) 269
The Sport of the Gods (Dunbar) 160
Spring and the Untimely Return of Winter (Aho) 164
Ein springender Brunnen (Walser) 291
Springtime (Achchygyya) 212
The Sputnik Sweetheart (Murakami) 294
The Spy: A Tale of the Neutral Ground (Cooper) 102
S.S. San Pedro (Cozzens) 194
St. Ronan's Well (Scott) 103
St. Urbain's Horseman (Richler) 249
St. Valentine's Day; or, The Fair Maid of Perth (Scott) 105
Staccando l'ombra da terra (del Giudice) 284
Stalingrad (Plievier) 214
A Stamp Album (Sergeyev) 287
Star of Satan (Bernanos) 188
The Stars Look Down (Cronin) 200
Staying On (Scott) 256
Steppenwolf (Hesse) 189
Steps (Kosinski) 244
Stern (Friedman) 235
Still Life (Byatt) 265
Stone Bird (Delblanc) 252
The Stone Country (La Guma) 243
The Stone Diaries (Shields) 280, 283
Stonedial (Konrád) 296
The Store (Stribling) 197
The Stormy Sea (Pisemsky) 123
The Story of a New Zealand River (Mander) 180
The Story of a South African Farm (Schreiner) 135
The Story of Borge (Branner) 209
The Story of Gosta Berling (Lagerlöf) 142
The Story of the Abderites (Wieland) 82
The Story of the Water Channel (Jamalzadeh) 215
The Storyteller (Vargas Llosa) 270, 272
La strada per Roma (Volponi) 276
Strait Is the Gate (Gide) 167
The Strange Case of Dr. Jekyll and Mr. Hyde (Stevenson) 138
Strange Heaven (Coady) 291
The Strange Marriage (Mikszáth) 158
The Strange River (Green) 196
The Strange Story of Mammy Hunt (Taeko) 276
The Stranger (Camus) 155, 209
The Stranger (Kuncewicz) 202
The Stranger from the Seine (Harvath) 197
Strangers (Memmi) 225
Strangers and Brothers (Snow) 207
Strathmore (Ouida) 124
The Straw Man (Giono) 228
The Street (Petry) 213

novel *(continued)*

Streets of Laredo (McMurtry) 279

Strike the Father Dead (Wain) 235

The Struggle for Life (Baroja) 162

Stucco (Bang) 138

A Student of Weather (Hay) 295

The Stuff of Youth (Mauriac) 173

Det Stutte livet (Heggland) 278

The Subterraneans (Kerouac) 229

The Suburbs of Hell (Stow) 264

Such a Long Journey (Mistry) 276

Such Is Life (Furphy) 161

Such Is My Beloved (Callaghan) 199

A Sudden Brightness (Boisonneau) 282

El sueño de la historia (Edwards) 296

El sueño del señor (Gamerro) 296

The Sugar Mother (Jolley) 271

Suicidi dovuti (Busi) 287

Suject Angot (Angot) 292

Sula (Morrison) 250

The Sum of Things (Manning) 259

Summary (Gandlevsky) 296

A Summer Affair (Klima) 249

The Summer Before the Dark (Lessing) 251

A Summer to Decide (Johnson) 216

A Summons to Memphis (Taylor) 267, 268

The Sun Also Rises (Hemingway) 153, 188

The Sundial (Jackson) 229

The Sunlight Dialogues (Gardner) 250

The Surgeon's Daughter (Scott) 105

Svart due (Lie) 288

Svindel (Holmer) 289

The Swan Song (Galsworthy) 190

Swan's Way (Proust) 171

The Sweet Cheat Gone (Proust) 186

The Sweet Hereafter (Banks) 276

A Swiftly Tilting Planet (L'Engle) 257

The Switch (Leonard) 257

The Sword and the Distaff (Simms) 118

Sword of Honor (Waugh) 221, 234

Symbiotic Worm (Ryu) 296

Symposium (Spark) 274

Synden (Ranelid) 283

Tai-Pan (Clavell) 241

The Taking of Ismail (Shishkin) 296

Taking the Trend (Castel-Blum) 293

The Tale of Cross-Eyed Lefty from Tula and the Steel Flea (Leskov) 134

A Tale of Poor Lovers (Pratolini) 215

A Tale of Two Cities (Dickens) 90, 121

Tales of Summer (Beer) 64

Tales of the Genji (Murasaki Shikibu) 15

Tales of the South Pacific (Michener) 215, 216

The Talisman (Scott) 93, 104

Talking About O'Dwyer (Stead) 296

Tangi (Ihimaera) 251

Tan-Huang (Inoue) 231

Tar Baby (Morrison) 260

The Tartar Steppes (Buzzati) 207

Tarzan of the Apes (Burroughs) 173

The Taut Rope (Simon) 215

Tavshed i oktober (Grondahl) 286

Te de la vida entera (Valdés) 289

Teach Us to Outgrow Our Madness (Oe) 246

Tears and Regrets (Koyo) 146

Telepenia de Celia Cecilia Villalobo (Pombo) 285

Tell Me, Mom (Petrusevskaya) 283

Tell Me How Long the Train's Been Gone (Baldwin) 244

La tempestad (Prada) 289

The Temple of My Familiar (Walker) 272

The Temple of the Golden Pavilion (Mishima) 227

Temporary Kings (Powell) 251

The Temptation (Kreve) 219

The Temptation of Saint Anthony (Flaubert) 92, 130

Ten North Frederick (O'Hara) 225

The Ten Thousand Things (Demont) 225

The Tenant of Wildfell Hall (Brontë) 115

The Tenants (Malamud) 249

The Tenants of Time (Flanagan) 270

Tender Is the Night (Fitzgerald) 198

The Tenement (Smith) 266

The Tenth Man (Greene) 154, 266

Term of Office (Sczepanski) 274

Terms of Endearment (McMurtry) 253

La terra è di tutti (Camon) 287

Terrasse à Rome (Quignard) 296

The Terrible Twos (Reed) 261

Terror on the Mountain (Ramuz) 186

Tess of the D'Urbervilles; A Pure Woman (Hardy) 142

Le testament français (Makine) 284

The Testament of Cain (Gyllensten) 237

Teufelsbruck (Kronauer) 296

Texaco (Chamoiseau) 278

Thais (Mistral) 141

The Thanatos Syndrome (Percy) 269

Thanks for the Fire (Benedetti) 240

That Uncertain Feeling (Amis) 225

Their Eyes Were Watching God (Hurston) 203

Their Father's God (Rolvaag) 194

Their Wedding Journey (Howells) 128

Them (Oates) 246

Theophilus North (Wilder) 250

Theory of War (Brady) 282

Thérèse Desqueyroux (Mauriac) 189

Thérèse Raquin (Zola) 126

They Shall Inherit the Earth (Callaghan) 200

The Thief (Leonov) 189

The Thief (Mahfouz) 240

The Thief and the Dogs (Mahfouz) 233

The Thin Man (Hammett) 196

The Thin Red Line (Jones) 235

A Thing of Beauty (Cronin) 227

Things Fall Apart (Achebe) 229

The Thinker (Aldanov) 184

The Third Book About Achim (Johnson) 236

The Third Man (Greene) 154, 217

Thirst for Love (Mishima) 219

This Bed Thy Centre (Johnson) 200

This Earth of Mankind (Tur) 259

This Gun for Hire (Greene) 154

This Island Now (Abrahams) 241

This Land, This Time (Cosic) 250

This Particular Africa (Ikelle-Matiba) 237

This Side of Paradise (Fitzgerald) 180

This Sporting Life (Story) 232

This Sunday (Donoso) 242

Thomas Ripenseren (Ejrnaes) 288

A Thousand Acres (Smiley) 276, 277

Thousand Cranes (Kawabata) 156, 217, 218

A Thousand Souls (Pisemsky) 120

The Three Black Pennys (Hergesheimer) 176

The Three Clerks (Trollope) 120

Three Crosses (Tozzi) 180

The Three Leaps of Want-Lun (Doblin) 174

Three Lovers (O'Faolain) 247

The Three Marias (Quieroz) 206

Three Men in a Boat (Jerome) 140

The Three Musketeers (Dumas) 113

Three Soldiers (Dos Passos) 181

Three Times (Bitner) 285

Three Trapped Tigers (Cabrera Infante) 240

The Three-Cornered Hat (Alarcón) 130

The Three-Cornered World (Natsume) 93, 164

Through the Looking Glass (Carroll) 128

La tierra promitida (Guelbenzu) 277

The Tiger (Kumne) 177

A Tiger for Malgudi (Narayan) 263

Tiger Juan (Pérez de Ayala) 188

Tiger-Lilies (Lanier) 126

Til verdes ende (Faldbakken) 276

The Timber Valley: A Story of Culture (Koch) 172

The Time: Night (Petrushevskaya) 280

Time in a Red Coat (Brown) 264

The Time Machine (Wells) 145

The Time of Angels (Murdoch) 241

A Time of Evil (Cosic) 274

Time of Indifference (Moravia) 192

Time of Migration Northwards (Salih) 233

The Time of the Hero (Vargas Llosa) 237

Time Remembered (Proust) 190

Time to Embrace (Onetti) 253

Timequake (Vonnegut) 288

Time's Arrow (Amis) 276

The Tin Drum (Grass) 231

Tine (Bang) 140

Tired Men (Garborg) 142

The Titan (Dreiser) 173

Titan (Richter) 95

Tlacuilo (Rio) 278

To Be a Pilgrim (Cary) 209

To Become an Island (Wispelaere) 237

To Get to the Heart of the Matter (Choromanski) 245

To Have and Have Not (Hemingway) 153, 203

To Kill a Mockingbird (Lee) 232, 233

To Let (Galsworthy) 181, 182

To Live (Yu) 284

To the East of the Mediterranean (Mounif) 265

To the Land of the Cattails (Appelfeld) 268

To the Lighthouse (Woolf) 189

Tobacco Road (Caldwell) 196

Die Tochter (Grosz) 269

Den tolvte ritter (Michael) 279

Tom Brown's Schooldays (Hughes) 120

Tom Jones, a Foundling (Fielding) 78

Tom Sawyer (Twain) 92, 131

Tom-Cat Murr (Hoffman) 102

Tomorrow (Mitusaki) 262

Tomorrow Will Be Another Sunrise (Sathapanawat) 231

Ton beau capitain (Schwarze-Bart) 269

Tono-Bungoy (Wells) 166

Too Dear for My Possessing (Johnson) 207

Too Many Men (Brett) 295

The Tool (Raffi) 137

Topography of a Phantom City (Robbe-Grillet) 255

The Torrent (Abruquah) 244

Torrent (Ba) 207

The Torrent (Herbert) 219

Torrents of Spring (Turgenev) 129

Tortilla Flat (Steinbeck) 200

Touch the Water, Touch the Wind (Oz) 251

Tough Guys Don't Dance (Mailer) 264

Toward Chaos (Cong) 290

Toward the End of Time (Updike) 288

The Tower at the End of the World (Heinesen) 254

Tower of Ecological Treatment (Oe) 274

The Towers of Trebizond (Macaulay) 227

The Town (Faulkner) 228

The Town (Richter) 219

The Town and the City (Kerouac) 219

The Town Gate (Delblanc) 230

The Tragedy of Pudd'nhead Wilson (Twain) 92, 144

The Tragic Comedians (Meredith) 133

The Tragic Muse (James) 91, 141
The Train Home (Shreve) 279
The Train Was on Time (Böll) 218
The Transgressor (Green) 225
The Transient Hour (Aymé) 214
Transparence (Broger) 279
A Traveler from Altruria (Howells) 144
The Travels and Adventures of Benjamin the Third (Sefarim) 130
The Travels of Jamie McPheeters (Taylor) 230
Travesty (Hawkes) 255
Treasure Island (Stevenson) 135
The Treasure of Sierra Madre (Traven) 189
Tree Between the Walls (Pacheco) 246
The Trees (Richter) 207
Treinta años (Boullosa) 294
Tresjoereren Johannes (Stigen) 274
The Trespassers (Hobson) 210
The Trial (Kafka) 152, 187
The Trials of Brother Jero (Soyinka) 232
The Trials of Enoc Huws (Owen) 142
Trilby (Du Maurier) 144
Trilhos e quintais (Oliveira) 291
Trio (Lassen) 295
The Triple Echo (Bates) 247
Tríptico del carnaval (Pitol) 294
Triptych (Simon) 251
Tristan (Mann) 161
Tristessa (Kerouac) 232
Tristram Shandy (Sterne) 79
The Triumph of Death (D'Annunzio) 145
Trollbyen (Alnaes) 278
Tropic of Cancer (Miller) 198
Tropic of Capricorn (Miller) 205
Trotters and Dancers (Pérez de Ayala) 172
Trout Fishing in America (Brautigan) 243
The Truce (Benedetti) 233
True Confessions (Dunne) 256
True West (Shepard) 260
Trust (Ozick) 241
Truth and Justice (Tannsaare) 188
Tryllefløyten (Lange-Nielsen) 284
The Tunnel (Kellerman) 172
The Tunnel (Sábato) 217
The Tunnel of Love (De Vries) 223
The Turn of the Screw (James) 91, 148
The Turn (Pirandello) 154, 160
Turning Point (Jankovic) 285
Turning Wheels (Cloete) 203
Turtle Moon (Hoffman) 277
Tvillingfeber (Billdoen) 291
Twenty Thousand Streets Under the Sky (Hamilton) 200
Twenty Years After (Dumas) 114
The Two Admirals (Cooper) 112
Two Adolescents (Moravia) 211
Two Brothers (Pratolini) 215
Two Countesses (Ebner-Eschenbach) 137
Two on a Tower (Hardy) 135
Two Serious Ladies (Bowles) 210

Two Thousand Seasons (Armah) 251
The Two Towers (Tolkien) 225
Two Virgins (Markandaya) 251
Two Women (Moravia) 228
Two Years Ago (Kingsley) 120
Two Years Before the Mast (Dana) 111
The Twyborn Affair (White) 258
Typee (Melville) 114
Typhoon (Conrad) 155, 161
Tzili: the Story of a Life (Appelfeld) 263
U-Don Jade (Mqhayi) 192
Udsigten (Hesselholdt) 290
Uffizio delle tenebre (Garavini) 291
The Ugly American (Lederer, Burdick) 229
Ukigumo (Futabatei) 139
Uli the Farmhand (Gotthelf) 112
The Ultimate Intimacy (Klima) 290
O ultimo cais (Marques) 280
Ulysses (Joyce) 152, 182
Ummachi (Kuttikrishnan) 224
Unbekannt verzogen (Schulte) 284
An Unclaimed Inheritance (Chraibi) 236
Uncle Tom's Cabin (Stowe) 117
Unconditional Surrender (Waugh) 234
Under Fire (Barbusse) 175
Under i september (Ostergren) 283
Under Moses (Asch) 177
Under the Greenwood (Hardy) 129
Under the Net (Murdoch) 224
Under the Volcano (Lowry) 235
Under the Yoke (Yazov) 143
Under Two Flags (Ouida) 126
Under Western Eyes (Conrad) 155, 169
The Underground Game (Mallet-Joris) 251
The Underpainter (Urquhart) 288
Underworld (DeLillo) 288
Undine (Fouqué) 98
The Undiscovered Country (Howells) 133
Une belle journée d'avance (Lalonde) 268
The Unicorn (Walser) 242
The Universal Baseball Association, Inc., J. Henry Waugh, Prop. (Coover) 244
A Universal History of Infamy (Borges) 154
Unknown Pleasures (Cowley) 295
The Unknown Sea (Mauriac) 206
The Unnamable (Beckett) 154, 223
An Unpleasant Man (Nayman) 294
The Unspeakable Skipton (Johnson) 231
Unstete Leute (Viragh) 278
Untouchable (Anand) 200
The Unusual Life of Tristan Smith (Carey) 282
The Unvanquished (Faulkner) 204
Up Above the World (Bowles) 241
Up the Mountains (Sydykbekov) 203

The Uprising (Rebrenu) 196
The Uprooted (Blest Gana) 162
Upstairs, Downstairs (Choromanski) 243
Urbes luminosas (García Aguilar) 277
U.S.A. (Dos Passos) 189
Utsikt til paradiset (Ambjornsen) 280
V (Pynchon) 237
Va' dove ti porta il cuore (Tamaro) 282
Va Savoir (Ducharme) 282
La vaca sagrada (Eltit) 277
The Vagabond (Colette) 168
Vallmobadet (Brunner) 294
Valperga; or, The Life and Adventures of Castruccio, Prince of Lucca (Shelley) 103
The Van (Doyle) 276
Vaniglia e cioccolato (Modignani) 296
Vanillepigen (Michael) 284
Vanishing Point (West) 286
Vanity Fair (Thackeray) 115
Varddjuret (Hermanson) 285
Vargskinnet (Ekman) 294
Vasconselos (Simms) 118
Das Vaterspiel (Haslinger) 296
Vathek (Beckford) 85
Vattenorgel (Andersson) 281
Veien tlil Dhaka (Bjornstad) 288
Vendita galline Km 2 (Busi) 280
The Vendor of Sweets (Narayan) 243
The Vengeance of the Condor (García Calderón) 185
Venice Diary (Cheng) 281
Venice in Winter (Robles) 260
Un vent se léve qui eparpille (Dalpe) 296
De verbeelding (Franke) 293
Verden forswinner (Koltzow) 288
Die verlorene Geschichte (Walter) 280
Vermutengen uber die Liebe in einem fremden Haus (Langle) 291
Versuch uber die Jukebox (Handke) 274
Very Old Bones (Kennedy) 277
Vesuvius (Robles) 234
La via del ritorno (Palandri) 274
Via Gemito (Starnone) 296
Viaje a los olivos (Cham) 296
El viajero de Agartha (Posse) 274
The Vicar of Sorrows (Wilson) 280
The Vicar of Wakefield (Goldsmith) 80
The Victim (Bellow) 215
Victoria (Hamsun) 148
Victory (Conrad) 155
Vida (Piercy) 259
Vile Bodies (Waugh) 193
Villa Europa (Bjorstad) 278
The Village (Bunin) 169
Village Pictures (Pontoppidan) 135
Village Priest (Balzac) 110
Villette (Brontë) 118
Le Vin est tiré (Desnos) 210
Vineland (Pynchon) 273
Violence (Bausch) 277
La violencia del tiempos (Gutiérrez) 281

The Violent Bear It Away (O'Connor) 232
The Violent Land (Amado) 209
Viper's Tangle (Mauriac) 196
The Virgin in the Garden (Byatt) 257
The Virgin of Skalholt (Kamban) 193
Virgin Soil (Turgenev) 131
The Virginians (Thackeray) 120
Virginie: Her Two Lives (Hawkes) 261
Et virkelig liv (Koppenvag) 276
Las visiones de Lucrecia (María Merino) 287
Visions of Gerard (Kerouac) 237
The Visiting Physician (Shreve) 286
The Voice (Okara) 238
The Voice of God (Moretti) 181
Volcano (Endo) 231
The Volcano (Lowery) 215
Les voleurs de beauté (Bruckner) 288
Von allem Anfang an (Hein) 289
Vorgeschichten oder schone Gegend Probstein (Schutz) 250
The Vortex (Rivera) 185
Voss (White) 228
The Voyage Out (Woolf) 174
Voyage to the End of the Millennium (Yehoshua) 289
The Voyeur (Robbe-Grillet) 225
Wacousta (Richardson) 107
The Wages of Violence (Ouologuem) 245
Waiting (Ha) 295
Waiting for Childhood (Elliott) 269
Waiting for the Barbarians (Coetzee) 259
Waiting for the Mahatma (Naroyan) 225
Waiting to Exhale (McMillan) 277
Waldernacht (Rothmann) 282
A Walk on the Wild Side (Algren) 226
The Wall (Hersey) 219
Wallenstein (Doblin) 180
Wally the Doubter (Gutzkow) 109
A Wanderer in Love (Schendel) 165
The Wanderer (Waltari) 218
The Wandering Jew (Heym) 264
The Wandering Jew (Sue) 113
The Wapshot Chronicle (Cheever) 228, 238
War (Le Clezio) 247
War and Peace (Tolstoy) 90, 124
The Warden (Arnold) 119
Washington, D.C. (Styron) 243
Washington Square (James) 91, 133
The Water Witch (Cooper) 106
The Waterfall and the Bonfire (Hauge) 217
The Waterfalls of Slunj (Doderer) 237
The Water's Eye (Veiga) 270
The Waterworks (Doctorow) 282
Watt (Beckett) 154, 222
The Waverley (Scott) 93, 99
The Waves (Woolf) 194
The Way I Found Her (Tremain) 288

novel *(continued)*

A Way in the World (Naipaul) 282

The Way of a Man (Sillanpää) 196

The Way of All Flesh (Butler) 161

The Way of Living in the World (Zhou) 286, 288

Way of Migration (Najjar) 286

The Way to Rainy Mountain (Momaday) 246

The Way We Live Now (Trollope) 130

The Way West (Guthrie) 218

The Wayfarer (Natsume) 93, 171

The Ways of the Hour (Cooper) 116

The Wayward Bus (Steinbeck) 215

We Were the Mujlvaneys (Berriault) 286

The Web and ther Rock (Wolfe) 205

The Wedding (Kadare) 244

Weedpatch (Lehtonen) 178

Weekend de chasse a la mère (Brisac) 286

A Weekend with Claud (Bainbridge) 243

Weep Not Child (Ngugi) 24

The Weir of Hermiston (Stevenson) 146

Welcome to Hard Times (Doctorow) 232

The Well (Jolley) 267

The Well of Giningi (Abdulla) 245

The Well of Loneliness (Hall) 190

Westward Ho! (Kingsley) 119

What I Lived For (Oates) 282

What I'm Going to Do, I Think (Woiwode) 246

What Maisie Knew (James) 91, 147

What's Bred in the Bone (Davies) 266

When His Hour Came (Glyn) 168

When I Lived in Modern Times (Grant) 295

When I Whistle (Endo) 242

When She Was Good (Roth) 243

When the Light Is Out (Ngo) 206

When We Were Orphans (Ishiguro) 295

Where Angels Fear to Tread (Forster) 163

Where Shall I Go? (Disengomoko) 210

Where the Air Is Clear (Fuentes) 230

Whiskey Galore (Mackenzie) 215

White Deer Plains (Cheng) 288

White Fang (London) 164

The White Guard (Bulgakov) 246

The White Hotel (Thomas) 260

White Jacket; or, The World in a Man-of-War (Melville) 116

White Man Yellow Man (Endo) 225

The White Monkey (Galsworthy) 185

White Robes (Dudintsev) 271

White Teeth (Smith) 295

The White Youthfulness (Rodenbach) 138

The Wicker Work Woman (France) 147

Wickford Point (Marquand) 205

Wide Open (Barker) 295

Wide Sargasso Sea (Rhys) 241

Widecombe Fair (Phillpotts) 172

The Widow Fiorvanti (Moretti) 208

A Widow for One Year (Irving) 290

The Widow Lerouge (Gaboriau) 125

Widows (Dorfman) 263

The Wife of Claude (Dumas) 129

The Wild Ass's Skin (Balzac) 106

Wild Blew the Wind (Nokan) 236

The Wild Blue Yonder (Thomas) 273

The Wild Boys (Burroughs) 249

Wild Conquest (Abrahams) 220

The Wild Goose (Mori) 170

A Wild Sheep Chase (Murakami) 262

A Wilderness of Mirrors (Frisch) 239

Wildlife (Ford) 273

Wilhelm Meister's Apprenticeship (Goethe) 67, 87, 103

Wilhelm Meister's Apprenticeship (Carlyle) 103

Wilhelm Meister's Travels (Goethe) 102

The Will of Krishnakunta (Chatterjee) 132

The Wind (Simon) 228

A Wind in the Door (L'Engle) 250

Windswept Dawn (Heinesen) 198

The Wine of Astonishment (Lovelace) 261

Wing-and-Wing (Cooper) 112

The Wings of the Dove (James) 91, 160

Winner Take Nothing (Hemingway) 197

Winner Takes All (Wellershof) 263

Winnie Mandela's Football Team (Rabikovitz) 289

A Winter Journey (Benet) 250

Winter Lair (Delblanc) 253

The Winter of Our Discontent (Steinbeck) 234

Wise Blood (O'Connor) 221

The Witches of Eastwick (Updike) 264

With Fire and Sword (Sienkiewicz) 136

With Pleasure, Dear Sirs (Fula) 226

With the East Wind (Aldecoa) 227

Within a Budding Grove (Proust) 178

Without Reason (Chacel) 233

Wives and Daughters (Gaskell) 124

Woman in Her Prime (Saichi) 280

The Woman in the Dunes (Abe) 236

Woman in the Mirror (Meri) 237

The Woman in White (Collins) 121

The Woman of Rome (Moravia) 215

A Woman of the Pharisees (Mauriac) 208

The Woman Taken in Adultery (Fontane) 135

The Woman Thou Gavest Me (Caine) 172

Woman Triumphant (Blasco Ibáñez) 164

A Woman Who Devoted Her Entire Life to Love-Making (Ihara Saikaku) 64

The Woman Who Was Poor (Bloy) 147

Women in Love (Lawrence) 180

Women in the Wall (O'Faolain) 254

The Women of Brewster Place (Naylor) 261

Women on Gallows Hill (Hauge) 229

The Women Who Walked into Doors (Doyle) 286

Wonder Maid (Kosztolányi) 188

Wooden Clara (Conscience) 116

Wooden Icons (Arghezi) 193

Woodlanders (Hardy) 138

Woodstock; or, The Cavalier: A Tale of the Year 1651 (Scott) 104

A Word Child (Murdoch) 253

Workers, a Story of Hatred (Koch) 171

Working People (Kielland) 134

The World According to Garp (Irving) 257

World Enough and Time (Warren) 219

World Light (Laxness) 203

The World of Chance (Howells) 143

The World of Nagaraj (Narayan) 274

The World of Seven Wells (Storni) 199

The World of the Maharachias (Arévalo) 205

The World of the Thibaults (Martin du Gard) 182

The World of Wonders (Davies) 253

World's End (Boyle) 269

World's End (Sinclair) 207

World's Fair (Doctorow) 265

The World's Illusion (Wasserman) 178

The Wrath of the Ancestral Spirits (Jordan) 207

The Wreath at the Foot of the Mountain (Li) 261

A Wrinkle in Time (L'Engle) 235

Wuthering Heights (Brontë) 115

Wyandotte (Cooper) 113

Yama: The Pit (Kuprin) 168

Yasvantrav Khare (Hari Narayan Apti) 143

The Year Has No Spring (Hauge) 216

The Year in San Fernando (Anthony) 240

The Year of the Death of Ricardo Reis (Saramago) 280

The Year of the French (Flanagan) 258

The Year of the Frog (Simecka) 281

The Yearling (Rawlings) 204, 205

The Years (Woolf) 203

Years of Grace (Barnes) 194

The Years with Laura Diaz (Fuentes) 294

Yeast (Kingsley) 115

The Yellow Admiral (O'Brian) 286

Yellow Black Radio Broke Down (Reed) 246

The Yellow-Plush Correspondence (Thackeray) 109

The Yemassee (Simms) 108

Yesterday (Dermont) 220

Yet Another Wish (Muschg) 258

¡Yo! (Alvarez) 290

Yo soy la rumba (Infante) 281

The Yoke of Pity (Breda) 170

Yom haOr shel Anat (Megged) 278

Yoman shel Zug Me'ohav (Sened, Sened) 278

You Can't Do Both (Amis) 282

You Must Remember This (Oates) 269

The Young and the Old (Pirandello) 154

The Young Assassin (Goytisolo) 224

The Young Lions (Shaw) 216

Young Lonigan: A Boyhood in Chicago Streets (Farrell) 196

Young Man in Chains (Mauriac) 172

The Young Manhood of Studs Lonigan (Farrell) 198

Zakhar Berkut (Franko) 136

Zalacaín el aventurero (Baroja) 168

Zaynab (Haykal) 173

Zazie in the Metro (Queneau) 231

Zettel's Dream (Schmidt) 248

The Zigzag Child (Grossman) 282

Zone of Emptiness (Hiroshi) 221

Zorba the Greek (Kazantzakis) 214

Zucherman Unbound (Roth) 260

Zuleika Dobson (Beerbohm) 169

novella

The Actual (Bellow) 288

Agostino (Moravia) 211

All Our Yesterdays (Ginzburg) 221

Almost Transparent Blue (Ryu) 255

Aquis Submersus (Storm) 131

The Aspern Papers (James) 139

The Ballad of the Sad Café (McCullers) 220

The Beauty of Life (Popov) 274

The Bellarosa Connection (Bellow) 272

Blind Dog (Hristow) 275

Bloodshed and Three Novellas (Ozick) 254

Breakfast at Tiffany's (Capote) 229

The Canker (Mao) 193

The Castaway (Cozzens) 198

Castle Durant (Eichendorff) 110

Cavalleria rusticana (Verga) 133

The Colonel's Daughter (Meri) 241

The Death of Ivan Ilyich (Tolstoy) 90, 138

The Dry Heart (Ginzburg) 215

Five Stories of Ferrara (Bassani) 227

Fraulein Else (Schnitzler) 185

Guilt (Idris) 230

The Headmaster (Ahmed) 230

Heart of Darkness (Conrad) 160
Hilarion and the Dwarf (Gubin) 289
In the Castle (Storm) 122
In the Penal Colony (Kafka) 152
An Italian Story (Pratolini) 240
The Jew's Birch Tree (Droste-Hülshoff) 112
The Judgment (Kafka) 152, 175
Kaputt (Malaperte) 211
Legends of the Fall (Harrison) 258
Look for My Obituary and First Love (Garro) 287
Looking Backward (Bellamy) 139
Love and Longing in Hing Kong (Wang) 281
The Marquis of O (Kleist) 97
M'liss (Harte) 121
The Moorland Cottage (Gaskell) 116
Mozart's Journey from Vienna to Prague (Morike) 119
The Old Man the Sea (Hemingway) 153, 221, 222
Passover/A Guest Who Came from Afar (Kometani) 266
The Promontory (Kenji) 255
Raise High the Roof Beam, Carpenters/Seymour: An Introduction (Salinger) 237
The Rider on the White Horse (Storm) 139
The Royal Game (Zweig) 209
The Saint (Meyer) 133
Satan in Goray (Singer) 201
Seize the Day (Bellow) 226
Sin (Idris) 235
The Slave (Singer) 236
Sogrim et ha Yam (Katzir) 274
Sonatas (Valle-Inclán) 160
To the Aegean Sea (Masuo) 257
Tonio Kroger (Mann) 152, 161
Tristan (Mann) 152
A Woman of Means (Taylor) 219
Women with Men (Ford) 288

O

ode
    "Alexander's Feast, or the Power of Music; An Ode in Honour of St. Cecilia's Day" (Dryden) 66, 71
    "The Bard" (Gray) 79
    "The Descent of Odin: An Ode" (Gray) 81
    "The Fatal Sisters: An Ode" (Gray) 81
    "Ode: Intimations of Immortality" (Wordsworth) 92, 96
    "Ode on a Distant Prospect of Eton College" (Gray) 76
    "Ode on a Grecian Urn" (Keats) 101
    "Ode on Indolence" (Keats) 101
    "Ode on Melancholy" (Keats) 101
    "Ode on the Death of the Duke of Wellington" (Tennyson) 118
    "Ode on the Spring" (Gray) 76
    "Ode to a Nightingale" (Keats) 101
    "Ode to Adversity" (Gray) 76
    "Ode to Autumn" (Keats) 101
    "Ode to Duty" (Wordsworth) 96
    "Ode to Fancy" (Wharton) 77
    "Ode to Joy" (Schiller) 67

    "Ode to Liberty" (Pushkin) 90, 102
    "Ode to Liberty" (Shelley) 93, 102
    "Ode to Psyche" (Keats) 101
    "Ode to the Confederate Dead" (Tate) 188, 201
    Ode to the Deity (Derzhavin) 84
    Ode to the Fatherland (Aribau) 107
    "Ode to the West Wind" (Shelley) 93, 101
    Odes (Horace) 4
    Odes (Klopstock) 81
    Odes (Ronsard) 33, 38
    Odes and Songs (Hagedorn) 76
    Odes Modernas (Quental) 124
    Odes to Several Descriptive and Allegoric Subjects (Collins) 77
    On the Death of Prince Meshchersky (Derzhavin) 83
    The Procession (Gibran) 178
    The Unknown Eros (Patmore) 131
opera
    Albion and Albanius (Dryden) 64
    The Duena (Sheridan) 82
    H.M.S. Pinafore (Gilbert) 132
    The Jolly Beggars: A Cantata (Burns) 88
    The Mikado (Gilbert) 136
    The Mother of Us All (Stein) 215
    The Pirates of Penzance (Gilbert) 132
    The Rise and Fall of the City of Mahogonny (Brecht) 153, 193
    St. Patrick's Day; or, The Scheming Lieutenant (Sheridan) 82
    The Three-Penny Opera (Brecht) 153, 190

P

parable
    One Ship—Laura Blair (Divis) 281
philosophy   *See also* treatise
    Adam in Paradise (Ortega y Gasset) 169
    The Archeology of Knowledge (Foucault) 246
    Being and Nothingness (Sartre) 210
    Being and Time (Heidegger) 189
    Beyond Good and Evil (Nietzsche) 114, 138
    The Birth of Tragedy (Nietzsche) 129
    Christian Discourses (Kierkegaard) 91
    The Concept of Dread (Kierkegaard) 91
    Concluding Unscientific Postscript (Kierkegaard) 91
    Critique of Practical Reason (Kant) 85
    Critique of Pure Reason (Kant) 84
    Dissemination (Derrida) 250
    The Ear of the Other (Derrida) 262
    Edifying Discourses on Diverse Spirits (Kierkegaard) 91
    Either/Or (Kierkegaard) 91, 113
    Fear and Trembling (Kierkegaard) 91, 113
    The House of Intellect (Barzun) 231

    Jeg har hort et stierneskud (Jensen) 290
    Lettres philosophiques (Voltaire) 68
    The Life of Reason (Santayana) 163
    Madness and Civilization (Foucault) 234
    Margins of Philosophy (Derrida) 250
    Matter and Memory (Bergson) 146
    Meditations on Quixote (Ortega y Gasset) 173
    The Order of Things: An Archeology of Human Science (Foucault) 241
    The Outsider (Wilson) 227
    Philosophical Essays Concerning Human Understanding (Hume) 77
    Philosophical Fragments (Kierkegaard) 91, 113
    Philosophical Thoughts (Diderot) 77
    Principia Mathematica (Russell, Whitehead) 168
    Psyche: Inventions of the Other (Derrida) 269
    The Psychological Outlook on Life (Jaspers) 178
    Repetition (Kierkegaard) 91
    The Revolt of the Masses (Ortega y Gasset) 192
    The Sickness Unto Death (Kierkegaard) 91
    Social Contract (Rousseau) 68, 80
    Stages on Life's Way (Kierkegaard) 91
    Thus Spake Zarathustra (Nietzsche) 135
    Time and Freewill (Bergson) 140
    Tractatus Logico Philosophicus (Wittgenstein) 181
    The Tragic Sense of Life (Unamuno) 172
    Training in Christianity (Kierkegaard) 91
    A Vision (Yeats) 186
    Works of Love (Kierkegaard) 91
    The World as Will and Idea (Schopenhauer) 101
    Young Men and Fire (Maclean) 277
    Zadig (Voltaire) 77
picaresque novel
    The Confessions of Felix Krull (Mann) 224
    Hampels Fluchten (Kumpfmuller) 296
    The Useless Life of Pito Perez (Romero) 205
    De var engang (Holten) 279
picture book
    Orbis Sensualium Pictus (Commenius) 59
play   *See also* comedy; drama; melodrama; morality play; social drama; tragedy; verse play
    Abe Lincoln in Illinois (Sherwood) 204
    Acharnians (Aristophanes) 3
    Across the Bridge (Vega) 32
    Acts Without Words (Beckett) 154
    Adam in Exile (Vondel) 60
    The Adding Machine (Rice) 184

    The Admirable Crichton (Barrie) 160
    The Adventurer and the Singer (Hofmannsthal) 149
    The Affected Young Ladies (Molière) 47, 59
    The African Continent (Nenekhaly-Camara) 248
    After the Fall (Miller) 238
    Agamemnon (Lemercier) 86
    Agésilas (Corneille) 48, 61
    Agnes Bernauer (Hebbel) 117, 119
    Ah, Wilderness! (O'Neill) 153, 197
    Ajax (Sophocles) 3
    Alain and Elise (Kaiser) 207
    The Alchemist (Jonson) 51
    All Citizens Are Soldiers (Vega) 32
    All for Love (Dryden) 49
    All for the Best (Pirandello) 180
    All My Sons (Miller) 214
    All's Well That Ends Well (Shakespeare) 50
    Amadeus (Shaffer) 258
    Amadís de Gaula (Vicente) 37
    American Blues (Williams) 205
    American Buffalo (Mamet) 253
    American Dream (Albee) 230, 233
    The Ancestors (Grillparzer) 100
    And Pippa Dances (Hauptmann) 164
    And They Put Handcuffs on the Flowers (Arrabel) 246
    Andorra (Frisch) 234
    Androcles and the Lion (Shaw) 153, 175
    Andromède (Corneille) 48, 58
    Anger (Menander) 3
    The Animal Kingdom (Barry) 196
    Anna Christie (O'Neill) 153, 182
    Anne of the Thousand Days (Anderson) 216
    Annibal (Marivaux) 74
    The Anniversary (Chekhov) 92
    Another Country (Mitchell) 261
    Another Part of the Forest (Hellman) 213
    Antony and Cleopatra (Shakespeare) 50
    The Apple Cart (Shaw) 153
    The Architect and the Emperor of Assyria (Arrabel) 243
    Ariadne (Tsvetayeva) 185
    Ariadne and Naxos (Ernst) 171
    Arms and the Man (Shaw) 153
    As You Like It (Shakespeare) 45
    Ascension of the Frog (Juji) 220
    The Ascent of F6 (Auden, Isherwood) 201
    The Assumption of Hanneles (Hauptmann) 144
    At the Hawk's Well (Yeats) 152
    Atlanta in Calydon (Swinburne) 124
    Attila (Corneille) 48, 61
    Attila, King of the Huns (Werner) 97
    Auchindrane; or, The Ayurshire Tragedy (Scott) 106
    Aunt Virike (Heiberg) 136
    Aureng-Zebe (Dryden) 49, 62
    Axel (Villiers de L'Isle-Adam) 137, 141
    Baal (Brecht) 153

play (continued)
Bacchae (Euripides) 2, 8
The Bachelor Party (Chayefsky) 223
Back to Methuselah (Shaw) 153, 181
O baile de mascaras (Rasi) 276
Bailegangaire (Murphy) 267
The Balcony (Genet) 225, 227
The Balcony (Heiberg) 145
The Bald Soprano (Ionesco) 219
Baltasar (Gómez de Avellaneda) 121
Bánk bán (Katona) 100
The Bankrupt (Bjørnson) 130
Barbera Blomberg (Zuckmayer) 218
Barefoot in the Park (Simon) 237
Barrier to the Northwest (Bontempelli) 184
The Basement Window (Buero Vallejo) 243
The Battle of Coxinga (Chikamatsu) 48
The Battle of Herman (Kleist) 98
The Bear (Chekhov) 92
The Beatification of Area Boy (Soyinka) 284
Becket, or the Honor of God (Anouilh) 231
Before Dawn (Hauptmann) 140
Beggar on Horseback (Kaufman) 185
The Beggar's Opera (Gay) 74
Benilde, or the Virgin Mother (Regio) 215
La Bergeries (Racan) 52
Bertrand and Raton; or, The Art of Conspiracy (Scribe) 107
Betrayal (Pinter) 257
Between the Battles (Bjørnson) 120
Beyond Human Endurance (Bjørnson) 135
Beyond the Horizon (O'Neill) 153
Birds (Aristophanes) 3
Birthday Party (Pinter) 229, 231
A Bitter Lot (Pisemsky) 121
The Blacks (Genet) 230
Blanchette (Brieux) 143
The Blind Beggar of Alexandria (Chapman) 45
Blithe Spirit (Coward) 208
The Blue Bird (Maeterlinck) 166
The Blue Stockings (Molière) 48
The Bluebird (Maeterlinck) 167
The Bluff (Labiche) 122
Bodas de sangre (Blood Wedding) (García Lorca) 155, 198
Boeto (Hooft) 52
A Bond Honored (Osborne) 241
The Bonds of Interest (Benavente y Martínez) 165
The Boors (Goldoni) 79
Bopha (Mtwa) 267
Both Your Houses (Anderson) 197
Bothwell, a Tragedy (Swinburne) 130
Bound East for Cardiff (O'Neill) 153
The Bourgeois Gentleman (Molière) 48, 62
The Boy with a Cart (Fry) 219
A Boy's Will (Frost) 172
Bradamante (Garnier) 42

Brand (Ibsen) 94, 125
The Bride of Messina (Schiller) 68, 96
Bride Price (Appa) 147
The Bridge (Herczeg) 187
Brief Moment (Behrman) 194
The Broken Pitcher (Kleist) 97
The Brothers (Terence) 5
The Browning Version (Rattigan) 216
Buried Child (Sheperd) 257
Bus Stop (Inge) 225
Butley (Gray) 249
Byzantium (Herczeg) 162
Cabal and Love (Schiller) 67, 84
Caesar and Cleopatra (Shaw) 153, 159
Caius Marius (Otway) 63
California Suite (Simon) 254
Caligula (Camus) 155, 211
Camino Real (Williams) 222
Cancionero (Encino) 29
Candida (Shaw) 148, 153
Captain Broussard's Conversion (Shaw) 153
The Caretaker (Pinter) 232
The Carriers (Vicente) 36
La casa de Bernarda Alba (García Lorca) 155
The Castilian Soul (Martínez Ruiz) 158
The Castle (Klima) 238
Cat on a Hot Tin Roof (Williams) 225
The Catafalque (Heiberg) 172
Catalina (Kurnberger) 119
The Catalyst (Duncan) 229
The Catered Affair (Chayefsky) 225
Cathy from Heilbronn; or, The Trial by Fire (Kleist) 97
Catilina (Ibsen) 94, 117
The Caucasian Chalk Circle (Brecht) 153, 216
Cavalleria rusticana (Verga) 136
The Chairs (Ionesco) 221
The Chalk Garden (Bagnold) 225
The Changeling (Middleton, Rowley) 59
Chapter Two (Simon) 255
Charles IX; or, La Sainte-Barthelemy (Chénier) 85
Chatterton (Vigny) 108
The Cheats of Scapin (Molière) 62
The Cherry Orchard (Chekhov) 92, 162
The Children's Hour (Hellman) 198
The Chinese Wall (Frisch) 215
A Chorus Line (Bennet, Kirkwood, Dante, Hamlisch, Kleban) 253
A Chorus of Disapproval (Ayckbourn) 267
Christina's Journey Home (Hofmannsthal) 168
The City Whose Prince Is a Child (Montherlant) 220
The Civil War (Montherlant) 240
The Claw (Bernstein) 164
The Clembaj Family (Krleza) 196
Cléopâtre captive (Jodelle) 39
The Clique (Scribe) 110
Clouds (Aristophanes) 3, 7
The Coat of Arms of the City of Coimbra (Vicente) 36

The Cocktail Party (Eliot) 152
The Colleen Bawn (Boucicault) 121
Columbine (Mackenzie) 180
Come and Go (Beckett) 154
Come Back, Little Sheba (Inge) 219
Comedy of Calisto and Melibea (Rojas) 30, 34
The Comedy of Errors (Shakespeare) 31, 43
The Comic Illusion (Corneille) 55
The Coming of Peace (Hauptmann) 141
Comrades (Strindberg) 92
The Condemned (Dagerman) 217
The Confidential Clerk (Eliot) 223
The Conquest of Granada by the Spaniards (Dryden) 49, 61
The Constant Couple; or a Trip to the Jubilee (Farquhar) 69
The Constant Prince (Calderón de la Barca) 48, 54
Coriolanus (Shakespeare) 51
Counselor-at-Law (Rice) 194
Count Oederland (Frisch) 234
The Countess Cathleen (Yeats) 143, 152
The Countess of Charolais (Beer-Hofmann) 163
The Country Wife (Wycherley) 62
The Coward (Lenormand) 186
The Crafty Widow (Goldoni) 77
The Creditors (Strindberg) 92, 141
Crime on Goat Island (Betti) 219
Crimes of the Heart (Henley) 258
Criminals in Love (Walker) 264
The Cross on the Baltic Sea (Werner) 97
Cross Purposes (Camus) 155
The Crucible (Miller) 222
Crusts (Claudel) 177
Cupid's Revenge (Beaumont, Fletcher) 51
The Curse of Rebellious Susan (Jones) 144
Cymbeline (Shakespeare) 51
Cyrano de Bergerac (Rostand) 147
The Dam (Butler) 222
Dame de Pique (Boucicault) 117
A dança final (Marcos) 291
The Dance of Death (Strindberg) 92, 159
Danger Memory! Two Plays (Miller) 270
The Dark at the Top of the Stairs (Inge) 228
The Dark Is Light Enough (Fry) 223
The Dark Tower (MacNeice) 215
The Daughter of Jorio (D'Annunzio) 162
The Daughter of the Air (Calderón de la Barca) 48, 59
The Dead Spot (Popovic) 285
Dear Brutus (Barrie) 176
Death and the Fool (Hofmannsthal) 144
Death and the King's Horseman (Soyinka) 252
Death of a Salesman (Miller) 217
The Death of Abel (Gessner) 79
The Death of Balder (Ewald) 82
The Death of Satan (Duncan) 223
The Death of Titian (Hofmannsthal) 143

Deathwatch (Genet) 218
The Deformed Transformed (Byron) 103
Deirdra (Yeats) 152, 165
Deirdra of the sorrows (Synge) 168
A Delicate Balance (Albee) 241
Le Demi-Monde (Dumas) 119
The Deputy (Hochhuth) 237
Design for Living (Coward) 197
Desire Under the Elms (O'Neill) 153, 185
Destan About Ali of Kesan (Taner) 239
Detective Story (Kingsley) 217
The Determination of a House (Cruz) 64
The Devil and the Good Lord (Sartre) 220
The Devil's Disciple (Shaw) 153
The Devil's General (Zuckmayer) 214
Dialogues des Carmelites (Bernanos) 218
Der Dibuk (Ansky) 173, 180
Dido, Queen of Carthage (Marlowe) 33, 44
The Difficult Man (Hofmannsthal) 181
The Difficult Times (Bourdet) 199
Dinner at Eight (Kaufman) 196
The Dirge of the Medidian (Kinoshita) 256
Dirty Linen (Stoppard) 255
Division Street (Tesich) 259
The Doctor's Dilemma (Shaw) 153, 164, 169
A Doll's House (Ibsen) 94, 132
Don Alvaro; or, The Power of Fate (Saavedra) 109
Don Carlos (Otway) 62
Don Carlos (Schiller) 67, 85
Don Sanche d'Aragon (Corneille) 48
Dorottya (Csokonai) 88
Double Suicide at Amijima (Chikamatsu) 48
The Dove Returns (Butler) 227
Dr. Faustus (Marlowe) 33
Drayman (Hauptmann) 148
The Dream Eater (Lenormand) 182
A Dream Is Life (Grillparzer) 108
The Dream on Monkey Mountain (Walcott) 241
A Dream Play (Strindberg) 92, 160
Driving Miss Daisy (Uhry) 269
Drums in the Night (Brecht) 153, 182
The Duel (Sedaine) 80
The Duke of Guise (Dryden and Lee) 64
The Dumb Waiter (Pinter) 228, 231
Dutchman (Baraka) 238
The Dwarfs (Pinter) 273
The Dybbuk (Ansky) 173, 180
Each in His Own Way (Pirandello) 154, 185
The Eagle Has Two Heads (Cocteau) 214
The Eaglet (Rostand) 158
The Earth (Sharqawi) 223
Earth Spirit (Wedekind) 145
East of Suez (Maugham) 182
Easter (Strindberg) 159

Echo and Narcissus (Calderón de la Barca) 48, 60
The Editor (Bjørnson) 130
Edufa (Sutherland) 243
Edward II (Brecht) 153
Edward II (Marlowe) 33, 44
The Effect of Gamma Rays on Man-in-the-Moon Marigolds (Zindel) 240
Eight New Comedies and Eight New Interludes (Cervantes) 32
Electra (Euripides) 2, 7
Electra (Sophocles) 3
The Emperor Jones (O'Neill) 153, 179, 181
Endgame (Beckett) 228
Endimion, the Man in the Moone (Lyly) 43
An Enemy of the People (Ibsen) 94, 135
The Entertainer (Osborne) 228
Epitaph for George Dillon (Osborne, Creighton) 229
Equus (Shaffer) 251
Erasmus Montanus (Holberg) 74
Erectheus (Swinburne) 131
Esther (Racine) 48, 65
Eugénie (Beaumarchais) 81
The Eunuch (Terence) 5
Every Good Day Deserves Favor (Stoppard) 256
Everyman (Hofmannsthal) 170
The Evil Doers of Good (Benavente y Martínez) 163
Exit the King (Ionesco) 237
Eyvind of the Hills (Sigurjonsson) 170
The Failures (Lenormand) 180
The Fair and Wise Father (Marivaux) 71
The Faithful Shepherd (Calderón de la Barca) 48
The False Accusation (Caragiale) 141
False Delicacy (Kelly) 81
A False Saint (Curel) 143
The Family Shakespeare (Bowdler) 97
Farewell, Liars (Popovic) 285
The Fatal Marriage (Southerne) 66
The Fateful Prong (Plater) 104
The Father (Strindberg) 92, 139
Faust (Goethe) 67, 97, 107
Faust, ein Fragment (Goethe) 67
The Female Joseph (Calderón de la Barca) 48, 56
Fences (Wilson) 265
The Feud of the Schroffensteins (Kleist) 96
Fiesco; or, The Conspiracy of Genoa (Schiller) 84
Fifty Comedies and Tragedies (Fletcher, Beaumont) 63
The Fire Bringer (Moody) 162
The Firebugs (Frisch) 230
Five-Finger Exercise (Shaffer) 232
The Flame of Life (D'Annunzio) 158
The Follies of Marianne (Musset) 107
Fool for Love (Shepard) 262
The Force of Habit (Bernhard) 252
Forefather's Eve (Mickiewicz) 103, 108

Forest of Deceits (Vicente) 37
Four Plays for Dancers (Yeats) 152
Free Game (Schnitzler) 146
Frogs (Aristophanes) 3
From Morn to Midnight (Kaiser) 175
The Front Page (MacArthur) 190
Fuente ovejuna (Vega) 32, 52
The Fugitive (Galsworthy) 172
Fugitives (Kivi) 126
The Funeral; or, Grief A-la-Mode (Steele) 70
The Funny Man (Holberg) 74
The Gallery of Mirrors (Bernstein) 185
The Galley Slaves (Alvarez Quintero) 158
Game of Life (Sofronov) 178
The Game of Madness and Prudence (Theotokos) 234
The Gardener of Toulouse (Kaiser) 204
The Gardener's Dog (Vega) 32
Gas (Kaiser) 176
Gas II (Kaiser) 180
Geeraert van Velsen (Hooft) 51
Le Gendre de Monsieur Poirier (Sandeau, Augier) 117
The Gentleman Dancing Master (Wycherley) 62
The Gentleman in Grey (Mackenzie) 164
The Ghost Sonata (Strindberg) 92, 165
Ghosts (Ibsen) 94, 134
Gideon (Chayefsky) 233
The Gin Game (Coburn) 254
The Girl with the Jug (Vega) 32
The Glass Menagerie (Williams) 211, 212
The Glass of Water; or, Causes and Effects (Scribe) 111
Glengarry Glen Ross (Mamet) 264
The Glittering Gate (Dunsany) 167
The God of the Mountain (Dunsany) 169
The God of Vengeance (Asch) 165
Golden Boy (Odets) 203
The Golden Chain (Peretz) 169
The Golden Gate (Davíd) 208
The Good Hope (Heijermans) 158
The Good Woman of Setzuan (Brecht) 153, 210
Götz von Berlichingen (Goethe) 67, 82
Grandida (Hooft) 50
The Great God Brown (O'Neill) 153, 188
The Great Highway (Strindberg) 92, 168
The Great Salzburg Theater of the World (Hofmannsthal) 170
The Greatest Alcalde (Vega) 32
The Greatest Day of Days (Calderón de la Barca) 48
The Guest (Corel) 144
Gustav Vasa (Strindberg) 92, 149
Gyges and His Ring (Hugo) 119
The Hairy Ape (O'Neill) 153, 182
Haluk's Notebook (Fikret) 171
Hamlet (Shakespeare) 31, 50
The Hangman (Lagerkvist) 198
Hannibal (Kabbada) 216
Happy Days (Beckett) 234

The Happy Vineyard (Zuckmayer) 187
Harlequin Brightened by Love (Marivaux) 73
Harold (Tennyson) 131
Harvey (Chase) 211
Hay Fever (Coward) 186
Hayavadana (Karnad) 249
Heartbreak House (Shaw) 153, 178
Hearts of Oak (Jones) 132
Heaven and Earth (Byron) 103
Hedda Gabler (Ibsen) 94, 141
The Heidi Chronicles (Wasserstein) 270
Helen (Euripides) 7
Heliogobalus, or the Crowned Antichrist (Artaud) 199
A Hell of a Mess (Ionesco) 251
Henry IV (Pirandello) 154, 182
Henry IV (Shakespeare) 31, 44
Henry V (Shakespeare) 45
Henry VI (Shakespeare) 31
Henry VIII (Shakespeare) 51
Hernani (Hugo) 106
Herod and Marianne (Hebbel) 116
Herr Puntila and His Man Mutti (Brecht) 153
Hippolytus (Euripides) 2, 7
The Historical Register for the Year 1736 (Fielding) 75
Holiday (Barry) 190
The Homecoming (Pinter) 240
The Honest Whore (Dekker) 54
Honor (Sudermann) 140
The Hostage (Behan) 229
The Hostage (Claudel) 170
The Hour Glass (Yeats) 152
The House of Blue Leaves (Guare) 248
The Hunting Party (Bernhard) 252
Husband and Wife (Fredro) 103
I Have Been There Before (Priestley) 203
I Ought to Be In Pictures (Simon) 259
I Serve (Teirlinck) 185
I Will Defend My Country (Heiberg) 171
The Iceman Cometh (O'Neill) 153, 213
If You Know Not Me, You Know Nobody (Heywood) 50
The Imitation of the Father (Claudel) 180
In the Burning Darkness (Buero Vallejo) 219
In the Shadow of the Glen (Synge) 161
In the Zone (O'Neill) 153
Incident at Vichy (Miller) 240
The Incredible Play (Benavente y Martínez) 208
The Indian Emperour (Dryden) 49, 60
The Indian Exiles (Kotzebue) 85
The Infernal Machine (Cocteau) 199
The Inspector Calls (Priestley) 213
Intervalle (Butor) 251
Ion (Euripides) 2, 7
Iphigenia at Aulis (Euripides) 2, 8
Iphigenie auf Tauris (Goethe) 67, 85

Irene (Kisfaludy) 102
Iridion (Krasinski) 109
Isle of Reason (Marivaux) 74
Isle of Slaves (Marivaux) 73
Israel (Bernstein) 166
It Isn't Necessary to Promise Anything (Musset) 109
Italian Night (Horvath) 193
Jacques and His Master (Kundera) 260
J.B. (MacLeish) 229
Jean de France (Holberg) 73
Jeppe of the Hill (Holberg) 73
Jero's Metmorphosis (Soyinka) 250
The Jew of Malta (Marlowe) 33, 55
Joan of Lorraine (Anderson) 215
Joe Turner's Come and Gone (Wilson) 267
John Bull's Other Island (Shaw) 153
John Gabriel Borkman (Ibsen) 94
Joseph in Egypt (Vondel) 56
The Journalists (Freytag) 117
Journey's End (Sheriff) 192
Juana (Vega) 32
The Judgment (Kinoshita) 248
Judith (Hebbel) 111
Julius Caesar (Shakespeare) 31, 45
Juno and the Paycock (O'Casey) 185
Just Assassins (Camus) 155
Justice (Galsworthy) 168
Kadmus (Aql) 211
Kaspar (Handke) 245
Katherine of Heilbronn (Kleist) 98
Key Largo (Anderson) 205
The Killing Game (Ionesco) 247
The King (Vega) 32
The King and the Farmer (Vega) 32
King Arthur (Dryden) 49, 65
King John (Shakespeare) 44
King Lear (Shakespeare) 31, 50
King Rene's Daughter (Hertz) 114
The King's Mandate (Jarvis) 232
The King's Threshold (Yeats) 152
The Knight from Olmedo (Vega) 32
Knights (Aristophanes) 3
Knock; or, The Triumph of Medicine (Romains) 184
Kozma (Kornis) 278
Krapp's Last Tape (Beckett) 229
The Ladies-in-Waiting (Buero Vallejo) 233
The Lady (Tamayo y Baus) 118
The Lady from Maxim's (Feydeau) 149
The Lady from the Sea (Ibsen) 94, 139
The Lady Nit-Wit (Vega) 32
The Lady of Lyons (Bulwer-Lytton) 110
The Lady of the Dawn (Casona) 212
Lady Windermere's Fan (Wilde) 143
The Lady's Not for Burning (Fry) 216
The Land of Heart's Desire (Yeats) 144, 152
Landscape (Pinter) 244
The Landslide (Betti) 198

play (continued)
The Lark (Anouilh) 222
The Last Days of Humanity (Kram) 182
Last Loves (Sillitoe) 273
The Last of the Red Hot Lovers (Simon) 245
Last Poems and Two Plays (Yeats) 152
The League of Cambrai (Platen) 107
The Learned Ladies (Molière) 62
A Legend of Florence (Hunt) 111
Lessness (Beckett) 154
The Lesson (Ionesco) 220, 223
Let Man Live (Lagerkvist) 218
The Liars (Jones) 147
A Life in the Theater (Mamet) 256
Life Is a Dream (Calderón de la Barca) 48, 55
Life of Galileo (Brecht) 153
Liliom (Molnár) 167
The Lion and the Jewel (Soyinka) 237
The Lion's Meal (Curel) 147
Little Eyolf (Ibsen) 94, 145
The Little Foxes (Hellman) 205
Little Lord Fauntleroy (Burnett) 137
The Little Theater of the World (Hofmannsthal) 147
London Assurance (Boucicault) 112
Lonely Lives (Hauptmann) 142
Long Day's Journey into Night (O'Neill) 153, 226
The Long Voyage Home (O'Neill) 153
Look Back in Anger (Osborne) 228
The Lord's Vineyard (Calderón de la Barca) 48
The Lost Cause (Mackenzie) 194
Lost in Yonkers (Simon) 276
A Lost Letter (Caragiale) 136
Louis XI (Delavigne) 107
The Love That Passes (Alvarez Quintero) 162
Love Without Stockings (Wessel) 82
The Lover's Melancholy (Ford) 54
The Lovers of Teruel (Hartzenbusch) 110
Love's Comedy (Ibsen) 94
Love's Labour's Lost (Shakespeare) 31, 44
The Loyal Subject (Fletcher) 52
Lucifer (Vondel) 59
Lucky Peter's Travels (Strindberg) 92
Luther (Osborne) 234
Lysistrata (Aristophanes) 3
Ma Rainey's Black Bottom (Wilson) 264
Macbeth (Shakespeare) 31, 50
The Mad Woman of Chaillot (Giraudoux) 212
Madame Devil-May-Care (Moreau, Sardou) 144
The Madman and the Nun (Witkiewicz) 187
Madman or Saint (Echegaray y Eizaguirre) 131
Madmen and Scientists (Soyinka) 241

The Madness of Love (Tamayo y Baus) 119
Madonna Dianora (Hofmannsthal) 147
The Magnificent Cuckold (Crommelynck) 180
The Maid of Orleans (Schiller) 68, 95
Maiden's Vows (Fredro) 108
The Maids (Genet) 215
The Maid's Tragedy (Beaumont, Fletcher) 51
Major Barbara (Shaw) 153, 163, 165
Malatesta (Montherlant) 214
The Malcontent (Marston) 50
Malvaloca (Alvarez Quintero) 171
Man and His Phantoms (Lenormand) 185
Man and Superman (Shaw) 153
Man and the Masses (Toller) 180
Man Is Insane (Nu) 210
The Man of Destiny (Shaw) 153
The Man She Hated (Menander) 3
The Man Who Had All the Luck (Miller) 205
The Man Without a Body (Teirlinck) 186
The Man Without a Soul (Lagerkvist) 202
Maria Magdalena (Hebbel) 112
Maria Stuart (Schiller) 68, 95
Mariana Pineda (García Lorca) 155
Mark Antony, or Cleopatra (Mairet) 55
The Marquis of Keith (Wedekind) 159
Marriage A-la-Mode (Dryden) 49, 62
Marriage by the Calendar (Bohomolec) 81
Marriage for Money (Scribe) 105
The Marriage of Sobeide (Hofmannsthal) 149
Martin Luther; or The Consecration of Strength (Werner) 97
Marty (Chayefsky) 222
The Massacre at Paris (Marlowe) 33
The Master Builder (Ibsen) 94, 143
The Master of Santiago (Montherlant) 215
Master Olof (Strindberg) 92
The Matchmaker (Wilder) 223
The Mayor of Zalamea (Calderón de la Barca) 48, 56
Measure for Measure (Shakespeare) 50
Medea (Euripides) 2, 7
The Melody That Got Lost (Abell) 205
The Melting Pot (Zangwill) 166
The Memorandum (Havel) 240
The Merchant of Venice (Shakespeare) 31, 44
The Merchant's Ship (Calderón de la Barca) 48
The Merry Wives of Windsor (Shakespeare) 45
Merry-Go-Round (Schnitzler) 147
Meteor (Behrman) 192

The Meteor (Durrenmatt) 242
Michael and His Lost Angel (Jones) 146
Midas (Lyly) 44
Mine Hostess (Goldoni) 78
The Minor (Fonvizin) 84
Misanthrope (Menander) 3
Le Misanthrope (Molière) 48, 61
Le Misanthrope et Lauvergnat (Labiche) 117
The Misfits (Miller) 234
Mister Bahram (Patel) 271
The Mistress of the Inn (Goldoni) 78
The Monkey Wrench Gang (Abbey) 253
A Month in the Country (Turgenev) 117, 119
A Moon for the Misbegotten (O'Neill) 153, 210, 221
Moon in Shanghai (Hisashi) 276
The Moratorium (Andrade) 226
More Stately Mansions (O'Neill) 238
Mother Courage and Her Children (Brecht) 153, 208, 218
The Mother-in-Law (Terence) 5
Mourning Becomes Electra (O'Neill) 153, 194
The Mousetrap (Christie) 221
Mr. Leonida (Caragiale) 132
Mrs. Warren's Profession (Shaw) 143, 153
Much Ado About Nothing (Shakespeare) 31, 45
Mule Bone (Hurston) 194
Murder in the Cathedral (Eliot) 200
A Mystery Play of the Sufferings of Israel (Sachs) 220
The Nabob (Daudet) 131
Napoleon, or the Hundred Days (Grabbe) 106
Nathan the Wise (Lessing) 69, 83
The Natural Son; or, The Proofs of Virtue (Diderot) 79
Nekrassov (Sartre) 225
The New Colony (Marivaux) 74
A New Drama (Tamayo y Baus) 126
The New Idol (Curel) 145
The New Kingdom (Strindberg) 92
The New Shelter for the Poor (Calderón de la Barca) 48
The New Tenant (Ionesco) 225
The Newlyweds (Griboyedov) 100
Nicomède (Corneille) 48, 58
Die Niebelungen (Hebbel) 123
'Night, Mother (Norman) 262
Night and Day (Stoppard) 257
The Night of the Iguana (Williams) 234
The Night of the Tribades (Enquist) 252
No caração do Brasil (Falabella) 278
No Exit (Sartre) 211
No Man's Land (Pinter) 253
Noah (Vondel) 61
Not I (Beckett) 252
Numantia (Cervantes) 32
The Octoroon; or, Life in Louisiana (Boucicault) 121
The Odd Couple (Simon) 240
Offending the Audience (Handke) 242

Okinawa (Kinoshita) 234
Old Times (Pinter) 249
On Baile's Strand (Yeats) 152
On Trial (Rice) 173
The Only Jealousy of Emer (Yeats) 178
Oresteia (Aeschylus) 2, 6
Orestes (Euripides) 8
The Orphan (Otway) 63
Orpheus (Cocteau) 188
Othon (Corneille) 48, 60
Our Goddess (Bontempelli) 187
Our Lady's Tumbler (Duncan) 220
Our Power and Our Glory (Grieg) 200
Our Town (Wilder) 204
Ovonramwen Nogbaisi (Rotimi) 250
The Painter of His Dishonor (Calderón de la Barca) 48, 57
Palamedes, or Murdered Innocence (Vondel) 54
Panchali's Vow (Bharati) 171
Pandora's Box (Wedekind) 162
Paola and Francesca (Phillips) 158
Papinianus (Gryphius) 59
The Pariah (Strindberg) 92, 140
Paris Bound (Barry) 189
Parricide (Bronnen) 180
A Party for Boris (Bernhard) 245
Party in Autumn (Dorst) 233
The Passion Flower (Benavente y Martínez) 172
The Passion of Joseph D. (Chayefsky) 238
A Patriot for Me (Osborne) 240
Pavel (Merezhkovsky) 166
Pedro, the Artful Dodger (Cervantes) 52
Peer Gynt (Ibsen) 94, 126
Pelleas and Melissande (Maeterlinck) 143
Penthesilia (Kleist) 97
The People's Council (Heiberg) 147
Peribanez and the Commander of Ocana (Vega) 32, 51
Pericles, Prince of Tyre (Shakespeare) 51
Perola (Rasi) 285
The Persecution and Assassination of Jean-Paul Marat, as Performed by the Inmates of the Asylum of Charenton Under the Directio of the Marquis de Sade (Weiss) 239
Persians (Aeschylus) 2
Pertharite (Corneille) 48
The Petrified Forest (Sherwood) 200
Phaedra (Tsvetayeva) 189
Phantom Lady (Calderón de la Barca) 54
The Phantom Lover (Kaiser) 190
The Philadelphia Story (Barry) 205
Philaster (Beaumont, Fletcher) 51
Philoctetes (Sophocles) 3, 7
A Phoenix Too Frequent (Isherwood) 213
Phormio (Terence) 5
The Physicists (Durrenmatt) 236
The Piano Lesson (Wilson) 269
Picnic (Inge) 222

The Pilgrimage of the Aggrieved (Vicente) 37
Pillars of Society (Ibsen) 94, 131
Le Ping-Pong (Adamov) 225
The Plain Dealer (Wycherley) 63
The Plants (Sternheim) 170
Play of Fame (Vicente) 32, 35
The Playboy of the Western World (Synge) 165
Playing with Love (Schnitzler) 146
Plays for Bleecker Street (Wilder) 235
Plays of Marionettes (Bergman) 177
Plaza Suite (Simon) 244
Pleasure Reconciled to Virtue (Jonson) 52
The Plebians Rehearse the Uprising (Grass) 242
The Plough and the Stars (O'Casey) 188
The Political Tinker (Holberg) 73
Polly (Gay) 74
Polyeucte (Corneille) 56
The Poor of New York (Boucicault) 120
Port Royal (Montherlant) 224
Portrait of a Planet (Durrenmatt) 248
Poverty Is No Disgrace (Ostrovsky) 118
The Power of Darkness (Tolstoy) 90
The Pretenders (Ibsen) 94, 124
The Price (Miller) 244
The Priest of Kirchfield (Anzengruber) 127
The Prince of Homburg (Kleist) 98
The Prisoner of Second Avenue (Simon) 248
Private Jokinen's Marriage Leave (Meri) 240
Private Lives (Coward) 193
The Profligate (Pinero) 140
The Proposal (Chekhov) 92
Pulchérie (Corneille) 48, 62
Pygmalion (Shaw) 153, 172
The Quare Fellow (Behan) 224
Quarrels of Honor (Tamayo y Baus) 123
Quarry of the Soul (Andrade) 230
The Queen and the Rebels (Betti) 220
Queen Mary (Tennyson) 130
Queen of Scotland (Della Valle) 43
The Queen's Defeat (Chedid) 264
Quoat-Quoat (Audiberti) 214
A Raisin in the Sun (Hansberry) 231
Ralph Roister Doister (Udall) 40
Raquel (García de la Huerta) 83
The Real (Tamayo y Baus) 123
The Recruiting Officer (Farquhar) 70
Reputable Men (Tamayo y Baus) 128
Request Concert (Kroetz) 250
Responsibilities: Poems and a Play (Yeats) 152, 173
Restoration (Bond) 260
The Return of Philip Latinowicz (Krleza) 196
The Revenge, a Tragedy (Young) 73

Rhinoceros (Ionesco) 231
Richelieu; or, The Conspiracy (Bulwer-Lytton) 110
The Ride Across Lake Constance (Handke) 249
Riders to the Sea (Synge) 161
Right You Are—If You Think You Are (Pirandello) 154, 176
The Rival Ladies (Dryden) 60
The Rivals (Sheridan) 82
The Road (Soyinka) 240
The Road Back (Andrade) 243
The Robbers (Schiller) 67, 84
Rockaby (Beckett) 154
The Roman Actor (Massinger) 54
The Romantic Oedipus (Platen) 106
Romeo and Juliet (Shakespeare) 31, 44
The Rose Garden (Popovic) 285
The Rose Tattoo (Williams) 220
Rosencrantz and Gildenstern Are Dead (Stoppard) 241
Rosmersholm (Ibsen) 94, 138
Rough Crossing (Stoppard) 266
The Rover, or the Banished Cavaliers (Behn) 63
The Royal Hunt of the Sun (Shaffer) 238
R.U.R. (Čapek) 179
The Sacrifice of Abraham (Kornáros) 55
The Saga of the Folkings (Strindberg) 92, 149
Saint Joan (Shaw) 153, 184
The Sandbox (Albee) 231
Santa Cruz (Frisch) 215
Sarmistha (Datta) 120
The Satin Slipper (Claudel) 192, 193
Saturday Night (Benavente y Martínez) 161
The Schism of England (Calderón de la Barca) 48
Schlageter (Johst) 197
The School for Husbands (Molière) 60
School for Mothers (Marivaux) 73
The School for Scandal (Sheridan) 83
The School for Wives (Molière) 47–48, 60
Scratch (MacLeish) 248
The Screens (Genet) 234
The Seagull (Chekhov) 92, 146, 162
Seascape (Albee) 253
The Second Man (Behrman) 189
The Second Mrs. Tanqueray (Pinero) 143
The Secret (Bernstein) 172
The Self-Tormentor (Terence) 5
Separate Tables (Rattigan) 223
La Sérénade (Regnard) 66
Sertorius (Corneille) 48, 60
Seven Against Thebes (Aeschylus) 2
The Sex Fable (Bourdet) 195
The Shadow of a Gunman (O'Casey) 184, 186
She Stoops to Conquer (Goldsmith) 82
Shenandoah (Schwartz) 208
The Shield (Menander) 3
The Ship of Love (Vicente) 36
Ship's Talk (Huygens) 54

The Shoemaker and the King, Part II (Zorrilla y Moral) 112
The Shoemaker and the King, Part III (Zorrilla y Moral) 111
The Shoemaker's Holiday (Dekker) 50
Shoemakers of the Hearth (Kivi) 124
Shore Acres (Herne) 143
Siddhartha: Man of Peace (Chattopadhyay) 227
Siegfried (Giraudoux) 190
The Sign in Sidney Brustein's Window (Hansberry) 238
Sigurd Slembe (Bjørnson) 123
Silence (Pinter) 246
The Silver Cord (Howard) 188
The Silver King Play (Jones) 135
The Silver Tassel (O'Casey) 188
The Simoom (Lenormand) 180
Singing from the Depths (Machado) 171
Six Characters in Search of an Author (Pirandello) 154, 181
The Skin of Our Teeth (Wilder) 209
The Slave (Baraki) 238
The Slaying of Kicak (Khadilkar) 169
A Sleep of Prisoners (Fry) 220
The Slow Motion Picture (Teirlinck) 182
The Sniper (Krige) 235
The Snow Maiden (Ostrovsky) 129
Soga Heir (Chikamatsu) 48, 62
Soldiers (Hochhuth) 243
The Solid Gold Cadillac (Kaufman, Teichman) 222
Song of a Goat (Clark) 234
The Sons of Jacob (Rainis) 185
The Sons of the Valley (Werner) 96
The Spanish Tragedie (Kyd) 44
Den Spieghel der Salicheit van Elckerlijk (Diest) 29, 35
The Splits (Ritter) 257
Spreading the News (Gregory) 162
Spring's Awakening (Wedekind) 142
The Springtime of Others (Bernard) 185
Squaring the Circle (Stoppard) 264
St. Joan of the Stockyards (Brecht) 196
The Stars Turn Red (O'Casey) 207
The Star-Spangled Girl (Simon) 241
The State of Innocence and Fall of Man (Dryden) 63
State of Siege (Camus) 155
The Statue of Prometheus (Calderón de la Barca) 48, 61
Still Life (Coward) 202, 213
A Stormy Night (Caragiale) 133
The Story of a Staircase (Buero Vallejo) 217
Strange Interlude (O'Neill) 153, 190
The Stranger (Kotzebue) 85
Stratton (Duncan) 217
Street Scene (Rice) 192
A Streetcar Named Desire (Williams) 215

A Stroll in the Air (Ionesco) 237
The Strong Bread (Soyinka) 237
Sturm und Drang (Klinger) 83
Successful Kagekiyo (Chikamatsu) 64
Suddenly Last Summer (Williams) 229
The Suitors (Kisfaludy) 100
The Sulky Fire (Bernard) 181
Summary of the History of God (Vicente) 36
Summer and Smoke (Williams) 216
Summer of the Seventh Doll (Lawler) 226
Sunday in the Park with George (Sondheim, Lapine) 264
The Sunrise (Cao) 201
The Sunshine Boys (SImon) 250
Suppliants (Aeschylus) 6
The Surgeon of His Honor (Calderón de la Barca) 48, 55
The Swamp Dwellers (Soyinka) 237
Sweeney Agonistes (Eliot) 152
Sweet Bird of Youth (Williams) 231
Take Root or Die (Butler) 247
Tales from the Vienna Woods (Horvath) 193
Talley's Folly (Wilson) 258
Tamburlaine the Great (Marlowe) 33, 43
The Tartars in Hungary (Kisfaludy) 98
Tea and Sympathy (Anderson) 222
Teahouse of the August Moon (Patrick) 222
The Tempest (Shakespeare) 31, 51
The Temple of Apollo (Vicente) 36
The Tenth Man (Chayefsky) 231
The Burgomaster of Stilmonde (Maeterlinck) 177
Le Théâtre de la Revolution (Rolland) 162
There Shall Be No Night (Sherwood) 207
Théroigne de Méricourt (Hervieu) 144
They Knew What They Wanted (Howard) 185
A Thread in the Dark (Haasse) 236
Three Plays for Puritans (Shaw) 153
Three Sisters (Chekhov) 92, 159
Three Tall Women (Albee) 282
The Thunderstorm (Ostrovsky) 121
Thy Neighbor's Wife (O'Flaherty) 184
Thyestes (Seneca) 5, 12
Time and the Conways (Priestley) 203
The Time of Your Life (Saroyan) 205
Timon of Athens (Shakespeare) 51
Tiny Alice (Albee) 240
'Tis a Pity She's a Whore (Ford) 54
Titus Andronicus (Shakespeare) 43
To Clothe the Naked (Pirandello) 154, 184

play *(continued)*
  To Damascus (Strindberg) 93, 148
  Tobia Commedia (Petrie) 38
  Toller (Dorst) 245
  Tom Jones (Osborne) 237
  Tonight We Improvise (Pirandello) 154, 193
  The Tooth of Crime (Shepard) 250
  La Tosca (Sardou) 138
  Toward Heaven and the Altars (Benavente y Martínez) 191
  The Tower (Hofmannsthal) 187
  Tower of Victory (Luzzatto) 74
  Trachiniae (Sophocles) 3
  The Traffic of Algiers (Cervantes) 32
  The Tragedies of Faith (Rolland) 172
  The Tragedies of Love (Gunnarsson) 162
  The Tragedy of Al-Hallaj (Abdassabur) 240
  The Tragedy of Chabot, Admiral of France (Chapman) 56
  The Tragedy of King Christophe (Césaire) 237
  The Tragedy of Othello, Moor of Venice (Shakespeare) 50
  The Tragic Engagement (Chenet) 245
  The Tragical History of the Life and Death of Doctor Faustus (Marlowe) 50
  Translations (Friel) 259
  Traveler Without Luggage (Anouilh) 202
  Tre borgerliga kvartetter (Noren) 279
  Trelawney of the "Wells" (Pinero) 148
  Tribute (Slade) 257
  Triumph of Winter (Vicente) 37
  Troilus and Cressida (Dryden) 63
  Troilus and Cressida (Shakespeare) 50
  Trojan Women (Euripides) 2, 7
  The Troubadour (García Gutiérrez) 109
  The Tutor; or, the Advantages of Private Education (Lenz) 82
  Twelfth Night, or What You Will (Shakespeare) 50
  The Twelve-Pound Note (Barrie) 168
  The Twenty-fourth of February (Werner) 98
  Twilight Crane (Kinoshita) 218
  The Two Friends; or, The Merchant of Lyons (Beaumarchais) 81
  The Two Gentlemen of Verona (Shakespeare) 44
  The Two Klingsbergs (Kotzebue) 95
  The Two Lamps (Krige) 238
  The Two Lovers of Heaven (Calderón de la Barca) 48, 56
  Two Women (Sarabhai) 221
  Tyrannick Love (Dryden) 49, 61
  The Unanimous Life (Romains) 166
  Uncle Vanya (Chekhov) 92, 147
  The Undivine Comedy (Krasinski) 109

  The Universal Heir (Regnard) 71
  The Unquiet Spirit (Bernard) 188
  Vain Entertainment (Neguse) 183
  Vengeance (Fredro) 108
  Venice Preserved (Otway) 64
  Venus Observed (Fry) 219
  Vicious Circle (Agustín) 253
  Victoria Regina (Housman) 199
  Vietnam Discourse (Weiss) 245
  A View from the Bridge (Miller) 225
  Vinterhagen (Vik) 274
  Virginie (Mairet) 55
  The Vise (Pirandello) 154
  The Visit: A Tragi-Comedy (Durrenmatt) 227
  Vladimir Reborn (Kheraskov) 85
  The Voice of Blood (Makonnen) 208
  Volpone, or the Fox (Jonson) 50
  Le Voyage de Monsieur Perrichon (Labiche) 122
  The Vultures (Becque) 135
  Waiting for Godot (Beckett) 154, 223
  Waiting for Lefty (Odets) 200
  The Wall of Death (Krige) 241
  Wallenstein's Camp (Schiller) 88
  Wallenstein's Death (Schiller) 88
  The Waltz of the Toreadors (Anouilh) 221
  Wandering Through Three Times (Abashidze) 234
  The Ward Wants to Be a Guardian (Handke) 246
  The Warrior's Battle (Kleist) 102
  Wasps (Aristophanes) 3
  Watch on the Rhine (Hellman) 208
  The Water Hen (Witkiewicz) 181
  The Way of the World (Congreve) 69
  The Way to the Tomb (Duncan) 212
  Wealth (Aristophanes) 3
  The Weather Cock (Holberg) 73
  The Weavers (Hauptmann) 143
  The Wedding (Chekhov) 92
  Weep Not for Me (Edwards) 260
  What Price Glory? (Anderson) 185
  When Love Is Young (Halbe) 144
  When the War Was Over (Frisch) 218
  When We Are Married (Priestley) 204
  When We Dead Awaken (Ibsen) 94, 149
  The Whirlwind (Bernstein) 163
  The White Devil (Webster) 51
  The White Fan (Hofmannsthal) 147
  White Wings (Barry) 188
  Who's Afraid of Virginia Woolf? (Albee) 235
  Widower's Houses (Shaw) 153
  Wild Beasts Are Tamed by Love (Calderón de la Barca) 48, 61
  The Wild Duck (Ibsen) 94, 136
  The Wild Gallant (Dryden) 49, 60
  The Will of the People (Sarabhai) 210
  William Tell (Schiller) 68, 96
  Wind in the Pines (Zeami Motokiyo) 15
  The Winter's Tale (Shakespeare) 31, 51

  Within the Gates (O'Casey) 197
  Woe from Wit (Griboyedov) 103
  A Woman Killed with Kindness (Heywood) 51
  The Woman Killer and the Hell of Oil (Chikamatsu) 73
  The Woman of Andros (Terence) 5, 9
  The Woman of Samos (Menander) 3
  The Woman's Prize, or the Tamer Tamed (Fletcher) 54
  Women at the Ecclesia (Aristophanes) 3
  Women at the Thesmophoria (Aristophanes) 3
  Women Beware Women (Middleton) 53
  The Wonder-Working Magician (Calderón de la Barca) 48, 56
  The Wood Nymph, or the Living Corpse (Mairet) 54
  Words in the Sand (Buero Vallejo) 218
  The World (Munk) 196
  Writings of a Prisoner (Gaediaty) 166
  Wupper River (Lasker-Schuler) 167
  A Yard of the Sun (Fry) 247
  Yellow Jack (Howard) 198
  Yerma (García Lorca) 155, 199
  Yesterday (Hofmansthal) 142
  Yorubus, You Must Think (Ogunde) 239
  You Can't Take It With You (Hart, Kaufman) 201
  You Never Can Tell (Shaw) 153
  The Youth of the Cid (Castro y Bellvís) 52
  The Zoo Story (Albee) 231
poem *See also* ballad; elegy; epic; epigram; epistolary poem; hymn; limerick; narrative poem; ode; prose poem; sonnet
  17-57 Poems (Bojic) 278
  18 Poems (Thomas) 199
  20 Digte (Larkin) 212
  XX Poems (Larkin) 212
  XLI Poems (cummings) 186
  77 Dream Songs (Berryman) 238, 239
  1914 (Brooke) 174
  À la frontière (Butor) 286
  A lume spento (Pound) 155, 166
  "A Silvia" (Leopardi) 91
  "Abou Ben Adhem" (Hunt) 113
  Above the River (Wright) 273
  Absalom and Achitophel (Dryden) 49, 63
  Adon Menuha (Yeshurun) 274
  "Adonais" (Shelley) 93, 102
  Adult Bookstore (Shapiro) 254
  The Adventuress (Augier) 115
  Aeneid (Virgil) 4, 11
  Africa (Petrarch) 14
  Africa Sings (Osadebay) 221
  After Russia (Tsvetayeva) 191
  The Afternoon of a Faun (Mallarmé) 131
  The Age of Anxiety (Auden) 215, 216
  Agenda (Hierro) 277
  Airplane Dreams: Compositions from Journals (Ginsberg) 244
  Aklake Mohseni (Kashefi) 29

  Al Aaraaf (Poe) 105
  Alastor; or, The Spirit of Solitude (Shelley) 100
  Album Verses (Lamb) 106
  Alcools (Apollinaire) 172
  Alive Together: New and Selected Poems (Mueller) 288
  All for Love, or, A Sinner Well Saved (Southey) 105
  All Sentiments (Mulla Vajhi) 55
  All the Poems (Caproni) 263
  "L'Allegro" (Milton) 48, 55
  Almost Spring (Ball) 293
  Alone (Nobre) 143
  Along the Way (Verhaeren) 142
  Amana Gras (Silkin) 249
  Amaranth (Robinson) 198
  America: A Prophecy (Blake) 68
  American Primitive (Oliver) 262, 263
  American Soul (Chocano) 164
  Among the Hills (Whittier) 127
  Amores (Ovid) 4
  Amores Folk (Celtis) 34
  The Amorous Vision (Boccaccio) 14
  "Amour" (Verlaine) 139
  Les Amours (Ronsard) 33
  Les Amours de Marie (Ronsard) 33
  Les Amours de P. de Ronsard Vandomoys, Ensemble de Bocages (Ronsard) 39
  Anabasis (Perce) 185
  Anapus Gaiso Eilerasciati (Juskaitis) 270
  An Anatomy of the World: The First Anniversary (Donne) 51
  An Ancient Book (Pavlovic) 278
  And Suddenly It's Evening (Quasimodo) 209
  "Andrea del Sarto" (Browning) 119
  The Angel (Lermontov) 107
  The Angel of History (Forché) 282
  Angeles de Compostela (Diego) 207
  Animal at Bottom (Jiménez) 215
  Animalia (Kilpi) 269
  Animals Arrival (Jennings) 246
  "Annabel Lee" (Poe) 116
  Annie Allen (Brooks) 217, 218
  "The Anniversary" (Donne) 49
  Annus Mirabilis (Dryden) 49, 61
  Another Life (Walcott) 251
  Another September (Kinsella) 229
  Another Song for America (Hensen) 268
  Another Time (Auden) 207
  Antartic Traveler (Pollitt) 261
  Anvare Soheyli (Kashefi) 34
  "Approach of Death" (Leopardi) 91, 109
  Arcadia (Sannazaro) 34
  Archy and Mehitabel (Marquis) 189
  Ariel (Plath) 240
  Aristophanes' Apology (Browning) 130
  The Arkansas Treatment (Walcott) 269
  Armarinho de miudezas (Salamao) 280
  Arquipelago (Barbosa) 200
  Ars amatoria (Ovid) 4, 11
  Ars poetica (Horace) 4, 11

Ars Vivendi eller de syv Jevmater (Johannesen) 292
The Art of Poetry (Boileau) 62
Ash and Honey (Szlosarek) 289
Ash Wednesday (Eliot) 193
Ashes (Bely) 168
Ashes and 7 Years from Somewhere (Levine) 258
Asolando (Browning) 140
Astraea Redux (Dryden) 49, 60
At the End of the Open Road (Simpson) 238
At the Fire of Controversy (Luzi) 257
An Atlas of the Difficult World, Poems, 1988–1991 (Rich) 275
Atta Troll (Heine) 113
Attempt of the Infinite Man (Neruda) 155
Audubon: A Vision (Lowell) 245
"Auld Lang Syne" (Burns) 68
Aurora Leigh (Browning) 120
Auroras of Autumn (Stevens) 218
Austrias (Latino) 41
"Autumn" (Thomson) 74
Autumn Leaves (Hugo) 106
Autumn Music (Preil) 258
Autumn Tranquility (Zollinger) 206
The Avenue Bearing the Initial of Christ into the New World: Poems, 1946–1964 (Kinnell) 252
The Avoiding and Other Poems (MacNeacail) 267
Babbling April (Greene) 154
Babi Year (Yevtushenko) 234
"The Bait" (Donne) 49
Balaustion's Adventure (Browning) 128
Balder Dead (Arnold) 118
"Balin and Balan" (Tennyson) 137
A Ballad from Beyond (Czechowicz) 196
The Ballad of Reading Gaol (Wilde) 148
The Ballad of the Figures (Eguren) 175
The Ballad of the Harp-Weaver (Millay) 183
Ballad of the Mari Lwyd and Other Poems (Watkins) 208
Ballads and Other Poems (Longfellow) 111
Ballads and Other Poems (Tennyson) 133
Ballads and Poems (Masefield) 168
Ballads and Poems of Tragic Life (Meredith) 138
Ballads and Songs (Davidson) 144
Baltics (Transtromer) 253
Bang-e Dara (Iqbāl) 185
Banquet (Dante) 14
Barbarian Prayer (Csoori) 272
"Bark" (Popa) 223
Barnabees Journal (Brathwaite) 56
Barrack-Room Ballads (Kipling) 143
"Batter My Heart" (Donne) 49
Be Angry at the Sun (Jeffers) 208
Beacons (Cruze Sousa) 158
The Bean Eaters (Brooks) 232
The Beautiful Changes and Other Poems (Wilbur) 214

The Bedroom (Bertolucci) 264
Belated Crown (Weinheber) 202
The Belfry of Bruges and Other Poems (Longfellow) 114
Belgium's Agony (Verhaeren) 174
The Bell Jar (Plath) 237
"Bells" (Poe) 116
Bells and Pomegranates (Browning) 114
Bells in Winter (Milosz) 257
"The Beloved's Exile" (Upadhyay Hariaudh) 173
Beneath Your Clear Shadow and Other Poems (Paz) 203
Beniowski (Słowacki) 112
Beppo (Byron) 93, 101
Beside the River Sar (Castro) 136
The Best Poems (Campos) 278
Between Gods and Demons (Weinheber) 204
Between Here and Now (Thomas) 260
Between the Coronation and the Sword (Alberti) 208
Between Two Rivers: Selected Poems, 1956–1984 (Kenny) 268
Bhuridat Lingagyi (Rahtathara) 28
Bhuridat Zatpaung Pyo (Rahtathara) 29
Big Work (Parra) 246
Birthday Letters (Hughes) 290
Birthplace (Haavikko) 225
Bishop Blougram's Apology (Browning) 119
Bitter Angel (Gerstler) 275
Black City (Lundkvist) 194
Black Feeling, Black Talk (Giovanni) 244
Black Label (Damas) 227
Black Pearls (Nervo) 148
Black Poems (Lima) 215
Black Sonnets (Sebastian) 166
The Black Venus (Baudelaire) 92
Black Zodiac (Wright) 290
"The Blessed Damozel" (Rossetti) 116
Blizzard of One (Strand) 292
Blood and Family (Kinsella) 271
Blood for a Stranger (Jarrell) 209
Blood-Red Sonnets (Hviezdoslav) 174
"The Bloody Throne" (Payrav) 194
A Blot in the 'Scutcheon (Browning) 113
Blue (Darío) 139
The Boatmen (Klonowic) 44
Bocages (Ronsard) 33
Bodenlos (Kirsch) 286
Bodenloser Sstz (Braun) 274
The Book of Ahania (Blake) 68, 87
The Book of Day and the Book of Night (Iwaszkiewicz) 182
Book of Exercises (Seferis) 207
Book of Folly (Sexton) 250
The Book of Good Love (Ruiz) 25
The Book of Hours (Rilke) 155, 163
The Book of Imaginary Beings (Borges) 154, 243
The Book of Landscapes (Lugones) 176
The Book of Los (Blake) 68, 87
Book of Mercy (Cohen) 264

The Book of Nightmares (Kinnell) 248
Book of Poems (García Lorca) 155
Book of Seven Days (Johannes) 225
The Book of Songs (Drachmann) 140
The Book of Songs (Heine) 93
Book of the Duchess (Chaucer) 14
Book of the Poor (Kasprowicz) 175
The Book of Urizen (Blake) 68, 86
The Borderers (Wordsworth) 87, 92
The Bothie of Tober-na-Vuolich (Clough) 115
The Bouge of Court (Skelton) 29
Bouquets and Prayers (Desbordes-Valmore) 113
The Boys (Lenngren) 87
Bozena Nemcova's Fan (Seifert) 207
Brajangana (Datta) 122
Brand (Ibsen) 122
The Breath of Copper (Enckell) 213
Breatijs (Boutens) 166
Brebeuf and His Brethren (Pratt) 207
The Bridal of Triermain (Scott) 99
The Bride of Abydos (Byron) 93, 99
The Bridge (Crane) 193
Bright Ambush (Wurdemann) 200
The Brightness of Life (Viélé-Griffin) 147
Britannia Rediviva (Dryden) 65
The British Prison Ship (Freneau) 84
Broken Country (Brodsky) 284
Broken Pitchers (al-Bayati) 223
The Broken Verse (Prudhomme) 125
"The Bronze Horseman" (Pushkin) 90, 110
Brother to Dragons: A Tale in Verse and Voices (Warren) 222
"The Brothers" (Wordsworth) 92
Brothers, I Love You All (Carruth) 257
Buch der Leider (Heine) 105
The Buck in the Snow (Millay) 190
Buckdancer's Choice (Dickey) 240
Bucolicum carmen (Boccaccio) 14
The Buried Lake (Tate) 222
Burning Brambles Selected Poems, 1944–1979 (Mathias) 263
The Burning Bush (Faesi) 190
The Burning Mystery of Anna in 1951 (Koch) 258
Burnt Norton (Eliot) 202
Butterflies (Spitteler) 140
"The Cachalot" (Pratt) 188
Cain (Leconte de Lisle) 127
"Calamiterror" (Barker) 203
Calçada de Verao (Figueiredo) 274
Calendau (Mistral) 126
Call (Nasir) 221
The Call (Vörösmarty) 110
Calligrammes (Apollinaire) 177
"The Campaign" (Addison) 70
Campo Santo (Wood) 277

"The Canonization" (Donne) 49
The Canterbury Tales (Chaucer) 14, 26
I Canti (Leopardi) 91, 106
Canticle (Guillén) 191
Cantos (Pound) 155, 174
Cantos No. 1–117, 120 (Pound) 247
Canzoni (Leopardi) 91, 103
Capital of Sorrow (Éluard) 188
Captain Quiros (McAuley) 238
Captain Sword and Captain Pen (Hunt) 108
"The Captive" (Echeverría) 110
Carmina de Laudibus Estensium (Boiardo) 27
The Carrier of Ladders (Merwin) 247, 248
Casi una leyenda (Rodríguez) 277
The Castaway (Cowper) 88
The Castle of Indolence (Thomson) 77
Casualties: Poems, 1966–1968 (Clark) 247
The Cathedral (Lowell) 127
Causes (Callimachus) 4
Cavender's House (Robinson) 191
Cawdor (Jeffers) 190
Centuries of Meditations (Traherne) 166
Ceremony and Other Poems (Wilbur) 219
Changing Light at Sandover (Merrill) 262
Chanticleer's Morsel (Popovic) 276
The Chapel of the Hermits, and Other Poems (Whittier) 118
Char Divan (Nava'i) 29
Charcoal Burner's Ballad and Other Poems (Andersson) 211
"Charge of the Light Brigade" (Tennyson) 93, 118
The Chestnut Tree (Tyler) 103
Chicago (Sandburg) 173
Chicago Poems (Sandburg) 175
Childe Harold's Pilgrimage (Byron) 93, 98
Children of Nature (Claussen) 138
Children of the Night (Robinson) 147
"Children of Wrath" (Alonso) 212
Child's Garden of Verses (Stevenson) 137
Child's Songs (Aicard) 131
Chills and Fever (Ransom) 185
The Chinese Insomniacs (Jacobsen) 260
The Chinese Nightingale and Other Poems (Lindsay) 176
"Christabel" (Coleridge) 100
Christmas Eve and Easter (Browning) 116
Chronique (Perse) 232
Church Poems (Betjeman) 260
Cinders (Amrouche) 199
Circles in the Water: Selected Poems (Piercy) 261
The Circus in the Attic (Warren) 216
The Cistern (Seferis) 196
"The City of Dreadful Night" (Thomson) 130
Clamor (Guillén) 229

poem (continued)
Clarel (Melville) 131
Clay Medals (Régnier) 158
The Closed Door (Bosschere) 176
"The Cloud" (Shelley) 93
A Cloud in Trousers
    (Mayakovsky) 174
A Coast of Trees (Ammons) 260
The Coat Without a Seam (Ku-
    nitz) 252
The Cold Green Element (Layton)
    225
Cold Morning Sky (Zaturenska)
    204
Collected Early Poems, 1950–1970
    (Rich) 279
Collected Poems (Aiken) 222
Collected Poems (Betjeman) 229
Collected Poems (Binyon) 194
Collected Poems (Crane) 197
Collected Poems (Davie) 250
Collected Poems (Freneau) 98
Collected Poems (Frost) 194
Collected Poems (Graves) 216
Collected Poems (Hartnett) 264
Collected Poems (Jennings) 243
Collected Poems (Larkin) 272
Collected Poems (Lenau) 114
Collected Poems (Lewis) 223
Collected Poems (MacCaig) 274
Collected Poems (Moore) 220,
    221
Collected Poems (Nemerov) 255,
    256
Collected Poems (Plath) 261
Collected Poems (Prince) 258
Collected Poems (Robinson) 182
Collected Poems (Sassoon) 215
Collected Poems (Seeger) 175
Collected Poems (Stevens) 223, 225
Collected Poems (Stubbs) 271
Collected Poems (Van Doren) 206
Collected Poems (Wright) 248,
    249
Collected Poems, 1917–1952
    (MacLeish) 222
Collected Poems, 1928–1953
    (Spender) 225
Collected Poems, 1930–1993 (Sar-
    ton) 279
Collected Poems, 1934–1952
    (Thomas) 221
Collected Poems, 1946–1991 (Car-
    ruth) 277
Collected Poems, 1947–1980
    (Ginsberg) 264
Collected Poems, 1948–1984 (Wal-
    cott) 267
Collected Poems, 1948–1998 (En-
    right) 290
Collected Poems of H.D. (Dolittle)
    186
Collected Poetry (Hope) 241
Collected Shorter Poems (Auden)
    241
Collected Verse (Hillyer) 198
Collected Works of Billy the Kidd:
    Left-Handed Poems (Ondaatje)
    247
The Colloquies (Gozzano) 170
Color (Cullen) 186
The Colossus (Plath) 232
The Coming Out Book (Susko)
    276
The Compass Flower (Merwin)
    256

The Complaint; or, Night Thoughts
    on Life, Death and Immortality
    (Young) 76
The Complaint of a Poor Little
    Child (Kosztolányi) 169
The Complete Poems (Jarrell) 245
Complete Poems (Sandburg) 219
Complete Works (Crémazie) 135
Concerning the Angels (Alberti)
    192
A Coney Island of the Mind (Fer-
    linghetti) 229
The Congo and Other Poems
    (Lindsay) 173
Los conjurados (Borges) 266
Conquistador (MacLeish) 196
Constantly Singing (Simmons)
    259
Contact Highs: Selected Poems,
    1957–1987 (Ansen) 270
Continuation des Amours (Ron-
    sard) 33
The Cooper's Hell (Denham) 57
Cor Ardens (Ivanov) 170
Corn Huskers (Sandburg) 178
The Corsair (Byron) 93, 99
Count Julian (Landor) 98
"Count Nulin" (Pushkin) 90, 105
Country (Desnos) 211
Country Music: Selected Early
    Poems (Wright) 262
The Courtship of Miles Standish
    (Longfellow) 120
"The Cranes of Ibycus" (Schiller)
    68
Credo des san-mélé ou je veux
    chanter la France (Gratiant) 216
"The Cretan" (Solomos) 107
Crimean Sonnetsi (Mickiewicz)
    104
A Critical Fable (Lowell) 182
Cross Hollows (Einar) 193
"Crossing the Bar" (Tennyson)
    140
Crossing the Water (Plath) 248
Crow: From the Life and Songs of
    the Crow (Hughes) 247
The Crow and the Heart (Carruth)
    230
A Cry and Landscapes (Ungaretti)
    221
Crypt (Torres Bodet) 203
Cryptogamen (Achterberg) 213
Cuaderno de Nueva York (Hierro)
    292
Cuttlefish Bones (Montale) 187
A Cycle of the West (Neihardt)
    217
The Cypresse Grove (Drummond)
    53
Dal silenzio delle campagne
    (Comon) 293
Dance of Death: A Baroque Poem
    (Rozewicz) 291
Dance of Death and Poems of the
    Times (Kaschnitz) 215
Dance of the Dead (Jouve) 176
The Dancing Bears (Merwin) 223
Dangerous Love (Okri) 288
Dark Fields of the Republic (Rich)
    284
Day After Day (Quasimodo) 215
A Day Book (Creeley) 250
Day by Day (Lowell) 256
A Day Lie Every Day (Czecho-
    wicz) 193

The Days (Torres Bodet) 184
The Dead Kingdom (Montague)
    263
The Dead Lecturer (Baraka) 238
"Death, Be Not Proud" (Donne)
    49
Death of a Naturalist (Heaney)
    241
"Death of a Poet" (Lermontov)
    110
The Death of Abel (Gessner) 79
The Death of Oneone, Akbar's
    Dream and Other Poems (Ten-
    nyson) 93
Death of the Seasons (Ungaretti)
    243
Deaths and Entrances (Thomas)
    213
Death's Jest-Book; or, The Fool's
    Tragedy (Beddoes) 116
Les Débâcles (Verhaeren) 139
Deep River Talk (Tuwhare) 282
Deep Shadows (Storm) 124
La Défense de Tartuffe (Jacob)
    178
The Defense of Guenevere and
    Other Poems (Morris) 120
"Dejection: An Ode" (Coleridge)
    96
Delie: Object of Highest Virtue
    (Scève) 38
The Delirious Heart (Torres
    Bodet) 183
Delphic Utterance (Sikelianós)
    189
Demeter and Other Poems (Ten-
    nyson) 93, 140
Departmental Ditties (Kipling)
    137
Departures (Justice) 251
Les Derniers Vers (Ronsard) 33
Description (Dragomoshchenko)
    296
The Deserted Village (Goldsmith)
    81
Desolation (Mistral) 183
Dess ande kysst (Johnsson) 279
Destruction (Mistral) 205
Destruction or Love (Aleixandre)
    200
The Dew Trapper (Nijlen) 214
"Dialogue of Insight" (Aleixan-
    dre) 253
The Diamond Cutters and Other
    Poems (Rich) 225
Diana's Hunt (Boccaccio) 14
Diary of My Father's Death (Issa)
    95
The Dice Box (Jacob) 176
Dikter (Södergran) 175
"Dipsychus" (Clough) 127
Discourse on the Miseries of These
    Times (Ronsard) 33
The Dismissal of the Greek Envoys
    (Kochanowski) 41
Distant Gardens (Jiménez) 163
Divan of Tamarit (García Lorca)
    155
Divan-e-Shams (Rūmī) 15
"The Diver" (Schiller) 68
Divine Comedies (Merrill) 255
Divine Comedy (Dante) 13
Doctor Copernicus (Banville) 255
The Doer (Borges) 233
The Dog Without Feathers (Melo
    Neto) 219

The Dogs (Aspenstrom) 224
Doine si Lacrimioare (Alecsandri)
    118
The Dolphin (Lowell) 252
A Dome of Many-Colored Glass
    (Lowell) 171
Don Juan (Byron) 93, 101
Don Juan Tenorio (Zorrilla y
    Moral) 114
Door into the Dark (Heaney) 246
The Double Man (Auden) 208
A Dove in Santiago: A Novella in
    Verse (Yevtushenko) 262
Downstream (Kinsella) 235
A Draft of XXX Cantos (Pound)
    197
"The Dragon and the Unicorn"
    (Rexroth) 221
Dramatis Personae (Browning)
    124
Dramen (Canetti) 239
"The Dream" (Byron) 100
Dream Flower (Yosano) 164
The Dream of Eugene Aram
    (Hood) 105
A Dream of Mind (Williams) 277
The Dream of the Unified Field
    (Graham) 286
The Dream Songs (Berryman) 245
Dream Variation (Hughes) 188
Dreams in Twilight (Terian) 166
The Dreamtigers (Borges) 154
Dressed in Light (Seifert) 207
Driving into the Storm: Selected
    Poems (Wedde) 269
Drommebroer (Nordbrandt) 295
Drowning with Others (Dickey)
    235
"Drum-Taps" (Whitman) 124
"The Drunken Boat" (Rimbaud)
    94, 128
Dry Salvages (Eliot) 208
Duino Elegies (Rilke) 155, 184
The Dumbfounding (Avison) 241
The Dust Which Is God (Benét)
    209
The Eagle (Král') 114
Eagle Nests (Bojic) 278
Eagle or Sun (Paz) 220
Earth Erect (Popa) 250
Earthly Paradise (Morris) 126
East Coker (Eliot) 207
East Slope (Paz) 249
"Easter 1916" (Yeats) 152, 175
The East-West Wind (Shvarts)
    289
Echoes and Traces (Transtromer)
    242
Eclogues (Virgil) 4
Education by Stone (Cayrol) 241
Effort at Speech: New and Selected
    Poems (Meredith) 288
Egyptian Nights (Pushkin) 90,
    109
Eight Sonnets in American Poetry,
    1922: A Miscellany (Millay) 183
Eldflugorna (Isakson) 292
"Eleanora: A Panegyrical Poem to
    the Memory of the Countess of
    Abingdon" (Dryden) 65
Elegy for an Exit (Herbert) 274
"Elegy Upon the Death of Rev-
    erend Mr. Thomas Shepard"
    (Oakes) 63
"Elegy Written in a Country
    Churchyard" (Gray) 78

"Elegy XX: To His Mistress Going to Bed" (Donne) 49
Eloisa to Abelard (Pope) 72
Elvira (Echeverría) 107
Embracing Defeat (Williams) 295
Empedocles on Etna and Other Poems (Arnold) 117
The Empire of Stupidity (Lista) 88
Enamels and Cameos (Gautier) 117
Endymion (Keats) 101
The English Pilot (Wergeland) 114
Enoch Arden (Tennyson) 93, 124
The Enthusiastic Slingshooter (Neruda) 155
"The Eolian Harp" (Blake) 87
The Epic of Sheikh Badruddin (Hikmet Ran) 202
Epipsychidion (Shelley) 93, 102
An Epistle to Dr. Arbuthnot (Pope) 69, 75
Epistle to Several Persons (Pope) 75
Epistle to the Heroines (Ovid) 4
Epistles (Horace) 4
Epodes (Horace) 4
Erato e Apollion (Quasimodo) 202
Eros (Ivanov) 165
Escape from Solitude (Csoori) 236
The Espousals (Patmore) 119
An Essay on Criticism (Pope) 69, 71
An Essay on Man (Pope) 69, 75
Essay on Rime (Shapiro) 212
Eugene Onegin (Pushkin) 90, 108
Europe: A Prophecy (Blake) 68
Europe and Other Bad News (Layton) 260
Evangeline, a Tale of Acadie (Longfellow) 115
"The Eve of St. Agnes" (Keats) 101
Ève (Péguy) 172
Evening (Akhmatova) 171
Evening Album (Tsvetayeva) 169
The Evening Hours (Verhaeren) 169
Evening Light (Ivanov) 212
Evening Star (Bandeira) 237
The Evening Star (Eminescu) 136
"An Evening Walk" (Wordsworth) 86
The Everlasting Gospel (Blake) 68
The Evil Poem (Machado) 168
The Excursion (Southey) 99
The Exhortation to War (Vicente) 32
Exile (Torres Bodet) 193
The Exile and Other Poems (Perse) 209
"Experimenting with an Amen" (Thomas) 267
Ezo Vikolinsky (Hviezdoslav) 141
The Fable of the Bees; or Private Vices, Public Benefits (Mandeville) 72
Fables, Ancient and Modern (Dryden) 66
Fábula de fuentes (Juárez) 271
The Faces of Life (Verhaeren) 149
Fageljagarna (Sjogren) 289
The Fair World (Tomas) 198
The Fairy Council (Laforgue) 138
Fairy Good Fortune (Lahuti) 217
The Fall of Princes (Lydgate) 29

Fallen Flower (Kumaran Asan) 167
The Far Field (Roethke) 238
Farewell (Drummond) 287
Fausto (Campo) 125
Feast Days (Burnside) 278
Feather Fall (Post) 282
The Feeling of Time (Ungaretti) 198
"Fern Hill" (Thomas) 213
The Fertile Eyes (Éluard) 202
Fervor in Buenos Aires, Poems (Borges) 154
Fêtes galantes (Verlaine) 127
A Few Figs from Thistles (Millay) 179, 183
Fiddler's Farewell (Speyer) 189
Field Work (Heaney) 258
Fifine at the Fair (Browning) 129
The Fifth of May (Manzoni) 102
Fighting Terms (Gunn) 223
Fire of Rose (Muradabadi) 224
The First Epistle of the Second Book of Horace to Augustus (Pope) 75
First Fruits of the Desert (Luzi) 221
First Gold of the Indies (Chocano) 199
First Loves (Verhaeren) 162
First Person Plural (Blandina) 239
First Songs (García Lorca) 155
Five Great Odes (Claudel) 168
Five Southern Poets (Marechal) 203
Flagons and Apples (Jeffers) 171
The Flemish (Verhaeren) 135
Flesh (Benn) 176
Flesh and Blood (Williams) 269
Floating Foam (Castro Alves) 127
Der Flohatz (Fischart) 41
Flood for the Muse's Springs (Cruz) 65
Flora Och Bellona (Karlfeldt) 178
Flora Och Pomona (Karlfeldt) 164
Flower, Fist and Bestial Wail (Bukowski) 231
Flower Herding on Mount Monadnock (Kinnell) 238
Flowering Rifle: A Poem from the Battlefields of Spain (Campbell) 206
The Flowering Stone (Dillon) 195
Flowers from the Volcano (Alegría) 262
The Flowers of Evil (Baudelaire) 92, 120
The Flutist's Happiness (Enckell) 186
The Flying Change (Taylor) 265, 267
Foot on the Neck (Belli) 239
For levande och doda (Transtromer) 275
For Love: Poems, 1959–1960 (Creeley) 235
For the Baptism of Our Fragments (Luzi) 266
For the Time Being (Auden) 212
For the Union Dead (Lowell) 238
Forberedelser for wintersasongen (Gustafsson) 275
Foreign Sky (Gumilyov) 171
The Forest (Jonson) 52
The Forest of Anyksciai (Baranauskas) 120

Forms (Nijhoff) 185
Forskjellig (Berg) 284
The Fortunate Traveler (Walcott) 260
The Fortune of Yakutsk (Elley) 215
The Fountain of Bakhchsaray (Pushkin) 90, 103
The Four Quartets (Eliot) 152
The Four Zoas: The Torment of Love and Jealousy in the Death and Judgment of Albion (Blake) 87
"Fra Lippo Lippi" (Browning) 119
Fragmenta Aurea (Suckling) 57
La Françiade (Ronsard) 33
Fredmans Epistlar (Bellman) 86
Fredy Neptune (Murray) 293
"The Free Besieged" (Solomos) 105
The Freeing of the Dust (Levertov) 253
The French Revolution (Blake) 68
Frequencies (Thomas) 257
The Friar (Melo Neto) 263
Frida's Book (Sjöberg) 183
Fridolin's Pleasure Garden (Karlfeldt) 159
Fridolin's Songs (Karlfeldt) 148
Frights (Varuzhan) 164
From Princeton One Afternoon: Collected Poems, 1950–1986 (Weiss) 293
From the Bottom of the Field (Luzi) 240
From the Days of Sorrow (Franko) 158
From the Surge (Faesi) 176
Frontiers (Torres Bodet) 224
Frost (Leino) 166
The Fudge Family in Paris (Moore) 101
A Further Range (Frost) 201, 203
Galician Songs (Castro) 123
Games—Tough and Divine (Régnier) 147
Garbage (Ammons) 279
"The Garden" (Marvell) 63
"Gareth and Lynette" (Tennyson) 129
A Gate in the Cloud (Stojcevski) 280
The Gathering Storm (Empson) 207
Gaudy Observations (Södergran) 179
Gay Shipwrecks (Ungaretti) 179
Gedichte (Heine) 102
Gedichte (Lenau) 107
Gedlichten, 1904–1938 (Nijlen) 204
Gelenging Tekad (Notodijo) 218
General William Booth Enters into Heaven and Other Poems (Lindsay) 172
Geography III (Bishop) 254
Georgics (Virgil) 4
Germany, a Winter's Tale (Heine) 114
"Gerontion" (Eliot) 152
Ghost Ship (Martinson) 192
The Giaour (Byron) 93, 99
Gītāñjalī (Tagore) 153, 168
Gilgamesh 1
Ginestra (Leopardi) 91
Il Giorno (Parini) 80

Gipsy Ballads (García Lorca) 191
Glass Puddles (Reverdy) 192
The Gleam of a Clear Dawn Approached (Král') 122
The Glittering Flint (Vaughan) 58
Glory to the Children and Olives (al-Bayati) 226
"The Glove" (Schiller) 68
Glowing Embers (Lundkvist) 191
"Go, Lovely Rose" (Waller) 57
Goblin (Rossetti) 123
God's Trombones (Johnson) 189
Gold in Azure (Bely) 162
The Golden Horns (Oehlenschläger) 95
The Golden Qishalq (Mirshakar) 209
The Good Flight (Kinsella) 251
The Good Move (Belli) 270
Gothic Notebook (Luzi) 215
Le Grand Testament (Villon) 27
Grass and Bell (Spitteler) 164
The Grave (Blair) 76
The Graves (Palamas) 147
Grazing into the Wall (Weöres) 269
Grazyna (Mickiewicz) 103
The Great Hunger (Kavanagh) 209
The Great Restlessness (Zollinger) 206
The Great Songbook (Bredero) 53
"Green Grow the Rashes, O" (Burns) 68
The Green Hamlet and Other Poems (Yeats) 168
Green Leaves (Singh) 202
Green Song (Sitwell) 211
The Green-Eyed Venus (Baudelaire) 92
Grief (Ungaretti) 215
Ground Work (Duncan) 264
Ground Work III: In the Dark (Duncan) 269
The Grumbling Hive; or, Knaves Turned Honest (Mandeville) 70
Guide to the Underworld (Ekelof) 244
Gunpowder (O'Donoghue) 286
Guttilaya (Vetteve) 27
"The Gypsies" (Pushkin) 90, 104
The Gypsy Ballads (García Lorca) 155
The Habitant and Other French-Canadian Poems (Drummond) 147
Haft Owrang (Jāmī) 27
Halley's Comet (Seifert) 242
Hallucinated City (Andrade) 183
A Halt in the Wasteland (Brodsky) 248
Hamasah (Abū Tammām) 19
A Handful of Sand (Ishikawa) 169
Hands Behind My Back: Selected Poems (Sorescu) 278
Hanna (Runeberg) 109
"Happiness" (Prudhomme) 139
Happy Ending (Podrimja) 270
The Hard Hours (Hecht) 244
Harlem (Hughes) 220
Harmonium (Stevens) 184
Harmony and Pastels (Montale) 236
The Haw Lantern (Heaney) 269
The Hawk in the Rain (Hughes) 228

poem *(continued)*

Healing Song for the Inner Ear (Harper) 265

Heartbreak (Aragon) 208

The Heart's Needle (Snodgrass) 231, 232

Heaven and Earth (Goldbarth) 277

Hecale (Callimachus) 4

The Heights of Machu Picchu (Neruda) 215

Hekigoto Kushu (Kawahigashi) 175

Helicon's Flowers (Johansson) 65

Hellas (Shelley) 93, 103

Hello: A Journal (Creeley) 257

Hello, Darkness: The Collected Poems of L. E. Sussman (Sussman) 257

The Helmet of Clay (Seifert) 212

Helmets (Dickey) 238

Here and Now (Levertov) 228

Here I Am, in Perfect Leaf Today (Dubarova) 279

Heretics (Kitahara) 179

Hermann and Dorothea (Goethe) 87

Hero and Leander (Marlowe) 33

"Herodias" (Mallarmé) 127

Heroic and Elegiac Song for the Lost Second Lieutenant of the Albanian Campaign (Elytis) 213

Heroics (Claussen) 186

Hesperides (Herrick) 58

Hexaemeron (Arrebo) 54

High and Low (Betjeman) 241

The High Tide in the Garden (Adcock) 249

High Windows (Larkin) 252

The Hind and the Panther (Dryden) 49, 64

"His Majesty's Escape at St. Andre" (Waller) 54

History of the Destruction of Troy (Colonno) 24

History of the Heart (Aleixandre) 224

Den hogsta kasten (Rydberg) 289

The Hollow Hill and Other Poems, 1960–1964 (Raine) 240

"The Hollow Men" (Eliot) 186

The Holy Flame (Drachmann) 149

"The Holy Grail" (Tennyson) 127

The Holy Stone (Blackburn) 223

Homage to Clio (Auden) 232

"Homage to Mistress Bradstreet" (Berryman) 216

Homage to Mistress Bradstreet (Berryman) 226

"Homage to Sextus Propertius" (Pound) 155

Homage to Sextus Propertius (Pound) 178

Honeymoon Ride (Seifert) 204

Honor of Truth (Luzi) 228

The Horn of Autumn (Karlfeldt) 189

Horses Make a Landscape Look More Beautiful (Walker) 264

Hot Ashes (Jastrun) 227

Hothouses (Maeterlinck) 140

"The Hound of Heaven" (Thompson) 139, 143

Hours (Castro) 142

Hours of Idleness (Byron) 97

The House (Torres Bodet) 184

House of Fame (Chaucer) 14

The House of the Customs Officer and Other Poems (Montale) 196

The House of Titans and Other Poems (AE) 199

How the Heart Is Torn Apart (Siktanc) 273

Howl, and Other Poems (Ginsberg) 226

Hudibras (Butler) 60

Hugh Selwyn Mauberley (Pound) 155, 179

Human Bodies: New and Collected Poems, 1987–1999 (Bowering) 293

Human Landscapes (Hikmet Ran) 242

Human Poems (Vallejo) 206

Human Verses (Diego) 187

Hungerfield and Other Poems (Jeffers) 223

"The Hunting of the Snark" (Carroll) 131

Hutten's Last Days (Meyer) 128

"I Sing the Body Electric" (Whitman) 119

I vantan pa pendeltaget (Vennberg) 275

"I Wandered Lonely as a Cloud" (Wordsworth) 96

Iambi (Callimachus) 4

Iambs and Anapaests (Palamas) 147

Ibis (Callimachus) 4

The Idea of Order at Key West (Stevens) 200

Idilli (Leopardi) 91

Idylls of the King (Tennyson) 93, 121

Iliad (Homer) 2, 51

Les Illuminations (Rimbaud) 94, 129, 138

The Imitation of Our Lady of the Moon (Laforgue) 138

Imitations (Lowell) 234

Implements in their Places (Graham) 256

In a Vast Domain (Aleixandre) 236

In Country Sleep (Thomas) 221

In Her Own Image (Boland) 259

"In Memoriam, A.H.H." (Tennyson) 116

In Memoriam (Tennyson) 93

In My Own Home (Ludens) 270

In Parenthesis (Jones) 203

In Praise of Sky, Sea, Earth and Heroes (D'Annunzio) 149

In the American Grain (Williams) 186

In the Clearing (Frost) 235

In the Harbor (Longfellow) 135

In the Line of Fire (Mihailovic) 283

In the Mecca (Brooks) 244

In the Midst of My Fever (Layton) 223

In the Seven Woods (Yeats) 161

In Time Like Air (Sarton) 229

In Wartime and Other Poems (Whittier) 124

The Incident Book (Adcock) 267

The Incomparable Earth (Quasimodo) 230

The Indian Hut (Bertolucci) 220

Indonesia, Land of My Birth (Yamin) 192

El infierno es un decir (Hernández) 283

Inhabited Heart (Andrade) 266

In the Magma (Luzi) 234

Inland and Other Poems (Hashimi) 271

The Inn Album (Browning) 130

The Inner Harbor (Adcock) 258

Inni Sacri (Manzoni) 99

The Intermezzo of Poems (D'Annunzio) 136

The Invention of Orpheus (Lima) 222

Ipotesi d'Amore (Cima) 264

The Iron Gate (Gripenberg) 163

The Island (Byron) 103

The Island in Winter (Young) 293

The Island of the Holy Name (Tenreiro) 209

It Exists Somewhere (Petri) 274

An Italian Visit (Day-Lewis) 222

Ixion's Wheel (Gustafson) 246

Jacklight (Erdrich) 264

Jadis et Naguerre (Verlaine) 136

Jan Van Huysum's Flowerpiece (Wergeland) 111

"Jana Gana Mana" (Tagore) 153

Jersey Rain (Pinsky) 295

Jerusalem (Blake) 68

"A Jew from Lublin" (Glatstein) 242

The Jew (Wergeland) 112

Jocoseria (Browning) 135

"John Anderson, My Jo" (Burns) 68

John Brown's Body (Benét) 190, 191

Joined Hands (Mauriac) 167

The Journey (Manner) 227

Journey (Meireles) 206

The Journey, and Other Poems (Winters) 194

The Joys (Viélé-Griffin) 140

The Joys of Rungsted (Ewald) 82

Judas Sack (Klonowic) 50

Julian and Maddalo (Shelley) 93

Jumping the Train Tracks with Angela (Durcan) 264

La Justice (Prudhomme) 132

Kaddish and Other Poems (Ginsberg) 234

Kanhadade Prabandha (Padmanabhan) 27

Kantapuranam (Sivakariyar) 54

King Arthur (Bulwer-Lytton) 116

The King's Flute (Palamas) 169

Kjoerlighetsdikt (Mehren) 289

A Knife All Blade (Melo Neto) 227

Kogan Pyo (Rahtathara) 36

Kokinshu (Tsurayuki Ki) 20

Konrad Wallenrod (Mickiewicz) 105

Korn (Lundqvist) 266

"Kubla Khan" (Coleridge) 100

Kumarasambhava (Kālidāsa) 15

Kung Fjalar (Runeberg) 113

Kuyil's Song (Bharati) 171

"La Drama de Marchaterre" (Brierre) 193

La Laboratoire central (Jacob) 181

The Lady of Maldoro (Lautréamont) 126

"The Lady of Shalott" (Tennyson) 93, 107

The Lady of the Lake (Scott) 93

Lake Lyrics and Other Poems (Campbell) 140

Lalla Rookh (Moore) 100

"Lament for the Death of a Bullfighter" (García Lorca) 155, 200

"The Lament of Tasso" (Byron) 100

Lamia (Keats) 101

Land, Land in Sight (Stojicic) 294

The Land of Silence (Sarton) 222

Land of the Heather (Kivi) 125

Land's End (Montale) 210

Landscape with Figures (Diego) 227

Language (Jouve) 221

Languor (Storni) 180

Lanzen im Eis (Schacht) 274

Lara (Byron) 93, 99

The Lark of Truth (Diego) 208

The Last Knight (Grun) 106

The Last Lantern (Kristensen) 223

Last Loves (Desportes) 42

Last Poems (Gonçalves Dias) 117

Last Poems (Laforgue) 141

Last Poems and Two Plays (Yeats) 152, 206

Last Songs (Ledwidge) 177

The Last Summer (Moretti) 246

"The Last Tournament" (Tennyson) 128

The Lay of the Last Minstrel (Scott) 93

Lays of My Home and Other Poems (Whittier) 113

The Lazy Steppe (Mirshakar) 234

Leaves, Pages (Haavikko) 230

Leaves in the Wind (Casal) 141

Leaves of Grass (Whitman) 119

Leaves of Hypnos (Char) 214

Leaves of Three Autumns (Bian) 197

"Leda and the Swan" (Yeats) 184

Legend of Good Women (Chaucer) 14

La Legende d'un Peuple (Fréchette) 138

Legends of New England in Prose and Verse (Whittier) 106

The Less Deceived (Larkin) 225

Less Than One (Brodsky) 268

Let There Be Light (Chocano) 166

Letters to Live Poets (Beaver) 241

La Lettrice di Isasca (Richelmy) 268

The Levant (Cartarescu) 276

Levia gravia (Carducci) 126

Libertinism (Bandeira) 193

Liberty (Thomson) 75

Lies and Secrets (Fuller) 258

The Life and Death of Jason (Morris) 126

Life and Poetry of Joseph Delorme (Saint-Beuve) 105

"Life and the Ideal" (Schiller) 68

Life Immovable (Palamas) 162

The Life of the Virgin Mary (Rilke) 155, 172

Life Studies (Lowell) 231

Life Supports; New and Collected Poems (Bronk) 261

Life That Strives to Be a Poem (Bagravana) 281

The Light Around the Body (Bly) 244

The Light-Shadowed (Sikelianós) 167

Like Most Revelations (Howard) 282

The Lincoln Relics (Kunitz) 257

"Lines Composed a Few Miles Above Tintern Abbey" (Wordsworth) 88, 92

Litany (Aspenstrom) 222

Little Friend, Little Friend (Jarrell) 212

Little Gidding (Eliot) 209

"The Little Mariner" (Elytis) 268

"Little Orphan Annie" (Riley) 135

Live or Die (Sexton) 241, 242

Lock of Berenice (Callimachus) 4

"Locksley Hall"(Tennyson) 93, 107, 112

Logbook I (Seferis) 207

London: A Poem (Johnson) 75

Un long Dimanche de fiancailles (Japrisot) 276

Long Live Man (Corso) 235

Longings for Heaven (Castro) 149

A Looking-Glass for the Times (Folger) 62

Loose Leaves (Deus) 131

Lord of the Isles (Scott) 93

Lord Weary's Castle (Lowell) 213, 214

Loss of Sons (Skallagrimsson) 20

Lost (Ibarbourou) 219

The Lost Son, and Other Poems (Roethke) 216

The Lost World: New Poems (Jarrell) 240

"The Lotos-Eaters" (Tennyson) 93, 107

Love Poems (Antonio) 233

Love Poems (Sexton) 246

"The Love Song of J. Alfred Prufrock" (Eliot) 152, 174

Love Songs (Teasdale) 177

Love Struck (Boccaccio) 14

Loves of the Angels (Moore) 103

Lucidities (Jennings) 247

"Lucy" (Wordsworth) 92

"Lucy Gray, or Solitude" (Wordsworth) 88

Ludus Dianae (Celtis) 34

Luise (Voss) 87

Lustra (Pound) 175

Lycidas (Milton) 48, 56

Lycksalighetens (Atterbom) 105

Lydia i lampans sken (Eggehorn) 275

Lyric Poems (Bacchelli) 173

Lyrical Ballads (Wordsworth, Coleridge) 88, 92

Lyrics of Lowly Life (Dunbar) 146

Lyrisches Intermezzo (Heine) 103

Mac Flecknoe (Dryden) 49, 64

Madoc (Southey) 96

The Magnetic Mountain (Day-Lewis) 197

Man (Ivanov) 206

The Man Against the Sky (Robinson) 175

The Man Who Died Twice (Robinson) 185, 186

The Man Who Lurks (Hernández) 206

The Man with the Blue Guitar (Stevens) 203

The Man with the Hoe and Other Poems (Markham) 149

Mānasī (Tagore) 141, 153

Manfred (Byron) 93, 100

The Manifest Splendor (Verhaeren) 164

A Manual of Piety (Brecht) 153

The Map of Love (Thomas) 206

Maria Nefeli (Elytis) 257

"Mariana" (Tennyson) 93, 106

Marilia de Dirceau (Gonzaga) 86

Marmion (Scott) 93

The Marriage of Heaven and Hell (Blake) 68, 86

Mask and Trefoil (Storni) 204

The Mask of Snow (Blok) 165

Maternal Primer (Deus) 131

The Matins of the Night (Herrera y Reissig) 160

"Matthew" (Wordsworth) 92

Maud (Tennyson) 93, 119

Mazeppa (Byron) 101

"Me" (Anwar) 218

The Meadow (Leśmian) 180

Meditaçao sore reinas (Judice) 285

"The Mediterranean" (Tate) 196

"Meghaduta" (Kālidāsa) 15

Memento Mori (Heinrich von Melk) 22

Memorials of a Tour on the Continent (Wordsworth) 103

Memories (Kitahara) 170

Memory of Snow (Csoori) 263

Men and Women (Browning) 119

"Mending Wall" (Frost) 173

Mercian Hymns (Hill) 249

The Merry Festival (Lenngren) 87

Meslanges (Ronsard) 33, 39

Message (Pessoa) 199

Metai (Donelaitis) 101

Metamorphoses (Ovid) 4

"Methought I Saw My Late Espoused Saint" (Milton) 59

Metrical Letters (Petrarch) 14, 25

Mexico City Blues (Kerouac) 231

"Michael" (Wordsworth) 92, 95

Michael Robartes and the Dancer (Yeats) 180

Midnight Salvage (Rich) 293

Midsummer (Walcott) 264

"Miniver Cheevy" (Robinson) 168

The Minstrel (Beattie) 81

Minted Coins (Launko) 269

Mireio: A Provençal Poem (Mistral) 121

A Mirrour for Magistrates (Ferrers, Baldwin) 40

Miscellaneous Poems (Browning) 107

Miscellanies (Cowley) 59

"Miss Kilmansegg and Her Precious Leg, a Golden Legend" (Hood) 112

Missal (Cruz e Sousa) 144

Missing Forever (Kosuke) 289

The Mistress (Cowley) 58

Mizan al-Awzan (Nava'i) 29

Modern Love (Meredith) 123

Moll Pitcher (Whittier) 106

Moly (Gunn) 249

The Moment Before Dawn (Krasinski) 113

Moments of Grace (Jennings) 258

O monhe das cobras (Knopfli) 289

The Monks (Verhaeren) 138

Mont Blanc (Shelley) 93, 100

Montage of a Dream Deferred (Hughes) 220

The Moon of Shiraz (al-Bayati) 264

The Moonstruck Countrysides (Verhaeren) 144

Morgue and Other Poems (Benn) 171

Morning in the Burned House (Atwood) 284

The Morning of the Poem (Schuyler) 260

Morning Songs (Agustini) 169

Morning Star (Bandeira) 202

"Morte d'Arthur" (Tennyson) 93, 112

Mosada (Yeats) 138

Mount Zion (Betjeman) 197

Mountain Interval (Frost) 175

Mountains and Rivers Without End (Snyder) 286

Mountains of Gold (Lagones) 147

The Moving Target (Merwin) 237

"Mr. Flood's Party" (Robinson) 181

Muses (Stiernhielm) 61

Music of the Future (Kaschnitz) 219

My Alexandria (Doty) 279

"My Heart Leaps Up When I Behold" (Wordsworth) 96

"My Last Duchess" (Browning) 112

My Voice Because of You (Salinas) 198

Le mystère des saints innocents (Péguy) 171

Mysteries of Selfessness (Iqbāl) 177

Mysterious Weddings (Jouve) 186

Mystery of the Charity of Charles Péguy (Hill) 263

Mystical Poems and Songs (Verdaguer) 128

Mythistorema (Myth-History) (Seferis) 200

Nach den Satiren (Grunbein) 293

Nameless (Obstfelder) 143

Napló (Radnóti) 274

Nar vagen vander (Espmark) 279

The Narrow Road to the Deep North (Bashō) 49, 66

Nattsol (Mehren) 278

Near Changes (van Duyn) 275

Near the Ocean (Lowell) 243

Nedjma, Poem or Knife (Yacine) 216

The Need to Hold Still (Muller) 260

The Negro of Peter the Great (Pushkin) 90, 105

The Negro Speaks of Rivers (Hughes) 181

Neon Vernacular (Komunyakaa) 281, 282

The Never Ending Lightning (Hernández) 202

The Never Silent Bells (Sevak) 230

New and Collected Poems (MacLeish) 254

New and Collected Poems (Wilbur) 270, 272

New and Collected Poems, 1941–1995 (Curnow) 286

New and Selected Poems (Meredith) 269

New and Selected Poems (Oliver) 277

New and Selected Poems (Warren) 265

New and Selected Poems, 1940–1986 (Shapiro) 269

New Hampshire (Frost) 184, 185

The New Life (Dante) 14, 24

The New Medley (Castro) 133

New Morning (Hadobian) 167

New Poems (Ady) 164

New Poems (Arnold) 126

New Poems (Fröding) 145

New Poems (Heidenstam) 174

New Poems (Heine) 93, 114

New Poems (Kinsella) 251

New Poems (Nijhoff) 198

New Poems (Rilke) 155

New Poems (Yeats) 152

New Songs (Machado) 185

New Weddings (Jouve) 188

Next: Two Poems (Clifton) 269

"Niagara" (Heredia) 104

Night Diary (Dimitrova) 275

Night Light (Justice) 243

The Night Search (Khlebnikov) 181

The Nightingale Sings Out of Tune (Siefert) 187

Nightmare Abbey (Peacock) 101

A Nip in the Air (Betjeman) 252

No Man's Grove (Lim) 259

Noble Numbers; or, His Pious Pieces (Herrick) 58

Nobleness and Extinction (Weinheber) 199

North (Heaney) 254

North Amerikkan Blues (Hyde) 249

North and South (Bishop) 213

North of Boston (Frost) 173

The North Ship (Larkin) 212

The Northern Flowers (Fréchette) 132

Notebook, 1967–1968 (Lowell) 246

Nouvelle Continuation des Amours (Ronsard) 33

Now and Then: Poems, 1976–1978 (Warren) 258

"O Captain! My Captain!" (Whitman) 124

Oberon (Wieland) 83

Obras Completas (Castilho) 110

Observations (Moore) 185

The Occasions (Montale) 206

Ocher (Storni) 187

The October Night (Musset) 110

Ode (Jouve) 219

Ode for Man and Woman (Marechal) 192

Odyssey (Homer) 2

Of Being Numerous (Oppen) 245

Of Divine Love (Waller) 64

Of Sepulchres (Foscolo) 97

"Of the Last Verses Written in His Book" (Waller) 64

The Offender (Montale) 242

Office Poems (Benedetti) 227

Oh Cybernetic Fairy (Belli) 234

Old and New Gods (Drachmann) 134

"The Old Familiar Faces" (Lamb) 88

"Old Ironsides" (Holmes) 106

An Old Man's Notebook (Ungaretti) 233

poem (continued)
Old Road to Paradise (Widdemer) 178
Old Spookses' Pass, Malcolm Katie and Other Poems (Crawford) 136
Olney Hymns (Cowper, Newton) 83
The Olympic Spring (Spitteler) 168
Omrade aldrifastlagt (Mjelve) 282
On Glassy Wings: New and Selected Poems (Lowther) 288
On Roads and Through Space (Jankovic) 283
"On Shakespeare" (Milton) 54
On the Brink (Nervesen) 266
On the Death of Goethe (Baratynsky) 107
"On the Morning of Christ's Nativity" (Milton) 54
On This Island (Auden) 202
On Windy Nights (Haavikko) 222
One and Other Poems (Kinsella) 258
The One Day (Hall) 270
One Hundred Springs (Binkis) 188
One Ship—Laura Blair (Divis) 281
"One Thousand Seven Hundred Thirty Eight. A Dialogue Something Like Horace" (Pope) 76
"Oneone" (Tennyson) 107
Opened Ground: Poems, 1956–1996 (Heaney) 291
Opéra: Oeuvres Poétiques (Cocteau) 189
Operette Morali (Leopardi) 91
Opus Maccaronicum (Folengo) 35
Or Else: Poem (Warren) 253
The Orators (Auden) 196
The Orchard (Sa'dī) 23
Orlando Furioso (Ariosto) 35
Orphic Hymns (Manner) 232
Orphic Songs (Campana) 173
Our Ground Time Here Will Be Brief (Kumin) 261
"Out of the Cradle Endlessly Rocking" (Whitman) 121
Over the Brazier (Bridges) 175
Over the Waves of TSF (Siefert) 186
Overijssel Songs and Poems (Revius) 54
"The Owl and the Pussycat" (Lear) 128
Painful Joy (Pirandello) 154
The Palice of Honour (Douglas) 34
La paloma de vuelo popular: Elegias (Guillén) 231
Pan Cogito (Herbert) 253
The Panorama and Other Poems (Whittier) 119
The Panther and the Lash: Poems of Our Times (Hughes) 243
Paracelsus (Browning) 108
Paradise Regained (Marsman) 189
Parijatapahanannamu (Timanna) 36
The Parish Register (Crabbe) 97
"Parisi'na" (Byron) 100
The Parlement of Foules (Chaucer) 14, 26

Partial Accounts: New and Selected Poems (Meredith) 270
Passage to India (Whitman) 128
Passing Through: Later Poems, New and Selected (Kunitz) 284
Passion Flowers (Howe) 118
The Passion Hymns (Petursson) 61
The Passionate Shepheard (Breton) 50
Passport to the War (Kunitz) 211
Pastorals (Pope) 71
Paterson (Williams) 213
"Paul Revere's Ride" (Longfellow) 123
Pauline (Browning) 107
Paulownia Blossom (Kitahara) 172
The Peacock Feather (Kristensen) 182
Pedestrian (Mukopadhyay) 207
The Pennsylvania Pilgrim and Other Poems (Whittier) 128
"Il Penseroso" (Milton) 48, 55
The People, Yes (Sandburg) 201
The People's Other World (Murray) 264
Persian Eclogues (Collins) 76
Personae (Pound) 155, 167
Le Petit Testament (Villon) 27
Pharsalia (Lucan) 5
Phocas the Gardener (Viélé-Griffin) 148
The Photographer in Winter (Szirtes) 267
Pictures from Breughel (Williams) 235, 236
Pieces (Creely) 246
"The Pied Piper of Hamelin" (Browning) 112
Pig Earth (Berger) 258
Pilgrimage and Wander (Heidenstam) 139
The Pillar of Fire (Gumilyov) 181
Pilot Stars (Ivanov) 161
Pippa Passes (Browning) 112
The Pisan Cantos (Pound) 155, 216
Plain Themes (Neruda) 135
Plains of Castile (Machado) 171
A poeira levada pelo vento (Magalhaes) 283
A Poem of One Hundred Links Composed by Three Poets at Minase (Sogi) 28
Poem of the Cante Jondo (García Lorca) 155
Poemas híbridos (Atxaga) 273
Poèmes de Provence (Aicard) 130
Poèmes saturnines (Verlaine) 126
Poems (Arnold) 118
Poems (Bradstreet) 63
Poems (Brontë, Brontë, and Brontë) 114
Poems (Browning) 113
Poems (Bryant) 102
Poems (Bull) 167
Poems (Chatterton) 83
Poems (Cowper) 84
Poems (Cruz) 65
Poems (Davith) 193
Poems (de la Mare) 164
Poems (Dickinson) 141
Poems (Droste-Hülshoff) 110
Poems (Dugan) 235
Poems (Eliot) 152, 178, 180

Poems (Freneau) 85
Poems (Gómez de Avellaneda) 112
Poems (Graves, ed.) 177
Poems (Heidenstam) 145
Poems (Holmes) 109
Poems (Jennings) 222
Poems (Key) 120
Poems (Kinsella) 227
Poems (Lowell) 113
Poems (Meredith) 117
Poems (Milton) 48
Poems (Moore) 181
Poems (Oehlenschläger) 96
Poems (Poe) 106
Poems (Rossetti) 127
Poems (Rydberg) 135
Poems (Storm) 117
Poems (Tennyson) 93
Poems (Vigny) 103
Poems (Whittier) 116
Poems (Zollinger) 197
Poems, 1901–43 (Jensen) 210
Poems, 1913 (Brennan) 173
Poems, 1924–1933 (MacLeish) 197
Poems, 1940–1953 (Shapiro) 222
Poems, Chiefly in the Scottish Dialect (Burns) 68, 85
Poems, Chiefly Lyrical (Tennyson) 93, 106
Poems, Chiefly of Early and Late Years (Wordsworth) 92, 112
Poems, First Cycle (Wergeland) 106
Poems: North and South 226
Poems: North and South—A Cold Spring (Bishop) 225
Poems and Antipoems (Para) 224
Poems and Ballads (Swinburne) 125, 132
Poems and Songs (Bjørnson) 127
Poems from a Voyage Across the Sound (Haavikko) 251
Poems from Prison (Soyinka) 246
Poems in Prose (Baudelaire) 127
Poems in Two Volumes (Wordsworth) 97
Poems of a Jew (Shapiro) 229
Poems of Consummation (Aleixandre) 245
Poems of Dedication (Spender) 215
Poems of Haikai Tsuji (Masao) 287
Poems of Stanley Kunitz (Kunitz) 258
Poems on Slavery (Longfellow) 112
Poesie (Quasimodo) 204
Poet in New York (García Lorca) 155
Poetic Edda 13
Poetic Meditations (Lamartine) 102
Poetical Blossomes (Cowley) 55
Poetical Sketches by Mr. W.B. (Blake) 68, 84
Poetical Works (Moore) 95
Poetical Works (Senghor) 274
Poetry for Supper (Thomas) 229
Poetry in Prose and Verse (Jiménez) 196
Poetry (Mickiewicz) 103
Politian, A Tragedy (Poe) 108
"Poltava" (Pushkin) 90, 106
The Pond (Morris) 251

Poor Flowers (Desbordes-Valmore) 111
Poppy and Memory (Celan) 221
"The Power of Song" (Schiller) 68
Powers of Congress (Fulton) 273
Praise to the End! (Roethke) 220
The Prelude, or, Growth of a Poet's Mind (Wordsworth) 88, 116
The Prelude (Wordsworth) 92
The Price of Stone and Earlier Poems (Murphy) 266
Primevères (Hasselt) 108
The Prince's Progress (Rossetti) 125
The Princess, a Medley (Tennyson) 115
The Prinzhorn Collection (Coles) 261
"The Prisoner of Chillon" (Byron) 93, 100
A Prisoner of Grace (Cary) 221
The Prisoner of the Caucasus (Pushkin) 90, 102
A Private Mythology (Sarton) 241
Profane Hymns and Other Poems (Darío) 146
The Progress of the Soul: The Second Anniversary (Donne) 51
Prologue to Life (Sikelianós) 176
Prometheus and Epimetheus (Spitteler) 134
Prometheus Unbound (Shelley) 93, 102
The Promised Land (Ungaretti) 219
Promises: Poems, 1954–1956 (Warren) 228, 229
The Proof (Winters) 193
The Prophecy of Dante (Byron) 93
Prose Edda 13
Providence (Popovski) 284
Prufrock and Other Observations (Eliot) 176
The Psalms of Struggle and Liberation (Cardenal) 239
The Public Rose (Éluard) 199
Public Speech: Poems (MacLeish) 201
The Punishments (Hugo) 118
Pure Elegies (Jiménez) 166
The Pyre (Gumilyov) 177
"The Quaker Graveyard in Nantucket" (Lowell) 213
Queen Mab (Shelley) 93, 99
Quia Pauper Amavi (Pound) 155
Quiet Fires (Mihalic) 265
Radiation (Sachiko) 284
Raghuvamsa (Kālidāsa) 14–15
Rain-Charm for the Duchy (Hughes) 278
The Rape of Lucrece (Shakespeare) 31, 44
The Rape of the Bucket (Tassoni) 53
"The Raven" (Poe) 91
The Raven and Other Poems (Poe) 114
Reality and Desire (Cernuda) 239
Recruit (Král') 114
"Red, Red Rose" (Burns) 68
Red Candle (Wen) 183
Red Cotton Night-Cap Country (Browning) 129
A Red Moon in Her Face (Hiroshi) 215

Red Roses for Me (O'Casey) 209
Rediscovery and Other Poems (Awoonor) 238
Rejse for en fremmed (Aidt) 295
Relationships (Jennings) 250
Le Reliquaire (Coppée) 126
Remains of Elmet (Hughes) 258
Remedia amoris (Ovid) 4
Renascence and Other Poems (Millay) 176
Repair (Williams) 295
The Republic of Babin (Lechon) 181
Res amissa (Caproni) 276
Rescue (Milosz) 213
Rescue the Dead (Ignatov) 244
Residence on Earth (Neruda) 155, 198
The Residual Years: Poems 1934–1948 (Everson) 244
"Resolution and Independence" (Wordsworth) 96
Responsibilities: Poems and a Play (Yeats) 152, 173
"Responsibility: The Pilots Who Destroyed Germany, Spring 1945" (Spender) 217
Restless Early Summer (Gömöri) 264
The Retrieval System (Kumin) 257
Return, Pinus Succinifera (Kaplinski) 264
Rhymes (Bécquer) 128
Rhymes to Be Traded for Bread (Lindsay) 171
Rhythms of My Heart (Balance) 207
Richard Cory (Robinson) 147
The Ride of Eldis (Viélé-Griffin) 144
Rider (Rudman) 282
Rienzi the Tribune (Acuña) 131
Rights of Passage (Brathwaite) 243
Rimas (Camões) 32
Rime (Carducci) 120
"The Rime of the Ancient Mariner" (Coleridge) 88
Rings (Neruda) 155
Rise, Magyar (Petőfi) 115
The Rise of the Winds (Ibarbourou) 194
"The River Duddon" (Wordsworth) 92
Rivers Among Rocks (Gustafson) 232
The Rivers Run Toward the Sea (Lundkvist) 199
"The Road Not Taken" (Frost) 174
The Road We Have Walked (Adiga) 221
Roan Stallion, Tamar and Other Poems (Jeffers) 186
The Robber Brothers (Pushkin) 90, 102
Robert und Guiscard (Eichendorff) 119
The Rock of Rushan (Zarian) 193
Roderick, the Last of the Goths (Southey) 99
Rokeby (Scott) 93, 99
Roman Elegies (Goethe) 67, 87
Romanzero (Heine) 93, 117
The Room and Other Poems (Day-Lewis) 240

Rosary (Akhmatova) 173
The Rose Altar (Södergran) 179
The Rose Garden (Sa'dī) 24
Rough and Ride (Melo Neto) 266
The Rough Field (Montague) 250
The Royal Domain (Viélé-Griffin) 184
Rubaiyat of Omar Khayyam (FitzGerald) 121
Rummet innanför (Arvidsson) 294
Rural Sports (Gay) 72
Ruslan and Ludmila (Pushkin) 90, 102
Russian Woman (Nekrasov) 128
Ruy Blas (Hugo) 110
Sabbaths (Berry) 269
Le Sacrifice imperial (Jacob) 192
"Sailing to Byzantium" (Yeats) 152, 189
Saint Matoral (Jacob) 167
The Saint's Tragedy (Kingsley) 115
Salmagundi, or The Whim-Whams and Opinions of Launcelot Langstaff, Esq., and Others (Irving) 97
Salome and Other Poems (Castro) 146
Sammanhang (Trotzig) 287
The Sand for the Urns (Celan) 216
"Santa Filomena" (Longfellow) 120
Satires (Horace) 4
Satires (Juvenal) 4
Satura (Montale) 236
Savage Moon (Paz) 198
The Scarlet Poem (Lechon) 180
A Scattering of Salts (Merrill) 284
The Scenic Route (Adcock) 252
Scent of Eucalyptus (Quasimodo) 198
Das Schlaraffenland (Sachs) 37
"The Scholar-Gipsy" (Arnold) 118
Scots Unbound and Other Poems (MacDiarmid) 196
Scrambled Eggs and Whiskey: Poems, 1991–1995 (Carruth) 286
Sea Grapes (Walcott) 255
Sea Marks (Perse) 220
The Seamless Tunic (Lima) 204
The Seaside and the Fireside (Longfellow) 116
A Season in Hell (Rimbaud) 94, 129
The Seasons (Thomson) 73, 74
Seasons of the Soul (Tate) 210
Second April (Millay) 181
"The Second Coming" (Yeats) 152, 180
Secondary Heaven (Popa) 245
Secret Star (Amrouche) 203
Secrets of the Self (Iqbāl) 174
Secrets on the Way (Transtromer) 230
Secular Hymns (Horace) 4
Seeing Through the Sun (Hogan) 265
Selected Poems (Aiken) 193
Selected Poems (Eberhart) 241
Selected Poems (Fletcher) 205
Selected Poems (Illyés) 249
Selected Poems (Jarrell) 273

Selected Poems (Justice) 259
Selected Poems (Kinnell) 261, 262
Selected Poems (Livesay) 228
Selected Poems (Mahon) 274
Selected Poems (Rexroth) 264
Selected Poems (Tate) 277
Selected Poems, 1928–1958 (Kunitz) 230
Selected Poems, 1933–1980 (Faludy) 266
Selected Poems, 1970–1983 (Henson) 265
Selected Poetry (Amichai) 268
Self-Portrait in a Convex Mirror (Ashbery) 253, 254
The Sense of Movement (Gunn) 228
"The Sensitive Plan" (Shelley) 102
Sentimental Lunar Almanac (Lugones) 168
"September 1, 1939" (Auden) 207
The September Lyre (Södergran) 178
The Seraphim and Other Poems (Browning) 110
Sestinas and Other Poems (Belli) 248
Seuls Demeurent (Char) 212
The Seven Deadly Sins (Boge) 209
The Seven-League Crutches (Jarrell) 220
Seventy Tombstones (Ryya'i) 291
Shabbytown Calendar (Shapcott) 255
The Shadow of the Future (Södergran) 180
Shadow of the Night (Chapman) 44
Shadows in the Grass (Gustafson) 276
Shaker, Why Don't You Sing? (Angelou) 262
Shapes (Gorakhpuri) 215
The Shark (Solomos) 116
"She Was a Phantom of Delight" (Wordsworth) 96
The Shepherd's Week (Gay) 72
The Shield of Achilles (Auden) 225
Shields (Cruz e Sousa) 144
Shining Solitude (Ahti) 264
A Shropshire Lad (Housman) 146
"The Siege of Corinth" (Byron) 100
The Siege of Thebes (Lydgate) 34
Silberne Saiten (Zweig) 159
El silencio de la luna (Pacheco) 283
Silesian Songs (Bezruč) 226
Silver and Black (Lechon) 185
Silvas americanas (Bello) 104
Simo the Bloodhound (Leino) 162
The Simple Truth (Levine) 282, 283
Simulacrum (Leiris) 186
The Singing Flesh (Layton) 234
The Sinking of the Titanic (Enzensberger) 258
Sir Eustace Grey (Crabbe) 97
Siste dikt (Orvil) 280
Sita's Story (Kumaran Asan) 179
Skunk Hour (Lowell) 231
The Sky (Maksimovic) 289

"The Skylark" (Shelley) 102
Sleepers Joining Hands (Bly) 250
A Slow Fuse (Weiss) 264
"A Small House in Kolomna" (Pushkin) 90, 108
Smooth Seas (Benediktsson) 164
Snapshots of a Daughter in Law: Poems, 1954–1962 (Rich) 237
The Snow Birds (Fréchette) 132
Snow Legend (Aspenstrom) 218
Snow-Bound (Whittier) 125
"The Soldier" (Brooke) 174
"The Solitary Reaper" (Wordsworth) 96
Solitude (Prudhomme) 127
Solitudes (Machado) 161
Solo on a Burning Trumpet (Shvarts) 217
Solstices (MacNeice) 234
Some Unease and Angels (Feinstein) 256
"Song" (Donne) 48, 55
Song for a Birth or a Death (Jennings) 234
Song for St. Cecilia's Day (Dryden) 64
The Song of Eternity (Iqbāl) 174
The Song of Hiawatha (Longfellow) 119
Song of Hildebrand 13
"A Song of Italy" (Swinburne) 126
"The Song of Los" (Blake) 68, 87
"Song of Myself" (Whitman) 119
Song of Semblance and Substance (Eeden) 145
"Song of the Open Road" (Whitman) 119
The Song of the Rhone (Mistral) 147
"The Song of the Shirt" (Hood) 113
The Song of Those Who Drink the Sun (Hikmet Ran) 191
Song Without a Name (Král') 114
Songs (Béranger) 99
Songs (García Lorca) 155
Songs (Leopardi) 100
Songs (Uhland) 99
Songs Before Sunrise (Swinburne) 128
Songs for the People (Claudius) 83
Songs from the Wings of Sorrow (Rynell) 291
Songs of Experience (Blake) 68, 86
Songs of Innocence (Blake) 68, 85
Songs of Labor (Whittier) 116
Songs of the Cold (Sitwell) 212
Songs of the Fatherland (Ihland) 100
Songs of Wilderness and Love (Karlfeldt) 145
Songs Without Words (Verlaine) 130
Sordello (Browning) 111
Sorgegondolen (Transtromer) 287
Sorgen per capita (Brunner) 275
The Soul (Machado) 160
The Sovereign Sun (Elytis) 249
The Spaniard (Wergeland) 107
Specimen Days (Whitman) 135
The Spider and the Flie (Heywood) 39
The Spirit Level (Heaney) 286
The Spirit of Man (Graves) 175
Spiritual Couplets (Rūmī) 15

poem *(continued)*

Splashes of Grail (Fröding) 148

Spoon River Anthology (Masters) 174

The Spring (Kleist) 78

"Spring" (Thomson) 74

Spring and All (Williams) 184

Spring and Fall (Hopkins) 133

Spring Moon (Boutens) 175

Springtime of Death (Bousoño) 214

Les Stances (Moreas) 149

Stanzas (Pushkin) 90, 104

Stanzas Begun for the Tournament of the Magnificent Giuliano de Medici (Politian) 28

Stanzas for the Death of His Father (Manrique) 29

Starlit Early Morning (Zollinger) 202

"The Star-Spangled Banner" (Key) 99

Static Poems (Benn) 216

Station Island (Heaney) 264, 266

Steeple Bush (Frost) 215

"The Stepchildren" (Elytis) 252

Steps to the Temple (Crashaw) 57

Still Centre (Spender) 205

Stone and Sky (Jiménez) 179

Stony Limits (MacDiarmid) 199

"Stopping by Woods on a Snowy Evening" (Frost) 184

Stories and Poems (Benediktsson) 147

The Storm and Other Poems (Montale) 227

The Story of Rimini (Hunt) 100

Strange Holiness (Coffin) 201

Stranger Music: Selected Poems and Songs (Cohen) 280

Stranger to Europe (Butler) 221

Straw into Gold (Stead) 288

The Strayed Reveller (Arnold) 116

A Street in Bronzeville (Brooks) 212

Street Songs (Sitwell) 209

Stubborn Hope: New Poems and Selections from China Poems and Strains (Brutus) 257

The Student of Salamanca (Espronceda y Delgado) 111

Suitable Words (Arghezi) 189

Sumerian Vistas (Ammons) 269

Summa de Magroll el Gaviero (Mutis) 275

"Summer" (Thomson) 74

Sun Stone (Paz) 228

Sun Under Wood (Hass) 286

Sunderland Capture (Bacon) 208

Sunken Oboe (Quasimodo) 196

The Sunlit Hours (Verhaeren) 146

Sunrise (Hazard) 259

Surgical Precision (Baranczak) 291

The Swans (Viélé-Griffin) 138

The Swan's Camp (Tsvetayeva) 228

Sweat of Blood (Jouve) 200

Sweet Injury (Storni) 178

The Sweet Secret (Ivanov) 171

The Swimmers and Other Selected Poems (Tate) 248

Switch off the Light (Seifert) 204

Sword Blades and Poppy Seed (Lowell) 173

Symbolism (Eguren) 170

Tada uti Mawgun (Rahtathara) 29

The Tale of Paraguay (Southey) 104

Tale of the Fiesole Nymph (Boccaccio) 14

Tales of a Wayside Inn (Longfellow) 123

Tam O'Shanter (Burns) 86

Tamar and Other Poems (Jeffers) 185

Tamerlane and Other Poems (Poe) 91, 105

Tangled Hair (Yosano) 159

Tanim shel Mora (Gil) 276

The Task (Cowper) 84

The Tears (Valmore) 107

"The Tears of Scotland" (Smollett) 77

The Temple (Herbert) 55

Ten Burn Offerings (MacNeice) 221

Tenderness (Mistral) 185

The Tent on the Beach and Other Poems (Whittier) 126

The Terrible Threshold (Kunitz) 252

Terror and Decorum (Viereck) 217

The Testament of Beauty (Bridges) 192

The Testing Tree (Kunitz) 249

Thalaba the Destroyer (Southey) 95

"Thanatopsis" (Bryant) 100

Theory of Flight (Rukeyser) 200

They Shall Not Pass (Paz) 203

They Think So (Petri) 266

They Want Bone (Pinsky) 273

Thickets (Abu Madi) 206

Things of This World (Wilbur) 226, 228

Third Vigil (Bryusov) 158

This Earth, My Brother (Awoonor) 249

This Is Not a Letter and Other Poems (Boyle) 265

This Time: New and Selected Poems (Stern) 290

Thomas and Beulah (Dove) 267, 268

Those Were the Mermaid Days (Young) 276

Threnodia Augustalis (Dryden) 64

Threny (Kochanowski) 42

Through the Woods Below (Belli) 242

Thrush (Seferis) 215

Thurso's Landing and Other Poems (Jeffers) 196

Thus Changed the Seasons (Manner) 239

"Thyrsis" (Arnold) 125

Tiepolo's Hound (Walcott) 296

Tigers (Adcock) 243

Tilottamsambhab (Datta) 121

Timbuctoo (Tennyson) 105

Time and Eternity (Mendes) 200

Time and Money (Matthews) 284

Time's Power (Rich) 272

Times Three: Selected Verse from Three Decades (McGinley) 233

Tiriel (Blake) 130

To a Dying World (Kasprowicz) 159

"To a Skylark" (Shelley) 93

"To a Water Fowl" (Bryant) 101

"To Althea, from Prison" (Lovelace) 58

To an Athlete Dying Young (Housman) 146

To Give and to Have and Other Poems (Quasimodo) 242

"To His Coy Mistress" (Marvell) 63

To His Sacred Majesty (Dryden) 49

"To Lucasta, Going to the Wars" (Lovelace) 58

"To My Friends" (Pushkin) 90, 105

To Stay Alive (Levertov) 249

"To the Nightingale" (Finch) 72

To the Sound of the Marimbas (Bessa Victor) 210

Tomorrows (Régnier) 137

Tongues of Diamond (Ibarbourou) 179

Too Late for This World (Nijlen) 228

Touch (Gunn) 243

The Tower (Yeats) 152, 190

The Town Down the River (Robinson) 168

Trade Winds (Martinson) 213

Tradet (Sonnevi) 277

Tragedy of My Country (Palamas) 138

A Tragic State (Kumaran Asan) 184

Tragiques (Aubigné) 52

Transformations (Sexton) 249

Transit (Dimitrova) 275

Translucency (Ivanov) 162

Transparent Gestures (Jones) 272

Travel Dice (Shapcott) 269

Travel Memoirs from the Summer of 1860 (Vinje) 122

The Traveller; or, A Prospect of Society (Goldsmith) 80

The Tree of Laughing Bells (Lindsay) 163

Trees (Kilmer) 172

Trial by Terror: Sri Lankan Poems (Arasanayagam) 269

Trial of a Poet and Other Poems (Shapiro) 215

Trials (Prudhomme) 125

Tristam of Lyonesse (Swinburne) 135

Tristia (Ovid) 4

Tristram (Robinson) 189, 190

The Triumph of Achilles (Gluck) 265

The Triumph of Life (Shelley) 93

Troilus and Creseyde (Chaucer) 14

The Troy Book (Lydgate) 35

Tsar-Maiden (Tsvetayeva) 183

The Tumultuous Force (Verhaeren) 160

The Tunnynge of Elynour Rummyng (Skelton) 35

The Turning Point (Seferis) 195

Turtle Island (Snyder) 252, 253

Tusindfodt (Tadrup) 292

The Twelve Lays of the Gypsy (Palamas) 165

Twentieth Century (Emin) 247

Twenty Love Poems and a Song of Despair (Neruda) 155, 185

Twilight in the Garden (Lugones) 163

"The Two Voices" (Tennyson) 93

Two Waters (Melo Neto) 226

The Twopenny Post Bag (Moore) 99

Tydverdryf/Pastime (Eybers) 288

Uber Berge Kam Ich (Walsdorf) 269

"Ulalume" (Poe) 91, 115

"Ulysses" (Tennyson) 93, 112

Uncle Remus: His Songs and Sayings (Harris) 134

Uncollected Poems (Betjeman) 261

Under Mausolaeet (Nordbrandt) 268

Under the Windows and Other Poems (Lowell) 127

Untitled Subjects (Howard) 246, 247

Unworldly (Shuntaro) 280

Up Country (Kumin) 250

"Upon the Death of Lord Hastings" (Dryden) 58

Uraniia (Brodski) 270

Urdargaldur (Porsteinn) 269

Urn (Bely) 168

U.S. 1 (Rukeyser) 204

Uvatzfifut (Bar-Yosef) 274

"A Valediction Forbidding Mourning" (Donne) 49, 55

The Valley of a Thousand Hills (Dhlomo) 208

Varias Rimas ao Bom Jesus (Bernardez) 44

Venus and Adonis (Shakespeare) 31

Venus and the Rain (McGuckian) 264

The Veritable Years (Everson) 257

Versek (Petófi) 112

Verses (Dowson) 146

Verses About the Lady Beautiful (Blok) 162

Verses and Poems (Brodsky) 240

Verses of the Salon (Parra) 236

Verses to Blok (Tsvetayeva) 183

Versi (Leopardi) 104

The Very Same Day (Gutmane) 271

Verzen (Gorter) 141

Vice (Ai) 293

Victoria Deorum (Klonowic) 43

Victorian Voices (Thwaite) 259

The Victories of Love (Patmore) 123

The Village (Crabbe) 84

Village Court (Rodrigues Lobo) 52

Violet Poems (Herrera y Reissig) 164

The Virgin of Paris (Jouve) 211

"The Vision of Sin" (Tennyson) 93

The Vision of Sir Launfal (Lowell) 115

Visions of the Daughters of Albion (Blake) 68

A Visit from St. Nicholas (Moore) 103

Visitations (MacNeice) 228

V-Letter and Other Poems (Shapiro) 211, 212

Voices (Boutens) 165

Voices of My Song (Jiménez) 213

Voices of Spring (Maironis) 188
Voices of the Night (Longfellow) 110
"Voyelles" (Rimbaud) 94
The Waggoner (Wordsworth) 101
Waiting for Saskatchewan (Wah) 266
Wake Me Yesterday (Donkov) 295
The Wakeful State (Desnos) 210
The Waking: Poems, 1933–1953 (Roethke) 222, 223
"The Walk" (Schiller) 68
Wanderings of Oisin and Other Poems (Yeats) 140, 152
War Poems (Sassoon) 178
The Waste Land (Eliot) 152, 182
The Waterfall (Derzhavin) 86
Waters and Land (Quasimodo) 193
Waves (Benediktsson) 172
Waxing Moon and Waning Moon (Johannes) 248
The Way of It (Thomas) 256
A Way of Looking (Jennings) 225
Way of the Cross (Diego) 195
We Are Still Married (Keillor) 272
The Weary Blues (Hughes) 188
Wessex Poems (Hardy) 148
West Eastern Divan (Goethe) 101
West of Your City (Stafford) 232
West Wind (Oliver) 288
The Western Approaches: Poems, 1973–1975 (Nemerov) 255
Western Star (Benét) 211
West-Running Brook (Frost) 190
What a Kingdom It Was (Kinnell) 232
What Work Is (Levine) 276
What's O'Clock (Lowell) 187
Wheat in Motion (Verhaeren) 171
When One Has Lived a Long Time Alone (Kinnell) 273
The Whispering Roots (Day-Lewis) 247
White (Paz) 243
The White Book (Agustini) 165
White Buildings (Crane) 188
The White Woman (Baudelaire) 92
The White-Footed Deer and Other Poems (Bryant) 113
Whither Gone? And Where's the Window? (Sosnora) 296
Whitsongs (Leino) 161
Who Can Be Happy and Free in Russia? (Nekrasov) 125
Whole Life Star (Bandeira) 240
The Whole Motion (Dickey) 277
Why Did You Leave the Horse Alone? (Darwish) 281
A Wife (Overbury) 52
Wild Earth (Colum) 165
Wild Flowers (Deus) 126
Wild Gratitude (Hirsch) 267
The Wild Iris (Gluck) 279
Wild Root (Ibarourou) 183
The Wild Rose Bush (Kasprowicz) 148
"The Wild Swans at Coole" (Yeats) 176
The Wild Swans at Coole (Yeats) 152
The Will to Change: Poems, 1968–1970 (Rich) 249

"Wille Brew'd a Peck o'Maut" (Burns) 68
Willow Pipes (Claussen) 149
The Winding Stair (Yeats) 152
Winds (Perse) 214
Windsor Forest (Pope) 72
Wine (Gay) 71
Wine from These Grapes (Millay) 199
The Wine Press (Mistral) 224
The Winged Legend of Wieland the Blacksmith (Viélé-Griffin) 158
The Winged Sandal (Régnier) 164
Wings of Knives and Nails (Csoori) 260
"Winter" (Thomson) 73
Winter Night (Leino) 163
Winter Trees (Plath) 250
"Wintering Out" (Heaney) 250
With Eyes at the Back of Our Heads (Levertov) 231
Withered Leaves (Franko) 138
Without Remedy (Storni) 179
Without Truce (Torres Bodet) 228
A Witness Tree (Frost) 209, 210
Die Wittenbergische Nachtigall (Sachs) 36
Wolf's Salt (Popa) 254
The Woman at the Washington Zoo: Poems and Translations (Jarrell) 232, 241
The Women at Point Sur (Jeffers) 189
Women in Love (Daudet) 120
Wonderful Night in Paris (Grupac) 292
Word after Word (Rzewic) 283
Word over All (Day-Lewis) 210
Words for Music, Perhaps, and Other Poems (Yeats) 196
Words for the Wind (Roethke) 228
Works (Pope) 76
The World Doesn't End (Simic) 273
"The World Is Too Much with Us" (Wordsworth) 97
The World of the Ten Thousand Things: Poems 1980–1990 (Wright) 273
Worship Company of Fletchers (Tate) 282
Worthy It Is (Elytis) 231
Woyzek (Büchner) 110, 132
"The Wreck of the Deutschland" (Hopkins) 130, 177
"The Wreck of the Hesperus" (Longfellow) 111
Xenia (Montale) 242
Yarrow Revisited and Other Poems (Wordsworth) 92
"Ye Banks and Braes o'Bonnie Doon" (Burns) 68
The Year of the Soul (George) 147
A Year's Life, and Other Poems (Lowell) 111
Yellow Sparks (Bacovia) 188
Yesteryear and Yesterday (Verlaine) 136
Yin: New Poems (Kizer) 264, 265
"You Are Men" (Jouve) 174
The Young Fate (Valery) 176
Your Silence, My Voice (Kaschnitz) 236
Yusuf u Zulaikha (Jāmī) 28

Zapolya (Coleridge) 100
Zero Hour and Other Documentary Poems (Cardenal) 232
Zero Hour (Nijhoff) 209
The Zodiac (Dickey) 255
Zone Journals (Wright) 271
Zukunftsmusik (Enzensberger) 276
Zulu Poems (Kunene) 248
The Zurich Idyll (Faesi) 166
poetic drama
　The Tidings Brought to Mary (Claudel) 171
prophecy
　Centuries (Nostradamus) 39
prose *See also* nonfiction
　Aklake Mohseni (Kashefi) 29
　The Allegory of Love (Lewis) 201
　Ameto's Story of the Nymphs (Boccaccio) 14
　The Anatomy of Melancholy (Burton) 53
　André del Sarto (Musset) 107
　Annotations in Pandectas (Budé) 34
　Appreciations (Pater) 140
　Arcadia (Sannazaro) 34
　The Arcadia (Sidney) 43
　Areopagitica (Milton) 48, 57
　Art (Bell) 173
　Aspects of the Novel (Forster) 189
　The Battle of the Books (Swift) 70
　Between Three Borders (Klima) 232
　The Bloody Tenet of Persecution for the Cause of Conscience (Williams) 57
　The Book of Imaginary Beings (Borges) 243
　Book of the City of Ladies (Christine de Pisan) 26
　Books on Matters to Be Remembered (Petrarch) 14, 25
　Borderliners (Hoeg) 282
　Candide (Voltaire) 68, 79
　La Celestina (Rojas) 30
　The Compleat Angler, or the Contemplative Man's Recreation (Walton) 59
　Confession (Tolstoy) 90
　Considerations of the Causes of the Grandeur and Decadence of the Romans (Montesquieu) 75
　Il Cortegiano (Castiglione) 36
　The Crucial Scene (Jouve) 200
　De Sacramento Matrimonii (Sánchez) 44
　The Death of Abel (Gessner) 79
　Democratic Vistas (Whitman) 128
　The Deserted World (Jouve) 189
　Devotions upon Emergent Occasions (Donne) 49, 53
　La Diana (Montemayor) 39
　The Dogs Bar: Public People and Private Place (Capote) 251
　Don Quixote (Cervantes) 32, 50
　Drapier's Letters (Swift) 68, 73
　Elegy on Madonna Fiammetta (Boccaccio) 14
　Endimion, The Man in the Moone (Lyly) 43
　Euphues: The Anatomy of Wit (Lyly) 41
　Exemplary Tales (Cervantes) 32, 52

　La Galatea (Cervantes) 42
　Gargantua (Rabelais) 32, 37
　Gerardo, the Unfortunate Spaniard (Céspedes y Meneses) 53
　Gulliver's Travels (Swift) 68, 73
　The Hessian Messenger (Büchner) 108
　The Human Province (Canetti) 251
　Ideas (Multatuli) 123
　Institutio Principis Christiani (Erasmus) 35
　Iron John: A Book About Men (Bly) 273
　Klosterheim (De Quincey) 107
　The Labors of Pesiles and Sigismunds: A Northern Story (Cervantes) 32
　Laments for the Living (Parker) 193
　The Law of War and Peace (Grotius) 53
　The Legend of Thyl Ulenspiegel (Coster) 126
　Legends of Guatemala (Asturias) 193
　Lessness (Beckett) 247
　Let Us Now Praise Famous Men (Agee) 208
　Letters of Espriella (Southey) 97
　Light of Eyes (Rossi) 41
　Loci Communes (Melanchthon) 36
　Lorenzaccio (Musset) 108
　The Love Afflicted (Boccaccio) 14
　Miami and the Siege of Chicago (Mailer) 244
　Midas (Lyly) 43
　A Modest Proposal (Swift) 68, 74
　Moroccan Letters (Cadalso y Vázquez) 86
　Le Morte d'Arthur (Malory) 28
　Music for Chameleons: New Writings (Capote) 259
　The New Life (Dante) 24
　News of a Kidnapping (García Márquez) 287
　Of a Fire on the Moon (Mailer) 247
　Of the Principles of Human Knowledge (Berkeley) 71
　On the Origin of the Species by Means of Natural Selection (Darwin) 121
　Pantagruel (Rabelais) 32, 37
　Parayana Wuthtu (Shin) 35
　Paulina (Jouve) 186
　Pensées (Pascal) 48, 61
　Pericles and Aspasia (Landor) 109
　Philosophical Thoughts (Diderot) 77
　A Poet's Notebook (Sitwell) 210
　A Priest to the Temple (Herbert) 58
　Provincial Letters (Pascal) 48, 59
　Rasselas, Prince of Abyssinia (Johnson) 79
　The Raw and the Cooked (Lévi-Strauss) 239
　Remains of Elmet (Hughes) 258
　Rosalynde (Lodge) 43
　The Shaving of Shagpat; an Arabian Entertainment (Meredith) 119
　Silent Spring (Carson) 237
　Sleepers Joining Hands (Bly) 250

prose (continued)
    Songlines (Chatwin) 269
    The Supposes (Gasciogne) 40
    Tablets (Callimachus) 4
    Tajik Vengeance (Niyazi) 215
    A Tale of a Tub (Swift) 68, 70
    Tale of the Horse (Dalin) 76
    Ten Days That Shook the World
      (Reed) 178
    The Test (Marivaux) 76
    Theodicee (Leibniz) 71
    Timber, of Discoveries Made Upon
      Men and Matter (Jonson) 56
    To the Finland Station (Wilson)
      207
    Today and Tomorrow (Musa) 189
    The Triumph over Life
      (Lagerkvist) 189
    Two Cultures and the Scientific
      Revolution (Snow) 231
    The Very Same Day (Gutmane)
      271
    The White Goddess (Graves) 216
    A World on the Wane (Lévi-
      Strauss) 225
    Young Men and Fire (Maclean)
      277
prose poem
    Amadís de Gaula (Montalvo) 34
    Axel (Villiers de L'Isle-Adam)
      137, 141
    Eureka (Poe) 115
    Gaspard of the Night (Bertrand)
      112
    Hymns to the Night (Novalis) 95
    The Northern Symphony (Bely)
      160
    Petersburg (Bely) 173
psychology
    The Theory of Psychoanalysis
      (Jung) 171
    Totem and Taboo (Freud) 172

R

religious text/writing See also sermon
    Address to the Nobility of the Ger-
      man Nation (Luther) 36
    Audi Filia (Juan de Avila) 39
    Bible 1, 37, 51
    The Book of Martyrs (Foxe) 40
    The Christian Socrates (Balzac)
      58
    City of God (Augustine) 13, 18
    Collected Works (Calvin) 52
    Concordance to the Holy Scriptures
      (Cruden) 75
    De los nombres de Cristo (León)
      42
    De Sacramento Matrimonii
      (Sánchez) 44
    Devotions upon Emergent Occa-
      sions (Donne) 49, 53
    Dialogues de Dom Frei Amador
      Arraiz (Arrais) 43
    Eleutheria (Mather) 66
    Enchiridion Militis Christianae
      (Erasmus) 34
    A Faithful Narrative of the Supris-
      ing Work of God (Edwards) 75
    Freedom of the Will (Edwards) 78
    The Grammar of Assent (New-
      man) 127
    Mere Christianity (Lewis) 210
    Milk for Babies, Drawn Out of the
      Breasts of Both Testaments (Cot-
      ton) 57

    New Testament (translation) 42
    The Pilgrim's Progress (Lewis) 197
    The Quest for Historical Jesus
      (Schweitzer) 164
    Rig-Veda 1
    The Saints Everlasting Rest (Bax-
      ter) 58
    Sermons (Swift) 77
    Sic et Non (Abélard) 22
    Sinners in the Hands of an Angry
      God (Edwards) 76
    Spiritual Exercises (Loyola, Ig-
      natius) 38
    A Treatise Concerning Religious
      Affections (Edwards) 77
    Tres Thomae (Stapleton) 43
    Tripitaka 1
    The Whole Booke of Psalmes
      (Sternhold, Hopkins) 38
    The Wonders of the Invisible World
      (Mather) 65
    Yijing (Wenwang) 1
roman à clef
    Pasado presente (García Ponce)
      283
roman-fleuve
    A Mountain of Fire (Yuko) 291

S

saga
    The Christian Georgics (Jammes)
      170
satire
    Absalom and Achitophel (Dryden)
      49
    The Adventures of Hajji Baba of Is-
      phahan (Morier) 103
    The Adventures of Telemachus
      (Fénelon) 66
    The Battle of the Books (Swift) 70
    Bertrand and Raton; or, The Art of
      Conspiracy (Scribe) 107
    Candide (Voltaire) 68, 79
    The Character, or Manners of the
      Age with the Characters of
      Theophrastus (La Bruyère) 65
    The Descendants (Immermann)
      109
    The Devil's Dictionary (Bierce)
      164
    Diviani Mataibat (Mushfiqi) 39
    Eloisa to Abelard (Pope) 72
    Exquisitely Foolish (Huygens) 53
    The Fable of the Bees; or Private
      Vices, Public Benefits (Mandev-
      ille) 72
    Der Flohatz (Fischart) 41
    Gargantua (Rabelais) 32, 37
    Grobianus (Dedekind) 38
    The Grumbling Hive; or, Knaves
      Turned Honest (Mandeville) 70
    Gulliver's Travels (Swift) 68, 73
    Henno (Reuchlin) 29
    The Historical Register for the Year
      1736 (Fielding) 75
    The History of a Town (Saltykov-
      Shchedrin) 127
    History of the Famous Preacher
      Fray Gerundio of Campazas,
      alias Zotes (Isla) 79
    "Holy Willie's Prayer" (Burns) 88
    Horribilicribrifax (Gryphius) 60
    The Itching Parrot (Fernández de
      Lizardi) 100
    The Life of Jonathan Wild the
      Great (Fielding) 76

    Mac Flecknoe (Dryden) 49, 64
    Memoirs of Martinus Scriblerus
      (Pope, Arbuthnot) 76
    Le Mercure galant (Boursault) 64
    The Misfortunes of Elphin (Pea-
      cock) 105
    A Modest Proposal (Swift) 68, 74
    Das Narrenschiff (Brant) 29
    The New Dunciad (Pope) 69, 74,
      76, 84
    Oblomov (Goncharov) 121
    Pantagruel (Rabelais) 32, 37
    Pasquin (Fielding) 75
    The Praise of Folly (Erasmus) 32,
      35
    Regrets (Bellay) 39
    The Ship of Fools (Barclay) 34
    Spaccio della Bestia Trionfante
      (Bruno) 42
    The Story of the Abderites
      (Wieland) 82
    A Tale of a Tub (Swift) 68, 70
    The Temptation (Kreve) 219
    The Universal Passion; or, The
      Love of Fame (Young) 73
    Visions (Quevedo y Villegas) 54
    What D'Ye Call It (Gay) 72
science fiction
    2010 Odyssey Two (Clarke) 261
    Always Coming Home (Le Guin)
      265
    Around the World in Eighty Days
      (Verne) 129
    Childhood's End (Clarke) 222
    A Citizen of the Galaxy (Heinlein)
      228
    Concrete Island (Ballard) 252
    Crash (Ballard) 251
    Dandelion Wine (Bradbury) 228
    Death Is a Lonely Business (Brad-
      bury) 265
    The Dispossessed (Le Guin) 252
    The Door into Summer (Heinlein)
      228
    Double Star (Heinlein) 226
    Dune (Herbert) 240
    Earthlight (Clarke) 225
    Fahrenheit 451 (Bradbury) 222
    A Fall of Moondust (Clarke) 234
    Fantastic Voyage (Asimov) 241
    Foundation (Asimov) 220
    Friday (Heinlein) 261
    From the Earth to the Moon
      (Verne) 124
    The Green Hills of Earth (Hein-
      lein) 220
    High Rise (Ballard) 253
    Hothouse (Aldiss) 235
    I Will Fear No Evil (Heinlein) 247
    The Illustrated Man (Bradbury)
      220
    The Invisible Man (Wells) 147
    The Island of Dr. Moreau (Wells)
      146
    A Journey to the Center of the
      Earth (Verne) 124
    Last and First Men (Stapledon)
      193
    The Left Hand of Darkness (Le
      Guin) 245
    The Martian Chronicles (Brad-
      bury) 219
    Methuselah's Children (Heinlein)
      229
    The Moon Is a Harsh Mistress
      (Heinlein) 241

    The Mysterious Island (Verne)
      130
    Nemesis (Asimov) 272
    The Number of the Beast (Hein-
      lein) 259
    Out of the Silent Planet (Lewis)
      204
    Prelandra (Lewis) 210
    Rendevous with Rama (Clarke)
      251
    Second Foundation (Asimov) 222
    Slaughterhouse Five; or, The Chil-
      dren's Crusade (Vonnegut) 246
    Something Wicked This Way
      Comes (Bradbury) 235
    Starship Troopers (Heinlein) 231
    Stranger in a Strange Land (Hein-
      lein) 234
    That Hideous Strength (Lewis)
      212
    Twenty Thousand Leagues Under
      the Sea (Verne) 127
    Vermilion Sands (Ballard) 249
    The War of the Worlds (Wells)
      148
    A Wizard of Earthsea (Le Guin)
      244
    The Word for World's Forest (Le
      Guin) 250
scientific thesis
    Creative Evolution (Bergson) 165
    Foundation and Empire (Asimov)
      221
screenplay
    An Englishman Abroad (Bennett)
      261
sermon See also religious text/writing
    A Faithful Narrative of the Supris-
      ing Work of God (Edwards) 75
    Sermons (Swift) 77
    Sinners in the Hands of an Angry
      God (Edwards) 76
short story See also detective story;
    tale/story
    Across the Bridge: Stories (Gallant)
      279, 280
    Adultery and Other Choices
      (Dubus) 255
    The Adventures of Sherlock Holmes
      (Doyle) 142
    African Stories (Lessing) 238
    After You've Gone (Adams) 272
    The Afterlife and Other Stories
      (Updike) 282
    Ajol and Laor (Czycz) 287
    The Aleph and Other Stories
      (Borges) 154
    Alexander in the Streetcar
      (Reznicek) 281
    The Alhambra (Irving) 107
    All the Faces of Death (An-
      dreevski) 284
    "Anaconda" (Quiroga) 181
    L'angelo nero (Tabucchi) 276
    Arabesques (Gogol) 91, 109
    "Ariadne" (Chekhov) 92
    An Armful of Blossoms (Karim)
      228
    "Armored Train 14-69" (Ivanov)
      183
    At the Bottom of the River (Kin-
      caid) 264
    "Babette's Feast (Dinesen) 218
    "Ball of Fat" (Maupassant) 133
    The Ballad of the Sad Café (Mc-
      Cullers) 220

"Bartleby the Scrivener" (Melville) 118

Bayou Folk (Chopin) 144

The Beach of Falesa (Stevenson) 143

"The Beast of the Jungle" (James) 161

Beasts and Super Beasts (Saki) 173

"The Black Cat" (Poe) 91

"The Black Monk" (Chekhov) 92, 145

The Black Prince, and Other Stories (Grau) 225

Bliss, and Other Stories (Mansfield) 180

Bloodshed and Three Novellas (Ozick) 254

The Book of Sand (Borges) 154, 254

The Bride of Innisfallen (Welty) 225

The Brigadier and the Golf Widow (Cheever) 238

The Burning House (Beattie) 261

Call to Arms (Lu) 156, 183

Can Such Things Be? (Bierce) 143

La casa di chiaccio (Vitale) 296

"The Cask of Amontillado" (Poe) 91, 114

"The Celebrated Jumping Frog of Calaveras County" (Twain) 92, 124

The Cheapest Night (Idris) 223

"Chelkash" (Gorky) 145

A Child's Christmas in Wales (Thomas) 224

The Chronicle of Clovis (Saki) 169

The Circus in the Attic (Warren) 215

City Life (Barthelme) 247

"A Clean Well-Lighted Place" (Hemingway) 153

Clipped Wings (Pontoppidan) 134

Close Range (Proulx) 293

The Coast of Chicago (Dybek) 273

Collected Stories (Calisher) 253

Collected Stories (Lessing) 257

Collected Stories (Porter) 240, 241

Collected Stories (Singer) 262

Collected Stories (Stafford) 247

Collected Stories (Trevor) 279

Collected Stories (Welty) 259

Collected Stories of Mavis Gallant (Gallant) 286

Colored Winds (Ivanov) 183

Come Back, Dr. Caligari (Barthelme) 238

Condensed Novels and Other Papers (Harte) 125

Contes cruels (Villiers de L'Isle-Adam) 135

A Country Doctor (Kafka) 152, 178

Country of Origin (Bakin) 287

The Country of the Blind (Wells) 169

The Crime of Batista the Student (Ribeiro Couto) 183

A Curtain of Green (Welty) 208

De Vitor ao Xadres (Torrado) 264

"The Dead" (Joyce) 173

"A Deal in Wheat" (Norris) 160

The Death of Methuselah and Other Stories (Singer) 271

"The Deceived Wives' Club" (Ribeiro Couto) 198

Los desterrados (Quiroga) 188

"The Devil and Daniel Webster" (Benét) 203, 205

"The Diamond as Big as the Ritz" (Fitzgerald) 182

"Diary of a Madman" (Gogol) 91, 109

"The Diary of a Madman" (Lu) 156

The Diary of a Superfluous Man (Turgenev) 119

Doce cuentos peregrinos (García Márquez) 278

"Dr. Heidegger's Experiment" (Hawthorne) 109

The Dream and the Desert (Krige) 222

"The Dream of a Ridiculous Man" (Dostoyevsky) 131

Dream Stuff (Malouf) 295

Dreams (Tagore) 153, 158

Droll Stories (Balzac) 91, 107

Dubliners (Joyce) 152, 173

The Earth Is Laughing (Khin) 226

The Easing of Fate (Berberova) 218

Eight Men (Wright) 233

The Encantadas (Melville) 118

The Enormous Radio and Other Stories (Cheever) 223

Evening Verses from Gunung (Iesmaniasita) 230

Everything That Rises Must Converge (O'Connor) 240

Fables for Our Time (Thurber) 207

Fair Haven and Foul Strand (Strindberg) 93, 160

"Falk" (Conrad) 155

"The Fall of the House of Usher" (Poe) 91, 110

Female and Male (Choromanski) 231

"A Fiddler Crab" (Kiyoko) 291

The Fifth Column and the First Forty-Nine Stories (Hemingway) 153, 204

The Finer Grain (James) 168

Fireman Flower and Other Stories (Sansom) 211

"The Five-Storied Pagoda" (Rohan) 142

Flowering Judas (Porter) 193

Franny and Zooey (Salinger) 233

Friend of My Youth (Munro) 273

"The Furnished Room" (Henry) 164

The Garden Party and Other Stories (Mansfield) 182

The Gentleman from San Francisco (Bunin) 175

"The Gift of the Magi" (Henry) 163

"Gimpel the Fool" (Singer) 213

Gimpel the Fool (Singer) 229

Go Down, Moses (Faulkner) 209

A Goat Who Wouldn't Be Mounted (Rosic) 270

God's Face (Drzezdzon) 264

"The Gods of Pegave" (Dunsany) 163

"The Gold Bug" (Poe) 91, 113

The Golden Apples (Welty) 217

The Golden Boat (Tagore) 143, 153

A Good Man Is Hard to Find (O'Connor) 225

Goodbye, Columbus (Roth) 231

Gorilla, My Love (Bambara) 250

The Great Wall of China (Kafka) 152

Groucho in Green (Mattsson) 270

Growing Up (Ichiyo) 145

Guys and Dolls (Runyan) 196

Heart of a Boy (De Amicis) 138

Heat and Other Stories (Oates) 276

"Herodias" (Flaubert) 92

High Song (Pontoppidan) 146

The Highway (Radichkov) 292

"Hills Like White Elephants" (Hemingway) 153, 189

Home Truths (Gallant) 266

The Horla (Maupassant) 137

Hot Hot Dogs (Shaham) 280

The Hotel and the House and Other Pieces (Evangelou) 266

The House by the Churchyard (Le Fanu) 123

How Much Is Belgrade (Dimic) 296

How to Write Short Stories (Lardner) 185

The Hunchbacks (Arlt) 198

A Hunger Artist (Kafka) 152, 185

Icelandic Loves (Gudmundsson) 185

Idiots First (Malamud) 237

If the River Was Whiskey (Boyle) 272

The Image, and Other Stories (Singer) 267

In Love and Trouble (Walker) 250

In the Absence of Angels (Calisher) 220

In the Days of the Counselor (Andersen) 147

In the Penal Colony (Kafka) 178

Isobars (Hospital) 276

"The Jackpot" (Jackson) 216

"Janet's Repentance" (Eliot) 120

The Jests of Life and Death (Pirandello) 154

Joe Wilson and His Mates (Lawson) 159

The Jungle Book (Kipling) 144

Just So Stories (Kipling) 160

"Lady Macbeth of the Mtsensk District" (Leskov) 125

The Lady or the Tiger? (Stockton) 136

"The Last Leaf" (Henry) 165

Late Harvest (Tagore) 153

Later the Same Day (Paley) 265

The Leaning Tower (Porter) 211

"The Legend of Saint Julian the Hospitaller" (Flaubert) 92

"The Legend of Sleepy Hollow" (Irving) 101

Letters from My Mill (Daudet) 127

Die Leute von Seldwyla (Keller) 119

Licks of Love (Updike) 295

"Ligeia" (Poe) 91, 110

The Little Karoo (Smith) 186

"Little Liza" (Karamzin) 86

"The Little Man" (Sefarim) 124

Living Wills (Macdonald) 276

Lost in the Funhouse (Barth) 244

Love, Action, Laughter and Other Sad Tales (Schulberg) 272

The Love Nest and Other Stories (Lardner) 188

Loves Without Love (Pirandello) 154

"The Luck of the Roaring Camp" (Harte) 126

The Magic Barrel (Malamud) 229

The Main Traveled Roads (Garland) 142

La Maison Tellier (Maupassant) 134

Makar's Dream (Korolenko) 137

Man Descending (Vanderhaeghe) 261

Man Is Good (Frank) 177

The Man That Corrupted Hadleyburg (Twain) 92, 149

"The Man Who Would Be King" (Kipling) 139

Many Thousands Gone (Bishop) 194

Mar al fondo (Sampedro) 281

Married (Strindberg) 93, 136

The Masked Days (Fuentes) 242

"The Masque of the Red Death" (Poe) 91, 112

The Matador of the Five Towns (Bennett) 171

Memoirs of Hecate County (Wilson) 213

The Memoirs of Sherlock Holmes (Doyle) 144

Men Without Women (Hemingway) 153, 189

The Middle Man and Other Stories (Mukherjee) 270

Mirgorod (Gogol) 91, 109

Mogens (Jacobsen) 128

"The Monkey's Paw" (Jacobs) 160

Montevideanos (Benedetti) 231

Moon Deluxe (Barthelme) 262

"The Moonstone" (Collins) 126

More Shapes Than One (Chapell) 276

The Morning Star (Dabrowska) 226

Mosby's Memoirs and Other Stories (Bellow) 244

Mosses from an Old Manse (Hawthorne) 114

Mount Taibai (Jia) 275

Mr. Balcer in Brazil (Konopnicka) 143

"Mr. Gilfil's Love-Story" (Eliot) 120

"A MS. Found a Bottle" (Poe) 91, 107

"The Murder" (Chekhov) 92

"The Murders in the Rue Morgue" (Poe) 91, 111

Museums and Women and Other Stories (Updike) 250

My First Loves (Klima) 265

My Life and Hard Times (Thurber) 197

My Name Is Aram (Saroyan) 207

"Neighbors" (Chekhov) 92

The Neon Wilderness (Algren) 215

New Stories, Frydenberg (Borgen) 240

A Night in Acadie (Chopin) 147

The Night of the Mad Cock (Oliveiro) 268

Nine Stories (Salinger) 222

short story *(continued)*

No One Writes to the Colonel and Other Stories (García Márquez) 243
Noon Wine (Porter) 203
Noturnos: contos (Miranda) 294
Le Novelle (Bandello) 39
Noveller i samling (Koltzow) 291
Obabakoak (Atxaga) 273
"An Occurrence at Owl Creek Bridge" (Bierce) 142
Odessa Tales (Babel) 195
The Old Adam (Pontoppidan) 145
"The Old Forest" (Taylor) 265
The Old Forest and Other Stories (Taylor) 265, 267
Old Tales Retold (Lu) 156, 201
One-Minute Letters (Örkény) 280
Open All Night (Morand) 182
"The Open Boat" (Crane) 148
"The Open Window" (Saki) 173
The Orphan of the Desert (Krige) 243
Our Old Home (Hawthorne) 123
"The Outcasts of Poker Flat" (Harte) 127
"The Overcoat" (Gogol) 91, 112
The Ox of Frankfurt (Yuryev) 289
Pale Horse, Pale Rider (Porter) 205
Paradis (Eriksson) 287
Partisans (Ivanov) 181
"Paul's Short Case" (Cather) 163
"The Peasants" (Chekhov) 92
The People and Uncollected Stories (Malamud) 272
The Periodic Table (Levi) 254
Piacevoli notti (Straparola) 38
The Piazza (Melville) 120
Pig Earth (Berger) 258
Pigeon Feathers (Updike) 235
Pinocchio: The Story of a Puppet (Collodi) 135
"The Pit and the Pendulum" (Poe) 91, 113
Pole Vault (Mihajlovski) 284
Portrait of the Artist as a Young Dog (Thomas) 207
Prelude (Mansfield) 177
"The Premature Burial" (Poe) 91, 113
The Price of Thebes (Lasker-Schuler) 173
Pricksongs and Descants (Coover) 246
Proud Are the Dead (Oe) 230
"The Purloined Letter" (Poe) 114
"Q.E.D." (Stein) 161
Quando Dio usci chiesa: Vita e fede in un borgio istriano del cinquecento (Tomizza) 269
"The Queen of Spades" (Pushkin) 90, 108
"The Ransom of Red Chief" (Henry) 168
"Rappaccini's Daughter" (Hawthorne) 113
Rare and Endangered Species (Bausch) 282
"Rashomon" (Akutagawa) 174
The Red Pony (Steinbeck) 203
Reginald (Saki) 162
Reginald in Russia (Saki) 168
Rise Up, O Young Men of the New Age (Oe) 263

The River of Life (Kuprin) 164
The Roaring Girl (Hollingshed) 284
"Roger Malvin's Burial" (Hawthorne) 107
Sacrifice (Tagore) 153, 159
"The Sad Fortune of the Rev. Amos Barton" (Eliot) 120
Saentieri sotto la neve (Stern) 291
Sagarana (Guimares Rosa) 214
Scenes from Private Life (Balzac) 91, 106
Scenes of Bohemian Life (Murger) 115
Schimpf und Ernst (Pauli) 36
"The Sea of Grass" (Richter) 201
The Season Ticket (Haliburton) 121
Sensitiva Amorosa (Hansson) 139
Seven Gothic Tales (Dinesen) 198
"The Shadow Line" (Conrad) 155
Ship Fever and Other Stories (Barrett) 286
A Short Bunch of Stories (Tagore) 153
"The Short Happy Life of Francis Macomber" (Hemingway) 153, 201
The Sign of Four (Doyle) 141
The Silence of Colonel Bramble (Maurois) 177
"A Simple Heart" (Flaubert) 92
Simple Stories (Schulze) 291
Sixty Tales (Buzzati) 230
The Sketch Book (Irving) 101
Sketches by Boz (Dickens) 109
Sleep It Off Lady (Rhys) 255
The Sleeping Lord and Other Fragments (Jones) 252
The Snow Image, and Other Tales (Hawthorne) 117
"The Snows of Kilimanjaro" (Hemingway) 153, 204
A Soldier's Embrace (Gordimer) 259
Someone to Watch over Me (Bausch) 293
Something Happened Here (Levine) 276
The Son of the Wolf (London) 158
Spinoza of Market Street (Singer) 234
St. Godhard Railway and Other Stories (Yoko) 287
Stars of the New Curfew (Okri) 272
Stories and Pictures (Peretz) 158
Stories and Poems (Benediktsson) 147
Stories from Mala Strava (Neruda) 132
Stories in an Almost Classical Mode (Brodkey) 270
The Stories of John Cheever (Cheever) 257, 258
The Stories of Muriel Spark (Spark) 266
The Stories of Vladimir Nabokov (Nabokov) 284
Stories Toto Told Me (Rolfe) 148
A Study (Doyle) 138
The Suitcase (Alavi) 199
Tale from Two Pockets (Čapek) 191
Tales (Achchygyya) 203
Tales (Poe) 114
Tales (Strindberg) 93

Tales of a Traveler (Irving) 103
Tales of Mountains and Steppes (Aytmatov) 237
Tales of Soldiers and Civilians (Bierce) 142
Tales of the Grotesque and Arabesque (Poe) 91, 111
Tales of the Jazz Age (Fitzgerald) 182
Tales of the O'Hara Family (Banim) 104
Tanzstunde (Trampe) 268
"Taras Bulba" (Gogol) 91, 109
"The Tell-Tale Heart" (Poe) 91, 113
There Was Once—Or Was There? (Jamalzadeh) 181
Thranes metode (Lonn) 283
Three Tales (Flaubert) 92
A Tired Horse Trots On (Nguyen) 265
"To Build a Fire" (London) 166
"Tobermory" (Saki) 169
The Troll Garden (Cather) 163
"Twenty-Six Men and a Girl" (Gorky) 149
Twice-Told Tales (Hawthorne) 109
The Two Drovers (Scott) 105
Two Little Misogynists (Spitteler) 165
Uncle Silas (Le Fanu) 124
Uncle Tom's Children (Wright) 204
Untitled Field (Moore) 161
Verik (Aleichem) 166
Vermilion Sands (Ballard) 249
Verso Paola (Sanvitale) 276
Very Happy Marriage (Belohradska) 290
Wandering (Lu) 156, 187
"Ward Number Six" (Chekhov) 92, 143
The Way Some People Live (Cheever) 210
We Are Still Married (Keillor) 272
Where I'm Calling From: New and Selected Stories (Carver) 270
Where the Jackals Howl and Other Stories (Oz) 240
Whilomville (Crane) 158
"Why I Live at the P.O." (Welty) 208
The Wide Net (Welty) 210
Will You Please Be Quiet, Please? (Carver) 255
Winesburg, Ohio (Anderson) 178
Winner Take Nothing (Hemingway) 153
Winter's Tales (Dinesen) 209
With Women's Names (Palau i Fabre) 270
Without a Hero (Boyle) 282
The Wonder Rabbi of Barcelona (Lasker-Schuler) 181
The World Is a Wedding and Other Stories (Schwartz) 216
Worlds, Mirrors, Magics (Chedid) 271
"The Yellow Wallpaper" (Gilman) 149
"Young Goodman Brown" (Hawthorne) 108
Youth and the Bright Medusa (Cather) 180
Zenobias liv (Reich) 292

social criticism
After Many a Summer Dies the Swan (Huxley) 205
The Lost Steps (Carpentier) 223
A Rhetoric of Motives (Burke) 219
social drama
The Silver Box (Galsworthy) 167
soliloquy
Solomon on the Vanity of the World (Prior) 72
sonnet
Amoretti (Spenser) 44
Les Amours de P. de Ronsard Vandomoys, Ensemble de Bocages (Ronsard) 39
Astrophel and Stella (Sidney) 43
Ballads and Sonnets (Rossetti) 134
Berryman's Sonnets (Berryman) 242
The Chimeras (Nerval) 118
The Dolphin (Lowell) 251
Eight Sonnets in American Poetry, 1922: A Miscellany (Millay) 183
Fatal Interview (Millay) 194
Garland of Sonnets (Preseren) 108
"The Growth of Love" (Bridges) 131
The Holy Sonnets (Donne) 49, 51, 55
"On First Looking into Chapman's Homer" (Keats) 100
"Ozymandias" (Shelley) 101
"Pied Beauty" (Hopkins) 132
Roman Sonnets (Ivanov) 188
Romantic Sonnets (Correia) 276
Songs and Sonnets (Ronsard) 39
Sonnets (Shakespeare) 51
Sonnets (Wordsworth) 92
Sonnets from the Portuguese (Browning) 116
Sonnets pour Hélène (Ronsard) 33
Sonnets to Orpheus (Rilke) 155, 182
Sonnets to Sophia (Marechal) 207
Spiritual Sonnets (Jiménez) 175
To Byron (Keats) 99
Les Trophées (Heredia) 144
Vowels (Rimbaud) 136
Winter Sonnets (Ivanov) 181
"The Windhover" (Hopkins) 131
"Yet I Do Marvel" (Cullen) 186
spy novel
From Russia with Love (Fleming) 228
Goldfinger (Fleming) 231
The Honorable Schoolboy (Le Carré) 256
The Ipcress File (Deighton) 235
The Little Drummer Girl (Le Carré) 263
The Russia House (Le Carré) 272
Smiley's People (Le Carré) 259
The Spy Who Came in from the Cold (Le Carré) 237
The Tailor of Panama (Le Carré) 286
Thunderball (Fleming) 234

T

tale/story *See also* short story
The Abbasids (Platen) 108
The Age of Chivalry (Bulfinch) 120

The Age of Fable (Bulfinch) 119
Black Forest Village Stories (Auerbach) 113
The Canterbury Tales (Chaucer) 14, 26
Confessio Amantis (Gower) 26
Contes et Faceties (Nerval) 117
Decameron (Boccaccio) 14, 25
The Devil's Elixir (Hoffman) 99
Ecatommiti (Giraldi) 40
The Elegant Buddha (Rohan) 140
Exemplary Tales (Cervantes) 32, 52
Extramundana (Spitteler) 135
Fables (Gay) 74
Fables (Saltykov-Shchedrin) 137
Fables: Selected Fables in Verse (La Fontaine) 61
Fables and Stories (Gellert) 77
Fairy Tales (Andersen) 108
Girls of Fire (Nerval) 118
Grimm's Fairy Tales (Grimm and Grimm) 98
Hans Brinker; or, The Silver Skates (Dodge) 124
The Happy Boy (Bjørnson) 122
Heidi (Spyri) 133
Late Harvest (Tagore) 146
Leonce and Lena (Büchner) 109
Mother Goose Tales (Perrault) 66
Mrs. Leicester's School (Lamb and Lamb) 98
Norwegian Folk Tales (Asbjørnsen, Moe) 117
The Parent's Assistant (Edgeworth) 87
Il Pentamerone (Basile) 62
Peter Schlemihl (Chamisso) 99
Popular Tales (Edgeworth) 96
Ragged Dick (Alger) 126
Sayahatnameye Hateme Tai (Kashefi) 28
The Serapion Brothers (Hoffman) 101
A Shabby Genteel Story (Thackeray) 111
Shock-Headed Peter (Hoffmann) 115
Slovenly Peter (Hoffmann) 114
A Sportsman's Sketches (Turgenev) 118
"The Story of a Bad Boy" (Aldrich) 127
Strange Stories from a Chinese Studio (Pu) 63
Strange Stories (Hoffman) 100
The Swiss Family Robinson (Wyss) 99
Sylvie and Bruno (Carroll) 140
The Tale of Rosamund Gray and Old Blind Margaret (Lamb) 88
Tales and Novels in Verse (La Fontaine) 60
Tales from Shakespeare (Lamb and Lamb) 97
Tales of a Manor (Lagerlöf) 148
Tales of Hoffman (Hoffman) 99
Tales of the Late Ivan Petrovich Belkin (Pushkin) 90, 106
Tales of the Rainy Moon (Ueda) 81
The Water Babies (Kingsley) 123
Zadig (Voltaire) 77
Zanoni (Bulwer-Lytton) 112
theatrical criticism
The World of Drama (Kerr) 177

thriller
Alte Kameraden (Skagen) 274
The Day of the Jackal (Forsyth) 249
The Dogs of War (Forsyth) 252
The Four Just Men (Wallace) 163
The Odessa File (Forsyth) 250
tragedy
Abufar (Ducis) 87
Adrienne Lecouvreur (Scribe and Legouvé) 116
Alexander the Great (Racine) 60
Amboyna (Dryden) 62
Andrea of Hungary, Fra Rupert, and Giovanna of Naples (Landor) 110
Andromaque (Racine) 48, 61
Antigone (Alfieri) 83
Antigone (Anouilh) 209
Antigone (Sophocles) 3
Appius and Virginia (Webster, Heywood) 51
Athalie (Racine) 48, 65
Atreus and Thyseus (Crébillon) 71
Bajazet (Racine) 48, 62
Bánk bán (Katona) 100
Becket (Tennyson) 136
Bérénice (Racine) 48, 61
Blood Wedding (García Lorca) 155, 198
Boris Godunov (Pushkin) 90, 104, 106
Brennoralt (Suckling) 57
Britannicus (Racine) 48, 61
Caesar and Pompey (Chapman) 55
Cain (Byron) 93, 102
Cardenio und Celinde (Gryphius) 59
Carolus Stardus (Gryphius) 59
Catharina von Georgien (Gryphius) 59
Cato (Addison) 72
The Cenci (Shelley) 101
Charles Stuart, or Majesty Murdered (Gryphius) 58
Le Cid (Corneille) 48, 56
Cinna (Corneille) 48, 56
Count Julian (Landor) 98
The Count of Carmagnola (Manzoni) 102
The Covetous Knight (Pushkin) 90, 109
Danton's Death (Büchner) 109
The Death of Caesar (Voltaire) 75
The Death of Pompey (Corneille) 48, 57
Deirdra (Yeats) 152, 165
Deirdra of the Sorrows (Synge) 168
Don Juan and Faust (Grabbe) 105
Don Sebastian (Dryden) 49
The Duchess of Malfi (Webster) 52, 53
Edward and Eleanore (Thomson) 76
Egmont (Goethe) 67, 85
Electra (Crébillon) 71
Emilia Galotti (Lessing) 69, 82
The Envious Man (Dalin) 76
Faust (Goethe) 67, 97, 107
Feast in the Time of Plague (Pushkin) 90, 107
Fifty Comedies and Tragedies (Fletcher, Beaumont) 63

Fredegonde and Brunehaut (Lemercier) 102
The Golden Fleece (Grillparzer) 102
Hakon Jarl (Oehlenschlager) 97
Hamlet (Shakespeare) 31, 50
Hannibal (Grabbe) 109
Henry VIII (Chénier) 86
Heraclius (Corneille) 48
Horace (Corneille) 48, 56
Horsztynski (Słowacki) 109
The House of Bernarda Alba (García Lorca) 202
Idoménée (Crébillon) 70
The Indian Queen (Dryden) 49, 60
Iphigénie en Aulide (Racine) 48, 62
Irene (Johnson) 78
Irène (Voltaire) 83
Jephthah, or The Promised Sacrifice (Vondel) 59
John Woodvil (Lamb) 96
Julius von Tarent (Leisewitz) 83
Kaiser Friedrich Barbarossa (Grabbe) 106
King Lear (Shakespeare) 31, 50
King Ottocar: His Rise and Fall (Grillparzer) 104
Kullervo (Kivi) 122
Leo Arminius (Gryphius) 57
The Love Suicide at Sonezaki (Chikamatsu) 70
The Love Suicides at Amijimi (Chikamatsu) 72
Macbeth (Shakespeare) 31, 50
The Maid's Tragedy (Beaumont, Fletcher) 51
Marino Faliero (Byron) 93, 102
Marino Faliero, Doge of Venice (Swinburne) 135
Médée (Corneille) 48
Merope, a Tragedy (Arnold) 120
Mérope (Voltaire) 76
Miss Julie (Strindberg) 92, 139
Miss Sara Sampson (Lessing) 69, 79
Mithridate (Racine) 48, 62
The Mourning Bride (Congreve) 66
Mozart and Salieri (Pushkin) 90, 106
The Mysterious Mother (Walpole) 81
Oedipus (Voltaire) 72
Oedipus at Colonus (Sophocles) 3
Oedipus at the Home of Admetus (Ducis) 83
Oedipus Rex (Sophocles) 3
Orazia (Aretino) 38
Orbecche (Giraldi) 37
Osorio (Coleridge) 87
Phèdre (Racine) 48, 63
Pinto (Lemercier) 133
Pizarro (Sheridan) 88
Ployeucte (Corneille) 48
Queen Jane (Mistral) 141
Ralf Krage (Ewald) 81
The Revenge of the Bussy D'Amboise (Chapman) 52
Rhadamistus and Zenobia (Crébillon) 71
Richard II (Shakespeare) 31, 44
Richard III (Shakespeare) 31, 44
Rodogune (Corneille) 48, 57
Romeo and Juliet (Shakespeare) 31, 44

Roxana (Alabaster) 55
Samson Agonistes (Milton) 48, 62
Sappho (Grillparzer) 101
Sardanapalus (Byron) 93, 102
Sofonisma (Trissino) 35
Sophonisbe (Mairet) 55
The Stone Guest (Pushkin) 90, 111
Strafford (Browning) 109
Suréna (Corneille) 48
Tancred and Sigismunda (Thomson) 77
The Thebans, or the Enemy Brothers (Racine) 60
Theodore (Corneille) 48
Tiger at the Gates (Giraudoux) 200
Torquato Tasso (Goethe) 67, 85
The Tragedy of Man (Madách) 122
The Tragedy of Othello, Moor of Venice (Shakespeare) 50
The Tragical History of the Life and Death of Doctor Faustus (Marlowe) 50
The Twins (Klinger) 82
The Two Foscari (Byron) 93, 102
Le Véritable Saint Genest (Rotrou) 57
The Waves of the Sea and Love (Grillparzer) 106
Werner (Byron) 103
Zaire (Voltaire) 75
tragicomedy
Clitandre (Corneille) 48
The Devil's Law Case (Webster) 53
Love Triumphant (Dryden) 49, 66
The Maidservant (Corneille) 48
Mélite (Corneille) 48, 54
Il pastor fido (Guarini) 43
The Queenes Arcadia (Daniel) 50
The Royal Place (Corneille) 48
Secret Love, or the Maiden Queen (Dryden) 49, 61
The Soldiers (Lenz) 82
The Widow (Corneille) 48
The Widow's Tears (Chapman) 51
travel narrative
American Notes (Dickens) 112
At Home and Abroad (Pritchett) 272
Balkan Ghosts (Kaplan) 279
The Bible in Spain (Barrow) 112
Black Lamb and Grey Falcon (West) 209
Chita: A Memory of Last Island (Hearn) 140
Diverse Voyages Touching the Discovery of America (Hakluyt) 42
Following the Equator (Twain) 147
The Great Railway Bazaar (Theroux) 253
The Green Hills of Africa (Hemingway) 200
The Innocents Abroad (Twain) 92, 127
Jeg har hort et stierneskud (Jensen) 290
Journal of a Tour of the Hebrides, with Samuel Johnson (Boswell) 84
A Journey to the Western Islands of Scotland (Johnson) 82

travel narrative (continued)
   Letters of a Russian Traveler (Karamzin) 85
   Il libro della prima navigazione per oceano alle terre de'negri della Bassa Ethiopia (Cadamosto) 34
   Mogg Megone (Whittier) 109
   The Narrow Road to the Deep North (Bashō) 49, 66
   North of South: An African Journey (Naipaul) 258
   The Old Patagonian Express: By Train Through the Americas (Theroux) 258
   The Path to Rome (Belloc) 160
   Pictures of Travel (Heine) 104
   Pillars of Hercules: A Grand Tour of the Mediterranean (Theroux) 284
   The Road to Wigan Pier (Orwell) 203
   Roughing It (Twain) 92, 128
   Tanzstunde (Trampe) 268
   A Tramp Abroad (Twain) 92, 133
   Travels with a Donkey in the Cevennes (Stevenson) 132
   Travels with Charley in Search of America (Steinbeck) 235
   Viaggio all'India Orientali (Balbi) 43
   Xiyou Ji (Wu) 44
treatise See also essay
   Address to the Nobility of the German Nation (Luther) 36
   The Advancement of Learning (Bacon) 50
   The Age of Reason (Paine) 86
   Annotations in Pandectas (Budé) 34
   Beyond Good and Evil (Nietzsche) 114, 138
   The Birth of Tragedy (Nietzsche) 129
   The Bloody Tenet of Persecution for the Cause of Conscience (Williams) 57
   A Century of Dishonor (Jackson) 134
   Christian Discourses (Kierkegaard) 91
   City of God (Augustine) 13, 18

   Civilization and Its Discontents (Freud) 193
   Collected Works (Calvin) 52
   The Concept of Dread (Kierkegaard) 91
   Concerning Vernacular Eloquence (Dante) 14
   Concluding Unscientific Postscript (Kierkegaard) 91
   Critique of Practical Reason (Kant) 85
   Critique of Pure Reason (Kant) 84
   De Arte Poetica (Vida) 36
   De Augmentis Scientiarum (Bacon) 53
   De Cive (Hobbes) 57
   De Homine (Hobbes) 59
   De Orbe Novo (Peter Martyr) 35
   De Revolutionibus Orbium Coelestium (Copernicus) 38
   De Sacramento Matrimonii (Sánchez) 44
   The Decay and Restoration of Civilization (Schweitzer) 184
   The Descent of Man (Darwin) 128
   Dialogues de Dom Frei Amador Arraiz (Arrais) 43
   Digression on Ancients and Moderns (Fontenelle) 65
   Discours de la méthode (Descartes) 56
   Edifying Discourses on Diverse Spirits (Kierkegaard) 91
   The Education of the Human Race (Lessing) 69
   Either/Or (Kierkegaard) 91, 113
   Eleutheria (Mather) 66
   Emile; or, On Education (Rousseau) 68, 80
   The Epistle to the Romans (Barth) 178
   Fear and Trembling (Kierkegaard) 91, 113
   Freedom of the Will (Edwards) 78
   The Genius of Christianity (Chateaubriand) 95
   The Grammar of Assent (Newman) 127
   Gravity and Grace (Weil) 215
   The Hessian Messenger (Büchner) 108
   I and Thou (Buber) 184

   The Interpretation of Dreams (Freud) 149
   Das Kapital (Marx and Engels) 126
   Laocoon: An Essay on the Limits of Painting and Poetry (Lessing) 69, 80
   The Leviathan (Hobbes) 58
   Liber de Arti Distellandi (Hieronymous Brunschwig) 34
   Love and Death (Mushanakoji) 206
   Magnalia Christi Americana (Mather) 70
   Mathematical Principles of Natural Philosophy (Newton) 64
   Matter and Memory (Bergson) 146
   The Modern Theme (Ortega y Gasset) 184
   The Need for Roots (Weil) 218
   The New Atlantis (Bacon) 54
   De los nombres de Cristo (León) 42
   The Notebooks of Don Rigoberto (Vargas Llosa) 292
   Novum Organum (Bacon) 53
   Objections to the Spirit of the Age (Costa) 103
   Of the Principles of Human Knowledge (Berkeley) 71
   On Monarchy (Dante) 14
   On the Reckoning of Time (Bede) 14
   On the Search after Truth (Malebranche) 62
   On the State (Cicero) 4, 10
   On Time (Bede) 14
   The Passion (Saneatsu) 188
   The Passions of the Soul (Descartes) 58
   Philosophical Essays Concerning Human Understanding (Hume) 77
   Philosophical Fragments (Kierkegaard) 91, 113
   Plastik (Herder) 83
   The Prince (Machiavelli) 35
   The Problem of Pain (Lewis) 207
   Reflections on the Revolution in France (Burke) 85
   Repetition (Kierkegaard) 91

   Resignation (Young) 80
   The Rights of Man (Paine) 86
   The Saints Everlasting Rest (Baxter) 58
   The Seven Lamps of Architecture (Ruskin) 116
   Sic et Non (Abélard) 22
   The Sickness Unto Death (Kierkegaard) 91
   The Spirit of the Laws (Montesquieu) 77
   Stages on Life's Way (Kierkegaard) 91
   Thus Spake Zarathustra (Nietzsche) 135
   Time and Freewill (Bergson) 140
   Training in Christianity (Kierkegaard) 91
   The Treason of the Intellectuals (Benda) 189
   A Treatise Concerning Religious Affections (Edwards) 77
   Treatise on the Education of Girls (Fénelon) 64
   Tres Thomae (Stapleton) 43
   The Two Sources of Morality and Religion (Bergson) 196
   A Vindication of the Rights of Woman (Wollstonecraft) 86
   Women in the Nineteenth Century (Fuller) 114
   The Wonders of the Invisible World (Mather) 65
   Works of Love (Kierkegaard) 91
   The World as Will and Idea (Schopenhauer) 101

V

verse novel
   The Golden Gate (Seth) 267
verse play
   Cathleen ni Houlihan (Yeats) 160
   Elektra (Hofmannsthal) 161
   Monna Vanna (Maeterlinck) 160
   Murder in the Cathedral (Eliot) 152

W

western novel
   Riders of the Purple Sage (Grey) 171
   The Virginian (Wister) 160

LANGUAGE INDEX

Entries in the index are filed word for word.

A

Acholi
  Song of Lawino (p'Bitek) 241
Afrikaans
  Citations About a Revolution (Ferreira) 265
  With Pleasure, Dear Sirs (Fula) 226
Albanian
  Broken April (Kadare) 261
  Dossier H (Kadare) 273
  The General of the Dead Army (Kadare) 236
  The Great Winter (Kadare) 255
  Happy Ending (Podrimja) 270
  The Monster (Kadare) 239
  The Palace of Dreams (Kadare) 260
  The Wedding (Kadare) 244
Amharic
  A Fictional Story (Gabra Iyasus) 166
  Good Example (Germasaw) 208
  Hannibal (Kabbada) 216
  I Went Abroad (Walda) 225
  The New World (Heruy) 186
  Vain Entertainment (Neguse) 183
  The Voice of Blood (Makonnen) 208
Arabic
  Arab
    Hamasah (Abū Tammām) 19
  Egyptian
    Baina al-Qasraym (Mahfouz) 226
    The Beginning and the End (Mahfouz) 220
    The Cairo Trilogy (Mahfouz) 226
    The Cheapest Night (Idris) 223
    The Earth (Sharqawi) 223

    An Egyptian Childhood (Taha Hussain) 195
    The Fellah (Sharqawi) 247
    Guilt (Idris) 230
    Ibrahim the Writer (al-Mazini) 194
    The Lamp of Umm Hashim (Haqqi) 211
    Love in Exile (Baha' Tahir) 283
    Midaq Alley (Mahfouz) 214
    Miramar (Mahfouz) 242
    People of the Cave (al-Hakim) 197
    The Return of the Spirit (al-Hakim) 197
    Sarāh (al-Aqqad) 204
    Sin (Idris) 235
    The Thief (Mahfouz) 240
    The Thief and the Dogs (Mahfouz) 233
    Today and Tomorrow (Musa) 189
    The Tragedy of Al-Hallaj (Abdass-abur) 240
    Zaynab (Haykal) 173
  Iraqi
    Broken Pitchers (al-Bayati) 223
    Doctor Ibrahim (Ayyub) 206
    Glory to the Children and Olives (al-Bayati) 226
    The Hand, the Earth and the Water (Ayyub) 216
    The Moon of Shiraz (al-Bayati) 264
  Jordanian
    To the East of the Mediterranean (Mounif) 265
  Lebanese
    The Broken Wings (Gibran) 182
    Dear Mr. Kawabata (ad-Daif) 284
    The Flute and the Wind (Hawi) 233

    I Live (Ba'albakki) 229
    Kadmus (Aql) 211
    The Procession (Gibran) 178
    Spirits Rebellious (Gibran) 179
    A Tear and a Smile (Gibran) 173
  Moroccan
    Harrouda (Ben Jelloun) 251
  Palestinian
    In Search of Walid Massoud (Jabra) 295
    Why Did You Leave the Horse Alone? (Darwish) 281
  Sudanese
    Time of Migration Northwards (Salih) 233
  Syrian
    Thickets (Abu Madi) 206
  Tunisian
    Barq al-Layl (Khurayyif) 233
    Decline; or, Your Love Has Destroyed Me (Khurayyif) 228
    The Mountain of Broom (Bourbane) 235
    The Slave Merchant (Bujah) 284
Armenian
  Abudulala Mahari (Isahakian) 169
  "Caravans Are Still Marching" (Kaputikian) 238
  The Companions of Vardan (Demirtichian) 210
  David Bele (Raffi) 133
  Dreams in Twilight (Terian) 166
  Frights (Varuzhan) 164
  The Golden Cockerell (Raffi) 134
  Jalaleddin (Raffi) 132
  The Never Silent Bells (Sevak) 230
  New Morning (Hadobian) 167
  The Rock of Rushan (Zarian) 193
  Sad People (Zorian) 177
  Samuel (Raffi) 137

  Sparks (Raffi) 135
  The Tool (Raffi) 137
  Twentieth Century (Emin) 247
Awadhi
  Ramacaritmanas (Tulsīdās) 41

B

Baluchi
  Call (Nasir) 221
Basotho
  Charles: An Historical Romance (Mofolo) 186
Basque
  Obabakoak (Atxaga) 273
  Poemas híbridos (Atxaga) 273
Bengali
  Andanda Math (Bannerjee) 134
  Birangana (Datta) 122
  Brajangana (Datta) 122
  The Chieftain's Daughter (Chatterjee) 124
  Dreams (Tagore) 153, 158
  Gītāñjali (Tagore) 153, 168
  The Golden Boat (Tagore) 143, 153
  Gora (Tagore) 153, 165
  "Jana Gana Mana" (Tagore) 153
  Late Harvest (Tagore) 146, 153
  Mānasī (Tagore) 141, 153
  Meghnadbadh (Datta) 122
  Pedestrian (Mukopadhyay) 207
  The Poison Tree (Chatterjee) 129
  Sacrifice (Tagore) 153, 159
  Sarmistha (Datta) 120
  A Short Bunch of Stories (Tagore) 153
  Song of the Road (Pather Panchali) (Bandyopadhyay) 191
  Tilottamsambhab (Datta) 121
  The Will of Krishnakunta (Chatterjee) 132
Bulgarian
  Blind Dog (Hristow) 275
  The Gangster War (Petrunova) 292

Bulgarian (continued)

Here I Am, in Perfect Leaf Today (Dubarova) 279

The Highway (Radichkov) 292

A Lassie Was Cracking Hazelnuts (Terziev) 292

Life That Strives to Be a Poem (Bagravana) 281

A Natural Novel (Gospodinov) 292

Sitting Duck (Radichkov) 290

Transit (Dimitrova) 275

Under the Yoke (Yazov) 143

Wake Me Yesterday (Donkov) 295

Burmese

Bhuridat Lingagyi (Shin) 28

Bhuridat Zatpaung Pyo (Shin) 29

The Earth Is Laughing (Khin) 226

Kogan Pyo (Shin) 36

Man Is Insane (Nu) 210

Modern Monk (Thein) 201

Parayana Wuthtu (Shin) 35

Pauper Tyetko (Banmo) 222

The Peasant Nga Ba (Maun) 214

Tada uti Mawgun (Shin) 29

C

Catalan

With Women's Names (Palau i Fabre) 270

Chagatai Turkish

Char Divan (Nava'i) 29

Mizan al-Awzan (Nava'i) 29

Chinese

The August Sleepwalker (Bei) 270

Black Snow (Liu) 279

Caisangzi (Ye) 295

Call to Arms (Lu) 156, 183

The Canker (Mao) 193

The Carnival Season (Wang) 295

The Centennial Sea-Wolf (Wang) 290

"The Diary of a Madman" (Lu) 156

Dream of the Red Chamber (Cao) 69, 80, 191

Father Murdering (Zeng) 290

Hometown Noodles and Flower (Liu) 290

Jin Ping Mei (Anonymous) 52

Leaden Wings (Zhang) 259

Leaves of Three Autums (Bian) 197

Living (Yu) 281

Love and Longing in Hing Kong (Wang) 281

Ma Qiao Dictionary (Han) 286

Mount Taibai (Jia) 275

Old River Daydreams (Liu) 279

Old Sites (Li) 279

Old Tales Retold (Lu) 156, 201

One the Margins (Go) 281

Outstanding Talent—Yang Du (Tang, Zhu) 288

Pallid Night (Jia) 284

The Piano Tuner (Cheng) 272

Rainbow (Mao) 277

Red Candle (Wen) 183

The Red Room Tavern (Ye) 281

Red Sorghum (Mo) 273

The Republic of Wine (Mo) 295

Rice (Su) 275

Rickshaw Boy (Lao) 216

A Season for Falling in Love (Wang) 279

Shijing 1

Silver City (Li) 290

The Sobbing Lancang River (Zhu) 273

Strange Stories from a Chinese Studio (Pu) 63

The Sunrise (Cao) 201

To Live (Yu) 284

Torrent (Ba) 207

Toward Chaos (Cong) 290

Venice Diary (Cheng) 281

Wandering (Lu) 156, 187

War and People (Wang) 288

The Way of Living in the World (Zhou) 286, 288

White Deer Plains (Cheng) 288

The Wreath at the Foot of the Mountain (Li) 261

Xiyou Ji (Wu) 44

Yijing (Wenwang) 1

Circassian

Attack (Charasha) 191

Croatian

An Angel Offsides (Feric) 295

The Clembaj Family (Krleza) 196

Fording the Stream of Consciousness (Ugresic) 277

The Museum of Unconditional Surrender (Ungresic) 292

Note About the Author (Matanovic) 295

Osman (Gundulić) 54

Quiet Fires (Mihalic) 265

The Return of Philip Latinowicz (Krleza) 196

Czech

Against the Wall (Jirásek) 144

Alexander in the Streetcar (Reznicek) 281

Alone Against the Night (Tatarka) 275

Between the Currents (Jirásek) 142

Between Three Borders (Klima) 232

The Book of Laughter and Forgetting (Kundera) 258

Bozena Nemcova's Fan (Seifert) 207

Brotherhood (Jirásek) 149

The Camel Through the Needle's Eye (Langer) 183

Cape of Good Hopelessness (Martinek) 281

The Castle (Klima) 238

Cat's Lives (Kriseova) 288

Closely Watched Trains (Hrahbel) 240

Colette (Lustig) 277

The Confessions of Mr. K. (Brackman) 265

Darkness (Jirásek) 174

Death by Seconds (Brousek) 284

Departure from the Castle (Putik) 292

Dressed in Light (Seifert) 207

The End of the Patriarchate (Pavlicek) 277

The Excursion Participants (Viewegh) 286

F. L. Vek (Jirásek) 139

Glorious Lousy Years (Viewegh) 279

The Good Soldier Schweik (Hašek) 179

Grandmothers (Sabach) 292

Gypsies (Macha) 108

Halley's Comet (Seifert) 242

The Helmet of Clay (Seifert) 212

Honeymoon Ride (Seifert) 204

Hordubal (Čapek) 197

How the Heart Is Torn Apart (Siktanc) 273

Identity (Kundera) 290

Immortality (Kundera) 273

Jacques and His Master (Kundera) 260

The Joke (Kundera) 242

The Jury (Klima) 245

Love and Litter (Klima) 273

May (Mácha) 109

The Memorandum (Havel) 240

Meteor (Čapek) 198

My Cheerful Mornings (Klima) 273

My First Loves (Klima) 265

Night Tango: A Novel of One Summer of the End of the Century (Kratochvil) 292

The Nightingale Sings Out of Tune (Siefert) 187

One Ship—Laura Blair (Divis) 281

Orbis Sensualium Pictus (Commenius) 59

An Ordinary Life (Čapek) 198

Over the Waves of TSF (Siefert) 186

Passion (Hercikova) 290

Plain Themes (Neruda) 135

R.U.R. (Čapek) 179

Silesian Songs (Bezrůc) 226

Stories from Mala Strava (Neruda) 132

A Summer Affair (Klima) 249

Switch off the Light (Seifert) 204

Tale from Two Pockets (Čapek) 191

The Ultimate Intimacy (Klima) 290

The Unbearable Lightness of Being (Kundera) 264

Very Happy Marriage (Belohradska) 290

The Year of the Frog (Simecka) 281

D

Danish

20 Digte (Lavgesen) 277

Ars Vivendi eller de syv Jevermater (Johannesen) 292

"Babette's Feast" (Dinesen) 218

Bang (Willumsen) 286

The Book of Songs (Drachmann) 140

Borderliners (Hoeg) 282

Brev til manen (Michael) 284

Broder Jacob (Stangerup) 275

Byen og verden (Hultberg) 279

Children of Nature (Claussen) 138

Children of Wrath: A Hired Man's Saga (Aakjaer) 162

Christian Discourses (Kierkegaard) 91

Clipped Wings (Pontoppidan) 134

Clouds (Pontoppidan) 141

The Concept of Dread (Kierkegaard) 91

Concluding Unscientific Postscript (Kierkegaard) 91

The Death of Balder (Ewald) 82

Denied a Country (Bang) 164

Dodningeuret (Gronfeldt) 275

Drommebroer (Nordbrandt) 295

Dyr (Preisler) 279

Edifying Discourses on Diverse Spirits (Kierkegaard) 91

Either/Or (Kierkegaard) 91, 113

Elskede ukendte (Thorup) 282

En Route to Myself (Pontoppidan) 210

Engel (Rifbjerg) 268

Erasmus Montanus (Holberg) 74

Fairy Tale of My Life (Andersen) 114

Fairy Tales (Andersen) 108

The Fall of the King (Jensen) 158

Fear and Trembling (Kierkegaard) 91, 113

Fortoellinger om natten (Hoeg) 275

Fru Astrid Grib (Jensen) 275

The Funny Man (Holberg) 74

Genspejlet (Madsen) 295

The Gods of the North (Oehlenschlager) 101

The Golden Horns (Oehlenschläger) 95

The Good Hope (Heineson) 238

Det gronne oje (Guldager) 292

Hakon Jarl (Oehlenschlager) 97

Havoc (Kristensen) 193

Her i noerheden (Christensen) 282

Heroics (Claussen) 186

Hexaemeron (Arrebo) 54

High Song (Pontoppidan) 146

Hjertelyd (Grondahl) 292

The Holy Flame (Drachmann) 149

Hovedstolen (Hesselholdt) 292

I See a Wondrous Land (Kamban) 201

Ida Brandt (Bang) 146

Jean de France (Holberg) 73

Jeg har hort et stierneskud (Jensen) 290

Jeppe of the Hill (Holberg) 73

Jonatan's Journey (Hansen) 208

The Joys of Rungsted (Ewald) 82

King Rene's Daughter (Hertz) 114

The Last Lantern (Kristensen) 223

The Liar (Hansen) 218

The Long Journey (Jensen) 166

The Lost Musicians (Heinesen) 218

Love Without Stockings (Wessel) 82

Lucca (Grondahl) 290

Lucky Kristoffer (Hansen) 212

Lucky Peter (Pontoppidan) 148

Mea Culpa (Holt) 288

Mellen himlen og verden (Tetevide) 295

The Melody That Got Lost (Abell) 205

Men Jorden star til evig tid (Helle) 288

Minna (Gjellerup) 140

Mogens (Jacobsen) 128

Nar fisken fanger solen (Winge) 288

Nattens rygrad (Krasilnikoff) 295
Niels Lynne (Jacobsen) 133
Night Guard (Pontoppidan) 144
The Old Adam (Pontoppidan) 145
Old and New Gods (Drachmann) 134
Om natten i Jerusalem (Kosovic) 292
Out of Africa (Dinesen) 203
The Peacock Feather (Kristensen) 182
Pedar Paars (Holberg) 72
Philosophical Fragments (Kierkegaard) 91, 113
The Pilgrim Kamanita (Gjellerup) 164
Pledged (Drachmann) 141
Poems (Oehlenschläger) 95
Poems, 1901–43 (Jensen) 210
The Political Tinker (Holberg) 73
Prins (Michaels) 288
Prioritaire (Hermann) 290
The Promised Land (Pontoppidan) 142
Ralf Krage (Ewald) 81
Ravnen (Goldsmith) 125
Rejse for en fremmed (Aidt) 295
Rejsen med Emma (Svendsen) 286
Repetition (Kierkegaard) 91
Det rigtige (Gronfeldt) 295
Serpent and Bull (Hansen) 221
Seven Gothic Tales (Dinesen) 198
Severe Passions (Holm) 248
The Sickness Unto Death (Kierkegaard) 91
Sidste sommer (Skou-Hansen) 277
Det skabtes vaklen Arabesker (Thomsen) 286
Skumring e Praha (Carling) 288
Skyggen i dit sted (Grondahl) 275
Slangen i Sydney (Larsen) 290
Spiritual Chorus (Kingo) 62
Stages on Life's Way (Kierkegaard) 91
The Story of Borge (Branner) 209
Stucco (Bang) 138
Svart due (Lie) 288
Tavshed i oktober (Grondahl) 286
Thomas Ripenseren (Ejrnaes) 288
Tine (Bang) 140
Den tolvte ritter (Michael) 279
The Tower at the End of the World (Heinesen) 254
Training in Christianity (Kierkegaard) 91
Transparence (Broger) 279
Trio (Lassen) 295
Tusindfodt (Tadrup) 292
Udsigten (Hesselholdt) 290
Under Mausolaeet (Nordbrandt) 268
Valdemar Afterdag (Hauch) 122
Vanillepigen (Michael) 284
De var engang (Holten) 279
Veien tlil Dhaka (Bjornstad) 288
Verden forswinner (Koltzow) 288
Village Pictures (Pontoppidan) 135
The Virgin of Skalholt (Kamban) 193
The Weather Cock (Holberg) 73
Willow Pipes (Claussen) 149
Windswept Dawn (Heinesen) 198
Winter's Tales (Dinesen) 209

Works of Love (Kierkegaard) 91
The World (Munk) 196
Zenobias liv (Reich) 292
Dutch
Adam in Exile (Vondel) 60
The Assault (Mulisch) 261
Back to Ina Damman (Vestdijk) 198
Boeto (Hooft) 52
Breatijs (Boutens) 166
Het bureau (Voskuil) 288, 290
The Count of Talavera (Lennep) 111
The Country of Rembrandt (Busken Huet) 134
Cryptogamen (Achterberg) 213
The Deeps of Deliverance (Eeden) 158
The Destruction of the First Creation (Bilderdijk) 102
The Destruction of the First World (Bilderdijk) 98
The Dew Trapper (Nijlen) 214
The Discovery of Heaven (Mulisch) 293
Ecstasy (Couperus) 143
Eline Vere (Couperus) 140
Exquisitely Foolish (Huygens) 53
Forms (Nijhoff) 185
Gedlichten, 1904–1938 (Nijlen) 204
Geeraert van Velsen (Hooft) 51
The Good Hope (Heijermans) 158
Grandida (Hooft) 50
The Great Songbook (Bredero) 53
The Grumbling Hive; or, Knaves Turned Honest (Mandeville) 70
Gysbreght von Aemstel (Vondel) 56
Het hof van barmhartigheid (Heijden) 288
The House in Haarlem (Schendel) 200
The House of Joy (Ammers-Küller) 182
I Serve (Teirlinck) 185
Ideas (Multatuli) 123
In a Dark Wood Wandering (Haasse) 217, 272
In the Dutch Mountains (Nooteboom) 264
Jephthah, or The Promised Sacrifice (Vondel) 59
The Johanna Maria (Schendel) 193
Joseph in Egypt (Vondel) 56
Last Call (Mulisch) 272
A Lost Wanderer (Schendel) 165
Lucifer (Vondel) 59
The Man in the Mirror (Teirlinck) 225
The Man Without a Body (Teirlinck) 186
Max Havelaar (Multatuli) 122
The Mountain of Light (Couperus) 164
Mr. Visser's Journey Through Hell (Vestdijk) 201
New Poems (Nijhoff) 198
Noah (Vondel) 61
Objections to the Spirit of the Age (Costa) 103
Overijssel Songs and Poems (Revius) 54
Palamedes, or Murdered Innocence (Vondel) 54

Paradise Regained (Marsman) 189
De Passievrucht (Loon) 293
Plankton (Voskuil) 290
De procedure (Mulisch) 293
Publieke werken (Rosenboom) 295
The Rebel Generation (Ammers-Küller) 186
Reinke de Vos (Alkmaar) 29
Rituals (Nooteboom) 259
The Scarlet City (Haasse) 221
Ship's Talk (Huygens) 54
The Slow Motion Picture (Teirlinck) 182
Song of Semblance and Substance (Eeden) 145
A Song of Truth and Semblance (Nooteboom) 260
Den Spieghel der Salicheit van Elckerlijk (Diest) 29, 36
Spring Moon (Boutens) 175
Teeuwis the Peasant (Coster) 51
The Ten Thousand Things (Demont) 225
Terug uit Irkoetsk (Vries) 282
A Thread in the Dark (Haasse) 236
Too Late for This World (Nijlen) 228
Tydverdryf/Pastime (Eybers) 288
De verbeelding (Franke) 293
Verzen (Gorter) 141
Voices (Boutens) 165
A Wanderer in Love (Schendel) 165
Yesterday (Dermont) 220
Zero Hour (Nijhoff) 209

E
English
American
XLI Poems (cummings) 186
The 42nd Parallel (Dos Passos) 193
77 Dream Songs (Berryman) 238
1876 (Vidal) 254
1919 (Dos Passos) 196
A lume spento (Pound) 155, 166
The Abduction (Kumin) 247
Abe Lincoln in Illinois (Sherwood) 204
Above the River (Wright) 273
Absalom, Absalom! (Faulkner) 201
Across the Bridge (Gallant) 279
Across the River and Into the Trees (Hemingway) 218
Active Service (Crane) 149
The Actual (Bellow) 288
Ada (Nabokov) 155, 245
The Adding Machine (Rice) 184
Adult Bookstore (Shapiro) 254
Adultery and Other Choices (Dubus) 255
The Adventures of Augie March (Bellow) 222
The Adventures of Huckleberry Finn (Twain) 92, 136
The Adventures of Tom Sawyer (Twain) 92, 131

Afloat and Ashore (Cooper) 113
After Rain (Trevor) 286
After the Fall (Miller) 238
After You've Gone (Adams) 272
The Afterlife and Other Stories (Updike) 282
Against Interpretation (Sontag) 241
The Age of Chivalry (Bulfinch) 120
The Age of Fable (Bulfinch) 119
The Age of Innocence (Wharton) 179
The Age of Reason (Paine) 86
The Aguero Sisters (Garcia) 288
Ah, Wilderness! (O'Neill) 153, 197
AIDS and Its Metaphors (Sontag) 270
The Air Conditioned Nightmare (Miller) 212
Airplane Dreams: Compositions from Journals (Ginsberg) 244
Al Aaraaf (Poe) 105
Albany Cycle (Kennedy) 277
The Algerine Captive; or, The Life and Adventures of Dr. Updike Underhill (Tyler) 87
The Alhambra (Irving) 107
Alice Adams (Tarkington) 181
All God's Children Need Traveling Shoes (Angelou) 267
All My Pretty Ones (Sexton) 235
All My Sons (Miller) 214
All Rivers Run to the Sea (Wiesel) 284
All the King's Men (Warren) 213
All the Pretty Horses (McCarthy) 277
An Almanac for New England for the Year 1639 (Pierce) 56
Almanac of the Dead (Silko) 275
Alnilam (Dickey) 268
Always Coming Home (Le Guin) 265
Amaranth (Robinson) 198
The Ambassadors (James) 91, 161
The American (James) 91, 131
American Appetites (Oates) 270
American Blues (Williams) 205
American Buffalo (Mamet) 253
An American Dictionary of the English Language (Webster) 105
American Dream (Albee) 230, 233
An American Dream (Mailer) 240
The American Language (Mencken) 178

English
American *(continued)*
American Pastoral (Roth) 288
American Primitive (Oliver) 262
The American Renaissance (Matthiessen) 208
The American Scene (James) 165
An American Tragedy (Dreiser) 186
America's Coming of Age (Brooks) 174
Among the Hills (Whittier) 127
The Anatomy Lesson (Roth) 262
The Ancient Child (Momaday) 272
Ancient Evenings (Mailer) 262
Andersonville (Kantor) 225
The Andromeda Strain (Chrichton) 245
Angel Landing (Hoffman) 259
The Angel of History (Forché) 282
Angela's Ashes: A Memoir (McCourt) 286, 288
Angle of Repose (Stegner) 248
Animal Dreams (Kingsolver) 273
The Animal Kingdom (Barry) 196
Anna and the King of Siam (Landon) 211
Anna Christie (O'Neill) 153, 182
Anna of the Five Towns (Bennett) 160
"Annabel Lee" (Poe) 116
Anne of the Thousand Days (Anderson) 216
Annie Allen (Brooks) 217
Annie John (Kincaid) 265
Annie Kilburn (Howells) 140
Another Part of the Forest (Hellman) 213
Another Song for America (Hensen) 268
Antartic Traveler (Pollitt) 261
Anthem (Rand) 204
Any Woman's Blues (Jong) 272
Appointment in Samarra (O'Hara) 198
Archy and Mehitabel (Marquis) 189
Are You a Bromide? (Burgess) 164
Ariel (Plath) 240
Around the Bedroom Wall: A Family Album (Woiwode) 253
Arrowsmith (Lewis) 186
Arthur Merwyn (Brown) 88
As I Lay Dying (Faulkner) 193
Ashes and 7 Years from Somewhere (Levine) 258
Ashes to Ashes: America's Hundred Year Cigarette War, the Public Health and the Unabashed Triumph of Philip Morris (Kluger) 288

The Aspern Papers (James) 139
The Assassins (Oates) 253
Assignment in Brittany (MacInnes) 209
The Assistant (Malamud) 228
At Heaven's Gate (Warren) 210
At Play in the Fields of the Lord (Matthiessen) 226
At the Bottom of the River (Kincaid) 264
An Atlas of the Difficult World, Poems, 1988–1991 (Rich) 275
Atlas Shrugged (Rand) 228
Atticus (Hansen) 286
Audubon: A Vision (Lowell) 245
Auroras of Autumn (Stevens) 218
The Autobiography (Franklin) 81
The Autobiography of Alice B. Toklas (Stein) 197
The Autobiography of an Ex-Colored Man (Johnson) 171
The Autobiography of Malcolm X (Malcolm X) 240
The Autobiography of Miss Jane Pittman (Gaines) 248
The Autocrat of the Breakfast-Table (Holmes) 120
The Avenue Bearing the Initial of Christ into the New World: Poems, 1946–1964 (Kinnell) 252
The Awakening (Chopin) 149
The Awkward Age (James) 91, 149
Axel's Castle (Wilson) 194
Babbitt (Lewis) 182
The Bachelor Party (Chayefsky) 223
Bailey's Café (Naylor) 277
Balisand (Hergesheimer) 185
Balkan Ghosts (Kaplan) 279
The Ballad of the Sad Café (McCullers) 220
Ballads and Other Poems (Longfellow) 111
Band of Angels (Warren) 225, 226
Bang the Drum Slowly (Harris) 226
Barefoot in the Park (Simon) 237
Barren Ground (Glasgow) 186
"Bartleby the Scrivener" (Melville) 118
Bayou Folk (Chopin) 144
Be Angry at the Sun (Jeffers) 208
The Bean Eaters (Brooks) 232
The Bean Trees (Kingsolver) 270
The Bear (Faulkner) 200
"The Beast of the Jungle" (James) 161
Beauchampe (Simms) 112
The Beautiful and Damned (Fitzgerald) 182
The Beautiful Changes and Other Poems (Wilbur) 214

Because It Is Bitter and Because It Is My Heart (Oates) 273
Bech: A Book (Updike) 247
Bech at Bay (Updike) 290
Bech Is Back (Updike) 261
Beggar on Horseback (Kaufman) 185
Being There (Kosinski) 247
The Belfry of Bruges and Other Poems (Longfellow) 114
A Bell for Adano (Hersey) 211, 212
The Bell Jar (Plath) 237
The Bellarosa Connection (Bellow) 272
Bellefleur (Oates) 259
"Bells" (Poe) 116
Beloved (Morrison) 268
Bend Sinister (Nabokov) 155, 214
Ben-Hur: A Tale of the Christ (Wallace) 133
Benito Cereno (Melville) 119
Berryman's Sonnets (Berryman) 242
Between Two Rivers: Selected Poems, 1956–1984 (Kenny) 268
Beyond Culture (Trilling) 240
Beyond the Horizon (O'Neill) 153
The Big Money (Dos Passos) 201
The Big Rock Candy Mountain (Stegner) 210
The Big Sleep (Chandler) 205
The Bigelow Papers (Lowell) 114, 115
Billy Bathgate (Doctorow) 272
Billy Budd, Foretopman (Melville) 185
Birds of America (McCarthy) 248
Birdy (Wharton) 258
Black Boy (Wright) 212
"The Black Cat" (Poe) 91
Black Elk Speaks (Neihardt) 196
Black Feeling, Black Talk (Giovanni) 244
The Black Prince, and Other Stories (Grau) 225
Black Spring (Miller) 201
Black Thunder (Bontemps) 201
Bless Me Ultima (Anaya) 250
The Blithedale Romance (Hawthorne) 117
Blood for a Stranger (Jarrell) 209
The Blood Oranges (Hawkes) 248
Blood Ties (Settle) 257
Bloodshed and Three Novellas (Ozick) 254
The Bloody Tenet of Persecution for the Cause of Conscience (Williams) 57
The Bluest Eye (Morrison) 247
Body and Soul (Conroy) 279
Bone by Bone (Matthiessen) 293
The Bonfire of Vanities (Wolfe) 268

A Book of Common Prayer (Didion) 255
The Book of Daniel (Doctorow) 248
Book of Folly (Sexton) 250
The Book of J (Bloom) 273
The Book of Nightmares (Kinnell) 248
The Border Trilogy (McCarthy) 290
Born Brothers (Woiwode) 270
Boston Adventure (Stafford) 211
The Bostonians (James) 91, 137
Both Your Houses (Anderson) 197
Bound East for Cardiff (O'Neill) 153
A Boy's Town (Howells) 141
A Boy's Will (Frost) 172
The Bravo (Cooper) 106
Breakfast at Tiffany's (Capote) 229
Breakfast of Champions: or, Goodby Blue Monday (Vonnegut) 251
The Breast (Roth) 250
Breathing Lessons (Tyler) 270
The Bride of Innisfallen (Welty) 225
The Bridge (Crane) 193
The Bridge of San Luis Rey (Wilder) 189
The Bridges at Toko-Ri (Michener) 222
Brief Moment (Behrman) 194
The Brigadier and the Golf Widow (Cheever) 238
Broke Heart Blues (Oates) 293
Broken Country (Brodsky) 284
Bronx Primitive: Portaits in a Childhood (Simon) 261
Brother to Dragons: A Tale in Verse and Voices (Warren) 222
Brotherly Love (Dexter) 275
Brothers, I Love You All (Carruth) 257
The Buccaneers (Wharton) 204
The Buck in the Snow (Millay) 190
Buckdancer's Choice (Dickey) 240
Bullet Park (Cheever) 245
The Bulwark (Dreiser) 213
Buried Child (Sheperd) 257
The Buried Lake (tATE) 222
Burning Daylight (London) 168
The Burning House (Beattie) 261
Burning (Johnson) 248
The Burning Mystery of Anna in 1951 (Koch) 258
Burr (Vidal) 251
Bus Stop (Inge) 225
Butterfield 8 (O'Hara) 200
By Love Possessed (Cozzens) 228
Cabot Wright Begins (Purdy) 238

Cadillac Jack (McMurtry) 261

The Caine Mutiny (Wouk) 220

California Suite (Simon) 254

Call at Corazon (Bowles) 270

The Call (Hauge) 213

Call It Sleep (Roth) 198

The Call of the Wild (London) 160

Camino Real (Williams) 222

Campo Santo (Wood) 277

Can Such Things Be? (Bierce) 143

Cannery Row (Steinbeck) 212

The Cannibal Galaxy (Ozick) 262

Cannibals and Missionaries (McCarthy) 258

Can't Quit You, Baby (Douglas) 270

Cantos (Pound) 155, 174

Cantos No. 1–117, 120 (Pound) 247

Carpenter's Gothic (Gaddis) 267

The Carrier of Ladders (Merwin) 247, 248

"The Cask of Amontillado" (Poe) 91, 114

Cass Timberlane (Lewis) 212

Cast a Cold Eye (McCarthy) 219

The Castaway (Cozzens) 198

The Cat in the Hat (Seuss) 228

Cat on a Hot Tin Roof (Williams) 225

Catch-22 (Heller) 233

The Catcher in the Rye (Salinger) 220

The Catered Affair (Chayefsky) 225

The Cathedral (Lowell) 127

The Catherine Wheel (Stafford) 221

Cat's Cradle (Vonnegut) 237

Cavender's House (Robinson) 191

Cawdor (Jeffers) 190

"The Celebrated Jumping Frog of Calaveras County" (Twain) 92, 124

The Centaur (Updike) 237

Centennial (Michener) 252

A Century of Dishonor (Jackson) 134

Ceremony and Other Poems (Wilbur) 219

A Certain Measure (Glasgow) 210

The Chainbearer (Cooper) 114

A Chance Acquaintance (Howells) 129

Changing Light at Sandover (Merrill) 262

The Chapel of the Hermits, and Other Poems (Whittier) 118

Chapter Two (Simon) 255

Charlemont (Simms) 119

Charlotte's Web (White) 221

A Charmed Life (McCarthy) 225

Charming Billy (McDermott) 290

Chesapeake (Michener) 257

The Chestnut Tree (Tyler) 103

Chicago (Sandburg) 173

Chicago Poems (Sandburg) 175

Children of the Night (Robinson) 147

The Children's Hour (Hellman) 198

Childworld (Oates) 254

Chills and Fever (Ransom) 185

Chimera (Barth) 250

The Chinese Nightingale and Other Poems (Lindsay) 176

Chita: A Memory of Last Island (Hearn) 140

A Chorus Line (Bennet, Kirkwood, Dante, Hamlisch, Kleban) 253

The Chosen (Potok) 242

Chosen Country (Dos Passos) 220

The Chosen Place, the Timeless People (Marshall) 245

The Cider House Rules (Irving) 265

Circles in the Water: Selected Poems (Piercy) 261

The Circular Staircase (Rinehart) 166

The Circus in the Attic (Warren) 215, 216

Cities of the Plain (McCarthy) 290

A Citizen of the Galaxy (Heinlein) 228

City Life (Barthelme) 247

City of Glass (Auster) 269

Clara Howard (Brown) 95

Clarel (Melville) 131

"A Clean Well-Lighted Place" (Hemingway) 153

Cleng Peerson (Hauge) 244

Clock Without Hands (McCullers) 233

Close Range (Proulx) 293

The Closing of the American Mind (Bloom) 268

Closing Time (Heller) 282

Cloudsplitter (Banks) 290

The Coast of Chicago (Dybek) 273

A Coast of Trees (Ammons) 260

The Coat Without a Seam (Kunitz) 252

Cold Mountain (Frazier) 288

Collages (Nin) 238

Collected Early Poems, 1950–1970 (Rich) 279

Collected Poems (Aiken) 222

Collected Poems (Crane) 197

Collected Poems (Freneau) 98

Collected Poems (Moore) 220

Collected Poems (Nemerov) 255, 256

Collected Poems (Plath) 261

Collected Poems (Seeger) 175

Collected Poems (Stevens) 223

Collected Poems (Wright) 248

Collected Poems, 1930–1993 (Sarton) 279

Collected Poems, 1946–1991 (Carruth) 277

Collected Poems, 1947–1980 (Ginsberg) 264

Collected Poems of H.D. (Dolittle) 186

Collected Short Stories (Porter) 240

Collected Stories (Calisher) 253

Collected Stories (Trevor) 279

Collected Stories (Welty) 259

Collected Stories of Mavis Gallant (Gallant) 286

The Colleen Bawn (Boucicault) 121

Color (Cullen) 186

The Color Purple (Walker) 261

The Colossus (Plath) 232

The Colossus of Maroussi (Miller) 205

Come Back, Dr. Caligari (Barthelme) 238

Come Back, Little Sheba (Inge) 219

Common Sense (Paine) 83

The Compass Flower (Merwin) 256

The Complete Poems (Jarrell) 245

Complete Poems (Sandburg) 219

The Complete Prose (Moore) 267

Compulsion (Levin) 226

Condensed Novels and other Papers (Harte) 125

The Condor Passes (Grau) 248

The Conduct of Life (Emerson) 121

A Coney Island of the Mind (Ferlinghetti) 229

The Confessions of Nat Turner (Styron) 243

The Confidence Man (Melville) 120

The Congo and Other Poems (Lindsay) 173

A Connecticut Yankee in King Arthur's Court (Twain) 92, 140

Conquest: Montezuma, Cortes and the Fall of Old Mexico (Thomas) 282

Conquistador (MacLeish) 196

Consenting Adult (Hobson) 253

Consider This, Señora (Doerr) 279

Contact Highs: Selected Poems, 1957–1987 (Ansen) 270

Contending Forces (Hopkins) 158

The Contrast (Tyler) 85

The Corsican Brothers (Boucicault) 115

Counselor-at-Law (Rice) 194

The Counterlife (Roth) 268

Country Music: Selected Early Poems (Wright) 262

The Country of the Pointed Firs (Jewett) 146

The Coup (Updike) 254

Couples (Updike) 244

The Courtship of Miles Standish (Longfellow) 120

The Crack-Up (Fitzgerald) 212

The Crater (Cooper) 115

The Cream of the Jest (Cabell) 176

Creation (Vidal) 260

A Crime in the Neighborhood (Berne) 293

Crimes of the Heart (Henley) 258

A Critical Fable (Lowell) 182

The Crossing (McCarthy) 282

Crossing the Water (Plath) 248

The Crow and the Heart (Carruth) 230

The Crucible (Miller) 222

The Cruise of the Snark (London) 169

The Crying of Lot 49 (Pynchon) 241

A Curtain of Green (Welty) 208

The Custom of the Country (Wharton) 172

A Cycle of the West (Neihardt) 217

Daisy Miller (James) 91, 132

Damascus Gate (Stone) 290

Dame de Pique (Boucicault) 117

The Damsel of Darien (Simms) 110

The Dancing Bears (Merwin) 223

Dandelion Wine (Bradbury) 228

Danger Memory! Two Plays (Miller) 270

The Dangerous Summer (Hemingway) 265

The Dangling Man (Bellow) 211

The Daring Young Man on the Flying Trapeze (Saroyan) 198

The Dark at the Top of the Stairs (Inge) 228

Dark Fields of the Republic (Rich) 284

Daughter Mine (Gold) 295

David Harum: A Story of American Life (Westcott) 148

A Day Book (Creeley) 250

Day by Day (Lowell) 256

The Day of Doom (Wigglesworth) 60

The Day of the Locust (West) 205

The Dead Father (Barthelme) 253

The Dead Lecturer (Baraka) 238

"A Deal in Wheat" (Norris) 160

The Dean's December (Bellow) 261

Death, Sleep and the Traveler (Hawkes) 252

Death Comes to the Archbishop (Cather) 189

Death in the Afternoon (Hemingway) 153, 196

English
American *(continued)*

A Death in the Family (Agee) 228

Death Is a Lonely Business (Bradbury) 265

"The Death of a Hired Man" (Frost) 173

Death of a Salesman (Miller) 217

Deception (Roth) 273

The Deer Park (Mailer) 225

The Deerslayer (Cooper) 111

A Delicate Balance (Albee) 241

Delta Wedding (Welty) 211, 213

Democracy (Didion) 264

Democratic Vistas (Whitman) 128

Departures (Justice) 251

Desert Meditations (Abbey) 244

Desert of the Heart (Rule) 238

Desire Under the Elms (O'Neill) 153, 185

Desire's Baby (Chopin) 147

The Destinies of Darcy Dancer, Gentleman (Donleavy) 256

Detective Story (Kingsley) 217

"The Devil and Daniel Webster" (Benét) 203, 205

The Devil Finds Work (Baldwin) 254

The Devil's Dictionary (Bierce) 164

The Dharma Bums (Kerouac) 229

"The Diamond as Big as the Ritz" (Fitzgerald) 182

The Diamond Cutters and Other Poems (Rich) 225

Dinner at Eight (Kaufman) 196

The Dispossessed (Le Guin) 252

A Distant Mirror: The Calamitous Fourteenth Century (Tuchman) 257

A Distant Trumpet (Horgan) 232

Division Street (Tesich) 259

Do with Me What You Will (Oates) 251

Dodsworth (Lewis) 192

The Dogs Bar: Public People and Private Place (Capote) 251

The Dolphin (Lowell) 251

A Dome of Many-Colored Glass (Lowell) 171

Don Juan in the Village (DeLynn) 273

The Door into Summer (Heinlein) 228

Double Indemnity (Cain) 201

Double Star (Heinlein) 226

Dr. Breen's Practice (Howells) 134

"Dr. Heidegger's Experiment" (Hawthorne) 109

A Draft of XXX Cantos (Pound) 197

"The Dragon and the Unicorn" (Rexroth) 221

Dragon Seed (Buck) 209

Dragon's Teeth (Sinclair) 209

A Dream of Mind (Williams) 277

The Dream of the Unified Field (Graham) 286

The Dream Songs (Berryman) 245

Dream Variation (Hughes) 188

Dreamer (Johnson) 290

Dred: A Tale of the Great Dismal Swamp (Stowe) 119

Driving Miss Daisy (Uhry) 269

The Drowning Season (Hoffman) 258

Drowning with Others (Dickey) 235

Drums at Dusk (Bontemps) 205

"Drum-Taps" (Whitman) 124

Duluth (Vidal) 262

Dune (Herbert) 240

Duplications (Koch) 256

Dust Tracks on a Road (Hurston) 209

The Dust Which Is God (Benét) 208

Dutch Shea, Jr. (Dunne) 261

Dutchman (Baraka) 238

Early Autumn (Bromfield) 188

The Earthsea Trilogy (Le Guin) 244

East of Eden (Steinbeck) 221

East of the Mountains (Guterson) 293

Echo House (Just) 288

Edgar Huntley (Brown) 88

The Education of Henry Adams (Adams) 164, 177

The Education of Hyman Kaplan (Kaplan) 203

The Effect of Gamma Rays on Man-in-the-Moon Marigolds (Zindel) 240

Effort at Speech: New and Selected Poems (Meredith) 288

Eight Men (Wright) 233

The Eighth Day (Wilder) 243

"Elegy Upon the Death of Reverend Mr. Thomas Shepard" (Oakes) 63

Eleutheria (Mather) 66

Elmer Gantry (Lewis) 189

Embracing Defeat (Williams) 295

The Emperor Jones (O'Neill) 153, 179, 181

Empress of the Splendid Season (Hijuelos) 293

The Encantadas (Melville) 118

The End of the Road (Barth) 229

The Enormous Radio and Other Stories (Cheever) 223

Entered from the Sun (Garrett) 273

Esperanza's Box of Saints (Escandón) 290

Essay on Rime (Shapiro) 212

Essays (Emerson) 111

Ethan Frome (Wharton) 169

Eureka (Poe) 115

Eutaw (Simms) 119

Evangeline, a Tale of Acadie (Longfellow) 115

Everything That Rises Must Converge (O'Connor) 240

Evidence of Love (Grau) 256

The Executioner's Song (Mailer) 258

Exodus (Uris) 229

Exterminator! (Burroughs) 250

A Fable (Faulkner) 223

Fables for Our Time (Thurber) 207

Fahrenheit 451 (Bradbury) 222

A Fairy Tale of New York (Donleavy) 251

A Faithful Narrative of the Suprising Work of God (Edwards) 75

Falconer (Cheever) 256

The Fall of a Sparrow (Hellenga) 290

"The Fall of the House of Usher" (Poe) 91, 110

Falling in Place (Beattie) 259

Fanny: Being the True History of the Adventures of Fanny Hack-about-Jones (Jong) 259

Fanshawe (Hawthorne) 105

Fantastic Voyage (Asimov) 241

The Far Field (Roethke) 238

Far Tortuga (Matthiesson) 253

Farewell, My Lovely (Chandler) 207

A Farewell to Arms (Hemingway) 153, 192

Fatal Interview (Millay) 194

The Fault of Angels (Horgan) 197

The Feast of Love (Baxter) 295

Fences (Wilson) 265

A Few Figs from Thistles (Millay) 179, 183

The Fifth Column and the First Forty-Nine Stories (Hemingway) 153, 204

Fifty-Two Pickup (Leonard) 252

Final Payments (Gordon) 257

The Financier (Dreiser) 171

The Finer Grain (James) 168

The Fire Bringer (Moody) 162

The Fire Next Time (Baldwin) 237

The Fixer (Malamud) 226, 241

Flagons and Apples (Jeffers) 171

Flesh and Blood (Williams) 269

The Floating Opera (Barth) 226

Flood (Warren) 238

Flower, Fist and Bestial Wail (Bukowski) 231

Flower Herding on Mount Monadnock (Kinnell) 238

Flowering Judas (Porter) 193

The Flowering of New England (Brooks) 201, 203

Fly Away Home (Piercy) 264

The Flying Change (Taylor) 265

Following the Equator (Twain) 147

Fool for Love (Shepard) 262

For Kings and Planets (Canin) 290

For Love: Poems, 1959–1960 (Creeley) 235

For the Union Dead (Lowell) 238

For Whom the Bell Tolls (Hemingway) 153, 207

The Forayers; or, The Raid of the Dog Days (Simms) 119

A Foregone Conclusion (Howells) 130

Foreign Affairs (Lurie) 264

The Forerunner (Gibran) 179

Fortune's Daughter (Hoffman) 265

Foundation (Asimov) 220

Foundation and Empire (Asimov) 221

The Fountainhead (Rand) 210

The Franchiser (Elkin) 254

Franny and Zooey (Salinger) 233

Freedom of the Will (Edwards) 78

The Freeing of the Dust (Levertov) 253

Friday (Heinlein) 261

A Frolic of His Own (Gaddis) 282

From Here to Eternity (Jones) 220

From Princeton One Afternoon: Collected Poems, 1950–1986 (Weiss) 269

From the Terrace (O'Hara) 229

The Front Page (MacArthur) 190

"The Furnished Room" (Henry) 164

A Further Range (Frost) 201

Galapagos (Vonnegut) 265

Garbage (Ammons) 279

A Garden of Earthly Delights (Oates) 243

The Garden of Eden (Hemingway) 267

Gardens in the Dunes (Silko) 293

Gather Together in My Name (Angelou) 252

General William Booth Enters into Heaven and Other Poems (Lindsay) 172

Generation Without Farewell (Boyle) 232

The Genius (Dreiser) 174

Gentleman's Agreement (Hobson) 215

Geography III (Bishop) 254

George Mills (Elkin) 261

Gertrude and Claudius (Updike) 295

The Ghost Writer (Roth) 258

Ghosts (Auster) 269
Giant (Gerber) 221
The Giant's House (Mc-
Cracken) 286
Giants in the Earth (Rolvaag)
189
The Gift (Nabokov) 203
"The Gift of the Magi"
(Henry) 163
Giles Goat-Boy (Barth) 241
The Gin Game (Coburn) 254
The Ginger Man (Donleavy)
225
Giovanni's Room (Baldwain)
226
Girls (Busch) 288
The Glass Menagerie
(Williams) 211, 212
Glengarry Glen Ross (Mamet)
264
Go Down, Moses (Faulkner)
209
Go Tell It on the Mountain
(Baldwin) 222
God Bless You, Mr. Rosewater
(Vonnegut) 240
The God That Failed (Wright)
219
God's Grace (Malamud) 261
God's Little Acre (Caldwell)
197
God's Snake (Spanidou) 267
God's Trombones (Johnson)
189
"The Gold Bug" (Poe) 91,
113
The Golden Apples (Welty)
217
The Golden Bowl (James) 91,
162
Golden Boy (Odets) 203
Gone With the Wind
(Mitchell) 201
The Good Earth (Buck) 194
Good Evening Mr. and Mrs.
America and All the Ships at
Sea (Bausch) 286
A Good Man Is Hard to Find
(O'Connor) 225
A Good Scent from a Strange
Mountain (Butler) 279
A Good Woman (Bromfield)
189
Goodbye, Columbus (Roth)
231
Gorilla, My Love (Bambara)
250
Gospel (Barnhardt) 279
A Grammar of Motives (Lit-
tle) 212
The Grand Design (Dos Pas-
sos) 217
The Grapes of Wrath (Stein-
beck) 205
The Grass Harp (Capote) 220
Graustark (McCutcheon)
159
Gravity's Rainbow (Pynchon)
250
The Great American Novel
(Roth) 250
The Great Gatsby (Fitzgerald)
186
The Great God Brown
(O'Neill) 153, 188

The Great Meadow (Roberts)
193
The Great Railway Bazaar
(Theroux) 253
The Great Train Robbery
(Crichton) 253
The Green Bay Tree (Brom-
field) 185
Green Hills of Africa (Hem-
ingway) 153, 200
The Green Hills of Earth
(Heinlein) 220
Green Mansions (Hudson)
162
Grendel (Gardner) 250
Ground Work (Duncan) 264
Ground Work III: In the Dark
(Duncan) 269
The Group (McCarthy) 237
The Groves of Academe (Mc-
Carthy) 221
Growing Up (Baker) 261
Guard of Honor (Cozzens)
216
Guide to Kulchur (Pound) 204
The Guns of August (Tuch-
man) 235
Guy Rivers (Simms) 108
Guys and Dolls (Runyan) 196
H. M. Pulham, Esq. (Mar-
quand) 208
The Hairy Ape (O'Neill) 153,
182
The Hamlet (Faulkner) 207
Hans Brinker; or, The Silver
Skates (Dodge) 124
The Hard Blue Sky (Grau)
229
The Harder They Fall (Schul-
berg) 215
Harlem (Hughes) 220
Harlot's Ghost (Mailer) 275
Harmonium (Stevens) 184
Harvey (Chase) 211
Hawaii (Michener) 231
A Hazard of New Fortunes
(Howells) 141
The Headman; or, The Abbaye
des Vignerons (Cooper)
107
Healing Song for the Inner Ear
(Harper) 265
The Heart Is a Lonely Hunter
(McCullers) 207
The Heart of a Woman (An-
gelou) 260
Heart of Aztlan (Anaya) 254
The Heart's Needle (Snod-
grass) 231, 232
The Heartsong of Charging Elk
(Welch) 295
Heat and Other Stories
(Oates) 276
Heaven and Earth (Gold-
barth) 277
The Heidenmauer; or, The
Benedictines (Cooper) 107
The Heidi Chronicles
(Wasserstein) 270
Helen Halsey; or, The Swamp
State of Conelachita
(Simms) 114
Hello: A Journal (Creeley) 257
Hello, Darkness: The Collected
Poems of L. E. Sussman
(Sussman) 257

Helmets (Dickey) 238
Hence (Leithauser) 272
Henderson the Rain King
(Bellow) 231
Her Son's Wife (Fisher) 188
The Here and Now (Cohen)
286
Here and Now (Levertov)
228
A Hero Ain't Nothing but a
Sandwich (Childress) 250
The Hero with a Thousand
Faces (Campbell) 217
Herzog (Bellow) 238
"Hills Like White Elephants"
(Hemingway) 153, 189
A History of New York (Irv-
ing) 98
Holiday (Barry) 190
"Homage to Mistress Brad-
street" (Berryman) 216
Homage to Mistress Bradstreet
(Berryman) 226
"Homage to Sextus Proper-
tius" (Pound) 155
Homage to Sextus Propertius
(Pound) 178
Hombre (Leonard) 233
Home as Found (Cooper)
110
Home Ballads and Other
Poems (Whittier) 121
Home to Harlem (McKay)
190
The Hoosier Schoolmaster
(Eggleston) 128
Horseman, Pass By (Mc-
Murtry) 234
Horses Make a Landscape
Look More Beautiful
(Walker) 264
The Hotel New Hampshire
(Irving) 260
The Hours (Cunningham)
293
House Made of Dawn (Mo-
maday) 244
The House of Blue Leaves
(Guare) 248
The House of Earth (Buck)
200
The House of Five Talents
(Auchincloss) 232
House of Incest (Nin) 201
The House of Intellect
(Barzun) 231
The House of Mirth (Whar-
ton) 163
The House of the Seven Gables
(Hawthorne) 117
The House on Coliseum Street
(Grau) 234
How German Is It? (Abish)
259
How to Save Your Life (Jong)
256
Howl, and Other Poems
(Ginsberg) 226
Huckleberry Finn (Twain) 92,
136
Hugh Selwyn Mauberley
(Pound) 155, 179
The Human Comedy
(Saroyan) 210
The Human Stain (Roth) 295
Humboldt's Gift (Bellow) 253

Hungerfield and Other Poems
(Jeffers) 223
Hyperion (Longfellow) 110
I, the Jury (Spillane) 215
I Know Why the Caged Bird
Sings (Angelou) 247
I Ought to Be In Pictures
(Simon) 259
"I Sing the Body Electric"
(Whitman) 119
I Will Fear No Evil (Heinlein)
247
The Iceman Cometh (O'Neill)
153, 213
The Idea of Order at Key West
(Stevens) 200
The Ides of March (Wilder)
216
Idiots First (Malamud) 237
If Beale Street Could Talk
(Baldwin) 252
If He Hollers, Let Him Go
(Himes) 212
If the River Was Whiskey
(Boyle) 272
Illumination Night (Hoff-
man) 269
The Illustrated Man (Brad-
bury) 220
Imitations (Lowell) 234
In Another Country (Baldwin)
235
In Cold Blood (Capote) 241
In Defense of Reason (Win-
ters) 215
In Dubious Battle (Steinbeck)
201
In Love and Trouble (Walker)
250
In the Absence of Angels (Cal-
isher) 220
In the American Grain
(Williams) 186
In the Clearing (Frost) 235
In the Harbor (Longfellow)
135
In the Mecca (Brooks) 244
In the Name of Salomé (Al-
varez) 295
In the Zone (O'Neill) 153
In Time Like Air (Sarton) 229
In Wartime and Other Poems
(Whittier) 124
Incident at Vichy (Miller) 240
Incidents in the Life of a Slave
Girl Written by Herself (Ja-
cobs) 122
Independence Day (Ford) 284
Indian Summer (Howells) 137
The Innocents Abroad
(Twain) 92, 127
Intruder in the Dust
(Faulkner) 216
Invisible Man (Ellison) 221
Invitation to a Beheading
(Nabokov) 204
The Iron Heel (London) 165,
166
Iron John: A Book About Men
(Bly) 273
Ironweed (Kennedy) 262
Islands in the Stream (Hem-
ingway) 247
Israel Potter: His Fifty-five
Years of Exile (Melville)
119

English
  American (continued)
    It Can't Happen Here (Lewis) 200
    Jack Tier (Cooper) 115
    Jacklight (Erdrich) 264
    "The Jackpot" (Jackson) 216
    Jailbird (Vonnegut) 258
    Jane Talbot (Brown) 95
    Java Head (Hergesheimer) 178
    Jazz (Morrison) 277
    J.B. (MacLeish) 229
    Jennie Gerhardt (Dreiser) 169
    Jeremy's Vision (Purdy) 247
    Jersey Rain (Pinsky) 295
    Jesus Saves (Steinke) 288
    Joan of Lorraine (Anderson) 215
    Joe (Brown) 276
    Joe Hill (Stegner) 219
    Joe Turner's Come and Gone (Wilson) 267
    John Brown's Body (Benét) 190
    John Dollar (Wiggins) 272
    Journey (Michener) 272
    The Journey, and Other Poems (Winters) 194
    The Joy Luck Club (Tan) 272
    Judgment Day (Farrell) 200
    Julian (Vidal) 238
    Juneteenth (Ellison) 293
    The Jungle (Sinclair) 164
    Jurgen (Cabell) 178
    The Just and the Unjust (Cozzens) 209
    Just Looking: Essays on Art (Updike) 272
    Kaddish and Other Poems (Ginsberg) 234
    Kadisz (Grynberg) 269
    Kate Vaiden (Price) 267
    Katherine Walton (Simms) 117
    Kavanagh (Longfellow) 116
    The Keepers of the House (Grau) 238
    Key Largo (Anderson) 205
    Killer Angels (Shaara) 252
    The Killing Man (Spillane) 272
    The King of Babylon Shall Not Come Against You (Garrett) 286
    Ko; or, A Season on Earth (Koch) 231
    Kwaiden (Hearn) 162
    The Lady of the Aroostook (Howells) 132
    The Lady or the Tiger? (Stockton) 136
    Lake Wobegon Days (Keillor) 265
    Laments for the Living (Parker) 193
    The Land of Little Rain (Austin) 161
    The Land of Silence (Sarton) 222
    The Landlord at Lion's Head (Howells) 147
    Language and Silence: Essays on Language, Literature and the Inhuman (Steiner) 243
    The Last Adam (Cozzens) 197

    The Last Days of Louisiana Red (Reed) 252
    Last Exit to Brooklyn (Selby) 238
    The Last Hotel for Women (Covington) 286
    The Last Hurrah (O'Connor) 226
    "The Last Leaf" (Henry) 165
    The Last of the Mohicans (Cooper) 104
    The Last of the Red Hot Lovers (Simon) 245
    The Last Picture Show (McMurtry) 248
    The Last Puritan (Santayana) 200
    The Last Thing He Wanted (Didion) 286
    The Last Tycoon (Fitzgerald) 208
    The Late George Apley (Marquand) 203
    Later the Same Day (Paley) 265
    Lays of My Home and Other Poems (Whittier) 113
    The Leaning Tower (Porter) 211
    Leaves of Grass (Whitman) 119
    Leaving Cheyenne (McMurtry) 237
    The Left Hand of Darkness (Le Guin) 245
    The Legend of La Llorona (Anaya) 264
    "The Legend of Sleepy Hollow" (Irving) 101
    The Legend of Svein and Maria (Hauge) 244
    Legends of New England in Prose and Verse (Whittier) 106
    Legends of the Fall (Harrison) 258
    Less Than One: Selected Essays (Brodsky) 267
    A Lesson Before Dying (Gaines) 279
    Let It Come Down (Bowles) 221
    Let Us Now Praise Famous Men (Agee) 208
    Libra (DeLillo) 270
    Licks of Love (Updike) 295
    Lie Down in Darkness (Styron) 220
    A Life in the Theater (Mamet) 256
    The Life of Reason (Santayana) 163
    Life on the Mississippi (Twain) 92, 135
    Life Studies (Lowell) 231
    Life Supports: New and Collected Poems (Bronk) 261
    Life with Father (Day) 200
    "Ligeia" (Poe) 91, 110
    The Light Around the Body (Bly) 244
    Light in August (Faulkner) 196
    The Light Possessed (Cheuse) 273
    Like Most Revelations (Howard) 282

    Lime Twig (Hawkes) 234
    The Lincoln Relics (Kunitz) 257
    The Lion and the Throne (Bowen) 226
    The Little Foxes (Hellman) 205
    Little Friend, Little Friend (Jarrell) 212
    Little House on the Prairie (Wilder) 200
    Little Men (Alcott) 128
    "Little Orphan Annie" (Riley) 135
    Little Women (Alcott) 126
    Live or Die (Sexton) 241
    Lives of the Poets (Untermeyer) 232
    The Living End (Elkin) 258
    Living Wills (Macdonald) 276
    The Locked Room (Auster) 269
    Lolita (Nabokov) 155, 225
    Lonesome Dove (McMurtry) 265
    Long Day's Journey into Night (O'Neill) 153, 226
    Long Live Man (Corso) 235
    The Long Voyage Home (O'Neill) 153
    Lonsome Dove (McMurtry) 273
    Look Homeward, Angel (Wolfe) 192
    Looking Backward (Bellamy) 139
    Looking for Mr. Goodbar (Rossner) 253
    A Looking-Glass for the Times (Folger) 62
    Loon Lake (Doctorow) 259
    Lord Weary's Castle (Lowell) 213
    Losing Battles (Welty) 247
    Lost Horizon (Hilton) 197
    Lost in the Funhouse (Barth) 244
    A Lost Lady (Cather) 184
    Lost Man's River (Matthiessen) 288
    The Lost Son, and Other Poems (Roethke) 216
    The Lost World: New Poems (Jarrell) 240
    Love, Action, Laughter and Other Sad Tales (Schulberg) 272
    Love and Death in the American Novel (Fiedler) 232
    Love in the Ruins (Percy) 248
    The Love Nest and Other Stories (Lardner) 188
    Love Poems (Sexton) 246
    Loving Hands at Home (Johnson) 244
    Lucidities (Jennings) 247
    "The Luck of the Roaring Camp" (Harte) 126
    Lustra (Pound) 175
    Lying Low (Johnson) 257
    Lyrics of Lowly Life (Dunbar) 146
    Ma Rainey's Black Bottom (Wilson) 264
    The Madman (Gibran) 177

    Maggie: A Girl of the Streets (Crane) 143
    The Magic Barrel (Malamud) 229
    The Magic Kingdom (Elkin) 265
    Magnalia Christi Americana (Mather) 70
    The Magnificent Ambersons (Tarkington) 177
    Main Currents in American Thought (Parrington) 189, 190
    Main Street (Lewis) 179
    The Main Traveled Roads (Garland) 142
    The Maine Woods (Thoreau) 124
    The Making of Americans (Stein) 169
    Malcolm (Purdy) 231
    The Maltese Falcon (Hammett) 193
    The Mambo Kings Play Songs of Love (Hijuelos) 273
    The Man Against the Sky (Robinson) 175
    Man Crazy (Oates) 288
    A Man in Full (Wolfe) 290
    The Man That Corrupted Hadleyburg (Twain) 92, 149
    The Man Who Came to Dinner (Hart, Kaufman) 205
    The Man Who Died Twice (Robinson) 185
    The Man Who Had All the Luck (Miller) 211
    The Man with the Blue Guitar (Stevens) 203
    The Man with the Golden Arm (Algren) 217
    The Man with the Hoe and Other Poems (Markham) 149
    Manhattan Transfer (Dos Passos) 186
    The Mansion (Faulkner) 231
    Many Thousands Gone (Bishop) 194
    Many Waters (L'Engle) 267
    Mao II (DeLillo) 276
    The Marble Faun (Hawthorne) 121
    Mardi (Melville) 116
    Marjorie Morningstar (Wouk) 225
    The Married Man (White) 295
    Marry Me: A Romance (Updike) 254
    The Martian Chronicles (Bradbury) 219
    Martin Dressler (Millhauser) 288
    Martin Eden (London) 167
    Martin Faber (Simms) 107
    Marty (Chayefsky) 222
    Marya: A Life (Oates) 267
    Mason & Dixon (Pynchon) 288
    "The Masque of the Red Death" (Poe) 91, 112
    The Matchmaker (Wilder) 223, 225
    Mating (Rush) 276

McTeague (Norris) 149

Meditations Divine and Moral (Bradstreet) 60

"The Mediterranean" (Tate) 196

The Medusa and the Snail (Thomas) 260

Meet Me in the Green Glen (Warren) 248

Mellichampe, a Legend of the Santee (Simms) 109

Melville Godwin U.S.A. (Marquand) 220

The Member of the Wedding (McCullers) 213

Memoirs of a Catholic Childhood (McCarthy) 228

Memoirs of Hecate County (Wilson) 213

The Memory of Old Jack (Berry) 252

Men Without Women (Hemingway) 153, 189

"Mending Wall" (Frost) 173

Mercedes of Castile (Cooper) 111

Mercy of a Rude Stream (Roth) 282

Meridian (Walker) 254

Merlin (Robinson) 176

Messiah (Vidal) 223

The Messiah of Stockholm (Ozick) 269

Meteor (Behrman) 192

Methuselah's Children (Heinlein) 229

Mexico City Blues (Kerouac) 231

Miami and the Seige of Chicago (Mailer) 244

Midcentury (Dos Passos) 234

The Middle Man and Other Stories (Mukherjee) 270

Middle Passage (Johnson) 273

Midnight Mass (Bowles) 260

Midnight Salvage (Rich) 293

Mila 18 (Uris) 234

Mildred Pierce (Cain) 208

Miles Wallingford (Cooper) 113

Milk for Babies, Drawn Out of the Breasts of Both Testaments (Cotton) 57

The Minister's Charge; or, The Apprenticeship of Lemuel Barker (Howells) 138

"Miniver Cheevy" (Robinson) 168

The Mirror and the Lamp: Romantic Theory and Critical Tradition (Abrams) 222

The Misfits (Miller) 234

"Miss Kilmansegg and Her Precious Leg, a Golden Legend" (Hood) 112

Miss Lonelyhearts (West) 197

M'liss (Harte) 121

Moby-Dick; or, The Whale (Melville) 117

A Modern Instance (Howells) 135

Modus Vivendi (Levinson) 264

Mogg Megone (Whittier) 109

Moll Pitcher (Whittier) 106

The Monikens (Cooper) 108

The Monk and the Hangman's Daughter (Bierce) 143

The Monkey Wrench Gang (Abbey) 253

Montage of a Dream Deferred (Hughes) 220

A Month of Sundays (Updike) 253

Mont-Saint-Michel and Chartres (Adams) 172

Moon Deluxe (Barthelme) 262

A Moon for the Misbegotten (O'Neill) 153, 210, 221

The Moon Is a Harsh Mistress (Heinlein) 241

The Moon Is Down (Steinbeck) 209

More Die of Heartbreak (Bellow) 269

More Shapes Than One (Chapell) 276

More Stately Mansions (O'Neill) 238

Mosby's Memoirs and Other Stories (Bellow) 244

Mosses from an Old Manse (Hawthorne) 114

Mother Night (Vonnegut) 234

The Mother of Us All (Stein) 215

Motherkind (Phillips) 295

Le Mouchoir (Cooper) 113

Mountain Interval (Frost) 175

Mountain Standard Time (Horgan) 235

Mountains and Rivers Without End (Snyder) 286

Mourning Becomes Electra (O'Neill) 153, 194

A Moveable Feast (Hemingway) 153, 238

The Moviegoer (Percy) 234

The Moving Target (Merwin) 237

"Mr. Flood's Party" (Robinson) 181

Mr. Sammler's Planet (Bellow) 247

Mrs. Stevens Hears the Mermaids Singing (Sarton) 240

Mrs. Ted Bliss (Elkin) 284

"A MS. Found a Bottle" (Poe) 91, 107

Mule Bone (Hurston) 194

Mulligan Stew (Sorrentino) 258

"The Murders in the Rue Morgue" (Poe) 91, 111

Museums and Women and Other Stories (Updike) 250

Music for Chameleons: New Writings (Capote) 259

Mutiny on the Bounty (Nordhoff) 196

My Alexandria (Doty) 279

My Antonia (Cather) 177

My Kinsman, Major Molineaux (Hawthorne) 107

My Life and Hard Times (Thurber) 197

My Life as a Man (Roth) 252

My Name Is Aram (Saroyan) 207

My Ten Years in a Quandary and How They Grew (Benchley) 201

Myra Breckinridge (Vidal) 244

Mystery (Hauge) 243

The Naked and the Dead (Mailer) 216

The Naked Lunch (Burroughs) 231

The Narrative of Arthur Gordon Pym, of Nantucket (Poe) 110

Native Son (Wright) 207

The Natural (Malamud) 221

Nature (Emerson) 109

Near the Ocean (Lowell) 243

The Need to Hold Still (Muller) 260

The Negro Speaks of Rivers (Hughes) 181

Nemesis (Asimov) 272

Neon Vernacular (Komunyakaa) 282

The Neon Wilderness (Algren) 215

The Nephew (Purdy) 232

New and Collected Poems (MacLeish) 254

New and Collected Poems (Wilbur) 270

New and Selected Poems (Meredith) 269

New and Selected Poems (Oliver) 277

New and Selected Poems (Warren) 265

New and Selected Poems, 1940–1986 (Shapiro) 269

The New Criticism (Ransom) 208

New Hampshire (Frost) 184, 185

The New York Trilogy (Auster) 269

The New Yorkers (Calisher) 246

Next: Two Poems (Clifton) 269

'Night, Mother (Norman) 261

A Night in Acadie (Chopin) 147

Night Light (Justice) 243

The Night of the Iguana (Williams) 234

Night Rider (Warren) 205

Nightwood (Barnes) 201

Nine Stories (Salinger) 222

No, But I Saw the Movie (De Vries) 221

No One Knows the Day (Hauge) 225

Nobody Knows My Name (Baldwin) 234

Noon Wine (Porter) 203

North and South (Bishop) 213

North of Boston (Frost) 173

Northwest Passage (Roberts) 203

Notebook, 1967–1968 (Lowell) 246

Notes of a Native Son (Baldwin) 225

Nova Express (Burroughs) 238

Nowhere Else on Earth (Humphreys) 295

The Number of the Beast (Heinlein) 259

Number One (Dos Passos) 210

"O Captain! My Captain!" (Whitman) 124

O Pioneers! (Cather) 172

The Oak Openings; or, The Bee Hunter (Cooper) 115

The Oasis (McCarthy) 217

Observations (Moore) 185

"An Occurrence at Owl Creek Bridge" (Bierce) 142

October Light (Gardner) 254

The Octopus (Norris) 159

The Octoroon; or, Life in Louisiana (Boucicault) 121

The Odd Couple (Simon) 240

"Ode to the Confederate Dead" (Tate) 188, 201

Of a Fire on the Moon (Mailer) 247

Of Mice and Men (Steinbeck) 203

Of Time and the River (Wolfe) 194, 200

Oh What a Paradise It Seems (Cheever) 261

Oil! (Sinclair) 189

"The Old Forest" (Taylor) 265

The Old Forest (Taylor) 267

"Old Ironsides" (Holmes) 106

The Old Man and the Sea (Hemingway) 153, 221

The Old Patagonian Express: By Train Through the Americas (Theroux) 258

Old Soldier (Bourjaily) 273

Omoo, a Narrative of Adventures on the South Seas (Melville) 115

On Native Grounds (Kazin) 209

On the Farm (Updike) 240

On the Road (Kerouac) 228

On Trial (Rice) 173

One Dark Body (Sherman) 279

The One Day (Hall) 270

One Flew Over the Cuckoo's Nest (Kesey) 235

One of Ours (Cather) 182

One Writer's Beginnings (Welty) 265

The Onion Eaters (Donleavy) 241

"The Open Boat" (Crane) 148

Operation Shylock (Roth) 279

The Opposing Self (Trilling) 225

The Optimist's Daughter (Welty) 250

Or Else: Poem (Warren) 253

Ormond (Brown) 88

Orphic Sayings (Alcott) 111

Oswald's Tale (Mailer) 284

Other Voices, Other Rooms (Capote) 216

Our Gang (Roth) 248

Our Ground Time Here WIll Be Brief (Kumin) 261

English
  American (continued)
    Our Old Home (Hawthorne)
      123
    Our Town (Wilder) 204
    "Out of the Cradle Endlessly
      Rocking" (Whitman) 121
    "The Outcasts of Poker Flat"
      (Harte) 127
    Outerbridge Reach (Stone) 277
    The Outmost Dream
      (Maxwell) 272
    The Outsider (Wright) 222
    The Ox-Bow Incident (Clark)
      207
    Paco's Story (Heinemann)
      269
    The Painted Bird (Kosinski)
      240
    Pale Fire (Nabokov) 155, 235
    Pale Horse, Pale Rider
      (Porter) 205
    Palimpsest (Vidal) 284
    The Panorama and Other
      Poems (Whittier) 119
    The Panther and the Lash:
      Poems of Our Times
      (Hughes) 243
    Paradise (Morrison) 290
    Paris Bound (Barry) 189
    The Partisan (Simms) 108
    Passage to India (Whitman)
      128
    Passing Through: Later Poems,
      New and Selected (Kunitz)
      284
    The Passion Artist (Hawkes)
      258
    Passion Flowers (Howe) 118
    The Passion of Joseph D.
      (Chayefsky) 238
    Passport to the War (Kunitz)
      211
    Paterson (Williams) 213
    The Pathfinder (Cooper) 111
    Patriotic Gore (Wilson) 235
    "Paul Revere's Ride" (Long-
      fellow) 123
    "Paul's Short Case" (Cather)
      163
    Peace Breaks Out (Knowles)
      259
    Peder Victorious (Rolvaag)
      190
    The Pennsylvania Pilgrim and
      Other Poems (Whittier)
      128
    Penrod (Tarkington) 173
    The People, Yes (Sandburg)
      201
    The People and Uncollected
      Stories (Malamud) 272
    The People of the Abyss (Lon-
      don) 161
    Personae (Pound) 155, 167
    The Personal Recollections of
      Joan of Arc (Twain) 146
    The Petrified Forest (Sher-
      wood) 200
    Philadelphia Fire (Wideman)
      273
    The Philadelphia Story
      (Barry) 205
    The Piano Lesson (Wilson)
      269
    The Piazza (Melville) 120

    Picnic (Inge) 222
    Pictures from Breughel
      (Williams) 235
    Pictures of Fidelman (Mala-
      mud) 246
    Pieces (Creely) 246
    Pierre; or, The Ambiguities
      (Melville) 117
    Pigeon Feathers (Updike) 235
    Pigs in Heaven (Kingsolver)
      279
    Pilgrim at Tinker Creek (Dil-
      lard) 252
    Pillars of Hercules: A Grand
      Tour of the Mediterranean
      (Theroux) 284
    The Pilot (Cooper) 103
    The Pioneers; or, The Sources
      of the Susquehanna Frontier
      (Cooper) 103
    Pippa Passes (Browning) 112
    The Pisan Cantos (Pound)
      155, 216
    The Pistol (Jones) 229
    "The Pit and the Pendulum"
      (Poe) 91, 113
    A Place to Come To (Warren)
      256
    Plains Song (Morris) 260
    Plainsong (Haruf) 293
    Play It as It Lays (Didion)
      247
    Player Piano (Vonnegut) 221
    Plays for Bleecker Street
      (Wilder) 235
    Plaza Suite (Simon) 244
    Plum and Jaggers (Shreve)
      295
    Pnin (Nabokov) 155, 228
    Poems (Bradstreet) 63
    Poems (Bryant) 102
    Poems (Dickinson) 141
    Poems (Freneau) 85
    Poems (Holmes) 109
    Poems (Key) 120
    Poems (Lowell) 113
    Poems (Moore) 181
    Poems (Poe) 106
    Poems (Whittier) 116
    Poems, 1924–1933
      (MacLeish) 197
    Poems, 1940–1953 (Shapiro)
      222
    Poems: North and South—A
      Cold Spring (Bishop) 225,
      226
    Poems of a Jew (Shapiro) 229
    Poems of Stanley Kunitz (Ku-
      nitz) 258
    Poems on Slavery (Longfel-
      low) 112
    Point of No Return (Mar-
      quand) 217
    Politian, A Tragedy (Poe) 108
    The Ponder Heart (Welty)
      223
    The Poor of New York (Bouci-
      cault) 120
    Poor Richard's Almanack
      (Franklin) 75
    The Poorhouse Fair (Updike)
      231
    Poppa John (Woiwode) 260
    Porgy (Heyward) 186
    Portnoy's Complaint (Roth)
      246

    Portrait in Brownstone (Auch-
      incloss) 235
    The Portrait of a Lady (James)
      91, 134
    Possessing the Secret of Joy
      (Walker) 277
    Possession (Bromfield) 186
    Postcards (Proulx) 279
    The Postman Always Rings
      Twice (Cain) 198
    Powers of Congress (Fulton)
      273
    The Prairie (Cooper) 105
    Praise to the End! (Roethke)
      220
    Praisesong for the Widow
      (Marshall) 262
    A Prayer for Owen Meany
      (Irving) 272
    Precaution (Cooper) 102
    "The Premature Burial"
      (Poe) 91, 113
    The Price (Miller) 244
    Pricksongs and Descants
      (Coover) 246
    The Prince and the Pauper
      (Twain) 92, 134
    The Prince of Tides (Conroy)
      269
    The Princess Cassmassima
      (James) 91, 137
    The Prisoner of Second Avenue
      (Simon) 248
    A Private Mythology (Sarton)
      241
    The Professor of Desire (Roth)
      256
    The Professor's House
      (Cather) 186
    The Progress of Love (Munro)
      267
    The Promised Land (Antin)
      171
    Promises: Poems, 1954–1956
      (Warren) 228
    The Proof (Winters) 193
    The Prophet (Gibran) 184
    The Public Burning (Coover)
      256
    Public Speech: Poems
      (MacLeish) 201
    "The Purloined Letter" (Poe)
      114
    The Puttermesser Papers
      (Ozick) 288
    Pylon (Faulkner) 200
    "Q.E.D." (Stein) 161
    "The Quaker Graveyard in
      Nantucket" (Lowell) 213
    Quia Pauper Amavi (Pound)
      155
    Rabbit, Run (Updike) 232
    Rabbit at Rest (Updike) 273
    Rabbit Is Rich (Updike) 260
    A Rage to Live (O'Hara) 217
    Ragged Dick (Alger) 126
    Ragtime (Doctorow) 253
    Raise High the Roof Beam,
      Carpenters/Seymour: An In-
      troduction (Salinger) 237
    A Raisin in the Sun (Hans-
      berry) 231
    Ramona (Jackson) 136
    Random Harvest (Hilton) 208
    "The Ransom of Red Chief"
      (Henry) 168

    "Rappaccini's Daughter"
      (Hawthorne) 113
    Rare and Endangered Species
      (Bausch) 282
    Ratner's Star (DeLillo) 254
    "The Raven" (Poe) 91
    The Raven and Other Poems
      (Poe) 114
    Reader's Block (Markson) 286
    The Real Life of Sebastian
      Knight (Nabokov) 155, 208
    The Recognition (Gaddis) 225
    The Rector of Justin (Auchin-
      closs) 238
    The Red, White and Blue
      (Dunne) 269
    The Red Badge of Courage
      (Crane) 145
    The Red Pony (Steinbeck)
      203
    The Red Rover (Cooper) 105
    Redburn (Melville) 116
    The Redskins (Cooper) 114
    Reflections in a Golden Eye
      (McCullers) 208
    The Reivers (Faulkner) 235
    Remembrance Rock (Sand-
      burg) 216
    Renascence and Other Poems
      (Millay) 176
    Requiem for a Nun (Faulkner)
      220
    Rescue the Dead (Ignatov)
      244
    The Residual Years: Poems
      1934–1948 (Everson) 244
    The Retrieval System (Kumin)
      257
    A Rhetoric of Motives (Burke)
      219
    Rhymes to Be Traded for
      Bread (Lindsay) 171
    Richard Carvel (Churchill)
      149
    Richard Cory (Robinson) 147
    Richard Hardis; or, The
      Avenger of Blood (Simms)
      110
    Rider (Rudman) 282
    Riders of the Purple Sage
      (Grey) 171
    The Rights of Man (Paine) 86
    The Rise and Fall of the Third
      Reich (Shirer) 232
    The Rise of Silas Lapham
      (Howells) 137
    The Rise of the Dutch Republic
      (Motley) 119
    Riven Rock (Boyle) 290
    The Road Home (Harrison)
      290
    "The Road Not Taken"
      (Frost) 174
    Roadwalker (Grau) 282
    Roan Stallion, Tamar and
      Other Poems (Jeffers) 186
    The Robber Bridegroom
      (Welty) 209
    Roderick Hudson (James) 91,
      130
    "Roger Malvin's Burial"
      (Hawthorne) 107
    Roger's Version (Updike) 267
    The Romany (Borrow) 120
    Rootabaga Stories (Sandburg)
      182

Roots: The Saga of an American Family (Haley) 254

The Rose Tattoo (Williams) 220

The Rosy Crucifixion: Nexus (Miller) 232

Roughing It (Twain) 92, 128

Rum Punch (Leonard) 277

Rummies (Benchley) 272

The Runaway Soul (Brodkey) 276

Rushes (Rechy) 258

Sabbaths (Berry) 269

Sabbath's Theater (Roth) 284

The Saddest Summer of Samuel S. (Donleavy) 241

Salmagundi, or The Whim-Whams and Opinions of Launcelot Langstaff, Esq., and Others (Irving) 97

Samuel Johnson (Bate) 257

Sanctuary (Faulkner) 194

The Sandbox (Albee) 231

"Santa Filomena" (Longfellow) 120

Sapphira and the Slave Girl (Cather) 207

Sartosis (Faulkner) 192

Satanstoe (Cooper) 114

The Scarlet Letter (Hawthorne) 116

A Scattering of Salts (Merrill) 284

Schultz (Donleavy) 258

The Scout; or, The Black Riders of Congaree (Simms) 118

Scrambled Eggs and Whiskey: Poems, 1991–1995 (Carruth) 286

Scratch (MacLeish) 248

The Sea Lions (Cooper) 115

"The Sea of Grass" (Richter) 201

The Sea Wolf (London) 162

Seascape (Albee) 253

The Seaside and the Fireside (Longfellow) 116

Seasons of the Soul (Tate) 210

Second April (Millay) 181

The Second Coming (Percy) 259

Second Foundation (Asimov) 222

The Second Man (Behrman) 189

Second Marriage (Barthelme) 264

The Second Skin (Hawkes) 238

The Second Tree from the Corner (White) 223

Seduction of the Minotaur (Nin) 234

Seeing Through the Sun (Hogan) 265

Seize the Day (Bellow) 226

Selected Poems (Jarrell) 273

Selected Poems (Kinnell) 261

Selected Poems (Rexroth) 264

Selected Poems, 1970–1983 (Henson) 265

Self-Portrait in a Convex Mirror (Ashbery) 253

A Separate Peace (Knowles) 231, 259

Set for Life (Freeman) 276

Seven Storey Mountain (Merton) 216

The Seven-League Crutches (Jarrell) 220

Seventeen (Tarkington) 175

Shadow and Act (Ellison) 238

The Shadow Knows (Johnson) 252

Shadows on the Rock (Cather) 194

Shaker, Why Don't You Sing? (Angelou) 262

The Shawl (Ozick) 272

She Drove Without Stopping (Gordon) 273

Shelter (Phillips) 282

The Sheltering Sky (Bowles) 216

Shenandoah (Schwartz) 208

Ship Fever and Other Stories (Barrett) 286

Ship of Fools (Porter) 235

A Shooting Star (Stegner) 234

Shore Acres (Herne) 143

"The Short Happy Life of Francis Macomber" (Hemingway) 153, 201

Show Boat (Ferber) 188

The Sign in Sidney Brustein's Window (Hansberry) 238

Silent Spring (Carson) 237

The Silver Chalice (Costain) 221

The Silver Cord (Howard) 188

The Simple Truth (Levine) 282

Sincerely, Willis Wayde (Marquand) 225

Singin' and Swingin' and Gettin' Merry Like Christmas (Angelou) 255

A Singular Man (Donleavy) 237

Sinners in the Hands of an Angry God (Edwards) 76

Sirens of Titan (Vonnegut) 231

Sister Carrie (Dreiser) 158

Skating in the Dark (Kaplan) 276

The Sketch Book (Irving) 101

The Skin of Our Teeth (Wilder) 209

Skunk Hour (Lowell) 231

Slaughterhouse Five; or, The Children's Crusade (Vonnegut) 246

The Slave (Baraki) 238

Sleepers in Moon-Crowded Valleys (Purdy) 247

Sleepers Joining Hands (Bly) 250

Slouching Toward Bethlehem (Didion) 244

A Slow Fuse (Weiss) 264

Smiles on Washington Square (Federman) 265

Snapshots of a Daughter in Law: Poems, 1954–1962 (Rich) 237

Snow Falling on Cedars (Guterson) 282

The Snow Image, and Other Tales (Hawthorne) 117

Snow White (Barthelme) 243

Snow-Bound (Whittier) 125

"The Snows of Kilimanjaro" (Hemingway) 153, 204

So Big (Ferber) 185

So Long, See You Tomorrow (Maxwell) 261

Soldier's Pay (Faulkner) 188

A Soldier's Play (Fuller) 260

The Solid Gold Cadillac (Kaufman, Teichman) 222

Some Came Running (Jones) 228

Some Freaks (Mamet) 272

Someone to Watch Over Me (Bausch) 293

Something Wicked This Way Comes (Bradbury) 235

A Son of the Circus (Irving) 282

Son of the Morning (Oates) 257

The Son of the Wolf (London) 158

The Song of Hiawatha (Longfellow) 119

"Song of Myself" (Whitman) 119

Song of Solomon (Morrison) 256

Song of the Lark (Cather) 174

"Song of the Open Road" (Whitman) 119

Songs of Labor (Whittier) 116

Sophie's Choice (Styron) 258

The Sot-Weed Factor (Barth) 232

The Sound and the Fury (Faulkner) 192

The Source (Michener) 240

The Southpaw (Harris) 222

Spartina (Casey) 272

Speak, Memory (Nabokov) 155, 220

Specimen Days (Whitman) 135

The Spectator Bird (Stegner) 255

Speedboat (Adler) 255

The Spider's House (Bowles) 225

The Spirit of Romance (Pound) 168

The Spoils of Poynton (James) 91, 147

Spoon River Anthology (Masters) 174

The Sport of the Gods (Dunbar) 160

Spring and All (Williams) 184

The Spy: A Tale of the Neutral Ground (Cooper) 102

S.S. San Pedro (Cozzens) 194

Starship Troopers (Heinlein) 231

"The Star-Spangled Banner" (Key) 99

The Star-Spangled Girl (Simon) 241

Steeple Bush (Frost) 215

Steps (Kosinski) 244

Stern (Friedman) 235

Stick (Leonard) 262

Still Life (Byatt) 265

A Stillness at Appomattox (Catton) 231

The Stone Diaries (Shields) 282

"Stopping by Woods on a Snowy Evening" (Frost) 184

Stories in an Almost Classical Mode (Brodkey) 270

The Stories of John Cheever (Cheever) 257

The Stories of Vladimir Nabokov (Nabokov) 284

"The Story of a Bad Boy" (Aldrich) 127

The Story of a Staircase (Buero Vallejo) 217

Strange Interlude (O'Neill) 153, 190

Stranger in a Strange Land (Heinlein) 234

The Stranger in Lowell (Whittier) 114

A Street in Bronzeville (Brooks) 212

The Street (Petry) 213

Street Scene (Rice) 192

A Streetcar Named Desire (Williams) 215

Streets of Loredo (McMurtry) 279

Stuart Little (White) 212

Styles of Radical Will (Sontag) 246

The Subterrraneans (Kerouac) 229

Suddenly Last Summer (Williams) 229

Sula (Morrison) 250

Sumerian Vistas (Ammons) 269

Summer and Smoke (Williams) 216

A Summons to Memphis (Taylor) 267

The Sun Also Rises (Hemingway) 153, 188

Sun Under Wood (Hass) 286

Sunday in the Park with George (Sondheim, Lapine) 264

The Sundial (Jackson) 229

The Sunlight Dialogues (Gardner) 250

Sunrise (Hazard) 259

The Sunshine Boys (Simon) 250

Swag (Leonard) 255

Sweet Bird of Youth (Williams) 231

The Sweet Hereafter (Banks) 276

A Swiftly Tilting Planet (L'Engle) 257

The Swimmers and Other Selected Poems (Tate) 248

The Switch (Leonard) 257

The Sword and the Distaff (Simms) 118

Sword Blades and Poppy Seed (Lowell) 173

Tales (Poe) 114

Tales of a Traveler (Irving) 103

Tales of a Wayside Inn (Longfellow) 123

Tales of Soldiers and Civilians (Bierce) 142

English
  American *(continued)*
    *Tales of the Grotesque and
      Arabesque* (Poe) 91, 111
    Tales of the Jazz Age (Fitzger-
      ald) 182
    Tales of the South Pacific
      (Michener) 215
    Talley's Folly (Wilson) 258
    Tamar and Other Poems (Jef-
      fers) 185
    Tamerlane and Other Poems
      (Poe) 91, 105
    Tar Baby (Morrison) 260
    Tarzan of the Apes (Bur-
      roughs) 173
    Tea and Sympathy (Ander-
      son) 222
    Teahouse of the August Moon
      (Patrick) 222
    *Tell Me How Long the Train's
      Been Gone* (Baldwin) 244
    "The Tell-Tale Heart" (Poe)
      91, 113
    The Temple of My Familiar
      (Walker) 272
    *Ten Days That Shook the
      World* (Reed) 178
    Ten North Frederick (O'Hara)
      225
    The Tenants (Malamud) 249
    The Tenants of Time (Flana-
      gan) 270
    Tender Buttons (Stein) 173
    Tender Is the Night (Fitzger-
      ald) 198
    *The Tent on the Beach and
      Other Poems* (Whittier) 126
    The Tenth Man (Chayefsky)
      231
    Terms of Endearment (Mc-
      Murtry) 253
    The Terrible Threshold (Ku-
      nitz) 252
    The Terrible Twos (Reed) 261
    The Testing Tree (Kunitz) 249
    "Thanatopsis" (Bryant) 100
    The Thanatos Syndrome
      (Percy) 269
    *Their Eyes Were Watching
      God* (Hurston) 203
    Their Father's God (Rolvaag)
      194
    Their Wedding Journey (How-
      ells) 128
    Them (Oates) 246
    Theophilus North (Wilder)
      250
    There Shall Be No Night
      (Sherwood) 207
    *They Knew What They
      Wanted* (Howard) 185
    They Want Bone (Pinsky)
      273
    The Thin Man (Hammett)
      196
    The Thin Red Line (Jones)
      235
    The Things of This World
      (Wilbur) 226, 228
    *This Is Not a Letter and Other
      Poems* (Boyle) 265
    This Side of Paradise (Fitzger-
      ald) 180
    *This Time: New and Selected
      Poems* (Stern) 290

Thomas and Beulah (Dove)
  267
A Thousand Acres (Smiley)
  276
The Three Black Pennys
  (Hergesheimer) 176
Three Soldiers (Dos Passos)
  181
Three Tall Women (Albee)
  282
*Thurso's Landing and Other
  Poems* (Jeffers) 196
The Tiger in the Grass (Doerr)
  284
Tiger-Lilies (Lanier) 126
Time and Money (Matthews)
  284
The Time of Your Life
  (Saroyan) 205
Timequake (Vonnegut) 288
Time's Power (Rich) 272
Tiny Alice (Albee) 240
The Titan (Dreiser) 173
"To a Water Fowl" (Bryant)
  101
To Be Young, Gifted and Black
  (Hansberry) 246
"To Build a Fire" (London)
  166
To Have and Have Not (Hem-
  ingway) 153, 203
To Kill a Mockingbird (Lee)
  232
To Stay Alive (Levertov) 249
To the Finland Station (Wil-
  son) 176, 207
Tobacco Road (Caldwell) 196
Tom Sawyer (Twain) 92, 131
The Tooth of Crime (Shepard)
  250
Tortilla Flat (Steinbeck) 200
Tough Guys Don't Dance
  (Mailer) 264
Toward the End of Time (Up-
  dike) 288
The Town (Faulkner) 228
The Town (Richter) 219
The Town and the City (Ker-
  ouac) 219
The Town Down the River
  (Robinson) 168
*The Tragedy of Pudd'nhead
  Wilson* (Twain) 92, 144
The Tragic Muse (James) 91,
  141
The Train Home (Shreve) 279
A Tramp Abroad (Twain) 92,
  133
Transformations (Sexton)
  249
Transparent Gestures (Jones)
  272
A Traveler from Altruria
  (Howells) 144
*Travels with Charley in Search
  of America* (Steinbeck) 235
Travesty (Hawkes) 255
*A Treatise Concerning Religious
  Affections* (Edwards) 77
The Tree of Laughing Bells
  (Lindsay) 163
Trees (Kilmer) 172
The Trees (Richter) 207
The Trespassers (Hobson) 210
*Trial of a Poet and Other
  Poems* (Shapiro) 215

Tristessa (Kerouac) 232
Tristram (Robinson) 189
The Triumph of Achilles
  (Gluck) 265
The Troll Garden (Cather)
  163
Tropic of Cancer (Miller) 198
Tropic of Capricorn (Miller)
  205
Trout Fishing in America
  (Brautigan) 243
True Confessions (Dunne)
  256
True West (Shepard) 260
The Trumpet of the Swan
  (White) 247
Trust (Ozick) 241
The Tunnel of Love (De Vries)
  223
The Turn of the Screw (James)
  91, 148
Turtle Island (Snyder) 252
Turtle Moon (Hoffman) 277
Twentieth Century (Hecht)
  196
Twice-Told Tales
  (Hawthorne) 109
The Two Admirals (Cooper)
  112
Two Serious Ladies (Bowles)
  210
Two Years Before the Mast
  (Dana) 111
Typee (Melville) 114
The Ugly American (Lederer,
  Burdick) 229
"Ulalume" (Poe) 91, 115
*Uncle Remus: His Songs and
  Sayings* (Harris) 134
Uncle Tom's Cabin (Stowe)
  117
Uncle Tom's Children
  (Wright) 204
*Under the Windows and Other
  Poems* (Lowell) 127
Underworld (DeLillo) 288
The Undiscovered Country
  (Howells) 133
*The Universal Baseball Associ-
  ation, Inc., J. Henry Waugh,
  Prop.* (Coover) 244
Untitled Subjects (Howard)
  246
The Unvanquished (Faulkner)
  204
Up Above the World (Bowles)
  241
U.S. 1 (Rukeyser) 204
U.S.A. (Dos Passos) 189
V (Pynchon) 237
*The Varieties of Religious Ex-
  perience* (James) 160
Vasconselos (Simms) 118
The Veritable Years (Everson)
  257
Very Old Bones (Kennedy)
  277
Vice (Ai) 293
The Victim (Bellow) 215
Vida (Piercy) 259
A View from the Bridge
  (Miller) 225
Vineland (Pynchon) 273
Violence (Bausch) 277
The Violent Bear It Away
  (O'Connor) 232

The Virginian (Wister) 160
Virginie: Her Two Lives
  (Hawkes) 261
The Vision of Sir Launfal
  (Lowell) 115
Visions of Gerard (Kerouac)
  237
A Visit from St. Nicholas
  (Moore) 103
The Visiting Physician
  (Shreve) 286
Voices of the Night (Longfel-
  low) 110
The Volcano Lover (Sontag)
  277
Waiting (Ha) 295
Waiting for Lefty (Odets) 200
Waiting to Exhale (McMillan)
  277
Wake-Robin (Burroughs)
  128
*The Waking: Poems,
  1933–1953* (Roethke) 222,
  223
Walden; or, Life in the Woods
  (Thoreau) 118
A Walk on the Wild Side (Al-
  gren) 226
The Wall (Hersey) 219
The Wapshot Chronicle
  (Cheever) 228, 238
Washington, D.C. (Styron)
  243
Washington Square (James)
  91, 133
Watch on the Rhine (Hell-
  man) 208
The Water Witch (Cooper)
  106
The Waterfall and the Bonfire
  (Hauge) 217
The Waterworks (Doctorow)
  282
The Way Some People Live
  (Cheever) 210
The Way to Rainy Mountain
  (Momaday) 246
The Ways of the Hour
  (Cooper) 116
The Wayward Bus (Steinbeck)
  215
We (Lindbergh) 189
We Are Still Married (Keillor)
  272
We Were the Mujlvaneys
  (Berriault) 286
The Weary Blues (Hughes)
  188
The Web and ther Rock
  (Wolfe) 205
Weep Not for Me (Edwards)
  260
Welcome to Hard Times
  (Doctorow) 232
West of Your City (Stafford)
  232
West Wind (Oliver) 288
*The Western Approaches:
  Poems, 1973–1975* (Ne-
  merov) 255
Western Star (Benét) 210
West-Running Brook (Frost)
  190
What a Kingdom It Was (Kin-
  nell) 232
What I Lived For (Oates) 282

What I'm Going to Do, I Think (Woiwode) 246

What Maisie Knew (James) 91, 147

What Price Glory? (Anderson) 185

What Remains (Delblanco) 295

What Work Is (Levine) 276

"When Lilacs Last in the Dooryard Bloom'd" (Whitman) 124

When One Has Lived a Long Time Alone (Kinnell) 273

When She Was Good (Roth) 243

Where I'm Calling From: New and Selected Stories (Carver) 270

Whilomville (Crane) 158

White Buildings (Crane) 188

White Fang (London) 164

White Jacket; or, The World in a Man-of-War (Melville) 116

White Wings (Barry) 188

The White-Footed Deer and Other Poems (Bryant) 113

The Whole Motion (Dickey) 277

Who's Afraid of Virginia Woolf? (Albee) 235

"Why I Live at the P.O." (Welty) 208

Wickford Point (Marquand) 205

The Wide Net (Welty) 210

A Widow for One Year (Irving) 290

Wieland; or, The Transformation (Brown) 88

The Wild Boys (Burroughs) 249

Wild Gratitude (Hirsch) 267

Wildlife (Ford) 273

The Will to Change: Poems, 1968–1970 (Rich) 249

Will You Please Be Quiet, Please? (Carver) 255

A Wind in the Door (L'Engle) 250

Wine from These Grapes (Millay) 199

Winesburg, Ohio (Anderson) 178

Wing-and-Wing (Cooper) 112

The Wings of the Dove (James) 91, 160

Winner Take Nothing (Hemingway) 153, 197

The Winter of Our Discontent (Steinbeck) 234

Winter Trees (Plath) 250

Winterset (Anderson) 200

Wise Blood (O'Connor) 221

The Witches of Eastwick (Updike) 264

With Eyes at the Back of Our Heads (Levertov) 231

Without a Hero (Boyle) 282

A Witness Tree (Frost) 209

A Wizard of Earthsea (Le Guin) 244

The Woman at the Washington Zoo: Poems and Translations (Jarrell) 232, 241

A Woman of Means (Taylor) 219

The Women at Point Sur (Jeffers) 189

Women in the Nineteenth Century (Fuller) 114

The Women of Brewster Place (Naylor) 261

Women on Gallows Hill (Hauge) 229

Women with Men (Ford) 288

The Wonderful Wizard of Oz (Baum) 158

The Wonders of the Invisible World (Mather) 65

The Word for World's Forest (Le Guin) 250

Words for the Wind (Roethke) 228

The World According to Garp (Irving) 257

The World Doesn't End (Simic) 273

World Enough and Time (Warren) 219

The World Is a Wedding and Other Stories (Schwartz) 216

The World of Chance (Howells) 143

The World of the Ten Thousand Things: Poems 1980–1990 (Wright) 273

World's End (Boyle) 269

World's End (Sinclair) 207

World's Fair (Doctorow) 265

Worship Company of Fletchers (Tate) 282

The Wound and the Bow (Wilson) 208

"The Wreck of the Hesperus" (Longfellow) 111

A Wrinkle in Time (L'Engle) 235

A Writer's American: Landscape in Literature (Kazin) 270

The Writing Life (Dillard) 272

Wyandotte (Cooper) 113

Yankee from Olympus (Bowen) 211

The Year Has No Spring (Hauge) 216

The Year of the French (Flanagan) 258

The Yearling (Rawlings) 204

A Year's Life, and Other Poems (Lowell) 111

Yeast (Kingsley) 115

Yellow Black Radio Broke Down (Reed) 246

Yellow Jack (Howard) 198

"The Yellow Wallpaper" (Gilman) 149

The Yemassee (Simms) 108

"Yet I Do Marvel" (Cullen) 186

Yin: New Poems (Kizer) 264

¡Yo! (Alvarez) 290

You Can't Take It With You (Hart, Kaufman) 201

You Must Remember This (Oates) 269

"Young Goodman Brown" (Hawthorne) 108

The Young Lions (Shaw) 216

Young Lonigan: A Boyhood in Chicago Streets (Farrell) 196

The Young Manhood of Studs Lonigan (Farrell) 198

Young Men and Fire (Maclean) 277

The Younger Son (Shapiro) 271

Youth and the Bright Medusa (Cather) 180

The Zodiac (Dickey) 255

Zone Journals (Wright) 271

The Zoo Story (Albee) 231

Zucherman Unbound (Roth) 260

Australian

Ahasuerus in Rome (Hamerling) 125

Billy Sunday (Jones) 286

Bring Larks and Heroes (Keneally) 243

Caesar: Let the Dice Fly (McCullough) 288

Captain Quiros (McAuley) 238

Captivity Captive (Hall) 269

Careful, He Might Hear You (Elliott) 237

The Cave and the Spring: Essays on Poetry (Hope) 240

The Chant of Jimmie Blacksmith (Keneally) 250

Coda (Astley) 282

Collected Poetry (Hope) 241

The Confederates (Keneally) 258

Coonardoo: The Well in the Shadow (Prichard) 192

Cry of the Rain Bird (Bird) 284

Dark Palace (Moorhouse) 295

The Devil's Advocate (West) 231

Dream Stuff (Malouf) 295

Drylands (Astley) 295

The Essence of the Thing (St. John) 288

The Eye of the Storm (White) 250

Flaws in the Glass: A Self-Portrait (White) 260

The Fortunes of Richard Mahoney (Richardson) 193

Foxybaby (Jolley) 265

Fredy Neptune (Murray) 293

Heart of the Country (Matthews) 267

His Natural Life (Clarke) 130

Jack Maggas (Carey) 288

Jacko: The Great Intruder (Keneally) 282

Joe Wilson and His Mates (Lawson) 159

Julia Paradise (Jones) 269

Kisses of the Enemy (Hall) 271

Leaves from Australian Forests (Kendall) 127

Letters to Live Poets (Beaver) 241

The Man Who Loved Children (Stead) 207

Memoirs of Many in One (White) 267

Miss Peabody's Inheritance (Jolley) 263

The Montforts (Boyd) 190

Morgan's Run (McCullough) 295

Mr. Scobie's Riddle (Jolley) 263

My Father's Moon (Jolley) 272

On the Beach (Shute) 228

The People's Other World (Murray) 264

The Pioneers (Prichard) 174

The Playmaker (Keneally) 269

Poems, 1913 (Brennan) 173

Remembering Babylon (Malouf) 280, 286

Riders in the Chariot (White) 234

The Riders (Winton) 284

A River Town (Keneally) 284

Schindler's Ark (Keneally) 261

Shabbytown Calendar (Shapcott) 255

The Shoes of the Fisherman (West) 240

Shogun (Clavell) 253

The Solid Mandala (White) 241

Songlines (Chatwin) 269

The Suburbs of Hell (Stow) 264

Such Is Life (Furphy) 161

The Sugar Mother (Jolley) 271

Summer of the Seventh Doll (Lawler) 237

Tai-Pan (Clavell) 241

This Island Now (Abrahams) 241

Too Many Men (Brett) 295

Travel Dice (Shapcott) 269

The Twyborn Affair (White) 258

The Unusual Life of Tristan Smith (Carey) 282

Vanishing Point (West) 286

Voss (White) 228

Waiting for Childhood (Elliott) 269

The Well (Jolley) 267

Barbadian

Christopher (Drayton) 231

Magical Realism (Brathwaite) 290

Rights of Passage (Brathwaite) 243

Roots (Brathwaite) 267

Belizean

North Amerikkan Blues (Hyde) 249

British

XX Poems (Larkin) 212

1914 (Brooke) 174

1984 (Orwell) 217

2010 Odyssey Two (Clarke) 261

Aaron's Rod (Lawrence) 182

"Abou Ben Adhem" (Hunt) 113

Absalom and Achitophel (Dryden) 49, 63

The Absentee (Edgeworth) 98

An Accidental Man (Murdoch) 249

English
  British (continued)
    Act of Darkness (King) 263
    Adam Bede (Eliot) 121
    "Adonais" (Shelley) 93, 102
    The Advancement of Learning (Bacon) 50
    The Adventures of a Younger Son (Trelawny) 106
    The Adventures of Captain Singleton (Defoe) 72
    The Adventures of Hajji Baba of Isphahan (Morier) 103
    The Adventures of Harry Richmond (Meredith) 127
    The Adventures of Sherlock Holmes (Doyle) 142
    The Adventures of Ulysses (Lamb) 97
    The Affair (Snow) 231
    The African Queen (Forester) 200
    African Stories (Lessing) 238
    African Witch (Cary) 201
    After Julius (Howard) 240
    After Many a Summer Dies the Swan (Huxley) 205
    Afternoon Men (Powell) 194
    The Age of Anxiety (Auden) 215
    Agnes Grey (Brontë) 115
    Alastor; or, The Spirit of Solitude (Shelley) 100
    Albion and Albanius (Dryden) 64
    Album Verses (Lamb) 106
    The Alchemist (Jonson) 51
    "Alexander's Feast, or the Power of Music; An Ode in Honour of St. Cecilia's Day" (Dryden) 66, 71
    The Alexandria Quartet (Durrell) 228, 229, 232
    Alice's Adventures in Wonderland (Carroll) 124
    All for Love, or, A Sinner Well Saved (Southey) 105
    All for Love (Dryden) 49
    All Passon Spent (Sackville-West) 194
    All the Conspirators (Isherwood) 190
    Allan Quatermain (Haggard) 138
    The Allegory of Love (Lewis) 201
    "L'Allegro" (Milton) 48, 55
    All's Well That Ends Well (Shakespeare) 50
    Alma, or the Progress of the Mind (Prior) 72
    Alms for Oblivion (Raven) 238
    Alton Locke, Tailor and Poet (Kingsley) 116
    Amadeus (Shaffer) 258
    Amana Gras (Silkin) 249
    The Amazing Marriage (Meredith) 145
    Amboyna (Dryden) 62
    Amelia (Fielding) 78
    America: A Prophecy (Blake) 68
    American Notes (Dickens) 112
    An American Visitor (Cary) 197
    Amoretti (Spenser) 44

    Amphitryon (Dryden) 49, 65
    Amrita (Jhabvala) 225
    Amsterdam (McEwan) 290
    An Englishman Abroad (Bennett) 261
    The Anatomy of Melancholy (Burton) 53
    An Anatomy of the World: The First Anniversary (Donne) 51
    "Andrea del Sarto" (Browning) 119
    Andrea of Hungary, Fra Rupert, and Giovanna of Naples (Landor) 110
    Angel in the House (Patmore) 118
    Angel Pavement (Priestley) 193
    Animal Farm (Orwell) 212
    Animals Arrival (Jennings) 246
    "The Anniversary" (Donne) 49
    Ann Veronica (Wells) 167
    Annus Mirabilis (Dryden) 49, 61
    Another Country (Mitchell) 261
    Another Part of the Wood (Bainbridge) 244
    Another Time (Auden) 207
    Antic Hay (Huxley) 184
    Antonina; or, The Fall of Rome (Collins) 116
    Antony and Cleopatra (Shakespeare) 50
    Any Old Iron (Burgess) 271
    Apologia Pro Vita Sua (Newman) 124
    An Apologie for Poetrie (Sidney) 42
    An Apology for the Life of Mrs Shamela Andrews (Fielding) 76
    Appius and Virginia (Webster and Heywood) 51
    Appreciations (Pater) 140
    Arcades (Milton) 55
    The Arcadia (Sidney) 43
    Areopagitica (Milton) 48, 57
    Aristophanes' Apology (Browning) 130
    Art (Bell) 173
    As You Like It (Shakespeare) 45
    The Ascent of F6 (Auden, Isherwood) 201
    Ash Wednesday (Eliot) 193
    Asolando (Browning) 140
    Aspects of the Novel (Forster) 189
    Astraea Redux (Dryden) 49, 60
    Astrophel and Stella (Sidney) 43
    Astrophel (Spenser) 42
    At Home and Abroad (Pritchett) 272
    Atlanta in Calydon (Swinburne) 124
    Aureng-Zebe (Dryden) 49, 62
    Aurora Leigh (Browning) 120
    Autobiography (Hunt) 116
    Autobiography, 1872–1914 (Russell) 243

    "Ave Atque Vale" (Swinburne) 126
    An Avenue of Stone (Johnson) 215
    An Awfully Big Adventure (Bainbridge) 273
    Ayala's Angel (Trollope) 134
    Babbling April (Greene) 154
    "The Bait" (Donne) 49
    Balaustion's Adventure (Browning) 128
    Balder Dead (Arnold) 118
    "Balin and Balan" (Tennyson) 137
    The Balkan Trilogy (Manning) 232
    "The Ballad of Bouillabaisse" (Thackeray) 116
    Ballads and Other Poems (Tennyson) 133
    Ballads and Poems (Masefield) 168
    Ballads and Poems of Tragic Life (Meredith) 138
    Ballads and Sonnets (Rossetti) 134
    Balthazar (Durrell) 229
    Barchester Towers (Trollope) 120
    "The Bard" (Gray) 79
    Barnabees Journal (Brathwaite) 56
    Barnaby Rudge (Dickens) 90, 112
    Barrack-Room Ballads (Kipling) 143
    Bartholomew Fair (Jonson) 52
    "Batter My Heart" (Donne) 49
    The Battle Lost and Won (Manning) 257
    The Battle of the Books (Swift) 70
    Beasts and Super Beasts (Saki) 173
    Beau Geste (Wren) 185
    The Beautiful Visit (Howard) 219
    Becket (Tennyson) 136
    The Beggar's Opera (Gay) 74
    Behind the Scenes at the Museum (Atkinson) 286
    Being Dead (Crace) 293
    Belinda (Edgeworth) 95
    "La Belle Dame sans Merci" (Keats) 101
    Bells and Pomegranates (Browning) 114
    Beowulf, 13, 19
    Beppo (Byron) 93, 101
    The Berlin Stories (Isherwood) 205, 213
    Betrayal (Pinter) 257
    Bible (Coverdale translation) 37
    Bible (King James version) 51
    The Bible in Spain (Barrow) 112
    Biographia Literaria (Coleridge) 100
    Birthday Letters (Hughes) 290
    Birthday Party (Pinter) 229, 231

    Bishop Blougram's Apology (Browning) 119
    Bitter Angel (Gerstler) 275
    Black Beauty (Sewell) 131
    Black Dogs (McEwan) 278
    Black Lamb and Grey Falcon (West) 209
    Black Mischief (Waugh) 196
    Black Narcissus (Godden) 205
    The Black Prince (Murdoch) 251
    Blasting and Bombardiering (Waugh) 203
    Bleak House (Dickens) 90, 117
    "The Blessed Damozel" (Rossetti) 116
    The Blessing (Mitford) 220
    The Blind Beggar of Alexandria (Chapman) 45
    Blithe Spirit (Coward) 208
    A Blot in the 'Scutcheon (Browning) 113
    The Blue Afternoon (Boyd) 280
    The Boat (Hartley) 217
    A Bond Honored (Osborne) 241
    The Book and Brotherhood (Murdoch) 269
    The Book of Ahania (Blake) 68, 87
    The Book of Los (Blake) 68, 87
    Book of Margery Kempe (Kempe) 27
    The Book of Martyrs (Foxe) 40
    Book of Nonsense (Lear) 114
    Book of the Duchess (Chaucer) 14
    The Book of Thel (Blake) 68, 85
    The Book of Urizen (Blake) 68, 86
    Books Do Furnish a Room (Powell) 249
    The Borderers (Wordsworth) 87, 92
    The Borough (Crabbe) 98
    The Bothie of Tober-na-Voulich (Clough) 115
    Bothwell, a Tragedy (Swinburne) 130
    The Bouge of Court (Skelton) 29
    The Boy with a Cart (Fry) 219
    Brave New World (Huxley) 196
    Brave New World Revisited (Huxley) 229
    Brennoralt (Suckling) 57
    The Bride of Abydos (Byron) 93, 99
    Brideshead Revisited (Waugh) 212
    Briefing for a Descent into Hell (Lessing) 249
    Bright Day (Priestley) 213
    Brighton Rock (Greene) 154, 204
    Britannia Rediviva (Dryden) 65
    The British Prison Ship (Freneau) 84

Brothers and Sisters (Compton-Burnett) 192

"The Brothers" (Wordsworth) 92

Browning, Robert, 112

The Browning Version (Rattigan) 216

Bruno's Dream (Murdoch) 246

The Bull from the Sea (Renault) 235

Burmese Days (Orwell) 199

Burnt Norton (Eliot) 202

A Burnt-Out Case (Greene) 154, 234

Butley (Gray) 249

A Buyer's Market (Powell) 221

Caesar and Pompey (Chapman) 55

Cain (Byron) 93, 102

Caius Marius (Otway) 63

Cakes and Ale (Maugham) 193

"Calamiterror" (Barker) 203

Call for the Dead (Le Carré) 232

Callista (Newman) 119

"The Campaign" (Addison) 70

"The Canonization" (Donne) 49

Canopus in Argus: Archives (Lessing) 258

The Canterbury Tales (Chaucer) 14, 26

Captain Sword and Captain Pen (Hunt) 108

Captains Courageous (Kipling) 147

The Careless Husband (Cibber) 70

The Caretaker (Pinter) 232

Casanova (Miller) 290

Casanova's Chinese Restaurant (Powell) 232

The Case Book of Sherlock Holmes (Doyle) 163

Casino Royale (Fleming) 222

The Castaway (Cowper) 88

The Castle of Otranto (Walpole) 80

Castle Rackrent (Edgeworth) 95

The Castle Spectre (Lewis) 88

The Catalyst (Duncan) 229

Catherine (Thackeray) 111

Cato (Addison) 72

The Cave (Warren) 230

Cecilia, or Memoirs of an Heiress (Burkey) 84

The Cenci (Shelley) 101

Centuries of Meditations (Traherne) 166

The Chalk Garden (Bagnold) 225

Chance (Conrad) 172

The Changeling (Middleton, Rowley) 59

"Charge of the Light Brigade" (Tennyson) 93, 118

Childe Harold's Pilgrimage (Byron) 93, 98

Childhood's End (Clarke) 222

Children of the Mist (Phillpotts) 148

The Children of the New Forest (Marryat) 115

Children of Violence (Lessing) 223, 229

The Chimes (Dickens) 113

A Chorus of Disapproval (Ayckbourn) 267

"Christabel" (Coleridge) 100

The Christian Hero (Steele) 70

Christie Johnstone (Reade) 118

A Christmas Carol (Dickens) 90, 113

Christmas Eve and Easter (Browning) 116

The Chronicle of Clovis (Saki) 169

Chronicles (Holinshed) 41

Church Poems (Betjeman) 260

The Circle (Maugham) 181

The Citadel (Cronin) 203

Citizens: A Chronicle of the French Revolution (Shama) 272

The City Heiress (Behn) 64

Clarissa Harlowe (Richardson) 77

The Clayhanger Family (Bennett) 186

Clea (Durrell) 232

A Clip of Steel (Blackburn) 246

A Clockwork Orange (Burgess) 235

The Clockwork Testament (Burgess) 252

The Cloister and the Hearth (Reade) 122

Close Quarters (Golding) 269

"The Cloud" (Shelley) 93

The Cocktail Party (Eliot) 152

A Coffin for Demetrios (Ambler) 205

Cold Comfort Farm (Gibbons) 196

Collected Poems (Betjeman) 229

Collected Poems (Binyon) 194

Collected Poems (Davie) 250

Collected Poems (Graves) 216

Collected Poems (Jennings) 243

Collected Poems (Larkin) 272

Collected Poems (Lewis) 223

Collected Poems (Sassoon) 215

Collected Poems (Stubbs) 271

Collected Poems, 1928–1953 (Spender) 225

Collected Poems, 1948–1998 (Enright) 290

Collected Shorter Poems (Auden) 241

Collected Stories (Lessing) 257

The Collector (Fowles) 237

The Comedians (Greene) 154, 241

The Comedy of Errors (Shakespeare) 31, 43

Coming Up for Air (Orwell) 205

The Common Reader (Woolf) 186

The Complaint; or, Night Thoughts on Life, Death and Immortality (Young) 76

The Compleat Angler, or the Contemplative Man's Recreation (Walton) 59

Comus (Milton) 48, 55

Concrete Island (Ballard) 252

Confessions of an Opium Eater (De Quincey) 102

The Confidential Agent (Greene) 154, 205

The Confidential Clerk (Eliot) 223

Coningsby (Disraeli) 113

The Conquest of Granada by the Spaniards (Dryden) 49, 61

The Conscience of the Rich (Snow) 229

The Conscious Lovers (Steele) 73

The Contenders (Wain) 229

The Cooper's Hell (Denham) 57

Coriolanus (Shakespeare) 51

Cork Street, Next to Hatter's (Johnson) 240

The Corsair (Byron) 93, 99

Count Julian (Landor) 98

The Country of the Blind (Wells) 169

The Country Wife (Wycherley) 62

Cousin Rosamund (West) 265

Cranford (Gaskell) 117

Crash (Ballard) 251

The Cricket on the Hearth (Dickens) 90, 114

The Crisis (Churchill) 159

The Critic (Sheridan) 83

Crome Yellow (Huxley) 181

Cross Channel (Barnes) 286

Crossing River (Phillips) 280

"Crossing the Bar" (Tennyson) 140

Crotchet Castle (Peacock) 106

Crow: From the Life and Songs of the Crow (Hughes) 247

The Cruel Sea (Montserrat) 220

Culture and Anarchy (Arnold) 127

The Cupboard (Tremain) 260

Cupid's Revenge (Beaumont, Fletcher) 51

The Curse of Rebellious Susan (Jones) 144

The Cutter of Coleman Street (Cowley) 57

Cymbeline (Shakespeare) 51

Cynthia's Revels (Jonson) 50

The Daisy Chain (Yonge) 119

A Dance to the Beginning of Time (Burgess) 220

Dance to the Music of Time (Powell) 220, 221, 235, 241, 244, 249

The Danger Tree (Manning) 256

Daniel Deronda (Eliot) 131

Daniel Martin (Fowles) 256

The Dark Is Light Enough (Fry) 223

The Dark Tower (MacNeice) 215

Daughters of the House (Roberts) 278

David Copperfield (Dickens) 90, 116

The Day of the Jackal (Forsyth) 249

The Day of the Scorpions (Scott) 244

De Cive (Hobbes) 57

De Homine (Hobbes) 59

A Dead Man in Deptford (Burgess) 280

"Death, Be Not Proud" (Donne) 49

Death of a Hero (Aldington) 192

The Death of Oneone, Akbar's Dream and Other Poems (Tennyson) 93

The Death of Satan (Duncan) 223

The Death of the Author (Adair) 278

The Death of the Heart (Bowen) 204

Death on the Nile (Christie) 203

Death's Jest-Book; or, The Fool's Tragedy (Beddoes) 116

Decline and Fall (Waugh) 190

The Deemster (Caine) 138

Deerbrook (Martineau) 111

The Defense of Guenevere and Other Poems (Morris) 120

The Deformed Transformed (Byron) 103

"Dejection: An Ode" (Coleridge) 96

Demeter and Other Poems (Tennyson) 93, 140

Demos (Gissing) 137

Departmental Ditties (Kipling) 137

The Descent of Man (Darwin) 128

"The Descent of Odin: An Ode" (Gray) 81

The Deserted Village (Goldsmith) 81

Design for Living (Coward) 197

Desperate Remedies (Hardy) 128

Deveroux (Bulwer-Lytton) 105

The Devil Is an Ass (Jonson) 52

The Devil's Law Case (Webster) 53

Devotions upon Emergent Occasions (Donne) 49, 53

Diana of the Crossways (Meredith) 137

Diary (Pepys) 104

A Dictionary of the English Language (Johnson) 79

Dido, Queen of Carthage (Marlowe) 33, 44

"Dipsychus" (Clough) 127

Dirty Linen (Stoppard) 255

The Disowned (Bulwer-Lytton) 105

English
    British *(continued)*
        Diverse Voyages Touching the Discovery of America (Hakluyt) 42
        The Doctor Is Sick (Burgess) 232
        Doctor Thorne (Trollope) 120
        The Dogs of War (Forsyth) 252
        Dombey and Son (Dickens) 115
        Don Carlos (Otway) 62
        Don Juan (Byron) 93, 101
        Don Sebastian (Dryden) 49
        The Double Dealer (Congreve) 66
        The Double Man (Auden) 208
        Down and Out in Paris and London (Orwell) 197
        Down by the River (O'Brien) 288
        Dr. Criminale (Bradbury) 278
        Dr. Faustus (Marlowe) 33
        Dramatis Personae (Browning) 124
        Drapier's Letters (Swift) 68, 73
        "The Dream" (Byron) 100
        The Dream of Eugene Aram (Hood) 105
        A Dream of John Ball (Morris) 139
        The Drummer (Addison) 72
        Dry Salvages (Eliot) 208
        The Duchess of Malfi (Webster) 52, 53
        The Duena (Sheridan) 82
        The Duke of Guise (Dryden and Lee) 64
        The Duke's Children (Trollope) 133
        The Dumb Waiter (Pinter) 228, 231
        The Dwarfs (Pinter) 273
        The Dynasts, an Epic Drama of the War with Napoleon (Hardy) 161, 168
        Earthlight (Clarke) 225
        Earthly Paradise (Morris) 126
        Earthly Powers (Burgess) 259
        East Coker (Eliot) 207
        East of Suez (Maugham) 182
        The Edge of Day (Lee) 231
        Edward II (Marlowe) 33, 44
        The Edwardian (Sackville-West) 193
        "Eleanora: A Panegyrical Poem to the Memory of the Countess of Abingdon" (Dryden) 65
        "Elegy Written in a Country Churchyard" (Gray) 78
        "Elegy XX: To His Mistress Going to Bed" (Donne) 49
        The Elements of Style (Strunk, White) 231
        Elizabeth and Essex (Strachey) 190
        Eloisa to Abelard (Pope) 72
        Emilia in England (Meredith) 124
        Eminent Victorians (Strachey) 177

        Emma (Austen) 91, 99
        Empedocles on Etna and Other Poems (Arnold) 117
        Empire of the Sun (Ballard) 264
        The End of the Affair (Greene) 154, 220
        The End of the House of Alard (Kaye-Smith) 184
        Enderby Outside (Burgess) 244
        Enderby Trilogy (Burgess) 252
        Endimion, the Man in the Moone (Lyly) 43
        Ending Up (Amis) 252
        Endymion (Keats) 101
        Enoch Arden (Tennyson) 93, 124
        The Entertainer (Osborne) 228
        "The Eolian Harp" (Blake) 87
        Epicoene, or the Silent Woman (Jonson) 51
        Epipsychidion (Shelley) 93, 102
        An Epistle to Dr. Arbuthnot (Pope) 69, 75
        Epistle to Several Persons (Pope) 75
        Epitaph for George Dillon (Osborne, Creighton) 229
        Equus (Shaffer) 251
        Erectheus (Swinburne) 131
        Erewhon (Butler) 128
        Ernest Maltravers (Bulwer-Lytton) 109
        The Espousals (Patmore) 119
        An Essay on Criticism (Pope) 69, 71
        An Essay on Man (Pope) 69, 75
        Essays, Critical and Historical (Macaulay) 113
        The Essays of Elia (Lamb) 103
        Eugene Aram (Bulwer-Lytton) 107
        Euphues: The Anatomy of Wit (Lyly) 41
        Europe: A Prophecy (Blake) 68
        The Eustace Diamonds (Trollope) 129
        Evan Harrington (Meredith) 121
        The Eve of Saint Venus (Burgess) 238
        "The Eve of St. Agnes" (Keats) 101
        Evelina; or, A Young Lady's Entrance into the World (Burney) 83
        "An Evening Walk" (Wordsworth) 86
        The Everlasting Gospel (Blake) 68
        Every Good Day Deserves Favor (Stoppard) 256
        Every Man for Himself (Bainbridge) 286, 288
        Every Man in His Humour (Jonson) 45
        Every Man Out of His Humour (Jonson) 45

        Everyman, 13, 35
        Except the Lord (Cary) 222
        The Excursion (Southey) 99
        Eyeless in Gaza (Huxley) 202
        The Fable of the Bees; or Private Vices, Public Benefits (Mandeville) 72
        Fables (Gay) 74
        Fables, Ancient and Modern (Dryden) 66
        The Faerie Queene (Spenser) 43, 51
        Fair Stood the Wind for France (Bates) 211
        "Falk" (Conrad) 155
        Falkland (Bulwer-Lytton) 105
        A Fall of Moondust (Clarke) 234
        The Fall of Princes (Lydgate) 29
        False Delicacy (Kelly) 81
        The Family Reunion (Eliot) 205
        A Family Romance (Brookner) 280
        The Family Shakespeare (Bowdler) 97
        Fanny Hill, Memoirs of a Woman of Pleasure (Cleland) 77
        Far from the Madding Crowd (Hardy) 130
        Farina, a Legend of Cologne (Meredith) 120
        "The Fatal Sisters: An Ode" (Gray) 81
        Fathers and Sons (Gosse) 165
        Feast Days (Burnside) 278
        Felix Holt the Radical (Eliot) 125
        The Fellowship of the Ring (Tolkien) 223
        Fifine at the Fair (Browning) 129
        The Fifth Child (Lessing) 271
        Fifty Comedies and Tragedies (Fletcher, Beaumont) 63
        Fighting Terms (Gunn) 223
        Fire Down Below (Golding) 272
        Fireman Flower and Other Stories (Sansom) 211
        The First Epistle of the Second Book of Horace to Augustus (Pope) 75
        The Fitzboodle Papers (Thackeray) 112
        Five-Finger Exercise (Shaffer) 232
        Flying to Nowhere (Fuller) 263
        The Folks That Live on the Hill (Amis) 273
        For the Time Being (Auden) 212
        The Forest (Jonson) 52
        Forsyte Saga (Galsworthy) 164, 182, 188
        The Four Just Men (Wallace) 163
        The Four Quartets (Eliot) 152
        The Four Zoas: The Torment of Love and Jealousy in the Death and Judgment of Albion (Blake) 87

        The Four-Gated City (Lessing) 246
        A Foxglove Saga (Waugh) 234
        "Fra Lippo Lippi" (Browning) 119
        Fragmenta Aurea (Suckling) 57
        Frankenstein; or, the Modern Prometheus (Shelley) 101
        Frankenstein Unbound (Aldiss) 251
        The French Lieutenant's Woman (Fowles) 246
        The French Revolution (Blake) 68
        From Russia with Love (Fleming) 228
        The Fugitive (Galsworthy) 172
        The Funeral; or, Grief A-la-Mode (Steele) 70
        Gabriel's Lament (Bailey) 267
        "The Garden" (Marvell) 63
        "Gareth and Lynette" (Tennyson) 129
        The Gates of Angels (Fitzgerald) 273
        The Gathering Storm (Empson) 207
        Gebir (Landor) 88
        A General Theory of Employment, Interest and Money (Keynes) 202
        The Gentleman Dancing Master (Wycherley) 62
        "Gerontion" (Eliot) 152
        Getting It Right (Howard) 261
        The Ghost of Abel (Blake) 103
        The Ghost Road (Barker) 284
        The Giaour (Byron) 93, 99
        Gil Blas (Lesage) 72
        A Girl in Winter (Larkin) 215
        "Go, Lovely Rose" (Waller) 57
        The Go-Between (Hartley) 222
        Goblin (Rossetti) 123
        The Goblins (Suckling) 56
        Godolphin (Bulwer-Lytton) 107
        The Golden Bough (Frazier) 141
        The Golden Notebook (Lessing) 235
        Goldfinger (Fleming) 231
        The Good Companions (Priestley) 192
        Good Morning, Good Night (Rhys) 205
        The Good Natur'd Man (Goldsmith) 81
        The Good Soldier: A Tale of Passion (Ford) 174
        The Good Terrorist (Lessing) 265
        Goodbye, Mr. Chips (Hilton) 199
        Goodbye to All That (Graves) 192
        Goodbye to Berlin (Isherwood) 205
        Grace Abounding to the Chief of Sinners (Bunyan) 61
        Grace Notes (MacLaverty) 288

The Grammar of Assent (Newman) 127

The Grass Is Singing (Lessing) 219

The Great Duke of Florence (Massinger) 55

Great Expectations (Dickens) 90, 121

The Great Hoggarty Diamond (Thackeray) 112

Great Morning (Sitwell) 215

The Great Tradition (Leavis) 216

The Green Hat (Arlen) 185

The Green Man (Amis) 246

Green Song (Sitwell) 211

The Green Years (Cronin) 211

"The Growth of Love" (Bridges) 131

Gulliver's Travels (Swift) 68, 73

A Gun for Sale (Greene) 202

Hadrian the Seventh (Rolfe) 162

Hamlet (Shakespeare) 31, 50

A Handful of Dust (Waugh) 199

Hard Times (Dickens) 90, 118

Harold (Tennyson) 131

Harold, the Last of the Saxon Kings (Bulwer-Lytton) 115

Harriet Said (Bainbridge) 250

Harry Potter and Prisoner of Azkaban (Rowling) 295

Harry Potter and the Chamber of Secrets (Rowling) 293

Harry Potter and the Sorcerer's Stone (Rowling) 290

Hatter's Castle (Cronin) 194

The Haunted Man and the Ghost's Bargain (Dickens) 115

The Hawk in the Rain (Hughes) 228

Hay Fever (Coward) 186

He Knew He Was Right (Trollope) 127

The Headlong Hall (Peacock) 100

Hearing Secret Harmonies (Powell) 253

Heart of Darkness (Conrad) 155, 160

The Heart of the Day (Bowen) 217

The Heart of the Matter (Greene) 154, 216

Hearts of Oak (Jones) 132

Heat and Dust (Jhabvala) 253

Heaven and Earth (Byron) 103

The Heir of Redclyffe (Yonge) 118

Heleconia Winter (Aldiss) 266

Hellas (Shelley) 93, 103

Hemlock and After (Wilson) 221

Henry and Cato (Murdoch) 255

Henry IV (Shakespeare) 31, 44

Henry V (Shakespeare) 45

Henry VI (Shakespeare) 31

Henry VIII (Shakespeare) 51

Hereward the Wake (Kingsley) 125

Hero and Leander (Marlowe) 33

Hers (Alvarez) 252

Herself Surprised (Cary) 208

Hesperides (Herrick) 58

High and Low (Betjeman) 241

High Rise (Ballard) 253

The High Tride in the Garden (Adcock) 249

A High Wind in Jamaica (Hughes) 192

High Windows (Larkin) 252

The Hind and the Panther (Dryden) 49, 64

"His Majesty's Escape at St. Andre" (Waller) 54

The Historical Register for the Year 1736 (Fielding) 75

The History of Henry Esmond (Thackeray) 117

The History of Henry VII (Bacon) 53

The History of Pendennis (Thackeray) 115

The History of Sir Charles Grandison (Richardson) 78

The History of Susan Spray, Female Preacher (Kaye-Smith) 194

The History of the Decline and Fall of the Roman Empire (Gibbon) 83

The History of the World (Raleigh) 52

H.M.S. Pinafore (Gilbert) 132

The Hobbitt (Tolkien) 203

The Hollow Hill and Other Poems, 1960–1964 (Raine) 240

"The Hollow Men" (Eliot) 186

"The Holy Grail" (Tennyson) 127

The Holy Sonnets (Donne) 49, 51, 55

The Holy Stone (Blackburn) 223

The Holy War (Bunyan) 64

Homage to Catalonia (Orwell) 204

Homage to Clio (Auden) 232

The Homecoming (Pinter) 240

The Honest Whore (Dekker) 54

The Honorable Schoolboy (Le Carré) 256

The Honorary Consul (Greene) 154, 251

The Horse's Mouth (Cary) 211

Hotel du Lac (Brookner) 264

Hothouse (Aldiss) 235

"The Hound of Heaven" (Thompson) 139, 143

The Hound of the Baskervilles (Doyle) 159

Hours of Idleness (Byron) 97

A House in Order (Denis) 241

The House in Paris (Bowen) 200

House of Fame (Chaucer) 14

How Far Can You Go? (Lodge) 259

How the Dead Live (Self) 295

Howards End (Forster) 168

Hudibras (Butler) 60

The Human Factor (Greene) 154, 257

"The Hunting of the Snark" (Carroll) 131

Hurry on Down (Wain) 222

"Hymn to Intellectual Beauty" (Shelley) 93, 100

Hypatia; or, New Foes with an Old Face (Kingsley) 118

Hyperion (Keats) 102

I, Claudius (Graves) 199

I Have Been There Before (Priestley) 203

"I Wandered Lonely as a Cloud" (Wordsworth) 96

The Idea of a Christian Society (Eliot) 152, 205

Idylls of the King (Tennyson) 93, 121

If You Know Not Me, You Know Nobody (Heywood) 50

Iliad (Chapman, tr.) 51

Imaginary Conversations (Landor) 103, 118

Imperial Palace (Bennett) 193

In Chancery (Galsworthy) 180, 182

In Every Face I Meet (Cartwright) 284

In Hazard (Hughes) 204

"In Memoriam, A.H.H." (Tennyson) 116

In Memoriam (Tennyson) 93

In Parenthesis (Jones) 203

In This House of Brede (Godden) 246

In Transit (Brophy) 246

Incline Our Hearts (Wilson) 272

Incognita (Dryden) 65

The Indian Emperour (Dryden) 49, 60

The Indian Queen (Dryden) 49, 60

The Industry of Souls (Booth) 290

Ingenious Pain (Miller) 293

The Inheritor (Golding) 225

The Inn Album (Browning) 130

The Inner Harbor (Adcock) 258

Inquiry Time (Bainbridge) 256

Inside Mr. Enderby (Burgess) 237

The Inspector Calls (Priestley) 213

Insular Passion (Mo) 267

The Invisible Man (Wells) 147

The Ipcress File (Deighton) 235

Irene (Johnson) 78

The Island (Byron) 103

The Island of Dr. Moreau (Wells) 146

It Is Never Too Late to Mend (Reade) 119

The Italian (Radcliffe) 87

The Italian Girl (Murdoch) 234

An Italian Visit (Day-Lewis) 222

The Jacaranda Tree (Bates) 216

Jacob's Room (Woolf) 182

The Jake's Thing (Amis) 257

Jane Eyre (Brontë) 115

"Janet's Repentance" (Eliot) 120

Jeame's Diary (Thackeray) 114

Jerusalem (Blake) 68

The Jew of Malta (Marlowe) 33, 55

The Jewel in the Crown (Scott) 241

Jill (Larkin) 213

Jocoseria (Browning) 135

John Woodvil (Lamb) 96

Joseph Andrews (Fielding) 76

Journal of a Tour of the Hebrides, with Samuel Johnson (Boswell) 84

A Journal of the Plague Year (Defoe) 73

Journal to Stella (Swift) 68, 71

A Journey to the Western Islands of Scotland (Johnson) 82

Journey Without Maps (Greene) 202

Journey's End (Sheriff) 192

Jude the Obscure (Hardy) 144

The Judge (West) 182

Julian and Maddalo (Shelley) 93

Julius Caesar (Shakespeare) 31, 45

The Jungle Book (Kipling) 144

Just So Stories (Kipling) 160

Justice (Galsworthy) 168

Justine (Durrell) 228

Kangaroo (Lawrence) 184

Keep the Apisdistra Flying (Orwell) 202

The Kellys and the O'Kellys (Trollope) 115

The Keys of the Kingdom (Cronin) 209

Kim (Kipling) 159

A Kind of Loving (Barstow) 232

The Kindly Ones (Powell) 235

The Kindness of Women (Ballard) 276

King Arthur (Bulwer-Lytton) 116

King Arthur (Dryden) 49, 65

King John (Shakespeare) 44

King Lear (Shakespeare) 31, 50

The King Must Die (Renault) 229

The King of Schnorrers (Zangwill) 144

King Solomon's Mines (Haggard) 137

Kipps (Wells) 163

English
  British *(continued)*
    The Kitchen God's Wife (Tan) 276
    Klosterheim (De Quincey) 107
    Knowledge of Angels (Walsh) 282
    "Kubla Khan" (Coleridge) 100
    Lady Chatterley's Lover (Lawrence) 190
    The Lady of Lyons (Bulwer-Lytton) 110
    "The Lady of Shalott" (Tennyson) 93, 107
    The Lady's Not for Burning (Fry) 216
    "The Lament of Tasso" (Byron) 100
    Lamia (Keats) 101
    The Lances of Lynwood (Yonge) 119
    Landlocked (Lessing) 240
    Landscape (Pinter) 244
    Landscape and Memory (Schama) 284
    A Laodicean (Hardy) 134
    Lara (Byron) 93, 99
    Last and First Men (Stapledon) 193
    The Last Chronicle of Barset (Trollope) 125
    The Last Days of Pompeii (Bulwer-Lytton) 108
    Last Loves (Sillitoe) 273
    The Last Man (Shelley) 104
    The Last of the Barons (Bulwer-Lytton) 113
    The Last of the Wine (Renault) 226
    Last Orders (Swift) 286
    "The Last Tournament" (Tennyson) 128
    Laughter in the Next Room (Sitwell) 216
    Lavengro (Borrow) 117
    Lays of Ancient Rome (Macaulay) 112
    "Lead, Kindly Light" (Newman) 107
    Left Hand, Right Hand (Sitwell) 211
    A Legend of Florence (Hunt) 111
    Legend of Good Women (Chaucer) 14
    The Less Deceived (Larkin) 225
    Letters of Espriella (Southey) 97
    Letters to Sister Benedicta (Tremain) 257
    The Leviathan (Hobbes) 58
    The Liars (Jones) 147
    Lies and Secrets (Fuller) 258
    The Life and Adventures of Martin Chuzzlewitartin Chuzzlewit (Dickens) 113
    The Life and Adventures of Robinson Crusoe (Defoe) 72
    The Life and Death of Jason (Morris) 126
    Life at the Top (Braine) 235
    Life of Christ (Farrar) 130
    The Life of Horatio Nelson (Southey) 99

    The Life of Jonathan Wild the Great (Fielding) 76
    The Light of Asia (Arnold) 132
    The Light That Failed (Kipling) 141
    The Light Years (Howard) 273
    "Lines Composed a Few Miles Above Tintern Abbey" (Wordsworth) 88, 92
    Little Dorrit (Dickens) 90, 119
    The Little Drummer Girl (Le Carré) 263
    Little Gidding (Eliot) 209
    Little Lord Fauntleroy (Burnett) 137
    The Lives of the English Poets (Johnson) 83
    Lives of the Fathers, Martyrs and Other Principal Saints (Butler) 79
    Liza of Lambeth (Maugham) 147
    "Locksley Hall" (Tennyson) 93, 107, 112
    The Lodger (Lowndes) 172
    London: A Poem (Johnson) 75
    London Assurance (Boucicault) 112
    Londoners (Duffy) 263
    The Loneliness of the Long Distance Runner (Sillitoe) 231
    The Long View (Howard) 226
    The Longest Journey (Forster) 165
    Look at the Harlequins! (Nabokov) 252
    Look Back in Anger (Osborne) 228
    The Looking Glass (Roberts) 295
    The Loom of Youth (Waugh) 176
    Lord Hornblower (Forester) 213
    Lord Jim (Conrad) 155, 158
    Lord of the Flies (Golding) 223
    The Lord of the Rings (Tolkien) 223, 225, 227
    Lord Ormont and His Aminta (Meredith) 144
    Lord Rochester's Monkey, Being the Life of John Wilmot, Earl of Rochester (Greene) 252
    Lorna Doone (Blackmore) 127
    Lost Empires (Priestly) 240
    Lost in Yonkers (Simon) 276
    "The Lotos-Eaters" (Tennyson) 93, 107
    Love, Again (Lessing) 286
    Love and Mr. Lewisham (Wells) 158
    Love for Love (Congreve) 66
    Love in a Cold Climate (Mitford) 217
    Love in a Wood (Wycherley) 62
    "The Love Song of J. Alfred Prufrock" (Eliot) 152, 174

    Love Triumphant (Dryden) 49, 66
    The Loved One (Waugh) 216
    The Lover's Melancholy (Ford) 54
    Love's Labour's Lost (Shakespeare) 31, 44
    Love's Riddle (Cowley) 56
    The Loyal Subject (Fletcher) 52
    The Luck of Barry Lyndon, a Romance of the Last Century by Fitzboodle (Thackeray) 113
    Lucky Jim (Amis) 223
    Lucretius (Tennyson) 126
    "Lucy" (Wordsworth) 92
    "Lucy Gray, or Solitude" (Wordsworth) 88
    Luther (Osborne) 234
    Lycidas (Milton) 48, 56
    The Lying Lover (Steele) 70
    Lyrical Ballads (Wordsworth, Coleridge) 88, 92
    Mac Flecknoe (Dryden) 49, 64
    Macbeth (Shakespeare) 31, 50
    The Macdermots of Ballycloran (Trollope) 115
    Madoc (Southey) 96
    A Maggot (Fowles) 266
    Magnetic Lady, or Humours Reconciled (Jonson) 55
    The Magnetic Mountain (Day-Lewis) 197
    Magnyfycens (Skelton) 35
    Maid Marian (Peacock) 103
    The Maid's Tragedy (Beaumont, Fletcher) 51
    The Malcontent (Marston) 50
    A Man Could Stand Up (Ford) 188
    The Man of Property (Galsworthy) 164, 182
    The Man Who Was Thursday (Chesterton) 166
    "The Man Who Would Be King" (Kipling) 139
    The Man Within (Greene) 154, 192
    Manfred (Byron) 93, 100
    Mansfield Park (Austen) 91, 99
    Mantissa (Fowles) 261
    "Mariana" (Tennyson) 93, 106
    Marino Faliero (Byron) 93, 102
    Marino Faliero, Doge of Venice (Swinburne) 135
    Marius the Epicurean (Pater) 137
    Marlborough: His Life and Times (Churchill) 197
    Marnie (Graham) 234
    Marriage A-la-Mode (Dryden) 49, 62
    The Marriage of Heaven and Hell (Blake) 68, 86
    Martha Quest (Lessing) 221
    Martin Chuzzlewit (Dickens) 90
    Mary, Queen of Scots (Fraser) 246
    Mary Barton, a Tale of Manchester Life (Gaskell) 115

    The Massacre at Paris (Marlowe) 33
    Master Georgie (Bainbridge) 290
    The Masters (Snow) 220
    The Matador of the Five Towns (Bennett) 171
    Mathematical Principles of Natural Philosophy (Newton) 64
    "Matthew" (Wordsworth) 92
    Maud (Tennyson) 93, 119
    Maurice (Forster) 249
    The Maxman (Caine) 144
    May Day (Chapman) 51
    The Mayor of Castorbridge (Hardy) 137
    Mazeppa (Byron) 101
    Measure for Measure (Shakespeare) 50
    Melincourt; or, Sir Oran Haut-ton (Peacock) 100
    The Melting Pot (Zangwill) 166
    Memoirs (Gibbon) 87
    Memoirs of a Cavalier (Defoe) 72
    Memoirs of a Fox-Hunting Man (Sassoon) 190
    The Memoirs of a Survivor (Lessing) 252
    Memoirs of Martinus Scriblerus (Pope, Arbuthnot) 76
    The Memoirs of Sherlock Holmes (Doyle) 144
    The Memorial (Isherwood) 196
    Memorials of a Tour on the Continent (Wordsworth) 103
    Men and Women (Browning) 119
    Men at Arms (Waugh) 221
    The Merchant of Venice (Shakespeare) 31, 44
    Mercian Hymns (Hill) 249
    Mere Christianity (Lewis) 210
    Merope, a Tragedy (Arnold) 120
    The Merry Wives of Windsor (Shakespeare) 45
    The Messiah (Pope) 71
    "Methought I Saw My Late Espoused Saint" (Milton) 59
    "Michael" (Wordsworth) 92, 95
    Michael and His Lost Angel (Jones) 146
    Midas (Lyly) 44
    Middlemarch, a Study of Provincial Life (Eliot) 128
    A Midsummer Night's Dream (Shakespeare) 31, 44
    The Mikado (Gilbert) 136
    The Military Philosopher (Powell) 244
    The Mill on the Floss (Eliot) 121
    Mine Own Executioner (Balchin) 212
    The Ministry of Fear (Greene) 154, 210
    A Mirrour for Magistrates (Ferrers, Baldwin) 40

Miscellaneous Poems (Browning) 107
Miscellanies (Cowley) 59
The Misfortunes of Elphin (Peacock) 105
The Mistress (Cowley) 58
Modern Love (Meredith) 123
A Modest Proposal (Swift) 68, 74
Moll Flanders (Defoe) 73
Moly (Gunn) 249
A Moment in Time (Bates) 238
Moments of Grace (Jennings) 258
Money (Bulwer-Lytton) 111
The Monk (Lewis) 87
"The Monkey's Paw" (Jacobs) 160
Monsignor Quixote (Greene) 154, 261
Mont Blanc (Shelley) 93, 100
The Moon and Sixpence (Maugham) 178
"The Moonstone" (Collins) 126
The Moorland Cottage (Gaskell) 116
Le Morte d'Arthur (Malory) 28
"Morte d'Arthur" (Tennyson) 93, 112
Moths (Ouida) 133
Mount Zion (Betjeman) 197
Mountolive (Durrell) 229
The Mourning Bride (Congreve) 66
The Mousetrap (Christie) 221
"Mr. Gilfil's Love-Story" (Eliot) 120
Mr. Midshipman Easy (Marryat) 109
Mrs. Dalloway (Woolf) 186
Mrs. Leicester's School (Lamb and Lamb) 98
Much Ado About Nothing (Shakespeare) 31, 45
Murder in the Cathedral (Eliot) 152, 200
The Murder of Roger Ackroyd (Christie) 188
Murder on the Orient Express (Christie) 197
Music and Silence (Tremain) 293
"My Heart Leaps Up When I Behold" (Wordsworth) 96
My Lady Ludlow (Gaskell) 120
"My Last Duchess" (Browning) 112
My Novel; or, Varieties in English Life (Bulwer-Lytton) 118
The Mysterious Affair at Styles (Christie) 180
The Mysterious Mother (Walpole) 81
The Mystery of Edwin Drood (Dickens) 90, 127
Mystery of the Charity of Charles Péguy (Hill) 263
The Napoleon of Notting Hill (Chesterton) 162
National Velvet (Bagnold) 200

A Natural Curiosity (Drabble) 272
The Nature of Passion (Jhabvala) 226
The Near and the Far (Myers) 207
The New Atlantis (Bacon) 54
The New Dunciad (Pope) 69, 74, 76, 84
New Grub Street (Gissing) 142
The New Machiavelli (Wells) 169
The New Men (Snow) 223
New Poems (Arnold) 126
New Testament (translation) 42
The Newcomes (Thackeray) 108, 118
News from Nowhere (Morris) 141
The Nice and the Good (Murdoch) 244
Nicholas Nickleby (Dickens) 90, 110
The Nigger of the "Narcissus" (Conrad) 147, 155
Night and Day (Stoppard) 257
Night and Day (Woolf) 178
Nightmare Abbey (Peacock) 101
A Nip in the Air (Betjeman) 252
No Man's Land (Pinter) 253
No More Parades (Ford) 186
No Other Life (Moore) 280
Noble Essences (Sitwell) 219
Noble Numbers; or, His Pious Pieces (Herrick) 58
The Noël Coward Diaries (Coward) 261
None but the Lonely Heart (Llewellyn) 210
North and South (Gaskell) 119
The North Ship (Larkin) 212
Northanger Abbey (Austen) 91, 100
Nostromo (Conrad) 155, 162
Notes Toward the Definition of Culture (Eliot) 152, 216
Novum Organum (Bacon) 53
The Occasion of Poetry: Essays in Criticism and Autobiography (Gunn) 261
Odd Girl Out (Howard) 250
"Ode: Intimations of Immortality" (Wordsworth) 92, 96
"Ode on a Distant Prospect of Eton College" (Gray) 76
"Ode on a Grecian Urn" (Keats) 101
"Ode on Indolence" (Keats) 101
"Ode on Melancholy" (Keats) 101
"Ode on the Death of the Duke of Wellington" (Tennyson) 118
"Ode on the Spring" (Gray) 76
"Ode to a Nightingale" (Keats) 101
"Ode to Adversity" (Gray) 76

"Ode to Autumn" (Keats) 101
"Ode to Duty" (Wordsworth) 96
"Ode to Fancy" (Wharton) 77
"Ode to Liberty" (Shelley) 93, 102
"Ode to Psyche" (Keats) 101
"Ode to the West Wind" (Shelley) 93, 101
Odes to Several Descriptive and Allegoric Subjects (Collins) 77
The Odessa File (Forsyth) 250
Of Divine Love (Waller) 64
Of Human Bondage (Maugham) 174
"Of the Last Verses Written in His Book" (Waller) 64
Officers and Gentlemen (Waugh) 225
The Old Bachelor (Dryden) 66
The Old Curiosity Shop (Dickens) 90, 111
"The Old Familiar Faces" (Lamb) 88
Old Times (Pinter) 249
The Old Wives' Tale (Bennett) 166
Oliver Twist (Dickens) 90, 109
Olney Hymns (Cowper and Newton) 83
"On an Infant Dying as Soon as It Is Born" (Lamb) 105
"On First Looking into Chapman's Homer" (Keats) 100
"On Liberty" (Mill) 121
On Murder as One of the Fine Arts (De Quincey) 105
On Poetry and Poets (Eliot) 228
On Reading Turgenev (Trevor) 276
"On Shakespeare" (Milton) 54
"On the Death of a Fair Infant Dying of a Cough" (Milton) 54
"On the Morning of Christ's Nativity" (Milton) 54
On the Origin of Species by Means of Natural Selection (Darwin) 121
On This Island (Auden) 202
On Translating Homer (Arnold) 122
The Once and Future King (White) 229
One of Our Conquerors (Meredith) 121
"One Thousand Seven Hundred Thirty Eight. A Dialogue Something Like Horace" (Pope) 76
"Oneone" (Tennyson) 107
"The Open Window" (Saki) 173
The Orators (Auden) 196
The Orchard on Fire (Mackay) 286
The Ordeal of Gilbert Pinfold (Waugh) 228

The Ordeal of Richard Feverel (Meredith) 121
Orient Express (Greene) 154, 196
Orlando (Woolf) 190
Orley Farm (Trollope) 122
Ormond (Edgeworth) 100
Oroonoko, or the History of the Royal Slave (Behn) 63
The Orphan (Otway) 63
Osorio (Coleridge) 87
Otherwise Engaged (Gray) 253
Our American Cousin (Taylor) 120
Our Lady's Tumbler (Duncan) 220
Our Man in Havana (Greene) 154, 229
Our Mutual Friend (Dickens) 90, 124
Out of the Silent Planet (Lewis) 204
The Outline of History (Wells) 180
The Outsider (Wilson) 227
Over the Brazier (Bridges) 175
"The Owl and the Pussycat" (Lear) 128
"Ozymandias" (Shelley) 101
Painted Roofs (Richardson) 174
A Painter of Our Time (Berger) 229
A Pair of Blue Eyes (Hardy) 129
Palmerin of England (Southey) 97
Pamela; or, Virtue Rewarded (Richardson) 76
Paola and Francesca (Phillips) 158
The Paper Men (Golding) 264
Paracelsus (Browning) 108
Parade's End (Ford) 185, 186, 188, 219
Paradise Lost (Milton) 48, 61
Paradise Regained (Milton) 48, 62
The Parent's Assistant (Edgeworth) 87
The Parish Register (Crabbe) 97
"Parisi'na" (Byron) 100
The Parlement of Foules (Chaucer) 14, 26
Pasmore (Storey) 250
Pasquin (Fielding) 75
A Passage to India (Forster) 185
The Passionate Shepheard (Breton) 50
Pastorals (Pope) 71
Pastors and Masters (Compton-Burnett) 186
The Path to Rome (Belloc) 160
A Patriot for Me (Osborne) 240
Patronage (Edgeworth) 99
Paul Clifford (Bulwer-Lytton) 106
Pauling (Browning) 107
Peg Woffington (Reade) 118

English
    British (continued)
        Pelham; or, The Adventures of
            a Gentleman (Bulwer-
            Lytton) 105
        "Il Penseroso" (Milton) 48,
            55
        Pericles, Prince of Tyre
            (Shakespeare) 51
        Pericles and Aspasia (Landor)
            109
        Persian Eclogues (Collins) 76
        A Personal History (Taylor)
            263
        Persuasion (Austen) 91, 100
        Peter Ibbetson (du Maurier)
            142
        Philaster (Beaumont,
            Fletcher) 51
        Phineas Finn (Trollope) 126
        Phineas Redux (Trollope) 130
        A Phoenix Too Frequent (Ish-
            erwood) 213
        The Photographer in Winter
            (Szirtes) 267
        Pickwick Papers (Dickens)
            90, 109
        Pieces of Light (Thorpe) 290
        "Pied Beauty" (Hopkins) 132
        "The Pied Piper of Hamelin"
            (Browning) 112
        Pig Earth (Berger) 258
        Pilgrimage (Richardson) 174,
            243
        The Pilgrim's Progress (Lewis)
            197
        The Pilgrim's Progress, from
            This World to What Which
            Is to Come (Bunyan) 63
        Pincher Martin (Golding)
            227
        The Pirates of Penzance
            (Gilbert) 132
        Pizarro (Sheridan) 88
        The Plain Dealer (Wycherley)
            63
        The Plain Speaker (Hazlitt)
            104
        Pleasure Reconciled to Virtue
            (Jonson) 52
        Pleasured (Hensher) 290
        The Plumed Serpent
            (Lawrence) 188
        Poems (Arnold) 118
        Poems (Brontë, Brontë, and
            Brontë) 114
        Poems (Browning) 113
        Poems (Chatterton) 83
        Poems (Cowper) 84
        Poems (de la Mare) 164
        Poems (Eliot) 152, 178, 180
        Poems (Graves, ed.) 177
        Poems (Jennings) 222
        Poems (Meredith) 117
        Poems (Milton) 48
        Poems (Rossetti) 127
        Poems (Tennyson) 93
        Poems, Chiefly Lyrical (Ten-
            nyson) 93, 106
        Poems, Chiefly of Early and
            Late Years (Wordsworth)
            92, 112
        Poems and Ballads (Swin-
            burne) 125, 132
        Poems in Two Volumes
            (Wordsworth) 97

        Poems of Dedication
            (Spender) 215
        Poetical Blossomes (Cowley)
            55
        Poetical Sketches by Mr. W.B.
            (Blake) 68, 84
        A Poet's Notebook (Sitwell)
            210
        Point Counter Point (Huxley)
            190
        Polly (Gay) 74
        Polonius (FitzGerarld) 117
        Popular Tales (Edgeworth) 96
        Possession (Byatt) 273
        The Posthumous Papers of the
            Pickwick Club (Dickens)
            90, 109
        The Power and the Glory
            (Greene) 154, 207
        Prancing Novelist (Brophy)
            251
        Precious Bane (Webb) 185
        Precious Thing (Kenway) 295
        Prelandra (Lewis) 210
        The Prelude (Wordsworth)
            92
        The Prelude, or, Growth of a
            Poet's Mind (Wordsworth)
            88, 116
        Pride and Prejudice (Austen)
            91, 99
        A Priest to the Temple (Her-
            bert) 58
        The Prime Minister (Trol-
            lope) 131
        Prince Hohensteil-Schwangau
            (Browning) 128
        The Prince's Progress (Ros-
            setti) 125
        The Princess, a Medley (Ten-
            nyson) 115
        Principia Mathematica (Rus-
            sell, Whitehead) 168
        "The Prisoner of Chillon"
            (Byron) 93, 100
        The Prisoner of Zenda (Hope)
            144
        Private Lives (Coward) 193
        The Private Papers of Henry
            Ryecroft (Gissing) 161
        The Problem of Pain (Lewis)
            207
        The Professor (Brontë) 120
        The Profligate (Pinero) 140
        The Progresse of the Soul: The
            Second Anniversary
            (Donne) 51
        Prometheus Unbound (Shel-
            ley) 93, 102
        A Proper Marriage (Lessing)
            223
        The Prophecy of Dante
            (Byron) 93
        Prufrock and Other Observa-
            tions (Eliot) 176
        The Pumpkin Eater (Martin)
            235
        The Purple Plain (Bates) 213
        The Pursuit of Love (Mitford)
            212
        The Pyramid (Golding) 243
        Quarantine (Crace) 288
        Queen Mab (Shelley) 93, 99
        Queen Mary (Tennyson) 130
        Queen Victoria (Strachey)
            181

        The Queenes Arcadia (Daniel)
            50
        The Quest for Corvo (Rolfe)
            199
        A Question of Upbringing
            (Powell) 220
        The Quiet American (Greene)
            154, 225
        Quinx; or, The Ripper's Tale
            (Durrell) 266
        Rabbi Ben Ezra (Browning)
            124
        The Radiant Way (Drabble)
            269
        The Rainbow (Lawrence) 174
        Rain-Charm for the Duchy
            (Hughes) 278
        The Raj Quartet (Scott) 241,
            244
        Ralph Roister Doister (Udall)
            40
        The Rape of Lucrece (Shake-
            speare) 31, 44
        The Rape of the Lock (Pope)
            69
        Rasselas, Prince of Abyssinia
            (Johnson) 79
        Rates of Exchange (Bradbury)
            263
        Raw Material (Sillitoe) 250
        The Razor's Edge (Maugham)
            211
        The Reader (Schlink) 288
        Rebecca (du Maurier) 204
        Rebecca and Rowenna: A Ro-
            mance Upon Romance
            (Thackeray) 116
        Red Cotton Night-Cap Coun-
            try (Browning) 129
        The Redundancy of Courage
            (Mo) 276
        Reflections on the Revolution
            in France (Burke) 85
        Reginald (Saki) 162
        Reginald in Russia (Saki) 168
        Relationships (Jennings) 250
        Religio Laici, or a Layman's
            Faith (Dryden) 64
        Religio Medici (Browne) 57
        Remains of Elmet (Hughes)
            258
        The Remains of the Day
            (Ishiguro) 272
        Rendevous with Rama
            (Clarke) 251
        Resignation (Young) 80
        "Resolution and Indepen-
            dence" (Wordsworth) 96
        "Responsibility: The Pilots
            Who Destroyed Germany,
            Spring 1945" (Spender)
            217
        Restoration (Bond) 260
        The Return of the King
            (Tolkien) 227
        The Return of the Native
            (Hardy) 132
        The Revenge, a Tragedy
            (Young) 73
        Revenge for Love (Lewis) 203
        The Revenge of the Bussy
            D'Amboise (Chapman) 52
        Riceyman Steps (Bennett)
            184
        Richard II (Shakespeare) 31,
            44

        Richard III (Shakespeare) 31,
            44
        Richelieu; or, The Conspiracy
            (Bulwer-Lytton) 110
        Rienzi; or, The Last of the Tri-
            bunes (Bulwer-Lytton) 108
        "The Rime of the Ancient
            Mariner" (Coleridge) 88
        The Ring and the Book
            (Browning) 126
        The Ripple from the Storm
            (Lessing) 229, 231
        Rites of Passage (Golding) 259
        The Rival Ladies (Dryden) 60
        The Rivals (Sheridan) 82
        The River (Godden) 213
        "The River Duddon"
            (Wordsworth) 92
        Rivers Among Rocks
            (Gustafson) 232
        The Riverside Willas Murder
            (Amis) 251
        The Road to Wigan Pier (Or-
            well) 203
        Roderick, The Last of the
            Goths (Southey) 99
        Rokeby (Scott) 99
        The Roman Actor (Massinger)
            54
        Romeo and Juliet (Shake-
            speare) 31, 44
        Romola (Eliot) 123
        The Room and Other Poems
            (Day-Lewis) 240
        Room at the Top (Braine) 228
        A Room of One's Own
            (Woolf) 192
        A Room with a View (Forster)
            166
        Rosalynde (Lodge) 43
        Rosencrantz and Gildenstern
            Are Dead (Stoppard) 241
        Rough Crossing (Stoppard)
            266
        The Rover, or the Banished
            Cavaliers (Behn) 63
        Roxana; or, the Unfortunate
            Mistress (Defoe) 73
        The Royal Hunt of the Sun
            (Shaffer) 238
        Rubaiyat of Omar Khayyam
            (FitzGerald) 121
        Rule a Wife and Have a Wife
            (Fletcher) 53
        Rural Sports (Gay) 72
        The Russia House (Le Carré)
            272
        Russian Thinkers (Berlin) 257
        Ruth (Gaskell) 118
        The Sacred and Profane Love
            Machine (Murdoch) 252
        Sacred Hunger (Unsworth)
            278
        The Sacred Wood (Eliot) 152,
            180
        "The Sad Fortune of the Rev.
            Amos Barton" (Eliot) 120
        Sadler's Birthday (Tremain)
            255
        The Saints Everlasting Rest
            (Baxter) 58
        The Saint's Tragedy (Kings-
            ley) 115
        Sally Bowles (Isherwood) 203
        Samson Agonistes (Milton)
            48, 62

Samuel Johnson (Bate) 256
Samuel Johnson (Wain) 252
The Sandcastle (Murdoch) 228
Sanditon (Austen) 100
Sandra Belloni (Meredith) 124
Sardanapalus (Byron) 93, 102
Sartor Resartus (Carlyle) 107
Saturday Night and Sunday Morning (Sillitoe) 229
Saville (Storey) 255
Scar Tissue (Ignatieff) 280
The Scarlet Pimpernel (Orczy) 163
The Scarlet Tree (Sitwell) 213
The Scenic Route (Adcock) 252
"The Scholar-Gipsy" (Arnold) 118
The School for Scandal (Sheridan) 83
Scoop (Waugh) 204
The Screwtape Letters (Lewis) 208
The Sea, the Sea (Murdoch) 257
The Sea Change (Howard) 231
The Search (Snow) 199
The Second Curtain (Fuller) 222
The Second Mrs. Tanqueray (Pinero) 143
The Secret Agent (Conrad) 155, 165
The Secret Garden (Burnett) 169
Secret Love, or the Maiden Queen (Dryden) 49, 61
Sense and Sensibility (Austen) 91, 98
The Sense of Movement (Gunn) 228
"The Sensitive Plan" (Shelley) 102
A Sentimental Journey Through France and Italy (Sterne) 81
Separate Tables (Rattigan) 223
"September 1, 1939" (Auden) 207
The Seraphim and Other Poems (Browning) 110
Sermons (Swift) 77
Setting the World on Fire (Wilson) 259
The Seven Lamps of Architecture (Ruskin) 116
The Seven Pillars of Wisdom (Lawrence) 188
Seven Types of Ambiguity: A Study of Its Effects on English Verse (Empson) 193
A Severed Head (Murdoch) 234
A Shabby Genteel Story (Thackeray) 111
"The Shadow Line" (Conrad) 155
Shadow of the Night (Chapman) 44
Shakespearean Tragedy (Bradley) 162

The Shape of Things to Come (Wells) 197
The Shaving of Shagpat; an Arabian Entertainment (Meredith) 119
She (Haggard) 138
She Stoops to Conquer (Goldsmith) 82
"She Was a Phantom of Delight" (Wordsworth) 96
The Shepheard's Calendar (Spenser) 41
The Shepherd's Week (Gay) 72
The Shield of Achilles (Auden) 225
The Ship of Fools (Barclay) 34
Shirley (Brontë) 116
The Shoemaker's Holiday (Dekker) 50
The Shrimp and the Anemone (Hartley) 211
A Shropshire Lad (Housman) 146
"The Siege of Corinth" (Byron) 100
The Siege of Thebes (Lydgate) 34
The Sign of Four (Doyle) 141
Silas Marner (Eliot) 122
Silence (Pinter) 246
A Silence of Desire (Markandaya) 232
The Silmarillion (Tolkien) 256
The Silver Box (Galsworthy) 167
The Silver King Play (Jones) 135
A Silver Spoon (Galsworthy) 188
The Singapore Grip (Farrell) 257
A Single Man (Isherwood) 238
Sir Eustace Grey (Crabbe) 97
Skellig (Almond) 293
Sketches by Boz (Dickens) 109
"The Skylark" (Shelley) 102
Sleep It Off Lady (Rhys) 255
A Sleep of Prisoners (Fry) 220
The Sleeping Lord and Other Fragments (Jones) 252
The Small Black Room (Balchin) 210
The Small House in Allington (Trollope) 123
Small World (Lodge) 264
Smiley's People (Le Carré) 259
Sohrab and Rustim (Arnold) 117
"The Soldier" (Brooke) 174
The Soldier's Art (Powell) 241
The Soldier's Fortune (Otway) 63
"The Solitary Reaper" (Wordsworth) 96
Solomon on the Vanity of the World (Prior) 72
Some Do Not (Ford) 185
Some Unease and Angels (Feinstein) 256
Something in Disguise (Howard) 246

Son of the Morning (Phillpotts) 158
"Song" (Donne) 48, 55
Song for a Birth or a Death (Jennings) 234
Song for St. Cecilia's Day (Dryden) 64
"A Song of Italy" (Swinburne) 126
"The Song of Los" (Blake) 68, 87
"The Song of the Shirt" (Hood) 113
Songs Before Sunrise (Swinburne) 128
Songs of Experience (Blake) 68, 86
Songs of Innocence (Blake) 68, 85
Songs of the Cold (Sitwell) 212
Sonnets (Shakespeare) 51
Sonnets (Wordsworth) 92
Sonnets from the Portuguese (Browning) 116
Sons and Lovers (Lawrence) 172
Sordello (Browning) 111
A Sort of Life (Greene) 154
The Spanish Fryar (Dryden) 63
The Spanish Tragedie (Kyd) 44
A Spell in WInter (Dumore) 286
The Spider and the Flie (Heywood) 39
Spider Web: A Novel (Lively) 290
The Spire (Golding) 238
The Spirit of Man (Graves) 175
The Spirit of the Age (Hazlitt) 104
Spring and Fall (Hopkins) 133
The Spy Who Came in from the Cold (Le Carré) 237
Squaring the Circle (Stoppard) 264
St. Patrick's Day; or, The Scheming Lieutenant (Sheridan) 82
A Staple of News (Jonson) 54
The Stars Look Down (Cronin) 200
The State of Innocence and Fall of Man (Dryden) 63
Staying On (Scott) 256
Steps to the Temple (Crashaw) 57
Still Centre (Spender) 205
Still Life (Coward) 202, 213
A Stitch in Time (Lively) 255
The Stories of Venice (Ruskin) 117
Stories Toto Told Me (Rolfe) 148
The Story of Dr. Dolittle (Lofting) 180
The Story of Rimini (Hunt) 100
The Story of Sigurd the Volsung and the Fall of the Niblungs (Morris) 131
Strafford (Browning) 109

Strangers and Brothers (Snow) 207
Strathmore (Ouida) 124
Stratton (Duncan) 217
The Strayed Reveller (Arnold) 116
Street Songs (Sitwell) 209
Strike the Father Dead (Wain) 235
A Study (Doyle) 138
A Study of History (Toynbee) 199
The Sum of Things (Manning) 259
The Summer Before the Dark (Lessing) 251
A Summer to Decide (Johnson) 216
Summoned by Bells (Betjeman) 232
The Supposes (Gascoigne) 40
Surprised by Joy: The Shape of My Early Life (Lewis) 225
The Swan Song (Galsworthy) 190
Sweeney Agonistes (Eliot) 152, 188
Sword of Honor (Waugh) 221, 234
Sylvie and Bruno (Carroll) 140
Table Talk; or, Original Essays on Men and Manners (Hazlitt) 102
The Tailor of Panama (Le Carré) 286
A Tale of a Tub (Jonson) 55
A Tale of a Tub (Swift) 68, 70
The Tale of Paraguay (Southey) 104
The Tale of Peter Rabbit (Potter) 160
The Tale of Rosamund Gray and Old Blind Margaret (Lamb) 88
A Tale of Two Cities (Dickens) 90, 121
Tales from Shakespeare (Lamb and Lamb) 97
Tamburlaine the Great (Marlowe) 33, 43
The Taming of the Shrew (Shakespeare) 31, 44
The Task (Cowper) 84
The Tempest (Shakespeare) 31, 51
The Temple (Herbert) 55
Temporary Kings (Powell) 251
The Tenant of Wildfell Hall (Brontë) 115
The Tender Husband (Steele) 70
The Tenement (Smith) 266
Tennyson, Alfred, 121
The Tenth Man (Greene) 154, 266
Tess of the D'Urbervilles; A Pure Woman (Hardy) 142
The Testament of Beauty (Bridges) 192
Thalaba the Destroyer (Southey) 95
That Hideous Strength (Lewis) 212
That Uncertain Feeling (Amis) 225

English
British *(continued)*
Theory of War (Brady) 282
These Enchanted Woods (Massie) 280
A Thing of Beauty (Cronin) 227
The Third Man (Greene) 154, 217
This Bed Thy Centre (Johnson) 200
This Gun for Hire (Greene) 154
This Sporting Life (Story) 232
The Three Clerks (Trollope) 120
Three Men in a Boat (Jerome) 140
The Three Voices of Poetry (Eliot) 222
Threnodia Augustalis (Dryden) 64
Through the Looking Glass (Carroll) 128
Thunderball (Fleming) 234
"Thyrsis" (Arnold) 125
Tigers (Adcock) 243
Timber, of Discoveries Made Upon Men and Matter (Jonson) 56
Timbuctoo (Tennyson) 105
Time and the Conways (Priestley) 203
The Time Machine (Wells) 145
The Time of Angels (Murdoch) 241
Time's Arrow (Amis) 276
Timon of Athens (Shakespeare) 51
Tiriel (Blake) 130
'Tis a Pity She's a Whore (Ford) 54
Tithonus (Tennyson) 121
Titus Andronicus (Shakespeare) 43
"To a Skylark" (Shelley) 93
"To Althea, from Prison" (Lovelace) 58
To an Athlete Dying Young (Housman) 146
To Be a Pilgrim (Cary) 209
To Byron (Keats) 99
"To His Coy Mistress" (Marvell) 63
To His Sacred Majesty (Dryden) 49
To Let (Galsworthy) 181, 182
"To Lucasta, Going to the Wars" (Lovelace) 58
To the Lighthouse (Woolf) 189
"To the Nightingale" (Finch) 72
"Tobermory" (Saki) 169
Tom Brown's Schooldays (Hughes) 120
Tom Jones (Osborne) 237
Tom Jones, a Foundling (Fielding) 78
Tom Thumb, a Tragedy (Fielding) 74
Tono-Bungoy (Wells) 166
Too Dear for My Possessing (Johnson) 207
Touch (Gunn) 243
The Towers of Trebizond (Macaulay) 227

The Tragedie of Philotas (Daniel) 50
The Tragedy of Chabot, Admiral of France (Chapman) 56
The Tragedy of Othello, Moor of Venice (Shakespeare) 50
The Tragic Comedians (Meredith) 133
The Tragical History of the Life and Death of Doctor Faustus (Marlowe) 50
The Traveller; or, A Prospect of Society (Goldsmith) 80
Travels with a Donkey in the Cevennes (Stevenson) 132
Trelawney of the "Wells" (Pinero) 148
Tres Thomae (Stapleton) 43
Trilby (Du Maurier) 144
The Triple Echo (Bates) 247
Tristam of Lyonesse (Swinburne) 135
Tristram Shandy (Sterne) 79
The Triumph of Life (Shelley) 93
Troilus and Creseyde (Chaucer) 14
Troilus and Cressida (Dryden) 63
Troilus and Cressida (Shakespeare) 50
The Troy Book (Lydgate) 35
The Tunnynge of Elynour Rummyng (Skelton) 35
Twelfth Night, or What You Will (Shakespeare) 50
Twenty Thousand Streets Under the Sky (Hamilton) 200
Two Cultures and the Scientific Revolution (Snow) 231
The Two Foscari (Byron) 93, 102
The Two Gentlemen of Verona (Shakespeare) 44
Two on a Tower (Hardy) 135
The Two Towers (Tolkien) 225
"The Two Voices" (Tennyson) 93
Two Years Ago (Kingsley) 120
Typhoon (Conrad) 155, 161
Tyrannick Love (Dryden) 49, 61
"Ulysses" (Tennyson) 93, 112
Uncollected Poems (Betjeman) 261
Unconditional Surrender (Waugh) 234
Under the Frog (Fischer) 280
Under the Greenwood (Hardy) 129
Under the Net (Murdoch) 224
Under the Volcano (Lowry) 235
Under Two Flags (Ouida) 126
Under Western Eyes (Conrad) 155, 169
Undertones of War (Blunden) 190
The Universal Passion; or, The Love of Fame (Young) 73

The Unknown Eros (Patmore) 131
Unknown Pleasures (Cowley) 295
The Unspeakable Skipton (Johnson) 231
"Upon the Death of Lord Hastings" (Dryden) 58
The Use of Poetry and the Use of Criticism (Eliot) 152
Utopia (More) 35
"A Valediction Forbidding Mourning" (Donne) 49, 55
The Valley of Bones (Powell) 238
The Valley of Fear (Doyle) 174
Valperga; or, The Life and Adventures of Castruccio, Prince of Lucca (Shelley) 103
Vanity Fair (Thackeray) 115
Vathek (Beckford) 85
Venice Preserved (Otway) 64
Venus and Adonis (Shakespeare) 31
Venus Observed (Fry) 219
Vermilion Sands (Ballard) 249
Verses (Dowson) 146
The Vicar of Sorrows (Wilson) 280
The Vicar of Wakefield (Goldsmith) 80
Victoria Regina (Housman) 199
Victorian Voices (Thwaite) 259
The Victories of Love (Patmore) 123
Victory (Conrad) 155
Vile Bodies (Waugh) 193
The Village (Crabbe) 84
Villette (Brontë) 118
A Vindication of the Rights of Woman (Wollstonecraft) 86
The Virgin in the Garden (Byatt) 257
The Virginians (Thackeray) 120
"The Vision of Sin" (Tennyson) 93
Visions of the Daughters of Albion (Blake) 68
V-Letter and Other Poems (Shapiro) 211
The Volcano (Lowery) 215
Volpone, or the Fox (Jonson) 50
The Voyage Out (Woolf) 174
The Waggoner (Wordsworth) 101
The War of the Worlds (Wells) 148
War Poems (Sassoon) 178
The Warden (Arnold) 119
The Warrior Queens (Fraser) 272
The Waste Land (Eliot) 152, 182
The Water Babies (Kingsley) 123
The Waves (Woolf) 194
The Way I Found Her (Tremain) 288
The Way of All Flesh (Butler) 161
A Way of Looking (Jennings) 225

The Way of the World (Congreve) 69
The Way to the Tomb (Duncan) 212
The Way We Live Now (Trollope) 130
Ways of Escape (Greene) 154
A Weekend with Claud (Bainbridge) 243
The Well of Loneliness (Hall) 190
Werner (Byron) 103
Wessex Poems (Hardy) 148
West with the Night (Markham) 209
Westward Ho! (Kingsley) 119
What D'Ye Call It (Gay) 72
When His Hour Came (Glyn) 168
When I Lived in Modern Times (Grant) 295
When We Are Married (Priestley) 204
When We Were Orphans (Ishiguro) 295
Where Angels Fear to Tread (Forster) 163
The Whispering Roots (Day-Lewis) 247
The White Devil (Webster) 51
The White Goddess (Graves) 216
The White Hotel (Thomas) 260
The White Monkey (Galsworthy) 185
White Teeth (Smith) 295
The Whole Booke of Psalmes (Sternhold, Hopkins) 38
Wide Open (Barker) 295
Wide Sargasso Sea (Rhys) 241
Widecombe Fair (Phillpotts) 172
The Widow Lerouge (Gaboriau) 125
The Widow's Tears (Chapman) 51
A Wife (Overbury) 52
The Wild Gallant (Dryden) 49, 60
Wilhelm Meister's Apprenticeship (Carlyle, tr.) 103
"The Windhover" (Hopkins) 131
Windsor Forest (Pope) 72
Wine (Gay) 71
Winnie the Pooh (Milne) 188
The Winter's Tale (Shakespeare) 31, 51
Witness for the Prosecution (Christie) 222
Wives and Daughters (Gaskell) 124
The Woman in White (Collins) 121
A Woman Killed with Kindness (Heywood) 51
The Woman Thou Gavest Me (Caine) 172
The Woman's Prize, or the Tamer Tamed (Fletcher) 54
Women Beware Women (Middleton) 53
Women in Love (Lawrence) 180

Woodlanders (Hardy) 138

A Word Child (Murdoch) 253

Works (Pope) 76

"The World Is Too Much With Us" (Wordsworth) 97

"The Wreck of the Deutschland" (Hopkins) 130, 177

Wuthering Heights (Brontë) 115

A Yard of the Sun (Fry) 247

Yarrow Revisited and Other Poems (Wordsworth) 92

The Years (Woolf) 203

The Yellow Admiral (O'Brian) 286

The Yellow-Plush Correspondence (Thackeray) 109

You Can't Do Both (Amis) 282

Zanoni (Bulwer-Lytton) 112

Zapolya (Coleridge) 100

Zuleika Dobson (Beerbohm) 169

Cameroonian

Agatha Moudio's Sons (Bebey) 243

A Few Nights and Days (Dipoko) 241

Canadian

The Acrobat (Richler) 223

Across the Bridge: Stories (Gallant) 280

Alias Grace (Atwood) 286

Almost Spring (Ball) 293

Angel Walk (Govier) 286

Anil's Ghost (Ondaatje) 295

The Apprenticeship of Duddy Kravitz (Richler) 228

Barney's Version (Richler) 288

Be Sure to Close Your Eyes (Hood) 280

The Blind Assassin (Atwood) 295

Book of Mercy (Cohen) 264

The Bookseller (Cohen) 280

Borderline (Hospital) 266

Brebeuf and His Brethren (Pratt) 207

Burridge Unbound (Cumyn) 295

"The Cachalot" (Pratt) 188

The Canadian Brothers (Richardson) 111

Caprice (Bowring) 269

Cargo of Orchids (Musgrove) 295

Cat's Eye (Atwood) 271

The Chinese Insomniacs (Jacobsen) 260

A Choice of Enemies (Richler) 228

The Chrome Suite (Birdsell) 278

Close to the Sun Again (Callaghan) 256

Cocksure (Richler) 244

The Cold Green Element (Layton) 225

Collected Works of Billy the Kidd: Left-Handed Poems (Ondaatje) 247

Criminals in Love (Walker) 264

The Cunning Man (Davies) 282

The Cure for Death by Lightning (Anderson-Dargat) 286

Dead Men's Watches (Hood) 284

The Deptford Trilogy (Davies) 247, 250, 253

A Discovery of Strangers (Wiebe) 282

The Dumbfounding (Avison) 241

The Electrical Field (Sakamoto) 290

Elizabeth and After (Cohen) 293

The English Patient (Ondaatje) 278

Eriksdottir: A Tale of Dreams and Luck (Clark) 282

Europe and Other Bad News (Layton) 260

Evening Light (Horwood) 288

Fall from Grace (Wright) 276

The Fifth Business (Davies) 247

A Fine Balance (Mistry) 286

Freedom's Just Another Word (Hamilton) 290

Friend of My Youth (Munro) 273

Fugitive Pieces (Michaels) 286

A Gift of Rags (Boyarsky) 284

The Girl with the Botticelli Face (Valgardson) 278

Girlfriend in a Coma (Coupland) 293

Gloria (Maillard) 293

The Golden Dog (Kirby) 131

A Good House (Burnard) 293

Graven Images (Thomas) 280

The Habitant and Other French-Canadian Poems (Drummond) 147

The Handmaid's Tale (Atwood) 266

Head Hunter (Findley) 280

The Healer (Hollingshead) 290

Home Truths (Gallant) 266

Human Bodies: New and Collected Poems, 1987–1999 (Bowering) 293

In a Glass House (Ricci) 280

In Praise of Older Women: Amorous Recollections of Andras Vajada (Vicinczy) 240

In the Midst of My Fever (Layton) 223

In the Skin of a Lion (Ondaatje) 269

In Transit (Gallant) 272

The Incomparable Atuk (Richler) 237

The Invention of Truth (Brewster) 276

The Island in Winter (Young) 293

Isobars (Hospital) 276

Isolation Booth (Hood) 276

Ixion's Wheel (Gustafson) 246

Kitchen Music (Foran) 282

Lake Lyrics and Other Poems (Campbell) 140

Larry's Party (Shields) 288

The Last Magician (Hospital) 278

The Love of a Good Woman (Munro) 291

The Loved and the Lost (Callaghan) 220

The Lyre of Orpheus (Davies) 271

Man Descending (Vanderhaeghe) 261

The Manticore (Davies) 250

The Mark of the Angel (Huston) 293

Mercy Among Children (Adams) 295

Morning in the Burned House (Atwood) 284

Mother Love (Wright) 284

Murther & Walding Spirits (Davies) 276

My Happy Days in Hell (Faludy) 235

The New Age (Hood) 273

Old Spookes' Pass, Malcolm Katie and Other Poems (Crawford) 136

On Glassy Wings: New and Selected Poems (Lowther) 288

Open Secrets (Munro) 282

Other Women (Wau) 284

A Passion in Rome (Callaghan) 234

The Pegnitz Junction (Gallant) 251

The Prinzhorn Collection (Coles) 261

Property and Value (Hood) 273

The Rain Ascends (Kogawa) 284

The Rebel Angel (Davies) 260

A Recipe for Bees (Dargatz) 291

The Roaring Girl (Hollingshed) 284

The Robber Bride (Atwood) 280

Roses Are Difficult Here (Mitchell) 273

Rules of Chaos; or, Why Tomorrow Doesn't Work (Vizinczey) 246

The Rules of Engagement (Bush) 295

Salterton Trilogy (Davies) 220

The Season Ticket (Haliburton) 121

Selected Poems (Livesay) 228

Selected Poems, 1933–1980 (Faludy) 266

The Shadow Boxer (Heighten) 295

Shadows in the Grass (Gustafson) 276

Shoeless Joe (Kinsella) 261

The Singing Flesh (Layton) 234

Solomon Gursky Was Here (Richler) 273

Something Happened Here (Levine) 276

Son of a Smaller Hero (Richler) 225

The Splits (Ritter) 257

St. Urbain's Horseman (Richler) 249

Still Stands the House (Ringwood) 205

The Stone Diaries (Shields) 280

Strange Heaven (Coady) 291

Stranger Music: Selected Poems and Songs (Cohen) 280

A Student of Weather (Hay) 295

Such a Long Journey (Mistry) 276

Such Is My Beloved (Callaghan) 199

A Sudden Brightness (Boisonneau) 282

They Shall Inherit the Earth (Callaghan) 200

Those Were the Mermaid Days (Young) 276

The Trade (Stenson) 295

Tribute (Slade) 257

The Underpainter (Urquhart) 288

Wacousta (Richardson) 107

Waiting for Saskatchewan (Wah) 266

What's Bred in the Bone (Davies) 266

The Wild Blue Yonder (Thomas) 273

The World of Wonders (Davies) 253

Dominican

The Orchid House (Allfrey) 222

Egyptian

The Map of Love (Soueif) 293

Ethiopian

The Afersata (Selassie) 246

Oda Oark Oracle (Gabre-Madhin) 240

Filipino

Po-on (Jose) 264

Ghanaian

The Beautiful Ones Are Not Yet Born (Armah) 244

Edufa (Sutherland) 243

Ethiopia Unbound (Hayford) 169

The Gab Boys (Duodo) 243

Rediscovery and Other Poems (Awoonor) 238

This Earth, My Brother (Awoonor) 238

The Torrent (Abruquah) 244

Two Thousand Seasons (Armah) 251

Guyanese

Black Label (Damas) 227

De Silva (Harris) 256

Morning at the Office (Mittelholzer) 219

Moscow Not My Mecca (Carew) 238

Son of Guyana (Apple) 251

Song of the Sugarcanes (Sadik) 253

Indian

The Autobiography of an Unknown Indian (Chadhuri) 220

Avadheshwari (Punekar) 269

English
    Indian *(continued)*
        The Circle of Reason (Ghosh)
            267
        Coolie (Anand) 202
        The English Teacher
            (Narayan) 212
        An Equal Music (Seth) 293
        The God of Small Things
            (Roy) 288
        The Golden Gate (Seth) 267
        Golden Honeycomb (Markan-
            daya) 256
        The Grand Man (Bhoosnur-
            math) 264
        The Ground Beneath Her Feet
            (Rushdie) 293
        The Guide (Narayan) 229
        Kanthapura (Rao) 204
        Light of Day (Desai) 259
        The Man Eaters of Malgudi
            (Narayay) 234
        Midnight's Children
            (Rushdie) 260
        Mister Bahram (Patel) 271
        The Moor's Last Sigh
            (Rushdie) 284
        Nectar in a Sieve (Markan-
            daya) 224
        Plans for Departure (Sahgal)
            266
        The Satanic Verses (Rushdie)
            271
        The Serpent and the Rope
            (Rao) 232
        Shalimar (Markandaya) 263
        Siddhartha: Man of Peace
            (Chattopadhyay) 227
        A Suitable Boy (Seth) 280
        A Tiger for Malgudi
            (Narayan) 263
        Two Virgins (Markandaya) 251
        Two Women (Sarabhai) 221
        Untouchable (Anand) 200
        The Vendor of Sweets
            (Narayan) 243
        Waiting for the Mahatma
            (Naroyan) 225
        The Whole Sky (Yadav) 232
        The Will of the People (Sarab-
            hai) 210
        The World of Nagaraj
            (Narayan) 274
    Irish
        Amongst Women (McGahern)
            274
        Androcles and the Lion (Shaw)
            153, 175
        Another September (Kinsella)
            229
        The Apple Cart (Shaw) 153
        Arms and the Man (Shaw)
            144, 148, 153
        At the Hawk's Well (Yeats)
            152
        Autumn Journal (MacNeice)
            204
        Back to Methuselah (Shaw)
            153, 181
        Bailegangaire (Murphy) 267
        The Ballad of Reading Gaol
            (Wilde) 148
        The Battle of the Books (Swift)
            70
        The Beaux's Stratagem (Far-
            quhar) 71

Bird Alone (O'Faolain) 202
The Black Soul (O'Flaherty)
    185
Blood and Family (Kinsella)
    271
The Bog of Stars (O'Grady)
    143
Borstal Boy (Behan) 229
Breakfast on Pluto (McCabe)
    291
The Brook Kerith (Moore) 175
Caesar and Cleopatra (Shaw)
    153, 159
Candida (Shaw) 148, 153
*Captain Broussard's Conver-
    sion* (Shaw) 153
The Captains and Kings
    (Johnston) 250
Cathleen ni Houlihan (Yeats)
    160
Chat Show (White) 269
The Christmas Tree (John-
    ston) 260
The Circus Animals (Plun-
    kett) 274
Cock-a-Doodle-Dandy
    (O'Casey) 218
Collected Poems (Hartnett)
    264
Come Back to Erin (O'Fao-
    lain) 207
*The Constant Couple; or a
    Trip to the Jubilee* (Far-
    quhar) 69
Constantly Singing (Sim-
    mons) 259
The Countess Cathleen (Yeats)
    143, 152
The Country Girls Trilogy
    (O'Brien) 232
De Profundis (Wilde) 163
"The Dead" (Joyce) 173
The Dead Kingdom (Mon-
    tague) 263
Death of a Naturalist
    (Heaney) 241
Deirdra (Yeats) 152, 165
Deirdra of the sorrows (Synge)
    168
The Devil's Disciple (Shaw)
    153
Doctor Copernicus (Banville)
    255
The Doctor's Dilemma (Shaw)
    153, 164, 169
Door into the Dark (Heaney)
    246
Downstream (Kinsella) 235
Dracula (Stoker) 147
Drapier's Letters (Swift) 68,
    73
Dubliners (Joyce) 152, 173
"Easter 1916" (Yeats) 152,
    175
The Epicurean (Moore) 105
Esther Waters (Moore) 144
Famine (O'Flaherty) 203
The Fatal Marriage (South-
    erne) 66
Field Work (Heaney) 258
Finnegan's Wake (Joyce) 152,
    206
The Flight of the Eagle
    (O'Grady) 147
The Fool's Sanctuary (John-
    ston) 269

Four Plays for Dancers (Yeats)
    152
The Fudge Family in Paris
    (Moore) 101
The Glittering Gate (Dun-
    sany) 167
The God of the Mountain
    (Dunsany) 169
"The Gods of Pegave" (Dun-
    sany) 163
The Good Flight (Kinsella) 251
The Great Hunger (Ka-
    vanagh) 209
*The Green Hamlet and Other
    Poems* (Yeats) 168
Gulliver's Travels (Swift) 68,
    73
Gunpowder (O'Donoghue)
    286
Happy Days (Beckett) 234
The Haw Lantern (Heaney)
    269
Heartbreak House (Shaw)
    153, 178
The Hostage (Behan) 229
The Hour Glass (Yeats) 152
The House by the Churchyard
    (Le Fanu) 123
*The House of Titans and
    Other Poems* (AE) 199
How Many Miles to Babylon?
    (Johnston) 252
*The Importance of Being
    Earnest* (Wilde) 145
In Her Own Image (Boland)
    259
In the Seven Woods (Yeats)
    161
In the Shadow of the Glen
    (Synge) 161
The Informer (O'Flaherty)
    186
The Invisible Worm (John-
    ston) 276
John Bull's Other Island
    (Shaw) 153
Journal to Stella (Swift) 68,
    71
*Jumping the Train Tracks with
    Angela* (Durcan) 264
Juno and the Paycock
    (O'Casey) 185
The King's Threshold (Yeats)
    152
Krapp's Last Tape (Beckett)
    229
Lady Windermere's Fan
    (Wilde) 143
Lalla Rookh (Moore) 100
The Land of Heart's Desire
    (Yeats) 144, 152
Last Poems and Two Plays
    (Yeats) 152, 206
Last Songs (Ledwidge) 177
"Leda and the Swan" (Yeats)
    184
Lessness (Beckett) 247
Lies of Silence (Moore) 274
*The Lonely Passion of Judith
    Hearne* (Moore) 225
Lovers of Their Time (Trevor)
    257
Loves of the Angels (Moore)
    103
The Luck of Ginger Coffey
    (Moore) 232

Madonna and Other Poems
    (Kinsella) 276
Major Barbara (Shaw) 153,
    163, 165
Man and Superman (Shaw)
    153
The Man of Destiny (Shaw)
    153
Mefisto (Banville) 267
Melmoth the Wanderer (Ma-
    turin) 102
*Michael Robartes and the
    Dancer* (Yeats) 180
Mister Johnson (Cary) 206
A Modest Proposal (Swift) 68,
    74
Mosada (Yeats) 138
Mrs. Warren's Profession
    (Shaw) 143, 153
Murphy (Beckett) 154, 204
New Poems (Kinsella) 251
New Poems (Yeats) 152
No Country for Young Men
    (O'Faolain) 259
North (Heaney) 254
Not Honour More (Cary)
    225
The Obedient Wife (O'Fao-
    lain) 261
*Of the Principles of Human
    Knowledge* (Berkeley) 71
The Old Jest (Johnston) 258
On Baile's Strand (Yeats)
    152
One and Other Poems (Kin-
    sella) 258
The Only Jealousy of Emer
    (Yeats) 178
*Opened Ground: Poems,
    1956–1996* (Heaney) 291
Paddy Clarke Ha Ha Ha
    (Doyle) 283
People Dust (O'Casey) 207
Philadelphia, Here I Come
    (Friel) 238
The Picture of Dorian Gray
    (Wilde) 141
*The Playboy of the Western
    World* (Synge) 165
The Plough and the Stars
    (O'Casey) 188
Poems (Kinsella) 227
Poetical Works (Moore) 95
*A Portrait of the Artist as a
    Young Man* (Joyce) 152,
    175
*The Price of Stone and Earlier
    Poems* (Murphy) 266
A Prisoner of Grace (Cary)
    221
Pygmalion (Shaw) 153, 172
The Quare Fellow (Behan)
    224
The Railway Station Man
    (Johnston) 264
Reading in the Dark (Deane)
    286
The Recruiting Officer (Far-
    quhar) 70
Red Roses for Me (O'Casey)
    209
*Responsibilities: Poems and a
    Play* (Yeats) 152, 173
Riders to the Sea (Synge) 161
The Rough Field (Montague)
    250

"Sailing to Byzantium" (Yeats) 152, 189
Saint Joan (Shaw) 153, 184
Salome (Wilde) 143
"The Second Coming" (Yeats) 152, 180
Selected Poems (Mahon) 274
Sermons (Swift) 77
The Shadow of a Gunman (O'Casey) 184, 186
Shadows on Our Skin (Johnston) 256
The Silver Tassel (O'Casey) 188
Skerret (O'Flaherty) 196
Solstices (MacNeice) 234
The South (Toibin) 274
The Spirit Level (Heaney) 286
Spreading the News (Gregory) 162
The Stars Turn Red (O'Casey) 207
Station Island (Heaney) 264, 266
A Tale of a Tub (Swift) 68, 70
Tales of the O'Hara Family (Banim) 104
Ten Burn Offerings (MacNeice) 221
Three Lovers (O'Faolain) 247
Three Plays for Puritans (Shaw) 153
Thy Neighbor's Wife (O'Flaherty) 184
The Tower (Yeats) 152, 190
Translations (Friel) 259
The Twopenny Post Bag (Moore) 99
Ulysses (Joyce) 152, 182
Uncle Silas (Le Fanu) 124
Untitled Field (Moore) 161
The Van (Doyle) 276
Venus and the Rain (McGuckian) 264
A Vision (Yeats) 186
Visitations (MacNeice) 228
Wanderings of Oisin and Other Poems (Yeats) 140, 152
Watt (Beckett) 154, 222
Widower's Houses (Shaw) 153
Wild Earth (Colum) 165
"The Wild Swans at Coole" (Yeats) 152, 176
The Winding Stair (Yeats) 152
"Wintering Out" (Heaney) 250
Within the Gates (O'Casey) 197
Women in the Wall (O'Faolain) 254
The Women Who Walked into Doors (Doyle) 286
Word over All (Day-Lewis) 210
Words for Music, Perhaps, and Other Poems (Yeats) 196
You Never Can Tell (Shaw) 153
Jamaican
    The Pond (Morris) 251
    San Gloria (Redcam) 180
Kenyan
    Weep Not Child (Ngugi) 24

Malawian
    No Bride Price (Rubadiri) 243
Malaysian
    No Man's Grove (Lim) 259
New Zealand
    Bliss, and Other Stories (Mansfield) 180
    The Bone People (Hulme) 263
    Deep River Talk (Tuwhare) 282
    Driving into the Storm: Selected Poems (Wedde) 269
    The Garden Party and Other Stories (Mansfield) 182
    The Incident Book (Adcock) 267
    The Matriarch (Ihimaera) 267
    New and Collected Poems, 1941–1995 (Curnow) 286
    Plumb (Green) 257
    Prelude (Mansfield) 177
    The Story of a New Zealand River (Mander) 180
    Straw into Gold (Stead) 288
    Talking About O'Dwyer (Stead) 296
Nigerian
    Africa Sings (Osadebay) 221
    Anthills of the Savannah (Achebe) 269
    The Beatification of Area Boy (Soyinka) 284
    Casualties: Poems, 1966–1968 (Clark) 247
    Chief of the Honorable Minister (Aluko) 247
    The Concubine (Amadi) 243
    Dangerous Love (Okri) 288
    Death and the King's Horseman (Soyinka) 252
    Efuru (Nwapa) 243
    The Famished Road (Okri) 276
    The Flights (Conton) 269
    From Zia, with Love (Soyinka) 278
    The Great Ponds (Amadi) 246
    Infinite Riches (Okri) 291
    The Interpreters (Soyinka) 240
    Isara: A Voyage Round Essay (Soyinka) 272
    Jagua Nana (Ekwensi) 234
    Jero's Metmorphosis (Soyinka) 250
    The Joys of Motherhood (Emecheta) 258
    Kongi's Harvest (Soyinka) 243
    The Last Imam (Tahir) 264
    The Lion and the Jewel (Soyinka) 237
    Madmen and Scientists (Soyinka) 241
    Man of the People (Achebe) 243
    Minted Coins (Launko) 269
    No Longer at Ease (Achebe) 232
    Oil Man of Oanje (Munonye) 247
    Ovonramwen Nogbaisi (Rotimi) 250
    The Palm-Wine Drinkard (Tutuola) 222

People of the City (Ekwensi) 224
Poems from Prison (Soyinka) 246
The Road (Soyinka) 240
Season of Anomy (Soyinka) 251
The Slave (Amadi) 257
Song of a Goat (Clark) 234
Stars of the New Curfew (Okri) 272
The Strong Bread (Soyinka) 237
The Swamp Dwellers (Soyinka) 237
Things Fall Apart (Achebe) 229
The Trials of Brother Jero (Soyinka) 232
The Voice (Okara) 238
Pakistani
    Ice Candy Man (Sidhwa) 271
    Inland and Other Poems (Hashimi) 271
Saint Lucian
    Another Life (Walcott) 251
    The Arkansas Treatment (Walcott) 269
    Collected Poems, 1948–1984 (Walcott) 267
    The Dream on Monkey Mountain (Walcott) 241
    The Fortunate Traveler (Walcott) 260
    Midsummer (Walcott) 264
    Nor Any Country (St. Omer) 246
    Omeros (Walcott) 274
    Sea Grapes (Walcott) 255
    The Star-Apple Kingdom (Walcott) 258
    Tiepolo's Hound (Walcott) 296
Scottish
    The Abbess of Crewe (Spark) 252
    The Abbot (Scott) 93, 102
    The Admirable Crichton (Barrie) 160
    The Adventures of Ferdinand, Count Fathom (Smollett) 78
    The Adventures of Peregrine Pickle (Smollett) 78
    The Adventures of Roderick Random (Smollett) 77
    Alfred (Thomson, Mallet) 76
    Anne of Geierstein; or, The Maiden of the Mist (Scott) 105
    The Antiquary (Scott) 93, 100
    Auchindrane; or, The Ayurshire Tragedy (Scott) 106
    "Auld Lang Syne" (Burns) 68
    The Avoiding and Other Poems (MacNeacail) 267
    Ballads and Songs (Davidson) 144
    The Beach of Falesa (Stevenson) 143
    The Black Dwarf (Scott) 93, 100
    The Bridal of Triermain (Scott) 99
    The Bride of Lammermoor (Scott) 93, 101

The Bruce (Barbour) 26
Castle Dangerous (Scott) 106
The Castle of Indolence (Thomson) 77
Child's Garden of Verses (Stevenson) 137
"The City of Dreadful Night" (Thomson) 130
Collected Poems (MacCaig) 274
Columbine (Mackenzie) 180
The Comforters (Spark) 228
Concordance to the Holy Scriptures (Cruden) 75
The Conservationist (Gordimer) 252
Count Robert of Paris (Scott) 106
Curriculum Vitae (Spark) 278
Cyclopaedia, or, an Universal Dictionary of Arts and Sciences (Chambers) 74
The Cypresse Grove (Drummond) 53
Dear Brutus (Barrie) 176
Docherty (McIlvanney) 254
The Driver's Seat (Spark) 247
Edward and Eleanore (Thomson) 76
The Expedition of Humphrey Clinker (Smollett) 81
The Fall of Kelvin Walker: A Fable in the Sixties (Gray) 266
A Far Cry from Kensington (Spark) 271
The Fortunes of Nigel (Scott) 93, 103
The Gentleman in Grey (Mackenzie) 164
The Girls of Slender Means (Spark) 237
The Grave (Blair) 76
"Green Grow the Rashes, O" (Burns) 68
Guy Mannering (Scott) 93, 99
Harold the Dauntless (Scott) 100
The Heart of Midlothian (Scott) 93, 101
The Highland Widow (Scott) 105
History of the French Revolution (Carlyle) 109
"Holy Willie's Prayer" (Burns) 88
How Late It Was, How Late (Kelman) 282
Implements in their Places (Graham) 256
Ivanhoe (Scott) 93, 101
"John Anderson, My Jo" (Burns) 68
The Jolly Beggars: A Cantata (Burns) 88
Kenilworth (Scott) 93, 102
Kidnapped (Stevenson) 138
The Lady of the Lake (Scott) 93, 98
The Lay of the Last Minstrel (Scott) 93, 96
A Legend of Montrose (Scott) 93, 101
Liberty (Thomson) 75

English
    Scottish *(continued)*
        The Life of Samuel Johnson
            (Boswell) 86
        The Little Minister (Barrie) 142
        Lord of the Isles (Scott) 93, 99
        The Lost Cause (Mackenzie)
            194
        The Man of Feeling (Macken-
            zie) 81
        The Mandelbaum Gate
            (Spark) 240
        Marmion (Scott) 93, 97
        The Master of Ballantrae
            (Stevenson) 140
        The Minstrel (Beattie) 81
        *Minstrelsy of the Scottish Bor-
            der* (Scott) 96
        Momento Mori (Spark) 229
        The Monarch of the Glen
            (Mackenzie) 208
        The Monastery (Scott) 93, 102
        Old Mortality (Scott) 93, 100
        *On Heroes, Hero-Worship and
            the Heroic in History* (Car-
            lyle) 112
        The Only Problem (Spark) 264
        The Palace of Honour (Dou-
            glas) 34
        Past and Present (Carlyle) 113
        *Peter Pan; or, The Boy Who
            Wouldn't Grow Up* (Barrie)
            162
        Peveril of the Peak (Scott) 103
        *Philosophical Essays Concern-
            ing Human Understanding*
            (Hume) 77
        The Pirate (Scott) 93
        *Poems, Chiefly in the Scottish
            Dialect* (Burns) 68, 85
        The Prime of Miss Jean Brodie
            (Spark) 234
        Quentin Durward (Scott) 93,
            103
        "Red, Red Rose" (Burns) 68
        Redgauntlet (Scott) 93, 103
        Rob Roy (Scott) 93, 100
        Rokeby (Scott) 93
        *Scots Unbound and Other
            Poems* (MacDiarmid) 196
        The Seasons (Thomson) 74
        Sir Launcelot Greaves (Smol-
            lett) 79
        South Wind (Douglas) 176
        St. Ronan's Well (Scott) 103
        *St. Valentine's Day; or, The
            Fair Maid of Perth* (Scott)
            105
        Stony Limits (MacDiarmid)
            199
        The Stories of Muriel Spark
            (Spark) 266
        *The Strange Case of Dr. Jekyll
            and Mr. Hyde* (Stevenson)
            138
        "Summer" (Thomson) 74
        The Surgeon's Daughter
            (Scott) 105
        Symposium (Spark) 274
        The Talisman (Scott) 93, 104
        Tam O'Shanter (Burns) 86
        Tancred and Sigismunda
            (Thomson) 77
        "The Tears of Scotland"
            (Smollett) 77
        Temora (Macpherson) 80

        The Thirty-Nine Steps
            (Buchan) 174
        Time in a Red Coat (Brown)
            264
        Treasure Island (Stevenson)
            135
        The Twelve-Pound Note (Bar-
            rie) 168
        The Two Drovers (Scott) 105
        Virginibus Puerisque (Steven-
            son) 134
        The Waverley (Scott) 93, 99
        The Weir of Hermiston
            (Stevenson) 146
        Whiskey Galore (Mackenzie)
            215
        "Wille Brew'd a Peck o'Maut"
            (Burns) 68
        The Wind in the Willows (Gra-
            hame) 166
        "Winter" (Thomson) 73
        *Woodstock; or, The Cavalier: A
            Tale of The Year 1651*
            (Scott) 104
        A Would-Be Saint (Jenkins)
            257
        "Ye Banks and Braes o'Bonnie
            Doon" (Burns) 68
    Somalian
        Secrets (Farah) 291
    South African
        The Beginners (Jacobson) 240
        Black Swan (Hope) 269
        Blame Me on History (Modis-
            ane) 237
        Bopha (Mtwa) 267
        Burger's Daughter (Gordimer)
            258
        Cape Town Theatrical Props
            (Stockenstrom) 269
        Collected Poems (Prince) 258
        The Confessions of Josef Baisz
            (Jacobson) 256
        Country of My Skull (Krog)
            293
        Cry, the Beloved Country
            (Paton) 216
        The Dam (Butler) 222
        Disgrace (Coetzee) 293
        Don't Forget (Malherbe) 172
        The Dove Returns (Butler)
            227
        Down Second Avenue
            (Mphahlele) 231
        The Dream and the Desert
            (Krige) 222
        The Emergency (Rive) 238
        The Essential Gesture
            (Gordimer) 271
        Feather Fall (Post) 282
        *Flowering Rifle: A Poem from
            the Battlefields of Spain*
            (Campbell) 206
        From the Heart of the Country
            (Coetzee) 256
        God's Stepchildren (Millin)
            185
        Her Story (Jacobson) 269
        Hidden in the Heart (Jacob-
            son) 276
        The House Gun (Gordimer)
            291
        Kruger's Alp (Hope) 264
        Life and Times of Michael K.
            (Coetzee) 262, 263
        The Little Karoo (Smith) 186

        The Lying Days (Gordimer)
            222
        The Master of Persburg (Coet-
            zee) 282
        Mating Birds (Nkosi) 267
        Memory of Snow and of Dust
            (Breytenbach) 272
        The Miller (Malherbe) 202
        Mine Boy (Abrahams) 213
        My Son's Story (Gordimer)
            274
        None to Accompany Me
            (Gordimer) 282
        On the Contrary (Brink) 282
        The Orphan of the Desert
            (Krige) 243
        The Rape of Tamar (Jacob-
            son) 247
        The Rhythm of Violence
            (Nkosi) 238
        The Rights of Desire (Brink)
            296
        Road to Ghana (Hutchinson)
            232
        A Season in Paradise (Breyten-
            bach) 255
        Serenity House (Hope) 278
        The Sniper (Krige) 235
        A Soldier's Embrace
            (Gordimer) 259
        A Sport of Nature (Gordimer)
            269
        The Stone Country (La Guma)
            243
        *The Story of a South African
            Farm* (Schreiner) 135
        Stranger to Europe (Butler)
            221
        *Stubborn Hope: New Poems
            and Selections from China
            Poems and Strains* (Brutus)
            257
        Take Root or Die (Butler) 247
        Turning Wheels (Cloete) 203
        The Two Lamps (Krige) 238
        Waiting for the Barbarians
            (Coetzee) 259
        The Wall of Death (Krige)
            241
        Wild Conquest (Abrahams)
            220
        *The Wrath of the Ancestral
            Spirits* (Jordan) 207
    Sri Lankan
        Reef (Gunasekara) 282
        The Sandglass (Gunasekara)
            291
        *Trial by Terror: Sri Lankan
            Poems* (Arasanayagam) 269
    Tanzanian
        Dying in the Sun (Palangyo)
            244
    Trinidadian
        A Bend in the River (Naipaul)
            258
        A Brighter Sun (Selvon) 221
        A Casual Brutality (Bissoon-
            dath) 272
        Crick Crack Monkey (Hodge)
            247
        The Games Were Coming (An-
            thony) 237
        Green Days by the River (An-
            thony) 243
        A House for Mr. Biswas
            (Naipaul) 234

        The Humming Bird Tree (Mc-
            Donald) 246
        *North of South: An African
            Journey* (Naipaul) 258
        Pan Beat (Jones) 251
        A Way in the World (Naipaul)
            282
        The Wine of Astonishment
            (Lovelace) 261
        The Year in San Fernando
            (Anthony) 240
    Virgin Island
        The King's Mandate (Jarvis)
            232
    Welsh
        18 Poems (Thomas) 199
        All Things Betray (Thomas)
            218
        Autobiography of Rhys Lewis
            (Owen) 137
        *Ballad of the Mari Lwyd and
            Other Poems* (Watkins) 208
        Between Here and Now
            (Thomas) 260
        *Burning Brambles: Selected
            Poems, 1944–1979* (Math-
            ias) 263
        A Child's Christmas in Wales
            (Thomas) 224
        Collected Poems, 1934–1952
            (Thomas) 221
        The Dark Philosophers
            (Thomas) 213
        Deaths and Entrances
            (Thomas) 213
        *Dreflan, Its People and Its Af-
            fairs* (Owen) 134
        "Experimenting with an
            Amen" (Thomas) 267
        "Fern Hill" (Thomas) 213
        Frequencies (Thomas) 257
        The Glittering Flint (Vaughan)
            58
        How Green Was My Valley
            (Llewellyn) 206
        In Country Sleep (Thomas)
            221
        The Map of Love (Thomas)
            206
        Poetry for Supper (Thomas)
            229
        *Portrait of the Artist as a Young
            Dog* (Thomas) 207
        The Trials of Enoc Huws
            (Owen) 142
        Under Milk Wood (Thomas)
            224
        The Way of It (Thomas) 256
    Zimbabwean
        On Trial for My Country
            (Samkange) 241
Estonian
    Blowing Sand/A Winter Journey
        (Kangro) 266
    Kalevipoeg (Kreutzwald) 96, 120
    Return, Pinus Succinifera (Kaplin-
        ski) 264
    Truth and Justice (Tannasaare)
        188

F

Finnish
    Animalia (Kilpi) 269
    Anti Kepler's Laws (Katz) 269
    The Birds (Vesaas) 228
    Birthplace (Haavikko) 225

Black Sonnets (Sebastian) 166
The Breath of Copper (Enckell) 213
The Colonel's Daughter (Meri) 241
A Cripple in Love (Lehtonen) 182
The Dark Angel (Waltari) 221
Dikter (Södergran) 175
The Egyptian (Waltari) 212
The Etruscan (Waltari) 225
The Family (Meri) 244
The Flutist's Happiness (Enckell) 186
Frost (Leino) 166
Fugitives (Kivi) 126
The Fugitives (Linnankoski) 166
Hanna (Runeberg) 109
Incidents (Meri) 232
The Iron Gate (Gripenberg) 163
The Journey (Manner) 227
Juha (Aho) 169
Kalevala (Lönnrot) 108
Kullervo (Kivi) 122
Kung Fjalar (Runeberg) 113
Land of the Heather (Kivi) 125
Leaves, Pages (Haavikko) 230
The Maid Silja (Sillanpää) 195
The Manilla Rope (Meri) 228
Meek Heritage (Sillanpää) 178
On Windy Nights (Haavikko) 222
Orphic Hymns (Manner) 232
Panu (Aho) 147
People in Summer Night (Sillanpää) 199
Poems from a Voyage Across the Sound (Haavikko) 251
Private Jokinen's Marriage Leave (Meri) 240
The Railway (Aho) 136
The Roman (Waltari) 239
Seven Brothers (Kivi) 127
Shining Solitude (Ahti) 264
Shoemakers of the Hearth (Kivi) 124
Simo the Bloodhound (Leino) 162
The Song of the Blood-Red Flower (Linnankoski) 163
Spring and the Untimely Return of Winter (Aho) 164
Thus Changed the Seasons (Manner) 239
The Wanderer (Waltari) 218
The Way of a Man (Sillanpää) 196
Weedpatch (Lehtonen) 178
Whitsongs (Leino) 161
Winter Night (Leino) 163
Woman in the Mirror (Meri) 237
Flemish
    Blind (Conscience) 116
    The Conscript (Conscience) 116
    A Day on the Ground (Wispelaere) 247, 254
    De geruchten (Claus) 288
    I Have No Home Now (Wispelaere) 262
    The Land of Gold (Conscience) 123
    Letters from Nowhere (Wispelaere) 267
    The Lion of Flanders (Conscience) 110
    My Living Shadow (Wispelaere) 240
    Paul Against Paul (Wispelaere) 247

The Poor Gentleman (Conscience) 117
To Become an Island (Wispelaere) 237
Wooden Clara (Conscience) 116
French
Algerian
    1,001 Years of Nostalgia (Boudjedra) 258
    The Big House (Dib) 221
    Cinders (Amrouche) 199
    Forgotten Hill (Mammeri) 221
    Last Impression (Haddad) 230
    Nedjma, Poem or Knife (Yacine) 216
    Secret Star (Amrouche) 203
    The Sleep of the Just (Mammeri) 225
Armenian
    Le Ping-Pong (Adamov) 225
Belgian
    Allegra (Mallet-Joris) 255
    Along the Way (Verhaeren) 142
    The Angel's Wink (Mallet-Joris) 263
    Belgium's Agony (Verhaeren) 174
    The Black Torches (Verhaeren) 141
    Blindness and Insight: Essays in the Rhetoric of Contemporary Criticism (De Man) 249
    The Blue Bird (Maeterlinck) 166
    Bruges, the Dead City (Rodenbach) 143
    The Closed Door (Bosschere) 176
    Les Débâcles (Verhaeren) 139
    Divine (Mallet-Joris) 276
    The Faces of Life (Verhaeren) 149
    The Favorite (Mallet-Joris) 232
    First Loves (Verhaeren) 162
    The Flemish (Verhaeren) 135
    Hothouses (Maeterlinck) 140
    The Illusionist (Mallet-Joris) 220
    Kamouraska (Hébert) 247
    King Dickie (Mallet-Joris) 258
    Laura's Daughter (Mallet-Joris) 266
    A Letter to Myself (Mallet-Joris) 237
    The Life of the Bee (Maeterlinck) 159
    The Little Man of God (Lemonnier) 160
    The Magnificent Cuckold (Crommelynck) 180
    A Male (Lemonnier) 134
    The Manifest Splendor (Verhaeren) 164
    The Monks (Verhaeren) 138
    Monna Vanna (Maeterlinck) 160
    The Moonstruck Countrysides (Verhaeren) 144
    Pelleas and Melissande (Maeterlinck) 143
    Primevères (Hasselt) 108

Les Quatre incarnations du (Hasselt) 123
The Right of the Strongest (Buysse) 144
The Sadness of the Kite (Mallet-Joris) 271
The Sunlit Hours (Verhaeren) 146
The Burgomaster of Stilmonde (Maeterlinck) 177
The Tumultuous Force (Verhaeren) 160
The Underground Game (Mallet-Joris) 251
Wheat in Motion (Verhaeren) 171
The White Youthfulness (Rodenbach) 138
Beninese
    The Endless Trip (Quenum) 232
    Snares Without End (Quenum) 232
Cameroonian
    Africa, We Do Not Pay Attention to You (Matep) 227
    Amours sauvages (Beyala) 293
    Mission Accomplished (Betti) 216
    This Particular Africa (Ikelle-Matiba) 237
Canadian
    Am I Disturbing You? (Hébert) 293
    Un ange cornu ave des ailes de tole (Tremblay) 282
    The Child Bordered with Dreams (Hébert) 278
    Children of the Black Sabbath (Hébert) 254
    Complete Works (Crémazie) 135
    Cristoforo (Thomas) 288
    La demarche du crabe (LaRue) 284
    L'ecureuil noir (Poliquin) 282
    The First Garden (Hébert) 271
    Gros mots (Decharme) 293
    In the Shadow of the Wind (Hébert) 262
    L'ingratitude (Chen) 284
    La legende d'un peuple (Fréchette) 138
    Noces de sable (Leclerc) 284
    The Northern Flowers (Fréchette) 132
    The Outlander (Guèvremont) 219
    La petite fille qui aimait trop les allumettes (Soucy) 291
    The Silent Rooms (Hébert) 230
    The Snow Birds (Fréchette) 132
    The Torrent (Herbert) 219
    Une belle journée d'avance (Lalonde) 268
    Va Savoir (Ducharme) 282
    Un vent se léve qui eparpille (Dalpe) 296
Congolese
    The Crocodile (Lomami-Tshibamba) 216
    Where Shall I Go? (Disengomoko) 210

Egyptian
    The Queen's Defeat (Chedid) 264
    Worlds, Mirrors, Magics (Chedid) 271
French
    The 120 Days of Sodom (Sade) 85
    À la frontière (Butor) 286
    Abufar (Ducis) 87
    The Abyss (Yourcenar) 245
    L'Abyssin (Rufin) 288
    The Acacia (Simon) 272
    Acts Without Words (Beckett) 154
    Aden (Garat) 278
    Adolphe (Constant) 100
    Adrienne Lecouvreur (Scribe and Legouvé) 116
    The Adventures of Telemachus (Fénelon) 66
    The Adventuress (Augier) 115
    The Affected Young Ladies (Molière) 47, 59
    The Afternoon of a Faun (Mallarmé) 131
    Against the Grain (Huysmans) 136
    Agamemnon (Lemercier) 86
    Agésilas (Corneille) 48, 61
    Aimée (Rivière) 182
    Alcools (Apollinaire) 172
    Alexander the Great (Racine) 60
    Aline, Queen of Golkonda (Boufflers) 80
    All in a Night (Cayrol) 224
    All Men Are Mortals (Beauvoir) 214
    Un aller simple (Cauwelaert) 282
    The Amethyst Ring (France) 149
    The Amorous Follies (Regnard) 70
    The Amorous Quarrel (Molière) 59
    "*Amour*" (Verlaine) 139
    Amour noir (Noguez) 288
    Les Amours (Ronsard) 33
    Les Amours de Marie (Ronsard) 33
    Les Amours de P. de Ronsard Vandomoys, Ensemble de Bocages (Ronsard) 39
    Un an (Echenoz) 288
    Anabasis (Perce) 185
    Anchise (Desbiolles) 293
    André del Sarto (Musset) 107
    Andromaque (Racine) 48, 61
    Andromède (Corneille) 48, 58
    Anielka (Taillandier) 293
    Annibal (Marivaux) 74
    Annotations in Pandectas (Budé) 34
    Antigone (Anouilh) 209
    Antiques Cabinet (Balzac) 91
    Approximate Man, and Other Writings (Tzara) 195
    L'arbre de rêve (Quiring) 269
    The Archeology of Knowledge (Foucault) 246
    Around the World in Eighty Days (Verne) 129
    The Art of Poetry (Boileau) 62

French

French *(continued)*

Artemenes; or, the Grand Cyrus (Scudéry) 58

Atala (Chateaubriand) 95

Athalie (Racine) 48, 65

Atreus and Thyseus (Crébillon) 71

Attila (Corneille) 48, 61

Au Soleil de Juillet (Adam) 161

Les aubes (Le) 296

Aurora (Leiris) 214

Autobiography of an Egotist (Stendhal) 143

Autumn Leaves (Hugo) 106

Avarice House (Green) 188

Axel (Villiers de L'Isle-Adam) 137, 141

Babu du Montparnasse (Philippe) 159

Bajazet (Racine) 48, 62

The Balcony (Genet) 225, 227

The Bald Soprano (Ionesco) 219

"Ball of Fat" (Maupassant) 133

The Barber of Seville (Beaumarchais) 82

La bataille (Rambaud) 288

The Battle of Pharsalus (Simon) 246

Becket, or the Honor of God (Anouilh) 231

Being and Nothingness (Sartre) 210

Bel ami (Maupassant) 137

The Bells of Basel (Aragon) 199

Bérénice (Racine) 48, 61

La Bergeries (Racan) 52

Bertrand and Raton; or, The Art of Conspiracy (Scribe) 107

The Black Rose (Montherlant) 245

The Black Sheep (Balzac) 91

Black Tulip (Dumas) 116

The Black Venus (Baudelaire) 92

The Blacks (Genet) 230

Blanchette (Brieux) 143

Blesse, ronce noire (Combet) 284

The Blue Flowers (Queneau) 240

The Blue Stockings (Molière) 48

The Bluebird (Maeterlinck) 167

The Bluff (Labiche) 122

The Blunderer (Molière) 59

Bocages (Ronsard) 33

The Bond (Borel) 240

Bonjour Tristesse (Sagan) 224

The Book Beside Me (Reverdy) 216

The Book of Masques (Gourmont) 146

The Book of Monelle (Schwob) 144

Bouborouche (Courteline) 144

Bouquets and Prayers (Desbordes-Valmore) 113

The Bourgeois Gentleman (Molière) 48, 62

The Boys in the Back Room (Romains) 172

Bradamante (Garnier) 42

Break at Noon (Claudel) 164

The Bridge over the River Kwai (Boulle) 221

The Brightness of Life (Viélé-Griffin) 147

Britannicus (Racine) 48, 61

The Broken Verse (Prudhomme) 125

The Bullfighters (Montherlant) 188

Cain (Leconte de Lisle) 127

Calendau (Mistral) 126

Caligula (Camus) 155, 211

Calligrammes (Apollinaire) 177

Candide (Voltaire) 68, 79

The Candlestick (Musset) 108

Le cant silencieux des chouettes (Bensoussan) 291

Capital of Sorrow (Éluard) 188

Captain Fracasse (Gautier) 123

The Captive (Proust) 184

Carmen (Mérimée) 114

Carrot Top (Renard) 144

Casimir mene la grande (Ormesson) 288

The Castle of Argol (Gracq) 204

The Cat (Colette) 197

La Cathédrale (Huysmans) 148

Centuries (Nostradamus) 39

C'est tout (Duras) 284

C'etait toute une vie (Bon) 284

The Chairs (Ionesco) 221

Les champs d'honneur (Rouaud) 274

Chandos (Ouida) 125

La Chanson de Roland, 13, 21

The Character, or Manners of the Age with the Characters of Theophrastus (La Bruyère) 65

Charles IX; or, La Sainte-Barthelemy (Chénier) 85

Charles XII (Voltaire) 68

The Charterhouse of Parma (Stendhal) 111

La chasseur zero (Roze) 286

Chatterton (Vigny) 108

The Cheats of Scapin (Molière) 62

Cheri (Colette) 180

Le Chevalier des touches (Barbey d'Aurevilly) 124

The Child at the Balustrade (Boylesve) 161

A Child of Our Time (Castillo) 228

The Children of the Earth (Queneau) 204

Children of the Game (Cocteau) 192

Child's Songs (Aicard) 131

The Chill of the Sun (Cayrol) 237

The Chimeras (Nerval) 118

Les Chouans (Balzac) 91, 105

The Christian Georgics (Jammes) 170

The Christian Socrates (Balzac) 58

Christophe Colomb (Lemercier) 98

Chronique des Pasquier (Duhamel) 193

Chronique (Perse) 232

Le Chute (Camus) 155

Le Cid (Corneille) 48, 56

Cinna (Corneille) 48, 56

Cinq-Mars (Vigny) 104

Cities of the Interior (Nin) 231

Cities of the Plain (Proust) 181

City Heights (Robles) 216

The City Whose Prince Is a Child (Montherlant) 220

The Civil War (Montherlant) 240

La classe de neige (Carrère) 284

Claude Gueux (Hugo) 108

The Claw (Bernstein) 164

Clay Medals (Régnier) 158

Clélie: Histoire romaine (Scudéry) 59

Cléopâtre captive (Jodelle) 39

The Clique (Scribe) 110

Clitandre (Corneille) 48

The Closed Garden (Green) 189

Collected Works (Calvin) 52

Colomba (Mérimée) 111

Come and Go (Beckett) 154

The Comic Illusion (Corneille) 55

Comme des anges (Boyer) 282

Comme ton père (Le Touze) 282

The Conceited Count (Destouches) 75

La conference de Cintegabelle (Salvayre) 293

Confession of a Child of the Century (Musset) 109

Confessions (Rousseau) 68, 84, 85

Confidence pour confidence (Constant) 291

Considerations of the Causes of the Grandeur and Decadence of the Romans (Montesquieu) 75

Constance (Bazin) 221

Contes cruels (Villiers de L'Isle-Adam) 135

Contes et Faceties (Nerval) 117

Continuation des Amours (Ronsard) 33

La conversation (Nobecourt) 291

Corinne (Staël) 97

Les corps celestes (Brehal) 280

The Count of Monte Cristo (Dumas père) 113

The Counterfeiters (Gide) 188

Country (Desnos) 211

The Country Doctor (Balzac) 91, 107

The Country Waif (Sand) 115

Cousin Bette (Balzac) 91, 114

Cousin Pons (Balzac) 91, 115

The Coward (Lenormand) 186

Creative Evolution (Bergson) 165

Credo des san-mélé ou je veux chanter la France (Gratiant) 216

The Crime of Olga Arbyelina (Makine) 293

The Crime of Sylvestre Bonnard (France) 134

Crispin, Rival of His Master (Lesage) 71

Critical Essays (Barthes) 239

Cromwell (Hugo) 105

Cross Purposes (Camus) 155

The Crowning of Spring (Simon) 224

The Crucial Scene (Jouve) 200

Crusts (Claudel) 177

Cuisine Novella (Laurent) 269

The Cult of the Self (Barres) 139

Cyrano de Bergerac (Rostand) 147

Daily Bread (Boylesve) 159

Dance of the Dead (Jouve) 176

Dangerous Liaisons (Laclos) 84

Dans ces bras-la (Laurens) 296

The Dark Journey (Green) 192

The Daughters of Calvary (Combescot) 276

Dawn on Our Darkness (Robles) 221

Days of Contempt (Malraux) 200

Days of Hope (Malraux) 203

De coeur et de l'affection (Teboul) 282

De Guerre lasse (Sagan) 266

Death of a Nobody (Romains) 170

The Death of Caesar (Voltaire) 75

The Death of Pompey (Corneille) 48, 57

Death on the Installment Plan (Céline) 202

Deathwatch (Genet) 218

Deborah et les anges dissipés (Jacques) 276

La declaration (Salvayre) 274

La Défense de Tartuffe (Jacob) 178

Degrees (Butor) 232

Delie: Object of Highest Virtue (Scève) 38

Delphine (Staël) 96

La démence du boxeur (Weyergans) 278

Le Demi-Monde (Dumas) 119

Democracy in America (Tocqueville) 108

The Demon of Good (Montherlant) 203

La dérive des sentiments (Simon) 276

Les Derniers Vers (Ronsard) 33

Des anges mineurs (Volodine) 293

Desert (Le Clezio) 259
The Desert of Love (Mauriac) 218
The Deserted World (Jouve) 189
Destroy, She Said (Duras) 246
The Devil and the Good Lord (Sartre) 220
The Devil in the Flesh (Radiguet) 184
The Devil Upon Two Sticks (Lesage) 71
The Devil's Pool (Sand) 114
Diabolus in musica (Apperry) 296
Dialogues de Dom Frei Amador Arraiz (Arrais) 43
Dialogues des Carmelites (Bernanos) 218
Diary of a Country Priest (Bernanos) 202
The Diary of My Times (Bernanos) 204
The Dice Box (Jacob) 176
The Difficult Times (Bourdet) 199
Digression on Ancients and Moderns (Fontenelle) 65
The Discipline (Bourget) 140
Discours de la méthode (Descartes) 56
Discourse on the Miseries of These Times (Ronsard) 33
Discourse on the Origin of Inequality (Rousseau) 68
Discourse on the Sciences and the Arts (Rousseau) 68, 78
Discourse on Universal History (Bossuet) 63
Dissemination (Derrida) 250
The Distant Lands (Green) 269
Le dit de Tianyi (Cheng) 291
The Diving Bell and the Butterfly (Bauby) 288
Djinn (Robbe-Grillet) 260
The Dog of Montargis; or, The Forest of Bundy (Pixérécourt) 99
Dominique (Fromentin) 123
Don Juan (Molière) 48, 60
Don Sanche d'Aragon (Corneille) 48
Donatienne (Bazin) 161
Down Stream (Huysmans) 135
Down There (Huysmans) 142
The Dram Shop (Zola) 131
The Dream Eater (Lenormand) 182
The Dreamer (Green) 199
Droll Stories (Balzac) 91, 107
"The Drunken Boat" (Rimbaud) 94, 128
Du plus loin de l'oubli (Modano) 286
The Duel (Sedaine) 80
The Duo (Colette) 199
The Durandeau Brothers (Soupault) 185
The Dying (Soupault) 199
The Dying Earth (Bazin) 149
The Eagle Has Two Heads (Cocteau) 214
The Eaglet (Rostand) 158

The Ear of the Other (Derrida) 262
Eclats de sel (Germain) 286
Education by Stone (Cayrol) 241
The Eiffel Tower and Other Mythologies (Barthes) 239
Electra (Crébillon) 71
Elle et Lui (Sand) 121
The Elm Tree in the Mall (France) 147
Eloges, and Other Poems (Perse) 170
Emile; or, On Education (Rousseau) 68, 80
En Route (Huysmans) 145
Enamels and Cameos (Gautier) 117
The Enchanted Soul (Rolland) 182
Encyclopédie 78
Endgame (Beckett) 228
L'enfant léopard (Picouly) 293
L'enfant roi (Rolin) 268
The Erasers (Robbe-Grillet) 222
L'espace anterieur (Trassard) 280
Essais (Montaigne) 32–33, 42
Esther (Racine) 48, 65
Un été memorable (Perol) 291
Etincelles dans les tenebres (Dai) 269
Eugénie (Beaumarchais) 81
Eugenie Grandet (Balzac) 91, 107
Ève (Péguy) 172
L'Eve Future (Villiers de L'Isle-Adam) 138
The Evening Hours (Verhaeren) 169
The Executioner (Boulle) 224
The Exile and Other Poems (Perse) 209
Exit the King (Ionesco) 237
The Fable and the Flesh (Aymé) 210
Fables: Selected Fables in Verse (La Fontaine) 61
The Failures (Lenormand) 180
The Fair and Wise Father (Marivaux) 71
The Fairy Council (Laforgue) 138
The Fall (Camus) 227
False Confessions (Marivaux) 75
A False Saint (Curel) 143
The Fashionable Bourgeois Ladies (Dancourt) 65
The Father of the Family (Diderot) 79
The Fertile Eyes (Éluard) 202
Fêtes galantes (Verlaine) 127
Fever (Le Clezio) 240
La fille de gobernator (Constant) 286
The Firm of Nucingen (Balzac) 91
Five Great Odes (Claudel) 168
The Flanders Road (Simon) 233

The Flight of Icarus (Queneau) 245
The Flood (Le Clezio) 241
The Flowers of Evil (Baudelaire) 92, 120
La folle allure (Bobin) 284
The Follies of Marianne (Musset) 107
For a New Novel (Robbe-Grillet) 237
For and Against (Lacretelle) 214
The Forced Marriage (Molière) 60
Foreign Bodies (Cayrol) 231
The Fortunate Peasant (Marivaux) 75
The Fortunes of the Rougon-Macquart Family (Zola) 128
La Françiade (Ronsard) 33
Les frères romance (Colombier) 274
From Honey to Ashes (Lévi-Strauss) 241
From the Earth to the Moon (Verne) 124
Fromont the Younger and Risler the Elder (Daudet) 130
The Frontenac Mystery (Mauriac) 197
Frou-Frou (Meilhac, Halevy) 127
Fru Marie Grubbe (Jacobsen) 131
Un gachis (Darley) 288
The Game of Love and Chance (Marivaux) 74, 75
Games—Tough and Divine (Régnier) 147
The Gamester (Regnard) 66
Gargantua (Rabelais) 32, 37
Gaspard of the Night (Bertrand) 112
Le Gendre de Monsieur Poirier (Sandeau, Augier) 117
The Genius of Christianity (Chateaubriand) 95
Gentrix (Mauriac) 184
Germinal (Zola) 137
The Giants (Le Clezio) 251
Gigi (Colette) 211
The Girls (Montherlant) 202
Girls of Fire (Nerval) 118
The Glass of Water; or, Causes and Effects (Scribe) 111
Glass Puddles (Reverdy) 192
The Gods Are Athirst (France) 171
The Gold Seeker (Le Clezio) 266
The Golden Fleece (Corneille) 48, 60
Golden Fruits (Sarraute) 237
Good Will (Diallo) 188
Le Grand Testament (Villon) 27
La grande beune (Michon) 286
The Grass (Simon) 230
The Graveyard by the Sea (Valery) 182
Gravity and Grace (Weil) 215
The Great Fear of the Well-Possessed (Bernanos) 195

The Green Mare (Aymé) 197
The Green-Eyed Venus (Baudelaire) 92
The Guermantes Way (Proust) 180
The Guest (Corel) 144
The Half Virgins (Prévost) 144
"Happiness" (Prudhomme) 139
Harlequin Brightened by Love (Marivaux) 73
A Harlot High and Low (Balzac) 91, 111
Head Against the Wall (Bazin) 218
Heartbreak (Aragon) 208
Heliogobalus, or the Crowned Antichrist (Artaud) 199
A Hell of a Mess (Ionesco) 251
La Henriade (Voltaire) 68, 73
Henry VIII (Chénier) 86
Heraclius (Corneille) 48
L'heritage de Tante Carlotta (Jacques) 269
Hernani (Hugo) 106
"Herodias" (Flaubert) 92
"Herodias" (Mallarmé) 127
High Bridges (Lacretelle) 196
Hilda (Ndiaye) 293
Historical and Critical Dictionary (Bayle) 66
The Holy Terrors (Cocteau) 192
L'homme ignore (Targowla) 274
Horace (Corneille) 48, 56
The Horla (Maupassant) 137
The Horsehair Glove (Reverdy) 189
The Horseman on the Roof (Giono) 221
The Hostage (Claudel) 170
House of Incest (Nin) 202
The Human Comedy (Balzac) 90–91
Hymnes (Ronsard) 33, 39
I Will Live the Love of Others (Cayrol) 215
Ibrahim, of the Illustrious Bassa (Scudéry) 57
Ici (Sarraute) 284
Les idées heureuses (Lapaque) 293
Idoménée (Crébillon) 70
If I Were You (Green) 215
If It Die (Gide) 180
The Iliad; or, The Poem of Force (Weil) 207
Les Illuminations (Rimbaud) 94, 129, 138
The Illustrious Gaudissart (Balzac) 91
The Imaginary Invalid (Molière) 48, 62
The Imitation of Our Lady of the Moon (Laforgue) 138
The Imitation of the Father (Claudel) 180
Immaculate Conception (Breton) 193
Immobile dans le courant de fleuve (Berger) 282
The Immoralist (Gide) 160
Impressions of Africa (Roussel) 168

French

French (continued)

In the Labyrinth (Sarraute) 231

In the Name of the Son
(Bazin) 233

Indiana (Sand) 107

The Infernal Machine
(Cocteau) 199

Ingrid Caven (Schuhl) 296

The Interrogation (Le Clezio)
237

Intervalle (Butor) 251

L'invention du monde (Rolin)
280

Iphigénie en Aulide (Racine)
48, 62

Irène (Voltaire) 83

L'Irréparable (Bourget) 136

Isis (Villiers de L'Isle-Adam)
123

An Island Fisherman (Loti)
138

Isle of Reason (Marivaux) 74

Isle of Slaves (Marivaux) 73

Israel (Bernstein) 166

It Isn't Necessary to Promise
Anything (Musset) 109

Italian Spring (Robles) 247

An Italian Straw Hat
(Labiche) 117

"J'Accuse" (Zola) 148

Jadis et Naguerre (Verlaine)
136

Jealousy (Robbe-Grillet) 228

Jean Christophe (Rolland)
162

Joan of Arc (Péguy) 147

Joined Hands (Mauriac) 167

The Journal of Jules Renard
(Renard) 186

A Journey to the Center of the
Earth (Verne) 124

Journey to the End of the Night
(Céline) 196

The Joys (Viélé-Griffin) 140

Les Juives (Garnier) 42

Julie; or, The New Eloise
(Rousseau) 68, 80

Just Assassins (Camus) 155

La Justice (Prudhomme) 132

Justine (Sade) 86

The Killing Game (Ionesco)
247

King Ubu (Jarry) 146

The Kiss to the Leper (Mauriac) 182

Knock; or, The Triumph of
Medicine (Romains) 184

La Laboratoire central (Jacob)
181

The Lady from Maxim's (Feydeau) 149

The Lady of Maldoro
(Lautréamont) 126

The Lady of the Camelias
(Dumas) 115

Lambeaux (Juliet) 284

Language (Jouve) 221

La langue maternelle (Alexakis) 284

The Lark (Anouilh) 222

The Last Domain (Fournier)
172

Last Loves (Desportes) 42

Last Nights of Paris
(Soupault) 190

The Last of Cheri (Colette)
188

The Last of the Just (Schwarz-
Bart) 231

Last Poems (Laforgue) 141

The Lay Monk (Huysmans)
161

The Learned Ladies (Molière)
62

Leaves of Hypnos (Char) 214

"The Legend of Saint Julian
the Hospitaller" (Flaubert)
92

The Legend of Thyl Ulen-
spiegel (Coster) 126

Lélia (Sand) 107

The Lepers (Montherlant)
206

Lessness (Beckett) 154

The Lesson (Ionesco) 220,
223

Letters from My Mill (Daudet)
127

Lettres philosophiques
(Voltaire) 68

The Liar (Corneille) 48, 57

Life and Adventures of Salavin
(Duhamel) 180

Life and Poetry of Joseph Delorme (Saint-Beuve) 105

The Life of Henry Brulard
(Stendhal) 141

The Life of Marianne (Marivaux) 74

The Lion's Meal (Curel) 147

The Litigants (Racine) 48, 61

Little Fadette (Sand) 116

The Little Prince (Saint-
Exupéry) 210

Lives of Gallant Women
(Brantôme) 60

The Living and Their Shadows
(Lacretelle) 256

Un long Dimanche de fian-
cailles (Japrisot) 276

Lorenzaccio (Musset) 108

Lost Illusions (Balzac) 91, 110

Louis XI (Delavigne) 107

Le loup Mongol (Homeric)
291

The Lover (Duras) 278

Lucien Leuwen (Stendhal)
144

Ma vie folle (Morgieve) 296

The Mad Woman of Chaillot
(Giraudoux) 212

Madame Bovary (Flaubert)
92

Madame Devil-May-Care
(Moreau, Sardou) 144

Madame Gervaisais
(Goncourt and Goncourt)
127

Mademoiselle Cloque
(Boylesve) 149

Mademoiselle de Maupin
(Gautier) 108

Madness and Civilization
(Foucault) 234

The Maid of Orleans
(Voltaire) 79

The Maids (Genet) 215

The Maidservant (Corneille)
48

La Maison Tellier (Maupassant) 134

La maladie de Sachs (Win-
kler) 291

Malatesta (Montherlant) 214

Malone Dies (Beckett) 154

Man and His Phantoms
(Lenormand) 185

The Mandarins (Beauvoir)
224

Manon Lescaut (Prévost d'Exiles) 74

Man's Estate (Malraux) 197

La manuscrit de Port-Ebène
(Bona) 291

Margins of Philosophy (Derrida) 250

Marianna (Sandeau) 111

Marion de Lorme (Hugo)
105

Mark Antony, or Cleopatra
(Mairet) 55

Marriage for Money (Scribe)
105

The Marriage of Figaro; or,
The Madness of a Day
(Beaumarchais) 84

The Married Philosopher
(Destouches) 74

A Married Priest (Barbey
d'Aurevilly) 124

Martereau (Sarraute) 223

The Martyrs (Chateaubriand)
98

The Master of Santiago (Montherlant) 215

Matter and Memory (Berg-
son) 146

Mauprat (Sand) 110

Maxims (La Rochefoucauld)
60

Médée (Corneille) 48

Mélite (Corneille) 48, 54

Mémoires (Comines) 29

Mémoires (Saint-Simon) 132

Memoirs (Chateaubriand)
116

Memoirs of a Dutiful Daughter (Beauvoir) 230

Memoirs of a Father (Mar-
montel) 96

Memoirs of Hadrian (Yourcenar) 220

Memoirs of Mistral (Mistral)
164

Men of Goodwill (Romains)
196

Le m'en vais (Echenoz) 293

Le Mercure galant (Boursault)
64

Mérope (Voltaire) 76

Meslanges (Ronsard) 33, 39

The Methods of History
(Bodin) 40

Midday Midnight (Cayrol)
241

Midnight (Green) 202

Mireio: A Provençal Poem
(Mistral) 121

Le Misanthrope (Molière) 48,
61

Le Misanthrope et Lauvergnat
(Labiche) 117

The Miser (Molière) 48, 61

Les Misérables (Hugo) 123

Mithridate (Racine) 48, 62

Moderato Cantabile (Duras)
230

Molloy (Beckett) 154, 220

Mon grand appartement
(Oster) 293

Le monde retrouve de Louis-
François Pinagot (Corbin)
291

Monsieur Bergeret in Paris
(France) 159

La morseure (Villemin) 288

Mother Goose Tales (Perrault)
66

Music Hall Sidelights (Colette) 172

Le mystère des saints innocents
(Péguy) 171

The Mysteries of Paris (Sue)
112

The Mysterious Island (Verne)
130

Mysterious Weddings (Jouve)
186

The Myth of Sisyphus
(Camus) 155, 209

Mythologies (Barth) 228

The Nabob (Daudet) 131

Nadja (Breton) 190

La naissance des fantomes
(Darrieussecq) 291

Nana (Zola) 133

The Natural Son; or, The
Proofs of Virtue (Diderot)
79

Nausea (Sartre) 204

The Need for Roots (Weil)
218

The Negro (Soupault) 189

Nekrassov (Sartre) 225

Nerto (Mistral) 136

The New Colony (Marivaux)
74

The New Idol (Curel) 145

The New Tenant (Ionesco)
225

New Weddings (Jouve) 188

Nicomède (Corneille) 48, 58

Night (Wiesel) 230

Ninety-Three (Hugo) 130

No Exit (Sartre) 211

Not I (Beckett) 252

Nothing Important Ever Dies
(Gary) 233

Nôtre-Dame de Paris (Hugo)
106

Nous sommes eternels (Fleutiaux) 274

Nouvelle Continuation des
Amours (Ronsard) 33

An Obscure Man (Yourcenar)
266

The October Night (Musset)
110

O.D.C. (Aster) 293

Ode (Jouve) 219

Odes (Ronsard) 33, 38

Odeur d'encre, odeur d'îles
(Jacq) 276

Oedipus (Voltaire) 72

Oedipus at the Home of Admetus (Ducis) 83

Oedipus Rex (Cocteau) 189

L'oeil du silence (Lambron)
280

L'oeuvre postume de Thomas
Pilaster (Chevillard) 293

L'offrande sauvage (Mila-
vanoff) 293

Old Goriot (Balzac) 108

On Love (Stendhal) 103

On the Search after Truth (Malebranche) 62

On the Track of God (Rivière) 186

On vient chercher Monsieur Jean (Tardieu) 274

Onitsha (Le Clezio) 276

Open All Night (Morand) 182

Opéra: Oeuvres Poétiques (Cocteau) 189

The Order of Things: An Archeology of Human Science (Foucault) 241

L'Ordre (Arland) 192

L'organization (Rolin) 286

The Origin of Table Manners (Lévi-Strauss) 245

Orlanda (Harpma) 286

Orpheus (Cocteau) 188

The Other One (Green) 249

Othon (Corneille) 48, 60

Our Lady of the Flowers (Genet) 211

Pantagruel (Rabelais) 32, 37

Parôle de sige (Cahuzac) 274

Les particules élémentaires (Houellebecq) 291

La pas si lent de l'amour (Bianciotti) 284

Pasquier Chronicle (Duhamel) 197

Passing Time (Butor) 227

The Passions of the Soul (Descartes) 58

Paul et Virginie (Bernardin de Saint-Pierre) 85

Paulina (Jouve) 186

Les Paysans (Balzac) 114

Le Peau de chagrin (Balzac) 106

Pendant la chaleur du jour (Pradier) 293

Penguin Island (France) 166

Pensées (Pascal) 48, 61

Le Père Goriot (Balzac) 91

Perou (Braudeau) 291

Persian Letters (Montesquieu) 73

Pertharite (Corneille) 48

Le Petit chose (Daudet) 126

Le Petit Testament (Villon) 27

The Phantom of the Opera (Leroux) 168

Phèdre (Racine) 48, 63

Philosophical Dictionary (Voltaire) 80

Philosophical Thoughts (Diderot) 77

Phocas the Gardener (Viélé-Griffin) 148

The Physiology of Marriage (Balzac) 91

Pierrot (Queneau) 210

Pinto (Lemercier) 133

Pity for Women (Montherlant) 202

The Plague (Camus) 155, 215

Planet of the Apes (Boulle) 237

Play of St. Nicholas (Bodel) 23

Ployeucte (Corneille) 48

Poèmes de Provence (Aicard) 130

Poèmes saturnines (Verlaine) 126

Poems (Vigny) 103

Poems in Prose (Baudelaire) 127

Poetic Meditations (Lamartine) 102

The Poetry Craze (Piron) 76

Poisson d'or (Le Clezio) 288

Polyeucte (Corneille) 56

Poor Flowers (Desbordes-Valmore) 111

Port Royal (Montherlant) 224

Porte disparu (Arrabal) 296

Portrait of a Man Unknown (Sarraute) 216

Port-Royal (Saint-Beuve) 111

The Princess of Montpensier (La Fayette) 60

La Princesse de Clèves (La Fayette) 63

Provincial Letters (Pascal) 48, 59

Psyche: Inventions of the Other (Derrida) 269

The Public Rose (Éluard) 199

Pulchérie (Corneille) 48, 62

The Punishments (Hugo) 118

The Pure and the Impure (Colette) 208

Les quartières d'hiver (Pancrazi) 274

Queen Jane (Mistral) 141

Querrelle of Brest (Genet) 215

Quoat-Quoat (Audiberti) 214

Rameau's Nephew (Diderot) 80

Rarahu (Loti) 133

The Ravishing of Lol V. Stein (Duras) 239

The Raw and the Cooked (Lévi-Strauss) 239

The Rebel (Camus) 155, 220

The Red and the Black (Stendhal) 106

Le regard de Vincent (Philippe) 269

A Regicide (Robbe-Grillet) 257

Regrets (Bellay) 39

Le Reliquaire (Coppée) 126

Remembrance of Things Past (Proust) 171, 178, 180, 181, 184, 186, 190

Remise de peine (Modiano) 271

Le Rendez-vous (Robbe-Grillet) 258

René (Chateaubriand) 97

Renée Mauperin (Goncourt and Goncourt) 124

The Residuary Legatee (Regnard) 71

Retable, Reverie (Chawaf) 252

Les reveries de la femme sauvage (Cixous) 296

Rhadamistus and Zenobia (Crébillon) 71

Rhinoceros (Ionesco) 231

The Ride of Eldis (Viélé-Griffin) 144

The Ripening Seed (Colette) 184

The Roads to Freedom (Sartre) 212

Rockaby (Beckett) 154

Rodogune (Corneille) 48, 57

Le roi du bois (Michon) 286

Roland Barthes (Barthes) 254

Le Roman comique (Scarron) 58

The Romance of a Poor Young Man (Feuillet) 120

The Royal Domain (Viélé-Griffin) 184

The Royal Place (Corneille) 48

Rules of the Game (Leiris) 255

Ruy Blas (Hugo) 110

Sa femme (Bernheim) 280

Sabine (Lacretelle) 196

Le Sacrifice imperial (Jacob) 192

Saint Matoral (Jacob) 167

Salammbô (Flaubert) 92, 123

Sappho (Daudet) 136

The Satin Slipper (Claudel) 192, 193

Scenes from Private Life (Balzac) 91, 106

Scenes of Bohemian Life (Murger) 115

The School for Husbands (Molière) 60

School for Mothers (Marivaux) 73

The School for Wives (Molière) 47–48, 60

A Scrap of Paper (Sardou) 122

The Screens (Genet) 234

Sea Marks (Perse) 220

A Season in Hell (Rimbaud) 94, 129

The Second Sex (Beauvoir) 218

The Secret (Bernstein) 172

La Semaine (du Bartas) 41

Sentimental Education (Flaubert) 92, 127

The Separation (Franck) 276

Les sept noms du peintre (Le Guillou) 288

La Sérénade (Regnard) 66

Sertorius (Corneille) 48, 60

Seuls Demeurent (Char) 212

Seven Strings of the Lyre (Sand) 111

The Sex Fable (Bourdet) 195

A Shady Business (Balzac) 91

Sido (Colette) 193

Le Siècle de Louis XIV (Voltaire) 68

Siegfried (Giraudoux) 190

Un silence d'environ une demi-heure (Schreiber) 286

The Silence of Colonel Bramble (Maurois) 177

Silsie (Redonnet) 274

The Simoom (Lenormand) 180

"A Simple Heart" (Flaubert) 92

Simulacrum (Leiris) 186

Social Contract (Rousseau) 68, 80

Le soleil des mourants (Izzo) 293

Solitude (Prudhomme) 127

The Song of the Rhone (Mistral) 147

The Song of the World (Giono) 199

Songs (Béranger) 99

Songs and Sonnets (Ronsard) 39

Songs Without Words (Verlaine) 130

Sonnets pour Hélène (Ronsard) 33

Sophonisbe (Mairet) 55

Sous l'étoile du chien (Puech) 276

Southern Mail (Saint-Exupéry) 192

The Spirit of the Laws (Montesquieu) 77

Spiridion (Sand) 111

The Springtime of Others (Bernard) 185

Les Stances (Moreas) 149

Star of Satan (Bernanos) 188

State of Siege (Camus) 155

Strait Is the Gate (Gide) 167

The Strange River (Green) 196

The Stranger (Camus) 155, 209

The Straw Man (Giono) 228

A Stroll in the Air (Ionesco) 237

The Sulky Fire (Bernard) 181

Suréna (Corneille) 48

The Swans (Viélé-Griffin) 138

Swann's Way (Proust) 171

Sweat of Blood (Jouve) 200

The Sweet Cheat Gone (Proust) 186

Tales and Novels in Verse (La Fontaine) 60

Tartuffe (Molière) 48, 60

The Taut Rope (Simon) 215

The Tears (Valmore) 107

The Temptation of Saint Anthony (Flaubert) 92, 130

Terrasse à Rome (Quignard) 296

Terror ont he Mountain (Ramuz) 186

The Test (Marivaux) 76

Le testament français (Makine) 284

Thais (Mistral) 141

Le Théâtre de la Revolution (Rolland) 162

The Thebans, or the Enemy Brothers (Racine) 60

Theodore (Corneille) 48

Thérèse Desqueyroux (Mauriac) 189

Thérèse Raquin (Zola) 126

Théroigne de Méricourt (Hervieu) 144

The Thief's Journal (Genet) 218

The Three Dorothys (Scarron) 57

The Three Musketeers (Dumas père) 113

Three Tales (Flaubert) 92

The Tidings Brought to Mary (Claudel) 171

French
  French (continued)
    Tiger at the Gates (Girau-
      doux) 200
    Time and Freewill (Bergson)
      140
    Time Remembered (Proust)
      190
    Tlacuilo (Rio) 278
    Tomorrows (Régnier) 137
    Topography of a Phantom City
      (Robbe-Grillet) 255
    La Tosca (Sardou) 138
    The Tragedies of Faith (Rol-
      land) 172
    Tragiques (Aubigné) 52
    The Transgressor (Green) 225
    The Transient Hour (Aymé)
      214
    Traveler Without Luggage
      (Anouilh) 202
    The Treason of the Intellectu-
      als (Benda) 189
    Treatise on the Education of
      Girls (Fénelon) 64
    Trials (Prudhomme) 125
    Triptych (Simon) 251
    Les Trophées (Heredia) 144
    Turcaret; or, The Financier
      (Lesage) 71
    Twenty Thousand Leagues
      Under the Sea (Verne) 127
    Twenty Years After (Dumas)
      114
    The Two Friends; or, The Mer-
      chant of Lyons (Beaumar-
      chais) 81
    The Two Sources of Morality
      and Religion (Bergson) 196
    The Unanimous Life (Ro-
      mains) 166
    Under Fire (Barbusse) 175
    The Unexpected Wager
      (Sedaine) 81
    The Universal Heir (Regnard)
      71
    The Unknown Sea (Mauriac)
      206
    The Unnamable (Beckett)
      154, 223
    The Unquiet Spirit (Bernard)
      188
    The Vagabond (Colette) 168
    Venice in Winter (Robles) 260
    Le Véritable Saint Genest
      (Rotrou) 57
    Vesuvius (Robles) 234
    Village Priest (Balzac) 110
    Le Vin est tiré (Desnos) 210
    Viper in the Fist (Bazin) 216
    Viper's Tangle (Mauriac) 196
    The Virgin of Paris (Jouve)
      211
    Virginie (Mairet) 55
    Les voleurs de beauté (Bruck-
      ner) 288
    Vowels (Rimbaud) 136
    Le Voyage de Monsieur Perri-
      chon (Labiche) 122
    "Voyelles" (Rimbaud) 94
    The Voyeur (Robbe-Grillet)
      225
    The Vultures (Becque) 135
    Waiting for God (Weil) 219
    Waiting for Godot (Beckett)
      154, 223

    The Wakeful State (Desnos)
      210
    The Waltz of the Toreadors
      (Anouilh) 221
    The Wandering Jew (Sue) 113
    War (Le Clezio) 247
    Weekend de chasse a la mère
      (Brisac) 286
    The Whirlwind (Bernstein)
      163
    The White Woman (Baude-
      laire) 92
    The Wicker Work Woman
      (France) 147
    The Widow (Corneille) 48
    The Wife of Claude (Dumas)
      129
    The Wild Ass's Skin (Balzac)
      106
    Wind, Sand and Stars (Saint-
      Exupéry) 206
    The Wind (Simon) 228
    Winds (Perse) 214
    The Winged Legend of
      Wieland the Blacksmith
      (Viélé-Griffin) 158
    The Winged Sandal (Régnier)
      164
    Within a Budding Grove
      (Proust) 178
    Woman of Paris (Becque)
      137
    A Woman of the Pharisees
      (Mauriac) 208
    The Woman Who Was Poor
      (Bloy) 147
    Women in Love (Daudet) 120
    The Wood Nymph, or the Liv-
      ing Corpse (Mairet) 54
    The World of the Thibaults
      (Martin du Gard) 182
    A World on the Wane (Lévi-
      Strauss) 225
    The Would-Be Gentleman
      (Molière) 61
    Yesteryear and Yesterday
      (Verlaine) 136
    The Yoke of Pity (Breda) 170
    "You Are Men" (Jouve) 174
    The Young Fate (Valery) 176
    Young Man in Chains (Mau-
      riac) 172
    Zadig (Voltaire) 77
    Zaire (Voltaire) 75
    Zazie in the Metro (Queneau)
      231
  Guadeloupean
    Moi, Tituba, sorcière noire de
      Salem (Condé) 268
    Ton beau capitain (Schwarze-
      Bart) 269
  Guinean
    The African Continent
      (Nenekhaly-Camara) 248
    I Was a Savage (Paris) 228
    The Radiance of the King
      (Laye) 224
  Guyanese
    Bozambo's Revenge: Colonial-
      ism Inside Out (Juminer)
      245
  Haitian
    "La Drama de Marchaterre"
      (Brierre) 193
    Masters of the Dew (Rou-
      mains) 211

    Rhythms of My Heart (Bal-
      ance) 207
    The Tragic Engagement
      (Chenet) 245
  Ivorien
    Allah n'est pas oblige (Kou-
      rouma) 296
    A Negro in Paris (Dadie) 231
    Wild Blew the Wind (Nokan)
      236
  Lebanese
    La Ocher de Tanios (Maalouf)
      280
    Way of Migration (Najjar) 286
  Malian
    The Wages of Violence (Ouo-
      loguem) 245
  Martinican
    Texaco (Chamoiseau) 278
    The Tragedy of King
      Christophe (Césaire) 237
  Moroccan
    Chronicle of Loneliness (Ben
      Jelloun) 255
    L'Enfant de sable (Ben Jel-
      loun) 266
    La nuit de lerreur (Ben Jel-
      loun) 289
    The Simple Past (Chraibi)
      224
    An Unclaimed Inheritance
      (Chraibi) 236
  Senegalese
    God's Bits of Wood (Sembene)
      233
    Karim, roman Sénégalais
      (Diop) 200
    Poetical Works (Senghor) 274
  Swiss
    Journal intime (Amiel) 136
  Tunisian
    Agar (Memmi) 225
    The Desert (Memmi) 256
    The Pharaoh (Memmi) 271
    The Pillar of Salt (Memmi)
      223
    The Scorpion or the Imaginary
      Confession (Memmi) 246
    Strangers (Memmi) 225

G

Georgian
  From Footpath to Railway Line
    (Lortkipanidze) 190
  The Goatibex Constellation (Iskan-
    der) 241
  Kvachi Kvachantiradze
    (Javakhishvili) 185
  Sandro of Chegem (Iskander) 257
  Wandering Through Three Times
    (Abashidze) 234
German
  Austrian
    The Adventurer and the Singer
      (Hofmannsthal) 149
    The Albigensians (Lenau) 112
    Amerika (Kafka) 152, 189
    The Ancestors (Grillparzer) 100
    The Ascension (Bahr) 175
    Belated Crown (Weinheber)
      202
    Between Gods and Demons
      (Weinheber) 204
    Beware of Pity (Zweig) 204
    The Capuchin Tomb (Roth)
      204

    The Castle (Kafka) 152, 188
    Catalina (Kurnberger) 119
    The Child of the Parish
      (Ebner-Eschenbach) 138
    Christina's Journey Home
      (Hofmannsthal) 168
    Civilization and Its Discon-
      tents (Freud) 193
    Collected Poems (Lenau) 114
    Correction (Bernhard) 254
    The Countess of Charolais
      (Beer-Hofmann) 163
    A Country Doctor (Kafka)
      152, 178
    Death and the Fool (Hof-
      mannsthal) 144
    The Death of the Tenant
      Farmer, Ignaz Hajek
      (Haslinger) 266
    The Death of Titian (Hof-
      mannsthal) 143
    The Death of Virgil (Broch)
      212
    Demian (Hesse) 178
    The Demons (Doderer) 227
    Derangement (Bernhard) 243
    The Difficult Man (Hof-
      mannsthal) 181
    Don Juan (Lenau) 117
    A Dream Is Life (Grillparzer)
      108
    Elektra (Hofmannsthal) 161
    Everyman (Hofmannsthal)
      170
    The Evil Spirit Lumpazi-
      vagabundus, or the Roguish
      Frio (Nestroy) 107
    Flight into Darkness (Schnit-
      zler) 195
    The Force of Habit (Bernhard)
      252
    Fraulein Else (Schnitzler) 185
    Free Game (Schnitzler) 146
    The Gallery of Mirrors (Bern-
      stein) 185
    The Golden Fleece (Grill-
      parzer) 102
    Der Golem (Meyrink) 174
    Grand Hotel (Baum) 192
    The Great Salzburg Theater of
      the World (Hofmannsthal)
      182
    The Great Wall of China
      (Kafka) 152
    He Intends to Have a Fling
      (Nestroy) 112
    Herod's Children (Aichinger)
      216
    A Hunger Artist (Kafka) 152,
      185
    The Hunting Party (Bern-
      hard) 252
    Illywhacker (Carey) 266
    In the Penal Colony (Kafka)
      152, 173, 178
    Inexpiable (Ebner-
      Eschenbach) 141
    The Interpretation of Dreams
      (Freud) 149
    Jakob der Letzte (Rosegger)
      139
    The Judgment (Kafka) 152,
      175
    Kampi; or, The Millionairess
      and the Seamstress (Ne-
      stroy) 117

The King of Zion (Hamerling) 127

King Ottocar: His Rise and Fall (Grillparzer) 104

The Lass from the Suburbs; or, Honesty Is the Best Policy (Nestroy) 112

The Last Days of Humanity (Kram) 182

The Last Knight (Grun) 106

Lay Down Your Arms (Suttner) 140

The Lime Works (Bernhard) 248

The Little Theater of the World (Hofmannsthal) 147

Lottie, the Watchmaker (Ebner-Eschenbach) 132

Madonna Dianora (Hofmannsthal) 147

Malina (Bachmann) 249

Man Full of Nothing (Nestroy) 114

The Man Without Qualities (Musil) 193

The Marriage of Sobeide (Hofmannsthal) 149

Meditation (Kafka) 152

Merry-Go-Round (Schnitzler) 147

The Metamorphosis (Kafka) 152, 174

Der Nachsommer (Stifter) 120

Nobleness and Extinction (Weinheber) 199

None but the Brave (Schnitzler) 159

The Other Side (Kubin) 167

A Party for Boris (Bernhard) 245

Playing with Love (Schnitzler) 146

The Priest of Kirchfield (Anzengruber) 127

The Psychological Outlook on Life (Jaspers) 178

Radetzky March (Roth) 195

The Road to the Open (Schnitzler) 166

The Royal Game (Zweig) 209

Sappho (Grillparzer) 101

Savonarola (Lenau) 110

Silberne Saiten (Zweig) 159

The Song of Berndotte (Werfel) 208

Totem and Taboo (Freud) 172

The Tower (Hofmannsthal) 187

Tractatus Logico Philosophicus (Wittgenstein) 181

The Trial (Kafka) 152, 187

The Triumph and Tragedy of Erasmus Rotterdamus (Zweig) 199

Two Countesses (Ebner-Eschenbach) 137

Das Vaterspiel (Haslinger) 296

Vermutengen uber die Liebe in einem fremden Haus (Langle) 291

The Waterfalls of Slunj (Doderer) 237

The Waves of the Sea and Love (Grillparzer) 106

The White Fan (Hofmannsthal) 147

The World's Illusion (Wasserman) 178

Yesterday (Hofmansthal) 142

German

The Abbasids (Platen) 108

Abschied von den Feinden (Jirgl) 284

Absence (Handke) 269

The Absurda Comica, or Master Peter Squentz (Gryphius) 59

Acquainted with the Night (Böll) 223

Adam, Where Art Thou? (Böll) 219

Address to the Nobility of the German Nation (Luther) 36

Agathon (Wieland) 80

Agnes Bernauer (Hebbel) 117, 119

Alain and Elise (Kaiser) 207

Alan Turing (Hochhuth) 269

All Quiet on the Western Front (Remarque) 192

Am kurzeren Ende der Sonnenallee (Brussig) 293

The Ancestors (Freytag) 129

And Pippa Dances (Hauptmann) 164

Animal triste (Maron) 286

Anniversaries: From the Life of Gesine Cresspahl (Johnson) 248

Anschlag (Neumann) 293

The Antichrist (Broch) 195

Der Antiquar (Schertenlieb) 278

Aquis Submersus (Storm) 131

Ariadne and Naxos (Ernst) 171

Army Chaplain Schmelzle's Journey (Richter) 98

The Assumption of Hanneles (Hauptmann) 144

Atta Troll (Heine) 113

Attila, King of the Huns (Werner) 97

Auto-da-Fé (Canetti) 200

Baal (Brecht) 153

Babylonian Wandering (Doblin) 199

Bambi (Salten) 184

Barbera Blomberg (Zuckmayer) 218

The Battle of Herman (Kleist) 98

The Beaver Coat (Hauptmann) 144

Before Dawn (Hauptmann) 140

Before the Rainy Season (Hoffmann) 271

Before the Storm (Fontane) 132

Being and Time (Heidegger) 189

The Beloved Returns (Mann) 152

Berlin Alexanderplatz (Doblin) 192

Beyond Good and Evil (Nietzsche) 114, 138

Billiards at Half-Past Nine (Böll) 231

The Birth of Tragedy (Nietzsche) 129

Bitte nicht sterben (Wohmann) 280

Black Forest Village Stories (Auerbach) 113

The Black Swan (Mann) 152, 223

Blackie the Fool (Klabund) 177

Blaubarts Shatten (Hahn) 276

The Blue Angel (Mann) 163

The Blue Band (Kellerman) 204

Bodenlos (Kirsch) 286

Bodenloser Sstz (Braun) 274

The Book of Hours (Rilke) 155, 163

The Book of Songs (Heine) 93

Die Braut im Park (Quadflieg) 278

The Bride of Messina (Schiller) 68, 96

The Broken Pitcher (Kleist) 97

Buch der Leider (Heine) 105

Die Buchhandlerin (Bohme) 293

Buddenbrooks (Mann) 152, 159

Cabal and Love (Schiller) 67, 84

Calendar Histories (Graf) 192

The Call of the Toad (Grass) 278

The Captain of Kopenick (Zuckmayer) 195

Cardenio und Celinde (Gryphius) 59

Carl and Anna (Frank) 188

Carolus Stardus (Gryphius) 59

The Case of Sergeant Grischa (Zweig) 189

Caspar Hauser (Wasserman) 166

Castle Durant (Eichendorff) 110

Cat and Mouse (Grass) 234

Catharina von Georgien (Gryphius) 59

Cathy from Heilbronn; or, The Trial by Fire (Kleist) 97

The Caucasian Chalk Circle (Brecht) 153, 216

Charles Stuart, or Majesty Murdered (Gryphius) 58

The Chaste Joseph (Grimmelshausen) 61

Cherubin Hammer und Cherubin Hammer (Bichsel) 293

The Chief (Mann) 187

Children of the World (Heyse) 129

The Clown (Böll) 237

The Coming of Peace (Hauptmann) 141

The Confessions of Felix Krull (Mann) 224

Countess Faustine (Hahn-Hahn) 112

"The Cranes of Ibycus" (Schiller) 68

Critique of Practical Reason (Kant) 85

Critique of Pure Reason (Kant) 84

The Cross on the Baltic Sea (Werner) 97

Dame (Sudermann) 138

Damon; or, True Friendship (Lessing) 69

The Dance of Death (Kellerman) 216

Dance of Death and Poems of the Times (Kaschnitz) 215

Danton's Death (Büchner) 109

Death and the Ploughman (Johannes von Tepl) 26

Death in Venice (Mann) 152, 171

The Death Ship (Traven) 188

Debit and Credit (Freytag) 119

The Decay and Restoration of Civilization (Schweitzer) 184

The Decline of the West (Spengler) 177

Deep Shadows (Storm) 124

The Deputy (Hochhuth) 237

The Descendants (Immermann) 109

The Devil's Elixir (Hoffman) 99

The Devil's General (Zuckmayer) 214

The Diary of a Young Girl (Frank) 215

"The Diver" (Schiller) 68

Doctor Faustus (Mann) 152, 215

Dog Years (Grass) 237

Don Carlos (Schiller) 67, 85

Don Juan and Faust (Grabbe) 105

Dorf uterm Wind (Schenk) 280

Dr. Katzenberger's Journey to the Spa (Richter) 98

Dramen (Canetti) 239

Drayman (Hauptmann) 148

Drums in the Night (Brecht) 153, 182

Duino Elegies (Rilke) 155, 184

Early Sorrow (Mann) 152

Earth Spirit (Wedekind) 145

Eduards Heimkehr (Schneider) 293

The Education of the Human Race (Lessing) 69

Edward II (Brecht) 153

Effi Briest (Fontane) 145

Egmont (Goethe) 67, 85

Emanuel (Laederach) 274

Emilia Galotti (Lessing) 69, 82

Eneit (Heinrich von Veldeke) 22

Entanglements (Fontane) 139

Er oder ich (Nadolny) 293

"Erkling" (Goethe) 67, 84

The Essence of Christianity (Feuerbach) 112

The Exile (Wagner) 271

Fables and Stories (Gellert) 77

The Fateful Prong (Plater) 104

German
   German (continued)
      Faust (Goethe) 67, 97, 107
      Faust, ein Fragment (Goethe)
         67
      Felix Krull (Mann) 152
      The Feud of the Schroffensteins
         (Kleist) 96
      Field of Violets (Hoffmann)
         268
      Fiesco; or, The Conspiracy of
         Genoa (Schiller) 84
      Die Flaterrzunge (Delius) 293
      Flesh (Benn) 176
      Der Flohatz (Fischart) 41
      The Flounder (Grass) 256
      The Flower, Fruit and Thorn
         Pieces (Richter) 87
      The Fool in Christ, Emanuel
         Quint (Hauptmann) 168
      The Forty Days of Musa Dagh
         (Werfel) 197
      Die Frau in den Kissen (Kro-
         nauer) 274
      Frauen vor Flusblandschaft
         (Böll) 266
      Fredegonde and Brunehaut
         (Lemercier) 102
      The Free Thinker (Lessing) 69
      From Morn to Midnight
         (Kaiser) 175
      Der Fuchs war damals schon
         der Jager (Muller) 278
      The Gardener of Toulouse
         (Kaiser) 204
      Gas (Kaiser) 176
      Gas II (Kaiser) 180
      Gedichte (Heine) 102
      Gedichte (Lenau) 107
      Germany, a Winter's Tale
         (Heine) 114
      Giganten (Doblin) 196
      "The Glove" (Schiller) 68
      Das Gluck (Hoffmann) 280
      The Goalee's Anxiety at the
         Penalty Kick (Handke) 248
      The Good Woman of Setzuan
         (Brecht) 153, 210
      Götz von Berlichingen
         (Goethe) 67, 82
      Green Henry (Keller) 132
      Grimm's Fairy Tales (Grimm
         and Grimm) 98
      Grobianus (Dedekind) 38
      Group Portrait with Lady
         (Böll) 249
      Gyges and His Ring (Hugo)
         119
      Hampels Fluchten (Kumpf-
         muller) 296
      Hannibal (Grabbe) 109
      The Happy Vineyard (Zuck-
         mayer) 187
      Heart on the Left (Frank) 221
      Heinrich von Otterdingen
         (Novalis) 88
      Hemingard of the Oak Burial
         Mounds (Drost) 107
      Henry of Ofterdingen (No-
         valis) 88
      The Heretic of Soana (Haupt-
         mann) 177
      Hermann and Dorothea
         (Goethe) 87
      Herod and Marianne
         (Hebbel) 116

Herr Puntila and His Man
   Mutti (Brecht) 153
Herzwand (Hartling) 274
Hesperus (Richter) 86
The Hessian Messenger (Büch-
   ner) 108
Der Himmel des Humoristen
   (Pivonas) 264
The History of Lady Sophia
   Sternhelm (La Roche) 82
History of the Thirty Years'
   War (Schiller) 68
The Holy Sinner (Mann) 152,
   220
Honor (Sudermann) 140
Horribilicribrifax (Gryphius)
   60
The Human Province
   (Canetti) 251
Hymns to the Night (Novalis)
   95
Hyperion (Holderllin) 87
I and Thou (Buber) 184
Ich (Hilbig) 280
In einer dunken Nacht gig ich
   aus meinen stillen Haus
   (Handke) 289
In the Castle (Storm) 122
The Invisible Lodge (Richter)
   86
Iphigenie auf Tauris (Goethe)
   67, 85
Italian Night (Horvath) 193
Iwein (Hartmann von Aue)
   23
Japhthah and His Daughters
   (Feuchtwanger) 228
The Jew (Lessing) 69
Jew Suss (Feuchtwanger) 187
The Jewish War (Feucht-
   wanger) 196
The Jew's Birch Tree (Droste-
   Hülshoff) 112
The Jews of Zirndorf (Wasser-
   man) 147
Joseph and His Brothers
   (Mann) 152, 197
The Journalists (Freytag) 117
The Joyful Wisdom (Niet-
   zsche) 135
Judith (Hebbel) 111
Julius von Tarent (Leisewitz)
   83
Kaiser Friedrich Barbarossa
   (Grabbe) 106
Das Kapital (Marx, Engels)
   126
Kaspar (Handke) 245
Katherine of Heilbronn
   (Kleist) 98
Kerkhoven's Third Existence
   (Wasserman) 199
Kopfjager (Timm) 276
Landschaft mit Dornen
   (Saeger) 280
Lanzen im Eis (Schacht) 274
Laocoon: An Essay on the Lim-
   its of Painting and Poetry
   (Lessing) 69, 80
The League of Cambrai
   (Platen) 107
The Left-Handed Woman
   (Handke) 255
Lenins Hirn (Spengler) 276
"Lenore" (Burger) 82
Leo Arminius (Gryphius) 57

Leonce and Lena (Büchner)
   109
Liber de Arti Distellandi (Hi-
   eronymous Brunschwig) 34
Lievesfluchter (Schlink) 296
The Life of the Virgin Mary
   (Rilke) 155, 172
"Life and the Ideal" (Schiller)
   68
Life of Galileo (Brecht) 153
Life of Quintus Fixelin, Ex-
   tracted from 15 Letter Boxes
   (Richter) 87
Little Man, What Now? (Fal-
   lada) 196
A Little Organum for the The-
   ater (Brecht) 154
Local Anesthetic (Grass) 246
Lonely Lives (Hauptmann)
   142
The Lost Honor of Katerine
   Blum (Böll) 252
The Lost Manuscript (Freytag)
   124
Lucinde (Schiller) 88
Ludwig muss sterben
   (Hettche) 274
Luise (Voss) 87
Lyrisches Intermezzo (Heine)
   103
The Magic Mountain (Mann)
   152, 185
Magister Ludi (The Glass Bead
   Game) (Hesse) 210
Mahoganny (Brecht) 193
The Maid of Orleans (Schiller)
   68, 95
Main Currents in Nineteenth-
   Century Literature Criticism
   (Brandes) 129
Man and the Masses (Toller)
   180
Man Is Good (Frank) 177
A Manual of Piety (Brecht)
   153
Maria Magdalena (Hebbel)
   112
Maria Stuart (Schiller) 68, 95
Mario and the Magician
   (Mann) 152
The Marquis of Keith
   (Wedekind) 159
The Marquis of O (Kleist) 97
Martin Luther; or The Conse-
   cration of Strength
   (Werner) 97
Master Arthur (Raabe) 128
Master Timpe (Kretzen) 139
The Maurizius Case (Wasser-
   man) 190
Medea: Stimmen (Wolf) 286
Mein Hund, meine Sau, mein
   Leben (Stadler) 282
Mein Kampf (Hitler) 187
Mein Stuck Zeit (Brezan) 274
Melodien (Krausser) 280
Memento Mori (Heinrich von
   Melk) 22
The Messiah (Klopstock) 77
Minna von Barnhelm; or, A
   Soldier's Fortune (Lessing)
   69, 81
The Misogynist (Lessing) 69,
   79
Miss Sara Sampson (Lessing)
   69, 79

Morbus Kitahara (Ransmayr)
   284
Morgue and Other Poems
   (Benn) 171
Mother Courage and Her
   Children (Brecht) 153, 208,
   218
Mozart (Hildesheimer) 256
Mozart's Journey from Vienna
   to Prague (Morike) 119
Munchausen (Immermann)
   110
Music of the Future (Kasch-
   nitz) 219
My Century (Grass) 293
My Heart (Lasker-Schuler)
   171
My Life (Wagner) 170
Nach den Satiren (Grunbein)
   293
Napoleon, or the Hundred
   Days (Grabbe) 106
Narcissus and Goldmund
   (Hesse) 193
Das Narrenschiff (Brant) 29
The Narrow Road to Happi-
   ness (Ernst) 162
Nathan the Wise (Lessing)
   69, 83
New Poems (Heine) 93, 114
New Poems (Rilke) 155
Die Niebelungen (Hebbel)
   123
The Night of the Generals
   (Kirst) 236
The Ninth of November
   (Kellerman) 181
The Northern Lights (Daubla)
   168
The Notebook of Malte Lau-
   rids Brigge (Rilke) 155, 168
The Nuremberg Chronicle
   (Schedel) 29
Oberon (Wieland) 83
"Ode to Joy" (Schiller) 67
Odes (Klopstock) 81
Odes and Songs (Hagedorn)
   76
Offending the Audience
   (Handke) 242
The Old Maid (Lessing) 69
The Opermanns (Feucht-
   wanger) 197
Otto the Marksman (Kinkel)
   114
Our Conquest (Hoffmann)
   264
Painter Nolten (Morike) 107
Pandora's Box (Wedekind)
   162
Papas Koffer (Kopf) 280
Papinianus (Gryphius) 59
The Parable of the Blind
   (Hoffmann) 266
Pargfrider (Heym) 291
Parricide (Bronnen) 180
Party in Autumn (Dorst) 233
Die Passionfrucht (Piwitt)
   280
The Patrioteer (Mann) 177
Pawels Briefe (Maron) 293
Penthesilia (Kleist) 97
The Persecution and Assassi-
   nation of Jean-Paul Marat,
   as Performed by the Inmates
   of the Asylum of Charenton

Under the Direction of the Marquis de Sade (Weiss) 239

Peter Camenzind (Hesse) 162

Peter Schlemihl (Chamisso) 99

The Phantom Lover (Kaiser) 190

The Piccolomini (Schiller) 88

The Plants (Sternheim) 170

Plastik (Herder) 83

The Plebians Rehearse the Uprising (Grass) 242

Poems (Droste-Hülshoff) 110

Poems (Storm) 117

The Poor (Mann) 176

Poppy and Memory (Celan) 221

"The Power of Song" (Schiller) 68

The Price of Thebes (Lasker-Schuler) 173

The Prince of Homburg (Kleist) 98

The Prodigy (Hesse) 163

The Proprietor of the Sun Inn (Kurz) 119

Das Provisorium (Hilbig) 296

The Quest for Historical Jesus (Schweitzer) 164

Raabe Baikal (Strittmatter) 274

The Rat (Grass) 268

The Realist (Broch) 196

The Rebellion of the Hanged (Traven) 202

Rebus (Rosei) 274

Reflections of a Nonpolitical Man (Mann) 177

Request Concert (Kroetz) 250

Richard Savage (Gutzkow) 111

The Ride Across Lake Constance (Handke) 249

The Rider on the White Horse (Storm) 139

The Rise and Fall of the City of Mahogonny (Brecht) 153

The Robbers (Schiller) 67, 84

Robert Guiskard (Kleist) 97

Robert und Guiscard (Eichendorff) 119

Roman Elegies (Goethe) 67, 87

The Romantic (Broch) 195

The Romantic Oedipus (Platen) 106

Romanzero (Heine) 93, 117

Der Rote Ritter (Muschg) 280

Das rote Schiff (Mand) 282

Die Sache mit Randow (Schelsinger) 286

The Sand for the Urns (Celan) 216

Schiller's Homeland Years (Kurz) 113

Schimpf und Ernst (Pauli) 36

Schlageter (Johst) 197

Das Schlaraffenland (Sachs) 37

Selige Zeiten, burchige Welt (Menasse) 278

The Serapion Brothers (Hoffman) 101

Shock-Headed Peter (Hoffmann) 115

Show Your Tongue (Grass) 272

The Sick Woman (Furchtegott) 77

Siddhartha (Hesse) 182

Simple Stories (Schulze) 291

Simplicissmus the Vagabond, that is the Life of a Strange Adventurer Named Melchio Sternfels von Fuchsheim (Grimmelshausen) 61

The Sinking of the Titanic (Enzensberger) 258

The Sleepwalkers (Broch) 195, 196

Slovenly Peter (Hoffmann) 114

Soldiers (Hochhuth) 243

The Soldiers (Lenz) 82

Song of Hildebrand, 13

Songs (Uhland) 99

Songs for the People (Claudius) 83

Songs of the Fatherland (Ihland) 100

Sonnets to Orpheus (Rilke) 155, 182

The Sons (Feuchtwanger) 200

The Sons of the Valley (Werner) 96

A Sorrow Beyond Dreams (Handke) 250

The Sorrows of Young Werther (Goethe) 67, 82

The Spectacle at the Tower (Hoffmann) 262

The Spell (Broch) 223

The Spring (Kleist) 78

Ein springender Brunnen (Walser) 291

Spring's Awakening (Wedekind) 142

St. Joan of the Stockyards (Brecht) 196

Stalingrad (Plievier) 214

Static Poems (Benn) 216

Steppenwolf (Hesse) 189

The Story of the Abderites (Wieland) 82

Strange Stories (Hoffman) 100

The Stranger (Kotzebue) 85

The Stranger from the Seine (Harvath) 197

Sturm und Drang (Klinger) 83

Tales from the Vienna Woods (Horvath) 193

Tales of Hoffman (Hoffman) 99

Tales of Summer (Beer) 64

Tanzstunde (Trampe) 268

Teufelsbruck (Kronauer) 296

Theodicee (Leibniz) 71

The Third Book About Achim (Johnson) 236

The Three Leaps of Want-Lun (Doblin) 174

The Three-Penny Opera (Brecht) 153, 190

Thus Spake Zarathustra (Nietzsche) 135

The Tin Drum (Grass) 231

Titan (Richter) 95

Die Tochter (Grosz) 269

Toller (Dorst) 245

Tom-Cat Murr (Hoffman) 102

Tonio Kroger (Mann) 152, 161

Torquato Tasso (Goethe) 67, 85

The Train Was on Time (Böll) 218

The Treasure of Sierra Madre (Traven) 189

Tristan (Mann) 152, 161

The Tunnel (Kellerman) 172

The Tutor; or, the Advantages of Private Education (Lenz) 82

The Twenty-fourth of February (Werner) 98

The Twins (Klinger) 82

The Two Klingsbergs (Kotzebue) 95

Two People (Dehmel) 161

Uber Berge Kam Ich (Walsdorf) 269

"Über das Erhabene" (Schiller) 68

"Über naive und sentimentalische Dichtung" (Schiller) 68

Unbekannt verzogen (Schulte) 284

Undine (Fouqué) 98

The Unicorn (Walser) 242

Unstete Leute (Viragh) 278

The Valentine (Freytag) 114

Die verlorene Geschichte (Walter) 280

Versuch uber die Jukebox (Handke) 274

Vietnam Discourse (Weiss) 245

Von allem Anfang an (Hein) 289

Vorgeschichten oder schone Gegend Probstein (Schutz) 250

Waldernacht (Rothmann) 282

"The Walk" (Schiller) 68

Wallenstein (Doblin) 180

Wallenstein's Camp (Schiller) 88

Wallenstein's Death (Schiller) 88

Wally the Doubter (Gutzkow) 109

The Wandering Jew (Heym) 264

The Ward Wants to Be a Guardian (Handke) 246

The Warrior's Battle (Kleist) 102

The Weavers (Hauptmann) 143

West Eastern Divan (Goethe) 101

When Love Is Young (Halbe) 144

Wilhelm Meister's Apprenticeship (Goethe) 67, 87, 103

Wilhelm Meister's Travels (Goethe) 102

William Tell (Schiller) 68, 96

Winner Takes All (Wellershof) 263

Die Wittenbergische Nachtigall (Sachs) 36

The Woman Taken in Adultery (Fontane) 135

The Wonder Rabbi of Barcelona (Lasker-Schuler) 181

The Wooers (Eichendorff) 107

The World as Will and Idea (Schopenhauer) 101

The World of Drama (Kerr) 177

Woyzeck (Büchner) 110, 132

Wupper River (Lasker-Schuler) 167

The Year of the Soul (George) 147

Your Silence, My Voice (Kaschnitz) 236

Zettel's Dream (Schmidt) 248

Zukunftsmusik (Enzensberger) 276

Swiss

Andorra (Frisch) 234

Autumn Tranquility (Zollinger) 206

The Ballad of Typhoid Mary (Federspiel) 262

Bluebeard: A Tale (Frisch) 262

The Burning Bush (Faesi) 190

Butterflies (Spitteler) 140

The Chinese Wall (Frisch) 215

Conrad de Leutnant (Spitteler) 148

Count Oederland (Frisch) 234

Daphnis (Gessner) 78

The Death of Abel (Gessner) 79

The Epistle to the Romans (Barth) 178

Extramundana (Spitteler) 135

The Firebugs (Frisch) 230

From the Surge (Faesi) 176

Grass and Bell (Spitteler) 164

The Great Restlessness (Zollinger) 206

Green Henry (Keller) 117

Heidi (Spyri) 133

Hutten's Last Days (Meyer) 128

I'm Not Stiller (Frisch) 224

Jakob von Gunten (Walser) 167

The Joys and Sorrows of a Schoolmaster (Gotthelf) 110

Lachweill Stories (Federer) 170

Leonard and Gertrude (Pestalozzi) 84

Die Leute von Seldwyla (Keller) 119

The Meteor (Durrenmatt) 242

Mirror of the Peasants (Gotthelf) 110

Montauk (Frisch) 254

Mountains and Men (Federer) 170

Needs of the Poor (Gotthelf) 111

The Olympic Spring (Spitteler) 168

German
  Swiss (continued)
    The Physicists (Durrenmatt) 236
    Poems (Zollinger) 197
    Pope and Emperor in the Village (Federer) 187
    Portrait of a Planet (Durrenmatt) 248
    Prometheus and Epimetheus (Spitteler) 134
    Saint Francis of Assisi (Federer) 166
    The Saint (Meyer) 133
    Santa Cruz (Frisch) 215
    Sixtus and Sesto (Federer) 172
    Starlit Early Morning (Zollinger) 202
    The Swiss Family Robinson (Wyss) 99
    The Theory of Psychoanalysis (Jung) 171
    Two Little Misogynists (Spitteler) 165
    Uli the Farmhand (Gotthelf) 112
    The Visit: A Tragi-Comedy (Durrenmatt) 227
    When the War Was Over (Frisch) 218
    A Wilderness of Mirrors (Frisch) 239
    Yet Another Wish (Muschg) 258
    The Zurich Idyll (Faesi) 166
Greek
  Acharnians (Aristophanes) 3
  Achillea's Fiancé (Zei) 269
  Ajax (Sophocles) 3
  Alcibiades (Plato) 3
  Anabasis (Xenophon) 2
  Anger (Menander) 3
  Antigone (Sophocles) 3
  Apology (Plato) 3
  Argo (Theotokos) 202
  Babylonians (Aristophanes) 3
  Bacchae (Euripides) 2, 8
  The Beggar (Karkavitsas) 149
  Birds (Aristophanes) 3
  Book of Exercises (Seferis) 207
  Causes (Callimachus) 4
  Charmides (Plato) 3
  The Cistern (Seferis) 196
  Clouds (Aristophanes) 3, 7
  Cratylus (Plato) 3
  "The Cretan" (Solomos) 107
  Critias (Plato) 3
  Crito (Plato) 3
  Delphic Utterance (Sikelianós) 189
  Electra (Euripides) 2, 7
  Electra (Sophocles) 3
  Epinomis (Plato) 3
  Euthymedemus (Plato) 3
  Euthyphoron (Plato) 3
  "The Free Besieged" (Solomos) 105
  Freedom or Death (Kazantzakis) 219
  Frogs (Aristophanes) 3
  The Game of Madness and Prudence (Theotokos) 234
  Gorgias (Plato) 3
  The Graves (Palamas) 147
  The Greek Passion (Kazantzakis) 224

Hecale (Callimachus) 4
Helen (Euripides) 7
Heptamychos (Pherecydes) 2
Heroic and Elegiac Song for the Lost Second Lieutenant of the Albanian Campaign (Elytis) 213
Hipparchus (Plato) 3
Hippias Major (Plato) 3
Hippias Minor (Plato) 3
Hippolytus (Euripides) 2, 7
History (Herodotus) 3
History of the Peloponnesian War (Thucydides) 3
The Hotel and the House and Other Pieces (Evangelou) 266
"Hymn to Liberty" (Solomos) 103
Hymns (Callimachus) 4
Iambi (Callimachus) 4
Iambs and Anapaests (Palamas) 147
Ibis (Callimachus) 4
Iliad (Homer) 2
Ion (Euripides) 2, 7
Iphigenia at Aulis (Euripides) 2, 8
The King's Flute (Palamas) 169
Knights (Aristophanes) 3
Laches (Plato) 3
The Last Tempatation of Christ (Kazantzakis) 225
Life Immovable (Palamas) 162
The Light-Shadowed (Sikelianós) 167
"The Little Mariner" (Elytis) 268
Lock of Berenice (Callimachus) 4
Logbook I (Seferis) 207
Lovers (Plato) 3
Lysis (Plato) 3
Lysistrata (Aristophanes) 3
The Man She Hated (Menander) 3
Maria Nefeli (Elytis) 257
Medea (Euripides) 2, 7
Menexeums (Plato) 3
Meno (Plato) 3
Metai (Donelaitis) 101
Misanthrope (Menander) 3
The Murderess (Papadiamantis) 171
Mythistorema (Myth-History) (Seferis) 200
Nomoi (Plato) 3
Odyssey (Homer) 2
Oedipus at Colonus (Sophocles) 3
Oedipus Rex (Sophocles) 3
The Old Man with the Kites (Ritsos) 266
Oresteia (Aeschylus) 2, 6
Orestes (Euripides) 8
Parmedides (Plato) 3
Peace (Aristophanes) 3, 7
Persians (Aeschylus) 2
Phaedo (Plato) 3
Phaedrus (Plato) 3
Philebus (Plato) 3
Philoctetes (Sophocles) 3, 7
Prologue to Life (Sikelianós) 176
Protagoras (Plato) 3
Republic (Plato) 3
The Sacrifice of Abraham (Kornáros) 55
Seven Against Thebes (Aeschylus) 2
The Shark (Solomos) 116
The Shield (Menander) 3
Slaves in Their Chains (Theotokis) 182

Sophist (Plato) 3
The Sovereign Sun (Elytis) 249
Statesman (Plato) 3
"The Stepchildren" (Elytis) 252
Suppliants (Aeschylus) 6
Symposium (Plato) 3
Tablets (Callimachus) 4
Theaetetus (Plato) 3
Thrush (Seferis) 215
Timeaus (Plato) 3
Trachiniae (Sophocles) 3
Tragedy of My Country (Palamas) 138
Trojan Women (Euripides) 2, 7
The Turning Point (Seferis) 195
The Twelve Lays of the Gypsy (Palamas) 165
Wasps (Aristophanes) 3
Wealth (Aristophanes) 3
The Woman of Samos (Menander) 3
Women at the Ecclesia (Aristophanes) 3
Women at the Thesmophoria (Aristophanes) 3
Worthy It Is (Elytis) 231
Zorba the Greek (Kazantzakis) 214

H

Hausa
  Shaihu Umar (Balewa) 225
Hebrew
  Abyss (Appelfeld) 280
  Ad haSof (Shamir) 276
  Adon Menuha (Yeshurun) 274
  Ahayat David (Kanuik) 274
  Alleles (Heffner) 282
  As a Few Days (Shalev) 282
  Ashmat Shomeron (Mapu) 124
  Autumn Music (Preil) 258
  Avishag (Schutz) 274
  Badenheim 1939 (Appelfeld) 258
  Black Box (Oz) 269
  The Bridal Canopy (Agnon) 179
  Bridal Veil (Shamir) 264
  Christus shel haDagim (Hoffmann) 274
  Clouds (Tsalka) 282
  The Conversion (Appelfeld) 291
  The Crime of Writing (Lapid) 291
  The Day Before Yesterday (Agnon) 216
  The Deserter (Abush) 286
  Discovering Elijah (Yizhar) 293
  Don't Pronounce It Night (Oz) 282
  Early Grace (Megged) 293
  Elef Levavot (Tsalka) 276
  For Every Sin (Appelfeld) 272
  Four Mothers (Horn) 293
  Gladiator, or a Note on the Military Police (Navot) 280
  The God of Vengeance (Asch) 165
  A Guest for the Night (Agnon) 204
  Hamatzav baShlishi (Oz) 276
  The Heart of Tel Aviv (Shaham) 286
  Hot Hot Dogs (Shaham) 280
  The Ice Mine (Appelfeld) 289
  The Immortal Bartfuss (Appelfeld) 271
  In the Desert of a Lodging Place (Sened, Sened) 291
  In the Wilderness (Appelfeld) 237

The Iron Tracks (Appelfeld) 291
A Journey into Winter (Appelfeld) 296
Katerina (Appelfeld) 272
Kidesh Halem (Asch) 179
Kneller's Happy Campers (Keret) 291
haLaila shebo Meta ha Tsionut (Almog) 274
Laish (Appelfeld) 282
Leil Zikharon (Ha'meiri) 274
Li viti Ota baDerekh leVeita (Kahana-Carmon) 276
Likro la 'Atalefim (Bat Shahar) 274
Love After All (Magen) 296
Lovely Malcomia (Yizhar) 291
Mar Mani (Yehoshua) 274
Mesilat Barzel (Appelfeld) 276
Mikdamot (Yizhar) 278
Mottke the Thief (Asch) 175
My Michael (Oz) 245
My Skin (Dromer) 286
A Night in Santa Paulina (Orpaz) 289
Our Wedding (Rabinyan) 293
Panim baA'nan (Birstein) 276
Persephone Remembers (Megged) 296
Post Mortem (Kaniuk) 278
The Pure Element of Time (Be'er) 293
Restoring Former Loves (Kenaz) 291
Return from India (Yehoshua) 282
A Room (Shimoni) 293
The Same Sea (Oz) 291
Sarah, Sarah (Matalon) 296
See Under: Love (Grossman) 272
Sefere haMeforash (Heffner) 276
Selected Poetry (Amichai) 268
Shining Lights (Yizhar) 280
Smile of the Lamb (Grossman) 268
Sogrim et ha Yam (Katzir) 274
Someone to Run With (Grossman) 296
Taking the Trend (Castel-Blum) 293
Tanim shel Mora (Gil) 276
To the Land of the Cattails (Appelfeld) 268
Touch the Water, Touch the Wind (Oz) 251
Tower of Victory (Luzzatto) 74
Tzili: the Story of a Life (Appelfeld) 263
Under Moses (Asch) 177
Uvatzfifut (Bar-Yosef) 274
Voyage to the End of the Millennium (Yehoshua) 289
Where the Jackals Howl and Other Stories (Oz) 240
Winnie Mandela's Football Team (Rabikovitz) 289
Yom haOr shel Anat (Megged) 278
Yoman shel Zug Me'ohav (Sened, Sened) 278
Zemah David (Gans) 44
The Zigzag Child (Grossman) 282
Hindi
  Arena (Prem) 185
  "The Beloved's Exile" (Upadhyay Hariaudh) 173

Bharatbharati (Gupta) 171
The Drop and the Sea (Nagar) 227
Embezzlement (Prem) 190
Forgotten Pictures (Varma) 231
The Gift of a Cow (Prem) 202
The House of People (Pant) 239
Kamayani (Prasad) 200
Lakshmibai, Queen of Jhansi (Varma) 214
Love Retreat (Prem) 182
The Lying Truth (Yospal) 230
Past Lucknow (Sharar) 173
Seed (Ray) 223
Hungarian
Arrival and Departure (Koestler) 210
Bánk bán (Katona) 100
Barbarian Prayer (Csoori) 272
The Black City (Mikszáth) 169
The Bridge (Herczeg) 187
Byzantium (Herczeg) 162
The Call (Vörösmarty) 110
The Children of Death (Babits) 189
The Complaint of a Poor Little Child (Kosztolányi) 169
Darkness at Noon (Koestler) 207
Dorottya (Csokonai) 88
Escape from Solitude (Csoori) 236
The Gates of Life (Herczeg) 179
The Gladiators (Koestler) 206
Grazing into the Wall (Weöres) 269
The Gyurkovics Girls (Herczeg) 144
A Hungarian Nabob (Jókai) 118
Hungary in 1514 (Eötvös) 115
In the Draft (Mándy) 280
Irene (Kisfaludy) 102
It Exists Somewhere (Petri) 274
János the Hero (Petőfi) 114
Kozma (Kornis) 278
Liliom (Molnár) 167
Man of Gold (Jókai) 129
Memory of Snow (Csoori) 263
Napló (Radnóti) 274
New Poems (Ady) 164
The Noszty Boy and Mary Tóth (Mikszáth) 166
One-Minute Letters (Örkény) 280
The Paul Street Boy (Molnár) 165
People of Puszta (Illyés) 202
The Prisoner of Urga (Krasznahorkai) 280
Restless Early Summer (Gömöri) 264
Rise, Magyar (Petőfi) 115
Selected Poems (Illyés) 249
Stonedial (Konrád) 296
The Strange Marriage (Mikszáth) 158
The Suitors (Kisfaludy) 100
The Tartars in Hungary (Kisfaludy) 98
They Think So (Petri) 266
Thorns and Flowers (Kazinczy) 98
Toldi (Arany) 115
Toldi's Evening (Arany) 118
Toldi's Lane (Arany) 116
The Tragedy of Agis (Bessenyei) 82
The Tragedy of Man (Madách) 122
Versek (Petőfi) 112
Wings of Knives and Nails (Csoori) 260
Wonder Maid (Kosztolányi) 188
Zalán futása (Vörösmarty) 104

I

Icelandic
Book of Seven Days (Johannes) 225
The Borg Family Papers (Gunnarsson) 171
Christianity at a Glacier (Laxness) 245
Cross Hollows (Einar) 193
Days with Monks (Laxness) 269
Eyvind of the Hills (Sigurjonsson) 170
The Fair World (Tomas) 198
The Fish Can Sing (Laxness) 228
Flying Blind (Omar) 269
The Golden Gate (Davíd) 208
The Great Weaver from Kashmir (Laxness) 189
Gunnladar Saga (Svava) 269
Icelandic Loves (Gudmundsson) 185
Iceland's Bell (Laxness) 210
Independent People (Laxness) 198
Lad and Lass (Thoroddsen) 116
Loss of Sons (Skallagrimsson) 20
Mother Iceland (Guthmundur) 213
Paradise Regained (Laxness) 233
The Passion Hymns (Petursson) 61
Poems (Davith) 193
Poetic Edda 13
Prose Edda 13
Salka Valka (Laxness) 195
Smooth Seas (Benediktsson) 164
Stories and Poems (Benediktsson) 147
The Tragedies of Love (Gunnarsson) 162
Urdargaldur (Porsteinn) 269
Waves (Benediktsson) 172
Waxing Moon and Waning Moon (Johannes) 248
White Nights (Gudmundsson) 199
World Light (Laxness) 203
Indonesian
Atheist (Mihardja) 218
A Child of All Nations (Tur) 259
Evening Verses from Gunung (Iesmaniasita) 230
Footsteps (Tur) 266
Gelenging Tekad (Notodijo) 218
Guerrilla Family (Tur) 227
House of Glass (Tur) 271
Indonesia, Land of My Birth (Yamin) 192
"Me" (Anwar) 218
The Paralyzed (Tur) 220
Sitti Nurbaja (Rusli) 182
This Earth of Mankind (Tur) 259
Italian
Adriatico (Nigro) 291
After the Divorce (Deledda) 160
Agostino (Moravia) 211
All for the Best (Pirandello) 180
All Our Yesterdays (Ginzburg) 221
All the Poems (Caproni) 263
Alonso e i visionari (Ortese) 286
Ameto's Story of the Nymphs (Boccaccio) 14
Aminta (Tasso) 42
The Amorous Vision (Boccaccio) 14
And Suddenly It's Evening (Quasimodo) 209

L'angelo nero (Tabucchi) 276
Anima mundi (Tamaro) 289
Annales Ecclesiastici (Baronius) 43
The Annals of Italy (Muratori) 77
Antigone (Alfieri) 83
"Approach of Death" (Leopardi) 91, 109
Arcadia (Sannazaro) 34
Arcodamore (De Carlo) 282
The Art of War (Machiavelli) 36
Arturo's Island (Morante) 228
Ashes (Deledda) 162
At the Fire of Controversy (Luzi) 257
Attesa sul mare (Biamonti) 282
Il bacio della Medusa (Mazzucco) 287
Banquet (Dante) 14
The Baron in the Trees (Calvino) 228
Barrier to the Northwest (Bontempelli) 184
The Bedroom (Bertolucci) 264
The Beneficent Grouch (Goldoni) 82
The Betrothed (Manzoni) 104
Book of the City of Ladies (Christine de Pisan) 26
The Boors (Goldoni) 79
Bread and Wine (Silone) 225
Bucolic Song (Petrarch) 14, 25
La Calandria (Dovizi) 35
Candido; or a Dream Dreamed in Sicily (Sciascia) 256
Canone inverso (Maurensig) 286
Cantare ne buio (Corti) 276
I Canti (Leopardi) 91, 106
Canzoni (Leopardi) 91, 103
Il cardillo addorlorato (Ortese) 280
Carmina de Laudibus Estensium (Boiardo) 27
Carossa (Marabini) 274
La casa a nort-est (Maldini) 278
La casa di chiaccio (Vitale) 296
La Cassaria (Ariosto) 34
The Castle of Crossed Destinies (Calvino) 251
Cavalleria rusticana (Verga) 133, 136
The Children of Pleasure (D'Annunzio) 148
La chimera (Vassalli) 274
Christ Stopped at Eboli (Levi) 213
I cieli di vetro (Conti) 293
La città del dotor Malagui (Pazzi) 280
La Città e la Casa (Ginzburg) 264
The Cloven Viscount (Calvino) 221
The Coffee-House (Goldoni) 78
The Colloquies (Gozzano) 170
The Comic Theater (Goldoni) 78
Concerning Vernacular Eloquence (Dante) 14
The Conformist (Moravia) 220
Il Cortegiano (Castiglione) 36
The Count of Carmagnola (Manzoni) 102
The Crafty Widow (Goldoni) 77
Crime on Goat Island (Betti) 219
A Cry and Landscapes (Ungaretti) 221
Cuttlefish Bones (Montale) 187
Dal silenzio delle campagne (Comon) 293

The Daughter of Jorio (D'Annunzio) 162
Day After Day (Quasimodo) 215
Death of the Seasons (Ungaretti) 243
Decameron (Boccaccio) 14, 25
Di vento e di fuoco (Pressburger) 296
Diana's Hunt (Boccaccio) 14
Diletta Constanza (Garavini) 286
Disobedience (Moravia) 216
Divine Comedy (Dante) 13, 14, 24
Dolce per se (Maraini) 289
Il doppio regno (Capriolo) 276
The Dry Heart (Ginzburg) 215
Due di due (De Carlo) 274
Each in His Own Way (Pirandello) 154, 185
Ecatommiti (Giraldi) 40
Elegy on Madonna Fiammetta (Boccaccio) 14
Elias Portulu (Deledda) 161
Emergency Exit (Silone) 240
The Empty Canvas (Moravia) 233
Erato e Apollion (Quasimodo) 202
L'età perfetta (Cotroneo) 293
The Faithful Lover (Bontempelli) 223
The Feeling of Time (Ungaretti) 198
The Fifth of May (Manzoni) 102
First Fruits of the Desert (Luzi) 221
Five Stories of Ferrara (Bassani) 227
The Flame of Life (D'Annunzio) 158
Fontano da case (Ferrucci) 286
For the Baptism of Our Fragments (Luzi) 266
La forza del passato (Veronesi) 296
Fouchi (Ferrucci) 280
The Four Books of Architecture (Palladio) 40
From the Bottom of the Field (Luzi) 240
The Garden of the Finzi-Cortinis (Massano) 236
Gay Shipwrecks (Ungaretti) 179
The Gentle Language (De Amicis) 163
Ghisola (Tozzi) 179
Giaconda a dama con la luna (Morandini) 287
I giardini della favorita (Campana) 278
Ginestra (Leopardi) 91
Il Giorno (Parini) 80
Gothic Notebook (Luzi) 215
Grief (Ungaretti) 215
A Handful of Black Berries (Silone) 221
Harmony and Pastels (Montale) 236
Heart of a Boy (De Amicis) 138
Henry IV (Pirandello) 154, 182
The Heron (Bassani) 245
History: A Novel (Morante) 252
History of the Destruction of Troy (Colonno) 77
Honor of Truth (Luzi) 228
The House by the Medlar (Verga) 134
The House of the Customs Officer and Other Poems (Montale) 196

Italian (continued)

Idilli (Leopardi) 91

If Not Now, When? (Levi) 262

If on a Winter's Night a Traveler (Calvino) 258

If This Is a Man (Levi) 215

Limpresa senza (Barbaro) 293

In Praise of Sky, Sea, Earth and Heroes (D'Annunzio) 149

In Purissimo Azzurro (Fiore) 268

In the Magma (Luzi) 234

Incerti di viaggio (Pazzi) 287

The Incomparable Earth (Quasimodo) 230

The Indian Hut (Bertolucci) 220

Inni Sacri (Manzoni) 99

The Intense Life (Bontempelli) 180

The Intermezzo of Poems (D'Annunzio) 136

The Intruder (D'Annunzio) 143

Invisible Cities (Calvino) 250

Ipotesi d'Amore (Cima) 264

L'Italia liberata dai Goti (Trissino) 38

An Italian Story (Pratolini) 240

It's a Hard Life (Biancardi) 236

Jack Frusciante e uscito dal gruppo (Bruzzi) 284

Jerusalem Delivered (Tasso) 41

The Jests of Life and Death (Pirandello) 154

Kaputt (Malaperte) 211

Land's End (Montale) 210

The Landslide (Betti) 198

The Last Summer (Moretti) 246

The Late Mattia Pascal (Pirandello) 154, 162

The Leopard (Lampedusa) 227

La Lettrice de Isasca (Richelmy) 268

Levia gravia (Carducci) 126

Il libro della prima navigazione per oceano alle terre de'negri della Bassa Ethiopia (Cadamosto) 34

Life of Christ (Papini) 181

The Life of Solitude (Petrarch) 14, 25

Light of Eyes (Rossi) 41

The Little World of the Past (Fogazzaro) 146

The Lives of the Most Eminent Italian Architects, Painters and Sculptors (Vasari) 38

The Love Afflicted (Boccaccio) 14

Love Struck (Boccaccio) 14

Loves Without Love (Pirandello) 154

Lune (Meldini) 293

La lunga de vita Marianna Ucria (Maraini) 274

La lunga notte (Tadini) 269

Lyric Poems (Bacchelli) 173

The Maidens of the Rocks (D'Annunzio) 146

Man in the Labyrinth (Alvaro) 188

A Man—Finished (Papini) 171

Marco e Mattio (Vassalli) 278

The Marriage of Cadmus and Harmony (Calasso) 271

Mastro-don Gesualdo (Verga) 140

Memoirs of Casanova (Casanova) 104

Metrical Letters (Petrarch) 14, 25

Mezza di transporto (Rasy) 280

Microcosmi (Magris) 289

The Military Life (De Amicis) 126

The Mill on the Po (Bacchelli) 204

Mine Hostess (Goldoni) 78

The Mistress of the Inn (Goldoni) 78

The Mother (Deledda) 180

The Naked Streets (Pratolini) 213

The Name of the Rose (Eco) 259

Nati due volte (Pontiggia) 296

Nel momento (Carlo) 296

The New Life (Dante) 14, 24

Ninfa plebea (Rea) 280

The Nonexistent Knight (Calvino) 231

Nottetempo, casa per case (Consolo) 278

Le Novelle (Bandello) 39

The Occasions (Montale) 206

Ocean Sea (Baricco) 293

Of Sepulchres (Foscolo) 97

The Offender (Montale) 242

The Old and the Young (Pirandello) 172

The Old Man of the Mountain (Deladda) 158

An Old Man's Notebook (Ungaretti) 233

On Illustrious Men (Petrarch) 14, 25

On Monarchy (Dante) 14

On Religious Idleness (Petrarch) 14, 25

One, None, and a Hundred Thousand (Pirandello) 154, 187

Operette Morali (Leopardi) 91

Orazia (Aretino) 38

Orbecche (Giraldi) 37

Orlando Furioso (Ariosto) 35

Orpheus (Politian) 28

Orphic Songs (Campana) 173

Our Goddess (Bontempelli) 187

The Outcast (Pirandello) 154, 159

Painful Joy (Pirandello) 154

La palude definitiva (Manganelli) 276

Passaggio in ombra (Di Lascia) 284

Il pastor fido (Guarini) 43

The Path to the Nest of Spiders (Calvino) 215

Il Pentamerone (Basile) 62

People in Time (Bontempelli) 203

The Periodic Table (Levi) 254

Petrarch's Secret (Petrarch) 14

Piacevoli notti (Straparola) 38

Pinocchio: The Story of a Puppet (Collodi) 135

Poesie (Quasimodo) 204

Posillipo (Rasy) 289

The Prince (Machiavelli) 35

Private Renaissance (Bellonci) 272

Progetto Burlamacchi (Duranti) 282

The Promised Land (Ungaretti) 219

Quando Dio usci chiesa: Vita e fede in un borgio istriano del cinquecento (Tomizza) 269

The Queen and the Rebels (Betti) 220

Queen of Scotland (Della Valle) 43

The Rape of the Bucket (Tassoni) 53

The Reawakening (Levi) 237

Res amissa (Caproni) 276

Revolt in Aspromonte (Alvaro) 193

Revolution of the Sun (Bontempelli) 208

Right You Are—If You Think You Are (Pirandello) 176

Rime (Carducci) 120

Il Rinaldo (Tasso) 40

Ruin (Fenoglio) 224

Saentieri sotto la neve (Stern) 291

Lo sapsimo de Palermo (Consolo) 293

Satura (Montale) 236

Saturday Sun (Moretti) 165

Scent of Eucalyptus (Quasimodo) 198

The Seed Beneath the Snow (Silone) 207

Separazione (Sanvitale) 289

Serena Cruz (Ginzburg) 274

Seta (Baricco) 287

Il silenzio (Lagorio) 280

"A Silvia" (Leopardi) 91

Six Characters in Search of an Author (Pirandello) 154, 181

Sixty Tales (Buzzati) 230

The Skin (Malaparte) 218

Sofonisma (Trissino) 35

Sogni mancini (Duranti) 289

Il sole e innocenti (Camarca) 278

Sonetti e Canzoni (Sannazaro) 37

Songs (Leopardi) 100

Sostiene Pereira (Tabucchi) 282, 284

Spaccio della Bestia Trionfante (Bruno) 42

The Squabbles at Chioggia (Goldoni) 80

Staccando l'ombra da terra (del Giudice) 284

Stanzas Begun for the Tournament of the Magnificent Giuliano de Medici (Politian) 28

The Storm and Other Poems (Montale) 227

La strada per Roma (Volponi) 276

Suicidi dovuti (Busi) 287

Sunken Oboe (Quasimodo) 196

Gli Suppositi (Ariosto) 40

A Tale of Poor Lovers (Pratolini) 215

Tale of the Fiesole Nymph (Boccaccio) 14

The Tartar Steppes (Buzzati) 207

La terra è di tutti (Camon) 287

Three Crosses (Tozzi) 180

The Three Slaves of Julius Caesar (Bacchelli) 230

Time of Indifference (Moravia) 192

To Clothe the Naked (Pirandello) 154, 184

To Give and to Have and Other Poems (Quasimodo) 242

Tonight We Improvise (Pirandello) 154, 193

The Triumph of Death (D'Annunzio) 145

The Turn (Pirandello) 154, 160

Two Adolescents (Moravia) 211

Two Brothers (Pratolini) 215

Two Women (Moravia) 228

Uffizio delle tenebre (Garavini) 291

Va' dove ti porta il cuore (Tamaro) 282

Vaniglia e cioccolato (Modignani) 296

Vendita galline Km 2 (Busi) 280

Versi (Leopardi) 104

Verso Paola (Sanvitale) 276

La via del ritorno (Palandri) 274

Via Gemito (Starnone) 296

Viaggio all'India Orientali (Balbi) 43

The Vise (Pirandello) 154

The Voice of God (Moretti) 181

Waters and Land (Quasimodo) 193

The Widow Fiorvanti (Moretti) 208

The Woman of Rome (Moravia) 215

Xenia (Montale) 242

The Young and the Old (Pirandello) 154

J

Japanese

An Account of My Hut (Kamo Chomei) 23

Almost Transparent Blue (Ryu) 255

Amorous Confessions of Two Nuns (Koyo) 140

Ascension of the Frog (Juji) 220

Ask the Flowers (Jakucho) 278

At 0 A.M. in Buenos Aires (Shu) 291

The Battle of Coxinga (Chikamatsu) 48

Beautiful Days (Nobuo) 289

The Bed (Tayama) 166

Before the Dawn (Toson) 200

Botchan: Master Darling (Natsume) 93, 164

Box Man (Abe) 251

The Bullfight (Inoue) 218

Burnt Metopolis (Otohiko) 287

The Chronicle of the Screw Turning Bird (Murakami) 284

Coeval Games (Oe) 258

Confessions of a Mask (Mishima) 218

The Cutter and Captain Shigemoto's Mother (Tanizaki) 218

Dark Painting (Hiroshi) 214

Deep River (Endo) 278

Descendants of Cain (Arishima) 176

Diary of a Mad Old Man (Tanizaki) 234

Diary of My Father's Death (Issa) 95

The Dirge of the Medidian (Kinoshita) 256

The Doctor's Wife (Sawako) 248

Double Suicide at Amijima (Chikamatsu) 48

Double Suicides Committed at Forty-Eight Waterfalls in Akame (Chokitsu) 291

The Downfall of Macias Giri (Natsuki) 280

Dream Flower (Yosano) 164

Dream of Yudotei Enmoku (Noboru) 296

The Elegant Buddha (Rohan) 140

Endless Fiesta (Tsuji) 287

Fantastic Gallery (Yumiko) 276

"A Fiddler Crab" (Kiyoko) 291
Fires on the Plain (Shohei) 220
Five Women Who Chose Love
    (Ihara Saikaku) 64
"The Five-Storied Pagoda"
    (Rohan) 142
Floating Bridge (Kunie) 278
Floating Cloud (Hayashi) 220
Fly, Kylin (Noboru) 294
Forbidden Colors (Mishima) 224
The Gate (Natsume) 93, 169
Germanium Nights (Mangetsu)
    291
Giving Life (Shun) 296
The Glorious Life of Saigyo
    (Kunio) 284
The Golden Demon (Koyo) 147
Grass on the Wayside (Natsume)
    93
Growing Up (Ichiyo) 145
Hamkampu (Arai) 70
A Handful of Sand (Ishikawa) 169
Hashish Gang (Kunio) 294
Hear the Wind (Murakami) 258
Hekigoto Kushu (Kawahigashi)
    175
Heretics (Kitahara) 179
Hiroshima (Minoru) 260
House in the Shadow (Gengetsu)
    296
I Am a Cat (Natsume) 93, 163
The Izu Dancer (Kawabata) 156
The Judgment (Kinoshita) 248
The Key (Tanizaki) 191
Kokinshu (Tsurayuki Ki) 20
Kokoro (Natsume) 93, 173
Life (Miri) 296
The Life of an Amorous Man
    (Ihara Saikaku) 64
Lights Thinning Tree (Nobuko)
    294
Love and Death (Mushanakoji)
    206
The Love Suicide at Sonezaki
    (Chikamatsu) 70
The Love Suicides at Amijimi
    (Chikamatsu) 73
The Makioka Sisters (Tanizaki) 210
Memories (Kitahara) 170
Michikusa (Natsume) 174
Mirage of Fire (Hideo) 274
Missing Forever (Kosuke) 289
Moon in Shanghai (Hisashi) 276
A Mountain of Fire (Yuko) 291
Musashi (Yoshikawa) 200
My Grandpa (Yasutaka) 296
Naked Feet and Seashell (Taku)
    296
Nanso Satomi Hakken (Bakin)
    112
Naomi (Tanizaki) 185
The Narrow Road to the Deep
    North (Bashō) 49, 66
Never-Setting Sun (Toyoko) 294
Norwegian Wood (Murakami)
    269
Notes of a Student Examinee
    (Maso) 175
Okinawa (Kinoshita) 234
Ori-Taku-Shiba (Arai) 72
Paradise Lost (Jun'ichi) 289
The Passion (Saneatsu) 188
Passover/A Guest Who Came from
    Afar (Kometani) 266
Paulownia Blossom (Kitahara)
    172

The Perfumed Pillow (Koyo) 141
Pinch Runner's Record (Oe) 230
Pluck the Bird and Destroy the Off-
    spring (Oe) 230
A Poem of One Hundred Links
    Composed by Three Poets at Mi-
    nase (Sogi) 28
Poems of Haikai Tsuji (Masao)
    287
Promise in Summer (Chuya) 296
The Promontory (Kenji) 255
Proud Are the Dead (Oe) 230
Radiation (Sachiko) 284
Rain Afterwards Rain? (Keiko)
    296
Rainbow Promontory (Tsuji) 282
"Rashomon" (Akutagawa) 174
A Red Moon in Her Face (Hiroshi)
    215
Requiem (Kyoko) 274
Ring of Youth (Hiroshi) 218
Rise Up, O Young Men of the New
    Age (Oe) 263
The Road Sign at the End of the
    Street (Abe) 217
The Samurai (Endo) 259
Satomi and the Eight Dogs (Bakin)
    99
Scandal (Endo) 242
The Sea and Poison (Endo) 228
The Sea of Fertility (Mishima)
    240
The Secret Record of Naruto
    (Yoshikawa) 188
The Setting Sun (Dazai) 215
The Shipwreck (Kume) 182
Silence (Endo) 242
The Silent Cry (Oe) 230
The Sky of September (Michit-
    suna) 257
Snow Country (Kawabata) 156,
    217
The Snow Dance (Yoshiko) 269
Soga Heir (Chikamatsu) 48, 62
Solar Eclipse (Heiichiro) 294
Some Prefer Nettles (Tanizaki)
    191
The Sound of the Mountain
    (Kawabata) 156, 221
The Sound of Waves (Mishima)
    224
South of the Border, West of the
    Sun (Murakami) 294
The Sputnik Sweetheart (Mu-
    rakami) 294
St. Godhard Railway and Other
    Stories (Yoko) 287
The Strange Story of Mammy
    Hunt (Taeko) 276
Successful Kagekiyo (Chikamatsu)
    64
Symbiotic Worm (Ryu) 296
Tales of the Genji (Murasaki Shi-
    kibu) 15
Tales of the Rainy Moon (Ueda)
    81
Tangled Hair (Yosano) 159
Tan-Huang (Inoue) 231
Teach Us to Outgrow Our Madness
    (Oe) 246
Tears and Regrets (Koyo) 146
The Temple of the Golden Pavilion
    (Mishima) 227
Thirst for Love (Mishima) 219
Thousand Cranes (Kawabata)
    156, 217, 218

The Three-Cornered World (Nat-
    sume) 93, 164
The Tiger (Kumne) 177
To the Aegean Sea (Masuo) 257
Tomorrow (Mitusaki) 262
Tower of Ecological Treatment
    (Oe) 274
The Transmission of the Flower of
    Acting Style (Zeami Motokiyo)
    15
Twilight Crane (Kinoshita) 218
Ukigumo (Futabatei) 139
Unworldly (Shuntaro) 280
Volcano (Endo) 231
The Wayfarer (Natsume) 93, 171
When I Whistle (Endo) 242
White Man Yellow Man (Endo)
    225
The Wild Goose (Mori) 170
A Wild Sheep Chase (Murakami)
    262
Wind in the Pines (Zeami Mo-
    tokiyo) 15
Woman in Her Prime (Saichi) 280
The Woman in the Dunes (Abe)
    236
The Woman Killer and the Hell of
    Oil (Chikamatsu) 73
A Woman Who Devoted Her En-
    tire Life to Love-Making (Ihara
    Saikaku) 64
The Year of My Life (Issa) 101
Zone of Emptiness (Hiroshi) 221

K
Kannada
    A Child of the Kudiyas (Karanta)
        220
    Hayavadana (Karnad) 249
    The Road We Have Walked
        (Adiga) 221
Kazakh
    Abay's Road (Auezov) 214
Kikongo
    Kinzoni and His Grandson
        Makundu (Bahele) 217
Kirghiz
    Tales of Mountains and Steppes
        (Aytmatov) 237
    Up the Mountains (Sydykbekov)
        203
Kriolu
    The Water's Eye (Veiga) 270
Kurdish
    Dimdim (Shamo) 245

L
Latin
    Aeneid (Virgil) 4, 11
    Africa (Petrarch) 14
    Amores (Ovid) 4
    Amores Folk (Celtis) 34
    Annales (Tacitus) 5
    Ars amatoria (Ovid) 4, 11
    Ars poetica (Horace) 4, 11
    Austrias (Latino) 41
    Bellus Helveticum (Pirkheimer)
        30
    Books on Matters to Be Remem-
        bered (Petrarch) 14, 25
    The Brothers (Terence) 5
    Brutus (Cicero) 4
    Bucolicum carmen (Boccaccio) 14
    City of God (Augustine) 13, 18
    Concerning Famous Women (Boc-
        caccio) 14

Confessio Amantis (Gower) 26
Danish History (Saxo Grammati-
    cus) 13
De Arte Poetica (Vida) 36
De Augmentis Scientiarum
    (Bacon) 53
De beneficiis (Seneca) 5
De clementia (Seneca) 5
De ira (Seneca) 5
De Orbe Novo (Peter Martyr) 35
De otio (Seneca) 5
De Partu Virginis (Sannazaro) 36
De Revolutionibus Orbium
    Coelestium (Copernicus) 38
De tranquillitate animi (Seneca) 5
Ecclesiastical History of the English
    Nation (Bede) 13, 14, 19
Eclogues (Virgil) 44
Enchiridion Militis Christianae
    (Erasmus) 34
Epistle to the Heroines (Ovid) 4
Epistles (Horace) 4
Epitome Rerum Germanicarum
    (Wempfeling) 34
Epodes (Horace) 4
The Eunuch (Terence) 5
Georgics (Virgil) 4
Germania (Tacitus) 5
Henno (Reuchlin) 29
Historiae (Tacitus) 5
Institutio Principis Christiani
    (Erasmus) 35
The Law of War and Peace
    (Grotius) 53
The Life of Julius Agricola (Taci-
    tus) 5
Loci Communes (Melanchthon)
    36
Ludus Dianae (Celtis) 34
Metamorphoses (Ovid) 4
Moral Epistles (Seneca) 5
The Mother-in-Law (Terence) 5
Odes (Horace) 4
On Duties (Cicero) 4
On the Different Conceptions of the
    Chief Good and Evil (Cicero) 4
On the Fates of Famous Men (Boc-
    caccio) 14
On the Genealogy of the Gods of
    the Gentiles (Boccaccio) 14
On the Nature of Gods (Cicero) 4
On the Orator (Cicero) 4, 10
On the Reckoning of Time (Bede)
    14
On the State (Cicero) 4, 10
On Time (Bede) 14
Opus Maccaronicum (Folengo) 35
Orator (Cicero) 4
Pharsalia (Lucan) 5
Phormio (Terence) 5
The Praise of Folly (Erasmus) 32,
    35
Proverbs (Erasmus) 32, 34
Remedia amoris (Ovid) 4
Roxana (Alabaster) 55
Satires (Horace) 4
Satires (Juvenal) 4
Secular Hymns (Horace) 4
The Self-Tormentor (Terence) 5
Sergius (Reuchlin) 29
Thyestes (Seneca) 5, 12
Tristia (Ovid) 4
The Tuscan Disputations (Ci-
    cero) 4
The Woman of Andros (Terence)
    5, 9

Latvian
    In My Own Home (Ludens) 270
    The Sons of Jacob (Rainis) 185
    The Very Same Day (Gutmane) 271
Lithuanian
    Anapus Gaiso Eilerasciati (Juskaitis) 270
    The Forest of Anyksciai (Baranauskas) 120
    One Hundred Springs (Binkis) 188
    The Temptation (Kreve) 219
    Voices of Spring (Maironis) 188

M

Macedonian
    Alexander and Death (Mickovic) 284
    All the Faces of Death (Andreevski) 284
    A Gate in the Cloud (Stojcevski) 280
    History of a Black Love (Mickovic) 291
    Pole Vault (Mihajlovski) 284
    Providence (Popovski) 284
Malay
    Abdullah's Story (Abdullah) 116
    Burnt to a Cinder (Shahnon) 240
    The Minister (Shahnon) 243
    Premier (Shahnon) 246
    Princess Nur al-Nin (al-Hadi) 192
Malayalam
    Childhood Friend (Bashir) 211
    Fallen Flower (Kumaran Asan) 167
    Shrimps (Pillai) 227
    Sita's Story (Kumaran Asan) 179
    A Tragic State (Kumaran Asan) 184
    Ummachi (Kuttikrishnan) 224
Maori
    Tangi (Ihimaera) 251
Marathi
    Mi (Hari Narayan Apti) 144
    The Slaying of Kicak (Khadilkar) 169
    Yasvantrav Khare (Hari Narayan Apti) 143

N

Norwegian
    Afensang (Staalesen) 296
    Allegretto (Stigen) 284
    Alte Kameraden (Skagen) 274
    En annen vei (Carling) 287
    Arnjot Jelline (Bjørnson) 127
    Aske (Brekke) 294
    Aunt Virike (Heiberg) 136
    Avlosning (Ulven) 280
    The Balcony (Heiberg) 145
    Baldershawn (Stigen) 264
    The Bankrupt (Bjørnson) 130
    Barnevakt (Bjornstad) 282
    The Barque Future (Lie) 129
    Beretninger om beskyttelse (Hansen) 291
    Between the Battles (Bjørnson) 120
    Beyond Human Endurance (Bjørnson) 135
    Bikubers song (Grytten) 294
    The Bird and the White Table Cloth (Abrahamsen) 266
    Brand (Ibsen) 94, 122, 125
    Brodrene Henrikson (Enger) 296
    The Catafalque (Heiberg) 172
    Catilina (Ibsen) 94, 117
    Creation, Man and Messiah (Wergeland) 106
    A Doll's House (Ibsen) 94, 132
    Drift (Bjornstad) 287
    The Editor (Bjørnson) 130
    Efter ar og dag (Hamsun) 274
    Elsi Lund (Vik) 282
    Elsk meg i morgen (Ambjornsen) 294
    An Enemy of the People (Ibsen) 94, 135
    Engelen din, Robinson (Hoem) 280
    The English Pilot (Wergeland) 114
    The Family at Gilje (Lie) 136
    The Ferry (Hoem) 253
    Forforeren (Kjaerstad) 280
    Fulgedansen (Ambjornsen) 284
    Garman and Worse (Kielland) 133
    Ghosts (Ibsen) 94, 134
    The Great Hunger (Bojer) 175
    Grenser (Jacobsen) 294
    The Growth of the Soil (Hamsun) 176
    The Gunpowder Tower (Bjornboe) 246
    The Happy Boy (Bjørnson) 122
    Hedda Gabler (Ibsen) 94, 141
    Hunger (Hamsun) 141
    Hutchinsons effekt (Pollen) 291
    I knolvannet (Petterson) 296
    I Will Defend My Country (Heiberg) 171
    Ibsens Italia (Naess) 289
    Images in a Mirror (Undset) 156, 176
    In God's Way (Bjørnson) 140
    In the Days of the Counselor (Andersen) 147
    Injustice (Borgen) 266
    Jan Van Huysum's Flowerpiece (Wergeland) 111
    Jenny (Undset) 156, 170
    The Jew (Wergeland) 112
    John Gabriel Borkman (Ibsen) 94
    Jorparadiset Varherres nedfallsfrukt (Heggland) 284
    Julie (Elstad) 280
    Kan hende ved em bredd (Carling) 294
    Karjana (Heggland) 274
    Kastanjetid (Larsen) 278
    Katedralen (Stigen) 270
    Kjoerlighetsdikt (Mehren) 289
    Kristin Lavransdatter (Undset) 156, 180
    Kron og mynt (Flogstad) 291
    The Lady from the Sea (Ibsen) 94, 139
    The Last of the Vikings (Bojer) 181
    Lillelord (Bergen) 262
    Little Eyolf (Ibsen) 94, 145
    Love's Comedy (Ibsen) 94
    Lyhamar (Heggland) 276
    Lykkens sonn (Wassmo) 278
    Lystreise (Nilsen) 284
    Maren Gripes nodwendige ritualer (Lonn) 294
    The Master Builder (Ibsen) 94, 143
    The Master of Hestviken (Undset) 156, 187
    Moment of Freedom (Bjorneboe) 242
    Mysteries (Hamsun) 143
    Nameless (Obstfelder) 143
    Nar jeg ser deg (Faldbakken) 287
    Nattsol (Mehren) 278
    New Stories, Frydenberg (Borgen) 240
    Norwegian Folk Tales (Asbjørnsen, Moe) 117
    Noveller i samling (Koltzow) 291
    Omrade aldrifastlagt (Mjelve) 282
    Omvei til Venus (Schgerven) 284
    On the Brink (Nervesen) 266
    One Day in October (Hoel) 195
    One of Life's Slaves (Lie) 136
    Oppdageren (Kjaerstad) 294, 296
    Ormens ar (Faldbakken) 280
    Our Power and Our Glory (Grieg) 200
    Pa St. Jorgen (Skram) 145
    Pan (Hamsun) 145
    Peace (Garborg) 143
    Peasant Students (Garborg) 136
    Peer Gynt (Ibsen) 94, 126
    The People of Juvik (Dunn) 177
    The People's Council (Heiberg) 147
    Pillars of Society (Ibsen) 94, 131
    Poems (Bull) 167
    Poems, First Cycle (Wergeland) 106
    Poems and Songs (Bjørnson) 127
    Poplene pa St. Hanshaugen (Vik) 276
    Portland Valley (Flogstad) 256
    The Pretenders (Ibsen) 94, 124
    Road to the World's End (Hoel) 198
    Rosmersholm (Ibsen) 94, 138
    Salame ved reisens slutt (Hansen) 276
    Seierherrene (Jacobsen) 276
    The Ship Sails On (Grieg) 185
    Sigurd Slembe (Bjørnson) 123
    The Silence (Bjorneboe) 251
    Sinners in Summertime (Hoel) 189
    Siste dikt (Orvil) 280
    Skammen (Haff) 287
    Solformokelson (Enger) 283
    Som dine dagerer (Elstad) 284
    The Spaniard (Wergeland) 107
    Det Stutte livet (Heggland) 278
    Thranes metode (Lonn) 283
    Til verdes ende (Faldbakken) 276
    Tired Men (Garborg) 142
    Travel Memoirs from the Summer of 1860 (Vinje) 122
    Tresjoereren Johannes (Stigen) 274
    Trollbyen (Alnaes) 278
    Tryllefloyten (Lange-Nielsen) 284
    Tvillingfeber (Billdoen) 291
    Utsikt til paradiset (Ambjornsen) 280
    Victoria (Hamsun) 148
    Villa Europa (Bjornstad) 278
    Vinterhagen (Vik) 274
    Et virkelig liv (Koppenvag) 276
    When We Dead Awaken (Ibsen) 94, 149
    The Wild Duck (Ibsen) 94, 136
    Working People (Kielland) 134

O

Ossetian
    Writings of a Prisoner (Gaediaty) 166

P

Pashto
    An Armful of Blossoms (Karim) 228
Persian
    Aklake Mohseni (Kashefi) 29
    Anvare Soheyli (Kashefi) 34
    The Blind Owl (Hedāyat) 203
    The Blindfold Horse: Memories of a Persian Childhood (Guppy) 272
    The Book About Absent People (Modarressi) 268
    The Custodian of the Divan (Jamalzadeh) 214
    Divan-e-Shams (Rūmī) 15
    Diviani Mataibat (Mushfiqi) 39
    Fairy Good Fortune (Lahuti) 217
    Haft Owrang (Jāmī) 27
    The Headmaster (Ahmed) 230
    Her Eyes (Alavi) 221
    The Husband of Ahu Khanom (Mohammad) 234
    The Mad House (Jamalzadeh) 209
    Mysteries of Selfessness (Iqbāl) 177
    Nahafat al-Uns (Jāmī) 28
    The Orchard (Sa'dī) 23
    Pele-Mele (Dehkhoda) 230
    The Pilgrim's Rules of Etiquette (Modarressi) 272
    The Rose Garden (Sa'dī) 24
    Salaman u Absal (Jāmī) 28
    Sayahatnameye Hateme Tai (Kashefi) 28
    Seventy Tombstones (Ryya'i) 291
    Shah-nameh (Firdawsī) 20
    Spiritual Couplets (Rūmī) 15
    The Story of the Water Channel (Jamalzadeh) 215
    The Suitcase (Alavi) 199
    Tazkerat Osh-sho-Ara (Daulatshah) 28
    There Was Once—Or Was There? (Jamalzadeh) 181
    Yusuf u Zulaikha (Jāmī) 28
Polish
    The Adventures of Nicholas Try-All (Krasicki) 83
    Afterimages: Young Men from Those Years (Nowakowski) 285
    Ajol and Laor (Czycz) 287
    Alone Among Men (Brzozoski) 170
    Always a Fragment (Rozewicz) 291
    The Ascension (Konwicki) 237
    Ash and Honey (Szlosarek) 289
    Ashes and Diamonds (Andrzejewski) 217
    A Ballad from Beyond (Czechowicz) 196
    The Barbarian in the Garden (Herbert) 236
    Bells in Winter (Milosz) 257
    Beniowski (Słowacki) 112
    Between the Wars (Brandys) 217
    Black Seasons (Glowisnki) 291
    The Boatmen (Klonowic) 44
    The Book of Day and the Book of Night (Iwaszkiewicz) 182
    Book of the Poor (Kasprowicz) 175

Carnival and Lent (Nowakowski) 274

Chlopi (Reymont) 162

The Comedienne (Reymont) 146

Crimean Sonnetsi (Mickiewicz) 104

Dance of Death: A Baroque Poem (Rozewicz) 291

Day Home, Night Home (Tokarczuk) 294

A Day Lie Every Day (Czechowicz) 193

The Deluge (Sienkiewicz) 138

The Dismissal of the Greek Envoys (Kochanowski) 41

Downstream (Siwertz) 180

A Dreambook of Our Time (Konwicki) 237

Elegy for an Exit (Herbert) 274

Female and Male (Choromanski) 231

Ferdydurke (Gombrowicz) 203

Forefather's Eve (Mickiewicz) 103, 108

God's Face (Drzezdzon) 264

Grazyna (Mickiewicz) 103

The Hag (Irzykowski) 161

Horsztynski (Słowacki) 109

Hot Ashes (Jastrun) 227

Husband and Wife (Fredro) 103

Iridion (Krasinski) 109

The Issa Valley (Milosz) 226

Jealousy and Medicine (Choromanski) 196

Judas Sack (Klonowic) 50

Konrad Wallenrod (Mickiewicz) 105

Kordian and the Churl (Kruczkowski) 196

A Little Side-Road Dog (Milosz) 289

The Madman and the Nun (Witkiewicz) 187

Maiden's Vows (Fredro) 108

Marriage by the Calendar (Bohomolec) 81

The Marshes (Konwicki) 227

Master Thaddeus (Mickiewicz) 108

The Meadow (Leśmian) 180

The Meeting (Reymont) 147

The Moment Before Dawn (Krasinski) 113

The Morning Star (Dabrowska) 226

Mr. Balcer in Brazil (Konopnicka) 143

Night and Day (Dabrowska) 196

Pan Cogito (Herbert) 253

Pan Michael (Sienkiewicz) 139

Peacock's Feathers (Kruczkowski) 200

Poetry (Mickiewicz) 103

Quo Vadis? (Sienkiewicz) 145

The Republic of Babin (Lechon) 181

Rescue (Milosz) 213

Return from the Stars (Lem) 234

Rotten Wood (Berent) 161

Salt of the Earth (Wittli) 202

The Scarlet Poem (Lechon) 180

Silence (Stryjkowski) 280

Silver and Black (Lechon) 185

The Stranger (Kuncewicz) 202

Surgical Precision (Baranczak) 291

Term of Office (Sczepanski) 274

Three Times (Bitner) 285

Threny (Kochanowski) 42

To a Dying World (Kasprowicz) 159

To Get to the Heart of the Matter (Choromanski) 245

The Undivine Comedy (Krasinski) 109

Upstairs, Downstairs (Choromanski) 243

Vengeance (Fredro) 108

Victoria Deorum (Klonowic) 43

The Water Hen (Witkiewicz) 181

The Wild Rose Bush (Kasprowicz) 148

With Fire and Sword (Sienkiewicz) 136

Word after Word (Rzewic) 283

Portuguese

  Angolan

    To the Sound of the Marimbas (Bessa Victor) 210

  Brazilian

    Achados e perdidos (Garcia-Roza) 291

    Agosto (Fonseca) 276

    Alcacer Quibir (Olinto) 289

    Amor que faz o mundo girar (Quintella) 276

    The Apple in the Dark (Lispector) 234

    Armarinho de miudezas (Salamao) 280

    O baille de mascaras (Rasi) 276

    Beacons (Cruze Sousa) 158

    The Best Poems (Campos) 278

    Black Poems (Lima) 215

    Boca do Inferno (Miranda) 274

    Brida (Coelho) 274

    O buraco ne parede (Fonseca) 287

    Calçada de Verao (Figueiredo) 274

    Calunga (Lima) 200

    Canaan (Graça Aranha) 160

    Canteiros de saturno (Machado) 278

    A confraria des espadas (Fonseca) 294

    A dança final (Marcos) 291

    Dead Fire (Rego) 211

    The Devil to Pay in the Backlands (Rosa) 227

    A Doce de Caetana (Pinon) 270

    The Dog Without Feathers (Melo Neto) 219

    Dom Casmurro (Machado de Assis) 149, 158

    Epitaph for a Small Winner (Machado de Assis) 134

    Eu, tiradentes (Motta) 278

    Evening Star (Bandeira) 237

    Farewell (Drummond) 287

    Floating Foam (Castro Alves) 127

    The Friar (Melo Neto) 263

    Gabriela, Clove and Cinnamon (Amado) 230

    O Guaranai (Alencar) 120

    Hallucinated City (Andrade) 183

    Uma historia de familia (Santiago) 278

    The Hour of the Star (Lispector) 256

    Inhabited Heart (Andrade) 266

    The Invention of Orpheus (Lima) 222

    Iracema (Alencar) 124

    Jantando com Melvin (Coelho) 291

    João Miguel (Quieroz) 196

    Journey (Meireles) 206

    A Knife All Blade (Melo Neto) 227

    Last Poems (Gonçalves Dias) 117

    Lealdade (Souza) 289

    Libertinism (Bandeira) 193

    Living Water (Lispector) 251

    Macunaima (Andrade) 191

    Madrugada (Steen) 280

    Manuscritos de Felipa (Prado) 294

    Memoirs of a Militia Sergeant (Almeida) 118

    Memoirs of the Notary Public Isaias (Lima Barreto) 167

    Missal (Cruz e Sousa) 144

    The Moratorium (Andrade) 226

    Morning Star (Bandeira) 202

    The Mulatto (Azevedo) 134

    Nao es tu, Brasil (Rubens Paiva) 287

    Near to the Savage Heart (Lispector) 212

    The Night of the Mad Cock (Oliveiro) 268

    Nine, Novena (Lins) 242

    No caração do Brasil (Falabella) 278

    Noturnos: contos (Miranda) 294

    The Obscure Woman (Lima) 206

    Os Tambores de São Luis (Montello) 254

    Panteros (Pignatari) 280

    The Passion According to G.H. (Lispector) 239

    Perola (Rasi) 285

    Perversas familias (Assis Brasil) 291

    Philosopher or Dog? (Machado de Assis) 142

    Plantation Boy (Rego) 196

    Prosopeya (Pinto) 50

    Quarry of the Soul (Andrade) 230

    O Que Agora Me Inquieta (Coutinho) 266

    The Queen of the Grecian Jails (Lins) 230

    Rebellion in the Backlands (Cunha) 160

    The Road Back (Andrade) 243

    The Rocky Road (Quieroz) 203

    Rough and Ride (Melo Neto) 266

    Sagarana (Guimares Rosa) 214

    Sangue na floresta (Olinto) 280

    São Bernardo (Ramos) 199

    The Seamless Tunic (Lima) 204

    Sentimental Memoirs of João Miramar (Andrade) 185

    Shields (Cruz e Sousa) 144

    Sonhos tropicais (Scliar) 278

    The Three Marias (Quieroz) 206

    Time and Eternity (Mendes) 200

    Trilhos e quintais (Oliveira) 291

    Two Waters (Melo Neto) 226

    A ultima quimera (Miranda) 285

    O Uruguia (Gama) 81

    The Violent Land (Amado) 209

    Whole Life Star (Bandeira) 240

  Cape Verdean

    Arquipelago (Barbosa) 200

  Portuguese

    All the Names (Saramago) 291

    Alone (Nobre) 143

    Auto de la Barca de la Gloria (Vicente) 35

    Auto de la Barca do Purgatorio (Vicente) 35

    Auto de la Barca (Vicente) 35

    Auto de la Sibilla Cassandra (Vicente) 35

    A barragem (Moreira) 280

    Um beijo dado mais tarde (Ilansol) 276

    Benilde, or the Virgin Mother (Regio) 215

    Blindness (Saramago) 287

    Caramuru (Durão) 84

    A casa da cabeça de cavalo (Gersao) 287

    As contadoras de historias (Botelho) 294

    Cousin Basilio (Eça de Queirós) 132

    The Crime of Batista the Student (Ribeiro Couto) 183

    De Vitor ao Xadres (Torrado) 264

    "The Deceived Wive's Club" (Ribeiro Couto) 198

    Un deus passeando pela brisa da tarde (Carvalho) 285

    Emigrants (Ferreira de Castro) 191

    An English Family (Dinis) 126

    O Evangelho segundo Jesus Cristo (Saramago) 278

    The Exhortation to War (Vicente) 32

    Exortaçao aos crocodilos (Lobo Antunes) 296

    Ferias de verao (Moreira) 294

    Filodemo (Camões) 32

    A God Strolling in the Cool of the Evening (Carvalho) 289

    The Golovlev Family (Saltykov-Shchedrin) 131

    Hours (Castro) 142

    Insania (Correia) 296

    The Jungle (Ferreira de Castro) 191

    King Seleucus (Camões) 32

Portuguese

Portuguese (continued)

*Life of Archbishop Dominican
   Friar Bartolomeu dos Mar-
   tires* (Sousa) 52
Litoral (Ramos) 278
Longings for Heaven (Castro)
   149
Loose Leaves (Deus) 131
Love Poems (Antonio) 233
Os Lusíadas (Camões) 32, 41
The Maias (Eça de Queirós)
   139
Marilia de Dirceau (Gonzaga)
   86
Maternal Primer (Deus) 131
Meditaçao sore reinas (Judice)
   285
Message (Pessoa) 199
O monhe das cobras (Knopfli)
   289
Mulheres de sombra (Ferreira)
   285
Na tua face (Ferreira) 283
Obras Completas (Castilho)
   110
Odes Modernas (Quental) 124
Outrora agora (Abelaira) 289
A paixao (Faria) 294
Partes de Africa (Macedo)
   278
Pedro e Paula (Macedo) 291
A poeira levada pelo vento
   (Magalhaes) 283
The Prince with Donkey Ears
   (Regio) 209
De profundis valsa lenta (Car-
   doso Pires) 289
Pupils of the Dean (Dinis) 126
A quintas das virtudes (Calu-
   dio) 276
Rimas (Camões) 32
Romantic Sommets (Correia)
   276
Salome and Other Poems
   (Castro) 146
The Sibyl (Besse Luis) 224
The Sin of Father Amaro (Eça
   de Queirós) 131
The Two Amphitryons
   (Camões) 32
O ultimo cais (Marques) 280
Varias Rimas ao Bom Jesus
   (Bernardez) 44
Village Court (Rodrigues
   Lobo) 52
Wild Flowers (Deus) 126
*The Year of the Death of Ri-
   cardo Reis* (Saramago) 280

São Tomean

The Island of the Holy Name
   (Tenreiro) 209

Punjabi

Green Leaves (Singh) 202

R

Rajasthani

Kanhadade Prabandha (Padmanabhan) 27

Romanian

Black Gate (Arghezi) 193
Doine si Lacrimioare (Alecsandri)
   118
The Evening Star (Eminescu) 136
The Fairy at the Bottom of the Lake
   (Davidescu) 171

The False Accusation (Caragiale)
   141
First Person Plural (Blandina) 239
*Hands Behind My Back: Selected
   Poems* (Sorescu) 278
The Levant (Cartarescu) 276
A Lost Letter (Caragiale) 136
Mr. Leonida (Caragiale) 132
A Stormy Night (Caragiale) 133
Suitable Words (Arghezi) 189
The Uprising (Rebrenu) 196
Wooden Icons (Arghezi) 193
Yellow Sparks (Bacovia) 188

Russian

Adventures of an Iron and a Boot
   (Petrushevskaya) 291
After Russia (Tsvetayeva) 191
Altar of Victory (Bryusov) 172
And Quiet Flows the Don
   (Sholokhov) 199
The Angel (Lermontov) 107
Anna Karenina (Tolstoy) 90, 130
The Anniversary (Chekhov) 92
The Anti-Soviet Soviet Union
   (Voinovich) 266
Arabesques (Gogol) 91, 109
Ardobiola (Yevtushenko) 265
"*Ariadne*" (Chekhov) 92
Ariadne (Tsvetayeva) 185
"*Armored Train 14-69*" (Ivanov)
   183
The Artamonov Business (Gorky)
   187
Ashes (Bely) 168
At Daggers Drawn (Leskov) 127
August 1914 (Solzhenitsyn) 154,
   249
Babi Yar (Kuznetsov) 242
Babi Year (Yevtushenko) 234
The Badgers (Leonov) 185
The Bear (Chekhov) 92
The Beauty of Life (Popov) 274
A Bitter Lot (Pisemsky) 121
"*The Black Monk*" (Chekhov)
   92, 145
The Block (Aitmatov) 270
Boris and Gleb (Buyda) 289
Boris Godunov (Pushkin) 90, 104,
   106
Bread Givers (Yezierska) 187
"*The Bridegroom*" (Pushkin) 90,
   104
"*The Bronze Horseman*"
   (Pushkin) 90, 110
The Brothers Karamazov (Dos-
   toyevsky) 90, 133
Budda's Little Finger (Pelevin)
   296
The Burn (Aksyonov) 259
The Cage (Azolsky) 289
Cancer Ward (Solzhenitsyn) 154,
   245
The Captain's Daughter (Pushkin)
   90, 109
Cathedral Folk (Leskov) 129
Cement (Gladkhov) 187
Chariot of Wrath (Leonov) 212
"*Chelkash*" (Gorky) 145
The Cherry Orchard (Chekhov)
   92, 162
*Childhood Years of Grandson
   Bagrov* (Aksakov) 120
Children of the Arbat (Rybakov)
   272
Christ and Antichrist
   (Merezhkovsky) 146

The Clay Machine Gun (Pelevin)
   294
The Closed Down Theater
   (Okudzhava) 283
A Cloud in Trousers
   (Mayakovsky) 174
A Collective Notebook (Morozov)
   294
Colored Winds (Ivanov) 183
Confession (Tolstoy) 90
Cor Ardens (Ivanov) 170
The Cossacks (Tolstoy) 90, 123
"*Count Nulin*" (Pushkin) 90
Country of Origin (Bakin) 287
The Courtyard (Lvov) 272
The Covetous Knight (Pushkin)
   90, 109
The Craft (Dovlatov) 266
Crime and Punishment (Dos-
   toyevsky) 90, 125
The Curly-Haired Lieutenant
   (Muraveva) 283
*The Day Lasts More Than a Hun-
   dred Years* (Aitmatov) 274
Dead Souls (Gogol) 91, 112
"*Death of a Poet*" (Lermontov)
   110
The Death of Ivan Ilyich (Tolstoy)
   90, 138
December the Fourteenth
   (Mereazhkovsky) 177
The Defense (Nabokov) 155
The Demon (Lermontov) 112
Description (Dragomoshchenko)
   296
Despair (Nabokov) 155
The Devense (Nabokov) 193
"*Diary of a Madman*" (Gogol)
   91, 109
The Diary of a Superfluous Man
   (Turgenev) 119
Dobrovsky (Pushkin) 90
Doctor Zhivago (Pasternak) 228
The Double (Dostoyevsky) 90,
   115
*A Dove in Santiago: A Novella in
   Verse* (Yevtushenko) 262
Dream of a Tree (Bakin) 291
"*The Dream of Ridiculous Man*"
   (Dostoyevsky) 131
The Dust and Ashes (Rybakov) 283
The Dybbuk (Ansky) 180
The Easing of Fate (Berberova)
   218
The East-West Wind (Shvarts)
   289
Egyptian Nights (Pushkin) 90,
   109
The Embezzler (Katayev) 188
Enchanted Wanderer (Leskov)
   129
Eros (Ivanov) 165
The Escort Angel (Pelevin) 291
Eugene Onegin (Pushkin) 90, 108
Evening (Akhmatova) 171
Evening Album (Tsvetayeva) 169
Evening Light (Ivanov) 212
*The Extraordinary Adventures of
   Julio Jurenito and His Disciples*
   (Ehrenburg) 183
Fables (Saltykov-Shchedrin) 137
The Fall of Paris (Ehrenburg) 208
Fathers and Sons (Turgenev) 123
Fear (Rybakov) 278
Feast in the Time of Plague
   (Pushkin) 90, 107

The Fiery Angel (Bryusov) 166
The Fifth Seal (Aldanov) 206
The First Circle (Solzhenitsyn)
   154, 245, 257
A Foreign Letter (Morozov) 291
Foreign Sky (Gumilyov) 171
The Forest (Ostrovsky) 128
Forever Flowering (Grossman) 239
The Fountain of Bakhchsaray
   (Pushkin) 90, 103
Freedom (Butov) 294
The Friend of the Family (Dos-
   toyevsky) 90, 121
From Another Shore (Herzen) 117
A General and His Army (Vladi-
   mov) 285
The Gentleman from San Francisco
   (Bunin) 175
The Gift (Nabokov) 155
Gold in Azure (Bely) 162
The Government Inspector (Gogol)
   91, 109
Gulag Archipelago (Solzhenitsyn)
   154, 251
"*The Gypsies*" (Pushkin) 90, 104
A Halt in the Wasteland (Brodsky)
   248
He Who Gets Slapped (Andreyev)
   175
The Heart of a Dog (Bulgakov)
   187, 270
A Hero of Our Times (Lermontov)
   111
Hilarion and the Dwarf (Gubin)
   289
The History of a Town (Saltykov-
   Shchedrin) 127
A History of Pugachov (Pushkin)
   90
The History of Russia (Karamzin)
   100
*The History of the Village of
   Gorykhina* (Pushkin) 90
The Holy Well (Katayev) 243
House of the Dead (Dostoyevsky)
   90, 122, 123
The Idiot (Dostoyevsky) 90, 126
The Inspector General (Gogol) 91,
   109
The Insulted and the Injured (Dos-
   toyevsky) 90, 122
Invitation to a Beheading (Nab-
   okov) 155
The Iron Flood (Serafimovic) 185
The Island of Crimea (Aksyonov)
   261, 274
"*A Jew from Lublin*" (Glatstein)
   242
Kangaroo (Aleshkovsky) 268
King, Queen, Knave (Nabokov)
   155, 191
The Kreutzer Sonata (Tolstoy)
   141
"*Lady Macbeth of the Mtsensk
   District*" (Leskov) 125
The Last Bow (Astafyev) 278
A Lear of the Steppes (Turgenev)
   127
Less Than One (Brodsky) 268
Letters of a Russian Traveler
   (Karamzin) 85
Life (Petrovich) 62
*The Life and Extraordinary Adven-
   tures of Private Ivan Chonkin*
   (Voinovich) 254
Lines of Fate (Kharitonov) 280

"Little Liza" (Karamzin) 86
Long Is Our Way (Makanin) 276
A Love Interest (Nayman) 294
The Lower Depths (Gorky) 160
Lyudmila (Zhukovsky) 97
The Magic Ring (Sefarim) 125
Makar's Dream (Korolenko) 137
Man (Ivanov) 206
Manhole (Makanin) 276
Mary (Nabokov) 155
The Mask of Snow (Blok) 165
The Master and Margarita (Bulgakov) 193, 242
Metro: A Novel of the Moscow Undergound (Kaletski) 266
The Minor (Fonvizin) 84
Mirgorod (Gogol) 91, 109
Mitya's Love (Bunin) 187
A Month in the Country (Turgenev) 117, 119
Mother (Gorky) 164
Mozart and Salieri (Pushkin) 90, 106
"The Murder" (Chekhov) 92
My Childhood (Gorky) 172
The Negro of Peter the Great (Pushkin) 90, 105
"Neighbors" (Chekhov) 92
The New Sweet Style (Aksyonov) 291
The Newlyweds (Griboyedov) 100
The Night Search (Khlebnikov) 181
Nikita's Childhood (Tolstoy) 181
The Northern Symphony (Bely) 160
Notes from Underground (Dostoyevsky) 90, 124
November 1916 (Solzhenitsyn) 280
The Novice (Lermontov) 111
Nowhere to Go (Leskov) 124
Oblomov (Goncharov) 121
"Ode to Liberty" (Pushkin) 90, 102
Ode to the Deity (Derzhavin) 84
Odessa Tales (Babel) 195
The Odyssey (Fyodorov) 285
An Official Tale (Pavlov) 285
The Old Man (Trifonov) 257
On the Death of Goethe (Baratynsky) 107
On the Death of Prince Meshchersky (Derzhavin) 83
On the Eve (Turgenev) 122
One Day in the Life of Ivan Denisovich (Solzhenitsyn) 154, 236
Oranges from Morocco (Aksyonov) 237
"The Overcoat" (Gogol) 91, 112
The Ox of Frankfurt (Yuryev) 289
Partisans (Ivanov) 181
Pavel (Merezhkovsky) 166
"The Peasants" (Chekhov) 92
A Person Not to Be Trusted (Otroshenko) 296
Peter the Great (Tolstoy) 192
Petersburg (Bely) 173
Phaedra (Tsvetayeva) 189
The Pillar of Fire (Gumilyov) 181
Pilot Stars (Ivanov) 161
"Poltava" (Pushkin) 90, 106
Poor Folk (Dostoyevsky) 90, 115
The Possessed (Dostoyevsky) 90, 129

Poverty Is No Disgrace (Ostrovsky) 118
The Power of Darkness (Tolstoy) 90
The Precipice (Goncharov) 127
The Prisoner of the Caucasus (Pushkin) 90, 102
The Proposal (Chekhov) 92
Pryasliny: A Saga of Peasant Life (Abramov) 253
The Pyre (Gumilyov) 177
"The Queen of Spades" (Pushkin) 90, 108
The Red Wheel (Solzhenitsyn) 154, 249, 280
Resurrection (Tolstoy) 90, 149
The Returnee (Maramzin) 294
The River (Yermakov) 294
The River of Life (Kuprin) 164
The Road to Calvary (Tolstoy) 181, 214
The Road to Nowhere (Grin) 193
The Robber Brothers (Pushkin) 90, 102
Roman Sonnets (Ivanov) 188
The Romance of Leonardo da Vinci (Merezhkovsky) 159
Rosary (Akhmatova) 173
The Rout (Fadeyev) 189
Rudin (Turgenev) 119
Ruslan and Ludmila (Pushkin) 90, 102
A Russian Beauty (Yerofeyev) 274
Russian Epic (Kheraskov) 82
A Russian Schoolboy (Aksakov) 119
Russian Woman (Nekrasov) 128
Sanine (Artsybasheff) 165
The Seagull (Chekhov) 92, 146, 162
The Settlement of Centaurs (Kim) 278
"A Small House in Kolomna" (Pushkin) 90, 108
Smoke (Turgenev) 126
The Snow Maiden (Ostrovsky) 129
Solitary Thoughts (Rozanov) 171
Solo On a Burning Trumpet (Shvarts) 217
A Sportsman's Sketches (Turgenev) 118
A Stamp Album (Sergeyev) 287
Stanzas (Pushkin) 90, 104
The Stone Guest (Pushkin) 90, 111
The Stormy Sea (Pisemsky) 123
The Story of a Life (Paustovsky) 239
Summary (Gandlevsky) 296
The Swan's Camp (Tsvetayeva) 228
The Sweet Secret (Ivanov) 171
The Taking of Ismail (Shishkin) 296
The Tale of Cross-Eyed Lefty from Tula and the Steel Flea (Leskov) 134
Tales of the Late Ivan Petrovich Belkin (Pushkin) 90, 106
"Taras Bulba" (Gogol) 91, 109
Tell Me, Mom (Petrusevskaya) 283
The Thief (Leonov) 189
The Thinker (Aldanov) 184
Third Vigil (Bryusov) 158

A Thousand Souls (Pisemsky) 120
Three Sisters (Chekhov) 92, 159
The Thunderstorm (Ostrovsky) 121
The Time: Night (Petrushevskaya) 280
"To My Friends" (Pushkin) 90, 105
Torrents of Spring (Turgenev) 129
Translucency (Ivanov) 162
Tsar-Maiden (Tsvetayeva) 183
The Twelve (Blok) 177
"Twenty-Six Men and a Girl" (Gorky) 149
Uncle Vanya (Chekhov) 92, 147
An Unpleasant Man (Nayman) 294
Urania (Brodski) 270
Urn (Bely) 168
Verik (Aleichem) 166
Verses About the Lady Beautiful (Blok) 162
Verses and Poems (Brodsky) 240
Verses to Blok (Tsvetayeva) 183
The Village (Bunin) 169
Virgin Soil (Turgenev) 131
Vladimir Reborn (Kheraskov) 85
Wake for a Red Bitch (Petkavich) 217
War and Peace (Tolstoy) 90, 124
"Ward Number Six" (Chekhov) 92, 143
The Waterfall (Derzhavin) 86
The Wedding (Chekhov) 92
What Is Art? (Tolstoy) 90
The White Guard (Bulgakov) 246
White Robes (Dudintsev) 271
Whither Gone? And Where's the Window? (Sosnora) 296
Who Can Be Happy and Free in Russia? (Nekrasov) 125
Winter Sonnets (Ivanov) 181
Woe from Wit (Griboyedov) 103
Yama: The Pit (Kuprin) 168

S

Sanskrit
Abhijñanasakuntala (Kālidāsa) 14, 15
Kumarasambhava (Kālidāsa) 15
Malavikagnimitra (Kālidāsa) 14
"Meghaduta" (Kālidāsa) 15
Raghuvamsa (Kālidāsa) 14–15
Vikramorvasi (Kālidāsa) 14
Serbian
17-57 Poems (Bojic) 278
Albion Albion (Moravcevic) 285
An Ancient Book (Pavlovic) 278
"Bark" (Popa) 223
Bottomless (Velmar-Jankovic) 287
Bread and Fear (Savic) 278
Chanticleer's Morsel (Popovic) 276
The Coming Out Book (Susko) 276
The Deat Spot (Popovic) 285
Dictionary of the Khazars (Pavic) 271
Divisions (Cosic) 234
Druid from Sindidun (Bajac) 296
Eagle Nests (Bojic) 278
Early Sorrows (Kis) 292
Earth Erect (Popa) 250
Far Away Is the Sun (Cosic) 220
Farewell, Liars (Popovic) 285

Fear of the Bell (Bratic) 278
A Goat Who Wouldn't Be Mounted (Rosic) 270
Half Brothers (Radulovic) 270
How Much Is Belgrade (Dimic) 296
In the Line of Fire (Mihailovic) 283
The Inner Side of the Wind (Pavic) 281
Land, Land in Sight (Stojicic) 294
Landscape Painted with Tea (Pavic) 281
Looney Tunes (Basara) 289
Lure (Albahari) 289
Mexico (Arsenijevic) 296
On Roads and Through Space (Jankovic) 283
A Premeditated Murder (Selenic) 283
Roots (Cosic) 224
The Rose Garden (Popovic) 285
Secondary Heaven (Popa) 245
The Sinner (Cosic) 274
The Sky (Maksimovic) 289
This Land, This Time (Cosic) 250
A Time of Evil (Cosic) 274
Turning Point (Jankovic) 285
Wolf's Salt (Popa) 254
Serbo-Croatian
The Bridge on the Drina (Andric) 217
Sesotho
Chaka (Mofolo) 195
Sinhalese
Guttilaya (Vetteve) 27
Slovak
Blood-Red Sonnets (Hviezdoslav) 174
The Eagle (Král') 114
Ezo Vikolinsky (Hviezdoslav) 141
The Game-Keeper's Wife (Hviezdoslav) 138
The Gleam of a Clear Dawn Approached (Král') 122
Recruit (Král') 114
Song Without a Name (Král') 114
Wonderful Night in Paris (Grupac) 292
Slovene
Baptism by the Slavica (Preseren) 109
Circles on the Water (Semolic) 296
Garland of Sonnets (Preseren) 108
Spanish
Argentine
The Abattoir (Echeverría) 128
Adán Buenosayres (Marechal) 217
The Aleph and Other Stories (Borges) 154
All Green Shall Perish (Mallea) 208
Amalia: A Romance of the Argentine (Mármol) 134
The Angel of the Shadow (Lugones) 188
La astucia de la razón (Feinmann) 274
The Banquet of Severo Arcangelo (Marechal) 240
Betrayed by Rita Hayworth (Puig) 245

Spanish
Argentine (continued)
Bomarzo (Mujica Lainez) 236
The Book of Imaginary Beings
(Borges) 154, 243
The Book of Landscapes (Lugones) 176
The Book of Sand (Borges)
154, 254
"The Captive" (Echeverría)
110
The Centaur (Marechal) 207
El cielo dividido (Roffe) 287
Los conjurados (Borges) 266
Days Like Arrows (Marechal)
188
El décimo infierno (Giardinelli) 294
The Departure of Martín
Fierro (Hernández) 129
Diario de Andrés Fava
(Cortázar) 285
Diary of the War of the Pig
(Bioy Casares) 246
The Doer (Borges) 233
Don Segundo Sombra (Güiraldes) 188
Dr. Brodie's Report (Borges)
154, 248
The Dream of Heroes (Bioy
Casares) 224
The Dreamtigers (Borges) 154
Elvira (Echeverría) 107
El evangelio según Van Hutten
(Castillo) 294
False Love (Arlt) 196
El farmer (Rivera) 287
Fausto (Campo) 125
Fervor in Buenos Aires, Poems
(Borges) 154
Five Southern Poets (Marechal) 203
The Flame Throwers (Arlt)
195
The Glory of Don Ramiro
(Rodríguez Larreta) 166
Guerra conyugal (Russo) 296
History of Eternity (Borges)
202
El Hombre que llegó a un
pueblo (Tizón) 274
Hopscotch (Cortázar) 237
The Hunchbacks (Arlt) 198
The Invention of Morel (Bioy
Casares) 207
Kiss of the Spider Woman
(Puig) 230
Languor (Storni) 180
La madriguera (Mercado)
287
Mask and Trefoil (Storni) 204
Mountains of Gold (Lagones)
147
La muerte como efecto secundario (Shua) 289
Nuestra señora de la noche
(Denevi) 289
Ocher (Storni) 187
Ode for Man and Woman
(Marechal) 192
On Heroes and Tombs (Sábato) 234
The Rabid Toy (Arlt) 188
La resistencia (Sábato) 296
Santo oficio de la memoria
(Giardinelli) 281

Se esconde tras los ojos
(Toledo) 296
Sentimental Lunar Almanac
(Lugones) 168
The Seven Madmen (Arlt)
192
Sonnets to Sophia (Marechal)
207
El sueño del señor (Gamerro)
296
Sweet Injury (Storni) 178
The Tunnel (Sábato) 217
Twilight in the Garden (Lugones) 163
A Universal History of Infamy
(Borges) 154
El viajero de Agartha (Posse)
274
Without Remedy (Storni) 179
The World of Seven Wells
(Storni) 199
X-Ray of the Pampa
(Martínez Estrada) 198
Chilean
Los años de la serpiente (Ostornol) 277
Ardiente paciencia (Skarmeta)
266
Arithmetic in Love (Blest
Gana) 122
Attempt of the Infinite Man
(Neruda) 155
Better Than Wine (Rojas) 230
Big Work (Parra) 246
Born Guilty (Rojas) 220
Brother Asno (Barrios) 183
Coronation (Donoso) 228
Daughter of Fortune (Allende)
294
Desolation (Mistral) 183
Destruction (Mistral) 205
A Down-and-Outer (Barrios)
178
During the Reconquest (Blest
Gana) 147
The Enthusiastic Slingshooter
(Neruda) 155
Fantasmas de carne y hueso
(Edwards) 281
The Garden Next Door (Donoso) 278
General Song (Neruda) 156,
219
Grand Gentleman and a Big
Rascal (Barrios) 217
The Heights of Machu Picchu
(Neruda) 215
Hell Has No Limits (Donoso)
242
The House of the Spirits
(Allende) 262
Javiera Carrera, madre de la
patria (Vidal) 296
The Love-Crazed Boy (Barrios) 174
Martín Rivas (Blest Gana)
123
Match Ball (Skarmeta) 275
The Obscene Bird of Night
(Donoso) 248
Of Love and Shadows
(Allende) 265
Otro baile en Paris (Lafourcade) 296
Persona Non Grata (Edwards)
251

Poems and Antipoems (Para)
224
Portrait in Sepia (Allende)
296
Portrait of a Paladin (Huidobro) 192
Residence on Earth (Neruda)
155, 198
Rings (Neruda) 155
Shadows Against the Wall
(Rojas) 239
Shining Tip (Rojas) 233
El sueño de la historia (Edwards) 296
Tenderness (Mistral) 185
This Sunday (Donoso) 242
Twenty Love Poems and a
Song of Despair (Neruda)
155, 185
The Uprooted (Blest Gana)
162
La vaca sagrada (Eltit) 277
Verses of the Salon (Parra)
236
The Wine Press (Mistral) 224
Colombian
Araucaima Mansion (Mutis)
251
Asuntos de un hidalgo disoluto
(Abad Faciolince) 283
The Autumn of the Patriarch
(García Márquez) 254
Capolas negras (Vallejo) 287
Cartas cruzadas (Jaramillo
Agudelo) 285
The Chronicle of a Death
Foretold (García Márquez)
261
Doce cuentos peregrinos (García Márquez) 278
Los felinos del canciller
(Moreno-Dorani) 270
The General in His Labyrinth
(García Márquez) 272
El gran jaguar (Valderrama
Andrade) 277
Una lección de abismo (Cano
Gaviria) 281
Long Ago (Corrasquilla) 200
Love in the Time of Cholera
(García Márquez) 266
The Marchioness of Yolombo
(Cairasquilla) 191
Maria: A South American Romance (Isaacs) 126
El mensajero (Vallejo) 277
News of a Kidnapping (García
Márquez) 287
No One Writes to the Colonel
and Other Stories (García
Márquez) 243
Of Love and Other Demons
(García Márquez) 285
Los ojos del basilisco (Espinosa) 281
One Hundred Years of Solitude (García Márquez) 243
La otra selva (Salazar) 277
Por el sendero de los ángeles
caídos (Hoyos) 275
The Promised Land (Rivera)
181
El río del tiempo (Vallejo)
294
El rumor del astracán (Bibliowicz) 277

Sinfonía desde el Nuevo
Mundo (Espinosa) 275
Summa de Magroll el Gaviero
(Mutis) 275
Urbes luminosas (García
Aguilar) 277
The Vortex (Rivera) 185
Cuban
Baltasar (Gómez de Avellaneda) 121
Cocuyo (Sardy) 275
Delito por bailar el chachacha
(Cabrera Infante) 285
Explosion in a Cathedral
(Carpentier) 236
Farewell to the Sea: A Novel of
Cuba (Arenas) 262
Heroes Are Grazing in My
Garden (Padilla) 262
Holy Smoke (Cabrera Infante)
268
The Kingdom of This World
(Carpentier) 218
Leaves in the Wind (Casal)
141
The Lost Steps (Carpentier)
223
"Niagara" (Heredia) 104
La paloma de vuelo popular:
Elegias (Guillén) 231
Paraíso (Lima) 242
Poems (Gómez de Avellaneda) 112
Querido primer novio
(Valdés) 294
Reasons of State (Carpentier)
253
Sonetos (Oliver Labra) 292
Te de la vida entera (Valdés)
289
Three Trapped Tigers (Cabrera Infante) 240
Ecuadorean
Catilinarians (Montalvo) 133
Chapters Forgotten by Cervantes (Montalvo) 137
Guatemalan
The Cyclone (Asturias) 219
The Eyes of the Interred
(Asturias) 233
The Green Pope (Asturias)
224
Legends of Guatemala
(Asturias) 193
Men of Maize (Asturias) 218
The Office of Peace on Orolandia (Arévalo) 187
The President (Asturias) 214
The World of the Maharachias
(Arévalo) 205
Honduran
The Ships (Quesada) 278
Mexican
1492: Life and Times of Juan
Cabezon de Castilla (Aridjis) 266
A la salud de la serpiente
(Sainz) 277
Amphitryon (Padilla) 296
Beneath Your Clear Shadow
and Other Poems (Paz) 203
Black Pearls (Nervo) 148
The Buried Mirror (Fuentes)
279
Los caciques (Azuela) 176
La campana (Fuentes) 275

A Change of Skin (Fuentes) 243

Christopher Unborn (Fuentes) 270

Constancia y otras novelas para vírgenes (Fuentes) 275

Crypt (Torres Bodet) 203

The Crystal Frontier (Fuentes) 287

The Days (Torres Bodet) 184

The Delirious Heart (Torres Bodet) 183

Deserted Cities (Agustín) 262

Diana: The Goddess Who Hunts Alone (Fuentes) 283

Distant Relations (Fuentes) 260

The Eagle and the Serpent (Guzmán) 191

Eagle or Sun (Paz) 220

East Slope (Paz) 249

Estrellita marinera (Esquivel) 294

Exile (Torres Bodet) 193

The Five Suns of Mexico (Fuentes) 296

Freedom Under Parole (Paz) 218

Frontiers (Torres Bodet) 224

The Good Conscience (Fuentes) 231

El gran lector (Solares) 281

La guerra de Galico (Aguilar Camín) 277

Guerra en el paraíso (Montemayor) 277

The House (Torres Bodet) 184

Human Mourning (Revueltas) 211

The Hydra Head (Fuentes) 257

El infierno es un decir (Hernández) 283

La insólita historia de la santa de Cabora (Domecq) 275

The Itching Parrot (Fernández de Lizardi) 100

Look for My Obituary and First Love (Garro) 287

Mal de amores (Mastretta) 289

The Masked Days (Fuentes) 242

Las moscas (Azuela) 178

El naranjo, o los círculos del tiempo (Fuentes) 281

News from Empire (Paso) 270

Ninguna eternidad como la mía (Mastretta) 294

The Old Gringo (Fuentes) 266

Pasado presente (García Ponce) 283

Quien como Dios (González) 292

Rasero (Robelledo) 283

Savage Moon (Paz) 198

El señor de los mil días (Aridjis) 283

The Shadow of the Leader (Guzmán) 192

Signals from the Flames (Pacheco) 260

El silencio de la luna (Pacheco) 283

Las soldaderas (Poniatowska) 294

Sun Stone (Paz) 228

They Shall Not Pass (Paz) 203

Tinísima (Poniatowska) 279

Tree Between the Walls (Pacheco) 246

Treinta años (Boullosa) 294

Tríptico del carnaval (Pitol) 294

The Useless Life of Pito Perez (Romero) 205

Viaje a los olivos (Cham) 296

Vicious Circle (Agustín) 253

Where the Air Is Clear (Fuentes) 230

White (Paz) 243

Without Truce (Torres Bodet) 228

The Years with Laura Diaz (Fuentes) 294

Nicaraguan

Blue (Darío) 139

Flowers from the Volcano (Alegría) 262

El pacto (Palma) 289

Profane Hymns and Other Poems (Darío) 146

The Psalms of Struggle and Liberation (Cardenal) 239

Zero Hour and Other Documentary Poems (Cardenal) 233

Paraguayan

Los hochos de Zacarías (Morón) 277

I, the Supreme (Roa Bastos) 253

Son of Man (Roa Bastos) 233

Peruvian

American Soul (Chocano) 164

La amigdalitis de Tarzán (Bryce Echenique) 294

Aunt Julia and the Scriptwriter (Vargas Llosa) 256

The Ballad of the Figures (Eguren) 175

Broad and Alien Is the World (Alegría) 208

Color of Blood (García Calderón) 195

Los cuadernos de don Rigoberto (Vargas Llosa) 289

The Cubs, and Other Stories (Vargas Llosa) 243

Deep River (Arguedas) 230

La fiesta del chivo (Vargas Llosa) 296

First Gold of the Indies (Chocano) 199

Foot on the Neck (Belli) 239

The Good Move (Belli) 270

Human Poems (Vallejo) 206

An Invincible Memory (Ubaldo Ribeiro) 272

Let There Be Light (Chocano) 166

Lituma en los Andes (Vargas Llosa) 281

The Notebooks of Don Rigoberto (Vargas Llosa) 292

Oh Cybernetic Fairy (Belli) 234

Play by Play (Goldemberg) 266

The Real Life of Alejandro Mayta (Vargas Llosa) 266

Sestinas and Other Poems (Belli) 248

The Sixth One (Arguedas) 234

The Storyteller (Vargas Llosa) 270, 272

Symbolism (Eguren) 170

Through the Woods Below (Belli) 242

The Time of the Hero (Vargas Llosa) 237

The Vengeance of the Condor (García Calderón) 185

La violencia del tiempos (Gutiérrez) 281

Spanish

Abel Sánchez (Unamuno) 176

Acropolis (Chacel) 265

Across the Bridge (Vega) 32

Adam in Paradise (Ortega y Gasset) 169

Agenda (Hierro) 277

All Citizens Are Soldiers (Vega) 32

El alquimista impaciente (Silva) 297

Amadís de Gaula (Montalvo) 34

Amadís de Gaula (Vicente) 37

El amante lesbiano (Sampedro) 297

El amargo don de la belleza (Moix) 287

AMDG (Pérez de Ayala) 169

And They Put Handcuffs on the Flowers (Arrabal) 246

Angeles de Compostela (Diego) 207

Animal at Bottom (Jiménez) 215

El año del deluvio (Mendoza) 279

Los años indecisos (Torrente Ballester) 289

La Araucana (Ercilla y Zúñiga) 40

Arcadia (Vega) 45

The Architect and the Emperor of Assyria (Arrabel) 243

El asesinato, el perdedor (Cela) 283

La Atlántida (Verdaguer) 131

Atlas de geografía humana (Grandes) 294

Audi Filia (Juan de Avila) 39

Azul (Regas) 283

The Basement Window (Buero Vallejo) 243

Beatriz y los cuerpos celestes (Etxebarria) 292

Belarmino and Apolonio (Pérez de Ayala) 181

Bernardo; or the Victory at Roncesvilles (Balbuena) 53

Beside the River Sar (Castro) 136

Between the Coronation and the Sword (Alberti) 208

Blood and Sand (Blasco Ibáñez) 166

Blood Wedding (Bodas de sangre) (García Lorca) 155, 198

The Bonds of Interest (Benavente y Martínez) 165

Bonfires (Alos) 239

The Book of Good Love (Ruiz) 25

Book of Poems (García Lorca) 155

The Bottom of the Glass (Ayala) 236

The Brightness and the Blood (Aldecoa) 224

El caballero de Sajonia (Benet) 277

Caballeros de fortuna (Landero) 283

La caída de Madrid (Chirbes) 297

Cancionero (Encino) 29

Canticle (Guillén) 191

Carajicomedia (Goytisolo) 296

La cárcel de amor (San Pedro) 29

The Carriers (Vicente) 36

Casi una leyenda (Rodríguez) 277

The Castilian Soul (Martínez Ruiz) 158

La Celestina (Rojas) 30

Children of Chaos (Goytisolo) 226

"Children of Wrath" (Alonso) 212

Los círculos del tiempo (Sampeda) 281

The City of Marvels (Mendoza) 271

Clamor (Guillén) 229

The Coat of Arms of the City of Coimbra (Vicente) 36

Comedy of Calisto and Melibea (Rojas) 30, 34

Compassion (Pérez Galdós) 147

Concerning the Angels (Alberti) 192

The Constant Prince (Calderón de la Barca) 48, 54

Corazón tan blanco (Marías) 279

The Court of Miracles (Valle-Inclán) 189

El Crimen del cine Oriente (Tomeo) 285

Crónica sentimental en rojo (Ledesma) 265

La cruz en la espada (Luján) 287

Cuaderno de Nueva York (Hierro) 292

La cuadratura del círculo (Pombo) 294

The Cypresses Believe in God (Gironella) 223

The Darkness at the Top (Pérez de Ayala) 165

The Daughter of the Air (Calderón de la Barca) 48, 59

De Sacramento Matrimonii (Sánchez) 44

Death as a World of Life (Ayala) 230

The Deceiver of Seville and the Stone Guest (Tirso de Molina) 54

Spanish

Spanish *(continued)*

Destruction or Love (Aleixandre) 200

The Determination of a House (Cruz) 64

El diablo cojuelo (Vélez de Guevara) 57

"Dialogue of Insight" (Aleixandre) 253

La Diana (Montemayor) 39

Diario de 360° (Goytisolo) 296

Días contados (Madrid) 281

El dios dormido (Rubio) 292

Disdain Turned Against Disdain (Moreto y Cabaña) 59

The Disinherited (Castillo) 230

The Disinherited Lady (Pérez Galdós) 134

Distant Gardens (Jiménez) 163

Divan of Tamarit (García Lorca) 155

Don Alvaro; or, The Power of Fate (Saavedra) 109

Don Juan Tenorio (Zorrilla y Moral) 114

Don Quixote (Cervantes) 32, 50

Doña Luz (Valera) 133

Doña Perfecta (Pérez Galdós) 131

La Dragontea (Vega) 45

The Dream of Sarajevo (Rojas) 262

A Dreamer for the Nation (Buero Vallejo) 230

Echo and Narcissus (Calderón de la Barca) 48, 60

Eight New Comedies and Eight New Interludes (Cervantes) 32

The Elusiveness of Truth (Ferrater Mora) 271

El embrujo de Shanghai (Marse) 281

Episodios nacionales (Pérez Galdós) 129

The Evil Doers of Good (Benavente y Martínez) 163

The Evil Poem (Machado) 168

Exemplary Tales (Cervantes) 32, 52

Fábula de fuentes (Juárez) 271

The Faithful Shepherd (Calderón de la Barca) 48

The Family of Pascal Duarte (Cela) 209

The Female Joseph (Calderón de la Barca) 48, 56

El filibusterismo (Rizal) 142

Firmly Rooted (Rovira) 170

First Songs (García Lorca) 155

Flood for the Muse's Springs (Cruz) 65

Forest of Deceits (Vicente) 37

La forja de un ladrón (Umbral) 289

Fortunata y Jacinta (Pérez Galdós) 138

The Four Horsemen of the Apocolypse (Blasco Ibáñez) 175

The Fox's Paw (Pérez de Ayala) 171

Fuente ovejuna (Vega) 32, 52

La Galatea (Cervantes) 42

Galician Songs (Castro) 123

Galindez (Vázquez Montalbán) 277

The Galley Slaves (Alvarez Quintero) 158

The Gardener's Dog (Vega) 32

Gerardo, the Unfortunate Spaniard (Céspedes y Meneses) 53

Gipsy Ballads (García Lorca) 191

The Girl with the Jug (Vega) 32

The Glories of Querétaro (Sigüenza y Góngora) 63

The Grandeur of Mexico (Balbuena) 50

The Greatest Alcalde (Vega) 32

The Greatest Day of Days (Calderón de la Barca) 48

Guzmán de Alfarache (Alemán) 45

The Gypsy Ballads (García Lorca) 155

The Healer of His Honor (Pérez de Ayala) 188

El hereje (Delibes) 292

La hija del caníbal (Montero) 289

His Only Son (Alas) 141

Las historias de Marta y Fernando (Martín Garzo) 294

History of the Famous Preacher Fray Gerundio of Campazas, alias Zotes (Isla) 79

History of the Heart (Aleixandre) 224

The Hive (Cela) 220

Honeymoon, Bittermoon (Pérez de Ayala) 184

The House of Bernarda Alba (García Lorca) 155, 202

Human Verses (Diego) 187

Hurrah to the Hilt (Valle-Inclán) 191

The Iberian Circle (Valle-Inclán) 189

In a Vast Domain (Aleixandre) 236

In Praise of the Stepmother (Cela) 271

In the Burning Darkness (Buero Vallejo) 219

The Incredible Play (Benavente y Martínez) 208

Irse de casa (Martín Gaite) 292

El jardín de las dudas (Savatar) 281

El jinete polaco (Muñoz Molina) 277

Juana (Vega) 32

Juanita la Larga (Valera) 145

The King (Vega) 32

The King and the Farmer (Vega) 32

The Knight from Olmedo (Vega) 32

The Knight of Saxony (Benet) 277

El laberinto griego (Vázquez Montalbán) 277

The Labors of Pesiles and Sigismunds: A Northern Story (Cervantes) 32

The Labors of Urbano and Simona (Pérez de Ayala) 184

The Ladies-in-Waiting (Buero Vallejo) 233

The Lady (Tamayo y Baus) 118

The Lady Nit-Wit (Vega) 32

The Lady of the Dawn (Casona) 212

"Lament for the Death of a Bullfighter" (García Lorca) 155, 200

Landscape with Figures (Diego) 227

El lapiz del carpintero (Rivas) 292

The Lark of Truth (Diego) 208

Life Is a Dream (Calderón de la Barca) 48, 55

The Life of Buscon (Quevedo y Villegas) 54

Life of Squire Marcos of Obregon (Espinel) 52

Limpieza de sangre (Pérez Reverte) 289

The Lord's Vineyard (Calderón de la Barca) 48

Love and Pedagogy (Unamuno) 160

The Love That Passes (Alvarez Quintero) 162

The Lovers of Teruel (Hartzenbusch) 110

Luna de Lobos (Llamazares) 266

Madera de boi (Cela) 294

Madman or Saint (Echegaray y Eizaguirre) 131

The Madness of Love (Tamayo y Baus) 119

Malvaloca (Alvarez Quintero) 171

The Man Who Lurks (Hernández) 206

Mañana en la batalla piensa (Marías) 283

El manuscrito carmesí (Gala) 275

Mar al fondo (Sampedro) 281

The Maravillas District (Chacel) 230

Mariana Pineda (García Lorca) 155

Martha and Mary (Palacio Valdés) 136

Más allá del jardín (Gala) 285

The Mayor of Zalamea (Calderón de la Barca) 48, 56

Mazurka for Two Dead People (Cela) 263

A Meditation (Benet) 246

Meditations on Quixote (Ortega y Gasset) 173

Melocotones helados (Freire) 294

Los melomanos (Amo) 297

Memoirs of Leticia Valle (Chacel) 213

The Men Cry Alone (Gironella) 268

The Merchant's Ship (Calderón de la Barca) 48

El metro de platino iridiado (Pombo) 277

Mientras vivimos (Torres) 297

La mirada del alma (Díez) 289

La mirada del otro (Delgado) 285

Mist (Unamuno) 173

The Modern Theme (Ortega y Gasset) 184

Las moras agraces (Jodra Davo) 294

Moroccan Letters (Cadalso y Vázquez) 86

Mother Nature (Pardo Bazán) 139

Mr. Witt Among the Rebels (Sender) 200

My Voice Because of You (Salinas) 198

Mystical Poems and Songs (Verdaguer) 128

Natural Sciences (Chacel) 271

Nazarín (Pérez Galdós) 145

The Never Ending Lightning (Hernández) 202

A New Drama (Tamayo y Baus) 126

The New Medley (Castro) 133

The New Shelter for the Poor (Calderón de la Barca) 48

New Songs (Machado) 185

El nido de los sueños (Montero) 279

Noli Me Tangere (Rizal) 139

De los nombres de Cristo (León) 42

Nothing (Laforet) 217

La novia de Matisse (Vincent) 297

Nubosidad variable (Martín Gaite) 279

Numantia (Cervantes) 32

O Cesar o nada (Vásquez Montalbán) 292

Occidental Paradise (Sigüenza y Góngora) 64

Ode to the Fatherland (Aribau) 107

Olvidado Rey Gudu (Matute) 289

One Million Dead (Gironelda) 234

La otra orilla de la droga (Tomás García) 266

The Painter of His Dishonor (Calderón de la Barca) 48, 57

Las palabras de la vida (Díez) 297

La pasión turca (Gala) 281

The Passion Flower (Benavente y Martínez) 172

Patas arriba (Galeano) 292

Peace After the War (Gironella) 242

Pedro, the Artful Dodger (Cervantes) 52

Pepe Carvalho (Vázquez Montalbán) 277

Pepita Jiménez (Valera) 130
Pequeñas infamias (Posada) 292
El pequeño heredero (Martín Garzo) 289
Peribanez and the Commander of Ocana (Vega) 32, 51
Phantom Lady (Calderón de la Barca) 54
La piel del tambor (Pérez Reverte) 287
The Pilgrimage of the Aggrieved (Vicente) 37
Plains of Castile (Machado) 171
Play of Fame (Vicente) 32, 35
Plenilunio (Muñoz Molina) 289
Poem of the Cante Jondo (García Lorca) 155
Poems (Cruz) 65
Poems of Consummation (Aleixandre) 245
Poet in New York (García Lorca) 155
Poetry in Prose and Verse (Jiménez) 196
Propalladia (Torres Naharro) 35
La prueba del laberinto (Sánchez Drago) 279
Pure Elegies (Jiménez) 166
Quarrels of Honor (Tamayo y Baus) 123
Quien Metanarrative (Canique) 289
Raquel (García de la Huerta) 83
Lo raro es vivir (Martín Gaite) 287
The Real (Tamayo y Baus) 123
Real sitio (Sampedro) 281
Reality and Desire (Cernuda) 239
The Regentess (Alas) 136
La reina de las nieves (Martín Gaite) 283
Reputable Men (Tamayo y Baus) 128
Requiem for a Spanish Peasant (Sender) 223
Return to Region (Benet) 243
The Revolt of the Masses (Ortega y Gasset) 192
Rhymes (Bécquer) 128
Rienzi the Tribune (Acuña) 131
La ruina del cielo (Díez) 297
Saint Manuel the Good Martyr (Unamuno) 198
San Camilo (Cela) 246
Sancho Saldana (Espronceda y Delgado) 108
Saturday Night (Benavente y Martínez) 161
The Schism of England (Calderón de la Barca) 48
Sea of Histories (Pérez de Guzmán) 35
The Seagull (Caballero) 116
El sentimiento (Guelbenzu) 285
The Ship of Love (Vicente) 36
The Shoemaker and the King, Part II (Zorrilla y Moral) 112

The Shoemaker and the King, Part III (Zorrilla y Moral) 111
Singing from the Depths (Machado) 171
El sol de Breda (Pérez Reverte) 294
La soledad era esto (Millas) 275
Solitudes (Machado) 161
La sombra del angel (Mayoral) 297
Son de mar (Vincent) 294
Sonatas (Valle-Inclán) 160
Songs (García Lorca) 155
The Soul (Machado) 160
Spiritual Exercises (Ignatius of Loyola) 38
Spiritual Sonnets (Jiménez) 175
Springtime of Death (Bousoño) 214
Stanzas for the Death of His Father (Manrique) 29
The Statue of Prometheus (Calderón de la Barca) 48, 61
Stone and Sky (Jiménez) 179
The Struggle for Life (Baroja) 162
The Student of Salamanca (Espronceda y Delgado) 111
Summary of the History of God (Vicente) 36
The Surgeon of His Honor (Calderón de la Barca) 48, 55
Telepenia de Celia Cecilia Villalobo (Pombo) 285
La tempestad (Prada) 289
The Temple of Apollo (Vicente) 36
The Three-Cornered Hat (Alarcón) 130
La tierra promitida (Guelbenzu) 277
Tiger Juan (Pérez de Ayala) 188
Toward Heaven and the Altars (Benavente y Martínez) 191
The Traffic of Algiers (Cervantes) 32
The Tragic Sense of Life (Unamuno) 172
Triumph of Winter (Vicente) 37
Trotters and Dancers (Pérez de Ayala) 172
The Troubadour (García Gutiérrez) 109
Truth Under Suspicion (Ruiz de Alarcón) 54
The Two Lovers of Heaven (Calderón de la Barca) 48, 56
La vieja sirena (Sampedro) 275
Las visiones de Lucrecia (María Merino) 287
Visions (Quevedo y Villegas) 54
Voices of My Song (Jiménez) 213
Way of the Cross (Diego) 195

Wild Beasts Are Tamed by Love (Calderón de la Barca) 48, 61
A Winter Journey (Benet) 250
With the East Wind (Aldecoa) 227
Woman Triumphant (Blasco Ibáñez) 164
The Wonder-Working Magician (Calderón de la Barca) 48, 56
Words in the Sand (Buero Vallejo) 218
Yerma (García Lorca) 155, 199
The Young Assassin (Goytisolo) 224
The Youth of the Cid (Castro y Bellvís) 52
Zalacaín el aventurero (Baroja) 168
Uruguayan
  "Anaconda" (Quiroga) 181
  A Brief Life (Onetti) 219
  Buzón de tiempo (Benedetti) 294
  Death and the Little Girl (Onetti) 252
  Los desterrados (Quiroga) 188
  Lost (Ibarbourou) 219
  The Matins of the Night (Herrera y Reissig) 160
  Montevideanos (Benedetti) 231
  Morning Songs (Agustini) 169
  No Man's Land (Onetti) 209
  Office Poems (Benedetti) 227
  The Rise of the Winds (Ibarbourou) 194
  The Shipyard (Onetti) 234
  Solitude (Acevedo Díaz) 145
  Thanks for the Fire (Benedetti) 240
  Time to Embrace (Onetti) 253
  Tongues of Diamond (Ibarbourou) 179
  The Truce (Benedetti) 233
  Violet Poems (Herrera y Reissig) 164
  The White Book (Agustini) 165
  Wild Root (Ibarourou) 183
Venezuelan
  La carujada (Romero) 275
  Pieles de leopardo (Mata) 281
  Silvas americanas (Bello) 104
  Viejo (González León) 285
  Yo soy la rumba (Infante) 281
Sumerian
  Gilgamesh 1
Swahili
  The Home of the Spirits of the Ancestors (Abdulla) 233
  The Well of Giningi (Abdulla) 245
Swedish
  Agnar (Delblanc) 281
  Alone (Strindberg) 93
  Amorina (Anderberg) 294
  Anna, Hanna, och Johanna (Frederiksson) 283
  Baltics (Transtromer) 253
  Barabbas (Lagerkvist) 219
  Det bla skapet och andra berattelser (Alfven) 294

Black Banners (Strindberg) 93, 165
Black City (Lundkvist) 194
Bobinack (Johnson) 196
The Boys (Lenngren) 87
A Burnt Child (Dagerman) 217
By the Open Sea (Strindberg) 141
The Cassock (Delblanc) 237
The Castrati (Delblanc) 254
The Cave in the Desert (Gyllensten) 252
Charcoal Burner's Ballad and Other Poems (Andersson) 211
Cinnamoncandy (Ahlin) 223
Comrades (Strindberg) 92
The Condemned (Dagerman) 217
The Creditors (Strindberg) 92, 141
The Dance of Death (Strindberg) 92, 159
The Days of His Grace (Johnson) 233
The Death of Socrates (Gyllensten) 233
Dess ande kysst (Johnsson) 279
The Diary of Selma Lagerlöf (Lagerlöf) 196
Doctor Glas (Söderberg) 163
The Dogs (Aspenstrom) 224
A Dream Play (Strindberg) 92, 160
Drivvd fran Ardadien (Radstrom) 294
The Dwarf (Lagerkvist) 212
Easter (Strindberg) 159
Echoes and Traces (Transtromer) 242
Edith (Brunner) 279
Eftertradaren (Erkelius) 279
Eldflugorna (Isakson) 292
The Emigrants (Moburg) 218
The Empire of Stupidity (Lista) 88
The Envious Man (Dalin) 76
The Eternal Smile (Lagerkvist) 180
Exterminate the Brutes (Lindqvist) 279
Fageljagarna (Sjogren) 289
Fair Haven and Foul Strand (Strindberg) 93, 160
The Father (Strindberg) 92, 139
Flora Och Bellona (Karlfeldt) 178
Flora Och Pomona (Karlfeldt) 164
Det florentisski vidsvinet (Ahlin) 277
Flowering Nettle (Martinson) 201
For levande och doda (Transtromer) 275
Forberedelser for wintersasongen (Gustafsson) 275
Forskjellig (Berg) 284
Fredmans Epistlar (Bellman) 86
Frida's Book (Sjöberg) 183
Fridolini's Pleasure Garden (Karlfeldt) 159
Fridolin's Songs (Karlfeldt) 148
Frithjofs Saga (Tegner) 104
Fungi (Pleijel) 281
Fuskaren (Evander) 277
Gaudy Observations (Södergran) 179
Ghost Ship (Martinson) 192
The Ghost Sonata (Strindberg) 92, 165
Glowing Embers (Lundkvist) 191
God's Beautiful World (Koch) 175

Swedish (continued)
    Gor mig levande (Ekman) 287
    The Great Highway (Strindberg) 92, 168
    Groucho in Green (Mattsson) 270
    Guest of Reality (Lagerkvist) 187
    Guide to the Underworld (Ekelof) 244
    Gustav Vasa (Strindberg) 92, 149
    The Hangman (Lagerkvist) 198
    Hatet (Espmark) 285
    Helicon's Flowers (Johansson) 65
    Hemligheter kring vatten (Ekman) 283
    Hercules (Stiernhielm) 59
    Det himmselska gastabudet (Gyllensten) 277
    His Grace's Will (Bergman) 169
    Historien med hunden (Gustafsson) 281
    Den hogsta kasten (Rydberg) 289
    The Horn of Autumn (Karlfeldt) 189
    Hummelhonung (Lindgren) 285
    I vantan pa pendeltaget (Vennberg) 275
    Inferno (Strindberg) 93, 147
    Infor nedrakningen (Myrdal) 281
    The Island of the Doomed (Dagerman) 214
    Israpport (Aspenstrom) 289
    Jerusalem (Lagerlöf) 159
    En kakelsattares eftermiddag (Gustafsson) 277
    Kapten Nemos (Enquist) 277
    Korn (Lundqvist) 266
    Lacemaker Lekholm Has an Idea (Hellstrom) 189
    En lampa som gor morker (Odensten) 294
    Let Man Live (Lagerkvist) 218
    Lifsens rot (Lidman) 287
    Litany (Aspenstrom) 222
    Livlakarens besok (Enquist) 294
    Ljuset ur Skuggornas varld (Gyllensten) 285
    The Long Ships (Bengtisson) 213
    Lotus in Hades (Gyllensten) 242
    Lucky Peter's Travels (Strindberg) 92
    Lycksalighetens (Atterbom) 105
    Lydia i lampans sken (Eggehorn) 275
    Magic Lantern (Bergman) 270
    Man i min alder (Claesson) 279
    The Man Without a Soul (Lagerkvist) 202
    The March of the Musicians (Enquist) 257
    Maria Alone (Delblanc) 266
    Married (Strindberg) 93, 136
    Martin Birck's Youth (Söderberg) 159
    Master Olof (Strindberg) 92
    The Memorial (Delblanc) 248
    Memories of My Childhood (Lagerlöf) 194
    The Merry Festival (Lenngren) 87
    Min salig bror Jean Hendrich (Burman) 281
    Minnena ser mig (Transtromer) 281
    The Miracles of Antichrist (Lagerlöf) 147
    Miss Julie (Strindberg) 92, 139

    Mitt namn skall vara Stig Dagerman (Ranelid) 281
    Modern Myths (Gyllensten) 218
    A Molna Elegy (Ekelof) 233
    Mozarts tredje hjarna (Sonnevi) 287
    Mrs. Marianne (Benedictsson) 139
    Muses (Stiernhielm) 61
    My Death Is My Own (Ahlin) 213
    A Mystery Play of the Sufferings of Israel (Sachs) 220
    Nar vagen vander (Espmark) 279
    The New Kingdom (Strindberg) 92
    New Poems (Fröding) 145
    New Poems (Heidenstam) 174
    Night in the Market Town (Ahlin) 229
    The Night of the Tribades (Enquist) 252
    Och jag grep arorna och rodde (Lillpers) 292
    Oskuldens minut (Lidman) 294
    Palatsbarnen (Collarp) 294
    Paradis (Eriksson) 287
    The Pariah (Strindberg) 92, 140
    The People of Hemso (Strindberg) 93, 139
    Pigan i Arras (Claeson) 281
    Pilgrimage and Wander (Heidenstam) 139
    Pippi Longstocking (Lindgren) 213
    Plays of Marionettes (Bergman) 177
    Poems (Heidenstam) 145
    Poems (Rydberg) 135
    Poetens liv (Mattson) 294
    The Queen's Diadem (Almqvist) 108
    Rain at Daybreak (Johnson) 198
    The Rain Bird (Lidman) 230
    The Red Room (Strindberg) 92, 133
    Return to Ithaca (Johnson) 214
    The Rivers Run Toward the Sea (Lundkvist) 199
    The Road (Martinson) 217
    The Rose Altar (Södergran) 179
    Rummet innanfor (Arvidsson) 294
    Rymdvarktaren (Nilson) 285
    The Saga of the Folkings (Strindberg) 92, 149
    Sammanhang (Trotzig) 287
    Secrets on the Way (Transtromer) 230
    Sena sagor (Jersild) 292
    Sensitiva Amorosa (Hansson) 139
    The September Lyre (Södergran) 178
    The Serious Game (Söderberg) 171
    The Seven Deadly Sins (Boge) 209
    The Seven Seas (Martinson) 192
    The Shadow of the Future (Södergran) 180
    Skimmer (Tunstrom) 287
    The Snake (Dagerman) 213
    Snow Legend (Aspenstrom) 218
    The Son of a Servant (Strindberg) 93, 138
    Songs from the Wings of Sorrow (Rynell) 267
    Songs of Wilderness and Love (Karlfeldt) 145

    Sorgegondolen (Transtromer) 287
    Sorgen per capita (Brunner) 275
    Splashes of Grail (Fröding) 148
    Stone Bird (Delblanc) 252
    The Story of Gosta Berling (Lagerlöf) 142
    The Story of San Michael (Munthe) 192
    Suject Angot (Angot) 292
    Svindel (Holmer) 289
    Swedenhielms (Bergman) 187
    Synden (Ranelid) 283
    Tale of the Horse (Dalin) 76
    Tales (Strindberg) 93
    Tales of a Manor (Lagerlöf) 148
    The Testament of Cain (Gyllensten) 237
    The Timber Valley: A Story of Culture (Koch) 172
    To Damascus (Strindberg) 93, 148
    Tobia Commedia (Petrie) 38
    The Town Gate (Delblanc) 230
    Trade Winds (Martinson) 213
    Tradet (Sonnevi) 277
    Tre borgerliga kvartetter (Noren) 279
    The Triumph over Life (Lagerkvist) 189
    Under i september (Ostergren) 283
    Unter tiden (Turnstrom) 281
    Vallmobadet (Brunner) 294
    Varddjuret (Hermanson) 285
    Vargskinnet (Ekman) 294
    Vattenorgel (Andersson) 281
    The Way Out (Martinson) 202
    Widows (Dorfman) 263
    Winter Lair (Delblanc) 253
    Workers, a Story of Hatred (Koch) 171

T

Tagalog
    Rays and Sunrise (Santos) 164
Tajik
    "The Bloody Throne" (Payrav) 194
    Daughter of Fire (Ikromi) 236
    Fire of Rose (Muradabadi) 224
    The Golden Qishalq (Mirshakar) 209
    Gulru (Jalil) 208
    I Am Guilty (Ikromi) 230
    The Lazy Steppe (Mirshakar) 234
    Loyalty (Niyazi) 224
    The Morning of Our Lives (Ulughzoda) 224
    The Mountain Village (Ayni) 190
    Tajik Vengeance (Niyazi) 215
Tamil
    Kamalampal; or, The Fatal Rumor (Rajam Iyer) 144
    Kantapuranam (Sivakariyar) 54
    Kuyil's Song (Bharati) 171
    Mother Came (Janakiraman) 240
    Panchali's Vow (Bharati) 171
    Son (Ramamitram) 240
Telugu
    Bride Price (Appa) 147
    Kalapurnodayamu (Suranna) 42
    Parijatapahanannamu (Timanna) 36
Thai
    The Prostitute (Surangkhanang) 203

    Tomorrow Will Be Another Sunrise (Sathapanawat) 231
Turkish
    Bosphorus Fortress (Gursel) 285
    Call Me Crimson (Kemal) 292
    The Clown and His Daughter (Adivar) 201
    Dangerous Tales (Altan) 287
    Destan About Ali of Kesan (Taner) 239
    The Devil Within (Ali) 207
    The Epic of Sheikh Badruddin (Hikmet Ran) 202
    The Forbidden Love (Usakligil) 187
    Haluk's Notebook (Fikret) 171
    Human Landscapes (Hikmet Ran) 242
    Look, the Euphrates Is Flowing Bloody (Kemal) 289
    Night (Karasu) 283
    Palace to Let (Karamosmanoglu) 183
    Ruined Mountains (Nadi) 285
    The Song of Those Who Drink the Sun (Hikmet Ran) 191
Turkmen
    Determined Step (Kerbabayev) 207

U

Ukrainian
    Boryslav Laughs (Franko) 135
    Crooked Paths (Franko) 158
    Fata Morgana (Kotsyubinsky) 162
    From the Days of Sorrow (Franko) 158
    Pillars of Society (Franko) 145
    Withered Leaves (Franko) 138
    Zakhar Berkut (Franko) 136
Urdu
    All Sentiments (Mulla Vajhi) 55
    Bang-e Dara (Iqbāl) 185
    Defeat (Chander) 206
    Fire (Ahmed) 214
    Flight (Ahmed) 213
    The Ocean of Night (Ali) 239
    River of Fire (Haidar) 231
    Secrets of the Self (Iqbāl) 174
    Shapes (Gorakhpuri) 215
    A Solid Sheet (Bedi) 236
    The Song of Eternity (Iqbāl) 174
Uzbek
    Obid Ketman (Qodiriy) 201

V

Vietnamese
    Ivory and Opium (Bach) 267
    A Tired Horse Trots On (Nguyen) 265
    When the Light Is Out (Ngo) 206

X

Xhosa
    The Ochre People: Scenes from a South African Life (Jabavu) 237
    U-Don Jade (Mqhayi) 192

Y

Yakut
    The Fortune of Yakutsk (Elley) 215
    Game of Life (Sofronov) 178
    Springtime (Achchygyya) 212
    Tales (Achchygyya) 203

Yiddish
  The Agunah (Grade) 234
  The Brothers Ashkenazi (Singer)
    202
  Chaim Lederer's Return (Asch) 190
  Collected Stories (Singer) 262
  *The Death of Methuselah and
    Other Stories* (Singer) 271
  Der Dibuk (The Dybbuk) (Ansky)
    173
  Enemies: A Love Story (Singer) 250
  The Estate (Singer) 246
  The Family Moskat (Singer) 213

  Fathers and Sons (Sefarim) 123
  "Gimpel the Fool" (Singer) 213
  Gimpel the Fool (Singer) 229
  The Golden Chain (Peretz) 169
  The Image, and Other Stories
    (Singer) 267
  In My Father's Court (Singer) 242
  Judge Not (Asch) 188
  "The Little Man" (Sefarim) 124
  The Magician of Lublin (Singer)
    231
  The Manor (Singer) 244
  The Nazarene (Asch) 206

  The Penitent (Singer) 263
  Satan in Goray (Singer) 201
  Shosha (Singer) 257
  The Slave (Singer) 236
  Spinoza of Market Street (Singer)
    234
  Stories and Pictures (Peretz) 158
  *The Travels and Adventures of
    Benjamin the Third* (Sefarim)
    130
Yoruban
  The Forest of a Thousand Daemons
    (Fagunwa) 205

  Yorubus, You Must Think
    (Ogunde) 239

Z

Zulu
  An African Tragedy (Dhlomo)
    191
  The Valley of a Thousand Hills
    (Dhlomo) 208
  Zulu Poems (Kunene) 248